Anonymus

Polk's (Trow's) New York copartnership and corporation directory, boroughs of Manhattan and Bronx

Anonymus

Polk's (Trow's) New York copartnership and corporation directory, boroughs of Manhattan and Bronx

ISBN/EAN: 9783742801159

Manufactured in Europe, USA, Canada, Australia, Japa

Cover: Foto ©Andreas Hilbeck / pixelio.de

Manufactured and distributed by brebook publishing software (www.brebook.com)

Anonymus

Polk's (Trow's) New York copartnership and corporation directory, boroughs of Manhattan and Bronx

THE TROW CITY DIRECTORY CO.'S

(FORMERLY WILSON'S)

Copartnership and Corporation

DIRECTORY

OF

NEW YORK CITY.

GIVING THE PARTNERS AND SPECIAL PARTNERS OF EACH
FIRM; THE OFFICERS, CAPITAL AND DIRECTORS OF THE
BANKS, BUSINESS AND MANUFACTURING CORPORA-
TIONS AND INSURANCE COMPANIES; TRADE NAMES
AND PROPRIETORS THEREOF; ALSO FOREIGN
FIRMS DOING BUSINESS IN NEW YORK, WITH
THE LOCATIONS OF THEIR HOME OFFICES
AND THE NAMES OF THEIR NEW YORK
REPRESENTATIVES OR AGENTS.

VOL. XXXVIII.

MARCH, 1890.

PUBLISHED BY

THE TROW CITY DIRECTORY COMPANY
11 UNIVERSITY PLACE, NEW YORK.

Printed and Bound by
TROW'S PRINTING AND BOOKBINDING COMPANY,
201-213 EAST TWELFTH STREET, NEW YORK.

PRICE FIVE DOLLARS.

PREFACE TO THE THIRTY-EIGHTH VOLUME

OF THE

COPARTNERSHIP AND CORPORATION DIRECTORY.

THIS is the thirty-eighth volume published since 1849. The first volume contained 66 pages and the names of about 6,000 firms. The present volume contains 386 pages and the names of about 24,000 firms, corporations, etc., an increase of business firms, etc., of 300 per cent. in 40 years.

In a city having such varied and vast commercial and financial interests as New York, the Copartnership and Corporation Directory is as essential in its sphere as a Business or General Directory, and to many the services of the two latter could be more easily dispensed with. The aim of this volume is to furnish to Lawyers, Bankers, Brokers, Insurance Companies, Trust Companies, Merchants, Capitalists, and Investors, the following information, viz.: To give the correct firm or corporate name, the names of the members of each firm, both general and special, where there are limited firms the names of the special partners and amount of special capital, the term of its duration; the names of the various Banks, Insurance, and Trust Companies, their Capital, Officers, and Directors; the Capital, Officers, and Directors of the numerous Manufacturing and Mercantile Companies; the various Trade names and who are the proprietors thereof, and finally, grouped by themselves at the last of the work, the names of the foreign houses located in New York, and giving in connection with each the location of the Home Office, the name of its New York representative, and the location of its New York Office; the whole arranged in alphabetical order, making it a work of easy comprehension and great utility. And the Publishers feel confident that the information they impart is as accurate and reliable as a perfect system, long experience, and human hands and brains can make it.

A FEW POINTS IN USING THE COPARTNERSHIP DIRECTORY.

1st. Its arrangement is strictly alphabetical.

2d. The word "(dissolved)" after a name denotes that this particular name appeared in the General Directory of 1889, and the dissolution has occurred since May 1, 1889.

3d. The words "(no inf.)" after a name signify that the firm or corporation so quoted was not found at the address printed, and that definite information as to their present location was unobtainable.

4th. The words "(inf. unattainable)" signify that, notwithstanding diligent effort was made on our part, we were unable to secure the desired information.

5th. (Example) Henderson Theodore & Co. (Theodore Henderson jr. & John Barnutz, only). The word "only," in this example, signifies that some person whose name appears in the style of the firm is not at present a member; in this particular case Theodore Henderson, Sr., has retired, although his name appears in the firm.

6th. For Foreign Firms, see page 336. For New Firms, Corrections, etc., too late for insertion in their proper place, see page 335.

Respectfully,
THE TROW CITY DIRECTORY CO.

THE CALIGRAPH WRITING MACHINE,
HARTFORD, CONN.

THE TROW CITY DIRECTORY CO.'S
(FORMERLY WILSON'S)
NEW YORK CITY
COPARTNERSHIP AND CORPORATION
MARCH, 1890.   **DIRECTORY.**   **VOL. XXXVIII.**

For Names of Foreign Houses and their Representatives, and Names Received too Late for Regular Insertion, see last pages.

* NOTE. The words "(no Inf.)" after a name signify that the firm or corporation so quoted was not found at the address printed, and that definite information as to their present location was unattainable; the words "(Inf. unattainable)" signify that, notwithstanding due effort was made on our part, we were unable to secure the desired information.

ABC	ABS

A

A. B. C. Motor Co. (Inf. unattainable) 44 Gold

Aaron Louis & Co. (Louis Aaron, Co. refused) 239 Division

Aaron Brothers (Isaac & Edward Aaron) 801 Eighth av.

Aarons & Co. (George S. & James Aarons) 510 B'way

Aarons & Feder (Ellis Aarons & Charles J. Feder) 95 Prince

Abberley & Son (John & Elias T. Abberley) 41 Madison

Abbett & Fuller (Leon Abbett, William J. A. Fuller, Henry Schmitt & William F. & Leon Abbett jr.) 229 D'way

Abbey & Imbrie (Charles F. Imbrie, only) 18 Vesey

Abbey, Schoeffel & Grau (Henry E. Abbey, John B. Schoeffel & Maurice Grau) 1212 B'way

Abbiati Brothers (Joseph & Constantino Abbiati) 97 Thompson

Abbot-Downing Co. (Lewis Downing jr., Pres.; Frank L. Abbot, Sec.; Edward A. Abbot, Treas. Capital, $400,000. Directors: Lewis Downing jr. Edward A. & Frank L. & Joseph H. Abbot, Samuel C. Eastman, R. M. Morgan, J. C. A. Hill) 142 Prince

Abbott Jore & Co. (Jaro Abbott, Austin A. Wheelock, Gordon Abbott & Eban B. Clarke) 23 Cliff

Abbott W. & J. (dissolved) 37 N. Moore

Abbott Brothers (William A. & Albert A. Abbott) 71 D'way

Abbott & Co. (Charles A. Abbott, no Co.) 60 Ann

Abbott & Teal (Charles Abbott & Don Teal) 1108 B'way

Abbott's M., Sons (Philip H. & Charles L. & Richard H. Abbott) 187 Eighth av.

Abbott's William, Sons (Charles E. & Robert B. Abbott) 257 D'way & 884 Third av.

Abeel Brothers (George & John H. Abeel jr.) 190 South & 865 Water

Abegg, Daenikee & Co. (Henry Abegg, Henry H. Daeniker & Adolph Rusch) 80 Grand

Abel Bernard & Co. (Bernard Abel & Melvin Whispell) 191 Reade

Abel C. C. & Co. (Christian C. Abel & Henry Pluysers) 19 Whitehall

Abel G. & Co. (George Abel, no Co.) 9 W. 4th

Abell E. C. & Co. (Ernatus C. Abell & Robert W. Webb) 60 D'way

Abell & Morton (dissolved) 181 Duane

Abels & Co. (ensola) (Ignatz & Henry Abels) 237 Mercer

Abels & Co. (leather) (Henry J. Abels & George Wolf) 242 & 244 E. 80th

Abendroth Brothers (William P. Abendroth, Pres.; John W. Abendroth, Sec.; John F. Mills, Treas. Capital, $150,000 ; further inf. unattainable) 282 Pearl & 109 Beekman

Abendroth & Root Mfg. Co. (John Abendroth, Pres.; William H. Leitch, Sec.; A. Howard Abendroth, Treas. Capital, $300,000. Directors: John & A. Howard Abendroth, William H. Leitch, Ernest C. Webb, A. Oldrin Salter) 28 Cliff

Abenheim M. & Co. (Max Abenheim & Baruch Kaufmann) 4 Stone

Abingdon Knitting Mills (Oliver Lamson, propr.) 507 W. 5Cth

Abingdon Tea & Coffee Co. (Cornelius L. Ryan, propr.) 588 Hudson

Ablowich J. & Co. (Julius & Alfred & Israel Ablowich & David Dreeben) 403 D'way

Abraham Brothers (Samuel & Philip Abraham) 473 Sixth av.

Abrahams H. & Co. (Henry Abrahams & Louis Kaufmann) 64 Bowery

Abrahams M. & Son (Morris & Mark L. Abrahams) 274 Seventh av.

Abrahams & Grunauer (Louis Abrahams & Reuben Grunauer) 451 Sixth av.

Abrahams & Schwarz (Nathan Abrahams, Maurice Schwarz & Michael M. Abrahams) 127 Grand

Abrams B. & Co. (Bernard Abrams, William Osten jr. & Nathan Langschur) 113 W. B'way

Abrams & Brother (Joseph & Jacob Abrams) 49 Wooster

Abrams & Kellar (Nathan Abrams & Isaac Kellar) 112 Spring

Abrams & Vesell (Harris Abrams & Meyer Vesell) 41 Division

Abramson & Jacoby (Solomon Abramson & Elias Jacoby) 237 Bleecker

Abstein & Schaffer (Jacob Abstein & George Schaffer) 319 W. 40th

COMPILED WITH ACCURACY AND DESPATCH. } **CLASSIFIED BUSINESS LISTS.** { THE TROW CITY DIRECTORY CO. 11 University Place.

ACA 4 ADD

Acadia Coal Co. (Ltd.) (James W. Clendenin, Pres.; Philip P. Harris, Sec.; capital, $4,000,-000; further inf. unattainable) 1 B'way

Accident Ticket Box Co. (Ltd.) (Edmund Dwight jr. Pres.; Abram M. Kirby, Sec. Capital, $300,000. Directors: Edmund Dwight jr.; Abram M. Kirby, Samuel Appleton, Henry B. Dwight, Thomas Adams jr., J. B. Weir, J. Scott Boyd jr.) 51 Cedar

Achor & Co. (Servetus T. Achor, Co. refused) 40 Dey

Acker J. & Co. (James W. Acker & Henry W. Rosenberg) 175 W. 46th

Acker J. W. & Co. (James W. & Albert Acker) 259 Sixth av.

Acker & Co. (John C. & Charles H. Acker) 145 Front & 71 South

Acker, Merrall & Condit (William J. Merrall, John W. Condit, Charles L. & Franklin Acker & William B. & Albert E. Morrall) 126 Chambers, 62 Warren, 1473 B'way & 1010 Sixth av.

Ackerman J. E. & Co. (John E. Ackerman & John F. Rodarmor) 603 W. 28th

Ackerman J. H. & Co. (John H. Ackerman, no Co.) 240 Pearl

Ackerman P. D. & Brother (Peter D. & Jacob D. Ackerman) Pier 34 E. R.

Ackerman & Co. (dissolved) 369 Washn. mkt.

Ackerman & Murphy (Peter I. Ackerman & Michael H. Murphy) 276 Washn.

Ackerman & Roberts (Thomas J. Ackerman & Graham Roberts) 202 E. 112th

Ackerman & Son (Jacob E. & Berthold Ackerman) 5 N. William

Ackerman, Bicker & Manvel (Lawrence L. Ackerman, Henry K. Bicker & Frederick C. Manvel) 6 Maiden la.

Ackerman, Deyo & Hilliard (Benjamin G. Ackerman, Peter Q. Deyo & John G. Hilliard) 41 Pine

Ackerman's Steam Carpet Cleaning Works (Frederick Ackerman, propr.) 133 W. 32d & 2424 Eighth av.

Ackermann Brothers (William & Christopher & Julius H. Ackermann) 701 G'wich

Ackert & Schroeder (no inf.) 233 W. 32d

Acme Bottling Co. (dissolved) 14 State

Acme Co. (not inc.; further inf. refused) 49 John

Acme Composition Co (Arthur T. Groocock, propr.) 26 Frankfort

Acme Liquid Fuel Co. (John S. Andrews, Pres.; Samuel G. Dimmick. Sec. Capital, $3,000,000. Directors: John S. Andrews, Samuel G. Dimmick, Thomas Cornell, James Roberts) 146 B'way

Acme Oil Co. (John D. Archbold, Pres.; further inf. refused) 26 B'way

Acme Printing Co. (Capital, $30,000; further inf. unattainable) no address

Acme Rubber Works (Philip F. Molloy, propr.) r 43 Centre

Acme Stationery & Paper Co. (Samuel I. Knight, propr.) 59 Duane

Acme Steam Laundry (William Angevine & Co., proprs.) 1400 B'way & 326 Seventh av.

Acme Underwear Co. (Solomon Lissner, propr.) 38 Wooster

Acme Vault Cover Co. (Adam E. Schatz, propr.) 908 Third av.

Actina Co. (Charles W. Lewis, propr.) 56 Fifth av.

Adair & Aldred (James Adair & John Aldred) 359 Fourth av.

Adam J. & Co. (Jacob Adam, no Co.) 373 Grand

Adam J. J. & Co. (Julius J. Adam & James Michael) 67 Greene

Adam S. & Son (Hugo S. Adam, only) 132 S. 5th av. & 94 Thompson

Adamo & Mirabella (Dominick Adamo & Joseph Mirabella) 310 Canal

Adams Edwin W. & Co. (Edwin W. Adams & J. Oswald Jimonis) 114 Wall

Adams Express Co. (John Hoey. Pres.; Clarence A. Seward, Sec.; William L. Hubbell, Treas. Capital, $12,000,000. Directors: John Hoey, Clarence A. Seward, C. Spooner, Henry Sanford, William B. Dinsmore, L. C. Weir, J. Q. A. Herring, Waldo Adams) 59 B'way

Adams Hugh W. & Co. (Hugh W. Adams & Daniel L. Cobb) 56 Pine

Adams Peter, Co.(Henry H. Bowman, Pres.; Frank B. Adams, Sec. Capital, $200,000. Trustees: Henry H. Bowman, Frank B. Adams, Frank C. Bishop, James D. Pickles, William Bishop, James N. Shaffer, Patrick A. Harvey, James Booth, Thomas Duncan) 88 Park row

Adams Power Fence Machine Co. (Louis M. Howland, Pres.; Henry K. Gilman, Sec. Capital $100,000. Directors: Louis M. Howland, Henry L. Shippy, Henry K. Gilman, J. H. Montgomery, George Q. Adams) 10 Wall

Adams Richard H. & Co. (Richard H. Adams & Jacob M. Frank) 11 E. 4th

Adams Safford & Co. (Safford Adams, no Co.) 41 St. Jones

Adams Walter & Co. (Walter Adams & George A. Elwood) 105 William

Adams F. T. & Co. (Frederick T. Adams & William E. Pearl) 104 B'way

Adams J. & W. (John & William)340 W. 40th

Adams L. H. & Co. (Lyman H. Adams & I. B. Storms) 294 E. 121st

Adams R. & H. (Robert & Henry) 16 Greene

Adams T. W. & Co. (Thomas W. & James W. & Robert W. Adams) 14 John

Adams & Barron (dissolved) 180 W 53d

Adams & Bishop Co. (Henry H. Bowman, Pres.; Frank C. Bishop, Sec. Capital, $200,000. Trustees: Henry H. Bowman, Frank C. Bishop, Patrick A. Harvey, Thomas Duncan, William Bishop) 88 Park row

Adams & Bogert (Lyman H. Adams & Charles Bogert) 460 E. Houston

Adams & Co. (drygds.) (Samuel Adams & John Flaulgnn) 339 Sixth av.

Adams & Co. (leather) (William B. Adams, no Co.) 27 Spruce

Adams & Co. (publishers) (George H. & Louis M. Adams) 59 Beekman

Adams & Co. (wines) (Frank & William E. & Harry C. Adams) 220 Front

Adams & Howe (Aaron Adams & John I. Howe) 329 Washn.

Adams & Hyde (Percy D. Adams & James W. Hyde) 59 Liberty

Adams & McIvor (dissolved) 4 W. 28th

Adams & Ritchie (Alexander Adams & Gordon Ritchie) 1695 B'way

Adams & Robar (dissolved) 268 G'wich

Adams & Westlake Co (J. McGregor Adams. Pres.; William N. Campbell, Sec. Capital, $1,000,-000. Directors: J. McGregor Adams, Lyman I. Todd, William N. Campbell, J. M. Flower, Norman Williams, Charles H. Hitchcock, A. Weinberg) 115 B'way

Adams, Lay & Comstock (Thatcher M. Adams, George C. Lay & Frederick H. Comstock) 36 Wall

Adams, Valentine & Osborne (John P. Adams, Samuel W. Valentine & Samuel D. Osborne) 206 B'way

Adams, Victor & Co. (Orville J. Victor, only) 98 William

Adamson Brothers (James & Alexander Adamson) 258 Pearl

Adder Co. (dissolved) 58 Cedar

MERCHANTS EXCHANGE NAT. BANK OF THE CITY OF N. Y.
SOLICITS YOUR ACCOUNT. 257 Broadway.
PHINEAS C. LOUNSBURY, President.   ALLEN S. APGAR, Cashier.

ADD   5   AIM

Addison & Pennsylvania Railway Co. (Thomas C. Platt, Pres.; James E. Jones, Sec.; George R. Sheldon, Treas. Capital, $600,000. Directors: Thomas C. Platt, William Brookfield, George R. Sheldon, James E. Jones, Charles L. Puttison, James Horton, John W. Hammond, Augustus C. Gurnee, Frank H. Platt, Henry P. DeGraaf, Frank M. Baker, Theodore F. Wood, Royal W. Clinton) 49 B'way

Addoms William H. & Co. (William H. & Samuel K. Addoms) 99 Gold

Addressing, Duplicating & Mailing Co. (Ltd.) (Thomas N. Bolles, Pres.; Leslie Gilbert. Sec. Capital, $50,000. Directors: Augustus W. Dunning, Margaret E. Siebart, Matilda A. & Thomas Bolles) 40 Dey

Adee Fred & Co. (Fred Adee & Benjamin C. Smith) 90 Beekman

Adelphi Silver Plate Co. (John Schimpf & Son, proprs.) 62 John

Aderer A. & Co. (Adolph Aderer & Frederick Jelenko:—special partner, Jacob Jelenko, *Charleston. W. Va.*, $4,000; terminates 1st Jan. 1895) 480 B'way

Adhesive Gimp Co. (Ltd.) (James P. Hoffernan, Pres.; Charles M. Kellogg, Treas.; Joseph W. Hayward, Sec. Capital, $8,500. Directors: James P. Hoffernan, Charles M. Kellogg, Joseph W. Hayward, Leonard J. Rossmini, Alfred R. Ostrom) 120 Walker

Adickes E. H. & Son (Elbe H. & William H. Adickes) 5 Gansevoort

Adirondack Railway Co. (R. Suydam Grant, Pres.; Charles A. Walker, Sec. Capital, $4,000,000. Directors: William W. Durant, Warner Miller, Freling H. Smith, Edward L. Molineux, William L. Strong, David Willcox, Chester Griswold, James Roosevelt, Horace G. Young, R. Suydam Grant, Robert Olyphant, James C Hartt, Frederick Dillings) 21 Cortlandt

Adkins & Allison (dissolved) 116 W. 27th

Adler Jacob & Co. (Alfred Adler, William J. Stitt, Benjamin Lichtenberg & Charles Adler, only) 471 B'way & 44 Mercer

Adler A. & Co. (crayons) (no inf.) 18 Clinton pl.

Adler A. & Co. (flour) (Adolph Adler & Herman Gampert) 12 Front

Adler J. & S. (no inf.) 55 Thompson av. W Washn. mkt

Adler L. & Co. (Leopold & Jacob Adler) 44½ Maiden la.

Adler S. & Sons (dissolved) 197 Pearl

Adler Brothers (hats) (Emil & Leopold Adler) 305 E. Houston

Adler Brothers (meat) (Benjamin & John & Louis Adler) 802 First av.

Adler & Herrman (Simon Adler & Henry S. Herrman) 155 B'way

Adler & Mendelson (Elias J. Adler & Louis Mendelson) 84 E. Houston

Adler & Sommer (Adolph Adler & Adolph Sommer) 58 E. 118th

Adler, Summer & Co. (Arnold Adler, Adolph Summer & Nathan Solomon) 1840 Ninth av.

Adler's S. Sons (Albert S. & Millard F. & Leon N. Adler) 197 Pearl

Adrian George S. & Co. (George S. Adrian, Co. refusal) 97 Water

Adriance, Platt & Co. (John P. Adriance, Pres.; Frederick D. Somers, Sec.; Isaac S. Platt, Treas. Capital, $500,000. Directors: John P. Adriance, Frederick D. Somers, Isaac S. Platt, John E. Adriance, Roland R. Dennis) 165 G'wich

Advance Electric Co. (no inf.) 17 B'way

Advance Mfg. Co. (dissolved) 16 Dey

Advance & Discount Co. (W. Rodman Winslow, propr.) 132 Nassau

Aeolian Organ & Music Co. (James Morgan, Pres.; J. Herbert Chase, Sec.; William B. Tremaine, Treas. Capital, $150,000. Directors: James Morgan, William B. Tremaine, George B. Kelly, John L. Given, William A. Webber, J. Herbert Chase, George R. Curtis) 831 B'way

Aeschlimann & Pellarin (Charles Aeschlimann & Vincent Pellarin) 231 E. 28th

Aetna Grate Bar Co. (Salamander Grate Bar Co. proprs.) 110 Liberty

Aetna Publishing Co. (Stratton & Hudson, proprs.) 26 Church

Affleck William & Co. (William Affleck & Elbert Hallock) 601 W. 93d

Afreck & Brother (Julius & Simon Afreck) 65 Suffolk

African Methodist Episcopal Book Concern (dissolved) 183 Bleecker

Agar, Ely & Fulton (John G. Agar, Alfred Ely & Louis M. Fulton) 20 Nassau

Agar, Hamblin & Co. (Alexander Agar, Wolcott G. Hamblin, Alexander Agar jr. & Felix J. S. Kyle) 292 B'way

Agency Security & Guaranty Co. (R. Carman Combes, Pres.; Henry C. Robinson, Treas.; William D. Chandler, Sec. Capital, $100,000. Directors: R. Carman Combes, William D. Snow, Henry C. Robinson, William D. Chandler) 233 B'way

Agents Novelty Mfg. Co. (no inf.) 50 Bond

Agnew William & Sons (John T. & Alexander McL. Agnew, only) 284 Front

Aguan Navigation & Improvement Co. (Luther E. Shinn, Pres.; Henry A. Kirkham, Sec. Capital, $5,000,000. Directors: Luther E. Shinn, Sheppard Homans, George S. McCulloh, Stephen W. Fullerton, Stephen G. Clarke, Halsey J. Boardman, Ellery H. Wilson, C. Robinson Griggs, John Bigelow) 120 B'way

Ahearn D. & Co. (Dennis Ahearn & John Fitzgerald) 46 Jefferson

Ahorn & Bentley (Michael J. Ahorn & Thomas H. Bently) 20 South, 20 Front & 130 Broad

Ahlers & Wer-ebe (Frederick Ahlers & Louis Wersebe) 1740 Lex. av.

Ahles Jacob, Brewing Co. (Frederick J. Ahles, Pres.; Max Ahles, sec. Capital, $150,000. Directors: Frederick J. & Max & Jacob Ahles jr., E. Steinmetz) 153 E. 54th

Ahles & Raymond (John W. Ahles & Arthur B. Raymond) 4 Stone

Ahlstrom Otto R. & Co. (Otto R. Ahlstrom, no Co.) 233 W. 46th

Ahrenfeldt Charles & Son (Charles & Charles J. Ahrenfeldt) 50 Murray

Ahrens John C. & Co. (John C. Ahrens, no Co.) 110 Washn. mkt

Ahrens L. W., Stationery & Printing Co. (Ahrens & Goldsmith, proprs.) 85 Liberty

Ahrens & Goldsmith (Lawrence W. Ahrens & Clara Goldsmith) 88 Liberty

Ahrens & Whitehead (Charles E. Ahrens & William R. Whitehead) 1014 W. 14th

Ahrens' G., Sons (Alexander A. & William G. & Charles E. Ahrens) 70 Dey

Ahsler & Staab (Philip C. Ahsler & John Staab jr.) 145 E. 23d

Aich Hermann (Hermann Aich:—special partner, Joseph Deckel, $10,000, terminates 30th April 1891) 46 Murray

Aiello & Co. (Frank Aiello & Celestino Tambelle) 180 Worth

Aikin, Lambert & Co. (James C. Aikin, Henry A. Lambert & John B. Shea) 23 Maiden la.

Aikman S. M. & Co. (E. Hazard Aikman & estate of Samuel M. Aikman) 261 Pearl

Aimone C. A. & Brother (Carlo A. & Raimondo Aimone) 30 B. 5th av. & 151 Bleecker

SNOW, CHURCH & CO. {ESTABLISHED 1874.

AIN 6 ALF

Ainsworth Boiler Covering Co. (Edward K. Hayt, Pres.; Frank D. Karr, Sec. Capital, $75,000. Directors: Edward K. Hayt, Frank D. Karr) 171 B'way

Ainsworth Brass Mfg. Co. (James Ainsworth, propr.) 44 Murray & 119 Walker

Airtight Wrapper Co. (refused) 491 B'way

Aisenstein & Woronock (Morris Aisenstein & Morris Woronock) 51 Spring

Aitken, Son & Co. (John W. Aitken, Archibald McLintock, George Taylor & George Shaw, only) 873 B'way, 218 E. 26th & 523 W. 46th

Ajax Envelope Co. (Henry J. Howlett, Pres.; Edward S. Cornwall, Sec. Capital, $100,000. Trustees: Henry J. Howlett, Abel T. Howard, Edward S. & W. W. Cornwall, Daniel L. Taylor) 519 Broome

Akbar Mfg. Co. (Thomas Goodenough, Pres., Augustus C. Maas, Sec. Capital, $8,000; Directors: Thomas Goodenough, Augustus C. Maas) 59 Fifth av.

Akin Automatic Advertising Clock Co. (William Akin, Pres.; William T. B. Milliken, Sec. Capital, $200,000. Trustees: William Akin, William T. B. Milliken, Thomas B. Chass) 7 Murray

Alabama Mineral Land Co. (Edmund D. Randolph, Pres.; Philip J. Goodhart, Sec. Capital, $1,000,000. Directors: Edmund D. Randolph, Emanuel Lehman, Daniel S. Appleton, Edwin Einstein, John T. Atterbury, Philip J. Goodhart, J. E. Fisher) 7 Nassau

Alart & McGuire (James F. McGuire & estate of Peter Alart) 70 Madison

Albany Baking Co. (Edward Mason, propr.) 2025 Third av.

Albany Baking Co. (Joseph Leriognr, propr.) 2795 Third av. & Lincoln av. & E. 180th

Albany Day Line Steamboats (Hudson River Line, proprs.) Pier 39 (old) N. R.

Albany Lubricating Compound & Cup Co. (Adam Cook, propr.) 313 West

Albany Perforated Wrapping Paper Co. (no inf.) 1475 D'way

Albemarle Soapstone Co. (James H. Serene, Pres.; Adolphus D. Pape, Sec.; Daniel J. Carroll, Treas. Capital, $200,000. Trustees: James H. Serene, Daniel J. Carroll, Frank Felter, Adolphus D. Pape) 525 W. 14th

Albert Nail Co. (Jacob Silberman, Pres.; Ludwig Silbermann, Sec.; Bernard Dreyfuss, Treas. Capital, $75,000. Trustees: Jacob & Ludwig Silbermann, Bernard Dreyfuss) 79 Duane & 300 Monroe

Albert William & Co. (William & Louis Albert) 326 E. 48th

Albert, Haager & Co. (Henry C. Albert & Charles Haager, no Co.) 876 B'way

Alberta Bronze Ink Co. (Albert Higgons, propr.) 146 Reade

Alberti J. & Co. (James Alberti, no Co.) 417 E. 12th

Alberti & Co. (Lawrence S. Alberti & George Brendstetter) 655 Third av.

Albertype Co. (Adolph Wittemann, Pres.; Louis Scherzinger, Sec. Directors: Adolph Wittemann, Frederick Lang, Louis Scherzinger) 58 Reade

Albo Carbon Light (William M. Crane & Co, proprs.) 766 B'way

Albrecht William & Co. (William Albrecht & Harry B. Young) 197 Wooster

Albrecht H. & Son (Henry & Charles R. Albrecht) 62 Fulton

Albrecht & Stucky (Lorenz Albrecht & Carl Stucky) 11 Seventh

Albright & Steindler (Charles H. Albright & Joseph Steindler) 530 B'way

Albro & Brothers (Samuel Palmer, only) 156 Bowery

Alcott C. W. & Son (Charles W. & Delafield S. Alcott) 311 Av. B

Alcott & Hall (dissolved) 606 W. 43d

Alden Evaporated Fruit Co. (inoperative) 79 Park pl.

Alden Publishing Co. (Frank Tracy, Pres.; Albert Christianson, Sec.; Henry B. Durand, Treas. Capital, $500,000. Directors: Frank Tracy, Albert Christianson, Henry B. Durand) 393 Pearl

Alden A. B. & Co. (Arthur B. Alden & David T. Hartshorn) 905 B'way

Alden & Sterne (William H. Alden & Morris E. Sterne) 9 E. 14th

Alderman I. & Co. (Isaac Alderman, George Pyser & Henry Wolesin) 486 Grand

Alderney Ice Cream Co. (not Inc.) (Chileon D. Decker, Edward M. Morgan & George B. Deane jr.) 86 Bank

Alderson & Sons (Thomas B. & Algernon B. & Henry E. Alderson) 220 B'way

Aldine Art Publishing Co. (dissolved) 27 Bond

Aldrich, Iddings & Clifton (James H. Aldrich, William F. Iddings, Junius A. Clifton & Robert E. Anthony) 256 Church

Ale Brewers' Assn. of the States of N. Y. & N. J. (Edward Underhill, Pres.; Alfred E. J. Tovey, Sec.; John H. Ballantine, Treas.) 24 Park pl.

Alexander H. & Co. (dissolved) 100 Greene

Alexander L. & A. Amans (no inf.) 446 Washn

Alexander L. & Co. (dissolved) 88 Clinton

Alexander L. D. & Co. (Lawrence D. Alexander & H. Raymond Munger) 44 B'way

Alexander R. & Co. (Rudolph Alexander, no Co.) 1280 Third Av.

Alexander W. J. & C. C. (William J. & Charles C.) 8 York

Alexander Brothers (cigars) (Henry & Jacob & Nathan Alexander) 140 Allen, 143 Orchard & 87 Rivington

Alexander Brothers (toys&c.) (Adolph & Emanuel Alexander) 227 Grand

Alexander Brothers (furniture) (Abraham & Lewis & Joseph Alexander) 107 Bowery

Alexander Brothers (furniture) (Max & Oscar Alexander) 93 Bowery

Alexander Brothers (tailors) (Jacob & Moritz Alexander) 102 Lewis

Alexander Brothers (tobacco) (Magnus D. & Julius D. Alexander) 212 Pearl

Alexander & Ash (Peter Alexander & Mark Ash) 234 B'way

Alexander & Co. (felts) (James Alexander & Howard W. Walgrove) 13 University pl.

Alexander & Co. (perfumers) (no inf.) 471½ W. 3d

Alexander & Green (Henry M. Alexander, John J. McCook, Charles B. Alexander, William C. Gulliver & William W. Green) 120 B'way

Alexander & Hanover (dissolved) 115 Spring

Alexander & Levy (Gilbert Alexander & Abraham Levy) 413 Broome

Alexander & Lewin (dissolved) 709 B'way

Alexander & Vanderamissen (Otto Alexander & Gilbert Vanderamissen) 1356 & 1388 Third av.

Alexander & Wood (dissolved) 89 Nassau

Alexander-Rosenfeld Co. (Leopold Alexander, Pres.; Joseph Kepce, Sec.; further inf. unattainable) 88 Clinton

Alexandre F. & Sons (dissolved) 31 B'way

Alford C. G. & Co. (Charles G. Alford & Frederick G. Thornbury) 200 D'way

Alford & Berkele Co (Alonzo Alford, Pres.; Henry Berkele, Sec.; Jonathan G. Davenport, Treas. Capital $25,000. Directors: Alonzo Alford, Henry Berkele, Jonathan G. Davenport, William Calhoun, J. W. Wilson) 77 Chambers

WATER METERS, GAS ENGINES, | **NATIONAL METER CO.**
FOR PUMPING AND POWER. | 252 Broadway, N. Y.

ALF 7 ALT

Alford & Lucas (Henry G. Alford & William C. Lucas) 73 Nassau

Aliano Antonio & Brother (Antonio & Raphael Aliano) 95 Crosby & 23 Marion

Alkan & Fogel (Henry Alkan & Ilabe R. Fogel) 401 B'way

Allan, McIntosh & Co. (James Allan, Jessie McIntosh & James W. Shaw) 149 Eleventh av.

Allard & Sons (Jules & George & Fernand Allard) 804 Fifth av.

Allegretti Refrigerator Co. (William J. Dudley, propr.) 599 Sixth av, & 15 Thirteenth av.

Allen George E. & Co. (dissolved) 83 Leonard

Allen George M. & Co. (George M. Allen, no Co.) 192 Water

Allen Henry & Co. (Henry Allen & Edward L. Norton) 81 New

Allen Henry G., Co. (Henry G. Allen. Pres. Capital $100,000. Directors: Henry G. Allen, Jacob R. Casselberry) 789 B'way

Allen Paper Car Wheel Co. (Richard N. Allen, Pres.; John W. Doane, Treas.; Charles H Antes, Sec. Capital $1,250,000. Directors: James C. Beach, William F. Finhrer, Richard N. Allen, G. Lee Stout, Horace Porter, John E. Gillette, Samuel Elliott, John W. Doane, Frederick T. Brown) 81 D'way

Allen Portable Pneumatic Riveting Machine Co., (Hope & Allen, proprs.) 221 Rider av.

Allen Richard H. & Co. (Richard H. & Thomas H. & Harry & Thomas H. Allen jr.) 81 Broad

Allen William & Co. (William Allen, Albert S. Clement & Melville C. Robinson) 470 B'way

Allen William L. & Co. (William L. & Edwin L. Allen) 104 Warren

Allen B. F. & Co. (Benjamin F. Allen & William N. Janvier) 805 Canal

Allen G.W. & Co. (Albert R. Sies, only) 133 William

Allen J. & B. (John & Benjamin) 85 Thomas

Allen J. & Son (John & Charles D. Allen) 7 W. 33d

Allen J. C. & Co. (no inf.) 56 New

Allen P. & Son (Patrick & Thomas F. Allen) 89 South

Allen R. J., Son & Co. (Richard J. & Rowland D. Allen, no Co.) 28 Barclay

Allen R. M. & Co. (Robert M. Allen, no Co.) 35 Beaver

Allen W. L. & Co. (Winslow L. Allen, Co. refused) 654 Sixth av.

Allen Brothers (Thomas & Patrick J. Allen) 1278 Third av.

Allen & Brother (Elishu M. Allen & estate of Ethan Allen) 144 Duane

Allen & Co.(Ferdinand W. Hofele, receiver) 140 E. 41st

Allen & Dykman (Samuel Allen & August Dykman) 22 W. Houston

Allen & Stevens (Ira A. Allen & Henry E. Stevens) ft. W. 47th

Allen, Talmage & Allen (Horatio P. Allen, John B. Talmage & Augustus H. Allen) 320 D'way

Allentown Passenger Railway Co. (National Improvement Co., proprs.) 32 Nassau

Allerton & Co. (William H. Merritt, assignee) ft. E. 27th

Alles & Gretsch (William Alles & Louis Gretsch) 78 Murray

Alley & Rosenberg (Alexander B. Alley & George H. Rosenberg) 81 Grand

Alley, Dowd & Co. (William S. Alley & William B. Dowd :—special partners, Ferdinand T. Hopkins, N. Y., & Thomas H. Thomas, New Utrecht, N. Y. each $25,000 ; terminates 30th April, 1891) 70 D'way

Alliance Ins. Assn. (James Yereance, Pres.; Armstrong Multzie, Sec. Capital $200,000. Directors: Frederick H. Parson, Herman Mosenthal, E. R. Craft, John H. Rieger, Albert Willcox, James W. Barbour, Aaron Josephic, James Yereance, Edward H. Betts, James G. Alden, J. Q. A. Williamson, M. Tanenbaum, Charles H. Price, Cornelius DuBois, George H. Smith, W. E. Lowe, Robert H. Gordon, John T. Baker, Robert P. Lethbridge, R. Bleecker Rathbone, George H. Leonard) 32 Nassau

Allen Henry V. & Co. (Laurent H. & Louis S. Allen, & estate of Henry V. Allen) 788 B'way

Alling & Co. (William R. & John D. Alling) 170 B'way

Allison Charles & Co. (Charles Allison, Herbert J. Frost & George F. Allison) 202 Fulton

Allison George & Co. (George Allison & Edwin R. Butler) 209 Washn.

Allison & Hearn (Charles M. Hearn, only) 841 B'way

Allison & Wilson (Henry L. Allison & J. Willson Wilson) 16 W. 125th

Allison, Stilson & Smith (Andrew Allison, Henry J. Stilson & David P. Smith) 178 Seventh av.

Allman Mfg. Co. (refused) 80 Fifth av.

Allman & Welsh (dissolved) 394 G'wich

Allouez Mining Co. (William C. Stuart, Pres.; John R. Stanton, Sec. Capital $2,000,000. Directors: William C. Stuart, Albert S. Sworts, John Bantz, H. R. Treadwell, Leonard Lewisohn, Joseph K. Gay, John Stanton, Fred Smith, John H. Stanton, 76 Wall

Almirall & Co.(Joseph J. Almirall, George B. Jenkinson & Enrique Conill) 10 Cedar

Almy Frederick & Co. (dissolved) 53 Leonard

Almy H. S. & Co. (Harvey S. & George W. Almy) 42 Park pl & 27 Barclay

Almy & Sulzer (Edwin R. Almy & Alfred Sulzer) 1930 Third av. & 311 E. 127th

Alnor Henry & Son (Henry & Peter Alnor) 119 Ninth av.

Alonso G., Palacios & Co. (Geronimo Alonso, Manuel C. Palacios, no Co.) 27½ Whitehall

Alpaugh E. S. & Co. (Edward S. Alpaugh, no Co.) 20 Bloomfield, W. Washn. mkt

Alpers & Mott (Henry F. Alpers, James W. Mott & George W. Alpers) 65 Beaver & 20 Exchange pl.

Alpers & Swarthout (dissolved) 1 B'way

Alpha Glass & Metal Co. (William H. Bellamy, Pres.; William G. Richards, Sec.; James G. Pennyouick, Treas. Capital, $1,000,000. Directors: William H. Bellamy, Edward F. McCaskie, James G. Pennyouick, John T. Pennycook, William G. Richards) 67 D'way

Alps Cons. Mining Co. (Frederic Prentice, Pres.; Howell Smith, Sec. Capital, $10,000,000. Directors: Frederic Prentice, Howell Smith, William S. Williams, Miller A. Smith, Scoville C. Williams) 44 B'way

Alsberg, Picbes & Jacobson (Solomon Alsberg, Frederick Piebes, Siegmund Jacobson & John Piebes) 51 Greene

Alsfeld's Christian, Sons (Christian jr. & Henry & William Alsfeld) 235 Delancey

Alsing J. R., Co. (John Q. Preble, Pres.; Gustave F. Perrenoud, Sec.; Theodore W. Bayand, Treas. Capital $20,000. Directors: John Q. Preble, Gustave F. Perrenoud, Theodore W. Bayaud) 60 New

Althause S. B. & Co. (Samuel B. Althause, Elijah P. Leonard & Walton C. Althause) 161 Thompson

Altheimer & Hirsch (Ferdinand Altheimer & Lazarus Hirsch) 1070 Second av. & 5 Av. C

Altheimer & Nill (Joseph Altheimer & Conrad Nill) 110 Reade

Altman Summer Neckwear Co. (Solomon Denzer, Pres.; Ignatz Altman, Sec. Capital $15,000. Directors: Solomon Denzer, Ignatz Altman, Mayer Meyer) 481 B'way

EXCELSIOR BIRD FOOD. The recognized standard. The most reliable for your Canary. Use no other. Insist upon getting it.
Packed only by C. ROSENSTEIN & CO., 373 Washington Street, New York.

ALT 8 AME

Altman B. & Brother (Bernhard & Samuel Altman) 791 B'way
Altman B. & Co. (Benjamin Altman, no Co.) 361 Sixth av.
Altman & Co (dissolved) r 195 Rivington
Altmayer Brothers (Nathaniel & Abraham E. Altmayer) 317 Church
Altschul T. & Co. (Theodore & Rudolph Altschul) 58 College pl.
Alturas Sonora Mining Co. (Lewis Edwards, Pres.; Willoughby Weston, Treas.; Henry Weston, Sec. Capital, $2,000,000. Directors: Lewis Edwards, John C. Barron, J. Aug. Johnson, James Woolworth, Lester M. Clark, Willoughby Weston, William M. Lawrence) 50 Exchange pl.
Aluminium Product Co. (refused) 468 Cherry
Alva's Brazilian Blood Specific Co. (Antonio Escandon, Pres.; Gabriel Escandon, Sec. Capital, $300,000. Directors: Antonio Escandon, Thomas Braniff, Antonio Basagoiti) 5 Wall
Alvarez & Llopis (dissolved) 156 Front
Amateur Sportsman Co. (not inc., further inf. unattainable) 4 College pl.
Ambrun Mfg. Co. (Charles Ambrun, propr.) 3 E. 13th
Amend E. & B. (Eliza & Barbara) 2006 Third av.
Am. Accident Indemnity Assn. (Thomas A. Ireland, Pres.; Arthur M. Sanders, Treas.; Charles L. Tompkins, Sec. Directors: A. B. Garner, George E. Glines, Thomas A. Ireland, Alfred E. Paillard, Arthur M. Sanders, W. D. Stevens, Frederick A. Stokes, Charles L. Tompkins, A. G. Wheeler) 5 Beekman
Am. Accumulator & Traction Co. (James H. Lancaster, propr.) 171 B'way
Am. Acme Advertising Co. (Ernest A. Des Marets, propr.) 50 B'way
Am. Advertising Agency (C. A. Montgomery & Co. proprs.) 7 Murray
Am. Agnol & Pyrodene Paint Co. (Spencer H. Smith, Pres.; Andrew J. Robinson, Sec.; Henry Naylor, Treas. Directors: Spencer H. Smith, Andrew J. Robinson, Henry Naylor, W. M. Onderdonk, Thomas Griffiths, Charles H. Talbot, Charles V. Moore) 424 W. 15th
Am. Art Assn. (not inc.) (James F. Sutton, Thomas E. Kirby & R. Austin Robertson) 6 E. 23d
Am. Art Metal Works (Hamline Q. French, propr.) 235 Fifth av. & 154 W. 29th
Am. Art Plating Works (George Richter, propr.) 59 Duane
Am. Artistic Gold Stamping Co. (Basil D. Vassiliades, Pres.; Constantine Vassiliades, Sec. Capital, $20,000. Directors: Basil D. & Constantine Vassiliades, Edward & Louise Lagarde) 58 Church
Am. Assn. of Public Accountants (John Heins, Pres.; William H. Veysey, Sec.) 21 Nassau
Am. Automatic Spray Perfume Co. (J. Edgar Leaycraft, Pres.; William S. Gilbert, Sec.; George Gehe, Treas. Capital, $20,000. Directors: J. Edgar Leaycraft, William S. Gilbert, George Gehe) 45 B'way
Am. Automaton Weighing Machine Co. (Erastus Wiman, Pres.; Leroy W. Baldwin, Sec. Capital, $500,000. Directors: Erastus Wiman, Sherburne D. Eaton, E. Holbrook Cushman, Eugene H. Lewis, O. S. Wood) 283 B'way
Am. Axle & Wheel Co. (Edward P. Bullard, Pres.; Benjamin L. Amerman, Treas. Capital, $100,000. Directors: Edward P. Bullard, J. Nelson Harris, Benjamin L. Amerman, James Stewart, W. L. Amerman) 92 College pl. & 72 Warren
Am. Baking Co. (Sarah J. Ashton, propr.) 201 & 341 First av.
Am. Baking Co. (James W. Castle, propr.) 1526 First av, 1134 Second av. & 752 Tenth av.

Am. Baking Co. (William H. Hale, propr.) 66 New Chambers, 411 Grand, 74 Roosevelt & 2259 Third av.
Am. Baking Co. (George F. Harris, propr.) 577 Ninth av. & 624 & 645 Second av.
Am. Baking Co. (Louis Homrod, propr.) 726 Eleventh av.
Am. Baking Co. (Sidney H. Lewis, propr.) 502 Second av.
Am. Baking Co. (May & Riggius, proprs.) 43 Av. D
Am. Baking Co. (Nicholas J. Tonner, propr.) 634 Courtlandt av.
AM. BAKING CO. (LTD.) (Ephraim J. Jennings, Pres.; John C. Beatty, Treas.; Charles H. Dalrymple, Sec. Capital, $10,000; further inf. unattainable) office, 68 Wall street
Am. Baking Powder Co. (Edward A. Powers, Pres.; William E. Irving, Sec. Capital, $10,000. Directors: William E. Irving, Edward A. Powers) 231 Fulton
Am. Ballast Log Co. (Edward H. Hobbs, Pres.; James McCaldin, Sec Capital, $250,000. Directors: Edward H. Hobbs, James McCaldin) 79 Broad
Am. Bank Note Co. (James Macdonough, Pres.; Theodore H. Freeland, Sec. Trustees: James Macdonough, Augustus D. & Elliott F. Shepard, J. Touro Robertson, Theodore H. Freeland, John E. Currier, Jared K. Myers, Philcore C. Lounsbury, Timothy H. Porter, Joseph S. Stout, William J. Arkell, Edmund C. Converse, James B. Ford) 78 Trinity pl.
Am. Bankers' Assn. (Charles Parsons, Pres.; William B. Greene, Sec.; George F. Baker, Treas.) 128 B'way
Am. Beef & Provision Co. (Arthur Wagenfuhr, propr.) 271 W. 47th
Am. Belgian Lamp Co. (Guillaume Reusens, Pres.; Jules Dawans, Sec.; Alphonse de Braekeleer, Treas. Capital, $00,000. Directors: Guillaume Reusens, John Dawans, Alphonse de Braekeleer, Charles Mali, Louis C. Linderman) 31 Barclay & 36 Park pl.
Am. Bible Soc. (Enoch L. Fancher, Pres.; Edward W. Gilman, Alexander McLean & Albert S. Hunt, Secs.; William Foulke jr., Treas.) 5 Bible h.
Am. Bituminous Rock Co. (Ivan Prowattain, Pres.; John F. Reynolds, Sec. Capital, $1,000,000, further inf. unattainable) 45 B'way
Am. Box Machine Co. (John Warner, Pres., Benjamin Finlayson, Sec.; Alonzo A. Deforest, Treas. Capital, $50,000. Directors: John Warner, Alonzo A. Deforest, Horace Inman, Titus Sheard, George Campbell) 429 W. 13th
Am. Branch Assn. of the North Holland Herd Book (Pierson K. Sanford Pres.; Frederick H. Beach, Sec.) 6 Harrison
Am. Bronze Powder Mfg. Co. (Henry Ahlborn, Pres.; Lewis M. Livingston, Sec. Capital, $60,000. Directors: Henry & August Ahlborn, Lewis M. Livingston) 6 Murray
Am. Cable Railway Co. (George S. Fields, Pres.; Frank B. Spalding, Sec. Capital, $3,000,000. Trustees: George S. Field, James Tillinghast, George W. Slatson, Charles H. Williams, Duncan D. Parmly, Arthur F. Willmarth, Francis B. Stockbridge, Edward R. & Arthur M. Tinker) 90 Nassau
Am. Capsule Co. (John C. Lackner, propr.) 56 W. 30th
Am. Car & Equipment Co. (Joseph D. Mitchell, Pres.; Charles S. Maynard, Sec.; Oren B. Colton, Treas. Capital, $75,000. Directors: Joseph D. Mitchill, Montford P. Sayce, Oren B. Colton, George H. Humphreys, Charles S. Maynard) 10 Wall
Am. Carbonate Co. (August Mietz, Pres.; August C. Hassey, Treas. Capital, $300,000. Directors: August Mietz, August C. Hassey, Emil Rueff) 428 E. 10th
Am. Cash Railway Co. (refused) 185 Stewart bldg.

IDEN & CO., University Place, 9th to 10th Sts., N.Y. | **MANUFACTURERS OF GAS FIXTURES AND ELECTROLIERS**

AME 9 AME

Am. Cattle Trust (inf. unattainable) 10 Wall
Am. Citizen Co. (dissolved) 132 Nassau
Am. Clasp & Steel Co. (Max Adler, Pres.; Ferdinand S. M. Binn, Treas.; Sely I. Mayer Sec. Capital, $1,000. Trustees: Max Adler, Moritz Cohn, Ferdinand S. M. Binn) 27 Walker
Am. Clock & Salt Co. (H. Danzig & Co., proprs.) 472 B'way & 36 Crosby
Am. Coal Briquette Co. (Heinrich Conried, Pres.; Ralph A. Weill, Sec.; Carl Herrmann, Treas. Capital, $1,000,000. Directors: Heinrich Conried, Carl Herrmann, Ralph A. Weill) 120 B'way
Am. Coal Co. (William DeL. Walbridge, Pres.; George M. Bowlby, Sec. Capital, $1,500,000. Directors: James A. Alexander, Sidney Wintringham, Benjamin Williamson, R. Suydam Grant, Alber J. Akin, David Stewart, Alexander M. White, Joseph E. Gay, William De L. Walbridge) 1 B'way
Am. Cold Storage & Refrigerating Co. (dissolved) 45 B'way
Am. Collecting Agency (Herbert A. Lee, propr.) 245 B'way
Am. Colonization & Industrial Bureaus (Andrew J. Rogers, Pres.; S. Henry Gage, Treas.; George F. Smith, Sec. Capital, $500,000. Directors: Andrew J. Rogers, Violn H. Gilbert, Peter Davidson, S. Henry Gage, George E. Smith) 245 B'way
Am. Commercial Co. (no inf.) 394 G'wich
Am. Composition Fuel Co. (dissolved) 35 William
Am. Conduit & Construction Co. (dissolved) 12 Cortlandt
Am. Contracting & Dredging Co. (Henry D. Slaven, Pres.; James J. Phelan, Sec.; Eugene Kelly, Treas. Capital, $2,000,000. Directors: Henry D. Slaven, William H. Farrell, James J. Phelan, Eugene Kelly, Charles M. Fry, Lawrence Ward, John Barker) 45 Exchange pl.
Am. Co-operative Savings, Loan & Building Assn. (William G. Knox, Pres.; Frank P. Crasto, Sec.; William C. Handa. Treas. Directors: James W. Cravin, George Brettell, William E. Benjamin, Horatio L. Braynard, Ellson W. Hurd, Jacob Doornbos, Walter H. Wagstaff, Henry T. Zimmerman, Zachary T. Benson) 2254 Third av.
Am. Copper Mining Co. (Josiah C. Reiff, Pres.; Sanford H. Steele, Sec. Capital, $500,000; further inf. refused) 40 Wall
Am. Corn Co. (inf. unattainable) 53 B'way
Am. Corn Food Co. (Frederick A. Wichelman, propr.) 52 Vesey
Am. Corn Harvester Co. (dissolved) 132 Nassau
Am. Corset Works (Lewis Schiele & Co., proprs.) 390 B'way
Am. Cotton Goods Co. (Clarkson Cowl, Pres.; C. H. Cowl, Sec.; Felix A. Canova, Treas. Capital, $10,000. Directors: Clarkson Cowl, Felix A. Canova, C. H. Cowl, George H. Schanck, William F. Hall) 292 Church
Am. Cotton Oil Trust (inf. unattainable) 45 B'way
Am. Cotton Seed Co. (no inf.) 68 Cotton Ex.
Am. Cow Milker Co. (Ebenezer B. Woodward, Pres.; A. Walter Durand, Sec. Capital, $300,000. Trustees: Ebenezer B. Woodward, Albert A. & A. Walter Durand, Charles H. Williams) 174 Chambers
Am. Dental Mfg. Co. (Joshua A. Hanway, Pres.; Oliver B. Dawson, Sec. Capital, $50,000; further inf. refused) 1300 B'way & 611 W. 36th
Am. Desk Manufactory (Peter Kehr, propr.) 3 Beekman
Am. Development Co. (Charles F. Crocker, Pres.; Frank S. Douty, Sec.; Isaac E. Gates, Treas. Capital, $5,000,000; further inf. unattainable) 15 Broad
Am. Development Co. (J. Bartlett Cooke, Pres.; Frederick M. Stevens, Sec.; Charles Wendell, Treas. Capital, $300,000. Directors: G. B. F. Cooper, William A. Miner. Townsend Percy, L. H. Wilson, Charles Wendell, J. Bartlett Cooke) 45 B'way
Am. Diamond Rock Boring Co. (Charles H. Tompkins, Pres.; Lewis F. Dostelmann, Sec. Capital, $150,000. Directors: Charles H. Tompkins, Richard Pancoast, Martin T. McMahon) 16 Cortlandt
Am. Directory Publishing Co. (refused) 65 Duane
Am. District Telegraph Co. (Thomas T. Eckert, Pres.; Charles S. Shivler, Sec. Capital, $2,000,000. Directors: Thomas T. Eckert, Charles A. Tinker, D. N. Crouse, E. A. Drake, George T. Bliss, James W. Clendenin, W. G. Oakman, Thomas C. Platt. H. K. & W. C. Sheldon, J. J. Patterson, George J. & Edwin Gould) 195 B'way & 8 Dey
Am. Dock & Improvement Co. (J. Rogers Maxwell, Pres.; Samuel Knox, Sec.; John W. Watson, Treas. Capital, $3,000,000. Directors: J. Rogers Maxwell, Austin Corbin, Edward D. Adams, George F. Baker, Harris C. Fahnestock, Henry W. Maxwell, Henry Graves) 119 Liberty
Am. Dock & Trust Co. (Medad W. Stone, Pres.; Alonzo C. Husey, Sec.; Frederick H. Pouch, Treas. Capital, $1,000,000. Directors: Medad W. & Medad E. Stone, Alfred J. & Frederick H. Pouch, Alonzo C. Husey) 50 Cotton Ex.
Am. Drug Mills (Crampton Brothers, proprs.) 8 Rutgers pl.
Am. Electric Arms & Ammunition Co. (George B. Satterlee, Pres.; Edmund W. Keese, Sec. Capital, $1,000,000. Trustees: Charles H. Tompkins, Robert S. Walker, Samuel Russell, George B. Satterlee,) 42 B'way
Am. Electric Construction Co. (Ltd.) (inoperative) 115 B'way
Am. Electric Illuminating Co. (inf. unattainable) ft. E. 24th
Am. Electric Mfg. Co. (dissolved) 18 Cortlandt
Am. Electric Motor Co. (Jesse H. Lippincott, Pres.; George H. Fitzwilson, Sec.; Thomas R. Lombard, Treas. Capital, $1,000,000. Directors: Jesse H. Lippincott, Thomas R. Lombard, George H. Fitzwilson, George S. Evans, Orazio Lugo, Charles A. DeWitt, Albert C. Woodworth) 115 B'way
Am. Embroidering Co. (Capital $8,000; further inf. unattainable) no address
Am. Emigrant Co. (not inc.) (James C. Savery & George H. Warner) 30 State
Am. Employment Agency (D. Gabrielle Sweet, propr.) 152 Sixth av.
Am. Encaustic Tiling Co. (Ltd.) (Benedict Fischer, Pres.; William G. Flammer, Sec. Capital, $150,000. Directors: Benedict Fischer, William G. & Charles A. Flammer, George R. Lansing, David Underhill, John Hoge, Andrew Blum) 140 W. 23d
Am. Envelope Machine Co. (dissolved) 177 Pearl
Am. Equitable Loan & Accumulating Fund Assn. (dissolved) 80 B'way
Am. Exchange in Europe (in liquidation) 102 B'way
Am. Exchange National Bank (George S. Coe, Pres.; Edward Burns, Ca-hier; William Ives Washburn, Notary. Capital, $5,000,000. Directors: George S. Coe, William C. Langley, Josiah M. Fiske, Henry K. Sheldon, Samuel D. Babcock, W. Bayard Cutting, Frederick Billings, Tuhn T. Terry, Dumont Clarke, J. Rogers Maxwell, John Claflin) 128 B'way
Am. Export & Trading Co. (inf. unattainable) 5 Bowling gr.
Am. Express Co. (James C. Fargo, Pres.; John N. Knapp, Sec.; Charles G. Clark, Treas. Capital, $18,000,000. Directors: James C. Fargo, John N. Knapp, Charles G. Clark, Theodore M. Pomeroy, Charles Fargo, Johnston Livingston, Edward B. Judson, Benjamin P. Cheney, William H. Seward) 65 B'way

CIRCULARS ADDRESSED TO ANY TRADE IN THE U. S. { Facilities
PROMPT, CAREFUL WORK } **THE TROW CITY DIRECTORY CO.,** { Unequalled.
AT MODERATE PRICES. } **11 University Place.**

AME   10   AME

Am. Facing Co, (Whitehead Brothers, proprs.) 515 W. 15th

Am. Family Library Assn. (not inc.; further inf. unattainable) 66 W. 23d

Am. Filtering Press Co. (Thomas Gaunt, propr.) 115 B'way

Am. Finance Co. (in liquidation) 96 B'way

Am. Fine Arts Soc. (Howard Russell Butler, Pres.; Charles R. Lamb, Treas.; Henry J. Hardenbergh, Sec. Capital, $50,000. Trustees: Howard Russell Butler, Frederic Crowninshield, Charles R. Lamb, Henry J. Hardenbergh, Daniel C. French, Horace Bradley, Louis C. Tiffany, Edward H. Kendall, Francis C. Jones, Edwin Howland Blashfield, Chester Loomis, J. Harrison Mills, Charles Broughton) 47 W. 42d

Am. Fire Ins. Co. (David Adee, Pres.; William H. Crolius, Sec. Capital, $400,000. Directors: David Adee, Le Grand B. Cannon, Robert W. Rodman, Thomas S. Young, James R. Taylor, Allan Hay, James H. Frothingham, Henry G. Marquand, John T. Terry, Henry Day, Frederick W. Downer, J. Hugh Peters, John F. Praeger, Alexander E. Orr, A. A. Low, Franklin Woodruff, Charles A. Davison, Jacob D. Vermilye, Osgood Welsh, John Sinclair) 146 B'way

Am. Forcite Powder Mfg. Co. (Hector de Castro, Pres.; William P. Ferguson, Sec. Capital, $300,000. Directors: Hector de Castro, William P. Ferguson) 1 B'way

Am. Gas Pressure Regulator Co. (William F. Widmayer, Pres.; Samuel J. Young, Sec. Capital, $30,000. Directors: William F. Widmayer, Bloomfield Brower, S. A. Beatty, Samuel J. Young) 1486 B'way

Am. Grain Ceiling Co. (McCaldin Brothers, proprs.) 79 Broad

Am. Grocer Publishing Assn. (Frank N. Barrett, Pres.; Erastus N. Root, Sec. Capital, $40,000. Directors: Francis B. & Horace K. Thurber, Albert E. Whyland, Frank N. Barrett, Erastus N. Root) 143 Chambers

Am. Guaranty Co (Ltd) (Thomas A. Ireland, Pres.; Charles L. Tompkins, Sec.; G. H. Kerr, Treas. Directors: Thomas A. Ireland, C. A. Grasselli, Charles L. Tompkins, G. H. Kerr, W. D. Stevens) 5 Beekman

Am. Hand-Sewed Shoe Co. (William B. Taylor, Pres.; Willets A. Eldridge, Sec. Capital $100,000. Trustees: William B. Taylor, Henry C. Wilson, Martin S. Shueffer, Willett A. Eldridge) 72 Reade

Am. Hard Rubber Co. (Fritz Achelis, Pres.; William W. Weitling, Sec.; Charles A. Hoyt. Treas. Capital, $400,000. Directors: Fritz Achelis, William W. Weitling, Charles A. Hoyt) 9 Mercer

Am. Hat Co. (N. Humbert & Co. proprs.) 239 Bowery

Am. Hoop Co. (dissolved) 200 Lewis

Am. Horse Exchange (Ltd.) (William K. Vanderbilt, Pres.; Frederic Bronson, Treas. Capital, $140,000. Directors: William K. Vanderbilt, Frederic Bronson, William Jay, Edward Lamontagne, James G. K. Lawrence, Frederick W. Vanderbilt, George Peabody Wetmore) 1694 B'way

Am. Horse Protector Co. (William H. Tregu, Pres.; William W. Tucker, Sec. Capital, $250,000 Directors: William H. Tregu, C. O. Lundberg, William W. Tucker, Edwin A. Taft, Gustavus St. Gem) 430 W. 14th

Am. Institute (J. Trumbull Smith, Pres.; James G. Powers, Sec.; Edward Schell, Treas. Trustees: Thomas Rutter, James Delamater, J. Trumbull Smith, Edward Schell, Charles McK. Leoser, William H. Gedney, Charles F. Allen, Walter Shriver, James G. Powers, Zachariah Dederick, William A. Camp, Alexander Knox) 19 Astor pl.

Am. Institute of Architects (Richard M. Hunt, Pres.; John W. Root, Sec.; Samuel A. Treat, Treas.) 18 B'way

Am. Institute of Electrical Engineers (Elihu Thomson, Pres.; Ralph W. Pope, Sec.; George M. Phelps, Treas.) 5 Beekman

Am. Institute of Mining Engineers (Richard Pearce, Pres.; Rossiter W. Raymond, Sec.; Theodore D. Rand, Treas.) 19 Burling sl.

Am. Insulator Co. (Daniel S. Roberson, Pres.; Henry C. Andrews, Sec. Capital, $120,000. Trustees: Daniel S. Robeson, Charles A. Edwards, Henry C. Andrews) 2 Wall

Am. Investment Co. (Charles V. Culver, Pres.; Walter R. Eaton, Sec.; John A. Bagley, Treas.; further inf. unattainable) 45 B'way

Am. Investment & Financial Co. (William A. Clark, Pres.; Clarence L. Healy, Sec. Capital, $100,000. Directors: William A. Clark, Clarence L. Healy) 45 B'way

Am. Jersey Cattle Club (Frederic Bronson, Pres.; Frederick W. Wicks, Sec.; John I. Holly, Treas. Directors: Edward Austen, Edward Burnett, George Cromwell, Walter J. G. Dean, George W. Farlee, Charles E. Hill, Herbert M. Howe, Matthew Mahorner, Archer N. Martin, J. J. Richardson, Rufus A. Sibley) 1 B'way

Am. Jockey Club (dissolved) 1 W. 25th

Am. Kindergarten Soc. (Emily M. Coe, Pres.; Emily D. Elton, Sec.; Sarah M. Story, Treas.) 87 W. 23d

Am. Laundry Co. (Wallach & Cohen, proprs.) 106 Seventh av., 200 W. 14th & 408 Sixth av.

Am. Lead Pencil Co. (Louis J. Reckendorfer, Pres.; Samuel J. Reckendorfer, Sec.; William Strauss, Treas. Capital, $252,000. Directors: Louis J. & Samuel J. Reckendorfer, William Strauss, Byron B. & Gustavus A. Goldsmith, James H. Hoffman) 50 Howard

Am. Leather Link Belt Co. (Charles A. Schieren, Pres.; G. H. Fisher, Sec.; Frederick A. M. Burrell, Treas. Capital, $25,000. Directors: Charles A. Schieren, G. H. Fisher, Frederick A. M. Burrell, Henry Bramm) 72 Cliff

Am. Legal Aid Soc. (no inf.) 599 B'way

Am. Linoleum Mfg. Co. (Joseph Wild, Pres.; Elijah Bliss, Sec.; John Cartledge, Treas. Capital, $450,000. Trustees: Joseph Wild, John Cartledge, Joseph A. Dean, Henry MacKay, John Cartlaige jr.) 82 Worth

Am. Literary Agency (dissolved) 82 Nassau

Am. Lithographer & Printer Co. (Frederick Buehring, Pres.; Theodore Buehring, Treas. Capital, $2,500; further inf. unattainable) 87 City Hall pl.

Am Lithographing Co. (George Krements, propr.) 20 Desbrosses

Am. Live Stock Express Co. (N. Y. & Ohio Railway Co., proprs.) 45 B'way

Am. Loan & Trust Co. (Octavius D. Baldwin, Pres.; James S. Thurston, Sec. Capital, $1,000,000. Directors: John L. Macauley, George S. Hart, Wallace C. Andrews, John I. Blair, William P. Anderson, Jules Aldige, John D. Kimmey, Charles Parsons, George A. Evans, Benjamin F. Tracy, Granville P. Hawes, James S. Thurston, John S. Silver, Thomas F. Goodrich, Payson Merrill, Homan Clark, George P. Slade, Thomas C. Platt, Octavius D. Baldwin) 113 B'way

Am. Lumber Co. of N. J. (George M. Grant, Pres.; J. Ralston Grant, Sec. Capital, $30,000. Directors: George M. & Charles B. & J. Ralston Grant) 55 Liberty & ft. W. 21st

Am. Machine Telegraph Co. (inf. unattainable) 5 Dey

Am. Machinist Publishing Co. (Horace B. Miller, Pres.; Lycurgus B. Moore, Sec. Capital, $50,000. Directors: Horace B. Miller, Lycurgus B. Moore) 96 Fulton

THE CALIGRAPH WRITING MACHINE,
HARTFORD, CONN.

Am. Manufacturers' Agency (John C. Geddes, propr.) 10 E. 14th

Am. Mfg. Co. (bagging) (David Nevins, Pres.; John D. Filley, Treas.; Appleton Sturgis, Sec. Capital, $1,944,000. Directors: David Nevins, Anderson Gratz, John D. Filley, Appleton Sturgis, Henry C. Nevins, James S. Murdoch, Benjamin B. Graham, Joel Wood) 15 Exchange pl.

Am. Mfg. Co. (umbrella matls.) (Asher T. Meyer, Pres.; Theodore A. Meyer, Sec. Capital, $50,000; further inf. refused) 713 E. 13th

Am. Mfg. Co. (Ltd.) (James H. Patterson, Pres.; H. W. Morford, Sec. Capital, $15,000; further inf. unattainable) 39 Dey

Am. Mfg. & Supply Co. (Ltd.) (dissolved) 10 Dey

Am. Mattress & Cushion Co. (H. Alfred Freeman, Pres.; Carl A. Sautter, Sec.; Nicholas P. Todd, Treas. Capital, $20,000. Directors: H. Alfred Freeman, Carl A. Sautter, Nicholas P. Todd) 100 Duane

Am. Meat Co. (no inf.) 45 B'way

Am. Mechanical Toy Co. (Leo Schlesinger & Co. proprs.) 129 Crosby

Am. Medical Digest Publishing Co. (Thomson P. McElrath, Pres.; P. F. McBreen, Sec.; Owen McBreen, Treas. Capital, $10,000. Trustees: Thomson P. McElrath, Howard Campbell, Owen & P. F. McBreen) 19 Park pl.

Am. Medical Preparation Co. (Ltd.) (F. M. F. Cazin, Pres.; M. E. Cazin, Treas.; further inf. refused) 7 Pearl

Am. Mercantile & Collection Assn. (Frederick H. Lawrence, Pres.; William Y. Kelly, Sec.; Henry C. Tallman, Treas. Capital, $30,000. Directors: Frederick H. Lawrence, Henry C. Tallman, William Y. Kelly) 234 B'way

Am. Metal Co. (Ltd.) (Jacob Langeloth, Pres.; Julius Goldmin, Sec.; Berthold Hochschild, Treas. Capital, $200,000. Directors: Jacob Langeloth, Julius Goldman, Berthold Hochschild) 80 Wall

Am. Meter Co. (George J. McGourkey, Pres.; William H. Down, Sec.; William N. Milstead, Treas. Directors: George J. McGourkey, William H. McFadden, William N. Milstead, William H. Down, Paul S. Merrifield, Thomas C. Hopper, Henry B. Cartwright) 512 W. 22d & 242 Sixth av.

Am. Midland R.R. Co. (William Thorpe, Pres.; George W. Ettenger, Sec. Capital, $5,000,000. Directors: William Thorpe, George W. Ettenger, Cornelius Fellowes, Davis Johnson, William A. Armstrong, Andrew A. Furman, H. E. McClure) 42 New

Am. Mining & Milling Co. (Silas B. Dutcher, Pres.; Winfield Bloodgood, Sec.; William C. McKean, Treas. Capital, $500,000. Trustees: Silas B. Dutcher, William C. McKean, Winfield Bloodgood, Jacob Ruppert, Frederick C. Linde, Mark K. Hamilton, Thomas Girvan) 11 Pine

Am. Missionary Assn. (William M. Taylor, Pres.; Michael E. Strieby, Sec.; Henry W. Hubbard, Treas. Directors: John H. Washburn, Addison P. Foster, J. E. Rankin, William H. Ward, J. W. Cooper, Edmond L. Champlin, Lyman Abbott, Charles A. Hull, Albert J. Lyman, Clinton B. Fisk, S.D. Halliday, Samuel Holmes, Samuel S. Marples, Charles L. Mead, Elbert D. Monroe) 56 Reade

Am. Mixed Paint Co. (Davidson & Knowles Co. proprs.) 180 Cherry

Am. Morocco Case Co. (not inc.) (Theodore G. Walpuski, Christian Rosberg & Theodore Kralt) 9 Bond

Am. Musician Publishing Co. (Horatio C. King, Pres.; J. Travis Quigg, Sec. Capital, $10,000. Directors: Horatio C. King, Stephen Fisko, J. Travis Quigg) 835 B'way

Am. Mutual Register Co. (Inf. unattainable) 24 Park pl.

Am. Net & Twine Co. (James S. Shepard, Pres.; Ivers W. Adams, Treas. Capital, $350,000; further inf. refused) 109 Fulton

Am. News Co. (Henry Dexter, Pres.; Charles K. Willmer, Sec.; Solomon W. Johnson, Treas. Directors: Henry Dexter, Solomon W. Johnson, Patrick Farrelly, William D. Dancker, Samuel S. Blood, Henry Taylor, Charles K. Willmer, Joseph E. Merrill, Stephen Farrelly, George I. Tyson, William H. Williams, Joseph A. Marsh) 39 Chambers

Am. Newspaper Advertising Co. (Ltd.) (George P. Rowell, Pres.; Oscar G. Moses, Sec.; further inf. refused) 10 Spruce

Am. Newspaper Publishers' Assn. (James W. Scott, Pres.; Robert H. Campe, Sec.; William M. Laffan, Treas.) 88 Park row

Am. Novelty Co. (Jebens & Co. proprs.) 287 S. 5th av.

Am. Oil Co. (Inf. unattainable) 45 B'way

Am. Ottoman & Hassock Co. (William B. Shaw, propr.) 119 Leonard

Am. Paper Bottle Co. (J. H. Cannon, Pres.; C. S. Osborn, Sec.; W. E. Smith, Treas. Trustees: J. H. Cannon, J. P. Whitney, R. J. Dean, W. E. Smith, E. Faber, A. DeCastro, W. H. Duckworth, Milo M. Belding, C. S. Osborn) 22 Church

Am. Paper Pail & Box Co. (Isidor Tahl, Pres.; Adolph S. Stiefel, Sec. Capital, $20,000. Directors: Isidor Tahl, Adolph S. Stiefel, Jacob W. Schwarts, Louis Schlesinger) 21 Rose

Am. Passimetre Co. (C. Ross Grubb, Pres.; Otto T. Bannard, Sec. Capital, $10,000. Trustees: C. Ross Grubb, Edward A. Bradford, Otto T. Bannard) 130 Worth

Am. Patent Agency (O. J. Bailey & Co. proprs.) 203 B'way

Am. Patent Portable House Mfg. Co. (Charles D. Leverich, Pres.; Walter H. Clarke, Sec. Capital, $50,000. Directors: Charles D. Leverich, Benjamin W. Strong, Walter H. Clarke, Earl Lee, George E. Gunvan) 48 Wall

Am. Pearl Works (F. J. Kaklenberg Co. proprs.) 210 E. 33d, 125 Fulton & 6 Astor h.

Am. Photo-Engraving Co. (William M. Fowler, Pres.; Russell D. Davis, Sec. Capital, $30,000. Directors: William M. Fowler, Russell D. Davis, Benjamin F. White) 15 Vandewater

Am. Photo-Lithographic Co. (Vincent M. Wilcox, Pres.; Frederick A. Anthony, Sec. Capital, $30,000. Director: Vincent M. Wilcox, Frederick A. & Richard A. Anthony) 591 B'way

Am. Pig Iron Storage Warrant Co. (George H. Hall, Pres.; John J. McCook, Sec.; Logan C. Murray, Treas. Capital, $1,500,000. Directors: George H. Hall, William Libbey, Logan C. Murray, Edward P. Thompson, John H. Inman, Eckstein Norton, John D. Probst, H. O. Armour, Thomas Rutter, John J. McCook, George F. Tyler, Morton McMichael, George T. Barns, Samuel R. Shipley, Enoch Ensley) 44 Wall

Am. Pin Co. (Theodore I. Driggs, Pres.; George A. Driggs, Sec. Capital, $100,000. Directors: Theodore I. Driggs, A. S. Chase, Chandler N. Weyland, J. S. Elton, H. H. Peck, F. J. Brown, F. D. Burnham) 214 Church

Am. Plate & Window Glass Co. (Henry W. Foote, propr.) 158 S. 5th av.

Am. Plush Ball Co. (Max Silberstein, propr.) 259 Canal

Am. Pneumatic Tool Co. (James S. MacCoy, Pres.; Charles A. Harvey, Treas.; N. P. T. Finch, Sec. Capital, $1,000,000. Directors: Frank H. Marsh, R. H. Ward, William H. Mailler, Andrew J. Macaulay, E. N. Foss, James S. MacCoy, Edward J. Berwind) 431 Eleventh av.

Am. Portrait Co. (Nathan Arnow, propr.) 18 Bible h.

SPECIAL ATTENTION PAID TO THIS CLASS OF WORK. **BANKERS' & BROKERS' CIRCULARS DELIVERED** **THE TROW CITY DIRECTORY CO. 11 University Place.**

AME 12 AME

Am. Press Assn. (Orlando J. Smith, Pres.; George W. Cummings, Sec. Capital, $800,000. Directors: Orlando J. Smith, George W. Cummings, F. K. Tracy, Paul Wilcox, W. S. Cappeller) 84 Vesey

Am. Press Information Bureau (George H. Spring, propr.) 52 John

Am. Pressed Tan Bark Co. (Asahel G. Darwin, Pres.; James C. Beach, Sec. Capital, $1,000,000. Directors: Asahel G. Darwin, James C. & Samuel H. Beach, James L. Hill, Henry W. Guernsey) 45 B'way

Am. Printing Co. (Singer & Co., proprs.) 206 Rivington

Am. Private Line Telephone Co. (George Gehe, Pres.; George T. Fox, Sec. Capital, $20,000. Directors: George Gehe, George T. Fox) 45 B'way

Am. Protective Tariff League (Edward H. Ammidown, Pres.; Henry M. Hoyt, Sec.; Chester Griswold, Treas.) 23 W. 23d

Am. Publishing Co. (Elisabeth B. Grannis, propr.) 53 E. 23d

Am. Publishing Co. (Gaylord Watson, propr.) 273 Pearl

Am. Publishing & Engraving Co. (inf. unattainable) 102 Chambers

Am. Pulverizer Co. (William M. Fuller, propr.) 171 B'way

Am. Rack Co. (dissolved) 18 Chambers

Am. Railway Equipment Co. (Osmer S. Barr, Pres.; Thomas R. White jr., Sec; A. S. Hatch, Treas. Capital, $1,000,000. Directors: Osmer S. Burr, A. S. Hatch, Thomas R. White jr., William Fullerton, Herbert S. Ogden, O. S. Stearns, George G. Saxe) 15 Cortlandt

Am. Railway Equipment Co. (Ltd.) (John S. Cameron, Pres.; O. Chandler Wells, Sec.; Charles A. Coutant, Treas. Capital, $10,000. Directors: John S. Cameron, O. Chandler Wells, Charles A. Coutant, Charles N. Morgan, C. C. Coe) 66 John

Am. Railway Publi-hing Co. (Emerson P. Harris, Pres.; Sherman J. Clark, Sec. Capital, $30,000. Directors: Emerson P. Harris, Mary S. Miles, Sherman J. Clark, Mrs. Sherman J. Clark, Mrs. Emerson P. Harry) 113 Liberty

Am. Rolling Stock Co. (inf. unattainable) 120 B'way

Am. Safe Co. (Willis B. Marvin, Pres.; Wright D. Pownall, Sec. Capital, $50,000. Trustees: Willis B. Marvin, Frank S. Pownall, Robert M. Hunting) 90 S. 5th av. & 205 B'way

Am. Safe Deposit Co. (Charles F. Cox, Pres.; Russell Raymond, Sec. Capital, $800,000. Trustees: Charles F. Cox, Russell Raymond, Alfred Skitt, Edward V. W. Rossiter, John B. Dutcher, William H. Paulding, John Carstensen, Francis S. Smithers, James Macdonough, John R. Brady, Augustus D. Shepard, William Irwin, E. H. Goodwin) 501 Fifth av.

Am. Sample Card Co. (Harry Mayer, propr.) 434 B'way

Am. Savings Bank (Daniel T. Hoag, Pres.; William Irwin, Sec.; Clarence Goadby, Treas. Trustees: Daniel T. Hoag, William Irwin, John R. Brady, Henry E. Russell, William L. Skidmore, Loomis L White, Moses H. Moses, Samuel Hall, Vincent Fisck, Myer Heilman, Myer S. Isaacs, Henry T. Bronson, Caldwell H. Blakeman, Herman Mendel, Edward V. Loew, Granville D. Smith, Henry T. Webb, Russell Raymond, Fessenden N. Otis, Adrian A. Pottier, John H. Timmerman, David H. Rowland, Warner Van Norden, Joseph T. Decker, William N. Cromwell, Samuel H. Rathbone, L. Bolton Bangs, Clarence Goadby) 501 Fifth av.

Am. Saw Co. (C. Upham Ely, Pres.; Isaac F. Bissell, Sec.; Samuel W. Putnam, Treas. Capital, $100,000. Trustees: John B. Woodward, C. Upham Ely, Samuel W. Putnam, Robert B. Woodward, A. W. Kellogg, T. F. Cummings,

Adam Hill, Charles N. Kent, D. A. Loomis) 35 Dey

Am. School Bureau (Julia E. Avery, propr.) 2 W. 14th

Am. Shipmasters' Assn. (Theophylact B. Bleecker jr., Pres.; Walter R. T. Jones, Sec.; William H. Moore, Treas.) 57 William

Am. Shoe Mfg. Co. (Herbert A. Smith, propr.) 86 Broad

Am. Shooting Assn. (Charles W. Dimick, Pres.; Elliott Smith, Sec.; Solomon Tarck, Treas.) 280 B'way

Am. Sign Co. (James D. Farrell, propr.) 438 W. 40th

Am. Silk Label Mfg. Co. (not Inc.) (George & Mary Hoy & Rosa Hurd) 420 Broome & 1820 Vanderbilt av. E.

Am. Soc. of Civil Engineers (William P. Shinn, Pres.; John Bogart, Sec.; George S. Greene jr., Treas. Directors: Charles D. Brush, Theodore Voorhees, Robert Van Buren, William Ludlow, William G. Curtis) 127 E. 23d

Am. Soc. of Mechanical Engineers (Oberlin Smith, Pres.; Frederick R. Hutton, Sec.; William H. Wiley, Treas.) 64 Madison av.

Am. Special Machine Co. (Ltd.) (Titus Sheard, Pres.; John H. Seed, Sec. Capital, $100,000. Directors: Titus Sheard, John H. Seed, William H. Boyer, Dennis Sweeney, John Warner, A. A. De Forest, Zerah S. Westbrook) 83 Reade

Am. Specialty Co. (refused) 192 Fifth av.

Am. Spiral Spring Butt Hinge Mfg. Co. (Capital, $100,000. Trustees: Cornelius S. Vanwagoner, William H. Williams; further inf. unattainable) 82 Beekman

Am. Stained Glass Works (Louis Borel, propr.) 1114 Park av

Am. Standard Ordnance Co. (no inf.) 10 Whitehall

Am. Star Capsule Works (no inf.) 54 Grove

Am. Steam Boiler Ins. Co. (William K. Lothrop, Pres.; Vincent R. Schenck, Sec.; R. K. Sheldon, Treas. Capital, $500,000. Directors: William K. Lothrop, Felix Campbell, George P. Sheldon, William Brinckerhoff, John H. Flagler, Edward E. Gedney, William R. Jackson. Albion K. Bolan, Edward H. Apgar, D. R. Satterlee, John M. Talbot, William K. Midgley, R. K. Sheldon, Vincent R. Schenck, Thomas F. Powers) 120 B'way & 79 John

Am. Steamship Co. (no inf.) 115 B'way

Am. Steel Barge Co. (Colgate Hoyt, Pres.; Charles W. Wetmore, Sec.; further inf. unattainable) 36 Wall

Am. Stone Co. (no inf.) 38 B'way

Am. Store Stool Co. (Angus L. Dobo, Pres.; Lois E. Bobo, Sec.; Albert E. Bobo, Treas. Capital, $25,000. Directors: Angus L. & Lois E. & Albert E. Bobo) 25 Howard

Am. Surety Co. (William L. Trenholm, Pres.; Frederick F. Nugent, Sec.; Samuel S. Colville, Treas. Capital, $1,000,000. Trustees: William A. Wheelock, Frederick W. Vanderbilt, William H. Leonard, John Jay Knox, Cornelius N. Bliss, Henry H. Cook, William B. Kendall, John A. McCall, John H. Inman, Henry B. Plant, Thomas C. Platt, George M. Pullman, William Dowd, Henry D. Welsh, John C. Bullitt, Charles J. Harrah, Jesse Spalding, Daniel M. Fox, John de Koven, Thomas S. Kirkwood, John N. Hutchinson, Robert Pitcairn, George S. Drake, Carlos S. Greeley, J. P. Spaulding, George W. Blabon, Charles F. Berwind, Daniel W. Caldwell, W. G. Deshler, Patrick Barry, G. P. Pomroy, George B. Sloane, Joshua D. Ripley, Ebenezer K. Sibley, Edward F. Browning, Charles L. Tiffany, James W. Pinchot, George F. Victor, Locke W. Winchester, Walter S. Gurnee, James A. Hayden, John J. McCook, M. W. Cooper, William L. Trenholm, Joel B. Erhardt, Walter S. Johnston, Charles H. Ludington, George S. Edgell, Edward N. Gibbs, Henry D. Lyman) 160 B'way

FOR THE BEST CO-PARTNERSHIP IN THE BEST CORPORATION SEE PAGE F IN BACK OF BOOK

Am. Swedenborg Printing & Publishing Soc. (Joseph K. Smyth, Pres.; Francis J. Worcester, Sec.; Mordaunt Bodine, Treas. Capital, $60,000. Managers; Joseph K. Smyth, G. W. Colton. Charles H. Mann, John Bigelow, Edwin A. Gibbens, Marston Niles, William C. Church, John Ellis, Daniel Pomeroy, Francis J. Worcester, Frank Curtis, John Sly, William A. Ilea, Mordaunt Bodine, Samuel S. Seward, Alexander J. Auchterlonie) 20 Cooper Union

Am. Tea & Coffee Co. (Charles Lutz & Co, proprs.) 155 First av.

Am. Telegraph & Cable Co. (Thomas T. Eckert. Pres.; Thomas F. Clark, Sec.; Roswell H. Rochester, Treas. Capital, $14,000,000. Directors; Jay Gould, Russell Sage, John T. Terry; Frederick L. Ames, Thomas T. Eckert) 195 B'way

Am. Telephone & Telegraph Co. (John E. Hudson, Pres.; Melville Egleston, Sec.; William R. Driver, Treas. Capital, $5,000,000. Directors; John E. Hudson, Howard Stockton, Charles P. Bowditch, Theodore N. Vail, Joseph P. Davis, William H. Forbes, Edward J. Hall jr.) 18 Cortlandt

Am. Temperance Life Ins. Assn. (George Merrill, Pres.; Frank Delano, Sec. Directors; George Merrill, Frank Delano, W. H. W. Young, John R. Stephenson, James H. Pettit, A. G. Mabee, Everett J. Esselstyn, Benjamin F. Coggwell, W. G. Ford jr.) 187 B'way

Am. Tin Mining Co. (Louis F. Payn, Pres.; Charles E. Cornell, Sec. Capital, $2,000,000; further inf. unattainable) 63 B'way

Am. Tontine Investment Union (Andrew S. Brownell, Pres.; Frank J. Havens, Sec. Directors; Andrew S. Brownell, J. Trumbull Smith, John C. Barnes, Joseph S. Case, Seth D. French, Charles C. Knowlton, George H. Sheldon, Frank C Havens, William H. Lyon jr., George A. Sterling, Edwin K. Martin, William H. Chickering, R. U. Hardeman, Paul Romarn, Martin F. Amorous, Charles C. Collier, J. Wesley Smith, John Parnas, William K. Bellis, James H. Smith, Lewis Hopicote, George D. Eldridge, John J. Harrison, Harmon Bell, Barry Baldwin, Charles K. Fish, George T. Hawley, Sidney M. Smith, Warren B. English, Edwin P. Danforth, William H. Bailey, H. M. Russell, D. McFarland J. V. Wachtel, Walton G. Hughes, W. B. Shaut, E. M. Arthur, George P. Frank, D. D. Oliphant, Frank M. Warren, Lewis Russell, John H. McGraw, H. G. Struve, George B. Adair, Lester Turner, J. S. Howell, W. J, Fife, Oscar Nuhn) 280 B'way

Am. Tontine Savings Union (dissolved) 280 B'way

Am. Tool Co. (John H. Patrick, Pres.; Richard Patrick 2d, Sec. Capital, $50,000; further inf. unattainable) 200 W. Houston

Am. Tract Soc. (William Strong, Pres.; John M. Stevenson, Sec.; Louis Tag. Asst. Treas. Executive Committee; John Hall, Amadeus A. Reinke, William M. Taylor, Talbot W. Chambers, L. W. Bancroft, Henry M. Sanders, William N. Blakeman, Titus B. Meigs, William A. Cauldwell, William S. Sloan, John P. Anderson, John N. Stearns, Caleb B. Knevals, Peter Donald, Wager Swayne. Roswell Smith, William M. Isaacs, William A. Wheelock) 150 Nassau

Am. Trading Co. (Frank E. Morgan, Pres.; George H. Mitchell, Sec.; William H. Stevens, Treas.; Capital, $250,000. Directors; Frank E. Morgan, James R. Morse, George H. Mitchell, A. Fuller Atkins, William H. Stevens) 184 Front

Am. Trading Soc. (Ltd.) (A. J. R. Landauer, Pres.; Frederick Vanriper, Sec.; Charles C. Cox, Treas. Capital, $200,000. Directors; Louis Rancur, A. J. R. Landauer, Simon Fatman, Charles C. Cox, Frederick Vanriper) 19 William

Am. Transit Co. (no inf.) Pier 6 N. R.

Am. Tube & Iron Co. (James Young, Pres.; Alvy W. Momeyer, Sec. Capital, $1,000,000. Directors; James Young, George Matheson, Alvy W. Momeyer, John J. Spowers, Adam S. Matheson) 98 John

Am. Ultramarine Works (Heller & Merz Co. proprs.) 55 Maiden ln.

Am. Uniform Time Co. (dissolved) 45 B'way

Am. Veterinary College (Faneuil D. Weisse, Pres.; William J. Coates, Sec.; H. A. Weeks, Treas. Directors; Faneuil D. Weisse, F. F. Vandervoer, F. Leroy Satterlee, Daniel M. Stinson, Samuel Marsh, George B. Satterlee, S. D. Ward, George A. Peters, Hamilton Bushey, H. A. Weeks, James W. Husted, James Stillman) 141 W. 54th

Am. Veterinary Hospital (Am. Veterinary College, proprs.) 141 W. 54th

Am. Vintage Co. (Tyson & Totton, proprs.) 24 Dey

Am. Watch Club Agency (Adolph Hass, propr.) 12 Maiden ln.

Am. Water Color Soc. (John G. Brown, Pres.; C. Harry Eaton, Sec.; James Symington, Treas.) 51 W. 10th

Am. White Metal Works (George D. Mackey, propr.) 64 Gold

Am. Window Ventilating Co. (Henry Wilson, Pres.; James W. McKinnon, Sec.; Thomas J. Wilson, Treas. Capital, $50,000. Directors; Henry Wilson, George H. Gaston. Thomas J. Wilson, James W. McKinnon, Frederick S. Morison) 335 B'way

Am. Wine Co. (Max J. Porges, propr.) 208 Canal & 36 Rivington

Am. Wood Powder Co. (Elliot Smith, Pres.; Edmund C. Stanton, Sec. Capital, $15,000. Trustees; Elliot Smith, Edmund C. Stanton, Paul L. Thebaud) 59 Wall

Am. Woodenware Co. (William J. Iles, Pres.; James F. Totman, Sec.; William P. Sandford, Treas.; further inf. unattainable) 93 Murray

Am. Writing Machine Co. (Hartford, Ct.) (see top lines)

Am. Zylonite Co. (Emil Kipper, Pres.; George V. A. Conger, Sec.; S. Warren Ingalls, Treas. Capital, $750,000. Directors; Levi L. Brown, Henry O. Hulbert, Charles A. Denny, James Renfrew jr., Joseph H. Smith, William L. Brown, Emil Kipper, S. Warren Ingalls, Edward F, Ingersoll, Thomas A. Mole) 561 B'way

Am. & Foreign Electrotype Agency (Estes & Lauriat, proprs.) 334 B'way

Am. & Foreign Teachers' Agency (Margaret J. Young-Fulton, propr.) 23 Union sq. W.

Americus Silver Mining Co. (Anson P. K. Safford, Pres.; Henry Bradstreet. Sec. Capital, $2,000,000; further inf. unattainable) 115 B'way

Amerman & Ford (Richard Amerman & Francis W, Ford) 8 James

Amerman & Patterson (William H. Amerman & Arthur W. Patterson) 68 Beaver & 50 Jay

Ames Daniel T. & Sons (Daniel T. & George J. Ames, only) 202 B'way

Ames & Co. (Caleb T. & Frank D. Ames & J. Elmer Briggs) 109 W. 34th & 201 W. 108d

Ames & Frost (no inf.) 166 Monroe

Amies Publishing Co. (in liquidation) 17 Murray

Ammermann Brothers (no inf.) 105 W. Houston

Ammidown & Smith (Edward H. Ammidown & Albert D. Smith) 58 Worth

Ammon & Blood (dissolved) 45 B'way

Ammunition Manufacturers' Assn. (Augustus Gaylord, commissioner) 138 Temple ct.

Amo, Perez & Co. (Jose M. Amo, Silverio Perez & Estanislao Ortiz) 213 Pearl

Amon's N., Son (George M. Amon) r 45 Ana

Ams Max, Preserving Co. (Max Ams, Pres.; Gustav Grafmueller, Sec. Capital, $100,000. Directors; Max Ams, Richard Weinacht, Gustav Grafmueller, Charles M. Ams) 372 G'wich

TYPEWRITING DONE BY THE TROW CITY DIRECTORY CO., 11 University Place.

Amsdell Brothers (George I. & Theodore M. Amsdell) 636 W. 34th
Amsinck G. & Co. (Gustav Amsinck, Gustave H. Gossler & August Lattmann) 148 Pearl
Amundson & Ward (John A. Amundson & Edwin C. Ward) 146 B'way
Amusement & Hotel Publication Co. (Charles F. Price, propr.) 104 Reade
Amy H. & Co. (Henry Amy, Gustav L. Hoppenstedt & Louis H. Amy) 31 Nassau
Analyst Publishing Co. (Henry Lessing, Pres.; Thomson P. McElrath, Sec. Capital, $10,000. Directors: Henry Lessing, Thomson P. McElrath) 19 Park pl. & 16 Murray
Ananthan & Co. (Moses Ananthan & Harry Oppenheimer :—special partner, Levi Samuels, $15,000, terminates 1st May, 1894) 305 B'way & 82 E. 14th
Anchor Brewing & Bottling Co. (Henry Leonhardt, propr.) 880 Eleventh av.
Anchor Color Mfg. Co. (William Slack & Sons, proprs.) 466 Cherry
Anchor Oil Co. (Lewis H. Smith, Pres.; Samuel Comfort, Sec. Capital, $1,000,000. Directors: Lewis H. Smith, John D. Archbold, H. Y. Pickering, J. J. Vandergrift, W. H. Johnson, Samuel Comfort, John H. Flagg, E. T. Johnston, T. P. Chambers) 18 B'way
Anderson C. F., Co. (dissolved) 61 Ann
Anderson H. James & Co. (H. James Anderson & H. F. Wright) 48 E. 19th
Anderson John & Co. (William H. Catlin, Pres.; Alfred Wagstaff, Sec. Capital, $50,000. Trustees: William H. Catlin, Alfred Wagstaff, George G. Barnard, George S. Floyd-Jones) 114 Liberty
Anderson John R., Co. (inf. unattainable) 150 Nassau
Anderson Rubber Co. (estate of Daniel D. Anderson, proprs.) 93 Duane
Anderson School Book Co. (dissolved) 65 Duane
Anderson B. C. & Co. (dissolved) 84 Pike
Anderson H. C. & Co. (Henry C. Anderson & Charles J. Herson) 124 W. B'way
Anderson J. F. jr. & Co. (John F. jr. & Franklin W. Anderson) 84 Beekman
Anderson N. & Co. (Niles Anderson & Thomas H. Johnston) B'way n Kingsbridge rd
Anderson P. & Co. (Philander Anderson & William H. Elting) r 207 E. 22d & 208 E. 23d
Anderson & Co. (John I. Anderson & Walter Doe) 704 Eighth av. & 2022 Third av.
Anderson & Crosby (Olof P. Anderson & Ansel Crosby) 20 Coenties sl.
Anderson & Howland (Henry H. Anderson, Henry F. Howland & George Welwood Murray) 85 Wall
Anderson & Jones (Thomas Anderson & John R. Jones) 184 Grand
Anderson & Krum Stationery Co. (inoperative) 806 B'way
Anderson & Man (E. Ellery Anderson & Frederick H. Man) 10 Wall
Anderson & Milligan (dissolved) 2022 Third av.
Anderson & Price (Edgar T. Anderson & Hiram K. Price) 77 Franklin
Anderson & Ryan (William H. Anderson & William Ryan) 225 E. 14th
Anderson & Stanton (Edward C. Anderson & George A. Stanton) 155 B'way
Anderson, Churchill & Co. (James G. Anderson & Newton Churchill, no Co.) 64 Leonard
Anderton & Chambers (Robert J. Anderton & Luther H. Chambers) 107 Fourth av.
Andover Shoe Co. (no inf.) 122 Duane
Andrade Joseph & Co. (Joseph Andrade, Emanuel M. Angel & Alfred L. Arone) 95 Bleecker

Andreas & Co. (Jeremiah J. Andreas, Edward E. Bruggerhof & William E. Sibell) 76 Broad
Andres & Gile (dissolved) 115 Clinton mkt
Andresen John & Son (John & Charles A. Andresen) 89 Gold
Andresen & Blatt Folding Bed Co. (no inf.) 61 W. 14th
Andress Paint & Color Co. (inf. unattainable) 15 Cortlandt
Andreu & Mochove (Frank Andreu & Simon Mochove) 116 Maiden la.
Andrews Mfg Co. (Melbert B. Cary, Pres.; John W. Cary jr. Sec. Capital, $1,000,000. Directors: Melbert B. Cary, Zephaniah S. Holbrook, William Bryce jr. William R. Adams, John W. & John W. Cary jr. Charles H. Ropes) 70 Fifth av.
Andrews William D. & Brother (William D. & George H. Andrews) 233 B'way
Andrews B. & Co. (dissolved) 42 Walker
Andrews & May (Sturges D. Andrews & John C. C. May) 790 Sixth av.
Andrews & Purdy (Lilian H. Andrews & Thomas J. Purdy) 132 Nassau
Andrews & Warner (John P. Andrews & Carlos S. Warner) 202 B'way
Andrews, Adams & Kellogg (Constant A. Andrews, William N. Adams, William C. Kellogg & Walter Mason.) 2 Wall
Andrews, Gulick & Sillcocks (John Andrews, Horace M. Gulick & Theodore W. Sillcocks) 144 Chambers
Andress & Groo (William W. Andress & Lines Groo) 236 Washn.
Andruss A. A. & Son (Abraham A. & Charles Andruss) 423 W. 43d
Angel & Smith (James R. Angel & Clarence M. Smith) 243 B'way
Angell M. G. & Co. (Harold G. Angell, no Co.) 17 Murray
Angell & Co. (Albert C. Angell, no Co.) 44 Hudson
Anger Brothers (John A. & Louis J. Anger) 389 Grand & 44 Suffolk
Anger & Egelhofer (Julius T. Anger & Henry Egelnofer) 181 William
Angevine George M. & Co. (George M. Angevine, no Co.) 109 E. 9th
Angevine William & Co. (William Angevine & William Dougherty) 1400 B'way, 828 Seventh av., 242 E. 31st, 201½ E. 89th, 137½ E. 56th & 138 Waverley pl.
Anglers' Publishing Co. (James A. Williamson, Pres.; William C. Harris, Sec. Capital, $10,000. Directors: James A. Williamson, D. W. Cross, H. H. Thompson, Henry R. & William C. Harris) 10 Warren
Anglo-Am. Drug Co. (refused) 217 Fulton
Anglo-Am. Dry Dock & Warehouse Co. (Jesse Boynton, Pres.; Cornelius J. Bushnell, Sec.; William F. Buckley, Treas. Capital, $1,500,000. Directors: Jesse Boynton, James E. Simpson, William F. Buckley, F. Gordon Dexter) 85 B'way
Anglo-Am. Electric Light Mfg. Co. (Orson Adams, Pres.; Lawrence B. Mott, Sec.; E. D. Woodruff, Treas. Capital, $2,500,000. Directors: Henry Steers, Julio Mertzbacher, Orson Adams, E. D. Woodruff, E. P. Sentenne, W. P. Ward, Henry E. Simmons, Harvey M. Mansell) 41 Park row & 420 W. 13th
Anglo-Am. Laundry (J. S. McNeal & Co., proprs.) 926 Sixth av.
Angraissola & Chacon (no inf.) 5 Carmine
Ankele C. & Co. (Rudolph Kampfer, only) 210 William
Annable George A. & Co. (George A. Annable, no Co.) 115 Warren

THADDEUS DAVIDS CO., WRITING INKS, SEALING WAX, MUCILAGE.
MAKE THE BEST

ANN 15 ARM

Annan & Co. (Edward Annan, Edward G. Burgess & John B. McCue) 101 Produce Ex.
Annan & Hoyt (Edward Annan & Jesse Hoyt) 102 Produce Ex.
Annin & Co. (Benjamin F. & John Annin) 99 Fulton
Anniston City Land Co. (inf. unattainable) 7 Nassau
Anrich E. L. & Co. (Emanuel L. Anrich & Emanuel M. de Frece) 24 Maiden la.
Ansanelli A. & Co. (Angelo Ansanelli & Thomas Tierno) 120 Mulberry
Ansbacher A. B. & Co. (Adolph B. Ansbacher & Maurice D. Eger) 4 Murray
Ansonia Brass & Copper Co. (William E. Dodge, Pres.; Alfred A. Cowles, Sec. Capital, $1,500,000. Directors: William E. Dodge, D. Willis James, Anson Phelps Stokes, Cleveland H. Dodge, Thomas Stokes, Henry James, Alfred A. Cowles) 19 Cliff
Anspach George (George Anspach:—special partner, Max Ams, $25,000, terminates 31st Dec., 1890) 64 N. Moore
Anspach & Hengst (dissolved) 207 Franklin
Anspacher Mfg. Co. (Leopold H. Anspacher, Pres.; Herman Rosenberg. Sec.; Siegfried Rosenberg, Treas. Capital, $75,000. Directors: Leopold H. Anspacher, Siegfried & Herman Rosenberg) 515 B'way & 84 Mercer
Anspacher L. H. & Brother (dissolved) 515 D'way
Anstett & Co. (Joseph Anstett, no Co.) 241 Fulton
Anthony E. & H. T. & Co. (Vincent M. Wilcox, Pres.; Frederick A. Anthony, Sec. Capital, $280,000. Directors: Vincent M. Wilcox, Frederick A. & Richard A. Anthony) 591 B'way
Anthony & Chew (Edward R. & Rowland C. Anthony, only) 16 Exchange pl.
Anti-Magnetic Shield & Watch Case Co. (no inf.) 1½ Maiden la.
Antony & Runk (Carl Antony & George S. Runk) 1090 Fifth av.
Antoxine Co. (inf. unattainable) 50 Park pl.
Anzelone P. & J. Curio (Peter Anzelone & Joseph Curio) 305 E. 111th
Apalachicola Lumber Co. (inoperative) 18 B'way
Aparicio J. & Co. (Juan Aparicio & Adrian Martinez) 101 Pearl
Apgar & Co. (Louis J. Apgar, Henry C. Woltemeyer & Edward H. Apgar) 78 Dey
Apgar & Garretson (Theodore B. Apgar & Lyman C. Garretson) 68 Dey
Apman, Creciman & Co. (Henry Apman, Albert Creciman & Charles Z. Wilson) 2138 Eighth av.
Appel S. & Co. (Solomon Appel & Gustav Basch) 10 Cath. sl.
Appel & Hirrlinger (Charles P. Appel & Charles W. Hirrlinger) 96 Fulton
Appel, Newwitter & Furst (Jacob Appel, Gustav J. Newwitter & Myron J. Furst) 80 Greene
Apple S. & L. Zwergbaum (Samuel Apple & Louis Zwergbaum) r 84 Suffolk
Apple Brothers (Louis W. & Morris Apple) 816 Canal
Apple & Co. (Herman Apple, no Co.) 57 Bleecker
Appleby & Co, (refused) 11 W. 25th
Appleton D. & Co. (William H. & Daniel S. & William W. & Daniel & Edward D. Appleton) 3 Bond
Appleton & Johnson (Randolph M. Appleton & Columbus O. Johnson) 10 Wall
Arabol Mfg. Co. (Julius Jungbluth, Pres.; Charles E. Seitz, Treas. Capital, $60,000. Directors: Julius Jungbluth, Edward Weingartner, Charles E. Seitz) 13 Gold
Arai R. (Rioichiro Arai & Samro Takaki) 46 Howard

Arbuckle Brothers (Charles & John Arbuckle) 111 Front
Arbuckle Brothers Coffee Co. (John Arbuckle, Pres.; Charles Arbuckle, Treas.; further inf. unattainable) 111 Front
Archambault & Co. (dissolved) 45 E. 12th
Archdeacon & Co. (Peter M. Archdeacon & John B. Grevatt) 55 Barclay
Archer Fuel Co. (William P. Watson, Pres.; William F. Chittenden, Sec.; Frederick Buess, Treas. Capital, $1,000,000; further inf. unattainable) 45 B'way
Archer Mfg. Co. (George W. Archer, Pres.; Henry C. White, Sec. Capital, $80,000. Directors: George W. & John W. Archer, Henry C. White, A. M. & M. A. Archer) 227 Canal
Archer I. H. & Co. (Isaac H. Archer, no Co.) 122 Pearl
Archer J. & G. (Joseph & George) 286 E. 35th
Archer & Pancoast Mfg. Co. (Archer V. Pancoast, Pres.; Benjamin F. Allen, Sec. Capital, $600,000. Trustees: Archer V. Pancoast, Clement M. & William C. Bickle, Benjamin F. Allen, Charles H. Fischer) 900 B'way & 886 First av.
Architectural Assistant Co. (Harry Howard, propr.) 7 Warren
Architectural Iron Works (J. G. & T. Dimond, proprs.) 209 W. 88J
Architectural Sheet Metal Works (not inc.) (Moritz F. Westergreen & Frederick L. Anderson) 202 Mercer
Architectural Wrought Iron Works (William H. Price, propr.) 433 Canal & 48 Watts
Arctander & Seabold (Arthur Arctander & Jacob Seabold) Willis av. n. B. 143d
Arctic Freezing Co. (not inc.) (Halsey W. Knapp, Daniel R. Vannostrand & Nicholas E. Hendrickson) 120 West
Aren & Hyman (Morris Aren & Nathan Hyman) 226 Seventh av.
Arendt & Fringant (Edward Arendt & Max Fringant) 151 Water
Arents Charles R. & Co. (Charles R. Arents, Co. refused) 49 Liberty
Arents & Young (George Arents & Albert Young) 3 Broad
Arfman G. & L. (George & Louis) 1131 First av.
Argand Grate Bar Works (Salamander Grate Bar Co. proprs.) 110 Liberty
Arguelles, Lopez & Brother (Facundo Arguelles & Joaquin & Celestino Lopez) 221 Pearl
Arguimbau & Ramee (Joseph L. Arguimbau & Louis C. Ramee) 2 Bridge
Arguimbau & Wallis (Daniel V. Arguimbau & William M. Wallis) 21 State
Argyle Press (Henry S. Allen, Pres.; Thomas D. Hurst, Sec. Capital, $80,000. Directors: Henry S. Allen, Samuel J. Kerr, Thomas D. Hurst) 265 Cherry
Arizona Commercial Co. (inoperative) 11 Pine
Arkell James & Co. (James & James W. Arkell) 10 Whitehall
Arkell & Douglass (William H. Douglas & Thomas M. Freeman, only) 19 Whitehall
Arlington Collar & Cuff Co. (Joseph R. France, Pres.; Henry S. Chapman, Sec. Capital, $90,000. Directors: Joseph R. France, Henry S. Chapman, Charles Lennig, E. Greenfield, E. N. Crane) 84 Leonard
Arlington Mfg. Co. (Joseph R. France, Pres.; Henry S. Chapman, Sec. Capital, $250,000. Directors: Joseph R. France, Charles Leanig, Henry S. Chapman) 84 Leonard
Arlington Novelty Co. (dissolved) 98 Duane
Arlington Skirt Mfg. Co. (Herman Stiefel, propr.) 457 Broome
Armanda Cigar Mfg. Co. (Ritter Brothers, proprs.) 743 E. 9th

COMPILED WITH ACCURACY AND DESPATCH. **CLASSIFIED BUSINESS LISTS.** **(THE TROW CITY DIRECTORY CO. 11 University Place.**

ARM 16 ART

Armeny & Marion (Gyulo Armeny & William C. Marion) 75 Nassau

Arming Francis M. & Co. (Francis M. Arming, no Co.) 81 New

Armitage & Hitchings (Charles Armitage & Edward W. Hitchings) 96 Spring

Armour H. O. & Co. (Herman O. Armour & Frederick V. Dare) 201 Produce Ex.

Armour & Osterhondt (Robert J. Armour & Alfred Osterhondt) 100 Beekman

Armour Brothers & Co. (Paul J. & Charles W. Armour, no Co.) 70 Wall

Armstrong Fire Ins. Co. (Philander B. Armstrong, Pres.; Joseph O. Hatle, Sec. Capital, $200,000. Trustees: Philander B. Armstrong, Oscar R. Meyer, Joseph Fox, John Dickson, Aaron F. Troescher, Otto Von Hein, Aaron Carter, Emil Calman, Charles S. Braisted, J. W. Mack, David Calman, Samson Lachman, J. Spencer Turner) 155 B'way

Armstrong Maitland & Co, (David Maitland Armstrong & Edwin O. Larned) 61 Washn. sq. S.

Armstrong Mfg. Co. (Frank Armstrong, Pres.; Charles Armstrong, Sec. Capital, $100,000. Directors: Frank & Charles & Elizabeth Armstrong) 242 Canal

Armstrong A. C. & Son (Andrew C. & J. Sinclair Armstrong) 714 B'way

Armstrong C. L. & Co. (Chauncey L. & William H. Armstrong) 110 Murray

Armstrong G. W. & Brother (George W. & Charles E. Armstrong) 127 Pearl & 80 Beaver

Armstrong L. W. & P. (Lorenzo & Charles P. & William F. & Roland D. Armstrong, only) 114 Wall

Armstrong Brothers (Abram T. & Thomas E. & Jackson Armstrong) 1026 Third av.

Armstrong & Co. (agents) (David & Andrew W. Armstrong) 554 Third av.

Armstrong & Co. (brokers) (Thomas H. Armstrong & Edward A. Yeoman) 50 Liberty

Armstrong & Knauer (Augustus Armstrong & Erhardt Knauer) 822 B'way

Armstrong & Knauer Publishing Co. (Armstrong & Knauer, proprs.) 822 B'way

Armstrong & Son (Susan M. & William H. Armstrong) 812 Seventh av.

Army Blanket Overcoat Co. (no inf.) 11 Wall

Arneel T. & Son (Thomas & William T. Arneel) 182 Charles

Arnold D. H. & Co. (Nathan & Benjamin & Walter C. Arnold, only) 519 B'way & 92 Mercer

Arnold F. R. & Co. (Francis R. Arnold, no Co.) 56 Murray

Arnold M. & Co. (Morris & Milton S. Arnold) 472 B'way & 80 Crosby

Arnold Brothers (William A. & George & Thomas J. Arnold) 141 W. B'way

Arnold & Aborn (Thomas L. Arnold & Benjamin Aborn) 89 Old sl.

Arnold & Bornheimer (Mary H. Arnold & Charles D. Bernheimer) 564 First av.

Arnold & Co. (brokers) (Benjamin G. & Francis B. Arnold & Frederick L. Emmons) 87 Wall

Arnold & Co. (tailors) (Max Arnold, no Co.) 37 Park row

Arnold & Conyers (Benjamin F. Arnold & W. Fred. Conyers) 2 Coenties sl.

Arnold & Elias (George T. Arnold & Albert J. Elias) 17 Union sq. W.

Arnold & Greene (Lemuel H. Arnold jr. & J. Warren Greene) 8 Broad

Arnold & Rowley (Charles D. Arnold & Edward H. Rowley) 28 Warren

Arnold & Schwalenberg (Edward Arnold & William Schwalenberg) 1805 Tenth av.

Arnold, Cheney & Co. (Benjamin R. & William H. Arnold, Frederick M. Cheney, William M. Vanderhoof & William G. Seeley) 158 Water & Pier 14 E. R.

Arnold, Cheney & Co.'s Australian Line (Arnold, Cheney & Co., proprs.) 108 Water & Pier 14 E. R.

Arnold, Constable & Co. (James M. & Frederick A. Constable & Hicks Arnold) 881 B'way & 115 Fifth av.

Arnoux & Hochhausen Electric Co. (Frederic A. Potts, Pres.; Allison Dodd, Sec. Capital, $100,000. Directors, Allison Dodd, Herman Bolsster, Frederic A. Potts) 26 B'way

Arnoux, Ritch & Woodford (William H. Arnoux, Thomas G. Ritch, Stewart L. Woodford, Haley Fiske, Christian N. Bovee jr. & William O. Wallace) 18 Wall

Arnson & Co. (Paula Arnson, no Co.) 78 Canal

Arnstaedt & Co. (Wilhelmina H. Arnstaedt, Clement H. Druel, Theodore W. Specht & Louis Daschnau) 63 Greene

Arnstein Albert & Co. (Albert Arnstein & Sigmund Messner) 95 S. 5th av.

Arnstein & Bonn (Solomon A. Arnstein & Herbert A. Bonn) 926 Third av.

Arnstein Brothers & Co. (Sigmund & Max & Emanuel & Samuel Arnstein;—special partner, Leopold Stern, $25,000; terminates 30th June, 1892) 37 Maiden la.

Aronson & Rosenthal (Gustav Aronson & Joseph Rosenthal) 73 Hester

Aronstein & Wolfers (Maurice Aronstein, Otto G. Wolfers & Theodore G. Well) 457 B'way

Arras Drapery & Novelty Co. (inf. unattainable) 51 Leonard

Arras Brothers (William & Charles Arras) 77 W. 125th

Arras & Wolf (Edward V. Arras & George Wolf) 830 Sixth av.

Arroyo Seco Gold Mining Co. (John M. Krohen, Pres.; George L. Knam, Sec. Capital, $100,000. Trustees: John M. Kochen, George Wellbrook, George L. Knam) no address

Art Interchange Co. (William Whitlock, Pres.; William McN. Purdy, Sec. Capital, $10,700. Directors: William Whitlock, Josephine Redding, William McN. Purdy, Dashe McE. Whitlock) 37 W. 22d

Art Pearl Co. (Emanuel M. Ikelheimer, propr.) 202 Canal

Art Photo. Engraving Co. (no inf.) 53 Franklin

Art Students' League of N. Y. (Edwin D. French, Pres.; Susan M. Ketcham, Sec.; William A. Marsh, Treas.) 143 E. 23d

Art Toilet Co. (A. C. Smith, propr.) 4 W. 14th

Art Trades Publishing & Printing Co. (William M. Halsted, propr.) 150 Nassau

Arteole Bric-a-Brac Co. (inf. unattainable) 404 West

Arthur Co. (James Arthur, Pres.; John F. Arthur, Sec.; Madeline Arthur, Treas. Capital, $10,000. Directors: James & Daniel & Madeline & John F. Arthur) 86 John

Arthur & Donnell (James Worrall Arthur, Frederick Mountain, Henry H. Arthur & Charles E. Marling, only) 55 Cedar

Arthur & Ketchum (Edward G. Arthur & Edmund Ketchum) 29 Wall

Artistic Bronze Co. (Foust & Wolf, proprs.) 6 E. 14th & Morris av. c. E. 155th

Artistic Decorating Co. (Henry Moltzen, propr.) 31 Second av.

Artistic Window Decorating Co. (Henry Herrmann, Pres.; Gustav Posschl, Sec.; further inf. unattainable) 368 Broome & 164 Mott

Artists' Union (George F. Dickinson, propr.) 10 E. 14th

Artman & Treichler (no inf.) 81 White

SPECIAL ATTENTION PAID TO THIS CLASS OF WORK } BANKERS' & BROKERS' CIRCULARS DELIVERED { THE TROW CITY DIRECTORY CO. 11 University Place.

ASB 17 ATL

Asbestos Faced Hair Felt Co. (Julius Delong, Pres.; Hiram W. French, Sec. Capital, $5,000. Directors: Julius Delong, Hiram W. French, James L. Reed) 128 Pearl

Asbestos Felting Works (Clara Hintze, propr.) 99 Maiden la.

Asbestos & Felt Mills (Edwin A. Hayes, propr.) 262 West

Asbury Glass Sign Co. (Francis B. Asbury, propr.) 71 William

Asbury Park Gas Co. (George H. Fletcher, Pres.; James W. Hodges, Sec. Capital, $150,000. Directors: Charles H. & George H. Fletcher, James W. Hodges, James A. Sherman) 170 B'way

Asch Brothers (William & Tobias Asch) 48 Spring

Asch & Jaeckel (Hugo Jaeckel, only) 11 W. Houston

Ascher Hyman & Co. (Hyman Ascher, no Co.) 88 Maiden la.

Ascher Leopold & Co. (dissolved) 221 Pearl

Asencio & Cossio (Thomas Asencio & Mariano F. de Cossio) 31 Pine

Ash Louis & Co. (Louis Ash, no Co.)779 Third av.

Ash Brothers (Magnus Ash, only) 61 W. 14th

Ash & Duckbee (John G. Ash & John Buckbee) 24 Spruce

Ash & Esler (Joseph Ash & Frederick C. W. Esler) 127 E. 53d

Ashcraft & Dumont (no inf.) 55 Liberty

Ashcroft John, Patent Grate Bar & Furnace Door Mfg. Co. (inf. unattainable) 73 Gold

Ashcroft Mfg. Co. (Eugene L. Maxwell, Pres.; Martin Luscomb, Sec.; Henry S. Manning, Treas. Capital, $200,000. Directors: Charles A. Moore, Henry S. Manning, Eugene L. Maxwell, Martin Luscomb) 111 Liberty

Ashe & Kramer (Edmund M. Ashe & Edward A. Kramer) 4 Bond

Ashelm & Edelmuth (Paul Ashelm & Louis Edelmuth) 133 Roosevelt

Ashforth A. & C. (Alfred A. & Charles A.) 22 Duane

Ashley & Bailey (Dwight Ashley & Peter Bailey) 72 Grand

Ashmall William E. & Co. (William E. & Alice Ashmall) 231 E. 60th

Ashman A. L. & Son (dissolved) 754 B'way

Ashton & Fromme (Samuel Ashton & Herman Fromme) 132 Nassau

Ashuelot R. R. Co. (inf. unattainable) 45 B'way

Ashwell & Co. (William C. Ashwell, no Co.) 30 Broad

Asiel L. N. & Co. (Leopold N. Asiel, Emil Salinger & Gustave Putzel) 466 B'way

Asiel & Co. (Elias Adel, Maurice Seligmann & Louis S. Frankenbeimer) 51 Exchange pl.

Askin & Co. (Patrick Askin & Mary Woods) 313 Third av.

Aspell & Co. (Gertrude S. Aspell, no Co.) 314 G'wich

Aspen Mining & Smelting Co. (Jerome B. Wheeler, Pres.; James L. Tilton, Sec.; Samuel S. Earle, Treas. Capital, $2,000,000. Directors: Robert S. Holt, Joseph R. Busk, William D. Sloane, William L. Heermance, Jerome B. Wheeler, Samuel S. Earle, James F. Sutton, Frederick G. Bulkley, J. H. Devereux, Thomas H. Edsall, James J. Hagerman) 54 Wall

Asphaltic Slag Paving & Roofing Co. (Fitz John Porter, Pres.; Robert S. Masterton, Sec.; Matthew M. Locram, Treas. Capital, $1,000,000. Directors: Fitz John Porter, Robert S. Masterton, Matthew M. Locram, George S. Lee, William F. Croft, Samuel H. Bates, Richard E. Preusser) 45 B'way

Aspinall's Enamel Agency (Edward Aspinall, propr.) 98 Beekman

Aspinwall Fruit Co. (Ltd.) (William L. Rathbun, Pres.; Eugene D. Miller, Sec.; Charles F. Lutz, Treas. Capital, $10,000. Directors: William L. Rathbun, Eugene D. Miller, Charles F. Lutz, Joshua Cromwell, Hipolito Dumois) 230 Fulton

Aspinwall T. & Son (Henry C. Aspinwall, only) 303 Fifth av.

Assets State Debenture Co. (Hildreth K. Bloodgood, Pres.; James S. Tait, Sec. Capital, $5,000,000. Directors: Hildreth K. & John Bloodgood, Leonidas M. Lawson, Rastus S. Ransom, H. L. Langhaar, William T. Lawson, Giles E. Taintor) 42 New

Associated Artists (Candace Wheeler, propr.) 115 E. 23d

Associated Press (William H. Smith, N. Y. manager) 195 B'way

Associated Publishing & Bookselling Co. (Edwin C. Siperly, propr.) 356 Pearl

Associated Railways of Virginia & the Carolinas (Horace P. Clark, agent) 229 B'way

Assn. Master Painters & Decorators (James F. Conley, Pres., Joseph Scott, Sec.; John Voetsen, Treas.) 3 Washn. sq. N.

Assn. of Experts & Specialists (dissolved) 26 Gt. Jones

Assn. of Importers & Jobbers of China, Glass & Earthenware (Isidor Straus, Pres.; Frank Haviland, Sec.; John M. Young, Treas.; David Felter, Actuary) 61 Park pl.

Assured Building Loan Assn. (Erastus Wiman, Pres.; Turner Ashby Beall, Sec.; Gabriel Morton, Treas. Directors: Erastus Wiman, J. H. Parker, Turner Ashby Beall, Gabriel Morton, Charles A. Deshon, Franklin Edson, J. Hobart Herrick, Touro Robertson, Edward A. Swain, David B. Jones, R. M. Johnson, Walter L. McCorkle) 108 Produce Ex.

Astarino Filippo & Brothers (Filipo & Francesco Astarino, only) 68 Carmine & 71 Hudson

Astheimer & Schoen (dissolved) 187 Norfolk

Aston Brothers (Samuel T. & George A. Aston) 108 Liberty

Astor Laundry (Julia E. Osborn, propr.) 897 Eighth av.

Astoria Ferry Co. (Cornelius Rapelye, Pres.; Samuel C. Ellis, Sec. Capital, $50,000. Directors: Cornelius Rapelye, Antony V. Winans, John S. & A. Vanhorne Ellis) 132 Front & ft. E. 92d

Astoria Veneer Mills (William H. Williams, Pres.; Alexander S. Williams, Sec. Capital, $100,000. Directors: William H. Williams, William Thatcher, Alexander S. Williams) 120 E. 13th

Atak Miguel & Co. (Miguel Atak & John Lee) 131 Park row

Atha & Hughes (Benjamin Atha & George H. Hughes) 111 Duane

Atherton J. M., Co. (no inf.) 55 Beaver

Athlophoros Co. (Robert N. Searies, Pres.; John E. Searies jr, Sec.; further inf. unattainable) 112 Wall

Atkins C. M. & Co. (Charles M. Atkins & O. W. Gross) 1267 B'way

Atkins & Durbrow (William E. Atkins & Walter Durbrow) 70 Wall

Atkinson Thomas & Co. (Thomas Atkinson, no Co.) 19 Whitehall

Atkinson & Co. (dissolved) 48 Broad

Atlanta & Charlotte Air Line Railway Co. (Eugene Kelly, Pres.; William N. Wilmer, Sec.; George Sherman, Treas. Capital, $1,700,000. Directors: Eugene Kelly, Pomeroy P. Dickinson, James H. Young, Richard Irvin, R. A. Lancaster, Hiram W. Sibley, Joseph Bryan, B. R. McAlpine, Skipwith Wilmer, Michael Jenkins, Charles S. Fairchild, Charles M. Fry) 46 Wall

Atlantic Ammunition Co. (Ltd) (C. Charles Tatham, Pres.; William F. Greene jr, Sec.; further inf. unattainable) 291 B'way

TYPEWRITING DONE BY THE TROW CITY DIRECTORY CO., 11 University Place.

ATL 18 AUS

Atlantic Chemical Co. (Wendell H. Cobb, Pres.; Francis A. Waters, Treas. Capital, $200,000. Directors: Edward E. Waters, Wendell H. Cobb, Francis A. Waters) 59 Park pl.

Atlantic Chemical Co. (Mass & Waldstein, proprs.) 81 G'wich & 44 Trinity pl.

Atlantic Cigar Factory (Deutsch Brothers, proprs.) 227 E. 56th & 400 E. 54th

Atlantic Coast, St. John & Indian River Railway Co. (James N. Smith, Pres.; Thornton N. Motley, Sec. Capital, $230,000. Directors: James N. Smith, C. W. Collins, H. H. Brown, Thornton N. & James M. Motley, C. H. Kinsley, C. F. Muir, A. S. Stevens, Peter Hall) 61 B'way

Atlantic Color Works (Pfeiffer & Lavanburg, proprs.) 525 W. 54th

Atlantic Dredging Co. (Ralph G. Packard, Pres.; J. S. Packard, Sec.; further inf. unattainable) 34 Pine

Atlantic Fire & Marine Ins. Co. (no inf.) 44 Pine

Atlantic Iron Works (Daniel D. Boyce, propr.) 700 E. 13th

Atlantic Mining Co. (Joseph E. Gay, Pres.; John R. Stanton, Sec. Capital, $1,000,000. Directors: Joseph E. Gay, Albert S. Swards, John Stanton, Isaac B. Crane, Edwin H. Mead, John R. Stanton) 76 Wall

Atlantic Mutual Ins. Co. (John D. Jones, Pres.; Joseph H. Chapman, Sec. Trustees: John D. Jones, William H. H. Moore, Anton A. Raven, Joseph H. Chapman, William Sturgis, John L. Riker, George Bliss, Horace Gray, Charles P. Burdett, Clifford A. Hand, Charles P. Leverich, William E. Dodge, Lawrence Turnure, James Low, William Degroot, Benjamin H. Field, N. Denton Smith, Ira Bursley, James A. Hewlett, George H. Macy, Christian de Thomsen, Leander N. Lovell, John D. Hewlett, William H. Webb, Edward Floyd-Jones, Anson W. Hard, Thomas Maitland, Joseph Agostini, George W. Campbell, Vernon H. Brown, James G. DeForest, Charles H. Marshall, Henry E. Hawley, Isaac Bell, Waldron P. Brown, George L. Nichols, Gustav Amsinck, William G. Boulton, Russell H. Hoadley) 51 Wall

Atlantic Oyster Co. (James F. Arundell, propr.) 101 N. Moore

Atlantic Publishing & Engraving Co. (inf. unattainable) 51 Chambers

Atlantic Shirt Co. (Bernstein Brothers & Gottlieb, proprs.) 525 B'way.

Atlantic Storage Warehouse (refused) 103 Fourth av.

Atlantic Sulphur Works (Nathaniel T. Cory, propr.) 119 Maiden la.

Atlantic Trust Co. (William H. Male, Pres.; James S. Suydam, Sec. Capital, $500,000. Directors: Louis C. Ledyard, Henry A. V. Post, Dean Sage, William H. H. Moore, Walter R. T. Jones, John L. Riker, William A. & Alexander M. White, Edward H. R. Lyman, Donald Mackay, Clifford A. Hand, Joseph H. Chapman, J. Langdon Ward, Anton A. Raven, William H. Male, Thomas Hitchcock, Edwin F. Knowlton, Henry H. Rogers, Charles D. Leverich, Alfred Wagstaff, Mathias Nicoll) 89 William

Atlantic Watch Case Co. (Keller & Untermeyer, proprs.) 192 B'way

Atlantic White Lead & Linseed Oil Co. (Romulus R. Colgate, Pres.; George W. Fortmeyer, Sec.; further inf. unattainable) 287 Pearl

Atlantic & Danville Railway Co. (Thomas Ewing, Pres.; Benjamin L. Fairchild, Sec.; Arthur E. Bateman, Treas. Capital, $3,170,000. Directors: Thomas Ewing, Arthur E. Bateman, J. E. D. Ryder, Isaac L. Rice, Jonas M. Libbey, Robert W. Stuart, Harvey A. Durand, Charles E. Coon, Charles B. Peck) 45 B'way

Atlantic & Pacific R. R. Co. (James A. Williamson, Pres.; Harrison W. Gardiner, Sec. Capital, $70,760,300. Directors: James A. Williamson, John B. Kerr, Jesse Seligman, William F. Buckley, Walter L. Frost, Bryce Gray, Edward H. Pardee, Allen Manvel, B. P. Cheney, George C. Magoun, John J. McCook, Alden Spoare, Levi C. Wade) 45 B'way

Atlas Mineral Releasing Co. (Luke Harrington, Pres.; Samuel R. Dummer, Sec.; Henry K. White, Treas. Capital, $500,000. Directors: Luke Harrington, Stewart Winslow, Samuel R. Dummer, Henry K. White, Norman A. Smith) 33 B'way

Atlas Rubber Co. (Doty & Herbert, proprs.) 68 Park pl. & 10 College pl.

Atlas Silk Co. (John G. Neeser, Pres.; John J. Gahde, Sec. Capital, $30,000; further inf. unattainable) 1 Greene & 525 W. 34th

Atterbury Brothers (Robert B. & Henry Atterbury) 140 Nassau & 73 Rutgers

Attwell Henry & Co. (Henry Attwell & James R. Whyte) 39 White

Atwood Mining Co. (Charles D. Ingersoll, Pres.; Charles A. Trowbridge, Sec. Capital, $500,000; further inf. unattainable) 170 B'way

Aube R. W. & Son (Reuben W. & Reuben W. Aube jr.) 125 Mott

Auburn Gold Mining Co. (Franklin E. Morse, Pres.; Addison B. Tuttle, Sec. Capital, $200,000. Directors: Henry Markell, Addison B. Tuttle, John A. Hilton, Franklin E. Morse, E. L. Hubbard, Charles L. Hardy) 171 B'way

Auchincloss Brothers (Edgar S. & John W. & Hugh D. Auchincloss) 47 White

Auchterlonie & Co. (Frances & William J. Auchterlonie) 27 Rose

Audel Theo. & Co. (Theodore Audel, no Co.) 91 Liberty

Auerbach Louis & Brother (Louis & Max Auerbach) 807 Ninth av.

Auerbach Simon & Co. (Simon Auerbach, Benjamin F. Cohen & Mayer Auerbach) 179 Pearl

Auerbach & Bloch (Samuel Auerbach & Leopold Bloch) 1882 Park av.

Auerbach & Newman (dissolved) 154 Reade

Auerbach & Silberberg (Julius Auerbach & Gustav Silberberg) 55 Beaver

Auffmordt C. A. & Co. (Clement A. Auffmordt, John F. & William Degener & Adolph W. Von Kessler; 33 Greene

Auffurth Brothers (Dederick H. & Henry T. Auffurth) 241 Third av.

August Brothers (Elias S. & Jacob S. & Abraham S. August) 512 B'way & 58 Crosby

August & Minzie (Elias & Henry E. August & Lossic Minzie) 2284 Third av.

Augusta, Tallahassee & Gulf R. R. Co. (Henry A. Blake, Pres.; M. W. Hayward, Treas.; further inf. unattainable) 10 Wall

Auld Robert & Co. (Robert & Thomas Auld jr.) 944 Eighth av.

Ausable Horse Nail Co. (Abraham Bussing, Pres.; James R. Romayn, Sec.; Edmond K. Baber, Treas.; futher inf. unattainable) 4 Warren

Austin Cons. Coal Co. (inoperative) 50 B'way

Austin Brothers (dissolved) 366 Third av.

Austin & Co. (Chauncey T. Austin, Co refused). 97 Barclay

Austin & Hoffman (James M. Austin & Charles H. Hoffman) 82 John

Austin & Magill (Samuel J. Austin & John Magill) 155 Fulton

Austin & Schaffner (Albert Austin & Lester Schaffner) 196 W. 42d

Austin, Bates & Wellington (Francis B. Austin, Harry O. Bates & Walter L. Wellington) 27 Thomas

Austin, Drew & Co. (Edward Austin, Robert N. Drew & Frederick Grundman) 122 Greene

THE CALIGRAPH WRITING MACHINE,
HARTFORD, CONN.

AUS   19   **BAB**

Ausin, Nichols & Co. (James E. Nichols, Louis Schott, Thomas M. McCarthy, Thomas W. Ormiston & William A. Buchanan, only) 55 Hudson

Australasian Publishing Co. (Oliver Watson, Pres.; Capital, $25,000. Directors: Oliver Watson, James H. Mayo; futher inf. unattainable) 49 W. B'way

Austrian Importing Co. (Fritz Andres, propr.) 25 Pearl

Austro-Hungarian Fairbanks Co. (William P. Fairbanks, Pres.; J. Adriance Bush, Sec.; further inf. refused) 311 B'way.

Autocopyist Co. (dissolved) 66 Pine

Autographic Register Co. of N. Y. (Alfred P. Boller, Pres.; James C. Shoup, Sec.; J. H. Shoup, Treas. Capital $150,000. Directors: Erastus Wiman, Alfred P. Boller, James C. Shoup, Joseph Swift, Samuel Shoup) 298 B'way.

Automatic Adjustable Car Truck Co. (dissolved) 261 B'way

Automatic Blow Testing Machine Co. (no inf.) 60 Park pl.

Automatic Bottle Stopper Co. (Harvey M. Munsell, Pres.; Charles Waite, Sec.; Eugene M. Sanger, Treas. Capital, $500,000. Directors: Harvey M. Munsell, J. M. Clark, Elijah S. Cowles, Chauncey T. Bowen, Charles Waite) 90 B'way

Automatic Coin Operated Door Lock Co. (Percival Everitt, propr.) 293 B'way

Automatic Co. (Edward N. Dickerson, Pres. Capital, $10,000. Trustees: Francis Seymour, William A. Pollock, Harry Coutant, Edward N. Dickerson, Anthony Gref, D. N. Maxon) no address

Automatic Delivery Co. (Harris H. Hayden, Pres.; Leander L. Frost, Treas.; G. Starke, Sec. Capital, $500,000. Directors: Harris H. Hayden, R. T. Van Boskerck, Leander L. Frost, F. W. Fitts, L. W. Frost, G. Starke, Eugene F. Endicott) 559 Hudson

Automatic Electric Light Co. (inoperative) 58 William

Automatic Fence Loom Co. (Samuel A. Duncan, Pres.; Leonard E. Curtis, Sec.; Allan W. Paige, Treas.; futher inf. unattainable) 120 B'way

Automatic Fire Alarm & Extinguisher Co. (Ltd.) (Seth G. Babcock, Pres.; Edward O. Richards, Sec.; Joseph P. Curtis, Treas. Capital, $300,000. Directors: Seth G. Babcock, Joseph P. Curtis, Benjamin L. Briggs, Elijah S. Cowles, Samuel Wyman jr., Edward O. Richards, Richard S. Bouts) 294 B'way

Automatic Fire Protection Co. (inf. unattainable) 58 Wall

Automatic Fire Shutter Co. (Charles C. Moore, Pres.; William A. Wilson, Treas.; John T. Law, Sec. Capital, $150,000. Directors: Charles C. Moore, William A. Wilson, John T. Law, John E. Bryant, John E. Briggs) 198 B'way

Automatic Opera Glass Co. (no inf.) 55 W. 33d

Automatic Perfume Fountain Co. (inf. unattainable) 293 B'way

Automatic Phonograph Exhibition Co. (inf. unattainable) 257 Fifth av.

Automatic Safety Burner Co. (Frederick P. Wilcox, propr.) 10 E. 14th

Automatic Spray Perfume Co. (dissolved) 36 W. 14th

Automatic Telegraph Railway Signal Co. (Octavius D. Baldwin, Pres.; Ernest L. Jones, Sec.; Thomas B. Musgrave, Treas. Capital, $300,000. Directors: Octavius D. Baldwin, Ernest L. Jones, Thomas B. Musgrave, Augustus D. Shepard, William H. Woolverton, William F. Allen, Louis C. Waehner, Charles E. Hubbel, Edward B. Harper, Henry J. Reinmund) 10 Wall

Automatic Telephone Exchange (Sanford H. Steele, Pres.; Antonio Knauth, Sec. Capital, $500,000. Directors: Sanford H. Steele, Antonio Knauth, Kendrick H. Wilson) 46 Wall

Automatic Type-Writer Co. (no inf.) 144 G'wich

Automatic Vending Box Co. (Max S. Stern, Pres.; George D. Dayand, Sec. Capital, $50,000. Directors: George D. Baynud, James M. O'Kelly, William A. Delong,——Reinstein) 60 New

Auxiliary Fire Alarm Co. (William A. Simmons, Pres.; Howard P. Simmons, Sec.; Uriah A. Pollard, Treas. Capital, $300,000. Directors: William A. & Howard P. Simmons, Uriah A. Pollard, Charles E. Bailey, Albert P. Sawyer) 260 B'way

Averell Insulating Conduit Co. of the U. S. (no inf.) 44 B'way

Avery Gas & Fuel Improvement Co. (Alfred Kimber, Pres.; Frederick H. Beck, Sec.; George B. Hulme, Treas. Capital, $100,000. Directors: Alfred Kimber, George B. Hulme, Richard B. Avery, Charles A. Andresen, Abraham Stein) 111 B'way

Avery L. & Co. (Susan Avery, only) 122 Clinton mkt

Avery & Pendleton (A. P. Avery & W. A. Pendleton) 43 Cedar

Avery, Pensbert & Co. (Henry A. Avery, only) 68 S. 5th av

Aviles Brothers (dissolved) 880 South

Avis William A. & Co. (William A. Avis, Ephraim Scudder & Henry E. Buermeyer) 63 & 91 Front, 104 & 336 Cherry & 552 Water

Avisador Hispano-Americano Publishing Co. (Robert W. Parsons, Pres.; Alfred T. Smith, Sec.; Henry P. Booth, Treas. Capital, $15,000. Directors: Robert W. Parsons, Alfred T. Smith, William T. H. Hughes, Henry P. Booth) 46 Vesey

Axios Co. (not inc.) (refused) 41 Park row

Axtell Frank P. & Co. (Frank P. Axtell, no Co.) 110 Front

Ayer, Houston & Co. (no inf.) 175 Greene

Ayers Patent Sash Holder Co. (no inf.) 260 B'way

Aylsworth, Fargo & Haskell (no inf.) 425 Broome

Ayres George L. & Co. (George L. Ayres, John G. Phyfe & E. Lewis Johnson) 75 Duy

Ayres P. & Son (Samuel E. Ayres, only) 424 Broome

Azema Arthur & Co. (in liquidation) 24 State

Aztec Land & Cattle Co. (Ltd.) (inf. unattainable) 15 Broad

B

Baab & Amend (Jacob W. Baab & Bernard F. Amend) 1536 Third av

Baar Frederick & Co. (dissolved) 149 West & 401 E. 34th

Baar & Tauby (Frederick Baar & Charles Tauby) 75 South

Babb, Cook & Willard (George F. Babb, Walter Cook & Daniel W. Willard) 55 B'way

Babcock H. H., Co. (Henry H. Babcock, Pres.; Frederick W. Babcock, Sec.; George H. Babcock, Treas. Capital $100,000. Directors: Henry H. & Frederick W. & George H. Babcock, Roswell P. Flower, Frank E. Babcock) 412 Broome

Babcock Seth G. & Co. (Seth G. & Paul Babcock) 371 Canal

Babcock J. A. & Co. (James A. Babcock & William Tuscano;—special partner, Frank M. Linnell, *Boston, Mass.*, $6,000, terminates 5th Jan. 1893) 71 John

Babcock & Cox (Wright Babcock, only) 26 B'way

Babcock & Kling (Sarah M. Babcock & Matilda Kling) 97 Seventh av.

CIRCULARS ADDRESSED TO ANY TRADE IN THE U. S. { Facilities
PROMPT, CAREFUL WORK } THE TROW CITY DIRECTORY CO.,
AT MODERATE PRICES. } 11 University Place. { Unequalled.

BAB 20 BAI

Babcock & Wilcox Co. (George H. Babcock, Pres.; Charles A. Miller, Sec.; Nathaniel W. Pratt, Treas. Capital, $450,000. Directors: George H. Babcock, Stephen Wilcox, Nathaniel W. Pratt, Charles A. Miller, E. H. Bennett, L. B. Miller) 30 Cortlandt

Babin E. & Co. (Emile & Eugene Babin) Eighth av. c. W. 135th

Babson & Harmon (George F. Babson & Ernest H. Harmon) 5 E. 17th

Babyhood Publishing Co. (Edward St. John, Pres.; Gustav Pollak, Sec.; Bernard Kaufmann, Treas. Capital, $25,000. Directors: Edward St. John, Bernard Kaufmann, Gustav Pollak, Thomas H. Delano, J. J. Murphy, Emanuel Loveman, George H. Richmond) 5 Beekman

Bach Elias & Son (Elias & Aaron J. & Isaac A. Bach) 101 Water

Bach J. & Sons (Joseph & Jules J. & Harry M. Bach) 30 Warren

Bacharach A. & Co. (no inf.) 705 B'way

Bacharach H. & Co. (Herman Bacharach, no Co.) 543 B'way & 114 Mercer

Bacharach Brothers (Henry & Julius Bacharach) 54 Av. D

Bacharach & Co. (Max Bacharach, no Co.) 350 G'wich

Bache Semon & Co. (Semon Bache, Solomon B. Ulmann, Sigmund J. Bach, Joe S. Ulmann & Leopold S. Bache) 443 G'wich

Bacheller & Co. (A. Irving Bacheller & James W. Johnson) 154 Nassau

Bachem C. H. & Co. (Conrad H. Bachem & Dederick Cely) 72 B'way

Bachmaier & Eppenbach (Joseph Bachmaier & William Eppenbach) 11 Rivington

Bachmau Brothers (Charles D. & Hollis W. Bachman) 102 Cedar

Bachmann William & Co. (dissolved) 329 Pearl

Bachmann & Derbling (Conrad W. Bachmann & John R. Derbling) 46 Hornlio

Bachrach S. & Sons (Solomon & Abram & Isaac Bachrach) 375 Grand

Bacigolopo & Nuce (John Bacigolopo & Nicholas Nuce) 142 Liberty

Backer A. & Co. (Abraham & Nathan C. Backer) 89 Worth

Backer & Cohen (Abraham Backer & Jacob G. Cohen) 89 Worth

Backert & Bach (Charles Backert & Anthony Bach) 598 B'way

Backstrom Centrifugal Separator Co. (Robert M. Taylor, Pres.; James A. Scott, Sec.; Charles E. Shepard, Treas. Capital, $500,000 ; further inf. unattainable) 50 W. 31st

Backus Peter & Son (Peter & Charles W. Backus) 133 W. 25th

Backus Portable Steam Heater Co. (Walter W. Bostwick, Pres.; Oscar R. Meyer, Sec.. Capital, $1,000,000. Directors: Walter W. Bostwick, Oscar R. Meyer, Quinby S. Backus, P. B. Armstrong, Samson Lachman) 22 Park pl.

Bacon J. & Sons (no inf.) 458 Broome

Bacon & Campbell (Richard S. Bacon & Benjamin H. Campbell) 34 E. 51st

Bacon & Eaton (Zadoc M. Bacon & William J. Eaton) 392 B'way

Bacon & Merritt (Henry Bacon & Joseph Merritt) 102 B'way

Bacon, Baldwin & Co (Francis M. Bacon, Edward Baldwin & Francis M. Bacon jr.) 94 Franklin

Badeau E. C. & Co. (Edward C. Badeau, no Co.) 92 Park pl.

Bader A. & Co. (Aaron Bader, no Co.) 436 Broome

Bader & Pflueger (dissolved) 445 W. 45th

Badger W. S. & Co. (Walter S. Badger, Charles B. Yardley & Thomas H. Langford) 105 Worth

Badgley J. D. & Son (Joseph D. & Howard G. Badgley) 72 Wall

Baeder Flint Paper Co. (not inc.) (William A Baeder & Howard R. Kern) 283 Pearl

Baeder William A., Glue Co. (not inc.) (William A. Baeder, Howard R. Kern & Louis C. Haughey) 283 Pearl

Baeder, Adamson & Co. (Benjamin F. Webb, Charles B. Baeder, Robert J. & William B. & Charles B. Adamson, William M. Scott & John K. Marshall) 67 Beekman

Baehr, Wictorowitz & Co. (dissolved) 48 Bleecker

Baer Morris B. & Co. (Morrie D. Baer & Morris B. Bronner) 72 W. 34th

MORRIS B. BAER & CO.,

Real Estate and Law Offices,

Management of Estates a Specialty.

70 & 72 West 34th Street.

MORRIS B. BAER, MORRIS B. BRONNER.
Counsellor-at-Law. Commissioner of Deeds.

Baer Brothers (Henry E. & Edmund G. Baer) 314 E. 21st

Baer, Kraemer & Hexter (Lucien Baer, David Kraemer & Charles D. Hexter) 617 W. 39th

Baerlein S. (Solomon Baerlein :—special partners, Lyman G. & Joseph B. Bloomingdale, each $10,000; terminates 31st Dec. 1892) 251 B'way

Baetjer & Meyerstein (Herman Baetjer jr. & Ludwig Meyerstein) 5 Dey

Baez & On. (dissolved) 34 Church

Baggaley J. & Co. (Joshua Baggaley, no Co.) 509 W. 59th

Bagley & Giesemann (dissolved) 97 Spring

Bagoe F. & Co. (Frederick Bagoe, no Co.) 423 Fourth av.

Bahan & Smith (Walter W. Bahan & Richard H. Smith) 261 W. 14th

Bahmann & Hoehu (dissolved) 44 College pl,

Bahr John F. & Co. (John F. Bahr, no Co.) 33 Dey

Bahr & Meyer (dissolved) 40 Eighth av.

Bahrenburg J. H., Brother & Co. (Gesche & Claus H. Bahrenburg & Henry H. Schulte, only) 108 Murray

Baier F. A. & Son (F. August & John A. Baier) 810 Fifth

Bailey Charles D. (Leonard H. Gates, only) 23 Catharine

Bailey Floyd & Son (Floyd & Charles C. Bailey) 71 Worth

Bailey Theodore W. & Co. (Theodore W. & Howard N. & Edward H. Bailey) 356 B'way

Bailey H. B. & Co. (Harry B. Bailey & Robert M. G. Walford) 51 South

Bailey & Marrow (dissolved) 240 Bleecker

Bailey & Sullivan (Charles H. Bailey & John J. Sullivan) 122 Bowery

Bailey's C. M., Sons & Co. (Charles M. & Charles J. & Elwood A. Bailey & Joseph E. Briggs) 81 Walker

Ballie Samuel & Son (Samuel & David J. Ballie) 211 & 314 E. 22d

Ballie H. C. & G. S. (Henry C. & George S.) 304 E. 22d

Baily George W. & Co. (George W. Baily & James A. Montgomery) 56 Cotton Ex.

Baily Leon E. & Co. (Leon E. Baily & James J. Etchingham) 702 Seventh av.

Bain E. & W. (Ellen & Winifred) 336 Bleecker

Bainbridge Henry & Co. (John G. Bainbridge, only) 99 William

Baird M. & J. (Matthew & James) 337 E. 63d

MERCHANTS EXCHANGE NAT. BANK OF THE CITY OF N. Y.
SOLICITS YOUR ACCOUNT. **257 Broadway.**
PHINEAS C. LOUNSBURY, President.   ALLEN S. APGAR, Cashier.

BAI 21 BAL

Baird W. C. & Co. (William C. Baird & William Friend) 234 B'way & 201 W. 11th

Baird & Gourlay (William M. Baird & Duncan Gourlay) 27 Depeyster

Baird & Levi (John H. Baird & Arthur C. Levi;—special partner, William D. Cochran, $25,000; terminates 1st March, 1893) 7 Dond

Bais & Wakeman (Jacob Bais & Abram Wakeman jr.) 102 Front

Baker Adjustable Bearing Co. (inoperative) 218 Water

Baker Castor Oil Co. (Conrad Braker jr. Pres.; William D. Faris, Sec.; further inf. unattainable) 215 Pearl

Baker Francis & Co. (Francis & Wendell Baker) 22 Thomas

Baker Heater Co. (William C. Baker, Pres.; Frank H. Andrews, Sec. Capital, $50,000. Directors: Edwin S. Greuley, William C. Baker, Frank H. Andrews, C. A. Baker, L. M. Andrews) 556 W. 34th

Baker James & Sons (James & Robert Baker, only) 20 W. 4th

Baker James H. G. & Brother (dissolved) 194 Chambers

Baker Transfer Co. (James H. G. Baker, Pres.; William F. Baker, Sec. Capital, $10,000. Directors: James H. G. & William F. Baker & Wilson R. Toll) 194 Chambers

Baker White Brass Co. (Samuel E. Whitenack, propr.) 3 York

Baker A. S. & Co. (Arthur S. Baker, no Co.) 18 B'way

Baker H. J. & Brother (Conrad jr. & Henry J. Braker & William D. Faris, only) 215 Pearl

Baker S. T. & Co. (Edwin H. Baker, only) 295 Pearl

Baker & Bergen (no inf.) 00 W. 70th

Baker & Carver (Howard M. Baker & George A. & Amos D. Carver) 29 South

Baker & Dubois (Charles Baker & William E. Dubois) 121 Maiden la.

Baker & Eaton (James H. Baker & Smith S. Eaton) 54 College pl.

Baker & Shay (George O. Baker & John Shay) 167 South

Baker & Taylor Co. (James S. Baker, Pres.; Nelson Taylor jr. Sec. Capital, $40,000. Directors: James S. Baker, Nelson & Nelson Taylor jr.) 740 B'way

Baker & Williams (Frederick Baker, James B. Williams, William H. Bench, Francis S. Phraner & Pierre F. Macdonald) 501 & 510 Wash. 441 G'wich, 45 Vestry, 86 Laight, 272 Front, 274, 285 & 300 Water & 72 Beaver

Baker, Kent & Ely (dissolved) 621 Madison av.

Baker, Smith & Co. (John J. & Charles H. & Elias D. Smith, only) 79 W. Houston

Baker, Voorhis & Co. (William H. Harrison, Pres.; Orlando P. Thomson, Sec.; further inf. unattainable) 66 Nassau

Bakers' Assn. (William Grevel, Pres.; Alfred Romer, Sec.; Christian Friedmann, Treas. Directors: William Grevel, Percy Rockwell, Christian Friedmann, Alfred Romer, J. F. Hildebrand, J. A. Dahn, Chilson B. Docker) 788 B'way & 78 E. 10th

Bakers' & Consumers' Compressed Yeast Co. (Thomas Fletcher, Pres.; Andrew T. Fletcher, Sec.; further inf. refused) 142 Second av.

Balance Valve & Steam Piston Packing Co. (Eugene Deberri, Pres.; Peter Milne, Sec. Capital, $100,000. Directors: Eugene Deberri, Peter Milne, Thomas R. Sharp, William C. Bowers, Samuel P. Halsey) 280 B'way

Balbin Brothers (Gabriel & Benigno Balbin) 103 Maiden la.

Balch A. W. & Co. (Alonzo W. Balch & George B. Lowarre) 84 Front

Balck & Roessle (Frederick O. Balck, only) 218 E. 59th

Balcom & Co. (dissolved) 143 Fulton mkt

Baldinger & Braun (Max Baldinger & Samuel Braun) 134 Ridge

Baldwin Austin & Co. (Austin P. & Radcliffe Baldwin) 58 B'way

Baldwin Eli & Son (Eli & Walter S. Baldwin) 139 Fulton

Baldwin E. E. & B. (dissolved) 80 Mercer

Baldwin F. J. & Co. (Fanning J. Baldwin; no Co.) 1191 B'way

Baldwin J. W. & Co. (Joseph W. Baldwin, Co. refused) 19 Beekman

Baldwin & Baker (Charles S. Baldwin & Josiah W. Baker) 5 & 7 W. 34th

Baldwin & Blackmar (Edwin Baldwin & Abel E. Blackmar) 85 Liberty

Baldwin & Carhart (dissolved) Pier 2 E. R.

Baldwin & Co. (servants) (dissolved) 621 Sixth av.

Baldwin & Co. (trunks) (Theodore F. Baldwin, no Co.) 1159 B'way

Baldwin & Gleason Co. (Ltd.) (Marcus W. Baldwin, Pres.; Thomas J. Gleason, Sec. Capital, $50,000. Directors: Marcus W. Baldwin, Thomas J. Gleason, Julius Waterman, Julius F. Toussaint, Atwood Porter, Elbridge G. Duvall jr.) 61 D'way

Baldwin Brothers & Co. (Austin P. & Radcliffe Baldwin & George B. Seymour) 58 B'way & 25 Water

Baldwin, Davidson & Wight (William D. Baldwin, Edward C. Davidson & Lloyd B. Wight) 41 Park row

Balfe & Co. (dissolved) 80 New Chambers

Balkans Mfg. Co. (William P. Ward, Pres.; Augustus C. Maas, Sec. Capital, $50,000. Trustees: William P. Ward, Augustus C. Maas) 50 Fifth av.

Balken W. S. & J. A. F. Hall (dissolved) 363 Bowery

Ball Electric Light Co. (William L. Brown, Pres.; Charles E. Ball, Sec.; James H. Breslin, Treas. Capital, $2,000,000. Directors: William L. Brown, James H. Breslin, Sherman H. Knevals, Charles E. Ball, Robert Dunlap, Solomon Sayles, W. W. Flannagan, John C. Noyes, George W. Cotterill, William S. Hopkins) 18 Cortlandt

Ball Electrical Illuminating Co. (Joseph J. Snow, Pres.; Michael Crane, Sec.; Lawrence E. Buckley, Treas. Capital $250,000. Trustees: Joseph J. Snow, Michael Crane, Lawrence E. Buckley) 131 W. 38th

Ball Thomas P. & Co. (Thomas P. & Edward A. Ball) 54 South

Ball E. M. & Co. (Elias M. Ball & John W. Day) 49 Leonard

Ball Brothers (no inf.) 1158 B'way

Ball & Co. (Samuel R. Ball & Lyman H. Dusenberry) 810 B'way

Ball & Lester (William E. Ball & Edward W. Lester) 106 Duane

Ball & Lussier (no inf.) 200 E. 115th

Ball & Ray (Thomas L. Ball & Charles E. Ray) 92 Bleecker

Ball, Florsheim & Co. (Thomas H. Ball & Simon Florsheim, no Co.) 402 B'way

Ball, Parker & Waters (Thomas F. Ball, William Parker & George L. Waters) 21 Cliff

Ballantine P. & Sons (John H. & Robert F. Ballantine, only) 134 Cedar

Ballantine & Co. (John H. & Robert F. Ballantine) 134 Cedar

Ballard Stephen & Co. (Stephen Ballard & Elias B. Brown) 123 Chambers

Ballard J. H. & A. (Joseph H. & Agnes) 38 Howard

CINCINNATI, BALTIMORE, PHILADELPHIA, | **SNOW, CHURCH & CO.** CORRESPONDENTS EVERYWHERE. | NEW YORK, BOSTON, CHICAGO, LOUISVILLE.

BAL 22 BAN

Ballenberg Samuel & Brother (dissolved) 136 E. 14th, 1211 B'way & 57 W. 42d
Ballin G. & J. (Gustav N. & Jacques) 855 B'way
Ballin Brothers (Morris & Louis Ballin & Julius P. Banmann) 14 Walker
Ballin & Berman (William Dallin & Emanuel Berman) 274 Church
Ballin & Co. (Oscar E. Ballin & David James King) 40 Wall
Ballin, Joseph & Co. (Julius Ballin, Elias Joseph, Ernest Werner & Edward Stieglitz) 96 Franklin
Ballou George William & Co. (George William Ballou, no Co.) 5 Wall
Balsamo A. & Brother (Antonio & Saverio Balsamo) 374 W. 65th
Balsan Brothers (Emile & Henry & Hillarion & Charles Balsan) 98 Grand
Balsells & Co. (Jose & Juan Balsells) 4 Stone
Baltimore Twine & Net Co. (dissolved) 235 Pearl
Baltimore & Ohio Express Co. (U. S. Express Co. proprs.) 49 B'way
Baltimore, Cincinnati & Western Railway (William T. Hart, Pres.; Edward K. Hayt, Sec.; George E. Horne, Treas. Directors: William T. Hart, Edward K. Hayt, George E. Horne) 171 B'way
Balz Brothers (Jacob & Adam Balz) 100 E. 14th
Bambach H. & Son (Henry & Edward W. Bambach) 108 Essex
Bamber Roger & Co. (William & Ellen Bamber, only) 87 Warren
Bamberg J. & Co. (Jacob & Wallace Bamberg & David Shoeline) 643 B'way
Bamberger G. & M. (Gilbert & Martin) 75 Greene
Bamberger S. & Co. (Samuel Bamberger & Jacob Benedict) 944 Third av.
Bamberger & Oberndorf (Herman Bamberger & Edward Oberndorf) 16 White
Bamman & Evers (Frederick Bamman & Frederick Evers) 2163 Third av.
Damman & Wohltman (Henry Bamman & Louis J. H. Wohltman) 2619 Tenth av.
Bamonte & Rizzo (Carmine Bamonte & Angelo Rizzo) 70 Crosby
Bampton F. W. & Co. (Frederick W. Bampton & Walter H. Beebe) 206 South & 401 Water
Bancel & Pastorini (Ferdinand Bancel & Liberato P. Pastorini) 1140 Third av.
Bancroft George & Co. (George & Aaron Bancroft) 60 B'way
Bandler Brothers (Max & William A. & Bernard Bandler) 506 B'way
Baney J. & Son (Jacob & Miles W. Baney) 19 Vestry
Bangs & Co. (Fletcher H. Bangs, no Co.) 739 B'way
Bangs, Stetson, Tracy & MacVeagh (Grover Cleveland, Francis Lynde Stetson, Charles W. Bangs, Charles Edward Tracy, Francis S. Bangs & Charles MacVeagh) 45 William
Bank for Savings (Merritt Trimble, Pres.; Robert S. Holt, Sec. Trustees: Merritt Trimble, Benjamin H. Field, James A. Roosevelt, Robert S. Holt, John T. Johnston, George DeF. Lord, Jacob D. Vermilye, Frederick D. Tappen, John J. Tucker, Adrian Iselin, John E. Parsons, John C. Brown, Alfred W. Spear, Carlisle Norwood, George M. Miller, Alfred M. Hoyt, Orlando B. Potter, Thomas Hillhouse, William A. Roe, William L. Andrews, Frederick W. Stevens, John M. Dodd jr., Oliver Harriman, Charles A. Sherman, Robert Winthrop, Henry W. DeForrest, William G. White, James Knowles, Richard L. Purdy) 67 Bleecker
Bank of America (William H. Perkins, Pres.; Dallas B. Pratt, Cashier; Frederic de P. Foster, Notary. Capital, $3,000,000. Directors: James M. Brown, William L. Jenkins, Samuel Thorne, Charles G. Landon, George A. Crocker, David S. Egleston, J. Hansen Rhoades, Augustus D. Juilliard, Oliver Harriman, Frederic P. Olcott) 46 Wall
Bank of Harlem (Charles H. Pinkham jr., Pres.; Charles E. Trotter, Cashier; John M. Roberts, Notary. Capital, $100,000. Directors: David F. Porter, John J. Sperry, Robert A. Hevenor, Frank Wanier, William H. Caldwell, Hanson C. Gibson, David M. Williams, William S. Gray, William W. Van Voorhis, Elliot Danforth, Charles H. Pinkham jr.) 242 W. 125th
Bank of New Amsterdam (Thomas C. Acton, Pres.; Nelson J. K. Edge, Cashier; Charles F. Devine, Notary. Capital, $250,000. Directors: John A. Stewart, Jacob D. Vermilye, Frederick D. Tappen, Jesse Seligman, George G. Haven, Thomas Denny, Samuel D. Babcock, James A. Roosevelt, John T. Terry, J. S. Barnes, Elihu Root, Thomas C. Acton, G. Hilton Scribner, Frank Curtiss, John L. Riker, Frank Tilford, Richard V. Lewis, George Jones, George W. Loss) 1434 B'way
Bank of New York (Charles M. Fry, Pres.; Ebenezer S. Mason, Cashier; Hanson C. Gibson, Notary. Capital, $2,000,000. Directors: James M. Constable, Charles M. Fry, Franklin Edson, Charles D. Leverich, George H. Byrd, James Moir, Gustav Amsinck, Anson W. Hard, Henry B. Laidlaw, Darius O. Mills, Eugene Kelly, John L. Riker, William M. Bradford) 48 Wall
Bank of North America (William Dowd, Pres.; Alvah Trowbridge, Cashier; Sidney Whittamore, Notary. Capital, $700,000. Directors: Henry A. Kent, William Dowd, John J. Donaldson, William D. Leonard, Henry H. Cook, Elihu Root, Stephen M. Clement, Salem H. Wales, David R. Houghtailing, Warner Van Norden, John H. Flagler, Henry D. Hyde, William F. Havemeyer) 25 Nassau
Bank of the Metropolis (Robert Schell, Pres.; Theodore Rogers, Cashier; John Deinhunty, Notary. Capital, $300,000. Directors: Samuel Sloan, William Steinway, Charles L. Tiffany, Joseph Park, Hicks Arnold, William B. Isham, William D. Sloane, Robert Schell) 29 Union sq. W.
Bank of the State of New York (Richard L. Edwards, Pres.; Beverley C. Duer, Cashier; Hanson C. Gibson, Notary. Capital, $1,200,000. Directors: Richard L. Edwards, James B. Colgate, David D. Withers, Charles M. Butler, Henry Hentz, Roosevell G. Rolston, James T. Olcmon, August Belmont jr, Eckstein Norton, James Swann, Benjamin C. Paddock, Edward T. Bedford) 35 William
Banker & Campbell (Albert C. Banker & William S. Campbell) 1768 B'way
Bankers' Publishing Assn. (George Marsland, propr.) 128 B'way
Bankers' Safe Deposit Co. (Harris C. Fahnestock, Pres.; Evander H. Schley, Sec.; James A. Garland, Treas. Capital, $100,000. Directors: Harris C. Fahnestock, George F. Baker, James A. Garland, Frederick F. Thompson, Fisher A. Baker) 4 Wall
Bankers' & Merchants' Alliance (Nathan Forbes, Pres.; Isaac B. Lewis, Sec.; Isaac L. V. Lewis, Treas. Trustees: Nathan Forbes, Edward R. Detts, Isaac L. V. & Isaac B. Lewis, D. S. Kimball, Andrew S. Hunter, Peter J. L. Searing, John A. Edwards, F. M. Stebbins, William J. Underwood, B. D. Southwick, Daniel A. Nesbitt, John Byers, John H. Rogers, Joshua Reeve jr., Charles A. Smith, A. L. Soulard) 185 B'way
Bankers' & Traders' Accident Assn. (Fletcher H. Bangs, Pres.; Joseph W. Abbott, Sec.; Oliver F. Berry, Treas. Directors: Fletcher H. & John K. Bangs, William M. Dean, Joseph W. Abbott, Oliver F. Berry, Andrew J. O. Foye, John Farr, John M. Korff, George C. Kobbe) 155 B'way

WATER METERS, GAS ENGINES, | **NATIONAL METER CO.**
FOR PUMPING AND POWER. | 252 Broadway, N. Y.

BAN 23 BAR

Banks A. & Co. (Augustine & William E. Banks) 66 B'way
Banks A. M. & Son (Ann M. & Orion Banks) 80 Park pl.
Banks H. W. & Co. (Henry W. Banks, D. Henderson Wells, James M. Montgomery, John D. Wells jr. & Henry W. Banks jr.) 111 Wall.
Banks Brothers (no inf.) 782 Second av.
Banks & Brothers (David & A. Bleecker Banks, only) 144 Nassau
Banks & Mackinney (dissolved) 1142 B'way
Bannan & Richter (Catharine R. Bannan & Elizabeth Richter) 146 Fifth av.
Banner Brothers (Simon & Peter Banner) 565 B'way
Bannigan P. & I. (Peter & Israel) 66 Greene
Banning & Monroe (Hubert A. Banning & Robert Grier Monroe) 140 Nassau
Banning, Bissell & Co. (William C. Banning & Edward H. Bissell, no Co.) 90 Reade
Bannon & Flanagan (Francis M. Bannon & Edward J. Flanagan) 218 Thompson
Bannon & Sullivan (John Bannon & Maurice J. Sullivan) 1506 Ninth av.
Bansbach & Mayberger (Christopher Bansbach & John Mayberger) 245 E. 37th
Banta George W. & Brothers (inf. unattainable) 19 Park pl. & 825 Sixth av.
Banta Brothers (E. & W. Banta) 82 Pearl
Baptist Review Assn. (Robert S. McArthur, Pres.; Henry C. Vedder, Sec.; James D. Squires, Treas. Capital, $5,000. Directors: Robert S. McArthur, Henry C. Vedder, James D. Squires, Washington Wilson, William M. Isaacs) 41 Park row
Barandon & Co. (Frederick Barandon & Henry Tatje) 120 Gwich
Barber Alfred & Son (dissolved) 377 Water
Barber Asphalt Paving Co. (Amzi L. Barber, Pres.; Joseph C. Hock, Sec.; Delos O. Wickham, Treas. Capital, $1,250,000. Directors: Amzi L. Barber, Francis V. Greene, Delos O. Wickham, E. Burgess Warren, Edmund Hayes, Frank H. Buell, William E. Barker) 1 B'way
Barber M. & Nephew (Marshall & Warren C. Barber) 65 Bayard
Barber & Co. (Herbert & James Barber) 35 B'way
Barber & Ziegler (Charles G. Barber & William H. Ziegler) 1 B'way
Barber's Alfred, Son (Henry G. Barber) 377 Water
Barbis E. & F. (Edward & Fernando) 900 Third av.
Barbour Flax Spinning Co. (Robert Barbour, Pres.; William Thompson, Sec.; William Barbour, Treas. Capital, $750,000. Directors: John D. & Robert & William Barbour, Garret A. Hobart, Alexander King, James S. Warren, E. T. Bell) 218 Church
Barhour A. E. & Co. (Adin E. & Aldin E. Barbour) 221 Pearl
Barbour Brothers Co. (William Barbour, Pres.; William Thompson, Sec.; Robert Barbour, Treas. Capital, $300,000. Directors: John D. & Robert & William Barbour, Garret A. Hobart, Alexander King, James S. Warren, E. T. Bell) 218 Church
Barbour, Brooke & Gardner (dissolved) 495 B'way
Barcalow & Minertzhagen (Richard G. Barcalow & Otto Minertzhagen) 76 Bowery
Barcelona Mining Co. (George Doyle, Pres.; Halsted C. Burnet, Sec.; George E. Righter, Treas. Capital, $5,000,000. Directors: Geo. Doyle, Halsted C. Burnet, George E. Righter) 18 B'way
Barchan & Son (Rebecca & Max Darchan) 193 Division.
Barclay Fibre Co. (William H. Parsons, Pres.; William H. Parsons, jr. Sec. Capital, $100,-000. Directors: John G. Myers, Charles A. Spalding, W. R. Sheffield, William H. & William H. Parsons jr.) 4 Warren
Barclay Street Refrigerating Warehouse Co. (Ltd.) (William S. Okie, Pres.; Julius D. Mahr, Sec.; Caspar Mahr, Treas. Capital, $40,000. Directors: William S. Okie, Charles Mulford, John Drohan, Caspar Mahr, R. L. Titus, John V. Inglee) 219 Washn.
Barclay & Co. (Reginald G. Barclay & Alexander Barrie) 44 & 15 Stone & 77 Pearl
Barclay & Livingston (Schuyler L. Mackie, only) 24 Beaver
Barclay & Parsons (Howard M. Barclay & Kenyon Parsons) 100 Water & 134 Pearl
Barclay, Macgregor & Co. (Samuel Barclay & James J. Macgregor, no Co.) 45 Exchange pl.
Bardillo Marble Mfg. Co. (William L. Strong, Pres.; Stephen D. Hatch, Sec. Capital, $100,-000. Directors: Charles B. Barker, Treas.; H. Herbert Howard, Sec. Capital, $55,000. Directors: William A. Abbott, Charles B. Barker, Charles & H. Herbert Howard, George H. Dieloch) 65 E. 9th
Bardsley Brothers (Joseph & William Bardsley) 118 Worth
Barger F. C. & Co. (Frederick C. Barger & Putnam H. Acres) 82 Warren
Barget & Birgel (Charles Barget & Henry F. Birgel) 2 Liberty
Barker C. B. & Co. (Ltd.) (William A. Abbott, Pres.; Charles B. Barker, Treas.; H. Herbert Howard, Sec. Capital, $55,000. Directors: William A. Abbott, Charles B. Barker, Charles & H. Herbert Howard, George H. Dieloch) 65 E. 9th
Barker D. & Son (Daniel & John B. Barker) 146 Reade
Barker D. P. & Co. (Daniel F. & Sophronia M. Barker) 254 Washn. mkt
Barker J. H. & Co. (Joseph H. Barker & Charles F. Chamberlaine;—special partners, Frederick Roosevelt & George B. Brown, each $10,000; terminates 1st Dec., 1891) 328 Cherry
Barker & Co. (brokers) (Edward Barker, George E. Brown & Samuel W. Thompson) 212 B'way
Barker & Co. (rubber gds.) (Stephen T. Barker, no Co.) 27 Maiden la.
Barker & Eggers Co. (Caleb Barker, Pres.; John R. Eggers, Sec. Capital, $25,000. Directors: Caleb Barker, John T. M. Brewster, John H. & Bernard C. Eggers) 6 Barclay
Barklage J. H. & Son (John H. & William H. Barklage) 617 Ninth av. & 539 W. 47th
Barkley Co. (not inc.) (John C. & J. M. Barkley) 492 S. Boulevard
Barlow & Bancroft (Charles A. Barlow & John M. Bancroft) 53 William
Barlow & Carman (dissolved) 206 B'way
Barlow & Wetmore (Francis C. Barlow & Charles W. Wetmore) 206 B'way
Barnard L. S. & Co. (Louis S. Barnard & Morris Levy) 103 Chambers
Barnard W. A. & Co. (William A. & Alfred Barnard) 171 Park row
Barnard & Olendorf (Frederick F. Barnard & Charles B. Olendurf) 234 B'way
Barnes A. C., Whip Co. (dissolved) 47 Warren
Barnes A. E. & Brother (Ambrose E. & Walter F. Barnes) 195 Canal
Barnes A. S. & Co. (Alfred C. & Henry B. & Charles J. & Edwin M. & Richard S. & William D. Barnes, only) 111 William
Barnes H. M. & Co. (Hollis M. Barnes, Co. refused) 52 E. 110th
Barnes Brothers (Davis & Howell H. Barnes) 18 New
Barnes Samuel T. & Co. (Samuel T. Barnes, Co. refused) 155 E. 110th

PROTECTION For Family, Home, Store, Factory, etc., by using only the "VULCAN" BRAND OF SAFETY MATCHES. Headquarters, 373 Washington Street, New York.

BAR 24 BAR

Barnes & Merritt (Theodore M. Barnes & Richard P. Merritt:—special partner, Edwin Thorne, $200,000; terminates 31st January, 1892) 55 Frankfort

Barnes & Scarff (Joseph B. Barnes & George S. Scarff) 207 E. 110th

Barnes, Hutchinson & Pierce (Charles D. Barnes, George Hutchinson & William D. Pierce) 46 White

Barnes, Taylor & Co. (dissolved) 123 Franklin

Barnet J. S. & Brother (Jonas S. & Morris S. Barnet) 27 Spruce

Barnett A. & Co. (Aaron Barnett, no Co.) 48 Leonard & 451 G'wich

Barnett F. & Co. (Flora Barnett & Lillian Pollak) 695 B'way

Barnett S. & Son (Solomon & Harry H. Barnett) 102 Water

Barnett & Co. (Moses Barnett & Nelson Crawford) 9 E. 12th

Barnett & Rosentall (Isaac Barnett & William Rosentall) 114 Nassau

Barney & Wells (Hiram Barney & Edward & Edward Wells jr.) 111 B'way

Barnston Tea Co. (Ltd.) (Lother W. Faber, Pres.; Charles H. Mundy, Sec.; C. Kennedy Hamilton, Treas. Capital, $5,000. Directors: Lother W. Faber, Charles H. Mundy, C. Kennedy Hamilton, Oscar Shulder, James G. Hamilton, Charles F. Polck, Herman Kings) 25 S. William

Barnum S. C. & Co. (Stephen C. Barnum & George Crosby) 8 Chatham sq.

Barnum & Co. (cards) (Susan E. Barnum, no Co.) 20 N. William

Barnum & Co. (clothing) (Edward C. & Edward H. Barnum & Albert J. Lyon) 110 Cherry

Barnum & Robhann (Edmund B. Barnum & Frederick W. Robhann) 115 Nassau

Barnum Brothers & Co. (Charles E. & Fayette S. Barnum, no Co.) 13 Walker

Barnutt & Diehl (John Barnutz & Peter Diehl) 148 Seventh av.

Baron M. & Brother (Max & Henry Baron) 83 Allen

Baron S. & Co. (Samuel & Theodore S. Baron & Max H. Straus) 90 Franklin

Barr Edward, Co. (Ltd.) (Albert L. Murphy, Pres.; Edward Barr, Sec. Capital $30,000. Directors: Albert L. Murphy, Edward Barr) 79 John

Barr Electric Mfg. Co. (inf. unattainable) 7 B'way

Barr & Co. (George Barr & Catharine Coop) 117 John, 97 Mercer, 313 Canal, & 153 W. B'way

Barr & Miller (b'khinders) (dissolved) 79 White

Barr & Miller (coffee) (Thomas M. Barr & Harry D. Miller:—special partner, Thomas T. Barr, B'klyn, N. Y. $50,000; terminates 31st Dec. 1890) 107 Front

Barranco M. & Co. (Manuel F. Barranco & Benjamin J. Guerra) 65 Barclay

Barratt & Cauldwell (J. Arthur Barratt & Thomas W. Cauldwell) 11 Pine

Barré Joseph & Co. (Joseph Barré, no Co.) 71 Fulton

Barren Island Oil & Guano Co. (Leon Rheinstrom, Pres.; Philip J. Goodhart, Sec.; O. D. Baldwin, Treas. Capital, $40,000. Directors: Leon Rheinstrom, Philip J. Goodhart, O. D. Baldwin) 89 S. William

Barrett Boiler Compound Co. (not inc.) (George N. Weston, manager) 111 B'way

Barrett F. A. & Co. (Peter A. & James P. Barrett) 460 W. 42d

Barrett W. S. & Co. (William Skidmore Barrett & George Palen) 1274 B'way & ft. E. 20th

Barrett Brothers (William C. & Hooper C. Barrett) 1492 B'way

Barrett & Carr (dissolved) 1539 Third av.

Barrett & Co. (James Barrett, Co. refused) 127 Broad

Barrett & Dooling (dissolved) 184 Front

Barrett & Jones (Thomas Barrett & John J. Jones) 202 E. 32d

Barrett & McGuire (Dennis J. Barrett & F. McGuire) 1447 Third av.

Barrett, Nephews & Co. (Charles W. Kennedy, V. Pres.; Charles E. Heal, Sec. Capital, $132,000. Directors: Clarence T. Barrett, Charles E. Heal, Charles W. Kennedy) 34 E. 14th, 12 John, 1190 B'way, 844 Sixth av., & 2390 Eighth av.

Barretts, Palmer & Heal Dyeing Establishment (Henry D. Palmer, Pres.; William H. Barrett, Sec. Capital, $112,000. Trustees: Reuben N. & William H. Barrett, Henry D. Palmer, Amos B. Heal) 346 Canal

Barres Charles & Co. (Charles Barres, S. Granville Beals & Charles H. Cavalli) 454 Broome

Barron James S. & Co. (James S. & William H. Barron) 141 Chambers & 2 Hudson

Barron H. J. & Co. (dissolved) 76 Cortlandt

Barron M. & J. (dissolved) 610 Ninth av.

Barron & Co. (dissolved) 82 B'way

Barrow & Anderson (David Barrow & John H. Anderson) 56 Worth

Barrows H. P. & Co. (Henry F. & Henry F. jr., & Ira Barrows) 1½ Maiden la.

Darrows & Gould (dissolved) 120 William

Barrows & Greene (Richard H. Barrows & John A. Greene) 41 Park row

Darry J. F. & Co. (John F. & F. S. Darry) 52 William

Barry Brothers (liquors) (dissolved) 2339 Third av.

Barry Brothers (waters) (Thomas J. & John & James Barry) 328 E. 88th

Barry & Keegan (John J. Darry & John J. Keegan) 1886 Vanderbilt av. W.

Barry & Piohatzuk (dissolved) 530 E. 14th

Barse, Smith & Co. (J. Frederick Barse, Frank J. Smith, no Co.) 68 Wall

Barstow Stove Co. (Amos C. Barstow. Pres.; Amos C. Barstow jr., Sec. Capital, $250,000. Directors: Amos C. & Amos C. Barstow jr., E. A. Stevens, Charles D. Hotchkiss) 230 Water

Barstow & Williams (Nathaniel Barstow & Walter S. Williams) 198 B'way

Bartelmes H. & Sons (Hartman Bartelmes, only) 401 Eighth

Bartelstone & Edelman (Harris Bartelstone & Jacob Edelman) 15 New Bowery

Bartens & Rice (Charles F. A. Bartens & Thomas E. Rice) 20 John

Barter & Kiernan (Albion K. Barter & Thomas F. Kiernan) 36 South

Barth & Dittmers (George Barth & Christal Dittmers) 50 Carmine

Bartholdi Hotel Co. (Robert Stafford, Pres.; Capital $50,000. Directors: Robert Stafford. J. P. Whittaker, W. C. Hall) 956 B'way

Bartholomae H. & Co. (Hugo Bartholomae & Edward E. Williams) 190 W. 33d

Bartholomew & Peckham (William H. Bartholomew & Henry M. Peckham) 18 Spruce

Bartlett George C. & Co. (George C. Bartlett & George V. A. Conger) 481 B'way

Bartlett Street Lamp Mfg. Co. (Gilbert S. Cook, Pres.; Thomas Davenport, Treas. Capital, $10,000. Trustees: Gilbert S. Cook, Thomas Davenport, George B. Barcalow) 42 College pl.

Bartlett E. B. & Co. (Edward D. Bartlett. Albert C. Woodruff & Henry E. Nitchie) 5 Hanover

Bartlett F. & C A. H. (Franklin & Clifford A. H.) 168 Nassau

Bartlett N. S. & Co. (Nelson S. Bartlett & George H. Curtis) 52 Wall

IDEN & CO.,
University Place, 9th to 10th Sts., N. Y.

MANUFACTURERS OF GAS FIXTURES AND ELECTROLIERS

BAR 25 BAV

Bartlett & Co. (Edward E. Bartlett & Theodore Vonderlinhe) 194 B'way
Bartlett & Plummer (Edward Plummer, only) 1300 B'way & 405 Fifth av.
Bartlett & Wood (dissolved) 310 Lenox av.
Bartlett, Wilson & Hayden (Edward T. Bartlett, Philip L. Wilson & Henry W. Hayden) 48 Wall
Bartmann & Co. (Theodore H. Bartmann, no Co.) 343 B'way
Barton J. C. & Co. (Josiah C. & Eula E. Barton) 318 B'way
Barton & Whittemore (George De Forest Barton & William I. Whittemore) 106 B'way
Bartow Theodosius & Sons (Theodosius & Theodosius jr. & Edward W. Bartow) 140 Nassau
Bartram F. S. & C. B. (Ferdinand S. & Charles B.) 126 William
Bartram Brothers (Joseph B. Bartram, only) 62 Pearl
Bartruff & Vanarsdale (Charles M. Bartruff & Stephen T. Vanarsdale) 150 West
Baruch H. & Son (Henry & Jacob Baruch) 21 Av. C
Barwise & Son (Charles A. & Charles A Barwise jr.) 110 Front
Barwood & Co. (Gustav & Lena Barwood) r 14 Wooster
Bas-Relief Advertising Sign Co. (Henry Fochteler, propr.) 1471 Park av.
Bas-Relief Mfg Co. (Salomon Salomon, Pres.; Hermann Kaufmann, Sec. Capital, $25,000. Directors: Salomon Salomon, Hermann Kaufmann, Gustav Salomon) 1220 Second av.
Basch E. & I. (dissolved) 302 Bowery
Basch & Greenfield Co. (Joseph Peder, Pres.; Charles J. Basch, Sec. Capital, $42,300; further inf. unattainable) 187 Duane
Basedow J. & Co. (Justus Basedow & Henry C. Herrmann) 120 Orchard
Baskerville's Paul, Sons (Thomas R. & William Baskerville) 617 G'wich
Basler & Bischoff (Louisa Basler & Henry J. Bischoff) 177 Third av.
Bass & Parker (dissolved) 63 Maiden la.
Bassett George F. & Co. (George F. Bassett, Edward F. Anderson & Frederick H. Doremus) 49 Barclay & 52 Park pl.
Bassett Jewelry Co. (Stephen W. Bassett, Pres.; George W. Bleecker, Sec. Capital, $50,000. Directors: William A. Copeland, Stephen W. Bassett, Theodore L. Parker, George W. Bleecker) 9 Maiden la.
Bassford H. A. & Co. (Henry A. Bassford, no Co.) 595 B'way & 162 Mercer
Bastable & Mannigan (Lawrence Bastable & James H. Mannigan) 926 B'way
Bastine & Co. (Andrew J. & Mary E. Bastine) 41 Warren
Batcheller & Beal (William H. Batcheller & Royal A. Beal) 47 Leonard
Batchelor W. A. & Co. (William A. Batchelor & Lewis C. Wilson) 30 E. 10th
Bate Refrigerating Co. (Richard Lacy, V. Pres.; Paul H. Bate, Sec. Capital, $60,000. Directors: Richard Lacy, Paul H. & J. Jay Bate) 5 Beekman
Bateman & Co. (Arthur E. Bateman & Charles E. Coon) 57 B'way
Bateman & Pollard (Charles E. Bateman & Horatio H. Pollard) 143½ E. 23d
Bates Edwin & Co. (Charles K. Bates, Charles B. Kidder & William T. Gilroy, only) 79 Spring
Bates J. Walker & Co. (no inf.) 47 Liberty
Bates James T. & Co. (James T. & John C. Bates) 11 Wall
Bates Mfg. Co. (Edwin G. Bates, propr.) 42 W. 23d

Bates Martin jr. & Co. (Charles S. & C. Francis Bates, Lewis H. Rogers & John B. Lingg, only) 163 Greene
Bates A. J. & Co. (Andrew J. & Jerome E. Bates) 202 Church & 50 Thomas
Bates E. C. & Co. (Edward C. & Rodney F. Bates) 2 Wall
Bates I. & Son (Isaac & George A. Bates) 65 South
Bates Brothers (Wells R. & Dewitt C. Bates) 11 Wall
Bates & Bacon (Joseph M. Bates & George M. Bacon) 196 B'way
Bateson & Armstrong (Charles E. Bateson & John J. Armstrong) 116 Franklin
Batjer H. A. & Co. (Henry Batjer, Alfred Leeb & Ferdinand Hartwig, only) 77 Water
Batopilas Mining Co. (George W. Quintard, Pres.; Andros B. Stone, Treas.; Lyndon H. Stevens, Sec. Capital, $9,000,000. Directors: George W. Quintard, Andros B. Stone, Louis H. Scott, Thomas L. Crittenden, Lyndon H. Stevens, John N. Hayward, Edward V. Loew, Samuel Elliott, William F. Mattingly, Juan M. Ceballos, William F. Davis, Bentley D. Hasall, Alexander R. Shepherd) 15 Broad
Battelle & Renwick (John G. Steenken, Edward J. Brockett & William C. Renwick, only) 163 Front
Batterson, See & Eisele (James G. Batterson, Walter F. See & John Eisele) 431 Eleventh av.
Battle House Hotel Co. (Ltd.) (dissolved) 11 Pine
Bauder Brothers (Arthur L. & William Bauder) 8 Fulton mkt
Bauendahl H. & Co. (Henry Bauendahl, no Co.) 76 Leonard
Bauer J. C. & Co. (Jacob C. Bauer & Isaac Porter jr.) 366 Canal
Bauer & Muller (Louis Bauer & Julius Muller) 376 E. Houston & 239 Second
Baum Charles S. & Co. (Charles S. Baum, Charles G. Yohn, Michael Baum & Michael Schiff) 654 B'way
Baum J. & Co. (no inf.) 869 Second av.
Baum L. & Son (Louis & M. C. Baum) 1692 Park av.
Baum & Friedman (Mayer Baum & Moses Friedman) 101 Nassau
Baum & Gross (Jacob S. Baum & William Gross) 2 Bowery
Baum & Mandel (Siegmund Baum & Louis Mandel) 54 Walker
Bauman & Sperling (Louis Bauman & Isidor Sperling) 58 Walker
Baumann Ludwig & Co. (Ludwig Baumann & David Frochlich) 514 Eighth av. & 22 E. 14th
Baumann J. & S. (Jacob & Samuel) 732 Eighth av.
Bauman S. & Brother (Samuel & Jacob Baumann, 39 W. 23d
Baumann Brothers (furniture) (Ludwig Baumann, only) 24 E. 14th & 21 E. 18th
Baumann Brothers (teas) (Albert & William Baumann) 16 Av. B
Baumbach J. & W. (dissolved) 335 E. 10th
Baumert F. X. & Co. (Christina Baumort, only) 26 Av. A
Baumgart & Co. (no inf.) 1459 Third av.
Baumgart & Kubel (Henry J. Baumgart & John Kubel) 1107 Third av.
Baumgarten M. & Co. (dissolved) 25 Lispenard
Baur & Byrne (dissolved) 344 E. 117th
Baur & Kocher (Eugene J. Baur & John H. Kocher) 52 Nassau
Baus & Co. (Augustus Baus & Charles Baumeister) 553 W. 30th
Bavarian Lithographic Stone Co. (Hermann, Schmidt & Co. proprs.) 65 Warren
Bavier, Meyer & Co. (refused) 452 Broome

TYPEWRITING DONE BY THE TROW CITY DIRECTORY CO., 11 University Place.

BAW 26 BEC

Bawo & Dotter (Francis H. Bawo:—special partner, Charles T. Dotter. $75,000; terminates 1st Jan. 1891) 80 Barclay

Baxter Electric Mfg. & Motor Co. (no inf.) 35 Park row

Baxter Wrecking Co. (John F. Baxter, propr.) 808 West

Baxter & Jones (William H. Baxter & Cyrus D. Jones) 15 Bond

Bay State Corset Co. (not Inc.) (Charles L. Olmstead & Albert D. Nason) 99 Franklin

Bay State Gas Co. (no inf.) 120 B'way

Bay State Shoe & Leather Co. (Charles E. Bigelow, Pres.; John B. Colton, Sec.; Frederick A. Neergaard, Treas. Capital, $400,000; further inf. unattainable) 91 Chambers & 78 Reade

Bay State Steam Carpet Cleaning Works (Sydney T. Johnson, propr.) 153 W. 24th

Bayaud & Stevens (Theodore W. Bayaud, only) 60 New

Bayer & Braun (Frank Bayer & Valentine Braun) 83 First av.

Bayer & Fletcher (Adolph Bayer & Frank Fletcher) 66 Beekmann

Bayer & Israel (dissolved) 46 Orchard

Bayer & Scherbner (Charles Bayer & Paul Scherbner) 449 W. 41st

Bayles J. H. & Co. (dissolved) 36 West

Bayles Brothers (no inf.) 121 Chambers

Baylis & Co. (Abraham D. & William Baylis & Alfred R. Kimball) 44 Exchange pl.

Bayne William & Co. (William & William jr. & Lawrence P. Bayne:—special partner, Daniel K. Bayne, $40,000; terminates 21st Oct. 1892) 59 Front

Baynes Tracery & Mosaic Co. (Frederic Shonnard, Pres.; Lockwood de Forest, Sec.; Charles H. Montague. Treas. Capital, $40,000. Directors: Frederic Shonnard, Charles H. Montague, George H. Holmes) 607 W. 36th

Bazzi & Fognazi (dissolved) 525 Sixth av.

Bazzoni & Wittkowsky (Francis E. Bazzoni & Herman Wittkowsky) 203 E. 88th

Beach J. C. & Brother (James C. & Robert J. Beach) 81 B'way

Beach & Sherwood (John Beach & Charles E. Sherwood) 139 Franklin

Beadle & Adams (William Adams, only) 98 William

Beadleston & Woerz (William H. & Alfred N. Beadleston, Ernst G. W. Woers & De Forest Fox) 291 W. 10th & 158 Charles

Beakes A. S. & Co. (Albert S. & Charles H. C. Beakes) 307 W. 44th

Beal William R., Land Improvement Co. (William R. Beal, Pres.; Alfred B. Hall, Sec.; John A. Norman, Treas. Capital, $300,000. Directors: William R. Beal, Wilber L. Molenaaux, William H. McCord. Francis B. Chedsey, John A. Norman, Franklin Lynch, Harry B. & Alfred D. Hall) 350 Alexander av.

Beals Railway Brake Co. (Thomas B. Atkins, Pres.; Robert W. Gilbert, Sec. Capital, $150,000. Directors: Thomas B. Atkins, Robert W. Gilbert, Henry B. Hammond, William D. Ellis, George Cochran) 53 B'way

Beals & Thomas (Leonard S. Beals & Philip Thomas) r 17 John

Beam Brothers (John & Walter Beam) 150 Crosby

Bean & Finnerty (John Dean & Joseph Flunerty) 393 Eighth av.

Bean & Sweetser (Chandler R. Bean & Edward R. Sweetser) 88 Leonard

Bear Creek Gold Mining Co. (Newcomb C. Barney, Pres.; J. Clement Uhler, Sec.; Daniel B. Horton, Treas. Capital, $250,000. Directors: Newcomb C. Barney, Daniel B. Horton) 32 B'way

Beard Samuel S. & Co. (Samuel S. & Eli Beard) 160 Duane

Beardsley's J. W., Sons (George A. & Samuel R. Beardsley) 179 West

Bearns Joseph H. & Co. (Joseph H. Bearns & John N. Cruelas) 253 Washn.

Beasley A. W. & Co. (Alfred W. Beasley, no Co.) 2 Wall

Beattie James & Co. (dissolved) 510 W. 15th

Beattie Robert & Sons (Robert & William Beattie, only) 85 White

Beattie & Green (dissolved) 601 Eighth av.

Beatty & Votteler (James B. Beatty & William Votteler) 103 West

Beattys & Low (George D. Beattys & Walter C. Low) 140 Nassau

Beauchamp & Sarnorna (dissolved) 1180 Lex. av.

Beaudet J. & E. P. (John & Ernest P.) 1983 Seventh av.

Beauvais & Bockwrath (Louise Beauvais & Annetta Bockwrath) 17 Abingdon sq.

Beaver & Dorf (no inf.) 816 Canal

Bebee R. W., Express Co. (Rial W. Bebee, propr.) 1061 B'way

Becerra's E. L., Nephew & Co. (Daniel Byrne, only) 38 Water

Becherer's Joseph, Son (Charles J. Becherer) 173 Suffolk

Bechstein F. & Son (Frederick & Frederick D. Bechstein) 132 West

Bechstein & Co. (Augustus C. Bechstein & William P. Ross) 100 Hudson & ft. W. 40th

Beck Charles F. & Son (Charles F. & William F. Beck) 1015 Sixth av.

Beck Fr. & Co. (Frederick Beck & Charles E. Runk) 534 Seventh av. 281 Fifth av. & 611 W. 30th

Beck Gottlieb & Son (Gottlieb & Edward Beck) 222 W. 80th

Beck Joseph & Co. (Joseph Beck & Bernhard Stahl) 183 Reade

Beck C. & F. (Charles & Frederick) 50 Av. A

Beck F. E. & Co. (Frank E. Beck, no Co.) 1001 Third av.

Beck J. & Son (Julius Beck, only) 10 Liberty pl.

Beck Brothers (meat) (Samuel & Frank Beck) 1720 Ninth av.

Beck Brothers (ribbons) (Don Alonzo & Theodore L. Beck) 889 Hudson

Beck & Braun (George Beck & Charles Braun) 547 Second av.

Beck & Egger (Gottfried Beck & Jacob Egger) 531 Courtlandt av.

Beck & Gersten (Hyman Beck & Morris Gersten) 112 Clinton

Beck & Graves (no inf.) 2506 Eighth av.

Beck & Kanitz (Max Beck & Adolph Kanitz) 302 Second av.

Beck & Steisner (dissolved) 430 E. 76th

Beckel Joseph & Co. (Joseph Beckel, Isaac Strauss & Benjamin F. Beckel) 394 B'way

Becker H. & Co. (Nicholas Bruel & Otto Goepel:—special partner, Christian H. Schultz, $50,000; terminates 31st Dec. 1892) 28 S. William

Becker H. & N. (Hyman & Nathan) 127 Stanton

Becker W. F. & Co. (William F. Becker & John Van Vorst) 172 W. B'way

Becker Brothers (engravers) (Philip & George Becker) 30 Gt. Jones

Becker Brothers (grocers) (John F. & Frederick W. Becker) 381 Park av.

Becker Brothers (lapidaries) (August & Charles Becker) 71 Nassau

Becker Brothers (liquors) (Julia Becker, only) 106 Eighth av.

Becker Brothers (provns.) (John & Adolph Becker) 1530 Second av.

**THE CALIGRAPH WRITING MACHINE,
HARTFORD, CONN.**

Becker Brothers (scales) (Christian Becker, only) 6 Murray
Becker & Co. (boxes) (dissolved) 8 Second
Becker & Co. (frames) (Francis & Frank Becker, jr.) 390 W. 35th
Becker & Downs (Alexander R. Becker & Wallace A. Downs) 1595 Ninth av.
Becker & Jacobi (Matilda Becker & Olga Jacobi) 207 E. 117th
Becker & Kohl (C. Adolph Becker & Daniel Kohl) 35 Ann
Beckermann & Co., (Dederick Beckermann & William Junghans) 274 Canal
Beckett Foundry & Machinery Co., (Frank A. Chapman, Sec. Capital, $150,000. Directors; Frank A. Chapman, J. L. Merriam, G. L. Hutchings, Joseph F. Sweezy, Ezra Osborn) 120 Liberty
Beckett & Bradford (James A. Beckett, only) 35 Vesey
Bedell C. C. & Co. (Caleb C. Bedell, James H. Ser & Rudolph Schaefer) 340 Fourth av.
Bedell D. B. & Co. (Charles E. Mosher, only) 866 B'way
Bedell & Brother Co. (not Inc.) (William A. & Francis M. Bedell) 1609 Fordham av.
Bedell & Merrell (Elizabeth A. Bedell & Azel F. Merrell) ft. Charles
Bedell & Parcels (dissolved) 128 Broad
Bedell & Trimmer (Alva A. Bedell & Samuel Trimmer) 514 E. 184th
Bedell & Wolf (Edward Bedell & August Wolf) 96 Canal
Bedford & Kellum (no inf.) 280 B'way
Bee Line Transp. Co. (Lehigh Valley R. R. Co. proprs.) 1 B'way
Beebe Warren & Co. (Warren & Leonard Beebe) 94 Front
Beebe Brothers (Clarence & Charles Beebe) 157 B'way
Beebe & Brother (Charles E. & Charles W. Beebe) 190 Water
Beebe & Saulnier (dissolved) 97 Front
Beeber M. & Co., (Max Beeber & Jacob Lehman) 475 B'way & 48 Mercer
Beech Creek Cannel Coal Co. (refused) 1 B'way
Beech Creek Railroad Co. (Allyn Cox, Sec. Capital, $5,000,000. Directors; Cornelius & William K. Vanderbilt, George J. Magee, Joseph M. Gazzam, George F. Baer, Marilu E. Olmsted) Grand Central depot
Beech & Shaw (Thomas Beech & George H. Shaw) 125 Fulton
Beecher & Benedict (Henry Barton Beecher, Seelye & Andrew C. Benedict & Henry W. Beecher) 145 B'way
Beeck & Klute (George A. Beeck & George Klute) 847 Seventh av.
Beeken & Geary (dissolved) 13 Park row
Beekman Publishing Co. (Julian Ralph, Pres.; John Ford, Sec.; John H. Duffy, Treas. Capital, $20,000. Directors: Julian Ralph, John Ford, John H. Duffy, Andrew W. Dillings) 12 Beekman
Beekman Brothers (Charles & Marcus Beekman) 1343 Third av.
Beekman & Blumenstok (Samuel Beekman & Max Blumenstok) 599 B'way & 174 Mercer
Beekman & Co., (dissolved) 189 E. 108th
Beerman Brothers (dissolved) 188 Greene
Beers J. B. & Co., (James B. & Frederick W. Beers) 36 Vesey
Beers Brothers (John M. & Samuel A. Beers) 1264 B'way
Beers, Ellis & Co. (dissolved) 26 Vesey
Beethoven Conservatory of Music, Elocution & Art (Philip R. Lee, propr.) 46 W. 23d

Beggs James & Co. (George N. Robinson, only) 9 Dey
Beggs E. J. & Co. (Eben J. & Jenny Beggs) 143 Maiden la.
Beggs & Still (Eben J. Beggs & John A. Still) 143 Maiden la.
Behning & Son (Henry & Henry Behning jr.) 150 E. 128th
Behr Herman & Co (Herman & Robert Behr & Gustav Heubach) 76 Beekman
Behr & Steiner (Gustavus E. Behr & Albert Steiner) 12 Cliff
Behr Brothers & Co. (Henry Behr, Pres.; further inf. unattainable) 15 E. 14th & 292 Eleventh av.
Behre F. & Brother (Frederick & John H. Behre) 255 Washn.
Behrend M. & Son (Moritz N. & Bernhard M. Behrend) 925 Second av.
Behrend & Triest (dissolved) 40 Cedar
Behrens Henry J. & Co. (Henry J. Behrens:— special partner, Hugo H. Hoenack, $10,000; terminates 31st Dec. 1893) 65 Pine
Behrens A. & Co. (Arend Behrens & Otto C. F. Kanzow) 3 S. William & 5 William
Behrens Brothers (beer) (Frederick & William Behrens) 2052 First av.
Behrens Brothers (liquors) (Nicholas & Richard Behrens) 360 Front
Behrens Brothers (mers.) (Sigmund & Benjamin Behrens) 46 Walker
Behrens & Arnemann (Albert C. Behrens & Martin Arnemann) 670 Eighth av.
Behrens & Goldgrabe (William Behrens & Richard Goldgrabe) 380 West
Behrens & Nebenzahl Brothers (Albert Behrens & Isaac & Jacob Nebenzahl) 263 Church
Behringer & McCoy (Edward A. Behringer & Henry J. McCoy) 90 Centre
Behsmann, Schroeder & Kahrs (George Behsmann, John F. Schroeder & Herman Kahrs) 413 E. 109th
Beiga Brothers (John & Francis Beiga) 363 Third av.
Beinecke & Co., (Bernhard Beinecke, Joseph Hesdorfer & Caspar F. Sondern) 196 Fulton
Beismer & Uffeln (Christian Beismer & William Uffeln) 135 Rivington
Belais H. & E. O. (Henry & Edward O.) 25 John
Belcher Mosaic Glass Co., (Henry F. Belcher, Pres.; J. Andrews Whittaker, Sec. Capital, $100,000. Directors: Henry F. & Charles Belcher, Eugene Crowell, Felix Gottschalk) 123 Fifth av.
Belcher & Emerson (Edward M. K. Belcher & Henry Emerson) 38 Ferry
Belden A. G. & Co., (Alfred G. Belden, no Co.) 145 Maiden la.
Belden & Dean (Milton B. Belden & Charles A. Dean) 166 Fulton
Belden & McTighe (dissolved) 52 B'way
Belding Brothers & Co., (Milo M. Belding, Pres.; Alvah N. Belding, Sec. Capital, $1,000,000. Directors: Milo M. & Alvah N. & Hiram H. & David W. Belding, John B. Emery, William A. Stanton, E. F. Crooks) 455 B'way
Belford Co. (Robert J. Belford, Pres.; William F. Squires, Sec.; Dederick J. Winkelmann, Treas. Capital, $50,000. Directors: Robert J. Belford, Dederick J. Winkelmann, William F. Squires, Edward Lange, Daniel B. Tresor) 22 E. 18th
Belford, Clarke & Co. (dissolved) 22 E. 18th
Beling, Niemeyer & Wessels (Nicholas Beling, Herman Niemeyer & John P. Wessels) 54 Broad
Belknap Standard Putty Works (E. S. Belknap's Son, propr.) 8 Gold

SPECIAL ATTENTION PAID TO THIS CLASS OF WORK. } **BANKERS' & BROKERS' CIRCULARS DELIVERED** { **THE TROW CITY DIRECTORY CO.** 11 University Place.

BEL 28 **BEN**

Belknap, Johnson & Powell (Willis H. Belknap, George K. Johnson jr. & Webster C. Powell) 428 B'way

Belknap's E. S., Son (Dayton O. Belknap) 8 Gold

Bell George A., Sons & Ward Phillips (George A. & R. Walter & Elmer Bell & Ward Phillips) 53 William

Bell George H. & Co. (George H. Bell, no Co.) 21 Beekman

Bell James M. & Co. (James M. Bell & Theodore E. Schmidt) 31 B'way

Bell James W. & Son (James W. & James W. Bell jr.) 172 Fifth av.

Bell John & Son (John & John J. Bell) ft. E. 115th & Lincoln av. n S. Boulevard

Bell Printing Press Exchange (George H. Bell & Co. propr.) 21 Beekman

Bell Publishing Co. (Mary E. G. Bell, Sec.| Capital, $1,000. Directors: F. H. Alfort, Mary E. G. & D. R. & Elizabeth Bell) 684 B'way

Bell William & Co. (William Bell & C. Seton Lindsay) 505 Produce Ex.

Bell J. & Co. (John & James Bell) 105 W. B'way

Bell Brothers (John P. & William R. Bell) Eleventh av. c W. 21st

Bell & Barber (George Bell & Robert P. Barber) 39 Vesey

Bell & Jones (dissolved) 21 Beekman

Bell & Kimball (Walter Bell & Cornelius V. Kimball) 8 Old sl.

Bell & Ryan (Joseph Bell & Cornelius Ryan) 1108 First av.

Bellamy & Winans (Albert Bellamy & Henry D. Winans) 659 Fifth av.

Belle & Therese (M. T. & B. McCann, proprs.) 343 Fifth av.

Belletti F. & Co. (dissolved) r 211 E. 54th

Belleville & Carondelet R.R. Co. (St. Louis, Alton & Terre Haute R.R. Co. lessees) 16 Broad

Belleville & El Dorado R.R. Co. (St. Louis, Alton & Terre Haute R.R. Co. lessees) 16 Broad

Belleville & Southern Illinois R.R. Co (St. Louis, Alton & Terre Haute R.R. Co. lessees) 16 Broad

Bellinger Brothers (Peter & John W. Bellinger) r 304 W. 36th

Bellmer John C. & Co. (dissolved) 2546 Eighth av.

Bellmer & Co. (Edward Bellmer & Dederick Schnaars) 659 Eleventh av.

Balloni & Co. (Louis J. jr. & Robert Balloni) 87 South

Bellows C. E. & Co. (Clifford E. Bellows & Charles J. Adams) 127 Front, 91 Pine, 65 South & 53d Water

Belmont August & Co. (August & August Belmont jr. & Walther Luitgen) 23 Nassau

Belt, Butler & Co. (Washington Belt & Elliott L. Butler, no Co.) 15 Duane

Beltaire, Larch & Co. (Mark A. Beltaire, Benjamin Larch & John C. Beltaire) 20 W. 3d

Belts & Large (Frederick Belts & Walter Large) 5 Beekman

Belvidere Iron Ore Co. (dissolved) 13 Park row

Bemak Brothers (William & Julius Bemak) 14 Bowery

Bemak & Co. (Louis Bemak & George Freeder) 872 Third av.

Bemis Car Box Co. (Sumner A. Bemis, Pres.; George B. Hewlett, Sec. Capital, $800,000, Trustees: Sumner A. Bemis, George M. Hoadley, Charles L. Seeger, Frederick P. Reed, Charles G. Stearns, Alexander K. Hackett, George B. Hewlett) 20 Platt

Ben Franklin Barge & Propeller Line (Toone Brothers, proprs.) Pier 24 (new) N. R.

Ben Franklin Press Co. (not inc.) (Milton T. Richardson, Matthew Gibb & James Stewart) 45 Rose

Benary's Henry, Sons (Albert E. & Robert H. Benary) 62 White

Benas & Otto (no inf.) 37 College pl.

Bencke H. Lithographic Co. (William Korn, Pres.; Herrmann E. Korn, Sec. Capital, $75,000, Directors: Herrmann E. & William & Felix Korn) 20 Howard

Bendelstein M. & H. Rosenberg (no inf.) 115 Essex

Bender Pb. J. & Sons (Philip J. & Jacob & George Bender) 95 Cliff

Bendheim Brothers & Co. (Adolph D. & Meier & Henry Bendheim :—special partners, Nathan Wise & Adolph M. Bendheim, each $37,500, & Julius G. Miller, $25,000 ; terminates 1st May, 1891) 254 Canal

Bendit, Drey & Co. (Louis A. Bendit, Max Drey & Sigmund L. Bendit) 159 Fifth av.

Bendix Herman & Co. (Herman Bendix & Moses H. Livingston) 811 B'way

Bendler J. Carl & Co. (no inf.) 627 Madison av.

Benedicks S. & Son (Barouy & Max S. Benedicks) 499 B'way

Benedict Coleman & Co. (dissolved) 2 Nassau

Benedict J. Irving & Son (J. Irving & Arthur I. Benedict) 142 Duane

Benedict' James A. & Co. (James A. Benedict & Myron D. Turner) 56 Wall

Benedict A. C. & Co. (Robert S. Ferguson, only) 23 Bowery

Benedict E. C. & Co. (Elias C. & Frederick H. & James H. Benedict) 20 Broad

Benedict J. H. jr. & Co. (James H. jr. & Howard R. Benedict) 50 Exchange pl.

Benedict Brothers (Read & Edwin P. Benedict) 171 B'way

Benedict & Brewer (R. C. Benedict & Solon Brewer) 219 Sixth av.

Benedict & Gaffney (Theodore H. Benedict & Hugh Gaffney) 131 Duane

Benedict & Highet (Williston H. Benedict & Robert B. Highet) 118 William

Benedict & Valentine (Stephen N. Benedict & John C. Valentine) 31 E. Houston

Benedict, Gaffney & Morton (dissolved) 181 Duane

Benedict, McIlroy & Fowler (Henry W. Benedict, William McIlroy & Robert A. Fowler) ft. E. 53d & ft. E. 54th

Beneke Brothers (William Beneke, only) 199 Canal

Benham & Boyesen (Boye C. Boyesen & Max M. Normann, only) 28 Bridge & 239 Fifth av.

Benjamin Alfred & Co. (Isaiah Joseph, Albert F. Hochstadter, Eugene S. Benjamin & David Hochstadter—special partners, Jesse & Samuel Rosenthal, jointly, $150,000 ; terminates 1st Jan., 1892) 104 Bleecker

Benjamin E. B., Mfg. Co. (not inc.) (Edmund B. Benjamin, George H. Davidson & Irving J. Benjamin) 6 Barclay & 12 Vesey

Benjamin John, Lee & Co. (John Benjamin, J. Bowers Lee, Frank P. Benjamin & Arthur Thomson :—special partner, Robert L. Cutting, $50,000 ; terminates 28th Feb, 1891) 19 William

Benjamin A. & Brother (Alexander & Morris Benjamin) 80 Wooster

Benjamin Brothers (dissolved) 52 New

Benjamin & Caspary (Waldemar Caspary, only) 465 Broome

Benjamin & Goldman (Israel S. Benjamin & William A. Goldman) 237 Centre

Benjamin & West (Pulaski Benjamin & Benjamin W. West) 1 Fulton fish mkt

Benkiser & King (Charles A. Benkiser & Robert J. King jr.) 64 Nassau

Benn & Poulson (Samuel B. Benn & George E. Poulson) 32 Nassau

FOR THE BEST CO-PARTNERSHIP IN THE BEST CORPORATION SEE PAGE F IN BACK OF BOOK

BEN 29 BER

Benn-Pitman Copying Co. (not inc.) (Lulu Alexander & Clara Honeywell) 239 B'way & 124 W. 23d

Benneche Edward & Brother (Edward & Henry Benneche) 25 Gt. Jones

Benner N. A. & Co. (Nathaniel A. Benner & Charles W. Pinkney) 19 Old sl.

Benner & Benner (Charles & Willis Benner) 62 Wall

Bennet J. A. & Co. (John A. Bennet & George S. Gilchrist) 76 Pine

Bennet & Co. (Napoleon T. Bennet, no Co.) 154 Monroe

Bennett Aubrey & Co. (Aubrey Bennett & Henry B. Reid) 111 Water

Bennett Frank P. & Co. (dissolved) 51 Leonard

Bennett I. P. (Irving P. Bennett;—special partner, Edward F. Randolph, $20,000; terminates 1st Feb. 1892) 208 Produce Ex.

Bennett John & Son (John & Albert J. Benactt) 4 Gt. Jones

Bennett A. & Co. (Alfred & Edwin Bennett) 156 West

Bennett D. & Son (David & William Bennett) 403 Third av.

Bennett H. C. & Co. (refused) 65 Wall

Bennett J. M. & Brother (James M. & Albert V. R. Bennett, jr.) 365 Washn.

Bennett & Gompper (George W. Bennett & Louis Gompper) 241 Centre

Bennett & Hall (George A. Bennett & Edward Hall) 161 West

Bennett & Maguire (Stephen M. Bennett & Lawrence P. Maguire) 3 E. 17th

Bennett & Vansile (dissolved) 369 Bleecker

Bennett, Day & Co. (Alfred & Edwin Bennett & Henry M. Day) 91 Park pl.

Bennett, Simpson & Co. (William D. Bennett & John A. F. & William R. Simpson) 167 Hudson

Bennett, Sloan & Co. (Philo S. Bennett, Alfred P. Sloan & Charles T. Ward) 44 W. B'way & 82 Thomas

Bennetts & Young (Thomas Bennetts & Robert A. Young) 359 Washn.

Bennewitz Charles & Co. (no inf.) 395 Front

Bennewitz & Niebuhr (dissolved) 485 Pearl

Beno & Co. (Joseph Bono, no Co.) 328 Church

Bensel W. P. & Son (Frank O. Bensel, only) 530 Washn.

Bensinger C. & Co. (Carl & Sigmund Bensinger) 5 Dey

Benson Charles O. (Charles O. Benson:—special partner, John J. K. Coard, $6,000; terminates 1st Jan. 1900) 1339 B'way

Benson & Nelson (Benjamin L. Benson & James J. Nelson) 165 Greene

Bent Samuel S. & Son (Samuel S. & Walter D. Bent) 111 Chambers

Bent G. W. & Co. (George W. Bent, no Co.) 171 Canal

Bent R. M. & Co. (Richard M. Bent, no Co.) 841 B'way & 780 Tenth av.

Bentham & McGowan (Meyer S. Bentham & John S. McGowan) 1267 B'way

Bentley-Knight Electric Railway Co. (Frank P. Slade, Pres.; Frank A. Rhue, Sec.; Henry D. Fuller, Treas. Capital, $1,000,000. Trustees; Frank P. Slade, Henry D. Fuller, Henry C. Adams, Herbert N. Curtis, William H. Randall) 25 Tenth av.

Benton Mfg. Co. (John B. Benton, Pres. Capital, $25,000; further inf. unattainable) 291 W. 11th

Bentzen & Wheeler (William A. Bentzen & Thomas Wheeler) 1182 Third av.

Benwood Loom Co. (Alonzo B. Cornell, Pres.; Charles E. Cornell, Sec.; R. E. Lester, Treas.; further inf. unattainable) 607 W. 36th

Benacery Brothers (dissolved) 1385 B'way

Benziger Brothers (Louis & Nicholas C. Benziger) 36 Barclay & 48 Dey

Benzinger, Graban & Co. (Frederick Benzinger, Hans E. Graban & Henry Ranken) 357 W. 40th

Berbecker Julius & Co. (Julius Berbecker, John J. Henderson, Thomas Morris & Carl M. W. Berbecker) 63 Duane

Berchman & Katz (dissolved) 16 Ludlow

Berean Tract Repository (James Knott, manager) 32 Bedford

Berel M. & A. (Martin & Arthur) 35 Av. D

Berenbroick & Martin (Frederick Berenbroick jr. & Max Martin) r 100 Wooster

Berg F. & Co. (Frederick jr. & Charles & Henry Berg) 20 W. 3d

Berg M. & Co. (Martin Berg, no Co.) 36 W. Houston

Berg Brothers (David & Julius & Isaac Berg) 44 Lispenard

Berg & Clark (Charles I. Berg & Edward H. Clark) 10 W. 23d

Berg & Meyers (Isidor Berg & Edward N. Meyers) 172 Duane

Berge J. & H. (John & Henry) 95 John

Bergel M. & Co. (Marcus Dergel & George H. Rubenstein) 48 Maiden la. & 35 Liberty

Bergen Electric Light, Heat & Power Co. (Samuel D. Haines, Pres.; Charles W. Price, Sec.; Louis Walsh, Treas.; further inf. unattainable) 14 Dey

Bergenport Chemical Co. (inf. unattainable) 20 B'way

Bergenport Sulphur Works (T. & S. C. White, proprs.) 30 Burling sl.

Bergenport Zinc Co. (inoperative) 24 State

Bergenstein Charles & Co. (Charles Bergenstein & Asher D. Box) 304 Canal & 57 Lispenard

Berger Edward & Co. (Edward & Leopold Berger) 703 B'way

Berger H., Sons (William & Adolph & Hugo Berger) 101 Fourth av.

Berger E. S. & Son (Elizabeth S. & Henry Berger) 1045 Park av.

Berger I. & Co. (Ignatz Berger, Co. refused) 84 Howard

Berger Brothers (cigars) (Max & Herman Berger) 67 Sheriff

Berger Brothers (novelties) (Oscar & Gustave Berger) 62 Reade

Berger & Co. (no inf.) 409 B'way

Berger & Greenstein (Pincus Berger & Simon Greenstein) 706 Sixth

Berger & Spelser (dissolved) 164 Ridge

Bergh B. F. & Co. (Dorg F. Bergh & Thomas E. Stubb) 259 Pearl

Bergin Brothers (Thomas & Patrick Bergin) 100 Broad

Bergmann Electric & Gas Fixture Co. (Sigmund Bergmann, Pres.; Philip H. Klein jr. Sec. Capital, $750,000. Directors: Sigmund Bergmann, Edward F. Caldwell, Philip H. Klein jr. E. H. Johnson, U. H. Painter) 527 W. 34th & 79 Fifth av.

Bergmann & Co. (Thomas A. Edison, Pres.; Joseph Hutchinson, Sec.; Samuel Insull, Treas. Capital, $750,000. Directors: Thomas A. Edison, Samuel Insull, Charles Batchelor) 65 Fifth av. 292 Av. B & 487 First av.

Bergmann & Southall (Adolph J. Bergmann & Morris Southall) 53 Ann

Bergstein & Son (August & Frederick W. Bergstein) 20 John

Beringer G. & Co. (Gerhard Beringer, no Co.) 1298 Third av.

CIRCULARS ADDRESSED TO ANY TRADE IN THE U. S. } Facilities
PROMPT, CAREFUL WORK } THE TROW CITY DIRECTORY CO., } Unequalled.
AT MODERATE PRICES. }   11 University Place.

BER   30   BET

Berkman P. & Co. (Pincus Berkman, no Co.) r 289 Madison
Berkovitz Brothers (Benjamin & Jacob Berkovitz) 2 Stanton
Berkowitz Max & Brother (Max & Benjamin Berkowitz) r 531 Fifth
Berkowitz Brothers (dissolved) 249 Stanton
Berkowitz & Co. (no inf.) 64 E. B'way
Berkshire Apartment Assn. (Edward M. Shepard, Pres.; William R. Barr, Sec. Capital, $120,000. Directors: Fletcher Harper, Hiram W. Sibley, William R. Barr, Edward M. Shepard, Theodore Burdell & Frederick V. Hamlin) 500 Madison av.
Berlin Banking Co.((not inc.) (Clara Schmidt & Ernest Reyman) 1800 B'way
Berlin Felting Co. (Aaron Brummer, propr.) 24 Cath. sl.
Berlin & Jones Envelope Co. (Henry C. Berlin, Pres.; J. Berlin, Treas.; further inf. unattainable) 136 William
Berliner Brothers (drygds.) (Solomon & Feist & Meyer Berliner) 78 Av. A & 73 Av. B
Berliner Brothers (liquors) (Abraham & Marcus Berliner) 1648 Second av.
Berliner & Strauss Mfg. Co. (Solomon Denzer, Pres.; Meyer Meyer, Sec. Capital, $25,000. Directors: Solomon Denzer, Meyer & Jacob Meyer, Bernhard Strauss, Isaac Meyer) 481 B'way
Berlinsky J. & Brother (Jacob & William Berlinsky) 206 Bowery
Berlitz School of Languages (Berlitz & Co. propers.) 1 W. 25th
Berlitz & Co. (Maximilian D. Berlitz, Nicholas A. Joly & Paul Rogen) 1 W. 25th
Berman & Budenbender (dissolved) 9 Av. A
Bermann C. & Son(Conrad & Frederick J. Berman) 6 Av. A
Bernard H. O., Mfg. Co. (Henry C. Bernard, Pres.; Frederick W. Patterson, Sec. Capital, $200,000. Directors; Henry O. Bernard, Frederick W. Patterson & Paul D. & Louise & Virginia Bernard) 573 B'way
Bernard Leo. & Co. (Leopold Bernard:—special partner, Charles Boorcherville, Paris, France, $40,000; terminates 31st Dec. 1897) 225 Pearl
Berner & Hamald (William Berner & John Hamaid) 256 Fulton
Bernet Frederick & Son (Frederick & Christian Bernet) 101 Second
Bernhard Joseph & Son (Elizabeth A. & Percival J. Bernhard, only) 827 B'way
Bernhard A. & Co. (Adolph Bernhard, no Co.) 2 Maiden la.
Bernhard B. & Son (Bernhard & Samuel Bernhard) 88 Walker
Bernhard & Schenck (Albert Bernhard & Adolph Schenck) 107 William
Bernheim H. & Co. (Henry Bernheim, Michael Dryfoos & Isaac Herrmann) 15 White
Bernheim J. & Son (Jacob & Isaac J. Bernheim) 100 Pearl
Bernheim S. & Sons (Solomon & Isaac & Matthew & Charles & Benjamin Bernheim) 1078 Third av.
Bernheim & Lewy (dissolved) 5 Gt. Jones
Bernheim, Bauer & Co. (Charles L. Bernheim, Felix L. Bauer & Abram C. & Julius C. Bernheim) 8 W. 3d
Bernheimer Herman, Son & Co. (Jerome Bernheimer, Marcus A. Bottman & Sanford & Meyer H. Bernheimer, only) 75 Leonard
Bernheimer Jacob S. & Brother (Jacob S. & Mayer S. Bernheimer) 81 White
Bernheimer & Schmid (Simon E. Bernheimer & Josephine Schmid) Ninth av. c W. 108th
Bernhols J. A. & Son (John A. & Louis F. Bernhols) 206 Washn.

Bernini J. & Co. (dissolved) 204 W. 15th
Bernius George D. & Son (George D. & George Bernius) 131 Washn. mkt
Bernor J. C. & Co. (Joseph C. Bernor, Co. refused) 418 Eighth av.
Bernstein D. & Son (Bennett & Max L. Bernstein) 69 Franklin
Bernstein H. & Son (Harris & David A. Bernstein) 84 E. B'way
Bernstein I. & Co. (dissolved) 442 B'way
Bernstein & Adler (Simon Bernstein & Caroline Adler) 390 B'way
Bernstein & Altmayer (no inf.) 456 B'way
Bernstein & Brown (William Bernstein & Louis Brown) 451 Washn. mkt
Bernstein & Co. (bankers) (no inf.) 44 Canal
Bernstein & Co. (trimmings) (Albert H. & Barbara Bernstein) 111 Mercer
Bernstein & Jacobs (Max Bernstein & Abraham H. Jacobs) 127 Division
Bernstein & Laske (Abraham Bernstein & Michaelis Laske) 95 Goerck
Bernstein & Meade (dissolved) 19 W. 26th
Bernstein Brothers & Gottlieb (Samuel & Charles Bernstein & Michael Gottlieb) 525 B'way
Berrent & Levinson (dissolved) 120 Division
Berrien & Halsey (Edward M. Berrien & Joseph B. Halsey) 88 Washn. pl.
Berry Cattle Co. (Ltd.) (Louis Gans, Pres.; Edward A. Meridan, Sec.; Emanuel Lehman, Treas. Capital $210,000. Directors: Louis Gans, Bernhard Berry, Solomon Fisher, Emanuel Lehman, Meyer Jonasson, Henry S. Boice, Edward A. Meridan) 23 Thomas
Berry, Wisner, Lohman & Co. (Samuel J. Berry jr. John Lohman & Franklin Whitney:—special partner, Henry Offerman, B'klyn, N. Y., $100,000; terminates 1st May, 1892) 265 G'wich
Bertaux C. W. & Co. (Charles W. Bertaux & William Porter) 10 Stone
Berteling T. & Co. (dissolved) 177 Bowery
Berthe, Schnorr & Co. (dissolved) 129 S. 5th av.
Berthel Louis & Son (Louis & George Derthel) 855 Second av.
Bertin Brothers (Charles & Eugene & Alfred Bertin) 1576 Vanderbilt av. E.
Bertine C. D. & Co., (Calvin D. Bertine & Lawrence Welker) 9 E. 19th
Berton & Nickel (Charles A. Berton & Frederick A. Nickel) 422 E. 23d
Bertuch Brothers (Henry & Moe Bertuch) 997 Second av.
Berutich & Spinetti (Arturo T. Berutich & Elbano Spinetti) 15 Irving pl.
Besoca M. & Co. (Manuel & Adolfo Besoca) 66 W. 125th
Bessemer Mining Co. (Levi M. Bates, Pres.; C. P. Bates, Sec. Capital, $60,000. Trustees: Levi M. Bates, A. D. Dickinson, C. P. Bates) 146 B'way
Bessey Frederick A. & Co. (Frederick A. Bessey & Frederick H. Wetmore) 975 Hudson
Best J. & W. (John & William) 274 Sixth av.
Best & Co. (Albert Best, Warren E. Smith & Thomas R. Tall) 60 W. 23d
Best & Mackie (no inf.) 41 W. 31st
Beste & Doscher (dissolved) 58 Broad & 70 Catharine
Besthoff Abraham & Son (Abraham & Charles S. Besthoff) 903 B'way
Beston R. S. & Co. (Robert S. Beston & Sarnco S. Leon) 242 G'wich
Betancourt & Rojo (Augustine Betancourt & Ramon Rojo) 767 Sixth av.
Betjeman & Betjeman (Nicholas jr. & John C. Betjeman jr.) 806 Third av.

THADDEUS DAVIDS CO., WRITING INKS, SEALING WAX, MUCILAGE.
MAKE THE BEST

BET   31   BIR

Bettelheim E. S. & Co. (Edwin S. Bettelheim & Willard S. Wright) 22 Ann

Bettelheim E. S. & F. C. (Edwin S. & Frederick C.) 22 Ann

Bettens & Lilienthal (Edward D. Bettens & Jesse W. Lilienthal) 30 Broad

Bettinberge & Parsont (Isaac Bettinberge & Bernard Parsont) 939 Second av.

Betting & Maszur (Louis L. Betting & Leon Maszur) 87 W. 4th

Bettman & Rocker (Isaac Bettman & Henry Rocker) 358 Canal

Betts & Co. (dissolved) 119 Pearl

Betts, Atterbury, Hyde & Betts (Frederic H. Betts, Charles L. Atterbury, J. B. Hindon Hyde & Samuel R. Betts) 120 B'way

Bettys J. Y. & Co. (John Y. Bettys, no Co.) 25 John

Beusse & Drunkhorst (dissolved) 106 Broome

Bevan J. M. & Co. (Jane M. & Jeremiah J. Bevan) 21 E. 17th

Beverforden G. F. C. & Co. (Gerhardt F. C. Beverforden & Robert Campbell) 332 W. 4th

Beverforden Brothers (Gerhardt F. C. & William Beverforden) 705 Tenth av.

Bevier & Co. (Charles Bevier, Co. refused) 606 First av.

Beyer L. & Co. (Leopold Beyer & Joseph Bruns) 131 Grand

Beyrich R. W. & Schnieba (dissolved) 476 Broome

Bianchi F. & Co. (Francisco Bianchi, Charles Beers & William F. Hill) 547 B'way & 118 Mercer

Bick Brothers (Philip & Joseph E. Bick) 81 Walker

Bickler John & Brother (Henry & Elizabeth Bickler, only) 186 Wooster

Bicknell A. J. & Co. (Amos J. Bicknell & Samuel W. Thrup) 115 B'way

Biddle Clement M. & Co. (Clement M. & William C. Biddle) 168 Church

Biddle J. & Son (John & Robert D. Biddle) 7 E. 14th

Biddle & Melville (no inf.) 217 G'wich

Biddle & Ward (A. Sydney Biddle, Henry G. Ward, J. Rodman Paul & Charles M. Hough) 150 B'way

Bidwell F. N. & Co. (dissolved) 98 Wall

Bidwell & French (Charles E. Bidwell & James M. French) 127 Water

Bieber J. & Brother (Julius & Morris Bieber) 667 B'way

Bieber L. & Son (Leopold & Joseph Bieber) 478 Grand

Biele C. F. & E. (Charles F. & Emil) 46 W. B'way

Bielefeld & Spahn (Albert Bielefeld & Louis Spahn) 93 Reade

Biemann & Bittel (August Biemann & John Bittel) 146 Baxter

Biemer S. & J. (Stephen J. & John V.) 127 Pearl & 90 Beaver

Bien Julius & Co. (Julius Bien & William M. Franklin) 139 Duane, 64 Thomas & 25 W. 30th

Biermann, Heidelberg & Co. (Isaac Biermann & Isaac N. Heidelberg, no Co.) 616 B'way & 150 & 153 Crosby

Biesenthal E. & Co. (Edward Biesenthal & Morris Kirstein) 56 Lispenard

Big Bend Hydraulic Co. (Philo S. Ely, Pres.; George W. Clark, Sec. Capital, $1,000,000. Directors: Philo S. Ely, Edwin Shufeldt, William Buck, E. P. Hoyt, A. W. Humphreys, George W. Clark, John Harney) 181 B'way

Bigelow Blue Stone Co. (Horace T. Caswell, Pres.; Howard C. Bogardus, Sec. Capital, $300,000. Directors: Horace T. & H. M. Caswell, Howard C. Bogardus, T. M. Warren, W. F. Wolfe) 65 Stewart bldg

Bigelow & Co. (no inf.) 7 Warren

Biggane & Kelly (Michael J. Diggane & Hugh A. Kelly) 847 Washn. mkt

Biggart James & Co. (James Biggart & Matthew McCroddan) Sedgwick av. c Wolf

Biggio & Cavagnaro (Luigi Biggio & Louis Cavagnaro) 82 Park pl.

Biglin & McMullan (dissolved) 589 Hudson

Biglow L. H. & Co. (L. Horatio Biglow, Henry E. Wheeler & Lucius H. Biglow jr.) 13 William & 24 Liberty

Biglow & Main (Lucius H. Biglow, only) 76 E. 9th

Bilhoefer & Gass (Christian Bilhoefer & Frank Gass) 326 E. 117th

Bill & Bill (Jefferson Davis & Edward Lyman Bill) 8 E. 14th

Bill & Caldwell (Edward W. Bill & Alexander Caldwell) 550 B'way

Billings F. Swift & Co. (dissolved) 142 Pearl & 108 Water

Billings Nickel Plating Works (not inc.) (Joseph N. Billings & William Flukenauer) 36 Fulton

Billings Pipe Bender Mfg. Co. (Matthew W. Hawes, Pres.; Charles S. Upton, Sec. Capital, $2,000. Directors: Charles S. & Rubin F. Upton, Matthew W. Hawes) 25 Warren

Billings J. & Son (Jeremiah & James Billings) r 550 W. 36th

Billings & Cardozo (Coles Morris, Oliver F. C. Billings & Michael H. Cardozo) 120 B'way

Billings & Endler (dissolved) 114 Sixth av.

Billings, Clark's Fork & Cooke City R. R. Co. (no inf.) 52 B'way

Bills & Davenport (James F. Bills & John N. Davenport) 50 Leonard

Billwiller Brothers (Charles J. & John W. Billwiller) 33 Walker

Bimberg M. & Son (Morris & Meyer R. Bimberg) 128 E. 15th

Bimstein & Friedman (Hyman Bimstein & Benjamin Friedman) 90 Forsyth

Bindernagel & Kaiser (Julius Bindernagel & Jacob Kaiser) 65 E. 9th

Bing Ferdinand & Co. (Ferdinand Bing, Arthur W. Gans & Charles G. Rathgunn) 106 Grand

Binge & Curie (Julius Binge & Charles Curie) 44 Exchange pl.

Binger & Neuberg (Otto D. Binger & William Neuberg) 181 Pearl

Bingham James & Co. (James Bingham & Herbert D. Clearman) 450 Produce Ex.

Bingham William & Co. (William & David A. Bingham) 110 Produce Ex.

Bingham & Co. (dissolved) 60 & 1196 B'way & 26 W. 20th

Bingham, Daley & O'Hara (Leander K. Bingham, Joseph D. Daley & Francis O'Hara) 51 Rose

Bingold J. & Son (John & John Bingold jr.) 248 W. 48th

Bininger & Hanson (E. D. Bininger & A. M. Hanson) 3 Broad & 45 Pine

Binney & Smith (Edwin Binney & Paul Smith) 17 Platt & 201 South

Binns D. W. & Co (no inf.) 47 B'way

Binswanger S. & Co. (Siegfried & Samuel Binswanger) 219 Canal

Birch John S. & Co. (dissolved) 182 Lewis

Birch & Co. (Isaac C. Birch, no Co.) 2406 Third av.

Bird William Edgar & Co. (William Edgar & Theodore L. Bird) 85 Dey & 52 Church

Bird T. R. & Co. (Tilghman R. Bird, John B. Breuniser & Walter E. Eunis) 74 Walker

Bird & Son (no inf.) 203 W. 104th

Birdsall Daniel & Co. (Daniel Birdsall & Richard A. Brown) 319 B'way

COMPILED WITH ACCURACY AND DESPATCH.	CLASSIFIED BUSINESS LISTS.	THE TROW CITY DIRECTORY CO. 11 University Place.
BIR	32	BLA

Birdsall & Bourne (Edward T. Birdsall & Frank Bourne) 115 B'way

Birdsall & Johnson (Theodore Birdsall & Samuel K. Johnson) 159 Crosby & 117 W. 25th

Birdseye & Co. (C. Edmund Birdseye & Edward A. McCormack) 185 Pearl

Birdseye, Cloyd & Bayliss (Lucien & Clarence F. Birdseye, James C. Cloyd & Benjamin H. Bayliss) 170 B'way

Birkenfeld, Curtin & Co. (Louis Birkenfeld & Margaret Curtin, no Co.) 38 Howard

Birmingham Electric Amalgamation Co. (inf. unattainable) 40 B'way

Birmingham Patent Metallurgical Co. (inf. unattainable) 40 B'way

Birmingham & Co. (Leo C. Evans, Pres.; Stephen S. Vreeland, Sec.; Ernest F. Birmingham, Treas. Capital, $5,000. Directors: Leo C. Evans, Stephen S. Vreeland, Ernest F. Birmingham) 2 Wall

Birmingham & Jackson (William G. Birmingham & William G. H. Jackson) 412 First av. & 177 Av. B,

Birmingham's Electro Chemical Gold & Silver Saving Co. (inf. unattainable) 40 B'way

Birnbaum M. & Co. (Morris Birnbaum & Isaac Goldberg) 135 Grand

Birnbaum Brothers (no inf.) 200 E. Houston

Bischoff Brothers (Henry & Bruno Bischoff) 483 Sixth av,

Bischoff & Meyerhoff (Cord Bischoff & Martin A. Meyerhoff) 829 Washn.

Bischoff, Adler & Co. (Max Bischoff & Leon A. & Joel Adler) 57 Walker

Bishop Gutta-Percha Co. (Samuel Boardman, Pres.; Henry A. Reed, Sec. Capital $50,000. Directors: Samuel Boardman, Helen E. Blitz, Ellen L. Anderson) 422 E. 25th

Bishop Victor & Co. (Marmaduke Richardson, only) 12 Maiden la.

Bishop & Crawford (dissolved) 19 W. Houston

Bishop & Gilligan (Joseph F. Bishop & John Gilligan) 194 Madison

Bishop & Hendrickson (Winfield S. Bishop & Charles S. Hendrickson) 196 Duane

Biskinty & Saba (dissolved) 79 Washn,

Bisland F. S. & Co. (dissolved) 5 Wall

Bisland & Holt (Edward S. & William A. Bisland & George B. Holt) 5 Wall

Bissinger Philip & Co. (Philip Bissinger, no Co.) 23 John

Bister & Schmitt (John Bister & Joseph Schmitt) 115 Worth

Bittel, Tepel & Ellers (Charles T. Bittel, William Tepel & Anton Ellers) 38 Spruce

Bitter Henry & Co. (Henry Bitter, no Co.) r 150 E. 33d

Bittner & Bendheim (Manheim Bittner & Heyman Bendheim) 523 Sixth av,

Bittner Andrew & Co. (Andrew Bittner, no Co.) 41 Ann

Bitz Henry J. & Co, (dissolved) 233 Centre

Bixby S. M. & Co. (Samuel M. Bixby, Pres.; William C. Carpenter, Sec.; Theodore W. Rich, Treas. Capital, $150,000. Directors: Samuel M. Bixby, Clarence Tucker, Theodore W. Rich, William C. Carpenter, Winthrop R. Tillotson) 194 Hester

Bjur Brothers (Warner G. & William L. Bjur) r 342 E. 34th

Black Foster, Co. (Ltd.) (Thomas Black, Pres.; James B. Pugh, Sec.; Foster Black, Treas. Capital $100,000. Directors: Thomas & Foster Black, James B. Pugh, William Sloane, Sarah B. Black) 279 Church

Black & King (Edward G. Black & David Bennett King) 71 Wall

Black, Starr & Frost (Robert C. Black, & Aaron V. Frost, only) 251 Fifth av.

Blackburn Edward & Co. (James N. McCall & Alfred D. Hewitt, only) 25 Beaver

Blackburn George & Co. (George Blackburn, no Co.) 12 Washn. mkt

Blackburn S. P. & Co. (Samuel P. Blackburn & Eugene H. Morse) 30 Whitehall

Blackford James M. & Son (James M. & William M. Blackford) 89 Burling sl,

Blackinton R. & Co. (Roswell Blackinton & Walter Ballou) 162 B'way

Blackinton W. & S. (William & Sumner & Louis A. Blackinton) 16 Maiden la.

Blackledge B. & Son (Benjamin & Charles E. Blackledge) 153 W. 18th

Blackledge & England (Peter J. Blackledge & Richard England) 54 W. 29th

Blackman Patent Pulp Co. (Henry Blackman, Pres.; Gustav L. Jaeger, Sec. Capital $100,000. Trustees: Henry Blackman, Gustav L. Jaeger) 136 Mulberry

Blackman H. & Son (Hyman & Max Blackman) 82 Bayard

Blackman J. J. & Co. (James J. & James S. Blackman & George W. Gardiner) 37 Water

Blackstone Co. (Clara B. Lorenze, propr.) 206 B'way

Blackwater & Greenbrier Valley R. R. Co. (no inf.) 45 B'way

Blackwell Wilson H. & Son (Wilson H. & Charles G. Blackwell) 67 Liberty

Blackwell Brothers (S. Howard Blackwell, only) 69 Park pl.

Blain F. J. & Co. (Frank J. Blain & William Miller) 63 Murray

Blair & Lawrence (inf. unattainable) 2534 Kingsbridge rd.

Blair & Rudd (Benjamin F. Blair & Frank Rudd) 162 B'way

Blair's George C., Son (George W. Blair) 23 South

Blake H. W. & Co. (Simeon Lyon Deyo, Henry D. Kingsbury & Frank M. Gilbert, only) 94 Reade

Blake R. M. & Co. (Richard M. & George L. Blake) 148 Front

Blake Brothers (Edward C. & Edward J. Blake) 346 Hudson

Blake & Co. (refused) 187 Barrow

Blake & Duffy (Thomas C. Blake & Francis Duffy) 517 W. 25th

Blake & Sullivan (Stephen S. Blake & Thomas J. Sullivan) 71 Centre

Blake & Williams (George W. Blake & Francis A. Williams) 197 Wooster

Blake & Wolff (Andrew Blake & Joseph C. Wolff) 80 Nassau

Blake Brothers & Co. (Arthur W. Blake, John P. Marquand, Joseph E. Brown, George M. Harris & Howland Davis, only) 5 Nassau

Blakslee E. G., Mfg. Co. (Joseph F. Moore, Pres.; Robert E. Carey, Sec.; Hiram A. Decker, Treas. Capital $60,000; further inf. unattainable) 76 Centre

Blakslee's E. G., Sons' Iron Works (Ebenezer G. Blakslee, Pres.; Thomas M. P. Mills, Sec. Capital, $50,000. Trustees: Ebenezer G. Blakslee, Frederick W. Barnes, Henry F. Lord, Andrew Elder & Thomas M. P. Mills) 144 Centre

Blancard & Co (Christian Blancard, no Co.) 85 John

Blanchard Electric Light & Power Co. (Virgil W. Blanchard, Pres. Capital, $10,000,000. Trustees: Virgil W. Blanchard, Robert D. Warner, George N. Wonson, Nahum W. Cady) no address

Blanchard C. A. & Co. (Charles A. Blanchard, no Co.) 1355 B'way

SPECIAL ATTENTION PAID TO THIS CLASS OF WORK. } BANKERS' & BROKERS' CIRCULARS DELIVERED { THE TROW CITY DIRECTORY CO. 11 University Place.

BLA 33 BLO

Blanchard R. A. & Co. (Herman A. Blanchard & Jonas Carr) 176 Water
Blanchard & Co. (no inf.) 258 B'way
Blanchard, Gay & Phelps (James A. Blanchard, Joseph G. Gay & George H. Phelps) 164 Nassau
Blanck D. & Co. (no inf.) 710 E. 13th
Blanck & Co. (William F. & Thomas J. Dianck) 16 Horatio
Blancke & Co. (Henry L. & Caroline Blancke) 97 Cedar, 194 Church & 9 Temple
Blandy C. G. & Co. (Charles G. Diandy, no Co.) 362 Province Ex.
Blaudy & Hatch (dissolved) 55 Liberty
Blank & Rothbel (Abraham Blank & Benjamin Rothbel) 2 Bond
Blanke & Doehle (Frederick H. Blanke & Daniel Doehle) 777 Third av.
Blanks & Hassinger (dissolved) 44 Sullivan
Blankmeyer & Burr (dissolved) 1692 Third av. & 162 Eleventh av.
Blapp & Zillig (dissolved) 326 E. 34th.
Blass & Menaker (Simon Blass & Solomon Menaker) 1699 Third av & 81 Essex
Blatz F. J. & Brother (Frederick J. & Anthony J. Blatz) 21 Spruce
Blauman & Gold (dissolved) 30 Orchard
Blaurock A. & J. (Andrew & Elizabeth Blaurock, only) 604 E. 17th
Blunt Brothers (dissolved) 226 Fulton
Blauvelt & Co. (drygds.) (Isaac Blauvelt & James A. Smith) 1858 Tenth av
Blauvelt & Co. (mast) (Orlando W. Blauvelt, no Co.) 235 Fourth av
Bleakley & Co. (dissolved) 161 W. 125th
Bleecker Augustus & Son (Augustus & Sherbrooke P. Bleecker) 48 South
Bleecker James & Son (James & William H. Bleecker) 150 B'way
Bleecker Street & Fulton Ferry R. R. Co. (John H. Selmes, Pres.; Thomas H. McLean, Sec. Capital, $900,000. [Directors: John H. Selmes, Isaac Hendrix, John Downey, Joseph Jacobs, Alexander E. Kurshoedt, Moses M. White, Matthew H. Beers, Samuel M. Smith, Otis W. Randall, Thomas H. McLean, Louis S. Brush, Samuel Rowland, A. S. Rosenbaum) 621 W. 23d
Bleekman & Gulick (no inf.) 73 Park row
Blendermann H. & J. (Henry & Jacob) 103 Washn. & 100 West
Blessing George A. & Co. (George A. Blessing & Henry Stein jr.) 52 Cliff
Bley & Harry (dissolved) 140 Maiden la.
Bleyer Brothers (Jacob S. & Simon F. & Emanuel Bleyer) 488 Broome
Bleyer & Brothers (Leopold & Herman & Joseph M. & Sigmund Bleyer) 255 E. Houston
Blickensderfer Mfg. Co. (George C. Blickensderfer, Pres.; Gwyn T. Jordan, Sec. Directors: Henry R. Towns, Charles A. Miller, James L Raymond, John Le Boutllier, C. L. Reid, Gwyn T. Jordan, George C. Blickensderfer) 841 B'way
Blinks George & Son (George P. Blinks, only) ft. W. 38th
Blinn & Galvin (Alexander F. Blinn & William J. Galvin) 2355 Eighth av.
Bliss E. A., Co. (Egerton A. Bliss, Pres.; George J. Dickinson, Treas. Capital, $50,000; further inf. refused) 176 B'way
Bliss John & Co. (John & George H. Bliss) 128 Front
Bliss Brothers (E. Frederick jr. & A. Edward Bliss) 294 First av.
Bliss & Schley (George Bliss & William T. Schley) 160 B'way

Bliss, Fabyan & Co. (Cornelius N. Bliss, George F. Fabyan, Jacob Edwards, Peder Olsen & Orlando H. Alford) 117 Duane & 32 Thomas
Bliven A. F. & Co. (no inf.) 80 B'way
Bliven & Bliven (Edward M. & William W. Bliven) 140 Nassau
Bliven, Carrington & Co. (John B. F. Bliven, Henry P. Carrington & James A. Fussell) 257 Front
Bloch A. & Brother (Arthur & Isidor Bloch) 222 W. 125th
Bloch A. & S. (Arthur & Samuel) 598 Park av.
Bloch H. M. & Brother (Henry M. & Louis Bloch) 41 Gt. Jones
Bloch J. & Co. (refused) 1457½ Third av.
Bloch S. E. & Brother (Samuel E. & Salomon M. Bloch) 92 Franklin
Bloch Brothers (Jacob & Meyer Bloch) 32 Av. C
Bloch Sisters (Regina & Henrietta Bloch) 119 Bleecker
Bloch & Baar (Edward Block & Morris Baar) 72 Grand & 38 Wooster
Bloch & Harrigan (dissolved) 197 Av. B
Bloch & Hecht (Arthur Bloch & Moses Hecht) 791 Park av.
Bloch & Kraus (no inf.) 504 E. 56th
Bloch & Piddlan (dissolved) 18 Grace av. W. Washn. mkt
Block D. L. & Co. (David L. Block, no Co.) 311 Church
Block J. & P. (Jacob & Peter) 165 Ridge
Block J. W. & Brother (John W. & Wesley S. Bloch) 9 Maiden la.
Block & Bergfels (Robert Z. Block & Julius Bergfels) 5 Maiden la.
Blodgett J. Q. & Son (John Q. & Ernest Blodgett) 1259 Lex. av.
Blohm Frederick & Co. (Frederick Blohm, no Co.) 278 Washn.
Blood R. T. & S. (Richard T. & Samuel) 81 John
Bloodgood John & Co. (John Bloodgood & John D. Slayback) 15 Broad
Bloodgood F. & W. E. (Freeman & William E.) 8 York
Bloom, Meyer & Rosenthal (dissolved) 649 B'way
Bloomberg C. & Co. (Caspar & William Bloomberg:—special partner, Max Weil, $10,000; terminates 10th Dec. 1890) 518 D'way & 75 Spring
Bloomer & Co. (Theophilus J. Bloomer, no Co.) 193 South
Bloomer & Simpson (Hiram Bloomer & John C. Simpson) 132 Fulton
Bloomfield J. C. & Co. (William King & Robert A. Lawrie, only) 14 Dey
Blooming Grove Park Assn. (Andrew J. Post, Pres.; Charles A. Billings, Sec.; William P. Roome, Treas. Directors: Andrew J. Post, Robert B. Lawrence, William P. Roome, Nathaniel B. Smith, Daniel D. Youmans, Thomas E. H. Curtis, Stephen M. Nash, Edward Bradley, Charles F. Hardy, Charles T. Wills, Charles B. Dunn) 102 B'way
Bloomingdale Beef Co. (Spengler & Schwaner, proprs.) 1611 Ninth av & 945 Tenth av.
Bloomingdale Graphite Co. (John Sloane, Pres.; Edward D. Johnes, Sec. Capital, $500,000. Trustees: John Sloane, Frederick Potter, Samuel M. Cauldwell, Louis J. Ryerson, Edward R. Johnes, Robert Milliken, Zabriskie Ryerson) 50 B'way
Bloomingdale Brothers (Lyman G. & Joseph B. Bloomingdale) 906 Third av & 50 Howard
Bloomingdale & Levy (Emanuel W. Bloomingdale & Arthur S. Levy) 18 Mercer
Blourock J. & Co. (Julius Blourock, no Co.) 5 Bond

3

TYPEWRITING DONE BY THE TROW CITY DIRECTORY CO., 11 University Place.

BLU 34 BOG

Blue Bird Mining Co. (Ltd.) (Ferdinand Van Zandt, Pres.; William G. Didrichsen, Sec. Capital, $5,000,000. Directors: Ferdinand & A. Van Zandt) 43 Exchange pl.

Blue Ledge Mining Co. (William W. Gibbs, Pres.; Robert A. C. Smith, Sec. Capital, $200,000. Directors: William W. Gibbs, Robert A. C. Smith, Charles P. Robinson) 40 Wall

Blum Gustave & Brother (Gustave & Emanuel Blum) 51 Walker

Blum Morris & Sons (Morris & Jacob & John Blum) 974 Second av

Blum A. jr's. Son (Morris Spiegel, only) 103 Broad

Blum B. & Co. (Benjamin & Alfred Blum) 5 Dey

Blum E. M. & Co. (Emile M. Blum, no Co.) 19 Whitehall

Blum G. & Son (George & Louis W. Blum) 680 Third av.

Blum Brothers (Theophilus & Marx & Leopold Blum, 65 & 191 Av. D & 81 Madison. Theophilus & Marx Blum & Emanuel Weisburger 566 Ninth av & 514 Tenth av.)

Blum & St. Goar (Charles Blum & Frederick St. Goar) 35 Wall

Blumauer & Co. (Simon Blumauer & Marcus A. Myers) 18 Liberty

Blumberg Brothers & Goldstein (no inf.) 105 Goerck

Blume W. F. & Co. (William F. Blume & Henry Slessenbuettel) 415 West

Blume & Co. (Joanna C. M. Blume, no Co.) 113 Water

Blumenberg & Floersheim (Marc A. Blumenberg & Otto Floersheim) 25 E. 14th

Blumenstiel & Hirsch (Alexander Blumenstiel & Morris J. Hirsch) 320 B'way

Blumenstock B. & Son (Bernard & Leon Blumenstock) 402 W. 30th

Blumenthal A. & S. (August & Sidney) 206 W. 67th

Blumenthal B. & Co. (Benjamin & Gustav Blumenthal) 984 B'way

Blumenthal F. & Co. (Ferdinand Blumenthal, Ludwig Roth & Julien S. Ulman) 19 Spruce & 193 William

Blumenthal S. & Co. (Gabriel Brunneman, only) 573 Eighth av.

Blumenthal Brothers (Samuel & Gabriel Blumenthal) 2184 Third av.

Blumenthal & Doss (Sigmund Blumenthal & Arthur E. Boas) 356 B'way

Blumenthal & Erdman (Nathan Blumenthal & Henry Erdman) 58 White

Blumenthal & Rosenblum (Abram Blumenthal & Isaac Rosenblum) 300 E. 57th

Blumenthal Brothers & Co. (Albert & Gustave Blumenthal & Gustave Rothenberg;—special partner, Jacob Scholle, $50,000; terminates 31st Dec. 1892) 482 B'way

Blumenthal's W., Sons (Isaac & August Blumenthal) 778 First av.

Blumlein C. & Co. (Abraham Blumlein, no Co.) 6 Durling sl.

Blüm F. S. M. & Co. (Ferdinand S. M. Blün & Sigmund Bendit) 18 Walker

Blun S. M. & Co. (dissolved) 18 Greene & 26 West

Blun & Co. (dissolved) 496 Cherry

Blün & Henius Mfg. Co. (inf. unattainable) 18 Walker

Bluxome & Co. (John D. Bluxome, no Co.) 30 West & 54 Washn.

Bluxome & Hamm (John D. Bluxome & James E. Hamm) 50 Wall

Blydenburgh Brothers (John B. & Harry D. Blydenburgh) 45 South

Blyn I. & Sons (Isaac & Louis & Nathan Blyn) 172 Chambers

Board of Missions of the Prot. Epis. Ch. (John Williams, Pres.; William S. Langford, Sec.; George Bliss, Trans.) 22 Bible h.

Board of Publication of the Ref. Ch. in America (Herman C. Berg, Pres.; Isaac D. Demarest, Sec.; Henry Vanbuskirk, Treas. Directors: William O. Perry, Henry Ward, George Seibert, L. R. Ladd, George W. Pool, Isaac D. Demarest, Henry Vanbuskirk) 26 Reade

Board of Underwriters of New York (John D. Jones, Pres.; James A. Whitlock, Sec.; Theophylact B. Bleecker jr. Treas.) 51 Wall

Boardman & Boardman (Samuel & Edward C. Boardman & James W. McDermott) 155 B'way

Boardman & Small (Gorham Boardman & Louis C. Small) 127 Water

Bocanema Gold & Silver Mining Co. (Lee R. Shryock, Pres.; James W. Thompson, Sec.; Capital, $1,250,000. Trustees: Lee R. Shryock, James S. Leeds, James W. Thompson, Santiago Perez-Triana, Charles W. Eldrid, Asbury Harpending jr. Richard H. Spencer) 45 B'way

Bock Brothers (dissolved) 129 Third av.

Bock & Co. (Louis Bock & David C. Andrews:—special partner, Alexander Nones, $10,000; terminates 31st Dec. 1891) 61 Pearl

Bock & Steckmest (dissolved) 59 Gansevoort, W. Washn. mkt

Bode Brothers (Christopher F. & Adolph H. & Herman A. Bode) 406 West, 135 & 394 Sixth av. & 403 Fourth av,

Bodenstein N. & M. (Nathan & Morris) r 110 Ridge

Bodine & Hutcheson (Abijah E. Bodine & Hugh Hutcheon) 28 Lawton av. W. Washn. mkt

Bodkin Martin R. & Son (Martin R. & Martin L. Bodkin) 10 Dey

Bodolea, Pressler & Reich (dissolved) no address

Boeddiker & Walter (Otto Borddiker & Anton Walter) 954 Sixth av.

Boedicker's J. D., Sons (John D. & Henry W. Boedicker) r 407 E. 24th

Boegler F. & Co. (Ferdinand Boegler, no Co.) 26 S. William

Boehm Samuel C. & Co. (Samuel C. & Gustav S. & Max S. Boehm) 241 Front

Boehm & Co. (Isaac & Eli & Moses H. Boehm & David Hoexter) 91 South & 210 First av.

Boehmcke F. E. & Co. (Frederick E. Boehmcke & William Hube) 125 Warren

Bochmer Adam & Co. (no inf.) 2505 Third av.

Boekell Julius & Son (Julius & Julius Boekell jr.) 54 Bond

Boericke & Tafel (Frank L. Boericke, Adolph J. Tafel & Felix A. Boericke) 145 Grand & 7 W. 42d

Boes Brothers (William & Henry Boes) 205 E. 129th

Boes & Brown (dissolved) 2416 First av.

Bosse C. & Q. W. (Clifford & Quincy Ward Boess) 280 B'way

Boetterling, Perts & Co. (William Boetterling & Hugo Perts, no Co.) 412 E. 68th

Boettger Charles & Son (Charles F. & Charles F. Boettger jr.) 209 E. Houston

Boettger & Hinse (Henry W. Boettger & Adolph Hinse) 82 Mercer & E. 144th n Brook av.

Bogardus Photographic Parlors (Sherman & McHugh, proprs.) 11 E. 42d

Bogardus Universal Eccentric Mill Co. (no inf.) 624 E. 14th

Bogardus, Ellaby & Ellsworth (Joseph A. Bogardus, Thomas Ellaby & T. Gardner Ellsworth) 177 West

Bogart P. S. & Co. (Peter S. Bogart & Jacob J. Moore) 170 Reade

THE CALIGRAPH WRITING MACHINE,
HARTFORD, CONN.

BOG   35   BOR

Bogart S. F. & Son (Carinus F. Bogart, only) 114 Warren
Bogart & Folsom (James H. Bogart & John F. Folsom) 25 South
Bogert & Teers (no inf.) 459 W. 42d
Bogert Albert G. & Brother (Albert G. & John G. Bogert) 113 Bank
Bogert R. R. & Co. (Rudolphus R. Bogert & Arthur E. Tuttle) 154 Nassau
Bogert S. M. & Co. (Seba M. Bogert & Mary C. Ford) 16 Broad
Bogert & Heydon (Abram B. Bogert & Clark A. Heydon) 204 Franklin
Boggs J. L. & R. (John L. & Robert) 285 Hudson
Bogle & Scott (William Y. Bogle & Alexander Scott) 67 Park pl.
Bogota City Railway Co. (Tunis G. Bergen, Pres.; Frank W. Allin, Sec. Capital, $500,000. Directors: Tunis G. Bergen, J. Henry & Mahlon C. Martin, Daniel D. Lathan, William A. Cauldwell, Frank W. Allin) 1 B'way
Bogota Coffee Co. (T. W. Kean & Co. proprs.) 46 Washn.
Bohemian Dry Goods Co. (Joseph Sommerich, propr.) 310 Church
Bohemian Glass Works (not inc.) (R. E. Hagerty & J. Deschan) 214 Pearl
Bohling J. & L. (John & Louis) 271 West
Bohling & Pahde (John C. Bohling & Charles A. Pahde) 234 West
Bohm Brothers (no inf.) 386 B'way
Bohm & Pfeiffer (Charles Bohm & Albert Pfeiffer) 545 E. 15th
Bohm & Stern (Samuel W. Bohm & Rosalie Stern) 301 E. 101st
Bohn A. & Charles Riedel (Albert Bohn & Charles O. Riedel) 1055 Third av.
Bohn H. & Brother (Henry M. J. & Martin Bohn) 1700 Park av.
Bohn Bothers (William & Charles Bohn) 2015 Third av.
Bohnenkamp & Schneider (William F. Bohnenkamp, jr & Henry Schneider) 11 E. 14th
Bohner Philip & Son (Philip & Philip Bohner jr.) 12 Warren
Bohnet John (John jr. & Edward & Frederick Bohnet) 188 Monroe & 74 Madison
Boisset P. & Son (Peter & Raphael Boisset) r 197 Greene
Bokens & Veeck (dissolved) 376 Seventh av.
Boker Hermann & Co. (Hermann & Herman Funke jr. & Ferdinand A. Boker, only) 101 Duane
Boland & Bauer (John Boland & John T. Bauer) 1151 Third av.
Boland & Co. (John Boland, John Taylor & Peter S. Terhune) 711 First av.
Boland & Sullivan (dissolved) 112 Park row
Boleman P. & Co. (no inf.) 43 Broad
Boleman & Co. (Pamella M. & Patrick Boleman) 14 Wooster
Bolen William J. & Co. (dissolved) 437 B'way
Bolen & Byrne (John Bolen & estate of John P. Byrne) 415 E. 54th
Bolger Thomas & Co. (Thomas Bolger & William O. Brewster) 51 Leonard
Bolger & Burke (dissolved) 1729 Second av.
Bollermann & Son (Arthur & Arthur M. Bollermann) 208 E. 117th
Boltwood & McKinney (Charles Boltwood & George A. McKinney) 105 Tenth av.
Bolz & Hass (George J. Bolz & Theodore M. Hass) 176 Centre
Bomzon & Rosenthal (Wolf Bomzon & Caspar Rosenthal) 20 Bleecker
Bonanza & Union Tunnel & Mining Co. (Paul A. Oliver, Pres.; Edward Guiager, Sec.; Theodore H. Becker, Treas. Capital, $2,000,000. Directors; Paul A. Oliver, Edward Guiager, Theodore H. Becker, Richard W. Swan) 171 B'way
Bonaventure & Co. (Edmond F. Bonaventure & Auguste C. Leroy) 2 Barclay
Bondy A. & Co. (Adolph Bondy, John Horstmann & John N. Jentz) 1868 Av. A
Bondy Brothers (dissolved) 295 Church
Bondy & Lederer (Charles Bondy, only) 1298 First av.
Bondy & Pick (Arthur Bondy & Henry Pick) 80 Nassau
Bonnel J. M. & Son (Joel M. & Charles L. Bonnel) 16 Cortlandt
Bonnell J. H. & Co. (Ltd.) (J. Harper Bonnell, Pres.; Albert S. Burlingham, Sec.; William D. Harper, Treas. Capital, $200,000. Directors: J. Harper Bonnell, William D. Harper, Alexander Bonnell, Albert S. Burlingham, Theodore Haight) 154 Nassau
Bonner E. H. & Co. (Edward H. Bonner & Edward E. Fraipont) 29 Wall
Bonner & Eisler (Julius Bonner & Isaac Eisler) r 17 John
Bonner & Margulondo (no inf.) 14 Beaver
Bonner & Rosen (Herman Bonner & Joseph Rosen) 85 Nassau
Bonner & Van Court (Thomas Bonner & Frederick K. Van Court) 483 W. 42d
Bonner's Robert, Sons (A. Alley & Robert Edwin & Frederick Bonner) 182 William
Bonnie C. R. & Co. (dissolved) 171 B'way
Boody, McLellan & Co. (David A. Boody, Charles W. McLellan, Reuben Leland & Henry T. Boody) 57 B'way
Bookhout Brothers (Edward jr. & Charles H. Bookhout) 48 Maiden la. & 85 Liberty
Bookwalter Steel & Iron Co. (John W. Bookwalter, Pres.; William A. Petts, Sec. Directors: John W. Bookwalter, William A. Petts, William A. Lown) 18 Cortlandt
Boom & Co. (Manrice Boom & James A. Wycherley) 513 Sixth av.
Boomer & Boechert Press Co. (George B. Boomer, Pres.; William D. Dunning, Treas. Capital, $250,000. Directors: George B. Boomer, William D. Dunning) 245 G'wich
Boonton Brass & Iron Works (no inf.) 59 John
Boorsem, Hamilton & Beckett (Louis V. Boorsem, William H. Hamilton & Charles H. Beckett) 160 B'way
Boorum & Pease (William B. Boorum & George L. Pease) 30 Reade
Boos F. & Brother (Frederick & George F. Boos) 449 B'way & 28 Mercer
Booth Samuel & Co. (Samuel Booth, no Co.) 199 Centre
Booth T. & G. (Thomas & George) 250 Washn. mkt
Booth & Campbell (Edgar H. Booth & Malcolm Campbell) 11 Wall
Booth & Co. (Alfred & Charles Booth & Thomas Fletcher) 15 Frankfort & 183 William
Booth & Fox (no inf.) 25 White
Booth & McGinnis (no inf.) 9 W. 14th
Booth Brothers & Hurricane Isle Granite Co. (William Booth, Pres.; John Donaldson, Sec.; John Booth, Treas. Capital, $250,000. Directors: William Booth, John Donaldson, John Booth, William S. White, Charles F. Ferguson) 60 Bank & R. E. 113th
Borchard L. & Co. (no inf.) 142 Centre
Borchardt S. & Co. (Samuel & Herman Borchardt) 217 S. 5th av.
Borck & Kohner (no inf.) 1614 Av. A
Berdeaux Cordial Co. (Samuels & Cohn, proprs.) 158 Chambers

SPECIAL ATTENTION PAID TO THIS CLASS OF WORK. } BANKERS' & BROKERS' CIRCULARS DELIVERED { THE TROW CITY DIRECTORY CO. 11 University Place.

Borden & Lovell (Leander N. Lovell, Charles A. Greene & Henry L. Freeland, only) 70 West & Pier 28 N. R.
Borden & Slater (Thomas H. Borden & Ephraim D. Slater) 5 Park pl.
Borden, Edwards & Co. (Cornelius T. Borden & Edward Edwards, Co. refused) 257 B'way
Bordollo & Hucksteth (dissolved) 209 Forsyth
Borcel Mining Co. (Hampton B. Denman, Pres.; Charles A. Cameron, Sec. Capital, $3,000,000. Directors: Hampton B. Denman, Richard C. Kerens. Thomas Moore jr. Richard C. McCormick) 1 B'way
Boremsky's E., Son (Charles Doremsky) 162 Pearl
Borg Simou & Co. (Simon Borg, Leo Speyer & Samuel Lichtenstadter) 20 Nassau
Borges L. & Co. (Louisa & Regina Borges) 110 W. 22d
Borges de Castro & Co. (Albert & Henry Borges de Castro) 735 B'way
Borgfeldt George & Co. (refused) 425 Broome
Bormann William H. & Co. (William H. Bormann & John Widder) 2456 Eighth av.
Born's F. A., Son (Osmr T. Born) 359 G'wich
Borne, Scrymser & Co. (John E. Borne, C. Howard Scrymser & Charles L. Tappin) 80 South
Bornemann Paul C. & Co. (Paul C. & Marie Bornemann) 13 Clinton pl.
Borner & Franzius (Theodore Borner & George Franzius) 230 E. 48d
Bornhoeft & Gollnik (Edward Bornhoeft & Adolph Gollnik) 502 E. 74th
Bornholz & Co. (Frederick Bornhols & James M. Lehmaler) 232 Front
Bornstein & Frank (Solomon Bornstein & Abraham Frank) 186 Bowery
Bornstein & Samuel (Isaac Bornstein & David Samuel) 490 Broome
Borst & Clausen (Adam J. Borst & William Clausen) 105 E. 9th
Borsum Brothers (Louis Dorsum & Frederick S. Williams, only) 98 Cliff
Bosch G. & Co. (dissolved) 34 Grace av. W. Washn. mkt
Boschen John H. & Brother (John H. & Charles F. Boschen) 101 Barclay
Boskowitz J. & A. (Ignatz & Adolph Boskowitz, only) 99 Prince
Boss Mfg. Co. (William L. Boss, Pres.; Washington I. Bartholomew, Treas. Capital, $2,000. Directors: William L. Boss, Washington I. Bartholomew) 30 Gold
Boss Steel Box Band Co. (Joseph C. Rogers, Sec.; further inf. unattainable) 188 E. 5th av.
Boss C. D. & Son (no inf.) 10 Old sl.
Bosse, Heath & Co. (dissolved) 34 Hudson
Boston Beef Co. (Herman Freund, 99 First av. Jacob Hock, 2066 Second av. Woods & Dreyfuss, 2284 First av. proprs.)
Boston Button Co. (Metcalf & McCleary, proprs.) 846 Canal
Boston Credit Clothing Co. (Anne Sugarman, propr.) 2 New Chambers
Boston Lamp Co. (no inf.) 712 B'way
Boston Mfg. Co. (inf. unattainable) 7 Murray
Boston Marine Ins. Co. (Ransom B. Fuller, Pres.; Thomas H. Lord, Sec. Capital, $1,000,000. Directors: William H. Hill, Ransom B. Fuller, H. J. Boardman, John B. Emery, P. H. Odiana, Frank B. Dole, M. F. Pickering, James Littlefield, George Hinman, Thomas H. Lord, Charles F. Perry, Charles O. Foster, William H. Lincoln, Enos C. Soule, William C Haskins, William H. Besse, Samuel Watts, Otis Hinman) 41 Wall
Boston Suspender Co. (no inf.) 712 B'way
Boston & N. Y. Cut Sole Co. (Samuel Engle, Pres.; John F. Harvey, Sec. Capital, $15,000.

Directors: Samuel Engle, John F. Harvey, Robert S. Engle) 87 Frankfort
Boston, Hoosac Tunnel & Western Railway Co. (Augustus Kountze, Pres.; Aaron T. Smith, Sec. Capital, $10,000,000. Directors: Augustus Kountze, John Q. Adams, Charles T. Crocker, Robert Codman, Rudolph Keppler, David P. Kimball, George A. Torrey, Cyrus J. Lawrence, Elijah B. Phillips, James, Renfrew jr. Francis Smith, Rodney Wallace) 120 B'way
Bostwick & Sheridan (George W. Bostwick & Albert D. Sheridan) 19 Bridge & 4 Stone
Bothfeld & Arnaud (F. Otto Bothfeld & estate of Gustavus P. Arnaud) 76 Broad
Botsford & Noe (Nelson J. Botsford & William R. Noe) 52 Park pl.
Botthof Brothers (dissolved) 7 Murray
Bottlers' Protective Union (Thomas Kavanagh, Pres.; William V. Keller, Sec.; Peter Byrne, Treas.) 27 Park row
Bouden & Jenkins (Thomas H. Bouden & Frank Jenkins) 48 & 40 Wall
Boughton & Terwilliger (John W. Boughton & Lorenzo Terwilliger) 3 W. 23d & 104 W. 24th
Bouker Contracting Co. (John A. Bouker, Pres.; Franklin Bouker, Sec.; Andrew A. Bouker, Treas. Capital, $10,000. Directors: John A. & Andrew A. & Franklin & Obadiah Bouker) 110 Wall
Bouker D. C. & Son (DeWitt C. & DeWitt C. Bouker jr.) 114 Wall
Boulevard Riding Academy (Emile Rohant, propr.) 5 Boulevard
Boulton, Bliss & Dallott (William G. & William B. Boulton, Ernest C. Bliss & John Dallott) 71 Wall & Pier 86 E. R.
Bour Mfg. Co. (Joseph N. Bour, propr.) 50 Bond
Bourdis J. & Co. (John Bourdis, no Co.) 53 Mercer
Bourke William & Co. (William Bourke, no Co.) 143 Centre
Bourke & Hughes (Margaret A. Bourke & Anne E. Hughes) 42 E. 19th
Bouthin J. & Son (dissolved) 187 Prince
Bouton A. F. & Co. (Adrian F. Bouton, no Co.) 118 Gansevoort
Boutwell, Fiero & Cornell (George S. Boutwell, William P. Fiero & Charles E. & Henry W. Cornell) 36 B'way
Bouve, Crawford & Co. (George F. Bouve, Harvey F. Crawford & Lander M. Bouve) 261 & 237 B'way & 218 W. 125th
Bouvier M. C. & Co. (dissolved) 16 Broad
Bowden J. B. & Co. (Joseph B. & M. Luther Bowden;—special partner, Joseph Bowden; further inf. refused) 102 B'way
Dowdoin Paper Mfg. Co. (William H. Parsons, Pres.; Marcella C. Parsons, Sec. Capital, $140,000. Directors : William H. & William H. Parsons jr. George F. Hicks) 4 Warren
Bower William J. & Co. (William J. Bower, no Co.) 489 Produce Ex.
Bower F. M. & Co. (Frank M. Bower & Edward E. Pierson) 155 Chambers
Bower-Barff Rustless Iron Co. (George W. Maynard, Pres.; Stephen V. White, Treas. Capital, $750,000. Directors : George W. Maynard, Stephen V. White, Rossiter W. Raymond, Wheaton B. Kinhardt, Charles C. Dodge, Nelis Poulson, John Bower) 35 B'way
Bowerman Brothers (William D. & Henry A. & Benjamin F. Bowerman) 97 Wall
Bowers B. O. & Co. (Benjamin O. Bowers & William Thompson) 96 Front
Bowers & Loy (Henry H. Bowers & John C. Loy) 111 Nassau
Bowery Bank (Henry P. De Graaf, Pres; Frank C. Mayhew, Cashier; William R. Kuran, Notary. Capital, $250,000. Directors: Henry

MERCHANTS EXCHANGE NAT. BANK OF THE CITY OF N. Y.
SOLICITS YOUR ACCOUNT. **257 Broadway.**
PHINEAS C. LOUNSBURY, President.   ALLEN S. APGAR, Cashier.

BOW   37   BRA

P. De Graaf, William R. Foster, Levi H. Mace, William E. Clark, John Q. Adams, Richard V. Harnett, Barak G. Coles, Richard Hamilton, Martin H. Sbrenkelsen, Abraham Kling, William W. Watson, Charles Gulden, Herman Strobel) 62 Bowery

Bowery Savings Bank (Edward Wood, Pres.; Robert Leonard, Sec. Trustees: John D. Hicks, Robert Haydock, Henry Darrow, John C. Chamberlain, Henry Lyles jr. Richard A. Storrs, Aaron Field, Edward Hincken, William H. S. Wood, Timothy H. Porter, Enoch Ketchum, William H. Parsons, William H. Hurlbut, William V. Brokaw, Benjamin F. Jackson, Samuel H. Seaman, Edward C. Sampson, William H. Bendleston, James W. Cromwell, John J. Sinclair, Joseph D. Lockwood, William Dowd, George Montague, George M. Olcott, Charles Kellogg, Charles Griffen, Alexander T. Van Nest, David S. Taber, Washington Wilson, Isaac S. Platt, Benjamin F. Romaine, Eugene Underhill, George E. Hicks, John W. Cochrane, Octavius D. Baldwin, Henry H. Cook, George H. Robinson, George Jeremiah, Robert Maclay, William L. Vennard) 128 Bowery

Bowes & Coombs (John Bowes & John Coombs) 435 E. 77th

Bowles M. L. & Co. (M. L. Bowles, Co. refused) 19 Old sl.

Bowles S. B. & Co. (Stephen B. Bowles, no Co.) 47 Liberty

Bowles & Smith (dissolved) 217 Lex. av. & 4 W. 28th

Bowman G. P. & Co. (George P. Bowman & Robert B. Gray) 601 W. 33d

Bowman S. & Co. (Solomon Bowman & William Friedlander) 115 Fulton & 384 & 691 Eighth av.

Bowman & Dock (dissolved) 194 Seventh av.

Bowne William R. & Co. (William R. & Samuel C. Bowne jr.) 182 Fifth av.

Bowne E. & Co. (Erastus Bowne & Clarence L. Funk) 238 Fulton

Bowne & Co. (Robert Bowne, no Co.) 124 Pearl

Bowring & Archibald (Thomas D. Bowring, Nicholas B. Stabb & Frederick C. Bowring, only) 18 B'way

Bowsky A. & Sons (Adolph & Adolph jr. & Max Bowsky) 220 E. 51st

Boyce & Hartshorne (George A. Boyce & William S. Hartshorne) 75 Broad

Boyd Edward A. & Sons (John F. & George H. Boyd, only) 61 Wooster & 167 S. 5th av.

Boyd James & Sons (James & George & William Boyd) 73 Thomas

Boyd Thomas & Co. (Thomas & Robert J. Boyd) 96 Reade

Boyd F. O. & Co. (Francis O. Boyd, no Co.) 59 Broad

Boyd J. E. & Brother (dissolved) 204 Produce Ex.

Boyd J. W. & Co. (John W. Boyd, further inf. unattainable) 142 G'wich

Boyd & Abbot Co. (John Scott Boyd, Pres.; Robert L. Boyd, Sec.; Edgar W. Abbot, Treas.; further inf. unattainable) 23 Warren

Boyd & Co. (William C. Boyd, no Co.) 2178 Seventh av.

Boyd & Gibson (John T. Boyd & John M. Gibson) 89 Nassau & 58 Liberty

Boyd & Hincken (James H. Boyd & Edward Hincken) 3 William

Boyd, Sutton & Co. (Robert M. Boyd, Henry K. Sutton & Charles A. Brown;—special partners, George B. Brown, Framingham, Mass. & Thomas H. Bird, Montclair, N. J., each $25,000; terminates 30th Nov. 1892) 61 Leonard

Boyd's City Dispatch (not inc.) (William & Mary Blackham & Edgar J. Williams) 5 Murray

Boyd's James, Son (John Boyd) 12 Franklin

Boyer's L., Sons (Charles H. & Frank W. Boyer) 90 Wall & Pier 35½ E. R.

Boylan Mfg. Co. (Ltd.) (John F. Boylan, Pres.; George R. Boylan, Sec.; James M. Jarvis, Treas. Capital, $20,000. Directors: John F. & George R. Boylan, James M. Jarvis, John Macaulay, William M. Murphy) 84 Howard

Boyland J. & Son (James & Edward J. Boyland) 2080 Third av.

Boyle John & Co. (John Boyle & William H. Macy) 208 Fulton

Boyle R. & Sons (Richard & John J. & Terence J. Boyle) 533 Eighth av.

Boyle & Co. (W. Lewis Boyle, no Co.) 48 Wall

Boylston Carriage Co. (Herbert S. Smith, propr.) 102 William

Boynton Bicycle Railway Co. (inf. unattainable) 32 Nassau

Boynton Co. (Ltd.) (dissolved) 253 Sixth av.

Boynton E. M., Saw & File Co. (no inf.) 99 Chambers

Boynton Furnace Co. (Nathaniel A. Boynton, Pres.; Edwin E. Dickinson, Sec.; Capital, $100,000. Directors: Nathaniel A. & Charles D. & Prudence W. Boynton, Edwin E. Dickinson, Joseph Wodell) 209 Water

Boynton & Vanwinkle (John H. Boynton & Harrison Vanwinkle) 129 Fifth av. & 151 Eleventh av.

Boys James & Co. (James & Robert J. Boys) 50 Exchange pl.

Bracher Ventilator Co. (James H. Hummel, propr.) 153 Fulton

Brackman & Levy (Henry Brackman & Sarah Levy) 11 W. 3d

Bradford & McDonald (William Bradford & Francis McDonald) 175 Christopher

Bradish & Kissam (G. Johnston Bradish & William A. Kissam) 1 B'way

Bradley Electric Power Co. (Francis O. French, Pres.; Luciano Fabbricotti, Sec.; Samuel H. Rathbone, Treas. Capital, $750,000. Directors: William C. Dreyer, Amos T. & Francis O. French, George Blagden, Francis D. Crocker, William Pennington, Charles S. Bradley) 68 B'way

Bradley Western Fuel & Gas Co. (George H. Smith, Pres.; Jesse W. Shepard, Sec.; John J. Gorman, Treas. Capital, $100,000. Directors: George H. Smith, Henry A. Bradley, John J. Gorman, Jesse W. Shepard) 2 W. 14th

Bradley Brothers (stationers) (James W. & Thomas F. Bradley) 563 Third av.

Bradley Brothers (trucks) (John E. & Henry J. Bradley) 505 W. 55th

Bradley & Co. (Catharine & John J. Bradley & Forbes Holland) 62 Union pl. & 8 E. 31st

Bradley & Currier Co. (Ltd.) Edwin A. Bradley, Pres.; John J. Hughes, Sec. Capital, $100,000. Directors: Edwin A. Bradley, George C. Currier, John J. Hughes, Thomas J. Morrow, Israel C. Shaylor) 303 Hudson

Bradley & Hubbard Mfg. Co. (Walter Hubbard, Pres.; Charles F. Linsley, Sec.; Nathaniel L. Bradley, Treas. Capital, $200,000. Directors: Walter Hubbard, Charles F. Linsley, Nathaniel L. Bradley) 26 Park pl. & 21 Barclay

Bradley & Poates (John F. Bradley & Leonard L. Poates) 114 Nassau

Bradley & Seabrook (Hawley Bradley & Charles H. Seabrook) 68 E. 125th

Bradley & Smith (James A. Bradley, only) 251 Pearl

Bradley & Sons (Daniel & James & John & Daniel J. R. Bradley) 50 Monroe

Bradley, Voorhees & Day Mfg. Co. (Ltd.) (Lyman H. Day, Pres.; Thomas C. Cassidy, Sec.; Malcolm H. Smith, Treas. Capital, $40,000. Directors: Lyman H. Day, Malcolm H. & Emma C. Smith, Thomas C. Cassidy, Francis E. Day) 83 White

SNOW, CHURCH & CO.,
265 & 267 BROADWAY.

COLLECTIONS IN ALL PARTS OF THE WORLD.
T. C. Campbell and Arthur Murphy, *Counsel.*
TELEPHONE, 736 MURRAY.

Bradstreet Co. (Charles P. Clark, Pres.; Henry C. Young, Sec.; Edward F. Randolph, Treas., Capital, $500,000. Directors: Charles F. Clark, Henry C. Young, Edward F. Randolph) 279 B'way

Bradstreet, Curtis & Co. (Albion G. Bradstreet, Sidney W. Curtis & Henry G. Romaine) 25 Pine

Brady Metal Co. (Daniel M. Brady, Pres.; Martin S. Paine, Sec. Capital, $25,000. Directors: J. E. French, Martin S. Paine, Charles Miller, D. L. Cobb, D. M. Brady) 115 B'way

Brady Philip & Co. (Philip Brady & John Gallagher) 868 Sixth av.

Brady M. F. & P. H. (Matthew F. & Philip H.) 1077 Third av.

Brady & Dolan (John J. Brady & Luke J. Dolan) 1726 Park av.

Brady & Doyle (Thomas Brady & John Doyle) 190 Bowery

Brady & McGrath (Patrick J. Brady & Thomas McGrath) 859 First av.

Brady & Masterson (Patrick Brady & Patrick Masterson) 1201 First av.

Brady & Messenkope (dissolved) 320 Fourth av.

Braemig Brothers (August J. & Nicholas Braemig) 129 Third

Braendly & Rose (Jean J. Braendly & Isidor Rose) 536 W. 14th

Bragdon E. O. & Co. (Edward O. Bragdon & Luther C. Valentine) 83 Pine

Braguglia & Carreno (Raimondo Braguglia & Aurelio Carreno) 18 B'way

Braid & Stine (George S. Braid & John R. Stine) 175 Greene

Braillard & Pfingsten (Francis F. Braillard & C. Gustav Pfingsten) 13 E. 17th

Brainard Dredging Co. (Morris F. Brainard, Pres., Louis E. Spencer, Sec. Capital, $350,000; further inf. unattainable) 68 Wall

Brainard Brothers (Morris F. & Elijah Brainard) 68 Wall

Brainerd & Armstrong Co. (Benjamin A. Armstrong, Pres.; Benjamin L. Cook, Sec. Capital, $240,000. Directors: Benjamin A. Armstrong, Leonard O. Smith, Benjamin L. Cook) 625 B'way & 192 Mercer

Brainerd & Co. (William F. Brainerd, no Co.) 97 Chambers

Brakeman Mfg. Co. (inf. unattainable) 18 Cortlandt

Brakmann Brothers (Ferdinand F. & Dederick Brakmann) 684, 685 & 686 Sixth av.

Braman Joseph D. & E. F. (Joseph D. & Ella F.) 120 & 1270 B'way

Braman, Ash & Darker (Hiram V. V. Braman, William McL. Ash & David S. Darker) 105 Franklin

Bramhall Brothers & Co. (George W. Bramhall & Carl R. Hieronymus;—special partner, Henry L. Einstein, $250,000; terminates 31st Jan. 1892) 59 Leonard

Bramhall, Deane & Co. (Royal E. Deane & George G. Brooks, only) 284 Water

Branchville Ore Milling Co. (Pomeroy P. Dickinson, Pres.; George A. Lawrence, Sec.; F. W. Hartwell, Treas. Capital, $150,000. Trustees: Pomeroy P. Dickinson, George A. Lawrence, F. W. Hartwell, J. Edward Mastin, Albert Storer) 7 Nassau

Brand John & Co. (John & George Brand & Andrew Curtin) 101 Pearl

Brand F. C. & Co. (dissolved) 81 Greene

Brand O. J. & Co. (Oscar J. Brand & John S. Ernst) 56 Wall

Brand Brothers (Charles W. & Joseph L. & Moses H. Brand) 507 & 1509 Second av. & 313 First av.

Brandeis L. & Co. (Leopold Wickert, only) 133 William

Brander & Boyd (dissolved) 650 W. 51st

Brander & Co. (William Brander & Emil Zehmisch) 550 W. 51st

Brandes William & Co. (William Brandes & Richard Kulze) 478 Fourth av.

Brandes Brothers (Dederick & August Brandes) 119 E. 42d

Brandis Mfg. Co. (Frederick E. Brandis, Pres.; William F. Widmayer, Treas.; Ernst A. Gieseler, Sec. Capital, $50,000. Directors: Frederick E. Brandis, William F. Widmayer, Ernst A. Gieseler) 55 Fulton

Brandon Isaac & Brothers (Isaac & David H. & Nathaniel Brandon) 35 B'way

Brandreth's D., Sons (George A. & Franklin & Ralph Brandreth) 274 Canal

Brandt J. & Son (John & Charles W. Brandt) 1444 Lex. av.

Brandt Brothers (Gustav & William & George Brandt) 100 Wooster

Brandt & Klenzler (George W. Brandt & Herman Klenzler) 76 William

Brandt & Robbins (dissolved) 140 Nassau

Brandus Silver Works (Edward Brandus, propr.) 529 B'way

Branford Granite Co. (William H. Murtha, Pres.; George W. Rice, Sec. Capital, $250,000. Directors: William H. Murtha, George W. Rice, Thomas A. Kerrigan) 203 B'way

Branford Lock Works (Alexander L. Dimyon, Pres.; Edward F. Jones, Sec.; further inf. unattainable) 94 Chambers

Brass Goods Mfg. Co. (William F. Hyatt, Pres.; Nicholas D. Redhead, Sec. Capital, $25,000; further inf. unattainable) 68 Chambers

Braumuller Co. (Otto L. Braumuller, Pres.; Wingult H. Taylor, Sec. Capital, $15,000; further inf. unattainable) 428 Eleventh av.

Braun Jacob & Co. (dissolved) 443 First av.

Braunsdorf & Gerstner (William Braunsdorf & Anthony W. Gerstner) 684 Eighth av.

Brautigam F. A. & Co. (Frederick A. Brautigam & Samuel E. Hingston) 41 W. B'way

Draveman & Saperstein (dissolved) 139 King

Brazil Coffee Co. (Ltd.) (dissolved) 108 Front

Brecher Philip & Son (Philip & Philip Brecher jr.) 497 Fifth

Brechin & Hefert (James Brechin & Frank M. Hefert) 1814 Third av.

Breck William P. & Co. (William P. Breck, no Co.) 59 John

Breckenridge Milling Co. (refused) 182 B'way

Bredt F. & Co. (Ernst Bredt & Anton Roesingh, only) 194 Fulton

Breece Mining Co. (Charles A. Rogers, Pres.; Henry Bradstreet, Sec. Capital, $5,000,000. Directors: Charles A. Rogers, Frank B. Whitfield, A. H. & Winthrop B. Rogers, N. Dana Whipple) 115 B'way

Breen & Nason (James R. Breen & Alfred G. Nason) 843 E. 80th

Breen & Taylor (William Breen & James Taylor) ft. W. 29th

Breese & Smith (William P. Smith, only) 6 Wall

Breidbach C. J. & Son (Caspar J. & Carl J. Breidbach) 895 Mott av.

Breier Brothers (Solomon & Morris Breier) 398 Tenth av.

Breier & Etler (Marcus Breier & Israel Etler) 59 Mulberry

Breisland & Foresman (Samuel Breisland jr. & William Foresman) 7 W. 14th

Breithaupt Brothers (William & Gustave Breithaupt) 451 Eighth av. 150 E. Houston & 2022 Third av.

Breitwieser M. & G. (dissolved) 778 Ninth av.

WATER METERS, GAS ENGINES, | NATIONAL METER CO.
FOR PUMPING AND POWER. | 252 Broadway, N. Y.

BRE 39 BRI

Bremer John L. & Co. (John L. Bremer, James S. & Henry F. Noyes, Charles B. Stewart, Theodore W. Bennett, Charles E. Perkins, John D. Gerrish & Charles L. Bansher) 64 Leonard

Bremer John P. & Co. (dissolved) 467 Tenth av.

Bremer H. & Son (Henry & John C. Bremer) 790 Eighth av.

Brenack & Co. (Emma F. & Thomas P. Brenack) 101 Park pl.

Brendel & May (Michael Brendel & William M. May) 600 W. 52d

Brendon & Higbie (dissolved) 1123 Park av.

Brennan Co. (John Brennan, propr.) 835 B'way

Brennan & Carr (Thomas F. Brennan & James L. Carr) 175 Greene

Brennan & Colligan (James Brennan & John Colligan) 20 Burling sl.

Brennan & Sullivan (Peter J. Brennan & Dennis Sullivan) 313 Third av.

Brennocks George & Co. (George & Henry Brennecke) Cotton Ex.

Brenner & Marks (Isaac Brenner & Adolph Marks) 167 Bowery

Brentano's (Angust Brentano, Pres.; Simon Brentano, Sec. Capital, $600,000; further information unattainable) 5 Union sq. W.

Brentini Joseph & Co. (Joseph Brentini & Rosa Toma) 228 Thompson

Brentwood Park Improvement Co. (inf. unattainable) 265 B'way

Bresha Joseph & Sons (Joseph & Pascale Bresha, only) 405 E. 113th

Breslin John & Son (John & John A. Breslin) 171 B'way

Breslin J. H. & Brother (James H. & Thomas Breslin) 1202 B'way

Breslin M. P. & Son (Michael P. Breslin, only) 402 E. 64th

Brett Lithographing Co. (M. L. Brett, Pres.; Charles V. Breit, Sec. Capital, $48,000. Directors: M. L. & Charles V. Brett, Frederick C. Brion) 49 Rose

Brett William & Sons (William & Thomas J. & John J. Brett) 76 Market

Brett G. A., Son & Co. (Gustavus A. & William G. & Pierre V. A. Drett) 41 South

Brett S. & Son (Sylvester & Morris Brett) 418 Broome

Brett & Ferguson (James J. Drett & Joseph H. Ferguson) 355 W. 59th

Brettell G. & Son (George & George W. Brettell) 2254 Third av.

Brettner & Moscovitz Jewelry Mfg. Co. (inf. unattainable) 64 Nassau

Brewer Mining Co. (Hosmer D. Parsons, Pres.; J. Clement Uhler, Sec. Capital, $250,000. Directors: Hosmer D. Parsons, William S. Todd, L. H. Scott, Emanuel Motz, N. C. Boynton) 30 B'way

Brewer H. & Brother (Henry & Nicholas Brewer) 76 Pearl

Brewer H. K. & Co. (Henry K. & John Brewer jr.) 26 Nassau

Brewer Brothers (Luther Brewer, only) 14 Ann

Brewers' Exchange of N. Y. & Vicinity (Monroe Eckstein, Pres.; Albert E. Seifert, Sec.; Emil Schaefer, Treas.) 2 Irving pl.

Brewers' Ice Co. (inf. unattainable) ft. E. 63d

Brewers' Indemnity Fund Assn. (Charles A. Schultz, Sec. Trustees: John B. Hasslocher, August Finck, Charles Gunther) 2 Irving pl.

Brewster J. B. & Co. (James B. Brewster, Pres.; R. Schuyler Tucker, Sec. Capital, $125,000. Directors: James B. Brewster, R. Schuyler Tucker, James S. Cone, Cairn-Cross Downey, Joseph C. Smith) 148 E. 25th & 506 Fifth av.

Brewster & Co. (Channing M. Britton, Charles J. Richter, & William Brewster :—special partners, Frances M. Britton, $100,000, & Henry D. Brewster, $50,000 ; terminates 9th July, 1892) 1581 B'way

Brice James E. & Co. (James E. Brice, Co. refused) 401 W. 27th

Brice & Johnson (Andrew Brice & James Johnson) 156 Bowery

Brickwedel C. & G. (Charles & George) 1553 Third av.

Bride A. J. & Co. (inf. unattainable) 51 Leonard

Bride J. & Co. (George W. Claflin & Co. proprs.) 122 Nassau

Bridge & Grant (Hamilton Bridge & Michael Grant) 406 Fourth av.

Bridgeport Knife Co. (Charles J. Healy, propr.) 106 Chambers

Bridgman, Birmingham & Co. (Herbert L. Bridgman, Pres.; Stephen S. Vreeland, Sec.; Ernest F. Birmingham, Treas. Capital, $10,000. Directors: Herbert L. Bridgman, Ernest F. Birmingham, Stephen S. Vreeland) 2 Wall

Brien H. & H. (Henry & Hugh) 480 & 762 Ninth av.

Brien & Jackson (John Brien & William J. Jackson) 300 W. 46th

Briesen & Knauth (Arthur V. Briesen & Antonio Knauth) 229 B'way

Briesen, Steele & Knauth (dissolved) 229 B'way

Brigg Brothers (Benjamin L. & John F. Brigg) 467 B'way

Brigg, Entz & Co. (dissolved) 467 B'way

Briggs Richard & Son (Richard & Augustus A. Briggs) 308 Washn. mkt

Briggs Warehouse Co. (S. Ellis Briggs, propr.) 552 Water & 300 Cherry

Briggs M. & Co. (Manasseh Briggs, no Co.) 180 Water

Briggs T. & R. (no inf.) 934 Tenth av.

Briggs T. L. & Co. (dissolved) 14 Lispenard

Briggs & Amsbury (dissolved) 107 Duane

Briggs & Dorland (dissolved) 621 Third av.

Briggs & Ellis Co. (Ltd.) (Wilbur D. Ellis, Pres.; George A. Ellis, Sec.; Ralph B. Briggs, Treas. Capital, $250,000. Directors: Theodore M. Leonard, Wilbur D. Ellis, Ralph B. Briggs, George A. Ellis, Milo M. Belding, William B. Putney, John Sparrenberger.) 157 Chambers

Briggs & Martens (no inf.) 18 Prince

Briggs & Son (dissolved) 606 W. 40th

Brigham & Baylis (Henry M. Brigham & Willard N. Baylis) 81 Nassau

Brigham & Mann (Dana D. Brigham & Frank Mann) 61 Leonard

Bright A. S. & J. L. (Aaron S. & Jacob L.) 187 B'way

Bright & Cameron (dissolved) 1560 Ninth av.

Dright, Church & Co. (Edward Dright, Robert Brady jr. Theodore Ryerson & estate of Pharcellus Church) 88 Park row

Brighton Laundry (Mary Keeney, propr.) 1485½ B'way

Brighton Mills (Charles Pratt, Pres.; Frank L. Babbott, Sec.; William Lyall, Treas.; further inf. unattainable) 68 Leonard & 541 W. 23d

Brighton Pharmaceutical Co. (N. Bradley Price propr.) 105 Chambers

Briglio & Co. (Antonio Briglio, no Co.) 57 Crosby

Brill A. & Co. (Abraham & William Brill) 317 Sixth av. 2 d W. 14th & 289 Grand

Brill Brothers (Morris & Samuel Brill) 45 Cortlandt & 211 Sixth av.

Brill & Doob (Isaac Brill & Moritz Doob) 443 B'way

Brinckerhoff & Co. (Daniel D. Brinckerhoff & Thomas S. Olive) 94 Elizabeth, 229 Grand & 42 Pearl

Brinckerhoff, Turner & Co. (J. Spencer & Thomas M. Turner, Jacob T. Van Wyck & Gilbert H.

EXCELSIOR BIRD FOOD. The recognized standard. The most reliable for your Canary. Use no other. Insist upon getting it. Packed only by **C. ROSENSTEIN & CO., 373 Washington Street, New York.**

BRI   40   BRO

Turner :—special partners, Elbert A. Brinckerhoff, *Englewood, N.J.,* & Henry D. Polhemus, *B'klyn, N. Y.,* each $100,000 ; terminates 31st Dec. 1890) 109 Duane

Briner Brothers (Emil & Henry Briner) 54 Rutgers

Brinker Henry & Co. (Henry Brinker & Andrew Icken) 190 West

Brinkerhoff W. H. & Co. (no inf.) 255 Wash'n.

Brisac S. & Co. (Solomon Brisac & John Delay) 751 B'way

Brissel John & Son (Marcus Brissel & Samuel B. Horan, only) 194 Park row

Bristol & Schultz (Lavius F. Bristol & Nicholas Schultz jr.) 47 Lispenard

Bristow, Peet & Opdyke (Benjamin H. Bristow, William Peet, William S. Opdyke, David Wilcox & William B. Bristow) 20 Nassau

British Am. Investment Co. (H. H. Warner, Pres.; T. A. Harris, Sec.; further inf. unattainable) 45 Wall

British & Irish Railway Joint Agency (Caesar A. Barattoni, agent) 852 B'way

Brittain, Richardson & Co. (dissolved) 339 B'way

Britten B. F. & Co. (Benjamin F. & Edwin F. Britten & F. Lawrence Uta) 27 Harrison

Britton & Burr (Reuben A. Britton & Melancthon Burr jr.) 58 New

Broadbent S. & Co. (Sarah Broadbent, Co. refused) 168 E. 64th

Broadnax & Bull (Amos Broadnax & J. Edgar Bull) 120 B'way

Broads & Aaronson (dissolved) 46 Walker

Broadway Dry Goods Co-operative Building & Loan Assn, (A. Judson Stone, Pres.; William H. Rawlins, Sec.; James A. Gilmour, Treas. Trustees : Walter P. Walsh, Alfred Foster, Peter B. Steele, R. G. Williams, F. W. Davison, William G. Wyatt, Benjamin F. Cromwell, George A. Trull, J. S. Bonnell, Joseph A. Rumrill, Thomas F. Larkin, Samuel J. Hague, John T. Breen, S. W. Kent) 335 B'way

Broadway Ins. Co. (Eugene B. Magnus, Pres.; Isaac Collord, Sec. Capital, $200,000. Directors : Bernard Smyth, Wilson G. Hunt, Alexander Masterton, James L. Stewart, James R. Hedges, George Forrester, William H. Stiles, William H. Albro, Henry Hannah, Crowell Hadden, Harvay F. Farrington, Amos C. Sherwood, Alfred W. White, Jesse G. Kays, John M. Crane, Theodore F. Vail, John W. Aitken, Harvey Farrington, Eugene B. Magnus, George H. Dayton, George H. Southard, Charles T. Van Santvoord, Stephen Valentine jr., Charles R. Dusenberry, Henry Demarest, Joseph S. Stout, Edgar B. Van Winkle, Theodore Magnus) 158 B'way

Broadway Savings Institution (Francis A. Palmer, Pres.; Horace F. Hutchinson, Sec.; Peter Cumming, Treas. Directors : Francis A. Palmer, Thomas Goadby, Peter Cumming, William H. Gedney, Jacob D. T. Hervey, James Talcott, Garrett Van Nostrand, Abraham F. Hazen, Francis P. Furnald, Jacob A. Geissenhainer, Edward P. Griffin, Horace F. Hutchinson, Caleb B. Knevals, David Jardine, John H. Rogers, Horace K. Thurber, John A. Carter, Warren A. Conover, J. Berre King, Joel E. Fisher, Eugene Britton, John Downey, Francis P. Furnald jr.) 4 Park pl.

Broadway Steam Laundry (Mary A. Roche, propr.) 1603 B'way

Broadway Theater Co. (Frank W. Sanger, Pres.; David B. Ogden, Sec. Capital, $250,000. Directors : Frank W. Sanger, David B. Ogden, Stephen P. Olin, T. Henry French, Elliott Zborowski) 1443 B'way

Broadway & Seventh Av. R. R. Co. (Henry Thompson, Pres.; Thomas F. Ryan, Sec. Capital $2,100,000. Directors : Henry Thompson. Thomas F. Ryan, B. M. Ewing, William H. Rockwell, John H. Murphy, Thomas J. O'Donohue, John J. Bradley, Charles Banks,

P. A. B. Widener, William L. Elkins, C. F. Frothingham, William B. Dinsmore, Daniel B. Hasbrouck) 761 Seventh av.

Broch & Co. (Charles L. Broch & William Dammeyer) 8 Warren

Brochon & Banvard (Peter C. Brochon & John C. Banvard) r 77 Nassau

Brock Boiler Co. (Capital, $20,000 ; further inf. unattainable) no address

Brock Brothers (James I. Brock, only) 814 Third av.

Brock & Co. (Max Brock, no Co.) 10 Cortlandt

Brock's Commercial Agency (Ltd.) (Henry Brock, Pres.; Thomas H. Wallace, Sec. Capital, $5,000 ; further inf. unattainable) 3 Broad

Brockington & Co. (dissolved) 438 B'way

Brockmann & Ihburg (dissolved) 163 Av. C

Brockner & Evans (Washington Brockner, only) 28 Vesey

Brockway & Davis (dissolved) 1997 Lex. av.

Brodbeck John & Son (John & John Brodbeck jr.) 815 Sixth

Brodek A. & Son (dissolved) 645 B'way

Brodek S. & Co. (Solomon Brodek & Siegfried Freudenthal) 727 Eighth av.

Brodek & Meyer (Herman A. Brodek & Henry Meyer) 645 B'way

Brodek, Freudenthal & Co. (Solomon Brodek, Siegfried Freudenthal & Julius Hilborn) 595 B'way & 168 Mercer

Broderick & Nearey (William J. Broderick & James F. Nearey) 156 Greene

Brodersen & Brandis (Henry W. Brodersen & William Brandis) 170 Wooster

Broderson & Day (no inf.) 608 B'way

Brodil Charles A. & Co. (Charles A. & Henry W. Brodil) 696 B'way

Brodsky Francis & Co. (Francis & Francis Brodsky jr. & Frank A. Sovak. 26 Av. C ; Francis & Francis Brodsky jr, Frank A. Sovak & Vincent Petrik, 1331 Second av.)

Brody M. & A. (no inf.) 150 Clinton

Brody & Chellmor (Isaac Brody & Jacob Chellmor) 132 Canal

Broegeler & School (dissolved) 106 Canal

Brogan Thomas & Son (Thomas & James K. Brogan) 434 Second av.

Brokaw Brothers (Isaac V. & William V. Brokaw) 30 Fourth av. & 62 Lafayette pl.

Brombacher Max H. C. & Co. (Max H. C. Brombacher & Anson Cuyler Banga) 15 Broad

Brombacher A. F. & Co. (Augustus F. Brombacher & William H. Hanna) 81 Fulton

Brombacher's Jacob, Sons (Augustus F. Brombacher, Pres.; M. A. Brombacher, Sec.; Max H. C. Brombacher, Treas. Capital, $25,000. Directors ; Augustus F. & M. A. & Max H. C. Brombacher) 20 Cliff

Bromell W. B. & Co. (William B. Bromell & Robert Kleiber) 87 Centre

Bromell & Bell (dissolved) 87 Centre

Bromfield Advertising Co. (not inc.) (Edward T. & George H. & Lawrence B. Bromfield) 658 B'way

Bromfield & Co. (Edward T. & Georgiana S. Bromfield) 658 B'way

Bromhorst & Co. (Louisa Bromhorst & Marie J. Bernhardt) 140 Attorney

Bronchialyne Tonicon Co. (not inc.) (Edward A. Phillips & Frank McIlorsh) 5 N. Y. & B'klyn bridge

Brook William B. & Co. (William B. & James F. Brook) 40 John

Brooke E. B. & Co. (Edwin B. Brooke & Frederick M. Lawrence) 120 Broad

Brooke & Brooke (Charles W. & Charles Lex Brooke) 111 B'way

IDEN & CO., MANUFACTURERS OF GAS FIXTURES AND ELECTROLIERS
University Place, 9th to 10th Sts., N. Y.

Brocker L. W. & Co. (Leonard W. Brocker & Philip Lynch) 164 W. 56th
Brocker & Lahey (Smith A. Brocker & James Lahey) 322 E. 60th, 1211 Ninth av. & 58 W. 125th
Brooklyn Art Embroidery Co. (Henry H. Bonnibr, propr.) 32 Howard
Brooklyn Brass & Copper Co. (William H. Davol, Pres.; Frank H. Davol, Sec.; further inf. unattainable) 100 John
Brooklyn Bridge Freezing & Cold Storage Co. (Thomas McLean, Pres.; William Fellowes Morgan, Sec. Capital, $50,000. Directors: Thomas McLean, William Fellowes Morgan, John B. Stewart, William E. Curtis, Charles P. Oudin, Juan M. Ceballos, Arnold C. Saportas, Edward F. Choate) 4 N. Y. & B'klyn bridge
Brooklyn Button Works (84th Brothers, proprs.) 413 E. 91st
Brooklyn Chemical Works (Ascher L. Piddian, Pres.; Philip Piddian, Sec. Capital, $5,000. Directors: Ascher L. & Philip Piddian, Leo Morgenstern, Joseph C. Rosenbaum, Abraham Meyer) 284 Pearl
Brooklyn Cooperage Co. (Lowell M. Palmer, Pres.; Julius A. Stursberg, Sec.; A. Ward Brigham, Treas. Capital, $100,000. Directors: Theodore A. & Henry O. Havemeyer, Julius A. Sturnberg, John E. Searles jr., John Jurgensen, Charles H. Senff, Lowell M. Palmer) 181 Front
Brooklyn Fire Ins. Co. (in liquidation) 4 Park pl.
Brooklyn Grain Warehouse Co. (Edward Annan, Pres.; Timothy L. Woodruff, Sec.; Richard H. Laimbeer, Treas.; further inf. refused) 108 Produce Ex.
Brooklyn Hills Improvement Co (John S. Long, Pres.; John S. Cain, Sec.; W. S. Wymond, Treas. Capital, $200,000. Directors: John S. Long, Attila Cox, Augustus S. & Louis C. Whiton, Charles Bell) 115 B'way
Brooklyn Improvement Co. (Edward H. Litchfield, Pres.; Levi S. Rhodes, Sec.; further inf. refused) 59 Wall
Brooklyn Knitting Co. (John H. Weber, Pres.; Oscar L. Baldwin, Sec.; Edward Y. Weber, Treas. Capital, $85,000. Directors: John H. Weber, Oscar L. Baldwin, Edward Y. Weber, Charles E. Hodge, Charles R. Baldwin) 74 Fifth av.
Brooklyn Life Ins. Co. (William M. Cole, Pres.; William Dutcher, Sec. Capital, $125,000. Directors: William M. Cole, William H. Wallace, William H. Lyon, Michael Chauncey, Augustus Ford, Arnold A Lewis, Jacob K. Olwine, Isaac Carhart, Felix Campbell, Hart B. Brundreth, Briton Richardson, Alonzo Slote, Charles T. Barney, Edward W. Mascord, Alexander Forman, Daniel Birdsall, William Dutcher, W. H. Ford) 51 Liberty
Brooklyn Mining Co. (Robert H. Parks, Pres.; Henry G. Romaine, Sec.; Sidney W. Curtis, Treas. Capital, $600,000. Directors: Robert H. Parks, Stephen B. French, F. L. Mathey jr., S. M. Hibbard, Sidney W. Curtis) 35 Pine
Brooklyn Railway Supply Co. (Charles D. Allyn, Pres.; John Allyn, Sec. Capital, $10,000. Directors: Charles B. & John Allyn, David W. Binns) 90 Chambers
Brooklyn Sugar Refining Co. (no inf.) 110 Wall
Brooklyn & N. Y. Ferry Co. (Joseph J. O'Donohue, Pres.; James Affleck, Sec.; John G. Jenkins, Treas. Capital, $3,000,000. Directors: Joseph J. O'Donohue, James Affleck, John G. Jenkins, William Ravesteyn, Jacob Hays, George Law, John Englis jr., Richard Poillon, Frank T. Wall, Seymour L. Husted jr.) ft. Grand; ft. Roosevelt & ft. E. 23d
Brookman H. D. & John U. (in liquidation) 43 Exchange pl.
Brooks Clarence & Co. (Clarence & Thomas B. Brooks) 403 W. 12th
Brooks Walter & Co. (Walter Brooks & Dwight M. Harris) 45 Exchange pl.
Brooks E. J. & Co. (Edward J. Brooks, Pres.; Leroy F. Hovey, Sec. Capital, $200,000. Directors: Edward J. Brooks, Leroy F. Hovey, A. D. Smith) 51 Dey
Brooks F. W. & Co. (dissolved) 40 Wall
Brooks S. & Son (Solomon & Abraham L. Brooks) 619 B'way
Brooks Brothers (John E. Brooks, Francis Wagner, Francis G. Lloyd & Frederick Brooks) 263 B'way
Brooks & Campbell (Clark Brooks & Alexander V. Campbell) 55 William
Brooks & Denton (Reuben R. Brooks & Harry M. Denton) 670 Sixth av.
Brooks & Foot (Erastus R. Brooks & Homer Foot) 23 Park row
Brooks & Goldstein (Thomas B. Brooks & Charles Goldstein) 145 E. B'way
Brooks & Klein (dissolved) 136 Chrystie
Brooks & Mendelowitz (Stephen A. Brooks & Jacob Mendelowitz) 42 Delancey
Brophy & Son (Patrick & William J. Brophy) 53 E. 11th
Brosnan T. J. & Brother (dissolved) 600 Third av.
Bross G. & J. (dissolved) 178 Seventh av.
Brotherhood Wine Co. (J. M. Emerson & Sons, proprs.) 20 Vesey
Brotherton & Co. (dissolved) 1848 Ninth av.
Brotman A. & Fortgang (no inf.) 96 Sheriff
Broun C. C. & Co. (Campbell C. Broun & Thomas Fleming) 66 Exchange pl.
Broun, Green & Adams (Heywood C. Broun, Edward B. Green & Eugene E. Adams) 40 Beaver
Brouwer & McGown (George H. Brouwer & George W. McGown) 2 Wall
Brower John & Co. (John & William W. Brower) 16 Water
Brower R. L. & Co. (Remsen L. & Marsh Brower & William Harris) 94 Barclay
Brower Brothers (mcrs.) (Abraham L. & Andrew S. Brower) 346 Washn.
Brower Brothers (stationers) (John V. & Bloomfield Brower) 289 B'way
Brown Charles & Co. (Charles Brown, no Co.) 202 Church
Brown Charles F. & Co. (Charles F. Brown & Richard S. Canfield) 94 Wall & 76 G'wich
Brown Charles S. & Co. (Charles S. & James P. Brown) 84 Warren
Brown Comb Co. (not inc.) (James T. & Samuel R. Brown) 392 B'way
Brown David S. & Co. (David S. & Delaplaine Brown) 8 Thomas & 101 Bank
Brown George & Clifford, 377 W. 12th & 171 Canal
Brown J, Romaine & Co. (J. Romaine Brown & Alexander P. W. Kinnan) 59 W. 33d
Brown James E. & Son (James E. & George Brown) 567 Eagle av.
Brown James M. & Co. (refused) 115 B'way
Brown John & Co. (John & James Brown) 140 W. 105th
Brown Joseph T. & Co. (Joseph T. Brown, no Co.) 121 Front
Brown Louis, Mfg. Co. (John E. White, Pres.; Reginald P. Sherman, Sec. Capital, $100,000. Directors: John E. White, Reginald P. Sherman, Louis Brown) 62 William
Brown Robert & Co. (Robert J. Brown & Sylvester G. Reybert) 101 Market
Brown Samuel J. & Co. (Samuel J. Brown, no Co.) 19 College pl.
Brown Standard Fire Arms Co. (John H. Brown, Pres.; Frederic A. Kursheedt, Sec. Capital,

$10,000. Trustees: John H. Brown, Alexander K. & Frederic A. Kursheedt) 190 S. 5th av.

Brown Thomas G. & Sons (Thomas G. & William A. & Thomas B. Brown) 680 B'way

Brown Vernon H. & Co. (Vernon H. & Albert H. & Vernon C. Brown & George F. Wilde, 28 Beaver; Vernon H. Brown, no Co. 4; Bowling gr. & Pier 40 (new) N. R.)

Brown Walston H. & Brothers (Walston H. & Frederic A. & Herbert P. Brown) 20 Nassau

Brown William A. & Co. (William A. Brown & James Callam) 122 Pearl

Brown A. & Co. (Abram Brown, no Co.) 214 Sixth

Brown A. & F. (Felix & Felix jr. & August F. Brown, only) 44 Park pl. & 59 Lewis

Brown A. E. & Co. (dissolved) 260 Washn. mkt

Brown C. F. & Co. (Charles F. Brown, no Co.) 96 Greene

Brown E. A. & Co. (Edwin A. Brown & Herman Greenberg) 178 Reade

Brown G. F. & C. E. & Co. (George F. & C. Edward & J. Warren Brown) 321 Canal

Brown H. & B. (Harris & Bernhardt) 622 B'way & 156 Crosby

Brown J. S. & W. (William Brown, only) 122 Produce Ex.

Brown L. D. & Son (Henry L. Brown, only) 486 B'way

Brown L. S. & Son (dissolved) Pier 32 E. R.

Brown M. & Co. (Marcus Brown & Samuel Broom:—special partner, Callman Rouse, $15,000; terminates 31st Dec. 1890) 40 White

Brown M. & Son (Michael & John J. Brown) 749 Third av. & 159 E. 52d

Brown R. C. & Co. (Robert C. Brown & Emma L. & Oliver R. Charlick) 21 Murray

Brown R. I. & Sons (Robert I. & Walter E. & William I. Brown) 3426 Third av.

Brown S. F. & Co. (dissolved) 202 B'way

Brown S. H. & Brothers (Stephen H. & Walter G. & Arthur Brown) 216 Washn. mkt

Brown T. D. & Co. (Theodore D. Brown, no Co.) 65 Wall

Brown T. D. & Son (Truman B. & William E. Brown) 14 Vesey

Brown W. L. & Co. (William L. Brown & George V. A. Conger:—special partners, Levi L. Brown, N. Adams, Mass., & Henry C. Halbert, B'klyn, N. Y., each, $50,000; terminates 1st July 1890) 361 B'way

Brown Brothers (liquors) (dissolved) 2521 Third av.

Brown Brothers (wharfingers) (Edwin M. & Joseph V. Brown) ft. E. 23d

Brown & Besson (dissolved) 518 Sixth av.

Brown & Biles (dissolved) 877 W. 12th & 171 Canal

Brown & Bower (D. William Brown & Lewis S. Bower) 72 E. B'way

Brown & Chapman (dissolved) 46 New

Brown & Collins (dissolved) 121 Front

Brown & Co. (lighters) (William Brown, no Co.) 22 South

Brown & Co. (waists) (Joseph & Jacob Brown) 628 B'way & 150 Crosby

Brown & Dewinter (Charles Brown & John Dewinter) 321 Washn.

Brown & Dexter (De Witt C. Brown & Frederick C. Dexter) 32 Nassau

Brown & Dorchester (Arnold W. Brown & Hoffman S. Dorchester) 41 Maiden la.

Brown & Evans (Harvey T. Brown & Thomas B. Evans) 1001 Sixth av.

Brown & Farnell (Charles R. Brown & Frederick W. Farnell) 238 Fourth av.

Brown & Fleming (Charles A. Brown & John Fleming) 129 Broad

Brown & Gilmore (William D. Brown & Howard D. Gilmore) 102 W. 27th

Brown & Golding (Gerald R. Brown & John N. Golding) 120 B'way & 703 Madison av.

Brown & Griswold (Henry T. Brown & James D. Griswold) 261 B'way

Brown & Keene (dissolved) 5 Counties sl.

Brown & Kurz (Theodore Brown & Richard Kurz) 46 W. 14th

Brown & Leviness (in liquidation) 59 Liberty

Brown & McElvare (dissolved) 12 Cortlandt

Brown & Matzenbacher (John Brown & John Matzenbacher) 88 White

Brown & Plympton (Mortimer Brown & Charles R. Plympton) 34 E. 14th

Brown & Pulverman (Lafayette J. Finch, only) 940 & 1228 B'way, 59 Liberty, 158 Fourth av., 270 W. 23d, 780 & 1020 Third av., 104 W. 42d, 1092 Ninth av, & 180 E. 125th

Brown & Rittenhouse (Moses Rittenhouse, only) 189 Reade

Brown & Sager (Charles A. Brown & William M. Sager) 636 Hudson

Brown & Seccomb (Edward M. Brown & Edward A. Seccomb) 26 State

Brown & Skinner (James A. Brown & James R. Skinner) 51 Liberty

Brown & Son (George B. & Henry Brown) 722 E. 175th

Brown & Wells (Willard Brown & Charles W. Wells) 105 B'way

Brown & Wetterer (dissolved) 121 Pearl

Brown & Wilkens (W. Schuyler Brown & Henry J. Wilkens) 260 Washn. mkt

Brown & Wilkinson (William R. J. Brown & Joseph Wilkinson) 27 Depeyster

Brown & Wilson (Enoch S. Brown & Henry C. Wilson) 28 Beekman

Brown & Withers (Thomas R. Withers & John D. Mills, only) 171 B'way

Brown Brothers & Co. (James M. & John C. & Alexander Hargreaves Brown, Sir Mark W. Collet, Francis A. Hamilton, Charles D. Dickey, Frederick Chalmers, Howard Potter, Waldron P. Brown & Charles D. Dickey jr.) 59 Wall

Brown, Draper & Co. (Joseph H. Brown & Frank E. Draper, no Co.) 542 B'way

Brown, Howard & Co. (Walston H. Brown, receiver) 20 Nassau

Brown, Place & Co. (dissolved) 115 Franklin

Brown, Silvers & Co. (inf. unattainable) 16 B'way

Brown's M., Son & Co. (Moses Brown, Edmund F. Krowson & Percy Lauderdale:—special partner, T. Wistar Brown jr. Phila., Pa.; further inf. unattainable) 286 Church

Brown's Stewart, Sons (Davison & George Alexander Brown) 64 B'way & 19 New

Browne William E. & Co. (William E. & Richard R. Browne) 26 Burling sl.

Brownes. McAllister & Co. (Jacob S. Browne, John McAllister & Thomas Couch) 431 W. 14th

Brownell H. C., Co. (Capital, $100,000; further inf. unattainable) no address

Brownell & Lathrop (Silas P. Brownell & William G. Lathrop jr.) 71 Wall

Brownell, Clark & Co. (Stephen E. Brownell & Samuel Clark, no Co.) 463 Eighth av.

Browning Brothers (William J. & Harry C. Browning) 1026 Third av.

Browning & Ward (Samuel Browning & John H. Ward) 271 Canal

Browning, King & Co. (William C. Browning, Henry W. King, Edward W. Dewey & John S. & William H. Browning) 408 Broome

Brownold & Co. (Charles & Bernhard Brownold, Meyer Hoffman & Jacob Lebenstein) 47 Walker

Brownson & Co. (dissolved) 22 College pl.
Bruce A. T. & Co. (John T. & Robert M. Bruce, only) 66 Pine
Bruce & Cook (Isabella B. Bruce, John C. Cook, Russell W. McKee & Spencer A. & Philander R. Jennings) 190 Water & 250 Pearl
Bruce & Hardy (Thomas K. Bruce & Samuel A. Hardy) 574 Second av.
Bruce, Busby & Bruce (Saunders D. Bruce, Hamilton Busby & Leslie C. Bruce) 251 B'way
Bruce's George, Son & Co. (David W. Bruce, no Co.) 13 Chambers & 3 City Hall pl.
Bruck George & Co. (George Bruck, Irving Alsberg & Ivan Frank) 722 D'way
Bruck & Gutmann (Louis J. Bruck & Jacques Gutmann) 57 B'way
Bruckheimer L. & Co. (Leopold & David Bruckheimer) 706 Second av.
Druckner Brothers & Lowenthal (Charles & Max P. Druckner & Isaac C. Lowenthal) 2307 Second av.
Bruder C. & Son (George & Frederick F. Bruder) 620 Ninth av.
Brudi & Betty (Alexander L. Brudi & Robert Betty) 1216 Third av.
Brueckner Richard & Co. (Richard Brueckner & James A. Stoothoff) 3 Platt
Brueggeman & Stemmen (Albert Brueggeman & Peter Stemmen) 144 Christopher
Brueggemann Albert & Co. (dissolved) 353 E. 33d
Bruen Brothers & Ritchey (Albert & Oscar H. Bruen & William P. Ritchey) 214 Fulton
Brügel & Bruckmann (John Brügel & Robert Bruckmann) 91 Duane
Brugh & DeKlyn (John H. Brugh & Charles B. DeKlyn) 1423 B'way
Brugman F. E. & Co. (Frank E. Brugman & James W. Griffith) 10 Old sl.
Bruhl Brothers & Co. (refused) 14 Maiden la.
Brull L. & Co. (Louis Brull & Louis Schoolhouse) 197 Lewis
Brumley's S. S., Son & Co. (Schuyler E. & Willard S. Brumley) 81 Moore
Brumme & Durstewitz (Anron Brumme & Anton Durstewitz) 732 B'way
Brummer L. & Co. (Louis & Marc A. Brummer) 486 E. 72d
Brummerhop Henry & Co. (dissolved) 85 Av. A
Brummerhop M. & Co. (Martin Brummerhop & Herman Will) 26 Coenties sl.
Brundage & Newton (dissolved) 40 College pl.
Brune & Ellerbrock (Henry Brune & Joseph Ellerbrock) 823 Broome
Bruner & Moore Co. (Montgomery B. Cowperthwait, Pres.; Peter F. Bruner, Sec.; further inf. refused) 43 W. 14th
Brunhild H. & Co. (Henry Brunhild & Dovy O. Sterns) 323 Pearl
Bruning & Pundt (William Bruning & John Pundt) 141 Eighth
Brunkhorst J. & F. (dissolved) 1026 First av.
Brunler Apparatus & Gas Co. (Capital, $20,500; further inf. unattainable) no address
Brunner Francis & Son (Francis & Alfred A. Brunner) 121 W. 26th
Brunner J. & H. (dissolved) 134 West
Brunner J. & Co. (William & Ann F. Brunner) 407 E. 12th
Brunner & Kahn (Henry Brunner & Louis Kahn) 440 Canal
Brunner & Tryon (Arnold W. Brunner & Thomas Tryon) 30 Union sq. W.
Brunner's Express Co. (Joseph G. Brunner, propr.) 344 Third av. 875 Sixth av. & Pier 24 E. R.
Brunner's J. Sons (Ferdinand H. & Otto & Robert J. Brunner) 146 Fulton & 18 Maiden la.

Bruno Publishing & Printing Co. (Paul Philippson, Pres.; Joseph O'Kelly, Treas.; Edward Nietack, Sec. Capital, $20,000. Directors: Paul Philippson, Joseph O'Kelly, Edward Nietack) 27 Beekman
Bruno C. & Son (Charles Bruno jr. only) 54 Maiden la. & 29 Liberty
Bruns Herman & Son (Herman & Henry Bruns) 31 Centre
Bruns H. & Son (Herman & Herman Bruns jr.) 330 Bowery
Brunssen George & Co. (George Brunssen & John Feldhusen) 146 Greene
Brunswick Briar Pipe Co. (A. Brunswick, propr.) 278 Ninth av.
Brunswick Gold Mining Co. (dissolved) 39 B'way
Brunswick Gold Mining Co. (of Nova Scotia) (Charles H. Adams, Pres.; Charles E. Hayden, Sec. Capital, $300,000. Directors: Charles H. Adams, James D. Fry, Joseph H. Parsons, Charles E. Hayden, William D. Whipple, T. L. Crittenden, John A. Spooner) 52 B'way
Brunswick Harbor & Land Co. (John I. Holly, Pres.; Edward P. Kennard. Sec.; John Sloane, Treas. Capital, $1,000,000. Directors: John I. Holly, John D. Gordon, John Sloane, Edward P. Kennard, Norman W. Dodge, Joseph W. Woolfolk) 81 New
Brunswick Land Reclamation Co. (John I. Holly, Pres.; Edward P. Kennard, Sec.; John Sloane, Treas. Capital, $200,000. Directors: John I. Holly, John D. Gordon, John Sloane, Edward P. Kennard, Norman W. Dodge, Joseph Hilton, Joseph W. Woolfolk) 81 New
Brunswick-Balke-Collender Co. (Hugh W. Collender, Pres.; Anthony F. Troescher, Sec. Capital, $1,500,000. Directors: Hugh W. Collender, Julius Balke, Anthony F. Troescher, Moses Boushiger, Leo Schmidt) 860 B'way
Brush Electric Illuminating Co. (William T. Moore, Pres.; Gaylord McFall, Sec. Capital, $1,000,000. Trustees: William T. Moore, Caleb H. Jackson, David L. Einstein, Samuel M. Schafer, Josiah M. Fiske, William M. Pomeroy, Julius Catlin, Paul D. Cravath, W. H. Browne, C. J. Marsh, F. F. Kobbé, Frederick Darlington) 210 Elizabeth
Brush-Swan Electric Light Co. of New England (William L. Strong, Pres.; Gaylord McFall, Sec. Capital, $2,000,000. Directors: William L. Strong, Augustus D. Juilliard, George W. Stockley, William A. Wheelock, Gaylord McFall, Lyman P. French, Joseph W. Sawyer, Edwin Einstein) 210 Elizabeth
Brussels Tapestry Co. (Hugh W. Collender, Pres.; Darrow B. Lyons, Sec.; Anthony F. Troescher, Treas. Capital, $100,000. Directors: Hugh W. Collender, Barrow B. Lyons, Anthony F. Troescher) 233 E. 42d & 58 Worth
Bryan Appliance Co. (Louis B. Jones, propr.) 231 B'way
Bryan Brothers (dissolved) 430 E. 70th
Bryan, Taylor & Co. (George J. Bryan, William Graham & Chauncey W. Brown, only) 757 B'way
Bryant Literary Union (Henry R. Heath, Pres.; George R. Carrington, Sec.; further inf. refused) 206 B'way
Bryant Solon, & Co. (no inf.) 440 B'way
Bryant M. B. & Co. (Monroe B. & William A. Bryant & James A. Smith) 10 Maiden la. & 26 Liberty
Bryant & Ondrak (William E. Bryant & Jacob A. Ondrak) 314 Fifth av.
Bryce William & Co. (dissolved) 280 B'way
Bryce & Hunter (dissolved) 111 W. 29th
Buchanan A. F. & Sons (Alexander P. & John U. & George W. & Andrew D. & Thomas S. Buchanan) 14 Thomas
Buchanan Brothers (coal) (David & Robert Buchanan) 210 Eleventh av. & 564 W. 25th

SPECIAL ATTENTION PAID TO THIS CLASS OF WORK.	BANKERS' & BROKERS' CIRCULARS DELIVERED	THE TROW CITY DIRECTORY CO. 11 University Place.
BUC	44	BUR

Buchanan Brothers (paper) (in liquidation) 23 Beekman

Buchanan & Co. (refused) 59 E. 9th

Buchanan & Lyall (William & Charles F. Buchanan & David C. Lyall) 101 Wall

Bucher Brothers (Charles & John Bucher) 1676 First av.

Buchman & Deisler (Albert Buchman & Gustav Deisler) 8 W. 29th

Buchner D. & Co. (David Buchner & Lewis Bockel) 133 Mulberry

Buck Richard F. & Co. (Daniel Barnes, George S. Underhill & John V. Barnes, only) 29 South

Buck Brothers (Gustav & Ferdinand Buck) 292 First av.

Buck & Webler (dissolved) 58 John

Buck, Steljes & Co. (William Buck, Martin Steljes & Frederick D. Burfeind) 104 South

Buckeye Basket Co. (David R. Saunders, propr.) 65 Watts

Bucki Charles L. & Co. (Charles L. Bucki & Charles S. Hirsch) ft. W. 13th & 18 B'way

Bucki L. & Son (Charles L. Bucki, only) 16 B'way

Buckingham C. & Son (Charles Buckingham, only) 43 Exchange pl.

Buckingham G. & Co. (Goodell Buckingham & Silas H. Moore) 15 Broad

Buckingham & Paulson (Oliver W. Buckingham & Leonard Paulson jr.) 68 Leonard

Buckley Brothers (Edward G. & Christopher J. Buckley) 490 Third av.

Buckley & Hotaling (Lawrence A. Buckley & Peter Hotaling) 232 Clinton

Buckley & Mahony (dissolved) 2271 Tenth av.

Buckley & Wood (Albion A. Buckley & Edwin C. Wood) 220 William

Bucklin, Crane & Co. (John A. & Isaac B. Crane, only) 45 South

Buckman I. & Son (dissolved) 158 Washn. mkt

Bucksmith & Blum (dissolved) 209 Forsyth

Budde & Westermann (Bernhard Budde & Carl Westermann) 50 Vesey

Budenbach O. & Co. (Oswald Budenbach & Henry F. Diefenthaler) 467 Eleventh av.

Budworth W. S. & Son (William S. & William S. Budworth jr.) 1 W. 14th & 624 W. 52d

Bueb & Co. (Otto J. Bueb & John H. & David M. Johnson) 122 W. 44th

Buehler & Dateman (dissolved) 148½ E. 23d

Buehler & Gehrig (Gustav Buehler & Anton Gehrig) 326 Church & 624 E. 102d

Buek Charles & Co. (Charles Buek & Henry F. Cook) 1167 Ninth av.

Buek G. H. & Co. (Gustave H. Buek & Leon Marie) 146 Centre

Buel Arthur, Mfg. Co. (John W. James, Pres.; Arthur Buel, Sec.; further inf. unattainable) 4 Burling sl.

Buel & Brevoort (dissolved) 206 B'way

Buel & Hansemann (dissolved) 152 South

Buell Electrical & Hydraulic Mfg. Co. (James G. Smith, Pres.; Charles E. Buell, Sec. Capital, $500,000. Directors: James G. Smith, Joseph W. & Charles E. Buell) 171 B'way

Buelow Brothers (Charles & Louis C. Buelow) 214 E. 111th

Buermann's A., Sons (Charles & Henry & August Buermann) 91 Columbia

Bues & Co. (William Bues & German Grob) 105 Rivington

Buffalo Acholene Co. (Harry J. Pierce, Pres.; Edward B. Stevens, Sec. Capital, $96,000. Directors: Harry J. & George N. Pierce, James M. Head, O. O. Smith, Edward B. Stevens) 105 Water

Buffalo Door & Sash Co. (not inc.) (James H. &

Franklin Lee, Nelson Holland & Charles S. Kendall) Ninth av. c. W. 124th

Buffalo, N. Y. & Erie R. R. Co. (Daniel N. Lockwood, Pres.; John Clinton Gray, Sec. Capital, $850,000. Directors: Daniel N. Lockwood, Thomas Brown jr., Henry H. Cook, John A. C. Gray, C. H. Daniels, J. A. Davenport, Augustus Frank, J. A. Manning, Samuel W. Milbank, C. M. Hunter, Henry Martin, F. S. Coit, John C. Gray) 115 B'way

Buffalo, Rochester & Pittsburgh Railway Co. (Adrian Iselin jr. Pres.; John R. Hocart. Sec.; John F. Dinkey.Treas. Capital, $12,000,000. Directors: Henry I. Barbey, Walston H. Brown, Henry Fatio, Adrian & Adrian Iselin jr., John H. Hocart, Wheeler H. Peckham, Auguste Richard, Alfred Roosevelt. Arthur W. Sherman, Alexander H. Stevens, Frederick D. Tappen, J. Kennedy Tod) 36 Wall

Buhler & Nans (Rudolph Buhler & Carl Nans) 182 B'way

Buhr F. & Son (dissolved) 324 W. 20th & 267 W. 27th

Building Material Exchange (James Rogers, Pres.; Joseph R. Van Valen, Sec.; Hiram Snyder, Treas.) 63 Liberty

Building & Loan News Co. (Thomas G. Hillhouse, Pres.; Samuel Marsh, Sec.; John C. Tencyek, Treas. Capital, $100,000, Directors: Louis H. Cornish, George B. Morris, Thomas G. Hillhouse, Samuel Marsh, John C. Tencyek) 2 Spruce

Bulen Watch-Clock & Electric Co. (dissolved) 265 B'way

Bulkley, Dunton & Co. (David G. Garabrant, Moses & Jonathan Dunkley & James S. Packard, only) 74 John

Bullard & Co. (Lewis H. Bullard & William H. Humphrey) 14 Ferry

Bullard & Wheeler (John L. Bullard & Henry H. Wheeler) 110 Maiden la.

Bullock & Co. (Thomas O. & L. P. Bullock) 120 Water

Bullock & Zaring (Charles E. Bullock & William C. Zaring) 91 Greene

Bullwinkel Brothers (George L. & August H. Bullwinkel) 267 Bleecker

Bulmer Stationery Co. (Benjamin L. Scott, propr.) 168 William

Bulmer & Co. (dissolved) 133 Water

Bunch H. S. & Co. (Higinio S. Bunch, no Co.) 4 Stone

Buning F. W. & Co. (Frederick W. Buning, no Co.) 58 Murray

Bunnell J. R. & Co. (Jesse R. Bunnell & Charles McLaughlin) 76 Cortlandt & 138 W. 24th

Bunnell & Eno Investment Co. (William B. Eno, Pres.; Luther D. Bunnell, Treas.; Matt. H. Ellis, Sec. Capital, $500,000. Directors: William B. Eno, S. E. Morse, Charles R. Otis, G. L. Morse, Frederic Shouinard, Adam C. Ellis, William H. Sweeny, Matt. H. Ellis, Luther D. Bunnell) 140 Nassau

Bonney Robert H. & Co. (Robert R. Banney & Frederick H. Norton) 180 Chambers

Bunzl J. & Sons (Victor & Gustave & Ernest Bunzl, only) 125 Water

Burberry W. & Co. (William Burberry, no Co.) r 40 E. 32d

Burbridge & Brother (James & Patrick Burbridge) 232 Eighth av.

Burchard & Co. (Lewis S. Burchard & William J. Leeds) 65 Cortlandt

Burchell & Hodges (John A. Burchell & John E. Hodges) 206 E. 56th

Burck & Groesbeck (dissolved) 478 Tenth av.

Burde Brothers (Julius & Paul Burde) 944 First av.

Burdett William V. & Co. (William V. Burdett & John Hechler) 13 State

FOR THE BEST CO-PARTNERSHIP IN THE BEST CORPORATION SEE PAGE F IN BACK OF BOOK

BUR 45 BUR

Burdett & Dennis (Daniel H. Burdett & Charles Dennis) 29 Burling sl.
Burdick Mfg. Co. (refused) 94 Liberty
Burdon Central Sugar Refining Co. (Henry J. Davison, Pres.; L. Murray Ferris, Sec.; Frank F. Jones, Treas. Capital, $100,000. Directors: Charles F. Dieterich, James Jourdan, Thomas J. Hayward, Henry M. Benedict, L. Murray Ferris, Henry J. Davison, Frank F. Jones) 2 Wall
Bureau of Audit (Charles Dutton, Pres.; George C. Wilde, Sec.; further inf. refused) 195 B'way
Barfeind F. D. & Co. (Frederick D. Barfeind & Mary Bosselmann) 322 West
Burgass & Co. (Ludwig Schildlower, only) 46 Cliff
Burger L. & Co. (Leopold & Maurice K. Burger) 83 Spring
Burger Brothers (dissolved) 191 Henry
Burger & Agar (Ray L. Burger & James Agar) 26 Bowery
Burger & Baumgard (Ferdinand Baumgard, only) 105 Chambers
Burger & Co. (Arthur H. E. & Gustav A. Burger) 59 Nassau
Burger & Lee (Theodore W. Burger & Henry A. Lee) 378 G'wich
Burgess W. H. & Co. (William H. Burgess, no Co.) 59 Greene
Burgess & Brother (Bernhard & William Burgess) 410 Fifth
Burgess & Goddard (William Burgess & Henry H. Goddard) 49 Barclay & 52 Park pl.
Burk Oil Co. (Mansfield B. Snevily, Pres.; Charles E. Hubbard, Sec. Capital, $30,000. Directors: Mansfield B. Snevily, Charles E. Hubbard, Alexander Moltrier) 27 Water
Burk C. & Co. (dissolved) 201 W. 40th
Burke Martin & Co. (Martin Burke, no Co.) 39 Little W. 12th
Burke Patrick J. & Son (Patrick J. & William E. Burke) 109 Sullivan
Burke L. A. & Co. (Luke A. Burke & Charles O. Perry) 40 Chambers & 286 E. 126th
Burke M. & E. (Margaret M. & Elisabeth M. J.) 103 E. 84th
Burke V. & Son (Victor & Charles Burke) 414 W. 41st
Burke Brothers (Thomas F. & James E. Burke) 414 Madison
Burke & Byrne (dissolved) 40 Chambers
Burke & Co. (Ulick W. C. Burke, Co. refused) 22 Jackson
Burke & Earle (dissolved) 506 W. 52d
Burke & Lynch (John G. Burke & Bernard Lynch) 1301 Third av.
Burke & McKeever (William F. Burke & Thomas F. McKeever) 84 W. 13th
Burkelman C. & C. (dissolved) 32 Sullivan
Burkhalter C. & Co. (Charles & John H. Burkhalter) 94 Hudson
Burkhardt's J. S., Sons (Robert E. & Gustave A. Burkhardt) 509 Ninth av.
Burkitt Brothers (refused) 2305 First av.
Burmeister & Kaiser (dissolved) 300 E. 70th
Burnaby G. R. & Co. (George R. Burnaby & Edward C. Halsey) 18 B'way
Burnap I. M. & Co. (dissolved) 519 G'wich
Burnet's John M., Sons (Charles C. Burnet, only) 52 Cedar
Burnett George B. & Son (George B. & William A. Burnett) 142 Greene
Burnett C. J. & Co. (Charles J. Burnett & Charles W. Honeyman) 485 D'way
Burnett & Co. (William Burnett, no Co.) 1916 Vanderbilt av. E.
Burnett & Whitney (Henry L. Burnett & Edward B. Whitney) 67 Wall

Burnham George H. & Co. (George H. & Edwin S. Burnham & Theodore R. Noyes) 188 W. Houston
Burnham S. J. & Co. (Sarah J. Burnham & William W. Hall) 756 Fifth av. & 251 W. 120th
Burnham & Meyer (dissolved) 23 Abingdon sq.
Burns Jabez & Sons (Jabez & Robert Burns, only) 3 Worth
Burns Milling Co (inoperative) 35 Liberty
Burns Brothers (Michael F. & Timothy A. Burns) 32 South, 25 East, ft. Delancey & 59 W. 42d
Burns & Knapp (Charles E. Burns & Edwin L. Knapp) 126 Chambers
Burns & Son (Charles De F. & George R. Burns) 744 B'way
Burnton & Co. (Maurice E. Burnton, no Co.) 94 Fourth av.
Burns & Co. (Eliza D. & Channing Burns) 24 Clinton pl.
Burr Brewing Co. (Herman B. Scharmann, Pres.; William H. Burr, Sec.; John M. Moser, Treas. Capital, $400,000. Directors: Herman B. Scharmann, William H. Burr, John M. Moser) 225 W. 18th
Burr George L., Co. (William E. Walkley, Pres.; George L. Burr, Treas. Capital, $600. Directors: William E. Walkley, George L. Burr) 142 Fulton
Burr Printing House (Frank D. Harmon, propr.) 18 Jacob
Burrage & Travis Paper Co. (not Inc.) (William B. Burrage & Josiah C. Travis) 20 Rose
Burres H. K. & Co. (Howard K. Burres & James S. Dearns) 2 Nassau
Burrell S. R. & Co. (Samuel R. & Frank R. Burrell) 307 West
Burrell & Corr (George A. Burrell & James J. Corr) 1 Lispenard
Burrill & Housman (William V. Burrill & Arthur A. Housman) 52 Exchange pl.
Burrill & Stitt (Edward L. Burrill & Charles H. Stitt;—special partner, Frederick F. Woodward, $15,000 ; terminates 1st May, 1890) 19 New
Burrill, Zabriskie & Burrill (John E. Burrill, George Zabriskie, Middleton S. Burrill & J. Archibald Murray) 21 Broad
Burris Elliott & Co. (Elliott Burris, no Co.) 60 Worth
Burroughs & Benson (John H. Burroughs & Nelson H. Benson jr.) 74 Wall
Burroughs & Chapman (John Burroughs & Charles J. Chapman) 61 Tenth av.
Burrows T. & Son (Thomas & Thomas Burrows jr.) 154 W. D'way
Burrows W. T. & Co. (William T. Burrows, no Co.) 19 Park pl. & 10 Murray
Burrows Brothers (John P. & James C. Burrows) 487 Tenth av. & 486 Ninth av.
Burrows & Co. (Edward O. & Caroline M. Burrows) 106 Beekman
Burrows & Smith (Thomas Burrows & Samuel Smith) r 307 E. 122d
Burt Edwin C. & Co. (Edward D. Burt, Henry R. Curtis & Edwin A. Goazer, only) 94 Centre
Burt & Mears (Charles E. Mears, only) 59 Reade
Burtis Brothers (James S. & Abram S. Burtis) 241 E. 51st
Burton Thomas & Son (Thomas & J. Charles Burton) 26 University pl.
Burton W. & Co. (Washington Burton & Jeremiah W. Perry) 77 Barclay
Burton & Davis (John J. Burton & James J. Davis) 311 G'wich
Burton Brothers & Co. (Frank V. & Robert L. Burton & Frank L. St. John) 70 Franklin
Burton, Price & Co. (James W. Burton, Theodore N. Price & Alvin Moore) 48 Lispenard

TYPEWRITING DONE BY THE TROW CITY DIRECTORY CO., 11 University Place.

Busch A. & Son (Andrew & George Busch) 232 W. 32d

Busch M. & Brother (Mary Busch, only) 86 Bedford

Busch Brothers (Robert & Carl Busch) 1312 First av.

Busch & Son (dissolved) 200 E. 42d

Busch & Tiedemann (Charles Busch & George Tiedemann) 229 W. 19th

Busch, Jaburg & Fuhs (Julia Busch, Frederick Jaburg & Louis Fuhs) 12 Wooster

Buse & Hattorff (dissolved) 106 Prince

Buse & Miller (Frederick Buse & Harman Miller) 100 Park row

Bush George W. & Co. (dissolved) 624 G'wich

Bush J. P., Mfg. Co. (Andrew J. Ditman, Pres. Capital, $10,000. Directors: Andrew J. Ditman, Henry T. Champney) 2 Barclay

Bush J. D. & Brother (no inf.) 844 Third av.

Bush & Denslow Mfg. Co. (Rufus T. Bush, Pres.; Abiel Wood, Sec. Capital, $300,000. Directors: Rufus T. Bush, John D. Archbold, Abiel Wood) 130 Pearl

Bush & Hollingsworth (George A. Bush & Edmund Hollingsworth) 23 Day

Bushnell George A. & Co. (inf. unattainable) 102 Chambers

Bushnell, Palmer & Co. (Albert E. Bushnell, Henry C. H. Palmer, no Co.) 132 Duane

Bushwick Glass Works (William Brookfield, propr.) 83 Fulton

Busick Brothers (Max & Samuel Busick) 864 Eighth av.

Business Address Co. (Robert W. Deforest, Pres.; H. H. Balch, Treas. Capital, $100,000; further inf. refused) 30 Vesey

Busk & Jevons (Thomas E. Jevons & George C. Allen, only) 301 Produce Ex.

Busoni & Burnet (Octavie Busoni & Anna Burnet) 46 E. 19th

Busse & Rabens (dissolved) 415 E. 100th

Busteed G. W. & Co. (George W. Busteed, no Co.) 162 E. 33d

Bustin & Co. (no inf.) 756 Seventh av.

Butcher John H. & Son (John H. & F. Edwin Butcher) 25½ Water

Butcher E. C. & Co. (dissolved) 250 W. 126th

Butchers' Hide & Melting Assn. (refused) ft. E. 45th

Butchers' Publishing Co. (dissolved) 805 Washn.

Butler Hard Rubber Co. (Richard Butler, Pres.; George R. Turnbull, Sec. Capital. $300,000. Directors: Richard Butler, George R. Turnbull, William Kell, George I. Seney, Frank Lyman, William H. Nichols, William Cary Sanger) 33 Mercer

Butler Hardware Co. (John H. Newman, Pres.; John W. Voorhis, Sec.; Edward V. D. Skillman, Treas. Capital, $66,000. Directors: Enoch M. Moore, Edward V. D. & Abram J. Skillman, John H. Newman, John W. Voorhis) 18 Warren

Butler E. & Son (Edwin & Michael E. & Philip A. Butler) 32 South

Butler O. H. & Co. (no. inf.) 54 Union pl.

Butler Brothers (Edward B. Butler, Pres.; Homer P. Knapp, Sec.; Charles C. Lloyd, Treas. Capital, $500,000. Directors: Homer P. Knapp, Charles C. Lloyd, Edward B. Butler, John R. Schofield) 380 B'way

Butler & Bauer (John W. Butler & John Bauer) 129 Washn. mkt

Butler & Bock (Henry L. Butler & Ferdinand Bock) 92 Centre

Butler & Johnson (Frederick Butler & Alfred E. Johnson) 44 Beekman

Butler & Kelley (Orlando W. Butler & Thomas W. Kelley) 126 Fulton

Butler & Sperry (James R. Butler & Frank Sperry) 81 Pine

Butler, Breed & Co. (Lewis C. Breed & Alfred Pierce, only) 92 Warren

Butler, Clapp & Co. (Henry L. Butler, Oliver M. Clapp, John T. Davies & John Hebertson) 355 B'way

Butler, Richards & Co. (Thomas A. Butler & James N. Richards:—special partners, Dalas Frere, Irlenz, Loire, France, $10,000; terminates 20th Dec. 1892) 88 Walker

Butler, Stillman & Hubbard (William Allen Butler, Thomas E. Stillman. Thomas H. Hubbard, John Notman, Adrian H. Joline, Wilhelmus Mynderse & William Allen Butler jr.) 54 Wall

Butman & White (Frederick P. Butman & Melvin L. White) 335 B'way

Butter Preservative Salt Co. (William J. Kellogg, Pres.; further inf. refused) 354 W. 11th

Butterfield Fred & Co. (Edward A. Price, Francis H. Inloes & Peters D. Worrall, only) 451 B'way

Butterick Publishing Co. (Ltd.) (Jonas W. Wilder, Pres.; Abner W. Pollard, Treas.; Ebenezer Butterick, Sec. Capital, $1,000,000. Directors: Jonas W. Wilder, Abner W. Pollard, Robert S. O'Loughlin. Joseph Plaut, Ebenezer Butterick) 9 W. 13th & 40 E. 14th

Butterworth & Judson (James Butterworth & Egbert Judson) 159 Front

Buttner Misses (Lillie Buttner & Edward B. Dickinson, only) 35 Wall

Button & Otley (dissolved) 71 Barclay

Button & Thurston (Eugene L. Button & Charles S. Thurston) 71 Barclay

Buttrick & Elliman (Charles A. Buttrick & William Elliman) 18 Wall

Buxton, Heins & Co. (George I Buxton, Charles L. Heins & Shepard Newton) 18 Spruce

Buys Cornelius & Co. (Cornelius Buys & Theodore O. Palme) 97 Water

Buz Brothers (Frederick H. & Oscar Buz) 193 Av. A

Buzzo P. & G. Rapuzzi (Pietro Buzzo & Giovanni Rapuzzi) 19 Baxter

Byers Joseph J., Epauletted Ventilation Co. (Joseph J. Byers, Pres.; Louis W. Frost, Sec.; Leander T. Powell, Treas. Capital, $100,000. Directors: Joseph J. Byers, Louis W. Frost, Leander T. Powell, Andrew R. Titus, George E. Hamlin, Paul Calvi) 280 B'way

Bynner John & Co. (John Bynner, no Co.) 80 Water

Byrne Joseph & Son (Joseph Byrne, only) 104 John

Byrne Brothers (liquors) (dissolved) 127 Cherry

Byrne Brothers (waters) (Peter Byrne, only) 278 Spring

Byrne & Co. (Patrick & Thomas Byrne) 60 Nassau

Byrne & Hartigan (William J. Byrne & Dennis J. Hartigan) 248 Fourth av.

Byrne & Tucker (Thomas J. Byrne & John Tucker) 253 Fourth av.

Byrne Brothers & Co. (George J. Byrne, only) 122 Liberty

Byrnes M. & Son (Matthew & Thomas J. Byrnes) 454½ W. 54th

Byrnes & Brady (Bernard Byrnes & Patrick Brady) 445 Seventh av.

Byrnes & Dultman (Thomas W. Byrnes & Albert H. Dultman) 580 Third av.

Byrnes & Wallace (dissolved) 446 Eighth av.

Byron & Duffy (dissolved) 165 Third av.

C

C. O. D. Printing House (Charles W. Sturges, propr.) 1651 Second av.

C. & C. Electric Motor Co. (Charles W. Gould, Pres.; Stanley Dwight, Sec.; George S. Mum-

THADDEUS DAVIDS CO., WRITING INKS, SEALING WAX, MUCILAGE.
MAKE THE BEST

CAB 47 CAM

ford, Treas. Capital, $200,000. Directors: Charles W. Gould, Charles T. Barney, George S. Mumford, William T. Buckley) 404 G'wich
Cabble William, Excelsior Wire Mfg. Co. (Elijah Cabble, Pres.; Emma Cabble, Treas.; Joseph C. Cabble, Sec. Capital, $60,000. Directors: Elijah & Emma & Joseph C. Cabble) 43 Fulton
Cable & Sons (Robert Cable, only) 550 W. 38th
Cable, Bailey & Co. (Thomas E. Cable, William R. Bailey & John M. Eastman) 130 B'way
Cabot, Ray & Co. (William Ray, only) 81 Water
Cadenas & Coe (Manuel Cadenas & Edward P. Coe; —special partner, Juan N. Luciani; further inf. refused) 58 William
Cadenas, Coe & Luciani (dissolved) 58 William
Cady J. C. & Co. (J. Cleveland Cady, L. Decoppet Berg & Milton See) 111 B'way
Cady & Nelson Co. (Ltd.) (Alfred Nelson, Pres.; L. Bertram Cady, Sec. Capital, $10,000. Directors: Alfred & Anna E. Nelson, L. Bertram & Ellen C. Cady, Alexander Wright) 226 Fifth av.
Caenen G. & Co. (no inf.) 1420 Av. A
Cæsar H. A. & Co. (Henry A. Cæsar & Frank Schlesinger:—special partners, Julius & Carl Niedick, Lobberich, Germany; terminates 31st Jan. 1891) 454 Broome
Cæsar Brothers (Frederick & Julius & August Cæsar) 11 Park row & r 232 E. 25th
Cæsar, Denis & Hauser (Jacob Cæsar, Otto Denis & Arnold E. Mauser) 53 Beekman
Caffrey, Murray & Wilson (Michael V. Caffrey, Thomas C Murray & estate of William Wilson) 410 Bleecker
Cagle Gold Mining Co. (Julius A. May, Pres.; Chalmer Overton, Sec.; Carleton Overton, Treas. Capital, $40,000; further inf. unattainable) 84 Vandam
Cagney T. J., Bindery Co. (Timothy J. Cagney, Pres.; Daniel Jackson, Sec.; Martin B. Brown, Treas. Capital, $20,000. Directors: Timothy J. Cagney, Daniel Jackson, Martin B. Brown, James H. English) 789 B'way
Cagney Brothers (David H. & Timothy G. Gagney) 156 & 387 B'way
Cahen J. P. & Brother (Julius P. & James P. Cahen) 24 Walker
Cahen L. & Son (Leon & Moses Cahen) 41 Canal
Cahn Hugo & Co. (Hugo Cahn & Joseph Brussel) 67 Murray
Cahn James M. & Brother (James M. & Charles Cahn) 555 B'way & 475 E. Houston
Cahn S. & Co. (Julius Cahn, only) 585 First av.
Cahn S. C. & Co. (Siegfried C. Cahn & Joseph & Leopold Gideon) 93 Prince
Cahn J. & Co. (dissolved) 18 Walker
Cahn & Co. (Jules S. Dache:—special partner, Leopold Cahn, $100,000; terminates 31st Dec. 1890) 45 Exchange pl.
Cahn & Davis (dissolved) 86 Second
Caboone & Wescott (Stephen Caboone & William P. Wescott) 13 Wall
Cain & Brother (Michael Cain, only) 229 E. 29th, 335 E. 31st & 331 E. 36th
Cairns William & Son (Charles L. Cairns, only) 93 Elizabeth
Cairns & Brother (Irving Cairns, only) 146 Grand
Calaum & Blackledge (Andrew H. Calaum & David W. Blackledge) 182 Duane
Caldwell & Bunker (Charles B. Caldwell, William R. Bunker & John G. Collingwood) 64 B'way & 19 New
Caldwell, Wilson & Calder (dissolved) 473 B'way & 46 Mercer
Calenberg & Vaupel (Henry S. Calenberg & Adam Vaupel) 440 Seventh av. & 533 W. 36th
Calhoun & Co. (John F. Calhoun & John D. Taylor jr.) 2013 Seventh av.

Calhoun, Robbins & Co. (Aaron S. Robbins, Olin G. Walbridge, Samuel Inslee, Matthew H. Beers, William F. King & Gerald N. Stanton, only) 410 B'way
Calla Michael & Son (Michael & Lorentio Calla) 172 Mulberry
California Distilling Works (Julius Cohen, propr.) 40 Water
California Vintage Co. (George Hamlin, Pres., Charles Roome Parmelo, Sec. Capital, $25,000; further inf. unattainable) 21 Park pl.
Caligraphic Type Writing Co. (F. Lyman Browne, propr.) 245 B'way
Calkin H. C. & J. H. (Hervey C. & Judson H.) 177 Christopher
Calkins, Strickland & Co. (Darius F. Calkins, Shalor S. Strickland & Henry L. Van Ness) 87 Warren
Callaghan Brothers & Co. (Arthur Callaghan, only) 161 Pearl
Callahan Charles & Son (Charles J. & Charles Callahan jr.) 66 Madison
Callahan George & Co. (George Callahan, Co. refused) 259 Front
Callahan Walter C. & Brother (Walter C. & Daniel L. C. Callahan) 404 Washn. mkt
Callahan W. & P. (William J. & Patrick J.) 26 Washn.
Callahan & Co. (clocks) (George W. Davis, only) 122 Chambers
Callahan & Co. (produce) (James Callahan, no Co.) 57 Dey
Callahan & Co. (supplies) (Cornelius & Jeremiah Callahan) 181 Reade
Callahan & Dempsey (William Callahan & John Dempsey) Eighth av. c W. 145th
Callahan & Gartlan (Thomas F. Callahan & James H. Gartlan) 30 Pine
Callahan & Maloney (Margaret E. Callahan & Mary A. Maloney) 710 Seventh av.
Callahan & Morrissy (Matthew Callahan & Thomas Morrissy) 43 W. 14th & 47 W. 13th
Callanan & Kemp (Lawrence J. Callanan & James A. Kemp) 41 Vesey
Callanan's Edward, Son (Michael J. & Thomas F. Callanan) 57 W. 44th
Callender Insulating & Waterproofing Co. (John R. Burdick, receiver) 47 Liberty
Callender A. M. & Co. (A. M. Callender, Co. refused) 42 Pine
Callender & Magnus (John R. Callender & Otto Magnus) 77 Cotton Ex.
Calman Emil & Co. (Emil & Gustave B. & Charles Calman) 209 Pearl
Calumet Fastener Co. (no inf.) 83 Leonard
Calvin & Breck (Delano C. Calvin & Charles J. Breck) 7 Nassau
Camacho-Roldan M. & Nephew (Miguel Camacho-Roldan & Gabriel Camacho) 17 Cotton Ex.
Cambell & Gardiner (Francis J. Cambell & Joseph H. Gardiner) 20 Exchange pl. & 65 Beaver
Cambridge & Batts (James A. Cambridge & Roger T. Batts) 2277 Eighth av.
Camerden & Forster (Charles C. Camerden, James V. Forster & Frank K. Hays) 1154 B'way
Cameron A. S., Steam Pump Works (Julia E. Cameron, propr.) 483 E. 23d
Cameron Iron Works (Margaret Cameron, propr.) 182 Sixth av.
Cameron Iron & Coal Co. (Edward M. Parrott, receiver) 41 Wall
Cameron A. J. & Co. (Alexander J. & Alpin J. Cameron & William F. Donegre) 83 Walker
Cameron D. & D. S. (D. Stuart Cameron, only) 2 Stone
Cameron J. C. W. & Co. (dissolved) 46 New

COMPILED WITH ACCURACY AND DESPATCH. } **CLASSIFIED BUSINESS LISTS.** { THE TROW CITY DIRECTORY CO. 11 University Place.

CAM 48 CAP

Cameron L, V. B. & Co. (Lambert V. B. Cameron, no Co.) 109 Water
Cameron R. W. & Co. (Roderick W. Cameron & William A. Street) 28 S. William & Pier 9 E. R.
Camis J. & Co. (Joseph Camis & Meyer Ball) 628 Eighth av.
Cammann H. R. & Co. (Herman H. Cammann & Newbold T. Lawrence) 51 Liberty
Cammann & Co. (Charles L. & Charles L. Cammann jr.) 11 Pine
Camp Hugh N. & Sons (Hugh N. & Frederic E. Camp, only) 55 Liberty
Camp John T. & Co. (in liquidation) 22 Howard
Campbell Alexander & Co. (Malcolm Campbell, only) 24 Pine
Campbell Engine Co. (James McLain, Pres.; Francis V. Greene, Sec. Capital, $10,000,000. Directors: James McLain, Joseph H. & Charles H. Campbell, F. Cooper Clarke, A. L. Barber, John W. Harper, Francis V. Greene) 55 Wall & 651 W. 46th
Campbell H., Co. (Howard Campbell, propr.) 140 Nassau
Campbell John & Co. (bkbinders' matls.) (George W. Garner & Ann E. & estate of John Campbell) 164 William
Campbell John & Co. (colors) (John Campbell, no Co.) 25 New Chambers
Campbell John W. jr. & Co. (John W. Campbell jr. & Martin K. Donohue) 49 Eighth av. & 282 W. 11th
Campbell Mining & Reducing Co. (inf. unattainable) 10 Wall
Campbell Printing Press & Mfg. Co. (John T. Hawkins, Pres.; Benjamin Farrington, Sec.; Ogden Brower, Treas. Capital, $100,000. Directors: John T. Hawkins, Benjamin Farrington, Ogden Brower, H. A. W. Wood, John L. Brower) 100 William
Campbell Ross & Co. (Eliza J. Campbell & William H. & Bushrod B. Bayne, only) 217 Church
Campbell Sash, Door & Moulding Co. (Ltd.) (Henry C. Campbell, Pres.; Enoch O. Bell, Sec.; John R. Campbell, Treas. Capital, $20,000. Directors: Henry O. Campbell, Enoch O. Bell, J. R. Campbell, Lewis H. Sawin, F. G. Swartwout, Marcus J. Sullivan, David A. Haynes) 435 E. 144th
Campbell William & Co. (William Campbell, no Co.) 514 W. 42d
Campbell D. & Co. (Bernard & Peter Campbell) 5 Lispenard
Campbell G. W. jr. & Co. (George W. Campbell jr. no Co.) 58 Wall
Campbell H. G. & Co. (Henry G. Campbell & J. Borden Harriman) 74 B'way & 9 New
Campbell J. & Co. (Joseph Campbell, no Co.) 59 Wall
Campbell J. F. & Co. (John E. Campbell & William O. Lefferts) 408 Washn.
Campbell J. W. & Son (John W. & Charles W. Campbell) 17 Fulton fish mkt.
Campbell Brothers (dissolved) 537 Third av.
Campbell & Co. (grocers) (Thomas A. Campbell & John Owens) 1622 Third av.
Campbell & Co. (storage) (Palmer Campbell, Pres.; William E. Campbell, Sec. Capital, $325,000. Directors: Edwin A. Stevens, C. B. Alexander, John Stevens, William E. & Palmer Campbell) 88 Water
Campbell & Elliott (William Campbell, John Elliott & Samuel S. Stewart) 52 White
Campbell & Gallon (George W. Campbell & Edward Gallon) 257 W. 42d
Campbell & Paige (Douglas Campbell & Edward Winslow Paige) 102 B'way
Campbell & Thayer (George W. & Moses T. Campbell & George A. & Arnold Thayer) 89 Maiden la.

Campbell & Vantassel (Andrew J. Campbell & William H. Vantassel) 553 & 558 W. 33d
Campbell, Nichols & Gwyer (Herbert P. Campbell, George Nichols & Charles D. Gwyer) 59 S. William & 420 W. 12th
Campfield & Wood (Alexander Campfield & Henry F. Wood) 20 Reade
Campos A. & Co. (Angel Campos & Edward Isarr) 81 B'way
Canada Atlantic Fast Freight Line (Frederick H. Goble, agent) 6 Coenties sl.
Canada Southern Railway Co. (Cornelius Vanderbilt, Pres.; Nicol Kingsmill, Sec.; Allyn Cox, Treas. Capital, $15,000,000. Directors: Cornelius & William K. Vanderbilt, James Tillinghast, Samuel F. Barger, Sidney Dillon, Edward A. Wickes, Anthony G. Dulman, Joseph E. Brown, Charles F. Cox) Grand Central depot
Canal Street Bank (Antonio Rasines, Pres.; James Blair, Cashier. Capital, $100,000. Directors: Simon Adler, David Block, P. Caponigri, Vernon M. Davis, William Hartsfield, S. Klingenstein, B. J. McCann, John S. McWilliam, Ernst L. Oppenheim, Antonio Rasines, James B. Byer, Edward F. Steers, John D. Simpson, A. Zuricalday) 206 Canal
Canal & Harbor Protection Union (Melville De Puy, Pres.; William Murphy, Sec.; Thomas Quigley, Treas. Directors: Melville De Puy, William Murphy, Fitch Raynsford, Thomas Quigley, Michael Kelly) 120 Broad
Cancemi Battista & Co. (Battista Cancemi & Luke De Mayo) 2131 Third av.
Canda & Kane (John M. Canda & John F. Kane) 14 Vesey, ft. Bank, ft. W. 51st, ft. W. 52d, ft. W. 96th, ft. B. 14th, ft. E. 122d, ft. E. 123d & ft. E. 134th
Candee Journal Bearing Co. (inf. unattainable) 171 B'way
Candee & Smith (Julius A. Candee & George Moore Smith) ft. E. 26th, 14 Vesey, ft. E. 53d & E. 185th n Third av.
Candelaria Water Works & Milling Co. (inf. unattainable) 7 Nassau
Candor & Munson (Addison Candor & C. La Rue Munson) 111 B'way
Canepa & Ferrotti (dissolved) 16 Baxter
Canfield Publishing Co. (dissolved) 19 Park pl. & 16 Murray
Canfield Rubber Co. (Ratcliffe Hicks, Pres.; Daniel M. Baldwin, Treas. Capital, $100,000. Directors: Ratcliffe Hicks, Daniel M. Baldwin, Chauncy Warren) 86 Leonard
Canfield & Thompson (Ira Canfield jr. & John F. Thompson) 98 Park row
Canning Reginald & Co. (Reginald Canning & John S. Dodge) 115 B'way
Cannon & Atwater (Sylvanus T. Cannon, Henry G. Atwater & Charles M. Cannon) 115 B'way
Cantel & Co. (no inf.) 186 E. 28th
Canter E. & S. (Eva & Sarah) 225 W. 42d
Canton Tea Co. (Wing & Lee, proprs.) 2610 Eighth av.
Cantoni & Co. (Salvatore Cantoni & Carlo Leoni) 25 Wall
Cantor & Van Schaick (Jacob A. Cantor & Eugene Van Schaick) 6 Wall
Capel E. & Sons (dissolved) 191 Mercer
Capel & McNulty (Henry A. Capel & William B. McNulty) 191 Mercer
Capen Edward A. & Co. (Edward Alexander Capen & Anthony Straubenmuller) 52 Maiden la.
Capen W. N. & Co. (dissolved) 140 Waverley pl.
Capen & Conklin (Charles H. Capen & Cornelius S. Conklin) 6 E. 23d
Capes & Ryan (Alice Capes & Charles T. Ryan) 18 Lafayette pl.

CAP 49 **CAR**

Capillaris Mfg. Co. (T. Hill Mansfield, propr.) 29 Park row

Caponigri & Cecire (Agostino Caponigri & Nicola Cecire) 38 Madison

Cappell H. & J. (Henry & John) 45 New Chambers

Carapiase Giuseppe & Sebastiano Bonienotte (dissolved) 214 Mott

Carbolic Soap Co. (David M. Thompson, Pres.; Daniel Scully, Sec.; George H. Thompson, Treas. Capital, $42,000. Directors: David M. Thompson, Daniel Scully, George H. Thompson, Edward Doll, William F. Kidder) 230 Pearl

Carbon Iron Co. (Charles M. Raymond, Pres.; William Brandreth, Sec.; John D. Slayback, Treas. Capital, $5,000,000. Directors: Charles M. Raymond, John D. Slayback, John G. McCullough, F. B. Robinson, Matthew Graff, William Brandreth, E. J. Brinner, Horace W. Lash, Edward F. Slayback) 35 Wall

Carbonaro & Mento (Frank Carbonaro & George Mento) 281 Av. A

Carbonate Diamond Drill Co. (inf. unattainable) 18 Broad

Carbonate Hill Mining Co. (refused) 111 B'way

Carbondale & Shawneetown R. R. Co. (St. Louis, Alton & Terre Haute R. R. Co. lessees) 16 Broad

Carbone & Gardella (James H. Carbone & Pasquale Gardella) 230 Centre

Card A. M. & G. (Albert M. & George) 98 Nassau

Card & Stuckey (Clark S. Card & William H. Stuckey jr.) 206 E. 101st & 2472 Third av.

Cardillo & Canale (Bernadino Cardillo & Ignatio Canale) 79 Mulberry

Cardwell & Reynolds (Edwin L. Reynolds, only) 532 Third av.

Carey E. L. & Co. (Catharine L. Carey, no Co.) 110 W. 19th

Carey Brothers (R. Davis & Theodore G. Carey & Thomas A. Young) 299 B'way

Carey & Sides (John S. Carey & Charles O. Sides) 126 Bowery

Carey, Yale & Lambert (William S. Lambert, only) 24 Beaver

Carey's William, Son (Lawrence J. Carey) 163 Washn.

Carfoot Brothers (William & estates of Arthur C. & George W. Carfoot) 15 Howard

Carhart & Brother (William B. & William E. Carhart) 49 Park pl.

Carhart & Stevens (William T. Carhart & Junius M. Stevens) 211 E. 10th

Carls John & Sons (John J. Carls, only) 153 Water

Carleton & Kissam (William F. Carleton & George Kissam) 41 Park row

Carleton & Moffat (L. Osgood Carleton & George B. Moffat) 132 Front

Carll S. Crosby & Co. (S. Crosby Carll, no Co.) 176 B'way

Carlozzi & Colavecchia (Joseph Carlozzi & Emil Colavecchia) 1375 Ninth av.

Carlozzi & Tully (dissolved) 1375 Ninth av.

Carman Nickel & Aluminum Mfg. Co. (William A. Carman, Pres.; William B. Carman, Sec. Capital, $30,000. Directors: William A. & William B. Carman, William A. Montrose) 462 E. 136th

Carman E. S. & T. D. (dissolved) 34 Park row

Carman & Hesse (Thomas G. Carman & Frederick Hesse) 326 Washn. mkt

Carman & Smith (Thomas Carman & William H. Smith) 117 John, 117 W. B'way, 31 Hudson & 280 & 313 Canal

Carmichael & Co. (David Carmichael, no Co.) 87 White

Carmichael & Neely (dissolved) 47 B'way

Carner & Daly (Mary F. Carner & Thomas J. Daly) 162 Washn. mkt

Carney F. M. & Co. (Frederick M. Carney, no Co.) 90 Broad

Carney R. M. & Co. (Richard M. & Joseph P. Carney) 2252 Seventh av.

Carney W. & F. (Winifred & Frances) 274 Third av.

Carnrick & Tice (David H. Carnrick & William H. Tice) 175 W. 48th

Caro J. & Son (Jacob & Henry Caro) 196 Canal

Caro & Brother (Henry & Michael Caro) r 631 Fifth

Carolina, Cumberland Gap & Chicago Railway Co. (Austin Gallagher, Pres.; George A. Evans, Treas. Directors: Austin Gallagher, George C. & George A. Evans, George A. Searles, J. Hugh Peters, Benjamin Watson, Charles F. Avery, John G. Evans, T. G. Croft, J. S. Cothran, Lewis Jones) 40 Wall

Carpender W. & J. N. (William & J. Neilson) 42 Pine

Carpenter Leonard J. (David Y. Swainson & Augustus H. & Emily E. Carpenter) 41 Liberty & 1151 Third av.

Carpenter & Mead (Silas S. & Charles M. Carpenter & Charles W. Mead) 51 Leonard

Carpenter & Mosher (James E. Carpenter & Joseph F. Mosher) 62 Wall

Carpenter & Pettengill (Francis M. Carpenter & James H. Pettengill) 408 W. 14th

Carpet Trade Assn. (William B. Kendall, Pres.; George E. Hamlin, Treas.; James F. Wardhaugh, Sec.) 115 Worth

Carpinter & Baker (William A. Carpinter & John T. Baker) 4 Hanover

Carpy & Maubec (Charles Carpy & Charles Maubec) 18 Cedar

Carr Alfred & Co. (no inf.) 36 Pine

Carr Walter & Co. (Walter & Dalwin B. Carr & William H. Sueckner) 160 Chambers

Carr A. & W. S., Co. (Adam Carr, Pres.; Samuel S. Sherwood, Sec. Capital, $75,000. Directors: Adam & William S. Carr, Samuel S. Sherwood) 138 Centre

Carr B. & J. (Samuel B. & Jeremiah) 32 Watts

Carr & Co. (Henry G. D. Carr & Philip H. W. Jones) 69 Wall

Carraher & Co. (James & Patrick Carraher jr.) 332 Monroe

Carraher & Connolly (dissolved) 209 Sixth av.

Carranza C. & Co. (Carlos Carranza & Felix L. de Castro) 60 Wall

Carrere & Haas (J. Maxwell Carrere & Charles Haas) 36 Park pl.

Carrere & Hastings (John M. Carrere & Thomas Hastings) 3 Bowling gr.

Carriage & Wagon Axle Mfrs'. Assn. (dissolved) 15 Cortlandt

Carrington Storage Warehouse (Robert N. Blackhall, propr.) 384 Third av.

Carrington & Co. (James H. Carrington, no Co.) 52 W. 22d

Carrington (George E. Carrington & Spencer C. Doty) 99 Nassau

Carrington & Emerson (Augustus B. Carrington & Howard L. Emerson) 115 B'way

Carroll Aluminum Mfg. Co. (Craft C. Carroll, Pres.; Coe E. Ellis, Sec. Capital, $1,000,000. Directors: Craft C. Carroll, William H. Dwinelle, Coe E. Ellis, Preston L. Belden, Elic S. Carroll, Albert Trego, Gurdon H. Wilcox) 391 Fifth av.

Carroll J. F. & Co. (John F. Carroll & Joseph N. Galway) 9 Vanderbilt av.

Carroll J. W. & Co. (dissolved) 18 Chambers

Carroll Brothers (John F. & William F. Carroll) 264 Canal

TYPEWRITING DONE BY THE TROW CITY DIRECTORY CO., 11 University Place.

CAR 50 CAS

Carroll & Meenan (refused) 364 Tenth av.
Carroll & Regan (Peter Carroll & William E. Regan) 306 Third av. & 711 Sixth av.
Carroll & Strong (dissolved) 322 W. 59th
Carson Alexander & Son (Alexander & Alexander H. Carson) 733 G'wich
Carson & Carroll (Minnie W. Carson & John J. Carroll) 167 E. 86th & 207 E. 120th
Carstens H. A. & Brother (Henry A. & William Carstens) 57 Pike
Carter E. C. (Eli C. Carter :—special partner, James S. Ogden, *Binghamton, N. Y.,* $3,- 500; terminates 31st Jan. 1891) 466 Broome
Carter Magnetic Ore Separating Co. (inf. unattainable) 254 Pearl
Carter Medicine Co. (Brent Good, Pres., Henry C, Hebbard, Sec. Directors; Henry C. Hebbard, Brent Good) 57 Murray
Carter Robert & Brothers (Peter & Robert Carter, only) 530 B'way
Carter White Lead Co. (Levi Carter, Pres.; Stewart B. Haydon, Sec. Capital, $500,000; further inf. unattainable) 5 Dutch
Carter H. C. & Co. (Henry C. Carter, no Co.) 140 Reade
Carter & Co. (Edward Carter, Co. refused) 194 Duane
Carter & Germond (dissolved) 479 E. 126th
Carter & Ledyard (James C. Carter, Lewis Cass Ledyard & George R. Balkam) 54 Wall
Carter & Lee (George Carter & Joseph H. Lee) Williamsbridge
Carter & Robertson (Manghan Carter & Alexander W. Robertson) 1201 Ninth av.
Carter & Varian (dissolved) Williamsbridge
Carter, Dinsmore & Co. (John W. Carter, only) 433 Pearl
Carter, Hawley & Co. (Henry R. Hawley, F. Griswold Heron & Edward W. Packard, only) 54 Wall
Carter, Hughes & Cravath (Walter S. Carter, Charles R. Hughes, Paul D. Cravath & John W. Houston) 120 & 346 B'way
Carter, Macy & Co. (Oliver S. Carter, George H. Macy, George S. Clapp & Arthur G. King) 108 Water & 142 Pearl
Carter, Shearman & Madden (William D. Carter, George Shearman & Stephen K. Madden) 171 Chambers
Carter, Sloan & Co. (Aaron Carter jr, Augustus K. Sloan, Courtland B. Hastings, George B. Howe & William T. Carter) 15 Maiden la.
Carteret Chemical Co. (Edward M. Cook, Pres.; Warren Delano jr. Sec. Capital, $200,000; further inf. unattainable) 115 B'way
Carthage & Adirondack Railway Co. (Ebenezer K. Sibley, Pres. Andrew Spotts, Sec. Capital, $500,000. Directors: Ebenezer K. Sibley, Duncan D. Parmly, John B. Garrett, John Greenough, Randolph Parmly, Henry Whelen, Robert H. Sayre, John Taylor, Thomas P. Fowler, Samuel A. & William S. Benson, Andrew Spotts) 168 B'way
Carupano Mining Co. (George E. Stevens, Pres.; Stephen Y. Myers, Sec.; William T. Hotchkiss, Treas. Capital, $200,000. Directors: George E. Stevens, Stephen Y. Myers, William T. Hotchkiss, M. I. Dupin, John H. Ammon, A. Solmans) 50 B'way
Carved Electrotype Plate Co. (Capital, $40,000 ; further inf. unattainable) no address
Carver & Rothmaler (Henry N. Carver & Emil Rothmaler) 23 South
Cary Henry & Sons (Robert F. Cary, only) 130 E. 129th
Cary Mfg. Co. (Spencer C. Cary, Pres.; further inf. unattainable) r 48 Centre
Cary Brothers (Ferris A. & Johnson S. Cary) 91 John

Cary & Moen Co. (Edward A. Moen, Pres.; Lewis R. Hurlbutt jr. Sec. Capital, $125,000. Directors: Edward A. Moen, Lewis R. Hurlbutt jr.) 234 W. 29th (*see adv. front cover*)
Cary & Whitridge (Clarence Cary, Frederick W. Whitridge, Edward C. Henderson & Edwin T. Rice jr.) 59 Wall
Casa Grande Improvement Co. (Ltd.) (inf. unattainable) 115 B'way
Casamajor Filter Co. (C. Odillon Mailloux, Pres.; Benjamin T. Rogers, Sec, Capital, $50,000. Directors: C. Odillon Mailloux, Paul Wilcox, Benjamin T. Rogers) 5 Beekman
Casano S. & Brother (Simon & Albert Casano) 255 Washn.
Casanova, Troconis & Co. (dissolved) 49 Cotton Ex.
Casas & Huygen (dissolved) 178½ Water
Casazza & Co. (Louis & Joseph & Charles Casazza) 466 Pearl
Case Commission Co. (Alfred W. Case, propr.) 194 Duane
Case Mfg. Co. (no inf.) 83 Nassau
Case A. L. & Co. (Alfred L. Case & Sayres Hadley) 330 Washn.
Case & Co. (dissolved) 47 John
Case, Dudley & Battelle (James B. Case, John L. Dudley & Eugene Battelle) 53 Worth
Case, Morris & Co. (James S. Case, Joseph C. Morris & Maurice Ahern) 30 White
Case's O. D., Sons (Gilbert D. Case & Cornelius L. Moore, only) 4 E. 20th
Casey Machine & Supply Co. (Jeremiah Casey, Pres.; James B. Lockwood, Sec. Capital, $100,000. Directors: Jeremiah Casey, Simon Strauss, Thomas G. Patterson, Michael E. Flaherty, Thomas J. Plunkett, James B. Lockwood, John Winterburn) 179 Lewis
Casey L. & J. (Lawrence S. Casey, only) 253 W. 49th
Casey Brothers (Thomas F. & Michael J. Casey) 564 Tenth av.
Cash J. & J. (Joseph & Sidney & Thomas A. Cash, only) 99 Greene
Caslin Brothers (dissolved) 447 Ninth av.
Casper & Brother (William & Gustave Casper) 185 Grand & 221 Centre
Casperfeld & Cleveland (dissolved) 144 Bowery
Cass & Mote (Frederick Cass & Henry Mote) 63 Pine
Cassagne & Vieu (Leocadie A. V. Cassagne & Frank L. Vieu) 3 W. 3d
Casse, Lackey & Co. (Alfred J. Casse, William J. Lackey & Alphonse Westee) 275 Canal
Cassebeer H. A. (Henry A. & Frederick Cassebeer) 1176 Ninth av.
Cassel L. B. & Co. (Isaac B. Cassel & Emma Goldman) 74, 176 & 274 Bowery
Cassidy H. (Mary A. Cassidy & Patrick A. Gaynor, only) 619 Washn.
Cassidy Hugh & Co. (no inf.) Pier 41 (old) N. R.
Cassidy Brothers (Michael J. Cassidy, only, 618 Tenth av. Patrick Cassidy, only, 560 Eighth av.)
Cassidy & Adler (Patrick Cassidy & L. Richard Adler) 490 Sixth av. & 531 W. 55th
Cassidy & Co. (James Cassidy, Abram B. Blashfield & George L. Drewer) 135 Front
Cassidy & McGee (James M. Cassidy & James H. McGee) 612 Eighth av.
Cassidy & Scannell (George Cassidy & Michael E. Scannell) 251 Mulberry
Cassidy & Son Mfg. Co. (John C. Cassidy, Pres.; James Beasley, Sec.; Edward P. Thomas, Treas. Capital, $200,000. Directors: John C. & John H. Cassidy, James Beasley & Edward P. Thomas) 133 W. 23d & 125 W. 24th
Castillo & Co. (Thomas Castillo, no Co.) 88 Dey

THE CALIGRAPH WRITING MACHINE,
HARTFORD, CONN.

Castle Braid Co. (Schloss & Sons, proprs.) 15 Mercer
Castle S. A. & Co. (James A. Sargent, Theodore A. Griggs & Samuel C. Kellogg, only) 50 Leonard
Castor George A. & Co. (George A. Castor & Charles S. Morley) 207 & 871 B'way
Caswell John & Co. (dissolved) 87 Front
Caswell F. B. & Co. (Fordyce B. Caswell, no Co.) 39 Dey
Caswell, Massey & Co. (John R. Caswell & William M. Massey, no Co.) 1121 B'way & 578 Fifth av.
Cataract Construction Co. (inf. unattainable) 15 Broad
Caterson & Brotz Co. (Samuel D. Hawley, Pres.; Leo Schlesinger, Treas.; William Mooney, Sec.; further inf. unattainable) 5 Jersey
Catholic Benevolent Legion (Bernard J. York, Pres.; Victor J. Dowling, Sec.; Edward J. Stapleton, Treas.) 250 B'way
Catholic Publication Soc. Co. (Joseph M. Hennessey, Sec. Capital, $45,000. Directors: Edward P. Slevin, J. P. Wentworth, Joseph M. Hennessey) 9 Barclay
Catlin & Co. (Julius Catlin, Dudley W. Van Ingen, Lowell Lincoln, & Thomas Motley jr.) 218 Church & 55 Thomas
Caton Brothers, Bixby & Co. (Edward & D. William & Thomas Caton, Charles L. Bixby & Robert W. Williamson) 506 B'way & 168 Mercer
Catskill Mountains Camp & Cottage Co. (Thomas M. Wheeler, Pres.; Henry Martin, Sec.; Francis B. Thurber, Treas. Capital, $50,000. Trustees: Thomas M. Wheeler, Henry Martin, Francis B. Thurber, Thomas Cornell, S. D. Coykendall) 116 Reade
Catskill & N. Y. Steamboat Co. (Ltd.) (inf. unattainable) Pier 33 (old) N. R.
Cattanach & Sons (James S. & John J. & Charles C. Cattanach) 32½ W. 44th
Cattell & Co. (Alexander G. Cattell jr. no Co.) 303 Produce Ex.
Cattelle & Decker (Wallis R. Cattelle & Wadsworth L. Decker) 20 Maiden la.
Cauchois F. A. & Co. (Frederic A. Cauchois, no Co.) 63 Fulton
Caulon John J. (Louise S. Caulon, only) 20 Vesey
Cavagnaro A. & F. Cuneo (Angelo Cavagnaro & Francesco Cuneo) 92 Murray
Cavagnaro J. & F. (John & Francis) 216 & 207 Centre
Cavanagh Brothers (Joseph Cavanagh, only) 66 Sheriff
Cavanagh & Co. (John F. Cavanagh & F. Robert Delury) 256 Bowery
Cavanagh & Welsh (James J. Cavanagh & Thomas Walsh) 387 W. 15th
Cavanagh, Sandford & Co. (John L. Cavanagh & Henry L. & Walter A. Sandford) 16 W. 23d
Cave Charles J. & Sons (Charles J. & Jackson O. & John W. Cave) 164 Fulton
Caw's Ink & Pen Co. (not inc.) (Marie Brown & Camille Quesnel) 157 B'way
Caxton Book Binding Co. (William P. Fogg, Treas.; Charles H. Thyng, Sec.; further inf. unattainable) 138 Mulberry
Ceballos J. M. & Co. (Juan M. Ceballos:—special partners, Jose N. Baro, *Havana, Cuba*, $300,000; Juan Pedro y Roig, *Havana, Cuba*, $200,000; terminates 31st Jan. 1892) 80 Wall & Pier 23 (old) N. R.
Cedar Falls & Minnesota R. R. Co. (J. Kennedy Tod, Pres.; Charles H. Booth, Sec. Capital, $1,586,500. Directors: J. Kennedy Tod, John Kean jr., William S. Tod) 45 Wall
Celenie & Co. (dissolved) 32 E. 20th
Celestial Tea Co. (Charles K. Hammitt, propr.) 34 Hudson

Cell Peter & Co. (Peter Cell, Cesare P. Falconi & Giovanni D. Ghetti) Woodlawn
Cella Brothers (Gerolamo & Domenico & Giovanni B. Cella) 33 S. 5th av.
Cellarius Charles & Brother (Charles & George Cellarius) 13 Baxter
Celler Brothers (Louis & David Celler) 236 E. 75th
Celluloid Brush Co. (William C. Smith, Pres.; Edwin A. Montell, Sec. Capital, $300,000. Trustees: Marshall C. Lefferts, Edwin A. Montell, William C. Smith, Joshua S. Cooley, Warren S. Silcocks, Collins L. Balch, William L. Vennard) 313 B'way
Celluloid Enamel Co. (no inf.) 1¼ Maiden la.
Celluloid Mfg. Co. (John A. Bartow, Pres.; Marshall C. Lefferts, Sec. Capital, $600,000; further inf. unattainable) 192 B'way
Celluloid Novelty Co. (Warren S. Silcocks, Pres.; Frederick R. Lefferts, Sec. Capital, $300,000. Directors: Warren S. Silcocks, Collins L. Balch, Joseph Larocque, Joshua S. Cooley, Frederick R. Lefferts) 313 B'way
Celluloid Piano Key Co. (Ltd.) (Henry Behning, Pres.; John Fischer, Sec.; Henry Morgenthau, Treas. Capital, $20,000. Directors: Henry Behning, Henry Morgenthau, John Fischer, Henry Behning jr., Cord H. Plump) 1 W. 14th
Celluloid Stereotype Co. (inoperative) 279 Front
Centaur Co. (Charles H. Fletcher, Pres.; John A. Sharp, Sec. Capital, $25,000; further inf. unattainable) 77 Murray
Centemeri P. & Co. (John A. Little & Frederick B. Marsh, Jonathon W. Bell & Joseph M. Stanford, only) 859 B'way
Centennial Am. Tea Co. (William Wilson, propr.) 49 Vesey
Centennial Beef Co. (Solomon Haas, propr.) 657 Second av.
Centennial Desk Mfg. Co. (not inc.) (Jacob Klemann, Adam Keller & Louis Mager) 588 E. 12th
Centennial Hat Co. (Ross Meyer, propr.) 19 Av. B & 334 E. Houston
Centennial Laundry (Leopold Stern, propr.) 521 Sixth av.
Centennial Transp. Co. (Caleb Haley, Pres.; George T. Moon, Sec. Capital, $15,000. Directors: Caleb Haley, H. E. Stillman, S. D. Miller, J. N. Gaskill, George T. Moon) 2 Fulton fish mkt
Central Am. Caoutchouc Co. (Ltd.) (inf. unattainable) 44 Beaver
Central Am. & Pacific Railway & Transp. Co. (Collis P. Huntington, Pres.; Gerritt L. Lansing, Sec.; Frank S. Douty, Treas. Capital, $1,000,000; further inf. unattainable) 23 Broad
Central Bureau of Engraving (Hespe & Gerland, proprs.) 30 Vesey
Central Crosstown R. R. Co. (George S. Hart, Pres.; Milton I. Masson, Sec.; B. Burton Hart, Treas. Capital, $600,000. Directors: George S. Hart, Addison Cammack, Homer A. Nelson, Milton I. Masson, B. Burton Hart, Charles B. Webster, Julius Benedict, Noah C. Rogers, Leroy W. Fairchild, John W. Sterling, Moores M. White) 335 Av. A
Central Electric Co. (George C. Lee, Pres.; Thomas Moore jr., Sec. Capital, $5,000,000; further inf. unattainable) 1 B'way
Central Electric Construction Co. (inf. unattainable) 34½ Pine
Central Electrical Co. (no inf.) 40 B'way
Central Electrotype Foundry (Clarence E. Reed, propr.) 49 Lafayette pl.
Central Elevated Transit Co. of N. J. (inf. unattainable) 74 Cortlandt
Central Exchange (no inf.) 66 W. 25th
Central Forge Works (Oliver B. Jennings, Pres.; Russell T. Bishop, Sec.; William F. Pinkham, Treas. Capital, $100,000. Directors: Oliver

B. Jennings, William D. & Russell T. Bishop, Joseph Park, William F. Pinkham) 81 Fulton

Central Gas Light Co. (William R. Beal, Pres.; Silas D. Gifford, Treas.; Amos Hadley, Sec. Capital, $500,000. Directors: William R. Beal, Jordan L. Mott, Isaac D. Fletcher, Silas D. Gifford, A. B. Hall, C. A. Stevens, Amos Hadley) 350 Alexander av. & E. 138th c Locust av.

Central Ice Co. (Kennedy, Reinhart & Campbell, proprs.) ft. W. 51st & 542 W. 39th

Central Iron Works (Charles L. Andrews, Pres.; Jacob Reis, Sec. Capital, $25,000. Directors: Charles L. Andrews, Jacob Reis, Albert Lorenzo) 203 E. 30th

Central Land Co. of W. Va. (Collis P. Huntington, Pres.; Herbert D. Lacey, Sec. Capital $600,000. Directors: Collis P. Huntington, A. A. Low, Isaac E. Gates, Richard Irvin, Edward P. Hatch) 23 Broad

Central Lard Co. (Jacob A. Chamberlain, Pres.; Stephen A. Condict, Sec.; Albert S. Roe, Treas. Capital, $400,000. Trustees: Jacob A. Chamberlain, Stephen A. Condict, Albert S. Roe, Orvill H. Blackmar, Frank W. Commiskey, William Mitchell, Christian F. Tietjen, Ebenezer Hurd, G. Morris Popham) 522 Produce Ex. & 517 W. 33d

Central Literary Press (inf. unattainable) 1 William

Central Lithographing & Engraving Co. (Julius Bien & Co. proprs.) 139 Duane, 64 Thomas & 25 W. 30th

Central Mfg. Co. (Edward Holmes, Pres.; James S. Holmes, Sec.; Benjamin H. Bennett, Treas. Capital, $300,000. Directors: Edward & Britain & James S. Holmes, Benjamin H. Bennett, Benjamin H. Bayliss, Edwin C. Cloyd) 42 Bleecker

Central Mining Co. (Joseph E. Gay, Pres.; John R. Stanton, Sec. Capital, $500,000. Directors: Joseph E. Gay, Robert Porterfield, John Stanton, William C. Sturges, Albert S. Swords, Edwin H. Mead) 76 Wall

Central National Bank (William L. Strong, Pres.; Edward Skillin, Cashier; William D. Page, Notary. Capital, $2,000,000. Directors: William A. Wheelock, William M. Bliss, Simon Bernheimer, James W. Smith, William L. Strong, Edward C. Sampson, William H. Beers, Eugene Higgins, James H. Dunham & Edwin & Woodbury Langdon) 320 B'way

Central N. E. & Western R. R. Co. (John S. Wilson, Pres.; William R. Carlile, Sec.; Arthur E. Newbold, Treas. Capital, $1,600,000. Directors: John S. Wilson, Arthur E. Newbold, Arthur Brock, Charlemagne Tower jr. William B. Scott, John W. Brock, William W. Gibbs, Charles Henry Hart, Henry C. Gibson, Charles C. Harrison, William T. Carter, Thomas Dolan, John T. Terry) 115 B'way

Central N. J. Land Improvement Co. (John Taylor Johnston, Pres.; Aaron D. Hope, Sec.; John R. Moore, Treas. Capital, $550,000. Directors: John Taylor & J. Herbert Johnston, Robert W. Deforest, R. W. Rodman, Warren Ackerman, John Kean, Loyall Farragut) 121 Liberty

Central Pacific R. R. Co. (Leland Stanford, Pres.; Edward H. Miller jr.; Timothy Hopkins, Treas. Capital, $68,000,000. Directors: Leland Stanford, Edward H. Miller jr. Timothy Hopkins, Charles F. Crocker, A. N. Towne, Charles E. Bretherton, Collis P. Huntington) 23 Broad

Central Park Improvement Co. (Simon Sterne, Pres.; William C. Orr, Sec.; John D. Criminus, Treas. Capital, $60,000. Trustees: Simon Sterne, Edward H. Ripley, Alexander P. Ketchum, Hiram Moore, Angelo L. Myers, John D. Criminius, Louis Stern, Daniel R. Kendall, Benjamin J. King, Louis S. Brush, William C. Orr) 29 William

Central Park, N. & E. R. R. R. Co. (G. Hilton Scribner, Pres.; Johnson L. Valentine, Sec. Capital, $1,800,000. Directors: G. Hilton Scribner, David Dows, Henry W. Smith, John T. Terry, Edward C. Smith, Charles Dana, C. Densmore Wyman, George S. Hart, C. H. Tucker, Henry K. Sheldon, Thomas C. Acton, Alonzo B. Cornell, James R. Cuming) 769 Tenth av.

Central Park Pickle Works (George E. Fuschsel, propr.) 507 B'way

Central Park Riding Academy (Cohn Brothers, proprs.) 936 Seventh av.

Central R. R. Co. of N. J. (J. Rogers Maxwell, Pres.; Samuel Knox, Sec.; John W. Watson, Treas. Capital, $18,563,200. Directors: J. Rogers Maxwell, Austin Corbin, Edward D. Adams, George F. Baker, Harris C. Fahnestock, Henry W. Maxwell, Henry Graves, James A. Garland, Charles Lanier) 119 Liberty & Pier 13 N. R.

Central Real Estate Assn. (Samuel D. Babcock, Pres.; George P. Slade, Treas. Capital, $225,000; further inf. unattainable) 110 Leonard

Central Real Estate Exchange (Hiram Torrey, propr.) 124 W. 23d

Central Refining Co. (Ltd.) (inf. unattainable) 26 B'way

Central Safe Deposit Co. (George F. Vail, Pres.; Spencer D. Jackson, Sec.; further inf. unattainable) 3 E. 14th

Central Stamping Co. (David H. James, Pres.; George W. Ketcham, Sec. Capital, $500,000. Directors: David H. James, George W. Ketcham, Walter M. Aikman, John H. Sprague) 25 Cliff

Central Steam Laundry (Edward Deyerberg, propr.) 105 Fourth av.

Central Stove Repair Co. (Albert W. Herche, propr.) 325 W. 38th

Central Trust Co. (Frederic P. Olcott, Pres; Charles H. P. Babcock, Sec. Capital, $1,000,000. Trustees: Samuel D. Babcock, James P. Wallace, Josiah M. Fiske, Henry F. Spaulding, John S. Kennedy, Samuel Thorne, Adrian Iselin jr. E. Francis Hyde, Benjamin G. Mitchell, David Dows, J. Pierpont Morgan, Charles Lanier, Charles G. Landon, William H. Webb, Frederic P. Olcott, Henry Talmadge, George Sherman, Augustus D. Juilliard, Abiel A. Low, Jacob D. Vermilye, William Allen Butler, Percy R. Pyne, William H. Appleton, George Macculloch Miller, Cornelius N. Bliss, Oliver Harriman) 54 Wall

Central & S. Am. Telegraph Co. (James A. Scrymser, Pres.; James R. Beard, Sec.; Samuel C. Blackwell, Treas. Capital, $6,000,000. Directors: Edward D. Adams, Michael F. Grace, William G. Hamilton, J. Pierpont Morgan, George S. Bowdoin, Charles Lanier, Theodore J. de Sabla, James A. Scrymser, Jose M. Munoz) 87 Wall

Centre Market Beef Co. (G. F. & E. C. Swift, proprs.) 5 Centre mkt

Century Co. (Roswell Smith, Pres; Frank H. Scott, Treas.; William W. Ellsworth, Sec. Capital, $50,000. Directors : Roswell Smith, Frank H. Scott, Charles F. Chichester, William W. Ellsworth) 33 E. 17th

Century Rubber Co. (inf. unattainable) 557 B'way

Ceramic Mfg. Co. (no inf.) 822 B'way

Cereals Mfg. Co. (Samuel B. Schieffelin, Pres.; Russel Stebbins jr. Sec. Capital, $300,000. Directors : Samuel B. Schieffelin, William N. Clark, William R. Schieffelin, Alfred C. Chapin, Russell Stebbins jr.) 88 Murray

Cernovsky & Co. (dissolved) 121 W. 40th

Chace Earl B. & Co. (Earl B. Chace, no Co.) 206 Water

Chacon Jose & Brother (Jose & Edward Chacon) 150 Bleecker

Chadwick John & Co. (John Chadwick, no Co.) 15 E. 18th

MERCHANTS EXCHANGE NAT. BANK OF THE CITY OF N. Y.
SOLICITS YOUR ACCOUNT. **257 Broadway.**
PHINEAS C. LOUNSBURY, President.   ALLEN S. APGAR, Cashier.

CHA

Chadwick I. L. & Co. (Isaac L. & Lewis B. & George B. Chadwick) 387 Washn.

Chadwick Brothers (James & Joseph Chadwick) 115 Worth

Challenge Press Co. (Napier Brothers, proprs.) 438 B'way

Challenor F. G. & Co. (Francis G. Challenor & George V. Maynard) 96 Wall

Challman & Schorquist (Charles I. Challman & Adolph W. Schorquist) 1847 Park av.

Chalmers-Spence Co. (Robert R. Martin, Pres.; Charles H. Van Nostrand, Sec. Capital, $150,000. Directors: James V. Chalmers, George E. Weed, John B. Roach, Robert H. Martin) 419 Eighth

Chamber of Commerce (Charles S. Smith, Pres.; George Wilson, Sec.) 32 Nassau

Chamberlain & Tracy (Bissell Chamberlain & Thomas J. Tracy) 269 W. 34th

Chambers James (Ltd.) (James McK. Graeff, Pres.; Henry R. Barcmore, Sec.; further inf. unattainable) 206 Church

Chambers St. & Grand St. Ferry R. R. Co. (Henry Thompson, Pres.; Charles E. Warren, Sec.; Thomas F. Ryan, Treas.; further inf. unattainable) Cherry c East

Chambers G. L. P. & Co. (George L. P. & Henry F. S. Chambers) 81 Pine

Chambers H. & Co. (refused) 91 Abingdon sq.

Chambers & Boughton (William P. Chambers & William H. Boughton) 59 Liberty

Chameroy & Finan (no inf.) 170 Bleecker

Champenois & Co. (Isaac & Charles C. Champenois) 5 Maiden la.

Champion Belt Hook Co. (John S. Bushnell, propr.) 120 Liberty

Champion Brewing Co. (Adolph Lucker, Pres.; Rudolph E. Krafft, Treas.; H. W. Monsees, Sec. Capital, $40,000. Directors: Adolph Lucker, Rudolph E. Krafft, H. W. Monsees) 15 Downing

Champion Burglar Alarm Co. (George A. Dowden, propr.) 841 D'way

Champion Feed Bag Co. (Dixie & Ritchie, proprs.) 381 Pearl

Champion Steam Laundry Co. (Wallach & Cohen proprs.) 108 Seventh av. 406, 420 & 749 Sixth av. 916 Ninth av. & 200 W. 14th

Champion Tea & Coffee Co. (Thomas Anderson, propr.) 239 First av.

Champion & Staddinger (Charles P. Champion & Charles R. Staudinger) 124 Pearl & 88 Water

Champlain Fibro Co. (Augustus G. Paine, Pres. Capital $130,000. Directors: Augustus G. Paine, William L. Pomeroy, Rufus H. Emerson, Julian O. Fuller, Augustus G. Paine jr.) 5 Beekman

Chandler W. H. & Co. (William H. & Frank T. Chandler) 71 Wall

Chandler, Sutton & Co. (Robert P. Chandler, Jesse M. Sutton & Walter H. Redman) 46 South

Chapin C. P. & Co. (Charles P. Chapin & Charles Delaplerre) 97 Front

Chapin E. S. & Co. (Edwin S. & Albert K. Chapin) 4 Exchange ct.

Chapin & Benson (Asahel Chapin & Frank B. Benson) 63 D'way

Chaplin Mfg. Co. (Michael Chauncey, Pres.; Robert A. C. Smith, Treas. Capital, $100,000. Directors: Michael Chauncey, David L. Bartlett, Herman G. Runkle, Robert A. C. Smith) 40 Wall

Chapman Derrick & Wrecking Co. (William E. Chapman, propr.) 70 South

Chapman R. J., Co. (Robert J. Chapman, Pres.; Henry Johnson, Sec. Capital, $21,000. Trustees: Robert J. Chapman, J. Noll, Henry Johnson) 24 E. 42d

CHA

Chapman C. J. & Co. (Charles J. Chapman & John Burroughs) 61 Tenth av.

Chapman E. J. & Son (Edward J. & Charles J. Chapman) 320 E. 28th

Chapman I. F. & Co. (Isaac F. Chapman & Albert G. Ropes) 62 South

Chapman & Bloemer (William Chapman & Edward Bloemer) 48 Fulton

Chapman & Bunting (Charles P. Chapman & James H. Bunting) 232 E. 125th

Chapman & Meehan (John M. Chapman, Thomas J. Meehan & Frank S. Aikman) 140 Franklin

Chapman & Selter (dissolved) 83 Cotton Ex.

Chapman & Wright (Samuel Chapman & William W. Wright) 147 Fulton

Chapman, Mitchill & Co. (George A. Chapman & William H. Mitchill, no Co.) 14 Water

Chapman's Seth, Son & Co. (Theodore R. Chapman & Robert E. Brady) 1 B'way

Chapman-O'Neill Mfg. Co. (William Chapman, Pres.; Peter McDermott, Sec.; Charles Curry, Treas. Capital, $10,000. Directors: William Chapman, Peter McDermott, Charles Curry) 508 E. 19th

Chappell & Seeley (Francis M. Chappell & Sarah C. Seeley) 59 Seventh av.

Chappell, Chase, Maxwell Co. (C. Will Chappell, Pres.; Benjamin E. Chase, Sec. Capital, $700,000. Trustees: C. Will Chappell, Benjamin E. Chase, John Maxwell) 27 Gt. Jones

Charavay & Bodvin (Marius Charavay & Napoleon F. Bodvin) 174 Worth

Chardon L. & Philippot (Louis Chardon & Peter Philippot) 18 W. 3d

Charig & Co. (Irving S. Charig, Co. refused) 116 Nassau

Charles John & Co. (John Charles, Nathan Bidwell & George S. Hanf) 158 Park row

Charles & Co. (Christopher D. Wallace, Emily Charles & John C. Clark) 50 E. 43d

Charleston Oil Co. (Edward Urquhart, Pres.; Joseph F. Ward, Sec. Capital, $60,000. Trustees: Caleb A. Dyer, Edward Urquhart, Ralph A. Broadbent) 45 B'way

Charleston, Cincinnati & Chicago R. R. Co. (Frank Coxe, Pres.; Henry K. Baker, Sec. Capital, $20,000,000. Directors: Frank Coxe, Wharton Barker, Chester W. Chapin, James A. Rumrill, William D. Bishop, William F. Weld, Amos Barnes, James T. Wilder, Pomeroy P. Dickinson, William L. Roddey, Peter J. Sinclair) 45 B'way

Charleston, Sumter & Northern R. R. Co. (John S. Silver, Pres.; Oliver M. Chace, Sec.; A. Ames Howlett, Treas. Directors: John B. Silver, John Harlin, A. Ames Howlett, Oliver M. Chace) 115 B'way

Charlotte, Columbia & Augusta R. R. Co. (V. E. McBee, Pres.; further inf. unattainable) 2 Wall

Chase Combination Car Spring Co. (Henry F. Tainter, Pres.; Charles C. Mills, Sec.; William R. Webster, Treas. Capital, $1,000,000. Directors: Henry F. Tainter, Charles C. Mills, William R. Webster, Harry G. Darwin, Thomas B. Chase) 45 B'way

Chase George C. & Co. (George C. Chase & Leveritt S. Cooper) 105 Front

Chase Machine Co. (dissolved) 100 Wall

Chase Medical Co. (S. B. Chase & H. M. Holdredge, proprs.) 228 W. 89th

Chase National Bank (Henry W. Cannon, Pres.; William H. Porter, Cashier; William H. Shepard, Notary. Capital, $500,000. Directors: Samuel Thomas, Edward Tuck, James J. Hill, Calvin S. Brice, John G. Moore, John Thompson, Henry W. Cannon) 15 Nassau

Chase Theodore B. & Co. (Theodore B. Chase & George Hollister) Eleventh av. c W. 34th

SNOW, CHURCH & CO. { ESTABLISHED 1874.

Chase L. C. & Co. (John Hopewell jr. Orrin F. Kendall & Frank Hopewell, only) 838 B'way

Chase S. B. & H. M. Holdredge (Sara B. Chase & H. M. Holdredge) 228 W. 59th

Chase S. B. & M. Macdonald (Sara B. Chase & M. Macdonald) 228 W. 59th

Chase & Higginson (Edward B. Chase, James J. Higginson, George Blagden & John E. Knapp) 24 Pine

Chase & North (no inf.) 8 Jacob

Chase, Talbot & Co. (Stephen C. & Lowell Talbot, only) 30 South

Chaskel James & Co. (James Chaskel, no Co.) 93 John

Chasmar A. E. & Co. (Alfred E. Chasmar & Joseph X. Arosemena) 833 B'way

Chateaugay Ore & Iron Co. (Smith M. Weed, Pres.; Henry M. Olmsted, Sec. Capital, $1,500,000; further inf. unattainable) 21 Cortlandt

Chatelard A. M. de & Co. (A. M. de Chatelard, Co. refused) 5 B'way

Chatfield Brothers (Thomas B. & Charles D. Chatfield) 2239 Seventh av.

Chatham National Bank (George M. Hard, Pres.; Henry P. Doremus, Cashier; Sanford H. Steele, Notary. Capital, $450,000. Directors: George M. Hard, Thomas W. Adams, Henry M. Anthony, Alfred S. Cross, Dan B. Smith, Henry Randel, John H. Washburn, Patrick H. Kelly, Henry P. Doremus, Sanford H. Steele, Henry W. Slocum) 192 B'way

Chatillon John & Sons (John P. & George H. Chatillon, only) 89 Cliff

Chatterton A. L. & Co. (Augustus L. Chatterton, no Co.) 73 Maiden la.

Chattin Medical Co. (William C. Chattin, Pres.; Joseph T. Farrington, Sec. Capital, $20,000. Directors: William C. Chattin & Joseph T. Farrington) 188 Grand

Chauncey & Gwynne Brothers (Daniel Chauncey & David E. & Abram E. Gwynne & Samuel S. Chauncey) 25 Broad

Chegwidden & Thomas (John Chegwidden & Olliffe W. Thomas) 167 Hudson

Chelimer S. & Son (Solomon & Morris B. Chelimer) 12 Division

Chelsea (The) (Andrew J. Campbell, Pres.; William H. Shepard, Sec.; John M. Chandler, Treas. Capital, $500,000. Trustees: Andrew J. Campbell, William J. Hoodless, Philip G. Hubert, John Ellis, William H. McCord, Edward B. Arnold, H. W. McElwee, William H. Shepard, Frank K. M. Rehn, Lewis W. Harrington) 222 W. 23d

Chelsea Jute Mills (Charles M. Pratt, Pres.; Frank L. Babbott, Sec. Capital, $100,000; further inf. unattainable) 819 B'way

Chelsea Steam Laundry (Long & Weeks, proprs.) 256 Eighth av.

Cheltenham Iron Works (George Bushell, propr.) 374 Second av.

Chemical Importing & Mfg. Co. (Emil C. Calm, Pres.; Marcus A. Josephi, Sec. Capital, $20,000. Directors: Emil C. & Charles B. Calm & Marcus Josephi) 23 Cedar

Chemical National Bank (George G. Williams, Pres.; William J. Quinlan jr. Cashier; Mortimer Bishop, Notary. Capital, $300,000. Directors: George G. Williams, James A. Roosevelt, Frederic W. Stevens, Robert Goelet, William J. Quinlan jr.) 270 B'way

Chemical Rubber Co. (John H. Cheever, Pres.; John D. Cheever, Sec. Capital, $150,000. Trustees: John H. & John D. Cheever, N. C. Mitchell, A. O. Bourn, R. J. Cummings) 15 Park row

Chemical Supply Co. (Capital $36,000; further inf. unattainable) no address

Cheney George W. & Son (dissolved) 477 E. 135th

Cheney Brothers (Frank Cheney, Pres.; Frank W. Cheney, Treas. Capital, $1,000,000; further inf. unattainable) 477 Broome

Cheney & Hewlett (Nathaniel Cheney & Charles Hewlett) 201 B'way

Cheney's Towing Line (Alfred C. Cheney, Pres.; George H. Robinson, Sec. Capital, $200,000; further inf. unattainable) ft. W. 20th

Cheriton T. F., Hardware Co. (Theodore F. Cheriton, propr.) 122 Chambers

Cherokee Land & Iron Co. (dissolved) 47 B'way

Cherouny Printing & Publishing Co. (Henry W. Cherouny, Pres.; L. B. Fahndrich Cherouny, Sec. Capital, $25,000. Directors: Henry W. & L. B. Fahndrich Cherouny, John P. Griffin) 23 Vandewater

Cherry Heat Welding Compound Co. (Cornelius S. Mitchill, Pres.; Neil R. Mitchill, Sec. Capital, $2,500. Directors: Cornelius S. & Neil R. Mitchill) 549 W. 22d

Chesapeake Dry Dock & Construction Co. (Calvin B. Orcutt, Pres.; Frank H. Davis, Sec.; Isaac E. Gates, Treas. Capital, $1,000,000. Directors: Collis P. Huntington, Calvin B. Orcutt, Frank H. Davis, Isaac E. Gates, A. A. Low) 23 Broad

Chesapeake & Nashville Railway Co. (Eugene Zimmerman, Pres.; Harvey M. Hoyt, Sec. Capital, $1,050,000. Directors: Isaac E. Gates, Richard T. Colburn, Edward H. Pardee, Frank R. Davis, Eugene Zimmerman, J. J. Turner, A. Evans, Harvey, M. Hoyt, H. E. Huntington) 23 Broad

Chesapeake & Ohio Grain Elevator Co. (no inf.) 108 Produce Ex.

Chesapeake & Ohio Railway Coal Agency (Chesapeake & Ohio Railway Co. proprs.) 1 B'way

Chesapeake, Ohio & Southwestern R. R. Co. (Collis P. Huntington, Pres.; Isaac E. Gates, Sec. Capital, $9,726,600. Directors: Collis P. Huntington, Eckstein Norton, Thomas C. Platt, Isaac E. Gates, William Mahl, John Echols, H. D. McHenry, Holmes Commins, Gabriel Morton) 23 Broad

Chesebro & Garnsey (John W. Chesebro & Willard N. Garnsey) 264 Canal

Chesebro & Whitman (Dennison P. Chesebro & William S. Whitman) 302 E. 54th

Cheesebrough Heating & Ventilating System (Robert A. Cheesbrough, propr.) 24 State

Cheesebrough Mfg. Co. (Cons.) (Robert A. Chesebrough, Pres.; James F. Willcox, Sec.; Capital, $500,000. Directors: Robert A. Cheesbrough, Henry H. Rogers, John D. Archbold, Ambrose M. McGregor, Charles Oendert, James Brand, Joseph J. Almirall, Charles C. Burke, Oswald N. Cammann) 24 State

Chostates Gold Co. (Frederick A. Neergaard, V. Pres.; Alexander B. Simonds, Sec. Capital, $100,000. Trustees, Frederick A. Neergaard, Charles E. Bigelow, Dache McE. Whitlock, Alexander B. Simonds) 51 Wall

Chestnut Hill Iron Ore Co. (Benjamin G. Clarke, Pres.; Charles E. Sturges, Sec.; further inf. unattainable) 52 Wall

Chiappa G. & Son (Giuseppe & Carlo Chiappa) 309 Mott

Chicago Artistic Boot & Shoe Repairing Co. (T. J. Nall & Co.) 178½ & 305 Bowery

Chicago Corset Co. (Ball, Floraheim & Co. proprs.) 409 B'way

Chicago Gas Trust Co. (inf. unattainable) 48 Exchange pl.

Chicago Loan Co. (Benjamin H. Tuthill, propr.) 713 B'way

Chicago Lumber Co. (no inf.) 45 B'way

Chicago Rubber Clothing Co. (no inf.) 835 B'way

Chicago & Georgia Mining Co. (L. H. Bullard, Pres.; Alexander B. Simonds, Sec.; Capital, $50,000. Trustees: L. H. Bullard, Charles E. Bigelow, Alexander B. Simonds) 51 Wall

WATER METERS, GAS ENGINES, | NATIONAL METER CO.
FOR PUMPING AND POWER. | 252 Broadway, N. Y.

CHI　　　　　55　　　　　CHR

Chicago & Grand Trunk Railway Co. (Joseph Hickson, Pres.; James H. Muir, Treas.; Capital, $6,600,000. Directors: Joseph Hickson, L. J. Seargeant, E. W. Meddaugh, James McMillan, W. J. Spicer, W. S. Shepard, W. C. Beardsley, F. A. Howe, J. H. Whitman, J. McCaffery, A. H. Dolton, W. Munro, R. Wright, DeF. Skinner, W. T. Mitchell) 271 B'way

Chicago & Northwestern Railway Co. (Marvin Hugitt, Pres.; Martin L. Sykes, Sec.; Capital, $48,700,390.58. Directors: Albert Keep, Marvin Hugitt, Nathaniel K. Fairbank, Horace Williams, David P. Kimball, Frederick L. Ames, William L. Scott, Anthony G. Dulman, Chauncey M. Depew, Samuel F. Barger, Hamilton McK. Twombley, William, K. & Frederick W. Vanderbilt, John M. Burke, Martin L. Sykes, Percy R. Pyne, John I. Blair) 52 Wall

Chicago & Ohio River R. R. Co. (Albert N. Parlin, Pres.; Everett R. Reynolds, Sec. Capital, $8,000,000. Directors: Austin Corbin, Albert N. Parlin, Berthold Schlesinger, C. W. Fairbanks, C. Kelsey, P. C. Hendricks, John A. Henry, William G. Beale. F. D. Tracy) 192 B'way

Chicago, Milwaukee & St. Paul Railway Co. (Roswell Miller, Pres.; Peter M. Myers, Sec.; Frederic G. Ranney, Treas. Capital, $61,296,261. Directors: Philip D. Armour, August Belmont jr. Frank S. Bond, Hugh T. Dickey, Peter Geddes, Frederick Layton, George O. Magoun, Joseph Milbank, Roswell Miller, William Rockefeller, Samuel Spencer, Alfred Van Santvoord, J. Hood Wright) 40 Wall

Chicago, Rock Island & Pacific Railway Co. (Ransom R. Cable, Pres.; Warren G. Purdy, Sec. Capital, $46,152,200. Directors: David Dows, James R. Cowing, Sidney Dillon, Roswell P. Flower, Benjamin Brewster, Heber R. Bishop, Henry M. Flager, Hugh Riddle, H. H. Porter, Marshall Field, Ransom R. Cable, George O. Wright) 18 William

Chicago, St. Louis & New Orleans R. R. Co. (inf. unattainable) 210 B'way

Chicago, St. Louis & Paducah Railway Co. (St. Louis, Alton & Terre Haute R. R. Co. lessees) 16 Broad

Chicago, St. Paul & Kansas City Railway Co. (Alphous B. Stickney, Pres.; M. C. Woodruff, Sec.; William B. Bend, Treas. Capital, $14,892,900. Directors: W. Lewis Boyle, C. W. Benson, William Dawson jr. Arnold Kalman, Ansel Oppenheim, Alpheus B. & Samuel C. Stickney) 45 Wall

Chicago, St. Paul, Minneapolis & Omaha Railway Co. (Marvin Hugitt, Pres.; Edwin E. Woodman, Sec.; Martin L. Sykes, Treas. Capital, $34,050,126.86. Directors: Albert Keep, Marvin Hugitt, J. H. Howe, Edwin W. Winter, John M. Whitman, John A. Humbird, David P. Kimball, Martin L. Sykes, Chauncey M. Depew, Cornelius & William K. Vanderbilt, Hamilton McK. Twombley, William L. Scott) 52 Wall & 409 B'way

Chickering & Sons (Charles F. Chickering, Pres.; George H. Chickering, Sec.; Peter J. Gildemeester, Treas. Capital, $1,000,000. Directors: Charles F. & George H. Chickering, Peter J. Gildemeester) 130 Fifth av.

Chidester William H. & Son (William H. & William H. Chidester jr.) 23 Bond

Chieves James & Co. (James & William Chieves) 240 Washn.

Chihuahua Mining Co. (John W. Shaw, Pres.; Alfred A. Spendlove, Sec.; Herbert L. Terrell, Treas. Capital, $600,000. Trustees: Oliver H. Payne, Charles T. Barney, John W. Shaw, Herbert L. Terrell, John R. Robinson) 76 B'way

Child O. W. & Co. (Orange W. Child, no Co.) 115 B'way

Child, Tappen & Brother (Alfred Child & Frank M. & A. Alfred Tappen) 97 Park pl.

Childs Charles M. & Co. (Charles A. Childs, only) 225 Pearl

Childs J. C. & Co. (John C. Childs & Charles H. Randall) 669 Third av.

Childs W. L. & Son (Walter L. Childs jr. only) 452 Pearl

Childs & Co. (Childs R. & Henry A. & Carl L. Childs) 308 W. 42d & 543 Tenth av.

Chilton Mfg. Co. (refused) 147 Fulton

China & Japan Trading Co. (Ltd.) (Horatio N. Twombly, Pres.; Robert Christie, Treas.; Darwin R. Aldridge, Sec. Capital, $700,000. Directors: Horatio N. Twombly, Robert Christie, Darwin R. Aldridge, Silas D. Webb) 85 Burling sl. & 167 Greene

Chinchorro Phosphate Co. (no inf.) 18 B'way

Chipman Medicine Co. (William P. Stevenson, Pres.; Edward G. Johns, Sec.; further inf. unattainable) 26 Church

Chippewa Valley Railway Co. (inf. unattainable) 150 B'way

Chisolm A. R. & Co. (Alexander R. Chisolm & William F. Carey) 61 B'way

Chittenden L. E. & H. H. (Lucius E. & Horace H.) 185 B'way

Chmellook Joseph F. & Co (dissolved) 1436 Av. A

Chovey Charles L. & Co. (Charles L. Chovey, Charles M. Shipman & Albert E. Schoch) 177 Washn.

Christensen & Bach (Rasmus Christensen & Elias Bach) 301 E. 82d

Christensen & Baker (no inf.) 105 W. 25th

Christian Alliance Publishing Co. (inf. unattainable) 692 Eighth av.

Christian at Work Publishing Co. (Eliphalet Remington, Pres.; Edgar W. Hawley, Sec.; Alonzo Alford, Treas. Capital, $5,000. Directors: Eliphalet Remington, Edgar W. Hawley, Alonzo Alford, John G. Davenport) 29 Park row

Christian Intelligencer Assn. (John M. Ferris, Pres.; Henry W. Bookstaver, Sec. Capital, $17,000. Directors: John M. Ferris, Henry W. Bookstaver, John B. Drury) 4 Warren

Christian Literature Co. (Burton D. Bagley, Pres.; Henry H. Bonnell, Sec. Capital, $50,000. Trustees: Burton D. Bagley, Henry H. Bonnell, Samuel M. Jackson) 85 Bond

Christian Science Publishing Soc. (no inf.) 138 Fifth av.

Christian Union Co. (refused) 80 Lafayette pl.

Christiansen & Co. (no inf.) 2448 Third av.

Christie D. I. & Co. (David I. Christie & Charles H. Soe) 220 W. Houston

Christie W. & Co. (Walter Christie, no Co.) 48 Thirteenth av.

Christie Brothers (James & Thomas Christie) 2690 Third av.

Christopher & Tenth St. R.R. Co. (Louis de Beblan, Pres.; George W. Linch, Sec.; Walter T. Hatch, Treas. Capital, $650,000. Directors: Louis de Beblan, Walter T. Hatch, John Feeney, Charles Phelps, George N. Curtis, George H. Prentiss, Elias Lewis jr. William H. Hazzard, Arthur Leary, Isaac V. Brokaw, Joel F. Freeman, James A. Richmond, George W. Linch) 174 Christopher

Chrolithion Handle Co. (Henry H. Childs, Pres.; Capital, $75,000. Trustees: Henry H. Childs, Daniel Seymour, Edward F. Coffin) no address

Chronicle Co. (Ltd.) (Charles H. Ford, Pres.; Franklin Webster, Sec. Capital, $15,000. Directors: Charles H. Ford, Franklin Webster, M. B. Hewitt, Lee Phillips, Clarence K. Valentine) 83 Pine

Chrysolite Silver Mining Co. (Rossiter W. Raymond, Pres.; Henry C. Cooper, Sec. Capital, $10,000,000. Trustees: Abram S. Hewitt, Edward Cooper, Walter S. Gurnee, Daniel S. Appleton, J. F. Tams, James Hall, Augustus C. Gurnee, A. F. Childs, Edwin F. Bedell, William Borden) 13 Burling sl.

PROTECTION For Family, Home, Store, Factory, etc., by using only the "VULCAN" BRAND OF SAFETY MATCHES. Headquarters, 373 Washington Street, New York.

CHR 56 CLA

Chrystal & Roy (James Chrystal & Ella Roy) 570 Hudson

Chrystie & Janney (John A. Chrystie & Samuel M. Janney;—special partner, William R. Stobbins, $50,000 ; terminates, 31st Dec. 1890) 6 Wall

Chubb & Son (Percy Chubb & Charles Myers, only) 77 Beaver & 5 Hanover

Chuck & Brother (Henry Chuck, only) 114 Greene

Chumar & Son (John A. & Charles H. Chumar) 251 Eighth av.

Church Record Co. (Charles G. Adams, Pres.; Willam S. Saunderson, Sec. Capital, $50,000. Directors : Charles G. Adams, William S. Saunderson, E. Livingston Wells) 258 Pearl

Church Review Co. (Henry Mason Baum, Pres.; Cotton W. Bean, Sec. Capital, $10,000. Directors: Arthur W. Chase, Henry Mason Baum, Cotton W. Bean) 21 Park row

Church W. C. & F. P. (William C. & Frank P.) 240 B'way

Church & Co. (James A. & E. Dwight Church) 82 Beaver & 129 Pearl

Church & Kissam (Louis K. Church & Edward H. Kissam) 32 Liberty

Church's C. M., Sons (John S. & Charles M, Church jr.) 120 Park row

Ciancimino's Towing & Transp. Co. (Alrick H. Man, Pres.; James T. Nelson, Treas. Capital, $25,000. Directors: James Fox, B. D. Lawrence, James T. Nelson, Alrick H. Man, William Herbert, Peter Ciaucimino) 127 Broad

Ciaramello M. & Co. (Michael A. & Frank Ciaramello) 51 & 55 Crosby

Ciccone E. & Co. (Ella Ciccone, no Co.) 52 W. 30th

Cilley J. K. & Co. (John K. & Joseph L. Cilley) 76 Gold

Cimiotti Brothers (Gustav & Ferdinand F. Cimiotti) 54 Bond

Cincinnati, Hamilton & Dayton R. R. Co. (Julius Dexter, Pres.; F. H. Short, Sec. Capital, $4,000,000. Directors : Julius Dexter, Sidney Dillon, Russell Sage, M. O, Martin, Alfred Sully, Edward E. Cole, Eugene Zimmerman, George W. Davis, M. D. Woodford) 40 Wall

Cincinnati, Jackson & Mackinaw R. R. Co. (Walston H. Brown, Pres.; Frank B. Swayne, Sec.; Dannistoun Wood, Treas. Capital, $16,- 350,000. Directors: Walston H. Brown, John T. Martin, J. O. Moss, Charles McGhee, George F. Stone, George R. Sheldon, Samuel Thomas, J. Kennedy Tod, R. T. Wilson, F. A. Anable, F. B. Drake, Dan F. Sells, F. L. Hamner, Oscar Sheppard, H. Waters, W. T. Carrington) 20 Nassau

Cincinnati, Selma & Mobile Railway Co. (Frederick Wolffe, Pres.; Max Meyer, Sec.; H. M. Abbett, Treas. Capital, $1,500,000. Directors: Frederick Wolffe, Theodore Cooke, Edgar M. Johnson, Thomas T. Gaff, Louis Krohn, Thomas R. Roulhac, C. M. Shelly, Samuel A. Carlton, Max Meyer, H. M. Abbett) 35 William

Ciofalo & Co. (dissolved) 246 Washn.

Cirina A. & Co. (no inf.) 24 State

Citizens' Coal Co. (George W. Gregory, propr.) ft. W. 40th

Citizens' Ins. Co. (Edward A. Walton, Pres.; Frank M. Parker, Sec. Capital, $300,000. Directors : James M. McLean, William J. Valentine, Edward Schell, Amos F. Eno, John D. Jones, Edward A. Walton, DeWitt O. Hays, Edward King, George H. McLean, James W. Smith, Benjamin L. Swan jr. George F. Baker, Garrett A. Hobart) 156 B'way & 100 Fourth av.

Citizens' Mutual Life Ins. Assn. (Levi M. Bates, Pres.; Charles Bell, Sec.; further inf. refused) 115 B'way

Citizens' Savings Bank (Edward A. Quintard, Pres.; Charles W. Held, Cashier ; Henry Hasler, Sec. Trustees: Edward A. Quintard, Frederick Kühne, John W. Pirsson, Daniel

Butterfield, George W. Odell, William E. Clark, Henry Kloppenburg, Ferdinand Traud, George H. Penniman, Barak G, Coles, Charles P. Burdett, John L. Dudley, E. Benedict Oakley, Thomas L. James, Marvelle W. Cooper, Charles H. Steinway, Locke W. Winchester, Courtlandt D. Moss, James R. Townsend, Douglas Taylor) 56 Bowery

Citizens' Savings & Loan Assn. (inf. unattainable) 247 W. 125th

Citizens' Steamboat Co. (Joseph Cornell, Pres.; Thomas D. Abrams, Sec. Capital, $250,000. Directors : William Kemp, Horace K. Thurber, N. D. Squires, H. H. Darling, A. M. Church, Joseph Cornell, George W. Horton, Thomas D. Abrams, D. F. Stiles, D. M. Greene, C. L. McArthur, G. W. Gibson, C. H. Garretson) Pier 46 (new) N. R.

Cittadino J. & Co. (Joseph Cittadino & Joseph Vetter) 201 E. 104th

City Button Works (Erlanger & Liebmann, proprs.) 238 Canal

City Dispatch Express Co. (James Welsh, propr.) 167 Washn. & 346 W. 42d

City Dressed Beef Co. (Henry Zahn, Pres.; Bernhard Beinecke, Treas.; Solomon Sayles, Sec. Capital, $5,000. Directors ; Julius Schuster, Louis Doctor, Henry Bauer, Henry Zahn, Bernhard Beinecke) ft. E. 44th

City Fire Ins. Co. (Samuel Townsend, Pres.; David J. Blauvelt, Sec. Capital, $210,000. Directors: John A. Stewart, Henry Barrow, Samuel Townsend, Edwin Hyde, Sylvanus S. Townsend, Henry Camerdon jr, David B. Powell, David J. Blauvelt, Thomas Hitchcock, Samuel H. St. John, William R. Thurston, William R. Woodward, E. Francis Hyde) 111 B'way

City Office Toilet Supply Co. (Capital, $10,000 ; further inf. unattainable) no address

City Railway Co. (inf. unattainable) 1 W. 25th

City Trade Mercantile Agency (John V. Alexander, propr.) 29 Harrison

City & Harlem Express (George Reiss, propr.) 85 Reade, 200 Franklin & 236 E. 118th

Claflin Aaron & Co. (Henry A. & Charles F. Claflin, only) 196 Church

Claflin George W. & Co. (George W. Claflin, no Co.) 122 Nassau

Claflin H. B, & Co. (Edward E. Eames, Dexter N. Force, Horace J. Fairchild, Daniel Robinson & John & estate of Horace B. Claflin) 224 Church

Clairmont & Co. (Joseph J. Clairmont, Co, refused) 303 Fourth av.

Clancey J. J. & W. J. (John J. & William J.) 1015 Sixth av.

Clancy John J. & Co. (John J. Clancy & Benjamin F. Frey) 1783 B'way

Clapp & Co. (brokers) (Osro W. & Dwight O. Clapp) 60 B'way

Clapp & Co. (jewelers) (Jacob Adler, Pres.; David H. Engel, Sec.; Isaac Lightstone, Treas. Capital, $10,000. Directors: Jacob Adler, David H. Engel, Isaac Lightstone) 18 Liberty

Clapp & Mason (John H. Clapp & Jarvis W. Mason) 2 Wall

Clarendon M. F. & Son (Matthew E. & James F. Clarendou) 78 Gold

Clarendon, Moore & Co. (dissolved) 78 Gold

Clark Electric Co. (James H. Seymour, Pres.; Abedell Benjamin, Sec. Capital, $3,000,000. Directors : James H. Seymour, Abodell Benjamin, Ernest P. Clark) 192 B'way & 478 Pearl

Clark George & Co. (George & George Clark jr.) 104 Murray

Clark George A. & Brother (John & Stewart & William Clark, only) 400 B'way

Clark J. Shephard, Co. (J. Shephard Clark, Pres.; Francis B. Clark, Sec. Capital, $10,000. Directors: J. Shepherd & Burnet L. & Francis B. Clark) 176 B'way

Clark John J. & Co. (John J. Clark & Frank R. Swackhamer) 438 B'way

Clark John T. & Co. (John T. Clark, no Co.) 111 Broad

Clark Mrs. N. B. & Co. (Nannie B. Clark & Fannie S. Dayne) 62 Wall

Clark Pneumatic Motor Co. (John Wood, Pres.; Leonidas C. Pressley, Sec. Capital, $10,000. Trustees: Leonidas C. Pressley, John Wood, William M. O'Regan, Charles F. Fogg, Perry Vanderlip, George Whittaker, Horatio C. King, Joseph J. Walton, George E. Carhart) 40 B'way

Clark William E. & Brother (William E. & Charles H. & William H. Clark) 164 Elizabeth

Clark A. H. & Son (Andrew & Thomas F. & Theodore F. Clark, only) 129 Washn. mkt

Clark A. J. & Co. (no inf.) 41 Mercer

Clark D. W. & J. D. (Dwight W. & James D.) 162 Chambers

Clark E. & A. (Ella C. & Anne L.) 927 B'way

Clark F. J. & Co. (Frank J. Clark, no Co.) 658 B'way

Clark H. & J. (Henry L & John E.) 18 Wall

Clark J. W. & Co. (John W. Clark & Mark H. Glynn) 119 Worth

Clark S. & A. (Samuel & Alexander) 430 Fourth av.

Clark Brothers (bags) (John T. Clark, only) 61 Ann

Clark Brothers (eating-h.) (John & Joseph Clark) 120 Fulton, 340 Canal & 603 B'way

Clark Brothers (engravers) (John & Samuel Clark) 60 University pl.

Clark Brothers (liquors) (John J. & Thomas J. Clark) 179 Varick

Clark & Allen (Adoniram Clark & Edward A. Allen) ft. E. 23d

Clark & Bull (Lester W. Clark & Harcourt Bull) 10 Exchange pl.

Clark & Co. (hats) (dissolved) 455 Sixth av.

Clark & Co. (salt) (Frank A. & Charles B. Clark & Smith Pine) 154 E. 35th

Clark & Co. (tailors) (Henry W. & Emma Clark) 1129 B'way ft. E. 32d

Clark & Dolan (Robert F. Clark & Hugh Dolan) ft. E. 32d

Clark & Hopps (Gilbert A. Clark & Lewis W. Hopps) 73 W. 125th & 177 E. 112th

Clark & Lynde (Rollin H. Lynde, only) 81 Pine

Clark & Lyon (Andrew J. Clark & Clarence M. Lyon) 41 Centre

Clark & McLaughn (Christina Clark & Joanna McLaughn) 261 W. 23d

Clark & Marmion (George W. Clark & Frank J. Marmion) 55 Barclay & 22 Barling st.

Clark & Sanborn (Jefferson Clark & Edwin W. Sanborn) 32 Nassau

Clark & Sowdon (Edgar O. Clark & William Sowdon) 7 Dutch

Clark & Wilkins (George M. Clark & Hartwell A. Wilkins) West c W. 11th & ft. E. 126th

Clark & Zugalla (Edmond Clark & Albert H. Zugalla) 39 Gold

Clark Brothers & Co. (John & Joseph Clark & Patrick F. Byrne, 502 Sixth av.; John & Joseph Clark & Thomas F. Hickey, 256 W. 125th)

Clark, Dodge & Co. (George C. & David C. & Louis C. Clark, only) 51 Wall

Clark, Holly & Ketchum (Frederick C. Clark, Henry H. Holly, Erastus W. Ketchum & Edwin A. Clark) 177 Duane

Clark, O'Brien & Westbrook (Heman Clark, John O'Brien & John D. Westbrook) 40 Wall

Clark, Ward & Co. (J. F. A. Clark & Reginald H. Ward, no Co.) 15 Broad

Clark's Luke, Son (John F. Clark) 209 W. 23d

Clarke David & Son (David & Gilmore & Marshall Clarke) Boulevard n W. 79th

Clarke William & Sons (William & James & Hudson & William Clark jr.) 96 Park row

Clarke Brothers (William J. & Thomas Clarke) 325 W. 25th

Clarke & Bibb (Edward P. Clarke & William Garritt Bibb) 18 B'way

Clarke & Culver (R. Floyd Clarke & Frederic F. Culver) 146 B'way

Clarkson Floyd & Son (Floyd & John V. B. Clarkson) 39 B'way

Clarkson M. & H. (Montgomery H. & Howard) 44 Wall

Clarkson T. S. & Co. (Thomas S. & David A. & Clermont L. Clarkson) 55 Liberty

Clarkson Brothers (Frederick & Augustus L. Clarkson) 80 Pine

Clarkson & Allan (James Clarkson & James Allen) 52 Eighth av.

Clarkson & Ford (Ashton C. Clarkson & William F. Ford) 224 Front

Clasp Envelope Co. (Dunphy & Gorman, proprs.) 30 W. B'way

Clatworthy F. & W. (Frank & William) 32 Chambers

Clausen H. & Son Brewing Co. (Henry Clauson, Pres.; Peter V. Stockey, Sec. Capital, $800,000.; further inf. unattainable) 309 E. 47th

Clausen & Dollmer (Herman F. Clausen jr. & Henry Bollmer) 20 Fulton & 655 Sixth av.

Clausen & Hoffmeyer (Hans C. Clausen & Anton W. Hoffmoyer) 533 E. 15th

Clausen & Price Brewing Co. (Charles C. Clausen, Pres.; John Riofe, Sec. Capital, $150,000. Directors: Charles C. Clausen, Walter J. Price, John Riofe) W. 50th c Eleventh av.

Clawson & Biglow (dissolved) 59 Prince

Clayton Air Compressor Works (James Clayton, propt.) 48 Dey

Clayton C. H. & Co. (Clarence H. Clayton & Charles E. Bogert) 157 Pearl

Cleanfast Hosiery Co. (William H. Peck, Pres.; Edward W. Peck, Sec.; Frank B. Colton, Treas. Capital, $75,000.; further inf. unattainable) 64 W. B'way, 927 B'way & 2 W. 14th

Clearfield Bituminous Coal Corporation (William D. Kelly, Pres.; L. P. Miller, Sec.; M. H. Arnot, Treas. Capital, $1,050,000. Directors: Charles J. Langdon, F. W. Kennedy, E. R. Peale, Chauncey M. Depew, H. McK. Twombly, C. C. Clarke) 1 B'way

Clearfield Cons. Coal Co. (dissolved) 1 B'way

Cleary & Donnelly (Thomas Cleary & William J. Donnelly) 458 E. Houston

Clegg & Hyde (dissolved) 305 Broome

Clemens & Garing (George Clemens & Anton Garing) 422 E. 62d

Clemens & Keugh (Sarah M. Clemens & Anne E. Keugh) 434 Madison av.

Clement George & Co. (Elizabeth B. Grannis, only) 38 E. 23d

Clement & Stockwell (Jesse B. Clement & Leander W. Stockwell) 80 Beekman

Clendinning John & Co. (William W. Clendinning, only) 28 White

Cleveland A. B., Co. (Ltd.) (no inf.) 47 Cortlandt

Cleveland Baking Powder Co. (Cornelius N. Hoagland, Pres.; Charles O. Gates, Treas. Directors: Cornelius N. Hoagland, George P. Tangeman, Charles O. Gates) 81 Fulton

Cleveland Motor Co. (Charles A. Brayton, Pres.; Edward B. Gethin, Sec. Capital, $50,000. Directors: Charles A. Brayton, Edward B. Gethin) 241 Centre

CIRCULARS ADDRESSED TO ANY TRADE IN THE U. S. { Facilities
PROMPT, CAREFUL WORK } THE TROW CITY DIRECTORY CO., { Unequalled.
AT MODERATE PRICES. } 11 University Place.

CLE 58 COD

Cleveland Stone Co. (James M. Worthington, Pres.; George H. Worthington, Sec. Capital, $2,250,000. Directors: James M. Worthington, John Hay, Henry C. Ellison, George H. Worthington, John Huntington, J. Homer Wade jr. J. V. Painter, E. A. Merritt, James Nicholl) 51 Chambers

Cleveland Tin Mining Co. (Alonzo B. Cornell, Pres.; Scoville C. Williams, Sec. Capital, $1,000,000 ; further inf. unattainable) 53 B'way

Cleveland, Columbus, Cincinnati & Indianapolis Railway Co. (consolidated with the Cleveland, Cincinnati, Chicago & St. Louis Railway Co.) 5 Vanderbilt av. & 287 B'way

Cleveland, Putnam & Warrin (Cyrus Cleveland, Kingman N. Putnam & Frank L. Warrin) [16 Exchange pl.

Cleverdon & Putzel (Robert N. Cleverdon & Joseph Putzel) 529 B'way

Clews Henry & Co. (Henry & James B. Clews & Charles M. Foster) 15 Broad, 260 Church, 582 & 1103 B'way, 6 Harrison & 39 W. 31st

Climax Curry Comb Co. (Daniel B. Furry, Pres.; Samuel E. Furry, Sec.; Luis F. Emilio, Treas. Capital, $30,000. Directors: Daniel B. & Samuel E. Furry, Luis F. Emilio, William R. Snyder, Alonzo A. Bates) 796 Tenth av.

Climax Fuse Co. (Albert F. Andrews, Pres.; George A. Saunders, Sec.; Henry S. Chapman, Treas. Capital, $50,000. Directors: Albert F. Andrews, Henry S. Chapman, George A. Saunders) 35 B'way

Climax Rail Co. (Albert C. Hallam, propr.) 134 Water

Climax Stopper & Bottle Co. (Charles T. Nightingale, Pres.; Lemuel H. Wilson, Treas. Capital, $5,000 ; further inf. unattainable) 40 Murray

Cline J. W. & Son (Jacob W. & William R. Cline) 44 Ann

Clinton Apartment Co. (Jared D. Flagg, Pres.; Ernest N. Fonin, Sec.; James D. Woodward, Treas. Capital, $80,000, Trustees: Charles W. Clinton, Jared B. Flagg, James D. Woodward, H. Bolton Jones, Montague Flagg) 253 W. 42d

Clinton Bank (Douglass R. Satterlee, Pres.; David W. Harkness, Cashier; Lexow & Haldane, Notaries. Capital, $200,000. Directors: Jerome E. Bates, Augustus G. Bechstein, Nelson J. Gates, Eugene N. Howell, David Hunt, John R. Jacobs, John E. Leffingwell, Asbury Lester, Clarence Lexow, William E. Midgley, John H. Mohlman, James E. Morris, Frederick E. Pitkin, Alexander Pollock, James Pyle, Douglass R. Satterlee, Charles J. C. Schrader, George P. Sheldon, William E. Smith, William A. Tyler) 87 Hudson

Clinton Clothing Co. (William J. McCaffrey, Pres.; Abram Cane, Sec.; Henry W. Cane, Treas. Capital, $30,000. Directors; William J. McCaffrey, Henry W. & Abram Cane) 635 B'way & 166 Greene

Clinton Cornice, Skylight & Roofing Works (Anton Albonesi jr. propr.) 626 Water

Clinton Hall Assn. (Isaac H. Bailey, Pres.; Hugh N. Camp, Sec.; Matthew C. D. Borden, Treas. Trustees: Isaac H. Bailey, Hugh N. Camp, Daniel F. Appleton, Matthew C. D. Borden, Cornelius N. Bliss, Henry A. Oakley, Charles H. Isham) 19 Astor pl.

Clinton Mfg. Co. (L. A. Knight, propr.) 104 Reade

Clinton Metallic Paint Co. (James A. Armstrong, Pres.; William M. Bristol, Sec.; Frederick De Wolf Smyth, Treas. Capital, $30,000. Trustees: James A. Armstrong, William M. Bristol, Frederick De Wolf Smyth, John R. Myers) 229 Pearl

Clinton Storage Warehouses (Charles R. Saul, propr.) 243 E. 35th

Clirehugh & Co. (William S. Clirehugh, no Co.) 146 D'way

Clodius & Taschendorff (August Coldius & Paul Taschendorff) 4 Stone

Cloke Thomas & Co. (Thomas Cloke & James L. Doyle) 326 Spring

Close A. & Son (Aaron & Frank L. Close) 201 G'wich

Close, Robertson, Fanton & Donnelly (Odle Close, William H. Robertson, Hull Fanton & Henry D. Donnelly) 200 B'way

Closter Shading Co. (not inc.) (Joseph Schoessler & Harry J. Wiggin) 74 Grand

Clothiers' Assn. of N. Y. (Julius Hammerslough Pres.; Jacob Woog, Sec.) 90 Spring

Clothing Manufacturers' Assn. (Julius Hammerslough, Pres.; Samuel Fleischman, Sec.; Albert P. Hochstadter, Treas.) 96 Spring

Clough & Macconnell (William R. Clough & James M. Macconnell) 132 Nassau

Cloutier & Poirier (dissolved) 505 E. 70th

Clover Brothers (William C. & Henry E. & Francisco Clover) 121 Leonard

Clowes T. H. & Co. (Thomas H. & William E. Clowes, & John McCabe) 114 Maiden la.

Clucas Publishing Co. (Henry Clucas jr. Pres.; Charles Clucas, Treas. Capital, $10,000. Trustees: Henry jr. & M. B. & Charles Clucas) 6 Harrison

Cluett, Coon & Co. (George B. & J. W. A. & Robert Cluett, Daniel W. & John H. Coon, Henry C. Statzell & Frederick F. Peabody) 636 B'way

Clute J. & Co. (no inf.) 29 Park row

Clute & Cobb (Andrew M. Clute & E. Benedict Cobb) 111 B'way

Clyde S. S. Co. (William P. Clyde & Co. propr.) 5 Bowling gr. & Piers 18, 20 & 84 N. R.

Clyde William F. & Co. (William P. & Benjamin F. Clyde) 5 Bowling gr. & Piers 18, 20 & 84 E. R.

Clyde's Phila. & N. Y. Line (William P. Clyde & Co. propr.) 5 Bowling gr. & Pier 84 E. R.

Coal Economizer Mfg. Co. (Daniel K. Colborn, Pres.; Frank F. McAllister, Sec. Capital, $1,000,000 ; further inf. unattainable) 211 Centre

Coal & Stone Transp. Co. (Horace T. Caswell, Pres.; Walter J. Ford, Sec. Capital, $60,000. Directors: Horace T. Caswell, A. Bigelow Kellogg, Howard C. Bogardus, Herbert M. Caswell, W. F. Wolfe) 85 Stewart bldg.

Coast City Publishing Co. (refused) 49 Nassau

Coates H. T. & Co. (Henry T. Coates & Pierson C. Royce) 26 Cotton Ex.

Cobb F. H. & Son (Frank F. & Sarah M. Cobb, only) 409 Washn.

Cobb J. H. & Co. (dissolved) 21 Centre

Cobb & Co. (no inf.) 10 Union sq. E.

Coburn & Page (C. E. Coburn & A. D. Page) 140 Nassau

Coby E. P. & Co. (E. Parke Coby: special partner, William H. Baker, $15,000 ; terminates 1st April, 1891) 96 William

Cochran John C., & Co. (John C. Cochran, Pres.; Charles T. Root, Treas. Capital, $50,000. Directors: John C. Cochran, Franklin H. Tinker, Charles T. Root)

Cochran R. E. & Co. (Richard E. Cochran & Eugene M. Hanson) 96 Parl pl.

Cochran & Beale (Frederick D. Cochran & Charles E. Beale) 60 D'way

Cochran, Baird & Levi (dissolved) 7 Bond

Cochran, Ramsey & Co. (Robert L. Cochran, & William T. Ramsey, no Co.) 757 D'way

Cockran & Clark (dissolved) 120 B'way

Codd Hiram & Co. (Philip Hathaway & Thomas Rylands, only) 10 Park pl. & 16 Murray

Coddington T. B. & Co. (George L. Nichols, George L. Jewett & Henry Van B. Nash :—

THE CALIGRAPH WRITING MACHINE,
HARTFORD, CONN.

special partners, Fannie C. Browning, *Venice, Italy*, & Marie F. Coddington *each*, $62,500; terminates 31st Dec. 1892) 27 Cliff
Coddington & Cruikshank (Charles E. Coddington & Alfred B. Cruikshank) 137 B'way
Codington George F. & Son (George F. & Charles H. Codington) 159 Perry
Codorus Mining Co. (William W. Wickes, Pres. Capital, $250,000. Trustees: William W. Wickes, Benjamin F. Stephens, S. H. Herriman) no address
Cody Brothers (Thomas F. & Daniel P. Cody) r 867 Third av.
Coe T. J. & Son (dissolved) 606 B'way
Coe & Brandt (Edward P. Coe & John W. Brandt) 419 E. 48th
Coenen & Roos (Bernard Coenen & John Roos) 1420 Av. A
Coffee Exchange (John F. Scott, Pres.; Aubrey Bennett, Treas.; Louis Sellgsberg, Sec.) 53 Beaver
Coffey J. V. & Brother (John V. & Charles A. Coffey) 331 W. 37th
Coffin C. A. & Rogers (James A. Rogers & estate of Charles A. Coffin) 86 John
Coffin & Stanton (William E. Coffin, Walter Stanton & Charles F. Street) 72 B'way
Coffin, Altemus & Co. (Lemuel Coffin, Joseph B. Altemus, Edward A. Treat, Thomas D. Martin, Everett H. Converse & Edward J. Tiel) 79 Worth
Coffin, Redington & Co. (I. Sherwood Coffin, William P. Redington & Christian W. Smith;—special partner, Andrew G. Coffin, *B'klyn, N. Y.*, $150,000; terminates 31st Dec. 1892) 72 John
Coghan & Co. (refused) 153 W. 23d
Cohen Harris & Brother (Harris & Abraham Cohen) 4 Baxter & 168 Park row
Cohen Harris & Son (dissolved) 84 Baxter & 136 White
Cohen Louis & Brother (Louis & Max Cohen) 153 Mercer
Cohen Louis & Co. (Louis & Israel D. Cohen) 88 Chambers
Cohen Philip I. & Co. (Philip I. & Solomon I. Cohen) 127 Pearl
Cohen Saling & Co. (Herman Cohen, only) 66 Cortlandt
Cohen Samuel H. & Brother (Samuel H. & Maurice H. Cohen) 56 Lispenard
Cohen William H. & Co. (William H. Cohen & Simon Lichtenstein) 229 Washn.
Cohen A. & Co. (Adolph & Isidor Cohen & Gustave Saenger) 116 Spring
Cohen A. E. & Co. (Alexander E. & Benjamin M. Cohen & David & Max Yankauer) 18 Wooster
Cohen B. M. & Co. (Bernhard M. & Simon B. Cohen) 5 Mercer
Cohen D. & Sons (Dora & Jacob & Herman Cohen) 25 Lispenard
Cohen J. & Son (ins.) (Jacob & Samuel Cohen) 321 Pearl
Cohen J. & Son (men's furng.) (Joseph & Charles Cohen) 136 Park row
Cohen L. & Co. (Harris Levy, only) 525 B'way
Cohen L. & J. (Louis & Joseph) 63 Elizabeth
Cohen L. & M. (Lewis M. & Marx) 591 Eighth av.
Cohen M. & Co. (Morris Cohen & John Morrissey) 58 Walker
Cohen M. & I. (Morris & Isaac) 96 Canal
Cohen M. & Son (Marcus & Abraham Cohen) 29 Whitehall
Cohen R. & C. (Rebecca & Clara) 252 E. 51st
Cohen R. & Son (dissolved) 351 E. Houston
Cohen S. M. & Co. (Samuel M. & Harman M. Cohen) 101 Greene

Cohen W. & Co. (no inf.) 244 Canal
Cohen Brothers (clothiers) (Isidor & Simon Cohen) 96 Catharine
Cohen Brothers (liquors) (Isidor & Louis Cohen) 2055 Second av.
Cohen & Brody (Lipman Cohen & Nathan Brody) 101 Division
Cohen & Co. (refused) 27 Ann
Cohen & Isaacs (Isidor H. Cohen & Solomon Isaacs) 10 Chatham sq.
Cohen & Levy (Harris F. Cohen & Louis D. Levy) 155 Greene & 50 W. Houston
Cohen & Lewis (Lewis Cohen & Raphael Lewis) 20 Carmine
Cohen & McWilliam (Maurice S. Cohen & John S. McWilliam) 44 B'way
Cohen & Rosenfeld (Jacob Cohen & Moses L. Rosenfeld) 49 E. B'way
Cohen & Schlossberg (David Cohen & Morris Schlossberg) 68 Division
Cohen & Simon (Henry Cohen & Simeon Simon) 542 B'way
Cohen & Sommer (dissolved) 79 Suffolk
Cohen & Wischaneki (dissolved) 277 Church
Cohen Brothers & Co. (Samuel & Morris & Jacob E. Cohen) 81 Walker
Cohen, Endel & Co. (Bernard Cohen, Woolf & Jacob W. & Charles W. Endel & Julius Kaufman) 52 Walker
Cohen, Goldman & Co. (Hyman Cohen & William Goldman, no Co.) 5 Gt. Jones
Cohen's S. A., Son & Co. (Milton L. & Matilda Cohen) 36 E. Houston
Cohn Albert & Co. (Albert Cohn & Adolph F. Kallman) 1987 Third av.
Cohn Charles & Baeder (Charles Cohn & Franz Baeder) 253 Pearl
Cohn George & Co. (George & Abraham Cohn) 522 B'way
Cohn Joseph & Brother (Joseph & William Cohn) 85 Maiden la.
Cohn Joseph & Son (Joseph & Michael Cohn) 147 Hester
Cohn Philip & J. (Philip & Joseph) 61 Walker
Cohn Samuel & Brother (Samuel & Gottschalk Cohn) 271 Grand & 361 Sixth av.
Cohn A. & Co. (Abraham & Leopold Cohn) 142 Water
Cohn A. & Sons (Aaron & Robert & William Cohn) 44 Bowery
Cohn G. & Co. (Guttmann Cohn & Abraham S. Debarfald) 27 Fulton
Cohn I. & Brother (Isaac Cohn, only) 62 Gansevoort
Cohn J. & Co. (Jacob Cohn, no Co.) 92 Greene
Cohn J. & M. (Julius & Max) 8 Greene
Cohn M. & Co. (corsets) (Moritz Cohn, Benno Klopfer & Julius M. Cohn) 375 B'way & 218 W. 26th
Cohn M. & Co. (pipes) (Moyer Cohn & Adolph Goldman) 270 Pearl
Cohn M. L. & Co. (dissolved) 258 Canal
Cohn N. & J. (Nehemiah & Jacob) 12 Fulton
Cohn Brothers (imprs.) (Julius & Leopold S. Cohn) 101 Bleecker
Cohn Brothers (riding) (Louis & Siegmund & Albert B. Cohn) 936 Seventh av.
Cohn & Brown (no inf.) 27 E. Houston
Cohn & Leopold (Jacob Cohn & John Leopold) 160 Pearl
Cohn & Milheiser (Solomon A. Cohn & Frederick Milheiser) 526 Washn.
Cohn & Schlecstein (Lester Cohn & Bernhard Schlecstein) 253 Canal
Cohn, Ball & Co. (Isidor Cohn, Isidor Ball & Adolph H. King) 627 B'way & 194 Mercer

Cohn, Brown & Co. (Isidor Cohn, Henry C. Brown & David Cohn) 543 B'way

Cohn, Solomon & Co. (Walter J. Cohn, Ephraim Solomon & William I. Cohn) 629 B'way

Cohnfeld Co. (Isidor Cohnfeld, Pres.; Oscar Hathaway, Sec.; Joseph Periam, Treas. Capital, $25,000; further inf. unattainable) 53 Greene

Cohn A. B., Co. (Aaron B. Cohn, Pres.; George Backhouse, Sec. Capital, $50,000. Directors: Aaron B. Cohn, George Backhouse, H. M. Cohn) 197 Water

Coiled Wire Belting Co. (Hendrickson & Bartel, proprs.) 93 Cliff

Coit & Co. (no inf.) 18 Spruce

Coit & Francklyn (J. Minturn Coit & Reginald Francklyn) 5 S. William

Colbron, Chauncey & Co. (W. Townsend Colbron, Henry Chauncey jr. & Louis Gibbins) 16 New

Colburn Brothers (refused) 369 Washn.

Colby E. B. & Co. (Edward B. & Benjamin B. Colby) 227 Water

Colby F. G. & Co. (Franklin G. Colby & Alexander J. Kirkland) 60 New

Colby, Abbot & Hoyt, Trustees (not a firm) (Charles L. Colby, Edwin H. Abbot & Colgate Hoyt) 20 Wall

Colchis Mining Co. (Robert G. Ingersoll, Pres. Capital, $500,000. Directors: Robert G. Ingersoll, Charles D. Jenkins, Charles E. Coon, Nathan Cleaves, John W, Dyer, W. B. Felton) 45 B'way

Coldwell & Co. (John H. Coldwell & John W. Terhune) 193 Mercer

Cole Cyrus & Co (Cyrus & Charles E. Cole) 256 W. 28th

Cole Isaac I. & Son (Isaac I. & George O. Cole) 427 Eighth

Cole A. O. & J. W. (Alonzo O. & Joseph W.) 80 Laight

Cole J. F. & Co. (Jacob F. & Thomas H. Cole) 45 Exchange pl.

Cole W. L. & Co. (William L. Cole, no Co.) 585 Kingsbridge rd.

Cole & Carver (John R. Cole & Morris C. Carver) 2334 Eighth av.

Cole & Krum (dissolved) 113 West

Cole & Williams (Charles F. Cole & Alfred G. Williams) 41 John

Colegrove James B. & Co. (no inf.) 6 Wall

Coleman Brewing Co. (Matthew Coleman, Pres.; Bartholomew A. Greene, Sec. Capital, $100,000. Directors: Matthew Coleman, Bartholomew A. Greene) 456 W. 14th

Coleman Charles A. & Co. (Charles A. & Emma W. Coleman) 145 B'way

Coleman Patent Candy Mould Mfg. Co. (John S. Huyler, Pres.; Henry Huide, Treas.; Walter E. Coleman, Sec. Capital, $5,000. Directors: John S. Huyler, Henry Huide, Walter E. Coleman) 179 Franklin & 14 Harrison

Coleman E. W. & Co. (Edward W. Coleman & Ellen R. Parish) 214 Potomac sq.

Coleman R. L. & Co. (R. Lindsay & Thomas C. Coleman) 85 Barclay & 40 Park pl.

Coler W. N. & Co. (William N. & William N. jr. & Bird S. Coler & James W. Campbell) 11 Pine

Coles B. G. & Co. (Barak G. Coles, Willard J, Marshall & Roderick M. Gedney) 100 Forsyth

Coles & Co. (John E. Coles, no Co.) 332 Washn.

Colgan Mfg. Co. (Thomas Colgan, propr.) 234 West

Colgan & Co. (John B. Colgan & Albro Akin) 7 Water & 11 Moore

Colgate James B. & Co. (James B. Colgate, John B. Trevor & Colgate Hoyt) 36 Wall

Colgate & Co. (Samuel & Bowles & Richard M. Colgate) 55 John

Colhoun W. H. & Co. (William H. Colhoun & William W. Sharp) 3 Broad

Collamore Davis & Co. (Ltd.) (M. Davis Collamore, Pres.; Patrick D. C. Shell, Sec.; Sereno D. Bonfils, Treas. Capital, $100,000; further inf. unattainable) 921 B'way & 151 Fifth av.

Collamore Gilman & Co. (John J. Gibbons, only) 19 Union sq. W.

College of Electrical Engineering, Telegraphy & Stenography (Henry Greer, propr.) 122 E. 26th

Collegian Publishing Co. (James W. Brooks, Pres.; George S. Olmstead, Sec.; further inf. unattainable) 70 South

Collins Harry & Co. (Harry & Maria Collins) 2272 Seventh av. & 354 W. 125th

Collins Iron Works (William Collins & Son, proprs.) ft W. 21st

Collins James R. & Co. (James R. Collins, no Co.) 46 Harrison

Collins John & Son (John & John J. Collins) 29 Depeyster

Collins Mfg. & Chemical Co. (Hoster H. Collins, propr.) 27 Union sq. W.

Collins Varnish Co. (Lewis Collins, Pres.; Arthur J. Elwang, Sec.; Stuart H. Young, Treas. Directors: Lewis Collins, Lloyd W. Gates, Arthur J. Elwang, Stuart H. Young) 174 Front

Collins William & Son (William & William P. Collins) ft W. 21st

Collins D. P. & Son (Denmark P. & Henry W. Collins) 42 Bethune

Collins J. N. & Co. (Joseph N. & Frederick N. Collins) 32 W. 14th

Collins Brothers (Stephen J. Collins, only) 145 Eighth av.

Collins & Co. (refused) 212 Water

Collins & Corbin (Gilbert Collins & Charles L. & William H. Corbin) 160 B'way

Collins & Johnston (James Collins & Adam Johnston) 244 Canal

Collins & McIvor (dissolved) 200 Eighth av.

Collins & Mahoney (Thomas F. Collins & Dennis H. Mahoney) 40 Madison

Collins & Nuttall (Arthur Collins & John Nuttall) 418 W. 27th

Collins & Ryan (dissolved) 35 Nassau

Collins & Sesnon (George J. Collins & James P. Rappolyea, only) 57 Maiden la.

Collins, Baily & Co. (Patrick H. Collins Thomas H. Baily & Paul B. Lafreniere) 10 Peck sl.

Collins, Downing & Co. (Henry C. Collins, Silas Downing, Eugene Clark & Philo S. Hager) 680 B'way & 40 Crosby

Collins' Sheldon, Son & Co. (Lucy N. & W. Newton Collins & Smith R. Treadwell) 22 Frankfort

Colse & Kelly (Michael J. Colos & Lawrence Kelly) 1069 Third av.

Colomas Mining Co. (Capital, $1,000,000; further inf. unattainable) no address

Colombia Mining Co. (inoperative) 18 B'way

Colombia Navigation & Commercial Co. (Charles H. Green, Pres.; Herman Knubel, Sec. Capital, $1,000,000. Directors: Charles H. Green, Herman Knubel, Samuel Untermyer, James Flanagan, Henry Clausen jr. Frank M. & Eli Tiffany) 89 Church

Colon Cons. Gold Mining Co. (Lee R. Shryock, Pres.; Dominique F. Verdenal, Sec. Capital, $500,000. Directors: Alexander Westphal, James B. Clews Lee R. Shryock, Henry Clay Lockwood, Joseph Trent) 45 B'way

Colorado Central (Cons.) Mining Co. (James L, de Fremory, Pres.; William E. Mantius, Sec.; John K. Creavey, Treas. Capital $2,750,000. Directors: Herman R. Baltzer, James L. de Fremory, John K. Creavey, Charles Dana, G. W. Hall, William E. Mantius, Charles F. Tag,

FOR THE BEST CO-PARTNERSHIP IN THE BEST CORPORATION SEE PAGE F. IN BACK OF BOOK

COL   61   COM

Theodore H. A. Tromp, William A. Castle) 48 Exchange pl.

Colorado Coal & Iron Co. (Edward J. Berwind, Pres.; Thomas E. H. Curtis, Sec. Capital, $10,000,000. Directors: Edward J. Berwind, Henry S. Grove, Ernst Thalmann, Henry W. O. Edye, William A. Dick, Heman Clark, Henry K. McHarg, August Rutten, C. B. Wright jr.) 15 Broad

Colorado Oil Co. (refused) 280 B'way

Colorado Securities Co. (H. J. Aldrich, Pres.; E. A. Fay, Sec. Capital, $100,000. Directors; H. J. Aldrich, E. A. Fay, H. N. Reynolds, F. H. & J. H. Otley) 258 B'way

Colorado Smelting Co. (Nelson H. Davis, Pres.; Henry C. Cooper, Sec.; Walter S. Gurnee, Treas. Capital, $500,000. Directors: Nelson H. Davis, Walter S. Gurnee, A. G. Paine, Anton Eflers, William L. Pomeroy, Roadter W. Raymond, W. A. Barnes) 7 Nassau

Colorado & Texas Railway Construction Co. (dissolved) 1 B'way

Colt J. B. & Co. (James B. Colt & Charles Goodyear jr.) 16 Beekman

Colton Dental Assn. (not inc.) (Gardner Q. Colton & Lewis M. Slocum) 19 Cooper Union

Colton G. W. & C. E. & Co. (G. Woolworth & Charles B. & Charles L. Colton) 182 William

Colucci Brothers (Tomenici & Angelo Colucci) 2066 First av.

Columbia Bank (Joseph Fox, Pres.; David H. Rowland, Cashier; George Stoll, Notary. Capital, $200,000. Directors: Joseph Fox, Daniel T. Hoag, John H. Watson, Joseph F. Blaut, Henry Gitterman, John S. Foster, William L. Skidmore, Myer S. Isaacs, John A. Beyer, Charles Reed, Hoffman Miller, Louis J. Fitzgerald, J. W. Mack, Leonard Friedman, Max J. Lissauer, Thomas P. Fiske, David H. Rowland, Simeon Ford, Louis Sensongood, John W. Kilbreth) 501 Fifth av.

Columbia Button Works (Leopold H. Cohen, propr.) 145 Elm

Columbia Collection Assn. (W. C. Woodburn & Co. proprs.) 137 B'way

Columbia Dental Exchange (Trustee: Frank W. Leonard) 834 B'way

Columbia Instalment Co. (Isaac Silverman, propr.) 136 Bowery

Columbia Institute (not inc.) (Edwin Fowler & N. Archibald Shaw jr.) 729 Sixth av. & 104 W. 42d

Columbia Knitting Works (Celia Flesch, propr.) 71 Lispenard

Columbia Neckwear Co. (Fanny Lewine, Pres.; Philip Cohn, Sec. Capital, $5,000. Directors: Fanny Lewine, Philip Cohn, James J. Burke) 9 Gt. Jones

Columbia Oil Co. (Hugh King, Pres.; Peter McDonnell, Sec. Capital, $175,000. Directors: Hugh King, Thomas McGoey, Peter McDonnell) 25 Beaver

Columbia Press (Fiss & Corneille, proprs.) 11 Vandewater

Columbia Refining Co. (not inc.) (Frederick W. Gregory, Peter S. Jennings & William A. Towner) 155 B'way & 388 W. 12th

Columbia Rolling Mill Co. (no inf.) 132 Nassau

Columbia Steam Packing Box Factory (Michael Bayersdorf, propr.) 440 Eleventh av.

Columbia Steel & Iron Co. (inf. unattainable) 81 Fulton

Columbia Type Writer Co. (F. J. Freudenthal & Co. proprs.) 199 Crosby

Columbia & Greenville R. R. Co. (A. C. Haskell, Pres.; John Craig, Sec.; John C. B. Smith, Treas. Capital, $2,000,000. Directors: C. H. Saber, H. Beattie, George S. Scott, W. F. Clyde, R. L. McCaughrin, Joseph Walker, J. Ferguson, F. W. Huldekoper, John L. Young, A. C. & John C. Haskell, E. B. Murray) 2 Wall

Columbian Ins. Co. (John P. Paulison, receiver) 52 Wall

Colwell Iron Works (Augustus W. Colwell, Pres.; Leffert Lefferts, Sec. Capital, $30,000. Directors: Augustus W. Colwell, Leffert & John Lefferts) 74 Cortlandt

Colwell Lead Co. (B. Frank Hooper, V. Pres.; George L. Knox, Sec. Capital, $30,000. Trustees: Augustus W. Colwell, B. M. Dunham, George L. Knox, B. Frank & C. B. Hooper, M. J. Ilride, E. H. Blandy) 63 Centre, 524 Pearl & 081 Sixth av.

Colwell W. H. & Son (William H. & Jane A. Colwell, only) 2166 Third av., E. 129th n Second av. & ft. E. 130th

Colwell & Canning (dissolved) 115 B'way

Colyer & Judson (Isaac Colyer & George L. Judson) 104 Fulton

Combes E. & Co. (Edward Combes & Adam Greenfield) 203 Duane

Combes' Henry, Sons (no inf.) 148 West

Combs A. H. & Co. (Albert H. Combs & Homer A. Lattin) 15 Broad

Combs H. W. & Co. (H. Wheeler Combs & Harrison H. Brown) 58 Wall & 59 Pine

Comegys & Lewis (Henry C. Comegys & Jared E. Lewis) 15 Cortlandt

Comerbatch Brothers (dissolved) 226 Sullivan

Comerford Philip & Co. (dissolved) 83 Av. A

Comerford Brothers (Patrick H. & James & John J. Comerford) 437 & 1438 Second av. & 1514 First av.

Comerford & Finnegan (Michael B. Comerford & Henry Finnegan) 476 Second av.

Comet Mining Co. (James E. Reynolds, Pres.; Randolph F. Purdy, Sec. Capital, $50,000. Trustees: James E. Reynolds, Randolph F. Purdy) 25 Broad

Comey & Co. (John F. Comey & John W. Rogers) 577 B'way & 148 Mercer

Comfort Cons. Mining Co. (Thomas H. Wheeler, Pres.; Samuel Comfort, Treas.; Stephen Tydeman, Sec. Capital, $300,000. Directors: Thomas H. Wheeler, J. G. Newcomb, Samuel Comfort, George H. Hopper, J. H. H. Williams, Martin Snider, E. C. Foljambe) 26 B'way

Comfort & Ruppe (no inf.) 1285 B'way

Comins & Evans (Charles W. Comins & William M. Evans) 81 Fulton

Comly & Flanigan (Robert Comley & William A. Flanigan) 19 Harrison

Commercial Advertiser Assn. (Parke Godwin, Pres.; Harold Godwin, Sec.; A. Ludlow White, Treas. Capital, $14,000; further inf. refused) 126 Fulton

Commercial Cable Co. (John W. Mackay, Pres.; Edward C. Platt, Treas.; George G. Ward, Sec. Capital, $10,000,000. Directors: John W. Mackay, Hector de Castro, Albert B. Chandler, George B. Coe, Edward C. Platt, Richard V. Dey, Gardner G. Howland, Charles Nordhoff, E. J. Mathews, James Gordon Bennett, Jules de Castro, Richard Irwin, Alfred de Castro) 1, 220 & 1111 B'way, 19 Beaver, 1 & 10 Broad & 442 Broome

Commercial Cloak & Suit Co. (Ellen Byrne, propr.) 145 W. 22d & 108 W. 23d

Commercial Co. (Joseph J. Koch, Sec.; further inf. refused) 864 B'way

Commercial Despatch (Ltd.) (Oscar L. Richard, Pres.; Oscar Wagner, Sec.; Emil L. Boss, Treas. Capital, $10,000. Directors: Oscar L. Richard, Emil L. Boss, Edwin H. Richard, Francis Deimel, Oscar Wagner) 81 B'way

Commercial Despatch & Addressing Co. (C. S. & W. F. Vincent, proprs.) 41 Beekman

Commercial Fire Ins. Co. (in liquidation) 23 William

TYPEWRITING DONE BY THE TROW CITY DIRECTORY CO., 11 University Place.

COM 62 CON

Commercial Grain Elevator Co. (Milton Knapp, propr.) 207 Produce Ex.
Commercial Ivory Button Co. (Seckendorf, Ulrop & Young, proprs.) 1228 Second av.
Commercial Mutual Ins. Co. (W. Irving Comes, Pres.; Henry D. King, Sec. Trustees: Henry K. Bull, Alexander Nones, Samuel McLean, John Zimmermann, George L. Nichols, Daniel Barnes, Stephen W. Carey, George H. Tuttle, John D. Woodward, William Dupont, Edward L. Heidon, Richard S. Roberts, Hezekiah King, Abraham G. Munn jr., Darwin R. James, Daniel V. Argulmbau, Henry M. Taber, James McLean, Henry S Henry, W. Irving Comes, Joseph F. McCoy, John H. Lau, Emanuel Lehman, Dwight Stone, Francis Spies, C. A. Zoebisch, F. Doegler, William Floyd, Charles S. Whitney, Henry Small, Wainwright Hardie) 42 Wall
Commercial National Bank (Orson Adams, Pres.; William W. Flannagan, Cashier; John H. Carr, Notary. Capital, $500,000. Directors: Isaac Rosenwald, Kenneth M. Murchison, Edward B. Bartlett, Alden S. Swan, William W. Flannagan, J. D. Kurtz Crook, Walter S. Johnston, Felix Campbell, Orson Adams) 78 Wall
Commercial Steam Laundry Co. (Ltd.) (Anthony O. Rowe, Pres.; Joseph W. Felter, Sec. Capital, $9,000; further inf. refused) 545 W. 22d
Commercial Telegram Co. (inoperative) 18 B'way
Commercial Union Life Ins. Co. (John I. Holly, Pres.; Charles H. Bogert jr., Sec.; Morris H. Smith, Treas. Capital, $150,000. Directors: John I. Holly, Edward L. Finch, George A. Dowden, Josiah Lombard, Henry W. O. Edye, Marshall Ayers, Hubbard W. Mitchell, Norman W. Dodge, Morris H. Smith, Joseph Hilton, Richard L. Lulmbeer, W. Austin Goodman, T. C. Van Brunt, John H. McCracken, Edgar L. Pierson) 45 B'way
Commercial Warehouse Co. (in liquidation) 71 s⅔ B'way
Commercial & Financial Agency (inf. unattainable) 196 B'way
Commerford & Edgerton (Thomas F. Commerford & John Edgerton) 842 First av.
Common Sense Mfg. Co. (inf. unattainable) 30 Vesey
Commonwealth Ice Co. (Ransom Parker jr. propr.) 552 W. 11th
Commonwealth Ins. Co. (Milo M. Belding, Pres.; Charles S. Bartow, Sec. Capital, $500,000. Directors: Milo M. Belding, Joseph Larocque, John Claflin, Henry Hentz, Richard Arnold, Bryce Gray, Edward C. Rice, Samuel F. Engs, Frank Rees, William M. Halsted, Thomas T. Barr, Henry J. Davison, John E. Leech, George H. Macy, Francis B. Austin, Benjamin F. Romaine, George P. Perkins, James E. Vail jr., H. A. Rogers, Eberhard Faber, Robert Funger, John J. Riker, Charles S. Bartow, William W. Coffin, B. Aymar Sands, H. Walter Webb, William A. Nash, John H. Dwight, Charles E. Simrall, Robert B. Whittemore) 33 Nassau
Commonwealth Rubber Co. (Lewis Roberts, Pres.; Addison F. Roberts, Sec.; Samuel F. Randolph, Treas.; further inf. unattainable) 9 Murray
Communipaw Coal Co. (Charles Runyon, Pres.; William S. Halliday, Sec.; James F, Randolph, Treas. Directors: Charles Runyon, William S. Halliday, James F. Randolph) 111 & 1505 B'way & 631 Eleventh av.
Compania Electric de Cuba (Clarence Cary, Pres.; George M. Phelps jr. Sec. Capital, $250,000. Directors: Clarence Cary, James Merrihew, W. J. Holmes, A. B. Brewer, R. H. Bull, George M. Phelps jr., D. I. Carson, W. J. Armstrong, V. F. Butler) 195 B'way
Complete Electric Construction Co. (Horace K. Thurber, Pres.; James E. Taylor, Sec. Capital, $50,000. Directors: Horace K. Thurber

Henry E. Hawley, James A. Taylor, John A. Seely, Louis F. Roque, John F. Noonan, Charles R. Truax) 14 Cortlandt
Composite Cell Co. (inf. unattainable) 35 B'way
Composite Iron Works Co. (inoperative) 53 Roade
Comstock School (Lydia Day, propr.) 32 W. 40th
Comstock Tunnel Co. (Theodore Sutro, Pres.; Horace H. Thayer, Sec. Capital, $4,000,000. Directors: Theodore Sutro, Eugene Seligman, Hermann Stursberg, Edward W. Kinsley, Hermann Zadig, Otto Löwengard, Elisha Dyer 3d) 115 B'way
Comstock O. & Co. (Cornelius Comstock, no Co.) 190 Front
Comstock & Brown (Albert Comstock & Everit Brown) 44 B'way
Conaghan & Co. (Patrick Conaghan, no Co.) 110 W. 14th
Conant Mfg. Co. (boxes) (not inc.) (Walter S. Conant & Edward A. & John R. Schlach) 20 Walker
Conant Mfg. Co. (hardware) (Henry G. Elliott, Pres.; John Cooper, Sec. Capital, $75,000. Directors: Henry G. Elliott, John Cooper, William S. Macfarlane) 162 W. 27th
Conaty & Spencer) James Conaty & John C. Spencer) 53 Cedar
Concave Elliptic Spring Co. (William H. Stanford, Pres.; Charles W. Minor, Sec. Capital, $250,-000. Directors: William H. Stanford, William T. Minor, William Davison) 11 Pine
Conckliin & Ernet (Walter W. Concklin & Horatio S. Ernet) 56 Worth & 39 Thomas
Concord Co-operative Printing Co. (Ltd.) (Philip J. Scannell, Pres.; Thomas McCormack, Sec.; Peter J. Flanagan, Treas. Capital, $5,500. Directors: Abram Pietoh, Walter W. Stone, Thomas McCormack, Edward Meagher, Philip J. Scannell, Charles G. Brown, Almond Pierce, Peter J. Flanagan) 104 Elm
Condell J. & Son (John & Henry J. Condell) 822 B'way
Condie & Smith (James Condie & Reuben E. Smith) 198 Ninth av.
Condon N. & M. (Mary M. & Catharine Condon, only) 692 Sixth av.
Cone C. H. & Co. (Charles H. Cone & Percy M. Comstock) 152 Beekman
Coney Island Jockey Club (Leonard W. Jerome, Pres.; James G. K. Lawrence, Sec.; John H. Bradford, Treas.) 945 B'way
Conforti N. & Co. (dissolved) 241 E. 106th
Conger Daniel & Son (Daniel & Dewitt Conger) 104 Broad
Congress Mfg. Co. (Weil, Dreyfus & Co. proprs.) 532 B'way
Conklin Jacob H. & Son (Jacob H. & George N. Conklin) Kingsbridge
Conklin W. & Co. (William Conklin & Jacob A. Melick) 199 Duane & 51 Christopher
Conklin W. D. & Co. (William D. & Ella C. Conklin) 24 State
Conklin & Boyle (dissolved) 390 West
Conlan Brothers (James F. & John J. Conlan) 480 Willis av.
Conley John & Son (John & John Conley jr.) 25 Bethune
Conlon & Moffitt (James Conlon & James Moffitt) 456 Fourth av.
Connecticut Clock Co. (inf. unattainable) 26 Church
Connecticut River Granite Co. (Charles E. Pratt, Pres.; George B. Molleson, Sec.; further inf. unattainable) 50 B'way
Connecticut Valley Paper & Envelope Co. (Lucian M. Stayner, propr.) 57 Beekman
Connecticut & Passumpsic Rivers R. R. Co. (no inf.) 45 B'way
Connell John & Sons (John & James & Thomas F. Connell) 30 Pell

THADDEUS DAVIDS & CO., WRITING INKS, SEALING WAX,
MAKE THE BEST MUCILAGE.

CON · 63 CON

Connell E. A. & Son (Eliza A. & John F. Connell) 133 W. 49th
Connell E. T. & Co. (Eugene T. Connell & Richard Markey) 171 Pearl
Connell & Co. (David J. Connell, no Co.) 115 Broad
Connelly Motor Co. (Charles H. Sprague, Pres.; E. Francis Eldredge, Sec.; Thomas E. Connelly, Treas. Capital, $1,000,000. Directors: Charles H. Sprague, Thomas E. Connelly, E. Francis Eldredge, John S. Connelly) 111 B'way
Connelly Street Railway Equipment Co. (John S. Connelly, Pres.; E. Francis Eldredge, Sec.; Thomas E. Connelly, Treas. Capital, $1,000,000. Directors: Charles H. Sprague, John S. Connelly, George F. Mellen, E. Francis Eldredge, Thomas E. Connelly, Emerson McMillin, Joseph W. Connelly) 111 B'way
Connelly M. & E. (Edmund Connelly, only) 88 Mangin
Connolly Brothers (James J. & Michael Connelly) 642 Second av. & 64 W. Houston
Connelly & Co. (John S. & Thomas E. & Joseph W. Connelly & Sterling F. Hayward) 111 B'way
Conner Brothers & Co. (John R. & Shelby W. Conner & Henry F. Trick) 112 Grand
Conner's James, Sons (Charles S. & Benjamin F. Conner & estate of James M. Conner) 26 Centre
Connett E. V. & Co. (Eugene V. Connett, William Read & Eugene V. jr. & Ernest R. Connett) 93 Bleecker & 197 Mercer
Connolly John & Son (John & Peter F. Connolly) 304 Eighth & 611 E. 12th
Connolly William & Son (William & William Connolly jr.) 1510 First av. & 406 E. 79th
Connolly Brothers (John J. & Joseph Connolly) 192 Water
Connolly & Co. (brokers) (no inf.) 43 Broad
Connolly & Co. (meat) (Thomas Connolly, no Co.) 6 Hewitt av, W. Washn, mkt
Connor John M. & Co. (John M. & Alexander C. Connor) 201 Mercer
Connor F. C. & Co. (dissolved) 201 Mercer
Connor G. C. & Brother (Gerald C. & Vincent J. Connor) 1888 Washn. av.
Connor T. & Co. (Thomas Connor & George W. Rifenburg) 755 Third av.
Connor & Co. (Ezra S. Connor & Anson G. F. Segur) 71 B'way
Conolly E. D. & Sons (Edward D. & Christopher J. & Frank J. & Henry A. Conolly) 676 Lex. av. & 1846 Second av.
Conolly & Dwyer (Hugh E. Conolly & Edward D. Dwyer) 12 W. 60th
Conover C. E., Co. (Charles E. Conover, Pres.; further inf. unattainable) 101 Franklin
Conover George W. & Co. (George W. Conover, no Co.) 45 Whitehall
Conover J. S. & Co. (James S. & Alonzo E. & William E. Conover & Hugh Young) 30 W. 23d & 82 Bank
Conover & Co. (Edwin K. Conover, Tunis R. Schenck & John D. Bird) 95 Liberty
Conover Brothers Co. (J. Frank Conover, Pres.; Samuel F. Prentiss, Sec.; George H. Conover, Treas. Capital, $200,000; further inf. refused) 402 W. 14th & 87 Ninth av.
Conradi Francis & Herman, 35 E. 19th
Conradi Mfg. Co, (Francis & Herman Conradi, propr.) 35 E. 19th
Conran & Lary (Charles S. Conran & George H. Lary) 105 Reade
Conried & Herrmann (Henry Conried & Carl Herrmann) 18 W. 42d
Conron & Quibell (Patrick H. Conron & Joseph W. Quibell) 18 Platt

Conrow Brothers (Theodore & William F. Conrow; —special partner, James W. Courow, S. Orange, N. J., $200,000 ; terminates 30th April, 1892) 33 Beekman
Conselyea & Lee (John P. Conselyea & Whitford J. Lee) 124 Bowery
Conservatory of Music of the City of N. Y. (Grand Conservatory of Music of the City of N. Y., propr.) 98 Fifth av
Consolidated Banking Co. (George Tarier, propr.) 35 B'way
Consolidated Buyers' Jobbing Co. (dissolved) 1 Cooper Union
Consolidated Carson River Dredging Co. (Peter Forrester, Pres., Clarence G. Christie, Asst. Sec.; Pearson Halstead, Treas. Capital, $100,000. Trustees: Peter Forrester, Clarence G. Christie, Pearson Halstead) 18 B'way
Consolidated Chemical Engine Co. (Alonzo B. Cornell, Pres.; Josef Veit, Sec.; William Schwind, Treas. Capital, $800,000. Directors: Alonzo B. Cornell, Anthony B. Bright, Chauncey B. Kendall, Josef Veit, William Schwind, Louis F. Payn, W. L. Bostwick) 50 B'way
Consolidated Cigarette Co. (Benjamin Lichtenstein, Pres.; Solomon K. Lichtenstein, Sec.; Adolph Moonelis, Treas. Capital, $25,000. Directors : Benjamin Lichtenstein, Adolph Moonelis, Solomon K. Lichtenstein) 148 Av. D
Consolidated Coupling Co. (dissolved) 45 B'way
Consolidated Electric Light Co. (Hugh R. Garden, Pres.; George H. Lewars, Sec. Capital, $2,500,000. Directors : Henry C. Davis, Hugh R. Garden, Jacob Hays, George Westinghouse jr. Amos Broadnax, Thomas B. Kerr, George H. Lewars) 82 Nassau & 516 W. 23d
Consolidated Express Co. of Newark, N. J. (George A. Hall, Pres.; Parke Burnett jr. Sec. Capital, $30,000. Directors: George A. Hall, Matthias Plum, Parke Burnett jr.) 117 John, 45 Church, 85 Reade & 812 Canal
Consolidated Fruit Jar Co. (Henry C. Wisner, Pres.; Alvin L. Fisher, Sec.; David D. Smith, Treas. Capital, $500,000. Directors : Henry C. Wisner, John J. Barnier, Alvin L. Fisher, Charles F. Buckley, Ralph W. Booth, Charles D. Ely, M. McFarlin) 49 Warren
Consolidated Gas Co. (James W. Smith, Pres.; Oscar F. Zollkoffer, Sec.; Harrison E. Gawtry, Treas. Capital, $35,430,000 ; further inf. unattainable) 4 Irving pl. 157 Hester, 300 Fourth av. 1547 B'way & 2054 Third av.
Consolidated Iron Works (Alexander Pollock, Pres.; William H. Harrison, Sec.; Joseph G. Harrison, Treas. Capital, $60,000. Directors : Alexander Pollock, William H. & Joseph G. Harrison, Andrew & William H. Fletcher, William T. Schultz) 212 West
Consolidated Knit Goods Co. (James P. Cumming, Pres.; James B. Hall, Sec.; Henry C. Becker, Treas. Capital, $20,000. Directors: James P. Cumming, James B. Hall, Henry C. Becker, Richard A. Nickerson, Weeks W. Culver) 275 Church
Consolidated Mercantile Agency (William H. Woods, Pres.; James J. Ovenden, Sec. Capital, $50,000. Directors: William H. Woods, James J. Ovenden) 401 B'way
Consolidated Patent Shirt Co. (Everett S. Tomlinson, Pres.; Alfred Poindexter, Sec.; J. Frank Supplee, Treas. Capital, $50,000. Directors : Everett S. Tomlinson, Henry Neustadter, J. Frank Supplee, William B. Hall, David W. Thompson) 712 B'way
Consolidated Purchasing Co. (Solomon M. Grouse, propr.) 61 Walker
Consolidated Railway Telegraph Co. (Charles E. Crowell, Pres.; Lucius J. Phelps, Sec. Capital, $2,500,000. Directors : Eugene & Charles E. Crowell, John Cochrane, Charles A. Okeever, Thomas A. Edison, William H. Hazzard, Abram E. Dailey, Felix Gottschalk, Corne-

lius Vanbrunt, Lucius J. Phelps, Philip J. Goodhart, S. R. Dingle, H. C. Townsend) 115 B'way

Consolidated Refrigerating Co. (Charles J. Canda, Pres.; George M. Hard, Sec.; Logan H. Roots, Treas. Capital, $6,000,000. Directors: Charles J. Conda, E. C. Gilman, Logan H. Roots, George M. Hard, B. D. Thornburgh, F. A. Boohman, Charles E. Simmons, P. A. Appleton, J. E. Fuller) 11 Pine

Consolidated Safety Pin Co. (Farmer & Jenkins, proprs.) 38 Bleecker

Consolidated Stock & Petroleum Exchange (Charles G. Wilson, Pres.; Rudolph Huban, Sec.; John S. Stanton, Treas.) 60 B'way

Consolidated Telegraph & Electrical Subway Co. (Edward Lauterbach, Pres.; William J. Sefton, Sec.; Joseph Kavanagh, Treas. Capital, $3,000,000. Directors: Edward Lauterbach, William H. Woolverton, Theodore N. Vail, Robert M. Gallaway, Frederick Lovejoy, Charles F. Cutler, Edward E. Gedney, Edward J. Hall jr.) 18 Cortlandt

Consolidated Ten Mile Mining & Reduction Co. (John Caplice, Pres.; Charles Tatham, Sec. Capital, $1,000,000. Directors: Benjamin & Edwin & Charles Tatham, Leonidas M. Lawson, John Caplice, Thomas R. Tutt, Samuel T. Hauser) 102 B'way

Consolidated Troy Laundry (Louis Marbe, propr.) 1021 Third av, & 289 Fourth av.

Consolidated Ultramarine Co. (Ltd.) (Henry Merz, Pres.; Charles F. Zentgraf, Sec.; Louis Dejonge, Treas. Capital, $200,000. Directors: Henry Merz, Louis Dejonge, Charles F. Zentgraf, Anna J. Heller, Louis Dejonge jr., Carl Merz) 55 Maiden la.

Constable Brothers (Howard & Stephenson Constable) 151 B'way

Constantine & Co. (Andrew J. & Richard B. & Louis & Robert Constantine) 290 Lewis

Constantine & White (dissolved) 710 Seventh av.

Consumers' Brewing Co. (Ltd.) (Herman H. Hingalage, Pres.; William P. Rinckhoff, Sec.; Henry L. Mayer, Treas. Capital, $600,000. Directors: Herman H. Hingalage, John Riefs, William P. Rinckhoff, Henry L. Mayer, Dederick Knabe, Henry Wellbrock, George Wehrenberg, John Von Glahn, Christoph F. Bode) 21 Park row

Consumers' Cigar Mfg. Co. (Ernst Stradtmann, Pres.; August Stradtmann, Sec.; Henry Menken, Treas. Capital, $100,000. Directors: Ernst Stradtmann, Henry Blendermann, Henry Monken, Max Marz, Henry Nobel) 226 E. 63d

Consumers' Coal Co. (in liquidation) 18 B'way

Consumers' Hygiene Ice Mfg. Co. (Ltd.) (George Fritz, Pres.; John Feierabend, Sec.; Joseph Grueninger, Treas. Capital, $250,000. Directors: George Fritz, Henry Arnold, Joseph Grueninger, John Feierabend, Henry Hollman, John N. Spaus, Victor Eckstein, Edwin Hots, A. Kramer, Paul Dochtermann, Charles Hechler, Henry Illemann, John A. Baumann) 78 E. 4th

Consumers' Ice Co. (Alexander M. Earle, Pres.; Stephen B. Colgate, Sec.; William P. Earle, Treas. Capital, $250,000. Trustees: Alfred B. Darling, William P. Earle, Gardner Wetherbee, George E. Weeks, William Ottmann, Alexander M. Earle, Joseph Park, Charles H. Kerner) 146 Horatio

Consumers' Journal Publishing Co. (Elisha Winter, Pres.; Albert E. Demott, Sec.; Richard Carpenter, Treas. Capital, $5,000. Trustees: Elisha Winter, Albert E. Demott, Richard Carpenter) 213 E. 23d

Contanseau Rapid Foreign Express Co. (Henry H. Yard, Pres.; William J. Gibson, Sec.; Heth Lorton, Treas. Directors: Henry H. Yard, William J. Gibson, Heth Lorton, Ludovic Contanseau, R. Morrison Gray) 71 B'way, & Hanover & 659 Sixth av.

Contanseau L. & Co. (Ludovic Contanseau, no Co.) 71 B'way

Content H. & Co. (Harry & Walter Content) 38 Broad

Continental Bank Note Co. (consolidated with Am. Bank Note Co.) 66 Trinity pl.

Continental Construction & Improvement Co. (William H. Hollister, Pres.; Daniel B. Hatch, Sec. Capital, $10,000,000. Directors: William H. Hollister, Daniel B. Hatch, Edward De Rose, Carll H. De Silver, Franklin M. Jones, Rudolph Keppler, Lewis May, William Mertens, A. S. Rosenbaum, Henry K. Sheldon, George Warren Smith, Christian von Hesse) 120 B'way

Continental Corset Works (Kellner & Strauss, proprs.) 372 B'way

Continental Dynamo Co. (Charles Schumacher, Pres.; Victor Schaller, Treas. Capital, $50,000. Directors: Charles Schumacher, Victor Shaller, Charles Stern) 68 B'way & 160 W. 27th

Continental Gas Engine Co. (inoperative) 2 Wall

Continental Ice Co. (Peter G. Kemp, propr.) 790 G'wich & ft. Spring

Continental Ins. Co. (Francis C. Moore, Pres.; Cyrus Peck, Sec. Capital, $1,000,000. Directors: William L. Andrews, Samuel D. Babcock, Hiram Barney, George Bliss, Charles H. Booth, Henry C. Bowen, John Cladin, John H. Earle, Henry Evans, James Fraser, Aurelius B. Hull, William H. Hurlbut, Bradish Johnson, H. H. Lamport, William G. Low, Edward Martin, Richard A. McCurdy, F. C. Moore, Alexander E. Orr, Cyrus Peck, Alfred Ray, William M. Richards, John L. Riker, Henry F. Spaulding, William H. Swan, Lawrence Turnure, Theodore F. Vail, J. D. Vermilye, Jacob Wendell) 100 & 1273 B'way, 77 Broad, 10 Cooper Union & 2261 & 2662 Third av.

Continental Line (Baltimore & Ohio R. R. Co. proprs.) 415 B'way, Pier 20 (old) N. R. & Pier 27 E. R.

Continental Loan & Trust Co. (Edmund Kimball, Pres.; Albert S. Drake, Sec. Capital, $200,000. Directors: Edmund Kimball, Francis A. Fales, Albert A. Sampson, George A. Raymond, Albert S. Drake) 115 B'way

Continental National Bank (Edmund D. Randolph, Pres.; Alfred H. Timpson, Cashier ; Edwin F. Corey, Notary. Capital, $1,000,000. Directors: Edmund D. Randolph; John T. Agnew, C. C. Baldwin, Henry M. Taber, Charles H. Marshall, Frederic Taylor, Horace Porter, William C. Whitney, Benjamin Perkins) 7 Nassau

Continental Press (dissolved) 194 Water

Continental Railway Co. (inf. unattainable) 5 Beekman

Continental Silver Mining Co. of Nevada (Benjamin R. Western, Pres.; Henry M. Western, Sec.; Joseph A. Taylor, Treas. Capital, $500,000. Directors: Benjamin R. Western, Alfred M. Wilder, Joseph A. Taylor, Max Ahrens, Felix Brown, Robert H. Martin, Charles L. Rowland) 111 Liberty

Continental Wire Grip Co. (inoperative) 190 B'way

Contracting & Building Co. (Collis P. Huntington, Pres.; Edward St. John, Sec.; further inf. unattainable) 15 Broad

Contractors' Exchange (inf. unattainable) 280 B'way

Convers & Kirlin (Ebenezer B. Convers & Joseph F. Kirlin) 5 Beekman

Converse, Stanton & Cullen (Edmund W. Converse, Walter Stanton, Thomas H. Cullen & Edmund W. Converse jr.) 63 Worth

Conway John M. & Co. (John M. Conway & Edmond H. Hamilton) 118 Worth

Conway & Co. (Edward Conway, no Co.) 203 E. 76th

Conway & Son (dissolved) 140 Elm

Conyngham & Josephine (dissolved) 287 Fifth av.

SPECIAL ATTENTION PAID TO THIS CLASS OF WORK } BANKERS' & BROKERS' CIRCULARS DELIVERED { THE TROW CITY DIRECTORY CO. 11 University Place.

COO 65 COR

Coogan Brothers (James J. & Edward V. Coogan) 121 Bowery & 378 Third av.
Cook Henry C. & Brother (dissolved) 407 W. 38th
Cook A. S. & Co. (Alfred S. Cook & James T. Wilber) 110 Warren
Cook C. M. & Co. (Charles H. Cook & Arthur E. Krieger) 36 Pine
Cook F. L. & Co. (Elijah L. Cook & Frank M. McGilvery) 77 Warren
Cook J. K. & Co. (James K. Cook, Wesley A. Lyon & Eugene Dankwert) 12 Cortlandt
Cook & Bernheimer (Martin R. Cook & Jacques A. Bernheimer) 144 Franklin
Cook & Calhoun (Francis L. Cook & James Calhoun) 584 Park av.
Cook & Radley (Valentine Cook, only) 214 E. 87th
Cook & Schuck (Peter Cook & Albert M. Schuck) 49 Chambers
Cook & Smith (William H. Cook & Frederick B. Smith) 25 Park pl.
Cook & Sons (Shadruck & William & Shadrack Cook jr.) 120 W. 30th
Cook, Valentine & Co. (George J. Cook, John W. Valentine & William D. McCarthy) 32 Howard
Cook's Charles J., Son & Co. (Penelope Cook, only) 98 Sixth av.
Cook's L., Sons (T. Henry & Robert J. Cook) 777 Eighth av.
Cook-Brinkley Co. (Charles E. Cook, propr.) 1522 B'way
Cooke Charles D. & Co. (dissolved) 71 Worth
Cooke, G. K., Mfg. Co. (Peter R. Hoffman, propr.) 90 Chambers
Cooke E. B. & W. S. (Edward B. & William S.) 43 Carmine & 67 Eighth av.
Cooke Brothers (Henry C. & Charles A. Cooke) 159 Front
Cooke & Cobb Co. (William A. Cook jr. Pres.; Charles S. Cooke, Sec.; Sylvester R. Cobb, Treas. Capital, $40,000. Directors: Sylvester R. Cobb, William A. & William A. jr. & Charles S. Cooke) 147 Chambers
Cooke & Co. (James W. Cooke & Lydia S. Cooke, trustee) 22 Cortlandt
Cooke & Johnson (Alfred B. Cooke & James L. Johnson) 100 Front
Cooke & McCormack (James J. Cooke & Terence J. McCormack) 162 E. 35th
Cooke & Totten (Joseph S. Cooke & Francis E. Totten) 20 Jacob
Cooksey George B. & Co. (George B. Cooksey & George L. Stebbins) Produce Ex.
Coolbaugh, McMunn & Pomeroy (Frank W. Coolbaugh, Samuel W. McMunn & Lewis H. Pomeroy) 45 B'way
Cooley A. & Co. (Alfred Cooley, no Co.) 456 B'way
Coolidge & Bradhurst (Henry Coolidge & Henry M. Bradhurst :—special partner, Charles C. Bradhurst, $25,000; terminates 5th April, 1890) 5 Wall
Coombs R. T. & Brother (Richard T. & Charles L. Coombs) 58 John
Coombs, Crosby & Eddy (William J. Coombs & Ulysses D. Eddy :—special partner, Henry F. Crosby, *Montclair, N. J.*, $50,000 ; terminates 31st Dec. 1891) 76 South
Coan & Co. (dissolved) 838 B'way
Cooney Brothers (Michael J. & Patrick H. & Francis J. Cooney) 1644 Third av. & 2079 Second av.
Cooney, Eckstein & Co. (John J. Cooney & Joseph H. Eckstein, no Co.) 168 Pearl
Coons & Bradbury (Alfred Coons & James W. Bradbury) 208 E. 86th
Coons & Cole (Thomas H. Coons & Jonas J. Cole) 312 G'wich
Coop's Express Co. (Barr & Co. proprs.) 117 John, 97 Mercer, 313 Canal & 158 W. B'way

Cooper Charles & Co. (Jacob Kleinhans & John B. Stobaeus, only) 194 Worth
Cooper Henry & Son (dissolved) 281 Bowery
Cooper Henry Prouse & Co. (dissolved) 54 D'way
Cooper E. W. & Co. (Edward W. Cooper, no Co.) 83 Cedar
Cooper & Co. (Andrew Cooper, no Co.) 42 South
Cooper & Dockstader (dissolved) 78 Gold
Cooper & Dougherty (dissolved) 168 E. 24th
Cooper & Hulsemann (Allen B. Cooper & John C. Hulsemann) 356 W. 12th
Cooper & Jarvis (Stephen A. Cooper & estate of Joseph Jarvis) 54 D'way
Cooper & Saul (dissolved) 1841 Third av.
Cooper & Seaman (Alvah Cooper & Jonah L. Seaman) 175 W. 48th
Cooper & Wood (James Cooper & John M. Wood) r 223 E. 23d
Cooper, Hewitt & Co. (Edward Cooper, Abram S. Hewitt, James Hall & Edwin P. Bedell) 17 Burling sl.
Co-operative Building Bank (no inf.) 35 Liberty
Co-operative Building Plan Assn. (Robert W. Shoppell, Pres.; Louis Klopsch, Sec. Capital, $100,000. Directors : Robert W. Shoppell, Louis Klopsch, Arthur V. B. Lockrow) 63 B'way
Co-operative Land & Improvement Co. (Charles M. Russell, Pres.; Frank P. Norton, Sec.; Eldridge G. Rideout, Treas. Capital, $200,000. Directors : Charles M. Russell, Frank P. Norton, Eldridge G. Rideout, Robert H. C. Valentine, Joseph B. Stilwell) 45 B'way
Co-operative Tea & Coffee Co. (M. P. Langan & Co, proprs.) 426 Second av.
Copcutt J. & Co. (John Copcutt & William Booth) 440 Washn. 256 Canal & 166 Centre
Copeland George & Co. (George Copeland, Malcolm T. Maine & William Ray) 100 Water & 184 Pearl
Copeland Mfg. Co. (William C. Baird, V. Pres.; John L. Bickford, Sec.; further inf. refused) 234 B'way
Copeland & Bacon (C. Edward Copeland & Earle C. Bacon) 85 Liberty
Copeland & Blair (William H. Copeland & William F. Blair) 92 Fifth av. & 147 W. 42d
Copeland & Clarke (Herschel P. Copeland & Andrew A. Clarke) 18 Cortlandt
Copeland & Luce (Henry E. Copeland & Edward J. Luce) 82 Liberty
Copland P. H. & Co. (George W. Copland, only) 44 Water
Copley & Woolf (George W. Copley & James A. Woolf) 1920. Vanderbilt av, M. & 1650 W. Farms rd.
Copper Queen Cons. Mining Co. (James Douglas, Pres.; Joseph Van Vleck, Sec. Capital $1,400,- 000. Directors : D. Willis James, William E. Dodge, James Douglas, Joseph Van Vleck, Horace K. Thurber, Edward Smith, Clarence F. Birdseye) 52 William
Coppola G. & A. Cerriglio (no inf.) r 216½ Wooster
Corbett Brothers (John jr. & Joseph Corbett) 3199 Third av.
Corbett & Clemons (dissolved) r 45 Ann
Corbett & McAuliffe (Eugene Corbett & Patrick McAuliffe) 828 Seventh av.
Corbett, Muchmore & Co. (Hudson Muchmore & Dederick Stell, only) 165 Reade
Corbin Banking Co. (not Inc.) (Austin Corbin, Frederick W. Dunton & William G. Wheeler) 192 D'way
Corbit Joseph & Co. (Joseph Corbit & James A. McDowell) 212 Ninth av.
Corcoran D. & Co. (Daniel M. Corcoran, no Co.) 2261 Third av.
Cordelia Wine Co. (no inf.) 589 G'wich

5

TYPEWRITING DONE BY THE TROW CITY DIRECTORY CO., 11 University Place.

COR 66 COT

Cordero E., Brother & Co. (Emilio & Porfirio Cordero & Pedro de Cordoba) 214 Pearl
Cordes A. & H. (August H. & Henry) 95 James
Cordes E. D. & Co. (Albert Cordes & Armin Fritze, only) 44 Exchange pl.
Cordes Brothers (dissolved) 1847 Second av. & 145 E. 90th
Cordley & Hayes (Henry G. Cordley & James E. Hayes) 178 Duane
Cordner & Williamson (George Cordner & George M. Williamson) 32 Walker
Core & Herbert (Francis R. Core & George R. Herbert) 108 Front, 271 South & 415 W. 12th
Corell & Kerr (John J. Corell & William L. Kerr) 88 Commerce
Corkery, Dowling & Co. (Patrick J. Corkery, William Dowling, Charles J. McGuire & Albert Behreus) 295 Grand
Corliss & Hamill (no inf.) 127 W. 86th
Corliss, Macy & Co. (Charles A. jr. & Francis H. Macy jr. & William Herbert, only) 54 Liberty & 39 Nassau
Cormack & Co. (Marian C. Cormack :—special partner, John H. Dixon, Wahpeton, N. Dak. $5,000; terminates 31st Dec. 1891) 81 New
Corn Exchange Bag Co. (F. Loring Blanchard, Pres.; Lucius Bradley, Sec.; Charles W. Bigelow, Treas. Capital, $50,000. Directors: F. Loring Blanchard, Lucius Bradley, Charles W. Biglow, George S. Jewell, Charles McCaffrey) 29 Pearl
Corn Exchange Bank (William A. Nash, Pres.; Loftin Love, Cashier; Thomas Nash, Notary. Capital, $1,000,000. Directors: David Dows, William Harman Brown, Edwin R. Livermore, David Bingham, Thomas T. Barr, William A. Nash, Michael B. Fielding, Thomas A. McIntyre, James N. Platt, Henry J. Davison, Howland Davis) 13 William
Corn Samuel & Son (Samuel & Henry Corn) 84 Greene
Corn L. & Co. (Elizabeth Corn & William Morris, only) 127 Greene
Corn, Kalleke & Co. (Meyer Corn, Henry S. Kaliske & Max J. Platz) 144 W. 125th
Cornell Steamboat Co. (Thomas Cornell, Pres.; Richard G. Townsend, Treas. Capital, $500,000. Directors: Thomas Cornell, Samuel D. Coykendall, Isaac M. North, George Coykendall, Joseph Cornell) ft. Bethune
Cornell J. D. & J. M. (John M. Cornell, only) 141 Centre & 594 W. 26th
Cornell & Ward (Russell R. Cornell & Theodore H. Ward) 150 Duane
Cornell, Hiscox & Underhill (Charles G. Cornell jr. William T. Hiscox & Richard W. Underhill) 13 Gold
Cornell, Secor & Page (John T. Cornell, Horace Secor jr. & Charles D. Page) 182 Nassau
Corner Mfg. Co. (no inf.) 449 G'wich
Corner J. & Son (Margaret & William M. Corner, only) 651 Sixth av.
Corner Brothers & Co. (Thomas jr. & Richard C. Corner, only) 108 Pearl
Corneth & Clark (William N. Corneth & David Clark) 181 W. 18th
Cornett H. M. & Co. (no inf.) 313 W. 125th
Corning Edward & Co. (Edward Corning & Howard Cushman) 16 Cortlandt
Corning S. B. & Son (dissolved) no address
Corning & Co. (refused) 2281 Eighth av.
Cornish Mailing Agency (Louis H. Cornish, propr.) 2 Spruce
Cornish & Co. (publishers) (Louis H. Cornish & Joseph E. Rhodes) 2 Spruce
Cornish & Co. (smiths) (Frank W. Cornish & Samuel F. Mammel) 250 South
Cornish & Mead (Selah C. Cornish & George Mead) 70 Beaver

Cornwall & Smock (William M. Cornwall & Daniel F. Smock) 281 B'way
Cornwell Charles M., Co. (Charles M. Cornwell, Pres.; John B. Cornwell, Sec. Capital, $3,000. Directors: Charles M. & John B. Cornwell, John F. McIntyre) 166 William
Cornwell & Myers (William F. Myers & E. Lewis Smith, only) 16 Spruce
Corona & Trillard (dissolved) 409 Fifth av.
Coronet Corset Co. (no inf.) 115 Worth
Corporation Law Agency (Jacob E. Bloom, propr.) 194 B'way
Corr & Devlin (dissolved) 611 W. 47th
Corralitos Co. (Josiah F. Crosby, Pres.; S. Newton Smith, Treas. Capital, $000,000. Trustees: Josiah F. Crosby, Henry Day, H. E. Sheldon, A. G. Agnew, S. Newton Smith) 54 Exchange pl.
Corrao & Epp (Domenico Corrao & John M. Epp) 260 E. 90th
Corridon M. F. & Co. (dissolved) 89 Fourth av.
Corridon & Meyer (Michael F. Corridon & Edward O. Meyer) 89 Fourth av.
Corsi E. & Son (Emilio & Alcesto Corsi) 15 City Hall pl.
Corson & Son (Sarah & George H. Corson) 529 Hudson
Cort N. L. & Co. (Nicholas L. & Clark P. & Mortimer H. Cort) 245 Water
Cortis A. E. & Co. (Alfred E. Cortis & Henry B. Nostrand) 17 B'way
Corwin William F. & Co. (William F. Corwin & Isaac H. Ward) 109 Chambers
Cory Charles & Son (John F. & Charles Cory) 278 Division
Cory Uzal & Co. (Uzal Cory, no Co.) 210 Water
Cosgrove D. & Sons (Barnett & James F. & William R. Cosgrove) 30 Durling st. & 282 & 352 Front
Cosgrove J. & Son (James & Francis Cosgrove) 184 Maiden la.
Coshland G. F. & Co. (Gilbert F. Coshland & Adolph G. Marshuetz) 174 Water
Cosio & Co. (Joaquin Cosio, Co. refused) 105 John
Cosmopolitan Co. (Ltd.) (A. Frank Richardson, Pres.; Lee Phillips, Sec.; Samuel A. Echols, Treas. Capital, $10,000. Directors: Samuel A. Echols, A. Frank Richardson, E. Bechtoldt, C. S. Whittemore, Lee Phillips) 32 Vesey
Cosmopolitan Express Co. (Charles H. Burnell, propr.) 504, 920 & 1017 Ninth av. & 385 Eighth av.
Cosmopolitan Magazine Co. (John B. Walker, propr.) 1 W. 25th
Cosmopolitan Real Estate & Improvement Co. (inf. unattainable) 77 W. 125th
Cosmus C. T. & Son (Christian T. & George N. Cosmus) 227 Fulton
Costar Co. (Gilbert M. Richardson, Pres.; further inf. refused) 40 Clinton pl.
Costello J. & Son (Jeremiah Costello, only) 144 Fulton mkt
Costello P. C. & Co. (P. Carroll & Alfred & Patrick K. & John H. Costello) 91 Gold
Costello & McIlvaine (James B. Costello & John A. McIlvaine) 181 Eighth av.
Costello & Taylor (Thomas F. Costello & James L. Taylor) 971 Third av.
Coster & Martin (Charles Coster & William H. & Alfred T. Martin) 329 Produce Ex.
Cotes B. S. & Co. (Byron S. Cotes & Thomas L. Reynolds) 1894 Ninth av.
Cothenl & Co. (Eli B. Budd & Egbert Ward, only) 55 Beaver
Cotter & Walsh (Sylvester W. Cotter & Maurice F. Walsh) 1840 First st.
Cottier C. & Son (Charles & Jean G. C. Cottier) 171 B'way

Cottier & Co. (Daniel Cottier & James S. Inglis) 144 Fifth av. & 198 Seventh av.

Cottle S., Co. (Shubael Cottle, Pres. Capital, $10,-000. Directors: Shubael & Jethro C. Cottle; further inf. refused) 800 B'way

Cotton Oil Product Co. (Frederick H. Benedict, Pres.; James W. Tappin, Sec. Capital, $100,-000. Directors: R. F. Munro, Frederick H. Benedict, James W. Tappin) 60 Broad & 19 W. 42d

Cotton C. H. & Co. (Charles H. Cotton & William D. Dickie) 69 William

Cotton W. W. & Son (William W. & Clifton H. Cotton) r 41 Centre

Cottrell C. D. & Sons (Calvert B. & Edgar H. & Charles P. & Calvert D. Cottrell jr.) 8 Spruce

Cottrell & Denison (dissolved) 30 Cortlandt

Coty Antoine & Hackett Co. (not inc.) (Antoine Coty & Alexander K. Hackett) 20 Platt

Coudert Brothers (Frederic R. & Charles Coudert & Paul Fuller) 68 William

Couillard Brothers (Charles K. & Israel C. Couillard) 52 B'way

Coulter A. H. & Son (Alexander H. & Arthur H. Coulter) 1 Doyers

Country Club Land Assn. (James M. Waterbury, Pres.; Frederick W. Jackson, Sec.; John S. Ellis, Treas. Capital, $375,000. Directors: James M. Waterbury, John S. Ellis, Frederick W. Jackson, Edward C. Potter, John C. Furman, Charles C. Ingersoll, Moses T. Campbell, George D. French, Francis R. Wissmann) 132 Front

Coursen & Coursen (William A. & Alfred C. Coursen) 237 B'way

Courtenay & Trull (William Courtenay, only) 14 Dey

Courtney Thomas & Son (Thomas & Thomas Courtney jr.) 310 Spring

Convoisier, Wilcox Mfg. Co. (George N. Wilcox, Pres.; George Convoisier, Sec.; Thomas K. Benton, Treas.; further inf. refused) 43 Maiden la.

Couse C. & Co. (Charles & Charles W. Couse) 39 Dey

Cousins J. & T. (James & Thomas) 197 Grand

Coutrie & Son (inf. unattainable) 3 Hudson

Covert, Ris & Suydam (Alfred Covert, John Ris jr. & James G. Suydam) 244 Washn.

Cowan A. D. & Co. (Alexander D. Cowan & Theodore V. W. Hergen) 114 Chambers

Cowan & Graham (dissolved) 50 W. 14th

Cowdrey S. F., F. H. & Harry (Samuel F. & Francis H. & Harry) 81 Pine

Cowen N. & Son (Newman & George Cowen) 207 Canal

Cowen R. I. & Co. (Raphael I. & Mark Cowen & Isidor Cohen) 9 E. 4th

Cowen & Brant (Sidney J. Cowen & Henry L. Brant) 38 Park row

Cowing & Roberts (Herbert W. Cowing & Frederick E. Roberts) 416 Produce Ex.

Cowles E. B. & C. P. (Charles P. & Justus A. B. Cowles, only) 3 Broad

Cowles H. L. & Co. (no inf.) 1198 B'way

Cowles & Co. (Benjamin L. & N. Mills Cowles) 190 Fulton

Cowman Brothers (Henry & John P. Cowman) 255 W. 26th

Cowperthwait B. M. & Co. (Bernard M. & J. Howard Cowperthwait) 108 Park row

Cox Albion & Co. (Albion Cox & Clement F. Kross) 62 Front

Cox James H. & Co. (James H. & Robert W. Cox) 40 B'way

Cox Lewis S. & Co. (dissolved) 335 B'way

Cox William J. & Co. (inf. unattainable) 453 W. 28th

Cox C. P. & Co. (refused) 654 Third av.

Cox & Cameron (John Cox & William Cameron) 210 E. 51st

Cox & Co. (John W. Cox & Louis & Giuseppe Velotta) 4 E. B'way

Cox & Rockwell (James S. Cox & John W. Rockwell) 1 B'way

Cox & Sedgwick Mfg. Co. (Stephen P. Cox, Pres.; Clarence W. Sedgwick, Sec.; M. LeB. Cooper, Treas. Capital, $80,000. Trustees: Stephen P. Cox, Mary A. Sedgwick, M. LeB. Cooper, Clarence W. Sedgwick) 26 John

Cox & Sharp (E. Van Dyke Cox & Sidney W. Sharp) 35 Broad

Cox & Sons (Stephen J. & Howard & Stephen J. Cox jr.) 11 Park row

Cox, Parish & Unger (Charles H. Cox, Thomas Parish & Benjamin Unger) 53 Warren

Cox's A., Sons (John Cox, only) 25 Maiden la.

Coxe Charles L. & Co. (Charles L. Coxe & Astley Atkins) 180 Pearl

Coyle B. & F. (Bernard & Frank) 519 Second av. & 616 Eighth av.

Coyle & Sullivan (dissolved) 216 Spring

Coyne & Locke (Anne M. Coyne & Mary J. Locke) 6 W. 14th

Craets & Repper (Philip Craets & George Repper) 141 Attorney

Crager Edward & Co. (Edward Crager, Charles H. Doblin & Emil L. Lambert) 6 Gt. Jones

Craig R. G. & Co. (Horatio G. Craig & Alvah Miller) 132 Nassau

Craig & Lays (Robert Craig & Edward Lays) 79 Tompkins

Craigie Medical Clinic (refused) 35 Nassau

Cramer Jay C., Laundry Machinery Co. (dissolved) 45 Cortlandt

Cramer G. & Kaufeld (Gottlieb Cramer & Theodore Kaufeld) 64 White

Crampton Brothers (Edwin H. & Eugene W. Crampton) 8 Rutgers pl.

Crandall & Co. (refused) 569 Third av.

Crandall & Godley (William D. Godley & Lyman F. Pettee, only) 157 Franklin & 7 Leonard

Crane Cooperage (John C. Ross, propr.) 308 Water

Crane William M. & Co. (William M. Crane & George H. Warner) 766 B'way

Crane C. W. & Co. (Frank Vandevelde, only) 100 Nassau

Crane H. H. & Co. (Harrison H. & Josiah M. Crane) 38 Broad & 84 New

Crane M. & Son (Monroe & Monroe Crane jr.) ft. W. 39th

Crane U. O. & Co. (Uzal O. Crane & Jean Felix) 74 Wall

Crane & Clark (Hiram A. Crane & LeRoy Clark) 620 W. 30th

Craue & Co. (feathers) (Charles Crane & Charles A. Cushman) 5 W. 3d

Crane & Co. (woolens) (Mary L. & Charles E. Crane) 45 Lispenard

Crane & Lockwood (Alexander D. Crane & Stephen O. Lockwood) 41 Wall

Crane & McMahon (John Crane & William A. McMahon) 38 Park pl.

Crane & Stewart (John J. Crane & Robert Stewart) 74 B'way

Crane Brothers Mfg. Co. (dissolved) 40 Wall

Crane, Lockwood & Fowler (dissolved) 41 Wall

Cranitch Brothers (Jeremiah A. & James P. Cranitch) 297 Fifth av.

Cranston & Co. (Charles Cranston & Ezra J. Sterling) 59 Park

Crapo F. A. & Co. (Frank A. Crapo, no Co.) 100 Franklin

Crapulli P. & S. Calabrese (Peter Crapulli & Salvatore Calabreso) 245 Bowery
Crary & Bergen (Edward H. Bergen, only) 81 Cedar
Crary & Co. (William P. Crary & George P. Willey) 104 Front & 447 Water
Crasto M. E. & Son (Moses E. & Frank P. Crasto) 106 W. 125th
Crave & Martin (Claude Crave & Alexander Martin) 321 E. 2d
Crawford A. & Co. (Andrew Crawford & Alexander Calder) 312 Canal
Crawford D. O. & Co. (David O. Crawford & William J. Hamilton) 52 Fulton
Crawford E. M. & Son (Edgar M. Crawford, only) 163 Water
Crawford G. H. & F. L. (Gilbert H. & Frank L.) 229 B'way
Crawford J. & Co. (John & William E. Crawford) 10 John
Crawford J. W. & Son (John W. & John W. Crawford jr.) 218 W. 18th
Crawford W. H. & Co. (William H. & George H. Crawford) 401 B'way
Crawford's E. Sons (Franklin & Samuel Crawford) 27 Pine
Creamer W. G. & Co. (William G. & Harriet E. Creamer) 95 John
Creamer & Forbes (Michael W. Creamer & David Forbes) 167 W. 19th
Credit Clothing Co. (Albert D. Kagan, propr.) 287 Bowery
Credit Foncier Co. (Albert K. Owen, Pres., Davitt D. Chidester, Sec.; John W. Lovell, Treas., further inf. unattainable) 34 Nassau
Credit Indemnity Co. (Marvin F. Wood, Pres.; William Lisle, Sec. Capital, $1,000,000. Directors: Marvin F. Wood, Orlando M. Harper, William Lisle, J. Turner Moorehead) 335 B'way
Creed William R. & Co. (William R. Creed & Garret W. Cropsey) 16 Exchange pl.
Creeden & Gavagan (dissolved) Kingsbridge rd. n E. 189th
Crego Russel & Son (Oscar M. Crego, only) 165 Chambers
Creighton J. B. & Co. (Johnston B. Creighton, Henry H. Brigham & Schuyler Van Vechten) 72 B'way
Cremins & Roche (James Cremins & John W. Roche) 10 E. 22d
Crenshaw & Wisner (William G. Crenshaw jr. & John M. Wisner) 16 Exchange pl.
Creque Mfg. Co. (Allen P. Creque, Pres.; Theodore Clarkson, Sec. Capital, $250,000. Directors: Allen P. Creque, Theodore Clarkson, Homer H. Creque) 16 N. Y. & B'klyn bridge
Crescent Jewelry Co. (Alexander Harris, propr.) 650 B'way
Crevier A. E. & Co. (Augustus E. Crevier, no Co.) 56 Warren
Crevier & Woolley (Charles E. Crevier & Walter C. Woolley) 1616 B'way
Crichton & Co. (Thomas J. Crichton, no Co.) 221 Fulton
Crimmins J. D. & T. E. (John D. & Thomas E.) 1043 Third av. & 440 E. 69th
Criss M. & Son (Michael & Thomas B. Criss) 11 Wall
Crist Engine Co. (Richard B. Lawrence, Pres., further inf. unattainable) 149 B'way
Critic Co. (Charles E. Merrill, Pres.; Edwin C. Merrill, Sec.; Joseph B. Gilder, Treas. Capital, $10,000. Trustees: Charles E. Merrill, Joseph B. Gilder, Edwin C. Merrill) 743 B'way
Crittenton & Miller (William H. D. Crittenton & Nathaniel H. Miller) 120 Water
Crocker Henry H. & Co. (Henry H. Crocker, Ira A. Kip, David Crocker & William G. Gardner) 132 Pearl & 85 Beaver
Crocker C. H. & J. H. (dissolved) 144 Reade
Crocker Brothers (George A. Crocker, only) 32 Cliff
Crocker & Beck (Caroline Crocker & Maria H. Beck) 31 W. 42d
Crocker & Co. (Caroline B. & Frederick Crocker) 1 Winthrop pl.
Crocker, Wood & Co. (in liquidation) 52 South
Crocker-Wheeler Electric Motor Co. (Schuyler S. Wheeler, Pres.; William Geers, Sec.; William B. Baldwin, Treas. Capital, $100,000. Directors. Schuyler S. Wheeler, Francis D. & David Crocker, William B. Baldwin, Richard N. Peterson, H. Foster Higgins, S. K. Sloan) 324 Seventh av.
Crockett David B., Co. (Aquila Rich, Pres.; Theodore Obrig, Sec. Capital, $100,000. Directors: Aquila Rich, William D. Lent, David T. Crockett, C. F. Towner, E. M. Ezekiel, Theodore Obrig) 84 William
Crockett H. W. & Son (Hiram W. & Thomas A. Crockett) 1 Worth
Crockett & Weeks (Ellen Crockett & William Weeks) 6 E. 59th
Croft William F. & Co. (William F. Croft & Samuel Walters) 150 B'way
Croft Brothers (Frank D. & Silas C. Croft) 2159 Third av.
Crofut & Knapp (Andrew J. & James K, Crofut & James H. & Philip N. Knapp) 160 Greene
Crofut & White (Henry Crofut & Joseph H. White) 158 Greene
Croll & Ahrens (Samuel H. Croll & David H. Ahrens) 26 W. 125th
Crombie & McKean (George T. Crombie & John H. McKean) 1559 Third av.
Cromwell John & Co. (George W. Judson, only) 239 Fulton
Cromwell S. S. Line (Samuel H. Seaman, agent) Pier 9 N. R
Cromwell W. H. & Co. (dissolved) 77 Franklin
Cromwell Brothers (William H. & David W. & Albert Cromwell) 77 Franklin
Cron & Mulhall (George P. Cron & William F. Mulhall) 244 Third av.
Croney & Lent (John Brown & William H. Lotty, only) 292 Fifth av.
Cronheim G. & Co. (Gustavus Cronheim & Harry Beerwald) 316 Canal
Cronk & Co. (William H. Cronk, no Co.) 79 White
Crook J. B. & Co. (Jabez B. & Henry M. Crook) 50 Fulton
Crook & Perham (John D. Kurtz Crook & Aaron G. Perham) 1 B'way
Crooke John J., Co. (John J. Crooke, Pres.; Charles C. Emott, Sec.; Robert Crooke, Treas. Capital, $500,000. Trustees: John J. Crooke, Charles C. Emott, Robert Crooke, Augustus Doughty) 166 Grand
Crooke Smelting & Refining Co. (Oscar E. Schmidt, Pres.; Edward A. Le Roy, Sec.; August Hahn, Treas. Capital, $40,000. Trustees: Oscar E. Schmidt, William O. Loeschigk, Edward A. Le Roy, August Hahn) 22 Burling sl. & ft. W. 15th
Crooke & Co. (John J. & Robert Crooke) 166 Grand
Crooks Jane & E. (Jane & Elizabeth) 528 Third av.
Crooks Samuel & Co. (Samuel Crooks, Jacob Gumperz & John L. Kretzmer) 13 Harrison
Crosby Electric Co. (William L. Muller, Pres.; William J. Arkell, Treas. Capital, $1,000,000 ; Trustees: William L. Muller, William J. Arkell, S. C. Chandler) 110 Fifth av.
Crosby F., Co. (Merrick D. Lawrence, Pres.; William Baker, Sec. Capital, $3,000. Directors: W. F. Baker, L. J. Percy, Merrick D. Lawrence) 56 W. 25th

MERCHANTS EXCHANGE NAT. BANK OF THE CITY OF N. Y.
SOLICITS YOUR ACCOUNT. **257 Broadway.**
PHINEAS C. LOUNSBURY, President. ALLEN S. APGAR, Cashier.

CRO 69 CUN

Crosby Samuel D. (Samuel D. Crosby:—special partner, George F. Randolph, $30,000; terminates 1st July, 1890) 100 Broad

Crosby & Appell (no inf.) 237 Canal

Crosby & Co. (Charles W. & Frederick W. & Wellington Crosby) 60 Cotton Ex.

Crosby & Crosby (William B. & Ernest H. Crosby & Robert J. Hare Powel) 120 B'way

Crosley Thomas H. & Co. (Thomas H. Crosley, John T. Allaire & William F. Keables) 18 Rose

Crosley C. W. & Co. (Selina & Charles H. Crosley, only) 111 Broad

Cross & Beguelin (Alfred F. Cross & Henry B. Beguelin) 21 Maiden la.

Crossman Charles S. & Co. (Charles S. Crossman, Co. refused) 23 Maiden la.

Crossman W. H. & Brother (William H. & George W. Crossman) 77 Broad

Crossmond L. D. & Co. (Louis D. Crossmond & Alonzo Shotwell) 25 Liberty

Crosson James J. & Co. (James J. Crosson & Owen Smyth) 543 W. 22d

Croton Laboratory (John B. Hendrickson, propr.) 26 Cedar

Croton Magnetic Iron Mines (inoperative) 13 Park row

Croton Valley Railway Co. (Cecil Campbell Higgins, Pres.; Isaac Aaron, Sec. Capital, $250,000. Directors: Cecil Campbell Higgins, William F. Humphrey, Percival J. Parris, George C. Lee, Louis D. Beck, J. Wheeler Hurdley, James S. Cushman, Charles H. Scrymser, Hopper S. Mott, Charles A. Murphey, Gouverneur Morris, John C. Coleman, Isaac Aaron) 45 Wall

Crotty J. G. & Co. (John G. Crotty, no Co.) 184 Cherry

Crotty Brothers (John S. Crotty, only) 129 W. B'way

Crotty & Ryan (James Crotty & Joseph Ryan) 941 Sixth av.

Crouch & Fitzgerald (George Crouch, Winfield S. Gilmore & Edward W. & John D. Crouch, only) 14 Cortlandt, 556 B'way, 723 Sixth av. & 852 W. 41st

Crounse D. & Son (David & David R. Crounse) 601 Tenth av.

Crouse, Kuchler & Co. (Daniel W. Crouse & George W. Kuchler, no Co.) 146 Water

Crowe M. & R. (Mary A. & Rose) 1509 Av. A

Crown Chemical Co. (George A. Haynes, propr.) 62 Wall & 133 Water

Crown Knitting Mills (no inf.) 99 Franklin

Crown Point Iron Co. (Legrand B. Cannon, Pres.; Henry M. Olmsted, Sec. Capital, $1,500,000; further inf. unattainable) 21 Cortlandt

Crown Suspender Co. (C. Bloomberg & Co. proprs.) 518 B'way & 155 Greene

Cruger S. Van Rensselaer & Co. (S. Van Rensselaer Cruger & Henry W. McVickar) 187 Fulton

Cruikshank E. A. & Co. (Edwin A. & Augustus W. & Warren Cruikshank) 176 D'way

Cruikshank & McKinney (dissolved) 47 B'way

Crump Samuel, Label Co. (Samuel Crump, Pres.; Walter S. Benedict, Sec.; Nathan S. Colman, Treas. Capital, $50,000. Directors: Samuel Crump, Walter S. Benedict, Nathan S. Colman, Richard S. & Henry A. Dickle) 6 Harrison

Crusoe Mfg. Co. (George A. Colby, propr.) 126 Worth

Cryan Brothers (dissolved) 69 South, 50 Rutgers & 587 Grand

Crystal Lake Ice Co. (Israel O. Blake, propr.) 818 E. 63d

Crystal Mica Mining & Mfg. Co. (Richard H. Johnson, propr.) 95 Maiden la.

Crystal M. & Co. (Moses Crystal & Bernhard Krellerstein) 36 Clinton pl.

Cuba Marble Co. (no inf.) 45 B'way

Cucci Frank & Brother (Frank & Luciano Cucci) Tenth av. n W. 161st

Cuddeback Brothers (Herbert & William E. Cuddeback) 1583⁄4 Seventh av.

Cudlipp Charles & Sons (dissolved) 850 Seventh av.

Cudlipp & Co. (dissolved) 10 Old sl.

Cudlipp & Glover (Reuben H. Cudlipp & William E. Glover) 11 Pine

Cuff John & Son (John & William E. Cuff) 150 Jane

Culbert Brothers (John L. & Archibald Culbert) 311 W. 40th

Culbert & Co (Robert J. & James E. Culbert) 24 Maiden la.

Culbert & Seabury (Francis R. Culbert & Frederick C. Seabury) 7 Wall

Culbert & Taylor (Robert B. Culbert & William A. Taylor) 39 B'way

Cullen & Carey (Patrick Cullen & James Carey) r 212 West

Cullmans & Rosenbaum (Joseph F. & Jacob F. Cullman & Henry C. Rosenbaum) 175 Water

Culp Electric Brush Co. (Edwin G. Brooks, Pres.; Franklin J. Wall, Treas. Capital, $100,000. Directors: Edwin G. Brooks, Franklin J. Wall, J. D. Culp, Myron L. Justin) 2 W. 14th

Culver D. E., Co. (Delos E. Culver, Pres.; R. Floyd Clarke, Sec. Capital, $50,000. Directors: Delos E. Culver, C. De Clark, Frederic F. Culver) 146 B'way

Culverwell Medicine Co. (Ferdinand F. Mublert, propr.) 30 Ann

Cumberland Gold Mining Co. (Newcomb C. Darney, Pres.; J. Clement Uhler, Sec.; Daniel B. Horton, Treas. Capital, $250,000. Directors: Newcomb C. Barney, Daniel B. Horton, Henry Cranston) 39 B'way

Cumming & Becker (James P. Cumming & Henry C. Becker) 275 Church

Cumming & Clark (Charles Cumming & Elmore W. Clark) 258 Eighth av.

Cumming & Russell (dissolved) 88 Cotton Ex.

Cumming & Seeley (Thomas Cumming jr. & Edward H. Seeley) 12 Coenties sl.

Cummings W. A. & Co. (William A. Cummings, no Co.) 458 B'way

Cummings & Co. (brokers) George F. Cummings & John B. Van Gieson) 72 B'way

Cummings & Co. (contractors) (James F. Cummings, no Co.) 21 W. 62d

Cummings & Prentiss (dissolved) 7 Warren

Cummusky Brothers (William & Hugh Cammusky) 21 Third

Cundy Brothers (Robert & Isaac Cundy) 6 Old sl. & 91 Barclay

Cuneo & Podesta (Lorenzo Cuneo & John Podesta) 48 Clinton pl.

Cunningham James, Son & Co. (Joseph T. Cunningham, Pres.; Arthur R. Young, Sec.; Rufus K. Dryer, Treas. Capital, $800,000. Directors: Joseph T. Cunningham, Rufus K. Dryer, Charles H. Wilkin) 1576 B'way

Cunningham Winthrop & Sons (William T. & Graham P. & Winthrop R. Cunningham, only) 80 Wall

Cunningham J. W. & Brother (James W. Cunningham, only) 38 Nassau

Cunningham R. A. & Co. (Richard A. Cunningham & William H. Taylor) 345 E. 16th & ft. E. 21st

Cunningham Brothers (John J. & Michael A. & Daniel P. Cunningham) 52 Lawton av. W. Washn. mkt, 639 Second av. & 2134 Third av.

| CINCINNATI, BALTIMORE, PHILADELPHIA, | **SNOW, CHURCH & CO.** CORRESPONDENTS EVERYWHERE. | NEW YORK, BOSTON, CHICAGO, LOUISVILLE. |

CUN 70 DAI

Cannion James & Son (James & Frank P. Cannion) 58 John

Cannion Brothers (Lewis & Michael Cannion) 1176 Second av.

Cuppia L. A. (Lorenzo & Cæsar A. Cuppia, only) 42 E. 14th

Curado & Loeds (Joseph Curado & Loring L. Leeds) 23 Chambers

Curley J. & Brother (Terence F. Curley, only) 126 Nassau

Curran J. & Son (dissolved) 512 W. 52d

Current Literature Publishing Co. (refused) 80 W. 23d

Currey & Whitney (Jonathan B. Currey & James F. Whitney) 16 Beaver

Currier E. A. & W. D. (Edwin A. & William D.) 144 Fulton

Currier & Ives (Edward W. Currier & James M. Ives) 115 Nassau & 34 Spruce

Curry R. V. & Co. (dissolved) 60 Hewitt av. W. Washn. mkt

Curry T. & Co. (Thomas & Andrew Curry) 14 Loew av. W. Washn. mkt

Curry Brothers (grocers) (Bernard Curry, only) 484 Second av.

Curry Brothers (liquors) (Bernard & John Curry) 685 Second av.

Curry & Co. (Hart Curry & George W. Hart) 1 Chatham sq. 190 Park row & 2 James

Curry & Schuck (Thomas P. Curry & Frederick Schuck) 239 E. 58th

Curry & Smyer (Hart Curry & William Smyer) 401 E. 3d

Curtin, Larrazabal & Macnally (James C. Curtin, Carlos N. Larrazabal & Alexander S. Macnally) 24 Whitehall

Curtis Henry M. & Co. (Henry M. Curtis & William H. Coon) 26 Beaver

Curtis M. L. & Co. (Morgan L. Curtis & George A. Curtis) 1595 B'way

Curtis & Blaisdell (Grove D. Curtis & Walter F. Blaisdell) 1080 Av. A, ft. W. 23d, ft. W. 60th & ft. W. 190th

Curtis & Drown Mfg. Co. (Ltd.) (refused) 217 Fulton

Curtis & Buffett (Benjamin F. Curtis & William T. Buffett) 233 B'way

Curtis & Co. (Henry Aird, Matilda M. Curtis, James Morrison & John Don) 138 Centre

Curtis & Dean (Herbert N. Curtis & Clarence R. Dean) 115 B'way

Curtis & Wright (dissolved) 263 B'way

Curtis' S. M. Sons (Wilkie M. & Steward W. Curtis) 485 B'way

Curtiss Mfg. Co. (no inf.) 85 John

Curtiss & Co. (Frank Curtiss, Henry P. Staats & Charles G. Daser) 728 Washn.

Cushman C. & Co. (Ormando L. Cushman & Forrest L. Millington, only) 837 Eighth av.

Cushman H. B. & Co. (Horatio B. & Burritt A. Cushman, 18 G'wich av.; Horatio D. Cushman, no Co. 150 Eighth av.)

Cushman O. L. & Co. (Ormando L. Cushman & Philip D. Shook) 261 W. 125th

Cushman S. & Sons (Sylvester & Wilbur E. & John E. & Nathan A. & L. Arthur Cushman) 817 Sixth av. 806 Third av. 808 Ninth av. & 15 E. 42d

Cushman Brothers (Townsend & William Cruger Cushman) 186 Reade

Cushman & Denison (Joseph W. & Holbrook Cushman & Sylvester P. Denison) 172 Ninth av.

Cusimano & Co. (Epifanio Cusimano & Michelangelo Pettinato) 24 State

Cutajar William & Co. (William Cutajar, Co. refused) 74 Beaver

Cuthbert & Harwood (Harry J. Cuthbert & Waldo S. Harwood) 06 Duane

Cutietta G. & Co. (Giuseppe & Vincenzo Cutietta) 17 Moore

Cutter George L. & Co. (George L. Cutter & Walter Higenbotham) 801 W. 14th & 60 Liberty

Cutter John D. & Co. (John D. Cutter & Walter P. Long) 44 E. 14th

Cutting R. L. jr. & Co. (Robert L. Cutting, only) 19 William

Cyclone Pulverizer Co. (Erastus Wiman, Pres.; Lawrence S. Mott, Sec.; Hugh M. Morrow, Treas. Capital, $750,000. Directors: Erastus & William D. Wiman, Hugh M. Morrow, Lawrence S. Mott) 15 State

Cyclone Wrought Iron Paint Co. (Erastus Wiman, Pres.; Lawrence S. Mott, Sec.; Edmund W. Morrow, Treas. Capital, $100,000. Directors: Erastus Wiman, H. M. Munsell, Edmund W. Morrow, W. H. Davis, Terence D. Wilkins, Charles E. Cunningham, Richard T. Williams, Clarence G. Brown, Lawrence S. Mott) 115 B'way

Cyclostyle Co. (Augustus D. Klaber, propr.) 10 Cortlandt

Cylindrograph Co. (John R. Woodruff, Pres.; John Phillips, Treas.; further inf. unattainable) 84 Leonard

Cypress Chemical Works (Lesker Brothers, proprs.) 227 Pearl

Cypress Hills Cemetery (James Rodwell, Pres.; Frederick H. Way, Treas. Directors: James Rodwell, Frederick H. Way) 194 Bowery

Cypress Lumber Co. (Albert T. Stearns, Pres.; Frederick C. Moseley, Sec. Capital, $200,000. Trustees: Albert T. Stearns, Frederick C. Moseley, Charles N. Morgan, Frederick M. Stearns) 69 Wall

Cyriacks & Wendelken (Christian F. Cyriacks & John Wendelken) 56 Madison & 57 Laight

D

Dabelstein & Johansmeyer (Henry F. Dabelstein & Theodore C. Johansmeyer) 1189 Ninth av.

Dabritz & Zimmermann (Edward W. Dabritz & Charles Zimmermann) 446 Broome

Daft Electric Light Co. (Robert L. Belknap, Pres.; Henry M. Hawkesworth, Treas. Capital, $1,000,000. Directors: Robert L. Belknap, John C. Barron, Henry M. Hawkesworth, David Bingham, Leo Daft, J. Dwight Ripley, Appleton D. Palmer) 115 B'way

Dahin Brothers (Frederick & Louis Dahin) 85 Stanton

Dahl & Eckhardt (dissolved) 323 Canal

Dahlbender's M. Sons (Joseph & George & Martin Dahlbender) 371 Grand

Dahlman Brothers (Aaron & Henry Dahlman) 271 Canal

Dahnke H. & Brother (Henry & Charles Dahnke) 206 & 1525 Third av.

Dailey J. D. & Brother (James D. & John Dailey) 112 Broad

Dailey, Montague & Co. (Milan E. Dailey & Herbert L. Montague, no Co.) 251 Sixth av. & 251 W. 125th

Daily News Building, Savings & Loan Assn. (Charles O'C. Hennessy, Pres.; R. B. McIntyre, Sec.; H. R. Van Kauren, Treas. Trustees: Joseph P. Hennessy, John P. Dalton, Maurice F. Holahan, William N. Penney, Timothy J. Leary, Herman Mayer, David Healy, P. F. Vaughan, George A. Smith, Henry E. Lynch, Cyrus C. Adams, C. C. Fleury, George A. Knott, Francis J. O'Connor, William Reeves) 16 Fourth av.

Daily Register Printing & Publishing Co. (Anson G. McCook, Pres.; David S. Owen, Sec. Capital, $25,000. Directors: Anson G. McCook, David S. Owen) 308 B'way

**WATER METERS, GAS ENGINES, | NATIONAL METER CO.
FOR PUMPING AND POWER. | 252 Broadway, N. Y.**

DAK 71 DAU

Dakota Commercial Co. (Ltd.) (Harvey D. Winsor, Pres.; William E. Winsor, Sec. Capital, $25,000. Directors: Harvey D. & William E. Winsor) 44 B'way

Dakota Steam Laundry (Clark & Hoppe, proprs.) 73 W. 125th

Dakota Water Power Co. (Philo S. Ely, Pres.; George W. Clark, Sec. Capital, $2,000,000. Directors: Philo S. Ely, George W. Clark, Jonathan Odell, Luther N. Curtis, William H. Johnson, Julian W. Chadwick, Alburtus Richarde) 181 B'way

Dalbano V. & Co. (no inf.) 199 Mercer

Dale Leather Notion Works (Dale & Co. proprs.) 710 B'way

Dale Mfg. Co. (Henry I. Darlich, propr.) 20 Maiden la.

Dale Tile Mfg. Co. (Ltd.) (Charles E. Furman, Pres.; Elias Whitney, Sec.; Elliott P. Gleason, Treas. Capital, $50,000. Directors: Charles E. Furman, Elliott P. Gleason, Elias Whitney, Elliott G. Albee, Charles P. Read, Charles E. & Charles E. Spencer 2d) 308 Broome

Dale & Co. (Frederick E. Dale, no Co.) 710 B'way

Daley & Knob (Thomas J. Daley & Christopher Knob) 1688 B'way

Daley & Son (John J. & George J. Daley) 88 Dey

Dalton George & Co. (dissolved) 42 B'way

Dalton Brothers (Andrew J. & John J. Dalton) Kingsbridge rd c Webster av.

Dalton & Foley (John J. Dalton & Thomas H. Foley) 495 Eleventh av.

Dalton & Kloepfer (dissolved) 238 First av.

Daly James A. & Co. (James A. Daly & Patrick J. Garrity) 156 Water

Daly K. B. & Son (Kieran B. & Valentine B. Daly) 118 Wall

Daly & Ubert (Maurice Daly & Harvey J. Ubert) 111 B'way & 93 Trinity pl.

Daly, Hoyt & Mason (Charles P. Daly, Henry R. Hoyt, Alexander T. Mason & Robert Sturges) 44 Wall

Dalzell Steel & Iron Works (David Colville & Sons, proprs.) 115 B'way

Dam & DeRevere (Andrew J. Dam & George B. DeRevere) 18 Union sq. E.

Dame Moses, Co. (Charles M. Crittenton, Pres.; further inf. unattainable) 54 Ann

Dame & Townsend Co. (Augustus A. Dame, Pres.; Richard E. Townsend, Treas. Capital, $50,000. Directors: Augustus A. Dame, Richard E. Townsend, Michael O'Neill) 76 John & 31 Platt

Damico Saverio & Co. (Saverio Damico & Angelo M. Canade) 100 Norfolk

Damon & Peets (George Damon & Elias S. Peets) 44 Beekman

Damson L. A. & Co. (Leonard A. Damson, no Co.) 160 Canal

Dana William B. & Co. (William B. Dana & John G. Floyd) 102 William

Dana R. H. & Co. (Richard H. Dana, no Co.) 25 Beaver

Dana & Co. (Frank & Frederick A. Dana) 20 Nassau

Dane Charles F. & Co. (Charles F. & John Dane jr.) 261 B'way

Danenbaum Brothers (Charles & William Danenbaum) 72 W. 23d

Danenberg I. & W. & U. (Isaac & William & Ury) 83 Water

Danforth, Clark & Co. (Edmund S. & James W. Clark jr. & Edmund J. Barnard, only) 58 White

Daniel William F. & Brother (William F. & James J. Daniel) 60 D'way

Daniel M. & Son (Henrietta & Isidor Daniel, only) 402 B'way

Daniell John & Sons (John & George J. & John Daniell jr.) 781 B'way & 54 E. 9th

Daniels G. E. & Son (William H. Daniels, only) 548 Pearl

Daniels & Co. (John L. Daniels & John Wilshaw) 202 Centre, 186 Baxter, 213 Hester & 139 Goerck

Danish Am. Creamery Export Assn. (Ohly, Schmidt & Co., proprs.) 83 Warren

Danker Brothers (John & Charles Danker) 501 E. 118th

Danker & Schlukmeier (dissolved) 112 Spring

Dankwerts & Coleman (Minnie Dankwerts & Mary Coleman) 2054 Seventh av.

Dann A. & J. (Adolph & Jacob) 420 E. 34th

Dannat & Pell (Charles E. Pell & David S. Dannat) 24 Tompkins

Dannbacher & Stimis (Frank Dannbacher & William A. Stimis) 191 William

Dannenberg S. & Son (Solomon Dannenberg, only) 65 Walker

Dannenberg & Sichel (dissolved) 427 E. Houston

Dannmeyer Mfg. Co. (inf. unattainable) 6 City Hall pl.

Danville & E. Tenn. Railway Co. (Thomas Ewing, Pres.; A. E. Bateman, Treas.; Benjamin L. Fairchild, Sec. Directors: Thomas Ewing, John H. Schoolfield, W. T. Sutherlin, E. B. Withers, J. F. Rixon, A. E. Bateman, R. W. Stuart, Charles D. Peck, James P. Harrison) 45 B'way

Danzig H. & Co. (Herman Danzig & David Marx) 472 B'way & 36 Crosby

Danzig Brothers (Jacob & Joseph Dänsig) 232 Chrystie

Danzig & Stix (dissolved) 163 S. 5th av. & 61 Wooster

Darcy B. & Co. (Bridget Darcy & Rose Casey) 788 Third av.

Darcy Brothers (John J. & Thomas F. Darcy) 300 E. 89th

Darcy & Butler (Richard Darcy & Richard Butler) 140 Fourth av.

Darling C. A. & A. D. (Clarissa A. & Anna D.) 39 Ann

Darling Brothers (William Lee & Remsen Darling) 171 B'way

Darling & Co. (refused) 1332 B'way

Darling & Conley (Herbert T. Darling & George E. Conley) 175 W. 48th & 889 Tenth av.

Darling & Simcox (Eugene R. Darling & Benjamin J. Simcox) 32 Nassau

Darling & Son (James & Andrew Darling) 368 W. 18th

Darling, Noble & Dinsmore (James J. Darling, John W. Noble & William Dinsmore) 18 Cedar

Darmstadt & Scott (Louis F. Darmstadt & George Scott) 21 Centre & 319 Water

Darragh & Small (Henry Small, only) 177 Water

Darrow Rufus & Co. (Rufus Darrow, Ira A. Allen & Henry E. Stevens) ft. W. 47th

Darrow & Gregory (Charles H. Darrow & Robert H. Gregory) 36 Reade

Darrow & Vonderheide (Gilbert Darrow & August Vonderheide) 19 Old sl.

Dart Henry C. & Co. (Henry C. Dart & Clay J. Woodhouse) 18 D'way

Dasey, Mayer & Co. (dissolved) 95 S. 5th av.

Dattelbaum & Friedman (William Dattelbaum & Isaac Friedman) 4 Maiden la.

Dats & Guhl (Adam Dats & Hugo Guhl) 1507 First av.

Daub George & Son (George & Philip Daub) 102 Centre

Dauchy & Co. (Samuel T. & Frederick W. Dauchy & Stephen D. Smith) 27 Park pl. & 24 Murray

EXCELSIOR BIRD FOOD. The recognized standard. The most reliable for your Canary. Use no other. Insist upon getting it. Packed only by **C. ROSENSTEIN & CO.**, 373 Washington Street, New York.

Dauer & Co. (Christopher & Robert Dauer) 51 Attorney

Dauntless Press Works (Patrick J. Jennings, propr.) 783 First av.

Davega S. B. & Co. (Solomon B. Davega, Co. refused) 497 Third av.

Davenport George L. & Co. (George L. Davenport, Co. refused) 181 B'way

Davenport, W. J. & S. H. (William John & Stephen H. Davenport & Howard O. Lent) 94 Park pl.

Davenport & Klock (Gideon W. Davenport & Percy L. Klock) 32 Liberty

Davenport & Tracy Co. (John Davenport, Pres.; Daniel F. Tracy, Sec. Capital, $25,000. Directors: John Davenport, Daniel F. Tracy) 444 W. 16th

Davenport, Smith & Perkins (J. Alfred Davenport, George Putnam Smith & Edward C. Perkins) 115 B'way

Davey W. O. & Sons (Edmond H. Davey, only) 47 South

Davey & Mitchell (James Davey & Henry T. Mitchell) 10 New Bowery & 404 Pearl

Davey & Russell (Henry Davey & Joseph Russell) 64 Fulton

Davey, Burt & Co. (Frederick W. Davey & Charles F. Burt, no Co.) 70 Warren

David J. & Sons (Joseph & Samuel & Abraham David) 579 B'way

David Brothers (Jacob & Julius & Albert A. & Charles G. David) 687 B'way

David & Pincus (Adolph David & Leopold Pincus) 232 W. 26th

Davidge Fertilizer Co. (Robert C. Davidge, Pres.; Sydney F. Gibbons, Treas. Capital, $45,000. Directors: Robert C. Davidge, Sydney F. Gibbons, W. McKay Chapman) 121 Front

Davidow & Rosenthal (William H. Davidow & Harry Rosenthal) 40 Walker

Davids Register Co. (Charles H. Davids, propr.) 96 Maiden ln.

Davids Thaddeus, Co. (George Snyder, Pres., David F. Davids, Sec. Capital, $30,000. Directors: George Snyder, Cyrus F. Lontrel, M. V. D. Cruser) 127 William (see head lines)

Davids & Gilmore (dissolved) 106 Liberty

Davidsen Steam Pump Co. (Marshall T. Davidsen, Pres.; Richard K. Shaldon, Sec. Capital, $100,000; further inf. unattainable) 77 Liberty

Davidson J. & R. (dissolved) 237 B'way

Davidson L. & Son (Levi & Abram Davidson) 14 Ann

Davidson W. M. & Co. (William M. Davidson & Henry Bauman) 1 B'way

Davidson Brothers (Aaron & Philip Davidson) 145 Water

Davidson & Christie (Thomas Davidson jr. & Edward N. Christie) 97 William

Davidson & Knowles Co. (Frederick C. Knowles, Pres.; Thomas J. Knowles, Sec. Capital, $25,000. Directors: Frederick C. & Thomas J. Knowles, Charles Blondel) 180 Cherry

Davies Robert K. & Co. (William A. Wisdom, assignee) 606 B'way & 586 W. 23d

Davies A. M. & R. (Andrew M. & Albert & Lawrence Davies, only) 16 Walker

Davies J. H. & Co. (John H. Davies, Co. refused) 443 & 552 G'wich

Davies Brothers (Charles F. & Hopkin D. & Thomas J. Davies) 157 E. 23d, ft. E. 25th, 216 E. 42d, 897 Fifth av. & 763 Madison av.

Davies & Holmes (dissolved) 355 Hudson

Davies & Rapallo (Julien T. Davies, Edward S. Rapallo, Edward Lyman Short, Howard Townsend & Charles A. Gardiner) 32 Nassau

Davies & Wilinski (Barry Davies & Bernard Wilinski) 77 Greene

Davies, Turner & Co. (Alfred Davies, Richard J. Foster & Adolph E. Bacor, only) 84 B'way

Davis Adjustable Shade Co. (Melvin D. Compton, Pres.; Lyman L. Settel, Sec.; Henry M. Jacobs, Treas. Capital, $50,000. Directors: Melvin D. Compton, Henry M. Jacobs, Lyman L. Settel, Etna H. & Daniel Davis) 258 B'way

Davis Charles C. & Co. (Charles C. Davis, Max Boremsky & William Schlesinger) 417 E. 76th

Davis Charles H. & Co. (Charles H. Davis & May D. Hatch) 52 B'way

Davis Fellowes & Co. (Fellowes Davis & John Porter) 70 B'way & 16 New

Davis Forrest E. & Co. (no inf.) ft. E. 86th

Davis John H. & Co. (John H. Davis, Jennings S. Cox & Benjamin G. Talbert) 10 Wall

Davis Noah & J. Henry Work, 2 Wall

Davis Oil Co. (William Connell, Pres.; Charles W. Hand, Sec.; Henry S. Hand, Treas. Capital, $50,000. Directors: William Connell, Lewis Pugh, Charles W. & Henry S. & William J. Hand, Henry Dolin jr, William H. Bentley) 10 Old sl.

Davis Samuel D. & Co. (Samuel D. Davis & Charles D. Van Nostrand) 44 Wall

Davis Samuel I. & Co. (Samuel I. Davis, no Co.) 244 E. 75th

Davis Selina & Son (Selina & David Davis) 369 Washn. mkt

Davis Thomas J. & Co. (Thomas J. & T. Monroe Davis & Irving Angell) 55 Leonard

Davis William F. & Son (William F. & William F. Davis jr.) 52 B'way

Davis William H. & Son (Albert E. & Henry L. Davis, only) 157 W. Houston

Davis A. & D. (Aaron H. & Daniel) 191 E. 117th

Davis A. M. & Co. (Allen M. Davis, Thomas Caden & Charles D. Davis) 20 Washn. & 140 Water

Davis B. H. & Co. (Benjamin H. & Louis H. Davis) 41 Maiden ln.

Davis C. D. W. & Son (refused) 159 E. 48th

Davis D. & Son (Daniel & George P. Davis) 21 Hudson

Davis E. W. & Co. (Edward W. & Isaac A. & Edward W. Davis jr.) ft. W. 39th

Davis F. S. & Co. (Frank S. Davis, no Co.) 145 B'way

Davis J. & Co. (Joseph Davis, Co. refused) 124 E. 14th

Davis J. W. & Co. (brokers) (Joshua W. Davis, Samuel Barton & Frederick L. Rodewald) 66 B'way, 19 New & 80 E. 42d

Davis J. W. & Co. (machines) (dissolved) 40 Dey

Davis M. & Co. (dissolved) 96 Murray & 349 G'wich

Davis M. J. & Co. (Mary J. Davis, no Co.) 117 John

Davis S. & Brother (Samuel & Max Davis) 95 Pitt

Davis Brothers (fruit) (Meyer & Gustav Davis) 349 G'wich & 96 Murray

Davis Brothers (mers.) (Daniel H. D. & James B. Davis) 66½ Pine

Davis & Darr (Edward F. Davis & William Darr) 190 Ninth av.

Davis & Cohen (Abraham Davis & Joseph H. Cohen) 109 Division

Davis & Corson (Charles H. Corson, only) 39 Nassau

Davis & Elias (Joseph A. Davis & M. Angelo Elias) 19 Whitehall

Davis & Fay (John C. Davis & W. Lewis Fay) 89 Cortlandt & 70 Bedford

Davis & Fitzgerald (William H. Davis & James Fitzgerald) 24 Liberty

Davis & Isaacs (Charles C. Davis & Joseph Isaacs) 52 Vesey

IDEN & CO., MANUFACTURERS OF
University Place, 9th to 10th Sts., N. Y. | **GAS FIXTURES AND ELECTROLIERS**

DAV 73 DEC

Davis & Lakey (Samuel H. Davis & Charles D. Lakey) 115 Nassau

Davis & Marks (William Davis & Lazarus Marks) 87 Canal

Davis & Marshall (John H. Davis & Robert R. Marshall) 216 W. 125th

Davis & Martin (David Davis & Colin A. Martin) 132 Duane

Davis & Pickman (dissolved) 73 Now

Davis & Pollak (Charles J. Davis & Jacques Pollak) 86 White

Davis & Quick (Thomas J. Davis & Henry L. Quick) 408 Bleecker

Davis & Raphael (Louis B. Davis & Herman Raphael) 158 S. 5th av.

Davis & Treat (James W. Davis & Charles H. Treat) 1321 B'way

Davis & Vail (William L. Davis & Charles L. Vail) 1889 B'way

Davis & Walton (Joseph Davis & Arthur G. Walton) 46 Gold

Davis, Clark & Co. (William H. & John P. Davis, George H. Waters & H. Ethan Austin, only) 18 Dey

Davis, Wolf & Co. (Peter Wolf, only) 56 Pine

Davison Henry J. & Co. (Henry J. Davison & Frank F. Jones) 2 Wall

Davison A. R. & Co. (Alfred R. Davison & William H. Brown) 161 Maiden la.

Davison T. F. & Brother (Thomas F. & Asa R. Davison) 847 Washn.

Davison Brothers (William & George M. Davison) 158 South

Davison & Chapman (Charles Stewart Davison & Henry G. Chapman) 56 Wall

Davison & Fischer (Henry J. Davison jr. & Israel F. Fischer) 45 B'way

Davison & Pitcairn (James Davison & William S. Pitcairn) 12 Barclay

Davison, Quentin & Co. (dissolved) 531 B'way

Davitt & Co. (Elizabeth T. Davitt, no Co.) 140 Fulton mkt

Davol John & Sons (William H. & Frank H. Davol & John J. Williams, only) 100 John

Davoren & Kerwick (Patrick Davoren & John E. Kerwick) 853 & 935 Third av.

Davot A. & Stoerokel (Arthur Davot & Catharine Stoerokel) 478 Fourth av.

Dawson & Archer (John Dawson & William Archer) 286 E. 35th

Dawson & Co. (frames) (James & Robert B. Dawson) 15 E. 17th

Dawson & Co. (painters) (inf. unattainable) 434 B'way

Dawsonamel Co. (Theron Baldwin, Pres.; Evan G. Sherman, Treas. Capital, $25,000. Directors: Theron Baldwin, James Dawson, Evan G. Sherman) 9 E. 17th

Day John B. & Co. (John B. Day, Charles P. Abbey & Frederick J. Davis) 121 Maiden la.

Day M. N. & Co. (Henrietta W. Day & Charles H. Van Buren, only) 22 Beaver

Day & Brother (Peter S. Day, only) 351 E. 23d

Day & Clark (John C. Day & Samuel Clark) 10 Maiden la.

Day & Heston (Henry M. Day, William W. Heston & Frank W. Giffin) 6 Wall

Day & Russell (William F. Day & Charles G. Russell) 42 Barclay

Day & Son (Ezekiel & Charles L. Day) 153 Crosby

Dayton Albert & Co. (Albert & Chauncey B. Dayton) 23 South

Dayton & Close (John Dayton, David & Walter H. Close & Williford Dayton) 97 Bleecker

Dayton & Waldo (John R. Dayton & Roger W. Waldo) 114 Pearl

Deadwood-Terra Mining Co. (Richard P. Lounsbery, Pres.; A. Harrison, Sec. Capital, $5,000,000. Directors: Richard P. Lounsbery, A. Harrison, Abraham B. Baylis, Willard P. Ward, Ben Ali Haggin) Mills bldg.

Deaguero M. E. &. J. W. (Miguel E. & Joaquin W.) 60 B'way

Dealing B. B. & W. H. (Benjamin B. & William H.) 817 W. 42d

Dean James & Son (James & Frank P. Dean) 113 Baxter

Dean Linseed Oil Co. (Joseph A. Dean, Pres.; Charles N. Manchester, Treas. Capital, $250,000. Directors: Joseph A. & Arthur Dean, Charles N. Manchester) 181 Front

Dean Mathew & Co. (Mathew Dean & Albert S. Marten) 226 Washn.

Dean G. A. & Co. (George A. Dean, no Co.) 196 B'way

Dean J. A. & Co. (dissolved) 181 Front

Dean R. J. & Co. (Robert J. & Edward N. Dean & Alvin J. Donally) 802, 990, 492, 509 & 605 G'wich, 164 Chambers, 216 Duane, 185 Reade, 98 N. Moore, 95 Beach. 46 Clarkson, 26 West, 94 Thirteenth av. 548 W. 14th, 48 Jay, 12 Caroline & 304 Washn.

Dean W. G. & Son (William G. & Harry W. Dean) 351 Washn.

Dean & Westbrook (Caspar W. Dean, John A. Westbrook & J. Frank Dean) 32 Liberty

Deane Plaster Co. (Michael J. Deane, Pres.; George Peyton, Sec.; John H. Heer, Treas. Capital, $50,000. Trustees: Michael J. Deane, John H. Heer, George Peyton) 23 Dey

Dearborn & Co. (George S. Dearborn & Henry E. D. Jackson) 104 Wall & Pier 14 E. R.

Dearborn & Pressey (dissolved) 13 E. 42d

Debarbieri J. & Co. (dissolved) 145 Thompson

De Bary Bays Merchants Line (Frederick De Bary, Pres.; George Poggenburg, Sec. Capital, $200,000. Directors: Frederick De Bary, George Poggenburg, Adolphe De Bary, George Cecil, Frank L. Pommer) 43 Warren

De Bary Frederick & Co. (Frederick & Adolphe De Bary) 43 Warren

Debaun Peter & Co. (Peter Debaun, Thomas Claydon & Charles Debaun) 156 William

Debevoise & Kendall (Charles D. Debevoise & John F. Kendall) 31 Greene

Deblois & Co (William A Deblois & Ferdinand Bellut) 31 Union sq. W.

Deblois, Hunter & Eldridge (N. James Deblois, William R. Hunter & Henry F. Eldridge) 9 W. 27th

De Boer & Bligh (Christopher De Boer & Thomas J. Bligh) 21 Little W. 12th

Deboes B. H. & Co. (Bernhard H. Deboes & Jacob Janss) 1362 Third av. & 202 E. 77th

De Bruin William & Brother (William & Philip De Bruin) 4 Maiden la.

Decamp & Willson (William H. Decamp & Walter R. Willson) 88 Cortlandt

Decaranza & Sondheim (dissolved) 446 Canal

Decastro Alfred, Chemical Works (Alfred Decastro, propr.) 1 B'way

Decastro E. & Co. (Edward Decastro & Francis L. Palmieri) 7 William

Decastro & Donner Sugar Refining Co. (Henry O. Havemeyer, Pres.; Julius A. Stursberg, Sec. Capital, $250,000; further inf. refused) 117 Wall

Decatur R. W. & Son (Robert W. Decatur, only) 912 Eighth av.

Deckenbach & Schmid (William Deckenbach & William H. Schmid) 305 Third av.

Decker David H. & Son (David H. & Frederic H. Decker) 55 Whitehall

Decker Thompson W. & Sons (Thompson W. & Thompson W jr. & Henry E. Decker) 533 Park av. & 1158 Ninth av.

TYPEWRITING DONE BY THE TROW CITY DIRECTORY CO., 11 University Place.

DEC 74 DEL

Decker A. T. & Co. (Alonzo T. Decker, no Co.) ft. Dethune
Decker Brothers (John J. & William F. Decker) 33 Union sq. W. & 822 W. 86th
Decker & Co. (Philip A. & Mary Decker) r 62 Clinton, 314 Av. D & 505 E. 78th
Decker & Merten (dissolved) 971 Tenth av.
Decker & Son (cigars) (dissolved) 584 Tenth av.
Decker & Son, (pianos) (Myron A. & Frank C. Decker) 1650 Third av.
Decker & Tompkins (Elijah A. Decker & Frank W. Tompkins) 601 W. 33d
Decker, Howell & Co. (Joseph S. Decker, George H. Howell, William A. Williams & William Evans jr.) 44 B'way
Decker, Spies & Co. (Joseph F. Decker, William A. Spies & William H. Duckwitz) 451 Broome
Declat Mfg. Co. (Gustav May, Pres.;- Edward L. Milhau, Sec. Capital, $40,000. Trustees: Gustav May, Edward L. Milhau, Henry F. Keenan) 47 Murray
Deco-Emboss Wall Metal Co. (Burger & Lee, propra.) 378 G'wich.
Decoppet & Co. (Frederick & Edward J. Decoppet, Robert S. Barclay & Walter Weston) 50 B'way
Decorative Leather Co. (inoperative) 109 Suffolk
Decorative Stained Glass Co. (Charles H. Williams, Pres.; Louis M. Howland, Sec. Capital, $5,000. Directors: Charles H. Williams, Louis M. Howland, Thomas Cox) 11 Washn. pl.
Decordoba Pedro & Co. (Pedro Decordoba & Robert C. Maley) 180 Pearl
Decordova Alfred & Co. (Alfred Decordova & John B. Dunham) 38 Broad
Decordova Altamont & Son (Altamont & Aaron Decordova) 60 & 260 B'way
Decordova G. & Co. (dissolved) 4 Stone
Dee Brothers (Leonard W. & Edward W. Dee) 1534 Ninth av.
Deechan John & Co. (no inf.) 14 Platt
Deeley Robert & Co. (Robert & Thomas E. Deeley) 509 W. 32d
Deen & Dunning (no inf.) 32 Beaver
Deering, Milliken & Co. (Seth M. Milliken, Daniel A. Davis, William H. Milliken & William S. Johnson, only) 79 Leonard
Defiance Cigar Manufactory (D. Hirsch & Co., propra.) 229 E. 41st
Defiance Mfg. Co. (Ahrens & Goldsmith, propra.) 85 Liberty
Defina A. & Co. (no inf.) 17 Bond
Definna & Larenze (dissolved) 16 Thompson
Deforest & Wanner (George A. Deforest & George E. Wanner) 82 Warren
Deforest & Weeks (Francis H. Weeks, Robert W. & Henry W. Deforest & Frank L. Hall) 120 B'way
Deforth Brothers (Henry & Peter Deforth) 85 First av.
Defreitas & Brown (dissolved) 47 Liberty
Degan & Fallon (John F. Degan & Francis Fallon) 417 Pearl
De Garmo & Noble (George J. De Garmo & Gilbert L. Noble) 712 B'way
Degener R. & C., Co. (Ltd.) (Julius von Sachs, Pres.; John Mecha, Sec.; further inf. refused) 25 William
Degenhardt C. & Son (Christian & Martin Degenhardt) 123 Av. A
Degenhardt C. D. & Co, (Cord D. Degenhardt & Herman Prange) 105 South & 371 G'wich
Degenhardt & Bosche (William Degenhardt & Henry Bosche) 18 Av. A & 94 Av. D
Degnan & McNally (dissolved) 386 Seventh av.
Degraaf & Taylor Co. (Robert M. Taylor, Pres.;

William H. Degraaf, Sec. Capital, $100,000. Directors: Henry P. Degraaf, H. D. Cochrane, James J. Allen, Robert M. Taylor, William H. Degraaf) 47 W. 14th & 48 W. 15th
De Grauw, Aymar & Co. (Walter N. De Grauw jr. & George F. Schmid, only) 84 South
De Groff Lewis & Son (Lewis & Arthur L. De Groff) 47 Harrison
Degroot Electric Co. (refused) 66 Liberty
Degroot & Peck (Arza C. & John A. Peck, only) 124 Water
Degroot, Rawson & Stafford (Alfred Degroot, Sidney F. Rawson & Dewitt Stafford) 58 B'way
Dehnhoff & Co., (Richard F. Dehnhoff & Henry Schluz) 21 E. 15th
Deicke & Vogt (Frederick O. Deicke & Frederick Vogt) 476 Water
Deike D. F. & Son (Henry & Edward H. Deike, only) 662 W. 52d
Deike F. & Co. (Frederick Deike, no Co.) 58 West
Daile & Loesch (dissolved) 193 Av. C
Deimel R. & Brothers (Rudolph & Joseph & Simon Deimel) 18 E. 15th
Deininger A. & Co. (dissolved) 331 Sixth
Deininger & Tienken (John P. Deininger & William Tienken) 90 Murray
Deitsch Brothers (Charles & Edward J. Deitsch) 416 Broome
Dejonge Louis & Co. (Louis & Louis Dejonge jr. & Charles F. Zentgraf) 71 Duane
Dejonge & Co. (Max Herzog & Fitch W. Smith :— special partner, Solomon Dejonge $125,000 ; terminates 31st Oct. 1890) 48 Exchange pl.
Dekremen D. & Co. (Die Dekremen, no Co.) 12 Cortlandt
Delacy & Co. (dissolved) 38 Park row
Delafield Brothers (Rufus Delafield, only) 90 B'way
Delafield & Reardon (Rufus Delafield & Daniel O. Reardon) 103 Chambers
Delafield, McGovern & Co. (—— Delafield, Thomas B. McGovern & Frederick F. Carey) 91 Hudson
Delamare A. T. & Co. (Alpheus T. Delamare & Joseph Magill) 170 Fulton
Delamater Iron Works (William Delamater, Pres.; Henry F. Lytle, Sec.; Leander A. Bevin, Treas. Capital, $50,000. Directors : William Delamater, Leander A. Bevin, Thomas J. Rider) 31 Cortlandt & ft. W. 13th
Delamater C. H. & Co. (dissolved) 21 Cortlandt & ft. W. 13th
Deland T. & Co. (Horace C. Deland, only) 85 Beaver
De l'Andre Remedy Co. (Sara B. Chase & M. Macdonald, propra.) 226 W. 39th
Delaney Forest & Son (Forest & Joseph M. Delaney) 39 Vesey & 14 N. Y. & B'klyn bridge
Delaney Kyran H. & Co. (no inf.) 108 Ninth av.
Delaney Mfg. Co. (Forest Delaney & Son, propra.) 39 Vesey
Delaney D. & J. Fitzpatrick (dissolved) 1024 Tenth av.
Delano T. H., Publishing Co. (Thomas H. Delano, Pres.; Edward W. Field, Sec. Capital. $25,- 000. Directors: Thomas H. Delano, Edward W. Field, R. Delano, W. J. Lilley, W. F. White) 102 Chambers & 32 Warren
Delano's George, Sons (Stephen C. L. & James Delano) 140 Front
Delany & Co. (Theodore M. Delany & Henry Whitaker) 306 Pearl
Delany's James, Sons (James & John A. Delany) 371 Second av.
Delatille & Burette (Victorius Delatille & Leonie Burette) 33 W. 3d
Delaval Separator Co. (August W. Almqvist,

THE DE LA VERGNE
REFRIGERATING MACHINE CO.

MANUFACTURERS OF

Refrigerating and Ice Machines,
AND OF
ANHYDROUS AMMONIA.

Office and Works, Foot of East 138th Street,

NEW YORK.

JOHN C. DE LA VERGNE, PRESIDENT.   LOUIS E. DE LA VERGNE, VICE-PRESIDENT.
CHARLES H. CONE, SECRETARY.

279 Machines in successful operation, having a total capacity equal to the melting of **13,102 tons of ice per day** in Breweries, Abattoirs and Packing Houses, Ice Factories, Cold Storage Warehouses, Hotels, Chemical Works, Restaurants, Confectionery Manufactories, etc., etc.

(SEE NEXT PAGE.)

THE DE LA VERGNE REFRIGERATING MACHINE CO.

NEW YORK. (SEE PREVIOUS PAGE.)

Pres.; Jesse E. Folk, Sec. Capital, $100,000. Directors: August W. Almqvist, Frank J. Dupignac, Jesse E. Folk, John C. McNaughton, Robert H. McCurtor) 74 Cortlandt

Delavergne Refrigerating Machine Co. (John C. Delavergne, Pres.; Louis E. Delavergne, V. Pres.; Charles H. Cone, Sec. Capital. $350,000. Directors: John C. & Louis E. Delavergne, Charles H. Cone, Louis Block, John G. Gillig) ft. E. 138th (see leaf opposite.)

Delaware Butter Co. (Seely S. Brown, propr.) 90 Av. B

Delaware Oyster Co. (E. M. Dixon & Co. proprs.) 36 Peck sl.

Delaware & Hudson Canal Co. (Robert M. Olyphant, Pres.; F. Murray Olyphant, Sec.; James C. Hartt, Treas. Capital, $24,600,000. Directors: Abiel A. Low, Legrand B. Cannon, James Roosevelt, David Dows, Robert M. Olyphant, Benjamin H. Bristow, John A. Stewart, Frederick Billings, R. Suydam Grant, William B. Tillinghast, Johnston Livingston, Alfred Van Santvoord, George C. Clark) 21 Cortlandt

Delaware & North River R. R. Co. (Isaac N. Cox Pres.; Charles St. John, Sec. Capital, $500,000. Directors: Charles St. John, William E. Scott, Peter E. Farnam, O. P. Howell, Edward Lauterback, Louis Adler, Abram J. Hardenberg, L. E. Schoonmaker, Hugo Rothschild, Stephen Pehas, William N. Cohen, William Morris, Isaac N. Cox) 120 B'way

Delaware & Raritan Canal Steam Towing (Pennsylvania R. R. Co. proprs.) 129 Broad

Delaware, Lackawanna & Western R. R. Co. (Samuel Sloan, Pres.; Frederick F. Chambers, Sec.; Frederick H. Gibbons, Treas. Capital, $26,200,000. Board of Managers: John I. Blair, George Bliss, Percy R. Pyne, Wilson G. Hunt, Benjamin G. Clarke, Sidney Dillon, Russell Sage, Edgar S. Auchincloss, Andrew T. McClintock, William H. Appleton, William W. Astor, Henry A. C. Taylor, Eugene Higgins, William Rockefeller) 26 Exchange pl.

Delclisar John & Co. (John Delclisar & Peter J. Hughes) 16 Beaver

Deleeuw & Oppenheimer (Rudolph M. Deleeuw & Adolph Oppenheimer) 231 William

Delehanty & McGrorty (dissolved) 353 Eighth av.

Delemos & Cordes (Theodore Delemos & August W. Cordes) 146 B'way

Delfosse & Clegg (Edward Delfosse & Henry Clegg) 211 E. 30th

Delilma D. A. & Co. (David A. & Elias S. A. & Elias A. Delima) 68 William

Delisle Brothers (Armand & William Delisle) 113 Pearl, 56 Beaver & 92 Fulton

Delislé & Ranchifuss (Emile Delisle & Oscar A. B. Ranchfuss) 83 White

Delisser & Co. (George W. Delisser, Co. refused) 457 W. 26th

Delmonico's (Rosa & Charles C. & L. Crist & Josephine C. Delmonico) 2 S. William, 22 Broad, 341 B'way & 212 Fifth av.

Delmonte L. & Co. (dissolved) 88 B'way

Delong Brothers (Theodore & George Delong) 106 Broad

Delong & French (Julius Delong & Hiram W. French) 128 Pearl

Delong & Pearsall (dissolved) 7 Fulton mkt

Delong, Betts & Co. (William A. Delong & William C. Betts, no Co.) 119 Pearl

Delong, Mayer & Co. (dissolved) 18 Whitehall

Delorme E. H. & G. H. (Edward H. & George H.) 318 B'way

Deluze Francis O. & Co. (Francis O. Deluze & William B. Simonds) 18 S. William

Delventhal & Kroenke (Julius F. Delventhal & Henry Kroenke) 105 Pearl

Demand Brothers (Louis & Charles Demand) 596 Grand

Demare & Papeson (dissolved) 253 E. 105th

Demarest A. & Son (Abraham & Abraham Demarest jr.) 240 B'way

Demarest A. T. & Co. (Aaron T. Demarest, no Co.) 232 & 835 Fifth av.

Demarest C. B. & Co. (C. B. Demarest & William Warner) 25 W. 30th

Demarest N. J. & Co. (Nicholas J. Demarest, no Co.) 51 Warren

Demarest & Asche (James Demarest & Charles H. Asche) 3 Hanover

Demarest & Banta (James E. Demarest & David Banta) 328 W. 40th

Demarest & Carr (Frank Demarest & Frank A. Carr) 2633 Third av. & 282 Morris av.

Demarest & Joralemon (David M. Demarest & Nicholas H. Joralemon) 108 Barclay

Demarest's G. W., Sons (Peter J. Demarest & Albert W. Shaw, only) 148 Reade

Demartino Brothers (Frank Demartino, only) 90 E. 9th

Demaziere H. & Co. (Henry Demaziere & John L. McCabe) 41 Broad

Demilt H. R. & Co. (Henry R. Demilt & Albert E. Bieling) 298 Water

Deming & Logan (Horace R. Deming & Walter S. Logan) 68 William

Demmerie Charles & Son (Charles & Theodore Demmerie) 29 Bond

Demmert F. & Son (no inf.) 20 Maiden la.

Demond & Co. (Louis Demond, no Co.) 38 Cortlandt

Democrat Fashion & Sewing Machine Co. (Gerrit S. Scofield, Pres.; Frank M. Scofield, Sec. Capital, $300,000. Directors: Gerrit S. & Frank M. Scofield, C. L. Munson, W. L. Ryan, Ferdinand W. Keller) 17 B. 14th

Demorest W. R. & Co. (William R. & Albert H. Demorest) 35 Murray

Dempsey J. R. & Co. (dissolved) 208 Front

Dempsey & Carroll (John Dempsey, Pres.; George D. Carroll, Treas.; Charles A. Richardson, Sec. Capital, $250,000. Directors: John Dempsey, George D. Carroll, Silas D. Morrell, Charles A. Richardson) 38 E. 14th

Dempsey & Cherry (John J. Dempsey & Joseph Cherry) 47 Ann

Dempsey & Fredericks (dissolved) E. 113th c Pleasant av.

Demuth William & Co. (William Demuth, Ernest Ehrmann & Louis Demuth) 507 B'way & 78 Mercer

Demuth Brothers (Adolph & Vincent Demuth) 80 Walker

Denenfville & Co. (Jacob J. & August Denenfville) 35 Wall

Denig & Grant (George A. Denig & John B. Grant) 106 Duane

Denison W. B. & Co. (William B. Denison & Walter F. Baldwin) 482 Broome

Denmark Water Power & Iron Co. (Edwin P. Merritt, Pres.; William H. Clarkson, Sec.; Charles H. Merritt, Treas. Capital, $200,000. Directors: Edwin F. & Charles H. Merritt, William H. Clarkson) 115 B'way

Denner F. & Co. (Frank Denner, no Co.) 15 Fulton

Dennerlein P. & Sons (Peter & George H. & Albert T. Dennerlein) 167 Water

Denning E. J. & Co. (Edwin J. Denning, Henry Graham Hilton, John M. Hughes & Albert B. & Frederic Hilton) 734 B'way

Denning & Co. (Peter Denning & George Ripley) 140 E. 14th

Dennis Mfg. Co. (Ltd.) (dissolved) 16 Chambers

Dennis & Austin (George B. Dennis & Martin J Austin) 759 Third av.

SPECIAL ATTENTION PAID TO THIS CLASS OF WORK. } BANKERS' & BROKERS' CIRCULARS DELIVERED { THE TROW CITY DIRECTORY CO. 11 University Place.

DEN 76 DEW

Dennison Mfg. Co. (Henry B. Dennison, Pres.; Albert Metcalf, Treas. Capital, $400,000. Directors: Henry B. Dennison, Henry K. Dyer, Albert Metcalf) 198 B'way

Dennison & Brown (Charles M. Dennison & Hersey Brown) 2 Liberty

Denniston & Flynn (Robert F. Denniston & George Flynn) 120 W. B'way

Denny Thomas & Co. (Thomas & John T. Denny) 80 Pine

Denny Brothers (George H. & Edward B. Denny) 36 Park pl.

Denny Brothers Co. (George H. Denny. Pres.; Edward B. Denny, Sec. Capital $18,000. Directors: George H. & Edward B. & Louis B. Denny) 36 Park pl.

Denny, Poor & Co. (Daniel Denny, Edward E. Poor & James E. Dean) 114 Worth

Donamore E. & H. (Emmet & Helen) 58 W. 55th & 368 W. 28th

Dental Co. (Orlando E. Bradford, propr.) 514 Third av.

Denton Samuel H. & Son (Samuel H. & Samuel H. Denton jr.) 601 Sixth av.

Denton J. F. & Co. (Joseph F. Denton, ao Co.) 4 Stone

Denver & Rio Grande R. R. Co. (David H. Moffat, Pres.; William Wagner, Sec.; Joseph W. Gilluly, Treas. Capital, $61,050,000. Directors: George Coppell, Adolph Engler, Richard T. Wilson, John Lowber Welsh, Joseph R. Busk, Edmund Smith, David H. Moffat, Walter S. Cheesman, Charles M. Da Costa) 45 William

Denyse William & Sons (William & William T. & James H. & Morton Denyse) 13 Frankfort

Denzer, Goodhart & Co. (Emanuel & Albert Denzer, William Goodhart & Louis J. Well) 511 B'way

Denzer, Stern & Co. (dissolved) 541 B'way

Denzi & Phillips (Isaac F. Denzi & J. Knox Phillips) 24 Day

Depinna & Son (Alfred & Jose S. Depinna) 155 Greene & 44 & 50 W. Houston

Depositors' Guarantee Co. (no inf.) 120 B'way

Deppeler John & Son (John & John J. Deppeler) 184 Greene

Derago R. & Son (no inf.) 510 Broome

Derby W. E. & Co. (Warren E. Derby & William O. Raven) 92 Franklin

Derleth & Taubert (Charles Derleth & William H. Taubert) 501 S. Boulevard

Deronde Abram & Co. (Abram Deronde, Camden Rathbone & J. Monroe Jackson) 12 Cedar

Deronge A. H. & Charles (Alfred H. & Charles) 19 S. William

Derosa Joseph & Brothers (Joseph & Domenico & Frank Derosa) 2181 Third av. & 189 E. 115th

Desbrisay & Allen (H. S. Desbrisay & Joseph H. Allen) 61 Cotton Ex.

Descaizi Brothers (dissolved) 233 Washn.

Des Moines & Fort Dodge R. R. Co. (Charles N. Gilmore, Pres.; John Givin, Sec.; Warren G. Purdy, Treas. Capital, $5,041,260. Directors: Joseph E. Brown, John R. Dewey, Henry H. Hollister, Anson R. Flower, George W. Cable, Charles N. Gilmore, John Givin, Warren G. Purdy, Thomas S. Wright) 13 William

Desoto J. B. & Son (José B. & John J. Desoto) 208 Pearl

Despard H. & C. L. (Henry & Clement L.) 16 Exchange pl.

Despard & Platt (Henry Despard & Clayton Platt) 16 Exchange pl.

Dessart Brothers (Charles H. & Victor R. Dessart & John W. Vackiner) 110 Chambers

Desvernine & Zabriskie (Peter E. Desvernine jr. & John W. Zabriskie) 56 Stone

Detwiller & Street Fireworks Mfg. Co. (Jacob J. Detwiller, Pres.; William A. Turner, Sec.;

Charles G. Street, Treas. Capital, $100,000. Directors: Jacob J. Detwiller, William A. Turner, Charles G. Street, Hugh M. Funston) 173 Fulton.

Detzel & Co. (no inf.) 2427 Eighth av.

Deublein & Bausbach (dissolved) 525 W. 55th

Deutermann Brothers (William & George Deutermann) 147 Grand

Deutsch Brothers (Morris & Jacob Deutsch) 227 E. 56th & 400 E. 54th

Deutsch & Co. (Simon L. & Alexander Deutsch) 356 B'way

Deutschen R. & Co (dissolved) 710 Sixth

Dentz & Sanders (Solomon Dentz & Simon Sanders) 794 First av.

Devallieres & Negroponte (Hermann Devalliere & Paul F. Negroponte) 19 William

Devaney John & Co. (John Devaney, Co. refused) 560 W. 23d

Devanney D. & Brother (Daniel & James Devanney) 391 First av.

Devenoge & Galoupeau (Leon Devenoge & Jean C. Galoupeau) 37 S. William

Deverall Mfg. Co. (Adolph Wisel, Pres.; Morris Wisel, Sec.; Jacob Wisel, Treas. Capital, $20,000. Directors: Adolph & Jacob & Morris Wisel) 26 Cliff

Deville & Saur (James E. Deville & George W. Saur) 40 Fulton

Devine C. & B. (dissolved) 166 Washn. mkt

Devine Brothers (Thomas F. & Peter J. Devine) r 507 W. 55th

Devine & Rush (James Devine & Thomas Rush) 401 Washn.

Devinne Theodore L. & Co. (Theodore L. & Theodore B. Devinne) 12 Lafayette pl.

Devitt, Cavagnan & Co. (John J. Devitt, James Cavagnan & Witt D. Power) 601 W. 32d & Manhattan mkt

Devlin Thomas J. & Son (dissolved) 332 W. 145th

Devlin & Co. (Jeremiah Devlin, George H. Daley, William C. Phelps & George A. Jones) 276 B'way

Devling & Co. (Joseph & estate of George Devling) r 251 W. 19th

Devoe Mfg. Co. (James McGee, Pres.; Joseph H. Lesser, Sec.; William T. Wardwell, Treas. Capital, $800,000; farther inf. refused) 75 New

Devoe F. W. & Co. (Frederick W. Devoe, James F. Drummond & J. Seaver Page) 101 Fulton & 98 Horatio

Devournney Brothers (Andrew M. & Marcus L. Devournney) 389 Broome

Devoy Brothers (John W. & Charles S. Devoy) 56 Wall & 59 Pine

Devries John & Son (John & John Devries jr.) 24 W. 18th

Dewey D. B. & Co. (Charles H. Fletcher & estate of Demas B. Dewey) 77 Murray

Dewey H. T. & Sons (Hiram T. & George E. & Hiram S. Dewey) 136 Fulton

Dewey L. S. & Brother (Leroy S. & Sturges P. Dewey) 104 E. 126th

Dewing J., Publishing Co. (James Dewing, Pres.; George S. Hulburt, Sec.; George Spiel, Treas. Capital, $50,000. Directors: James Dewing, George S. Hulburt, George Spiel, Henry W. B. Howard, Oliver M. Dewing) 287 Canal

Dewing H. & Son (Hiram & Clark Dewing) 18 Wall

De Winter & Co. (John B. A. De Winter & Edward J. Fox) 99 Maiden la.

Dewitt Peter & Co. (Peter & Thomas D. Dewitt) 111 B'way, ft. W. 11th & ft. E. 49th

Dewitt Publishing House (R. H. Russell & Son, proprs.) 33 Rose

Dewitt Wire Cloth Co. (Francis J. Bartlett, Pres.; John G. Miller, Sec.; Cornelius Van Houten,

FOR THE BEST CO-PARTNERSHIP IN THE BEST CORPORATION SEE PAGE F IN BACK OF BOOK

DEW 77 DIL

Treas. Capital, $300,000. Directors: Francis J. Bartlett, John G. Miller, Robert Rogers, Cornelius Van Houten, Hoallngs Lippincott) 11 Murray

Dewitt, Lockman & Dewitt (George G. Dewitt jr. Jacob K. & John T. Lockman & William O. Dewitt) 88 Nassau

Dewolf D. R. & Co. (Joseph B. Dewolf, only) 108 Broad

Dexter Stock Indicator & Telegraph Co. (Robert W. Hawkesworth, Pres.; William B. Rankine, Sec. Capital, $850,000. Directors: Robert W. Hawkesworth, William Courtenay, William B. Rankine) 115 B'way

Dexter, Lambert & Co. (Catholina Lambert, Henry B. Wilson, Charles N. Starrett, William F. Suydam & Walter S. Lambert, only) 83 Greene

Day & Kugler (Wyckoff E. Day & Anderson B. Kugler) 56 Thompson av. W. Washn. mkt

Day & Somerville (Robert Dey & William Somerville) r 210 E. 123d

Deyo, Duer & Dauerdorf (Robert E. Deyo, William A. Duer & Charles F. Bauerdorf) 115 B'way

Diable Louis J. & Co. (Louis J. Diable, Wolf Blum & Moses Loeb) 196 Clinton & 5 Monroe

Diamond Bottling Co. (George H. Stetson, propr.) 255 W. 15th

Diamond Brick Co. (Ltd.) (Ira M. Hedges, Pres.; George H. Smith, Treas.; further inf. refused) 624 W. 30th

Diamond Chemical Works (Nelson Vandyke, propr.) 118 Pearl

Diamond Coal Co. (Seekamp Brothers, proprs.) 67 Gouverneur

Diamond Mills Paper Co. (Charles T. Raynolds, Pres.; George W. Thompson, Sec.; Henry K. Raynolds, Treas. Capital, $60,000. Directors: Charles T. & Henry K. Raynolds, George W. Thompson; 46 Murray

Diamond Quilting Co. (not inc.) (George R. Cullingworth & James Galbraith) 120 Walker

Diamond Soap Co. (Washington Haskell, propr.) 414 W. 28th

Diamond Steel Mat Co. (inoperative) 68 Murray

Diamond Brothers (Samuel & David Diamond) 66 W. 33d

Diatite Co. (inoperative) 51 Leonard

Diaz Medina & Co. (dissolved) 146 Front

Diaz A. & Co. (Andres & Manuel Diaz) 7 Burling sl.

Diaz B. & Co. (Bruno Diaz & Ricardo Rodriguez) 157 Water

Dick A. B., Co. (Albert B. Dick, propr.) 32 Liberty

Dick Dundas & Co. (Michael B. Finnigan, Pres.; James Hardie, Sec.; James Waldie, Treas. Capital, $75,000. Directors: Michael B. Finnigan, James Hardie, James Waldie) 112 White

Dick Brothers (dissolved) 17 Manhattan mkt

Dick & Charchill (George Dick & Thomas W. Churchill) 3 Coenties sl.

Dick & Fitzgerald (William B. Dick, only) 18 Ann

Dick & Meyer Co. (no inf.) 110 Wall

Dick & Stout (dissolved) 186 Washn.

Dick Brothers & Lawrence (William A. & Evans R. & Frank M. Dick & Walter B. Lawrence) 41 Wall

Dick's Popular Publishing House (Augustus J. Dick, Pres.; Charles H. Dick, Sec. Capital, $10,000. Directors: Augustus J. & Charles J. Dick) 37 Bond

Dickerson & Brown (Edmund A. Dickerson & Benjamin J. Brown) 92 Spring

Dickerson & Dickerson (Edward N. Dickerson, only) 5 Beekman

Dickerson, Van Dusen & Co. (John S. Dickerson, Samuel B. Van Dusen, Frank Dickerson, Lewis L. Abbott & S. Clinton Van Dusen) 29 Cliff

Dickinson A. S. & H. M. (Abisha S. & Henry M.) 448 W. 14th

Dickinson H. A. & Co. (Henry A. Dickinson & David I. Johnson) 15 Hudson

Dickinson & Alling (William H. Dickinson, Edward P. Alling & George F. Secor) 80 Pine

Dickinson & Co. (painters) (William Dickinson, no Co.) 152 Prince

Dickinson & Co. (pianos) (George F. Dickinson jr. no Co.) 10 E. 14th

Dickmann & Wintermeyer (dissolved) 50 New Bowery

Dickson J. & Brother (James & Alfred Dickson) 24 Beekman

Dickson J. & Son (James & Frederick W. & George M. Dickson) 88 Watts

Dickson's George H., Sons (J. Warren & George H. Dickson jr.) 738 Sixth av.

Dickson's James, Sons (Alfred & James Dickson jr.) 24 Beekman

Didlor J. H. & Son (dissolved) 151 Baxter

Dieckerhoff, Raffloer & Co. (Emil Dieckerhoff & Adolf & Rudolf Erbsloh, only) 384 B'way

Diecks Pharmaceutical Extract Co. (Clemens Diecks, Pres.; Henry Hahn, Sec.; Leopold Hahn, Treas. Capital, $15,000. Directors: Clemens Diecks, Henry & Leopold Hahn) 221 Fulton

Diefenbacher & Jaques (no inf.) 262 Third av.

Dieffenbach L. & M. Nussberger (Louis Dieffenbach & Marc Nussberger) 103 Bayard

Dieffenbach L. & M. Nussberger Iron Works (L. Dieffenbach & M. Nussberger, proprs.) 103 Bayard

Diehl & Curtiss (Daniel J. Diehl & Dwight W. Curtiss) 90 Broad

Dielmann & Lincke (William Dielmann & George Lincke) 517 W. 19th

Diestel H. & Co. (Herman Diestel & John Hill) 1568 Ninth av.

Dietrich J. & Brothers (Julius & Philip Dietrich, only) 154 Malden la.

Dietrich & Co. (Frank Dietrich & Bertha Shackman) 30 W. 4th

Dietrich & Fitzsimmons (Daniel W. Dietrich & John Fitzsimmons) 63 Reade

Dietz R. E., Co. (Robert E. Dietz, Pres.; Frederick Dietz, Treas.; John E. Dietz, Sec. Capital, $100,000. Directors: Robert E. & John E. & Frederick Dietz) 60 Laight & 76 Fulton

Dietz & Bierschenk (Carl Dietz & Henry Bierschenk) 147 Fulton

Dietz, Beckett & Co. (Joseph F. Dietz & John Beckett, no Co.) 323 E. 23d

Diffley C. & Son (Cecilia F. & John J. Diffley) 412 E. 16th

Digest Publishing Co. (Max Drey, Pres.; Christian Schierloh, Sec. Capital, $50,000. Trustees: Max Drey, Christian Schierloh, George Law) 320 B'way

Dilalla & Grasso (Joseph Dilalla & Leopold Grasso) 102 Mulberry

Dill, Chandler & Seymour (James B. Dill, Louis A. Chandler & Frederick Seymour) 31 Nassau

Dillaway, Davenport & Leeds (George W. Dillaway, John Sidney Davenport & Theodore B. Leeds) 18 Wall

Dillenback & Dewey (George Dillenback & George W. Dewey) 312 W. 50th

Dillenback & Peck (Louis S. Dillenback & Thaddous O. Peck) 601 W. 33d

Dillingham & Stockton (Ezra C. Dillingham & Harry M. Stockton) 47 Worth

Dillon Co. (not inc.; farther inf. refused) 35 Bond

Dillon Brothers (Thomas Dillon, only) 1082 Third av.

Dillon & Hayes (Michael Dillon & William J. Hayes) 150 E. 41st

Dillon & Sons (Anthony S. & Charles F. & James P. Dillon) 659 Sixth av.
Dillon & Swayne (John F. Dillon & Wager Swayne) 195 B'way
Dimatteo A. & S. (dissolved) 182 Grand
Dimock, Fink & Co. (Otis K. Dimock & Martin D. Fink, no Co.) 79 Malden la. & 212 E. 125th
Dimon J. & Co. (Mary A. Dimon & James L. Montgomery, only) 77 Warren
Dimond J. G. & T. (James G. jr. & Thomas) 209 W. 33d
Dingee M. H. & Co. (Montgomery H. Dingee & Avery Brumley) 230 Water
Dingee P. M. & Sons (Charles F. & John F. Dingee, only) 202 Lewis
Dingelstedt & Co. (Adolph & Rudolph Dingelstedt) 27 William
Dingfelder & Libko (Peter Dingfelder & Adolph Libko) 212 Pearl & 89 & 98 Fulton
Dinsmore & O'Rourke (no inf.) 19 W. 12th
Diossy & Co. (Charlotte M. & George S. Diossy, John J. Moffatt & George J. Schilling) 231 B'way
Dippel's J., Sons (John & Jacob Dippel) 57 First
Dipple's M., Son (dissolved) 130 Wooster
Dirlam & Schoeppner (Charles Dirlam & John Schoeppner jr.) 501 E. 70th
Dirlam, Schafer & Co. (dissolved) 501 E. 70th
Disbrow's J. P., Sons (J. Edwin & Thomas A. Disbrow) 28 Fulton mkt
Dissosway & Henderson (Cornelius D. Dissosway & James S. Henderson) 165 G'wich
Display Advertisement Co. (George Brunswick, propr.) 26 Church
District Telegraph & Burglar Alarm Co. of Harlem (John J. Sperry, Pres.; Franklin P. Crosto, Sec. Capital, $25,000. Directors: Joseph M. Devenu, Hanson C. Gibson, George A. Clement, E. Wells Sackett, John A. Eagleson, Thomas M. Robinson, George B. Brown, Isaac A. Shinn, David F. Porter, John J. Sperry) 104 W. 125th
Dithridge Flint Glass Co. (E. D. Dithridge, Pres.; F. C. Winship, Sec.; George W. Dithridge, Treas. Capital, $100,000. Trustees: E. D. Dithridge, F. C. Winship, M. M. Bartholomew, George W. Dithridge) 120 B'way
Ditore James & Co. (James Ditore & Agostino Palameo) 56 Centre
Ditson Charles H. & Co. (John C. Haynes, Pres.; Charles H. Ditson, Treas. Capital, $300,000. Directors: John C. Haynes, Charles H. Ditson, Charles C. Williams, Charles F. Smith, Moses Williams) 867 B'way
Dittenhoefer & Gerber (Abram J. Dittenhoefer, David Gerber & Irving M. Dittenhoefer) 6 Wall
Dittman S. & Co. (Semon Dittman, no Co.) 508 B'way
Dittmar & Jaeger (Joseph E. Dittmar & Abraham Jaeger) 210 Washn.
Dittmar & Sholfer (Lenis Dittmar & Noah S. Sheifer) 788 D'way
Dives Pelican Mining Co. (Norvin Green, Pres.; George C. Wilde, Sec.; Walter C. Humstone, Treas. Capital, $5,000,000; further inf. unattainable) 195 B'way
Dix & Cole (Henry Dix & William J. Cole) 49 John
Dix & Phyfe (Alfred P. Dix & John J. Phyfe) 27 Wall
Dixie & Ritchie (—— Dixie & James Ritchie) 381 Pearl
Dixon James & Co. (James & Hugh Dixon) 323 Eighth av.
Dixon Joseph, Crucible Co. (Edward F. C. Young, receiver) 65 Reade
Dixon E. M. & Co. (Edward M. Dixon, no Co.) 36 Peck sl.

Dixon R. W. & Son (Robert W. & Robert N. Dixon) 190 Duane
Dixon & Co. (no inf.) 143 West
Dixon & Keen (Courtlandt P. Dixon & Lucien B. Keen) 5 Counties al.
Dixon, Williams & Ashley (Edward H. Dixon, Mornay Williams & Clarence D. Ashley) 216 B'way
Dixson Brothers (no inf.) 41 Old sl.
Doak James jr. & Co, (no inf.) 75 Franklin
Doak & Beck (George F. Doak & Louis D. Beck) 58 Cedar & Kingsbridge rd. n W. 164th
Doane J. W. & Co. (John W. Doane, Henry M. Humphrey & John E. Doane) 87 Front
Doane & Brother (Henry P, & James P. Doane) 131 Pearl
Doane & Tufts (dissolved) 131 Pearl
Dobble & Co. (no inf.) 610 B'way
Dobbins & Duggan (James A. Dobbins & John Duggan) 1897 Park av.
Dobbins & Loeb (R. Percy Dobbins & Ferdinand G. Loeb) 120 B'way
Dobler A. & Sons (Anton & Charles Dobler, only) 333 W. 56th
Doblin R. & Co. (Benjamin Doblin & Adolph D. Engelsman) 552 B'way
Dobson John & James, 40 W. 14th & 353 B'way
Docherty Brothers (James H. & Edward J. Docherty) 210 E. 38th
Doctor & Co. (Max Doctor & Simon Hatch) 3 Thompson av. W. Washn. mkt
Dodd & Childs (no inf.) 296 Canal
Dodd, Mead & Co. (Frank H. Dodd, Edward S. Mead, Bleecker Van Wagenen & Robert H. Dodd) 755 B'way
Dodge A. M. & Co. (no inf.) 15 Cortlandt
Dodge E. P., Mfg. Co. (Elisha P. Dodge, Pres.; Henry B. Little, Treas. Capital, $200,000. Directors: Elisha P. Dodge, Henry B. Little, F. E. Taft, L. N. Kent, J. H. Ireland) 78 Reade & 177 Church
Dodge H. C. & Co. (Henry C. Dodge, no Co.) 605 W. 36th
Dodge S. P. & Co. (dissolved) 838 B'way
Dodge & Houston (Henry M. Dodge & Samuel Houston) 50 Wall
Dodge & Olcott (Richard J. Dodge, George M. Olcott, Francis K. Dodge & Francis H. Sloan) 60 William
Dodge, Meigs & Co. (George E. Dodge & Titus B. Meigs, no Co.) 72 Wall
Dods & Burnier (no inf.) 145 Elm
Doe Run Lead Co. (J. Wyman Jones, Pres.; Hugh N. Camp, Sec. Capital, $500,000. Directors: J. Wyman Jones, Hugh N. Camp, Charles B. Parsons, William H. Harris, Russell H. Hoadley, J. H. Crane, Furman Dealoga, Lewis F. Whitin, Frederick F. Camp) 55 Liberty
Doe, Bonnel & Co. (Walter S. Doe & Francis G. Bonnel, no Co.) 49 Catharine
Doehler & Embach's Sons (William Doehler & George Embach) 448 Sixth av.
Doelger & Eckert (Peter Doelger jr. & John A. Eckert) 251 Pearl
Doelger's Joseph, Sons (Jacob & Anthony Doelger) 223 E. 54th & 254 E. 55th
D'Oench & Simon (Albert F. D'Oench & Bernhard Simon) 10 William
Doerflinger & Lacy (dissolved) 24 State
Doernberg & Goodman (Julius Doernberg & Henry D. Goodman) 407 Eighth & 226 Lewis
Doggett Brothers (Hilton & Frederick W. E. Doggett jr.) 104 John
Dohan, Carroll & Co. (Alexander Forman, only) 117 Nassau
Doherr, Grimm & Co. (John B. Doherr, only) 57 Frankfort

THADDEUS DAVIDS CO., WRITING INKS, SEALING WAX,
MAKE THE BEST MUCILAGE.

DOH 79 DOR

Doherty Brothers (Patrick H. & Hugh Doherty) 2 Coentles sl.
Doherty & Co. (John F. Doherty & Lorenzo A. Evans) 587 Eighth av. & 165 Mott
Doherty, Durnin & Hendrick (Horace K. Doherty, Eugene Durnin & Peter A. Hendrick) 20 Nassau
Dohm & Rosa (Herman Dohm & Bruno Rosa) 59 Pearl
Dohnal John & Co. (no Inf.) 107 William
Dohrmann & Gerken (Henry Dohrmann & Mary Gerken) 166 West
Dolan P. & Nephew (Peter H. Dolan & John Smith) 8 Park row
Doll August jr. & Brother (August jr. & Ernst Doll) 20 Chrystie
Dollard T. E. & Brother (Theodore E. & William J. Dollard) 69 Broad
Dolphin Mfg. Co. (Otto T. Bannard, Pres. Capital, $300,000. Directors: John Taylor Johnston, Alexander T. Vannest, Robert W. Deforest, J. Herbert Johnston, Otto T. Bannard) 110 Worth
Domestic Sewing Machine Co. (Eli J. Blake, Pres.; James Blake, Sec.; Frederick A. Booth, Treas. Capital, $1,000,000 ; further Inf. refused) 558 B'way
Domestic Water Still Co. (Charles A. Cheever, Pres.; further Inf. unattainable) 15 Park row
Dominici & Marino (Giovanni Dominici & Francisco Marino) 15 State
Dominici's S., Sons (Napoleon Dominici, only) 81 New
Dominick & Dickerman (William G. & George F. & Bayard Dominick & Watson B. Dickerman) 74 & 3-16 B'way & 087 Fifth av.
Dominick & Haff (Henry B. Dominick & Le Roy D. Haff) 860 B'way
Don Enrique Mining Co. (George C. Magoun, Pres.; Charles T. Barney, Sec. Capital, $1,250,000. Directors: George C. Magoun, Walter Lambert, George F. Crane, Charles T. Barney, James C. Fargo) 84 B'way
Dona Maria Mining Co. (William H. Barnett, Pres. Capital, $250,000. Trustees: William H. Barnett, George D. Hedian, George D. Gorman) 62 Fulton
Donaghoe & McKenna (James Donaghoe & Owen McKenna) 1311 Third av.
Donald James & Co. (Charles D. & Robert Hogg & William Donald, only) 124 Maiden la.
Donald John A. & Co. (John A. Donald, no Co.) 84 Broad
Donald P. & Co. (Peter Donald, no Co.) 90 Franklin
Donald & Waldie (Robert Donald & James Waldie) 41 White
Donald, Gordon & Co. (William M. Donald, John W. Gordon & John D. Harris) 27 William
Donaldson Iron Co. (John Donaldson, Pres.; George Ormrod, Treas.; Harry L. Donaldson, Sec. Capital, $100,000. Directors: John Donaldson, David B. Duncan, A. S. Shimer, H. W. Peacock; Harry L. Donaldson) 1 B'way
Donaldson Brothers (Robert M. & George W. Donaldson & Charles K. Mills) 54 Park
Donaldson & Duncan (John Donaldson & David B. Duncan) 1 B'way
Donally M. E. & Co. (Melvin E. Donally, Co. refused) 160 Third av.
Donat & Michel (John Donat & John Michel) 130 Greene
Dondero & Son (John D. & Andrew Dondero) 75 Thompson
Dons Henry & Co. (Henry Dons & Charles M. Lembke) 855 G'wich
Donegan & Swift (Bartholomew Donegan & Edwin H. Swift) 174 Fulton
Donigan E. & E. (Emily T. & Ellen A.) 821 B'way

Donigan T. J. & Co (Thomas J. Donigan & John A. Stoothoff) 313 Hudson & 19 Centre
Donlan & McGarrigle (dissolved) 405 W. 51st
Donnell J. F. & Co. (John F. Donnell, no Co.) 150 Fifth av
Donnell, Lawson & Simpson (Robert W. Donnell, Leonidas M. Lawson & George E. Simpson) 102 B'way
Donnellon J. & T. (John J. & Thomas) 451 W. 140th
Donnelly Samuel & Co. (Samuel Donnelly, Co. refused) 419 E. 23d
Donnelly M. & Co. (Michael Donnelly & Peter J. McArdle) 184 Leroy & 5-48 Washn.
Donnelly & Johnson (Thomas W. Donnelly & Alexander G. Johnson jr.) 32 E. 59th
Donnelly & Kernlake (dissolved) 25 Fulton
Donnelly & McCaffery (Daniel Donnelly & James McCaffery) 18 Washn.
Donnelly & Malone (Edward Donnelly & Owen Malone) 346 Third
Donohoe & Clark (dissolved) 1454 B'way
Donohue J. & M. (John J. & Michael) 107 Willis av.
Donohue & Brothers (John H. & Lawrence F. Donohue, only) 158 Av. C
Donohue & Hugot (dissolved) 371 Second av.
Donohue & Quigley (Michael J. Donohue & John J. Quigley) 381 Tenth av.
Donohue, Newcombe & Cardozo (Charles Donohue, Richard S. Newcombe & Albert Cardozo jr.) 96 B'way
Donovan James J. & Co. (dissolved) 12 Barclay
Donovan D. & Son (Daniel & Joseph F. Donovan) 157 South
Donovan S. & Son (Simon & John M. Donovan) 92 Duane
Donovan & Londergan (Michael N. Donovan & James H. Londergan) 290½ Pearl
Donovan & Sons (dissolved) 27 West, W. Washn. mkt
Dooley Grinder Co. (no Inf.) 12 Beekman
Doppler & Hoffman (Paul Doppler & George J. Hoffman) 243 Centre
Doran & Flynn (Myles Doran & John Flynn) 148 Washn.
Doran & Wright Co. (Ltd.) (S. Gregor Doran, Pres.; Albert J. Stoddard, Sec. Capital, $100,000. Directors: S. Gregor Doran, Edward D. Weldon, Edgerton R. Williams, Albert J. Stoddard, A. H. Doran) 19 Wall
Dorcas Publishing Co. (Charles C. Hearne, Pres.; Warren N. Herrick, Sec. Capital, $6,000. Directors: Charles C. Hearne, Warren N. Herrick, Charles E. Robinson) 37 College pl.
Dorchester Union Free Stone Co. (John Dewsnap, Pres.; Gilbert P. Sherwood, Sec. Capital, $100,000. Directors: John Dewsnap, Gilbert P. Sherwood, John Furlong) 80 Pine
Doré Brothers (John L. & Downing L. & William C. & George S. & Harry D. & Benjamin F. & Alfred A. & Frank S. & Joseph S. Doré) 602 Sixth av.
Dorothy & Wadsworth (William S. Dorothy & Frederick S. Wadsworth) 357 West
Dorflinger C. & Sons (Christian & William F. & Louis J. & Charles H. Dorflinger) 36 Murray
Doring Folding Bed Co. (Ernst N. Doring, Pres.; Fred. Siemon, Sec.; John Siemon, Treas. Capital, $20,000. Directors: Ernst N. Doring, Fred. & John Siemon) 50 W. 14th
Dorlon A. & P. (Adelaide & Harry F. Dorlon & George H. Wood, only) 96 Fulton mkt
Dorlon & Shaffer (Caroline S. Dorlon & Thomas W. Wilson, only) 187 Fulton mkt & 207 Front
Dorn Charles & Smitzer (Charles Dorn & Jacob Smitzer) 370 Third av.

Dorn & Brother (George & Andrew Dorn jr.) 179 Seventh
Dornin W. C. & Co. (William C. Dornin & George B. Salisbury) 11 Wall
Dorr & Heinemann (John Dorr & Jacob Heinemann) 38 Rivington
Dorr Brothers & Bodell (George R. & Henry J. Dorr & William B. Bodell) 1997 Lex. av.
Dorr's J. O., Son Co. (George W. Dorr, Pres.; Albert H. Dorr, Sec.; Charles T. Wecks, Treas. Capital, $25,000 ; further inf. unattainable) 208 Franklin
Dorrain John J. & Son (John J. & John T. Dorrain) 242 E. 45th
Dorrance & Dorrance (Silas F. & Henry D. Dorrance) 17 W. 42d
Dorrance & Krugier (Edwin F. Dorrance & Frank H. Krugier) 194 B'way
Dorrance & Long (Julia E. Dorrance & Philip H. Long) 194 B'way
D'Orsay & Co. (J. Stanly D'Orsay, no Co.) 68 Bible h.
Dorsch William & Sons (William & Emile & William Dorsch jr.) 124 Duane
Dorsett A. & Co. (no inf.) 217 Duane
Dorsey Thomas H. & Co. (Thomas H. & George B. Dorsey) ft. Charles
Dort Brothers (Henry & John Dort) 1081 Second av.
Doscher John & Co. (John & Henry Doscher) 90 Warren
Doscher William C., Mfg. Co. (William C. Doscher, Pres.; George H. Stell, Sec. Capital, $75,000. Directors: William C. Doscher, George H. Stell, E. J. Benson) 404 E. 14th
Doscher C. & Son. (Claus & John R. Doscher) 168 West
Doscher Brothers (dissolved) 304 G'wich
Doscher & Meyer (John Doscher & William Meyer) 100 Church & 27 Barclay
Doscher & Otten (dissolved) 216 E. 86th
Dospassos Brothers (John R. Dospassos & Charles C. Shelton, only) 15 Broad
Dossert Detective Camera Co. (Dossert & Co. proprs.) 145 Elm
Dossert & Co, (John J. & Frank G. & Edward A. Dossert, Martin J. Erismann & Theodore A. Schulte) 145 Elm
Doty H. & C. (Harriet & Calista) 52 E. 54th
Doty & Herbert (John F. Doty & Eugene Herbert) 68 Park pl.
Doty & Scrimgeour (Ethan Allan Doty & James Scrimgeour) 70 Duane
Doty's A. W. Sons (Wheeler K. & Alfred D. Doty) 76 W. 35th
Donal Institute (William E. Scholl, propr.) 1509 B'way
Double Pointail Tack Co. (Henry L. Putnam, Pres.; further inf. unattainable) 108 Chambers
Dougall John & Co. (James D. Dougall, only) 150 Nassau & 11 Vandewater
Dongan John & Co. (John Dongan & John R. Hall) 364 B'way
Dongan Joseph & Co. (dissolved) 98 Gold
Dongan & Merritt (Joseph W. Dongan & Albert A. Merritt) 43 W. 61st
Dougherty E. H. & Co. (Edward R. Dougherty & William Hamilton) 355 Produce Ex.
Dougherty & Rist (dissolved) 406 Cherry
Dougherty, Elliot & Morison (Francis Dougherty, Henry A. Elliot & Robert S. Morison) 58 Wooster
Dougherty, Hertel & Co. (Theodore M. Dougherty, F. Ernst Hertel & Edwin W. Emery) 174 Fifth av.
Doughty & Cooper (dissolved) 6 Malden la.

Douglas David & Co. (William Douglas, only) 275 Church
Douglas George B. & Co. (Stephen H. Halstead, & estate of George B. Douglas) 286 G'wich
Douglas A. & E. (Anna & Emily) 95 Third av.
Douglas R. B. & Co. (Richard B. & George A. Douglas) 120 Lincoln av. & E. 139th c Third av.
Douglas & Henry (Harry J. Douglas & George W. Henry) 273 W. 23d
Douglas & Jones (John F. Douglas & Willard H. Jones) 72 B'way
Douglas & Steere (George Douglas & —— Steere) 5 Dey
Douglas, Berry & Co. (Henry Douglas, Edward Berry & William Cooper) 82 Franklin
Douglass John L., Co. (John L. Douglass, propr.) 580 Hudson & 29 Park row
Douglass & Co. (Alexander Douglass, no Co.) 208 Washn.
Douglass & Kissam (dissolved) 58 Liberty
Douglass & Minton (Benjamin Douglass jr. & Francis L. Minton) 314 B'way
Dontney Brothers (William B. & George P. Doutney) 489 B'way
Dow Andrew & Co. (Andrew Dow & George F. Cowell) 313 Canal
Dow, Jones & Co. (Harriet W. Dow, Edward D. Jones & Charles M. Bergstresser) 41 Broad
Dowd James & Co. (James & Dennis P. Dowd) 169 W. 18th
Dowd P. A. & Co. (Peter A. Dowd & George W. Larue) 239 B'way
Dowie & Canniff (Zenas Dowie & James R. Canniff) 428 Eighth av.
Dowling Brothers (John & James Dowling) 262 Elizabeth
Dowling & Co. (James Dowling & William Thompson) 19 Whitehall
Downes S. B. & Co. (Samuel B. & Joseph O. Downes) 189 Reade
Downes & Pell (Henry Downes & Albert W. Pell) 92 John
Downes & Slattery (James W. Downes & James E. Slattery) 2275 Third av.
Downey & Mathews (Nicholas Downey & John Mathews) 5 Bowery
Downing R. F. & Co. (Richard F. & Thomas H. Downing) 20 Exchange pl. & 65 Beaver
Downing & Lawrence (Edward Downing & Merrick D. Lawrence) 28 Coenties sl.
Downing, Keller & Co. (John C. Downing, Adam Keller, Frank A. Frey & Charles E. Mott) 5 & 52 Maiden la.
Downs & Finch (dissolved) 45 Leonard
Downs & Son (George A. Downs, only) 415 Pearl
Dows David & Co. (David Dows & Alexander E. Orr) Produce Ex.
Doxtater R. H. & Co. (dissolved) 86 Warren
Doyé & Beer (dissolved) 34 New & 38 Broad
Doyle James & Co. (James & Nathaniel Doyle) 50 Front
Doyle John B. & Co. (John B. Doyle & Patrick Reynolds) 296 Elizabeth
Doyle Brothers (Luke & Michael J. & John Doyle) 125 E. 109th
Doyle & Conroy (James A. Doyle & Robert F. Conroy) 59 Maiden la.
Doyle & Dillon (Thomas Doyle & Peter F. Dillon) 367 Ninth av.
Drachman & Nelson (Gustave S. Drachman & Abraham Nelson) 261 B'way
Drake Publishing Co. (John N. Drake, Pres.; Oliver Durfee, Sec. Capital, $25,000. Trustees: John N. Drake, Oliver Durfee, Frank C. Drake) 21 Park row

DRA 81 **DRY**

Drake J. A. & Son (Julius A. & George A. Drake) 45 B'way

Drake F. H. & Co. (William P. Ward, only) 59 Fifth av.

Drake Brothers (Edward A. & Samuel J. Drake) 64 B'way & 19 New

Drake & Stratton (John H. Drake & William D. Stratton) 71 B'way

Drake, Martin & Co. (James M. & Herbert H. Drake & J. Edward Mastin) 3 Broad

Drake's James H., Sons (Francis W. & Edwin F. Drake) 77 Fourth av.

Dramatic Press Clipping Bureau (E. S. Bettelheim & Co., proprs.) 22 Ann

Dramatic Publishing Co. (Alexander O. Milne, Pres.; George Milne, Sec.; Deshler Welch, Treas. Capital, $4,500. Trustees: Alexander O. & George Milne, Deshler Welch) 42 W. 23d

Draper Mfg. Co. (Daniel Draper, Pres.; Alfred L. Berthet, Sec.; Robert Howitt, Treas. Capital, $15,000. Directors: Daniel Draper, Alfred L. Berthet, W. L. Shriver, A. L. Botch) 152 Front

Draudt Henry & Son (Henry & William Draudt) 235 W. 64th

Drawbaugh Telephone Syndicate (John R. Bartlett, Pres.; Henry C. Andrews, Sec. Capital, $3,200,000. Directors: Frank Jones, J. F. Cook, Charles A. Sinclair, Marcus Marx, Henry C. Andrews, James Jourdan, J. Heron Crossman, J. B. Reynolds, John R. Bartlett, George C. Gorham, James Kirkham, Samuel R. Shipley, L. O. Robertson, B. C. Paddock, Albert F. Fisher) 2 Wall

Drechsler Joseph & Son (Joseph & Simon Drechsler) 713 B'way

Dredging Improvement Co, (inf. unattainable) 15 Cortlandt

Dresben & Shapiro (no inf.) 2147 Second av.

Dreher Mfg. Co. (Jordan L. Mott jr. Pres.; Abraham Lichtenhein, Sec. Capital, $150,000. Directors: Jordan L. jr. & Augustus W. Mott, Abraham Lichtenhein, Hiram J. Dreher) 37 Platt

Drein Thomas & Son (dissolved) 16 South

Dreisacker & Co. (John Dreisacker & Martha Henshel) 2287 Third av.

Dressel George C. & Co. (George C. Dressel, no Co.) 715 E. 173d & 37 Park pl.

Dresser & Olmsted (Horace E. Dresser & Wells Olmsted) 343 B'way

Dressler Oscar & Co, (no inf.) 112 Leonard

Drevet Mfg. Co. (Charles Marchand, Pres.; William H. Townley, Sec.; Joseph B. Rose, Treas. Capital, $100,000. Directors: Charles Marchand, William H. Townley, Joseph B. Rose) 10 W. 4th

Drew H. R. & Co. (Hosea R. Drew, no Co.) 1 W. 27th

Drew J. H. & Brother (John H. & Orrin H. Drew) 431 W. 17th

Drew & May (Henry F. Drew & John May) 308 E. 19th

Drew, Baldwin & Co. (George F. Drew, Frederick H. Baldwin, no Co.) 45 B'way

Drexel, Morgan & Co. (Anthony J. Drexel, J. Pierpont Morgan, J. Hood Wright, George S. Bowdoin, George C. Thomas, Edward T. Stotesbury, James W. Paul jr., Charles H. Coster & Anthony J. Drexel jr.) 23 Wall

Dreyer Brothers (John A. & Albert J. Dreyer) 151 W. 4th, 126 Clinton pl. & 131 Seventh

Droyer & Krug (Louis Dreyer & Arnold Krug) 41 Av. D

Dreyer, Rickiefs & Co. (dissolved) 41 Av. D

Dreyfus Henry & Co. (Henry Dreyfus:—special partner, Michael Block, Paris, France, $100,000; terminates 1st May, 1896) 25 Maiden la.

Dreyfus J. G. & Co. (Julius G. & Julius R. Dreyfus) 411 B'way

Dreyfus Brothers (Bernhard & Isidor Dreyfus) 52 Lispenard & 341 B'way

Dreyfus & Co. (Samuel Dreyfus & Baruch Frank) 100 Essex

Dreyfus, Kohn & Co. Aaron Kohn & Moses G. Rosenblatt, only) 35 Mercer

Dreyfuss & Toff (Julius Dreyfus & Maurice Toff) 7 Mercer

Driggs Elliott F. & Co. (Elliott F. Driggs, no Co.) 113 Water & 271 South

Driggs M. S. & Co. (dissolved) 276 South & 72 Beaver

Dritschel & Hahn (Michael Dritschel & Herman Hahn) 142 W. 31st

Droege & Root (August Droege & William O. Root) 102 William

Drohan & Co. (John & John jr. & Henry M. Drohan) 214 Washn.

Drouhn H. & P. (Hugo & Paul) 502 W. 18th

Drovin & Clery (George C. Drovin & Edward D. Clery) 110 Worth

Drucker Brothers (John & Philip Drucker) 310 Grand

Drucklieb J. C. & Co. (Julius C. Drucklieb, Co. refused) 11 Stone

Drummond D. M. & Co. (David M. Drummond, no Co.) 60 White

Drummond E. J. & Co. (Anne A. Drummond, only) 881 Grand

Drummond R. & Son (Richard & Thomas J. Drummond) 153 W. 53d

Drummond & Fiske (Francis S. Drummond & Robert T. P. Fiske) 24 State

Drummond & Neu (Robert Drummond & Theodore F. Neu) 3 Hague

Drummond's N. Y. Secret Service Agency (Andrew L. Drummond, propr.) 338 Stewart bldg.

Dry Dock Cornice Work (Anthony Schwoerer, propr.) 120 Av. D

Dry Dock Savings Institution (Andrew Mills, Pres.; Charles Miehling, Sec. Trustees: James J. Barnet, Henry E. Crampton, Guy Colgin, Jesse J. Davis, Charles T. Galloway, William H. Hollister, Sidney W. Hopkins, Richard L. Larremore, Abner B. Mills, William Murphy, Charles E. Poll, Henry C. Perley, George B. Rhoads, Arthur T. J. Iles, John A. Tacksberry, David J. Taff, John Tiebout, Stephen M. & Robert J. Wright, Frederick Zittel, Andrew Mills, Samuel P. Paterson) 343 Bowery

Dry Dock, E. B'way & Battery R. R. Co. (William White, Pres.; Richard Kelly, Sec. Capital, $1,200,000. Directors: William White, John M. Scribner, Richard Kelly, John E. Hoffmire, John Lowry, John Byrne, Charles A. Hotchkiss, Henry A. Morgan, Lansing Zabriskie, William Richardson, Joseph Jacobs, S. Sidney Smith, Peter J. Thorne) 606 Grand & 543 E. 14th

Dry Goods Chronicle Publishing Co. (William A. Pembrook, Pres.; John A. Tweedy, Sec.; Horace K. Thurber, Treas. Capital, $50,000. Directors: William A. Pembrook, John N. Beach, Horace K. Thurber, John A. Tweedy, Francis B. Thurber, George W. Bible) 143 Chambers

Dry Goods Commercial Agency (Wood & Co. proprs.) 336 B'way

Dry Goods Mutual Benefit Assn. (A. Judson Stone, Pres.; James P. Wardhaugh, Sec.; Benjamin F. Cromwell, Treas.) 1115 Worth

Dryden & Palmer (Noah Palmer & Isaac H. Archer, only) 19 Hudson

Dryfoos A. & Co. (Alphons Dryfoos & Feist Samuels) 150 Chambers

Dryfoos L. & Co. (Louis & Joseph Dryfoos) 274 Church

TYPEWRITING DONE BY THE TROW CITY DIRECTORY CO., 11 University Place.

Duane & Barry (——Duane & Thomas J. Barry) 55 Centre
Dubois Addison & Son (dissolved) 512 W. 30th
Dubois Mfg. Co. (Frederick N. Dubois, Pres. Capital, $50,000; further inf. refused) 246 Ninth av.
Dubois C. H. & Son (Charles H. & William A. Dubois) 61 Ann
Dubois & Helriegel (Chester & Sarah Dubois & Charles Helriegel) 21 Fulton mkt
Dubois & Trantum (dissolved) 119 South
Dubois' Henry, Sons (Charles & Henry E. & Abraham & James & Jacob Dubois) 110 South
Dubrul & Levy (dissolved) 314 E. 75th
Ducas B. P., Co. (Benjamin P. Ducas, Pres.; Isaac Dreyfuss, Sec. Capital, $15,000. Directors: Benjamin P. Ducas, Isaac Dreyfuss) 64 Front
Ducey J. M. & Co. (John M. & William S. Ducey) 332 W. 145th
Ducey & Diveny (Charles A. Ducey & Michael J. Diveny) 703 Sixth av.
Duches Jerome M. (Jerome M. Duches:—special partner, Richard Stokor, $3,000; terminates 8th Aug. 1894) E. 162d & Elton av.
Duchochois & Mardaga (Caroline Duchochois & Josephine Mardaga) 59 E. 11th
Ducker Portable House Co. (William M. Ducker, Pres.; George P. Sheldon, Sec. Capital, $800,000. Directors: William M. Ducker, Henry W. & Henry W. Slocum jr. George P. Sheldon, William Marshall) 220 B'way
Duden & Co. (Herman Duden, no Co.) 485 Broome
Dudensing Richard & Son (Richard & Frank Dudensing) 810 B. 20th
Dudley Mfg. Co. (not inc.) (Cory W. Dudley & Henry L. Bridges) 18 Bond
Dudley Shutter Worker & Burglar Alarm Co. (George W. Folsom, Pres.; Julian O. Fuller, Sec. Capital, $50,000. Directors: George W. Folsom, Francis H. Weeks, Edward F. Baker, Julian O. Fuller) 7 Beekman
Dudley U. H. & Co. (Uriah H. & William B. Dudley, Jacob Weis & Edward Materno) 4 Bridge
Dudley, Clapp & Doe (Josiah W. Dudley, Samuel H. Clapp & Nelson B. Doe) 180 Reade
Duetzmann H. & Son (Henry & August Duetzmann) 1008 B'way
Duff J. & Co. (John Duff, no Co.) 42 Nassau
Duff & Conger (Alexander D. Duff & George H. Conger) 1474 Third av.
Duffie & Wells (James H. Duffie & Milo M. Wells) 9 Little W. 12th
Duffy Michael & Sons (Michael & Thomas L. & James Duffy) 1836 Third av. & 205 E. 101st
Duffy C. & P. (Cornelius F. & Patrick J.) 649 Hudson
Duffy J. P. & Co. (James P. & Thomas F. Duffy) E. 138th n Railroad av.
Duffy P. H. & Sons (Patrick H. & John H. Duffy, only) ft. E. 90th
Duffy T. L. & Co. (dissolved) 1821 Third av. & 208 E. 101st
Duffy & Levy (dissolved) 335 W. 17th
Duffy & McConnell (John Duffy & Florence A. McConnell) 47 Bleecker
Duffy & McCue (John Duffy & Patrick McCue) 59 Jackson
Duffy & Murphy (Francis Duffy & Patrick Murphy) 498 Tenth av
Duffy & Rice (James Duffy & Patrick Rice) 537 First av.
Dugan M. & Son (Michael & John Dugan) 84 Scammel
Dugan & Hudson (William E. Dugan & Charles B. Hudson) 122 Duane
Duggan & Corrigan (John F. Duggan & John F. Corrigan) 344½ Bowery

Duhain L. jr. & Co. (Louis jr. & August D. Duhain) 585 B'way
Duhne John & Son (John & Henry Duhne) 2733 Eighth av.
Duignan J. L. & W. J. (dissolved) 1389 Second av.
Duke W., Sons & Co. (James B. Duke, Pres.; George W. Watts, Sec. Capital, $600,000. Directors: James B. Duke, George W. Watts, Benjamin N. & Washington & Brodie L. Duke) 709 Second av.
Duke, Hanna, Macmahon & Co. (John H. Duke, Joseph B. Hanna, Benjamin Macmahon & William Campbell) 27 White
Dulany Brothers (dissolved) 250 E. 124th
Dulberger M. & M. Eisenstein (Martin Dulberger & Moritz Eisenstein) 91 Delancey
Dule Jacob & Co. (Jacob Dule, David D. Reeve & Richard Vanriper) 46 Water
Duluth & Iron Range R. R. Co. (Heber R. Bishop, Pres.; Charles W. Hillard, Sec. Capital, $500,000. Directors: Heber R. Bishop, Henry H. Porter, Benjamin Brewster, M. J. Carpenter, Darius O. Mills, George C. Stone, Marshall Field, H. M. Flagler, George H. Ball, Roswell P. Flower, C. Tower jr. David Dows, P. H. Kelly) 15 Broad
Duluth, S. Shore & Atlantic Railway Co. (James McMillan, Pres.; Louis M. Schwan, Sec.; William A. C. Ewen, Treas. Capital, $24,000,000. Directors: George Stephen, Donald A. Smith, William C. Vanhorne, John W. Sterling, Richard J. Cross, Samuel Thomas, Calvin S. Brice, John G. Moore, George L. Seney, James McMillan, Thomas W. Pearsall) 10 Wall
Dumas & Slater (Matilda Dumas & Elise Schoonmaker) 47 Lex. av.
Dumbarton Iron Works (Alexander Reid, propr.) 167 Charles
Dumois H. & Co. (Hipolito & Simon Dumois) 41 South
Dumont Co. (John L. Dumont, Pres.; Charles A. Robbins, Sec.; Henry K. Dumont, Treas. Capital, $50,000. Trustees: John L. & Henry K. Dumont, Charles A. Robbins) 10 Old sl.
Dumont William H. & Co. (William H. Dumont & Albert I. Mann) 18 Exchange pl.
Dumont L. & E. Verpillier (Louis Dumont & Emile Verpillier) 19 John
Dun R. G. & Co. (Robert G. Dun, Erastus Wiman, Arthur J. King & Robert Dun Douglass) 314 B'way, 80 Wall & 110 E. 125th *(see adv, in front)*
Dunbar Box & Lumber Co. (Thomas T. Reid, Sec. Capital, $10,000; further inf. refused) 282 Eleventh av.
Dunbar M. P., Co. (Melzar P. Dunbar, Pres.; Edwin M. English, Sec.; Albert S. Holt, Treas. Capital, $20,000. Directors: Melzar P. Dunbar, Albert S. Holt, Edwin M. English) 18 B'way
Dunbar, Hobart & Co. (William H. Dunbar, Henry & James F. Hobart & Joseph Pottes jr.) 80 Warren
Duncan David & Son (David B. Duncan & John Donaldson, only) 1 B'way
Duncan Samuel & Co. (dissolved) 142 Fulton
Duncan W. J. & Co. (William J. Duncan & James C. Elliotz) 251 Washn.
Duncan & Anderson (David Duncan & William Anderson) 507 Tenth av.
Duncan & Johnston (William B. Duncan & William R. Johnston) 314 Fifth av.
Duncan, Curtis & Page (Samuel A. & Robert H. Duncan, Leonard E. Curtis & Parker W. Page) 190 B'way
Duncan's John, Sons (David & John P. Duncan) 48 Park pl.
Dundee Chemical Works (J. Zabriskie Ackerson, Pres.; William M. Johnson, Sec. Capital,

$60,000. Directors: William M. Johnson, J. Zabriskie Ackerson) 17 Cedar

Dunham Joseph T. & Co. (Joseph T. Dunham, no Co.) 59 John

Dunham Mfg. Co. (cocoanuts) (John S. Dunham, Pres.; James P. Wood, Sec. Capital, $50,000. Directors: John S. & Frank J. & R. F. Dunham) 7 James sl.

Dunham Mfg. Co. (liquors) (Crittenton & Miller, proprs.) 120 Water

Dunham Piano Co. (William H. Conkling, Pres.; Horace F. Baldwin, Sec. Capital, $15,000. Directors: William H. Conkling, Horace F. Baldwin, Richard W. Turner, Ferdinand W. Chivvis, William L. McDougall) 412 E. 23d

Dunham D. & C. E. (David & Charles E.) 411 W. 17th

Dunham H. B. & Son (Humphrey B. & Theodore L. Dunham) 161 B'way

Dunham & Wood (Frank J. Dunham & James P. Wood) 5 James sl.

Dunham, Buckley & Co. (James H. Dunham, William T. Buckley & Charles H. & William E. Webb) 340 B'way

Dunham, Mulford, Simmons & Williamson (Clarence E. Dunham, Charles Mulford, William H. Simmons & James Williamson) Eleventh av. n W. 15th

Dunham's Thomas, Nephew & Co. (refused) 68 South

Dankell Brothers (dissolved) 228 E. 120th

Dunkirk, Alleghany Valley & Pittsburgh R. R. Co. (Edwin D. Worcester, Pres.; Dwight W. Pardee, Sec.; Capital, $1,300,000. Directors: Cornelius & William K. & Frederick W. Vanderbilt, Edwin D. Worcester, Samuel F. Barger, Charles C. Clarke, Chauncey M. Depew, Horace J. Hayden, Dwight M. Pardee, Darwin Thayer, Oscar W. Johnson, Rasselas Brown) Grand Central depot

Dunlap A. J. & Son. (A. Judson & Cornell Dunlap) 86 Wooster, 97 Mercer, 117 W. B'way & 313 Canal

Dunlap R. & Co. (Robert Dunlap, no Co.) 130 Fifth av. & 181 B'way

Dunlap's Cable News Co. (Robert Dunlap, Pres.; Davidson Dalziel, Sec.; Gustavus C. Henry, Treas. Capital, $30,000. Directors: Robert Dunlap, Davidson Dalziel, Gustavus C. Henry) 80 Broad

Dunlevey A. L. & Co. (Ambrose Dunlevey & Eugene C. Mulhern, only) 71 South. Bargain men, New York City purchasing agency

Dunn A. (Marcella Dunn & Margaret & John Moonan, only) 427 West

Dunn Fire Escape Co. (no Inf.) 140 Nassau

Dunn John, Son & Co. (John & J. Carr Dunn & Charles A. McCollough) 76 Wall

Dunn L. A. & Brothers (no inf.) 126 Liberty

Dunn S. & Son (dissolved) 3631 Third av.

Dunn W. S. & Co. (Wilson S. Dunn & Lucius H. Dodge) 46 Murray

Dunn Brothers (Joseph H. & Charles B. & Robert M. & John G. Dunn) 40 Wall & 87 Pine

Dunn & Costello (Roderick Dunn & John Costello) Boulevard n W. 65th

Dunn & Darling (dissolved) 57 Gt. Jones

Dunn & Robertson (William Dunn & John Robertson) 5 Jones la.

Dunn & Sanders (no inf.) 1847 Park av.

Dunn & Smith (dissolved) 31 South

Dunn & Wilson (Thomas J. Dunn & Joseph J. T. Wilson) 151 Fulton

Dunne Lawrence & Son (Lawrence & Edward J. Dunne) 211 E. 47th

Dunne A. & Co. (Agnes Dunne, no Co.) 56 Reade

Dunne & Armstrong (Thomas Dunne & John D. Armstrong) Jerome av. c Kingsbridge rd.

Dunning & Fowler (Benjamin F. & Frank &

William F. Dunning & Thomas Powell Fowler) 67 Wall

Dunphy John & Sons (John & John J. & William H. Dunphy) 6 Ferry

Dunphy & Gorman (John Dunphy & Thomas J. Gorman) 39 W. B'way

Dunscomb & Co. (Godfrey Dunscomb & George P. Cammann) 80 Pine

Dunscomb & Frith (Richard T. Dunscomb & S. Archibald Frith) 40 Exchange pl.

Dunsing & Hoepfner (August Dunsing & Robert Hoepfner) 353 Fourth av.

Dunwald & Co. (Peter Dunwald, no Co.) 90 Fulton

Duparquet, Huot & Moneuse Co. (Elis J. Moneuse, Pros.; Alexander Hebert, Treas.; Capital, $350,000. Directors: Pierre Huot, Elis J. Moneuse, Alexander Hebert) 43 Wooster

Duplex Steam Heater Co. (Newell Universal Mill Co. propra.) 23 Bethune

Dupont Medical Toilet Co. (not inc.; further inf. refused) 44 W. 23d

Duprat & Co. (Felicie Duprat, no Co.) 349 Fifth av.

Durand & Co. (Wickliffe B. Durand, Joseph G. Ward & Wallace Durand) 44 E. 14th

Durand & Hawes (Frederick F. Durand & John B. Hawes) 18 W. 33d

Durant Land Improvement Co. (Frederick C. Durant, Pres.; Howard M. Durant, Treas.; Capital, $80,000. Trustees: Frederick C. & Howard M. Durant) 1 B'way

Durbrow & Ayers (William Darbrow & Henry E. Ayers) 111 B'way

Durbrow & Hearne (Alfred F. Durbrew & Robert J. Hearne) 369 Canal

Duren & Costigan (Henry Duren & Kyran E. Costigan) 184 Maiden la.

Durfee, Smith & Barber (John F. Durfee, William H. Smith & James F. Barber) 9 Bond

Durfey & Reynolds (Joseph P. Durfey & David L. Reynolds) 8 John

Durham House Drainage Co. (Caleb W. Durham, Pres.; Charles F. Whitney, Sec. Capital $200,000. Directors: F. B. Wilson, Henry J. Gielow, A. R. & Celeb W. Durham, Charles F. Whitney) 158 W. 27th

Durkee A. W. & Co. (dissolved) 45 B'way

Durkee E. R. & Co. (George H. Burgess, Eugene W. Durkee & David M. Moore, only) 187 Water

Durland Riding Academy Co. (Edward S. Stokes, Pres.; Dwight Townsend, Sec.; William Durland, Treas. Capital, $150,000. Directors: William Durland, Nathan M. Jewett, Edward S. Stokes) Grand Circle c Boulevard

Duross Automatic Link Coupler Co. (inoperative) 21 Murray

Duryea John & Co. (John & William H. Duryea) 29 Gansevoort, W. Washn. mkt

Duryea, Watts & Co. (Ltd.) (Charles H. Duryea, Pres.; William J. Watts, Sec.; William S. Weiss, Treas. Capital, $10,000. Directors: Charles H. Duryea, William J. Watts, William S. Weiss, George A. Watts) 19 Whitehall

Duryea's W. E., Sons (Charles M. & Andrew J. Duryea) 119 Warren

Duryee Peter & Co. (William H. Cowl, only) 215 G'wich & 68 Vesey

Duschnes Henry & Co. (Henry Duschnes & Charles Lieb) 68 Prince

Dusenbury H. & Co. (Henry & Joseph W. & J. Warren Dusenbury) 90 West

Dusenbury & Bond (C. Coles & Louis Dusenbury & William W. Bond) 11 Murray

Dusenbury's Thomas, Sons (estate of Thomas Dusenbury, only) 528 W. 34th

Dusinberre & Co. (Theodore L. Dusinberre, Robert E. Small & William H. Corss) 462 E. 136th

SPECIAL ATTENTION PAID TO THIS CLASS OF WORK } BANKERS' & BROKERS' CIRCULARS DELIVERED { THE TROW CITY DIRECTORY CO. 11 University Place.

DUT 84 EAS

Dutch A. & Son (Alfred & Alfred Dutch jr.) 62 South
Dutcher & Edmister (Silas B. Dutcher & Willard E. Edmister) 58 William
Dutell & Co. (dissolved) 1148 Third av.
Dutel & Holmes (dissolved) 7 Bridge
Dutton E. P. & Co. (Edward P. Dutton & Charles A. Clapp) 31 W. 23d
Dutton & Disbrow (dissolved) 165 Greene
Dutton & Rhodes (Charles R. Dutton, Benjamin F. Rhodes & Asa S. Dutton) 90 Bowery
Dutton & Townsend (Charles H. Townsend & Stephen C. Clarke, only) 46 Beaver & ft. Seventh
Dutton & Willets (Charles K. Dutton & Thomas W. Willets) 146 Front
Duval & Co. (Charles L. Duval, no Co.) 14 S. William
Duval & Eagan (Hortense A. Duval & Pierson R. Eagan) 16 W. 23d
Duvivier & Co. (Charles A. & Edward A. Duvivier) 49 Broad
Duxbury Co. (Thomas C. Snedeker, Pres.; Charles R. Duxbury, Sec. Capital, $100,000. Directors: Thomas C. & William R. Snedeker, Charles R. Duxbury) 116 Franklin
Dwight John & Co. (John & John B. Dwight & William I. Walker) 11 Old sl. & First av. c E. 112th
D'Wolf & Parsons (dissolved) 52 B'way
Dwyer Thomas N. & Co. (Thomas N. Dwyer & James Rorke) 40 Barclay
Dwyer Brothers (carpenters) (dissolved) 401 W. 33d
Dwyer Brothers (liquors) (Patrick & James E. Dwyer) 687 Second av.
Dwyer & Sands (James Dwyer & Richard L. Sands) 30 W. 4th
Dyck & Fuelling (Charles P. Dyck & William L. Fuelling) 187 William
Dye & Castree (John H. Dye & John W. Castree) 154 Sixth av.
Dyer H. B. & Co. (Henry B. Dyer, no Co.) 206 B'way
Dyer H. P. & Co. (Horatio P. Dyer & John W. Turtle) 194 Front
Dyer & Seely (Richard N. Dyer & Henry W. Seely) 40 Wall
Dyott & Co. (Charles G. Dyott & Edward B. Williams) 52 Wall

E

Eadie W. R. & A. R. (William R. & Andrew R.) 17 Lawton av. W. Washn. mkt
Eagan J. & Co. (John Eagan, no Co.) 155 Grand
Eagan & Leake (Michael Eagan & Austin Leake) 225 Spring & 9 Macdougal
Eager J. & J. (estate of Joseph Eager, only) 34 Cliff
Eagle Cloak Co. (Bischoff, Adler & Co. proprs.) 57 Walker
Eagle Embroidering Works (Edward H. Horner, propr.) 86 Walker
Eagle Fire Co. (Alexander J. Clinton, Pres.; Thomas J. Gaines, Sec. Capital, $300,000. Directors: James A. Roosevelt, Henry Meyer, Josiah S. Blossom, Frederic W. Stevens, Alexander J. Clinton, Augustus F. Holly, George G. De Witt jr., Joseph H. Choate, John D. Skidmore, George G. Williams, M. Bayard Brown, Charles De Rahm jr. Wilson G. Hunt) 71 Wall
Eagle Jet & Onyx Mfg. Co. (Joseph J. Cohn, propr.) 41 Maiden la.
Eagle Lock Co. (Mortimer C. Ogden, Pres.; Rollin J. Plumb, Sec. Capital, $600,000. Directors: Mortimer C. Ogden, R. D. H. Allen, Elisha Johnson, Rollin J. Plumb, R. H. Laimbeer, John S. Gray, O. D. Hunter) 93 Chambers
Eagle Machine Oil Co. (Israel M. Manson, propr.) 235 South
Eagle Novelty Works (refused) 137 Elm
Eagle Oil Co. (Charles C. Burke, Pres.; further inf. refused) 26 B'way
Eagle Paper Co. (not inc.) (Morris Adler, Isaac Liebmann, Lewis J. Trounstine & Morton L. Adler) 90 Walker
Eagle Pencil Co. (Emil Berolzheimer, Pres.; Leopold Ansbacher, Treas.; Charles S. Braisted, Sec. Directors: Emil Berolzheimer, Samuel Kraus, Leopold Ansbacher, Charles S. Braisted) 73 Franklin & 710 E. 14th
Eagle Refining Co. (George H. Moore, Pres.; Ernest H. Moore, Sec. Capital, $60,000. Directors: George H. Moore, Robert S. Turnbull, Ernest H. Moore) 154 Maiden la.
Eagle Tube Co. (Clarence Stephens, Pres.; Melvin Stephens, Sec. Capital, $160,000. Directors: Melvin Stephens, Uri M. Hazard, Allen W. Brainard, Joseph Richardson, Clarence Stephens) 41 Dey
Eagle Wire Works (Emil Battey, propr) 484 Sixth av. & 46 W. 30th
Eagle Wrought Iron Works (Hoffmann & Schuback, proprs.) 123 Horatio & 524 West
Ealy John W., Co. (John W. Ealy, propr.) 230 B'way
Eames Vacuum Brake Co. (John C. Thompson, Pres.; George R. Massey, Sec. Capital, $500,000. Directors: John C. Thompson, Royal C. Vilas, George R. Massey, Henry W. Boyer, Charles A. Starbuck, Thomas G. Carson, Prentiss W. Scudder, Henry M. Stevens, Edward C. Hodges, Abraham Avery, George A. Bagley, Asariah H. Sawyer, Dennis O'Brien) 115 B'way
Eames & Moore (Francis L. Eames, H. Ramsdell Moore & Peter A. Hardy) 30 New & 66 Exchange pl.
Eardenson R. & Co. (Robert Eardenson & Isaac Henris) 707 & 797 Eighth av.
Eardley & Winterbottom (Frederick W. Eardley & John J. Winterbottom) 12 Jacob
Earl & Son (Henry E. Earl, only) 1263 B'way
Earl & Wilson (William S. Earl, Washington & Arthur R. Wilson & Edgar K. Betts) 33 E. 17th
Earle Brothers (Joseph P. & William P. Earle) 136 Pearl
Earls & Co. (James G. Timolat, only) 59 S. 5th av.
Earle & Hoffmann (Franklin Earle & Charles Hoffmann) 506 W. 53d
Earley & Prendergast (Martin J. Earley & Laurance E. Prendergast) 229 B'way
Early John & Co. (John Early & Patrick Cavanagh) 5 Hudson, 145 Chambers & 127 Reade
Early & Kelly (Maria L. Early & Catharine E. Kelly) 293 Fifth av.
Easley Mfg. Co. (Delafield & Reardon, proprs.) 108 Chambers
E. Brooklyn Realty Co. (John S. Cain, Pres.; Paul Cain, Sec.; Harry Stucky, Treas. Capital, $20,000. Trustees: John S. Cain, Harry Stucky, Augustus S. & Louis C. Whiton, Charles Bell) 115 B'way
E. Jersey Water Co. (Elisha F. Wilbur, Pres.; David G. Baird, Sec.; Edward D. Adams, Treas. Capital, $3,000,000. Directors: Elisha F. Wilbur, Edward D. Adams, David G. Baird, Henry S. Drinker) 2 Wall
E. R. Electric Light Co. (Seymour G. Smith, Pres.; Edward Duffy, Sec. Capital, $1,000,000. Directors: Seymour G. Smith, John N. Hayward, Edward Duffy, John J. Moore, Z. J. Halpin, Meyer Thalmessinger, William H. Taylor) 425 E. 24th

MERCHANTS EXCHANGE NAT. BANK OF THE CITY OF N. Y.
SOLICITS YOUR ACCOUNT. **257 Broadway.**
PHINEAS C. LOUNSBURY, President.   ALLEN S. APGAR, Cashier.

EAS   85   ECK

E. R. Melting Co. (Joseph H. Ladew, propr.) ft. E. 44th

E. R. Mill & Lumber Co. (George H. Toop, Pres.; George T. Crombie, Sec. Capital, $75,000. Directors: John Hanson, George H. Toop, Homer J. Baudet) 425 E. 92d

E. R. National Bank (Charles Jenkins, Pres.; Zenas E. Newell, Cashier; Wilbur F. Smith, Notary. Capital, $250,000. Directors: David & Charles Banks, A. D. Porter, Charles Jenkins, William Phelps, Joseph Rogers, William H. Huma, Raymond Jenkins) 682 B'way

E. R. Oil Works (Hannah Michael, propr.) ft. E. 108d

E. R. Railway Co. (Benjamin S. Henning, Pres.; Otto Andreae jr. Sec. Capital, $100,000. Directors: Benjamin S. Henning, Otto Andreae jr. J. A. Patterson, H. C. Illmers, Robert Whitehill, Grinnell Burr, Charles H. Odell, J. C. O'Brien, C. W. Smith, Alexander Curtis) 15 Broad

E. R. Savings Institution (William H. Slocum, Pres.; Charles A. Whitney, Sec. Trustees: William H. Slocum, John W. Avery, Peter H. Titus, Thompson Pinckney, Charles F. Goodhue, Nathaniel M. Terry, John N. Hayward, Hamilton S. Searles, William Montrose, Henry L. Slote, John H. Waydell, Amasa H. Scoville, Alfred Barber, William C. Smith, Joshua H. Cort, Charles Frazier, Henry T. Nichols, Brinkerhoff Myers, Andrew J. Robinson, J. Sinclair Armstrong, George Abell) 3 Chambers

E. R. Steam Laundry (Frank A. Bates, propr.) 312 E. 22d

E. R., Central Park & N.R.R.R. Co. (Inf. unattainable) 49 Chambers

East Side Bank (Thomas R. Manners, Pres.; James S. Oakley, Cashier. Capital, $500,000. Directors: Walter Luttgen, James Doyle, John Overbeck, Samuel B. Clark, William N. Cromwell, Samuel M. Janney, George G. Hallock jr. G. Wessels, Alva Trowbridge, Christian Friedman, Charles G. Emery, D. S. Willard, Frederick Jones, D. O. Eshbaugh, Jesse C. Keys, Jacob Horowitz, Thomas S. Olliva, John Byrns, Thomas R. Manners) 459 Grand

East Side Building Assn. (Inf. unattainable) 189 Bowery

East Side Co-operative Building & Loan Assn. (no inf.) 77 W. 125th

East Side Tailoring Co. (S. Stein & Co. proprs.) 2086 Third av.

East Side Union Printing Co. (not inc.) (Frederick Schaerr & William Gottlob) 2 Spring

E. Tenn. Land Co. (Clinton B. Fisk, Pres.; Alphonso A. Hopkins, Sec.; Adam W. Wagnalls, Treas. Capital, $3,000,000. Directors: Clinton B. Fisk, James B. Hobbs, Ferdinand Schumacher, Francis W. Breed, Adam W. Wagnalls, William Silverwood, John Hopewell jr. J. R. Leeson, W. C. Harriman, Frederick Gates, Philip S. Mason, E. M. Goodall, Alphonzo A. Hopkins) 96 B'way

E. Tenn., Virginia & Georgia Railway Co. (Samuel Thomas. Pres.; Louis M. Schwan, Sec.; J. Nell Mitchell, Treas. Capital, $57,900,000. Directors: Samuel Thomas, Calvin S. Brice, George S. Scott, John H. Inman, John G. Moore, Thomas M. Logan, Edward J. Sanford, William S. Chisholm, John Greenough, William L. Bull, George Coppell, Charles M. McGhee, John R. Hall, Evan Howell, George J. Gould) 10 Wall

Eastern Distilling Co. (Maximilian Fleischmann, Pres.; Jacob P. Balter, Treas. Capital, $25,000; further inf. refused) 701 Washn.

Eastern Furniture Assn. (Joseph T. Lamm, Pres.; George R. Emerick, Sec.; Andrew J. Emerick, Treas.) 211 Canal

Eastern Furniture Mfg. Co. (Thomas Stacom, propr.) 2270 Third av.

Eastern Mfg. Co. (no inf.) 712 B'way

Eastman & Mandeville (James C. Eastman, only) 153 Maiden la.

Eastman's Co. (Timothy C. Eastman, Pres.; Henry Van Holland, Sec.; Joseph Eastman, Treas. Capital, $750,000. Directors: Timothy C. & Joseph Eastman, George G. Williams, George H. Taylor, Russell H. Monro) ft. W. 59th

Easton Electric Co. (inf. unattainable) 45 B'way

Easton & Co. (Newton C. Easton, no Co.) 229 & 1389 B'way

Easton & McMahon Transp. Co. (Owen Brady, Pres.; James T. Easton. Sec. Capital, $100,000. Directors: Owen Brady, James T. Easton) 2 Coenties sl.

Easton, Nichols & Co. (David A. Easton, Starr H. Nichols & Arthur I. Corner) 30 Broad

Easton's National Horse & Cattle Exchange (Ltd.) (William Easton, Pres.; Horace Theobald Sec.) 1129 B'way

Easy Starting Whiffletree Co. (Ltd.) (inoperative) 906 Third av.

Eaton George A. & Co. (inf. unattainable) 194 B'way

Eaton Mfg. Co. (Jacob New, Pres.; Frederick W. Ebert, Sec. Capital, $250,000. Directors: Jacob New, Frederick W. Ebert) 75 Greene

Eaton W. L. & Brother (William L. & Henry Eaton) 109 W. 10th

Eaton & Lewis (Sherburne B. Eaton & Eugene H. Lewis) 120 B'way

Eaton, Cole & Burnham Co. (John Eaton, Pres.; Edward H. Cole, Treas.; William H. Douglas, Sec. Capital, $850,000. Directors: John Eaton, Edward H. Cole, William H. Douglas, Edward G. Burnham) 62 Fulton

Eatontown Improvement Co. (George B. Smith, Pres.; Frank H. Brown, Sec.; Edwin V. Machette, Treas. Capital, $200,000. Directors: George B. Smith, Frank H. Brown, Edwin V. Machette, William H. B. Thomas, Charles M. Wilkins) 111 B'way

Eaves Costume Co. (Albert G. Eaves, Pres.; Charles F. Hallett, Sec. Capital, $100,000. Directors: Albert G. Eaves, Charles F. Hallett, Joseph Lublin) 63 E. 12th

Ebbecke & Stieuen (Philip J. Ebbecke & F. Stieuen) 258 W. 28th

Ebbets & Wright (dissolved) 124 E. 121st

Ebenstein S. H. & Son (Solomon H. & Alfred Ebenstein) 357 Grand

Eberhardt Charles A. & Co. (estate of Herman G. D. Meschendorf, only) 184 Duane

Eberhart Marcus & Son (Marcus & Francis Eberhart) 1402 First av.

Eberle J. & Sons (dissolved) 741 Second av. & 998 Tenth av.

Eberle & Fritsche (Herman Eberle & Max Fritsche) 191 Worth

Ebermayer A. & Co. Adolph Ebermayer, no Co.) 89 Hudson

Eberth & Ludwig (dissolved) 17 William, 86 Duane & Custom h.

Ebling Philip & William, Brewing Co. (Philip Ebling, Pres; William Ebling, Treas.; William Ebling 2d, Sec. Capital, 750,000. Directors: Philip & William & William Ebling 2d) 760 St. Ann's av.

Echo Telephone Co. (Charles E. Conyngham, Pres.; Redmond Conyngham, Sec.; W. W. Tucker, Treas.; further inf. unattainable) 79 Cedar

Eck N. & Co. (Nicholas Eck & Zerline Schwarz) E. 98th c First av.

Eckel August & Co. (dissolved) 36 White

Eckenroth Francis & Son (Francis & Henry C. Eckenroth) 622 Fifth

Eckert William & Son (William & Edward J. Eckert) 232 W. 41st

Eckert J. B. & Co. (Justus B. Eckert & Charles W. Henry) 168 Washn. mkt

**SNOW, CHURCH & CO.,
265 & 267 BROADWAY.**

COLLECTIONS IN ALL PARTS OF THE WORLD.
T. C. Campbell and Arthur Murphy, *Counsel.*
TELEPHONE, 785 MURRAY.

Eckert & Clark (John A. Eckert & Percy W. Clark) 62 Liberty

Eckford Ship Windlass Co. (John Gardner, Pres.; David W. McLean, Sec.; further inf. unattainable) 108 Cannon

Eckhardt & Co. (Martin Eckhardt, Kirby S. Blaut & Adam Fecher) 361 Rivington

Eckmeyer & Co. (Gustave D. Eckmeyer, no Co.) 42 Beaver

Eckstein Charles G. & Co. (Charles G. Eckstein & Frederick Gopper) 82 Liberty

Eckstein White Lead Co. (inf. unattainable) 100 Malden la.

Eckstein & Schrader (no inf.) 184 Canal

Eckstein & Wertheimer (Bernhard Eckstein & Emanuel & Emil Wertheimer) 529 B'way

Eclipse Electric Co. (Charles A. Hussey, propr.) 144 G'wich

Eclipse Wringer Co. (Henry Schaeberg, propr.) 19 Eighth av.

Economic Gas Engine Co. (George B. Post, Pres.; William H. Goadby, Sec. Directors: George B. Post, William H. Goadby, W. Y. Mortimer, Charles F. Stone, George M. Hopkins) 34 Dey

Economic Light & Fuel Co. (Henry Bradstreet, Pres.; Charles S. Carnaghan, Sec.; Thomas S. Smith, Treas. Capital, $250,000. Directors: Henry Bradstreet, E. Benjamin Ramsdell, Thomas S. Smith, George Ramsdell, Charles S. Carnaghan) 115 B'way

Economical Refrigerating Co. (Inoperative) 71 Beekman

Economist Press (Richard R. Bowker, Pres.; Adolph Growoll, Sec.; Daniel R. Bowker, Treas. Capital, $12,500. Trustees: Richard R. Bowker, Adolph Growoll, Daniel R. Bowker) 330 Pearl

Economy Clean Towel Supply Co. (Charles A. Maurice, propr.) 19 Park pl. & 18 Murray

Economy Refrigerating Co. (Charles D. Rhinehart, Pres.; Oliver E. Stanton Sec. Capital, $200,000. Directors: Charles D. Rhinehart, Oliver E. Stanton, P. R. Gray, John J. D. Trenor) 280 B'way

Eddison Fire Extinguisher Co. (dissolved) 51 John

Eddy S. & Co. (Samuel Eddy, no Co.) 145 B'way

Eddy & Jones (Herman J. Eddy jr. & Edward E. Jones) 320 B'way

Edelhoff & Rinke (Charles A. Edelhoff & Emil Rinke) 171 Greene

Edelman & Klein (Isidor Edelman & Abraham Klein) 11 Ann

Edelmann & Smith (dissolved) 102 Chambers

Edelmeyer & Morgan Hod Elevator Co. (William C. Morgan, Pres.; John H. Edelmeyer, Treas. Capital, $15,200. Directors: William C. Morgan, John H. Edelmeyer, Walter W. Youmans, Charles W. Morgan) 333 W. 49th

Eden Musée Am. Co. (Ltd.) (Theodore Heilman, Pres.; James W. Monk Sec.; Louis Windmuller, Treas. Capital, $130,000. Directors: Theodore Heilman, Abraham Van Santvoord, Louis Windmuller, James W. Monk, Joseph Keppler, George F. Victor, Count Kessler) 55 W. 23d

Eden H. W. & Co. (Harold W. Eden & John J. Voorhees) 197 Pearl

Edesheimer Brothers (Michael & Isaac Edesheimer) 622 G'wich

Edey Brothers (Charles L. & Henry Edey) 50 B'way

Edey & Connell (Charles C. Edey & James B. Connell) 105 Wall & 113 Front

Edgar & Dunn (William A. Edgar & James C. Dunn) 296 Wash'n.

Edgar & Lowrey (Newbold L. R. Edgar & Grosvenor Lowrey) 9 Broad

Edgar's George C., Sons (no inf.) 1269 Ninth av.

Edgerton C. A. & Son (Charles A. & C. Frederick Edgerton) 99 Franklin

Edge Hill Wine Co. (Ernest Dichman, Pres.; George A. Morrison, Sec. Capital, $250,000. Directors: Ernest Dichman, George Stoker, George A. Morrison, George W. Phillips, Edward A. Pierson) 19 Barclay

Edge W. C. & Sons (no inf.) 15 John

Edgewater Stk Co. (no inf.) 47 Leonard

Edinger Brothers & Jacobi (Morris B. Edinger, Michael Jacobi & Solomon M. Mandel, only) 2 N. Y. & B'klyn bridge

Edison Electric Illuminating Co. (George Foster Peabody, Pres.; James D. Skehan, Sec. Capital, $4,500,000. Directors: John I. Beggs, R. R. Bowker, Charles E. Crowell, C. H. Coster, Thomas A. Edison, J. Buchanan Henry, Edward H. Johnson, J. P. Marquand, George Foster Peabody, Frank S. Smithers, Spencer Trask, Henry Villard, J. Hood Wright) 16 Broad & 439 Fifth av.

Edison Electric Light Co. (J. Hobart Herrick, Pres.; Frank S. Hastings, Sec. Capital, $1,500,000. Trustees: Thomas C. Buck, Charles H. Coster, Noah Davis, John W. Doane, Thomas A. Edison, J. Hobart Herrick, Samuel Insull, Edward H. Johnson, Morris H. Smith, Frank S. Smithers, Spencer Trask, Henry Villard, J. Hood Wright) 44 Wall

Edison Electric Light Co. of Europe (Ltd.) (inf. unattainable) 19 Dey

Edison General Electric Co. (Henry Villard, Pres.; A. Marcus, Sec.; Edward Eden, Treas. Capital, $12,000,000. Directors: Charles H. Coster, J. Hobart Herrick, J. Hood Wright, Carl Soburz, Frank S. Smithers, Samuel Insull, Edward H. Johnson, Thomas A. Edison, Henry Villard, William D. Marks, A. Marcus) 44 Wall

Edison Machine Works (Thomas A. Edison, Pres.; W. E. Gilmore, Sec.; Samuel Insull, Treas. Capital, $750,000. Directors: Thomas A. Edison, Charles Batchelor, Samuel Insull, John Kruesi, H. M. Livor, J. Hutchinson) 19 Dey

Edison Spanish Colonial Light Co. (Thomas A. Edison, Pres.; Francis P. Lowry, Sec.; A. Arango, Treas. Capital, $100,000; further inf. unattainable) 71 B'way

Edison United Mfg. Co. (dissolved) 65 Fifth av.

Edman & Kramer, (Solomon Edman & Henry J. Kramer) 128 E. B'way

Edmiston W. R. & Co. (William R. Edmiston & George W. Perkins) 695 B'way

Edmonston's S. S., Brother (Peter H. Edmonston) 47 Broad

Edson Franklin & Co. (Franklin & Franklin Edson jr.) 485 Produce Ex.

Edson Brothers & Edison (A. D. & Frank & William D. Edson jr. & Theodore P. Gilman) 356 Wash'n.

Edwards Joseph & Co. (Joseph Edwards & James R. F. Kelly) 412 Water & 143 Cherry

Edwards A. E. & Co. (James H. Killough & Frank E. Stults, only) 249 Wash'n.

Edwards C. & Co. (Charles H. Edwards, no Co.) 85 Park pl.

Edwards H. H. & Co. (no inf.) 150 B'way

Edwards W. & Co.(cigars) (William & Andrew Edwards) 257 E. 127th

Edwards W. & Co. (gilders) (no inf.) 196 Worth

Edwards & Co. (brokers) (refused) 335 B'way

Edwards & Co. (elec. insts.) (Robert Edwards & Adam Lungen) 7 Dey & Railroad av. n E. 144th

Edwards & Malone (Richard Edwards & Dennis Malone) 282 Seventh av.

Edwards & Odell (Walter Edwards & Hamilton Odell) 120 B'way

Edwards & Wilson (Martin N. Edwards & James S. Wilson) 322 G'wich & 187 Duane

Edwards & Wright (Hosea M. Edwards & William H. Wright) 20 Manhattan mkt

Eells & Sargent (dissolved) 51 Exchange pl.

WATER METERS, GAS ENGINES, | NATIONAL METER CO.
FOR PUMPING AND POWER. | **252 Broadway, N. Y.**

EGA 87 ELE

Egan James & Co. (James Egan & William F. Newkirk) 367 Seventh av.
Egan K. & Co. (Kieran Egan & Michael J. Morris) 19 Barling sl.
Egan P. J. & Co. (Patrick J. Egan & Solomon Pulver) 54 Lispenard
Egan & Hallcey (John J. Egan & Daniel Hallcey) 318 E. 23d
Egbert & Case (Thomas K. Egbert & George W. Case) 50 Warren
Ege & Otis (Benjamin W. Otis, Jacob W. Ege & Henry C. Larowe) 78 Dey & 16 Hewitt av. W. Washn. mkt
Egerton William & Co. (William Egerton & Charles G. Adams) 2 Cooper Union
Eggebrecht & Bernhardt (Carl Eggebrecht & Siegmund Bernhardt) 48 Howard
Eggers Henry & Co. (Henry Eggers & Frederick Hambrock, 325 G'wich. Henry & Herman Eggers & Frederick Hambrock, 166 E. 129th)
Eggers Brothers (Conrad & Herman Eggers) 133 Hudson
Eggers & Heinlein (Otto J. Eggers & Hans Heinlein) 60 Stone & 97 Pearl
Eggers & Weisman (Carl A. Eggers & John Weisman) 653 Courtlandt av.
Eggert William & Co. (William & Edward Eggert) 245 Pearl & 20 Cliff
Eggert's D., Sons (John & Dominick B. Eggert) 74 Wall
Eggleston F. E. & Co. (Francis E. Eggleston & Augustus F. Tuthill) 46 New
Eginton & Co. (dissolved) 570 Hudson
Egleston Brothers & Co. (David S. Egleston & Andrew W. Nicholson, only) 267 Front & 166 South
Ehlers & Rosemeisl (Luer Ehlers & Joseph Rosemeisl) 109 E. 125th
Ehlers & Schmidt (John F. Ehlers & Frederick W. Schmidt) 866 Washn.
Ehlers & Weber (John W. F. Ehlers & Albert R. Weber) 44½ Malden la.
Ehmann & Co. (Gustave J. Ehmann, no Co.) 56 Warren
Ehrenreich Brothers (cigars) (dissolved) 61 Clinton
Ehrenreich Brothers(coal)(Moses & Berman Ehrenreich) ft. E. 63d, 201 E. 78th, ft. E. 107th & 209 E. 86th
Ehrentreu Philip & Son (Philip & Adolph Ehrentreu) r 266 E. Houston
Ehrhard & Hagen (Philip Ehrhard & Marcarius Hagen) 247 W. 28th
Ehrhardt H. F. & Co. (dissolved) 627 Madison av.
Ehrich Brothers (Samuel W. & Julius S. Ehrich) 367 Sixth av.
Ehrichs Brothers (Nicholas & Martin Ehrichs) 20 Stanton
Ehrler & Kaiser (Dominick Ehrler & Joseph Kaiser) 6 Chatham sq.
Ehrlich & Buchsbaum (no inf.) 1413 Second av.
Ehrman & Co. (dissolved) 853 B'way
Ehrsam & Harding (William F. Ehrsam & Alfred A. Harding) 284 E. 53d
Eibenschutz & Malter (dissolved) 419 B'way
Eichhold & Miller (Charles Eichhold & Edward A. Miller) 626 B'way & 160 Crosby
Eichler John, Brewing Co. (John Eichler, Pres.; Louis J. Heintz, Sec. Capital, $500,000. Directors: John Eichler, Jacob Siegel, Louis J. & John C. Heintz) 3582 Third av.
Eichler Brothers (Ignatz & David Eichler) 1054 Second av.
Eickemeyer Dynamo Machine Co. (Rudolf Eickemeyer, Pres; Edward A. Nichols, Sec. Capital, $60,000. Directors: Rudolf Eickemeyer, Samuel Shethar, Edward A. Nichols) 737 B'way

Eidlitz Marc & Son (Marc & Otto M. Eidlitz) 308 E. 59th & 123 E. 73d
Eidt & Lehnert (no inf.) 665 B'way
Eidt & Weyand (Jacob Eidt & Henry Weyand) 850 Second av.
Eifert Brothers (Frederick & Jacob Eifert) r 183 Attorney
Eiffert & Schultz (no inf.) 691 First av.
Eighth Av. R. R. Co. (George Law, Pres.; James Affleck, Sec. Capital, $1,000,000. Directors: Otis W. Randall, George Law, Jacob Hays, Joseph H. Goodwin, Joseph J. O'Donohue, Edward St. J. Hays, James T. Closson, Herman B. Wilson, S. H. Herriman, William Ravensteyn, G. Granville Wright, James & James G. Affleck) 828 Eighth av.
Eilshemius H. G. & F. E. (Henry G. jr. & Frederick E.) 265 B'way
Eimer & Amend (Bernard G. Amend, only) 207 Third av.
Einbigler & Adler (Rudolph Einbigler & Christian Adler) 435 Seventh av.
Einstein, Finn & Waxelbaum (Elias Einstein, Morris Finn & Joseph Waxelbaum) 548 B'way & 82 Crosby
Einstein, Wolff & Co. (Isaac D. Einstein & Emil Wolff, no Co.) 443 B'way
Eiseman Brothers (Samuel & Moses L. Eiseman) 73 Grand
Eisenberg & Koplowitz (Samuel Eisenberg & Joseph Koplowitz) 2 Birmingham
Eisenmann Brothers (Emil F. W. & Oscar F. & Gustav F. Eisenmann) 22 Malden la.
Eisenstein & Lewine (Julius D. Eisenstein & Asher Lewine) 57 E. B'way
Eising E. & Co. (Emanuel Eising & John C. Dyckhoff) 47 Front
Eisner M. H. & D. L. (Mark H. & David L.) 400 E. 46th & 818 First av.
Eisner & Mendelson Co. (Adolph W. Miller, Pres.; Moritz Eisner, Sec.; Joseph Mendelson, Treas. Capital, $200,000. Directors: Adolph W. Miller, Moritz Eisner, L. Rosskan, Joseph Mendelson, Frederick Ashenbach) 6 Barclay
Eisner & Singer (no. inf.) 1193 First av.
Eisner F. & Co. (Frederick Eisner & Albert Brunner) 19 Bible h.
El Chontaduro Mining Co. (inf. unattainable) r 25 William
El Cristo Gold & Silver Mining Co. (Santiago Perez-Triana, Pres.; James W. Thompson, Sec. Capital, $1,000,000. Trustees: Herbert B. Parsons, Edward Motz, Santiago Perez-Triana, James S. Leeds, Jonathan Brownell, Lee H. Shryock, James W. Thompson) 45 B'way
El Oro Mining Co. (William N. Thompson, Pres.; John E. Whitman, Sec. Capital, $10,000,000. Directors: William N. Thompson, William T. Hamilton, John A. Beall, Robert Patrick, John E. Whitman, Daniel Valentine) 16 Beaver
Elastic Truss Co. (refused) 822 B'way
Elcox H. & Co. (dissolved) 41 Malden la.
Elderd & Co. (dissolved) 2472 Third av.
Eldred & Haley (Charles H. Eldred & Irvin Haley) 9 Fulton fish mkt
Eldredge R. N. & Co. (Edward I. Eldredge, only) 327 Washn. mkt
Eldridge C. H. & Co. (Charles H. Eldridge & Edward J. Hartman) Pier 53 E. R.
Electric Age Publishing Co. (John B. Taltavall, Pres.; George E. Holbrook, Sec.; Thomas R. Taltavall, Treas.; further inf. unattainable) 5 Dey
Electric Automatic Instructor Co. (inf. unattainable) 186 Stewart bldg.
Electric Composite Co. (no inf.) 85 B'way

EXCELSIOR BIRD FOOD. The recognized standard. The most reliable for your Canary. Use no other. Insist upon getting it. Packed only by G. ROSENSTEIN & CO., 373 Washington Street, New York.

ELE 88 ELL

Electric Construction & Supply Co. (Herbert Torrey, Pres.; Henry G. Rice, Sec.; Robert D. Corey, Treas. Capital, $120,000. Directors: Henry G. Rice, Herbert Torrey, Samuel T. Hillman, Robert B. Corey) 18 Cortlandt

Electric Couch Co. (J. Barnes Schmalz, propr.) 127 Fifth av.

Electric Cutlery Co. (Louis C. Fuller, Pres.; Clifford B. Fuller, Sec. Capital, $50,000. Directors: Louis C. & Clifford B. Fuller, David Eastman) 91 Chambers & 73 Reade

Electric Engineering & Supply Co. (Capital, $25,000. Directors: John P. Moffett, Henry C. Hodgkins, John V. Clarke, Charles T. Moffett, Francis H. Leonard jr.) no address

Electric Fire Protective Co. (William A. Simmons, Pres.; Howard P. Simmons, Sec.; Charles W. Wilder, Treas. Capital, $300,000. Directors: William A. & Howard P. Simmons, Uriah A. Pollard, Charles W. Wilder) 280 B'way

Electric Furniture Polish Co. (Denniston & Flynn, proprs.) 120 W. D'way

Electric Letter Box Co. (Charles F. Harms, propr.) 140 Broad

Electric Light & Power Co. (Capital, $500,000; further inf. unattainable) 54 Wall

Electric Light & Supply Co. (Arthur H. Rennie, propr.) 171 B'way

Electric Mfg. Co. (inf. unattainable) 45 B'way

Electric Mfg. Co. (Moore Brothers, proprs.) 108 Liberty

Electric Power Co. (Henry M. Hawkesworth, Pres.; William P. Stevenson, Sec.; Cornelius B. Gold, Treas. Capital, $700,000. Directors: Henry M. Hawkesworth, Cornelius B. Gold, Robert L. Belknap, Robert W. Hawkesworth, J. Dwight Ripley, Francis H. Weeks) 115 B'way

Electric Power Publishing Co. (Ralph W. Pope, Pres.; Frank L. Blanchard, Sec. Capital, $10,000. Directors: George H. Stockbridge, Henry W. Pope, Frank L. Blanchard, Ralph W. Pope) 132 Nassau

Electric Railway Co. of U. S (Robert E. Deyo, V. Pres.; William Molloy, Sec. Capital, $2,000,000. Directors: Robert E. Deyo, F. S. Hastings, Frederick F. Thompson, Cyrus W. & Stephen D. Field, John H. McClemoni, Edward H. Johnson, Spencer Trask, Jacob H. Herrick) 1 B'way

Electric Railway Trust Co. (inf. unattainable) 15 Broad

Electric Reporting Co. (James G. Smith, Pres.; Jeremy G. Case, Sec. Capital, $200,000. Directors: James G. Smith, Jeremy G. Case) 171 B'way

Electric Signal Mfg. Co. (William Pierrepont Williams, Pres.; Andrew Z. Terhune, Treas. Capital, $1,000,000. Directors: E. P. Williams, G. J. Taube, E. P. Johnson, A. Z. Terhune, C. L. Browne, H. V. Cleaver) 45 B'way

Electric Stereopticon Advertising Co. (Emanuel L. S. Hart, propr.) 185 Fifth av.

Electric Sugar Refining Co. (in liquidation) 96 Cotton Ex.

Electric Time Co. (William P. Shinn, Pres.; Joseph A. Davidson, Sec. Capital, $500,000. Directors: William P. Shinn, Spencer Trask, Joseph A. Davidson, Wallace C. Andrews, Royal C. Peabody, Arthur W. Soper) 50 B'way

Electrical Accumulator Co. (inf. unattainable) 44 B'way

Electrical Review Publishing Co. (George Worthington, Pres.; Charles W. Price, Sec. Capital, $30,000. Trustees: George Worthington, Charles W. Price, Henry D. Lyman) 13 Park row

Electro Engraving & Printing Co. (inoperative) 66 Reade

Electro Light Engraving Co. (not Inc.) (Charles A. Breck, Benjamin W. Wilson jr. & Alfred M. Messer) 150 William

Electro Silicon Co. (Andrew G. Coffin, Pres.; Henry A. Schenck, Sec. Capital, $30,000. Directors: Andrew G. & Isaac S. Coffin, Henry A. Schenck) 72 John

Electro-Dynamic Light Co. (inoperative) 82 Nassau

Electro-Pneumatic Time Co. (Capital, $100,000. Trustees: Edward Uhl, Adolph Schwartzman, Paul Goepel, Louis C. Raegener, George Gehe ; further inf. unattainable) 45 B'way

Eleventh Ward Bank (Henry Steers, Pres.; Charles E. Brown, Cashier ; Joseph W. Swain, Notary. Capital, $100,000. Directors : Henry Steers, George W. Quintard, John Englis, Edward V. Loew, David H. & Edwin A. McAlpin, John R. Hoffmire, George E. Wood, Edward S. Knapp, James Gregory, Charles E. Brown) 147 Av. D

Elfelt A. B. & Co. (dissolved) 0 Desbrosses

Elfers J. H. & Co. (John H. Elfers & William & Otto Rank) 458 E. 10th

Elgar & Sheehan (Francis R. Elgar & Daniel F. Sheehan) 388 Hudson

Elias Harris & Son (Harris & Herman Elias) 65 E. B'way

Elias Henry, Brewing Co. (Edward Hanitzsch, Pres.; Henry J. Lippe, Sec. Capital, $500,000. Directors: Edward Hanitzsch, Henry Elias jr, Henry J. Lippe) 403 E. 54th & 404 E. 55th

Elias Brothers & Co. (Raphael & Henry F. & Robert F. Elias) 20 Walker

Eilsberg S. & Sons (Solomon & Elias & Benjamin Elisberg) 141 E. B'way

Elite Cloak & Suit Co. (James O'Flaherty, propr.) 470 B'way & 52 Mercer

Elite Works (Solomon Katz, propr.) 372 B'way

Elizabethport Cordage Co. (Elisha M. Fulton, Pres.; Elisha M. Fulton jr. Sec.; Willard F. Whitlock, Treas. Capital, $1,000,000. Directors: Elisha M. Fulton, Willard P. Whitlock, Edward M. & Elisha M. Fulton jr.) 46 South

Elizabethtown, Lexington & Big Sandy R. R. Co. (Joseph P. Lloyd, Pres.; William C. Emery, Sec.; Isaac E. Oates, Treas. Capital, $5,000,000. Directors: William C. Emery, Isaac E. Gates, George Watkins, Joseph P. Lloyd, Frank H. Davis, John Echols, Joseph S. Woolfolk, George O. Graves, George R. Nelson) 28 Broad

Elk Shirt Mfg. Co. (Oshinsky, Liberman & Co. proprs.) 11 White

Elkan S. & Co. (Siegfried Elkan & Morris Spiegel) 1862 Third av.

Elkeles S. & Co. (Samuel Elkeles, no Co.) 406 E. 104th

Elkins & Zerbe (Ira S. Elkins & James S. Zerbe) 298 B'way

Eller Maurice & Son (Maurice & Maurice Eller jr.) 183 Pearl

Ellery William P. & Brother (William P. & Charles K. Ellery) 30 Broad

Ellery & Garrison (dissolved) 500 Grand

Ellice John & Co. (John Ellice, no Co.) 81 Dey

Ellin, Kitson & Co. (Robert Ellin, John Henry & John W. Harrison, only) 510 W. 21st

Ellinger Julius & Co. (Julius Ellinger, no Co.) 51 Murray

Ellinger S. & Co. (dissolved) 83 Av. B

Ellinger Brothers (Lels & Max Ellinger) 1 B'way

Elliot & Rindlaub (Henry G. Elliot & John C. Rindlaub) 93 Barclay

Elliott James & Co. (linens) (James & John G. Elliott) 71 Leonard

Elliott James & Co. (paper) (dissolved) 12 James st. & 216 William

Elliott Mfg. Co. (inoperative) 41 John & 7 Dutch

Elliott William & Sons (William & William J. & Carl S. Elliott) 56 Dey

IDEN & CO., University Place, 9th to 10th Sts., N. Y. | **MANUFACTURERS OF GAS FIXTURES AND ELECTROLIERS**

ELL 89 EMP

Elliott & Co. (Alexander & George L. Elliott) 56 Wall
Elliott & Congle (Richard W. Elliott & William R. Congle) 52 Elizabeth
Elliott & Tompkins (J. Chetwood Elliott & F. Bianchi Tompkins) 62 D'way
Ellis John & Co. (John Ellis, Theodore M. Leonard & Wilbur D. Ellis) 187 Chambers
Ellis Mfg. Co. (not inc.) (Henry D. Harris & James W. Ellis) 71 D'way
Ellis A. C. & M. H. (Adam C. & Matthew H.) 140 Nassau
Ellis C. C. & Son (Christopher C. & Charles C. Ellis) 964 Third av.
Ellis & Co. (dissolved) 1686 Third av.
Ellis & Goltermann (Frederick L. Ellis & Herman Goltermann) 28 College pl.
Ellis & Macdonald (William H. Ellis & William G. Macdonald) 70 Park pl.
Ellis & Murray (William Ellis & John Murray) 642 Washn.
Ellis, Brooks & Co. (dissolved) 16 Clinton pl.
Ellis, Knapp & Co. (Abram B. & Waldo Ellis Knapp, only) 871 D'way
Ellison A. S. & Co. (Adolph S. Ellison & Samuel A. Ontner) 103 Greene
Ellison & Chambers (Thomas J. Ellison & Edwin J. Chambers) 2173 Seventh av.
Ellison & Pohlmann (John S. & Emma W. Ellison & Edward A. Pohlmann) 110 W. 19th
Ellison, Gill & Porteous (William D. Ellison, Charles C. Gill & Robert A. Porteous) 229 B'way
Ellor Brothers & Hall (Samuel & Joseph Ellor & William J. Hall) 160 Greene
Ellrodt & Co. (John C. Ellrodt, Co. refused) 858 Third av.
Ellsworth J. W. & Son (Joseph W. & William M. Ellsworth) 29 South
Elmenhorst & Co. (Frederick Elmenhorst, George Gravenhorst & Edgar A. Reincke) 123 Front
Elmira Bridge Co. (Ltd.) (Charles Kellogg, Pres.; William S. McCord, Sec.; Walter Hawxhurst, Treas. Capital, $100,000. Directors: Charles Kellogg, Walter Hawxhurst, William S. McCord, Robert Grimes, Everett E. Buchanan) 15 B'way
Elmira, Cortland & Northern R. R. Co. (Austin Corbin, Pres.; Everett R. Reynolds, Sec.; William G. Wheeler, Treas. Capital, $2,000,000. Directors: Henry W. Maxwell, Gilman S. Moulton, John R. Maxwell, Frederick W. Dunton, John P. Dosh, James D. Campbell, Thomas F. Ward, George S. Edgell, A. A. McLeod, James K. O. Sherwood, Austin Corbin, Everett R. Reynolds, William G. Wheeler) 192 B'way
Elsas, Kellar & Co. (Herman Elsas & David Keller, no Co.) 158 Franklin
Elsberg R. A. & Co. (Rebecca A. Elsberg & Ernest J. Kaltenbach) 213 Centre
Elstner J. M. & Co. (dissolved) 810 D'way
Elsworth J. & J. W., Co. (Joseph Elsworth, Pres.; J. Watson Elsworth, Sec. Capital, $30,000. Directors: Joseph & J. Watson & William E. Elsworth) ft. Charles
Elterich Art Tile Stove Works (George Meier, Pres.; G. Otto Elterich, Sec.; Henry Lindenmayr, Treas. Capital, $50,000. Trustees: George & Charles E. Meier, Otto P. & G. Otto Elterich, Gottlieb Gunther, Gustav L. Jaeger, Henry Lindenmayr) 805 Pearl
Elwell James W. & Co. (James W. Elwell, Thomas E. Sherwood & Charles F. Notman) 47 South
Elwood B. H. & E. E. (Byron H. & Ellsworth E.) 454 Broome
Ely Olin P. & Brother (Olin P. & Eugene Ely) 208 W. 125th

Ely Brothers (Charles C. & Alfred G. & Frederick Ely) 56 Warren
Ely & Co. (Alexander McIntyre & Charles A. Peck, only) 60 G'wich
Ely & Ramsay (Nathan L. Ely & Dick S. Ramsay) 247 Water
Ely & Walker (James R. Ely & Eugene Walker) 82 Nassau
Ely & Williams (Edward Ely & Edward P. Williams) 38 Park row
Ely & Wray (Griswold L. Ely & Edward M. Wray) 16 Warren
Emanuel E. F. & O. W. (dissolved) 48 Church
Emblem Book & Job Printing Co. (Isaacs & Blayer, proprs.) 400 Broome
Embossed Lumber & Fibre Co. (Inf. unattainable) 49 Liberty & ft. W. 20th
Emerald & Phœnix Brewing Co. of N. Y. (Thomas C. Lyman, Pres.; George H. Taylor, Sec.; Henry L. Greenman, Treas. Capital, $200,000. Directors: Thomas C. Lyman, Franz J. Kastner, Ely E. Goddard, Lucius T. Rossiter, Russell Henry Munro, Henry L. Greenman, George H. Taylor) 422 W. 38th
Emerson J. M. & Sons (Jesse M. & Edward R. & Jesse M. Emerson jr.) 26 Vesey
Emerson & Co. (Benjamin Emerson & Elias P. Roberts) 7 Thompson av. W. Washn. mkt
Emerson & Turnbull (William K. Bond Emerson & Ramsay Turnbull) 80 Broad
Emery & Forsyth (Alfred Emory & Alexander Forsyth) 2429 Riverdale av.
Emery & Price (Robert S. Emery & Harman Price) 42 South
Emery-Gates Sectional Ladder & Mfg. Co. (P. Tenney Gates, Pres.; R. H. Emery, Sec. Capital. $50,000. Directors: R. H. Emery, P. Tenney Gates) 83 Dey
Emigrant Industrial Savings Bank (Henry L. Hoguet, Pres.; John J. Milhau, Sec. Directors: James Olwell, Eugene Kelly, Henry L. Hoguet, Edward C. Donnelly, Bryan Lawrence, Robert J. Hoguet, James B. Floyd, William Lemmie, James A. G. Beales, Henry Amy, James McMahon, Arthur Leary, John J. Milhau, John C. McCarthy, James D. Lynch, P. H. Leonard, James Horke, Eugene Kelly jr.) 49 Chambers
Emken Chemical Co. (Frederick Emken, Pres.; Emil A. Riege, Sec. Capital, $10,000. Directors: Frederick Emken, Emil A. Riege) 96 Spring
Emmans John & Co (John Emmans & Washington Cockis) 93 Water
Emmerich F. J. & Son (dissolved) 43 Barclay
Emmerich & Vonderlehr (Rudolph F. Emmerich & Frederick Vonderlehr) 191 Worth
Emmet & Iselin (Henry C. Emmet & Isaac Iselin) 52 B'way
Emmet & Robinson (Richard S. Emmet & Robert E. Robinson) 52 Wall
Emmett & Co. (Harry J. Emmett & George W. Love) 309 Fourth av.
Emmons F. R. & Brother (Francis R. & James M. Emmons) 21 Warren
Emmons & Co. (Henry W. Emmons & John M. Tenney) 628 B'way
Empire Bottling Co. (Fitzpatrick & Prothero, proprs.) 47 Gt. Jones
Empire Brewery (Beadleston & Woerz, proprs.) 291 W. 10th
Empire Bustle Co. (no inf.) 115 Worth
Empire Chocolate Co. (Green & Blackwall, proprs.) 167 Duane
Empire City Beef Co. (Joseph Holm, propr.) 1625 First av.
Empire City Electric Co. (Oscar E. Madden, Pres.; Frederick Lines, Sec.; William T. Black jr. Treas. Capital, $100,000. Directors: Oscar E.

Madden, Ezra T, Gilliland, John C. Tomlinson, Henry L. Storke. John A. Sooly, F. C. Timpson, H. G. Madden) 15 Day

Empire City Fire Ins. Co. (Lindley Murray jr. Pres.; David J. Durtis, Sec. Capital, $200,000. Directors: Francis F. Marbury jr. Thomas Scott, John M. Burke, Mahlon Apgar, Charles H. Kerner, William Montanye, Nehemiah Tunis, Henry C. Mortimer, John W. Condit, Lindley Murray jr. Charles H. Lowerre. Roswell G. Rolston, Henry W. Curtiss, Charles H. Leland, Walter R. Wood, H. G. Eilshemius, David J. Durtis) 166 B'way

Empire City Pottery (Frank Lauferswelier, propr.) 519 W. 27th

Empire City Steam Carpet Beating & Renovating Works (Henry Haviland, propr.) 1597 B'way

Empire Cloak & Suit Co. (J. Silberman & Brother, proprs.) 94 Greene

Empire Clothing Co. (I. B. Cassel & Co., proprs.) 176 Bowery

Empire Coal Co. (refused) ft. Jackson

Empire Condensed Milk Co. (no inf.) 34 Hudson

Empire Co-operative Ass'n. (Frederick Gay, Pres.; Joseph B. Reycraft, Sec.; Emil Guth, Treas. Capital, $10,000. Directors: Emil Guth, Joseph B. Reycraft, Charles & John & Frederick Gay) 24 Reade

Empire Credit Clothing Co. (Levy & Horwitz, proprs.) 218 Sixth av.

Empire Crotchet Button Co. (B. Blumenthal & Co. proprs.) 384 B'way.

Empire Dress Trimming Co. (Jarmulowsky Brothers, proprs.) 260 Grand

Empire Embossing Works (William J. Andrus, propr.) 239 Centre

Empire Gas & Electric Light Co. (inf. unattainable) 45 D'way

Empire Granite Co. (Robert E. Difenderfer, Pres.; Dean La Banta, Sec.; F. Southworth, Treas. Capital, $50,000. Directors: Robert E. Difenderfer, Dean La Banta, F. Southworth) 425 E. 15th

Empire Hardware Co. (refused) 540 W. 14th

Empire Hydro-Carbon Co. (Ernest T. Fellowes, Pres.; George Howes, Sec.; James Francis, Treas. Capital, $500,000. Directors: Ernest T. Fellowes, Charles W. Mackey, Edgar M. Crawford, Philip M. Millspaugh, George Howes, James Francis) 18 Exchange pl.

Empire Improvement Co. (dissolved) 52 B'way

Empire Iron Works (George E. Tilford, propr.) 220 W. 80th

Empire Ivory Button Works (Albert Alsberg propr.) 645 B'way

Empire Lubricating Co. (refused) 8 Front

Empire Manganese & Iron Co. (Winfield S. Chamberlain, Pres.; James Gilfillan, Sec. Directors: James Gilfillan, N. T. Botsford, James D. Henderson. D. M. Yeomans, W. S. Chamberlain) 115 B'way

Empire Mfg. Co. (Laura D. Hull, propr.) 62 Varick

Empire Nitre Works (Knowles Brothers, proprs.) 62 William

Empire Novelty Co. (Alonzo A. Marr, propr.) 10 E. 14th

Empire Pants Co. (Cohn, Solomon & Co. proprs.) 628 B'way

Empire Paving & Construction Co. (Jacob Corlies, Pres.; Franklin Haines, Sec.; further inf. unattainable) 56 Liberty

Empire Print Works (Worthen & Aldrich, proprs.) ft. Jane & 25 N. Moore

Empire Printing Co. (Daniel D. Sherwood, propr.) 195 Water

Empire Real Estate Co. (Charles Gross, Pres.; George S. Reindel, Sec.; Ferdinand N. Neumann, Treas. Capital, $40,000. Directors: Charles Gross, George S. Reindel, Ferdinand

N. Neumann, Gustave Straubenmuller, Peter Lochman) 7 Rivington

Empire Refining Co. (Ltd.) (Albion K. Bolan, Pres.; Henry B. Riggs, Sec. Capital, $100-000. Directors: Albion K. Bolan, Henry B. Riggs) 26 D'way & 884 South

Empire Rubber Co. (A. H. Wiegandt, propr.) 885 B'way

Empire Safety Mfg. Co. (Joseph W. Oakman, Pres.; Alfred M. Rodriguez, Sec.; Henry B. Oakman, Treas. Capital, $120,000. Directors: Joseph W. Oakman, Alva G. Woodrow, Alfred M. Rodriguez, Henry B. Oakman) 68 B'way

Empire State Bank (James W. Conrow, Pres.; Charles H. Roberts, Cashier. Capital, $250,000. Directors: James W. Conrow, Eugene W. Connett, Henry W. Curtiss, Henry Newman, Granville F. Dailey, John H. Coop, Julius Hammerslough, William B. Thom, Leon Mandel, Jacob H. Loewenstine, Charles T. Wagner, Abraham Steinam, Elliott P. Gleason, Jacob Emsheimer, Charles H. Roberts) 640 B'way

Empire State Brewing Co. (refused) 143 W. 18th

Empire State Cigar Co. (Louis Schlesinger, Pres.; Edward Stiefel. Sec. Capital, $30,000. Directors: Louis Schlesinger. Edward & Theresa Stiefel, Henry M. Zeldenrust) 222 E. 87th

Empire State Gas Improvement Co. (James E. Hedges, Pres.; William H. De Hart, Sec. Capital, $500,000. Directors: James E. Hedges, George W. Harris, Alexander M. Sutherland, William H. Dellart) 115 B'way

Empire State Nail Co. (Thomas V. Johnson, Pres.; Theodore Boughner, Sec. Capital, $90,000. Directors: Thomas V. Johnson, Theodore Boughner, Charles Boyd, George W. Greenfield, William M. Cavanaugh) 227 Canal

Empire State Tea Co. (Charles B. Nelson, propr.) 95 Sixth av.

Empire State Type Founding Co. (Stillman R. Walker, Pres.; Patrick H. Brennan, Treas.; William H. Hubbard, Sec. Trustees: Stillman R. Walker, Patrick H. Brennan, William H. Hubbard) 15 Frankfort

Empire Steam Laundry Co. (Horace H. Brockway, Pres.; Henry F. Wood, Sec.; William Ottmann, Treas. Capital, $110,000. Directors: Horace H. Brockway, William Ottmann, Henry F. Wood, Robert L. Burnett) 122 W. Houston

Empire Storage Warehouses (H. O'Reilly & Co. proprs.) 890 Hudson & 268 W. Houston

Empire Suit Co. (William D. Savidge, propr.) 14 W. 14th

Empire Syringe Co. (William Platt, propr.) 40 Cortlandt

Empire Tea & Coffee Co. (Terence J. O'Connor, propr.) 76 Water

Empire Towage & Lighterage Co. (inf. unattainable) 75 South

Empire Warehouse Co. (Ltd.) (Edward B. Bartlett, Pres.; Henry E. Nitchie, Sec.; Mark W. Maclay. Treas. Capital, $100,000. Directors: Edward B. Bartlett, Henry E. Nitchie, Mark W. Maclay) 5 Hanover

Empire & Bay States Telegraph Co. (Wendell Goodwin. Pres.; George H. Wirth, Sec.; James A. G. Benies, Treas. Capital, $1,000,000. Directors: Wendell Goodwin, George R. Wirth, James A. G. Benies, Eugene Durnin, John Byrne, William F. Walworth, William H. Hurst, Joseph Leavy, Michael J. Newman, Henry B. Slaven, James J. Phelan) 34 B'way

Employers' Liability Ins. Co. of U. S. (inf. unattainable) 9 Pine

Employment Soc. Repository (Mrs. S. Sidney Smith, Pres.; Miss H. C. Butler, Sec.; Mrs. Nathan Chandler, Treas.) 146 E. 16th

Emrich E. jr. & J. Clemens (Edward Emrich jr. & Joseph Clemens) 182 E. 119th

**THE CALIGRAPH WRITING MACHINE,
HARTFORD, CONN.**

END 91 EQU

Enderlein & Callen (dissolved) 146 West
Endolithic Marble Co. of the U. S. (dissolved) 123 Fifth av.
Engel M. & Co. (Morris Engel & Herman Goldfarb) r 66 Wooster
Engel & Doering (William Engel & Herman Doering) 212 Centre
Engel & Gelb (dissolved) r 290 Third
Engel, Heller & Co. (Julius Engel & Bernard Heller, no Co.) 29 First av.
Engelage & Lies (George H. Engelage & George Lies) 9 Gansevoort
Engelberg A. & Co. (Arthur Engelberg, Co. refused) 192 Pearl
Engelfried, Braun & Weidmann (John V. Engelfried, John Braun & Robert Weidmann) 128 Fulton
Engelhard A. J. & Co. (Adam J. Engelhard & William H. Markgraf) 976 Ninth av.
Engelhard & Huber (Rudolph Engelhard & Daniel Huber jr.) 105 & 2126 Third av.
Engelke K. & M. (Catharine & Margaret) 1583 First av.
Engelke & Bull (John W. Engelke & William Bull) 10 South
Engelmann & Drachmann (dissolved) 143 Eldridge
Engineering News Publishing Co. (George H. Frost, Pres.; David McN. Stauffer, Sec. Capital, $50,000. Directors: George H. Frost, Arthur M Wellington, David McN. Stauffer) 154 Nassau
Engineers' Directory Publishing Co. (Edwin A. Hayes, propr.) 202 West
Englander S. & Brother (Solomon & Samuel Englander) 111 Mangin
Englert G. & Co. (Gustav Englert & Frederick Ungerland) 370 E. 76th
English Stock Food Co. (not inc.) (Henry & James M. Blnek) 289 W. 15th
English & Am. Mortgage Co. (Ltd.) (no inf.) 146 B'way
Enga P. W. & Sons (Edward L. Snyder & John Durke, only) 137 Front & 94 Pine
Enge R. L. & Brother (dissolved) 454 Produce Ex.
Eninger & Carson (dissolved) 201 E. 34th
Eninger & Unger (George J. Eninger & Ernest F. Unger) 201 E. 34th
Ennis & Co. (Andrew J. Ennis & Anderson C. Wilson) 62 New
Eno Steam Generator Co. (no inf.) 39 Dey
Enock Brothers (Arthur & Charles Enock) 460 Pearl
Enos H. K. & Co. (Henry K. Enos & Thomas C. Buck) 45 Wall
Enright P. & Sons (Peter & John A. & Martin S. Enright) 112 W. 19th
Enterprise Brush Co. (not inc.) (John F. Ebert & Daniel M. Robinson) 21 College pl.
Enterprise Crockery Co. (Morris Freldenberg, propr.) 1741 Ninth av. & 560 B'way
Enterprise Mfg. Co. (Kromm & Rosenthal, proprs.) 117 Leonard
Enterprise Printing Co. (Herron & Kunz, proprs.) 108 W. 42d
Enyard & Bain (Isaac S. Enyard & David Bain) 163 Chambers
Epileptic Remedy Co. (Edward A. Hulbert, propr.) 47 Broad
Epoch Publishing Co. (Dewitt J. Seligman, Pres.; Eugene Seligman, Sec. Capital, $5,000. Directors: Dewitt J. & George & Eugene Seligman) 80 Union sq. E.
Eppelsheimer & Co. (Henry & Peter R. Eppelsheimer) r 162 Bleecker
Eppens, Smith & Wiemann Co. (Ltd.) (John F. Pupke, Pres.; Leonard B. Smith, Treas. Capital, $500,000. Directors: John F. Pupke,

Thomas Reld, Frederick P. Eppens, Frederick Wiemann, Leonard B. Smith, Thomas C. Parkhill) 263 Washn. & 87 Front
Eppinger William & Son (William & William Eppinger jr.) 3611 Third av.
Eppinger & Amba (dissolved) 86 First av.
Eppinger & Russell (Isaac Eppinger & John K. Russell) 100 Water
Epple G. & Son (Gottlieb & Herman F. Epple) 20 & 322 E. 22d
Epstein S. & Sons (Samuel & Isidor & Louis W. Epstein) 147 Spring
Epstein & Vollweller (David Epstein & Herman Vollweller) 316 Fifth
Equitable Bank (Jacob B. Tallman, Pres.; Nathaniel A. Chapman, Cashier; William S. Mathews, Notary. Capital, $100,000. Directors: Jacob B. Tallman, Charles A. Gerlach, James S. Harris, Sigmund T. Meyer, Nathaniel S. Dailey, Eugene Ellery) 9 W. 28th
Equitable Electric Construction Co. (not inc.) (E. S. Sims & E. Hayward) 104 Front
Equitable Gas Light Co. (Robert M. C. Graham, Pres.; Harry Keene, Sec.; Jacob D. Vermilye, Treas. Capital, $4,000,000. Directors: E. C. Benedict, Jacob Berckshman, Samuel W. Boocock, Edward N. Dickerson jr. Charles M. Fry, William H. Gebhard, Robert M. C. Graham, Erazm J. Jerzmanowski, Eugene Kelly, John Sloane, Charles F. Tag, Jacob D. Vermilye, Jerome B. Wheeler) 340 Third av. & First av. c E. 80th
Equitable Jewelry Co. (A. L. Bamber, Pres.; William H. Payne, Sec. Capital, $5,000. Directors: A. L. Bamber, Philip Babcock, William Bamber) 175 B'way
Equitable Life Assurance Soc. (Henry B. Hyde, Pres.; William Alexander, Sec. Directors: Henry B. Hyde, Louis Fitzgerald, Henry A. Hurlbut, Henry G. Marquand, Wm. A. Wheelock, Henry Day, M. Hartley, H. M. Alexander, Chauncey M. Depew, Charles G. Landon, Cornelius N. Bliss, Alanson Trask, E. Boudinot Colt, Eugene Kelly, John D. Jones, John Sloane, S. Borrowe, D. Williamson, G. W. Carleton, E. W. Lambert, H. S. Terbell, Thomas S. Young, William M. Bliss, John J. McCook, D. F. Randolph, John A. Stewart, Levi P. Morton, George C. Magoun, Wm. B. Kendall, Daniel D. Lord, H. J. Fairchild, William Alexander, Horace Porter, C. B. Alexander, George De F. L. Day, J. F. De Navarro, Joseph T. Low, Edward W. Scott, Charles S. Smith, George H. Stuart, A. Van Bergen, T. DeWitt Cuyler, Oliver Ames, Eustace C. Fits, S. H. Phillips, Henry H. Wolcott, Gustav G. Pohl, John A. McCall, James H. Dunham, Daniel R. Noyes, Waldo Adams) 120 B'way
Equitable Mfg. Co. (Thomas Bracken, Pres.; Hugh O'Donnell, Treas.; Henry N. Hooper, Sec.; further inf. unattainable) 120 B'way
Equitable Mercantile Co. (Hosford B. Niles, Pres.; John M. Niles, Treas. Capital, $10,000. Directors: Hosford B. Niles, Alfred B. Kelsey, John M. Niles, Andrew J. Provost, Jacob Hey) 5 Beekman
Equitable Mortgage Co. (inf. unattainable) 203 B'way
Equitable Permanent Co-operative Building & Loan Assn. (John McDermott, Pres.; Joseph A. Turner, Sec.; James Noble, Treas.) 232 Sixth av.
Equitable Printing Co. (Weenage & Browne, proprs.) 120 Liberty
Equitable Reserve Fund Life Assn. (John von Glahn, receiver) 171 B'way
Equitable Trust Co. (in liquidation) 32 Pine
Equity Board of Grain Measurers & Inspectors (inf. unattainable) 40 Whitehall
Equity Mfg. Co. (inf. unattainable) 814 B'way
Equity Publishing Co. (William A. Baldwin, propr.) 9 W. 14th

SPECIAL ATTENTION PAID TO THIS CLASS OF WORK. } BANKERS' & BROKERS' CIRCULARS DELIVERED { THE TROW CITY DIRECTORY CO. 11 University Place.

ERD   92   **EUR**

Erdmann I. S. & Co. (Isaac S. & Jacob Erdmann & Nathan Hirschman) 69 Greene

Erff Brothers (Charles & George Erff) 11 Waverley pl. & 28 W. 23th

Erickson F. N., Newspaper Advertising Agency (Eric N. Erickson, propr.) 5 Beekman

Erickson, Stewart & Thayer (William T. Erickson, Charles Stewart & Herbert W. Thayer) 506 B'way & 132 Crosby

Ericsson Coast Defence Co. (George H. Robinson, Pres.; Cornelius J. Bushnell, Sec. Capital, $250,000. Directors: George H. Robinson, Cornelius S. Bushnell, E. S. Innet, William Williams, Ericsson F. & Cornelius J. Bushnell) 35 B'way

Erie Basin Iron Works (Krajewski & Pesant, proprs.) 35 B'way

Erie Boatmen's Transp. Co. (Ltd.) (Matthew McCormick, Pres.; Edward M. Clarkson, Sec.; William E. Cleary, Treas. Capital, $10,000. Directors: Matthew McCormick, Edward M. Clarkson, Francis J. Cassidy, Hugh Blair, William E. Cleary, Joseph Accles, John H. Armstrong, Jeremiah Baker, Joseph Laughlin) 17 South

Erie City Iron Works (not inc.) (George & George D. Selden & John H. Bliss) 9 Dey

Erlanger N. & Co. (dissolved) 453 Broome

Erlanger N., Blumgart & Co. (Nathan Erlanger, Louis Blumgart & Cyrus L. Sulzberger) 93 Prince

Erlanger & Liebmann (Max Erlanger & Rudolph Liebmann) 282 Canal

Eriwein & Jemm (George Eriwein & Emil Jemm) 250 E. 120th

Ernst J. H. & Co. (John R. Ernst, no Co.) 65 Warren

Ernst L. M. & Co. (Louis M. Ernst, no Co.) 42 Bond

Ernst M. L. & C. (Morris L. & Carl) 55 Liberty

Errico Brothers (Frank A. & Louis J. & Frederick J. Errico) 862 B'way

Erschell & Buchner (dissolved) 4 Gt. Jones

Erskine John & Co. (James M. & William B. & Charles W. Erskine, only) 478 Broome

Erstein L. & Brother (Leopold & Marx Erstein) 53 Greene

Erthellor M. & Son (Moritz & James Ertheiler) 141 Water

Escalante Brothers (dissolved) 37 Ann

Escande & Gentien (Eugene Escande & Joseph Gentien) 50 Vestry

Eschbach S. & Son (Sylvester Eschbach & Adelbert Rubor, only) r 348 W. 44th

Eschelbacher A. & Co. (Adolph Eschelbacher, Joseph Cohen & Meyer J. Wallach) 723 B'way

Eschelbacher & Mayer (Joseph Eschelbacher & Herman Mayer) 96 White

Eschmann & Co. (Balthasar Eschmann & Anthony Saffer) 211 E. 22d

Eschwege & Goldschmidt (dissolved) 73 Franklin

Eschwege & Schielsaner (dissolved) 43 Av. A

Espenscheid J. M. & Co. (John M. Espenscheid & John Walhizor) 158 Greene

Esperanza & Co. (Julio Esperanza, Stephen W. Cary & Julius Lichtenhein) 28 W. B'way

Espinal's P., Brother & Co. (Ricardo & Carlos Espinal) 26 William

Esselborn's George, Sons (Herman & Emil & George & William Esselborn) 519 W. 47th

Esselmann Brothers (Henry Esselmann, only) 1754 Ninth av.

Essen Iron Works (not inc.) (John A. Delves & John Kobler) 310 E. 110th

Essex Button Co. (John H. Leonhard, Pres.; Robert E. Vanhovenberg, Sec.; Alfred A. Vanhovenberg, Treas. Capital, $5,000. Directors: John H. Leonhard, Alfred A. & Robert E. & Martin & Martin H. R. Vanhovenberg,

Giles W. Dart, James J. Vanhovenberg) 304 B'way

Essex Market Beef Co. (G. F. & E. C. Swift, proprs.) Essex mkt

Essick Printing Telegraph Co. (F. S. Jennings, Pres.; Abner McKinley, Treas.; F. H. Wilkins, Sec. Capital, $5,000,000. Directors: F. S. Jennings, Abner McKinley, S. V. Essick, F. H. Wilkins, E. W. Gray, S. Johnson) 171 B'way

Esterbrook Steel Pen Mfg. Co. (Richard Esterbrook, Pres.; Francis Wood, Sec.; Alexander C. Wood, Treas. Capital, $300,000. Directors: Richard Esterbrook, Francis & Alexander C. Wood) 26 John

Esterly Brothers (John & Henry Esterly) 798 Eighth av.

Estes E. B. & Sons (Elihu B. & Webster C. Estes, only) 254 Pearl

Estey Piano Co. (Jacob Estey, Pres.; Julius J. Estey, Sec.; Robert Proddow, Treas. Capital, $60,000. Directors: Jacob Estey, L. K. Fuller, John B. Simpson jr. Robert Proddow, Stephen Drambach) 5 E. 14th, S. Boulevard c Lincoln av. & 403 E. 69d

Etowah Gold Mining Co. (no inf.) 40 B'way

Ettenborough & Sherer (John J. Ettenborough & John H. Sherer) 10 Reade

Ettinger Public Adjusting Bureau (refused) 35 Nassau

Ettinger Brothers (Herman L. & Seymour I. Ettinger) 64 E. B'way

Ettinger L. & Sons (Louis & Louis jr. & Frederick V. & Adolph & Charles F. Ettinger) 50 Nassau

Ettinger & Browning (dissolved) 119 Wooster

Ettore & De Fina (John Ettore & Antonio De Fina) 145 Pearl

Etzel Brothers (Joseph & Albert Etzel) 189 Varick

Etzel & Braun (Frank Etzel & Adam Braun) 329 Delancey

Eureka Button Co. (Emanuel Neuman, propr.) 703 B'way

Eureka Electric Co. (Charles C. Southard, Pres.; Francis E. Southard, Treas.; Charles M. Lyman, Sec. Capital, $50,000. Trustees: Charles C. Southard, George W. Dickerman, Francis E. Southard, John C. Howe, Charles M. Lyman) 18 B'way & 510 W. 30th

Eureka Fire Hose Co. (John Van D. Reed, Pres.; George A. Wies, Sec.; Junius Schenck, Treas. Capital, $500,000. Directors: John Van D. Reed, Junius Schenck, B. L. Stowe) 13 Barclay

Eureka Gas Generator Mfg. Co. (Ellis F. Edgar, Pres.; Allen G. N. Vermilya, Sec. Capital, $30,000. Directors: Napoleon Valentine, Allen G. N. Vermilya, Ellis F. Edgar) 5 Beekman

Eureka Mfg. Co. (James B. Crosby, propr.) ft. E. 26th

Eureka Mills (Nassau Trading Co. proprs.) 127 Front

Eureka Paper Novelty Co. (Sigmund Rosenbaum, propr.) 139 W. B'way

Eureka Reed Co. (inoperative) 166 Greene

Eureka Sign Co. (refused) 7 W. 28th

Eureka Silk Dye Works (William Meyer, propr.) r 519 W. 35th

Eureka Trick & Novelty Co. (Charles F. Shutts, Pres.; Clarence W. Shutts, Sec. Capital, $5,000; further inf. unattainable) 67 Warren

Eureka Urn Mfg. Co. (dissolved) 1263 B'way

European Express (Jacob Terkulle, propr.) 88 B'way

European Importing & Grocery Co. (Capital, $10,000. Trustees: Gustaf Blungran, Nilo Width, William Anderson, Werner Schatelowitz, Frederic Larsen) no address

FOR THE BEST CO-PARTNERSHIP IN THE BEST CORPORATION SEE PAGE F IN BACK OF BOOK

EUR 93 EXC

European Watch Co. (refused) 9 Murray

Eustace & Murphy (Mary V. Eustace & Emily J. Murphy) 40 W. 80th

Eustis Mfg. Co. (John P. Eustis, Pres.; William H. G. Rowe, Sec. Capital, $50,000. Directors: John P. Eustis, William H. G. Rowe, Frank J. Sprague) 12½ W. 24th

Evans George & Son (George W. Evans, only) 1 Jacob

Evans Joseph D. & Co. (no inf.) 19 Whitehall

Evans Q. N., Construction Co. (Quimby N. Evans, Pres.; William C. Adams, Sec. Capital, $25,-000. Directors: Quimby N. Evans, William C. Adams, Edward F. Haydon) 43 Dey

Evans C. H. & Sons (Cornelius H. & Robert W. & Cornelius H. Evans jr.) 127 Hudson

Evans J. O. & Co. (James O. Evans, no Co.) 404 W. 14th

Evans S. C. & Co. (Silas C. & Frank G. Evans) 36 South & Pier 10 E. R.

Evans & Co. (hats) (Lucian A. Chapin, only) 455 Sixth av.

Evans & Co. (meat) (dissolved) 38 & 47 Whitehall

Evans & Co. (real estate) (William Evans, Co. refused) 128 B'way

Evans & Curry (Timothy J. Evans & Charles Curry) 44 Rose

Evans & Finley (Alethea W. Evans & M. Elizabeth Finley) 38 Broad

Evans & Holmes (dissolved) 150 Nassau

Evansville & Terre Haute R. R. Co. (D. J. Mackey, Pres.; W. J. Lewis, Sec. Directors: William H. Payne, Edward V. Loew, Christopher C. Baldwin, Joseph M. De Vean, James Stillman, Herman Clark, T. W. Evans, Benjamin Russak, S. O. Nelson, William Heilman, Harry I. Nicholas, C. W. Hillard) 7 Nassau

Evansville, Dayton & Eastern R. R. Co. (inoperative) 56 B'way

Evarts, Choate & Beaman (William M. Evarts, Joseph H. Choate, Charles C. Beaman, J. Evarts Tracy, Treadwell Cleveland, Prescott Hall Butler & Allen W. Evarts) 52 Wall

Evener Spring Co. (Sebastian Mfg. Co. proprs.) 229 E. 43d

Evening Post Publishing Co. (Horace White, Pres.; Wendell P. Garrison, Sec. Capital, $100,000. Trustees: Horace White, Edwin L. Godkin, Frederick Sheldon, David A. Wells, Wendell P. Garrison) 210 B'way

Evening Star Mining Co. (Watson B. Dickerman, Pres.; Henry K. McHarg, Sec. Capital, $500,-000. Trustees: Watson B. Dickerman, George G. Nevers, W. Gayer Dominick, A. H. Porter, Henry K. McHarg, George B. Greer, Justin A. Edwards) 52 B'way

Everall Brothers (George Everall, only) 286 Fifth av. & 1158 B'way

Everdell W. K. & Brother (William K. & Henry G. Everdell) 227 Produce Ex.

Everett Board & Real Estate Agency (Elizabeth A. Dailey, propr.) 74 W. 35th

Everett D. B. & Co. (David B. Everett & Thomas Rose) 30 Old sl.

Everett H. W. & Co. (Henry W. Everett, no Co.) 22 Platt

Everett Brothers (Francis M. & Edward E. Everett) 2295 Third av.

Everitt Mfg. Co. (Percival Everitt, Pres.; Theodore H. Smith, Sec. Capital, $50,000; further inf. unattainable) 298 B'way & 14 Reade

Everitt & Co. (William J. & John N. Everitt) 46 Thompson av. W. Washn. mkt

Everitt & Pidcock (dissolved) ft. W. 59th

Everlasting Roofing Co. (Cornelius S. Bushnell, Pres.; Cornelius J. Bushnell, Sec. Capital, $5,000. Directors: Cornelius S. & Cornelius J. Bushnell, Harrison F. Wagner) 35 B'way

Everson W. Henry & Co. (W. Henry Everson, Co. refused) 18 Cortlandt

Everson & Reed (Charles Everson & Eli H. Reed) 241 B'way

Evory & Freeman (Peter Freeman, only) 290 & 299 E. 42d

Evory A. F. & Co. (Alexander F. Evory, no Co.) 106 G'wich

Ewen A. D. & Son (Austin D. & Arthur C. Ewen) 299 B'way

Ewing & Southard (Thomas Ewing & Milton I. Southard) 135 B'way

Excelsior Advertising Sign Co. (Joseph T. Commoss, propr.) 46 Vesey

Excelsior Beef Co. (Leopold Ehrmann, propr.) 34 Jones

Excelsior Button Co. (refused) 90 Walker

Excelsior Dynamite Co. (Samuel T. Apollonio, Pres; Willis Van Tine, Sec. Capital, $50,000. Directors: Samuel T. Apollonio, Willis Van Tine, Eben D. Crane) 45 B'way

Excelsior Egg & Butter Package Co. (A. L. Ellis, Pres.; William P. Sandford, Sec.; James F. Tolman, Treas.; further inf. unattainable) 56 Murray

Excelsior Electric Co. (Henry D. Fuller, Pres.; George D. Allen, Sec. Capital, $500,000. Directors: Henry D. Fuller, George D. Allen, William Hochhausen, Herbert N. Smith, Robert Maitland) 115 B'way

Excelsior Elevator Guard & Hatch Cover Co. (James R. Webb, Pres.; Robert E. Stoel, Sec. Capital, $25,000. Directors: James R. Webb, Robert E. Stoel, John Keir) 120 B'way & 141 Charles

Excelsior Embroidering Co. (Wohl & Branner, proprs.) 358 Canal

Excelsior Enamel Paint Co. (Davidson & Knowles Co. proprs.) 180 Cherry

Excelsior Engraving & Printing Co. (N. Solomon, propr.) 76 William

Excelsior Glass Sign Mfg. Co. (no inf.) 209 E. 10th

Excelsior Hardware Co. (Edward J. Brady, propr.) 56 Warren

Excelsior Lantern Co. (John M. Lawrence, propr.) 194 Water

Excelsior Life Saving Car Coupling Co. (Fitz John Porter, Pres. ; J. Hamilton Hunt, Sec. Capital, $1,000,000. Trustees: Fitz John Porter, J. Hamilton Hunt, James F. Wenman) Ninth av. c W. 72d

Excelsior Mailing Agency (Buckley & Wood, proprs.) 220 William

Excelsior Mfg. Co. (Hervey C. Calkin, Pres.; Herbert T. Ketcham, Sec. Capital, $50,000. Trustees: Hervey C. Calkin, Herbert T. Ketcham, Joseph Koch, M. R. Gray, James R. Davies) 13 Park row

Excelsior Perfumery & Novelty Co. (John H. Carmiencke, propr.) 142 W. 23d

Excelsior Playing Card Co. (Max J. Mayer, propr.) 328 Seventh av.

Excelsior Press Rooms & Publishing Co. (Isaac Harvey, Pres.; John T. Harvey, Sec. Capital, $20,000. Directors: Isaac & John T. Harvey, John J. Murphy, E. A. Buck, Lawrence Kehoe) 11 Frankfort

Excelsior Publishing House (refused) 29 Beekman

Excelsior Quilting Co. (Louis Schultz, Pres.; Charles T. Wagner, Sec. Capital, $100,000. Directors: Louis Scholts, Charles T. Wagner, William Wiess, M. P. Wilkins, Charles Hyams) 204 Greene

Excelsior Remedy Co. (Moses Namias, propr.) 35 Frankfort

Excelsior Rubber Stamp Works (J. Martin, propr.) 70 William

Excelsior Rubber Works (Henry Trann, propr.) 835 B'way

TYPEWRITING DONE BY THE TROW CITY DIRECTORY CO., 11 University Place.

Excelsior Sample Card Co. (Henckel & Bolan, proprs.) 91 Leonard
Excelsior Savings Bank (George C. Waldo, Pres.; John C. Griswold, Sec. Trustees: Norvin Green, John Dickson, Edward L. Merrifield, Michael P. Dreslin, Thomas S. Robertson, William J. Roome, James C. Gulick, Frederick D. Lawson, Robert Dunlap, Amaziah L. Ashman, George C. Currier, James H. Breslin, John C. Gulick, John Burke, James C. Matthews, Robert C. Brown, William D. Garrison, George C. Waldo, Richard A. Cunningham) 118 W. 23d
Excelsior Steam Carpet Cleaning Works (Hoffstaetter & Himmel, proprs.) 538 W. 46th
Excelsior Steam Power Co. (William T. Denyse, Pres.; Charles L. Helns, Treas. Capital, $240,000. Trustees: William T. Denyse, J. M. Crane, Charles L. Helns, W. Shepard Newton, Martin M. Brown, James A. Flack, James Stevenson) 37 Gold & 18 Spruce
Excelsior Suspender Co. (Mark Eisler, propr.) 75 Franklin
Excelsior Varnish Works (David J. Isaacs, propr.) 381 Pearl
Exchange Broadway Bath Co. (Ltd.) (Henry Imhof, Pres.; John D. Haas, Treas.; George J. Dohrenwend, Sec. Capital, $50,000. Directors: Henry Imhof, John D. Haas, George J. Dohrenwend, Hermann F. Kudlich, John Friedrich) 8 B'way
Exchange Fire Ins. Co. (R. Carman Combes, Pres.; George W. Montgomery, Sec. Capital, $200,010. Directors: R. Carman Combes, Rufus L. Todd, J. D. Brown, Silas Davis, Sigourney W. Fay, Lorenzo G. Woodhouse, Edward L. Kalbfleisch, Adon Smith, Edward F. Brown, George W. Montgomery, James Galway, Charles G. Emory, William K. Thorn, Franklin Chandler, Benjamin Park) 41 Pine & 46 William
Exchange Place Real Estate Co. (Charles F. Tag, Pres.; Samuel L. Parrish, Sec. Capital, $440,000. Trustees: Charles F. Tag, Samuel L. Parrish, Casimir & Albert Tag, James C. Parrish, Francis K. Pendleton) 44 B'way
Exchange Printing Co. (John Ryer, Pres.; Francis E. Fitch, Treas. Capital, $14,500. Directors: John Ryer, Francis E. & Cornelia K. Fitch) 47 Broad
Exchange Publishing Co. (Eugene Sheridan, propr.) 54 Broad
Export Lumber Co. (Ltd.) (Lewis A. Hall, Pres.; Wallace D. Flint, Sec.; Charles B. Fearing, Treas. Capital, $600,000. Directors: Lewis A. Hall, Wallace B. & Charles R. Flint, Charles B. Fearing, Andrew A. Buell) 142 Pearl
Eytinge Publishing Co. (William Fieron, propr.) 833 B'way

F

F. B. Q. Clothing Co. (Simon Mayer, Pres.; further inf. unattainable) 10 W. 3d
Fabbrini Brothers (Egisto & John J. & Silvio Fabbrini) 105 E. 125th & 105 W. 125th
Fabbrini & Coari (dissolved) 287 Washn. & 186 Chambers
Fabien & Mendy (Remy Fabien & Justin Mendy) 250 G'wich
Fabric Fire Hose Co. (Henry F. Wheeler, Pres.; Frank H. Wheeler, Sec.; Leonard Jacob jr. Treas. Capital, $100,000. Directors: Henry F. & Frank H. Wheeler, Leonard Jacob jr. William T. Baird, George W. Sayre) 5 Barclay
Fabric Measuring & Packaging Co. (Edward P. Watson, Pres.; Reginald Young, Sec.; George G. Williams, Treas. Capital, $50,000. Trustees: Edward P. Watson, James Henry Smith, Reginald Young, George G. Williams, R. W. Watson) 34 Thomas & 117 Duane
Fabrici F. & Co. (Felice Fabrici, no Co.) 24 Stone

Fabyan Knife Co. (Hubbell & Randal, proprs.) 80 Reade
Fach & Co. (Charles A. Fach & Herman Mundhenk) 29 Mercer
Fachiri P. & Co. (Pandelli A. & E. A. & N. A. Fachiri) 55 Beaver
Facile Bottle Stopple Co. (William F. Duncan, Pres.; Clarence W. Duncan, Sec. Capital, $1,000,000. Trustees: William F. & Clarence W. Duncan, John W. Stockton, G. A. Fullerton, George H. P. Flagg) 66 Murray
Fahnestock & Co. (William & Gibson Fahnestock) 2 Wall
Fahys Joseph & Co. (Joseph Fahys, Henry F. Cook & George E. Fuhys) 39 Maiden la.
Faience Mfg. Co. (Bernard Voit, Pres.; Joseph E. Baruch, Sec. Capital, $20,000. Directors: Bernard Voit, Joseph Offenbach, Joseph E. Baruch) 56 Murray
Fairbanks & Co. (William S. Wells, William P. Fairbanks & Samuel N. Brown) 311 B'way & 84 Thomas
Fairbanks & Parker (Thomas G. Fairbanks & William H. Parker) 381 Washn.
Fairbanks, Tull & Co. (dissolved) 231 Washn.
Fairchance Furnace Co. (George R. Sheldon, Pres.; William H. DeForest jr. Sec. Directors: George R. Sheldon, William H. DeForest jr. Robert L. Martin) 111 B'way
Fairchild Leroy W., Co. (Leroy W. Fairchild, propr.) 189 B'way
Fairchild & McCosker (dissolved) 260 Canal
Fairchild & Ryley (Clarence E. Fairchild & Rupert A. Ryley) 1 W. 25th
Fairchild & Yoran (Benjamin P. Fairchild & Frank Yoran) 171 B'way
Fairchild Brothers & Foster (Samuel W. & Benjamin T. Fairchild & Macomb G. Foster) 82 Fulton
Fairchild, Playter & Co. (dissolved) 30 Broad
Fairfax Hamilton R. & Co. (Hamilton R. Fairfax, no. Co.) 812 B'way
Fairfax Brothers (Lindsay & John W. Fairfax jr.) 812 B'way
Fairfield Chemical Works (Solomon Hexter, Pres.; Joseph D. Dillard jr. Sec. Capital, $250,000. Directors: Solomon Hexter, Louis S. Wolf, Joseph D. Dillard jr. Alexander Guiterman) 71 Wall
Fairies & Ollivier (no inf.) 17 B'way
Fairmount Printing Ink Works (J. K. Wright & Co. proprs.) 22 Spruce
Fairmount Upholstery Fringe Co. (Lazarus, Schwarz & Lipper, proprs.) 416 B'way
Faist & Son (Catharine & John George Faist) 234 E. 84th
Faith Cotton Oil Agency (Edwin L. Johnson, propr.) 26 Moore
Fajen Brothers (Henry & Herman Fajen) 14 South
Fajen & Co. (Henry & Herman Fajen & Behrend Geils) 17 South
Falaska Angelo & Co. (Angelo Falaska & Donato Zanna) 218 Av. A
Falck Art Glass Works (Edward P. Grout, propr.) 84 E. Houston
Falconer's William H., Son (William W. Falconer) 100 Fourth av.
Falconi & Ghetti (dissolved) Fordham av. c Tremont av.
Falk Joseph D. & Co. (Joseph B. Falk & Simon Dannenberg) 304 B'way
Falk A. & Sons (Abraham & David B. & Zachariah & Washington Falk) 676 B'way
Falk G. & Brother (Gustav & Arnold Falk) 171 Water
Falk I. L. & Co. (Isaac L. & George W. Falk) 691 B'way & 254 Mercer
Falk L. & Son (Louis & Max Falk) 104 Av. A

THADDEUS DAVIDS CO., WRITING INKS, SEALING WAX, MUCILAGE.
MAKE THE BEST

FAL 95 FEA

Falk & Co. (dissolved) 529 B'way
Falk & Dannenberg (Henry Falk & Moses Dannenberg) 536 Third av.
Falk & Lichtenberg (Max Falk & Henry Lichtenberg) 448 Sixth av.
Falk Brothers & Co. (Abraham & Zachariah & David D. & Washington Falk) 676 B'way
Falk Brothers & Friedman (dissolved) 430 W. 17th
Falkenau, Oppenheimer & Co. (Moritz Falkenau, David E. Oppenheimer & Joseph Hamerschlag) 40 Malden la.
Falkenberg Charles & Brother (Charles & Jacob Falkenberg) 332 B'way
Falkenberg & Lederer (Charles Falkenberg & Jacob Lederer) 34 Howard
Falkenhelm Brothers (dissolved) 106 Av. B
Fallon Owen & Son (Owen & Thomas F. Fallon) 92 Park
Fallon Brothers (John J. & James Fallon) 1159 First av.
Fallon, Brunnemer & Crandall (Joseph P. Fallon, John Brunnemer & Elbert Crandall) 93 Nassau
Family Fund Soc. (Inf. unattainable) 280 B'way
Fangemann & Heins (John Fangemann & Henry Heins) 565 Grand & 409 Madison
Fantel Brothers (Leopold & Marcus Fantel) 200 Av. A
Faraday Electric Co. (inoperative) 11 Gold
Farber Jacob & Co. (dissolved) 101 Lewis
Farber M. & L. Dillon (dissolved) 142 E. Dway
Farber & Co. (no inf.) 141 Stanton
Faris & Knight (dissolved) 60 B'way
Farjeon & Co. (Bessie & Jacques Farjeon) 25 John
Farlee J. S. & Brother (Jacob S. & Robert D. Farlee) 7 Nassau
Farley James & Co. (James Farley & John Coleman) 30 Water
Farley Brothers (Susan & Charlotte Farley, only) 17 E. 27th
Farley's Terence, Sons (John T. & James A. Farley) 1172 Ninth av.
Farmer Edgar & Co. (William H. Peck & William C. Farmer, only) 34 Cortlandt
Farmer Brothers (James W. Farmer, only) 424 W. 43d
Farmer & Jenkins (George P. Farmer & Joel J. Jenkins) 82 Bleecker
Farmer, Little & Co. (Aaron D. Farmer, Andrew Little, John Bentley & William W. Farmer) 65 Beekman
Farmers' Butter & Egg Co. (Leonard S. Burdick, Pres.; Leonard S. Burdick jr. Sec. Capital, $2,000; further inf. refused) 1822 Ninth av,
Farmers' Feed Co. (Charles V. Stehlin, Pres.; Ritter C. Hadley, Sec.; George E. Todd, Treas. Capital, $150,000. Directors: Charles V. Stehlin, Ritter C. Hadley, George E. Todd, John D. Kimmey, John Barthel, Joseph Stehlin) 200 E. 47th
Farmers' Loan & Trust Co. (Rosewell G. Rolston, Pres.; Edwin S. Marston, Sec. Capital, $1,000,000; further inf. unattainable) 20 William
Farnum F. L. & Co. (Frederick L. Farnum, no Co.) 338 B'way
Farquhar A. B. & Co. (Arthur B. Farquhar, Cornelius Dunkle & Percival Farquhar) 21 Cotton Ex
Farquhar N. & C. (no inf.) 23 State
Farragut Fire Ins. Co. (John E. Leffingwell, Pres.; Samuel Darbee, Sec. Capital, $200,000, Directors: William H. Beers, N. D. Morgan, Eckford Webb, Charles A. Denny, W. F. Shirley, E. R. Eames, Stewart L. Woodford, Everett Clapp, David M. Hildreth, George L. Fox, Thomas J. Atkins, M. P. Robins, Henry Tuck, John C. Furman, Robert McCafferty,

Martin V. Wood, Edwin J. Hanks, D. R. Salteries, John E. Leffingwell, Samuel Darbee) 340 B'way & 71 Liberty
Farrand & Everdell (Albert S. Farrand & Alfred E. Everdell) 253 Pearl
Farrar Coal Co. (George C. Farrar, Pres.; Charles Edmonds, Treas. Capital, $50,000. Directors: George C. Farrar, Charles H. Jones, Charles Edmonds) 68 Wooster
Farrar & Jones (Owen C. Farrar, Mills L. Eure & George F. Jones) 182 Pearl
Farrell Richard & Co. (Richard & William J. Farrell) 26 Harrison
Farrell M. P. & Co. (Martin P. Farrell, no Co.) 60 Little W. 12th
Farrell Brothers (William & James F. & Matthew J. Farrell) 253 & 255 W. 33d
Farrell & Drennan (William Farrell & William Drennan) W. 129th c Boulevard
Farrell & Cochran (dissolved) 206 Mercer
Farrell & Larsen (dissolved) 413 E. 124th
Farrington D. & Co. (Darius Farrington, no Co.) 103 Chambers
Farrington H. & G. B. & Co. (Harvey & George D. & Albert H. Farrington) 151 Front
Farrington J. & J. (John A. & Jonas S.) 352 Fourth av. & 81 W. 4th
Farrington & Quigley (Edward M. Farrington & George V. Quigley) 100 W. 70th
Farrington's George W., Sons (John M. & James W. Farrington) 24 Tomp. mkt
Farris M. & Co. (Matthew Farris, Richard F. Durke & Charles H. Simms) 56 Wall & 61 Pine
Farson, Leach & Co. (John Farson, Arthur B. Leach & Duke M. Furson) 2 Wall
Fashion Collar Co. (Heidelberger, Frank & Co. proprs.) 404 B'way
Fassbinder, Reiss & Co. (dissolved) 141 Attorney
Fatman & Co. (Solomon J. Fatman & Solomon Ranger) 70 Broad
Faubel & Hawk (Frederick Faubel & William C. Hawk) 67 Broad
Fauchere L. & Co. (Louis Fauchere & James H. Magown) r 184 W. 26th
Faulkner F. G., Co. (dissolved) 41 Dey
Faulkner & Blackburn (James A. Faulkner & Robert S. Blackburn) 1151 Sixth av.
Faulkner, Page & Co. (Henry A. Page, Joseph S. Kendall, Alfred W. Bates, Robert C. Dillinga, George M. Preston & Edward D. Page, only) 66 Leonard
Favilla G. & Co. (Giuseppe Favilla, no Co.) 146 E. 14th
Fawcett Henry & Son (dissolved) r 155 W. 30th
Fawcett, Benedict & Co. (James Benedict, only) 35 D'way
Fay John H. & Co. (dissolved) 308 Washn.
Fay A. J. & Co. (Andrew J. Fay & Thomas C. Sheppard) 814 B'way
Fay Brothers (Patrick H. Fay, only) 92 Monroe & 224 Cherry
Fay & Newton (Edwin R. Fay & Rollin C. Newton) Tenth av. n W. 158th
Fay & West (dissolved) 514 B'way
Fayen & Brockmeyer (Henry F. Fayen & William H. Brockmeyer) 100 W. 53d
Fayerweather & Ladew (Daniel B. Fayerweather & Edward R. & Joseph H. Ladew) 80 Spruce, 259 Eldridge & 161 E. Houston
Fayman & Sprague (William H. Fayman & Charles Sprague) 671 B'way
Fearn E. S. & Son (Edward S. & Charles C. Fearn) 363 W. 42d & 824 W. 45d
Fearn, De Friese & Bailey (Walker Fearn, Lafayette H. De Friese & John S. C. Bailey) 171 B'way

COMPILED WITH ACCURACY AND DESPATCH } **CLASSIFIED BUSINESS LISTS.** { THE TROW CITY DIRECTORY CO. 11 University Place.

FEA 96 FER

Fearon & Jenks (Edward J. Fearon & William H. Jenks) 158 South
Fearon, Low & Co. (Robert I. & James S. Fearon & Edward G. Low) 91 Wall
Featherston Brothers (dissolved) 537 Eleventh av.
Fechheimer, Goodkind & Co. (Martin S. Fechheimer, Henry Goodkind, Charles Fishel & Charles E. Adler) 748 B'way
Fechheimer, Rau & Co. (Sigmund Fechheimer & John Rau, no Co.) 361 B'way & 308 Hudson
Fechtoler Decorating Co. (Henry Fechteler, propr.) 1471 Park av.
Fechtman L. F. & Co. (L. Foreman & George H. & Frank W. Fechtman) 158 Canal
Feder H. & G. & Co. (Harry & Gustav & Isaac Feder) 873 B'way
Federal Co-operative Building & Loan Assn. (Robert M. Offord, Pres.; Stephen O. Sutton, Sec.; Ernest A. W. Soppett, Treas. Trustees: A. Hayward, J. E. Hubbell, George A. Hayunga, George V. Taylor, Wauhope Lynn, Henry Lowenhaupt, F. C. Driscoll, H. M. Lester, A. Firmin, Henry Warburg, W. H. M. Hick, Charles H. Ressler, T. C. Lauer, Charles Osborne) 258 B'way
Federal Valley Coal Co. (William R. Utley, Pres.; Charles T. Jung, Sec. Capital, $1,000,000. Trustees: William R. Utley, Robert E. Philips, William R. Utley jr. Aaron Carter jr. Edward Simpson, John C. Mertle, Samuel Snow) 7 Wall
Feeley James R. & Co. (no inf.) Astor h.
Feeley & Pollinger (Mary T. Feeley & John Pollinger) 26 W. 19th
Feeney William P. & Co. (William P. Feeney, Thomas J. Gilroy, Frederick H. Stevens & Samuel B. Moorhead) 21 Chambers & 201 Front
Feeney & Devanny (Patrick H. Feeney & Michael W. Devanny) 318 E. 23d
Fehring W. & Co. (William & Herman Fehring) 102 E. 125th
Feiermann & Hennefeld (Benjamin Feiermann & Louis Hennefeld) 225 S. 8th av.
Feigel Car Co. (Asa L. Rogers, Pres.; Frank L. Corwin, Sec. Capital, $25,000. Directors: Asa L. Rogers, Frank L. Corwin) 108 Wall
Feigel M. & Brother (Morris & Isaac Feigel) 149 Mercer & 519 W. 15th
Feigel & Co. (Philip Feigel jr. & Henry H. Giebelhouse) 102 Grand
Feinberg J. & Popkin Brothers (no inf.) 60 Mott
Feinberg Brothers (Michael & Herman Feinberg) 167 E. B'way
Feinberg & Cohen (Charles L. Feinberg & Samuel Cohen) 47 Prince
Feinberg & Koran (Abraham Feinberg & Joseph Koran) 228 Bowery
Feinberg & Shapiro (dissolved) 97 Clinton
Feist Brothers (Simon Feist, only) 62 Walker
Feitner & Beck (Thomas L. Feitner & Howard Beck) 56 Wall
Feld, Mayer & Siebrecht (dissolved) 11 Lawrence
Feldhusen K. & M. (Catharine M. & Mary) 746 Tenth av.
Fell Mfg. Co. (refused) 171 B'way
Fell & Vannees (Thomas Fell & Alida Vannees) 412 Second av. & 852 Third av.
Fellman Brothers (dissolved) 16 Lispenard
Fellowes, Johnson & Co. (dissolved) 70 B'way & 15 New
Fellows & Co. (John P. Fellows, no Co.) 17 Maiden la.
Felt Joseph P. & Co. (Joseph P. & Albert T. Felt) 26 Rose
Felton & Co. (A. L. Felton & August Hecker) 838 B'way

Femenella Brothers (Juan & Vincenzo Femenella) 171 Thompson
Fenn & Braxmar (William A. Fenn & Charles O. Braxmar) 47 Cortlandt
Fennell George & Co. (George & estate of Louis Fennell) 58 Av. A
Fennell & Pye (George Fennell & Henry B. Pye) 248 Grand & 2209 Third av.
Fennell & Sopher (William H. Fonnell & Drake Sopher) 224 South
Fenner Thomas & Co. (Thomas & Thomas R. Fenner) 140 Pearl & 108 Water
Fensterer & Schreitmiller (Gabriel Fensterer & William Schliensener;—special partner, Gustav Schreitmiller, $15,000; terminates 31st Dec., 1892) 21 Murray
Ferber J. C. & J. M. (John C. & Jacob M.) 1219 Union av.
Ferber & Feinknopf (dissolved) 137 Eldridge
Ferdinand Claude & Brother (Claude & Charles Ferdinand) 159 Wooster
Ferguson M. & Co. (Max Ferguson & Gabriel Spero) 70 Fulton
Ferguson George N. & Son (George N. & Frank Ferguson) 124 W. 53d
Ferguson William B. & Son (William B. & William M. Ferguson) 226 South
Ferguson A. S. & Co. (Anthony S. Ferguson & Robert J. Houston) 7 Barclay
Ferguson J. & S. (Walton Ferguson, only) 11 Pine
Ferguson Brothers (Louis & Henry & George W. Ferguson jr.) 440 W. 30th
Ferguson & Co. (Henry C. Ferguson, no Co.) 42 Pine
Ferguson & Fairchild (James A. Ferguson & David W. Fairchild) 44 B'way
Ferguson & Porter (dissolved) 169 E. 120th
Ferguson, Weller & Co. (Robert L. Ferguson & Charles H. Weller, no Co.) 103 Franklin
Fernandes G. & Co. (Genaro Fernandez, no Co.) 206 Pearl
Fernandez & Brother (Andres & Jose M. Fernandez) 122 Front
Fernoline Chemical Co. (Edmund W. McClave, Pres.; William A. Parke, Sec.; William G. Dominick, Treas. Capital, $1,000,000. Directors: Edmund W. McClave, William A. Parke, William G. Dominick, John B. McCue, George P. Greer) 18 B'way
Fernschild William & Son (no inf.) 73 E. 120th
Ferraioli & Cameron Biscuit Co. (Louis Ferraioli, Pres.; George H. Cannon, Sec.; William A. Cameron, Treas. Capital, $8,000. Trustees: Louis Ferraioli, George H. Cannon, William A. Cameron) 1127 Ninth av.
Ferris Edwin & Co (Edwin & Samuel S. & Franklin Ferris & Michael Curran) 185 Washn.
Ferris Eugene & Son (Eugene Ferris, only) 81 Nassau
Ferris George B. & Co. (George B. & Robert L. Ferris) 58 Pearl
Ferris A. M. & Kimball (A. Morton & Floyd Ferris & William A. Kimball) 68 B'way & 17 New
Ferris F. A. & Co. (Frank A. Ferris, John J. Cape & Eugene S. Hand) 264 Mott
Ferris Brothers (printers) (Alexander & Thomas & Robert Ferris) 325 Pearl
Ferris Brothers (waists) (Sherwood B. & Murray W. Ferris) 341 B'way
Ferris & Co. (refused) 57 Beekman
Ferris & Ketcham (William L. Ferris & Arthur C. Ketcham) 19 Whitehall
Ferris & Kitto (William Ferris & Albert Kitto) 324 Ninth av.
Ferris & Reehill (David J. Ferris & Joseph C. Reehill) 442 Fourth av.
Ferris & Sons (no inf.) 80 South

Ferris' Henry, Son (Charles W. Ferris) 249 Tenth av. & 504 W. 25th

Ferro P. & I. Zoogen (Philip Ferro & Israel Zoogen) 45 John

Ferronite Mfg. Co. (John E. White, Pres.; Reginald P. Sherman, Sec. Capital, $250,000. Directors: John E. White, Isaac W. Litchfield, Reginald P. Sherman, Louis Drown, William W. Ker) 62 William

Ferry & Holtzmann (Charles Holtzmann, only) 136 Dowery

Ferry & Napier (George J. Ferry & Ernest Napier) 121 Greene

Ferst M. & Co. (dissolved) 850 B'way

Feser Brothers (Anton & Valentine Feser) 260 Dowery

Fesler H. L. & Co. (Harry L Fesler, no Co.) 464 Broome

Fessler & Wolfart (dissolved) 829 W. 37th

Fest & Sons (Albert & Albert C. & Charles A. Fest) 415 W. 40th

Fett & Sengstak (Hugo C. Fett & Ernest P. E. Sengstak) 59 William

Fettretch, Silkman & Seybel (Joseph Fettretch, Theodore H. Silkman, Daniel E. Seybel & Darius G. Crosby) 99 Nassau

Feuchtwanger L. & Co. (Albert Uel Todd & William H. Oscanyan, only) 191 Fulton

Feuchtwanger & Co. (Henry & Jacob Feuchtwanger & Simon Danzig) 55 Exchange pl. & 260 Church

Feuchtwanger & James (Abraham H. Feuchtwanger & Frank James) 20 White

Feuerbach F. & J. (Frederick F. & John) 118 Clinton pl.

Fouerbach Brothers (dissolved) 271 Seventh av.

Feury John & Co. (Catharine V. Feury, Peter O'Toole & Patrick H. Gilgallon, only) 286 G'wich

Foust & Wolf (Sigmund Feust & David Wolf) 6 E. 14th & Morris av. c E. 155th

Fiala A. & E. (Andrew & Eugene) 207 Centre

Fibel L. & Brother (Louis & Adolph Fibel) 89 White

Fibrone Mfg. Co. (Louis Steinberger, Pres.; John H. Poppanburg, Treas. Capital, $60,000; further inf. unattainable) 300 Monroe

Fick & Breck (Nicholas Fick & Frank Breck) 965 Third av.

Ficke Brothers (William F. & Frank A. Ficke) 1596 Av. A

Ficken J. H. & G. (dissolved) 216 Bleecker

Ficken & Wiechman (Henry Ficken & John Wiechman) 132 Maiden la.

Ficker Brothers (no inf.) 665 E. 146th

Fidelity Indorsing & Guarantee Co. (not inc.) (Louis Smadbock, Isidor B. Brooks & Emanuel G. Buch) 155 B'way

Fidelity Loan & Trust Co. (of Sioux City, Ia.) (Joseph Sampson, Pres.; Frank W. Little, Sec.; William G. Clapp, Treas. Capital, $500,000. Directors: Cornelius C. Cuyler, William G. Clapp, Frank W. Little, John C. French, Joseph Sampson) 87 Wall

Fidelity Paper Co. (inf. unattainable) 140 Nassau

Fidelity Watch Case Co. (Charles Schwitter, Pres.; Adrian G. Funck, Sec. Capital, $125,000. Directors: Charles Schwitter, Adrian G. Funck, George Marchand, Martin Martins, Joseph Funck) 192 B'way, 90 Oliver & 382 Water

Fidelity & Casualty Co. (William M. Richards, Pres.; Robert J. Hillas, Sec. Capital, $250,000. Directors; George S. Coe, J. S. T. Stranahan, Alexander E. Orr, C. G. Williams, J. Rogers Maxwell, A. D. Hull, H. A. Hurlbart, Jacob D. Vermilye, John L. Riker, J. G. McCullough, T. S. Moore, William H. Male,

William M. Richards, George F. Seward) 216 D'way

Fiedler & Hanau (Frank Fiedler & Nathan A. Hanau) 92 Prince

Field Alfred & Co. (Harry C. Field & Alanson H. Saxton, only) 93 Chambers & 75 Reade

Field Engineering Co. (Cornelius J. Field, Pres.; Edward F. White, Sec.; further inf. unattainable) 15 Cortlandt

Field William & Son (William & William Field jr.) 130 Water

Field William Hildreth & Deshon (William Hildreth Field & Charles A. Deshon) 287 B'way

Field & Co. (L. E. Field, no Co.) 140 Nassau

Field & Harrison (William Hildreth Field & John B. Harrison) 287 B'way

Field & Wagener (Thomas Field & James W. Wagener) 115 Worth

Field, Chapman & Fenner (Aaron Field, Noah H. Chapman & William G. Fenner) 306 B'way

Field, Lindley & Co. (Edward M. Field, Daniel A. Lindley, Pope C. Tofft, John P. Truesdell, Edward S. Washburn & George Smith:— special partner, Cyrus W. Field, $500,000; terminates 30th March, 1891) 1 D'way

Fielding & Gwynn (Michael D. Fielding & Nicholas Gwynn) 42 Cotton Ex.

Fields & Co. (refused) 233 Centre

Fields & Grant (Joseph Fields & Richard Grant) 57 W. D'way

Fien & Klein (Bernhard Fien & John Klein) 142 Lincoln av.

Fifth Avenue Auction Rooms (Charles F. Wetmore, propr.) 240 Fifth av.

Fifth Avenue Bank (Algernon S. Frissell, Pres.; Thomas S. Vanvolkenburgh, Notary. Capital, $110,000. Directors: Algernon S. Frissell, Gardner Wetherbee, William R. Lee, Russell Sage, Charles S. Smith, John D. Dutcher, Joseph Thompson, Isaac Iokolheimer, James R. Plum, Edward H. Perkins jr, Samuel Shethar, John D. Crimmins, Edward A. Price, James G. Cannon) 530 Fifth av.

Fifth Avenue Carpet Co. (refused) 1 W. 14th

Fifth Avenue Railway Co. (Thomas B. Musgrave, Pres.; Ernest L. Jones, Sec.; Isaac B. Newcombe, Treas. Directors: Thomas B. Musgrave, Ernest L. Jones, Isaac B. Newcombe, Lewis Nay, Edward V. Loew, William H. Lee, Alfrederick S. Hatch) 10 Wall

Fifth Avenue Safe Deposit Co. (William C. Brewster, Pres.; George Montague, Treas. Capital, $100,000. Trustees; Henry A. Hurlbut, Alfred B. Darling, John L. Riker, William C. Brewster, George Montague, Charles B. Fosdick, George Sherman, George W. Carleton, Augustus C. Downing, William P. Eno, William P. St. John, Joseph S. Case, William R. Downe) 190 Fifth av.

Fifth Avenue Storage Warehouse (William P. Ryman, trustee; further inf. unattainable) 3 & 6 E. 18th

Fifth Avenue Transp. Co. (Ltd.) (William Wade, Pres.; William Irwin, Sec.; William B. Taylor, Treas. Capital, $250,000. Directors: Howell H. Barnes, William Irwin, Frank Baker, William B. Taylor, James H. Hendley, William T. Colbron, James Blewitt, Augustus D. Shepard, Robert C. Alexander, William L. Skidmore, Arnold Leo, William Wade, Charles C. Delmonico) 55 E. 38th, Fifth av. c E. 72d & 11 W. 100th

Fifth National Bank (Richard Kelly, Pres.; Andrew Thompson, Cashier; Richard B. Kelly & Thomas W. Smith, Notaries. Capital, $150,000. Directors; Richard Kelly, Napoleon J. Haines, T. W. Decker, James B. Brewster, Daniel D. Wylie, James Everard, Frederick Zittel, Richard B. Kelly, Andrew Thompson) 300 Third av.

Fiftieth St., Astoria Ferry & Central Park R. R.

TYPEWRITING DONE BY THE TROW CITY DIRECTORY CO., 11 University Place.

FIG　　　　98　　　　FIS

Co. (Charles E. James, Pres.; Frederick A. Bartlett, Sec. Capital, $500,000. Directors: Charles E. James, Frederick A. Bartlett, Horace M. Ruggles, F. R. Pemberton, John W. Mersereau, Robert A. Grescon, Jared F. Harris) 5 Beekman

Figaro Publishing Co. (Capital, $8,000; further inf. unattainable) no address

Figueredo & Milian (dissolved) 1554 Ninth av.

Files & Co. (Edward A. & Isaac Files) 151 E. 126th

Filmer John & Son (John & Herbert Filmer) 818 B'way

Finance Co. (Albert Lupton, Pres.; further inf. unattainable) 284 B'way

Financier Co. (Justus E. Ewing, Pres.; Charles T. Haviland, Sec. Capital, $30,000; further inf. unattainable) 5 B'way

Finch Stove Co. (no inf.) 117 Beekman

Finch Wells & Co. (Wells Finch & William L. Watson) 506 Produce Ex.

Finch's L. R., Sons (Edward L. & Henry T. Finch) 221 Produce Ex.

Finck A. & Son (August Finck, only) 825 W. 89th

Fincken E. & Son (Henry & John C. Fincken, only) 564 W. 23d

Findlay H. D. & Co. (Helen D. Findlay & Mary E. Gardner) 56 Reade

Findler & Wibel (Philip Findler & Ernest Wibel) 145 Nassau

Findley C. E. & Co. (no inf.) 862 Tenth av.

Fine A. & Son (Abraham & Joseph Fine) 91 E. B'way

Fine & Roth (dissolved) 91 E. B'way

Finegan & Muller (Peter E. Finegan & L. Edward Muller) 111 King & 560 Washn.

Finelite David & Son (dissolved) 426 Grand

Finelite J. & L. (Jacob & Lenn) 1 Baxter

Finelite & Margowski (Abraham Finelite & Max Margowski) 21 Centre

Finestone L. & Son (Louis & Morris A. Finestone) 119 E. B'way

Fink Joseph H. & Co. (Joseph H. & Rachel F. Fink) 25 Ann

Fink J. & Son (Joseph & Julius Fink) 639 Sixth

Fink S. & Co. (Simon & Samuel H. Fink) 21 Maiden la.

Fink & Abrams (Marcus Fink & Anne Abrams) 107 Grand

Fink, Bodenheimer & Co. (Samuel H. Fink, Henry Bodenheimer & Simon Fink) 8 Maiden la.

Finke Charles & Co. (Caroline A. Finke, Frank Buscher & John T. Mellor jr. only) 149 Water

Finkelstein J. & Co. (Jacob Finkelstein & Charles Cohen) 31 Bayard

Finkelstein L. & W. (no inf.) 63 Canal

Finkelstein M. & H. (Morris & Harris) 5 E. B'way

Finkelstein, Braciowsky & Co. (dissolved) 454 Seventh av.

Finkenaur & Co. (William Finkenaur & Paul Gantert) 1285 B'way

Finlay E. & W. S. (Elizabeth & Walter S.) 105 Prince

Finlay J. & Co. (James Finlay, Co. refused) 87 New

Finlay Brothers (John M. & Patrick M. Finlay) 564 Third av.

Finlay & Kendrick (dissolved) 111 B'way

Finley & Wotton (dissolved) 21 Park row

Finn L. & E. (Edward Finn, only) 211 & 314 Hudson & 28 Spring

Finnegan & Co. (John Finnegan, Co. refused) 92 Gold

Finney P. H. & Sons (Patrick H. & John F. & Timothy H. Finney) 859 Sixth av.

Finney & Fennell (Thomas J. Finney & Gerald M. Fennell) 250 B'way

Fire Assn. of N. Y. (Philander B. Armstrong, Pres.; Joseph C. Hatie, Sec. Capital, $300,000. Directors: Philander B. Armstrong, Oscar B. Meyer, Joseph Fox, John Dickson, Anton F. Troescher, Otto Von Hein, Aaron Carter, Emil Calman, William E. Lowe, Rudolph A. Loewenthal, Charles S. Braisted, J. W. Mack, Jacob H. Loewenstine, William Eggert, James Jourdan, Frederick Von Bernuth, David Calman, Samson Lachman, Nathan D. Bill, J. Spencer Turner, Lewis Friedman, Edward Barr, William B. Rice, Eberhard Faber, Benjamin Wendt, William P. Ridgely, Myer Hellman) 155 B'way

Fire Extinguisher Mfg. Co. (George H. Robinson, Pres.; Edward S. Innet, Sec. Capital, $200,000. Directors: George H. Robinson, Edward S. Innet, William H. H. Robinson, James H. Ferguson, Samuel A. Briggs) 15 Cortlandt & 351 Canal

Fireman's Publishing Co. (inf. unattainable) 819 B'way

Firemen's Ins. Co. (of N. Y.) (John F. Halsted, Pres.; Philander H. Oakley, Sec. Capital, $204,000. Directors: William G. Read, John F. Halsted, George F. Gantz, William H. Wallace, Alonzo Slote, Lucius H. Biglow, Arthur T. Sullivan, John H. Waydell, Wilson G. Hunt, S. D. Leverich, Joseph H. Gray, Edward A. Low, Francis R. Southwick, Philander H. Oakley, Alexander T. Vannest) 153 B'way

Firetag L. S. & Co. (Louis S. & Abraham Firetag) 66 Greene

Firm Printing Press Co. (Joseph L. Firm, Pres.; Louis H. Cramer, Sec. Capital, $100,000. Directors: Joseph L. Firm, Louis H. Cramer, Alexander Sutherland, Michael Crane, Charles B. Powell) 110 Fifth av.

First National Bank (George F. Baker, Pres.; Ebenezer Scofield, Cashier; Fisher A. Baker, Notary. Capital, $500,000. Directors: George F. Baker, Harris C. Fahnestock, James A. Garland, Ebenezer Scofield, Fisher A. Baker, Frederick F. Thompson, William Fahnestock) 2 Wall

First Vienna Bank (Edward Berger & Co. proprs.) 703 B'way.

First Vienna Window Cleaning Co. (Weiss & Heksch, proprs.) 300 Fifth

Firth & Foster Brothers (Thomas Firth & Joseph R. & John H. Foster) 851 Canal

Fischbach J. & Son (Jacob & Henry J. Fischbach) 26 St. Mark's pl.

Fischer George & Brother (George & Valentine Fischer) 209 Forsyth

Fischer Mills (B. Fischer & Co. proprs.) 325 G'wich

Fischer B. & Co. (Benedict Fischer, Charles E. Diefenthaler, Ernest Roloff & George T. Diefenthaler—special partner, George R. Lansing, $60,000; terminates 31st Dec. 1890) 325 G'wich & 165 Duane

Fischer C. H. & Co. (Charles H. Fischer, no Co.) 45 Harrison

Fischer J. & Brother (Joseph Fischer, only) 7 Bible h.

Fischer J. & C. (Charles S. Fischer, only) 110 Fifth av. & 417 W. 28th

Fischer J. A. & Co. (James A. & William A. Fischer) 131 Pearl

Fischer Brothers (cigars) (Frederick & William Fischer) 1390 Ninth av.

Fischer Brothers (drygds.) (Adolph & Samuel Fischer) 1550 First av.

Fischer Brothers (fcygds.) (no inf.) 293 First av.

Fischer Brothers (meat)(William & George Fischer) 941 Eighth av.

Fischer Brothers (printers) (Charles & Louis Fischer) 99 Mercer

**THE CALIGRAPH WRITING MACHINE,
HARTFORD, CONN.**

FIS 99 FLA

Fischer & Burnett Lumber Co. (Frederick Fischer, Pres.; Frederick Fischer jr, Sec. Capital, $100,000; further inf. unattainable) 193 Eleventh av.
Fischer & Decker (dissolved) 128 Delancey
Fischer & Deutsch (Solomon Fischer & Lipman Deutsch) 323 E. Houston
Fischer & Ewald (Frank Fischer & Otto Ewald) 8 Cedar
Fischer & Heinrichs (Anthony F. Fischer & Charles Heinrichs) 183 Duane
Fischer, Herrmann & Costello (Theodore Fischer, Otto E. Herrmann & Frank Costello) 47 Centre
Fischer, Schroeter & Co. (Ferdinand A. Fischer, F. August Schroeter & Oscar P. Pause) 1455 B'way
Fischl & Strauss (Joseph Fischl & Emanuel Strauss) 1368 Av. A
Fischlowitz & Konigsberg (Abraham J. Fischlowitz & Solomon Konigsberg) 183 Prince
Fish William jr. & Co. (William Fish jr. & John D. Reynolds) 60 Leonard
Fish A. W. & Co. (Andrew W. & Frederick K. Fish) 4 Stone
Fish J. D. & Co. (Sands H. & Silas Fish, only) 153 Maiden la.
Fishel Brothers (Isaac S. & Jacob L. & Abraham L. & William V. Fishel) 27 Walker
Fishel & Levy (Marks Fishel & Morris & Adolph L. & William Levy) 55 Dey
Fishel & Reid (Eugene Fishel & Willard P. Reid) 59 Liberty
Fishel, Adler & Schwartz (Aaron A. Fishel, Abraham I. Adler & Samuel Schwartz) 94 Fulton & 1149 B'way
Fishel, Nessler & Quitman (Henry W. Fishel, Louis D. Nessler & Maurice D. Quitman) 534 B'way
Fisher Frank L. & Co. (dissolved) 1269 & 1727 Ninth av.
Fisher John & Sons (no inf.) 541 E. 9th
Fisher Nathaniel & Co. (Irving R. & Nathaniel C. Fisher & George W. Davis, only) 31 Warren & 27 Murray
Fisher Robert C. & Co. (Robert C. Fisher & Edward B. Tompkins) 97 E. Houston
Fisher A. & Co. (Adolph Fisher & Otto E. Herrmann) 47 Centre
Fisher M. & Son (no inf.) 599 B'way
Fisher R. W. & A. J. (Robert W. & Andrew J.) 182 Cherry
Fisher T. H. & Co. (Tillmon H. Fisher & George H. Rache) 60 B'way
Fisher Brothers (barbers) (Samuel & Michael Fisher) 94 Norfolk
Fisher Brothers (butter) (no inf.) 177 E. 110th
Fisher Brothers (cigars) (Henry & Samuel Fisher) 836 Third av.
Fisher Brothers (hangings) (dissolved) 1569 Ninth av.
Fisher & Drucker (Emanuel Fisher & Henry Drucker) 429 E. Houston
Fisher & Rittenhouse (Charles H. Fisher & George M. Rittenhouse) 154 Reade
Fisher & Sons (James J. & Edward & Edward J. Fisher) 1 Maiden la.
Fisher's Island Steamboat Co. (Ltd.) (James H. Lyles, Pres.; William M. Hoes, Sec. Capital, $10,000. Directors: James H. Lyles, Edmund M. Ferguson, William P. Ketcham, Henry Bowers, George H. Bartlett, Archibald Mitchell) 89 Wall
Fishermen's Mutual Benefit Assn. (George H. Case, Pres.; Edward Longbotham, Sec.; Hiram Burnet, Treas. Directors; George H. Case, George F. Barker, George T. Moon, Hiram Burnet, Edward Longbotham, Pulaski Benjamin, David I. Robinson, Willis Rogers, Luke S.

Wilson, H. E. Stillman, Horace Geyer) 2 Fulton fish mkt
Fishkill & Matteawan Gas Works (Robert F. Mullins, propr.) 10 Wall
Fishman & Spiwak (Joseph Fishman & Louis Spiwak) 115 Hester
Fisk Harvey & Sons (Harvey & Harvey E. & Charles J. & Pliny Fisk) 29 Nassau
Fisk, Clark & Flagg (Henry G. Fisk, Thomas R. Clark & Thomas J. Flagg) 686 B'way
Fiske P. M. & Co. (no inf.) 20½ E. 42d
Fiske Brothers (Thomas P. & Frederick B. Fiske) 61 Water
Fiss & Corneille (George W. Fiss & William G. Corneille) 11 Vandewater
Fiss & Doerr (William Fiss & John B. Doerr) 153 E. 24th & 154 E. 25th
Fistere Brothers (Joseph & Charles Fistere) 488 Hudson
Fitch B. & Co. (Benjamin Fitch & Max Goldsmith) 59 Fourth av.
Fitch T. & S. H. (Theodore & S. Hedding Fitch) 5 Beekman
Fitch & Whitney (Halsey Fitch & Herbert C. Whitney;—special partner, Frederick W. Pitcher, $22,500; terminates 1st May, 1890) 170 Chambers
Fitchburg Steam Engine Co. (no inf.) 109 Liberty
Fithian Engine & Electric Light Co. (Benjamin H. Jessup, Pres. Capital, $1,250,000. Directors: Benjamin H. Jessup, Richard B. Fithian, Smith H. Freeman, Edward S. Peck) no address
Fithian J. H. & Co. (Josiah H. Fithian & Henry Searing) 61 Greene
Fitzgerald Brothers (brewers) (Edmund Fitzgerald, only) 439 Washn.
Fitzgerald Brothers (grocers) (James & Gerald Fitzgerald) 680 Tenth av.
Fitzgerald Brothers (shoes) (Patrick & Jeremiah Fitzgerald) 116 E. 63d
Fitzgibbon M. & Co. (Maurice Fitzgibbon & George B. Barcalow) 87 Crosby
Fitzgibbon & Co. (dissolved) 12 College pl.
Fitzmaurice & Reilly (dissolved) 2464 Third av.
Fitzpatrick A. C. & Co. (Austin C. Fitzpatrick & Watts C. Vanblercom;—special partner, Benjamin H. Howell, B'klyn, N. Y., $25,000; terminates 31st Dec. 1890) 112 Hudson
Fitzpatrick J. & Co. (Jeremiah & Charles J. & James J. Fitzpatrick) 28 N. Moore
Fitzpatrick J. G. & Co. (James G. Fitzpatrick & Thomas F. Somers) 58 Worth
Fitzpatrick T. & Son (Thomas & John H. Fitzpatrick) 126 W. 19th
Fitzpatrick & Cassidy (James F. Fitzpatrick & John Cassidy) 147 Fulton
Fitzpatrick & Ewen (William J. Fitzpatrick & John A. Ewen) 2 Stanton
Fitzpatrick & Prothero (Charles Fitzpatrick & David Prothero) 47 Gt. Jones
Fitzpatrick & Sharkey (dissolved) 542 Second av.
Fitzsimmons & Brogan (Patrick Fitzsimmons & Patrick F. Brogan) 100¼ W. 37th
Fitzsimons M. & Co. (Michael Fitzsimons & Frank Shiller) 214 W. 38th
Flaacke's Henry, Sons (Frederick W. & Christian F. Flaacke) 200 West
Flaccus F. & Son (Frederick & Charles Flaccus) 102 First av.
Flack J. A. & Son (James A. & William L. Flack) 3 N. William & 14 Frankfort
Flagg James H., Cutlery Co. (James H. Flagg, propr.) 148 Chambers
Flagg C. H. & Co. (Charles H. & Frank E. Flagg) 905 B'way

Flagg J. & Co. (no inf.) 25 E. 14th
Flagg Brothers (buttons) (Elisha & Francis F. Flagg) 113 Worth
Flagg Brothers (grocers) (George E. & Theodore Flagg) 1776 Lex. av.
Flagler A. & Co. (Albert Flagler, no Co.) 72 Reade
Flake Albert & Co. (Albert Flake, Co. refused) 239 B'way
Flam & Brandt (William Flam & Andrew G. Brandt) 508 Pearl
Flanagan B. & Son (J. Emmet Flanagan, only) 536 Sixth av.
Flanagan Brothers (Thomas & Richard Flanagan) 817 W. 112th & Boulevard n. W. 75th
Flanagan & Maguire (Thomas Flanagan & James Maguire) 54 New Chambers
Flanagan, Nay & Co. (James Flanagan, only) 262 Tenth av. & 448 W. 20th
Flanders Mfg. Co. (William G. Flanders, propr.) 20 Fourth av.
Flandrau A. S. & Co. (Seth C. Keyes & Daniel T. Wilson;—special partner, James W. Lawrence, *Mt. Vernon, N. Y.*, $25,000; terminates 15th Feb., 1893) 372 Broome
Flannery & Moran (Thomas & William H. Flannery & Michael Moran) 16 South
Flashner Brothers (Otto W. & Albert W. Flashner) 287 Seventh av.
Flax Seed Emulsion Co. (Arthur J. Cleveland, propr.) 85 Liberty
Fleck John W. & Son (John W. & Frederick F. Fleck) 199 Centre
Flegenheimer Brothers (Henry & David & Adolph Flegenheimer & Nathan V. Hammerschlag) 287 Eighth av. 483 Fifth & 1028 Second av.
Fleisch & Co. (Jacob H. & Nathan Fleisch) 516 B'way
Fleischhauer J. & Brother (Jacob & Julius Fleischhauer) 400 E. 45th
Fleischhauer M. & Sons (dissolved) 400 E. 45th
Fleischmann Brothers (Frederick L. & Morris Fleischmann) 863 First av.
Fleischmann & Co. (Charles & Maximilian Fleischmann) 701 Wash'n.
Fleischner, Mayer & Co. (Louis Fleischner, Mark A. Mayer, Alexander Schlussel, Solomon Hirsch & Samuel Simon) 361 B'way
Fleitmann & Co. (Herman & Ewald & Frederick T. & William M. Fleitmann) 460 Broome & 403 E. 91st
Flemer & Koehler (J. A. Henry Flemer & V. Hugo Koehler) 261 B'way
Fleming Cut Sole Co. (dissolved) 126 Chambers
Fleming Philip J. & Co. (Philip J. Fleming & James O'Reilly) 69 University pl.
Fleming William G. & Co. (William G. & Robert B. Fleming) 38 Wall
Fleming C. R. & Co. (Charles R. & George Fleming) r 75 Nassau
Fleming H. & Co. (dissolved) 144 Reade
Fleming & Kimball (William R. Fleming & George C. Kimball) 17 Day
Fleming & Peters (John Fleming & Philip Peters) 68 Little W. 12th
Fleming & Pierce (Archibald Fleming & John Pierce) 98 Duane
Fleming, Brewster & Alley (dissolved) 288 Second av.
Fless & Ridge (Louis Fless & Richard R. Ridge) 110 Fifth av.
Fletcher Bottle Packing Co. (George Shearman, Pres.; William D. Carter, Sec. Capital, $10,000. Directors: George Shearman, Abram Gitsky, William D. Carter) 172 Chambers
Fletcher John A. & Co. (John A. Fletcher & Alphonso de Risathal) 8 Warren

Fletcher W. & A., Co. (Andrew Fletcher, Pres.; Samuel Putnam, Sec. Capital, $60,000. Directors: Andrew Fletcher, Samuel Putnam, Stevenson Taylor, William H. Fletcher, Edwin R. Mead) 266 West
Fletcher W. H. & Co. (William H. Fletcher & Joseph S. Shaw) 345 B'way
Fletcher & Co. (Charles A. Fletcher & John Berger) 7 Warren
Fletcher & Hotze (John G. Fletcher & Peter Hotze) 6 Cotton Ex.
Fleurmont & Co. (dissolved) 72 Nassau
Fliedner & Bindewald (Edward Fliedner & Louis Bindewald) 474 B'way
Fliess William M. & Co. (refused) 47 B'way
Flinn James R. & Co. (dissolved) 39 Harrison
Flint George C., Co. (George C. Flint, Pres.; Frederick Pullman, Sec.; Montgomery B. Cowperthwait, Treas. Capital, $50,000. Directors: George C. Flint, Montgomery B. Cowperthwait, Frederick Pullman) 104 & 111 W. 14th, 154 W. 19th & 304 West
Flint & Co. (Benjamin & Charles R. & Wallace B. Flint) 142 Pearl
Flint, Blood & Co. (William W. Flint & Joseph F. Blood, no Co.) 196 B'way
Flock N. S. & Co. (Nelson S. Flock, Co. refused) 291 B'way
Flockhart Brothers (no inf.) 58 Centre
Flognus & Thompson (Rosa Flognus & Robert G. Thompson) 149 E. 130th
Flomar Brothers (dissolved) 1631 Av. A
Flomerfelt J. A. & Co. (James A. Flomerfelt, no Co.) 177 B'way
Florence Dale Coal Co. (Charles H. Bass, propr.) 17 B'way
Florence Soap Co. (Russell W. Chace, Pres.; David S. Wood, Sec. Capital, $25,000. Directors: David S. Wood, Russell W. Chace, Henry L. Gilsen) 386 B'way & 745 E. 11th
Florencia Mining & Milling Co. (Daniel D. Conover, Pres.; Thomas Clark, Sec. Capital, $2,500,000; further inf. unattainable) 45 William
Florentine Art Co. (dissolved) 51 Warren
Flores R. de & Co. (Rafael de Flores & Julien de Pionza) 511 Pearl & 24 Stone
Florida Central & Peninsular R. R. Co. (H. Raimon Duval, Pres.; Edgar R. Hoadley, Sec.; William N. Thompson, Treas. Capital, $29,082,003. Directors: W. Bayard & R. Fulton Cutting, H. Raimon Duval, Edward N. Dickerson, Adolph Engler, Lucius K. Wilmerding, Jonathan K. Gapen, Wayne MacVeagh, F. W. Peck, D. E. Maxwell, John A. Henderson) 84 Nassau
Florida Construction Co. (inf. unattainable) 10 Wall
Florida Land & Improvement Co. of N. J. (inf. unattainable) 42 New
Florida Line (N. A. Bennar & Co. proprs.) 19 Old sl. & Pier 11 E. R.
Florida Ocean & Gulf Canal Co. (James C. Spencer, Pres.; Charles L. Anderson, Sec.; John H. Mooney, Treas. Capital, $60,000,000. Directors: James C. Spencer, Horace A. Hurlbut, Charles L. Anderson, John H. Mooney, Heman Clark) 230 B'way
Florida Railway & Navigation Co. (no inf.) 85 Wall
Florida Tobacco Producing & Trading Co. (Robert C. Brown, Pres.; Peter Miller, Sec. Capital, $100,000. Directors: Robert C. Brown, George & Henry Storm, Peter Miller, William M. Corry) 203 E. 27th
Florida West Coast Improvement Co. (Joshua L. Chamberlain, V. Pres.; Alexander C. Quarrier, Sec.; Henry H. Man, Treas. Capital, $300,000. Directors: Joshua L. Chamberlain, Henry K. Man, Alexander C. Quarrier, James G. Gardiner, William M. Allee) 56 Wall

MERCHANTS EXCHANGE NAT. BANK OF THE CITY OF N. Y.
SOLICITS YOUR ACCOUNT. **257 Broadway.**
PHINEAS C. LOUNSBURY, President.   ALLEN S. APGAR, Cashier.

Flos Shade Roller Co. (Charles Flos, Pres.; Frank B. Wightman, Sec.; Francis Briggs, Treas. Capital, $100,000. Trustees: Charles Flos, Frank H. Wightman, Francis Briggs) 468 Cherry

Flower R. P. & Co. (Roswell P. & Anson R. & John D. & Frederick S. Flower & Williston B. Lockwood) 52 B'way & 5 Exchange ct.

Floyd James R. & Sons (James R. & Frederick W. & Henry E. Floyd) 539 W. 20th

Floyd Brothers (Edward E. & Charles O. Floyd) 84 W. B'way

Floyd & Co, (dissolved) 229 Fulton

Floyd & Newins (William Floyd & E. Smith Newins) 177 South

Floyd-Jones R. B. & Co. (dissolved) 62 William

Floyd-Jones & Robison (William C. Floyd-Jones & William Robison) 52 B'way & 2 Exchange ct.

Flukiger Brothers (John A. & Albert Flukiger) 203 Bleecker

Flushing Steamboat Line (L. Boyer's Sons, proprs.) 90 Wall & Pier 35½ E. R.

Foehrenbach F. & Co. (Francis & Michael Foehrenbach) 229 & 440 W. 46th

Foerster William & Co. (William Foerster, Siegfried Berja & Oscar O. Friedlaender) 127 Duane

Foerster J. & Son (Joseph & Oscar Foerster) 806 Fifth

Foerster Brothers (no inf.) 52 First

Fogarty & Brother (Michael & Patrick J. Fogarty) 110 Wasbn mkt

Fogg & Scribner (John C. Fogg & Gilbert H. Scribner jr.) 52 B'way

Foland & Co. (Russell & Charles H. Foland) 431 Eighth av. & 471 Sixth av.

Folds Brothers (no inf.) 389 E. 77th

Folding Trunk Co. (Russell P. Hoyt, Pres.; James Gwatkin, Sec.; Ira C. Whitehead, Treas. Capital, $40,000. Trustees: Russell P. Hoyt, Ira C. Whitehead, Edward O. Oppenheim) 319 B'way

Foley Gold Pen Co. (dissolved) 300 B'way

Foley James & Co. (James Foley & Michael Lanney) 160 Washn. mkt

Foley John R. & Son (John R. & John R. Foley jr.) 153 B'way

Foley D. F. & Co. (Daniel F. Foley & Henry S. Alkin) 22 Maiden la. & 587 Hudson

Foley Brothers (carriages) (Robert M. & Daniel W. Foley) 239 E. 127th

Foley Brothers (liquors) (John W. & James P. Foley) 745 Second av. & 427 First av.

Foley & Condon (John C. Foley & Patrick W. Condon) 205 First av.

Folin C. V. & Son (Caius V. & Washington L. Folin) Webster av. n E. 182d

Folk & Fritz (John H. Folk & Charles Fritz) 47 Warren

Folkard & Lawrence (Robert D. Folkard & George F. Lawrence) 482 Broome

Follett George & Co. (George & Austin W. & William J. Follett) 144 Duane

Follmer, Clogg & Co. (Charles J. Follmer, Levin H. Clogg, Theophilus Butts jr. & James L. Brown) 414 B'way

Follprecht William & Son (no inf.) 333 E. 60th

Folmer & Schwing (William F. Folmer & Walter E. Schwing) 391 B'way

Folsom H. & D., Arms Co. (David Folsom, Pres.; Henry T. Folsom, Sec.; Thomas T. More, Treas. Capital, $80,000. Directors: David & Henry T. Folsom, Thomas T. More) 15 Murray

Folsom Brothers (Samuel D. & Thomas W. & William H. Folsom) 834 B'way

Folsom & Mayer (George Folsom & Arthur Mayer) 115 Nassau

Fonda Lake Paper Co. (Inf. unattainable) 52 Broad

Fonda Thomas & Co. (Thomas Fonda & Charles & James Rosoll) 601 W. 33d

Fontaine Allen & Co. (dissolved) 1339 B'way

Foote Warren & Son (Warren & Francis S. Foote) 9 South

Foote A. W. & Co. (Arthur W. Foote & Edward Eggort) 125 Maiden la.

Foote & Co. (no inf.) 24 Stone

Foote & Knevals (Horace A. Foote & Stephen M. Knevals) 109 Water

Foppes & Partisch (Gustav Foppes & Otto Partisch) 30 Vesey

Forbell & Bragaw (Isaac W. Forbell & Jacob Bragaw) 10 Fulton

Forbes H. A. & Co. (Harold A. Forbes, no Co.) 180 Water

Forbes P. D. & Co. (Peter D. Forbes, no Co.) 609 Sixth av.

Forbes R. W. & Son (Robert W. & William J. Forbes) 14 S. William

Force William A. & Co. (William A. Force & Pearre E. Crowl) 60 Beekman

Force B. H. & Brother (dissolved) 34 N. Moore

Force & Fingold (dissolved) 425 Eighth av.

Ford Martin J. & Son (Martin J. & Martin A. Ford) 420 E. 55th

Ford A. E. & R. E. (Austin E. & Robert E.) 17 Barclay & 45 Warren

Ford F. A. & Co. (dissolved) 59 Murray

Ford Brothers (James & John Ford) 620 Eighth av.

Ford & Hirschberg (dissolved) r 21 Bowery

Ford & Kruger (John Ford & Adolph Kruger) 663 Sixth av.

Ford & McCabe (John J. Ford & John J. McCabe) 1 Forsyth

Ford, Rowell & Hone (Charles H. Ford, Edward Rowell & Robert G. Hone) 38 Pine

Fordham Co-operative Building & Loan Assn. (Charles Dunlop, Pres.; William H. Coffin, Sec.; Josiah A. Briggs, Treas. Directors: John V. Black, James Baillie, Thomas Casey, George Gade, W. H. Bassett, Michael Roiily, F. Saggermann, John H. Eden, William Coogan, Bernard Kelly, John J. Clinton, James Keene) 2511 Vanderbilt av. W.

Fords, Howard & Hulbert (John R. Howard, Pres.; George S. Hulbert, Treas.; Frank H. Bell, Sec. Capital, 40,000. Trustees: John R. Howard, George S. Hulbert, Frank H. Bell) 30 Lafayette pl.

Fordyce & Himpler (Alexander R. Fordyce & Francis G. Himpler) 145 B'way

Foreign Express Co. (Ltd.) (James L. Skillin, Pres.; Isaac F. Rooea, Treas. Capital, $50,000 ; further inf. unattainable) 172 Fulton

Foreign Fruit Exchange (Dominious Wegman, Pres.; William Rose, Sec.; Frederick S. Robinson, Treas.) 34 State

Foreign Trade Agency (Ltd.) (dissolved) 128 Pearl

Forest & Stream Publishing Co. (George Bird Grinnell, Pres.; Edward R. Wilbur, Sec. Capital, $9,000. Directors: George B. & George Bird Grinnell, Edward R. Wilbur) 318 B'way

Forester W. & T. G. (William & Thomas G.) 47 Murray

Formel & Co. (Julius Z. Formel & Francisco Lavandeyra) 607 B'way

Formica & Winner (Gaetano F. Formica & Isaac C. Winner) 87 S. 5th av.

Formosa Tea Co. (Charles M. Burke, propr.) 213 Mulberry

Fornes C. V. & Co. (Charles V. & John Fornes) 458 B'way & 123 Grand

SNOW, CHURCH & CO. {ESTABLISHED 1874.

FOR 102 FOW

Forrest H. A. & Co. (Henry A. Forrest & William E. Lucas) 104 John

Forrest & Sullivan (dissolved) 415 E. 34th

Forschner Charles & Son (Charles & George S. Forschner) 46 Rivington

Forst Brothers (Ambrose & Albin Forst) 1385 Third av.

Forster & Speir (Frederic P. Forster & Francis Speir jr.) 58 Wall

Forster, Hotaling & Klenke (William Forster, George P. Hotaling & William H. Klenke) 86 Wall

Forstmann & Co. (Louis Schreiber & Adolf Gansel:—special partner, Juline Forstmann, *Lins, Germany*, $150,000; terminates 31st Dec. 1890) 61 Worth

Forsythe & Co. (George & James Forsythe) 648 W. 48th & 2 Bond

Fort Lee Park & Steamboat Co. (inf. unattainable) Pier 41½ N. R.

Fort Madison Water Co. (G. D. L'Hullier, Pres.; H. M. Gilligan, Sec. Capital, $150,000. Trustees: G. E. Taintor, G. D. L'Hullier, F. Hopkinson Smith, H. M. Gilligan, D. A. Morrison, George IL Holt, Dudley Betts) 11 Wall

Fortune & Peterson (T. Thomas Fortune & Jerome B. Peterson) 4 Cedar

Forty-second St. & Grand St. Ferry R. R. Co. (George Green, Pres.; Charles P. Emmons, Sec.; Ralph J. Jacobs, Treas. Capital, $750,000. Directors: George Green, George C. Mitchell, Charles B. Hogg, Henry A. Hurlbut, George A. Heinrich, F. H. Smith, F. P. Lussis, Ralph J. Jacobs, Charles P. Emmons, J. M. Calhoun, Jordan L. Mott jr. N. Brewster, M. F. Thompson) 658 W. 42d

Forty-second St., Manhattanville & St. Nicholas Av. Railway Co. (John S. Foster, Pres.; Charles F. Naething, Sec.; Alfred Skitt, Treas. Capital, $2,500,000. Directors: Arthur Leary, Alfred Skitt, Alfred Wagstaff, John B. Dutcher, Charles Phelps, Daniel D. Conover, James Matthews, Joseph Haight, Jacob Fleischhauer, Charles F. Naething, William R. Foster, Richard W. Harnett, John S. Foster) 119 E. 42d

Forum Publishing Co. (Isaac L. Rice, Pres.; Nathan Bijur, Sec.; Moses Bruhl, Treas. Capital, $100,000. Trustees: Isaac L. Rice, Nathan Bijur, Lorettus S. Metcalf) 253 Fifth av.

Fosdick C. B. & Son (Charles B. & C. Baldwin Fosdick) 26 Spruce

Foss W. & Morris (Wolf Foss & Morris Ocheman) 70 Chrystie

Fossil Meal Co. (August Giese, propr.) 2 Cedar

Foster John E. & Co. (John E. Foster, no Co.) 17 Elizabeth

Foster William R. & Co. (William R. & John S. Foster & Emil C. Roever) 25 Canal

Foster B. B. & Co. (inf. unattainable) 521 W. 30th

Foster J. H. & A. E. (John H. & Albert E.) 18 Wall

Foster J. M. & Co. (John M. Foster & Hugh McConnell) 81 Fulton

Foster Brothers (hotel) (Alonzo W. & Augustus C. Foster) 917 B'way

Foster Brothers (h t'urng.) (dissolved) 779 & 1047 Third av.

Foster & Bailey (Theodore W. Foster & Samuel H. Bailey) 176 B'way

Foster & Co. (Elizabeth J. Foster & John B. D'Homergue) 194 Front

Foster & Foster (Edgar P. & Walter C. Foster) 132 Nassau

Foster & Freeman (Charles E. Foster & Frank L. Freeman) 38 Park row

Foster & Gannon (dissolved) 402 Water

Foster & Nolan (George Foster & John F. Nolan) 40 Cortlandt

Foster & Stephens (Walter J. Foster & George W. Stephens) 132 Nassau

Foster & Thomson (James Thomson, only) 52 Wall

Foster & Totten (John Foster & John A. Totten) 24 Dey

Foster & Wilson (James P. Foster & Andrew Wilson) 5 Beekman

Foster, Brown & Co. (Peil W. Foster, Edward W. Brown & James W. Shaw) 146 B'way

Foster, Duffee & Co. (Charles Foster & Charles P. Duffee, no Co.) 74 Pine

Foster, Hilson & Co. (Myer Foster & Edward & Max Hilson) 677 First av. & 225 E. 68d

Foster, Paul & Co. (William F. Foster, Pres.; Thomas N. Foster, Sec.; Samuel F. Paul, Treas. Capital, $200,000. Directors: William F. & Thomas N. Foster, Samuel F. Paul, Charles A. Reed, Livingston Gifford) 459 B'way

Foster's J. S., Sons (John W. & Charles O. Foster) 725 Ninth av.

Fotheringhams George & Son (George & Spencer M. C. Fotheringhams) r 350 W. 18th

Fougera E. & Co. (William R. Woodward & Emile Heydenreich, only) 30 N. William

Foulke & Co. (George B. Lockhart, only) 25 Beaver

Foulke & French (William B. Foulke & Luke B. French) 165 B'way

Foulkes & White (John Foulkes & Joseph A. White) r 189 Seventh av.

Fountain Ink Co. (Francis C. Brown, Pres.; A. Burr Chalmers, Sec.' Capital, $30,000. Trustees: Francis C. Brown, Thomas Cleland, A. Burr Chalmers) 167 B'way

Fournier Felix & Knopf (Felix Fournier & August E. Knopf) 36 Spruce

Fourteenth Street Bank (George F. Vail, Pres.; William J. Worrell, Cashier; Morris E. Sterne, Notary. Capital, $100,000. Directors: Henry A. Hurlbut, Richard I. Brewster, Charles I. Hudson, Benjamin H. Hertz, William Harris Roome, Frauk W. Kingman jr. Charles Schneider, Daniel B. Halstead, Charles P. Rogers, Frederick S. Howard, George Green, Morris E. Sterne, J. Romaine Brown, Frederick A. O. Schwarz) 3 E. 14th

Fourteenth Street Bargain House (Oscar Alexander, propr.) 6 E. 14th

Fourth National Bank (J. Edward Simmons, Pres.; Charles H. Patterson, Cashier; Benjamin P. Lee, Notary. Capital, $3,200,000. Directors: J. Edward Simmons, Frederick Mead, Cornelius N. Bliss, Charles S. Smith, John H. Inman, Robert W. Stuart, Richard T. Wilson, Marcus A. Bettman, James G. Cannon) 14 Nassau (*see adv. in back*)

Fowler Anderson, Co. (Anderson Fowler, Pres.; William F. Moffett, Sec.; Charles S. Walker, Treas. Capital, $500,000. Directors: Anderson & Emily Fowler, Charles S. Walker, William F. Moffett, Robert L. Scoles) 111 Produce Ex.

Fowler Mfg. Co. (Ltd.) (Calvin M. Cram, Pres.; Samuel H. Mills jr. Sec. Capital, $150,000; further inf. unattainable) 500 W. 23d & 2286 Second av.

Fowler William A. & Co. (William A. Fowler & Frank N. O'Brien) 540 Grand

Fowler J. & G. (James D. & George M.) 134 Pearl

Fowler W. & Co. (inf. unattainable) 6 City Hall pl.

Fowler Brothers (grocers) (Otis L. & John P. Fowler) 2077 Boston rd.

Fowler Brothers (grocers) (Thomas P. & John J. Fowler) 260 W. 125th

Fowler Brothers (jewelers) (Charles A. & Jeremiah D. Fowler) 166 B'way

Fowler Brothers (provns) (Anderson & Robert D. Fowler) 112 Produce Ex.

WATER METERS, GAS ENGINES, | **NATIONAL METER CO.**
FOR PUMPING AND POWER. | **252 Broadway, N. Y.**

FOW 103 FRA

Fowler & Co. (agents) (J. Odell & William Fowler) 165 B'way
Fowler & Co. (clothing) (Benjamin W. Fowler & Clarence Hubbard) 241 Fifth av.
Fowler & Fowler (Albert C. & Charles D. & Willie Fowler) 5 Beekman
Fowler & Rockwell (Charles S. Fowler & Lucius A. Rockwell;—special partners, Thomas Wilson & John L. Garvoy; further inf. refused) 9 Elizabeth
Fowler & Wells Co. (Charlotte F. Wells, Pres.; Henry S. Drayton, Sec.; Albert Turner, Treas. Capital, $20,000. Directors: Charlotte F. Wells, Nelson Sizer, Henry S. Drayton, Albert Turner, Lester A. Roberts) 775 B'way
Fowler's Rice Co. (Ltd.) (Charles R. Fowler, Pres.; Emanuel J. Ametrano, Sec. Capital, $500,000; further inf. unattainable) 83 Beaver
Fownes Brothers (dissolved) 134 Park Row
Fox George & Son (George Fox, only) 509 W. 34th
Fox William B. & Brother (William B. & Stephen T. Fox) 97 Chambers & 81 Reade
Fox C. A. & Co. (dissolved) 170 Worth
Fox D. & Co. (Denis Fox; — special partner, Richard H. Fraenckel, $50,000; terminates 24th Feb. 1891) 243 Sixth av.
Fox M. & Co. (Michael & Charles J. & G. Louis Fox) 1 Maiden la.
Fox M. J. & Brother (Michael J. & Joseph Fox) 158 E. 117th
Fox S. G. & Co. (dissolved) 54 Worth
Fox S. K. & Co. (Stephen K. Fox, no Co.) 225 Produce Ex.
Fox T. M. & J. M. (Teresa M. & Julia M.) 36 W. 34th
Fox Brothers (hardware) (dissolved) 632 Eighth av.
Fox Brothers (tailors) (Robert C. Fox, only) 58 W. 4th
Fox & Kerner (dissolved) 215 Av. A
Fox & Kronengold (Henry Fox & Adolph Kronengold) 234 Third av. & 251 Third
Fox & Stallknecht (James Fox & Harry S. Stallknecht) 5 Beekman
Fox, Leonard & Co. (James W. Fox & Clarence E. Leonard, no Co.) 43 B'way
Foy Brothers (Hugh Q. & Patrick Q. Foy) 269 W. 12th
Foy, Harmon & Chadwick (James H. Foy, George M. Harmon & Charles N. Chadwick) 60 White
Fraaker, Willard & Co. (dissolved) 18 W. 4th
Fradley J. F. & Co. (Joseph F. Fradley, Pres., Dudley P. Mygatt, Sec. Capital, $40,000. Directors: Joseph F. Fradley, Dudley P. Mygatt, Frank M. Mathews) 29 John
Fradley J. G. & Co. (Joseph G. Fradley & William E. Williamson) r 17 John
Frame & Shade (Emlen P. Frame & Charles R. Shade) 206 D'way
Francesconi & Co. (Giuseppina Francesconi & Javier Eguiguren) 17 B'way
Francis E. E. & Co. (Edward E. Francis & Ellsworth Doane) 22 W. Houston
Francis & Loutrel (Cyrus F. Loutrel, only) 45 Maiden la.
Francis & Muller (George H. Francis & Adolph Muller) 64 Leonard
Francklyn R. & Co. (Reginald & Cyril Francklyn) 5 S. William
Franco-Am. Agency for Dramatic Literature (Ltd.) (Alfred de Castro, Pres.; Nathan Bijur, Sec.; S. D. Rosenbaum, Treas. Capital, $60,000; further inf. unattainable) 1 B'way
Franco-Am. Food Co. (Alphonse Blardot, Pres.; William H. Seidel, Sec.; Octave Blardot, Treas. Capital, $35,000. Directors: Alphonse & Ernest & Octave Blardot, William H. &

Henry B. Seidel, Edward C. Hazard) 42 W. B'way & 101 Warren
Franco-Am. Patent Can Opening Co. (Frederic Reiset, Pres; Gustave A. Waeber, Sec. Capital, $50,000; further inf. unattainable) 78 Hudson
Franco-Am. Wine & Brandy Co. (Jules Bertrand, Pres.; Eugene Goesds, Sec.; Louise Conti, Treas. Capital, $500,000. Directors: Jules & Louis Bertrand, Louise Conti, Eugene Goesds) 159 Ninth av. & 405 W. 53d
Francois B. & Co. (Benjamin Francois & Anna P. Read) 65 W. 14th
Francois J. & Co. (Joseph Francois & John B. Perrand) 106 Centre
Francois & Co. (Francklyn W. Howes & Mathilda Blum, only) 296 Fifth av.
Francolini Giuseppe & Co. (Giuseppe & Pasquale Francolini) 2133 First av. & 60 Spring
Frank Gustav & Co. (Gustav Frank, no Co.) 280 Grand
Frank Joseph & Sons (Joseph & Julius & Bernhard Frank) 56 John
Frank Lewis & Son (Lewis and Maurice Frank) 48 Leonard
Frank Philip & John, 89 Beaver
Frank Philip & Son (Philip & Henry Frank) 1423 Second av.
Frank B. & Sons (Bettie & Henry & Max Frank) 71 Gold
Frank E. & Brother (Ellis & Abraham Frank) 94 Canal
Frank E. L. & Co. (Elias L. Frank & Jonas Honigsberger) 25 Broad
Frank F. & Co. (Francis Frank & Daniel Weidman) 744 B'way
Frank F. & Son (dissolved) 290 Stanton
Frank F. A. & Co. (Francis A. & Christian Dilg) 316 E. 82d
Frank H. & Son (Herman & Samuel Frank) 962 Third av.
Frank I. & Brother (Isaac & Jay Frank) 347 B'way
Frank I. & Co. (Isaac Frank, Abraham Kahn & Edward Frank) 49 White
Frank M. & Co. (Ellen M. Griffin, only) 17 E. 17th
Frank & Brother (David & Max Frank) 97 Sixth av.
Frank & Co. (Marcus A. Frank, no Co.) 436 Broome
Frank & Dubois (Emil H. Frank & Cornelius & Cornelius D. Dubois) 58 William
Frank & Dugan (Joseph Frank & Thomas Dugan) 66 Greene
Frank & Gipport (Charles Frank & George Gipport) 749 G'wich & 1488 Ninth av.
Frank & Goldsmith (Seligman Frank & Morris M. Goldsmith) 695 B'way
Frank & Gutmann (Henry C. Frank & Henry Gutmann) 156 W. B'way
Frank & Lambert (Morris Frank & Julius J. Lambert) 167 Greene
Frank & Levy (no inf.) 12 Essex
Frank & Manner (Michael Frank & Charles Manner) 880 Wash'n.
Frank & Moeller (Jacob W. Frank & Charles F. Moeller) 968 Sixth av.
Frank & Sonneborn (David Frank & Leo Sonneborn) 425 B'way
Frank & Swartz (Elias Frank & Semon S. Swartz) 101 Reade
Frank & Weis (Morris Frank, only) 57 Leonard & 313 E. 22d
Frank, Kiernan & Co. (Albert Frank, John J. Kiernan & James Rascovar) 152 B'way
Franke Louis & Co. (Louis Franke & Henry W. Struss) 110 Grand

EXCELSIOR BIRD FOOD. The recognized standard. The most reliable for your Canary. Use no other. Insist upon getting it. Packed only by C. ROSENSTEIN & CO., 373 Washington Street, New York.

Franke & Co. (Johan & Otto Franke) 1127 B'way

Frankel Max & Son (Max & Albert H. Frankel) 34 Beaver

Frankel Suspender Co. (Neuman Frankel, propr.) 161 E. B'way

Frankel & Hirsch (Siegfried Frankel & Isidor Hirsch) 507 Pearl & 100 Roosevelt

Frankel's Joseph, Sons (David J. & Simon & John Frankel) 1 Maiden la.

Frankenbusch H. & A. (Hormino & Augusta) 381 E. 77th

Frankenheim Brothers (Jacob & Emanuel Frankenheim) 70 Av. B

Frankenstein A. & Co. (Alexander Frankenstein & Bernard & Nathan & Jacob Magen) 87 Delancey

Frankenstein & Schwerin (Samuel Frankenstein & Herman Schwerin) 800 Second av.

Frankenthal Brothers (Jacob & Adolph Frankenthal) 151 S. 5th av. & 87 Wooster

Frankenthaler's L., Sons (Benjamin & Joseph Frankenthaler) 10 Av. B

Frankfeld E. (Emanuel & Louis Frankfeld) 251 Third av.

Frankfield A. & Co. (Adolph A. & Emil Frankfield) 52 W. 14th

Frankish Joseph jr. & Co. (dissolved) 3 Water

Frankish & Snyder (Joseph & John K. Frankish & Mosier R. Snyder) 8 Water

Frankl Brothers (Frederick & Julian J. Frankl) 596 B'way

Franklin Bank Note Co. (Enos Wilder, Pres.; A. Claxton Cary, Sec.; James Bannister, Treas. Capital, $20,000; further inf. unattainable) 142 B'way

Franklin Coal Co. (refused) 137 Goerck

Franklin Glass Co. (Capital, $500,000; further inf. unattainable) no address

Franklin Laundry (Margaret Cronin, propr.) 1781 D'way

Franklin Photo.-Engraving Co. (John H. Eggers, Pres.; Winfield S. Russell, Sec. Capital, $20,000. Directors: John H. Eggers, Winfield S. Russell, B. C. Eggers, Stephen F. Russell) 6 Barclay

Franklin Savings Bank (Archibald Turner, Pres.; William G. Conklin, Sec.; George Crouch, Treas. Trustees: George M. Beyer, George Crouch, J. L. Campbell, W. M. McLaury, Welcome G. Hitchcock, John D. Robinson, John S. Sills, William H. Van Kleeck, Joseph H. Chapman, George G. Rockwood, John J. Smith, Archibald Turner, Bernard Karsch, Abram Ayres, John H. G. Hildebrand, James G. Cannon, J. Edgar Lenycraft, William T. Booth, William G. Conklin, Thomas C. Acton, Henry W. Cannon) 656 Eighth av.

Franklin Stationery Mfg. & Uncle Ben Publishing Co. (John O'Connor, Pres; Edward D. Browne, Sec.; Dudley P. Browne, Treas. Capital, $3,000; further inf. unnattainable) 93 Liberty

Franklin & Co. (clothing) (James R. Franklin, no Co.) 155 Fifth av.

Franklin & Co. (real estate) (Jacob A. Good, only) 219 W. 125th

Franklin & Lippman (Louis H. Franklin & Samuel W. Lippman) 25 Gt. Jones

Franklin's Benjamin, Detective Agency (Benjamin Franklin, propr.) 280 B'way

Frankoski Brothers (Ernst Frankoski, only) 29 Greene

Frankovits & Gaxda (George Frankovits & Andrew Gaxda) 197 Third

Franks Charles & Co. (Charles & Clarence S. Franks) 8 Harrison

Frasch C. F. & Co. (Ernst F. Frasch & Bernhard Schreiner, only) 175 Park row

Fraser Arthur C. & Co. (Arthur C. & George H. Fraser & Arthur S. Browne) 5 Beekman

Fraser George H. & Co. (George H. Fraser, William F. Leonard & Alfred R. Anthony) 284 Wasbn.

Fraser Tablet Triimrate Mfg. Co. (Horatio N. Fraser, Pres.; Giles A. Manwaring, Sec. Capital, $20,000. Trustees : Horatio N. Fraser, Erwin T. West, Giles A. Manwaring) 311 W. 40th

Fraser C. & Co. (Cauldwell Fraser & William F. Browne) 374 Eighth av.

Fraser T. E. & Co. (Thomas E. Fraser & Leslie A. Frasiok) 1024 Second av.

Fraser & Co. (Horatio N. Fraser, no Co.) 208 Fifth av. & 1180 B'way

Fraser & Minor (dissolved) 44 B'way

Fraser, Major & Co. (James Fraser, William Kevan Major & William A. & George S. Fraser) 92 Cliff

Frash & Co. (Christian G. & C. E. Frash) 87 Hudson

Frasse Peter A. & Co. (Peter A. Frasse & John L. Howe) 95 Fulton

Frause & Co. (Henry F. Frasse, Andrew H. Briggs & Sarah J. Frasse) 92 Park row

Fraternal Directory Publishing Co. (George A. Hyman, propr.) 183 Clinton

Fraternal Printing Co. (not inc.) (Thomas I. Furlong & John T. Fletcher) 23 Day

Fraternity Publishing Co. (Capital, $25,000; further inf. unattainable) no address

Frawley & Lyons (John Frawley & Thomas Lyons) 965 Forest av.

Frazeo & Co. (Jonathan A. & William Y. Frazee) 601 W. 33d & 624 W. 36th

Frazer Lubricator Co. (Richard Brown, Pres.; Robert Cawthorne, Sec. Capital, $600,000. Directors: Richard Brown, George B. Swift, William H. & James H. Moore, Charles T. Trego) 73 Murray

Frazer's John, Son (Alexander C. Frazer) 2 Broome

Frederick & Son (Solomon & Hyman Fredrick) 1280 Third av.

Free & Fowler (George E. Free & Frank S. Fowler) 487 Sixth av.

Freeborn's Thomas C., Son (George W. Freeborn) 2236 Third av. & 167 E. 122d

Freed & Maiga (James Freed & Victor Maiga) 54 Stone

Freedman Brothers (Charles L & Moritz Freedman) 832 Canal & 89 Lispenard

Freeland Mining Co. (Henry Rosener, Pres.; Dominique F. Verdenal, Sec. Capital, $5,000,-000. Directors: Henry Rosener, George Laing, Louis Rosenfeld, Joseph Wittgenstein, Dominique F. Verdenal) 45 B'way

Freeman Charles D. & Co. (Charles D. Freeman & Edward K. Cone) 7 Wall

Freeman Dynamo Electric Motor Co. (N. Denison Morgan, Pres.; Robert Webb Morgan, Treas. Capital, $250,000. Trustees: N. Denison Morgan, Louis Bauer, Julian W. Merrill, James H. Morgan, Warren F. Freeman, Robert Webb Morgan, Samuel C. Robinson) 89 Liberty

Freeman Electric Mfg. Co. (Warren F. Freeman, Pres.; Robert Webb Morgan, Sec. Capital, $50,000. Trustees : Warren F. Freeman, J. W. Robertson, William H. Cottorell, Robert Webb Morgan, S. Blovelt) 89 Liberty

Freeman Perfume Co. (William D. Freeman, propr.) 523 E. 152d

Freeman Water Motor Co. (Frederick L. Pierce, Pres.; George P. Benjamin, Sec. Capital, $600,000. Directors: Frederick L. Pierce, George P. Benjamin, Melvin P. Freeman, Walter S. Adams) 104 Chambers

Freeman B. S. & Co. (Benjamin S. & Benjamin S. Freeman jr.) 194 B'way

IDEN & CO., University Place, 9th to 10th Sts., N. Y. | MANUFACTURERS OF **GAS FIXTURES AND ELECTROLIERS**

FRE 105 FRI

Freeman F. P. & Co. (Francis P. & Frank M. Freeman) 43 Exchange pl. & E. 42d c. Madison av.
Freeman S. & Co. (no inf.) 116 Produce Ex.
Freeman W. B. & Co. (William D. Freeman & Frederick P. Schlesinger) 1884 Tenth av.
Freeman Brothers (Martin & Joseph Freeman) 594 B'way & 124 Crosby
Freeman & Gillies (dissolved) 85 W. 23d
Freeman & Green (John C. Freeman & John D. Green) 280 B'way
Freeman & Schwarz (Henry Freeman & William Schwarz) 249 E. 119th
Freeman, Monheimer & Co. (dissolved) 691 B'way & 254 Mercer
Freeman's Van & Express Co. (Freeman & Schwarz, proprs.) 249 E. 119th
Freiershansen Brothers (Frederick & Henry Freierhausen) 1712 Second av. & 450 E. 88th
Freiman Brothers (Joseph & Henry Freiman) 69 Nassau
Freitag Mfg. Co. (Bloch & Baar, proprs.) 72 Grand
Freitag M. & Co. (Minna Freitag & Anna Kronberg) 311 E. 52d
French Samuel & Son (Samuel & Thomas H. French) 29 W. 23d
French William S. & Co. (William S. French, no Co.) 15 Liberty
French G. W. & Co. (dissolved) 452 Sixth av.
French J. C. & Son (James C. & George E. French) 155 W. B'way
French & Boughton (John H. French & Arthur H. Boughton) 44 W. 14th
French & Co. (neckwear) (refused) 85 Howard
French & Co. (produce) (Nathan R. & Walter G. & Emile French) 556 G'wich
French & Davenport (dissolved) 42 College pl.
French & Purgold (Robert French & Alfred J. Purgold) 1506 Ninth av.
French & Stuart (George W. French & Albert Stuart) 432 Sixth av.
French & Ward (Charles H. French & Robert Ward) 99 Franklin
French, Dixon & Desaldern (C. Abbott French, Robert C. Dixon jr. & Arthur Desaldern) 1769 B'way
Frenchman's Bay & Mt. Desert Land & Water Co. (no inf.) 55 Liberty
Frepp & Kempf (Frank Fropp & Henry Kempf) 177 Hester
Frercks D. & H. (Daniel D. & Herman) 2143 Lex. av.
Frese Brothers (Christian H. D. & Frank H. Frese) r 178 Suffolk
Frese & Vocke (Frederick Frese & Frederick Vocke) 172 Front
Freud J. Richard & Co. (J. Richard Freud, no Co.) 440 B'way
Freudenthal J. & Co. (Julius & Ludwig B, Freudenthal) 129 Crosby
Freudenthal R. & Co. (Rachel Freudenthal & Laura Flash) 15 Liepenard
Freund Alexander & Co. (Alexander & Rosa Freund) 169 Av. A
Freund Harry E., Publishing Co. (refused) 88 Fifth av.
Freund Max & Co. (Max & Adolph S. & Henry Freund) 8 Maiden la.
Freund Victor & Son (Henry V. & Maurice V. & Samuel W. Freund, only) 177 B'way & 760 Third av.
Freund J. & Co. (Jacob & Moses Freund & Asher Foise) 839 Grand
Freund P. & Co. (Philip & Catharine Freund) 9 Av. B
Freund & Stein (Isidor Freund & Gerson Stein) 244 Canal

Freund, Foise & Co. (Jacob Freund, Asher Foise & Moses Freund) 102 Franklin
Freutel's A., Son (Charles J. Freutel) 147 Elm
Frey A. & Son (Amandus & Paul R. Frey) 2407 First av.
Frey F. & Brother (Francis jr. & Gustave Frey) 57 Allen & 61 Division
Frey S. & Son (Samuel & Isaac Frey) 1523 First av.
Frey & Adler (Emanuel Frey & Carl Adler) 38 Pearl
Frey & Forgotston (Augustus Frey & John S. Forgotston) 104 E. 125th
Frey Brothers & Co. (Daniel & Isidor Frey & Edward M. Scheider) 1404 Av. A
Freystadt J. & Sons (Jacob & Edward A. & William H. Freystadt) 475 B'way & 48 Mercer
Frias J. & Co. (dissolved) 816 Lenox av.
Fribourg E. & Son (Eugene & Gustave Fribourg) 66 Wall
Frick Jacob & Brother (Jacob & Frederick Frick) 61 Jackson & 684 Water
Fridman S. & Son (Solomon & David Fridman) 4 Forsyth
Fried E. & Co. (Emil Fried & Jacob Furst) 164 E. 110th
Friedberg Brothers (Simon S. & Robert Friedberg) 29 Murray & 38 Warren
Friedberger Leopold S. & Co. (Salvatore B. Segroe, only) 203 & 423 B'way
Friedemann & Co. (Rachel & Julius Sawalsky, only) 639 B'way
Friedensville Zinc Co. (Horatio W. Greenough, Sec.; William H. Osgood, Treas.; further inf. unattainable) 24 State
Friedenthal F. & Co. (Ferdinand & Gusta Friedenthal) 405 E. 12th
Frieder S. & Co. (Samuel Frieder & Louis Rosenberg) 553 Second av.
Friederich J. & Son (dissolved) 263 Second
Friedewald H. & Co. (Frank E. Duffy, only) 834 B'way
Friedheim & Co. (Emil Friedheim, no Co.) 543 B'way
Friedhof George H. & Son (George H. Friedhof, only) 262 Canal
Friedhoff & Meyer (John P, Friedhoff & Henry C. Meyer) 174 Av. B, 99 Av. A & 32 & 82 First av.
Friedl & Wiese (John Friedl & Albert Wiese) 412 Fourth av.
Friedland A. S. & Co. (Abram S. Friedland, no Co.) 41 Essex
Friedlander A. & Co. (Albert Friedlander & Marcus Marks) 377 B'way
Friedlander R. & L. (Richard & Louis) 65 Nassau, 264½ Bowery & 50 Bond
Friedlander Brothers (Aaron & George Friedlander) 141 Eighth av,
Friedlander & Basch (Julius Friedlander & Joseph Basch) 371 Canal
Friedman Leonard & Co. (Leonard Friedman, Lewis Cantor & Max Adler) 203 Pearl
Friedman Sol & Co, (Solomon & Lewis Friedman) 522 B'way
Friedman A. & Co. (Iscegda.) (Arnold Friedman, no Co.) 45 Liepenard
Friedman A. & Co. (soap) (Abraham Friedman & Henry Reinhardt) 430 W. 17th
Friedman L. & Co. (Lewis Friedman & William B. Act) 1 Fourth av.
Friedman M. & Co. (Moses Friedman & William Duschnes) 177 Grand
Friedman W. L. & Son (Wolf L. & Simon K. Friedman) 186 Division
Friedman Brothers (Adolph & Emil Friedman) 162 Essex

CIRCULARS ADDRESSED TO ANY TRADE IN THE U. S. } Facilities
PROMPT, CAREFUL WORK } THE TROW CITY DIRECTORY CO., } Unequalled.
AT MODERATE PRICES. } 11 University Place.

FRI 106 FUL

Friedman & Rosenblum (Edward Friedman & Abraham Rosenblum) 61 Bleecker
Friedman & Schuler (William Friedman & William Schuler) 170 Norfolk
Friedman & Zucker (dissolved) 582 B'way
Friedmann Mfg. Co. (Isidor Friedmann, Pres.; Henry Friedmann, Treas.; Samuel Ehrich, Sec. Directors: Isidor & Henry Friedmann, Samuel Ehrich) 402 E. 104th & 62 White
Friedmann & Feigenbaum (Samuel Friedmann & Reuben Feigenbaum) 272 E. Houston
Friedmann & Weiss (Max Friedmann & David Weiss) 1248 Second av.
Friedrich John & Brother (John & William Friedrich) 16 Cooper Union
Friedrich Brothers (dissolved) 52 W. 4th
Friedrich & Strahal (dissolved) 157 Fulton
Friedrich & Gartmayer (Christian Friedrich & Joseph Gartmayer) 238 Seventh av.
Friedsam, Coletti & Co. (Morris Friedsam, Emile Coletti & Charles Williamson) 291 B'way
Friel & Hand (John J. Friel & John F. Hand) 891 Third av.
Friend E. G. & Co. (Edward & Gustav & Leonard Friend) 129 Maiden la.
Friend S. & Son (Samuel & Samuel Friend jr.) 33 John
Friend & House (Emanuel M. Friend & Frederick B. House) 25 Chambers
Frinke & Co. (refused) 26 W. 29th
Frisbee-Lnoop Mill Co. (J. Frank Emmons, Pres.; Lester W. Clark, Sec.; Edwin P. Goodwin, Treas. Capital, $500,000. Directors: J. Frank Emmons, Lester W. Clark, Edwin P. Goodwin, Samuel F. Emmons, Gideon Frisbee) 145 B'way
Frisbie D., Co. (William M. Frisbie, Pres.; M. S. Frisbie, Sec. Capital, $32,000. Directors: William M. & M. S. Frisbie, James D. Scranton) 112 Liberty
Frisbie & Co. (Washington J. Frisbie, no Co.) 20 Coenties sl.
Frisbie & Co. (Frederick Frisch & Henry Seelig) 7 Burling sl.
Frisch F. & Co. (Frederick Frisch & Henry Seelig) 7 Burling sl.
Frisch Brothers (Nathan & Samuel Frisch) 112 Willett
Frischen & Schramm (Frederick W. Frischen & Joseph C. Schramm) 147 Water
Frischman & Schlesinger (no inf.) 112 Bowery
Frisco Line (St. Louis & San Francisco Railway Co. proprs.) 353 B'way
Fritz R. P. & Co. (Egbert P. & Michael Fritz) 624 Hudson & 753 G'wich
Fritz L. & Sons (Louis & John & Theodore Fritz) 413 W. 44th & 596 Ninth av.
Fritz & Back (Gabrielle A. Fritz & Augustine A. Back) 705 Sixth av.
Fritz & Nagel (Charles Fritz & Carl E. Nagel) 90 Barclay
Fritzsche Brothers (Herman T. & Ernest T. & Lucie Fritzsche & Sigmund Loerburger) 34 Barclay
Froeber John & Son (John & John G. Froeber) 46 E. 26th
Froehlich Henry & Co. (Henry Froehlich & Seymour W. Frohlichstein) 40 Maiden la.
Froelke & Maasel (dissolved) 1141 Park av.
Frohmann Brothers (Herman & David & Hugo Frohmann) 230 Eighth av. 389 & 1409 Second av. & 1672 Third av.
Froman Brothers (Nathan & Joseph Froman) 172 Chambers
Fromann Charles & Son (Charles Fromann, only) 306 Mott
Fromme Brothers (Isaac & Abraham L. Fromme) 287 B'way
Frommel Oscar & Brother (Oscar & Frank Frommel) 21 Tenth av.

Frontera Antonio & Co. (dissolved) 261 Delancey
Frost King Co. (Alanson A. Sumner, Pres.; Benjamin F. Warren, Sec. Directors: Alanson A. Sumner, Samuel Q. Brown, Robert D. Benson, Reuben E. Nichols, Benjamin F. Warren) 12 B'way
Frost Rufus S. & Co. (Rufus S. & Charles H. Frost, Rufus F. Greeley & Rufus H. & Albert P. Frost) 24 White
Frost I. T. & J. G. & Co. (Isaac T. Frost jr. only) 411 Produce Ex.
Frost M. S. & Son (dissolved) 50 B'way
Frost S. H. & E. H. (Samuel H. & Edward H.) 100 Park pl.
Frost & Coe (dissolved) 280 B'way
Frothingham C. F. & Co. (Charles F. Frothingham & George C. Thomas) 50 Exchange pl.
Frothingham, Baylis & Co. (John W. & Benjamin T. & John S. & Nathaniel Frothingham, only) 74 Broad
Fruchtenicht & Ullrich (John Fruchtenicht & Charles A. Ullrich) 379 G'wich
Frush Brothers (Charles & Albert & Stephen Frush) 1704 Ninth av.
Frugone & Balletto (Francis L. Frugone & Augustus Balletto) 178 Park row
Fruit Buyers' Union (Charles H. Parsons, Pres.; William D. Clarke, Sec.; Frederick R. Franke, Treas.) 24 State
Fruit Trade Journal Co. (Hon S. Hobbs, Pres.; Isaac Tuck, Treas. Capital, $6,000; further inf. unattainable) 24 State
Frumberg M. & Co. (Morris Frumberg & Joseph Lindy) 33 Hester
Fry Frank C. & Co. (Frank C. Fry & William P. Woodruff) 1359 B'way
Fry Brothers (Simon & Isaac Fry) 494 Grand
Frye Jed & Co. (Jed Frye, William S. Nichols & John W. Fitzsimons) 47 Water
Fuchs Ferdinand & Brother (Ferdinand & Rudolph Fuchs) 140 W. 23d
Fuchs Minnie & Brother (Wilhelmina Fuchs & Charles Schwartz, only) r 17 John
Fuchs & Co. (Frederick Fuchs, no Co.) 293 Grand
Fuchs & Kleinan (Herman Fuchs & August Kleinan) 304 G'wich
Fuchs & Kraus (dissolved) 1327 Av. A
Fuchs & Lang (John M. Fuchs & Julius C. F. Lang) 29 Warren
Fuerst & Wordtmann (Martin Fuerst & John Wordtmann) 894½ Bowery
Fuerste Brothers (George H. & Bernhard G. Fuerste) 963 Second av.
Fuess & Deicke (Emil T. Fuess & Irving O. Deicke) Rider av. n E. 139th
Fuld Brothers (Samuel & Seligman & Bernhard Fuld) 45 Walker
Fullencamp & Co. (Harry B. & George H. Fullencamp) 334 Fifth av.
Fuller Brothers (Joseph A. & William K. Fuller) 33 Chambers
Fuller & Pullen (Almon D. Fuller & William H. H. Pullen) 189 Washn.
Fuller & Son (John B. & Waldo E. Fuller) 168 W. 65th
Fuller Brothers & Co. (George & Horace W. & Charles D. Fuller) 130 G'wich
Fuller's Paterson Express (Guindon & Berlan, proprs.) 215 Duane, 167 Washn. 117 John, 1 Lispenard & 313 Canal
Fullerton & Rushmore (William & Stephen W. Fullerton & Charles E. Rushmore) 87 Wall
Füllkrug H. & Son (dissolved) 312 Eighth
Fulton Construction Co. (Edward Lauterbach, Pres.; Edward Selleck, Sec.; Augustus T. Docharty, Treas. Capital, $400,000. Directors: Edward Lauterbach, Alfred Wagstaff,

THE CALIGRAPH WRITING MACHINE,
HARTFORD, CONN.

FUL   107   **GAN**

Augustus T. Docharty, Charles F. MacLean, Edward Selleck) 45 William

Fulton County Gold Mining Co. (John B. Conkling, Pres.; Lindley Murray, Sec. Capital, $1,000,000. Directors: John B. Conkling, Levi H. Palmer, Lindley Murray, Egbert Howe, Charles B. Bellows, William Euclid Young, Edward B. Bellows) 6 Wall

Fulton Fish Co. (S. L. Storer & Co. proprs.) 15 Fulton fish mkt

Fulton Mfg. Co. (Charles N. Middleton, propr.) 18 Cortlandt

Fulton Wire Works (Wooley & Co. proprs.) 61 Fulton

Fulton T. A. & Co. (Thomas A. Fulton, no Co.) 1826 Ninth av.

Fulton & Bookstaver (dissolved) 295 Spring & 1550 B'way

Fulton, Wall St. & Cortlandt St. Ferries R. R. Co. (Edward Kearney, Pres.; DeWitt J. Apgar, Sec. Capital, $700,000. Directors: Edward Kearney, Daniel D. Conover, John S. Foster, Gilbert M. Speir jr. Patrick Keenan, Edward Selleck, DeWitt J. Apgar) 45 William

Funch, Edye & Co. (Henry W. O. Edye, William Volckens, Frederick Fortmann & Paul Gotthell, only) 27 S. William & 41 Stone

Funk & Wagnalls (Isaac K. Funk & Adam W. Wagnalls) 18 Astor pl.

Furey Robert & Son (Robert & James Furey) 104 Fulton mkt

Furlong & Furlong (Richard & Richard Furlong jr.) E. 184th n Third av.

Furman G. & Co. (William H. & John L. Furman, only) 2 West, W. Washn. mkt

Furman S. H. & Co. (Silas H. Furman & Austin Finegan) 187 B'way

Furman & Page (John E. Furman, only) 112 Warren

Furniture Loan Co. (Evans & Co. proprs.) 128 B'way

Furniture Trade Assn. (Frederick Mohr, Pres.; Robert P. Lyon, Sec.; Albert L. Baldwin, Treas.) 62 Dowery

Fusco J. & Starace (Joseph Fusco & Louis Starace) 353 E. 10th

Fussell Ice Cream Co. (Mordecai T. Fussell, Pres.; Jacob Fussell, Treas. Capital, $10,000. Trustees: Mordecai T. & Jacob & Isabelle D. Fussell) 760 & 1485 B'way

Fyfe John & Co. (John Fyfe & Charles McLeod) 469 West

G

Gabler Ernest & Brother (Emil & estate of Ernest Gabler) 214 E. 22d

Gabriel & Schall (Max Gabriel & Herman Schall) 205 Pearl

Gadsden & Co. (Henry A. Gadsden, no Co.) 19 Whitehall

Gaffney & Smith (Sarah A. Gaffney & Isabella Smith) 67 W. 21st

Gafney & Jackson (James H. Gafney & Charles A. Jackson) 72 John

Gage J. P., Mfg. Co. (Robert K. Thompson, Pres.; Henry D. Rolph, Sec. Capital, $15,000. Directors: Robert K. Thompson, Henry D. & William T. Rolph) 96 Dowery

Gage & Co. (William T. Gage & Frank A. Stevens) 841 W. 59th

Gage & Joost (dissolved) 243 Water

Gager O. A. & Co. (Frederick Haviland & Frank F. Abbot — special partners, Mary M. Gager, B'klyn, France, $50,000 & Emile Gerard, Limoges, France, $30,000; terminates 20th June, 1895) 29 Barclay

Gaines S. W. & H. W. (dissolved) 83 Fulton

Galzer & Schmiedt (Jacob Galzer & John Schmiedt) 421 E. 13th

Gale & Co. (James Gale & Abram Mundel) 85 Pearl

Gale Sisters (dissolved) 124 Lex. av.

Gall & Lembke (Charles F. Lembke, only) 21 Union sq. W.

Gallagher & Casey (dissolved) 440 B'way

Gallagher Brothers (Terence F. & Hugh J. Gallagher) 273 & 386 Tenth av.

Gallagher & Baor (dissolved) 50 Walker

Gallagher & Smith (Walter Smith, only) 16 B'way

Galland B. & A. (no inf.) 72 Worth

Galland Brothers & Co. (Eugene & George & Max Galland) 274 Church

Gallatin National Bank (Frederick D. Tappen, Pres.; Arthur W. Sherman, Cashier; Horatio L. Braynard, Notary. Capital, $1,000,000. Directors: Frederick D. Tappen, Alexander H. Stevens, William W. Astor, Adrian Iselin jr., Thomas Denny, Frederick W. Stevens, Alfred Roosevelt, Henry I. Darbay) 36 Wall

Gallaudet P. W. & Co. (Peter W. Gallaudet & Henry Fitch jr.) 2 Wall (see adv. front cover)

Galle S. & Co. (Samuel Galle & Samuel Karlen) 44 Jay

Galligan T. P. & Son (Thomas P. & Thomas P. Galligan jr.) 629 E. 17th

Gallison & Hobron Co. (Louis D. Gallison, Pres.; Frederick N. Mason, Sec.; Benjamin F. Hobron, Treas. Capital, $50,000. Directors: Louis D. Gallison, Benjamin F. Hobron, Frederick N. Mason, Charles T. Root, Franklin H. Tinker) 698 B'way

Gallo Joseph & Brother (Joseph & Saverio Gallo) 14 Marion

Gallt & Branch (William T. Gallt & William M. Branch : — special partner, Sylvester F. Best, B'klyn, N. Y., $10,000 ; terminates 3d Oct. 1892) 95 Franklin

Galpen Horace & Co. (Horace Galpen & Alexander Carmichael jr.) 9 White

Galt John & Sons (John & Clarence H. & William R. Galt) 52 John

Galvano Farmfo Mfg. Co. (Cornelius Vanhouten, Pres.; Willard B. Vanhouten, Sec ; further inf. unattainable) 300 Fourth av.

Galvanotype Engraving Co. (Sheffield & Ballestier, proprs.) 50 Beekman

Galveston. Harrisburg & San Antonio Railway Co. (Collis P. Huntington, Pres.; John Bagnal, Sec.; P. J. Huller, Treas. Capital, $27,003,012. Directors: Isaac E. Gates, Edward H. Pardee, Collis P. Huntington, Charles C. Gibbs, Charles Babbidge, Julius Kruttschnitt, W. G. Van Vleck) 23 Broad

Galveston, Houston & Henderson R. R. Co. (George A. Eddy, Pres.; R. B. Hawley, Sec. Capital, $1,000,000. Directors: George A. Eddy, R. C. Cross, D. P. McDonald, R. C. Foster, R. B. Hawley, S. H. H. Clark, Ira H. Evans, C. L. Slaughter) 195 B'way

Galway & Co. (William T. & Charles Galway) 50 B'way

Galwey & Feldmann (Edward T. Galwey & Ernst Feldman) 66 Broad

Gambee & Co. (Isaac T. & William Y. Gambee & William A. Burton) 1008 Forest av.

Gamble William & Co. (William & Andrew Gamble) 165 Reade

Gamble & Levy (William Gamble & Herman Levy) 158 Mercer

Gamewell Fire Alarm Telegraph Co. (Joseph W. Stover, Pres.; Charles W. Cornell, Sec. Capital, $750,000. Directors: William F. Allen, David H. Bates, Moses G. Crane, Samuel Carpenter, Dennis Doren, John N. Gamewell, James Merrihew, Otis T. Pettee, Samuel F. Pierson, Joseph W. Stover, William H. Woolverton) 1¾ Barclay

Gandolfi L. & Co. (Luigi Gandolfi & Hector Grassi) 104 S. 5th av.

SPECIAL ATTENTION PAID TO THIS CLASS OF WORK. } **BANKERS' & BROKERS' CIRCULARS DELIVERED** { THE TROW CITY DIRECTORY CO. 11 University Place.

GAN 106 GAR

Gane Brothers (Thomas F. & George A. Gane) 81 Duane

Gangel & Nelson (Max Gangel & Gustave Nelson) 318 Canal

Ganns F. & H. Meisel (Frank Ganns & Henry Meisel) 551 W. 52d

Gans L. L. & Brother (Levi L. & Clarence L. Gans) 349 B'way

Gans Brothers (dissolved) 42 Exchange pl.

Gans & Rosenzweig (Jacob Gans & Adolph Rosenzweig) 196 Second

Gans Brothers & Gutwillig (Ralph & Robert Gans & Henry Gutwillig) 316 Church

Gans Brothers & Rosenthal (Joseph S. Gans, Mayer Rosenthal & Max Gans) 150 Water

Gans' J. S., Son (Samuel J. Gans) 131 Water

Gansevoort Bank (Timothy C. Kimball, Pres.; Frank H. Skelding, Cashier; P. F. Hillery, Notary. Capital, $500,000. Directors: John Castree, Andrew Icken, Hugh King, Hazen Kimball, Frank Frommel, Francis McMulkin, C. E. Bigelow, Thomas J. Roberts, Alfred Bennett, Timothy C. Kimball) 356 W. 14th

Gansevoort Carriage Works (Perrin, Payson & Co. proprs.) 75 & 76 Little W. 12th

Gansevoort Freezing & Cold Storage Co. (Robert Hewitt, Pres.; William E. Mackey, Sec.; James J. Phelan, Treas. Capital, $50,000. Directors: Robert Hewitt, James J. Phelan, William E. Mackey, James S. Stearns, Charles R. Hewitt, Henry C. Wells) 515 West

Gansz D. F. & Son (dissolved) 23 Market

Ganter & Schwenk (John Ganter & Christian Schwenk) 89 Gt. Jones

Gantert Paul & Son (Paul & Edward A. Gantert) 482 Third av.

Gantz, Jones & Co. (George F. Gantz & John M. & Enos F. & Franklin B. Jones) 176 Duane

Ganun & Parsons (Stephen M. Ganun & George F. Parsons) 5 W. 42d

Garbade E. & Son (Emily & William Garbade) 84 W. Houston & 1702 Ninth av.

Garcia F., Brother & Co. (Francisco & Ramon Garcia:—special partner, Vincente Galarza, $100,000; terminates 1st Jan. 1892) 167 Water

Garcia & Vega (Alvaro Garcia & José Vega) 171 Pearl

Garcia, Pando & Co. (Secundino Garcia & Jose Pando, no Co.) 86 Maiden la.

Gard's S. H., Sons (Anson A. & D. Frank Gard) 206 Produce Ex.

Gardam William & Son (William & Joseph Gardam) 96 John

Garden Publishing Co. (Ltd.) (Lawson Valentine, Pres.; John De Wolf, Sec.; Edgar H. Libby, Treas. Capital, $25,000. Directors: Lawson Valentine, Charles Barnard, L. H. Bailey, John De Wolf, Edgar H. Libby) 10 Spruce

Garden & Forest Publishing Co. (Charles S. Sargent, Pres.; Frederick L. Ames, Sec.; Henry H. Hunnewell, Treas. Capital, $50,000. Directors: Charles S. Sargent, John L. Gardiner, Frederick L. Ames, Henry H. Hunnewell) 154 Nassau

Gardiner Binding & Mailing Co. (Edwin F. Waters, Pres.; Charles Whitaker, Sec.; Charles S. Young, Treas. Capital, $75,000. Directors: Edwin F. Waters, Charles Whitaker, A. D. S. Bell, Charles S. Young, Henry C. Miller, James E. Whitaker, R. W. Waters, Edwin W. Noyes, Hubert Gardiner) 13 Frankfort & 39 Gold

Gardiner A. K. & Brother (Arthur K. & Clement E. Gardiner) 1½ Cedar

Gardiner E. O. & Co. (no inf.) 605 B'way

Gardiner H. & Co. (dissolved) 39 Gold

Gardiner R. & H. (inf. unattainable) 410 Lenox av.

Gardiner & Boucher (James M. Gardiner & Henry Boucher) 77 Front

Gardiner & Estes (Hubert Gardiner & Charles A. Estes) 675 Hudson

Gardner Co. (Forsythe & Co., proprs.) 643 W. 48th & 2 Bond

Gardner A. S. & Co. (Avery S. Gardner & Henry B. Henson) 17 Maiden la.

Gardner E. & Son (Elijah & Howard D. Gardner) 249 E. 118th

Gardner I. & Son (Isaac S. & Rudolph Gardner) 1876 Lex. av.

Gardner J. B. & Son (John B. & Hermon H. Gardner) 147 Fulton

Gardner M. & Co. (Moses Gardner & Henry Glass) 302 Church

Gardner & Co. (John B. Gardner & Thomas Rhodes) 111 Franklin

Gardner & Hansmann (Robert W. Gardner & Sigmund Hansmann) 349 Eighth av.

Gardner & Vail (J. Wright Gardner & Mary L. Vail) 773 & 169 B'way

Garfield National Bank (Alfred C. Cheney, Pres.; Henry D. Northrop, Cashier. Capital, $200,000. Directors: Alfred C. Cheney, Hiram Hitchcock, James H. Breslin, Edward Holbrook, Henry Maillard, Samuel D. Styles, George H. Wyckoff) 370 Sixth av.

Garfield Safe Deposit Co. (Alfred C. Cheney, Pres.; Alonzo E. Conover, Sec.; Horace H. Brockway, Treas. Capital, $150,000. Directors: Benjamin Altman, James H. Breslin, Alfred C. Cheney, Silas B. Dutcher, Adolpho H. Fischer, Edward Holbrook, Hiram Hitchcock, Frank R. Lawrence, James McCutcheon, Thomas C. Sloane, William B. Stafford, Samuel D. Styles, James F. Sutton) 78 W. 23d

Garlic & Co. (no inf.) 539 Tenth av.

Garlick J. E. & J. (James E. & John) 254 Washn.

Garmendia B., Spalding de & Brother (B. Spalding & Martin J. S. de Garmendia) 73 Cotton Ex. & 257 G'wich

Garnar Thomas & Co. (Thomas Garnar & James V. Walsh) 151 William

Garner & Co. (William E. Thorn, only) 10 Worth

Garnsey E. D. & Brother (Erasmus D. & William H. Garnsey) 182 E. 28th

Garrecht C. & L. (no inf.) 308 E. 40th

Garretson & Eastman (Garret J. Garretson & Henry M. W. & George W. Eastman) 5 Beekman

Garrettson F. P. & Co. (Frederick P. Garrettson, no Co.) 156 Front

Garrettson & Harvey (Lyttleton G. Garrettson & Ashton Harvey) 85 B'way

Garrigues & Hencken (Robert L. Reade, receiver) 31 Nassau

Garrison Martin & Co. (inf. unattainable) 280 B'way

Garrison W. C., Mfg. Co. (Winton C. Garrison, Pres.; Henry Acker, Sec.; Frederick M. Lyon, Treas. Capital, $25,000. Directors: Winton C. Garrison, Henry Acker, Frederick M. Lyon) 75 Warren

Garry Brothers (Thomas & Michael J. Garry) 308 Grand

Garside A. & Sons (Abraham & John R. & Herbert Garside) 181 Duane

Garside & Busby (Lawton B. Garside & Winslow E. Busby) 60 B'way

Gartuer & Friedenhelt (Isidor Gartner & Isaac Friedenhelt) 111 Grand

Garvin Machine Co. (George K. Garvin, Pres.; Eugene E. Garvin, Treas.; Frank W. Garvin, Sec. Capital, $100,000. Directors: George K. & Eugene E. & Frank W. Garvin) Laight c Canal

Garvin E. E. & Co. (dissolved) Laight c Canal

FOR THE BEST CO-PARTNERSHIP IN THE BEST CORPORATION SEE PAGE F IN BACK OF BOOK

Garvin E. L. & Co. (James Gray, John L. Shea & George D. Jones, only) 45 William
Gary Typewriting Co. (Margaret Beaton, propr.) 15 Wall
Gas Consumers' Assn. of the State of N. Y. (no inf.) 55 Liberty
Gas Consumers' Benefit Co. of N. Y. (no inf.) 16 Murray & 19 Park pl.
Gas Consumers' Benefit Co. of the U. S. (Walter M. Jackson, Pres.; George T. Gaden, Sec. Capital, $750,000. Directors: Walter M. Jackson, Francis B. Thurber, Hiram Hitchcock, John W. Kilbreth, William B. Baldwin, Thomas R. Brown, George T. Gaden) 21 Jane
Gas Engine & Power Co. (Clement Gould, Pres.; John J. Amory, Sec. Capital, $100,000. Trustees: Clement Gould, John J. Amory, Edward V. Cary, W. Frank West, Hans Jansen) Morris Dock
Gas Saving Co. (Benjamin H. Senley, Sec. Capital, $200,000. Directors: Benjamin H. & Benjamin T. Senley, P. C. Adams) 171 B'way
Gaskell William & Son (William & Robert E. Gaskell) 483 E. 25th
Gaskell, Greenlie & Co. (dissolved) 499 Water & 253 South
Gaskill, Bauer & Condermann (dissolved) 355 Canal
Gasser Martin & Co. (John N. Spanss, only) 63 G'wich & 24 Trinity pl.
Gasser's M., Son (August J. Gasser) 18 G'wich
Gassin Brothers (Charles E. & Joseph R. Gassin) 174 Bleecker
Gast Lithograph & Engraving Co. (Ltd.) (Louis J. W. Wall, Pres.. Olin D. Gray, Sec. Capital, $40,000; further inf. unattainable) 0 Desbrosses & 36 Vestry
Gate City Stone Filter Co. (Alphonse de Riesthal, Pres.; Gustave E. de Riesthal, Sec. Capital, $250,000. Directors: Alphonse & Gustave E. de Riesthal, Samuel L. & Andrew J. McBride, Thomas C. Smith) 46 Murray
Gatehouse J. H. & Co. (dissolved) 115 Nassau
Gately & Williams (John Williams & estate of Michael R. Gately) 89 W. 14th & 136 W. 23d
Gates Church B. & Co. (Ephraim C. Gates, John F. Steeves, Henry H. Barnard & Bradley L. Eaton, only) 227 Mott av. & Webster av. n E. 187th
Gates F. Tenney & Son (F. Tenney & Frank W. Gates) 39 Dey
Gates Brothers (Samuel D. & Simon C. Gates) 504 W. 13th
Gathmann Brothers (John & Henry Gathmann) 278 Pearl
Gatjen & Ahlers (John Gatjen & Abrend Ahlers) 88 Beekman
Gatjen & Oost (John Gatjen & Henry Oost) 34 Whitehall
Gatto & Cattoni (Giacinto Gatto & Joseph Cattoni) 103 W. 38th
Gaudalupana Mining & Milling Co. (George A. Harris, Pres.; John F. Zebley, Sec. Capital, $300,000. Directors: George A. Harris, conduce G. Megrue, Julius A. Skilton, John F. Zebley, Samuel W. Smith, Edward M. Comos, George T. Hilton) 45 B'way
Gaunt & Janvier (James Gaunt & Walter R. Janvier) 365 Canal
Gaunt & Martinez (Thomas Gaunt & Manuel J. Martinez) 115 B'way
Gaussa & Muzzio (Dominick Gaussa & Andrew Muzzio) 19 Baxter
Gautier D. G. & Co. (Dudley G. Gautier & William C. Pearson) 114 John
Gautschy & Grieder (Henry Gautschy & Adolph Grieder) 259 W. 87th
Gavagan & Corbin (Joseph C. Gavagan & Frank Corbin) 551 Washn.
Gay William & Co. (dissolved) 27 Warren

Gay & Dickinson (George C. Gay & Charles H. Dickinson) 24 Broad
Gay Brothers & Co. (John & Charles jr. & Frederick Gay) 34 Reade & 27 Warren
Gayler E. & Co. (Ewald Gayler, no Co.) 639 B'way
Gaylord Don A. & Co. (dissolved) 507 W. 35th
Gaynor & Rankin (Thomas F. Gaynor & James Rankin) 1473 Ninth av.
Gazlay Brothers (John C. & George E. Gazlay) 157 William
Gazzolo P. & A. Persagnio (Paul Gazzolo & Antonio Persagnio) 54 Wash. sq. S.
Gazzolo & Sanlorenzo (dissolved) 219 Wooster
Gebert & Co. (Gustav & Mary Gebert) 2239 Third av.
Gebhard F. & Son (Frederick & John F. Gebhard) 462 Sixth av.
Gebhard & Darnum (Edward Gebhard & Henry A. Darnum) 26 Broad
Gebhard & Clayborne (Frederick W. Gebhard & William Clayborne) 251 Water
Gebuhr & Vonbuitzingelowen (Carl E. Gebuhr & Bruno Vonbuitzingelowen) 20 Church
Geddes & Smith (refused) 81 Nassau
Gedney W. H. & Son (William H. & William A. Gedney) 330 W. 40th
Gedney's Improved Patent Steam Carpet Beating & Renovating Works (estate of Charles Gedney, propr.) 247 W. 47th & 1858 B'way
Geerdes & Hafker (Cornelius Geerdes & Henry Hafker) 180 West
Geery David R. & Co. (David R. Geery, no Co.) 39 Gold
Gohlen F. & Sons (Feodore & Charles W. & William J. Gehlen) 104 E. 17th
Gehlert Edward & Son (Edward & Edward Gehlert jr.) 1843 Park av. & 2455 Eighth av.
Geib & Dorland (William H. Geib & Irving V. Dorland) 19 Whitehall
Geils & Schlottmann (no inf.) 433 Sixth
Geis A. & E. (Albert S. & Edward) 2665 Third av. & 687 E. 140th
Geis & Dietz (William Geis & Conrad Dietz) 151 Av. A
Geisenheimer & Co. (Otto & Theodore Geisenheimer & Theodore Graeven) 7 Cedar
Geismar D. & Co. (no inf.) 335 B'way
Geisenhainer Brothers (Jacob A. & Frederick W. Geisenhainer) 298 B'way
Geizler Brothers (David & Samuel Geizler) 191 G'wich
Gelb & Co. (Louis Gelb, no Co.) 194 South
Gelbaar Henry & Co. (dissolved) 871 Hudson
Gellin & Petersdorff (Gustave Gellin & Max Petersdorff) 337 E. 75th
Gelston & Bussing (William J. Gelston & John S. Bussing) 24 Pine
Gem Combined Ironing & Bosom Board Co. (John J. Sanders, propr.) 152 E. 110th
Gem Mfg. Co. (Holmes & Allen, proprs.) 587 Hudson
General Copying Apparatus Co. of Am. (Sidney Henry, Pres.; Hermann Klatter, Sec.; further inf. unattainable) 200 B'way
General Development Co. (refused) 45 B'way
Genesee Salt Co. (James Wood, Pres.; H. G. Morris, Sec.; W. H. Male, Treas. Capital, $125,000. Directors: James Wood, A. L. Loomis, W. H. Male, Henry G. Piffard, E. F. Fowler, H. G. Morris, R. H. Downing) 6 Harrison
Gennerich & Illiemann (Henry W. Gennerich & Emil A. Illiemann) 180 West
Gennerich & Vonbremen (George Gennerich & Henry Vonbremen) 15 Harrison

TYPEWRITING DONE BY THE TROW CITY DIRECTORY CO., 11 University Place.

Gennero L. & G. Parisio (Louis Gennero & Gasper Parisio) 248 Washn.
Gentles & Bradley (Lewis H. Gentles & William Bradley) 157 E. 125th
Geoffroy & Co. (Nicholas Geoffroy, only) 23 Maiden la.
George Henry & Co. (Henry & Richard F. George) 12 Union sq. E.
George C. H. & Co. (estate of Charles H. George, only) 299 Fifth av.
George E. & Co. (Edwin George, Henry A. Kessel & Edwin George jr.) 82 South
George's Creek & Cumberland R. R. Co. (Henry Loveridge, Pres.; William De L. Walbridge, Sec. Capital, $345,000. Directors: Henry Loveridge, James A. Alexander, Alexander M. White, George L. Kingsland, Sidney Wintringham, George P., Bangs, Benjamin Williamson) 85 B'way
Georgen & Hahn (William T. Georgen & John W. Hahn) 54 E. 23d
Georgens Mining Co. (inf. unattainable) 7 Nassau
Georgi & Haight (Otto H. Georgi & Oscar C. Haight) 3227 Third av.
Georgia Co. (inf. unattainable) 7 Nassau
Georgia Pacific Railway Co. (Joseph Bryan, Pres.; further inf. refused) 2 Wall
Gerard & Brown (Frank W. Gerard & Raymond F. Brown) 172 Pearl
Gerardi Joseph & Co. (Joseph Gerardi, Joseph & Nicholas Mariuello, Joseph & Rocco St. Angelo & Nicholas Ramingnani) 45 Crosby
Gerber F. & J. (John G. Gerber, only) 297 Duane
Gerbrach J. F. & G. (John F. & George G.) 119 W. 50th
Gerbracht & Co. (Eugene A. & Ernest W. Gerbracht) 11 Cannon
Gerdau Otto (Otto Gerdau:—special partner, Heinrich A. Meyer jr. *Hamburg, Germany*, $20,-000 ; terminates 31st Dec. 1892) 41 Day
Gerdes & Mengels (Martin Gerdes & William C. F. Mengels) 308 Washn.
Gerety E. & P. (Edward & Patrick) 380 Eighth av.
Gerety & Glidea (dissolved) 1746 Lex. av.
Gerhard Paul F. & Co. (Paul F. Gerhard & George H. Brewer) 84 Broad
Gerhards Brothers (Julius & Victor Gerhards) 177 Essex
Gerisch William & Son (William & Emile H. Gerisch) 260 W. 70th
Gerken B. C. & Co. (Benjamin C. Gerkin & Henry Niemeyer) 312 E. 75th
Gerken Drothers (dissolved) 1485 Third av.
Gerken & Burmeister (Henry N. Gerken & Charles H. Burmeister) 189 Reade
Gerken & Co. (dissolved) 504 Lenox av.
Gerli C. & E., Fratelli & Co. (Charles & Emanuel Gerli & Enrico Spasciani) 31 Wooster
Germ Proof Filter Co. (inf. unattainable) 5 B'way
German Am. Bank (Henry Rocholl, Pres.; John F. Fredericks, Cashier ; Julius J. Lyons, Notary. Capital, $750,000. Directors : Philip Bissinger, Theodore Droier, John F. Fredericks, Gottlob Gunther, Marcellus Hartley, Joshua Hendricks, Alexander Klingenberg, Emil Magnus, William Mertens, Emil Oelbermann, John F. Pupke, Henry Rocholl, Samuel M. Schafer, Herman Stutzer, Casimir Tag, Edward N. Teller, James M. Thorburn, Charles Unger, Frederick Von Bernuth, Charles A. Zoebisch) 50 Wall
German Am. Ins. Co. (Emil Oelbermann, Pres.; James A. Silvey, Sec. Capital, $1,000,000. Directors: C. F. Ackermann, F. J. Allen, Austin P. Baldwin, Joseph H. Choate, E. W. Corlies, Louis F. Dommerich, Hermann Funke, Gustav H. Gossler, Charles Haight, Otto Holzse, C. F. A. Hinrichs, Charles A. Hoyt, Charles H. Isham, Charles G. Landon, Woodbury Langdon, Lowell Lincoln, Charles Mali, John W. Murray, Emil Oelbermann, George T. Paterson jr. Charles Pfizer, Thomas E. Proctor, Ferdinand W. Roebling, Louis Schreiber, James A. Silvey, Charles S. Smith, Adolph A. Strohn, George W. Smith, Henry C. Ward, Hugo Wesendonck, A. R. Whitney, Louis Windmuller, F. Wiukhaus, William Wood) 115 B'way
German Am. Mfg. Co. (inf. unattainable) 796 Tenth av.
German Am. Mutual Warehousing & Security Co. (inoperative) 115 B'way
German Am. Real Estate Title Guarantee Co. (Andrew L. Soulard, Pres.; William Wagner, Treas.; Adolph Koppel, Sec. Capital, $500,-000. Directors: John A. Beyer, George C. Clausen, James Fellows, Charles Uusngst, Andrew L. Soulard, Adolph Koppel, Jacob F. Miller, John Stralton, George W. Quintard, Charles F. Tag, William Wagner) 34 Nassau
German Artistic Weaving Co. (refused) 120 Franklin
German Exchange Bank (Michael J. Adrian, Pres.; Charles L. Adrian, Cashier. Capital, $200,-000. Directors: Michael J. Adrian, Bernard G. Amend, Auke Dooper, H. Herold, Mosse Mehrbach, S. Borgmann, George Rothmann, Joseph Schaeffer, George Storm, John Schnugg, Henry Weller, D. Wetterau, William Wiske, C. Wynen) 380 Bowery
German Legal Aid Soc. (Arthur V. Briesen, Pres.; Charles K. Lexow, Sec.; Carl L. F. Rose, Treas.) 85 Nassau
German Peat Moss Co. (Loewenstein & Marcus, propr.) 99 Nassau
German Savings Bank (Philip Bissinger, Pres.; Gustav F. Amthor, Treas.; John B. Keiler, Cashier. Trustees: Philip Bissinger, Otto Ernst, Robert Schell, Ernst Bredt, Hugo Wesendonck, William Steinway, Emil Oelbermann, Carl Rose, Gottlob Gunther, George H. Moller, Charles Unger, Julius W. Brunn, Alfred Roelker, Karl Meissner, Ewald Fleitmann, Gustavus Haye, Charles A. Zoebisch, Walther Luctgen, E. Steiger) 100 E. 14th
Germania Bank (Marc Eidlitz, Pres.; John A. Morschhauser, Cashier.; Francis J. Miller, Notary. Capital, $200,000, Directors : Oscar Zollikoffer, Marc Eidlitz, David Brabacher, Henry W. Schmidt, John Lindenmeyr, John Rheinfrank, Conrad Stein, Edward C. Schaefer, Bernhard Beinecke, Henry E. G. Luytics, Charles A. King, Jacques Bach, Otto Hoppenhelmer, Gustav L. Jaeger, William Ottmann) 215 Bowery
Germania Fire Ins. Co. (Rudolph Garrigue, Pres.; Charles Ruykhaver, Sec. Capital, $1,000,000. Directors: Frederick Von Bernuth, Henry G. Eilshemius, Francis Doelting, Ernest Hall, Ferdinand A. Boker, Frederick J. Kaldenberg, Thomas Chatterton, Henry Kloppenburg, Staffen Dieckmann, P. H. Leonard, John Moller, Michael Lienau, Oswald Ottendorfer, Carl Victor, G. Ramsperger, Edward Scheltlin, Abraham Sondern, Marcus L. Ward, Charles A. Zoebisch, Rudolph Garrigue, Hugo Schumann, Charles Ruykhaver) 179 D'way & 287 Bowery
Germania Knitting Works (William Reichman, propr.) 71 Franklin & 440 Canal
Germania Life Ins. Co. (Hugo Wesendonck, Pres.; Cornelius Doremus, Sec. Directors: L. E. Aminck, H. R. Beltzer, Isaac Dornheimer. Francis Bolting, Ernst Bredt, Henry G. Eilshemius, Otto Heinze, Hermann Marcuse, Richard Maser, Emil Oelbermann, Albrecht Pagenstecher, Alfred Roelker, Carl Rose, Frederick Schwendler, Hermann Rose, Charles F. Tag, F. von Bernuth, Edward von der Heydt, Hugo Wesandonck, B. Westermann, Otto Wesendonck) 20 Nassau
Germania Publishing Co. (Paul Lichtenstein, Pres.; George Staber, Treas. Capital, $50,-000. Directors : Paul Lichtenstein, George

THADDEUS DAVIDS CO., WRITING INKS, SEALING WAX, MUCILAGE.
MAKE THE BEST

GER 111 GIL

Staber, Carl Meissner, Herman C. Kudilch, Julius Goebel) 132 Fulton
Germania Roofing Co. (Charles Durkelman, propr.) 82 Sullivan
Germann G. A. & F. (George A. & Frederick jr.) 395 Grand & 231 Division
Germann & Son (John & John M. Germann) 135 Rivington
Germany Peter A. & Co. (Peter A. Germany & George C. Baker) 845 B'way
Germicide Co. (Caspar L. Cohn, Pres.; Albert L. Cohn, Sec. Capital, $275,000. Directors: Casper L. & Albert L. Cohn & Henry Levy) 862 B'way
Gerner & Schaeffer (Charles Gerner & John C. Schaeffer) 143 Washn. mkt
Gernsheim M. & Co. (Michael Gernsheim & Eugene A. & Albert Loeb) 10 Wall
Gernshym Henry & Brother (Henry & Max Gernshym) 85 Franklin
Gerold & Imhoff (Frederick Gerold & Frederick Imhoff) 105 Elm
Gerry Allston & Co. (Allston Gerry & Joseph A. Flynn) 40 Wall
Gerry & Murray (Theodore L. C. Garry & Charles Murray) 26 Broad
Gershel H. & Son (Heyman & George Gershel) 112 Prince
Gershel L. & Brother (Leopold & Solomon Gershel) 191 Pearl
Gershwiller & Schneider (Melchior Gershwiller & Jacob Schneider) 518 E. 15th
Gerstenberg L. F. & F. (Louise F. & Frederick & Carl Gerstenberg) 178 E. 80th
Gerstendorfer Brothers (Max & Albert Gerstendorfer) 17 Barclay
Geratie R. H. & Brother (Rafael H. & Edward G. Geratle) 288 Bowery
Gessert C. F. & Co. (dissolved) 53 W. B'way
Gessler & Tansig (dissolved) 404 E. 91st
Gessner M. & Brother (Moses & Aaron Gessner) 250 E. 4th
Getgood William F. & George J. 2305½ Third av.
Gettlock & Smith (Henry Gettlock & Charles Smith) 55 Av. D & 350 Third
Ghiglione Angelo & Co. (Angelo & Marie Ghiglione) 195 Lewis & 807 Sixth
Ghilotti & Crosci (dissolved) 16 Roosev. lt
Ghio & Rovira (Apollonio P. Ghio & Benito Rovira) 251 E. 3'd
Ghirardelli G. & Co. (Giacomo Ghirardelli, no Co.) 232 Bleecker
Gibb Brothers & Moran (Matthew & Alexander W. & James A. Gibb & Michael Moran) 57 Rose
Gibbens & Beach (Edwin A. Gibbens & Dennis Beach) 20 W. 59th
Gibbons & Ryan (dissolved) 135 W. 125th
Gibbs R. H. & Co. (dissolved) 81 Pearl & 48 Stone
Gibbs & White (Thomas R. Gibbs & Thomas P. White) ft. W. 41st
Giblin & Shea (Charles Giblin & John Shea) 45 Liberty
Gibson Electric Co. (Henry S. Iselin, Pres.; Samuel F. Barry, Sec.; William S. Vernam, Treas. Capital, $200,000, Trustees: Henry S. Iselin, Francis P. Lowrey, C. A. Spofford, William S. Vernam, Samuel F. Barry, O. D. F. Gibson) 74 Cortlandt
Gibson Brothers (John W. & Thomas J. Gibson) 609 Madison av.
Gibson & Davis (William J. Gibson & Westmoreland D. Davis) 120 B'way
Gibson & Lange (Samuel Gibson & Henry Lange) 178 Chambers
Gibson & Wesson (Henry S. Gibson & Frank B. Wesson) 206 B'way

Gibson & Whiting (Hanson C. Gibson & John B. Whiting) 59 Wall
Gibson, Parish & Co. (no inf.) 115 Worth
Gibson's William, Sons (William & George H. Gibson) 142 E. 33d
Gidley & Raebaer (Jane Gidley & Rae Raebaer) 4 W. 22d
Giegerich J. & C. (John & Charles) 93 Pitt
Gieschen & Eggers (Henry Gieschen & Herman Eggers) 2217 Second av.
Giesecke H. & Son (Henry E. F. & Frederick H. G. Giesecke) 112 E. 11th
Giesoke & Barnefuer (dissolved) 101 Rivington & 1101 Second av.
Giesler C. J. & Son (Conrad J. & Jacob Giesler) 338 E. 43d
Giffin & Loomes (Thomas Giffin & Edward Loomes) 140 W. 55th
Giffing John C. & Son (John C. & William C. Giffing) 23 South
Gifford & Brown (Livingston Gifford & Edwin H. Brown) 32 Park pl.
Gila River Irrigation Co. (Wells H. Bates, Pres.; Sterling E. Edmunds, Sec.; DeWitt C. Bates, Treas. Capital, $5,000,000. Directors: Wells H. & DeWitt C. Bates, Henry B. & Francis A. James Cosgrove jr. Albert H. Smith, William P. Robeson, Ridgly C. Powers, Walter G. Bates, Sterling E. Edmunds, Benjamin S. Church, Seth Pinkham, Silas E. Fuller) 11 Wall
Gilbert Car Mfg. Co. (Edward G. Gilbert, Pres.; Frederick S. Young, Sec.; further inf. unattainable) 3 Broad
Gilbert Cut Lining Co. (Orlando P. Dorman, Pres.; Frank H. Gilbert, Sec. Capital, $10,000. Trustees: Orlando P. Dorman, William T. McIntire, Frank H. Gilbert) 346 B'way
Gilbert Mfg. Co. (Orlando P. Dorman, Pres.; Frank H. Gilbert, Sec. Capital, $25,000. Trustees: Orlando P. Dorman, William T. McIntire, Frank H. Gilbert) 346 B'way & 127 Centre
Gilbert & Bennett Mfg. Co. (Edwin Gilbert, Pres.; David H. Miller, Sec. Capital, $175,000. Directors: Edwin Gilbert, David H. & Leonard J. Miller, Elbert B. Monroe, Lewis G. Beers) 42 Cliff
Gilbert & Sweeney (Wright L. Gilbert & Michael Sweeney) 199 Duane
Gilbert & Taylor (Ellakim W. Gilbert & William W. Taylor) 732 Westchester av.
Gilbert, Sweet & Lyon (dissolved) 88 Chambers
Gilder, Farr & Co. (W. Howard Gilder, T. H. Powers Farr, John C. Kilbreth:—special partner, Henry Harbeck, $250,000; terminates 5th May, 1891) 81 Broad
Gildersleeve M. R. & Co. (Moses R. Gildersleeve & George M. Smith) Pier 24 E. R.
Gildersleeve, Palmer & Boothby (Henry A. Gildersleeve, Arthur C. Palmer & John W. Boothby) 280 B'way
Gilds Co. (Horace T. Kline, Pres. Capital, $12,000.; further inf. refused) 993 Sixth av.
Giles Co. (Ferdinand S. M. Blun, Pres.; George W. Averell, Sec.; Sigmund Bendit, Treas. Capital, $225,000. Directors: John R. Giles, Ferdinand S. M. Blun, Sigmund Bendit, Oscar L. Richard) 30 W. 18th
Giles Lithographic & Liberty Printing Co. (dissolved) 62 College pl. & 72 Warren
Giles & Hills (Stephen W. Giles & Edwin M. Hills) 84 Park pl.
Gilham S. W. & Son (Samuel W. & George L. Gilham) 159 W. 18th
Gilkinson & Co. (Arthur J. Gilkinson, no Co.) 331 G'wich
Gill R. & Sons (Robinson & Frank N. & William H. Gill) 59 E. 105th

Gill R. J. & Co. (Robert J. Gill & Harry Jackson) 104 Franklin
Gill & Shroh (dissolved) 97 Mercer
Gillender & Stolber (Augustus T. Gillender & Adolphus H. Stolber) 2 Nassau
Gillies & Moran (Archibald Gillies & John Moran) 1360 B'way & 500 Seventh av.
Gillespie Charles H. & Sons (Charles H. & Charles H. jr. & Louis C. Gillespie) 554 W. 25th
Gillespie S. W. & Co. (Samuel W. Gillespie, Farrington Hanford & Samuel S. Gillespie) 97 Front
Gillespie's J. W. Sons (Charles H. & James M. Gillespie) 52 John
Gillet Joseph Allston & Brother (Joseph Allston & Sully Gillet) 101 Front
Gillotte Barrel Co. (Paul Wilcox, Pres.; Isaac N. Falk, Sec.; Benjamin J. Falk, Treas. Capital, $600,000. Directors: Paul Wilcox, Arthur E. Johnstone, Isaac N. & Benjamin J. Falk, Theophilus M. Marc) 5 Beekman
Gillette Tap, Valve & Faucet Co. (Joseph L. Spofford, Pres.; Edward W. Milliken, Sec. Capital, $100,000. Trustees: Joseph L. Spofford, Edward W. Milliken) 31 B'way
Gillette C. F. & Co. (dissolved) 14 S. William
Gilley F. W. jr. & Co. (Franklin W. jr. & Edward S. Gilley) 64 B'way
Gillies Coffee Co. (Anna E. Gillies, propr.) 237 Washn.
Gillies Edwin J. & Co. (Edwin J. Gillies & James H. & William R. Schmelzel) 245 Washn.
Gillies James & Sons (James C. & John Gillies, only) ft. W. 50th
Gillies Wright & Brother (Wright & Homer R. Gillies) Tenth av. c W. 160th
Gilligan M. J. & Son (Matthew J. & Thomas J. Gilligan) 42 E. Houston
Gillings & Co. (Peter Gillings, no Co.) 3015 Third av. & 717 Elton av.
Gillis & Ford (John P. Gillis & Edward M. Ford) 145 B'way
Gillis & Geoghegan (Charles J. Gillis & Stephen J. Geoghegan) 116 Wooster
Gillies Brothers & Turnure (Walter & Frank Le Grand & Morton M. Gillies & Arthur B. Turnure) 402 W. 14th
Gillmann Frederick & Co. (Frederick Gillmann & Charles Fredericks) 477 Seventh av.
Gilman C. H. & Co. (Charles H. Gilman & William A. Batchelor) 1257 Ninth av.
Gilman & Co. (no inf.) 48 Broad
Gilman, Son & Co. (Theodore & Winthrop S. Gilman, no Co.) 68 Cedar
Gilmartin Thomas & Co. (Thomas Gilmartin & James J. Walsh) 25 Chambers
Gilmartin & Doyle (James Gilmartin & Patrick J. Doyle) 14 Lispenard
Gilmor J. D. & Co. (dissolved) 203 G'wich
Gilmore J. & Co. (John Gilmore, no Co.) 5 West & 8 Washn.
Gilmore & Sillery (John Gilmore & George Sillery) 328 Church
Gilmore & Tompkins (Edward G. Gilmore & Eugene Tompkins) 2 Irving pl.
Gingold & Abrams (Isaac Gingold & Isaac Abrams) 106 E. B'way
Ginn & Co. (Edwin Ginn, George A. Plimpton, Frederick B. Ginn & Justin H. Smith) 743 B'way
Ginna & Co. (Stephen A. Ginna & Richard A. Donaldson) 53 Beach
Ginnel Henry & Co. (Henry & William S. Ginnel & Francis R. Simmons) 81 Maiden la.
Giovannoni U. & B. (Ulass & Bernardo) 661 B'way
Gipner & Co. (refused) 228 E. 42d

Giro E. & Co. (no inf.) 2 W. 14th
Girolama P. & Co. (Pasquale & Joseph Girolama) 254 Ninth av.
Girondin Disinfectant Co. (William Brandreth, Pres.; Daniel E. Lancaster, Sec.; Henry King, Treas. Capital, $150,000. Trustees: William Brandreth, Daniel E. Lancaster, Henry King) 170 W. 25th
Gitsky Brothers (Joseph & William & Isaac Gitsky) 463 Second av.
Gittelsohn Brothers (no inf.) 155 E. 26th
Ginfrida & Pecoraro (dissolved) 26½ E. 42d
Givernaud Brothers (Louis & Etienne Givernaud & Emanuel Gerli) 31 Greene
Glaccum William & Sons (William & William Glaccum jr. only) 302 E. 45th
Glade & Michaels (Henry Glade & Louis Michaels) 326 Second av.
Gladstone Lamp Co. (James F. Place, propr.) 71 Park pl.
Gladstone & Colville (Matilda J. Gladstone & Catharine Colville) 144 E. 19th
Glaenzer Georgus A. & Co. (Georgus A. Glaenzer, Pres.; further inf. refused) 33 E. 20th
Glaeser Emanuel & Co. (dissolved) 14 Clinton pl.
Glaeizner & Brown (Otto Glaeizner & Frank M. Brown) 413 Park av.
Glancy & Trochases (dissolved) 1207 & 1215 Ninth av.
Glasco Ice Co. (not inc.) (Charles Mulford, William H. Simmons, James Williamson & Clarence K. Dunham) ft. W. 15th
Glaser Brothers (Max & Charles Glaser) 20 Fulton
Glaser & Schultz (dissolved) 20 Chambers
Glasgow Printing Co. (McNaught & Co. propr.) 107 Walker
Glass John & Son (John & John Glass jr.) 209 W. 21st
Glassheim & Spiegel (Nathan Glassheim & Charles Spiegel) 76 Orchard
Glatten & Pregenzer (Charles Glatten & Philip Pregenzer) 505 E. 11th
Glaze & McCreedy (George W. Glaze & Thomas Bell McCreedy) 15 E. 15th
Glazer & Karfunkel (dissolved) 130 E. B'way
Gleasing & Plush (Henry Gleasing & Peter Plush) 102 South
Gleason E. P., Mfg. Co. (Elliott P. Gleason, Pres.; Frank W. Belmont, &c.; John C. Granger, Treas. Capital, $25,000. Directors: Elliott P. & M. Wilfred Gleason, Frank W. Belmont, John C. Granger, Elliott G. Albee, Emil F. Goenert, Francis Billingham) 20 W. Houston
Gleason Knitting Mfg. Co. (Elliott P. Gleason, propr.) 20 W. Houston
Gleason Brothers (Charles R. & William S. Gleason) 426 Sixth av.
Gleason & Bailey Mfg. Co. (Ltd.) (Elliott P. Gleason, Pres.; Wallace Drew, Sec.; Warren C. Gleason, Treas. Capital, $100,000. Directors: Elliott P. Gleason, Pryce W. Bailey, Wallace Drew, Warren C. Gleason, Morton Sisson & Frank Beebe) 189 Mercer & 23 South
Gledhill Henry & Co. (Henry & William H. & James E. Gledhill & George H. Kelm) 524 W. 34th
Gleeson M. & Brother (Michael & Patrick Gleeson) 183 Christopher
Glen Cove Machine Co. (Ltd.) (William W. Underhill, Pres.; William E. Kroy, Sec. Capital, $150,000. Directors: Hiram & William & John & Louis T. Duryea, William W. Underhill, James F. Welch, Alfred B. Hutchinson, William E. Kroy, Augustus F. Samson) 208 South
Glen Cove Mfg. Co. (William Duryea, Treas.; William F. Reed, Sec. Capital $1,000,000; further inf. unattainable) 208 South

Glendinning, McLeish & Co. (Robert G. Glendinning, George McLeish & James R. Eccles) 42 White

Glenwood Mfg. Co. (inf. unattainable) 56 Park

Glick Brothers (Henry & Lipman Glick) 60 Pearl

Glick & Co. (Samuel Glick & H. Schneider) 124½ Cannon

Glimm Brothers (Christian F. & John E. Glimm) 321 Washn.

Globe Aniline Works (Heller & Merz Co. proprs.) 55 Maiden la.

Globe Carpet Cleaning Co. (A. D. Yetter & Son, proprs.) 305 E. 61st & 968 Ninth av.

Globe Clothing Co. (Hannah Loewenberg, propr.) 134 Bowery

Globe Curtain Pole Co. (Albert D. Field, Pres.; Samuel A. Chapman, Sec. Capital, $10,000; further inf. unattainable) 242 Canal

Globe Engraving Co. (Fischer, Herrmann & Costello proprs.) 47 Centre

Globe Filter Co. (Alfred Gorham, propr.) 9 Murray

Globe Fire Ins. Co. (James S. Eadie, Pres.; Charles E. W. Chambers, Sec. Capital, $200,000. Directors: James S. Eadie, John Castree, Wilson G. Hunt, T. G. Mathews, John J. Morris, James C. Gulick, Thomas Rood, Samuel T. Knapp, Edwin R. Livermore, John Kayser, Francis Jenkins, Charles H. Ludington, L. A. Jacobus, Washington L. Cooper, Valentine Kirby) 161 B'way

Globe Foreign Express (Morris European & Am. Express Co. (Ltd.) proprs.) 18 B'way

Globe Incandescent Light Co. (no inf.) 6 Wall

Globe Iron & Spring Works (Frank M. Andrews, propr.) 556 W. 34th

Globe Jewelry Mfg. Co. (Alkan & Fogel, proprs.) 401 B'way

Globe Laundry (Cornelius R. Eldridge, propr.) 640 Sixth av.

Globe Linseed Oil Co. (Joseph A. Bluxome, propr.) 43 Front

Globe Lubricating Co. (Jacob Pease, Pres.; Henry A. Macdonald, Sec.; Alexander Barclay, Treas. Capital, $20,000. Directors: Jacob Pease, L. M. Anway, Alexander Barclay, Henry A. Macdonald) 103 Maiden la.

Globe Machine Co. (Charles H. Lockett, propr.) 35 B'way

Globe Mutual Benefit Soc. (inf. unattainable) 18 B'way

Globe Print Works (William H. M. Marsh, propr.) 176 Worth

Globe Stationery & Printing Co. (Julian W. Merrill, Pres.; N. Denison Morgan, Sec. Capital, $20,000. Directors: Julian W. & Cyrus Merrill, N. Denison & James H. & Robert Webb Morgan) 89 Liberty

Globe Storage Warehouse & Moving Van Co. (A. B. Yetter & Son, proprs.) 805 E. 61st & 968 Ninth av.

Glore John A. P. & Co. (John A. P. Glore, no Co.) 80 Jay

Glover Frank & Son (Frank & George W. Glover) 89 Peck sl.

Glover G. & Co. (George G. & William H. Glover) 673 Tenth av.

Glover & Co.,(James A. Glover, no Co.) 141 B'way

Glover, Sweezy & Glover (John H. Glover, Richard L. Sweezy & Henry S. Glover) 81 Nassau

Gluck M. & Brother (Marcus & David Gluck) 1431 Second av.

Glucksman Brothers (Joseph & Herman Glucksman) 8 Manhattan

Gluth & Coyle (Conrad J. A. Gluth & James A. Coyle) 78 E. 13th

Glynn Martin J. & Co. (Martin J. Glynn & John McDonald) 70 Front & 79 Catharine

Goadby W. H. & Co. (William H. Goadby, Edward Bement & Charles T. Kilborne) 24 Broad

Goatcher & Young (Philip W. Goatcher & John H. Young) 844 & 1445 B'way & 541 W. 21st

Gobbi Brothers (John B. & Jerome Gobbi) 91 Third av. & 396 Fourth av.

Gobbi Brothers & A Negri (John B. & Jerome Gobbi & Angelo Negri) 213 E. 13th

Godbold James & Son (James & James W. Godbold) 19 James sl.

Goddard J. W. & Sons (Joseph W. & Warren N. & F. Norton Goddard) 816 B'way & 62 Crosby

Godet Henry T. & Co. (Henry L. Faris & N. Townsend Thayer, only) 88 Broad & 1300 B'way

Godfrey Joseph & Co. (Joseph Godfrey & Joshua T. Hicks) 3 Ferry

Godfrey William L. & Co. (dissolved) 87 Frankfort

Godfrey Wilson & Co. (Wilson Godfrey & Ralph E. Sumner) 91 Wall

Godwin R. J. & Sons (Richard J. & John D. & Allan W. Godwin) 65 Wall

Godwin & Co. (Thomas Godwin, no Co.) 1560 Ninth av.

Godwin & McCarthy (William M. Godwin & Mary F. McCarthy) 52 W. 34th

Godwin's Samuel, Sons (Richard J. jr. & Samuel A. Godwin) 46 William

Goebel J. & Co. (Julius Goebel, no Co.) 129 Maiden la.

Goebel & Schott (Andrew G. Goebel & Valentane Schott) 11b7 Railroad av.

Goedecke Brothers (Richard & Herman Goedecke) 212 Centre

Goepel & Raegener (Paul Goepel & Louis C. Raegener) 230 B'way

Goepel & Trube (Adolph Goepel & Carl Trube) 18 B'way

Goetz B., Mfg. Co. (not inc.) (Augustus L. Schryver & Charles D. Garvin) 172 & 227 Mercer

Goetz Brothers (Christian & Adam Goetz) 32 Delancey & 492 Second av.

Goetse Theodore & Co. (Theodore jr. & Charles Goetze, only) 256 Grand

Goetze F. A. & Brother (William J. Goetze, only) 46 Jay

Goetze & Zengen (dissolved) 821 Third av.

Goff & Pollock (John W. Goff & Francis W. Pollock) 229 B'way

Goffe C. C. & Co. (Charles C. Goffe & Edward T. Williams) 80 Broad

Gogorza E. & Co. (Eduardo Gogorza & Miguel D. Ferrer) 47 Liberty

Gohring Adolf & Co. (Adolf Gohring, no Co.) 202 William

Gohring & Pape (Ernest Gohring & William C. Pape) 122 W. 29th

Golcouria, Leroy & Co. (Albert V. de Golcouria, Frederick G. Leroy & Robert M. Heifenstein) 68 B'way

Golconda Gold & Silver Mining Co. (dissolved) 245 B'way

Gold Car Heating Co. (Edward E. Gold, Pres.; Samuel F. Gold, Sec.; Frederick W. Wright, Treas. Capital, $100,000. Directors: Frederick W. Wright, Edward E. & Samuel F. Gold, C. W. Osborne, F. G. Mensio, E. H. Gold) 6 N. Y. & B'klyn bridge

Gold Cliff Gold Mining Co. (inoperative) 46 Cliff

Gold Cup Mining & Smelting Co. (Emile Vatable, Pres.; George W. Crane, Sec. Capital, $500,000. Directors: Emile & Jules & Auguste Vatable, Charles E. Merritt, Hippolyte Dumois, George W. Crane, Jules H. Coffin) 59 Water

Gold & Stock Life Ins. Assn. (Richard J. Hutchinson, Pres.; William J. Denly, Sec.; Michael Breslin, Treas.) 195 B'way

TYPEWRITING DONE BY THE TROW CITY DIRECTORY CO., 11 University Place.

GOL 114 GOO

Gold & Stock Telegraph Co. (Norvin Green, Pres.; Abijah R. Brewer, Sec.; Roswell H. Rochester, Treas. Capital, $5,000,000. Directors: Norvin Green, William A. Wheelock, William M. Bliss, Jay Gould, Russel Sage, Charles G. Landon, John Vanhorne, Thomas T. Eckert, Charles A. Tinker, George J. Gould) 195 B'way, 16 Broad & 10 W. 23d

Gold, Barbour & Corning (Cornelius B. Gold, William D. Barbour & Edwin Corning) 18 Wall

Gold's Heater Mfg. Co. (dissolved) ft. E. 104th

Gohlbach S. & Co. (dissolved) 207 E. 101st

Goldberg Nathan & Co. (dissolved) 29 Norfolk

Goldberg C. H. & E. S. (Charles H. & Eugene S.) 826 Washn. & 29 Juy

Goldberg H. & Son (Harris & Hyman Goldberg) 117 Division

Goldberg I. & Co. (Israel Goldberg & Louise Goodman) 41 Walker

Goldberg I. & Son (Israel & Jacob Goldberg) 49 Essex

Goldberg M. & Sons (Moses & Meyer & Michael Goldberg) 124 E. B'way

Goldberg Brothers (Abraham & Joseph Goldberg) 233 E. 107th

Goldberg & Co. (Ellis Goldberg, no Co.) 715 Mercer

Goldberg & Jaffe (Joseph Goldberg & Julius Jaffe) 439 E. Houston

Goldberg & Samuels (dissolved) 438 E. Houston

Goldberg & Vorzimer (dissolved) 21 Gt. Jones

Goldberger S. & Co. (Samuel Goldberger & Sigmund Rosenwald) 13 Water & 14 Front

Golden Age Mining Co. (Samuel Eddy, Pres.; J. C. Sanders, Sec. Capital, $500,000. Directors: Samuel Eddy, J. C. Sanders) 145 B'way

Golden P. & Son (Patrick & Edward Golden jr.) 2245 First av.

Golden Brothers (John B. & Jason P. Golden) 940 B'way

Goldenberg Brothers & Co. (Simon & Julius L. & Joel & Samuel L. Goldenberg & Louis Seeberger) 470 Broome

Golderman P. S. & Co. (Philip S. Golderman & John L. Parker) 711 Tremont av.

Goldey W. H. & Co. (dissolved) 52 Vesey

Goldfarb Samuel & Son (no inf.) 200 E. B'way

Goldfarb & Blankstein (Joseph Goldfarb & Harris Blankstein) 47 Allen

Goldfogle & Cohn (Henry M. Goldfogle & Charles L. Cohn) 261 B'way

Golding Brothers (hats) (John J. & Stephen C. Golding, 140 & 428 Third av. Thomas F. Golding, only, 517 Eighth av.)

Goldman Brothers (Seligman & Herman & Theresa Goldman) 101 Greene

Goldman & Friedman (no inf.) 29 Attorney

Goldman, Sachs, & Co. (Marcus Goldman, Samuel Sachs, Ludwig Dreyfuss & Henry Goldman) 9 Pine & 10 Wall

Goldmann Brothers (Moses & Leopold Goldmann) 1516 Third av.

Goldmark & Conried (Leo Goldmark, Henry Conried & Carl Herrmann) 13 W. 42d

Goldsberry's L. D., Sons (dissolved) 2289 Third av.

Goldschmidt H. P. & Co. (Henry P. Goldschmidt, August Rütten & Joseph E. Heimerdinger) 53 Exchange pl.

Goldschmidt L. & Co. (Louis Goldschmidt, no Co.) 211 Pearl

Goldschmidt & Heinetnan (dissolved) 385 Grand

Goldschmidt & Koch (Jacob Goldschmidt, Joseph Koch) 182 Av. A

Goldschmidt, Bachrach & Co. (Daniel & Adolph M. Goldschmidt & David Bachrach) 15 Greene & 26 West

Goldschmidt, Hess & Co. (Isaac & Ascher Goldschmidt & Nathan Hess jr.) 142 Grand

Goldsmith Ingomar & Co. (Ingomar & Frederick Goldschmidt) 20 Maiden la.

Goldsmith Mining Co. (inoperative) 35 Liberty

Goldsmith Piano & Organ Mfg. Co. (inf. unattainable) 60 B'way

Goldsmith G. & Son (Gabriel & Samuel G. Goldsmith) 411 E. Houston

Goldsmith L. & Son (Levi & David Goldsmith) 920 Third av. & 861 Sixth av.

Goldsmith M. & Co. (Milton Goldsmith, no Co.) 194 Park av.

Goldsmith S. & Son (Simon & Charles S. Goldsmith) 306 Washn.

Goldsmith Brothers (Simon & Jerome S. Goldsmith) 408 Broome

Goldsmith & Davis (Jonas R. Goldsmith & David Davis) 39 First av.

Goldsmith & Doherty (Samuel J. Goldsmith & James E. Doherty) 820 B'way

Goldsmith & Plaut (dissolved) 472 B'way & 80 Crosby

Goldsmith & Wulf (Frederick T. Goldsmith & Theodore Wolf) 61 New

Goldsmith, Hoffman & Am. Collar Co. (Gustavus A. Goldsmith, Pres.; Charles L. Simms, Sec.; Julius Levine, Treas. Capital, $10,000. Directors: Gustavus A. Goldsmith, Julius Levine, James H. Hoffman) 52 Howard

Goldstein William H. & Co. (William H. & Sigmund Goldstein) 181 B'way

Goldstein E. A. & Co. (Elias A. Goldstein & Charles B. Schellenberg) 440 B'way

Goldstein L. & M. N. (Lewis & Meyer N.) 74 Division

Goldstein M. & Brother (dissolved) 129 Goerck

Goldstein M. H. & Co. (Morris H. Goldstein & Ephraim Grossman) 75 Nassau

Goldstein Brothers (Solomon & Morris Goldstein) 12 Suffolk

Goldstein & Bimberg (Louis Goldstein & Charles Bimberg) 35 E. 4th

Goldstein & Jaretzki (dissolved) 121 Spring

Goldstein & Schweizer (dissolved) 69 Clinton

Goldstein & Son (George & Louis Goldstein) 121 Spring

Goldstein & Sons (no inf.) 695 B'way & 266 Canal

Goldstein & Stern (Gerson Goldstein & Nathan Stern) 185 E. 108th

Goldsticker L. & M. (Louis & Martin & William Goldsticker) 162 Fulton

Goldstone Brothers (Henry & William Goldstone) 252 First av.

Goldwasser & Co. (dissolved) 159 W. B'way

Goll Henry & Co. (Henry Goll & Gaspard Schelker) 6 Liberty pl.

Golla & Berghorn (John Golla & Henry Berghorn) Boulevard c W. 130th

Golland's I., Sons (Jacob & Morris Golland) 811 B'way

Gombossy Brothers (Maximilian & Ignatz Gombossy) 34 Second av. & 224 Bowery

Gombossy & Co. (Max & William Gombossy) 294 Bowery

Gomez & Pearsall (Jose Gomez, Theodore F. Pearsall & Salvador N. Gomez) 168 Front & Pier 14 E. R.

Gomprecht's P., Sons (Gustav & Solomon & Benjamin Gomprecht) 999 Third av.

Gonnoud & Oeckler (Thomas E. Gonnoud & Frederick Oeckler) 836 W. 42d

Gonon & Macdonald (Paul F. Gonon & Ronald H. Macdonald) 41 W. 31st

Good Brent & Co. (Brent Good, no Co.) 57 Murray

Good Return Mining Co. (Charles H. Barkelow, Pres.; W. S. Estey, Sec. Capital, $100,-

000. Trustees: Charles H. Barkelew, J. B. Bowden, G. P. Chapman, W. H. Kays) no address

Goodale S. B. & Co. (Samuel B. Goodale & Edward D. Grant) 1180 B'way

Goodall & Veazie (Edwin Goodall & Henry A. Veazie) 38 Broad

Goodbody, Glyn & Dow (Robert Goodbody, William E. Glyn & Charles H. Dow) 80 Broad

Goodenough & Woglom Co. (Samuel J. Goodenough, Pres.; Edward Goodenough, Sec. Capital, $10,000. Trustees: Samuel J. & Catharine I. & Anne Goodenough) 122 Nassau

Goodeve & Elliot (James Goodeve & H. Randolph Elliot) 47 Broad

Goodfellow Car Holder Co. (Capital, $10,000; further inf. unattainable) no address

Goodfriend Brothers (Isaac & James Goodfriend) 1480 First av.

Goodhart P. J. & Co. (Philip J. & Albert R. Goodhart & Edward L. Heinsheimer) 24 Broad

Goodhart Brothers (dissolved) 132 Nassau

Goodhart & Phillips (Morris Goodhart & Albert L. Phillips) 45 William

Goodheart R. M. & Co. (Richard M. Goodheart, Charles W. Smith & William B. Hartley) 172 Reade

Goodkind & Jakobowic (dissolved) r 108 Delancey

Goodlatte Oil Cloth Co. (William Burgess, Pres.; Thomas A. R. Goodlatte, Sec. Capital $50,000. Directors: William Burgess, Thomas A. R. Goodlatte, Edo Kip, E. K. Goodlatte) 216 Church

Goodman B., Mfg. Co. (Leopold Rothschild, Pres.; Burkard Goodman, Treas.: John C. Hotchkiss, Sec. Capital, $75,000. Directors: Burkard Goodman, W. G. Lunburgh, Frederick A. Mason, John C. Cook, Leopold Rothschild, John C. Hotchkiss) 353 Canal

Goodman George L. & Co. (George L. & Henry J. Goodman) 234 B'way

Goodman B. & Son (Bernard & Moses Goodman) 980 Second av.

Goodman I. D. & Son (Israel D. & Barnett Goodman) 69 E. B'way

Goodman N. & Sons (Otto & Abraham Goodman, only) 173½ Division

Goodman Brothers (diamonds) (Henry & Leopold & Albert Goodman) 27 Maiden la.

Goodman Brothers (hosiery) (Joel B. & Benson H. Goodman) 51 Walker

Goodman & Co. (dissolved) 25 Whitehall

Goodman & Steinman (dissolved) 7 Ludlow

Goodman, Bastianelli & Co. (Edward Goodman, Adrian Bastianelli & Leo D. Honigsberg) 391 B'way

Goodman's Charles, Son (Max Goodman) 479 B'way & 52 Mercer

Goodnow Nathan D. & Co. (Nathan B. Goodnow, no Co.) 2 Nassau

Goodrich J. F. & Co. (Joseph F. Goodrich & Albert W. Adams) 634 B'way & 168 Crosby

Goodrich & Woodcock (Resolvert N. Goodrich & Edwin Woodcock) 20 Eighth av.

Goodrich, Deady & Goodrich (William W. Goodrich, John A. Deady & Henry W. Goodrich) 59 Wall

Goodridge, Victor & Co. (William E. Goodridge, Herman Victor, William C. L. Rubsamen & John Koester) 32 Liberty

Goodspeed H. S. & Co. (Albina E. Goodspeed, only) 180 Cherry

Goodstein Isaac & Sons (Isaac & David & Henry Goodstein) 9 Hester & 340 E. 62d

Goodstein & Rudich (no inf.) 8 Orchard

Goodwin Charles T. & Son· (Charles T. Goodwin, only) 228 Water

Goodwin F. & S. E. (Samuel E. Goodwin, only) 517 E. 17th

Goodwin Brothers (pottery) (Harvey B. & Wilbur E. & Newell E. Goodwin) 24 Park pl. & 19 Barclay

Goodwin Brothers (publishers) (Frederick S. & John Goodwin) 241 B'way

Goodwin & Cassidy (John Goodwin & Martin Cassidy) 76 University pl.

Goodwin & Co. (Charles G. Emery, only) ft. Grand

Goodwin & Gallagher (Edward Goodwin & Edward J. Gallagher) 220 Washr.

Goodwin, Strong & Co. (dissolved) 544 B'way & 533 W. 54th

Goodwin's G., Sons (Samuel T. & Alfred J. Goodwin) 406 E. 29th

Goodyear Buckle Co. (not Inc.) (Charles T. Deforest, Bernard Sprague & estate of Leonard A. Sprague) 265 B'way

Goodyear Gossamer Rubber Co. (Charles F. Becker, propr.) 165 Eighth av.

Goodyear Rubber Co. (Frederick M. Shepard, Pres.; Joseph A. Minott, Sec. Capital, $500,000. Directors: Frederick M. Shepard, Joseph A. Minott, James Kipp) 487 B'way & 49 Maiden la.

Goodyear Rubber Novelty & Para Rubber Mfg. Co. (G. O. Stanfield & Co. propra.) 28 E. 14th

Goodyear & McKay Sewing Machine Co. (dissolved) 265 B'way

Goodyear's India Rubber Glove Mfg. Co. (John D. Vermeule, Pres.; George M. Allerton, Sec. Capital, $500,000; further inf. unattainable) 503 & 205 B'way

Gordan H. G. & Boss (Herman G. Gordan & J. Frederick Boss) 181 Fourth av.

Gordon Press Works (Mary A. Gordon, propr.) 97 Nassau

Gordon Steam Pump Co. (Alexander Gordon, Pres.; Robert C. McKinney, Sec. Capital, $100,000. Directors: T. T. Gaff, James D. Parker, Alexander Gordon, Robert C. McKinney) 96 Liberty

Gordon E. D. & Brother (Edward B. & Charles A. Gordon) 63 E. 126th

Gordon S. T. & Son (Stephen T. & Hamilton S. Gordon) 13 E. 14th

Gordon Brothers (coal) (Robert & Joseph Gordon) 230 E. 42d

Gordon Brothers (elevators) (John & Andrew Gordon) 141 Spring

Gordon Brothers & Robinson (Charles W. & Joshua L. Gordon & Andrew Robinson) 79 Nassau

Gordon & Dilworth (Read Gordon, only) 555 G'wich

Gordon & Kerr (John S. Gordon & Joseph Kerr) 131 E. 49th

Gordon & Levin (no inf.) 63 Sheriff

Gordon & Levy (Louis Gordon & Barnett Levy) 70 Bayard

Gordon & Roberts (Robert H. Gordon & William J. Roberts) 43 Cedar & 59 W. 42d

Gordon & Wilson (Robert H. Gordon & Belvin T. Wilson) 268 Washn.

Gorman C. & H. (Catharine & Honora) 1406 Ninth av.

Gorrey & White (dissolved) 253 W. 47th

Gorth's Peter, Son (Peter Gorth) 109 Eldridge

Gorton Steamer Co. (Ltd.) (Benjamin S. Comstock, Sec. Capital, $30,000; further inf. refused) 126 William

Gorton S & W. (Simeon & William) r 259 W. 21st

Gorton & Hartling (dissolved) 609 E. 145th

Gorton & Lidgerwood Co. (John H. Lidgerwood, Pres.; Joseph A. Gorton, Sec.; Walter L. Pierce, Treas. Capital, $50,000. Directors: John H. Lidgerwood, Joseph A. Gorton, Walter L. Pierce) 96 Liberty

CIRCULARS ADDRESSED TO ANY TRADE IN THE U. S. { Facilities
PROMPT, CAREFUL WORK } **THE TROW CITY DIRECTORY CO.,** Unequalled.
AT MODERATE PRICES. } **11 University Place.**

GOR 116 GRA

Gorton & Pinet (Elizabeth P. Gorton & Anne Pinet) 3 W. 3d
Gosaman & Co. (dissolved) 2286 Third av.
Gotham Art Students (no inf.) 697 B'way
Gothberg H. & Son (dissolved) 87 College pl.
Gotthelf's A., Sons (Charles & Herman Gotthelf) 29 Willett
Gotthold & Co. (Frederick Gotthold & Maurice M. Berg) 561 B'way
Gotthold & Estabrook (dissolved) 42 Elizabeth
Gottlieb G. & Son (Gettel & Samuel Gottlieb) 85 Hester
Gottlieb H. & Bruder (Herman Gottlieb & Samuel Bruder) 277 Second
Gottlieb L. & Son (Leopold & Abraham J. Gottlieb) 260 Second
Gottlieb M. & Son (Mayer & Max Gottlieb) 267 E. Houston
Gottsberger W. S. & Co. (William S. Gottsberger & George G. Peck) 11 Murray
Gottsch Brothers (Joachim & Marx Gottsch) 346 G'wich
Gottscho I. & Brother (Isaac & Herman Gottscho) 20 Lispenard
Goubert Mfg. Co. (Francis O. Matthiessen, Pres.; Nathaniel W. Pratt, Sec.; August A. Goubert, Treas. Capital, $18,000. Directors: Francis O. Matthiessen, Nathaniel W. Pratt, August A. Goubert) 32 Cortlandt
Gouge Heating & Ventilating Co. (Henry A. Gouge, Pres.; William G. Fulton, Sec. Capital, $100,000. Directors: Henry A. Gouge, William G. Fulton, John F. Doty) 47 Beekman
Gougelmann & Co. (Peter Gougelmann & William T. Pape) 117 E. 12th
Gough Richard & Co. (Richard Gough & Adolph Furnans) 55 Beaver
Gough & Osborn (James W. Gough & John Osborn jr.) 332 B'way
Goulard, Rouse & Co. (Thomas Goulard & Martin Rouse, no Co.) 36 Whitehall & 514 Washn.
Gould John H., Publishing Co. (John H. Gould, propr.) 17 B'way
Gould Robert S., Co. (James Jackson, Pres.; Henry Reubel, Sec.; Charles W. Lawrence, Treas. Capital, $100,000. Directors: James Jackson, A. Gould, Charles W. Lawrence, Henry Reubel) 368 B'way & 239 E. 43d
Gould W. Reid (Margaret D. Gould, only) 139 Nassau & 120 B'way
Gould Brothers (dissolved) 644 Ninth av.
Gould & Clancy (no inf.) 162 E. 121st
Gould & Co. (George H. Gould, Thomas M. Buckley, & George F. Taylor) 85 Nassau
Gould & Henry (dissolved) 24 New
Gould's Elastic & Fireproof Paint Co. (Inf. unattainable) 250 St. Nicholas av.
Gould's J., Son (George T. Gould) 44 South
Gould's M., Son (William B. Gould) 105 Duane
Gouldsbury R. & Son (dissolved) 320 E. 23d
Gourd & Tournade (Henry E. Gourd & Jules E. Tournade) 25 S. William
Gousset & Eller (dissolved) 105 S. 5th av.
Gove & Heuss (Edgar A. Gove & Jacob Heuss) 918 Ninth av.
Gowan Mining Co. (Walter S. Logan, Pres.; Charles Robinson Smith, Sec. Capital, $1,000,000. Trustees: Walter S. Logan, Charles Robinson Smith, George W. Kenyon) 58 William
Gower C. H. & Co. (Charles H. Gower, Frank H. Traphagen & Stephen V. Lewis) 52 Lispenard
Gowing, Sawyer & Co. (Henry A. Gowing, Decatur M. Sawyer & Clinton H. Blake) 63 Leonard
Grace W. R. & Co. (William R. & Michael P. & John W. Grace) 1 Hanover sq. & Pier 13, E. R.

Gracie J. K. & Roosevelt (James K. Gracie & Elliott Roosevelt) 87 New
Gradler & Co. (Ernest Gradler & Charles Schaffer) 14 Bond
Grady J. W. & Co. (John W. & Thomas F. Grady, & William G. Thomas) 438 W. 31st
Grady & Liller (dissolved) 191 Elizabeth & 277 Greene
Grady & McKeever Co. (Clifford H. Thompson, Pres.; David M. Holdredge, Sec.; James C. King, Treas. Capital, $10,000. Directors: Clifford H. Thompson, C. A. McNichols, James C. King, David M. Holdredge) 219 W. 42d
Graef Charles & Co. (Charles & Anthony Graef, Francis Drax. Ludwig Roecke & Harry C. & C. Alfred Graef) 82 Beaver
Graef Cutlery Co. (Albrecht Graef, propr.) 98 Duane
Graef Walter H. & Co. (Walter H. Graef & Otto T. Schuller) 35 W. Houston
Graef & Schmidt (William R. Graef & Carl Schmidt) 29 Warren
Graef's H. A., Son (Edward L. Graef) 41 Platt
Graefenberg Co. (Charles E. Bridge, propr.) 111 Chambers
Graeser & Schreyer (Charles D. Graeser & August Schreyer) 709 First av.
Graf J. & Co. (Jacob Graf, no Co.) 256 Canal & 164 Elm
Graf L. & Son (Ludwig & John Graf) 182 Canal
Graf Brothers (butter) (August & Albert Graf) 303 Tenth av. & 2078 Third av.
Graf Brothers (hair) (Joseph L. & Alexander Graf) 302 Canal
Graff Brothers (Henry J. & George & Alfred Graff) 64 Broad
Graff & Blauvelt (William T. Graff & Hiram B. Blauvelt) 229 B'way
Graff & Co. (John M. Graff, William M. Seymour, & John H. Forshew) 208 Water
Graff & Robbins (Jacob A. Graff & Arthur K. Robbins) 54 Dey
Graham John & Co. (John Graham & David Forbes) 87 Franklin
Graham John H. & Co. (John H. & William A. Graham) 113 Chambers & 95 Reade
Graham Misses (Frances A. & Margaret W. Graham) 63 Fifth av.
Graham C. & Sons Co. (Charles Graham, Pres.; George G. Brooks, Sec.; John Graham, Treas. Capital, $400,000. Trustees: Charles Graham, George G. Brooks, John Graham, Alonzo E. Conover, Thomas Graham, George M. Smith, Samuel Clark, Benjamin A. Williams, John Toumey) 805 E. 43d
Graham J. C. & Co. (John C. Graham & Edwin Sbeild jr.) 44 Cotton Ex.
Graham & Co. (Edward L. Graham, no Co.) 63 Nassau
Graham & Conway (dissolved) 77 Front
Graham & Fortnam (dissolved) 64 Cedar
Graham & Murphy (Edward H. Graham & Joseph Murphy) 1845 Park av. & 47 W. 126th
Graham, Hinkley & Co. (William W. F. Bourne, William Graham, Frederick. W. Fell, William J. Hinkley & James Durand) 9 S. William
Graham's John, Sons (George W. & John B. & J. Franklin Graham) 516 W. 35th
Grainlet Co. (David W. Brainard, propr.) 191 Duane
Gramercy Co. (Richard H. Bull, Pres.; Alfred W. Law, Sec. Capital, $165,000. Directors: Richard H. Bull, Alfred W. Law, Charles A. Peabody jr. James M. Varnum, J. Monroe Taylor, Charles C. Parmelee) 84 Gramercy pk.
Gramercy Park School & Tool House Assn. (inoperative) 25 E. 21st

MERCHANTS EXCHANGE NAT. BANK OF THE CITY OF N. Y.
SOLICITS YOUR ACCOUNT. **257 Broadway.**
PHINEAS C. LOUNSBURY, President.   ALLEN S. APGAR, Cashier.

Gramm Brothers (dissolved) 17 W. 42d

Gramm's William, Sons (Emil & William Gramm jr.) 5 Marion

Granati & Fools (no inf.) 48 Mulberry

Granbery D. W. & Co. (dissolved) 189 B'way

Granbery W. H. & Co. (William H. Granbery & William Miller jr.) 19 New

Grand Army Publishing Co. (Joseph W. Kay, propr.) 96 Maiden la.

Grand Central Employment Agency (Charlotte J. King, propr.) 740 Sixth av.

Grand Central Wine Co. (Isaac Levy, propr.) 352 Grand

Grand Conservatory of Music of the City of N. Y. (Ernst Eberhard, Pres.; Henry C. Appleton, Sec.; George H. Cameron, Treas. Directors: Frank Roosevelt, George W. Skellen, P. D. Strauch, Asa Heinamann, George H. Cameron, Samuel Bornstein, James F. Milliken, Ernst Eberhard, Henry C. Appleton) 96 Fifth av.

Grand Conservatory Publishing Co. (Grand Conservatory of Music of the City of N. Y. proprs.) 96 Fifth av.

Grand Oil Stove Co. (r'ct inc.) H. H. jr. & D. S. & H. L. Smith) 106 Dockman

Grand River Coal & Coke Co. (Jerome B. Wheeler, Pres.; Samuel S. Earle, Sec. Capital, $2,000,000. Directors: John Sloane, C. G. Ramsey, Jerome B. Wheeler, William H. Rocca, Samuel S. Earle, H. Collman, Walter D. Devereux) 34 Wall

Grand Street Drug Co. (Frank W. Carmon, propr.) 223 Grand

Grand View Mining & Smelting Co. (inf. unattainable) 8 Broad

Grandeman W. & Sons (William & William C. & Charles F. Grandeman) 60 Dey

Graner Louis & Co. (Louis Graner, Robert S. Pyko & Hugo J. Potosky) 477 B'way & 50 Mercer

Granny Michael & Brothers (Michael & Martin & Patrick & John Granny) 96 Tenth av.

Granite Cutters' National Union (no inf.) 37 Frankfort

Granite Ready Roofing Co. (Edward Vanorden & Co. proprs.) 110 John

Granite State Provident Assn. (G. Loring Pierce, Pres.; John G. Lane, Sec.; Clark M. Eggleston, Treas. Capital, $500,000. Directors: G. Loring Pierce, Clark M. Eggleston, D. M. Shapleigh, Robert P. Gibson, Howard J. Forker) 171 & 835 D'way

Granitic Sidewalk Co. (inf. unattainable) 171 B'way

Granite S. & Brother (Salvador & Vincenzo Granito) 1277 B'way

Grano Metallic Stone Co. (W. M. Bennet, Sec. Capital, $1,000,000; further inf. unattainable) 8 Wall

Grant Locomotive Works (Richard S. Grant, Pres.; William W. Evans, Sec.; further inf. refused) 41 Wall

Grant Richard, Co. (Richard Grant, Pres.; Samuel O. Church, Sec. Capital, $250,000; further inf. unattainable) 181 Hudson

Grant Brothers (James & Frederick Grant) 56 B'way

Grant & Co. (Richard S. Grant, no Co.) 41 Wall

Grant & English (Raymond M. Grant & Melvin L. English) 2134 Eighth av.

Grant & Grant (George M. & Charles B. & J. Ralston Grant) 55 Liberty

Grant & Little (May C. Grant & Joanna N. Little) County C. H.

Graphic Process Co. (inf. unattainable) 63 B'way

Graphic Publishing Co. (in liquidation) 41 Park pl.

Grasmuck & Ostrander (Frederick Grasmuck & William H. Ostrander) 202 D'way

Grasmuck Brothers (Joseph & Edward Grasmuck, 120 Nassau, Martin & Joseph & Edward Grasmuck W. 155th n Eighth av.)

Grau Julius & Son (Julius & William Grau jr.) 701 Sixth

Grauer Moritz & Son (no inf.) 595 Grand

Graver & Palotte Publishing Co. (no inf.) 164 Fifth av.

Graves Cotton Harvester Co. (Isaac Blum, Pres. Capital, $50,000. Trustees: Isaac Blum. Isaac Alexander, Adolph Prochownick) 123 Duane

Graves Robert, Co. (Robert Graves, Pres.; Henry Durn, Treas. Capital, $240,000; further inf. refused) 453 Fifth av.

Graves & Steers (Henry C. Graves & Henry D. Steers) 19 Whitehall

Gravity Sign & Novelty Co. (Martin Lippmann, propr.) 56 Thomas

Gray A. R., Lighterage Co. (Malcolm Ramsay, Pres.; William H. Smith, Sec.; James B. Leeds, Treas. Capital, $65,000. Directors: Malcolm Ramsay, William H. Smith, James S. Leeds) 109 Produce Ex.

Gray Christopher & Co. (dissolved) 75 Franklin

Gray Thomas F. & Co (dissolved) 175 Pearl

Gray J. & Son (Jacob & Lewis Gray) 126 Leonard

Gray Brothers (brokers) (George F. & B. Morrison Gray) 4 Hanover

Gray Brothers (printers) (James & John & Robert & George Gray) 170 Fulton

Gray & Bender (dissolved) E. 135th n Rider av.

Gray & Gedney (Mary E. Gray & Caroline B. Gedney) 2148 Seventh av.

Gray & Gibbons (John A. Gray & Joseph L. Gibbons) 1829 B'way

Gray's Ferry Printing Ink Works (Robinson Brothers, proprs.) 27 Beekman

Graybill & Co. (George T. Graybill & Henry Gunson) 40 B'way

Graziano E. & A. (Emanuel & Andrea) 30 State

Great Am. Clothing Co. (Hein Brothers, proprs.) 312 Bowery

Great Am. Engraving & Printing Co. (Thomas R. Dawley. propr.) 57 Beekman

Great Am. Steam Carpet Cleaning Works (William H. Howden, propr.) 155 W. 29th

Great Am. Tea Co. (George F. Gilman, propr.) 31 Vesey

Great Atlantic & Pacific Tea Co. (George F. Gilman, propr.) 35 Vesey

Great Equator Cons. Gold Mining Co. (Charles H. Martin, Pres.; Frederick Baker, Sec. Capital, $2,000,000; further inf. refused) 206 B'way

Great Long Acre Agency (Ellen V. Hines, propr.) 705 Seventh av.

Great Northern Railway Co. (James J. Hill, Pres.; Edward T. Nichols, Sec.; Edward Sawyer, Treas. Capital, $40,000,000; further inf. unattainable) 40 Wall

Grant Overland Tea Co. (estate of James Ryan, propr.) 543 & 748 Second av. & 965 First av.

Great Republic Tea Co. (Patrick Gallinagh, propr.) 828 Tenth av.

Great Southern Freight & Passenger Lines (Theodore G. Eger, agent) 347 B'way, 5 Bowling gr. & Pier 29 E. R.

Great Western Beef & Provision Co. (Leopold J. Aumann, propr.) 172 & 834 Eighth av. & 88 G'wich av.

Great Western Ins. Co. (in liquidation) 75 Beaver

Greco C. & Co. (Cosmo Greco & Joseph Speciale) 90 Park pl.

Groeff & Co. (Emil & Bernhard Groeff & Philip B. Gallagher) 26 Greene

Greeley E. S. & Co. (Edwin S. Greeley, Pres.; James W. Sands, Sec. Capital, $250,000. Directors: Edwin S. Greeley, Arthur Parker, Joseph Bailey, E. S. Riggs) 5 Dey

| CINCINNATI, BALTIMORE, PHILADELPHIA, | SNOW, CHURCH & CO. CORRESPONDENTS EVERYWHERE. | NEW YORK, BOSTON, CHICAGO, LOUISVILLE. |

GRE 118 GRE

Green Charles M., Printing Co. (dissolved) 76 Beekman

Green Daniel & Co. (Daniel & William R. Green) 122 E. 13th

Green Lake & Lake Denmark Ice Co. (Edwin P. Merritt, Pres.; Charles H. Merritt, Sec. Capital, $300,000. Directors: Edwin P. & Charles H. Merritt, William H. Clarkson) 115 B'way

Green Mountain Gold Mining Co. (Francis H. Weeks, Pres.; Horace S. Bradford, Sec.; Capital, $1,250,000. Trustees; Francis H. Weeks, A. S. Comstock, Horace S. Bradford, William K. Lothrop, William D. Vernam) 120 B'way

Green Robert & Son (Robert & Robert Green jr.) 60 Cath. mkt

Green Samuel & Co. (Samuel Green & Henrietta Michels) 57 Prince

Green Shipton (Thomas John Shipton Green:—special partners, Robert Singlehurst & Robert & George W. & Henry & Septimus Brockiehurst, *Liverpool, Eng.*, each $15,000; terminates 19th Oct. 1890) 112 Pearl

Green Volney & Son (Volney & Frederick S. Green) 110 Front

Green Brothers (cotton) (David E. & Charles F. Green) 130 Pearl

Green Brothers (painters) (Patrick & Lawrence Green) 151 Madison

Green Brothers (real estate) (Emil & Maurice Green) 2 W. 4th

Green & Bateman (dissolved) 57 B'way

Green & Blackwell (Albert Green & Willis B. Blackwell) 167 Duane

Green & Hewlett (Joseph M. Green & George W. Hewlett) 180 South

Green & Putney (George Green & George T. Putney) 1459 B'way

Greenbaum & Co. (dissolved) 301 E. 125th

Greenberg L. & H. (Louis & Henry) 98 Baxter

Greenberg & Reuben (Henry Greenberg & Hyman J. Reuben) 426 Broome

Greenberg & Sondheim (Isidor Greenberg & Philip Sondheim) 2130 Third av.

Greenberger & Keck (Ernest Greenberger & Christian F. Keck) 951 Third av.

Greene George E. & Son (George E. Greene, only) 113 W. 28th

Greene J. Frank & Co. (J. Frank & Wilkins U. Greene) 80 Cliff

Greene Mfg. Co. (inoperative) 21 Cliff

Greene William C. & Co. (William C. & Byron Greene) 11 John

Greene F. E. & J. A. (Frank E. & J. Alonzo Greene) 35 W. 14th & 322 E. 63d

Greene & Hawley (Herbert W. Greene & Charles B. Hawley) 21 E. 14th

Greene, Tweed & Co. (J. Ashton & John W. Greene & Willard H. Platt, only) 83 Chambers & 85 Reade

Greenebaum F. & E. (Ferdinand & Edward) 13 Spruce & 117 Park row

Greenebaum H. & Co. (Henry Greenebaum & Nathan Marks) 1523 Flint av.

Greenebaum & Co. (Sigmund & Morris & Gussie Greenebaum & John B. Luther) 27 Walker

Greenfield E. T. & Co. (no Inf.) 324 W. 26th

Greenfield & Flynn (Adolph Greenfield & Thomas Flynn) 89 Grand

Greenfield's E., Son & Co. (Nelson Greenfield & August Schwarzschild;—special partner, Moritz Davidson, $25,000; terminates 31st Dec. 1890) 44 Barclay

Greenhall & Co. (Abraham Greenhall, no Co.) 230 Pearl & 30 Front

Greenhood & Bohm (Isaac Greenhood & Ferdinand Bohm) 61 Walker

Greenlie, Wyatt & Co. (William P. Greenlie, Robert S. Wyatt, Andrew A. Bremner & David Greenlie) 499 Water & 253 South

Greenpoint Towage & Lighterage Co. (not inc.) (James & Daniel & William McAllister, Henry Gillen & James McKillop) 128 Pearl

Greenstein Saul & Son (no inf.) 12 Rutgers st.

Greenthal Brothers (William Greenthal, only) 560 Seventh av.

Greenwald Isaac & Brother (Isaac & Abraham Greenwald) 34 Macdougal

Greenwald C. & Son (refused) 781 Second av.

Greenwald Brothers (Edward & Isaac Greenwald) 27 Av. C

Greenwald & Co (Louis Greenwald & James Gowdy) 202 B'way

Greenwald & Jacobs (Isaac Greenwald & Bernhard Jacobs) 291 Bleecker

Greenwall H. & Son (no inf.) 1145 B'way

Greenwich Bank (John S. McLean, Pres.; William A. Hawes, Cashier. Capital, $200,000. Directors: John S. McLean, John Harsen Rhoades, Clinton Gilbert, Albert G. Bogert, John M. Tilford, Charles Shultz, Peter A. Welch, Isaac Hendrix, William Moir) 402 Hudson

Greenwich Ins. Co. (Samuel C. Harriot, Pres.; Mason A. Stone, Sec. Capital, $200,000. Directors: Clinton Gilbert, John G. Davis, William H. S. Elting. Samuel C. Harriot, William J. Haddock, George Gordon, Quentin McAdam, Solomon W. Albro, James A. Roosevelt, Mason A. Stone, Allen S. Apgar. Abiel A. Low, Angustus C. Brown, William P. Douglas, Samuel W. Harriot, Samuel Raynor, James M. & William Brookfield) 161 B'way

Greenwich Mfg. Co. (inf. unattainable) 56 Vesey

Greenwich Savings Bank (John H. Rhoades, Pres.; Leonard D. White & Francis H. Leggett, Secs.; Clinton Gilbert, Treas. Trustees: Clinton Gilbert, John S. Dickerson, D. M. Morrison, William Remsen, John H. Rhoades, Samuel D. Van Duzen, Alexander McL. Agnew, John A. Stewart, Lowell Lincoln, Charles P. Daly, Joseph W. Goddard, John S. McLean, Edward Onthout, Joseph H. Gray, John Wilson, Charles G. Landon, William L. Jenkins, Charles A. Davison, James B. M. Grosvenor, Julius Catlin jr. William Moir, George Bliss, Arthur B. Graves, Edward N. Taller, John L. Riker, William B. Isham, Leonard D. White, George W. Smith, Francis H. Leggett, Algernon S. Frissell, William T. Wardwell, Joseph Thompson, Charles Stewart Smith) 71 Sixth av.

Green-wood Cemetery (Abiel A. Low,Pres.; Charles M. Perry, Comptroller. Trustees: James R. Taylor, Benjamin H. Field, Alexander M. White, John W. C. Leveridge, Benjamin D. Silliman. George Beekman, James M. Brown, George Masculloch Miller, Jasper W. Gilbert, Edmund L. Baylies, John J. Pierrepont, Samuel D. Babcock, Abiel A. Low, Charles M. Perry) 26 B'way

Greenwood Lake Improvement Co. (inf. unattainable) 120 Liberty

Greenwood Lake Steamboat Co. (inf. unattainable) 120 Liberty

Greenwood & Tupper (Henry C. Greenwood & Kimball I. Tupper) 16 Little W. 12th & 65 Gansevoort

Gregg & Class (Franklin N. Class, only) 20 Exchange pl.

Gregory James (James & William Gregory) 106 Cannon

Gregory Brothers (George Gregory, only) 119 Sixth av.

Gregory & Co. (Elisha Gregory & Dightman D. Bishop) 196 B'way

Gregory & Jennings (Julian C. Gregory & Horace N. Jennings) 403 Cherry

Gregory, Ballou & Co. (Charles Gregory, Maturin Ballou & Curtis F. Gately) 1 New

WATER METERS, GAS ENGINES, FOR PUMPING AND POWER. | **NATIONAL METER CO.** 252 Broadway, N. Y.

GRE 119 GRO

Grell, Wildermann & Co. (Ernest Grell & Charles Wildermann, no Co.) 11 Barclay
Greiner John & Co. (John Greiner & Samuel Rheinstrom) 433 W. 42d
Greiner B. & Son (Bruno & Oscar Greiner) 503 E. 82d
Gretsch & Leroy (dissolved) 12 Clinton pl.
Grenhart & Son (Marie & Henry Grenhart) 100 E. 02d
Gress & Palmer (John G. E. Gress & Herman Palmer) 171 E. 92d
Grether & Wahrenberger (Frederick Grether & Herman J. E. Wahrenberger) 427 E. 144th
Gretsch & Mayer (William Gretsch & Adolph Mayer) 96 Fulton
Greve Henry & Co. (Henry Greve, no Co.) 22 E. 13th
Gribble & Nash (Henry Gribble & David Nash) 184 Pearl & 100 Water
Gridley & Co. (Edward M. Gridley & Henry M. Polhemus) 87 Maiden la.
Grieco & Brother (Domenico & Frederick Grieco) 45 S. 5th av.
Grief & Koch (dissolved) 1684 Park av.
Griem Henry & Son (Henry Griem, only) 6 City Hall pl.
Grieme & Mahnke (dissolved) 2261 Second av.
Gries Sisters (Augusta & Louise Gries) 870 Ninth av.
Grifenhagen Brothers (Jacob B. & Max S. Grifenhagen) 101 W. 127th
Griffen Charles Field & Co. (Charles Field Griffen & George B. Moore) 132 Park av.
Griffen's John D., Son (John D. Griffen) 196 Chambers
Griffin John J. & Co. (John J. Griffin & John Gribbel) 52 Dey
Griffin Mfg. Co. (James K. Griffin, Pres.; George E. Righter, Sec.; Edwin C. Griffin, Treas.; further inf. unattainable) 74 Cortlandt
Griffin H. & Sons (Edward P. & Charles F. Griffin, only) 54 Duane
Griffin & Prior (Edward Griffin & John Prior) 60 W. 3d
Griffing & Debevoise (Joseph Griffing & Walter W. Debevoise) 323 E. 2d
Griffing's H. B., Sons & Co. (William H. & Edward R. Griffing & Edward P. Bellows) 70 Cortlandt
Griffith C. L. & Co. (Charles L. Griffith:—special partner, M. Griffith; further inf. refused) 89 Front
Griffith J. G. & Co. (Joseph G. Griffith & Joseph E. Saffery) 144 Centre
Griffith W. H. & Co. (Elizabeth F. Griffith, Pres.; William R. Griffith, Sec.; Richard Ross, Treas. Capital, $20,000. Directors: Elizabeth F. & William R. Griffith, Richard Ross) 10 Fourth av. & r 370 Bowery
Griffith & Co. (Albert R. Griffith, no Co.) 67 & 2241 Third av.
Griffiths John A. & Co. (John A. Griffiths & William C. Tragesor) 515 E. 19th
Griffiths R. A. & Co. (no inf.) 120 Water
Griffiths Brothers (Thomas M. & William A. Griffiths) 15 John
Griffiths & Greer (Frederick C. Griffiths & Austin M. Greer) 42 New
Griggs & Carleton (James M. Griggs & Charles A. Carleton) 202 B'way
Griggs & Co. (James M. & Isaac Griggs) 154 E. 55th, 1164 Third av. & 21 Jackson
Griggs & Crowley (Henry H. Griggs & Emmett Crowley) 190 Seventh av.
Grimes J. & M. F. (dissolved) 101 Broad
Grimm Charles & Co. (Charles Grimm, Co. refused) 119 S. 5th av.

Grimm Brothers (John & Henry Grimm) 251 Washn.
Grimm & Runge (dissolved) 119 S. 5th av.
Grimmer Brothers (Charles & John W. Grimmer) r 149 E. 22d
Grinberg P. J. & Co. (Paul J. & Lassar J. Grinberg) 155 South
Grinberg Brothers (dissolved) 155 South
Grinberg & Glauber (Adolf J. Grinberg & Nathan Glauber) 32 Maiden la.
Grinberg & Schans (Leopold Grinberg & Charles F. Schans) 32 Maiden la.
Grindal & Andresen (Augustine Grindal & John H. Andresen) 11 Water
Grinnell, Minturn & Co. (C. Edward Billqvist:— special partner, Robert S. Minturn, $100,000; terminates 1st Jan. 1893) 45 William
Grinnon Brothers (Hugh & Daniel J. Grinnon) 810 Eighth av.
Grissler & Son (Gottlieb & Henry G. Grissler) 934 E. 17th
Griswold H. & Co. (Harrison Griswold & Harry H. Treadwell) 87 Vestry
Griswold S. M. & F. J. (Stephen M. & Frederick J.) 18 John
Griswold & Co. (Catharine A. Griswold & Jerome D. & Martha M. Wygant & John B. & Julia B. Putnam) 928 B'way
Griswold & Gillett (Wayne Griswold & Jerome D. Gillett)-3 Wall
Griswold, Deuel & Griswold (Almon W. Griswold, Joseph M. Deuel & Almon W. Griswold jr.) 11 Pine
Grocers' Mercantile Agency (dissolved) 6 Harrison
Grode & Co. (Charles Grode & Carl Ehrhard) 102 E. 14th
Groeschel & Rosman (Elizabeth Groeschel & Daniel P. Rosman) 27 John & 97 Cliff
Grogan Brothers (Patrick & James Grogan) 479 Seventh av.
Groh & Reid (Jacob A. Groh & Andrew O. Reid) 91 Murray
Groh's Michael, Sons (Michael J. & John Groh) 242 W. 26th
Groht & Co. (Joseph H. Groht, Co. refused) 146 Reade
Grollmund & Rose (John Grollmund & Andrew Rose) 378 Seventh av.
Grolz & Co. (Charles Grolz & Catharine Roth) 511 Ninth av.
Groom L. J. & Son (Levi J. & Willard Groom) 1014 Third av.
Gross Philip C. & Co. (Philip C. Gross & Daniel Wolff) 89 Murray
Gross A. & Co. (Androw & Charles E. Gross & Emma V. Slevin) 78 Murray
Gross S. & Co. (Samuel Gross & Louis Klein) 8 Av. C
Gross Brothers (no inf.) r 164 Attorney
Gross & Rosenfeld (dissolved) 307 E. Houston
Gross & Wise (Albert H. Gross & Otto S. Wise) 523 B'way
Grossman Martin & Sons (George J. & Gustav Grossman, only) 193 Canal & 88 Clinton
Grossman & Brother (dissolved) 120 W. 17th
Grossman & Samilson (Barnet Grossman, Reuben Samilson) 7 Elizabeth
Grossmann H. & Son (Henry & Jacob Grossmann) 172 Attorney
Grosvenor & Carpenter (James B. M. Grosvenor & Charles M. Carpenter) 70 Worth & 23 Thomas
Grosvenor & Richards (John M. Grosvenor, only) 100 Fulton
Grote F. & Co. (Charles H. Steinway, receiver) 114 E. 14th

PROTECTION For Family, Home, Store, Factory, etc., by using only the "VULCAN" BRAND OF SAFETY MATCHES. Headquarters, 373 Washington Street, New York.

GRO 120 HAA

Grote & McMahon (Herman G. Grote & Bernard McMahon) 115 Rivington
Gruber Francis J. & Son (Francis J. & Leonard Gruber) 163 E. 44th
Gruber & Davidson (Arnold Gruber & Millie Davidson) 134 Park row
Gruber & Felbertaum (dissolved) 153 E. 110th
Gruber, Bard & Landon (Abraham Gruber, Frederic B. Bard & Henry L. Landon) 41 Park row
Gruelle & Francois (Eva Gruelle & Joseph D. Francois) 217 Sixth av.
Gruenfeld & Eisner (dissolved) 148 Attorney
Gruhn R. & Son (Rudolph & Solomon Gruhn) 41 Cortlandt & 18 Bowery
Grum & Son (dissolved) 11 Washn. mkt
Grumbach & Grote (Frederick H. Grote, only) 125 Hudson
Grumbach's J. E., Son (Hugo E. Grumbach) 227 William
Gruner Siegfried & Co. (Siegfried Gruner, Otto Arens & Henry Schaefer) 60 Broad
Granthal & Bohlen (Henry Bohlen, only) 39 Ninth av.
Guarantee Medical Attendance Assn. (no inf.) 41 Union sq. W.
Guaranty Mutual Accident Assn. (dissolved) 165 B'way
Guardian Fire Ins. Co. (Walter K. Paye, Pres.; James C. Stevens, Sec. Capital, $200,000. Directors: Bryce Gray, Walter K. Paye, Wilson G. Hunt, Theodore Timpson, Samuel A. Patterson, William King, Alexander T. Vannest, Charles F. Pond, David Crocker, John F. Plummer, Eugene F. O'Connor, Mitchell N. Packard, J. B. Woodward, William Barbour, James K. Murphy, James C. Stevens, John J. E. Rothery, Edward Smith) 153 B'way
Guastavino Fire Proof Construction Co. (Lindley M. Hoffman, Pres.; Wuffredo Uffreduzi, Sec. Capital, $150,000; further inf. unattainable) 35 B'way
Guayabillas Mining Co. (no inf.) 1 B'way
Gudewill & Bucknall (George Gudewill & Henry W. J. Bucknall) 123 Water
Guedalla & Co. (Aaron Gnedalla & Oscar Pfeiffer) 407 E. 70th
Guerber Brothers (Henry & August Guerber) 28 John
Guerineau & Drake (William S. Guerineau & William H. Drake) 11 Bible h.
Guerra Brothers (Vicente & Ramon Guerra) 172 Water
Guest & Co. (Isaac D. & Frank D. Guest) 744 Seventh av. & 306 W. 48d
Guest & Hill (dissolved) 55 Cotton Ex.
Guggenheim's M., Sons (Meyer & Isaac & Daniel & Morris & Solomon Guggenheim) 2 Wall
Guggenheimer & Steinhard (Samuel Guggenheimer & Samuel W. Steinhard) 25 E. Houston
Guggenheimer & Untermyer (Randolph Guggenheimer & Isaac & Samuel Untermyor) 46 Wall & 908 Third av.
Guida & Son (Vinanzo & Rafaele Guida) 702 Third av.
Guillem & Grimard (Eliza Guillem & Amelie Grimard) 145 W. 36th
Guinand & Son (Charles A. & Charles H. Guinand) 9 Peck sl.
Guindon & Berdan (Eugene W. Guindon & John H. Berdan) 117 John, 216 Duane, 167 Washn. 313 Canal & 1 Lispenard
Guion & Co. (Amanda Guion & Marie G. Barril) 39 B'way
Guiterman S. & Co. (Sigmund Guiterman & Sigmund Pulzer) 82 Broad
Guiterman Brothers (Simon Guiterman, only) 108 Grand

Gumpert Samuel & Co. (Samuel Gumpert & Samuel Klauber) 623 B'way & 190 Mercer
Gundling D. & Co. (David & Harry Gundling) 41 Maiden la.
Gunning & Brown (Edwin J. B. Dunning & Henry E. Brown) 114 Wall
Gunning & Holmes (William Gunning & Michael B. Holmes) 393 G'wich
Gunther C. B. & Brother (Charles B. & John J. Gunther) 40 Wall
Gunther & Co. (Louis & Charles Gunther & Charles Preusch) 65 Duane
Gunther & Oumme (Henry Gunther & Frederick W. Oumme) 25 Chambers
Gunther & Kahn (Isaac Gunther & Leopold Kahn) 1860 & 1905 Third av.
Gunther & Moll (dissolved) 217 S. 5th av.
Gunther's C. G., Sons (F. Frederic Gunther, Louis F. George & William H. jr. & Franklin L. & Ernest R. Gunther) 184 Fifth av.
Guns P. & Son (Protas & Charles Guns) 88 Essex
Gunsburger Brothers (David & Norbert Gunsburger) 25 Maiden la.
Gurell & Hanlon (dissolved) 244 Washn. mkt
Gurell & Schick (John C. Gurell & William Schick) 244 Washn. mkt
Gurnee W. S. jr. & Co. (Walter S. jr. & Augustus C. Gurnee) 7 Nassau
Guthrie & Co. (Samuel & John N. Guthrie) 225 Front
Gutman R. & Son (Regina & Jonas Gutman) 168 B'way
Gutman Brothers (Mayer & Abraham & Sanders Gutman) 452 B'way & 16 Crosby
Gutman Brothers & Seckel (Sigmund S. & Jacob Gutman & Abraham Seckel) 2236 Third av.
Gutmann N. & Co. (Nathan Gutmann & David Krakauer) 311 Third av.
Gutmann & Frank (dissolved) 30 Ferry
Gutmann & Leopold (Carl Gutmann & Samuel Leopold) 96 Spring
Gutta Percha & Rubber Mfg. Co. (Amadee Spadone, Pres.; Matthew Hawe, Treas. Capital, $500,000. Directors: Amadee Spadone, Dorman T. Warren, Charles G. Landon, Clay B. Pelton, William Scott, Henry E. Spadone) 35 Warren
Guttenberg J. B. & Son (Joseph B. & Max J. Guttenberg) 2194 Third av.
Guttermann E. & Co. (Henry Waldmann, Gustav Buxbaum, S. Kramer, S. Bamberger & Elkan Guttermann) 11 Stone
Gutwillig Brothers (Sigmund & Alois & Alfred Gutwillig) 405 B'way
Guy & Cloughen (James Guy & Joseph Cloughen) 1212 Tenth av.
Guyon C. F. & Co. (Charles F. Guyon, James H. Cutler & Rufus L. Woodrough) 99 Reade
Gusik & Roth (dissolved) 195 Second
Gwathmey & Bloss (James O. Bloss & James T. Gwathmey: — special partner, Archie B. Gwathmey, B'klyn. N. Y., $50,000; terminates 18th Sept. 1891) 128 Pearl
Gwillim & Meyers (Reese B. Gwillim & John G. H. Meyers) 21 Park row
Gwynne & Richardson (Richard Gwynne & Henry W. Richardson) 580 Hudson

H

Haaf John & Son (John & Edmonds W. Haaf) 162 William
Haag F. & G & Co. (Gustave K. Haag & J. Edward & George J. Jetter, only) 113 Canal & 101 Elm
Haake A. & C. Baasel (Albert Haake & Charles Baasel) 29 Rector

IDEN & CO., MANUFACTURERS OF
University Place, 9th to 10th Sts., N.Y. | **GAS FIXTURES AND ELECTROLIERS**

HAA   121   HAL

Haaker William, Co. (William Haaker, Pres.; Henry Jaburg, Treas.; William Kraft, Sec.; further inf. unattainable) 125 Hudson
Haaren & Meinken (John W. Haaren, Ernest A. Meinken & Ernest A. Haaren) 358 G'wich
Haas Henry & Son (Louis Haas, only) 402 E. 30th
Haas Leonard J. & Co. (Leonard J. Haas & Abraham Davis) 293 Church
Haas L. & Co. (Leopold Haas & Jacob K. & Leopold S. Weiner) 248 Canal
Haas S. & Co. (Simon Haas & Hugo Worms) 290 Church
Haas Brothers (sporting gds) (Samuel & William & Michael Haas) 60 W. 26th, 142 W. 25th & 13 Av. B
Haas Brothers (supplies) (Louis S. & Sidney & Benjamin Haas) 110 Reade
Haas & Abeles (Bertha Haas & Edmund Abeles) 2034 Third av.
Haas & Baier (Joseph Haas & Charles Baier) 269 Canal
Haas & Fried (Samuel H. Haas & Isidor W. Fried) 25 John, 22 Ann & 57 W. 30th
Haas & Hirschmann (Louis Haas & Charles Hirschmann) 157 Bowery
Haas, Ryttenberg & Co. (Henry W. Haas, Abraham Ryttenberg & David Tohalski) 510 B'way
Haas' A. Sons (Isaac & Simon & Felix Haas) 175 W. 48th & 373 Lenox av.
Haase & Co. (Gustave H. Haase & Joseph Aschauer) 64 G'wich
Haase & Meyer (Adolph Haase & Abraham Meyer) 180 Mercer
Haase & Moeller (Julius Haase & William H. Moeller) 1220 Tenth av.
Hackberry Mining Co. (refused) 11 Cliff
Hackenbroch & Selz (Theodor Seiz, only) 27 W. 125th
Hackett, Carhart & Co. (Corcellus H. Hackett, John B. Van Wagenen, Albert E. Colfax, Edmund H. Carhart & William H. Whitford) 422 B'way
Hadden & Co. (Harold F. & James B. Smith Hadden) 109 Worth
Haddock, Shonk & Co. (John C. Haddock, George W. Shonk & Edward B. Arnold) 1 B'way
Haddon & Co. (Henry Haddon, no Co.) 143 Centre
Haebler & Co. (Theodore Haebler & Oscar Fashrmann) 121 Pearl
Hachner E. & Co. (no inf.) 184 Bowery
Haff Mfg. Co. (Haff & Walbridge, propra.) 73 Leonard
Haff & Walbridge (Edward P. Haff & John H. Walbridge) 76 Leonard
Haffen J. & M. (John & Matthias jr.) 644 E. 152d
Haffner & Henley (dissolved) 250 E. 104th
Hafner & Kohart (Leopold Hafner & Frank C. Kohart) 21 John
Haft N. & Son (dissolved) 39 Malden la.
Hagan & Co. (Frank M. Hagan, no Co.) 80 West
Hagan & Duff (dissolved) 502 Ninth av.
Hage J. D. & Co. (Johannes D. Hage & Henry O. Tallmadge) 19 Whitehall
Hagedorn & Co. (Daniel Schnakenberg, only) 64 Beaver
Hagelstein Brothers (Philip & Charles Hagelstein) 142 Bowery
Hagemeyer George & Son (George & George Hagemeyer jr.) ft. F. 11th & ft R. 10th
Hagemeyer & Brunn (Francis E. Hagemeyer & Julius W. Brunn) 47 Pearl
Hagens & Stellmann (dissolved) 216 Church

Hagerty & Hynes (James Hagerty & James Hynes) 1909 Third av. & 1737 Second av.
Hagerty Brothers & Co. (Michael H. Hagerty, George M. Nichols & Anne J. Hagerty, only) 5 & 10 Platt
Haggerty Brothers (Dennis C. & Joseph F. & John F. & Francis J. Haggerty) 154 Malden la.
Hague A. J. & Co. (Ainsworth J. Hague & Francis R. Baker) 74 Franklin
Hahlo H. & Co. (Herman Hahlo, Joseph U. Hoexter, Hugo H. Hahlo, Mervyn Wolff & Julius H. & Henry G. Hahlo) 260 Church
Hahlo & Lindner (dissolved) 280 B'way
Hahn Charles J. & Co. (dissolved) 237 E. 115th
Hahn Henry & Brother (dissolved) 1452 First av.
Hahn Joseph & Son (Joseph & Myer Hahn) 212 Wash.
Hahn A. & Co. (Abraham Hahn, no Co.) 296 B'way
Hahn M. & Co. (Morris Hahn & Frank W. Struvy) 150 Chambers
Hahn Brothers (Berthold & George Hahn) 49 Warren
Hahn & Brunett (Paul Hahn & Henry F. Brunett) 262 G'wich
Hahn & Co. (Philip Hahn & August Schaffer) 41 Malden la.
Hahn & Erreger (Jacob Hahn & George Erreger) 304 Bowery
Hahn & Mann (Bernhard Hahn & Frederick E. Mann) 511 E. 85th
Hahn & Martin (Charles J. Hahn & Isaac N. Martin) 237 E. 115th
Hahn & Myers (Nathan L. Hahn & Emanuel J. Myers) 237 D'way
Hahn, Brussel & Co. (Morris Prochaska & James Brussel, only) 428 E. 63d
Hahns R. & Son (Robert & Oscar Hahne) 318 G'wich
Haiduven's J., Sons (Joseph J. & Richard J. & Edward S. Haiduven) 492 E. 134th
Haigh E. & L. (Emily & Louisa) 435 Fourth av.
Haight Charles & Co. (Charles Haight, Alfred A. Freeman & Henry Koper) 24 State
Haight G. L. & L. (Louis Haight & Edward H. Jewett, only) 26 Broad
Haight & Roberts (Willet M. Haight & Mortimer O. Roberts) 1798 D'way
Haincr & Saabye (Daniel W. Halner & William J. Saabye jr.) 23 William
Haines John H. J., Co. (John H. J. Haines, Pres.; E. S. M. Haines, Sec. Capital, $15,000; further inf. unattainable) 78 Malden la.
Haines S. A., Co. (Samuel A. Haines, Pres.; Anne E. Haines, Treas.; further inf. unattainable) 90 Chambers
Haines Brothers (Napoleon J. Haines, only) S. Boulevard c Alexander av.
Haines & Bishop (Henry A. Haines & Alfred G. Bishop) 70 Worth
Haire & Langer (Robert J. Haire & Oscar B. Langer) 23 Chambers
Hais Brothers (Charles F. & Frank J. & George Hais) 509 First av. 546 Second av. & ft. E. 10th
Hake John H. & Co. (John H. & John D. Hake) 98 Essex & 224 Av. A
Halbert Brothers (Henry C. & Charles F. Halbert) 110 Prince
Halbert & Millard (dissolved) 99 Nassau
Haldeman & Cleary (dissolved) 43 E. 12th
Haldy Frederick & Co. (Frederick & Marie Haldy) 242 Bleecker
Hale J. P., Co. (Charles H. Stone, Pres.; F. W. Cronkhite, Sec. Capital, $132,000. Directors: Charles H. & George C. Stone, John E. Thompson, F. W. Cronkhite) 523 W. 35th

TYPEWRITING DONE BY THE TROW CITY DIRECTORY CO., 11 University Place.

HAL 122 HAM

Hale & Co. (Henry A. Hale & William F. Smith) 304 Pearl
Hale & Totten (Edgar F. Hale & Harry W. Totten) 15 Jay
Hales & Galschiot (John Hales & William Galschiot) 97 Water
Haley Caleb & Co. (Caleb & Seabury N. Haley) 14 Fulton fish mkt
Haley C. C. & Co. (dissolved) 586 W. 41st
Haley C. J. & Co. (Christina J. Haley, no Co.) 897 B'way
Haley D. & Co. (Dudley & Albert Haley) 6 Fulton fish mkt
Haley J. S. & Co. (Josiah S. Haley, no Co.) 57 Elm
Halford & Benson (no inf.) 2074 Third av.
Halifax Street Railway Co. (Ltd.) (no inf.) 3 Broad
Halk John V. & Son (John V. & John Halk) 516 Pearl
Hall Alvah & Co. (Albert C. Hall & William N. Stevenson, only) 96 Franklin
Hall George P. & Son (George P. & James S. Hall) 157 Fulton
Hall Mfg. Co. (Edward K. Hall, propr.) 60 Barclay
Hall Peter & Co. (Peter Hall, no Co.) 111 Liberty
Hall Signal Co. (William P. Hall, Pres.; Winfield S. Gilmore, Treas. Capital, $4,000,000. Directors: William P. Hall, Winfield S. Gilmore, Aldah W. Hall, William F. Cochran, S. Marsh Young, Irving Ingraham, E. S. Hollister) 50 B'way
Hall Telephone Co. (inoperative) 744 B'way
Hall A. & Son (Alicia & Frank E. Hall) 73 Leonard & 208 West
Hall D. C. & Co. (Dewitt C. Hall, no Co.) 86 Leonard
Hall R. M. & D. P. (Rowland M. & David P.) 32 Liberty
Hall & Arbes (Ferdinand Hall & Joseph Arbes) 88 Bleecker
Hall & Buell (Lewis A. Hall & Andrew A. Buell) 140 Pearl
Hall & Co. (hats) (Belle J. Hall, Oliver Shepard & Percy H. Hall) 190½ Greene
Hall & Co. (publishers) (A. Wilford Hall, no Co.) 23 Park row
Hall & Furgason (Michael C. Hall & Lewis C. Furgason) 206 Duane
Hall & Hackett (dissolved) 211 Centre
Hall & Harvey (dissolved) 50 Exchange pl.
Hall & Henshaw (Henry H. Hall & William W. Henshaw jr.) 54 William
Hall & Johnston (dissolved) 265 B'way
Hall & Near (Herbert O. Hall & Mervin S. Near) 51 Cliff
Hall & O'Donoghue (dissolved) 202 B'way
Hall & Reppenhagen (George Hall & John W. Reppenhagen) 321 Broome
Hall & Ruckel (William H. Hall, only) 216 G'wich
Hall & Vaughan (Thomas W. Hall & Henry D. Vaughan) 18 Ferry
Hall's Bazar Form Co. (B. Ross Appleton, propr.) 683 B'way
Hall's H. B., Sons (Henry B. jr. & Charles D. & Alfred R. Hall & Edmund H. Knight) 23 Park pl.
Hall's Isaac, Son (William A. Hall) 194 Broad
Hall's Samuel, Son (Charles Hall) 239 W. 10th
Hall's William, Sons (Thomas B. A. & William H. Hall) ft. E. 108th
Hallahan & Allison (George L. Hallahan & Theodore Allison) 495 Hudson
Hallen Louis H. & Co. (Louis H. & Louis F. Hallen) 7 W. 125th

Hallenbeck & Hollis (John J. Hallenbeck & E. F. Hollis) ft. W. 59th
Haller & Son (dissolved) 749 E. 9th
Hallet & Breen (James Breen, only) 60 Fulton
Hallett A. F. & Son (Adam F. & Charles F. Hallett) 969 Park av.
Hallett & Co. (Adam F. Hallett & Louis H. Zocher) 1476 Third av.
Halley William & Co. (dissolved) 197 West
Halley, Atchison & Sinotte de Loiselle (William Halley, James I. Atchison & E. Sinotte de Loiselle) 869 B'way
Hallgarten & Co. (Sigmund Neustadt, Henry Budge, Bernhard Mainzer & Charles Wehrhane :—special partner, Charles L. Hallgarten, Frankfort-on-the-Main, Germany, $500,000; terminates 31st Dec. 1890) 23 Broad
Halliday A. & Co. (Alexander Halliday, no Co.) 17 Harrison
Halliday A. T. & Co. (dissolved) 81 Cedar
Halligan & Dalton (Thomas F. Halligan & William Dalton) 5 Hewitt av. W. Washn. mkt & 601 W. 89th
Halligan & Son (Thomas J. & John Halligan) 501 Eleventh av.
Hallock & Havens (dissolved) Williamsbrdge
Halm & Simon (Anton Halm & Joseph R. Simon) 936 First av. & 231 E. 51st
Halpin William & Co. (no inf.) 13 Murray
Halsey & Banta (Frank A. Halsey & Cornelius D. Banta) 117 West
Halsey & Pitcher (Charles C. Halsey & William R. Pitcher) 58 William
Halstead & Co. (Pearson & James W. Halstead & Ebenezer Hurd) 200 Forsyth & 427 Produce Ex.
Halsted E. S. & Co. (Ezekiel S. & Gilbert C. & William M. Halsted) 75 Pearl
Halsted & McLane (Richard H. Halsted & Henry R. McLane) 81 Broad
Halvorsen & Redlin (Thomas Halvorsen & Albert Redlin) 13 Market
Hamann & Koch (John A. Hamann & Peter Koch) 5 Maiden la.
Hamburger L. & Co. (Isaac & Solomon Hamburger) 174 Water
Hamburger & Co. (Simon Hamburger & Hymes W. Rosenbaum jr.) 416 Broome
Hamel's James, Sons (William & Isaiah Hamel) 214 E. 52d & 230 E. 63d
Hamerschlag M. & Co. (refusal) 129 Park row
Hamerschlag's J., Sons (refusal) 129 Park row
Hames John H. J., Co. (Capital, $15,000; further inf. unattainable) no address
Hamill & Booth (James Booth & estate of Robert Hamill) 96 Grand
Hamill & Vannes (Thomas Hamill & Harry I. Vannes) 110 W. 53d
Hamilton Bank (Lucien C. Warner, Pres.; Carroll St. John, Cashier; William A. Shelton, Notary, Capital, $150,000. Directors: Lucien C. Warner, Charles B. Fosdick, William P. St. John, William C. Browning, George Taylor, Mayer Lehman, Cyrus Clark, Emanuel Lauer, William C. Brewster, Samuel T. Peters, George Montague, Julius W. Tiemann, Joseph Milbank, Samuel Shethar, James M. Horton, George W. Crossman, Louis Strasburger, Welcome T. Alexander, Frederick R. Schenck) 278 W. 125th
Hamilton Bank Note Engraving & Printing Co. (Alexander R. Chisolm, Pres.; Nicholas F. Seebeck, Sec. Capital, $75,000. Directors: Alexander R. Chisolm, H. Cohen, J. W. Johnston, Charles E. Krack, William H. English, D. Calman, Nicholas F. Seebeck) 1 B'way
Hamilton Edward P. & Co. (Edward P. Hamilton, no Co.) 96 B'way

THE CALIGRAPH WRITING MACHINE,
HARTFORD, CONN.

Hamilton Fire Ins. Co. (Daniel D. Whitney, Pres.; David D. Leeds, Sec. Capital, $150,000. Directors: Charles Jenkins, Josiah M. & Daniel D. Whitney, Henry David, William H. Montanye, William Miles, David Mahony, Henry J Baringer, Nicholas Seagrist, John B. Blydenburgh, Frederick E. Willits, David D. Leeds, F. L. B. Mayhew) 155 B'way

Hamilton House Co. (dissolved) 19 E. 28th

Hamilton James & Brother (James & Charles W. Hamilton) 107 William

Hamilton Loan & Trust Co. (Moses E. Worthen, Pres.; Lucius F. Spencer, Sec.; William P. Aldrich, Treas. Capital, $225,000. Directors: Moses E. Worthen, George L. Whitman, Charles H. Wheeler, William F. R. Mills, John M. Thayer, William P. Aldrich, William O. Browning, William A. Wolff, Peter Reid, Frank W. Popple, John N. Beach, Frederick Y. Robertson, John T. Granger, Edward Forsythe, Lucius F. Spencer, Herbert Stevens, Thomas Scattergood) 150 B'way

Hamilton Park Co. (Harold G. Henderson, Pres.; W. Harrison Eisenbrey, Sec.; Charles T. Barney, Treas. Capital, $100,000. Trustees: Harold G. Henderson, Charles T. Barney, Alfred L. Loomis, W. Harrison Eisenbrey, Howard M. Durant) 8 Beekman

Hamilton Rubber Co. (Joseph Whitehead, Pres.; Frederick Whitehead, Sec. Capital, $200,000 ; further inf. unattainable) 10 Barclay

Hamilton Storage & Warehouse Co. (Frederick Vanriper, Pres.; Abner B. Vanriper, Sec. Trustees: Louis Banger, Wayland E. Benjamin, Abner B. & Frederick Vanriper, Charles C. Cox) 210 E. 125th

Hamilton Brothers (James G. & C. Kennedy Hamilton jr) 42 New

Hamilton & Bishop (Charles H. Hamilton & William F. Bishop) 96 B'way

Hamilton & Cholwell (John F. Hamilton & George C. Cholwell) 128 Front

Hamilton & Hamilton jr. (Ralph S. & Ralph S. Hamilton jr.) 192 B'way

Hamilton & McFadden (Joseph Hamilton & William A. McFadden) 716 Tenth av.

Hamilton & Myers (Mark E. Hamilton & Charles A. Myers) 56 B'way

Hamilton & Zippel (Frederick H. Hamilton & Charles J. Zippel) 38 Pine

Hamlin George E. & Co. (George E. & Albert O. Hamlin) 101 Duane & 10 Thomas

Hamlin & Co. (Frederick V. Hamlin & Isidor M. Stettenheim) 32 Nassau

Hammacher, Schlemmer & Co. (William Schlemmer & Charles F. Goepel, only) 209 Bowery, 8 & 15 Rivington & 221 Canal

Hammel J. & Son (Jacob & Valentine A. Hammel) 315 E. 115th

Hammel L. & Co. (Leo Hammel & Jacob W. Riglander) 35 Maiden la.

Hammen Brothers (Louis & Frederick Hammen) 199 Duane

Hammen & Gross (dissolved) 199 Duane

Hammerschlag Mfg. Co. (Siegfried Hammerschlag, Pres.; Charles A. Pierz, Sec. Capital, $300,000 ; further inf. refused) 234 G'wich

Hammerschlag Brothers (William & Isidore Hammerschlag) 120 Eighth

Hammerslough Brothers (Julius & Edward Hammerslough & Carl A. Lange) 482 & 636 B'way

Hammerslough, Saks & Co. (Samuel Hammerslough & Andrew & Isadore Saks) 96 Bleecker

Hammerstein & Ellison (Oscar Hammerstein & Lsmar S. Ellison) 2 Burling sl.

Hammill & Gillespie (Frederick R. Gillespie, only) 240 Front

Hammond Typewriter Co. (James B. Hammond, Pres.; John M. Bancroft, Sec.; William T. Phipps, Treas. Capital, $55,000. Directors: James B. Hammond, John M. Bancroft, William T. Phipps, William A, Hammond, L. J. Warner) 447 E. 52d, 77 Nassau & 292 Av. B

Hammond & Co. (sashes) (Alfred R. & Charles M. Hammond) 2390 Third av.

Hammond & Co. (stables) (A. P. & Thomas Hammond) 10 Seventh av.

Hammond & Hunter (James A. Hammond & Francis D. Hunter) 51 W. 30th

Hammond & Lobdell (dissolved) 12 Cliff

Hammond & Schild (Thomas R. Hammond & Charles M. Schild) 176 B'way

Hammond, Knowlton & Co. (George A. Hammond, Charles C. Knowlton & Louis Hauchhaus) 524 B'way

Hampden Corundum Wheel Co. (Willard P. Leshure, Pres.; James D. Safford, Treas. Capital, $16,000. Directors: Willard P. Leshure, George S. Graves, James D. Safford) 751 B'way

Hampson Edward P. & Co. (Edward P. Hampson & William F. Haring) 36 Curtlandt

Hamsley Metal Roofing Co. (not inc.) (Frederick L. Shoch, Millard F. Hamsley & Charles H. Kraft) 19 Cliff

Hanan & Son (James & John H. Hanan & John F. Edwards) 122 Centre & 207½ & 1203 B'way

Hance Brothers (William T. Hance, George B. McKowen & Robert H. Riddick, only) 68 Lawton av. W. Washn. mkt

Hanckel & Riordan (Thomas M. Hanckel & James & B. Rechfort Riordan) 8 Cotton Ex.

Hancock Coal Co. (Samuel W. Smith. Pres.; John F. Zebley, Treas. Capital, $80,000. Trustees, Samuel W. Smith, John F. Zebley, F, H. Smith, C. D. Turney) 20 Broad

Hand Gold Mining Co. (Nathan H. Hand, Pres.; Charles W. H. Hand, Sec. Capital, $1,000,000; further inf. refused) 206 B'way

Hand, Bonney, Pell & Jones (Clifford A. Hand, George B. Bonney, Frederick A. Pell, & Townsend Jones jr.) 51 Wall

Handren & Robins (John W. Handren & John N. Robins) 126 Washn.

Handy & Harman (Parker Handy, John F. Harman & Parker D. Handy) 24 Nassau

Hanft Brothers (John B. Hanft, only) 224 Fifth av.

Hanigan William T. & Co. (no inf.) 40 Perry

Hanken & Co. (Louis Hanken & George Baumgarten) 14 Av. C

Hanks Co. (Edmund F. Hanks, propr.) 203 Sixth av.

Hanlein & Co. (Henry Hanlein & Gottfried Oethinger) 321 E. 92d

Hanley John H. & Co. (John H. & George W. Hanley) 51 Jay

Hanlon & Goodman (John Goodman, only) 57 Fulton

Hanlon & Hayman (William H. Hanlon jr. & George W. Hayman) 4 White

Hanlon & Ortmann (Thomas Hanlon & George A. Ortmann) 54 Cliff

Hanlon & Ryan (Thomas Hanlon & Michael Ryan) ft. E. 51st

Hanly W. W. & Co. (William W. & Susan E. Hanly) 60 B'way

Hanly & Glynn (Mortimer Hanly & William A. Glynn) 59 Whitehall

Hanna W. C. & Son (William C. & William C. Hanna jr.) 1 Grand

Hannam William & Co. (William Hannam & Walter J. Katzé) 29 Union sq. W.

Hannigan & Bouillon (Patrick M. Hannigan & Michael L. Bouillon) 248 Grand & 2963 Third av.

Hanning George T. & Co. (George T. Hanning, no Co.) 79 Cedar

Hanover Aaron & Co. (no inf.) 19 Thirteenth av. W. Washn. mkt

HAN 124 **HAR**

Hanover Fire Ins. Co. (I. Remsan Lane, Sec. Capital, $1,000,000. Directors: James P. Wallace, William H. Lee, Henry Adams, Paul Worth, William A. Brown, Addison F. Roberts, E. L. Corning, Arthur B. Graves, Salem H. Wales, Isaac T. Smith, Samuel E. Howard, Russell H. Hoadley, Charles G. Landon, William D. Walcott, John L. Riker, I. Remsen Lane, Aretas Blood, Albert Mathews, Clarence F. Moulton, David S. Egleston, Samuel Thorne, George A. Crocker, David B. Flint, William D. Sloane, Samuel Shethar, Charles K. Wallace, Henry E. Hawley, William L. Strong, Joseph Haslehurst, William D. Leonard, Joseph T. Low, Augustus D. Juilliard) 40 Nassau, 105 B'way & 1 Third av.

Hanover National Bank (James T. Woodward, Pres.; James M. Donald, Cashier; John C. Ryer, Notary. Capital, $1,000,000. Directors: James T. Woodward, Vernon H. Brown, Signourney W. Fay, Martin S. Fechheimer, Mitchell N. Packard, William Rockefeller, James Stillman, Elijah P. Smith, Isidor Straus, James M. Donald) 9 Nassau

Hanrahan T. & Co. (Thomas Hanrahan, no Co.) 78 Nassau

Hanse James & Co. (James Hanse & John J. Deering) 93 Beekman

Hansen S. & Co. (Simon Hansen & Riewert M. Jappen) 81 Third av.

Hansen & Dieckmann (John Hansen & Stuffen Dieckmann) 308 Wash.

Hansen & Magee (Louis Hansen & Celia Magee) 144 E. 32d

Hansen & Tichenor (dissolved) 108 W. 23d

Hansmann & Van Glahn (August Hansmann & Henry Van Glahn) 152 South

Hanson Henry & Co. (Henry Hanson & William O. Saxton) 90 Warren

Hanson F. G. & Co. (Francis G. & Elizabeth A. Hanson) 169 Greene

Hanson W. J. & Son (dissolved) 194 Duane

Hanson & Green (Thomas E. Hanson & Louis A. Green) 91 Bleecker

Hanson & Hogan (William J. Hanson & Willard A. Hogan) 194 Duane

Hanson & Morrison (James S. Hanson & Richard H. Morrison) 1253 Third av.

Hanson, Van Winkle & Co. (Joseph Hanson, Abraham Van Winkle & Frederick S. Ward) 92 Liberty

Happersberger Philip & Son (Philip & Frederick Happersberger) 194 Elizabeth

Haran & Smith (Benjamin J. Haran & Henry Smith) 262 Wash.

Harbison & Loder (Edward Harbison & Noah Loder) 377 B'way

Harbor & Suburban Building & Savings Assn. (H. M. Haigh, Pres.; Jacob E. Bloom, Sec.; further inf. unattainable) 194 B'way

Harburg Rubber Comb Co. (Henry Trauu, propr.) 335 B'way

Harcourt & Co. (dissolved) 192 Water

Hard & Parsons (Bradley A. Hard & Samuel Parsons) 156 William

Hard & Rand (Anson W. Hard & George C. Rand) 107 Wall

Hard's Melvin, Sons (Melvin T. & Frank W. Hard) 25 Beekman

Hardee Brothers (Noble A. & Herbert P. Hardee) 2253 Seventh av.

Harden Acheson & Co. (James Harden, only) 107 Franklin

Hardenburg Henry B. & Co. (Henry B. Hardenberg & Charles J. Tiensch) 58 Centre

Harding George Edward & Co. (George Edward Harding & W. Tyson Gooch) 40 Exchange pl.

Harding J. M., Mfg. Co. (J. W. Fiske, Pres.; J. M. Fiske, Sec. Capital, $10,000. Directors:

J. W. & J. M. Fiske, J. M. Harding) 7 W. 14th

Harding F. W. & Co. (Philip W. Harding, no Co.) 16 Broad

Harding Brothers (Frank & George Harding) 229 Bowery

Harding & Co. (Edward E. Harding & Thomas F. McNulty) 80 Vesey

Harding & Heal (Theodore L. Harding & Harry E. Heal) 7 Cortlandt

Harding, Colby & Co. (dissolved) 80 Leonard

Harding, Whitman & Co. (Charles L. Harding, William Whitman & Edgar Harding) 80 Leonard

Hardman, Peck & Co. (Leopold Peck & Henry P. Sondheim, only) 183 Fifth av. & 643 W. 48th

Hardt J. P. & Co. (Jacob P. Hardt & Joseph Redegeld) 221 Park row

Hardt & Lindgens (William A. Hardt, Henry A. Lindgens & Christian H. Suckau) 58 Greene & 88 Worth

Hardt, Vonbernoth & Co. (Engelbert Hardt & Frederick A. & Emil Vonbernuth) 62 Greene & 76 Leonard

Hardware Board of Trade (Ltd.) (John C. Cook, Pres.; Edward H. Cole, Sec.; James H. Golday, Treas.) 4 Warren

Hardy H. C. & Co. (Horace C. Hardy & Henry E. Ide:—special partner Danford N. Darney, Farmington, Ct., $50,000; terminates 1st Feb. 1891) 50 Maiden la.

Hardy W. W. & Co. (William W. Hardy, no Co.) 402 E. 33d

Hardy & Caldwell (Francis Hardy & William H. Caldwell) 58 W. 125th

Hardy & Co (Thomas Hardy, no Co.) 585 Eighth av.

Hargrave & Gubelman (Arthur J. Hargrave & Theodore Gubelman) 38 W. 23d

Harkness Fire Extinguisher Co. (not Inc.) (James L. Wise, John J. Smith & William Harkness) 77 W. Houston

Harlam Brothers (Moses & Edward Harlam) 400 Hudson

Harlem Baking Co. (Walter M. Reynolds, propr.) 1946 Third av.

Harlem Beef Co. (G. F. & E. C. Swift, proprs.) ft. E. 127th

Harlem Beef Packing House (Richard Webber, propr.) 208 E. 120th & 213 E. 119th

Harlem Bridge, Morrisania & Fordham Railway Co. (Henry Spratley, Pres.; William Cauldwell, Sec. Capital, $350,000. Directors: Henry Spratley, William Remsen, William Cauldwell, Matthew H. Wynkoop, John J. Hallenbeck, John B. Haskin, Horace P. Whitney, Edwin Bedell, Henry Hart, Alfred B. Whitney, Edwin J. Hart, Elijah & Girard N. Whitney) Third av, n E. 170th, 115 B'way & 2349 Third av.

Harlem Coal Pockets (Robert Murray, Pres.; Herbert G. Straut, Sec. Capital, $5,000. Directors: Robert Murray, Herbert G. Straut, George W. Collins) ft. E. 119th, 261 W. 128th, 163 E. 94th & 2184 Third av.

Harlem Color Works (Catharine W. Hochstaetter, propr.) 533 E. 119th

Harlem Commons Syndicate (Henry P. O'Blenis, Pres.; Edward C. Burgess, Sec.; Frank H. Davies, Treas. Capital, $200,000. Trustees: Henry P. O'Blenis, Frank H. Davies, James C. Church, Edward C. Burgess, Samuel E. Cox, Father Columbia) 17 B'way

Harlem Conservatory of Music & Languages (Hermine Mathushek-Fischer, propr.) 63 E. 125th

Harlem Co-operative Building & Loan Assn. (Robert F. Johnston, Pres.; Louis W. Beardsley, Sec.; Edward F. Carr, Treas.) 79 W. 125th

Harlem Dental Assn. (Edmund R. Menscm, propr.) 2130 Third av.

FOR THE BEST CO-PARTNERSHIP IN THE BEST CORPORATION SEE PAGE F IN BACK OF BOOK

Harlem Exchange for Women's Work (Mrs. Charles C. Tyler, Pres.; Mrs. Joseph Keane, Sec.; Mrs. E. Wells Sackett, Treas.) 40 W. 125th

Harlem Iron Works (James R. Irons, propr.) E. 130th c Park av.

Harlem Loan Assn. (refused) 110 E. 125th

Harlem Manhattan Hat Co. (Martin M. Kahn, propr.) 249 W. 125th

Harlem News Co. (David Wilson & Son, proprs.) 8 Spruce & 206 E. 126th

Harlem Novelty Co. (Myers & Clark, proprs.) 1293 B'way

Harlem Real Estate Exchange (Louis Stern, propr.) 151 E. 125th

Harlem River Bank (Albert H. Leszynsky, Pres.; Jacob R. Demarest, Cashier. Capital $100,-000. Directors: Robinson Gill, John S. Ellis, William H. Burke, Jacob A. Cantor, James A. Blackman, Max E. Bernheimer, Henry Budelman, Albert H. Leszynsky, C. F. Schaue, Albert A. Stein, J. W. Barry jr.) 2007 Third av.

Harlem Roofing Co. (not inc.) (Benjamin F. Paddock, Richard Griffin, Charles Corson) 543 E. 115th

Harlem Savings Bank (Thomas B. Tappen, Pres.; L. Homer Hart, Sec. Trustees: Thomas B. Tappen, Edward A. Reid, Adam Harrmann, George Ebert, Charles B. Tooker, Isaac Rosenbourgh, Cornelius W. Van Voorhis, Silas A. Brush, Michael Duff, William H. Colwell, William E. Trotter, W. H. Paine, Richard Webber) 2281 Third av.

Harlem Tea & Coffee Co. (Mary O'Connor, propr.) 2219 First av.

Harlem Window Shade Co. (Hugo Wirth, propr.) 315 W. 125th

Harlem Wire Works (John Sullivan, propr.) 166 E. 124th

Harlem & Morrisania Cons. Transp. Co (G. A. & M. G. Wright, proprs.) ft. E. 130th & Pier 2d E. R.

Harlem & Son (Samuel & Isaac W. Harlem) 112 W. 31st

Harlem, Brook Av. & Woodstock R. R. Co. (Capital $1,000,000; further inf. unattainable) no address

Harlem, Mott Haven & Morris Av. R. R. Co. (Capital, $1,000,000; further inf. unattainable) no address

Harman & Strauss (dissolved) 391 Canal

Harmer, Hays & Co. (Charles G. Harmer & Henry Haunah, only) 72 Beekman

Harmon & Chapman (dissolved) 6 Wall

Harmon & Dixon (Harry W. Harmon & George U. Dixon) 118 Chambers

Harmony's P., Nephews & Co. (Miguel Garcia, William H. Speer, Miguel R. Martinus & Pedro R. de Flores) 63 B'way

Harms T. B. & Co. (Thomas B. & Alexander T. Harms) 819 B'way

Harms Brothers (Frederick D. & John F. H. Harms) 196 Eighth av.

Harned C. A. & Co. (Charles A. Harned & Frederick Currie) 15 Broad

Harness Soap Mfg. Co. (Inoperative) Av. D c E. 11th

Harnett Richard V. & Co. (Richard V. Harnett & Henry W. Donald) 73 & 58 Liberty (see adv. in front)

Harnett Brothers (Patrick W. & John W. Harnett) 2876 Third av.

Harney Peak Tin Mining, Milling & Mfg. Co. (Samuel Untermyer, Pres; Charles D. Deshler, Sec.; Lewis May, Treas. Capital, $15,000,-000. Directors: Samuel Untermyer, Charles D. Deshler, Lewis May, Henry Clausen, jr, William Hemsen, Daniel S. Appleton, William L. Flanagan, James Wilson, Lord Thurlow,

John Taylor, Edward S. Baring-Gould, Henry Seton Karr) 220 B'way

Harper Brothers (Thomas & William Harper) 16 Murray & 19 Park pl.

Harper & Brothers (Philip J. A. & Fletcher & Joseph W. & John W. & Joseph A. & Joseph Henry Harper) 331 Pearl

Harper & Vormilyea (James I. Harper & Francis H. Vermilyea) 229 W. 50th

Harper, Hollingsworths & Darby (George Harper, Loftus & Henry S. Hollingsworth & Albert B. Darby) 94 Greene

Harrell Leather Goods Co. (Andrew J. Kelley, Pres.; Bernardus Evertsen, Sec. Capital $10,-000. Directors: William H. Hoss, Andrew J. Kelley, Bernardus Evertsen, J. Henry Smith) 873 B'way

Harren & Farrell (Francis Harren & John Farrell) 1145 First av.

Harrigan Brothers (James C. & Daniel J. Harrigan) 1409 Lex. av.

Harriman & Co. (William M. & Oliver Harriman jr. & Nicholas Fish) 120 B'way

Harriman & Fessenden (George F. Harriman & James D. Fessenden) 88 Park row

Harriman, MacLee & Co. (dissolved) 457 Broome

Harrington E. G & Co. (Elbridge G. Harrington & Charles T. & William J. Sutton) 529 Seventh av.

Harrington J. & Co. (John & John J. Harrington) 772 First av.

Harrington & Doody (Edward C. Harrington & Christian J. Doody) 1215 & 1357 Ninth av.

Harrington & Goodman (Samuel & William E. & Joseph E. Goodman, only) 832 B'way

Harriot & Groesbeck (Samuel J. Harriot, Ernest Groesbeck & J. Bloomfield Harriot) 9 Broad

Harris Button-Hole Attachment Co. (Henry J. Davison, Pres; Charles M. Davison, Sec. Capital, $100,000. Directors: Justus O. Woods, Samuel Thorne, Henry J. Davison, James O. Sheldon, William F. Smith) 2 Wall

Harris Button-Hole Co. (Ltd.) (Edmund C. Smith, Pres.; Mahlon Buckman, Sec.; Charles T. Deforest, Treas. Capital, $24,000. Directors: Edmund C. Smith, Mahlon Buckman, Charles T. Deforest, John G. Cozine, Charles E. Spencer) 265 B'way

Harris Fluishing Co. (Mary E. Harris, propr.) 62 Vesey

Harris George S. & Sons (George S. & George T. & William T. & Frank S. Harris) 125 Bowery

Harris James & Co. (James Harris & Orlando Rockafellor) 212 Eighth av.

Harris Lewis & Brother (dissolved) 10 Sixth av.

Harris T. William & Co. (T. William Harris & Edward D. Bolton) 44 B'way

Harris A. S. & Co. (no inf.) 39 Grace av. W. Washn. mkt

Harris A. W. & Co. (Albert W. Harris, no Co.) 82 Cortlandt

Harris J. N. & Co. (James N. Harris & Earn R. Sammis) 3 Fulton fish mkt

Harris S. & Son (Simon & Max Harris) 2153 Third av.

Harris Brothers (clothing) (Jacob & Pincus & Moyer Harris) 87 E. B'way

Harris Brothers (gloves) (Sigmund & Albert Harris) 665 B'way

Harris Brothers (men's furng.) (Louis & Morris Harris) 176 B'way

Harris Brothers (pawnbrokers) (David J. & Isaac Harris) 692 Third av.

Harris & Alexander (dissolved) 376 Washn. mkt

Harris & Brother (Louis & Morris Harris) 235 Division

Harris & Calmer (Silverman Harris & Bernstein Calmer) r 12 Ludlow

Harris & Co. (refused) 107 Fourth av.
Harris & Co. (cement) (Charles M. & Walter R. Harris) 85 Liberty
Harris & Co. (cloaks) (Isaac K. Harris & Max Hurvich) 297 Sixth av.
Harris & Co. (express) (Henry W. Harris, no Co.) 174 Duane, 44 Beckman & 3402 Third av.
Harris & Co. (tailors) (Samuel E. Harris, no Co.) 216 & 1164 B'way
Harris & Corwin (Clinton S. Harris & John H. Corwin) 21 Park row
Harris & Crawford (dissolved) 207 Sixth av.
Harris & Fuller (Smith W. & John R. Harris & Henry C. Fuller) 56 B'way
Harris & Harper (Henry G. Harris & John Harper) 280 B'way
Harris & Kingsley (Jabez Harris & Cornelius L. Kingsley) 42 University pl.
Harris & Nixon (George Harris & Theodore T. Nixon) 18 W. 27th
Harris & Pfluger (John F. O. Harris & August W. Pfluger) 23 Liberty
Harris & Russak (Alfred Harris & Benjamin Russak) 14 Washn. pl.
Harris & Stien (Moses Harris & Francis J. Stien) 90 Crosby
Harris, Griffin & Co. (dissolved) 52 Dey
Harrison Charles & Co. (Charles Harrison & William P. Towne) 16 W. 4th
Harrison John & Co. (John Harrison & George O. Baker) 170 South
Harrison E. M. & Co. (Edwin M. & Nathan Harrison) 164 Dunne
Harrison M. & Son (Michael & Michael Harrison) 214 E. 52d
Harrison W. S. & Co. (Walter S. Harrison & F. Hill) 45 B'way & 14 Vesey
Harrison Brothers (Maurice H. & Nathan & Louis Harrison) 60 Nassau
Harrison & Co. (Daniel V. & Edwin M. jr. & Jared E. Harrison jr.) 45 Harrison
Harrison & Langdon (Jared F. Harrison & William Langdon) 5 Beekman
Harrison, Bostwick & Karples (Tosswill E. Harrison, Alfred W. Bostwick & Henry M. Karples) 21 Beaver
Harrison Brothers & Co. (John & George L. & Thomas S. Harrison) 117 Fulton & 52 Ann
Harrnach D. & Co. (Barbara & Henry Harrnach) 144 E. Houston
Harrold & White (James Harrold & James White) 202 W. 20th
Harrs & Schroeder (Charles Harrs & August T. Schroeder) 144 E. 112th
Hart A. H., Co. (John Hinde, Pres.; Thomas T. Allan, Sec. Capital, $225,000. Directors: John Hinde, William & Thomas T. Allan) 90 White & Eleventh av. o W 57th
Hart Bagging Co. (Nathaniel G. Hart, Pres.; Henry C. Hart, Sec. Capital, $160,000. Directors: Nathaniel G. & Henry C. Hart, James R. Townsend) 81 Cotton Ex.
Hart Brothers Land & Cattle Co. (Ltd.) (inf. unattainable) 45 B'way
Hart George S. & Co. (George S. Hart, Pres.; E. P. Post, Sec.; Charles J. Hart, Treas. Capital, $100,000. Directors: George S. Hart, E. F. Post, Charles J. Hart) 85 Pearl & 24 Bridge
Hart Lucius & Co. (Lucius Hart & Charles W. Tarbell) 150 Water & 8 Burling sl.
Hart William T. A. & Co. (William T. A Hart & Walter S. Martin) 2302 Seventh av.
Hart William T. A. & Son (William T. A. & William J. Hart) 67 Prince, 642 Third av. & 509 Madison av.
Hart & Brother (George W. & Benjamin F. Hart) 191 Chambers

Hart & Felbel (Arthur B. Hart & Dore Felbel) 19 B'way
Hart & Price (George H. Hart & Edmund E. Price) 280 B'way
Hart & Robertson (dissolved) 826 Sixth av.
Hart & Vonarx (no inf.) 16 Murray
Hart, Lewis & Co. (Alexander Hart, Julius Lewis & Abraham Jacobson) 63 Mercer
Hartell & Schilz (Oswald Hartelt & George Schilz) 444 E. 18th
Hartemann H. T. & Co. (Henry T. Hartemann & Henry Gleismer) 209 Eighth av.
Hartenstein Brothers (Frederick & Joseph I. Hartenstein) 536 Pearl
Harifield John C. & Son (John C. & John W. Hartfield) 92 Pine
Hartford & Connecticut Western R. R. Co. (John S. Wilson, Pres.; Edward R. Beardsley, Sec. Capital, $2,600,000. Directors: John S. Wilson, John W. Brock, William W. Gibbs, Charlemagne Tower jr. Arthur E. Newbold, Arthur Brock, William B. Scott, Henry Gay, Jaffrey O. Phelps, Julius H. Appleton, Henry A. Boisford, Frederick Miles, Edwin W. Spurr) 115 B'way
Hartley T. M. & Co. (Theodore M. Hartley, no Co.) 112 John
Hartley Brothers (Joseph Hartley, only) 7 Walker
Hartley & Coleman (Edward Hartley, Walter H. Coleman & I. Augustus Stanwood) 62 Wall
Hartley & Graham (Marcellus Hartley & Malcolm Graham) 17 Maiden la.
Hartling H. & Co. (Henry Hartling, no Co.) 609 E. 148th
Hartman H. & E. & Co. (Henry & Emanuel & Henry Hartman jr.) 656 First
Hartman M. & Co. (Max Hartman & David Kalherman) 179 Pearl
Hartman & Carson (Garrett Hartman & Joseph E. Carson) 61 Dey & 41 Thompson av. W. Washn. mkt
Hartman & Mendelsohn (Leopold Hartman & Lewis Mendelsohn) 266 Canal
Hartman & Rosenbaum (Morris Hartman & Morris Rosenbaum) 21 Wooster
Hartman & Wilcox (Emile Hartman & Thomas H. Wilcox) 51 Leonard
Hartman, Goldsmith & Co. (Ely Hartman & Aaron Goldsmith, no Co.) 45 Warren
Hartmann George F. & Son (George F. & Ferdinand H. Hartmann) 545 Eighth av.
Hartmann Brothers (Philip C. & Hudson C. Hartmann)120 Front
Hartmann & Co. (no inf.) 12 Old sl.
Hartmann & Hubbard (Augustus H. E. Hartmann & Frank H. Hubbard) 84 Beaver
Hartmann Brothers & Reinhard (Alfred & Rudolph Hartmann & Frederick Reinhard) 225 Bowery, 23 Union sq. W. & 514 E. 75th
Hartney & Dyer (no inf.) 1420 B'way
Harton Thomas A. & Co. (Thomas A. Harton, no Co.) 273 Church
Hartshorne J. M. & Brother (James M. & Richard B. & Sidney G. Hartshorne) 16 Wall
Hartt George S. & Co. (dissolved) 40 B'way
Hartt & Brother (Henry & William Hartt) 738 Tenth av.
Hartung C. E. & Co. (Charles E. Hartung, no Co.) 49 E. 10th
Hartwell H. E., Glass Works (Horace Edgar Hartwell, Pres.; Louisa M. Hartwell, Sec. Capital, $3,000. Trustees: Horace Edgar Hartwell, Frank E. Hipple) 20 E. 27th
Hartwig Brothers (Ernest Hartwig, only) 220 West
Hartwig & Frey (dissolved) 58 Third av.
Hartwig, Schrader & Co. (Louis Hartwig & Henry F. C. & Charles J. C. Schrader) 349 Washn.

THADDEUS DAVIDS CO., **WRITING INKS,**
MAKE THE BEST **SEALING WAX,**
MUCILAGE.

HAR 127 HAV

Harvey Furnace Co. (Harvey & Co. proprs.) 1225 B'way

Harvey William & Co. (William Harvey, Edward Osborn & Joseph & John Watts) 392 D'way

Harvey & Co. (Margaret D. & Charles E. Harvey & William Hodgson) 1325 B'way

Harvey & Outerbridge (Augustus W. Harvey & Eugenelus H. Outerbridge) 305 Produce Ex.

Harwny Dye-Wood & Extract Mfg. Co. (Frederick G. Pauly, Pres.; Israel J. Merritt jr. Sec. Capital, $100,000. Directors: Israel J. Merritt, E. Davison, Israel J. Merritt jr. Frederick G. Pauly) 184 Front

Harwood & Son (Samuel A. & Warren E. Harwood) 58 W. B'way

Hasberg & Co. (Nathan Hasberg, no Co.) 309 D'way

Hasbrouck J. L. & Son (John L. & Frank Hasbrouck) 75 Hudson

Hascall, Clarke & Vanderpoel (Theodore F. Hascall, John P. Clark & Herman W. Vanderpoel) 71 D'way

Hasell B. D. & Co. (Bentley D. Hasell;—special partner, James W. Quintard, Portchester, N. Y., $5,000; terminates 2d Jan. 1895) 66 Pine

Haseltine & Co. (George Haseltine, no Co.) 247 B'way

Haskins & Culver (dissolved) 1172 Ninth av.

Haslam & Monks (William Haslam & George L. Hunks) 99 Franklin

Haslehurst & Co. (Joseph Hastlehurst & Henry Jones) 82 Leonard.

Haslett's J. C., Sons (Charles O. & William Haslett) 45 Broad

Hasper & Co. (Bruno F. Hasper & Felix Brendieoke) 458 Pearl

Hassell Milling Co, (inf. unattainable) 25 Beaver

Hassell, Wilson & Hassell (Samuel Hassell, Penrose J. Wilson & Samuel Hassell jr.) 112 W. 38th

Hastings Card Co. (Ltd.) (Orlando B. Hastings, Pres.; Frederick C. Lounsbury, Treas. Capital, $25,000. Directors: Orlando B. Hastings, Frederick C. Lounsbury, Danforth L. Jones, Albert E. Evans, Henry B. Lounsbury) 26 Beekman

Hastings George & Co. (George Hastings & Edward Brandus) 30 Broad

Hastings Pavement Co. (Charles G. Palmer, Pres.; Charles R. Flint, Treas. Capital, $100,000. Directors: Charles G. Palmer, J. Baxter Upham, H. L. Sprague, Charles L. Work, George B. Upham) 140 Pearl & 108 Water

Hastings & Gleason (George S. Hastings & Albert H. Gleason) 265 D'way

Hastings & Hahn (Andrew K. Hastings & Philip J. Hahn) 72 Murray

Hat Sweat Mfg. Co. (John B. Stetson, Pres.; James Greenwood, Sec. Capital, $300,000. Directors: John B. Stetson, William B. Thom, Jerome Taylor, William T. Fray, Charles A. Wharton) 166 Greene

Hatch Lithographic Co. (no inf.) 49 Lafayette pl.

Hatch Rufus & Co. (Rufus Hatch, no Co.) 1 B'way

Hatch W. T. & Sons (Walter T. & Henry Prescott & Arthur Melvin Hatch) 14 Nassau

Hatch & Co. (cans) (Francis L. Hatch & Brace Hopkins) 495 G'wich

Hatch & Co. (shoes) (Joseph Hatch, no Co.) 133 Duane

Hatch & Foote (Daniel B. Hatch & Charles B. Foote) 7 Pine

Hatch & Kendall (William D. Hatch & William B. Kendall) 50 Exchange pl.

Hatch & Warren (Edward S. Hatch & Lyman B. Warren) 55 Liberty

Hatfield & Benson (Abraham Hatfield & Arthur Benson) 114 Water

Hatfield & Sons (Charles W. & Albert S. Hatfield, only) 239 Fifth av.

Hathaway & Montgomery (Henry D. Hathaway & William Montgomery jr.) 69 Wall

Hathaway, Soule & Harrington (Savory C. Hathaway, Rufus A. Soule & Herbert A. Harrington) 128 Duane

Hattemer Brothers (Valentine & Philip Hattemer) 621 Tenth av.

Hatton E. & Co. (Adolph Katzenstein, only) 61 Temple ct

Hatton L. D. & Co. (Loftus D. & Elizabeth H. Hatton) 35 W. 4th

Hatzel & Buehler (John C. Hatzel & Joseph Buehler) 29 W. 26th

Haubner & Heller (Oscar H. Haubner & William J. Heller) 75 Gold

Haubold A. & Co. (Arthur Haubold & Ignatz Rosenberg) 113 E. 14th

Haug A. & Co (Albert Haug & Robert Loercker) 106 Duane

Haughton & Lee (William A. Haughton & Mortimer M. Lee) 853 B'way

Haulenbeek & Mitchell (John W. Haulenbeek & William L. Mitchell) 170 Duane

Hauptner D. & A. (Bertha A. & Anna V.) 1298 B'way

Hauptner & Co. (Oscar A. Hauptner, no Co.) 1298 B'way.

Hauschild & Esche (Max Hauschild & Hugo Esche) 315 D'way

Hauschild & Nenke (Franz Hauschild & Otto Nenke) 200 Worth

Hauschildt F. & Co. (Frederick Hauschildt & Rebecca C. Tobelman) 456 E. Houston

Hauseman & Crawford (dissolved) 1186 Tenth av.

Hauser J. N. & Son (John N. & John W. Hauser) 537 Madison av. & 1012 Third av.

Hausling & Stonebridge (dissolved) 620 E. 14th

Havana Tobacco Co. (Ltd.) (Ernest Thalmann, Pres.; Max T. Rosen, Sec. Capital, $50,000. Directors: Ernest & Karl Thalmann, Oscar E. Tanchoot, William Roessler, Max T. Rosen) 144 Water

Havana & Key West Cigar Co. (Ltd.) (Max T. Rosen, Pres.; Julius Goldman, Sec.; Karl Thalmann, Treas. Capital, $50,000; further inf. unattainable) 144 Water

Havana & N. Y. Cigar Co. (Aarons & Co. propre.) 619 D'way

Havanagh & Co. (refused) 63 W. 44th

Havemeyer Sugar Refining Co. (no inf.) 112 Wall

Havemeyer & Vigelius (William Vigelius, only) 175 Pearl

Havemeyers & Elder Sugar Refining Co. (Henry O. Havemeyer, Pres.; Julius A. Stursberg, Sec. Capital, $500,000; further inf. unattainable) 117 Wall

Haven & Kenny (no inf.) 535 Eighth av.

Haven & Stout (Howard A. Haven & Wright C. Stout) 60 D'way

Havens J. H. & Son (James H. Havens, only) 825 Eleventh av.

Havens & Beebe (A. Britton Havens & Henry Warren Beebe) 18 Wall

Haveron & Brennan (John Haveron & Michael J. Drennan) 67 South

Haverstraw Water Co. (John Lockwood, Pres.; John C. Lockwood, Sec. Capital, $100,000. Directors: John & John C. & Frank G. Lockwood) 52 D'way

Haviland S. & D. F. (dissolved) 311 First av.

Haviland & Co. (Charles Edward & Theodore Haviland) 45 Barclay

Haviland & Williamson (dissolved) 526 Seventh av.

Haviland's S. C., Son (William F. Haviland) 201 West

COMPILED WITH ACCURACY AND DESPATCH } CLASSIFIED BUSINESS LISTS. { THE TROW CITY DIRECTORY CO. 11 University Place.

HAW 128 HAZ

Hawes Willard & Co. (Alpheus M. Hawes & Reuben Arkush, only) 210 Lewis
Hawk G. Z. & Son (George Z. & Charles T. Hawk) 84 Loew av. W. Washn. mkt
Hawk & Wetherbee (William S. Hawk, Gardner Wetherbee & Andrew R. Blakely) 571 Fifth av.
Hawke & Norman (Edward H. Hawke jr. & A. Livingston Norman) 45 William
Hawkes & Sullivan (Samuel L. Hawkes & J. P. Sullivan) 695 Morris av.
Hawkesworth J. A. (James A. Hawkesworth & George Weiss) 15 State
Hawkesworth & Rankine (Robert W. Hawkesworth & William D. Rankine) 115 B'way
Hawkins H. C. & Co. (dissolved) 1284 B'way
Hawkins & Norman (Frederick Hawkins & Thomas Norman) 319 E. 92d
Hawkins & Pannes (John B. Pannes, only) 154 Nassau
Hawkins & Pearson (dissolved) 168 Reade
Hawkins' C. P., Sons (George W. & Ellsworth F. Hawkins) 843 W. 41st
Hawks & Ogilvy (Thomas E. B. Hawks & Robert Ogilvy) 500 B'way
Hawley Box & Lumber Co. (Henry N. Doolittle, Pres.; Oscar F. Hawley, Sec. Capital, $40,000. Directors; Henry N. & O. S. Doolittle, Oscar F. Hawley) 40 Gold & ft. Corlears
Hawley William & Co. (William & Alan R. Hawley) 26 Broad
Hawley & Hoops (John S. Hawley & Herman W. Hoops) 271 Mulberry
Hawley, Hendel & Mohn (Samuel R. Hawley, John & George Hendel & John G. & Jeremiah G. & Richard Mohn) 145 Greene
Hawlowetz M. & Co. (dissolved) 44½ Sixth av.
Haws & Miller (Walter D. Haws & Harry D. Miller) 811 Nassau
Hawthorn & Co. (Daniel G. Hawthorn & James Fellows) 12 Cortlandt
Hawthorn & Finn (William J. Hawthorn & John J. Finn :—special partner, William Brabson, $1,000 ; terminates 7th Oct. 1894) 258 Eleventh av.
Hawthorne A. F. & Co. (A. F. Hawthorne, Luke W. Rickard & Martin Hubbe) 24 State
Hawver & Wilson (James E. Hawver & J. Marshall Wilson) 1028 Bathgate av.
Hay Allan, Co. (Allan Hay, Pres.; Ninian Stevenson, Sec.; Robert Hay, Treas. Directors : Allan & Robert & Thomas & James G. Hay, Ninian Stevenson) 621 W. 38th
Hay James & Co. (James & James Hay jr.) 145 Mulberry
Hay James G. & Co.(James G. & Thomas Hay) 521 W. 38th
Hay Lithographing Co. (Peter Hay, propr.) 58 Centre
Hay & Hunold (dissolved) 58 Centre
Hay & Straw Dealers' Assn. of the State of N. Y. (Willis Bullock, Pres.; William H. Falke, Sec.; Thomas W. Smith, Treas.) 74 Cortlandt
Hayden & Co. (no inf.) 108 Front
Hayden & Pickup (Howard L. Hayden & Francis Pickup) 104 Duane
Hayden's George, Son (Albert C. Hayden) 151 Fulton
Haydenville Mfg. Co. (Arad T. Foster, Pres.; John M. Peck, Sec. Capital, $150,000. Directors; Arad T. Foster, Henry F. & John M. & Oliver D. Peck, L. L. Camp) 18 Beekman
Haydock Pill & Export Co. (Joseph Haydock, Pres.; Theodore C. Wells, Sec. Capital, $10,000. Directors : Joseph Haydock, Theodore C. Wells) 68 Fulton
Haydock & Bissell (Robert R. Haydock & Eugene Bissell) 12 Murray & 15 Park pl.

Hayek F. & Co. (Francis & Francis Hayek jr. & Charles F. Boll) 619 Tenth av.
Hayes Duster Co. (Erastus Hayes, Pres.; Francis M. Hayes, Sec. Capital $10,000 ; further inf. unattainable) 51 Vesey
Hayes Mfg. Co. (no inf.) 74 Cortlandt
Hayes Timothy & Co. (Timothy Hayes & John Fox) 160 B'way
Hayes O. H. & Co. (Orrill H. Hayes, no Co.) 88 Leonard
Hayes & Codyre (George Hayes & Margaret Codyre) 237 Ninth av.
Hayes & Co. (Joseph Hayes, no Co.) 1 B'way
Hayes & Hessels (Michael H. Hayes & George Hessels) 840 W. 59d
Hayes & Pauly (Frank J. Hayes & Charles W. Pauly) 168 Greene
Hayes & Rothschild (Charles S. Hayes & Isaac Rothschild) 132 Nassau
Hayman Brothers (Ferdinand Hayman, only) 59 Pearl & 56 Stone
Hayman, Marx & Rosenthal (Morris H. Hayman, Joel M. Marx & Alexander Rosenthal) 234 B'way
Hayman's Louis, Sons (Leopold L. & Maurice L. Hayman) 202 E. 24th
Hayn & Day (John F. Hayn & Frank Day) 80 Dey
Haynes C. A. & Co. (Calvin A. Haurice & Lewis Saphar) 74 Beaver
Haynes D. W. & Co. (Dudley W. Haynes, no Co.) 271 B'way
Haynes Brothers (George A. & Frank E. Haynes) 23 West, W. Washn. mkt
Haynes & Boyle (Edward Haynes & William S. Boyle) 128 Pearl
Haynes & Flowers (dissolved) 88 Grace av. W. Washn. mkt
Hays Daniel & Co. (dissolved) 180 William
Hays David & Sons (David & Benjamin F. Hays, only) 561 Fifth av.
Hays B. St. John & Co. (B. St. John Hays & Joseph Tate) 11 Pine
Hays & Cleverley (Samuel Hays & John Cleverley) 206 Ninth av.
Hays & Greenbaum (Daniel P. Hays & Samuel Greenbaum) 170 B'way
Hayward Hand Grenade Co. (S. F. Hayward & Co. proprs.) 351 Canal
Hayward S. F. & Co. (Sterling F. Hayward, no Co.) 351 Canal
Hayward & Barron (William A. Hayward & Samuel H. Barron) 32 B'way
Hayward & Duffy (William T. Hayward & Edward Duffy) 484 E. 20th
Hazard Powder Co. (George Weightman, Sec.; William S. Colvin, Treas.; further inf. unattainable) 68 Pine
Hazard E. C. & Co. (Edward C. Hazard, Frank Green, John J. Blauvelt, Theodore Sterne & Eugene L. Froment) 117 Hudson & 74 Grove
Hazard & Parker (Charles Hazard & William N. Parker) 15 Broad
Hazard, Hazard & Co. (Horace K. Thurber, receiver) 1099 B'way, 324 Seventh av. & 672 Sixth av.
Hazazer & Stanley (Edgar W. Hazazer, Arthur F. Stanley & Harry Hill) 32 Frankfort
Hazeli & Patterson (Reginald T. Hazell & Samuel S. Patterson) 87 Walker
Hazelton Boiler Co. (Edward S. T. Kennedy, Pres.; Capital, $100,000. Trustees : John F. & Edward S. T. & William T. Kennedy) 716 E. 13th & 145 B'way
Hazelton Frederick & Co. (Frederick Hazelton & Charles B. Carr) 111 Franklin
Hazelton Brothers (Henry & John E. & Samuel Hazelton) 34 University pl.

SPECIAL ATTENTION PAID TO THIS CLASS OF WORK. } **BANKERS' & BROKERS' CIRCULARS DELIVERED** { THE TROW CITY DIRECTORY CO. 11 University Place.

HAZ 129 HEI

Hazelwood Ice Co. (Peter Green, Pres.; John M. Rogan, Sec. Capital, $20,000. Directors: Peter Green, Patrick C. Clark, Charles P. Geissler, John Doerr, John Corrigan, Charles W. & John H. Rogan) 309 Third & ft. Fifth

Hazen M. W.. Co. (Marshman W. Hazen, propr.) 66 W. 23d

Hazen & Co. (refused) 76 Vesey

Hazen & French (William L. Hazen & John W. French) 119 W. 125th

Hazzard & Brainard (Charles Hazzard & John L. Brainard) 60 South

Head Charles & Co. (Charles Head, S. Eliot Guild, Thomas L. Manson jr. Harris K. Smith, James S. McCobb, Harry V. Long & Herbert S. Carpenter) 17 Broad

Headley William O. & Son (Albert O. Headley, only) 388 B'way

Healey & Co. (Warren M. Healey & John H. Zabriskie;—special partners, Henry C. Valentine, $30,000 & William Williams, River Edge, N. J., $20,000; terminates 1st May, 1891) 1476 B'way & 315 W. 43d

Healey & Ellis (Martin H. Healey & Christopher C. Ellis) 304 G'wich

Health Food Co. (Frank Fuller, propr.) 74 Fourth av.

Health Lift (Lewis G. Janes, propr.) 55 Liberty

Health Restorative Co. (Francis B. Thurber, Pres.; Manfred Lanza, Sec.; Albert E. Whyland, Treas. Directors: Francis B. Thurber, Manfred Lanza, Albert E. Whyland) 10 W. 23d

Healy John & Co. (John Healy, Co. refused) 28 Loew av. W. Washn. mkt

Healy A. & Sons (Aaron & A. Augustus & Frank Healy) 5 Ferry

Healy J. & Co. (John Healy & Joel L. Isaacs) 80 Eighth av.

Healy N. jr. & Co. (Nicholas Healy jr. no Co.) Pier 5 N. R.

Healy Brothers (Dennis & Patrick Healy) 2058 First av.

Healy & Co. (Bryan Healy, no Co.) 214 Church

Healy & Earl (Nicholas Healy & George W. Earl) Pier 41 (old) N. R.

Healy & O'Brien (William J. Healy & David O'Brien) 4 Hewitt av. W. Washn. mkt

Heard Brothers & Co. (James B. & Benjamin F. Heard, no Co.) 81 Dey

Hearn James A. & Son (George A. & Arthur H. Hearn, only) 30 W. 14th & 27 W. 13th

Hearne & Co. (dissolved) 340 W. 125th

Hearne Improved Gas Meter Co. (Ltd.) (Charles Place, Chairman; Walter P. Elliott, Sec. Capital, $500,000. Directors: Charles Place, Joseph Flannery, John Hearne, Walter P. Elliott, Frank H. Cheyney) 11 Pine

Hearsey & Adams (dissolved) 335 B'way

Heasty Irwin & Co. (Irwin Heasty, Co. refused) 7 White

Heath & Co. (hats) (dissolved) 1522 Third av.

Heath & Co. (printers) (William H. Heath, no Co.) 117 John

Heather & Co. (George Heather & Elwood Carpenter) 28 W. 14th

Heatherton Thomas & Son (Thomas & Thomas jr. & William Heatherton) 97 Maiden la.

Heavenrich, Hirschberg & Co. (Julius Heavenrich, Julius Hirschberg & Karl Steinman) 689 B'way

Hebbard & Brother (refused) 860 B'way

Hebbard S, E. & Son (Southwick E. & Southwick Hebbard) 54 E. 23d

Hebel & Bruning (Peter Hebel & William Bruning) 563 Bleecker

Hebert Henry B. & Co. (Henry B. Hebert & Samuel Stenson) 110 Produce Ex.

Hebert John H. & Co. (John H. Hebert, no Co.) 108 Produce Ex.

Hebrew Emigrant House Assn. (dissolved) 141 Cedar

Hebrew Journal Co. (Joseph Davis, Pres.; Jesse Davis, Sec.; further inf. refused) 124 E. 14th

Hebrew Standard Co. (Jacob P. Solomon, Pres.; further inf. unattainable) 297 William

Hecht Jacob & Son (Jacob & Solomon Hecht) 46 Walker

Hecht Joseph & Sons (Joseph & Meyer & Aaron Hecht) 96 Cliff, ft. E. 45th & ft. W. 40th

Hecht S. L. & Co. (Samuel L. Hecht, no Co.) 46 Walker

Hecht Brothers (feygds.) (Bernard & Meyer Hecht) 455 B'way

Hecht Brothers (liquors) (Joseph & Benjamin Hecht) 2289 First av.

Hecht & Co. (Henrietta Hecht, no Co.) 116 Greene

Hecht & Livingston (Nettie Hecht & Albert Livingston) 155 Mercer

Hecht & Morris (Joseph M. Hecht & James N. Morris) 707 Eighth av.

Hecht & Newmark (Jonas Hecht & Bernhard Newmark) 76 Clinton

Heck O. & Co. (Otto Heck & Samuel M. Spedon) 317 B'way

Hecker George V. & Co. (estate of George V. Hecker, only) 205 Cherry

Heckler & Brockway (Augustus L. Heckler & Frank S. Brockway) 1257 B'way

Heckmuller & Jagy (John P. Heckmuller & John Jagy) 327 W. 38th

Heckscher & Toffer (dissolved) 211 E. 23d

Hecla Architectural Bronze & Iron Works (Poulson & Eger, proprs.) 210 W. 23d

Hecla Powder Co. (William Dupont, Pres.; Jerome E. Morse, Treas.; Ralph G. Morse, Sec. Capital, $200,000. Directors: William Dupont Jerome E. & Ralph G. & George F. Morse, J. J. Vall) 239 B'way

Hed-Ak-Kur Mfg. Co. (John G. Mercur, propr. 104 Bowde

Hedden V. J. & Sons (Vincr J. & Charles R. & Louis O. & Samuel S. Hedden) 18 Cortlandt

Hedden & Cairns (Eugene D. Hodden & Robert A. Cairns) 35 B'way

Hedenkamp D. & Son (Dederick & Henry H. Hedenkamp) 608 Grand

Hedges William S. & Co. (James Hedges, only) 170 B'way

Hedges A. J. & Co. (Andrew J. Hedges, no Co.) 6 Maiden la.

Heerbrandt Publishing Co. (inf. unattainable) 54 Beekman

Heerdt Brothers (Charles & Louis N. Heerdt) 925 Third av.

Heert Henry H. & Co. (Henry H. Heert & Frederick H. Ehlen) 175 Chambers

Heesch & Sibbert (John Heesch & Henry C. Sibbert) 131 Beekman

Heffernan James & Co. (James Heffernan, no Co.) 212 Grand, 209 Grand & 418 Water

Heffernan & Rossman (James P.. Heffernan & Leonard J. Rossman) 180 Fulton

Hefter & Stock (Caesar L. Hofter & Louis Stock) 529 B'way

Hegeman J. N. & Co. (Johnson Nevin Hegeman & Willard Ferrier) 756 & 1318 B'way

Hegeman & Co. (corporation of) (Henry T. Cutter, Pres.; George H. Cutter, Sec. Capital, $25,000. Directors: Henry T. & George H. Cutter) 203 B'way

Hegeman & Oliphant Filter Co. (inf. unattainable) 112 Liberty

Heichel & Co. (Frank J. Heichel, no Co.) 58 New Bowery

TYPEWRITING DONE BY THE TROW CITY DIRECTORY CO., 11 University Place.

Heidelbach, Ickelheimer & Co. (Alfred S. Heidelbach, Isaac Ickelheimer & Alfred Lichtenstein) 29 William

Heidelberger, Frank & Co. (Charles Heidelberger, Jacob M. Frank & David Heidelberger) 404 B'way

Heidelberger & Brother (Joseph & Isaac Heidelburger) 502 Hudson

Heidelheim J. & L. M. (Jacob & Leopold M.) 49 Columbia

Heidenheimer C. & L. (Charles & Louis) 13 Stone

Heidgerd William & Co. (William Heidgerd, Gustav Engelke & Franz Leinhos) 151 Leonard

Heidgerd D. & H. (Dederick A. & J. Herman Heidgerd) 270 Canal

Heilbronn & Blank (Justus Heilbronn & David Blank) 26 John

Heilbronner A. & Son (Abraham & Max Heilbronner) 50 Eighth av.

Heilmann Brothers (Joseph & Louis & Charles Heilmann) 210 W. 18th & 150 W. 17th

Heiner Percy & Son (Samuel Heiner, only) 1 B'way

Heiner & Son (Marcus B. Heiner, only) 1 B'way

Heiner & Strauss (Solomon Heiner & Henry S. & Samuel Strauss) 372 B'way

Heiner & Wolf (Emanuel Heiner & Mosca J. Wolf) 185 B'way

Heilshorn Brothers (Henry & George Heilshorn) 121 Eleventh av.

Heim Belting Co. (Cyrus H. Chatfield, Pres.; further inf. unattainable) 29 Ferry

Heim & Burt (dissolved) 53 Grand

Heim & Wolfe (Louis Heim & Henry S. Wolfe) 416 G'wich

Heiman, Ludwig & Co. (Gustave Heiman, Max Ludwig & Morris M. Levy) 53 Franklin

Heimann & Lichten (Joseph Heimann & Morris C. Lichten) 682 B'way & 69 Wooster

Hein H. & Co. (no inf.) 68 Grand

Hein Brothers (Hyman & Louis Hein) 312 Bowery

Heine Arnold B. & Co. (Arnold B. Heine & Jacob Rohner) 115 Franklin

Heine Paul & Son (Paul & Charles Heine) 190 E. Houston

Heine Co. (Oscar & Isidor J. Heine) 1306 Second av.

Heine & White (David R. Heine & John W. White jr.) 88 Walker

Heineman C. & Co. (dissolved) 42 B'way

Heineman M. & Co. (Mayer Heineman:—special partners, Daniel Proshitz & Asor Greenebaum. jointly $10,000; terminates 1st Jan. 1891) 64 Lispenard

Heineman Brothers (dissolved) 201 W. 58th

Heineman & Hopes (no inf.) 529 Broome

Heiner G. & A. Pfost (George Heiner & Albert Pfost) 15 Dutch

Heinig George & Son (George & George A. Heinig) 445 Ninth av.

Heinrich F. & Co. (Frederick Heinrich & Hannah Kohn) 6 Howard

Heins & Ehler (John E. Heins & Herman F. Ehler) 2226 Seventh av.

Heins & Hencken (John C. Heins & Charles Hencken) 172 Lewis

Heins & La Farge (George L. Heins & C. Grant La Farge) 6 Beekman

Heintz's William, Sons (Jacob & Christian & John P. Heintz) 952 Sixth av.

Heinze, Löwy & Co. (Otto Heinze, Maurice Löwy & Herrmann Schneider) 81 Franklin

Heinzelman & Silverstone (no inf.) 280 B'way

Heinzer & Miller (John Heinzer & Frederick Miller jr.) 171 Suffolk

Heipershausen Brothers (Philip & Henry & Frederick Heipershausen) 45 Tompkins

Heissenbuttel John D. & Son (dissolved) 1 B'way

Heissenbuttel & Grau (John D. Heissenbuttel & Jacob Grau) 744 E. 14th

Heissenbuttel & Mehrtens (Henry Heissenbuttel & Richard Mehrtens) 1385 Third av. & 1460 First av.

Heissenbuttel & Welson (dissolved) 2263 Second av.

Heisser's Jacob, Son (William H. Heisser) 511 Eighth av.

Heiter, Glen & Cawley (Henry L. Heiter, Samuel S. Glen & Samuel J. Cawley;—special partner, Simon Heiter, $50,000; terminates 31st Jan. 1891) 9 White

Hektograph Mfg. Co. (Charles H. Green, Pres.; John W. Paul, Sec. Capital, $150,000. Directors: Charles H. Green, John W. Paul, A. D. Dickenson) 82 Church

Helbing & Spenko (dissolved) 208 E. 12th

Helburn & Hagen (William Helburn & Oscar Hagen) 65 E. 9th

Held H. Max & Co. (H. Max Held & Charles E. Young) 115a Produce Ex.

Held A. & Co. (Adolph Held, no Co.) 15 John

Helfenstein H. E. & Co. (Herman E. Helfenstein, Henry J. Westbrook & Herman Bosch) 8 Wooster

Hell Gate Cigar Factory (Bernhard Kumm, propr.) 1818 Av. A

Hell Gate Dye Works (Joseph Schofield & Co. proprs.) 416 B'way

Hell Gate Oil Works (not inc.) (Frank Freund, Benno Gohlmann & Philip Knauerer) 62 Cliff

Hellenberg & Loewenstein (Adolph & Herman Hellenberg, only) 507 B'way

Heller Franz & Son (Franz & Franz Heller jr.) 405 Broome

Heller William & Son (William & Isaac Heller) 91 Chambers

Heller A. & Brother (Adolph Heller & Sigismund D. Wortmann, only) 1284 B'way

Heller E. & Co. (Emile Heller & Morris & Sigismund D. Wortmann) 807 E. 54th

Heller Brothers (Louis H. & Marcus Heller & Henry Oestreicher) 540 B'way

Heller & Bardel (Henry K. Heller & William Bardel) 22 Maiden la.

Heller & Merz Co. (Anna J. Heller, Pres.; Carl Merz, Sec.; Henry Merz, Treas. Capital, $200,-000. Directors: Anna J. Heller, Henry & Carl Merz) 55 Maiden la.

Heller, Hirsh & Co. (James E. Heller & Adolph Hirsh, no Co.) 104 Front

Hellman N. & Co. (Nathan Hellman & Simon Levy) 628 B'way & 180 Crosby

Hellman & Blaut (Myer Hellman & Joseph F. Blaut) 30 Nassau

Hellrung B. & Brother (Bernhard & Gustave Hellrung) 145 Bleecker

Helmer & Lietz (Barbara Helmer & Charles L. Lietz) 125 Fourth av.

Helmet Mountain Tunnel Co. (Inoperative) 80 William

Helmus & Dreyfuss (Adolph Helmus & Isidor Dreyfuss) 99 Mott

Helmuth's Charles, Son (George C. Helmuth) 80 Beaver & 127 Pearl

Heminway & Co. (Truman Heminway & Robert S. Sauzade) 70 B'way & 15 New

Hemken & Slayton (Hans Hemken & Emil Slayton) 14 Greene

Hemmel A. B. & Co. (Arthur E. Hemmel, no Co.) 1680 Ninth av.

Hemmerdinger L. & Co. (Louis Hemmerdinger, no Co.) 210 Centre

Hemsley Oswald T. & Co. (Oswald T. & Walter Hemsley) 121 Front

THE CALIGRAPH WRITING MACHINE,
HARTFORD, CONN.

Hencke M. & A. (dissolved) 1518 Third av.
Hencke & Moehlenbrock (August Hencke & Bernard Moehlenbrock) 1518 Third av.
Henckel & Bolan (Henry A. Henckel & Michael Bolan) 91 Leonard
Heneken & Co. (Haneke Heneken, Frederick H. Willenbrock, Christopher Wohltmann & Daniel Meyer) 410 E. 4th, ft. E. 4th, ft. Stanton, 1571 Third av. & ft. E. 94th
Heneken & Wohlken (Carsten Heneken & Luhr Wohlken) 386 Fourth av.
Hendelman & Lippman (Carl Hendelman & Samuel Lippman) 59 Division
Henderson Estate Co. (Charles R. Henderson, Pres.; Norman Henderson, Sec. Capital, $100,000. Trustees: Harold G. & Norman & Charles R. Henderson, William W. Donald, Gugy Æ. Irving) 741 B'way
Henderson Peter & Co. (Alfred & Charles Henderson, only) 35 Cortlandt
Henderson Robert & Co. (Robert & Charles H. Henderson) 7 Pearl & 24 State
Henderson Brothers (agents) (Richard Henderson, William Coverly, David W. McDonald, Allen C. Smith & David G. Henderson) 7 Bowling gr. & Pier 41 (new) N. R.
Henderson Brothers (painters) (George Richard & William Henderson :—special partner Wemyss Henderson, *Chicago, Ill.* $500; terminates 1st March 1890) 2 W. 125th
Henderson & Bird (Alexander Henderson, only) 88 Prince
Henderson & Briggs (George M. Henderson & William A. Briggs) 93 Cliff
Henderson & Son (Robert Henderson, only) 545 W. 21st
Henderson & Stoutenborough (dissolved) 270 Pearl
Henderson & Winter (James Henderson & Thomas W. Winter) 15 Maiden la.
Hendrick Press System Co. (Hendrick & Co. proprs.) 52 W. 14th
Hendrick P. & Son (Patrick & Frank J. Hendrick) 172 E. 123d
Hendrick & Co. (Otis M. & Susan M. Hendrick) 52 W. 14th
Hendricks Brothers (Joshua & Edmund & Francis & Harmon W. & Edgar Hendricks) 49 Cliff
Hendricks & Ford (dissolved) 115 Nassau
Hendrickson & Bartel (James G. Hendrickson & Rudolph Bartel) 98 Cliff
Henig Osias & Brother (Osias & Bernhard Henig) 20 Attorney
Henius Mfg. Co. (David Henius, Pres.; Charles C. Conn, Sec. Capital, $2,500; further inf. unattainable) 233 E. 102d
Henkle Incandescent Gas Burner Co. (John R. Van Wormer, Pres.; Matthew W. Hawes, Sec.; Charles B. Upton, Treas. Capital, $250,000. Directors: Leonard Henkle, Charles Upton, Matthew W. Hawes, John R. Van Wormer, Henry M. Brigham) 25 Warren
Henley & Golden (Margaret S. Henley & William D. Golden) 44 Ann
Henman & Co. (John L. N. Henman, Andrew P. Coles & William W. Wendler) 135 Pearl
Henn & Freeman (Charles Henn & Charles Freeman) 17 Fulton mkt
Hennemeier & Cassel (dissolved) 311 W. 145th
Hennessey James & Co. (James Hennessey & John T. Godfrey) 28 City Hall pl.
Hennessey James J. & Co. (James J. & James Hennessy,) 122 Dunne
Hennessy's Sample Tea Co. (Catharine M. Hennessy, propr.) 263 Pearl
Henning Charles & Co. (Alfred C. Henning & Hiram L. Austin, only) 18 Cedar
Henning Land & Investment Co. (Ltd.) (Capital, $5,000; further inf. unattainable) no address

Henning H. W. & Son (Henry W. & Emil F. Henning) 18 Cedar
Henning J. L. & Co. (Joseph L. Henning & John Rudman) 62 Fulton mkt
Henninger A. & Co. (August Henninger & William Spengler) 1625 Av. D
Henrich & Graves (dissolved) 35 Maiden la.
Henry John F. & Co. (John F. Henry & Henry E. Dowen) 24 College pl.
Henry H. S. & Son (Henry S. & Charles L. Henry) 48 Exchange pl.
Henry L. & Co. (William Henry & Arthur Gaffre, only) 588 B'way
Henry M. C. & Co. (Matthew C. Henry & John Gaynor) E. 70th n Av. A
Henry N. & Son (Nicholas & Adrian L. Henry) 40 W. 110th
Henry S. & Sons (Simon & David & John Henry) 402 E. 13th
Henry Brothers (brokers) (Howard H. & Frank L. & Ambrose D. Henry) 5 Wall
Henry Brothers (properties) (William & George E. Henry) r 226 E. 23d
Henry & Co. (John H. Henry, no Co.) 32 E. 14th
Henry & Foster (dissolved) 30 E. 14th
Henry-Bonnard Bronze Co. (Henry J. Newton, Pres.; Arthur Merritt, Sec. Capital, $45,000. Directors: Henry J. Newton, Eugene F. Aucaigne, Arthur Merritt) 432 W. 16th
Henschel & Spring (Max Henschel & Ernst Spring) 1451 Third av.
Hensel, Bruckmann & Lorbacher (Louis Bruckmann, Edmund Lorbacher, John A. Wolfenden & Andrew J. Hamilton, only) 25 William
Henshaw George A. & Son (George A. & George E. Henshaw, only) 50 Wall & Custom h.
Hensle George L. & Son (George L. & George L. Hensle jr.) 164 Varick
Hentz H. & Co. (Henry & Leonard S. Hentz, Theodore Kastmond, Peter A. Leman & David C. Hipkins) 8 S. William
Hepburn L. F. & Co. (Leonard F. Hepburn & James C. Livingston) 444 Broome
Hepe, Koven & Co. (Theodore Hope & William & Ludolph O. Koven) 18 Spruce
Hepner & Co. (Fabian Hepner :—special partner, Sophia ' Horwitz, $2,000; terminates 31st Dec. 1893) 84 Leonard
Heppe E. H. & Co. (Ernst H. & Adolph Heppe) 159 Chambers
Heppenheimer's F., Sons (Otto & Edward & Ernest J. Heppenheimer) 24 N. William & 225 William
Herald Employees' Building & Loan Assn. (James G. Lynes, Pres.; James J. Murphy, Sec.; W. H. Bailey, Treas.) 28 Ann
Herb V. & Co. (Victor Herb, no Co,) 38 John
Herbert Brush Co. (John T. Herbert, Pres.; George McClelland, Sec. Capital, $40,000; further inf. refused) 125 Chambers
Herbert D. & E. (Daniel Herbert, only) 427 E. 54th
Herbert H. L. & Co. (Henry L. & Gilbert I. Herbert) 71 B'way, ft. E. 20th & ft. E. 53d
Herbst Brothers (Robert Herbst & Lionel Hagenaers, only) 58 Stone & 93 Pearl
Herbst & Goldstein (Joseph Herbst & Moses F. Goldstein) 414 B'way
Herbst & Morrison (William Herbst & Morris Morrison) 101 Bowery
Herdtfelder & Specht (Jacob F. Herdtfelder & Francis P. Specht) 183 Rivington & 187 E. Houston
Herkert & Unkelbach (Carl Herkert & Joseph Unkelbach) 45 W. 31st
Herklotz & Zapke (dissolved) 860 E. 76th
Herklotz, Corn & Co. (John D. Herklotz & Charles O. Corn, no Co.) 52 New

SPECIAL ATTENTION PAID TO THIS CLASS OF WORK. } **BANKERS' & BROKERS' CIRCULARS DELIVERED** { THE TROW CITY DIRECTORY CO. 11 University Place.

HER 132 HES

Herkner & Stine (James W. Herkner & Jacob R. Stine) 8 Ferry
Herman & Guinzburg (Max Herman & M. Charles Guinzburg) 527 B'way
Herman & Liman (Charles Herman & George Liman) 28 E. 4th
Herman & Murphy (Theodore Herman, only) 68 Warren
Herman & Weber (dissolved) 30 Willett
Hermans & Scott (William F. Hermans & Seaman Scott) 83 Liberty
Hernandez & Tracy (dissolved) 39 Broad
Herold L. & F. (Leo & Frank) 102 E. 110th
Herold's H.. Sons (Ignatius & Hieronymus J. Herold) 87 Ferry
Herow & Co. (Joseph E. Herow & John Mackay) ft. E. 100th
Herow & Dube (dissolved) ft. E. 104d
Heroy & Marronnier (William W. & James H. Heroy, only) 124 S. 5th av. & 102 Thompson
Herrick J. H. & Co. (dissolved) 108 Produce Ex.
Herrick & Bergen (dissolved) no address
Herrick & Co. (inf. unattainable) 237 B'way
Herring & Co. (Frank O. Herring, John Farrel, John O. Sherman, Silas H. Ruston & John T. Farrel) 251 B'way & 375 South
Herrlein & Co. (Emil F. & Adolph Herrlein) 122 Liberty
Herrlich Jacob & Brother (Jacob & August Herrlich) 505 Sixth
Herrman Julius & Co. (Julius Herrman & Aaron Simon) 95 Bleecker
Herrman H., Sternbach & Co. (Charles Sternbach, Abraham Herrman, James Wilkinson, Daniel W. Herrman & Morris Sternbach, only) 476 B'way & 36 Crosby
Herrman & Co. (Solomon & Bettina Herrman) 364 Canal
Herrman & Diercks (dissolved) 618 Eighth av.
Herrman & Schneer (Samuel Herrman & Isaac Schneer; — special partner, Henry S. Herrman, $25,000; terminates 5th Jan, 1892) 506 B'way & 128 Crosby
Herrman's Philip, Son (James S. Herrman) 405 W. 14th
Herrmann Bureau Co. (Henry Herrmann, Pres.; Gustave Possehl, Sec.; further inf. refused) 608 Broome & 188 Mott
Herrmann Chamber Suit Furniture Co. (Henry Herrmann, Pres.; Gustave Possehl, Sec.; further inf. refused) 368 Broome & 188 Mott
Herrmann Desk Co. (Henry Herrmann, Pres.; Gustave Possehl, Sec.; further inf. refused) 368 Broome & 185 Mangin
Herrmann Dining Room Furniture Co. (Henry Herrmann, Pres.; Gustave Possehl, Sec.; further inf. refused) 868 Broome & 89 Crosby
Herrmann, Aukam & Co. (Adolph Herrmann, only) 81 Thomas
Herrmann Brothers & Co. (Uriah & Nathan & Max Herrmann) 80½ Pearl
Herrmann Brothers & Obermeier (Salomon & Leopold Herrmann & Charles Obermeier) 96 Greene
Herron James M. & Son (dissolved) 61 Park pl.
Herron Joseph & Son (Joseph & George D. Herron) 14 Water
Herron William & Co. (William Herron & James H. & Henry Dawson) 301 G'wich & 24 Harrison
Herron & Kunz (John Herron jr. & James M. Kunz) 103 W. 42d
Herschel & Conner (Celeste A. Herschel & Oscar T. Conner) 281 Sixth av.
Herschmann & Bleier (Ross Herschmann & David Bleier) 54 Av. C & 96 Columbia
Hershey & Co. (dissolved) 412 W. 28th

Hershfield L. & Brother (Levi & Reuben N. Hershfield) 532 B'way
Herskovits S. & Co. (Siegmund Herskovits: — special partner, Leopold Lehman, $2,000; terminates 31st Dec. 1890) no address
Herskovits & Roth (Albert Herskovits & Ignatz Roth) 180 Mercer
Herter Brothers (architects) (Peter & Frank W. Herter) 191 B'way
Herter Brothers (furniture) (William Baumgarten & William G. Nichols, only) 154 Fifth av. & 470 First av.
Herterich John & Co. (no inf.) 145 E. 23d
Herting William & Son (William & Emil Herting) 185 Elizabeth
Hertlein & Schlatter (Christopher F. Hertlein & Charles W. Schlatter) 31 Mercer & Brook av. c E. 148th
Herts D. & Co. (Daniel Herts, no Co.) 204 Fulton
Herts H. B. & Sons (Maurice A. & Jacques H. Herts, only) 242 Fifth av.
Herts Brothers (Isaac H. & Benjamin H. Herts) 594 B'way & 104 E. 82d
Herweg C. J. & Son (Charles J. & Joseph Herweg) r 171 Suffolk
Herz Brothers (Herman & Jacob L. Herz) 104 Water
Herzberg M. & L (dissolved) 1 Bowery
Herzberg & Co. (dissolved) 41 Bowery, 44 Division & 11 Delancey
Herzberg & Feistel (Leopold Herzberg & Edward Feistel) 41 Maiden la.
Herzfeld Brothers (drugs) (Herman & Alfred Herzfeld) 260 Seventh av.
Herzfeld Brothers (liquors) (no inf.) 127 Stanton
Herzfeld & Co. (brokers) (Felix Herzfeld & Lewis H. & Edward Strouse:—special partner, Joseph Herzfeld, Berlin, Germany, $50,000; terminates 31st Dec. 1890) 54 Exchange pl.
Herzfeld & Co. (trimmings) (Edward S. Herzfeld, no Co.) 862 Third av.
Herzig Albert, Sons & Co. (Albert & Samuel & Joseph Herzig & Morris Mayers) 109 Prince
Herzig F. & Co. (Frederick & Leopold Herzig) 42 Lispenard
Herzig Brothers (Simon & Philip Herzig) 188 Mercer
Herzog Electric Appliance Co. (F. Benedict Herzog, Pres.; Philip Herzog, Sec.; Capital, $140,000. Trustees: F. Benedict & Philip Herzog) 80 Broad
Herzog Louis & Co. (Louis Herzog & Alfred Frank) 32 Maiden la.
Herzog Telesome Co. (F. Benedict Herzog, Pres.; Philip Herzog, Sec. Capital, $1,400. Trustees: F. Benedict & Philip Herzog) 80 Broad
Herzog Telesome Co. of N. Y. State (F. Benedict Herzog, Pres.; Philip Herzog, Sec. Capital, $500,000. Trustees: F. Benedict & Philip Herzog, N. P. Deors) 80 Broad
Herzog William & Co. (William Herzog, Co. refused) 126 Maiden la.
Herzog S. & Son (Solomon & Alexander Herzog) 56 Walker
Herzog & Co. (Julius & Ely & Joseph Herzog) 88 Whitehall & 44 Fulton
Hespe & Gerland (William C. Hespe & Frederick J. M. Gerland) 30 Vesey
Hess Henry & Co. (Henry Hess & Michael M. Chorinsky) 121 Mercer
Hess D. S. & Co. (Louis J. Lesser, Albert L. Woarms & estate of David S. Hess) 870 B'way & 818 E. 75th
Hess Brothers (Jacob & Max Hess) 177 Franklin
Hess & Fries (Henry Hess & Julius Fries) 382 Broome
Hess & Harburger (Ferdinand Hess & Ludwig Harburger) 27 Spruce

MERCHANTS EXCHANGE NAT. BANK OF THE CITY OF N. Y.
SOLICITS YOUR ACCOUNT. **257 Broadway.**
PHINEAS C. LOUNSBURY, President.   ALLEN S. APGAR, Cashier.

HES   133   HIL

Hess & Morgenthau (Philip Hess & Moritz G. Morgenthau) 533 B'way

Hess & Son (Bernhard & Samuel Hess) 74 St Mark's pl.

Hess & Townsend (Charles A. Hess & William J. Townsend) 206 B'way

Hess & Wagner (dissolved) r 177 E. 75th

Hess & Wise (dissolved) 2212 Third av.

Hess Brothers & Co. (Henry & Jonas Hess, no Co.) 22 Nassau

Hess, Goldsmith & Co. (Leon Hess & Max & Louis Goldsmith) 99 Grand

Hesse & Baltinger (no int.) 118 Eighth av. & 1759 Ninth av.

Hesse & Ohlsen (Doderick Hesse & Charles Ohlsen) 48 Gansevoort, W. Washn. mkt

Hession William & Son (William & William J. Hession) 451 E. 54th

Hessler & Lamprecht (dissolved) 1846 Ninth av.

Hessman & Finck (John H. Hessman & John H. Finck) 176 Bank

Hester & Henry (John W. Hester & Isaac Henry) 131 Reade

Hettinger & Richards (John Hettinger & George Richards) 151½ Stanton

Hetzer Hermann & Co. (Hermann Hetzer & Charles F. Nahmmacher) 155 Greene & 50 W. Houston

Heuer Henry & Son (Henry & Henry Heuer jr.) 424 E. 121st

Heuer H. & Co. (Henry & Otto Heuer) 1507 Ninth av.

Heuman L. & Son (Leopold & Harry & Abraham Heuman) 406 E. 77th

Heumann Brothers (Hugo & Benno Heumann) 11 Howard

Heuser & Son (Frederick & Henry F. Houser) 250 Broome

Hewitt C. D. & Brothers (Charles D. & Edward G. & George F. Hewitt) 48 Beekman

Hewitt & Co. (real estate) (dissolved) 149 W. 40th

Hewitt & Co. (weighers) (Francis C. Hewitt, no Co.) 102 Wall

Hewitt & Hosier (Frederick A. Hewitt & John N. Hosier) 19 E. 14th

Hewlett & Hart (White Hewlett & John R. Hart) Sylvan pl. n E. 120th

Hewlett & Torrance (James A. Hewlett & Samuel Lea, only) 71 Wall

Hewson & White (John H. Hewson & Frank T. White) 39 Broad

Heydecker & Harris (Isaac Heydecker & Abraham Harris) 350 Third av.

Heyer Brothers (William & Gustav Heyer) 1115 Park av.

Heyl & Noethen (Charles Heyl & Joseph Noethen) 6 Bond

Heyman N. H. (firm of) (dissolved) 488 E. 59th

Heyman Solomon & Co. (Solomon Heyman & Henry Blumenthal) 996 Third av.

Heyman C. & Co. (Clara Heyman, no Co.) 22 Howard

Heyman Brothers (Morris & Simon & Abraham Heyman) 75 Murray

Heyman & Fischer (Leopold Heyman & Henry E. Fischer) 78 Broad

Heyman Brothers & Lowenstein (Edward E. & Samuel Heyman & Louis Lowenstein) 480 E. 59th

Heymann Charles M. & Co. (Charles M. Heymann, no Co.) 17 E. 42d

Heymann Edward & Co. (Edward Heymann, no Co.) 401 B'way

Heymann Brothers (David & Bernhard Heymann) 266 Broome

Heyne Nicholas & Son (dissolved) 340 Canal

Heyne F. W. & Brother (Frederick W. & John F. Heyne) 13 William

Heyne I. & Son (Isidore & François F. Heyne) 822 B'way

Heywood Walter, Chair Co. (not inc.; further inf. refused) 45 Elizabeth

Heywood Brothers & Co. (Henry & George H. Heywood, Amos Morrill, Alvin M. Greenwood, Calvin H. Hill, John D. Walsh) 207 Cherry & 197 Canal

Hibernia Iron Mining Co. (Edwin P. Merritt, Pres.; Charles H. Merritt, Treas.; William H. Clarkson, Sec. Directors: Edwin P. & Charles H. Merritt, William H. Clarkson, S. D. Patterson, L. W. Francis) 115 B'way

Hibson & Brother (James A. & Robert F. Hibson) 126 Fulton

Hickey T. & J. (Theresa H. & James) 209 South

Hickling & Co. (dissolved) 60 B'way

Hickman Hose Coupling Co. (William Boardman, Pres.; Archibald M. Pentz, Sec. Capital, $25,000. Directors: William Boardman, Archibald M. & William E. Pentz, Perry P. Williams, James A. Croker) 26 John

Hickok & Co. (William P. Hickok, no Co.) 317 B'way

Hickok & Johnson (John N. Hickok & William V. Johnson) 85 Murray

Hicks B. & Co. (Benjamin J. & William L. Hicks) 19 Whitehall

Hicks Brothers (Benjamin B. & G. Embree Hicks) 42 White

Hicks & Bell (George Bell, only) 68 South

Hicks & McCollough (William A. Hicks & Elwood C. McCollough) 281 Eighth av.

Hicks & Smith (Michael Hicks & Thomas Smith) 42 S. 5th av.

Higganum Mfg. Corporation (George M. Clark, Pres.; Clinton B. Davis, Sec. Capital, $200,000. Directors: George M. & Thomas J. Clark, Joseph & Clinton D. Davis) 190 Water

Higgins E. A. & A. M. (Eleanor A. Higgins & Alice M. Fleming, only) 140 Fifth av.

Higgins E. S. & Co. (Eugene Higgins & John D. Wood, only) 84 White & ft. W. 43d

Higgins Brothers (James & William H. Higgins) 124 W. 23d

Higgins & Seiter (Arthur S. Higgins & Charles J. Seiter) 52 W. 22d

Higgins & Son (James & Edward Higgins) 214 E. 121st

Higgins & Woodruff (no inf.) 418 Lex. av.

Higgins, Cox & Barrett, Attorneys (not a firm) (A. Foster Higgins, James Farley Cox & John D. Barrett) 50 Wall

Higgins, Fraser & Co. (Charles M. Higgins, Arthur C. & George H. Fraser & Arthur S. Browne) 5 Beekman

Higgins' S., Son (William F. Higgins) 430 Fourth av.

Higgs & Rooke (dissolved) 885 B'way

Highland Beach Improvement Co. (Ferdinand Fish, Pres.; John P. Hayward, Sec.; Wheaton S. Lowry, Treas. Capital, $100,000. Directors: Ferdinand Fish, John P. Hayward, Wheaton S. Lowry) 149 B'way

Highland Steamboat Co. (dissolved) 56 Wall

Highlands Chemical Co. (Eugene Waugh, Pres.; George V. N. Baldwin, Sec. Capital, $50,000; further inf. unattainable) 17 Cedar

Higley Sawing & Drilling Machine Co. (William B. Williams, Pres.; William S. Browning, Sec.; James H. Pratt, Treas. Directors: William B. Williams, James H. Pratt, Oren P. Browning) 45 B'way

Hilborn Harness Agency (Lena Hilborn, propr.) 112 Chambers

SNOW, CHURCH & CO.,
265 & 267 BROADWAY.

COLLECTIONS IN ALL PARTS OF THE WORLD.
T. C. Campbell and Arthur Murphy, *Counsel*.
TELEPHONE, 738 MURRAY.

HIL   134   HIR

Hilborn Brothers (dissolved) 508 B'way & 132 Crosby

Hildburgh Henry & Co. (Henry Hildburgh & Isidor Kahn) 206 B'way

Hiklebrand C. P. & Co. (Charles P. Hildebrand & Beverly R. Wood) 242 Washn.

Hildebrand F. & Co. (Frederick Hildebrand & Otto Eichler) 219 E. 93d

Hildebrand J. H. G. & Son (John H. G. & Dederick G. Hildebrand) 700 Eleventh av.

Hildebrant Jacob T. & Co. (Jacob T. Hildebrant, no Co.) 188 Eleventh av.

Hildreth Varnish Co. (Peter S. Jennings, Pres.; John W. Combs, Sec.; James Hildreth jr. Treas. Capital $100,000. Directors: Peter S. Jennings, John W. Combs, James Hildreth jr.) 155 D'way

Hildreth R. W. & Co. (Russell W. & Percy S. Hildreth) 10 Cedar

Hildreth & Allen (David M. Hildreth & Flavius J. Allen) 582 B'way

Hildreth & Nettleton (dissolved) 10 Cedar

Hildreth Brothers & Sogelken (Luther S. & Henry P. Hildreth & Henry Sogelken) 28 W. 37th

Hill Charles R. & Co. (Frank H. & Louis A. Hill & John C. Gregory) 23 South

Hill Glass Co. (Samuel McCracken, propr.) r 75 Nassau

Hill Mary E. & Co. (Mary E. Hill & Anne J. H. Fletcher) 5 Beekman & 98 Nassau

Hill Paper Bag Co. (George W. Hill, propr.) 388 Pearl

Hill A. F. & Co. (Alvin F. Hill & Henry L. Crane) 19 B'way

Hill E. & Co. (Eliza Hill, no Co.) 357 Sixth av.

Hill E. & S. (Elizabeth & Susan) 1452 Third av.

Hill J. A. & Co. (James A. Hill, no Co.) 44 E. 14th

Hill L. A. & Co. (Louis A. Hill & J. Odell Fowler jr.) 165 B'way

Hill W. C. & Co. (no inf.) 80 Wall

Hill Brothers (photographs) (no inf.) 56 W. 30th

Hill Brothers (strawgds.) (William H. & Sylvester C. & Stanley B. Hill) 564 B'way

Hill & Baldwin (dissolved) 93 Elizabeth

Hill & Co. (dissolved) r 75 Nassau

Hill & Harrison (dissolved) 816 Sixth av.

Hill & Langstroth (Adam Hill & Francis W. Langstroth) 70 Beekman

Hill & Stout (dissolved) 40 B'way

Hill's Edward, Son & Co. (Hugh Hill & George McDermott) 27 Cedar

Hillabrand & Dykes (George Hillabrand & Andrew F. Dykes) 76 Warren

Hillebrand & Co. (Gustav Hillebrand, no Co.) 15 Howard

Hillebrandt Brothers (Dederick & Christopher Hillebrandt) 246 Eighth av.

Hiller M. L. & Son (Michael L. & Hugo L. Hiller) 140 W. 23d

Hillier's R., Son Co. (George R. Hillier, Pres.; Isaac V. S. Hillier, Sec. Capital, $200,000. Directors: George E. Hillier, Francis A. Moore, Isaac V. S. Hillier) 46 Cedar

Hillin, Dearhope & Co. (Edward & Matthew Hillin & George Dearhope) 10 Ferry

Hillis Plantation Coffee Co. (inf. unattainable) 309 Washn.

Hillis & Abbott (no inf.) 10 E. 14th

Hillman Brothers (dissolved) 2326 First av.

Hills Brothers (John & William Hills) 79 Park pl.

Hillsdale Terrace Improvement Co. (not Inc.) (Chapin & Benson, managers) 63 B'way

Hillyer E. T. & Co. (Edward T. Hillyer, no Co.) 50 Leonard

Hilmers, McGowan & Co. (Herman C. Hilmers & Henry D. McGowan, no Co.) 38 Wall

Hilsmann & Hachmann (Frederick Hilsmann & Frederick H. Hachmann) 247 Seventh av.

Hilt & Staub (dissolved) 401 E. 47th

Hilton & Dodge Lumber Co. (Joseph Hilton, Pres.; Robert P. Paul, Sec. Capital, $1,000,000. Directors: Joseph Hilton, Norman W. Dodge, James L. Foster, Robert P. Paul) 81 New

Hilton & Paddock (no inf.) 2 W. 14th

Hilton & Son (James & George T. Hilton) 56 West

Hilton, Hughes & Denning (Henry Graham Hilton, John M. Hughes, Edwin J. Denning & Albert B. & Frederic Hilton) 784 B'way

Himrod Mfg. Co. (Himrod & Pinckney, proprs.) 191 Fulton

Himrod & Pinckney (Stephen B. Pinckney & estate of Peter Himrod) 101 Fulton

Hinchman W. H. & Co. (William H. Hinchman & Fridge Riach) 55 Leonard

Hinck Brothers (dissolved) 2062 Second av. & 87 E. 113th

Hinck & Ould (Henry J. Hinck & Thomas Ould; —special partner: Claus F. Hinck, $50,000; terminates 31st Dec. 1890) 55 Worth

Hinck & Wobbekind (John Hinck & August Wobbekind) 456 Pearl

Hindley Thomas & Son (John H. Hindley, only) 761 Sixth av.

Hinds Arthur & Co. (Arthur Hinds & G. Clifford Noble) 4 Cooper Union

Hinds, Ketcham Co. (Joseph F. Hinds, Pres.; Henry E. Ketcham, Sec. Capital, $250,000. Directors: Joseph E. Hinds, John Hogg, George D. Soth, Henry E. Ketcham, Walter A. Daniels, Peter F. Downey, Paul Weidmann jr.) 280 D'way

Hine Eliminator Co. (not Inc.) (Frank A. Hine & John W. Hull) 45 Cortlandt

Hine C. C. & Son (Charles C. & Thomas A. Hine) 137 D'way

Hine & Lynch (George M. Hine & Charles E. Lynch) 133 Dunne

Hine & Robertson (Frank A. Hine & James L. Robertson) 45 Cortlandt

Hines & Mansfield (William M. Hines & David H. Mansfield) 197 Chambers

Hingelage & Bunger (Herman H. Hingelage & John Bunger) 332 G'wich

Hingelage & Wellbrock (Herman H. Hingelage & Frederick Wellbrock) 170 Church & 85 Reade

Hinman William K. (William K. Hinman, Jacob C. Stamler & Frank Richard) 109 South

Hinman Brothers (William & Matthew Hinman) 359 B'way

Hinrichs B. & Sons (Bernard J. & Bernard C. & William J. Hinrichs) 49 Thompson av. W. Washn. mkt

Hinrichs & Co. (Louis Hinrichs & Albert C. Melsel;—special partner, Charles F. A. Hinrichs, $255,000; terminates 1st March, 1892) 31 Park pl.

Hinsdale & Sprague (Elizur B. Hinsdale & Edward E. Sprague) 192 B'way

Hinton & Fay (William M. Hinton & John H. Fay) 308 Washn.

Hintze J. C. & Son (John C. & Henry J. Hintze) 58 Gansevoort

Hippel, Tillard & Runk (Jacob Hippel, John W. Tillard & Mary E. Runk) 739 D'way

Hirsch David & Sons (David & Zachariah & Samuel Hirsch) Pleasant av. n E. 114th

Hirsch George & Son (George & Charles Hirsch) 30 Broome

Hirsch Isaac & Son (Isaac & Benjamin Hirsch) 114 Greene

WATER METERS, GAS ENGINES, | NATIONAL METER CO.
FOR PUMPING AND POWER. | 252 Broadway, N. Y.

HIR 135 HOE

Hirsch Joseph & Sons (Joseph & Nathan & Leon Hirsch & Adolph Forsheim) 79 Greene
Hirsch A. & Co. (no inf.) 97 Spring
Hirsch D. & Co. (David Hirsch:—special partner, William A. H. Stafford, $24,500; terminates 31st April, 1890) 229 E. 41st
Hirsch M. & Co. (Morris & Edward Hirsch) 729 Tremont av.
Hirsch S. & Co. (Simon Hirsch, Edward Marks & Adolph S. Amson) 427 B'way
Hirsch Brothers (Michael & Abraham Hirsch) 62 Walker
Hirsch & Co. (Rosa & Simon Hirsch) 139 Greene
Hirsch & Kahn (dissolved) 111 Bleecker
Hirsch & Klatthaar (Edward Hirsch & John P. Klatthaar) 103 S. 5th av.
Hirsch & Lyons (Ascher Hirsch & Albert Lyons) 400 Broome
Hirsch & Schwarzkopf (Isidor Hirsch & Isidor F. Schwarzkopf) 46 E. Houston
Hirsch, Victorius & Co. (Henry Hirsch, Morris Victorius & Bernhard Rosenblath) 159 Water
Hirsch's D., Sons (Aaron & Simon Hirsch) 149 Av. C
Hirschbein Brothers (Theodore & Henry Hirschbein) 1726 Park av.
Hirschberg & Co. (Gustav & Simon S. & Augusta & Hulda Hirschberg) 97 Greene
Hirschfelder & Co. (Sigmund Hirschfelder & Eliza Ettlinger) 599 B'way
Hirsh Leon & Sons (Leon & Charles L. & Abraham L. Hirsh) 370 G'wich
Hirsh A. & Co. (Albert A. Hirsh & Henry K. Culver) 647 B'way
Hirsh Brothers (Jacob & Louis Hirsh) 622 Tenth av. & 677 Eleventh av.
Hirsh & Brother (Mason & Henry & Alfred C. & Harry & William Hirsh & Otto J. Lang) 495 B'way
Hirsh & Co. (Samuel Hirsh, no Co.) 455 B'way
Hirsh & Eckstein (Jacob Hirsh & Simon Eckstein) 29 Lispenard
Hirsh & Gutstadt (dissolved) 66 Wooster
Hirsh & Lowenstein (Joseph Hirsh & Moses H. Lowenstein) 176 Chambers
Hirsh & Metzger (dissolved) 5 Malden la.
Hirsh & Park (Bernard Hirsh & Archibald Park) 570 B'way
Hirsh, Frank & Co. (no inf.) 708 B'way
Hirshfield Brothers (Siegfried & Paul Hirshfield) 1282 Third av.
Hirshkind & Co. (Emanuel Hirshkind, no Co.) 396 B'way
Hirzel, Feltmann & Co. (Charles Hirzel & Henry Feltmann:—special partner, Alexander Schweizer, Zurich, Switzerland, $20,000; terminates 31st Dec., 1891) 55 Beaver
Hiscox & Co. (David Hiscox, no Co.) 103 William
Historical & Statistical Publishing Co. (Capital, $5,000; further inf. unattainable) no address
Hitchcock Oliver & Son (Oliver & Oliver N. Hitchcock) 34 Park row
Hitchcock W. G. & Co. (Welcome G. Hitchcock, George J. Gear, A. Howard Hopping & Charles H. Lane) 453 Broome
Hitchcock & McCargo Publishing Co. (Ltd.) (Benjamin W. Hitchcock, Pres.; P. Randolph McCargo, Sec. Capital, $60,000; further inf. refused) 885 Sixth av.
Hitchcock, Darling & Co. (Himm Hitchcock, Alfred B. & Elmer A. Darling & Charles N. Vilas) 196 Fifth av.
Hitchcock, Dermody & Co. (John A. Dermody, G. Oscar Reynolds, Charles Gay, Edward Armstrong & Charles T. Raymond, only) 109 Greene

Hitchings & Co. (Thomas W. King, only) 233 Mercer
Hoadley & Co. (Russell H. Hoadley, Frederick Wesson & Chester C. Munroe) 77 William
Hoadly, Lauterbach & Johnson (George Hoadly, Edward Lauterbach, Edgar M. Johnson, William N. Cohen & Louis Adler) 120 B'way
Hoag W. H. & Co. (William H. & Russell Hoag) 32 Lawton av. W. Washn. mkt
Hoagland & Holmes (dissolved) 97 Cliff
Hoar & Day (Charles N. Hoar & Horatio B. Day) 52 E. 23d
Hoare J. & Co. (James & John Hoare & George L. Abbott) 49 Barclay
Hobart Frank B. & Co. (Frank B. Hobart, no Co.) 92 White
Hobart Henry L. (Henry L. Hobart:—special partner, Edward Rawson, Cinn., O., $10,000; terminates 31st Dec. 1890) 120 Front
Hobbs Charles W. & Co. (Charles W. Hobbs & George Gregory) 113 Sixth av.
Hobbs J. & Son (John & Henry Hobbs) 429 E. 68th
Hobbs & Gifford (Edward H. Hobbs & James M. Gifford) 58 William
Hobbs & Turnbull (dissolved) 15 State
Hobby, Akin & Hendrickson (Moses M. Hobby, William L. Akin & Nathaniel C. Hendrickson) 1473 B'way
Hobby's J. H., Son (George R. Hobby) 286 South & 371 Water
Hobby's John B., Son & Co. (J. Oakley & Charles F. Hobby) 112 Washn.
Hoberg & Fitschen (Peter W. Hoberg & Dederick Fitschen) 1356 Third av.
Hoblin's John W., Son (Henry G. Hoblin) 7 W. B'way
Hoboken Coal Co. (Charles Runyon, Pres.; William S. Halliday, Sec.; James F. Randolph, Treas. Directors: Charles Runyan, William S. Halliday, James F. Randolph) 111 B'way
Hoboken Land & Improvement Co. (Edwin A. Stevens, Pres., Samuel D. Dod, Sec. Capital, $1,500,000. Directors: Edwin A. & John Stevens, Samuel D. Dod, John J. McCook, Robert C. Livingston, William A. Macy, C. Albert Stevens) ft. Barclay, ft. Christopher & ft. W. 14th
Hobson & Co. (Moses S. Hobson & Clifton P. Worman) 4 Stone
Hochberger S. & Co. (Solomon Hochberger & David Heineman) 63 Crosby
Hochner & Zucker (David Hochner & Morris Zucker) 77 Av. A
Hochstadter Co. (B. Hochstadter, propr.) 31 Vandewater
Hockmeyer Brothers (Vincent & Otto Hockmeyer jr.) 127 Greene
Hoctor & Co. (no inf.) 1147 Ninth av.
Hodenpyl & Sons (Anthony J. G. & George H. & Anton Hodenpyl) 170 B'way & 95 Cliff
Hodge Alfred & Co. (Alfred Hodge & Frederick W. A. Pigou) 108 Broad
Hodgkins W. C. & Co. (Walter C. Hodgkins, Louis R. Menard, Charles M. Cobb & Michael Sullivan) 300 B'way
Hodgman Rubber Co. (George F. Hodgman, Pres.; George B. Hodgman, Sec. Capital, $250,000. Directors: George F. & Charles A. & George B. Hodgman) 461 B'way
Hodgson & Barwood (dissolved) 294 B'way
Hoe R. & Co (Robert & Peter S. Hoe, Stephen D. Tucker, Theodore H. Mead & Charles W. Carpenter) 504 Grand
Hoe's James C., Sons (William A. & George E. Hoe) 10 Liberty pl. & 52 Gansevoort
Hoebel & Bantelman (Louis Hoebel & Henry Bantelman) W. 152d n St. Nicholas av.

EXCELSIOR BIRD FOOD. The recognized standard. The most reliable for your Canary. Use no other. Insist upon getting it. Packed only by **C. ROSENSTEIN & CO.**, 373 Washington Street, New York.

HOE   136   HOL

Hoecker & Renken (Richard Hoecker & Charles Renken) 252 Clinton
Hoehn R. & Co. (Rudolph Hoehn, no Co.) 44 College pl.
Hoehle Brothers (Herman & John H. Hoehle) 75 W. B'way
Hoellerer M. & Son (dissolved) 141 Ludlow
Hooninghaus & Curtiss (Frederick Hooninghaus & Henry W. Curtiss) 473 Broome
Hoepfner & Co. (George Hoepfner & Henry Wuest) 47 Dayard
Hoertel's William, Sons (dissolved) 219 W. 31st
Hoff Brothers & Herring (Henry & Augustus Hoff & James Herring) 87 Fulton
Hoffman Aaron & Co. (Aaron Hoffman & Isidor Jacobs) 32 Walker
Hoffman Emanuel & Son (Joseph E. & Alexander E. Hoffman, only) 149 Water
Hoffman Press (Anna M. Hoffman, propr.) 380 Pearl
Hoffman Brothers (Charles F. jr. & William M. V. Hoffman) 4 Warren
Hoffman & Co. (Daniel Hoffman, no Co.) 45 B'way
Hoffman & Oculist (dissolved) 2308 Eighth av.
Hoffman & Oehninger (Robert Hoffman & Jacques Oehninger) 23 Warren
Hoffman & Woodward (dissolved) 52 B'way
Hoffmann Jacob, Brewing Co. (Jacob Hoffmann, Pres.; Philip Hoffmann, Sec.; William Hoffmann, Treas. Capital, $400,000. Directors: Jacob & Philip & William Hoffmann) 204 E. 55th
Hoffmann Joseph & Son (Joseph & Louis A. Hoffmann) 193 Third
Hoffmann F. W. & Sons (Frederick W. & Emil R. & Alfred W. Hoffmann) E. 161st c Third av.
Hoffmann & Rhode (Max Hoffmann & Charles Rhode) 442 Boulevard
Hoffmann & Schuback (Joseph Hoffmann & John Schuback) 122 Horatio & 524 West
Hoffmann's George A., Sons (William A. & Frank J. Hoffmann & Charles J. Senger) 178 Park row
Hoffmire John E. & Son (John E. & John D. Hoffmire) 808 Fifth
Hoffschmidt Brothers (Carl M. & Frank N. Hoffschmidt) 272 G'wich
Hoffstaetter & Himmel (John J. Hoffstaetter & Charles Himmel) 538 W. 46th
Hofheimer H. & Co, (Henry Hofheimer & Samuel Danziger) 630 B'way
Hofheimer N. & Co. (dissolved) 32 Beaver
Hofmann & Ellrodt (Florenz F. Hofmann & Christian Ellrodt) 91 Mercer
Hofmeister & Bidwell (dissolved) 306 W. 23d
Hofstatter Theodore & Co. (Theodore Hofstatter jr. & John Barnets, only) 628 B'way & 111 E. 11th
Hofstatter's Sons (Adolph G. & Theodore Hofstatter jr.) 111 E. 19th
Hogan T. & Sons (Timothy & Charles W. & Jefferson Hogan) 123 Front
Hogan & Son (Percy F. Hogan, only) 243 Pearl & 18 Cliff
Hogencamp John W. & Son (John W. & William M. Hogencamp) 136 W. 55th
Hogins & Lee (Henry H. Hogins & George C. Lee) 124 Pearl & 78 Beaver
Hogue J. Camillo & Co. (J. Camillo Hogue & Sigmund Gruenberg) 200 Av. A
Hoguet Robert J. & Co. (Robert J. Hoguet, James Morris & Charles G. Bornmann:—special partner, Henry L. Hoguet, $100,000 ; terminates 31st Dec. 1892) 61 White
Hoheb & Julien (Benjamin S. Hoheb & William J. Julien:—special partner, Norverto Oan, *Paris,*

France, $20,000 ; terminates 30th June, 1896) 24 State
Hohenstein H. & Sternbach (Hugo Hohenstein & Philip Sternbach) 11 Warren
Hohmann & Maurer (August B. Hohmann & Henry W. Maurer) 90 Fulton
Hojer & Graham (George W. Hojer & Gilbert Graham) 97 Duane
Holahan & Morrow (Anthony F. Holahan & S. Robinson Morrow) 187 B'way
Holbrook G. J., Co, (inf. unattainable) 88 Fifth av.
Holbrook Mfg. Co. (not Inc.) (John Dickson & George R. K. Smith) 410 Washn.
Holbrook H. J. & Co. (Henry J. Holbrook & Lewis H. Lawrence) 128 Duane
Holbrook Brothers (Isaac E. & Harry Holbrook) 85 Beekman
Holbrook & Co. (Edwin C. Holbrook, Co. refused) 42 Pine
Holder R. & J. (dissolved) 1894 Lex. av.
Holiday Publishing Co. (Edward S. Ellis, Pres.; further inf. unattainable) 19 Beekman
Holland Building Assn. (Robert B. Roosevelt, Pres.; George W. Van Siclen, Sec.; James B. Van Woert, Treas. Capital, $100,000. Trustees: Robert B. Roosevelt, William Remsen, John R. Planten, James B. Van Woert, John D. Vermeule, G. Van Nostrand, George W. Van Siclen) 7 Wall
Holland Coffee Co. (Ltd.) (Hasbrouck Bartow, Pres.; Charles Lange jr. Sec. Capital, $5,000. Directors : Hasbrouck Bartow, Charles Lange jr, F. J. Soaring, John M. Miner, E. G. Wright) 82 Water
Holland Peat Moss Co. (C. J. Schellings & Co., proprs.) 110 Pearl
Holland Trust Co. (Robert B. Roosevelt, Pres.; George W. Van Siclen, Sec. Capital, $500,000. Trustees: Benjamin F. Vosbargh, Joseph S. Stout, C. W. Hutchinson, Garrot A. Van Allen, Warner Van Norden, James B. Van Woert, Gardiner Van Nostrand, John R. Planten, Henry W. Bookstaver, William D. Van Vleck, Robert B. Roosevelt, George M. Van Horson, William Dowd, William Remsen, John D. Vermeule, John Van Voorhis, Tunis G. Bergen, William W. Van Voorhis, Charles F. Daly, George W. Van Siclen, George F. Hodgman, Jotham Goodnow, Augustus Van Wyck, Daniel A. Heald) 7 Wall
Holland William P. & Adams (Frank E. Adams, only) 91 Water
Holland T. & Sons (dissolved) r 211 E. 84th
Holland Brothers (Thomas G. & John L. Holland) 1790 Park av.
Hollander Oscar & Brother (dissolved) 11 Desbrosses
Hollander & Berkovitz (dissolved) 96 Cannon
Hollander & Werner (Aaron Hollander & Julius Werner) 5 Howard
Hollar Lock Inspection & Guaranty Co. (William H. Hollar, Pres.; Rollin M. Morgan, Sec. Capital, $50,000. Trustees: William H. Hollar, John J. Knox, Benjamin B. Comegys, Rollin M. Morgan, Alans R. Vedder) 187 B'way
Hollender Frederick & Co. (Frederick Hollender & Charles Tiolenics) 115 Elm, 2 Tryon row & 273 B'way
Hollender & Leiman (no inf.) r 168 Delancey
Holler John S. & Co. (August vom Dorp, only) 94 Duane
Hollerich George & Son (George & Henry Hollerich) 447 E. 114th
Holliday's R. Sons (Thomas & Robert & Edgar Holliday) 7 Platt
Hollingsworth J. H. & Co. (John H. & Thomas P. Hollingsworth) 552 B'way
Hollins Frank C. & Co. (dissolved) 11 Wall
Hollins H. B. & Co. (Harry B. Hollins, Fernando

IDEN & CO.,
University Place, 9th to 10th Sts., N. Y.
MANUFACTURERS OF GAS FIXTURES AND ELECTROLIERS

HOL 137 HOM

A., Ysnaga, Bernard J. Burke & Frederick Edey) 18 Wall & 5 Vanderbilt av.

Hollis Phototype Co. (dissolved) 18 Reade

Hollister Mfg. Co. (Robinson Gill, Pres.; Robert A. Hollister, Sec. Capital, $40,000. Directors: Albert E. Scott, Robinson Gill, Sebastian V. Hollister, Wallace R. Eickhoff) 152 W. 127th

Hollister H. H. & Co. (Henry H. Hollister & Nehemiah P. Howell) 42 New

Hollister & Co. (dissolved) 152 W. 127th

Hollister & Friedline (George K. Hollister & Samuel A. Friedline) 214 E. 47th

Hollister, Crane & Co. (George & John B. Hollister & William N. Crane) 90 Broad & 37 Water

Holly H. Hudson & Jolliff (H. Hudson Holly & Horatio F. Jolliff) 111 B'way

Holly Mfg. Co. (Thomas T. Flagler, Pres.; Charles G. Hildreth, Sec.; Horace H. Flagler, Treas. Capital, $500,000. Directors: Thomas T. Flagler, Charles G. Hildreth, Horace H. Flagler, James Jackson jr. George W. Bowen) 45 B'way

Holly Brothers (Charles W. & Edgar Holly) 932 Ninth av.

Hollywood Co. (William M. Fliess, Pres.; Richard Vom Hofe, Sec.; Baxter Barker, Treas. Directors: William M. Fliess, Baxter Barker, Richard Vom Hofe) 47 B'way

Holm & Robinson (Charles F. Holm & George Robinson) 21 Park row

Holman Liver Pad Co. (Frank Holman, Pres.; George W. Holman jr. Sec. Capital, $50,000. Directors: Frank & George W. & George W. jr. & H. E. Holman) 81 John

Holmes Burglar Alarm Telegraph Co. (inf. unattainable) 518 B'way

Holmes Electric Protective Co. (Edwin Holmes, Pres.; Edwin T. Holmes, Sec.; James Tomney, Treas. Capital, $1,000,000. Directors: Edwin Holmes, Charles A. Tinker, Edwin T. Holmes, James Tomney, Philip Bissinger, Aaron Carter jr. W. C. Finnstone, John F. Patterson, William G. Raemo) 518 B'way

Holmes Joseph jr. & Co. (dissolved) 7 Pearl

Holmes C. I. & E. F. (Clara L. & Emma F.) 137 B'way

Holmes Brothers (Theodore D. & William H. Holmes) 920 B'way

Holmes & Adams (Artemas H. Holmes & George H. Adams) 15 Broad

Holmes & Allen (Samuel J. Holmes & Eugene S. Allen) 587 Hudson

Holmes & Carry (Ellen Holmes & William Carry) 88 John

Holmes & Co. (framee) (Emma Holmes & Thomas R. Penketh) 18 Baxter

Holmes & Co. (ins.) (Frederick L. Holmes & Willard L. Candee) 13 Park row

Holmes & Coutts (John Holmes & George M. Coutts) 341 Washn. & 5 William

Holmes & Farnam (Robet A. Holmes & Eleanor M. Farnam) 21 W. Houston

Holmes & Ide (Henry Holmes & John C. Ide) 27 Greene

Holmes & Scott (William H. Holmes & Walter Scott) 96 Park pl.

Holmes, Booth & Haydens (Chandler N. Wayland, Pres.; George H. Benham. Sec. Capital, $400,000. Directors: Chandler N. Wayland, Thomas D. Kent, Henry E. Russell, Douglass W. & T. Brownell Durnham, George W. McGill, E. C. Lewis, James S. Elton, F. L. Adams) 26 Park pl. & 22 Murray

Holohan & O'Reilly (Patrick Holohan & Thomas O'Reilly) 1075 First av.

Holsten & Bischoff (John Holsten & Frederick Bischoff) 144 Reade

Holt Henry & Co. (Henry & Charles Holt) 29 W. 23d & 8 W. 24th

Holt A. L. & C. L. (Alfred L. & Charles L.) 169 Front

Holt Brothers (Henry T. & Chauncey Holt) 23 Vandewater

Holt & Butler (George C. Holt & Charles H. Butler) 111 B'way

Holt & Co. (no inf.) 19 B'way

Holt & Co. (flour) (Robert S. Holt, Leonard J. Busby & Charles W. McCutchen) 57 Water

Holt & Kooy (Alfred A. Holt & Jacob F. Kooy) 304 Canal

Holton & Pearson (Lewis M. Holton & Charles P. Pearson) 19 Beekman

Holtz L. & Son (Levy & Hyman Holtz) 33 E. B'way

Holtz & Freystedt (Christian F. Holtz & Bruno Freystedt) 349 B'way & 95 Dunne

Holworthy & Ellis (William T. Holworthy & David Ellis) 93 Wall

Holzapfel & Murphy (no inf.) 206 B'way

Holzinger A., Brother & Co. (Abraham & Samuel Holsinger & Moses Sichel) 82 Warren

Holzman Brothers (Elkan & Asher Holzman) 650 B'way

Holzmann & Deutschberger (Jacob Holzmann & Jacob Deutschberger) 201 E. 67th

Homan Andrew, Co. (Andrew Homan, Pres.; William Homan, Sec. Capital, $25,000; further inf. unattainable) 440 & 448 Water

Homan & Bonnell (Charles M. Homan & Judson B. Bonnell) 219 West

Homan Brothers & Conch (Samuel & Charles F. Homan & Samuel Conch) 206 Hester

Homans Publishing Co. (Albert S. Bolles, Pres.; Obadiah Banks, Sec. Capital, $50,000. Directors: Albert S. Bolles, Obadiah Banks) 251 B'way

Homans & Co. (Edward C. Homans, William B. Post, Nelson Robinson & William A. Putnam) 2 Wall

Homans & Wiley (Benjamin Homans & Theodore W. Wiley) 166 B'way

Homberger M. & Co. (Mayer Homberger & Morris Koenigsberger) 44 Walker

Home Bank (Edmund Stephenson, Pres.; Howard L. Bain, Cashier. Capital, $100,000. Directors: Edmund Stephenson, William Campbell, Edward Schweyer, G. Waldo Smith, George Starr, George E. Ketcham, William P. Esterbrook, Otto Wesseli, Francis Blessing, George Mulligan, James Fitzpatrick, Richard Kelly, Smiten V. Tripp, Henry Schwarzwalder) 303 W. 42d

Home Benefit Assn. (William A. Camp, Pres.; Frederick J. Brown, Treas.; Eugene A. Baker, Sec. Directors: William A. Camp, Henry C. Brownell, Frederick J. Brown, Eugene A. Baker, George D. Clift, John C. Moore, Joseph S. Case, Augustus M. Scriba. George H. Sheldon, J. Trumbull Smith) 187 B'way

Home Benefit Soc. (John F. H. King, Pres.; George W. Godward, Sec.; James J. Smith, Treas. Directors: T. M. Nichols, William H. Cromwell, Charles Mortimer, William A. Miner, L. F. Frazee, Evelyn L. Bissell, George W. Godward) 161 B'way

Home Ins. Co. (Daniel A. Heald, Pres.; William L. Bigelow & Thomas B. Greene, Sec's. Capital, $3,000,000. Directors: Isaac H. Frothingham, Levi P. Morton, Cornelius N. Bliss, Edmund F. Holbrook, John H. Washburn, John H. Inman, Walter H. Lewis, Francis H. Leggett, Benjamin Perkins, George E. Beguelin, George W. Smith, Frederic P. Olcott, J. Harsen Rhoades, George C. White jr. William H. Townsend, Oliver S. Carter, Henry M. Taber, Daniel A. Heald, David H. McAlpin, Andrew C. Armstrong, Elbridge G. Snow jr. William R. Fosdick, John R. Ford, William Sturgis, Henry A. Hurlbut) 119 B'way & 9 Cooper Union

Home Life Ins. Co. (George C. Ripley, Pres.; George H. Ripley, Sec.; Isaac H. Frothingham, Treas. Capital, $125,000. Directors: A. A. Low, Isaac H. Frothingham, J. S. T. Stranahan, George C. Ripley, John T. Martin, George A. Jarvis, S. E. Howard, Charles A. Townsend, John W. Frothingham, E. Lewis jr, William G. Low, Thomas H. Messenger, J. Warren Greene, John Claflin, John P. Atkinson, Henry E. Pierrepont, Lemuel H. Arnold jr, George H. Ripley) 254 B'way

Home Maker Co. (refused) 19 W. 23d

Home of Industry (John H. Boswell, Pres.; William R. Tilss, Sec.) 40 E. Houston

Home Provident Safety Fund Assn. (in liquidation) 80 Liberty

Home Reliance Co. (Capital, $10,000; further inf. unattainable) no address

Home Seeker Printing & Publishing Co. (Charles O'C. Hennessy, Pres.; C. S. May, Sec. Capital, $10,000; further inf. unattainable) 258 B'way

Home Topics Publishing Co. (David R. Doty, Pres.; Bernhard Osann, Sec. Cap'tal, $25,000. Trustees: David R. Doty, Bernhard Osann, Robert Hartman) 37 College pl.

Home Vapor Bath & Disinfector Co. (Alexander H. Reitlinger, Pres.; Augustus Nathan, Sec.; Joseph Stuart, Treas. Capital, $500,000. Directors: Alexander H. Reitlinger, John Pundir, Adolph L. Sanger, Joseph Stuart, Augustus Nathan) 15 Broad

Homer Lee Bank Note Co. (William L. Strong, Pres.; Henry A. Armstrong, Sec.; Homer Lee, Treas. Capital, $500,000 Directors: William L. Strong, William A. Wheelock, Calvin S. Brice, Samuel Thomas, Duncan D. Parmly, Homer Lee, A. D. Juilliard, Louis Fitzgerald, William A. Camp, Stephen B. Elkins, S. Perry Sturges, Henry A. Armstrong, W. M. Hoffer) 164 Nassau

Homestead Bank (J. Wesley Smith, Pres.; Peter Sunn, Cashier. Capital, $100,000. Directors: James A. & Elsworth L. Striker, J. Wesley Smith, Horace D. Russ, William H. Bellamy, Gary J. Moulton, Frederick Wood, William Mitchell, Eben Demarest) 785 Tenth av.

Homestead Co. (Cornelius V. Sidell, Pres.; Henry C. Stetson, Sec.; Ogden P. Pell, Treas. Capital, $50,000. Directors: Cornelius V. Sidell, William Fuller Tafts, Henry C. Stetson, Ogden P. Pell, C. B. Mesorole, J. H. Corpening) 47 Liberty

Homestead Material Co, (Capital, $10,000; further inf. unattainable) no address

Homœopathic Mutual Life Ins. Co. (Edwin M. Kellogg, receiver) 117 W. 42d

Honduras Commercial Co. (Andrew W. Kent, Pres.; Oliver G. Hilliard, Sec.; Joseph A. Garginlo, Treas. Capital, $1,000,000. Directors: Hector de Castro, Louis L. Lorillard, Andrew W. Kent, William A. Gay, Hiram G. Smith, John Cumming, Joseph A. Garginlo) 1 B'way

Hone Philip, Co. (Ltd.) (Leonidas Dennis, Pres.; William P. O'Brien, Sec.; Henry F. Wiegmnd, Treas. Capital, $4,500. Directors: Leonidas Dennis, William P. O'Brien, Henry F. Wiegmnd) 550 Pearl

Honenthal & Son (Charles F. L. & Frederick Honenthal) 857 Third av.

Honer & Mitchel (Martin Honer & William T. Mitchel) 431 Fifth av.

Honey J. F. & Son (John F. & James B. Honey) 110 W. 18th & 12 B'way

Honig Henry & Son (Henry & Joseph Honig) 170 B'way

Honigman & Prince (Isaiah Honigman & Louis A. Prince) 80 B'way

Honigman, Mack & Co. (J. Leo Honigman & Walter S. Mack, no Co.) 783 B'way

Hood H., Co. (dissolved) 88 Park pl.

Hooker W. H. & Co. (Walter H. & William Hooker) 46 W. B'way

Hooker & Lawrence (William A. Hooker & Benjamin B. Lawrence) 145 B'way

Hoole Machine & Engraving Works (Edward G. Black, propr.) 46 Centre

Hoole Mfg. Co. (William H. Woolverton, Pres.; Henry W. Lombaert, Sec.; William F. Allen, Treas.; further inf. refused) 46 Dond & 53 Gt. Jones

Hoole & Co. (dissolved) 1179 B'way

Hooper Co. (Frank B. Hooper, Pres.; Augustus J. Patterson, Sec.; Smith Mowry, Treas. Capital, $25,000. Directors: Frank B. Hooper, Augustus J. Patterson, Smith Mowry) 295 Pearl

Hooper & Gore (Richard A. Hooper & Calvin Gore:—special partner, Carlos Gore, B'klyn, N. Y., $10,000; terminates 1st Nov, 1891) 146 Greene

Hooven G. W., Mercantile Co. (George W. Hooven, Pres.; Rollin O. Hooven, Sec. Capital $75,000. Directors: George W. & Rollin O. Hooven, Elmer E. Hassan, Wilbur T. & Robert L. Hoovea) 6 Harrison

Hoover, Sulzer & Forster (Wilson W. Hoover, William Sulzer & Isaac S. Forster) 19 Barclay & 24 Park pl.

Hopcraft & Co, (Alfred Hopcraft, no Co.) 7 Warren

Hope Mining Co. (A. Francis Sutherland, Pres.; Clinton B. Fisk, Treas. Capital, $250,000. Trustees: A. Francis Sutherland, Jose F. Navarro, Clinton B. Fisk) 96 B'way

Hope & Allen (Walter E. Hope & John F. Allen) 221 Rider av.

Hopkins George E. & Co. (George E. Hopkins & Oscar J. Mendel) 154 E. 43d

Hopkins Joseph & Co. (Joseph Hopkins & Frederick Vogt) 100 W. 3d

Hopkins &. Blaut (Sydney B. Hopkins & Lazarus Blaut) 1 W. 16th

Hopkins & Co, (Eliza B. Hopkins & Thomas Angus) 90 W. B'way & 20 Harrison

Hopkins & Dickinson Mfg. Co. (Thomas H. O'Connor, Pres.; Erwin J. Crane, Treas. Capital $100,000. Directors: Thomas H. O'Connor, Erwin J. Crane, William T. Hume) 88 Reade

Hopkins & Ingalls (dissolved) 121 Front & 377 West

Hopkins & Rossell (Richard Hopkins & Randolph L. Rossell) 184 South

Hopkins, Dwight & Co. (Gustavus C. Hopkins, Charles D. Miller, Lucius Hopkins Smith & Samuel Hopkins, only) 52 Cotton Ex.

Hopkins, Lane & Hubbard (Lewis C. Hopkins, Nathan Lane & Clarence E. Hubbard) 48 South & 377 West

Hopkinson J. F. & Co. (George W. Hopkinson, only) 202 B'way

Hoppe A. & P. (Augustus & Pauline) 1334 Third av.

Hopper Jacob A. & Son (Francis M. & Jacob J. Hopper, only) 400 W. 17th

Hopper R. & L. (Rebecca & Elizabeth) 229 W. 25th

Hoppin & Coursen (dissolved) 141 Elm

Hoppin & Talbot (William W. Hoppin jr. & Charles N. Talbot) 111 B'way

Hopping & Campbeld (S. D. Hopping & Samuel L. Campbell) 333 G'wich

Hopwood T. & W. (dissolved) E, 168th n Boston rd.

Horenstein & Bloch (no inf.) 100 Second

Horgan & Slattery (Arthur J. Horgan & Vincent J. Slattery) 12 Roosevelt

Horgan & Wischors (refused) 210 Fulton mkt

Horicon Iron Co. (Cyrus Butler, Pres.; John L. Hubbard, Sec. Capital, $500,000. Directors: Cyrus Butler, further inf. unattainable) 24 Cliff

THE CALIGRAPH WRITING MACHINE,
HARTFORD, CONN.

HOR 139 HOU

Horler & McGrath (James Horler & Thomas McGrath) 40 E. 19th
Hörmann, Schütte & Co. (Rudolph Hörmann & William Schütte, only) 102 Greene
Horn Silver Mining Co. (Allan C. Washington, Pres.; Ambrose I. Harrison, Sec. Capital, $10,000,000. Directors: Allan C. Washington, Bache McK. Whitlock, Andrew R. Culver, P. T. Farnsworth, F. W. Jennings, Ambrose I. Harrison, Theodore B. Moore, John Sharpe jr.) 52 B'way
Horn C. W. & Co. (Charles W. Horn & William B. Brown) 239 E. 115th
Horn R. & Son (Reinhold & Robinson Horn) 54 E. 4th
Horn & Callohan (George Horn & Dennie Callahan) 115 Cherry
Horn & Fanshaw (Alfred E. Horn & William A. Fanshaw) 811 E. 9th
Horn & Faulder (May T. Horn & William H. Faulder) 42 Dey
Hornblower & Byrne (William B. Hornblower, James Byrne & Howard A. Taylor) 280 B'way
Hornby Robert & Co. (Robert Hornby, Robert H. Kelly & Thomas Webster) 31 E. Houston
Horner R. J. & Co. (Robert J. Horner & Thomas I. Dirkin) 63 W. 23d
Horns John & Brother (John & Frederick Horns) 72 Washn. sq. S.
Hornthal, Noble & Co. (Joseph Hornthal, William J. Noble & Moses Hatch) 81 Bond & 829 B. 53d
Hornthal, Whitehead, Weissman & Co. (Lewis M. Hornthal, Leopold Weissman, William E. Lauer, Leopold M. Whitehead, Simon R. Riem, Edwin Whitehead & Joseph Benjamin) 670 B'way
Hornum Brothers (dissolved) 150 E. 125th
Horowitz & Blank (dissolved) 2 Bond
Horowitz & Jacobson (Samuel Horowitz & Jacob Jacobson) 290 Elizabeth
Horr & Roseman (dissolved) r 531 Fifth
Horre William & Co. (William Horre & Edwin V. Holden) 1 B'way
Horst Brothers (hops) (Paul R. G. & Louis A. & E. Clemens Horst—special partner. Frank Jones, *Portsmouth, N. H.*, $25,000; terminates 22d June, 1892) 45 Pearl
Horst Brothers (setters) (Otto G. & Rudolph F. Horst) 65 Nassau
Horstmann F. & Sons (Frederick & Frederick jr. & Albert Horstmann) 4 Hall pl.
Horstmann Brothers (Dederick & George H. Horstmann) 77 Cortlandt
Horstmann, Vonhein & Co. (Charles J. Horstmann, Otto Vonhein & Charles Willenborg) 25 Mercer
Horton J. M., Ice Cream Co. (James M. Horton, Pres.; Joseph A. Cozino, Sec.; John J. Frech, Treas. Capital, $40,000. Directors: John J. Frech, Chauncey E. Horton, Hugh Stewart, James M. Horton, Joseph A. Cozino) 305 Fourth av., 536 Sixth av. 115 Park row. 110 E. 125th, 142 W. 125th & 1219 Ninth av.
Horton G. B. & Co. (Gurdon B. Horton & John D. Ratcliff) 78 Gold
Horton H. L. & Co. (Harry L. Horton, Frederick T. Brown, J. Frank Emmons & Edwin P. Goodwin) 56 B'way
Horton J. W. & Son (John W. & William E. Horton) 195 Water
Horton W. A. & S. (dissolved) 622 Sixth av.
Hortou & Co. (Gurdon B. & Eugene Horton) 78 Gold
Horton & Durland (Seymour Horton & George L. Durland) 622 Sixth av.
Horton & Fitzsimons (Augustus A. Horton & Philip Fitzsimons) 529 B'way
Horton & Headley (William G. Horton & Elwood Headley) 44 Gold

Horton, Crary & Co. (Webb & Walter & George & Isaac Horton & Jerry & Horace H. Crary) 76 Gold
Horwitz & Hershfeld (Otto Horwitz & Abraham Hershfeld) 280 B'way
Horwood E. H. & Co. (Edward H. & Charlotte L. Horwood) 51 Mercer
Hosford Furniture Mfg. Co. (dissolved) 2263 Eighth av.
Hosford & Sons (Henry & J. Spencer Hosford, only) 56 Cedar
Hosmann & Co. (Christopher Hosmann & Charles Fleet) 63 Gansevoort
Hospital Supply Co. (Hamilton E. Smith, Pres.; Albert W. Bailey, Sec.; Benjamin A. Dare, Treas. Capital, $100,000. Trustees: Hamilton E. Smith, Benjamin A. Dare, Albert W. Bailey) 30 Dey
Hossfeld & Wierl (Anton Wierl, only) 39 Broad
Hostetter Co. (D. Herbert Hostetter, Pres.; Milton L. Myers, Sec. Directors: D. Herbert & T. R. Hostetter, Milton L. Myers) 72 John
Hotaling & Knox (Herbert D. Hotaling & Louis A. Knox) Williamsbridge
Hotchkiss George & Co. (Ltd.) (George Hotchkiss, Pres.; William C. Jessup, Sec. Capital, $5,000; further inf. refused) 100 Gansevoort & Manhattan mkt
Hotchkiss Guy C., Field & Co. (dissolved) 624 E. 104th
Hotchkiss Horace L. & Co. (Horace L. Hotchkiss, Harvey D. Rich & Allen F. Hedges) 36 Wall & 190 & 571 Fifth av.
Hotchkiss C. T. & Co. (dissolved) 97 Pine.
Hotchkiss W. F. & Co. (William F. Hotchkiss, no Co.) 1293 B'way
Hotchkiss & Co. (Georgiana I. Hotchkiss, no Co.) 31 B'way
Hotchkiss & Reiley (Charles E. Hotchkiss & De Witt V. D. Reiley) 88 Park row
Hotel Bartholdi Co. (Robert Stafford, Pres.; H. Prescott Whittaker, Sec. Capital, $50,000. Directors: Robert Stafford, H. Prescott Whittaker, W. C. Hall) 956 B'way
Hotel Mail Publishing Co. (David M. Thayer, Pres.; Albert J. Leader, Sec. Capital, $20,000. Directors: David N. Thayer, Albert J. Leader) 89 Nassau
Hotel Register & Directory Publishing Co. (J. Legare Harrison, propr.) 7 Warren
Hotkies & Segall (dissolved) 147 Eldridge
Hotopp & Co. (William & Henry Hotopp & William F. Braun) 407 Canal
Hotze & Scharninghausen (dissolved) 81 Lispenard
Houchin Mfg. Co. (Thomas W. Houchin, Pres., Charles B. Riker, Sec.; Joseph C. Fegan, Treas. Capital, $100,000. Directors: Thomas W. Houchin, Edward J. Murray, Charles B. Riker, Joseph C. Fegan) 67 Park pl. & 746 E. 160th
Houghton E. W. (Edwin W. Houghton:—special partner, Catharine A. Beekman), $10,000; terminates 6th Sept. 1892) 101 Bleecker
Houghton, Mifflin & Co. (Henry O. Houghton, George H. Mifflin, Lawson Valentine, James M. Kay, Thurlow W. Barnes & Henry O. Houghton jr.) 11 E. 17th
Housatonic Brass Co. (Judson B. Underwood, Pres.; David L. Durand, Sec. Capital, $10,000. Directors: Judson B. Underwood, David L. Durand) 44 Park pl.
Housatonic Line (Housatonic R.R. Co. & N. E. Terminal Co. proprs.) 36 Wall, 266 South & Pier 49 E. R.
Housatonic R. R. Co. (William H. Starbuck, Pres.; Moad E. Stone, Sec. Capital, $3,000,000. Directors: William H. Starbuck, John L. Macaulay, Henry Hentz, Thomas Ratter, William H. Stevenson, S. E. Merwin, Phineas

C. Lounsbury, A. B. Myatt, William E. Downes) 30 Wall

House Corset Machinery Co. (James Alford House, Pres.; Emile H. Roth, Sec. Capital, $60,000. Directors: James Alford House, Emile H. Roth, Charles H. Dimond) 10 Walker

House Dr., N. Y. Elastic Truss Co. (George V. House, Pres.; Joseph A. House, Sec.; George V. House jr. Treas. Capital, $10,000. Trustees: George V. & Joseph A. & George V. House jr.) 744 B'way

Household Specialty Co. (Elkins & Zorbs, proprs.) 263 B'way

Household Utensil Mfg. Co. (inf. unattainable) 194 Front

Housewife Publishing Co. (inf. unattainable) 111 Nassau

Houston D. & Co. (David & Robert J. Houston) 22 Platt

Houston & Steinle (Thomas Houston & Frederick Steinle jr) 771 Sixth av.

Houston & Texas Central R. R. Co. (Charles Dillingham, Pres.; Horace Hall, Sec.; E. W. Cave, Treas. Capital, $10,000,000; further inf. unattainable) 29 Broad

Houston, West St. & Pavonia Ferry R. R. Co. (Daniel S. Lamont, Pres.; Daniel B. Hasbrouck, Sec. Capital, $250,000. Directors: Daniel S. Lamont, Henry Thompson, Daniel B. Hasbrouck, Thomas F. Ryan, William L. Elkins, Peter A. B. Widener, Charles E. Warren) 415 E. 10th

Hovey A. H. & Co. (no inf.) 29 Wall

How Hall J. & Co. (Hall J. How & Thomas S. Walker) 171 B'way

Howard Cutlery Co. (H. Herbert Howard, propr.) 65 E. 9th

Howard Ins. Co. (in liquidation) 56 Wall

Howard Mendel & Co. (Mendel Howard, no Co.) 26 Church

Howard C. N. & Co. (Charles N. Howard & Christian Christiansen) 141 Reade

Howard Brothers (Joseph B. & James Howard) 81 South

Howard & Childs (Robert H. Howard & Childs H. Childs) 522 W. 33d

Howard & Cockshaw (John T. Howard jr. & Herbert Cockshaw) 857 B'way

Howard & Co. (Joseph P. Howard, Pres.; Edward S. Newell, Sec. Capital, $500,000; further inf. refused) 264 Fifth av.

Howard & Morse (John W. Howard & David R. Morse) 45 Fulton

Howard & Son (Hiram & Stephen C. Howard) 176 B'way

Howard Brothers & Co. (Louis B. & William C. Howard, Robert H. Kellock & Walter C. Thompson) 19 Mercer

Howard's Detective Bureau (inf. unattainable) 7 W. 14th

Howe Frederick C. & Brother (Frederick C. & Charles T. Howe) 78 Hudson

Howe Insulated Wire & Cable Co. (no inf.) 198 B'way & 80 Cliff

Howe National Baking Co. (J. S. Purdy & Sons, proprs.) 1888, 1990, 2196 & 2890 Third av.

Howe National Baking Co. (Patrick C. Duffy, propr.) 302 Tenth av.

Howe National Baking Co. (Peter E. Henderson, propr.) 745 Third av. & 695 & 1126 Second av.

Howe J. D. & Co. (no inf.) 1278 B'way

Howe R. S. & Co. (Roble S. Howe, no Co.) 63 B'way

Howe S. L. & C. C. (refused) 1155 Ninth av.

Howe Brothers (Michael & Patrick Howe) St. Nicholas av. n W. 160th

Howe & Rummel (William F. Howe & Abraham H. Hummel) 89 Centre

Howe & Yasinski (dissolved) 2195½ Third av.

Howe, Balch & Co. (Lemuel R. Howe, Arthur S. Balch & Walter L. Bailey) 77 Water

Howe, Balch & Tay (dissolved) 77 Water

Howell Cold Air Refrigerating Co. (Capital, $30,000; further inf. unattainable) no address

Howell Condensed Milk & Cream Co. (James A. Howell. Pres.; Mark A. Howell, Treas. Capital, $100,000; further inf. unattainable) 205 E. 27th

Howell Mfg. Co. (D. B. Howell & Co. proprs.) 869 Broome

Howell Mining Co. (inf. unattainable) 102 Chambers

Howell B. H., Son & Co. (Benjamin H. & Thomas A. & Frederick H. & Henry B. Howell & James H. Post) 109 Wall & 254 Front

Howell D. B. & Co. (David B. Howell, no Co.) 520 Broome

Howell T. P. & Co. (Alfred Jenkins, Pres.; Samuel C. Howell, Sec.; Henry C. Howell, Treas. Capital, $800,000. Directors: Alfred Jenkins, Henry C. & Samuel C. Howell, William Clark, H. N. Conger) 77 Beekman

Howell & Co. (Josiah P. Howell & Irving L. Dragdon) 68 B'way

Howell & Demarest (Coe H. Howell & Frank P. Demarest) 6 Jeff. mkt

Howell & Vangelderen (Joseph Howell & Abraham Vangelderen) 307 Washn. mkt

Howell's M. H. Sons (Henry M. & Frank & William Howell) 309 W. 11th

Howells H. C. & Co. (Henry Crilk Howells, no Co.) 519 B'way & 94 Mercer

Howes Franklin & Son (Franklin & J. Lawrence Howes) 750 B'way

Howes & Williams (Benjamin Howes & William Williams) 62 Fulton

Howland Brothers (Theodore & George W. Howland) 52 South

Howland & Aspinwall (Lloyd Aspinwall & Marquis C. Gasper, only) 54 South

Howland & Lein (George W. Howland & Henry W. Lein) 102 W. 46th

Howser's J. C., Son (John B. Howser) 7 Charles

Howson & Howson (Charles & Henry & Hubert Howson) 38 Park row

Hoym & Ahrens (Paul E. Hoym & Frederick H. Ahrens) 501 G'wich

Hoyt Paper Tube Co. (Terence P. Ford, propr.) 95 Liberty

Hoyt William H. & Co. (William H. Hoyt, no Co.) 5 Vanderbilt av.

Hoyt A. E. & Co. (Adelbert E. & Charles H. Hoyt) 21 E. 42d

Hoyt A. M. & Co. (Alfred M. Hoyt & James W. Jackson) 1 B'way

Hoyt H. L. & Co. (Hazen L. Hoyt & Mark M. Stanfield) 4 W. 27th

Hoyt Brothers (William & Mark Hoyt) 72 Gold

Hoyt & Co. (Joseph A. Hoyt & William C. Cartwall) 187 B'way

Hoyt & Schell (James Otis Hoyt & Edward H. Schell) 158 B'way

Hoyt & Thomas (Charles H. Hoyt & Charles W. Thomas) 1164 B'way

Hoyt, Talcott & Co. (dissolved) 187 B'way

Hraba & Hopfensack (Louis W. Hraba & Barbara Hopfensack) 95 W. B'way

Huachuca Water Co. (Charles H. Stone, Pres.; Hugh Porter, Sec. Capital, $1,000,000; further inf. unattainable) 11 Pine

Hub Publishing Co. (Charles B. Beckwith, Pres.; John H. Eggers, Treas.; L. Fairbanks, Sec. Capital, $30,000. Directors: Charles B. Beckwith, John H. Eggers, George F. Swain, L. Fairbanks, George W. W. Houghton) 6 Barclay

FOR THE BEST CO-PARTNERSHIP IN THE BEST CORPORATION SEE PAGE F IN BACK OF BOOK

Hubbard Charles & Co. (Charles & Charles D. Hubbard) 46 Cliff
Hubbard G. W. & Co. (James S. Burroughs, only) 58 Pine
Hubbard & Rushmore (no inf.) 52 B'way
Hubbard, Price & Co. (Samuel T. Hubbard jr. Theodore H. Price & Walter C. Hubbard) Cotton Ex.
Hubbel & Schermerhorn (John H. Hubbel & Otis T. Schermerhorn) 623 W. 56th & 601 W. 53d
Hubbell Legal Directory Co. (John H. Hubbell, Pres.; Edward S. Terry, Sec. Capital, $50,000; further inf. unattainable) 317 B'way
Hubbell J. H. & Co. (John H. Hubbell, no Co.) 317 B'way
Hubbell & Randall (Frank D. Hubbell & Darley Randall) 80 Reade
Huber Dr., Dry Cell Pocket Battery Co. (inf. unattainable) 88 Fifth av.
Huber Henry & Co. (Henry Huber & Adolph C. Tiedemann) 81 Beekman & 481 E. 136th
Huber Brothers (dissolved) 511 W. 29th
Huber & Rengler (Amelia Huber & Herman Bengler) 62 G'wich
Huber & Schaerr (Charles Huber & Amelia Schaerr) 200 William
Huber & Betz (dissolved) ft. E. 79th
Hubert Apartment Ass'n (Lemuel Skidmore, Pres.; John Elderkin, Sec. Capital, $85,925. Trustees: Frank W. Kitching, John C. Mott, Willard Parsons, Dwight W. Tryon, John Elderkin, Lemuel Skidmore) 118 Warren & 230 W. 55th
Hubert, Pirsson & Hoddick (Philip G. Hubert & August O. Hoddick, only) 19 E. 28th
Huchting & Katt (John W. Huchting & Frederick B. Katt) 342 Canal
Hudnut's R., Pharmacy (James T. White, Pres.; Richard A. Hudnut, Sec. Capital, $25,000. Trustees: James T. White, Richard A. Hudnut, Andrew J. White) 925 B'way
Hudson Connecting R. R. Co. (dissolved) 115 B'way
Hudson Ice Co. (Herman Ropke, propr.) 180 Franklin
Hudson River Bank (William De Groot, Pres.; Peter Snyder, Cashier; William H. Fock, Notary. Capital, $200,000. Directors: William A. Nash, George A. Morrison, Joseph H. Parsons, H. Walter Webb, Charles L. Aokol, B. Aymar Sands, William De Groot, Ira Barsley, Bradish Johnson jr. Charles T. Barney, John W. Aitken, W. D. Ellis, Thomas A. McIntyre, William R. Peters) 1183 Ninth av.
Hudson River Reef Co. (Ltd.) (Thomas H. Wheeler, Pres.; Charles M. Webber, Sec.; Walter H. Wheeler, Treas. Capital, $10,000; further inf. unattainable) ft. W. 132d
Hudson River Blue Stone Co. (dissolved) 137 B'way
Hudson River Boot & Shoe Mfg Co. (Eugene N. Howell, Pres.; Leonard D. Christie, Sec. Capital, $300,000; further inf. unattainable) 116 Duane
Hudson River Broken Stone & Supply Co. (inf. unattainable) 41 Park row
Hudson River Building Co. (Everett D. Barlow, Pres.; George W. Schooley, Sec.; Sophia M. Hayward, Treas. Capital, $100,000. Directors: Everett D. Barlow, George W. Schooley, S. M. Hayward, William Hazen) 206 B'way
Hudson River Line (Alfred Vansantvoord, Pres.; Charles T. Vansantvoord, Treas. Capital, $125,000. Directors: Albert & Charles T. Vansantvoord, H. P. Farrington) 120 B'way & ft. Vestry
Hudson River Ore & Iron Co. (Howard H. Burden, Pres.; Henry M. Olmsted, Sec. Capital, $1,500,000; further inf. unattainable) 21 Cortlandt
Hudson River Telephone Co. (Joseph P. Davis, Pres.; Henry L. Storke, Sec. Capital, $2,000,000; further inf. unattainable) 18 Cortlandt

Hudson River & Maine Ice Co. (inf. unattainable) 385 Front
Hudson Suspension Bridge & New England Railway Co. (Edward W. Serrell, Pres.; George O. Bunch, Sec.; William G. Ladd, Treas. Capital, $10,000,000; further inf. unattainable) 38 Wall
Hudson Tunnel Construction Co. (inf. unattainable) ft. Morton
Hudson Tunnel Railway Co. (William M. Force. V. Pres.; Henry S. White, Sec. Capital, $10,000,000. Directors: William M. Force, Henry S. White, Frank P. Abbot, Charles Sooysmith, Albert B. Gibbs) 2 Nassau
Hudson Wagon Co. (Ezra Brown, propr.) 542 Hudson & 107 Charles
Hudson C. I. & Co. (Charles I. Hudson & Albert H. De Forest) 36 Wall & 945 B'way
Hudson & Co. (dissolved) 23 Park row
Hudspeth & Bruns (Robert S. Hudspeth & Werner Bruns) 243 B'way
Huebner D. & Son (Balthasar & Louis Huebner) 188 Second
Huebsch S. & D. (Samuel & Daniel) 820 Pearl
Huebsch & Sternberg (Morris Huebsch & Simon Sternberg) 2010 Third av.
Huebschmann Brothers (Morris J. & Jacob Huebschmann) 90 Cannon
Hueg Mary L. & Son (Mary L. & William Hueg) 407 First av.
Huesmann & Co. (Francis & Louis A. Huesmann) 83 Maiden la.
Hueston & Brother (Thomas & William F. Hueston) B'way c Lawrence
Huether & Co. (George Huether, Charles E. Duttsch & Charles Jonaoh) 120 William
Huffman Theodore P. & Co. (Theodore P. Huffman, no Co.) 649 W. 34th
Hufnagel & Sauer (Philip Hufnagel & John Sauer) 819 Bleecker
Hug & Boscowitz (Herman Hug & Charles M. Boscowitz) 58 Day
Higgins James & Brother (James & Joseph D. Higgins) 14 Warren
Higgins N. & S. J. (Nathaniel & Samuel J.) 129 Chambers
Hughes Yacht Agency (Owen L. Hughes, propr.) 34 New
Hughes B. G. & Brother (Brian G. & Hugh Hughes) 242 Centre
Hughes G. F. & Co. (George F. & William Hughes) 61 Leonard
Hughes H. & Co. (Henry Hughes & Joseph Goldstein) 24 New Bowery & 26 Chestnut
Hughes M. & R. (Raphael Hughes, only) 218 W. 40th
Hughes W. & Brother (dissolved) 24 New Bowery
Hughes Brothers (carpenters) (Frank J. & James F. Hughes) 2 W. 22d
Hughes Brothers (liquors) (Peter A. & Thomas J. & James J. Hughes) 2648 Third av. 688 S. Boulevard, 488 College av. & 421 Willis av.
Hughes Brothers (machinists) (Charles D. & Jesse G. & Theodore A. Hughes) 75 Frankfort
Hughes & Brother (Hugh & James Hughes) 14 Manhattan mkt
Hughes & Campbell (William D. Hughes & Patrick A. Campbell) 320 B'way
Hughes & Co. (Charles Hughes, no Co.) 1516 First av.
Hughes & Halladay (dissolved) 54 Fourth av.
Hughes & McLindon (James Hughes & Alexander McLindon) 211 Av. C
Hughes & McMahon (John Hughes & Bernard McMahon) 27 Ninth av. & 1406 Second av.
Hughes & Ross (James W. Hughes & William O. Ross) 47 B'way

TYPEWRITING DONE BY THE TROW CITY DIRECTORY CO., 11 University Place.

HUG 142 HUR

Hughes & Scanlon (James Hughes & Edward J. Scanlon) Av. A c E. 67th
Hughes' John, Sons (Peter F. & John M. & Thomas F. Hughes) 206 E. 12th
Hughson & Oudin (no inf.) 227 Canal
Huhn Brothers (Damian & Marcus Huhn) 1162 Second av.
Hulbert H. C. & Co. (Henry C. Hulbert & Joseph H. Sutphin) 53 Beekman
Hull C. R. & Co. (refused) 18 Cedar
Hull S. G. & Son (Samuel G. & William S. Hull) 391 Hudson
Hull W. H. H. & Co. (William E. H. Hull, Kossuth E. Bunnell & Charles G. Daus) 154 Nassau
Hull & Doorman (Henry Hull & Peter H. Doorman) 155 Seventh av.
Hull, Grippen & Co. (Belden J. Rogers, only) 310 Third av.
Hulse G. O. & L. S. (Gilbert O. & Levi S.) 120 B'way
Humason & Beckley Mfg. Co. (William L. Humason, Pres.; Harvey E. Case, Sec.; Virgil P. Humason, Treas. Capital, $ 65,000. Directors: William L. & Virgil P. Humason, Frank W. Beckley, Harvey E. Case, Morton C. Swift) 80 Chambers
Humberg W. G. & Co. (William G. Humberg & Philip Simon) 124 Greene
Humbert E. C. & Son (Elias C. & John J. C. Humbert) 74 B'way
Humbert N. & Co. (Nicholas Humbert & Jacob Cottick) 259 Bowery
Humbert & Wick (Theodore Humbert & Robert Wick) 151 Eleventh av.
Humbert, Hopkins & Bickley (William P. Humbert, Allison R. Hopkins & Lawrence W. Bickley) 40 Wall
Humble & Oaten (no inf.) 210 W. 51st
Hume A. W. & T. (dissolved) 459 Fifth av.
Hume & Mullen (James H. Hume & Andrew Mullen) ft. W. 59th
Hume & Weed (dissolved) r 48 Centre
Humfreville & Co. (dissolved) 47 B'way
Hummel Adam & Son (Adam & Henry Hummel) 145 E. Houston
Hummel J. M. & Son (John M. & Jacob C. Hummel) 90 Gold
Hummel & Steinmiller (Frederick P. Hummel & George A. Steinmiller) 444 E. 86th
Humphrey J. A., Son & Coe (Jeffrey A. & George G. Humphrey & James H. Coe) 76 Franklin
Humphrey W. M. & Co. (Sarah F. L. Taylor & estate of William M. Humphrey) 614 Madison av.
Humphreys & Co. (George W. Humphreys & Horace S. Godsoe) 657 Sixth av.
Humphreys & Sayce (George H. Humphreys & Montford P. Sayce) 10 Wall
Humphreys' Homoeopathic Medicine Co. (Frederick Humphreys, Pres.; Frederick H. Humphreys, Sec. Capital, $500,000. Directors: Frederick & Frederick H. & Frank L. Humphreys) 109 Fulton
Hundt & Puckhafer (Joseph Hundt & Charles Puckhafer) 343 G'wich
Huner John T. & Co. (dissolved) 174 Duane
Huner & Co. (inf. unattainable) r 505 W. 36th
Hungaria Publishing Co. (no inf.) 27 Centre
Hungerford Co. (George R. Hillier, Pres.; Frank P. Vansaun, Sec. Capital, $15,000. Directors: George R Hillier, Frank P. Vansaun, George S. Hungerford) 122 Broad
Hungerford & Martin (Theodore A. Hungerford & John Martin) 907 B'way
Hunningsen F. L. & Co. (dissolved) 275 Canal
Hunninghaus & Lindemann (Frederick L. Hunninghaus & Carl Lindemann) 245 Canal

Hunold & Faerber (John Hunold & Francis Faerber) 932 Sixth av.
Hunsicker Jacob & Co. (Jacob Hunsicker & Alexander Kaiser) 211 E. 4th
Hunt C. W., Co. (Charles W. Hunt, Pres.; John Allen, Sec.; George M. Luther, Treas. Capital, $94,000. Directors: Charles W. Hunt, George M. Luther, John Allen, John M. Blake, Charles C. King) 45 B'way
Hunt David & Co. (David & George W. Hunt) 150 Reade
Hunt Publishing Co. (inf. unattainable) 24 Beekman
Hunt Robert W. & Co. (Robert W. Hunt, George W. G. Ferris, Frank C. Osborn, John J. Cone & James C. Hallsted) 171 B'way
Hunt F. W. & Son (Francis W. & Charles F. Hunt) 69 Beekman
Hunt J. B. & Co. (James B. Hunt, no Co.) 272 Wash'n.
Hunt L. K. & Son (dissolved) 104 E. 28th
Hunt & Co. (William H. & Caroline O. Hunt) 1481 & 1616 Third av. & 435 E. 92d
Hunt & Dusenbury (James Hunt, only) 7 Astor h.
Hunt & Eaton (Sandford Hunt & Homer Eaton) 150 Fifth av.
Hunt & Fuller (George W. Hunt & Hugh E. Fuller) 78 Nassau
Hunt & Gregorius (Charles E. Hunt & George Gregorius) 437 Eighth av. & 259 First av.
Hunt & Leach (Richard R. Hunt & Adam C. Leach) 41 Beaver
Hunt & Voorhees (Josiah C. Hunt & John N. Voorhees) 179 Reade
Hunter Iron Works (T. & J. Hunter, propr's.) 419 E. 91st
Hunter T. & J. (Thomas & James) 419 E. 91st
Hunter T. F. & Co. (Theodore F. Hunter & Henry C. Willis) 33 Church
Hunter & Co. (John B. Hunter & Theodore Spencer) 155 Chambers
Hunter & Eyre (dissolved) 64 B'way & 131 William
Hunter & Wiener (Robert B. Hunter & Clarence B. Wiener) 41 Park row
Hunter, Walton & Co. (John J. Walton, Alexander D. Marks & Thomas A. Somerville, only) 104 Chambers
Hunting S. T. & Co. (Sinclair T. Hunting & Peter H. S. Vandervoort) 985 B'way
Hunting & Hammond (David S. Hammond & estate of Nathaniel L. Hunting) 112 Park av.
Huntingdon Mfg. Co. (George W. Dithridge, Pres.; James T. Goodfellow, Sec.; M. M. Bartholomew, Treas. Capital, $200,000. Trustees: George W. Dithridge, M. M. Bartholomew, E. J. Gardner, James T. Goodfellow) 120 B'way
Huntington Co. (no inf.) 81 Nassau
Huntington & Dorn (Charles P. Huntington, only) 108 Front
Huntington Brothers & Co. (Byron O. Huntington only) 398 Canal
Huntley E. A. & Co. (Edwin A. Huntley & William S. Stone) 187 Wash'n.
Huntoon M. & J. B. (Moses & John B.) 154 Jane
Hunsinger George & Son (George & George Hunsinger jr.) 328 W. 16th
Häpfel J. Christian G., Brewing Co. (J. Christian G. Höpfel, Pres.; Philip Hartenfels, Sec. Capital, $500,000. Directors: J. Christian G. Höpfel, Philip Hartenfels, Michael Fleck, Jacob Vix, Charles Nette) 229 E. 38th
Höpfel's A., Sons (Adolph G. Höpfel, only) St. Anne av. c E. 101st
Hurd George B. & Co. (George B. & Frank B. Hurd) 79 Beekman
Hurlbut W. W. & Co. (William W. Hurlbut & James R. Hall) 135 Pearl

THADDEUS DAVIDS CO., WRITING INKS, SEALING WAX, MUCILAGE.
MAKE THE BEST

HUR 143 HYM

Hurlbut Brothers (William P. & Henry A. Hurlbut jr.) 2452 Third av.
Hurlbut, Shethar & Sanford (William H. Hurlbut, Edwin H. Shethar & Charles G. Sanford) 737 B'way
Hurley Stone Co. (inf. unattainable) 1 B'way
Hurley & Duncan (Joseph B. Hurley & Adam Duncan) 169 Chambers
Hurst & Co. (Thomas D. Hurst, no Co.) 122 Nassau
Hurst & Tremor (dissolved) 547 W. 45th
Hurtado & Co. (in liquidation) 16 Exchange pl.
Hurwitz & Faine (dissolved) 68 E. D'way
Huser J. C. & Brother (John C. & Behrend W. Huser) 100 Duane
Huss & Brother (Charles & Henry Huss) 22 Harrison
Hussa & Co. (Jaroslav Hussa & A. Eugene Crosbie) 27 William
Hussey Battery Co. (A. E. Paillard, Pres.; further inf. unattainable) 144 G'wich
Hussey Re Heater & Steam Plant Improvement Co. (inf. unattainable) 15 Cortlandt
Hussey & Co. (Erwin A. Hussey & Harry Gay) 66 B'way & 19 New
Hussey's Special Message Express (Robert Easson, propr.) 61 Pine
Huston H. E. & Co. (Harvey E. Huston:—special partner, Joseph C. Everett, *Norfolk*, *Va*., $10,000; terminates 1st Sept. 1890) 67 Cotton Ex.
Huston & Corbitt (Adam Huston & James R. Corbitt) 909 Sixth av. & 406 W. 52d
Hutcheson & Bethel (Anna B. & Willis A. Hutcheson, only) 100 Front
Hutchings & Brother (William B. & Edward E. Hutchings) 96 South
Hutchins & Platt (Waldo & Augustus S. & Waldo Hutchins jr., only) 69 Wall
Hutchinson John & Son (John A. & John A. Hutchinson jr.) 840 E. 12th
Hutchinson John W. (John William Hutchinson; —special partners, John J. & Lewis H. Lapham, *each* $25,000; terminates 1st March, 1895) 173 Eighth av.
Hutchinson W. H. & Son (George O. & Charles G. Hutchinson, only) 99 Park pl.
Hutchinson & Co. (Samuel & Joseph Hutchinson) 184 Tenth av.
Hutchinson, Pierce & Co. (Gardiner S. Hutchinson, Henry B. Pierce, Ira Cole & Thomas J. Morison) 833 B'way
Huth & Kolm (Gustav Huth & Julius Kolm) 7 Second av.
Hutson G. & R. (George & Robert) 214 West
Huyck & Boswell (Minna S. Huyck & Helen V. Boswell) 13 Park row
Huyler's (John S. Huyler, Pres.; Charles J. Coulter, Treas. Directors: John S. Huyler, B. Frank De Klyn, Charles J. Coulter) 64 Irving pl. 150 & 863 B'way & 21 W. 42d
Hyams Misses (Leah & Rose Hyams) 16 Sixth av. & 350 Grand
Hyams William & Co. (William & Edward Hyams & Frank Pauson) 594 B'way & 124 Crosby
Hyams D. & Co. (David & Henry M. Hyams) 274 G'wich
Hyams J. & A. (dissolved) 16½ Carmine
Hyams M. & L. (Malvina & Lillie) 6 Av. C
Hyams Brothers (Albert & Samuel Hyams) 398 Third av.
Hyams & Myers (Benjamin Hyams & Frank Myers) 162 Pearl
Hyams & Schyf (Samuel Hyams & John Schyf) 102 W. Houston
Hyatt Co. (Edward H. Balley, Treas. Capital, $10,000; further inf. unattainable) 278 Canal

Hyatt Heights Land Office (Charles H. Goodsell, propr.) 47 Liberty
Hyatt Pure Water Co. (John W. Hyatt, Pres.; Orrin N. Baldwin, Sec.; David Blake, Treas. Capital, $500,000. Directors: John W. Hyatt, Orrin N. Baldwin, David Blake, John D. Harrison, Peter Kinnear, S. C. Westervelt) 18 Cortlandt
Hyatt S. G. & Co. (Stiles G. Hyatt & Noah S. Barnam) 1675 B'way
Hyatt & Darke (Charles E. Hyatt & B. Danby Darke) 68 D'way
Hyde Henry G. & Co. (Henry G. Hyde & Mark Foley) 174 B'way
Hyde A. G. & Sons (Albert G. & Seymour J. & Albert F. Hyde) 354 B'way
Hyde & Behman (Richard Hyde & Louis C. Behman) 1331 B'way
Hyde & Co. (dissolved) 48 Exchange pl.
Hyde & Robinson (dissolved) 206 W. 125th
Hyde & Wylie (William T. Hyde & Duncan S. Wylie) 60 B'way
Hyde's John E. Sons (Jonathan L. Hyde, only) 22 Maiden la.
Hydraulic Tube Well Construction Co. (inf. unattainable) 145 B'way
Hydraulic & Sanitary Plumber Publishing Co. (Ltd.) (John Byrns, Pres.; Edward Murphy, Sec.; Henry G. Gabay, Treas. Capital, $2,500. Directors: George D. Scott, John McCarron, William Young, Edward J. Brady, John Byrns, Henry G. Gabay, Edward Murphy) 24 Park row
Hydro-Carbon Gas & Fuel Co. (John J. Gorman, Pres.; Jesse W. Shepard, Sec. Capital, $500,000. Trustees: John J. Gorman, Jesse W. Shepard, Henry A. Bradley) 2 W. 14th
Hydro-Pneumatic Pump Co. (John H. Morrison, Pres.; Henry J. La Marche, Sec.; Frank H. Morrison, Treas. Capital, $10,000. Directors: John H. Morrison, Henry J. & Mathew J. La Marche, George B. Cullingworth) 101 Walker
Hydrogen Co. (of N. J.) (William J. Roe, Pres.; Cortlandt Parker jr., Sec.; Benjamin H. Franklin, Treas. Capital, $2,000,000. Directors: William J. Roe, R. Wayne Parker, Ethan Allen, Henry W. Levey, Benjamin H. Franklin, B. Franklin Clark, A. D. Stevens, W. H. Grenelle, Sidney De Kay, A. D. Palmer, Louis S. Phillips, Frederick W. Hadfield, Cortlandt Parker jr.) 85 B'way
Hydrogen Co. (of U. S.) (Henry E. Alexander, Pres.; Sidney De Kay, Sec. Capital, $2,000,000. Trustees: William H. Arnoux, Henry E. Alexander, Edward A. Pearson, Sidney De Kay, Joseph Pearson Gill) 115 D'way
Hydrogen Heater Co. (not inc.; further inf. unattainable) 102 B'way
Hydromass Mfg. Co. (inf. unattainable) 417 W. 24th
Hygeia Sparkling Distilled Water Co. (Edwin A. McAlpin, Pres.; Dudley B. Fuller, Sec. Capital, $150,000. Directors: Edwin A. McAlpin, Warren E. Dennis, R. Fulton Cutting, Dudley B. Fuller) 351 W. 14th
Hyland & Blackburn (Thomas A. Hyland & Andrew J. Blackburn) 89 W. Houston
Hyland & Meehan (Thomas F. Hyland & Patrick Meehan) 102 Centre
Hyland & Zabriskie (Josiah A. Hyland & Nelson Zabriskie) 45 B'way
Hyman Jacob & Son (Jacob Hyman & Leon Krieger, only) 25 Beekman
Hyman C. M. & Co. (Charles M. Hyman, no Co.) 100 Walker
Hyman & Baruch (dissolved) 375 Broome
Hyman & Meyers (Rose Hyman & Henry Meyers) 86 Worth & 564 W. 38th
Hyman & Spitz (dissolved) 43 Centre

Hyman, Stiner & Co. (Moses Hyman, Samuel Stiner & Abraham Goodkind) 25 E. Houston
Hyman's A., Son (refused) 149 Bowery
Hymes & Cohn (dissolved) 611 B'way
Hymes, Brother & Co. (dissolved) 329 B'way
Hyneman & Schmidt (Julius Hyneman & Alfred Schmidt) 548 Pearl
Hynes Peter & Son (Peter & Peter H. Hynes) 278 Seventh av.
Hynes T. W. & Co. (Thomas W. Hynes & Lorenzo Cutler) 991 B'way
Hynes & Hagerty (James Hynes & James Hagerty) 1737 Second av.

I

Ilu Brothers (dissolved) 36 Grand
Idaho Mining & Irrigation Co. (Charles H. Tompkins, Pres.; Lewis F. Bostelmann, Sec. Capital, $5,000,000. Directors: Charles H. Tompkins, Lewis F. Bostelmann, Burton N. Harrison) 15 Cortlandt
Ide George P. & Co. (George P. & James M. & Alba N. Ide & Frank B. Twining) 105 Franklin
Ideal Pen Co. (Lewis E. Waterman, propr.) 155 B'way
Iden & Co. (Henry Iden, no Co.) 26 University pl. (see head lines & adv. in back)
Identification Assn. (Jacob E. Bloom, Pres.; A Congreve, Sec.; further inf. unattainable) 104 B'way
Identification Card Co. (George H. Ward, Pres., George Brush, Sec. Capital, $10,000. Trustees: George H. Ward, Paul Fuller, George Brush) 30 Union sq. E.
Igniting Apparatus Co. (J. Spencer Smith, Pres.; Gilbert H. Tuthill, Treas.; James H. Ash, Sec. Directors; J. Spencer Smith, Gilbert H. Tuthill, James H. Ash) 6 Harrison
Ihlenburg & Son (Frederick & Edward A. Ihlenburg) 510 E. 76th
Ijams & Story (John T. Ijams & William C. Story) 69 Worth
Ilfelder D. & Co. (Leopold & Max Ilfelder & Sigmund Levy, only) 534 B'way
Illg & Howard (Gustave Illg & George Howard) 6 E. 14th
Illinois Beef Co. (Schatzman & Steiniger, proprs.) 1070 First av.
Illinois Central R. R. Co. (inf. unattainable) 214 B'way
Illinois Steel Co. (Jay C. Morse, Pres.; J. C. Stirling, Treas.; D. W. Perkins, Sec. Capital, $25,000,000. Directors: Orrin W. Potter, William J. Rolen, Edward C. Potter, Nathaniel Thayer, Francis Bartlett, H. H. Porter, William R. Stirling, Norman Williams, Jay C. Morse, A. J. Forbes Leith) 44 Wall
Illinois Watch Co. (Jacob Bunn, Pres.; George A. Bates, Sec. Directors: Jacob Bunn, George A. Bates, Jacob Bunn jr.) 11 John
Illuminated Sign Co. (no inf.) 5 Dey
Illustrated Am. Publishing Co. (Lorillard Spencer, Pres.; William Augustus Spencer, Treas.; Maurice M. Minton, Sec. Capital, $100,000. Directors: Lorillard & William Augustus Spencer, Maurice M. Minton, Andrew H. Mickle, Philip S. Minton) Bible h.
Illustrated Associated Press (no inf.) 73 Park row
Illustrative Press Bureau (John Filmer & Son, proprs.) 318 B'way
Ilsley S. A. & Co. (Silas A. & Stillman Ilsley) 173 Pearl
Ilsley, Doubleday & Co. (William C. Ilsley & Chester P. & Edwin S. Doubleday) 229 Front & 21 to Third av.
Imandt & Forger (Christian Imandt & William Forger) 550 Eighth av.

Imatara Iron Co. (George Turnbull, propr.) 81 B'way
Imbrie William Morris & Co. (William Morris Imbrie & Robert T. Currie) 56 B'way
Immediate Transp. Co. (Ltd.) (inf. unattainable) 12 B'way
Immich Brothers (William A. Immich, only) 662 Sixth av.
Imperial Chemical Mfg. Co. (inf. unattainable) 54 W. 23d
Imperial Life Ins. Co. (no inf.) 42 Wall
Imperial Medicated Rubber Co. (Abraham S. Jessarun, propr.) 25 White
Imperial Suspender Co. (Morris Brothers, proprs.) 277 Church
Imperial Type Writer Co. (Paschal R. Smith, Pres.; Ambrose S. Lynch, Sec.; Herbert Parsons, Treas. Capital, $250,000. Directors: Paschal R. Smith, Ambrose S. Lynch, Herbert Parsons, William Cahoon jr. Edward L. Le Fevre) 40 B'way
Impervious Paper Co. (Capital, $3,000; further inf. unattainable) no address
Importers' & Grocers' Exchange (in liquidation) 107 Water
Importers' & Traders' National Bank (Edward H. Perkins jr. Pres.; Edward Townsend, Cashier, Randolph W. Townsend, Notary. Capital, $1,500,000. Directors: Edward H. Ammidown, John Arbuckle, Julius Catlin, Henry C Hulbert, Isaac Ickelheimer, Edward A. Price, James R. Plum, Edward H. Perkins jr. Edward C. Rice, Russell Sage, Randolph W. & Edward Townsend, Horace K. Thurber, Edward Van Volkenburgh, Antony Wallach) 247 B'way
Importers' & Traders' Tea Co. (Hanly & Glynn, proprs.) 59 Whitehall
Improved Edible Nut Co. (inf. unattainable) 529 B'way
Improved Hat Blocking & Drying Co. (William H. Kendall, Pres.; Morris C. Lichten, Sec. Capital, $50,000. Directors: William H. & J. L. Kendall, J. Heimann S. Wolf, Morris C. Lichten) 632 B'way & 60 Wooster
Improved Horse Shoe Co. (William Duffy, Pres.; George G. Herriot, Sec. Capital, $500,000. Trustees: William Duffy, Charles A. Jenney, George G. Herriot, Adrian G. Hegeman) 58 William
Improved Light, Heat, Power & Mfg. Co. (Paul K. Ames, attorney) 102 B'way
Improved Patent Porous Cup Battery Co. (Ltd.) (Charles J. Hirlimann, Pres.; Gustav Phillipoteaux, Sec. Capital, $1,000. Directors: Charles J. Hirlimann, Julius M. Dubois, Joseph Well) nr 80½ Greene
Income & Life Assn. of America (Werner Bruns, Pres.; John N. Bruns, Sec.; George G. Read, Treas. Capital, $1,000,000. Directors: Werner Bruns, James L. Mills, William H. Bramhall, John N. Bruns, Evan F. Smith, George G. Read, Ansel Dailey, Edward P. Sanderson, Darwin S. Dolbear) 266 B'way
Independent Bung Co. (Peter Doelger jr. Pres.; Henry B. Wheatcroft, Sec Capital, $60,000. Directors: Peter Doelger jr. Henry B. Wheatcroft, J. O. G. Hüpfel, John G. Gillig, W. G. Abbott) 636 W. 48th
Independent Bung & Bushing Co. (dissolved) 635 W. 48th
Independent District Telegraph Co. (Clermont H. Wilcox, Pres.; James Wolff, Treas.; Joseph D. Baldwin jr. Sec. Capital, $25,000. Directors: Clermont H. Wilcox, James Wolff, Joseph D. Baldwin jr. Frederick F. Van Keuren) 9 New
Independent Dynamite Co. (John E. Alexander, Pres.; William H. Curtiss, Sec.; further inf. unattainable) 24 Park pl. & 19 Barclay
Independent Toilet Supply Co. (Samuel S. Rogers, propr.) 4 Warren

IND 145 INS

Indestructible Dress Shield Co. (Ash Brothers, proprs.) 61 W. 14th
India Rubber Comb Co. (Fritz Achelis, Pres.; William W. Weitling, Sec.; Charles A. Hoyt, Treas. Capital, $400,000. Directors: Fritz Achelis, William W. Weitling, Charles A. Hoyt) 9 Mercer
India Rubber Publishing Co. (Capital, $20,000; further inf. unattainable) no address
India Rubber & Gutta Percha Insulating Co. (inf. unattainable) 159 Front
India Wharf Storage Co. (in liquidation) 80 Wall
Indian Herb & Electric Pad Co. (no inf.) 247 Pearl
Indian River Land & Improvement Co. (Herbert M. Linnell, Pres.; John P. Salter, Sec. Capital, $200,000. Directors: Herbert M. Linnell, Robert B. Sherwood, John T. Salter, Charles E. Dustin, Alexander McDonald, Walter Z. Brown, Harry Willer) 45 B'way
Indiana Paint & Roofing Co. (George E. Glines, Pres.; Herbert H. Glines, Sec. Capital, $7,000. Directors: George E. & Herbert H. Glines) 42 W. B'way
Indiana Wood-Turning Co. (Wilson S. Dunn, Pres.; Lewis L. Carrington, Sec. Capital, $2,000. Directors: Wilson S. Dunn, Lewis L. & Raymond B. Carrington) 46 Murray
Indianapolis & St. Louis Railway Co. (consolidated with the Cleveland, Cincinnati, Chicago & St. Louis Railway Co.) 5 Vanderbilt av.
Indianapolis, Decatur & Western Railway Co. (Henry B. Hammond, Pres.; Thomas B. Atkins, Sec. Capital, $370,050. Directors: John D. Probst, Hiram Hitchcock, Henry B. Hammond, Horace L. Hotchkiss, Stephen H. Thayer, Charles C. Allen, Thomas B. Atkins, John K. Warren, Edward F. Leonard, John R. Elder, Robert B. F. Pierce) 2 Wall
Indicator Publishing Co. (Nathan W. Josselyn, Pres.; John S. Hanson, Sec. Capital, $100,000. Directors: Nathan W. Josselyn, John S. Hanson, Wilbur F. Barber) 58 Broad
Indig, Berg & Co. (Benjamin Indig, Hart E. Berg & Max M. Schwarcz) 888 B'way
Individual Underwriters (John B. Waters, attorney) 86 Worth
Indo European Art Co. (dissolved) 21 W. 42d
Indorf & Meyer (Jacob Indorf & John Meyer) 1741 Lex. av.
Indotype Co. (Walter G. Eliot, Pres.; further inf. unattainable) 115 B'way
Industrial Co-operative Building & Loan Assn. (inf. unattainable) 16 Fourth av.
Industrial Information Co. (Sidney W. Hopkins jr. Pres.; William T. G. Weymouth, Treas. Capital, $25,000. Directors: Sidney W. Hopkins jr, William T. G. Weymouth, Albert H. Ely) 78 Tribune bldg.
Industrial Light Co. (James A. Hudson, Pres.; Alfred Shedlock, Sec. Capital, $200,000. Trustees: J. Thomson Duncan, Alfred Shedlock, James A. Hudson) 5 Beekman
Industrial Publication Co. (John Phin, propr.) 9 Barclay
Industrial Record Co. (Ltd.) (Horace L. Congdon, Pres.; Charles S. McCulloh, Sec. Capital, $10,000. Directors: Horace L. Congdon, William O. Allison, Edward D. Congdon, Charles S. McCulloh) 140 Nassau
Inez Gold Mining Co. (Henry L. Benn, Pres.; James E. Coleman, Sec. Capital, $2,000,000. Directors: Henry L. Benn, Philip F. Harris, William H. Bibby, R. S. Foster, G. G. Ward, C. Irving, James R. Coleman) 32 Liberty
Infants' Outfitting Co. (Frankoski Brothers, proprs.) 29 Greene
Influence Machine Co. (not inc.) (Edward T. Birdsall, William H. Meadowcroft & F. K. Bourne) 115 B'way
Infusorial Earth & Silica Mining & Mfg. Co. (inoperative) 630 B'way

Ingalls & Keely (Charles H. Ingalls & William F. Keely) 121 Front & 340 West
Ingenito G. & Co. (Giuseppe Ingenito & Michele Consenza) 208 Sixth
Ingersoll Robert H. & Brother (Robert H. & Charles H. Ingersoll) 65 Cortlandt
Ingersoll & Glenney (David B. Ingersoll & William P. Glenney) 1129 B'way
Ingersoll-Sergeant Rock Drill Co. (Robert W. Chapin, Pres.; William L. Saunders, Sec.; John H. Moss, Treas. Capital, $800,000. Directors: Robert W. Chapin, Edward Earle, William H. Grace, John H. Moss, William L. Turner, H. B. Chapin, John I. Waterbury, Charles C. Noble, H. C. Sergeant, Frank Cunningham, William L. Saunders) 10 Park pl.
Ingraham D. Phœnix & Co. (D. Phœnix Ingraham & James S. McQuillon) 73 Cedar
Ingraham & Allen (Frederick Ingraham & James S. Allen) 192 B'way
Ingraham & Dean (Nathaniel O. Ingraham & Howard D. Dean) 73 B'way
Inland Transp. Line (not inc.) (George W. jr. & Julius B. Stilwell) 111 Broad & Pier 8 E. R.
Inman, Swann & Co. (John R. Inman, James Swann, Bernard S. Clark & Robert W. Inman) 11 Cotton Ex.
Innes & Kennedy (Charles E. Innes & George Kennedy) 102 W. 32d
Innes & McLean (no inf.) 225 W. 51st
Innes' John, Son (Andrew J. Innes) 454 West
Innes Thomas B. & Co. (dissolved) 115 B'way
Innis & Co (Hasbrouck & William R. Innis) 120 William
Inniss & Knight (dissolved) 2614 Third av.
Inquirer Publishing Co. (John B. Calvert, Pres.; Robert T. Middleditch, Treas.; Latham A. Crandall, Sec. Capital, $10,000. Managers: John B. Calvert, Robert T. Middleditch, Latham A. Crandall, Robert S. MacArthur, John Humpstone) 5 Beekman
Instalment Real Estate Agency (Jacob E. Bloom, propr.) 104 B'way
Instant Thill Coupling Co. (Jerome E. Morse, Pres.; Eldridge W. Morse, Sec. Capital, $50,000. Directors: Jerome E. Morse, William H. Coffin, Theodore Hanger, William C. Boone, Eldridge W. Morse) 239 B'way
Institution for the Savings of Merchants' Clerks (Andrew Warner, Pres.; William T. Lawrence, Cashier; George G. Williams, Treas. Trustees: William H. Guion, James M. Constable, George A. Robbins, Walter T. Miller, Andrew C. Armstrong, George G. Williams, Egerton L. Winthrop, Edward M. Townsend, Hewlett Scudder, Albert M. Patterson, Andrew Warner, N. Denton Smith, Thomas J. Davis, Robert M. Strobeigh, W. Emlen Roosevelt) 20 Union sq. E.
Insulated Fibrous & Water Proof Paint Co. (Edward L. Molineux, Pres.; Edward H. Raynolds, Sec.; Thomas D. Hidden, Treas. Capital, $24,000. Trustees: Edward L. Molineux, Thomas D. Hidden, Edward H. Raynolds, Aquila Rich, John Bagley, George M. Mather) 106 Fulton
Insulating Fibre Subway Co. (Horace J. Medbery, Pres.; George W. Rowan, Sec.; Henry C. Andrews, Treas. Capital, $32,400. Directors: Horace J. Medbery, Charles H. Sewall, D. Noble Rowan, Henry C. Andrews, L. S. Stone, David Young, Malcolm W. Niven) 17 B'way
Insulite Mfg. Co. (David H. Brandon, Pres.; Nathaniel Brandon, Sec.; further inf. unattainable) 85 B'way
Insurance Clerks' Mutual Benefit Assn. (inf. unattainable) 158 B'way
Insurers' Automatic Fire Extinguisher Co. (Antonio Raaines, Pres.; Lewis H. Newton, Sec. Capital, $50,000. Directors: Antonio Raaines, Lewis H. Newton, Jacob Jamer, De

TYPEWRITING DONE BY THE TROW CITY DIRECTORY CO., 11 University Place.

INT 146 INV

Witt C. Weld, T. E. D. Power, Charles W. Dayton, S. Howard Martin) 45 Pine

Inter-Ocean Improvement Co. (inf. unattainable) 50 B'way

Inter-State National Bank (Robert H. Weems, Pres.; Francis F. Stone, Cashier; William M. Thatcher, Notary. Capital, $200,000. Directors: Herbert G. Hull, William D. Lent, Henry E. Bowers, Edward H. Kellogg, H. Parrish, Armory S. Carhart, John G. Slonecker, John Francis, Robert H. Weems) 167 B'way

Interior Electrical Conduit Co. (Edward H. Johnson, Pres.; Walter A. Willard, Sec. Capital, $150,000. Directors: Edward H. Johnson, Edwin T. Greenfield, Jonathan H. Vail, Luther Stieringer, William J. Jenks) 154 W. 27th

International Art Publishing Co. (Edward S. Savage, Pres.; Charles D. Phelps, Treas. Capital, $125,000. Directors: Edward S. Savage, Charles D. Phelps, William J. Kelly) 126 Wooster

International Bank Note Co. (Clendenin Eckert, Pres.; William A. Robinson, Sec.; George D. Webber, Treas. Capital, $75,000. Directors: Henry M. Flagler, John G. Moore, Clendenin Eckert, George D. Webber, William A. Robinton) 18 B'way

International Banking Co. (not inc.) (Joseph M. & Arthur J. Koehler) 81 B'way

International Bell Telephone Co. (Ltd.) (Samuel D. Babcock, Pres.; Louis A. Von Hoffmann, Treas.; William F. Elliott, Sec. Capital, $1,700,000. Directors: Samuel D. Babcock, Louis A. Von Hoffmann, William F. Elliott) 32 Nassau

International Boiler Co. (Ltd.) (Allan Stirling, Pres.; Robert P. Orr, Sec. Capital, $100,000. Directors: Allan Stirling, Robert P. Orr, J. Townsend Borden, Robert L. Cutting, John Jardine, John F. Taylor, John F. Torrence) 74 Cortlandt

International Bow & Stern Dock Co. (Henry P. Kirkham, Pres.; Julian D. Shope, Sec.; further inf. unattainable) 78 Broad

International Commercial Co. (dissolved) 39 New Bowery

International Co. of Mexico (dissolved) 39 B'way

International Construction, Railway & Investors Co. (inf. unattainable) 40 Wall

International Contract Co. (Ltd.) (C. V. V. Sewell, Pres.; Cornelius C. Van Santen, Sec.; Robert Sewell, Treas. Capital, $10,000. Directors: C. V. V. Sewell, J. A. Hodge jr. F. L. Rondebush, N. C. Miller, F. J. Winston) 32 Nassau

International Etchers Publishing Co. (dissolved) 45 B'way

International Express Co. (dissolved) 101 Mercer

International Fraternal Alliance (William Baumgarten, Pres.; Daniel F. Penington, Sec. Directors: William Baumgarten, Charles H. Unversagt, August W. Schmitt, Mark H. Eisner, William D. Volger, Nathan Beauman & Samuel Glensor) 6 Union sq. E.

International Gas Co. (Charles G. Francklyn, Pres.; William F. Van Pelt, Sec. Capital, $500,000. Directors: Charles G. Francklyn, John Sickels, William F. Van Pelt, William L. Boyle, C. L. Morgan) 17 William

International Grain Elevating Assn. (Annan & Co., propr.) 101 Produce Ex.

International Graphophone Co. (inf. unattainable) 15 Broad

International Loan & Savings Soc. (William Baumgarten, Pres.; Joseph C. Legg, Sec. Capital, $100,000,000. Directors: Samuel Glensor, Joseph C. Legg, William Baumgarten, Charles H. Unversagt, August W. Schmitt, Nathan Beauman) 6 Union Sq. E.

International Mfg. Assn. (Edmund C. Stanton, Pres.; Henry K. Gilman, Sec.; Louis M. Howland, Treas. Capital, $50,000. Directors: Edmund C. Stanton, John H. Montgomery, Louis M. Howland, Henry K. Gilman, Harold B. Thorne) 10 Wall & 9 Pine

International Mercantile Agency & Collecting Co. (William P. Chase, Pres.; Daniel H. Denton, Sec. Capital, $10,000; further inf. unattainable) 322 B'way

International News Co. (Samuel S. Blood, propr.) 83 Duane

International Ocean Telegraph Co. (Norvin Green, Pres.; Thomas F. Clark, Sec.; Roswell H. Rochester, Treas. Capital, $8,000,000. Directors: Norvin Green, Thomas T. Eckert, John B. Van Every, John T. Terry, Robert C. Livingston, John Vanhorne, Russell Sage, Edwin & George J. Gould) 195 B'way

International Oyster Co. (Leon F. Blanchard, Pres.; Edwin Ingram, Sec.; William W. Blanchard, Treas. Capital, $250,000. Directors: Leon F. Blanchard, Edwin Ingram, J. R. Hart, H. M. Crowell, C. W. Meyer, William W. Blanchard) 74 Cortlandt

International Patent Agency (Renard & Co., propr.) 834 B'way

International Phosphate Co. (Lucien C. Warner, Pres.; Harris H. Haydon, Sec. Capital, $100,000. Directors: Lucien C. Warner, Harris H. Haydon, Walter V. Clark, Walter S. Pierce) 2 Stone

International Portelectric Co. (inf. unattainable) 254 Pearl

International Publishing Agency (not inc.) (William Borsodi :—special partner, Bernhard Weinberger, $1,000; terminates 1st Jan. 1895) 710 B'way

International Publishing Co. (dissolved) 102 Chambers

International Publishing & Portrait Co. (inf. unattainable) 74 Third av.

International Railway & Steamship Advertising Co. (Edward V. Skinner, Pres.; Charles A. Hess, Sec.; Timothy J. Campbell, Treas. Capital, $20,000. Directors: John J. Kiernan, Edward V. Skinner, Charles A. Hess, Jacob Wortheim, Timothy J. Campbell, Luke F. Cozans, William H. Williams) 206 B'way

International Restaurant Co. (Ltd.) (Capital, $25,000; further inf. unattainable) no address

International Secret Service (James N. Walter, Pres.; Marcus W. Bacon. Sec.; Wilbur M. Bates, Treas. Capital, $100,000. Directors: James N. Walter, Marcus W. Bacon, Wilbur M. Bates) 384 B'way

International Steam Laundry. (Edward Wilcke, propr.) 222 Eighth av.

International Steamship Propulsion Co. (inoperative) 18 B'way

International Tooth Crown Co. (Washington W. Sheffield, Pres.; Lucius T. Sheffield, Sec.; Edward N. Dickerson, Treas. Capital, $500,000. Directors: Washington W. & Lucius T. Sheffield, Edward N. Dickerson) 55 W. 33d

International Ultramarine Works (Ltd.) (Louis Dejonge, Pres.; Louis Dejonge jr. Sec.; Charles F. Zentgraf, Treas. Capital, $150,000. Directors: Louis & Louis Dejonge jr. Charles F. Zentgraf) 71 Duane

International & Great Northern R. R. Co. (Jay Gould, Pres.; D. S. H. Smith, Sec. Capital, $9,755,000. Directors: Russell Sage, A. L. Hopkins, Jay Gould, S. H. H. Clark, James A. Baker, F. A. Rice, Ira H. Evans, H. B. Kane, B. W. McCollough) 195 B'way

Interstate Despatch (N. Y., Lake Erie & Western R. R. Co. & N. Y., Chicago & St. Louis R. R. Co. proprs.) 347 B'way

Inventors' Mfg. Co. (inf. unattainable) 47 Barclay

Investigator Co. (Henry C. Raymond, Pres.; Howard H. Hamilton, Sec. Capital, $10,000, further inf. unattainable) 384 B'way

Investment Assn. (Sidney W. Hendrickson, Pres.;

THE CALIGRAPH WRITING MACHINE,
HARTFORD, CONN.

INV 147 ITA

William G. Rule, Sec.; Herbert A. Lee, Treas. Capital, $25,000. Directors: J. Herbert Potts, George L. Cole, Herbert A. Lee, George W. Morrill, William G. Rule, W. H. Jennings, Charles H. Lowerre, Sidney W. Hendrickson, W. S. Beckley) 248 B'way

Investors' Directory Co. (refused) 10 Wall

Investors' Publishing Co. (James H. Goodsell, Pres.; Clifford Thomson, Sec.; Samuel Elliott, Treas.; further inf. unattainable) 14 Cortlandt

Iowa Barb Wire Co. (Charles Douglass, Pres.; George S. Douglass, Sec. Capital, $300,000; further inf. unattainable) 98 Reade

Iowa Central Railway Co. (Russell Sage, Pres.; George R. Morse, Sec.; Edwin H. Perkins jr, Treas. Capital, $14,000,000. Directors: Russell Sage, H. J. Morse, A. D. Stickney, G. E. Taintor, E. E. Chase, Henry A. & James P. Gardner, Edward F. Lawrence, Robert D. Mofadon) 46 Wall

Ipp Samuel & Co. (dissolved) 155 E. 75th

Ireland-Benedict Co. (Ltd.) (no inf.) 157 B'way

Ireland-Speer Portable Electric Lighting System (not inc.) (John E. Ireland & Edward D. Speer) 35 B'way

Iron Car Co. (George W. Dithridge, Pres.; Wilson L. Baldwin, Sec. Capital, $2,500,000. Directors: George W. Dithridge, Wilson L. Baldwin, Robert M. Cushman, Jonathan Odell, Reuben Leland) 120 B'way

Iron Clad Mfg. Co. (Robert Seaman, Pres.; David D. Otis, Sec. Capital, $310,000. Directors: Robert Seaman, David D. Otis, Henry W. Shepard) 22 Cliff

Iron Line (Frederick W. Stark, Pres.; Frederick Grube, Sec. Capital, $10,000. Directors: Frederick W. Stark, Frederick Grube, Frederick H. Wilkins) 33 Coenties sl.

Iron Reduction Co. (Matthew Graff, Pres.; William Brandeth, Sec.; Charles M. Raymond, Treas. Capital, $10,000. Trustees: Charles M. Raymond, William Brandreth, Frank B. Robinson, John P. Slaybock, Matthew Graff) 35 Wall

Iron Silver Mining Co. (Ashley Pond, Pres.; Fremont Woodruff, Sec.; John M. Nichol, Treas. Capital, $10,000,000. Directors: Ashley Pond, W. G. Wiley, F. L. Smith, H. A. Taylor, Henry A. Hoyt, William H. Stevens, James McMillan, William A. Moore, L. K. Pierce, Parker W. Shepard, Parker D. Handy) 23 Broad

Iron Steamboat Co. (Samuel Carpenter, Pres.; John W. Gilbough, Treas.; Walter F. Parker, Sec. Capital, $2,000,000. Directors: G. M. Dodge, John W. Gilbough, Samuel Carpenter, W. H. Woolverton, S. N. Smith, L. O. Wachner, Oscar E. Ballin, J. Henry Alexandre, A. R. Culver, Emile Vatable, Thomas G. Rigney, J. H. Coffin, Frank C. White) Pier 1 N. R.

Ironton & Petersburgh Railway Co. (Charles H. Harman, Pres.; William Kerr, Sec. Capital, $100,000. Directors: Charles H. Harman, Orson Adams, W. H. Enochs, William Kerr, Dallas Flannagan) 32 Nassau

Irvin Richard & Co. (Richard Irvin, no Co.) 19 William

Irvine & Co. (inf. unattainable) 102 Chambers

Irving Charles & Son (Charles & Benjamin M. Irving) 509 Third av.

Irving George H. & Brother (George H. & Thomas J. Irving) 408 W. 24th

Irving Law & Collection Agency (James Forrest, propr.) 239 G'wich

Irving Mfg. Co. (John Irving & Co. proprs.) 297 Church

Irving Mfg. & Tool Co. (McCoy & Sanders, proprs.) 26 Warren

Irving National Bank (John L. Jewett, Pres.; George E. Souper, Cashier; Wilson C. King, Notary. Capital, $500,000. Directors: John Castree, William A. Thomson, John L. Jewett, Charles S. Brown, John Nix. Harry McBride, Charles F. Mattiage, William H. Montanye, John R. Waters, Arno H. Schoff, Charles Burkhalter) 287 G'wich

Irving Savings Institution (John Castree, Pres.; Clarence D. Heaton, Sec.; John L. Jewett, Treas. Trustees: Abram Wakeman, Joseph Rogers, John A. Hardenbergh, James E. Hedges, Ernest O. Korner, William Corey, Cornelius L. Blauvelt, William R. Mitchell, Frederick Meyer, Robert Seaman, William H. B. Totten, Henry Demarest, Martin Gerdes, Daniel B. Halstead, Thomas Stillman, John K. Lasher, Lloyd L. Seaman, C. W. Miller, David D. Moses, William H. Duckworth, Albert G. Bogert, Gilbert Oakley, Charles Burkhalter) 90 Warren

Irving & Hinds (Joseph S. Irving & John F. Hinds jr.) 161 B'way

Irving & Son (Joseph & George W. Irving) 118 W. 82d

Irwin Thomas & Sons (Henry & James D. Irwin, only) 49 Wall

Irwin R. J. & Co. (Robert J. Irwin & Michelangelo Pettinato) 24 State

Irwin & Co. (Thomas C. Irwin & Frederick Ernst) 79 Duane

Isaacs A. & B. (Abraham & Baron) 51 Whitehall

Isaacs A. & Co. (Max, Wertheimer, only) 79 William

Isaacs A. & Son (Abraham & Isidor Isaacs) 364 & 378 Bowery

Isaacs' G. W. & Son (dissolved) 145 West

Isaacs M. S. & I. S. (Myer S. & Isaac S.) 115 B'way

Isaacs R. & Brother (Reuben & Israel Isaacs) 555 B'way & 126 Mercer

Isaacs S. & Co. (Solomon Isaacs & Emil & Gustave B, Calman) 209 Pearl

Isaacs S. G. & Co. (dissolved) 295 G'wich

Isaacs S. L. & Ash (Samuel L. Isaacs & Simon A. Ash) 280 B'way

Isaacs & Blayer (Moses Isaacs & Bernhard Blayer) 409 Broome

Isaacs & Heineman (Moses Isaacs & Joseph Heineman) 189 William

Isaacs & Victor (Samuel G. Isaacs & Isaac Victor jr.) 295 G'wich

Isaacs, Vought & Co (Richard R. Vought & Frederick Berenbroick, only) 50 Wall

Isaacs' G. W., Son (Solomon Isaacs) 145 West

Isbell-Porter Co. (George G. Porter, Pres.; Charles W. Isbell, Sec. Capital, $400,000. Directors: George G. Porter, Charles W. & Arthur H. Isbell, A. F. Wehner, Samuel F. Hay) 245 B'way

Iselin A. & Co. (Adrian jr. & Columbus O'Donnell Iselin) 36 Wall

Iselin, Neeser & Co. (William E. Iselin, John G. Neeser & Alfred Vondermuhll;—special partner, Adrian Iselin, $300,000; terminates 30th Nov. 1891) 1 Greene

Iskiyan J. & Co. (no inf.) 113 Elm

Isler & Gaye (refused) 97 Prince

Ison & Co. (dissolved) 1197 Railroad av.

Israel Charles & Brother (Charles & Ernest W. Israel) 110 Hudson

Israel Hyman & Sons (Hyman & Julius I. & Joseph M. Israel) . 9 Bowery

Israel A. & Co. (Adolph Israel, no Co.) 248 Canal

Israel J. & Son (Julius & David Israel) 7 Rutgers pl.

Israel J. C. & Co. (Joseph C. Israel & Herman Cohn) 35 Maiden la.

Israel S. & Co. (Samuel & Harris Israel & Emanuel Weiss) 109 Canal

Isselbacher S. & Sons (Simon & Morris & Lazarus Isselbacher) 828 First av. & 1585 Second av.

Italian Chamber of Commerce in N. Y. (Louis

COMPILED WITH ACCURACY AND DESPATCH.	CLASSIFIED BUSINESS LISTS.	THE TROW CITY DIRECTORY CO. 11 University Place.

ITA 148 JAE

Centencin, Pres.; Michele Lemmi, Sec.; Salvatore Cantoni, Treas.) 24 State
Italo Am. Bank (Charles Barsotti, propr.) 4 Centre
Itschner Werner & Co. (Werner Itschner & H. Alfred Streuli) 57 Greene
Ivanhoe Paper Mills (no inf.) 120 B'way
Ivers M. J. & Co. (James Sullivan, only) 86 Nassau
Ives & Bonar (Ronald B. Bonar & estate of Dotius D. Ives) 441 B'way & 10 Crosby
Ives, Blakeslee & Co. (Edward R. Ives, Cornelius Blakeslee & Edward G. Williams) 294 B'way
Ivison, Blakeman & Co. (Birdseye Blakeman, David B. Ivison, George R. Cathcart, Louis H. Blakeman & Henry Ivison) 753 B'way
Ixen & Son (dissolved) 553 Eighth av.

J

Jaburg Brothers (John & Hugo Jaburg) 115 Hudson
Jackson Architectural Iron Works (William H. Jackson, Pres.; John Cooper, Sec.; John H. Hankinson, Treas. Capital, $225,000. Directors: William H. & Ebenezer C. Jackson, John Cooper, John H. Hankinson, Joseph Lantry) 315 E. 26th
Jackson Edwin A. & Brother (Edwin A. & William M. Jackson) 50 Beekman
Jackson Jacob & Son (dissolved) 740 B'way
Jackson Oswald & Brother (Oswald & Charles Carroll Jackson & Stephen Van Rensselaer) 21 S. William
Jackson Peter A. H. & Sons (Peter A. H. & Henry H. & Adrian H. Jackson) 103 E. 27th
Jackson William H. & Co. (William H. & Ebenezer C. Jackson & John H. Hankinson) 81 E. 17th & 36 E. 18th
Jackson H. B. & Co. (Hiram B. Jackson, no Co.) 103 Water
Jackson R. & E. (Rebecca & Eliza) 1196 Third av.
Jackson R. D. & Co. (Richard D. Jackson & Joseph W. Masters) 65 Beaver & 20 Exchange pl.
Jackson Brothers (furs) (Julius & Moritz Jackson) 109 Wooster
Jackson Brothers (trucks) (Jacob W. & Benjamin A. Jackson) 101 Chambers & 40 Crosby
Jackson & Co. (grocers) (Richard K. Jackson, John Emslie & August Lober) 114 W. 23d
Jackson & Co. (refrigerators) (John P. & Julia T. Jackson) 626 Tenth av.
Jackson & Ingraham (dissolved) 16 Exchange pl.
Jackson & Shuttleworth (Jerome A. Jackson & Edward Shuttleworth) First av. c. E. 94th
Jackson & Son (Henry W. & Richard E. Jackson) 60 Walker, 186 Mercer & 612 Water
Jackson James M., Son (Henry S. Jackson) 85 Murray.
Jackson's W. Sons (James L. & John W. Jackson) 246 Front & 208 Water
Jacksonville, Tampa, & Key West Railway Co. (Robert H. Coleman, Pres.; Charles C. Deming, Sec. Capital, $2,010,000. Directors: William H. Barnum, Robert H. Coleman, Charles C. Deming, Henry M. Flagler, James H. & Mason Young, Jacob Edwards, John W. Candler, Joseph R. Parrott) 10 Wall
Jacob Charles & Brother (Charles & Jacob Jacob) 60 Av. C
Jacob Gisella & Brother (Gisella & Isaac Jacob) 551 Grand
Jacob Brothers (pianos) (Charles & C. Albert Jacob) 400 Eighth
Jacob Brothers (shoes) (dissolved) 261 Rivington
Jacob & Grossman (Morris Jacob & Kolef Grossman) 30 Market
Jacobi & Co. (no inf.) 19 Barclay & 24 Park pl.

Jacobs Hyman & Son (Hyman & Moses Jacobs) 96 Canal & 29 Eldridge
Jacobs Lewis & Son (Lewis & Myer Jacobs) 409 B'way
Jacobs A. & Son (Adolph & Meyer C. Jacobs) 518 B'way
Jacobs A. W. & Co. (A. W. & R. C. Jacobs) 1162 B'way
Jacobs C. & Co. (Charles Jacobs & Isaac Wasserzug) 35 Lispenard
Jacobs J. L. & M. (Jacob L. & Mark) 89 Spring
Jacobs S. & Son (Samuel & Ralph Jacobs) 52 E. B'way
Jacobs Brothers (agents) (Mark & Henry Jacobs) 112 Canal
Jacobs Brothers (clothing) (Abraham L. & Joseph Jacobs) 110 Grand
Jacobs Brothers (lawyers) (Michael & Edward & Joseph A. Jacobs) 985 B'way
Jacobs Brothers (tailors) (Henry & Abraham & Charles & Moses & John & Nathan Jacobs) 229 & 1255 B'way & 152 Bowery
Jacobs Brothers (waters) (dissolved) 5 Elizabeth
Jacobs & Bernstein (Abraham Jacobs & Isaac Bernstein) 81 Eighth av.
Jacobs & Knapp (George Jacobs & August Knapp) 1050 Third av.
Jacobs & McCafferty (J. Samuel Jacobs & James McCafferty) 445 West
Jacobs & Schwartz (no inf.) 53 Attorney & 115 E. B'way
Jacobs & Steinberg (Samuel Jacobs & Marks Steinberg) 60 Canal
Jacobs & Sterzelbach (Philip Jacobs & Abraham Sterzelbach) 460 Broome
Jacobs, Peters & Knapp (dissolved) 1050 Third av.
Jacobs, Schwartz & Cohen (Nathan Jacobs, Moses Schwartz & Tobias Cohen) 412 Broome
Jacobsen John & Co. (dissolved) 177 E. Houston
Jacobsen A. & Co. (Adolph Jacobsen & Charles Rippert) 89 B'way
Jacobsen E. & Co. (Ernest O. Jacobsen & Arthur M. Edwards) 2 Stone
Jacobsen N. & Co. (ribbons) (dissolved) 55 Mercer
Jacobsen N. & Co. (trimmings) (Nathan Jacobsen, no Co.) 4 Bond
Jacobsohn A. & Son (Adolph & Lazar Jacobsohn) 114 E. B'way
Jacobson Brothers (clothing) (Max & Victor Jacobson) 105 Hester
Jacobson Brothers (diamonds) (Henry H. & Emanuel Jacobson) 10 Maiden la.
Jacobson & Gleitzman (Ferdinand Jacobson & Isaac Gleitzman) 18 E. B'way
Jacobson & Ziegel (Leopold Jacobson & Robert Ziegel) 532 b'way
Jacobus & Loewenstein (Herman Jacobus & Max Loewenstein) 40 Bleecker
Jacoby Morris & Co. (Morris & Charles Jacoby) 342 E. 58th
Jacoby S. & Co. (Sigmund & Gustav Jacoby) ft. E. 52d
Jacoby S. M. & Brother (no inf.) 145 Elm
Jacoby & Graswinckel (Max J. Jacoby & Arend Graswinckel) 314 E. 75th
Jacocks Joseph F. & Co. (Joseph F. & E. Jacocks) 10 Lispenard
Jacot & Son (Charles H. & Aristides H. Jacot) 298 B'way
Jacquelin John H. & Co. (John H. Jacquelin & Lawrence Jacob) 44 B'way & 45 New
Jacquin J. & Co. (Joseph J. & Jacob Rothschild, only) 68 W. 23d
Jaeger C. & Co. (Christian Jaeger & Megerdich Attarian) 145 Elm

MERCHANTS EXCHANGE NAT. BANK OF THE CITY OF N. Y.
SOLICITS YOUR ACCOUNT. **257 Broadway.**
PHINEAS C. LOUNSBURY, President.   ALLEN S. APGAR, Cashier.

JAE   149   JEN

Jaeger Brothers (cigars) (Adolph S. & Julius & Morris S. Jaeger) 1299 Av. A
Jaeger Brothers (grocers) (Richard & Henry F. Jaeger) 147 Washn. & 58 Oliver
Jaeger & Dieter (John J. Jaeger & Conrad Dieter) 112 Stanton
Jaeger & Kerkmann (William D. H. Jaeger & G. W. August Kerkmann) 207 Bleecker
Jaeger & Redmond (Christian Jaeger & Thomas W. Redmond) 145 Delancey & 311 Madison
Jaeger & Semcken (Henry Jaeger & Henry Semcken) 486 Cherry
Jaeger & Timme (Otto Jaeger & Edward F. Timme) 413 Broome
Jaeger & Wodiski (dissolved) 180 Av. B
Jaeger's Dr., Sanitary Woolen System Co. (Herman Schaeffer, Pres.; Ernst Benger, Treas. Capital, $300,000. Directors: Herman Schaeffer, Stephen V. White, John D. Godwin, William Hauff, W. C. Weber, Ernst Benger) 820 & 199 B'way
Jaffe O. & Pinkus (Frederick S. & Leopold Pinkus, only) 89 Leonard
Jaffray E. S. & Co. (Edward S. & Howard S. Jaffray, John H. P. Woodriff & Charles J. Hadfield) 330 B'way
Jahn Gustave A. & Co. (Gustave A. Jahn & William J. Griffiths) 98 Wall
Jahn Brothers (William & Herman Jahn) 760 D'way
Jakobi A. & Co. (Anselm & Manuel W. Jakobi) 18 Walker
Jakobi & Glendinning (Leo C. Jakobi & John Glendinning) 251 Canal
Jamaica International Exhibition Committee (Thomas Amor, Sec.) 280 B'way
Jamaica Water Supply Co. (John Lockwood, Pres.; John C. Lookwood, Sec. Capital $75,000, Directors: John & John C. & Frank G. Lookwood) 52 B'way
James F. E. Co. (refined) Tenth av. c W. 37th
James John S. & Co. (John S. & Warren T. James & Edward C. Kimball) 8 Broad
James William B. & Co. (William B. James, no Co.) 84 Nassau
James O. P. & Co. (Owen P. James & Edward F. Murphy) 608 B'way
James & Brink (Kate G. James & John W. Brink) 14 Walker
James & Holmstrom (Frederick P. James & Andrew Holmstrom) 236 E. 21st
James & James (J. King & Arthur H. James) 137 B'way
James & Mohlig (Charles James & Charles Mohlig) 106 W. 37th
James & Noble (no inf.) 350 E. 32d
Jameson, Smith & Co. (Joseph A. Jameson, James D. Smith, Franklin M. Jones & Archibald H. Smith) 28 Broad
Jamieson & Moss (Joseph B. Jamieson & Edgar A. Moss) 52 Leonard
Jandorf P. & Brothers (Pfeifer & Louis C. & Charles Jandorf) 34 Malden la.
Janes & Kirtland (Henry E. & Hurbert Janes, only) 242 Water, 112 Beekman & 774 Westchester av.
Janson & Co. (Jens & Peter Janson) 12 Bridge
Janson & Gordon (dissolved) 83 Bowery
Janssen & Co. (Frank G. & M. A. Janssen) 68 Broad
Janssen & Hilliers (Henry Janssen & Henry Hillers) 4 G'wich
Jantzen Brothers (Henry & John H. Jantzen) 606 Second av.
Janvrin & Walter (Louis B. Janvrin & Henry Walter) 1108 B'way
Japanese Fan Co. (Isaac J. Stiebel, propr.) 519 B'way & 94 Mercer

Japhe & Bondy (William E. Japhe & Simon M. Bondy) 714 B'way
Jaques & Marcus (George B. Jaques & William E. & Herman Marcus) 237 B'way
Jarboe J. W. & Son (John W. & George W. Jarboe) 521 E. 19th
Jardine George & Son (Edward G. & Joseph P. & Sarah E. Jardine, only) 316 E. 59th
Jardine D. & J. (David & John Jardine, Jav H. Van Norden & George E. Jardine) 1262 B'way
Jarecky Brothers (Bernard & Samuel R. Jarecky) 16 W. Houston
Jarmulowsky Brothers (Meyer & Elias Jarmulowsky) 260 Grand
Jaros J. N. & Co. (Julius N. & Alfred L. & Leopold Jaros) 52 W. 15th
Jarvis James L. & Son (James L. & John A. Jarvis) 16 South & 511 W. 20th
Jarvis F. W. & Co. (Frederick W. Jarvis & James W. & Forrest W. Gallison) 152 Front
Jarvis & Co. (Robert M. Jarvis & Samuel M. Schafer) 60 Broad & 286 South
Jay & Candler (William Jay & Flames B. Candler) 48 Wall
Jayne B. F. & Co. (Benjamin F. Jayne, no Co.) 66 South
Jayne S. F. & Co. (Samuel F. Jayne & Albert M. Oulner) 254 W. 23d & 59 Liberty
Jeanneret P. A. & Co. (Paul A: Jeanneret & Louis Hillart) r 75 Nassau
Jeannot & Shiebler (August A. Jeannot & Andrew K. Shiebler) 20 Maiden la.
Jeans & Taylor (Edward Jeans & John A. Taylor) 101 S. 5th av.
Jebens & Co. (Herman H. Jebens & John H. Elken) 237 S. 5th av.
Jefferson Ins. Co. (Samuel F. Belcher, Pres; William B. Flowery, Sec. Capital, $200,010. Directors: Nehemiah Tunis, Robert P. Lee, Samuel E. Belcher, Henry S. Terbell, Samuel T. Hubbard, Edward A. Hall, Thomas L. Smith, John N. Quirk, Albert J. Milbank, Robert D. Roosevelt, Walter M De Gruuw jr. Amos F. Eno, Robert P. Lee jr.) 111 B'way
Jefferson Real Estate Co. (Thomas Jefferson, Pres.; John J. Jefferson, Sec. Capital. $50,000. Trustees: Thomas & Susan & John J. Jefferson) 540 W. 58th
Jeffreys & Co, (Bernard Kreizer, only) 81 Cortlandt
Jeffreys & Son (Arthur & Arthur Edwin Jeffreys) 86 Fulton
Jelliff Hiram & Son (Hiram & Hiram L. Jelliff) 235 Ninth av.
Jelliff Wright & Co. (Taylor Jelliffe, James Wright & Frederick L. Jelliffe) 234 Washn., 22 Grace av. W. Washn. mkt. & ft. W. 60th
Jellinek & Jacobson (Marcell Jellinek & Gustave S. Jacobson) 13 E. 17th
Jemison E. S. & Co. (Elbert S. Jemison, no Co.) 23 William
Jenkins Co. (Theodore P. Jenkins, Pres.; Arthur C. Jenkins, Sec. Capital, $40,000. Directors: Arthur C. & Theodore P. & C. Jenkins) 37 Canal
Jenkins Marcus, Flour Co. (William Warbrick, Pres.; George Herkimer, Sec.; Marcus Jenkins, Treas. Capital, $5,000. Directors: William Warbrick, George Herkimer, Marcus Jenkins) 124 Warren
Jenkins T. W. & Co. (Thomas W. Jenkins & David Hammond) 99 Gold
Jenkins Brothers (brokers) (Henry E. & Guy R. Jenkins) 6 Cedar
Jenkins Brothers (valves) (Alfred B. & Charles Jenkins) 71 John
Jenkins & Co. (E. P. Jenkins & Oliver McCartney) 39 Dey

SNOW, CHURCH & CO. { ESTABLISHED 1874.

JEN 150 JOH

Jenkins & McCowan (Henry C. Jenkins & Archibald McCowan) 224 Centre

Jenkins & Tregarthen (William Jenkins & James Tregarthen) 41 South & Pier 52 E. R.

Jenkins & Williams (Henry B. Jenkins & Frank S. Williams) 601 W. 33d

Jenkins' Edward O., Son (Herbert Jenkins) 20 N. William

Jenks Brothers (Joseph & Benjamin & Julius Jenks) Pier 24 (new) N. R.

Jenks' H. E., Sons (Joseph C. & Benjamin D. Jenks) 41 Old sl.

Jenness-Miller Publishing Co. (Anna Jenness-Miller, Pres.; Mabel Jenness, Sec.; C. Miller, Treas.; further inf. refused) 363 Fifth av. & 121 W. 38th

Jenney S. & Son (Henry C. Jenney, only) 96 Maiden la.

Jennings Express (George P. Jennings, propr.) 85 Reade

Jennings Lace Works (Abraham G. Jennings, Pres.; Edwin W. Le Clear, Sec. Capital, $100,000. Directors: Abraham G. Jennings, Edwin W. Le Clear, Charles H. Smith, Foster D. Hendrickson, Walter L. Sackett, Albert Gould Jennings) 69 Greene

Jennings C. E. & Co. (Charles E Jennings & Francis B. Griffin) 97 Chambers & 51 Reade

Jennings F. C. & Co. (Frederick C. Jennings & William J. Butzfield) 107 Front

Jennings & Co. (Mary F. & Elizabeth F. Jennings:—special partner, Josephine H. Egan, London, Eng. $10,000; terminates 31st March, 1891) 56 E. 19th

Jennings & Russell (Frederic D. Jennings & Charles H. Russell jr.) 2 Nassau

Jennings & Welstead (Samuel M. E. Jennings & Thomas Welstead) 231 W. 55th & 1731 B'way

Jentes H. & Brother (Henry & Adolph Jentes) 779 B'way

Jerkowski & Ernst (Max Ernst, only) 526 B'way & 158 Crosby

Jeroloman & Arrowsmith (John Jeroloman & William Arrowsmith) 229 B'way

Jeroloman & Williams (Charles M. Jeroloman & William T. S. Williams) 30 Av. D

Jerome Avenue R. R. Co. (J. Romaine Brown, Pres.; John Whalen, Sec.; William Chapman, Treas. Capital, $200,000. Directors: J. Romaine Brown, Frank Youran, William B. Whitney, Henry Campbell, Moses Mehrbach, Adolph C. Horbacher, James H. Sullivan, William Chapman, John Whalen, Thomas E. Crimmins, Hugh N. Camp, Richard A. Cunningham, D. Lowber Smith) 206 B'way

Jerome Park Villa Site & Improvement Co. (William A. Duer, Pres.; Frederick A. Lovecraft, Sec. Capital, $1,000,000. Directors: William A. Duer, George B. Fearing, C. F. Bauerdorf, Theodore Moss, William R. Travers, Frederick A. Lovecraft) 945 B'way

Jerome & Nason (William Travers Jerome & Daniel Nason) 5 Bookman

Jersey City Casing Co. (Charles Bollow, propr.) 607 W. 36th

Jersey Embroidering & Mfg. Co. (inf. unattainable) 51 Leonard

Jersey Franklinite Co. (James L. Curtis, Pres.; Edward A. S. Man, Sec.; W. W. Hebbard, Treas.; further inf. refused) 62 William

Jarvis Clark & Co. (H. Clark S. & Frank T. Jarvis, only) 126 Fulton mkt

Jesselsohn & Co. (refused) 679 B'way

Jessup & Moore Paper Co. (Clarence B. Moore, Pres.; Frank W. McDowell, Sec.; Jacob B. Moore, Treas. Directors: Clarence B. Moore, Daniel W. Evans, Jacob B. Moore, Frank W. McDowell, William Luke, D. Lindsay) 99 Nassau & 9 Water

Jessup & Watkins (dissolved) 59 W. 26th

Jesup F. W. & Co. (Frank W. Jesup, no Co.) 171 B'way

Jesup & Lamont (James R. Jesup jr. & Lansing Lamont) 52 B'way

Jewel Cloak & Suit Co. (not Inc.) (Margaret & Mary A. Dolan) 439 B'way

Jewelers' Circular Publishing Co. (W. Nelson Cromwell, Pres.; Lewis J. Mulford, Sec.; Joseph W. Bencham, Treas. Capital, $37,500; further inf. refused) 189 B'way

Jewelers' Exchange (dissolved) 225 B'way

Jewelers' League (Henry Hayes, Pres.; William L. Sexton, Sec.) 170 B'way

Jewelers' Mercantile Agency (Ltd.) (Delold Safford, Pres.; Charles H. Swords, Treas. Capital, $20,000; further inf. refused) 216 B'way

Jewelers' Security Alliance of the U. S. (David C. Dodd jr. Pres.; George H. Hodenpyl, Sec.; Charles G. Lewis, Treas.) 170 B'way

Jewelers' Weekly Publishing Co. (Alonzo Rothschild, propr.) 41 Maiden la.

Jewelers' & Tradesmen's Co. (Gilbert T. Woglom, Pres.; Ephraim S. Johnson jr. Sec.; Samuel W. Saxton, Treas.) 84 John

Jewell Pure Water Co. (no inf.) 145 B'way

Jewett White Lead Co. (Benjamin C. Webster, Pres.; John A. Stevens, Sec.; Charles H. Jewett, Treas. Capital, $212,000. Directors: Benjamin C. Webster, John A. Stevens, Charles H. Jewett) 26 Burling sl.

Jimenes, Haustedt & Co. (Juan Y. Jimenes, Johannes Haustodt & Rafael Rodriguez) 5 S. William

Jimeson C. W. & Co. (Charles W. & Joseph H. Jimeson) 41 Jay

Joachim Morris P. & Co. (Morris P. & William Joachim) 1435 Second av.

Jochum & Jetter (Andrew Jochum & Gottlieb Jetter) 148 E. 50th

Jocuistita Mining Co. (Richard P. Lounsbery, Pres.; A. Harrison, Sec. Capital, $2,500,000. Directors: Richard P. Lounsbery, A. Harrison, Abraham B. Baylis, Willard P. Ward, Ben Ali Haggin) Mills bldg.

Joerges A. & Son (John H. Joerges, only) 14 Market

Johannsen Brothers (Christian & Theodore Johannsen) 810 Second av.

Johansen William & Co. (William Johansen & Jacob H. Himmelrich) 323 B'way

Johansmeyer & Koenke (John H. C. Johansmeyer & Bernard Koenke) 1232 Third av.

John Cinnamon Commission Merchant (John Cinnamon & Charles Borrall jr.) 19 Whitehall

Johnes & Willcox (Edward R. Johnes & Henry C. Willcox) 50 B'way

Johnes H. W., Mfg. Co. (Henry W. Johns, Pres.; George S. Curtis, Sec.; Charles H. Patrick, Treas. Capital, $150,000; further inf. refused) 87 Maiden la.

Johns R. C. & Brother (Richard C. Johns, only) 247 W. 47th

Johns & Co. (David J. & Edward A. Johns) 215 Bowery

Johnson Edward P. & Co. (Edward P. Johnson, no Co.) 312 G'wich

Johnson Extract Wool Co. (Pierrepont E. Johnson, Pres.; John G. Austin, Sec. Capital, $30,000. Directors: Pierrepont E. Johnson, John G. Austin) 88 Reade

Johnson Isaac G. & Co. (Isaac G. & Isaac B. & Gilbert H. & Elias M. Johnson) Spuyten Duyvil

Johnson James G. & Co. (James G. Johnson, Charles S. La Vake, Thomas J. Colton & James M. Bingham) 655 B'way

Johnson John & Co. (John & Samuel Henry Johnson & Christopher C. Hutchinson) 1 Franklin sq.

WATER METERS, GAS ENGINES, | **NATIONAL METER CO.**
FOR PUMPING AND POWER. | **252 Broadway, N. Y.**

Johnson Martin & Son (Martin & Edwin S. Johnson) 94 Murray
Johnson Milton C. & Co. (Milton C. Johnson & Samuel Williams) 32 Reade
Johnson Peerless Works (Henry Johnson, Pres.; William G. Hoagland, Sec.; George G. Dudley, Treas. Capital, $25,000. Directors: Henry Johnson, William G. Hoagland, George G. Dudley, M. Nicholas Johnson) 44 Beekman
Johnson Pneumatic Tube Co. (inf. unattainable) 187 B'way
Johnson Rowland (Joseph E. Busby & Peter A. Wolcott, only) 441 B'way
Johnson A. B. & Co. (Artemus B. & Josiah H. Johnson) First av, c E. 60th & 3 Broome
Johnson A. J. & Co. (William W. Johnson, only) 11 Gt. Jones
Johnson A. M. & Brother (Arthur M. & Joseph E. Johnson) 81 Nassau
Johnson A. P. & Co. (Andrew P. Johnson & Lawrence P. Carlson) 20 Beekman
Johnson B. S. & Co. (Burdell S. Johnson, Frank T. Dutson & Harry C. Dean) 39 B'way
Johnson E. S. & Co. (Ephraim S. Johnson, Pres.; Ephraim S. Johnson jr. Treas.; Henry V. Terbune, Sec. Capital, $200,000. Directors: Ephraim S. & Ephraim S. Johnson jr. Henry V. Terbune) 26 Malden la. & 55 Nassau
Johnson F. W. & Co. (Frederick W. Johnson, no Co.) 14 Moore
Johnson J. & Co. (John Johnson & Gustave Borkman) 125 Fulton
Johnson P. J. & Co. (Peter J. Johnson & Andrew J. Peterson) 46 Beekman
Johnson S. & Co. (Swan Johnson, no Co.) 124 Malden la.
Johnson S. M. & Brother (Samuel M. & Abram A. Johnson) 48 Wall, 177 B'way & 235 Pearl
Johnson Brothers (iron) (Isaac C. & John B. Johnson) 215 Grand
Johnson Brothers (lumber) (Russell & Boswell H. & estate of William M. Johnson) 8 Broome
Johnson Brothers (meat) (William & Edmund C. Johnson) Kingsbridge
Johnson & Barnes (George G. Johnson & Isabella A. Barnes) 2090 Seventh av.
Johnson & Boardman (S. Fisher Johnson & Lansdale Boardman) 16 Wall
Johnson & Brother (Thomas & William Johnson) 24 Washn. mkt
Johnson & Co. (M. J. Johnson & J. W. Shields) 61 W. 42d
Johnson & Eagles (Russell C. Johnson & James F. Eagles) 17 Water
Johnson & Faulkner (Edward H. & Edward D. & Francis E. Faulkner, only) 35 E. 17th & 44 E. 18th
Johnson & Fitzgerald (Thorkell Johnson & Thomas H. Fitzgerald) 1585 Second av.
Johnson & Fry (William S. Johnson & George Gardiner Fry) 111 B'way
Johnson & Higgins (Andrew Foster Higgins, William Kreba, John D. Barrett, John H. Gourlie jr. & James B. Dickson, only) 66 Wall
Johnson & Johnson (Robert W. Johnson. Pres.; Edward M. Johnson, Sec. Capital, $100,000. Directors: Robert W. & Edward M. & James W. Johnson) 92 William
Johnson & McKoy (dissolved) 28 John
Johnson & Morris (Richard M. Johnson & George H. Morris) 114 Leonard
Johnson & Prybill (Samuel Johnson & H. Daniel Prybill) 176 B'way
Johnson & Sawyer (Franklin F. Sawyer, only) 95 Liberty
Johnson & Sharp (Francis E. Johnson & James B. Sharp) 236 Church & 230 W. 30th

Johnson & Smith (dissolved) 166 Washn.
Johnson & Son (coopers) (William W. Johnson, only) 163 Malden la.
Johnson & Son (wagons) (Patrick & Thomas Johnson) 415 E. 23d
Johnson & Wilson (Charles B. Johnson & John J. Wilson) 45 B'way
Johnson, Cowdin & Co. (John E. Cowdin & Edward N. Herzog, only) 121 Spring
Johnson, Gallup & Hurry (J. Augustus Johnson, Albert Gallup & Randolph Hurry) 58 William
Johnson, Hammond & Co. (Robert Johnson jr. George L. Hammond & Henry Johnson) 189 Front
Johnston Chemical Co. (Henry S. Johnston, Pres.; Rider Johnston, Sec.; George L. Peck, Treas. Capital, $5,000. Directors: Henry S. Johnston, George L. Peck, John M. Prall) 147 E. 22d
Johnston Thomas J. & Co. (Thomas J. Johnston, no Co.) 360 B'way
Johnston W. J., Co. (Ltd.) (William J. Johnston, Pres.; Walter T. Hunt, Sec.; Clarence E. Stump, Treas. Capital, $25,000. Directors: William J. Johnston, Frank E. Knight, Walter T. Hunt, Clarence E. Stump, John J. Johnston) 41 Park row
Johnston A. & Co. (Alexander Johnston & Elbert Fleet) 54 W. 34th
Johnston C. H. & Co. (Coburn H. Johnston, no Co.) 41 Union sq. W.
Johnston E. L. & Co. (Edward L. Johnston & James Fulton) 53 Front
Johnston J. H. & Co. (John H. & Albert Edward Johnston;—special partner, William J. Johnston, *Greenwich, Ct.*, $30,000; terminates 1st Feb. 1894) 150 Bowery & 17 Union sq, W.
Johnston J. Y. & Co. (Joseph Y. Johnston & Samuel Smith) 23 Murray & 27 Warren
Johnston N. & Son (Nathan & William F. Johnston) 97 N. Moore
Johnston W. R. & Co. (no inf.) 15 B'way
Johnston Brothers (James W. & Artemas B. Johnston) 155 E. 113th
Johnston & Co. (refused) 3 Lispenard
Johnston & Johnston (Lewis & Edward W. S. Johnston) 8 Centre
Johnston & Lichtenstein (dissolved) 30 Gt. Jones
Johnston & North (Edward M. Johnston & A. Lincoln North) 21 Harrison
Johnston & Washington (John W. Johnston & George Washington) 865 Seventh av.
Johnston, Tallman & Co. (George R. Johnston & Stephen S. & George D. Tallman;—special partners, Edward D. Thurston, *N. Y.* & Edwin Spaeth, *Newark, N.J.*, each $10,000; terminates 31st Jan. 1892) 41 Barclay & 391 W. 12th
Johnstone & Buckley (Robert K. Johnstone & William C. Buckley) 87 Ferry
Johnstone & Smedley (dissolved) 328 Fifth av.
Joints Lime Co. (refused) 21 Cortlandt
Jolly C. & Son (Charles & Leon Jolly) 952 B'way & 61 E. 12th
Jonas Charles S. & Brother (Charles S. & Richard A. Jonas) 23 Beekman
Jonasson Meyer & Co. (Meyer Jonasson, no Co.) 358 B'way
Jones Charles H. & Co. (Charles H. Jones, John Wilkinson & Robert J. Johnston) 114 Fulton
Jones David, Co. (Patrick Kiernan, Pres.; Augustus T. Docharty, Sec. Capital, $200,000. Directors: Patrick Kiernan, Augustus T. Docharty) First av. c E. 44th
Jones Mfg. Co. (inf. unattainable) 110 Fifth av,
Jones Trevor F. & Co. (Trevor F. & Henry H. Jones) 404 Broome

PROTECTION For Family, Home, Store, Factory, etc., by using only the "VULCAN" BRAND OF SAFETY MATCHES. Headquarters, 373 Washington Street, New York.

JON 152 JUL

Jones William L. & Co. (William L. Jones, no Co.) 229 B'way
Jones C. A. & Co. (Charles A. Jones, no Co.) 50 South
Jones D. & Son (Dramin & Henry Jones) 21 Walker
Jones D. S. & Co. (David S. & Henry F. Jones) 26 South
Jones N. & Co. (Henry G. Bell, only) 96 Chambers
Jones T. & Sons (Theron & Theron B. & Clarence P. Jones) 7 Murray
Jones Brothers (drugs) (dissolved) 798 Ninth av.
Jones Brothers (jewelers) (John T. & Thomas Jones) 176 B'way
Jones Brothers (hats) (Frank S. & Cyrus D. & Charles F. Jones) 72 & 79 Front
Jones & Birdsall (John E. Jones & Samuel E. Birdsall) 208 West
Jones & Collins (David J. Jones & Henry A. Collins) 23 Old sl.
Jones & Co. (builders) (D. H. & Walter Jones) 58 W. 13th
Jones & Co. (flour) (Eugene & Frederick Jones) 37 Broome
Jones & Co. (printers) (William F. jr. & Samuel E. Jones & Emmet Vanburen) 48 Beaver
Jones & Co. (umbrellas) (refused) 45 Lispenard
Jones & Crane (William A. Jones jr. & Alden S. Crane) 182 Nassau
Jones & Faile (Edward C. Jones & George E. Faile) 137 B'way
Jones & Greeley (James Dann Jones & Edward A. & William B. Greeley) 1 B'way
Jones & Roosevelt (Charles Jones & John E. Roosevelt) 120 B'way
Jones & Skinner (Thomas L. Jones & Robert W. Skinner) 131 William
Jones & Smith (no inf.) 10 Chatham sq.
Jones & Whitlock (Walter R. T. Jones & James A. Whitlock) 51 Wall
Jones, French & Maury (William W. Strother Jones jr. George B. French & Charles W. Maury) 58 Exchange pl.
Jones, Gordon Co. (Ltd.) (Robert Gordon, Pres.; Thomas B. Kingsland, Sec. Capital, $5,000. Directors: Robert Gordon, Thomas B. Kingsland, Allen Goklic) 204 West
Jones, Kennett & Hopkins (Nathaniel S. Jones, Francis J. Kennett, George B. Hopkins & George Kirkland) 56 B'way & 7 Exchange ct.
Jones' C. C., Sons (George T. & Abraham D. Jones) ft. Charles
Jones' Owen, Son (Walter O. Jones) 179 Eighth av.
Jones' Thomas, Son (Howard S. Jones) 6 Howard
Jonson Foundry & Machine Co. (Julius Jonson, Pres.; Abraham Frank, Sec.; Julius Elson, Treas. Capital, $60,000. Directors: Julius Jonson, Julius Elson, Martin Grossarth) 541 E. 118th
Jordan Stationery Co. (Robert S. Jordan, Pres.; Richard M. Jordan, Sec. Capital, $20,000 ; further Inf. refused) 30 Liberty
Jordan & Co. (Charles Jordan & William A. Long) 221 Centre
Jordan & Giller (Julius Jordan & Louis Giller) 19 Park pl, & 16 Murray
Jordan & Hodges (Edward Jordan & Thorndike D. Hodges) 160 B'way
Jordan & McLean (dissolved) 100 Eleventh av.
Jordan & Moriarty (James Jordan & Thaddeus Moriarty) 207 Park row
Jordan, Hodges & Dix (dissolved) 160 B'way
Jordan's Kosmic Oil Co. (Frank Jordan, propr.) 31 B'way

Jordan-Mills Mfg. Co. (Henry W. Jordan, Pres.; Henry Miller jr. Sec.; further inf. unattainable) 18 Cortlandt
Jorges & Lehmann (George Jorges & Leonard Lehmann) 697 Eighth av.
Joseph & Ashton (dissolved) 290½ B'way
Josephie, Son & Simons (Aaron & Isaac Josephie & Henry Simons) 640 B'way
Josephs Samuel & Co. (Samuel & Joseph S. & Harry S. Josephs) 305 E. 71st
Josephs & Glaser (dissolved) 66 Cherry
Josephson & Wartovsky (Bernhard Josephson & Isaac Wartovsky) 57 Bayard
Josephthal Brothers (dissolved) 654 B'way
Josle E. & A. (Emily & Augusta) 203 Broome
Journal of Commerce (David M. Stone, Pres.; Charles O. Gates, Sec.; William C. Prime, Treas. Capital, $64,000. Directors: David M. Stone, William C. Prime, John N. Stickney, Charles O. Gates) 76 Beaver
Journal of Useful Inventions Publishing Co. (Edgar de V. Vermont, Pres.; Gaston de Fontenilliat, Sec. Capital, $20,000. Directors: Edgar de V. Vermont, Gaston de Fontenilliat, A. de V. Vermont, D. T. Kimball, S. T. Apollonia) 744 B'way
Journal Publishing Assn. (Edgar P. Ackerman, propr.) 88 Park row
Joyce Thomas & Son (Thomas & Maurice J. Joyce) 41 Henry & 106 W. 125th
Joyce Brothers (John H. Joyce, only) 495 E. 139th
Jube John P. & Co. (John P. & William U. Jube) 97 Bowery
Judd Orange, Co. (Edward H. Phelps, Pres.; Asa O. Crosby, Sec. Capital, $400,000. Trustees: Edward H. Phelps, George S. Graves, James D. Safford, Charles H. Post, Howard Mansfield) 751 B'way
Judd H. L. & Co. (Hubert L. Judd, Pres.; Albert L. Woodworth, Sec.; John Day, Treas. Capital, $350,000. Directors: Herbert L. Judd, John Day, W. N. Clark jr. W. H. Edsall, B. F. Burnett) 87 Chambers & 69 Reade
Judd J. R. & Co. (dissolved) 191 W. 30th
Judd & Co. (no inf.) 17 W. Houston
Judelovits & Pollack (no inf.) 2276 Third av.
Judge Publishing Co. (not inc.) (William J. Arkell & Bernhard Gillam) 110 Fifth av.
Judson Pneumatic Mining Tramway Co. (Robert W. Chapin, Pres.; William L. Saunders, Sec. Directors: Robert W. Chapin, Henry D. Cooke, William R. Grace, William L. Turner, Lewis Walker) 45 B'way
Judson Pneumatic Street Railway Co. (Whitcomb L. Judson, Pres.; Harry L. Earle, Sec. Capital, $2,500,000. Directors: Whitcomb L. Judson, Lewis Walker, James F. Williamson, William W. Dudley, Robert W. Chapin, Henry D. Cooke, Harry L. Earle) 45 B'way
Judson Power Co. (Robert W. Chapin, Pres.; Harry L. Earle, Sec. Capital, $5,000,000. Directors: Robert W. Chapin, Edward Lauterbach, John T. Brigham, Eben O. McNair, John J. Macfarlane, George W. Delamater, Lewis Walker, William W. Dudley, Frederick W. Huldekoper, Henry D. Cooke, Harry L. Earle) 45 B'way
Judson Printing Co. (dissolved) 16 Beekman
Judson H. I. & Co. (Henry I. Judson & William H. Burger) 6 Wall
Judson Brothers (Pixleo & Lewis H. Judson) 49 Bond
Juhre & Ingverson (no inf.) 4 W. 14th
Juilliard A. D. & Co. (Augustus D. Juilliard, Duncan E. Mackenzie & Joseph R. Quinby) 56 Worth
Julian H. G. & Co. (Henry G. & Henry G. Julian jr.) 107 Grand
Julien Electric Co. (William Bracken, Pres.; Henry R. Waite, Sec. Capital $1,000,000. Directors:

IDEN & CO., University Place, 9th to 10th Sts., N. Y. | **MANUFACTURERS OF GAS FIXTURES AND ELECTROLIERS**

JUL 153 KAN

Jullen Edouard de Onters, Edmund Jullen, William Bracken, Stephen D. Hatch, S. Marsh Young, E. J. Moore, John T. Hand, J Seaver Page, Benjamin F. Archer, Flemming Tuckerman) 120 D'way

Jullen Electric Traction Co. (William Bracken. V. Pres.; Henry Weston, Sec.; Edward O. Coles, Treas. Capital, $3,000,000, Directors; Charles E. Warburton, William Bracken, S. A. B. Abbott, Edward O. Coles, A. C. Smith, Willoughby Weston, Frederick G. Corning) 120 D'way & Madison av. n E. 85th

Julienthaller Mineral Spring Co. (Montgomery H. Schuyler, Pres.; Samuel M. Roosevelt, Sec. Capital, $150,000, Directors; Montgomery H. Schuyler, Samuel M. Roosevelt, J. Murray Mitchell, M. M. Howland) 55 Beaver

Jung H. & Co. (Henry & C. Girardin Jang) 98 S. 5th av.

Jung & Eichner (Christian Jung & Lorenz Eichner) 419 E. 10th

Jungbluth & Weingartner (Julius Jungbluth & Edward Weingartner) 13 Gold

Junge William & Co. (William Junge & Oscar & Gustave Uhlmann) 302 E. 40th

Jungo F. W. & Co. (Frederick W. Jungo, no Co.) 48 Broad & Custom h.

Junger Brothers (Emil & Theodore Junger) 23 E. 4th

Jungermann Brothers (John J. & George Jungermann) 240 W. 27th

Junior & Schultz (John S. Junior & Christopher Schultz) 186 Duane

Junker & Meyer (no inf.) 2402 Second av.

Junker & Schubiger (Alois Junker & Joseph L. Schubiger) 402 W. 38th

Jurgens H. & Brother (Henry & Charles Jurgens) 1 Duane & 220 William

K

"K" Oxygen Supply Co. (George H. Everett, propr.) 157 W. 23d

Kaatz Theodore & Co. (Theodore Kaatz & Morris Kornicker), 148 Wooster

Kadano & Levy (David L. Kadane & Simon J. Levy) 311.Church

Kadyschewitz & Levitt (Bernhard A. Kadyschewitz & David Levitt) 62 Canal

Kaelber & Co. (dissolved) 1814 Third av.

Kaemmer M. & C. Stoecklein (Minna Kaemmer & Cecilia Stoecklein) 121 St. Mark's pl.,

Kaempffer Brothers (dissolved) 208 W. 40th

Kaempffer & Kratz (Gustav Kaempffer & Jacob Kratz) 208 W. 40th

Kahler P. & Sons (Peter J. & Charles O. Kahler, only) 815 B'way

Kahn Joseph & Son (Joseph & Samuel Kahn) 2 Av. A

Kahn Louis J. & Co. (Louis J. & Joseph Kahn) 2213 Third av.

Kahn B. & Son (Benoit Kahn, only) 32 Maiden la.

Kahn J. & R. (Julius R. & Rachel) 80½ Sixth av.

Kahn L. & M. & Co. (Louis & Moses Kahn & Samuel H. Levy) 10 Maiden la.

Kahn Brothers (meat) (Tassard & Eugene Kahn) 340 Eighth av. & 403 W. 26th

Kahn Brothers (metal) (Isaac & Emanuel S. & Jacob & German Kahn) 325 E. 19th & 580 E. 20th

Kahn & Co. (Joseph Kahn & Adolph Baer) 91 Av. B

Kahn & Frank (Joseph Kahn & Jacob Frank) 56 Walker

Kahn & Sanford (dissolved) no address

Kahner L. & Co. (Lazarus Kahner & Leopold Sinsheimer) 202 E. 100th

Kahnweiler & Roeder (Carl Kahnweiler & Jacob S. Roeder) 411 B'way

Kahrs H. & Co (Herman Kahrs & Henry G. Doschen) 206 E. 26th

Kainer Hugo & Co. (Hugo Kainer, no Co.) 17 S. William

Kaiser Brothers (Jacob & George Kaiser) 70 Murray & 104 Sixth av.

Kaiser & King (Charles Kaiser & Theodore Klug) 303 E. 44th

Kajok & Tudross (dissolved) 19 Washn.

Kalbfell & Wright (Andrew Kalbfell & James Wright) 2232 First av.

Kalbfleisch's Martin, Sons Co. (George W. Kenyon, Pres.; Leander T. Savage, Sec. Capital, $750,000. Trustees: George W. Kenyon, Thomas J. Parker, Charles Robinson Smith, Thomas W. Lowell, George W. Dillaway) 55 Fulton

Kaldenberg F. J., Co. (Frederick J. Kaldenberg, Pres.; Eberhard Faber, Sec Capital, $500,-000; further inf. unattainable) 215 E. 334

Kaley M. & Brother (Michael & John J. Kaley) 39 Little W. 12th

Kallske T. & A. S. (Theodore Kallske, only) 9 Desbrosses

Kalisk L. & Son (Leopold & Frederick Kaliski) 514 Ninth av.

Kallenberg A. & Brother (Albert & Herman Kallenberg) r 157 Goerck

Kalley J. N. & Son (Julius N. & Frederick D. Kalley) 171 B'way

Kalley & Benner (dissolved) 171 D'way

Kallman Brothers (Arnold & Jacob Kallman) 1491 Third av. & 2283 Seventh av.

Kallmann Philip & Son (Philip & Henry D. Kallmann) 206 E. 21st

Kalmus & Levy (dissolved) 585 D'way

Kalmus & Myers (Philip Kalmus & Charles S, Myers) 585 D'way

Kamak Mfg. Co. (dissolved) 59 Duane

Kamuterer & Bookstoever (John J. Kammerer & Louis Bookstoever) 111 Greene

Kamp & Baecker (Michael Kamp & John Baecker) 89 South

Kamp & Engelman (dissolved) 89 South

Kampe & Grout (dissolved) 34 E. Houston

Kampfe Brothers (Frederick & Otto & Richard Kampfe) 8 Reade

Kampmann & Meyer (C. Ernst Kampmann & Charles Meyer) 142 Grand

Kanawha & Ohio Railway Co. (Grinnell Burt, Pres.; William P. Palmer, Sec. Capital, $12,-200,000. Directors: Grinnell Burt, E. K. Robinson, R. V. D. Wood, William P. Palmer, J. M. Townley, R. T. H. Halsey, J. H. Sterling, H. D. Whitcomb, C. O. Hunter, Albert Gallup, E. W. Knight) 2 Wall

Kane Edward & Son (Edward & Henry Kane) 200 Av. A

Kane Hugh & Son (Hugh & Hugh H. Kane) 372 Washn. mkt

Kane R. W. & Co. (Richard W. Kane, Bernard Lenahen & Patrick Cummings) Rider av. n E. 140th

Kane Brothers (Arthur V. & Thomas M. Kane) 340 Canal

Kane & Behrens (Marshall C. Kane & John F. Dehrens) 100 Pearl

Kane & Nash (dissolved) 831 Eighth av.

Kaus & Peebles (William H. Kane & Robert J. Peebles) 51 W. 125th

Kane & Wright (Michael Kane & Robert J. Wright) 417 E. 46th & ft. E. 105th

Kane's Nicholas, Sons (Edward J. & Daniel J. Kane) 171 South

Kanenbley Brothers (Herman F. & August Kanenbley jr.) 85 Columbia

CIRCULARS ADDRESSED TO ANY TRADE IN THE U. S. { Facilities
PROMPT, CAREFUL WORK } THE TROW CITY DIRECTORY CO., } Unequalled.
AT MODERATE PRICES. } 11 University Place.

KAN 154 KEC

Kangaroo Line (Mailler & Quigrean, proprs.) 51 Stone & Pier 10 E. R.
Kann N. & Son (Nathan & Joseph Kann) 768 First av.
Kannofsky J. & Co. (John Kannofsky & Samuel Hang) 329 Canal
Kansas Loan & Trust Co. (no inf.) 96 B'way
Kantor, Brooks & Goldstein (dissolved) 145 E. B'way
Kantrovits & Rosenblum (no inf.) 10 Lispenard
Kantrowitz A. I. & Co. (Abraham I. Kantrowtz & Charles A. Yonge) 120 William
Kaplan David & Co. (David & Abraham Kaplan) 5 Rutgers pl.
Kaplan Joseph & Co. (Joseph Kaplan & Nathan Cohen) 518 W. 47th
Kaplan & Cohen (no inf.) 85 Hester
Kaplan & Matthews (Louis Kaplan & James Matthews) 8 Pike
Kaplan & Phillips (Paul Kaplan & Robert Phillips) 71 Essex
Karatsonyi & Kmetz (Nicholas Karatsonyi & Adolph G. Kmetz) 76 Second av.
Karcher Ph. H. & Co. (Philip H. Karcher & William Mohrmann) 14 Cedar
Karcski & Steinberg (dissolved) 17 Essex
Karelsen F. (Jacques E. & Adolphus E. & Frank E. Karelsen, only) 16 Maiden la.
Karelsen's B., Sons (Jacques E. & Adolphus E. & Frank E. Karelsen) 211 Franklin & E. 107th n First av.
Karlein & Liebert (Oscar Karlein & Conrad Liebert) 26 G'wich
Karr George & Co. (George Karr & George W. Wanmaker) 844 West
Karrer J. V. & Son (John V. & George J. Karrer) 43 Madison
Karsch Brothers (Edward & George Karsch) 525 Eighth av.
Kasebier E. & Co. (Edward Kasebier & Carl Vigolius) 445 Water
Kaskel & Kaskel (Albert & Max Kaskel) 20 W. 23d
Kaskell & Smyth (dissolved) 295 Third av.
Kasner Noah & Son (Noah & Adolph Kasner) 217 G'wich
Kassubau Henry F. & Co. (Henry F. Kassebau, Co. refused) 275 Bowery
Kassel J. & Son (Joseph & Abraham Kassel) 62 Loew av. W. Washn. mkt
Kastner & Williams (Rudolph C. Kastner & Myron R. Williams) 99 Franklin
Kastor Adolph & Brothers (Adolph & Nathan & Sigmund Kastor) 126 Duane
Kastriner H. & Son (Herman & Max Kastriner) 380 Canal
Kathmann Brothers (Henry & Dederick Kathmann) 1636 Tenth av.
Katz Brothers (olgars) (Mayer Katz, only) 1471 Park av.
Katz Brothers (drygds) (Jacob & Siegmund Katz) 27 Av. D & 1404 Second av.
Katz & Co. (Aaron Katz & Edward Dinkelspiel) 827 Church
Katz & Goodman (Adolph L. Katz & Eli M. Goodman) 88 Howard
Katz & Hynes (dissolved) no address
Katzenberg M. & Co. (Moe Katzenberg & Charles M. Rosenthal) 404 B'way
Katzenberg M. & Sons (Mayer & Charles & Henry Katzenberg) 74 Reade
Katzenstein L. & Co. (Leopold Katzenstein, Co. refused) 357 West
Katzenstein S. & Son (Simon & Jacob Katzenstein) 432 E. Houston
Kaufman Isidor & Co. (Isidor Kaufman & Siegfried Isidor) 649 B'way

Kaufman Louis & Co. (Louis Kaufman & David Kutner) 52 Maiden la.
Kaufman F. & Co. (Felix Kaufman, no Co.) 176 William
Kaufman W. G. & Co. (William G. Kaufman, no Co.) 36 Harrison
Kaufman & Pollak (Herman Kaufman & Leopold Pollak) 14 First av.
Kaufman & Strauss (Charles Kaufman & Adolph Strauss) 628 W. 39th & 622 W. 40th
Kaufman & Zucker (Samuel Kaufman & Marcus Zucker) r 370 E. 4th
Kaufman Brothers & Co. (Abraham & Herman Kaufman & David Lachenbruch) 1050 Third av.
Kaufman, Giles & Co. (Leo Kaufman, Isaac Giles & Moritz Kaufman) 50 Prince
Kaufmann Ernst & Son (Ernst & Charles Kaufmann) 246 Seventh av.
Kaufmann Isaac & Brother (Isaac & Sigmund Kaufmann) 120 Crosby
Kaufmann Joseph & Co. (Joseph Kaufmann, no Co.) 28 Bond
Kaufmann Louis & Co. (Louis Kaufmann & Harry Abrahams) 150 Canal
Kaufmann L. & Co. (Louis Kaufmann, no Co.) 447 Sixth av.
Kaufmann Brothers (Samuel & Julius Kaufmann) 350 Washn. & 202 Franklin
Kaufmann & Arnow (Edward Kaufmann & Richard N. Arnow) 154 Nassau
Kaufmann & Co. (Alexander & Maurice Kaufmann) 107 Duane
Kaufmann & Sanders (dissolved) 5 Deckman
Kaufmann & Strauss (Charles Kaufmann, William Strauss & Solomon Kaufmann) 77 Duane
Kaufmann & Wagner (dissolved) 5 Deckman
Kaufmann Brothers & Bondy (Gustav Kaufmann & Max Mayer:—special partner, Leopold Kaufmann; further inf. refused) 129 Grand & First av. c E. 234
Kaupper, Keil & Co. (John W. Knupper & Henry & Henry W. Keil) 123 Brond
Kautzmann T. & W. Speck (Theodore Kautzmann & William Speck) 180 Grand
Kavanagh & McAleenan (Henry E. Kavanagh & Henry McAleenan jr.) 44 Exchange pl.
Kay James & Co. (James & Robert Kay) 150 Washn. mkt
Kay William G. & Co. (William G. Kay, no Co.) 34 Washn.
Kaye & Einstein (Charles Kaye & Moses Einstein) 555 B'way & 126 Mercer
Kayser Julius & Co. (Julius Kayser, no Co.) 33 Greene & 9 Desbrosses
Kayton & Feustman (dissolved) 1954 Third av.
Kean T. W. & Co. (Thomas W. Kean, Kilen De Nunes & Arthur S. Mahoney) 46 Washn.
Kean & Carter (dissolved) 426 First av.
Keane James R. & Co. (James R. Keane & James H. Hennessey) 1357 Third av.
Kearney & Co. (no inf.) 25 Gt. Jones
Kearney & Foot Co. (James D. Foot, Pres.; Sandford D. Foot, Sec. Capital, $250,000. Trustees: James D. Foot, James Kearney) 101 Chambers
Kearsarge Silver Mining Co. (A. W. Leisenring, Pres.; William Bush, Sec. Capital, $2,000,000. Trustees: A. W. & John R. & E. B. Leisenring, William Bush) no address
Keary P. J. & Brother (Charles Keary, only) 207 Canal & 49 Howard
Keasbey Robert A. & Co. (dissolved) 56 Warren
Keasbey & Mattison (Henry G. Keasbey & Richard V. Mattison) 76 Maiden la.
Keck, Mosser & Co. (Thomas Keck & James K. &

**THE CALIGRAPH WRITING MACHINE,
HARTFORD, CONN.**

KED   155   KEL

Henry S. & Jacob & George K. Mosser) 39 Frankfort

Kedenburg J. P. A. & Brother (John P. A. & Jacob Kedenburg) 335 E. 46th

Kedenburg & Siegmund (Herman Kedenburg & John Siegmund) 1587 Second av.

Kedian & Brother (James Kedian, only) 246 Third av.

Keefe & Decannon (Timothy J. Keefe & William H. Decannon) 157 B'way

Keehne & Reed (Edward Keehne & Robert F. Reed) 250 Washn. mkt

Keeler David D. & Co. (dissolved) 150 Nassau

Keeler & Greenman (George W. Keeler & William D. Greenman) 35 Liberty

Keen Sutterle Co. (Ltd.) (Frederick W. Sutterle, Pres.; William Helmrath, Sec.; Hans Reincke, Treas. Capital, $100,000; further inf. unattainable) 91 Gold

Keeler's G. F., Son (George Keeler) 25 Ninth av.

Keenan Andrew & Son (Andrew & Walter F. Keenan) 12 Elm

Keenan & Co. (masons) (dissolved) 12 Chambers

Keenan & Co. (woolens) (Patrick H. Keenan & Patrick H. Collins) 28 Howard

Keenan & McGuinness (dissolved) 1490 Tenth av.

Keene & Dixon (dissolved) 5 Counties sl.

Keeney F. G. & Co. (Frank G. & George A. Keeney) 146 Beekman

Keep Mfg. Co. (not Inc.) (Oliver H. & Leah H. Keep) 609 B'way

Keep & Keen (Charles W. Keep & Robert L. Keen) 15 Broad

Keer & Briggs (dissolved) 52 Nassau

Keese & Bailey (Edmund Keese & Frank L. Bailey) 2262 Third av.

Kohlenbeck R. & Co. (Richard Kohlenbeck & Frederick Emigholz) 1547 Av. A

Kehoe W. & Son (William & John J. Kehoe) 187 G'wich

Kehr A. & Co. (no inf.) 344 Sixth

Kehrmann Brothers (no inf.) 312 E. 4th

Keilholz Brothers (Charles C. & William F. Keilholz) 48 Exchange pl.

Keinath Charles & Son (Charles & Charles Keinath jr.) 6 S. William

Keith Mfg. Co. (Monroe J. Keith, propr.) 105 Franklin

Keith D. & Co. (Francis W. & Lucy A. & Frederick W. Keith, only) 75 William

Kek & Co. (George F. & John Kek) 341 W. 37th

Kelliher John J. & Co. (dissolved) 102 Centre

Kell & Co. (dissolved) 480 Broome

Kelland Philip & Co. (Philip Kelland & Henry W. Fischer) 178 Pearl

Kelleher Brothers (Michael I. & James J. Kelleher) 1619 B'way

Keller Charles & Co. (Charles Keller, no Co.) 192 B'way

Keller John J. & Co. (John C. Garnaus, attorney) 39 Beaver

Keller Mfg. Co. (E. J. Keller, propr.) 117 Walker

Keller Printing Co. (John Keller, Pres.; further inf. unattainable) 708 B'way

Keller F. K. & Son (Frederick K. & William C. Keller) 664 Sixth av.

Keller H. C. & Co. (refused) 1907 Third av.

Keller J. & Son (Joseph & George A. Keller) 139 W. 24th

Keller L. H. & Co. (Frederick J. Boesse, Adolph & Hugo P. Keller, only) 64 Nassau

Keller M. von & Co. (Max von Keller & Charles W. Offermann) 157 William

Keller Brothers (Theodore & Julius L. Keller) 70 Av. A

Keller & Co. (Charles Keller & Jacob Ackermann) 175 Second

Keller & Frey (Frank Keller & Charles Frey jr.) 52 Maiden la.

Keller & Lang (dissolved) 164 Eighth av.

Keller & McNally (Samuel J. Keller & William H. McNally) 253 E. 83d

Keller & Schroeder (dissolved) 124 Park av.

Keller & Untermeyer (David & Henry & Emanuel Untermeyer & Samuel Aufhauser, only) 192 D'way

Keller & Yager (Irving W. Keller & Harry C. Yager) 821 Seventh av.

Keller & Young Mfg. Co. (inf. unattainable) 51 W. 125th

Keller, Ettinger & Fink (David Keller, Isaac D. Ettinger & Henry J. Fink) 24 John

Kelley Albert & Co. (Albert & Albert T. & Austin F. Kelley & Charles E. Miller) 87 Wall

Kelley Benjamin F. & Son (Benjamin F. & Harry N. Kelley) 21 Liberty

Kelley A. P. & W. E., Co. (no inf.) 80 Wall

Kelley & Bliss (James E. Kelley & Chauncey S. Bliss) 15 W. 28th

Kellock J. & I. (Jessie & Isabella) 2433 Second av.

Kellogg Peter C. & Co. (Peter C. & Charles W. Kellogg) 107 John

Kellogg C. L. & W. A. (Charles L. & William A. Kellogg & George H. Hitchcock) 9 W. 29th

Kellogg E. H. & Co. (Edward H. Kellogg, George W. & David W. Bartlett & Edward C. Banzay) 243 South & 475 Water

Kellogg E. L. & Co. (Edward L. & Amos M. Kellogg) 25 Clinton pl.

Kellogg S. P. & Co. (dissolved) 55 Cedar

Kellogg & Bach (dissolved) 229 Park row

Kellogg & Kilgen (Melville A. Kellogg & George J. Kilgen) 15 Wall

Kellogg & Shedden (Edward Kellogg & William F. Shedden) 94 Gold

Kellogg, Hitchcock & Co. (William A. Kellogg, George H. Hitchcock & Charles L. Kellogg) 24 Park pl.

Kellogg's Laboratory (C. L. & W. A. Kellogg, proprs.) 9 W. 29th

Kelly Bernard & Son (William P. Kelly, only) 187 West

Kelly Charles A., Co. (Charles A. Kelly, Pres. Capital, $20,000; further inf. unattainable) 354 G'wich

Kelly Eugene & Co. (Eugene Kelly, Joseph A. Donohoe & Edward Kelly) 45 Exchange pl.

Kelly Henry & Son (Henry & Joseph Kelly) 424 W. 42d

Kelly Horace R. & Co. (Ltd.) (Horace R. Kelly, Pres.; John C. Jacobsohn, Sec. Capital, $250,000; further inf. refused) 26 S. William

Kelly Hugh (Hugh Kelly; — special partners, Franklin Farrell, Ansonia, Ct., $87,500 & Charles H. Pine, Ansonia, Ct., $12,600; terminates 9th Oct. 1894) 71 Wall

Kelly John & Son (John & Edward J. Kelly) 620 W. 55th

Kelly A. M. & Son (Anna M. Kelly & George F. Laubeudorfer, only) 180 Grand

Kelly D. J. & M. C. (no inf.) 115 B'way & 30 E. 14th

Kelly J. & M. J. (John & Michael J.) 520 Sixth av.

Kelly J. M. & Co. (John M. Kelly, Co. refused) 3 Crosby

Kelly J. W. & Co. (no inf.) 237 Fulton

Kelly T. P. & Co. (Thomas P. Kelly & Daniel J. Kane) 96 John & 19 Platt

Kelly W. A. & Co. (William A. Kelly & James S. Duffy) 48 Fulton mkt

SPECIAL ATTENTION PAID TO THIS CLASS OF WORK — **BANKERS' & BROKERS' CIRCULARS DELIVERED** — **THE TROW CITY DIRECTORY CO. 11 University Place.**

KEL 156 KEP

Kelly Brothers (liquors) (dissolved) 789 Eleventh av.
Kelly Brothers (real estate) (Oliver & Alexander C. Kelly) 189 B'way
Kelly Brothers (stables) (dissolved) 1403 Ninth av. & Boulevard c W. 75th
Kelly & Allard (Thomas Kelly & Robert J. Allard) 681 B'way
Kelly & Callan (Eugene Kelly & Philip Callan) 419 Pearl
Kelly & Co. (Patrick J. Kelly, no Co.) 436 Water
Kelly & Cummings (William H. Kelly & Patrick F. Cummings) 55 Market
Kelly & Gallagher (John Kelly & John J. Gallagher) 206 E. 34th
Kelly & Leamy (dissolved) 1877 Av. A
Kelly & Macrae (Richard B. Kelly & William F. Macrae) 237 B'way
Kelly & Power (Owen Kelly & John J. Power) 141 West
Kelly & Rogers (Hugh G. Kelly & Thomas Rogers) r 157 E. 85th
Kelly & Tighe (Thomas Kelly & Michael Tighe) 355 West
Kelly & Wefer (Edward J. Kelly & John M. Wefer) 17 Bond
Kelly, Tucker & Henderson (Eugene Kelly jr. Preble Tucker, Harold G. Henderson & Charles J. Hardy) b Beekman
Kelly's Henry, Son (William H. Kelly) 1004 Sixth av.
Kelty G. L. & Co. (Gibbons L. Kelty & Charles M. Aikman) 869 B'way
Kemeys & Babcock (Edward Kemeys & Henry D. Babcock;—special partners, George G. Haven & Samuel D. Babcock, each $100,000; terminates 30th April, 1892) 18 Wall
Kemp J. A. & Co. (John A. & John M. Kemp) 181 Seventh av.
Kemp & Byrnes (Henry Kemp & John J. Byrnes) 416 Washn. mkt
Kemp & Winne (dissolved) 790 G'wich & ft. Charlton
Kemp, Day & Co. (John H. Kemp, Edwin Sherman & Sidney Thursby, only) 116 Wall & 100 Murray
Kempler & Selfter (Solomon Kempler & Seigfried Selfter) 51 Canal
Kempner D. & Son (David & Nathan Kempner) 602 Eighth av.
Kempner S. & Brother (Samuel & Eli Kempner) 83 Nassau
Kempster James, Printing Co. (James Kempster, propr.) 56 Cedar
Kempton C. W. & Arthur Thacher (Charles W. Kempton & Arthur Thacher) 61 B'way
Kempton J. P. & Co. (John P. Kempton, no Co.) ft. Charles
Kendall Mfg. Co. (dissolved) 154 Chambers
Kennedy F. A. Co. (Frank A. Kennedy, Pres.; James W. Hazen, Treas. Capital, $150,000; further inf. unattainable) 122 Chambers
Kennedy James & Son (James & George A. Kennedy) 488 W. 17th
Kennedy G. H. & Co. (George H. Kennedy & Frank J. Foster) 22 Duane
Kennedy M. & J. (Michael & John) 196 Washn. mkt
Kennedy Brothers (James B. Kennedy, only) 417 Willis av.
Kennedy & Daine (Michael Kennedy & John R. Daine) 234 W. 41st
Kennedy & Ginsel (William E. Kennedy & August W. Ginsel) 820 Stanton
Kennedy & McDermott (David Kennedy & William McDermott) 851 Bleeker

Kennedy & Moon (Joseph S. Kennedy & William R. Moon) 55 Beaver
Kennedy & Wall (dissolved) 2508 Third av.
Kennedy, Reinhart & Campbell (James & Patrick Kennedy, William Reinhart & Bernard J. Campbell) 542 W. 38th & ft. W. 51st
Kennelly William & Brother (William & Bryan L. Kennelly) 45 Liberty
Kennesaw Route (Leigh J. Ellis, agent) 203 B'way
Kenneson, Crain & Alling (Thaddeus D. Kenneson, Thomas C. T. Crain, Asa A. Alling & Daniel L. Gibbens) 15 Broad
Kenney & Sullivan (dissolved) 445 W. 45th
Kenny James & Son (James & George J. Kenny) 80 E. Houston
Kenny & Levy (dissolved) 89 Loew av. W. Washn. mkt
Kenny & Ratcliffe (Peter Kenny & William Ratcliffe jr.) 200 B'way
Kenosha Milling Co. (inf. unattainable) 19 Whitehall
Kent Brothers (Nicholas Kent, only) 404 Broome
Kent & Angus (William F. Kent & John Angus) 5 E. 28th
Kent & Daly (William J. Kent & Thomas F. Daly) 91 Av. D
Kentucky Central Railway Co. (Isaac R. Gates, Pres.; Lewis Rood, Sec.; Frank H. Davis, Treas. Capital, $7,000,000. Directors; Isaac E. Gates, George Bliss, Samuel Thomas, Calvin S. Brice, M. F. Ingalls, Elliott H. Pendleton, H. E. Huntington) 27 Broad
Kentucky Coal, Iron & Development Co. (Capital, $2,000,000; further inf. unattainable) no address
Kentucky Union Railway Co. (Francis D. Carley, Pres.; Leon T. Rosengarten, Sec. Capital, $5,000,000. Directors; Francis D. Carley, Henry C. McDowell, St. John Boyle, Leon T. Rosengarten, Alexander P. Humphrey, William R. Belknap, John M. Atherton, George M. Davis, C. H. & R. P. Stoll) 35 Wall
Kentucky & Arkansas Land & Industrial Co. (William R. Bergholz, Pres.; Charles H. Odell, Treas.; W. Bonner, Sec. Capital, $2,500,000. Directors; James G. Caldwell, George L. Danforth, John D. Adams, J. F. O'Shaughnessy, Charles H. Odell, William R. Bergholz, W. Bonner) 15 Cortlandt
Kenworthy J. P. & Co. (James P. Kenworthy & Walter R. Gray) 116 Duane
Kenyon C. (Clarence Kenyon:—special partner, Seaman L. Pettit, Hempstead, N. Y., $50,000; terminates 31st Dec., 1890) 70 Bowery
Kenyon, Baldwin & Co. (David A. & George M. Kenyon, William Baldwin & William J. Severn) Manhattan mkt & ft. W. 23d
Kenzie & Leauwe (Thomas Kenzie & George Leauwe) 262 Seventh av.
Keogan & May (Thomas Keogan & George May) r 80 N. Moore
Keogh C. D. & Co. (Christopher D. Keogh & Henry C. Smith) 8 Howard
Keokuk & Des Moines Railway Co. (Benjamin Brewster, Pres.; A. Bridgman, Sec.; James R. Cowing, Treas. Capital, $4,125,000. Directors; Hugh Riddle, Ransom R. Cable, Edward Johnstone, Henry A. Darling, David Dows, Robert C. Geer, Benjamin Brewster, Theodore Gilman, James R. Cowing) 13 William
Keppel Frederick & Co. (Frederick Keppel & William Macbeth) 20 E. 16th
Keppler Rudolph & Co. (Rudolph Keppler & Edward R. Vollmer) 89 Broad
Keppler & Schwarzmann (Joseph Keppler, Pres.; Adolph Schwarzmann, Treas.; Henry Wimmel, Sec. Capital, $100,000. Directors: Joseph Keppler, Adolph Schwarzmann, Henry Wimmel) 89 E. Houston

FOR THE BEST CO-PARTNERSHIP IN THE BEST CORPORATION SEE PAGE F IN BACK OF BOOK

KER 157 KID

Ker E. Thomas & Co. (E. Thomas Ker & Calvin Campbell) 834 B'way
Kerbs D. & Brother (dissolved) 91 William, 676 Third av. & 1018 Second av.
Kerbs & Spiess (dissolved) 1018 Second av.
Kerbs & Summerfield (David & Joseph Kerbs & Isidor Summerfield) 232 E. 26th
Kerbs, Wertheim & Schiffer (Edward Kerbs, Jacob Wertheim & Joseph J. Schiffer) 1018 Second av.
Kerby & Brother (Daniel & Joseph Korby) 50 Fulton
Korby & Johnston (William H. Kerby & Robert Johnston) 244 Canal
Keresey John & Co. (John Keresey, Hugh M. Gartlan & James H. Butler) 85 Pearl & 52 Stone
Kerin & Co. (Daniel J. Kerin & James Corbett) 1985 Third av.
Kerkmann & Holscher (George Kerkmann & Charles Holscher) 635 Third av.
Kern A. & Co. (Adolph & Henry Kern) 81 New
Kern G. & Co. (Gustav Kern, no Co.) 229 Bowery
Kern & Frey (Frederick Kern & Charles Frey) 1 Park row
Kern & Obermiller (Peter Kern & August Obermiller) 388 Bowery
Kernan F. G. & Co. (Felix G. Kernan & Nathaniel Lott) 14 Ann
Kernan Brothers & Quin (John D. & Nicholas P. & Francis Kernan & William P. Quin) 10 Wall
Kerr J. & J. (dissolved) 335 E. 121st & 339 E. 122d
Kerr R. B. & T. H. (Robert B. & Thomas H.) 16 Broad
Kerr Brothers (Samuel & William H. & David Kerr) 736 Second av. & 616 Ninth av.
Kerr & Campbell (Thomas J. Kerr & Hudson Campbell) 31 Nassau
Kerr & Co. (Hugh Kerr & George L. Miller) 304 B'way
Kerr & Rosario (James M. Kerr & Stanislaus M. Rosario) r 229 W. 32d
Kertscher & Co. (Herman Kertscher & Theodore H. Marktbaler) 520 W. 24th
Kertscher & Tiedt (dissolved) 520 W. 24th
Kesler Mining Co. (inoperative) 120 B'way
Kessel & Chadil (Frederick A. Kessel & Joseph Chadil) 102 Grand & 401 E. 91st
Kesselring & Muller (Henry Kesselring & George J. Muller) 202 E. 26th
Kessler Robert & Son (Robert Kessler, only) 368 Seventh av.
Kessler William & Son (William & Emil Kessler) 616 Eighth av.
Kessler & Co. (bankers) (William & Edward Kessler & Gustavo E. Kissel) 54 Wall
Kessler & Co. (buttons) (Christian Kessler, Richard Knupp & Leopold M. Schwerin) 16 Howard
Kessler & Co. (imps.) (Samuel & Adolph Kessler) 58 Day
Kessler, Behringer & Co. (George A. Kessler, John J. Behringer & George A. Semel) 20 Beaver
Ketcham Charles F. & Co. (Charles F. Ketcham & Thomas Nolan) 27 Nassau
Ketcham David E. & Co. (dissolved) Tenth av. c W. 165th
Ketcham George E. & Co. (George E. & William P. & E. Dorland Ketcham & George W. Woolsey) Eleventh av. c W. 63d
Ketcham J. W. & Co. (James W. Ketcham, no Co.) 51 Beekman
Ketcham & Butler (John B. Ketcham & John A. Butler) 58 W. 125th
Ketcham & Doyle (John B. Ketcham & Edward Doyle) 302 W. 126th

Ketcham & McDougall (Edward W. Ketcham & Hugh McDougall) 108 B'way
Ketcham & Ryan (Philip R. Ketcham & Edward J. Ryan) 177 Washn. mkt
Ketterer & Co. (Charles P. Ketterer, no Co.) 514 W. 13th & 138 S. 5th av.
Keuffel & Esser Co. (William Keuffel, Pres.; Herman Esser, Treas.; William L. E. Keuffel, Sec. Directors: William Keuffel, Herman Esser, William L. E. Keuffel) 127 Fulton & 42 Ann
Keane A. & Sons (August & Adolph & Emil F. Keane) 59 Duane
Kentgen Brothers (William & Charles Kentgen) 329 B'way
Keveney T. J. & Co. (Thomas J. & Hugh Keveney) 329 B'way
Keyes & Wilson (Seth C. Keyes & Daniel T. Wilson;—special partner, James W. Lawrence, Mt. Vernon, N. Y., $30,000; terminates 15th Feb. 1893) 372 Broome
Keyport Steamboat Co. (Joseph Cornell, Pres.; George M. Lewis, Treas. Capital, $75,000. Directors: Thomas D. Abrams, Abram Barsell, Joseph & Samuel J. Cornell, George M. Lewis) Pier 44 (new) N. R.
Keys Jesse G. & Son (Jesse G. & Charles H. Keys) 260 Cherry & 529 Water
Keys & Lockwood (William A. Keys & Jared Lockwood) 869 B'way
Keyser A. & Son (dissolved) 180 Delancey
Keyser & Co. (William H. & George & Mary A. Keyser) 101 Washn. mkt
Keyser & Garraty (Maurice Keyser & John J. Garraty) 55 Nassau
Keystone Cement Co. (Antonio F. de Navarro, Pres.; Alfonso de Navarro, Sec.; Frederick W. Sharon, Treas. Capital, $150,000. Directors: Antonio F. & Alfonso de Navarro, Frederick W. Sharon, Francis G. Newland, Charles R. Shepard, George Collingworth, James Clyne) 71 B'way
Keystone Collar Co. (Henry J. White, propr.) 52 Howard
Keystone Construction Co. (consolidated with N. Am. Construction Co.) 171 B'way
Keystone Gold Mining Co. (Frederick W. Pitcher, Pres.; Alfred W. Gedney, Sec.; Conrad H. Abelman, Treas. Capital, $500,000. Directors: Charles W. Chase, Frederick W. Pitcher, Gustav H. Schwab, Conrad H. Abelman & William P. Wilder) 812 Washn.
Keystone Paper Co. (not inc.) (J. Harper Bonnell & Frederic R. Coffin) 164 Nassau
Keystone Seal & Press Co. (Ltd.) (James C. Beach, Pres.; Albert B. Schofield, Sec. Capital, $60,000. Trustees: James C. Beach, Albert B. & William H. Schofield) 170 B'way
Keystone Watch Club Co. (no inf.) 2 W. 14th
Khasan & Co. (Naum Khasan, no Co.) 115 Broome
Kibbe, Chaffee & Co. (Henry R. Kibbe, Edward J. Chaffee, Alexander Beach & Harry G. Kibbe) 45 Worth
Kidd George W. & Co. (George W. Kidd, no Co.) 35 Water
Kidd W. I. & Co. (Washington I. Kidd & William Gardner) 304 E. 95th
Kidder Jerome, Mfg. Co. (Established over 30 years, and incorporated 1881, under the laws of the State of New York; information refused only on account of collections on foreign money orders and drafts) 820 Broadway
Kidder A. M. & Co. (Amos M. Kidder, Horace J. Morse, Charles D. Marvin & William M. Kidder) 18 Wall
Kidder, Peabody & Co. (Francis H. & Oliver W. & Frank E. Peabody, George C. Magoun, Thomas Baring, Frank G. Webster, George F. Crane & Herbert L. Griggs) 1 Nassau

TYPEWRITING DONE BY THE TROW CITY DIRECTORY CO., 11 University Place.

KID　　　　　158　　　　　KIN

Kidney & Farlees (Alfred H. Kidney & George E. Farless) 20 Platt
Kiel & Sudhaus (dissolved) 72 Fulton
Kiemeyer F. & Co. (Frederick Kiemeyer & John Mayer) 241 South
Kieran & Lynch (Patrick Kieran & James Lynch) 232 & 1445 First av.
Kiernan News Co. (William G. Clapp, Pres.; Clarence F. Birdseye, Sec. Capital, $200,000. Trustees: William G. Clapp, Clarence F. Birdseye, Charles Tracy, John J. Kiernan) 30 Broad
Kierst & Co. (M. & John J. Kierst) 81 New & 215 E. 100th
Kiersted & Storm (dissolved) 196 B'way
Kies Brothers (inf. unattainable) r 428 W. 37th
Kiessel & Fachner (Jacob Kiessel & Leon E. Fachner) 4 E. 20th
Kiffe & Voges (Frederick W. Kiffe & Justus Voges) 51 Front
Kiggins & Tooker Co. (Isaac C. Kiggins, Pres.; Henry G. Kiggins, Sec.; Charles S. Kiggins, Treas. Directors: Isaac C. & Charles S. & Henry G. Kiggins, Emma Tooker) 128 William
Kihn C. E. & A. C. (Charles E. & Alfred C.) 26 Church
Kilborne A. W. & Co. (Allerton W. Kilborne & Clarkson Runyon) 40 Wall
Kildare & Son (James L. Kildare, only) 1177 Third av.
Killan Brothers (Theodore E. & William Killan) 157 W. 32d
Killan & Meyer (Adam Killan & George Meyer) 389 Broome
Killerlane & Ryder (Donald Killerlane & Thomas F. Ryder) 240 West
Killian & Vermilya (dissolved) 128 B'way
Killough J. H. & Co. (James H. Killough & Frank E. Stultz) 249 Washn.
Kilpatrick & Co. (dissolved) 589 Eleventh av. & 1586 B'way
Kimball Austin & Co. (Austin & Hazen Kimball) 155 West
Kimball Elias & Co. (Elias Kimball & Charles E. Erikeson) 406 W. 20th
Kimball William S. & Co. (William S. Kimball & James C. Hart) 11 Warren
Kimball R. S. & Co. (Robert J. Kimball & Alfred B. Lounsbery) 16 Broad
Kimball & Parker (Charles O. Kimball & Horace J. Parker) 49 W. 33d
Kimball Brothers & Co. (Richard C. Kimball & William Matter, only) 132 Reade
Kimball, Howell & Co. (dissolved) 68 B'way & 17 New
Kimbel A. & Sons (Anthony & Henry & Anthony Kimbel jr.) 7 E. 20th & 458 Tenth av.
Kimber Alfred & Co. (Alfred Kimber, no Co.) 111 B'way
Kimberly & Co. (A. L. Kimberly & Charles W. Johnson) 8 Bridge
Kimmel D. & Son (David & Osias Kimmel) 114 Division
Kimmel & Voigt (George R. Kimmel & Henry E. F. Voigt) 242 Canal
Kimmig Brothers (Peter & Louis Kimmig) 198 Eighth av.
Kimpel Brothers (George C. & John N. Kimpel) 556 Eighth av.
King Alexander & Co. (Alexander & George W. King) 54 Leonard
King D. Webster, Glue Co. (D. Webster King, Pres.; D. Webster Dow, Sec. Capital, $150,000. Directors: D. Webster King, D. Webster Dow, Walter K. Purington) 280 Pearl
King Herbert Booth & Brother (Herbert Booth & Frederic Louis King) 202 B'way

King Hugh & Co. (Hugh King, no Co.) 530 Hudson
King John & Son (John H. King, only) 141 Maiden la.
King Locomotive Works (Albert H. King, Pres.; J. H. Longstreet, Treas. Directors: Albert H. King, John Headden, J. H. Longstreet) 11 Wall
King Thomas & Son (Thomas & Thomas L. King) 64 W. 13th
King Wheel Co. (no inf.) 51 Barclay
King A. & Son (Abraham & Henry King) 208 Bowery
King A. H. & Co. (Adolph H. King, Isidor Cohn & Isidor Ball) 627 B'way & 194 Mercer
King B. & H. (Bernard & Hyman) 2 Bond
King C. M. & Co. (Clarence M. King & James W. Connor) 58 Frankfort
King J. B. & Co. (J. Berre & George R. King) 24 State
King J. O. & Co. (Jabe O. King, no Co.) 76 Franklin
King L. C. & Co. (Lewis C. & Eugene F. King & George E. D. Todd) 171 Front
King M. & Son (Michael & Jacob King) 88 E. Houston
King R. jr. & Co. (Richard King jr. & Reginald Fry) 67 Exchange pl. & 24 New
King V. C. & C. V. (Vincent C. & C. Volney King) 517 West
King W. A. & Co. (William A. King & Edwin Robinson) 514 G'wich
King & Clement (Horatio C. King & George A. Clement) 38 Park row
King & Golden (dissolved) 165 Bank, 5¼ Hudson & 6 Clinton pl.
King & Hargrave (Edward J. King & Thomas Hargrave) 346 Sixth av.
King & Purcell (William H. King & Thomas Purcell) 42 Nassau & 60 Cliff
King's Edward J. Sons (Bennett J. & Edward J. King jr.) 97 Greene
King's James G. Sons (A. Gracie & John Alsop & Frederick Gore King & James G. K. Duer) 53 William
King-Hinckley Co. (Walter F. Hinckley, Pres.; Charles E. King, Sec. Capital, $30,000. Directors: Walter F. Hinckley, Charles E. King, George W. Kenyon) 42 Bond
Kingan Provision Co. (refused) 329 G'wich
Kingdon C. & H. (Clara & Hannah) 1554 Ninth av.
Kingman & Campbell (dissolved) 264 Canal
Kings County Elevated Railway Co. (James Jordan, Pres.; Henry J. Robinson, Sec.; James H. Frothingham, Treas. Capital, $1,000,000. Directors: James Jordan, Wendell Goodwin, Edward A. Abbot, James O. Sheldon, Henry J. Davison, William A. Read, August Belmont jr., S. Newton-Smith, Henry J. Robinson) 15 Broad
Kings County Fire Ins. Co. (William E. Horwill, Pres.; Edward S. Terhune, Sec. Capital, $150,000. Directors: William E. Horwill, G. W. Griffith, Samuel S. Free, Edward North, Robert Irwin, John N. Hayward, James M. Brookfield, Samuel Longman, Adrian M. Suydam, William Brookfield, William H. Male, Martin Joost, Charles Longman, Lewis Hurst, Daniel Smith, Ezra B. Tuttle, Charles F. Pope) 139 B'way
Kings County Journal Publishing Co. (Michael J. McGrath, Pres.; Charles C. Overton, Sec. Capital, $6,000. Directors: Michael J. McGrath, Charles C. & Robert H. Overton, John Neville, William W. Smith) 163 Maiden la.
Kingsberg & Cohen (Abraham Kingsberg & Bernhard Cohen) 181 Spring
Kingsford's Oswego Starch Depot (Oswego Starch Factory, proprs.) 146 Duane

THADDEUS DAVIDS CO., WRITING INKS, SEALING WAX, MUCILAGE.
MAKE THE BEST

KIN .159 KLO

Kingsland A. C. & Sons (refused) 58 Broad
Kingsland & Comstock (Daniel F. Kingsland & James C. Comstock) 5 Fulton fish mkt
Kinney Tobacco Co. (Francis S. Kinney, Pres.; William H. Butler, Sec. Capital, $100,000. Directors: Francis S. & J. D. Kinney & William H. Butler) 513 W. 22d
Kinsman F. W. & Co. (Frank W. & Frank W. jr. & Frederick G. Kinsman) 343 Fourth av.
Kinstler Brothers (Louis Z. & August D. Kinstler) 452 Canal
Kip Henry & Co. (Henry Kip & Augustus W. Drake) 198 B'way
Kipling E. E. (Edward E. Kipling:—special partner, Juliette B. Kipling, $28,000; terminates 16th Feb. 1898) 182 B'way
Kipp Wagon Works (John L. Kipp, propr.) 209 Eldridge
Kipper, Vogel & Co. (Emil F. Kipper & Bernard Vogel, no Co.) 17 Malden la.
Kirby & Durckets (David D. Kirby & Charles H. Burckett) 24 Liberty
Kirby & Dwight (Abram M. Kirby & Edmund Dwight jr.) 51 Cedar
Kirby & Halsted (James H. Kirby & James M. Halsted) 87 Front
Kirchhof & Brown (William Kirchhof & Isaac J. Brown) 166 E. 82d
Kirchner George & Co. (George Kirchner & Arnold C. Rank) 33 W. 23d
Kirk David B. & Co. (David B. Kirk, no Co.) 81 New
Kirk E. K., Mfg. Co. (inf. unattainable) 68 Murray
Kirk H. B. & Co. (Harford D. Kirk & Peter J. L. Searing) 60 Fulton, 9 Warren & 1158 B'way
Kirk Brothers (George & Joseph Kirk) 849 Washn.
Kirk & Kelly (dissolved) 15 Downing
Kirker & Friedman (Charles F. Kirker & Lewis W. Friedman) 554 B'way & 92 Crosby
Kirkham H. P. & Son (Henry P. & George K. Kirkham) 76 Broad
Kirkland Brother (William H. Kirkland) 103 Front
Kirkman & Son (Ann & Alexander S. Kirkman) 30 Catharine
Kirkwood C. & Co. (dissolved) 197 Wooster
Kirmss E. & Co. (Edward Kirmss, Co. refused) 94 Clinton
Kirschbaum Brothers (George & Max Kirschbaum) 547 Ninth av. 301 Seventh av. & 2259 Second av.
Kirschbaum & Hunter (dissolved) 303 Seventh av. & 547 Ninth av.
Kirschbaum Brothers (Daniel & Morris Kirshbaum) 99 E. B'way
Kirtland Brothers & Co. (Herman C. Rose, only) 62 Fulton
Kirtland, Andrews & Co. (Ltd.) (William H. Kirtland, Pres.; Charles E. Ensign, Sec.; Edson H. Andrews, Treas.; further inf. refused) 49 Union sq. E.
Kisch Mfg. Co. (not inc.) (David Kisch, Ignats Modry & Louis Frankenstein) 22 & 46 Lispenard
Kissam & Allen (dissolved) 6 & 14 Park pl.
Kissam, Whitney & Co. (Samuel H. Kissam, Henry N. Whitney & Eugene R. Washburn) 11 Broad & 184 Park av.
Kistler's Stephen, Sons (Milo & Michael D. Kistler) 103 Gold
Kitchen George H. & Co. (George H. Kitchen, Pres.; Patrick F. Gibbons, Sec. Capital, $125,000. Trustees: George H. & John F. Kitchen, Patrick F. & John J. Gibbons) 78 University pl.
Kitching & Bicknell (Frank W. Kitching & George A. Bicknell) 94 Reade

Kittel J. & Co. (Joseph J. Kittel, no Co.) 111 D'way
Kittle & Co. (Jonathan G. Kittle & James Palache) 88 Wall
Klaber S. & Co. (Simon & James & Maurice Klaber) 47 W. 42d & 58 W. 43d
Klapper R. & B. Goodson (Roewy Klapper & Boris Goodson) 156 E. B'way
Klappert's C. W. & Sons (Emil W. & Frederick W. Klappert) 328 E. 25th
Klauberg C. & Brothers (Charles A. & William J. & Augustus H. Klauberg) 173 William
Klausman & Mayer (William Klausman & Rudolph J. Mayer) 2253 Third av.
Klausner & Stern (Elias Klausner & Aaron Stern) 101 Stanton
Klaw & Erlanger (Marc Klaw & Abraham L. Erlanger) 26 W. 30th
Klee Henry & Sons (Henry & Ernest & Henry Klee jr.) 58 Ninth av.
Klee J. & Co. (Jacob & Bernhard S. & Benjamin Klee) 628 B'way & 180 Crosby
Klee & Co. (Adam Klee & Michael J. Wolf) 1388 Ninth av.
Klein Henry & Co. (Henry Klein & Rudolph & William H. Jahr) 44 Cortlandt
Klein John G. & Co. (John G. Klein & Adam Gerhard) 247 G'wich
Klein F. & Son (Frederick & Frederick Klein jr.) 705 Sixth
Klein M. J. & Co. (dissolved) 21 Bond
Klein Brothers (Julius & Edward Klein) 81 Av. A
Klein & Co. (Eugene D. Klein & Max A. Kreielsheimer) 424 E. 50th
Klein & Grad (Carl Klein & Jacob Grad) 77 Av. C
Klein & Leventhal (Max J. Klein & Abraham Leventhal) 21 Bond
Klein, Harriman & Co. (Louis Klein, William E. Harriman & James Bogle:—special partners, Edouard Gros-Hartmann, Wesserling, Germany, $100,000; & Emanuel Brossel, Lyons, France, $150,000; terminates 30th Nov. 1892) 28 Greene
Kleiner George & Co. (George & Meyer Kleiner) 463 Third av.
Klenck E. T. & Son (no inf.) 88 Hudson
Klenen Martin & Co. (Martin Klenen, no Co.) 304 B'way
Klenk George M. & Co. (George M. Klenk & Arno Bley) 28 E. 14th
Klenke F. P. & H. C. (Frederick P. & Horatio C.) 1182 Ninth av. & 44 W. End av.
Klie Brothers (John D. & John F. Klie) 222 Washn.
Kliesrath & Koonts (Jacob Kliesrath & Anthony Koonts) 2653 Third av.
Klim, Linder & Bauer Lithographing Co. (refused) 10 Warren
Kling & Co. (dissolved) 101 Columbia
Kling, Guertin & Co. (Frederick Kling, Peter A. Guertin & George Kling) 540 Pearl
Klingenstein Brothers (clothing) (Sigmund & Henry Klingenstein) 83 Walker & 812 Grand
Klingenstein Brothers (shirts) (Bernhard & Jacob Klingenstein) 16 Walker & 47 Av. A
Klingenstein & Kaufman (Solomon Klingenstein & Louis Kaufman) 59 Av. A
Klingler S. & Brother (dissolved) 30 S. 5th av.
Kloeblen A. & Co. (Albert Kloeblen & George Biadel) 20 Thompson av. W. Washn. mkt
Kloepfer Brothers (no inf.) 446 E. 122d
Kloes F. J., Mfg. Co. (inf. unattainable) 260 Canal
Kloh William & Co. (William Kloh, no Co.) 629 D'way
Kloppenburg's H., Son (Frederick Kloppenburg) 404 W. 14th

COMPILED WITH ACCURACY AND DESPATCH. **CLASSIFIED BUSINESS LISTS.** **(THE TROW CITY DIRECTORY CO. 11 University Place.**

KLO — 160 — KNO

Kloth & Landwehr (Henry Kloth & . Dederick Landwehr) 16 Beaver

Klots Brothers (dissolved) 369 Rivington

Klots Felix S. & Co. (Felix S. Klots & Clarence C. Ross) 542 B'way

Klots Fred., Mfg. Co. (Frederick Klots & Co. propra.) 121 Prince

Klots Frederick & Co. (Frederick Klots & Herman Oswald) 121 Prince

Klots & Veit (Jacob S. Klots & Gustave Veit) 36 E. Houston

Klugkist, Power & Co. (dissolved) 34 Beaver

Klumpp & Hains (dissolved) 124 Elizabeth

Knab Brothers (Charles & Philip Knab) 366 Bowery

Knabe William & Co. (William Knabe & Co. Mfg. Co. propra.) 148 Fifth av.

Knabe D. & H. (Dederick & Henry) 112 & 184 Centre & 174 Grand

Knapp Mfg. Co. (Lucien Knapp, Pres.; William Waldenburg, Sec. Capital, $25,000. Directors: Lucien Knapp, William Waldenburg, F. W. Kalulusch) 22 Frankfort

Knapp Rubber Binding Co. (Sheppard Knapp, Pres.; Edward H. Bailey, Treas. Capital, $75,000. Directors: Sheppard & Charles E. Knapp, Edward H. Bailey) 273 Canal & 189 Sixth av.

Knapp Sheppard & Co. (Sheppard Knapp, no Co.) 188 & 189 Sixth av.

Knapp P. B. & Sons (Peter B. & Frank F. & Gilbert F. Knapp) 362 Hudson & 868 Eighth av.

Knapp S. T. & E. J. (Samuel T. & Edward J.) 202 West

Knapp Brothers (no inf.) 52 Fulton

Knapp & Co. (Joseph F. & Joseph P. Knapp) 50 Park pl.

Knapp & Gallagher (Ella A. Knapp & Margaret A. Gallagher) 4 W. 22d

Knapp & Griffin (Shepherd Knapp & Charles H. Griffin) 11 Wall

Knapp & Vannostrand (Halsey W. Knapp & Daniel R. Vannostrand) 208 & 216 Washn.

Knapp's C., Son & Co. (William T. Knapp, no Co.) 96 Murray

Knauth, Nachod & Kuhne (Percival Knauth, Frederick Nachod & Frederick Kuhne) 5 S. William

Knebel G. & K. (Gertrude & Katz) 309 E. 78th

Kneeland Henry T. & Co. (Henry T. & Franklin E. Kneeland ;—special partner, Edward W. Eames, Buffalo, N. Y., $50,000; terminates 8th Oct. 1891) 104 Produce Ex.

Kneeland, Stewart & Epstein (Stillman F. Kneeland, Ira B. Stewart, Jesse S. Epstein) 40 Chambers

Knevals & Perry (Sherman W. Knevals, James W. Perry & Edward J. Knauer) 52 Nassau

Knickerbacker H. & Co. (Henry Knickerbacker, no Co.) 70 B'way & 18 New

Knickerbocker Agency (Arthur D. Cochrane, propr.) 684 B'way

Knickerbocker Apartment Co. (Charles Macdonald, Pres.; Walter L. Oliphant, Sec.; James T. Woodward, Treas. Capital, $500,000. Trustees: Edward Bell, Alexander Galid, Levi Holbrook, Robert S. & Robert G. Hone, Henry S. Leech, Charles Macdonald, Henry O. May, William B. Ross, Edgar T. Welles, James T. Woodward) 347 Fifth av.

Knickerbocker Art Gallery (Albert C. Roosevelt, propr.) 8 W. 14th

Knickerbocker Brewing Co. (Maussell Van Rensselaer jr. Pres.; J. Edgar Hance, Sec. Capital, $500,000. Directors: Maunsell Van Rensselaer jr. James E. Granniss, J. Edgar Hance, Solomon Ranger) 336 W. 18th

Knickerbocker Catering Co. (William Fowler jr. Pres.; William Fowler, S.c. Capital, $6,000;

Directors: William & William Fowler jr. John L. Adams) 35 Carmine

Knickerbocker Conservatory (not Inc.) (Charles G. Doring & Charles C. Giegler) 44 W. 14th

Knickerbocker Express Co. (George Scott, propr.) 1 Lispenard, 318 Canal, 117 John & 31 Hudson

Knickerbocker Fire Ins. Co. (Edmund W. Albro, Pres.; William P. Bogert Sec. Capital, $210,000; further inf. unattainable) 64 Wall

Knickerbocker Guide Co. (William F. Allen, Pres.; Edwin S. Allen, Sec. Capital, $60,000; further inf. unattainable) 46 Bond

Knickerbocker Ice Co. (Robert Maclay, Pres.; Little O. Reeve, Sec.; Edmund A. Smith, Treas. Capital, $2,000,000. Trustees: Robert Maclay, Horace Dennett, Edward E. Conklin, Orrin Dennett, Moses B. Maclay, Reuben A. Compton, James Shindler, Robert McCullough, H. T. Farrington) 432 Canal

Knickerbocker Laundry (Marie L. Driggs, propr.) 439 Sixth av.

Knickerbocker Lumber Co. (Charles B. Barnes, Sec.; further inf. refused) 85 Wall

Knickerbocker Steamboat Co. (John E. Hoffmire, Pres.; John Englis jr. Treas. Directors: John E. Hoffmire, Stephen V. White, Adolph H. Borman, John jr. & Charles M. Englis, John D. Hoffmire) 116 South

Knickerbocker Storage Co. (Ltd.) (John J. Moore, Pres.; William H. Kelly, Sec. Capital, $10,000; further inf. unattainable) 6 E. 14th, 426 E. 24th & 922 Ninth av.

Knickerbocker Subscription Agency (J. Irving Burns, propr.) 132 Nassau

Knickerbocker Trust Co. (John P. Townsend, Pres.; Frederick L. Eldridge, Sec. Capital, $500,000. Directors: Joseph S. Auerbach, Charles T. Barney, James H. Breslin, I. Townsend Burden, Frederick G. Bourne, Samuel J. Colgate, Ira Davenport, Henry F. Dimock, William A. Duer, Jacob Hays, A. Foster Higgins, Harry B. Hollins, David H. King jr. Edward V. Loew, George J. Magee, Robert Maclay, Henry W. T. Mali, Robert G. Remsen, Andrew H. Sands, John S. Tilney, John P. Townsend, Charles F. Watson, Charles H. Welling) 234 Fifth av.

Knie F. & Son (Frederick Knie & Frederick Knie jr.) 347 E. 77th

Knieriem & Martens (dissolved) 163 E. 86th

Kniering & Souder (Conrad Kniering & James R. Souder) 179 Grand

Kniffin & Tooker (Thomas B. Kniffin & George W. Tooker) 48 Murray

Knight George D. & Co. (George D. Knight & Charles Loring) 208 E. 23d

Knight A. L. & Co. (dissolved) 7 Ferry

Knight J. N. & Son (James N. & James P. Knight) 755 Seventh av.

Knight Brothers (billiards) (refused) 474 Sixth av.

Knight Brothers (patents) (Herbert & Harry E. & Octavius Knight) 234 B'way

Knight & Bill (Robert T. Knight & Conrad Bill) 26 Ann

Knight & Garleck (Jacob & Joseph N. Knight, only) 315 Washn.

Knight-Bruce & Lionel Samuel (J. C. L. Knight-Bruce & Lionel Samuel) 91 Wall

Knighton & Sampson (Robert Knighton & Robert L. Sampson) 95 Dieroker

Knit Goods Trading Co. (dissolved) 25 Lispenard

Knobel H. & Co. (Herman Knobel & Sigmund Sommers) 513 B'way

Knobloch Philip & Son (Philip & Philip Knobloch jr.) 356 Bowery

Knobloch H. & Brother (Henry & Frederick Knobloch) 1098 Second av.

Knobloch H. & K. (Herman & K. Knobloch) 293 G'wich

SPECIAL ATTENTION PAID TO THIS CLASS OF WORK } **BANKERS' & BROKERS' CIRCULARS DELIVERED** { **THE TROW CITY DIRECTORY CO.** 11 University Place.

KNO   161   KOH

Knodel & Trostel (Adolph Knodel & Ferdinand Trostel) 105½ Second av.
Knoedler M. & Co. (John & Roland F. & Edmond L. & Charles L. Knoedler, only) 170 Fifth av
Knoeller & Schuetz (John A. Knoeller & Charles Schuetz) 61 Nassau
Knoll Brothers (Adam & Emil Knoll) 1228 Third av.
Knoll & Prichard (Louis Knoll & Nathaniel B. W. Prichard) 304 Washn. mkt
Knoop, Freriohs & Co. (Ludwig Knoop & Julius von Knoop, only) 3½ Cotton Ex.
Knothe Brothers (Adolf C. & Frank Knothe) 521 B'way
Knower W. & G. (William & George jr.) 104 W. 125th
Knower & Cooley (Benjamin Knower & James C. Cooley) 113 Duane & 26 Thomas
Knowles Frederick C. & Co. (Frederick C. Knowles & Patrick H. Kearney) 88 Desbrosses
Knowles Brothers (marble) (James H. & John J. Knowles) 57 Lafayette pl.
Knowles Brothers (saltpetre) (William F. Knowles, only) 62 William
Knowlton William & Sons (Edwin F. & George W. & Eben J. Knowlton, only) 564 B'way & 100 Crosby
Knowlton & Co. (D. Henry Knowlton & J. Sewell Tappan) 15 Broad
Knox Andrew & Son (Andrew & James C. Knox) 643 Sixth av.
Knox A. A. & Co. (Addison A. Knox, Co. refused) 52 E. 9th
Knox & Co. (dissolved) 817 B'way
Knox & Woodward (Charles H. Knox & Henry E. Woodward) 52 William
Knoxville & Ohio R. R. Co. (Edward J. Sanford, Pres.; Louis M. Schwan, Sec.; J. Neil Mitchell, Treas.; Capital, $1,123,000. Directors: Charles M. McGhee, Samuel Thomas, Calvin S. Brice, Edward J. Sanford, John G. Moore, John H. Hall, George S. Scott, John H. Inman, John A. Rutherford) 10 Wall
Knudson, Paterson & Co. (Morris F. Knudson, Robert W. Paterson, John T. Wilson & William S. Paterson) 154 Front
Kny Richard & Co. (Richard Kny & John Brune) 10 Cortlandt
Kobart & Wanmaker (dissolved) 6 W. 35th & 105 W. 81st
Koblenzer & Dasian (Morris Koblenzer & Moses Dasian) 78 Franklin
Kobre & Herschmann (Max Kobre & Samuel I. Herschmann) 40 Canal
Koch Andrew & Sons (Andrew & Frederick Koch, only) 455 First av.
Koch William A. & Brother (William A. & Frederick Koch) 59 E. 114th
Koch F. A. & Co. (F. August Koch & Ernest Stratmann) 100 Chambers
Koch H. C. F. & Co. (Henry C. F. Koch & Adolph Riesenberg) 319 Sixth av.
Koch L. & Co. (Leo Koch & Justus Rothschild) 60 Walker
Koch Brothers (Samuel & Meyer Koch) 117 First av. & 207 Av. B
Koch & Brahe (Paul Koch & Herman Brahe) 126 E. 129th
Koch & Co. (dressmkrs) (Adolph Koch & Herman Schlesinger) 37 W. 16th
Koch & Co. (real estate) (inf. unattainable) 38 Grand
Koch & Dreyfus (Nathan Koch, Leon Dreyfus & Jonas Koch) 22 John
Koch & Ebbecke (dissolved) 258 W. 26th
Koch & Semke (William C. Koch & John H. Semke) 185 Third av.

Koch, Sons & Co. (John V. Koch & William C. & Frederick W. Horn, only) 541 Pearl
Koedding Brothers (Andrew & John B. Koedding) 57 Sheriff
Koefler & Ritter (Frank A. Koefler & John E. Ritter) 116 Clinton pl.
Koehler Herman & Co. (Samuel Goldberger, only) 845 B. 20th
Koehler D. M. & Son (David M. & Martin D. Koehler) 202 E. 29th
Koehler J. M. & Co. (Joseph M. & Alfred Koehler) 204 E. 26th & 228 E. 121st
Koehler & Ottens (dissolved) 141 Av. A
Koell & Reinfeld (George Koell & George Reinfeld) 187 Washn. mkt
Koeller & Schmitz (Richard Koeller & E. Lothar Schmitz) 92 Reade
Koeller & Schmitz Cutlery Co. (Koeller & Schmitz, proprs.) 92 Reade
Koeliner H. & W. (Herman C. W. & William G.) 412 Sixth av. & 394 Third av.
Koelsch August & Son (August & Henry A. Koelsch) 838 Sixth av.
Koenen A. & Brother (Anton & John G. Koenen) 61 Nassau
Koenig H. & Co. (Herman Koenig, Ignatz Popper & Jacob Nusbaum) 220 Pearl
Koenig & Co. (grocers) (Herman A. Koenig, Co. refused) 101 E. 104th
Koenig & Co. (trimmings) (Henrietta Koenig & Thomas Ineson) 19 Walker
Koenig & Schuster (August Koenig & Carl Schuster) 350 G'wich & 68 Av. D
Koeppler & Cohen (dissolved) 130 E. 57th
Koerber Henry & Son (Henry & William Koerber) 55 Willett
Koerber, Giesohen & Co. (Rudolph C. Koerber, Henry Giesohen & Richard Voelkel) 807 Washn.
Koerner J. & Co. (John Koerner, no Co.) 83 Willett
Koernig Brothers (George & Frank Koernig) 416 Tenth av.
Kouster & Sievers (dissolved) 279 Sixth av.
Koevoets H. & C. (Henry C. & Cornelius G.) 183 B'way
Kohlbecker & Georgi (no inf.) 67 W. 13th
Kohlhepp Brothers (Adam J. & Charles F. Kohlhepp) 105 Sullivan, 63 Bedford & 1558 Ninth av.
Kohn Alois & Co. (Alois & Edmund & Arnold Kohn) 11 Maiden la.
Kohn Theodore A. & Son (Theodore A. & Albert M. & Emil W. Kohn) 56 W. 23d
Kohn H. & Son (Hosekiah & Harry N. Kohn, Louis Cohn, William H. Atlendorffer, Benjamin Speers & Herman Woschler) 722 B'way
Kohn & Daer (Max Kohn & Louis Daer) 79 Greene
Kohn & Bloch (dissolved) 382 Canal
Kohn & Robner (Julius C. Kohn & Titus Blatter, only) 73 Leonard
Kohn & Rosenthal (Sigmund Kohn & Mayer Rosenthal) 321 E. 63d
Kohn & Ruck (August Kohn & John M. Ruck) 38 Park row
Kohn & Tobias (Adolph Kohn & Michael Tobias) 34 Spring
Kohn & Young (Morris Kohn & Bertram L. Young) 518 B'way
Kohn Brothers & Co. (Sigmund & Gustav Kohn & Charles Boehme) 322 E. 45th
Kohn, Popper & Co. (David Kuhn, Edward Popper & William M. Kohn) 66 B'way & 19 New
Kohn's Fine Art Rooms (Lorenzo C. Delmonico, proprs.) 106 Fifth av.

TYPEWRITING DONE BY THE TROW CITY DIRECTORY CO., 11 University Place.

KOH 162 KRE

Kohnstamm Leo & Co. (Leo Kohnstamm, no Co.) 514 W. 19th
Kohnstamm H. & Co. (Heimon & Emanuel H. & Emil V. & Edward G. Kuhnstamm) 126 Chambers
Kojawsky J. & A. (Joseph & Abraham) 121 Ludlow
Kolb Bernhard & Son (Bernhard & Edmund A. Kolb) 316 E. 53d
Kolesch & Co. (Adolph Kolesch & Aline Daur) 155 Fulton
Kollberg & Hartmann (Eugene Kollberg & Louis Hartmann) 76 W. 125th
Kolyer & Richardson (Abram B. Kolyer jr. & William G. Richardson) 10 E. 14th
Kommell Brothers (dissolved) 51 Ludlow
Kon M. & Co. (Morris Kon, William Borsodi & Morris Bornstein) 710 B'way
Kon & Broski (dissolved) 384 Fifth
Konigsberg & Strauss (Felix B. Konigsberg & Philip L. Strauss) 53 Wooster
Konzelmann & Ford (dissolved) 1293 B'way
Koop Hermann & Co. (dissolved) 23 William
Koopman & Co. (Julius & Henry & Charles Koopman) 326 Fifth av.
Koopman & Hart (Anne L. Koopman & Mary E. Hart) 100 W. 39th
Kopankiewics & Dabrowski (Anton Kopankiewics & Vincent Dabrowski) 177 Grand
Kopetsky & Harris (Lena Kopetsky & Joseph Harris) 1142 Second av.
Kopp H. & Co. (Henry & William Kopp) 1706 Ninth av,
Koppel & Hagan (dissolved) 117 Nassau
Kopper & Jenks (Philip W. Kopper & William W. Jenks) 230 B'way
Korach & Geller (no inf.) r 255 Third
Korff A. & E. (Augusta & Emily) 28 E. 14th
Korff Brothers & Co. (Herman G. & Louis F. & Arthur L. Korff & James G. Armstrong) 107 Liberty
Korn S. W. & Co. (Samuel W. Korn, Isaac Schmeidler & Jacob Holzman) 622 B'way & 156 Crosby
Korn Brothers (David & Henry Korn) 479 B'way & 52 Mercer
Korne & Currie (dissolved) 683 Sixth av.
Korner & Schwabeland (E. Christian Korner & Henry Schwabeland) 187 West
Korting Gas Engine Co. (Ltd.) (George W. Sillcox, Pres., Maximo E. Mora, Sec. Capital, $200,000. Directors: George W. Sillcox, Maximo E. Mora, Arthur Kitson, Arthur H. Schultz, John Henry Hull) 74 Cortlandt
Kortjohn & Co. (Louis C. Kortjohn & Ernest A. Meinken) 1065 First av.
Koscherak Brothers (Emanuel & Ignatz Koscherak) 17 Warren & 1594 First av.
Kosches Brothers (no inf.) 1168 Second av.
Koshland J. & Co. (Joseph & Simon Koshland) 80 Reade
Koster John & Son (John & Henry Koster) 146 Reade
Koster & Bial (John Koster & Albert Bial) 115 W. 23d, 110 W. 24th & 38½ Sixth av.
Koster & Jachens (John D. Koster & John H. Jachens) 41 Rose
Koster, Bial & Co. (Maria Koster, Harriet Bial & David Rothschild) 196 Park row
Koth Henry C. & Co. (dissolved) 875 E. Houston
Kotlowsky & Levy (Philip Kotlowsky & Barnett Levy) 74 Henry
Kountze Brothers (Augustus & Luther & Herman & Charles B. Kountze) 120 B'way
Kraemer T. F. & Co. (David Horn, Pres.; Felix Kraemer, Sec. Capital, $50,000. Directors: William Steinway, Felix Kraemer, William F.

Hasse, Theodore Koven & David Horn) 105 E. 14th
Kraemer Brothers (Herman & Henry Kraemer) 45 Church & 312 Canal
Kraft T. V. & Co. (Thomas V. Kraft & George Russenbetler) 4 Vesey
Kraft Brothers (Herman A. & Ferdinand J. Kraft) 427 Grand
Kraft & Bach (dissolved) 73 W. 9th
Krahmer Brothers (August D. & Charles Krahmer) 178 E. 105th
Krajewski & Pesant (Thomas F. Krajewski & Alfonso Pesant) 85 B'way
Krakauer Brothers (David & Daniel Krakauer) 40 Union sq. E. & 159 E. 126th
Krakaur M. & Brother (Meyer & Henry G. Krakaur) 113 Delancey
Kraker Brothers (dissolved) 166 Front
Kramer L. & L. (Israel & Louis) 133 Lewis
Kramer J. & Son (Jacob & Philip Kramer) 974 Henry
Kramer S. & Levy (Samuel Kramer & Jacob Levy) 85 Lispenard
Kramer Brothers (carpenters) (Sylvester & Conrad Kramer) 651 E. 158th
Kramer Brothers (meat) (Abraham & Aaron Kramer) 1605 Second av.
Kramer & Johnson (dissolved) 1 Hanover sq.
Kramer & Schrader (dissolved) 180 West
Kranich & Bach (Helmoth Kranich & Jacques Bach) 237 E. 23d & 16 W. 125th
Kraus Joseph & Sons (Joseph & John & George Kraus) 546 Eighth av.
Kraus & Co. (Charles Kraus & Charles Weyrauch) 162 Seventh
Kraus & Harby (dissolved) 57 Ann
Kraus, Stetten & Co. (George H. Kraus & Joseph Stetten, no Co.) 24 State
Krause O. K. & Co. (Otto K. Krause & William Kothe) 98 Franklin
Krause Brothers (Charles & Jacob Krause) r 437 E. 53d
Krause & Livingston (Daniel Krause & Morris Livingston) 86 & 149 Park row & 10 Bowery
Krebaum T. & Co. (Theodore O. Krebaum & James S. Leslie) 735 Courtlandt av.
Krebs Brothers (Anselm Krassa, only) 31 Nassau
Kreines & Ginsberg (dissolved) 116 Canal
Kreischer B. & Sons (Charles C. & Edward B. & George F. Kreischer, only) 182 Mangin
Kreiss & Kuraner (dissolved) 158 Hester
Kreitsberg E. & J. Dittorf (Ernst Kreitsberg & John Dittorf) 264 Av. A
Kremelberg & Co. (J. George Kremelberg & Adolph Engler) 160 Pearl
Krements & Co. (George Krementz & Julius A. Lebkuecher) 162 B'way
Kremer H. & Son (dissolved) 127 Division
Kremer & Brody (Hillel Kremer & Jacob Brody) 128 Division
Krenrich & Kemmer (William Krenrich & John Kemmer jr.) 719 Fifth
Kress John, Brewing Co. (Susanna Kress, Pres.; Charles Gunther, Sec.; Henry M. Haar, Treas. Capital, $400,000. Directors: Susanna Kress, Henry M. Haar, Charles & Henry Gunther) 213 E. 54th
Kress Oscar & Co. (Oscar Kress & William Schoelles) 915 Sixth av.
Kress & Behrens (Oscar Kress & Herman L. Behrens) 1670 B'way
Kress & Co. (John H. Ernst, only) 56 Warren
Kretzschmar & Wagner (Charles Kretzschmar & Adolph Wagner) r 122 Elizabeth
Kreuder Ernst & Co. (Ernst & Adolph Kreuder) 53 First av.

Kreyer John G. & Son (John G. & John M. Kreyer) 390 Third av.
Krieg J. K. & Co. (John K. Krieg, Lemuel R. Mears, Charles O. Kuhnert & Louis C. Metzger) 39 Warren
Krieg & Denker (no inf.) 117 First
Krieger G. & N. (no inf.) 45 Hewitt av. W. Washn. mkt
Kriete Brothers (dissolved) 103 Rivington
Kriger A. & Co. (Abraham & Lena Kriger) 26 Orchard
Kroeber F., Clock Co. (Florence Kroeber, Pres.; Otto Bartel, Sec. Capital, $100,000. Trustees: Florence Kroeber, Otto Bartel, L. Skinkle) 360 B'way
Kroeck & Son (Catharine & Julius E. G. Kroeck) 868 Third av.
Kroeger & Sons (Henry & Henry jr. & Otto L. Kroeger) 360 Second av.
Kroh H. C. & Co. (Hiram C. Kroh & Dwight C. Finney) 678 B'way
Krohn & Co. (Christian E. W. Krohn, no Co.) 303 Bowery
Krombach Brothers (Joseph & William Krumbach) 383 Grand
Kromm & Rosenthal (Edward A. Kromm & Emanuel Rosenthal) 117 Leonard
Krone Brothers (Herman & Louis Krone) 105 Chambers
Kronoff Brothers (Frank O. & Peter M. Kronoff) 1251 B'way
Kronold & Co. (Adolph S. & Louisa Kronold) 4 Walker
Kronowitz & Klein (dissolved) 95 Columbia
Kronthal Brothers (Louis & Charles Kronthal) 314 Church
Krooglansky & Parsont (dissolved) 289 Second av.
Krouse Brothers (dissolved) 526 E. 11th
Krower & Sylvester (Louis Krower & Seamon Sylvester) 656 B'way
Krueger H. & Son (Herman T. & Herman T. Krueger jr.) 51 Beekman & 81 Ann
Krueger & Braun (Ernest Krueger & William Braun) 61 Goerck
Krug L. & Co. (Louis & Emma Krug) 96 Nassau
Krüger George W. & Co. (George W. Krüger & Christian F. Rust) 18 Beaver
Kruger S. & Co. (dissolved) 342 E. Houston & 34 Essex
Kruger Brothers (dissolved) 58 Market & 21 Pike
Krugler, Kimball & Co. (Charles L. Krugler, Charles H. Kimball & Charles L. Krugler jr.) 14 John
Krulewitch P. & Co. (Philip Krulewitch & Julius Feinberg) 63 Walker
Krull & Boyce (dissolved) 146 W. 17th
Krupp Mfg. Co. (refused) 427 E. 25th
Kruse Check & Adding Machine Co. (Charles Kruse, Pres.; James J. Kennedy, Sec.; Charles M. Barnes, Treas. Trustees: Charles Kruse, Charles M. Barnes, James J. Kennedy) 28 E. 14th
Kruse Mfg. Co. (Charles Kruse, propr.) 124 E. 14th
Kruse & Baron (Dederick Kruse & Albert L. Baron) 207 Centre
Kruse & Murphy Mfg. Co. (Lucius Lyon, Pres.; Charles Kruse, Sec.; Edward Murphy, Treas. Capital, $100,000. Directors: Lucius Lyon, Charles Kruse, Edward Murphy) 457 W. 26th
Krusius Brothers (August & Emil & Ewald Krusius) 373 B'way
Kubatz Mary & A. (dissolved) 44 First
Kubes J. & F. Holoubek (John Kubes & Frank Holoubek) 334 E. 73d
Kubie Isaac & Co. (Isaac Kubie, no Co.) 96 Malden la.
Kuecks & Tietgen (dissolved) 1580 First av.

Kuehn Brothers (refused) 2026 Lex. av.
Kuever Brothers (Henry J. & William C. Kuever) 33 Christopher & 163 W. 56th
Kugeler & Zellweger (Henry Kugeler & John J. Zellweger) 19 Seventh av.
Kugelmann & Co. (Julius A. Kugelmann;—special partners, Francisco Vasquez & Adolfo Casals, Gibraltar, each $15,000: terminates 6th Dec. 1892) 52 Stone
Kugelmann & Klein (Louis Kugelmann & Edward Klein) 1585 First av.
Kugler William & Son (no inf.) 389 W. 44th
Kugler H. & Co. (Herman Kugler & Theodore Münch) 10 Division
Kugler & Wollens (Ernst T. Kugler & William Wollens) 217 Bowery
Kuh E. S. & Toska (Emanuel S. Kuh & Irving M. Taska) 67 Pearl
Kuh's Alexander, Sons (Moses A. & Millard F. Kuh) 272 Sixth av. & 2407 Eighth av.
Kuhlke & Blank (Louis Kuhlke & Henry Blank) 105 Broad
Kuhn Brothers (John J. & Peter Kuhn) 2254 Third av.
Kuhn & Tobler (no inf.) r 154 E. 27th
Kuhn, Doerdlinger & Co. (Charles Kuhn jr. & George Doerdlinger, no Co.) 18 John
Kuhn, Loeb & Co. (Jacob H. Schiff & Lewis S. & Abraham A. Wolff;—special partner, Solomon Loeb, $500,000; terminates 31st Dec. 1892) 30 Nassau
Kuhn, Werner & Co. (Herman Kuhn, Max Werner & Samuel C. & Ferdinand Kuhn) 537 B'way & 108 Mercer
Kunath A. & A. (Augusta & Adele) 3 E. 76th
Kunath J. B. & Co. (dissolved) 104 John & 9 Platt
Kunhardt & Co. (Henry R. Kunhardt jr.' George H. Diehl & Rudolph W. R. Koester;—special partner, Henry R. Kunhardt, New Brighton, S. I., $300,000; terminates 31st Dec. 1891) 32 Beaver
Kunstadter Patent Screw Steering & Propelling Co. (I. Wall Wilson, Pres.; William H. Shepard, Sec.; Frederick T. Brown, Treas. Capital, $1,000,000. Directors: I. Wall Wilson, Matthew Tayler, Frederick T. Brown, William H. Shepard, Jacob J. Kunstadter, Ronald Taylor, T. Frederick Tama, Leoncio Julia, William Turnbull) 31 B'way
Kunstler William & Brothers (William & Adolph & Isidor Kunstler) 495 B'way
Kuntz Joseph, Brewing Co. (Frederick Dassori, Pres.; Frank Durwanger, Sec. Capital, $400,000. Trustees: Joseph Kuntz, Frank Durwanger, Philip Bunn, Frederick Dassori) 3526 Third av.
Kunz & Jost (Anton Kunz & John Jost) 1442 First av.
Kuper G. D. & Brothers (George D. & Jacob E. W. & Charles P. Kuper) 608 Washn. 25 William, Custom h. 80 Laight & Pier 42 (new) N. R.
Kupfer Otto & Co. (dissolved) 19 B'way
Kupfer F. & Co. (Frederick Kupfer & Anthony W. Hubner) 18 Chatham sq.
Kupfer Brothers (Bernhard & Leopold Kupfer) 61 Warren
Kupfer & Robitschek (Edward Kupfer & Max Robitschek) 10 Lispenard
Kurasch & Englander (Goodman Kurasch & Max Englander) 108 Stanton
Kurinsky & Levy (Solomon Kurinsky & Morris Levy) 91 Delancey
Kursheedt Mfg. Co. (Frederic A. Kursheedt, Pres.; Israel B. Kursheedt, Sec. Capital, $50,000. Trustees, Frederic A. & Alexander E. & Israel B. Kursheedt) 190 S. 5th av. 36 Thompson & 143 W. 19th

KUR 164 **LAK**

Kurtz Bag Co. (refused) 74 Pearl
Kurtz & Bloechle (Henry Kurtz & Joseph Bloechle) 57 University pl.
Kurtz & Graham (Julius Kurtz & William W. Graham) 1895 B'way, 131 W. 38th & 321 E. 64th
Korts, Stuboeck & Co. (Jutus A. Kurts & Christian Schmitz, only) 104 Greene
Kurtz's M., Son (John Kurtz) 679 First av.
Kurtzer & Rühl (William Kurtzer & Richard Rühl) 1 Third av.
Kursman M. & Son (Michael & Samuel Kursman) 291 Grand
Kursman Brothers (Max & Henry Kursman) 117 Pearl & 115 Warren
Kursman & Yeaman (Ferdinand Kursman & George H. Yeaman) 287 B'way
Kutner J. & Son (no inf.) 19 Division
Kutnow G. (Gustav & Herman & John Kutnow) 658 B'way
Kuttner & Fibel (Morris Kuttner & Jacob Fibel) 58 Walker
Kwadrite Electric Co. (James L. de Fremery, Pres.; William B. Baird, Sec. Capital, $10,-000. Trustees: James L. de Fremery, William B. Baird, Henri M. Suermondt) 44 B'way
Kydd J. & T. (James & Thomas) 86 Walker
Kyle James & Sons (James & John M. Kyle, only) 610 Third av.
Kyle Samuel & Co. (Samuel & Robert T. Kyle) 150 Barrow

L

La America Publishing Co. (Felix L. de Castro, Pres.; Edward Peres-Triana, Sec. Capital, $5,000. Directors: Felix L. de Castro, R. Farres Santiago & Edward Peres-Triana, J. R. Martinez) 16 Beaver
Labagh & Kemp (John Labagh & James L. Kemp) 5 Bedford
Labaree J. H. & Co. (Joseph H. Labaree, Arthur C. Gilman, Seymour S. Smith & Charles B. Holmes) 125 Front
Labate & Co. (Louis & Dominick Labate) 126 Mulberry
Labrook & Heckler (dissolved) no address
Lacentra Donato & Son (Donato & Joseph Lacentra) 324 Ninth av.
Lacerra M. & W. Lipari (Michael Lacerra & William Lipari) 59 Cortlandt
Lachenbruch N. & Brother (Nathan & Isaac & Matthias & Jonas Lachenbruch) 164 Water
Lachman S. & Co. (Samuel & Albert & Henry Lachman & Leo Metzger) 22 Elm
Lachman, Morgenthau & Goldsmith (Samson Lauhman, Henry Morgenthau & Abraham Goldsmith) 154 Nassau
Lackawanna Iron & Coal Co. (Edwin F. Hatfield, Pres.; Henry V. Vultee, Sec.; Theodore Sturges, Treas. Capital, $3,000,000; further inf. unattainable) 52 Wall
Lackey Hugh & Son (Hugh & Francis L. Lackey) 168 South
Lackey & Buckbee (Edwin D. Lackey & John Buckbee) 235 W. 51st
Lacovia Mfg. Co. (William H. Perrine, Pres.; John S. Owden, Sec. Capital, $1,000,000. Directors: William H. Perrine, John S. Owden, Albert Cordes, William H. & John Acken) 40 Exchange pl.
Lacrosse Gold Mining Co. (John Vanneat, Pres.; Henry Smith, Sec. Capital, $2,000,000. Directors: John Vanneat, Henry Smith, C. P. Sykes, Dudley Hall, W. W. Case, G. D. Munroe, E. F. Hollister) 59 William
Ladd Hermon W., Co. (dissolved) 57 W. 18th
Ladd & Coffin (John B. Ladd & Sturgis Coffin) 34 Barclay

Ladenburg, Thalmann & Co. (Adolf Ladenburg, Ernst Thalmann, Richard & estate of Abraham Limburger:—special partner, Gerson von Bleichröder, *Berlin, Prussia*, $400,000; terminates 31st Dec, 1890) 44 Wall
Laderer L. & Son (Samuel L. Laderer, only) 342 G'wich
Ladies' Art Assn. (Emma S. Maraldy, Pres.; Alice Donlevy, Sec.; Elizabeth C. Field, Treas.) 23 E. 14th
Ladies' Depository (Sarah B. Nevius, 1st Directress; Mrs. William Powell, Sec.; Cornelia S. Wray, Treas.) 27 E. 19th
Lafaye George E. & Co. (dissolved) 21 Park row
Lafayette Fire Ins. Co. (Samuel Van Wyck, Pres.; J. Philip Stark, Sec. Capital, $150,000. Directors: Samuel Van Wyck, James S. Buydam, Isaac Carhart, Harkort Napier, William H. Male, Joseph F. Sanxay, John J. Vanderbilt, Frederick L. Dubois, David F. Manning, James M. Leavitt, Albert P. Wells, James Reynold) 105 B'way
Lafferty Brothers (William R. & James M. Lafferty) 2454 Second av.
Laflin & Rand Powder Co. (Solomon Turck, Pres.; A. Wallace Higgins, Sec.; Edward Greene, Treas. Capital, $1,000,000 ; further inf. unattainable) 29 Murray
La Force Drug Co. (John F. Hammond, propr.) 624, B'way
Laforest & Eaton (dissolved) 60 Gold
Lager Beer Brewers' Board of Trade of N. Y. & Vicinity (William Hoffmann, Pres.; Albert E. Seifert, Sec.; Michael Groh, Treas.) 2 Irving pl.
Lagerman Typothetæ Co. (Lebbens H. Rogers, Pres.; Julian W. Chadwick, Treas.; Herbert H. Taylor, Sec. Capital, $1,000,000. Directors: Lebbeus H. Rogers, John A. Eagleson, Herbert H. Rogers, John M. Littell, Henry Smith, Julian W. Chadwick, Elliot W. Taylor) 189 B'way
Lagowitz J. & Co. (Arnold Tanzer & estate of Jacob Lagowitz) 473 B'way & 46 Mercer
La Hacienda Cigar Factory (not inc.) (Joseph E. Wood & Joseph Rosenthal) 78 William
Lahey Francis & Sons (Francis & William T. & Joseph & Francis G. Lahey) 162 E. 86th
Lahey & Dubord (Isaiah A. Lahey, Colin C. Duncan & John J. H. Dubord) 461 Broome
Lahnstein & Strauss (dissolved) 1193 Ninth av.
Laidlaw & Co. (Henry D. & Charles E. Laidlaw) 14 Wall
Laidlaw Brothers & Co. Alexander H. & George F. Laidlaw, no Co.) 137 W. 41st
Laing James B. & Co. (James B. Laing & William H. Healy) 193 Duane
Laird George W., Co. (Herman Hanneberger, Pres.; George W. Laird, Sec. Capital, $50,-000 ; further inf. unattainable) 39 Barclay
Laird & Gray (Alexander Laird & William Gray) 16 Exchange pl.
Lake Erie & Western R. R. Co. (Calvin S. Brice, Pres.; Louis M. Schwan, Sec. Capital, $23,-580,000. Directors: Columbus R. Cummings, Calvin S. Brice, George S. Stone, Samuel Thomas, John G. Moore, John B. Cobra, George F. Baker, Nelson Robinson, Edward Tuck) 10 Wall
Lake Hopatcong Steamboat Co. (George W. Campbell jr, Pres.; Henry N. Nimmons, Sec.; further inf. refused) 56 Wall
Lake Milk Co. (Jesse Durland, Pres.; James H. Crissey, Sec.; Alfred R. Holbert, Treas. Capital, $5,000. Directors: Jesse Durland, James H. Crissey, Alfred R. Holbert, John W. & Henry W. Houston, James D. & Henry Benedict) 57 Sixth av.
Lake Placid Improvement Co. (no inf.) 149 B'way
Lake Shore & Michigan Southern Railway Co. (John Newell, Pres.; Edwin D. Worcester,

MERCHANTS EXCHANGE NAT. BANK OF THE CITY OF N. Y.
SOLICITS YOUR ACCOUNT. **287 Broadway.**
PHINEAS C. LOUNSBURY, President.   ALLEN S. APGAR, Cashier.

LAK   165   LAN

Sec. Capital, $50,000,000. Directors: William K. & Cornelius & Frederick W. Vanderbilt, Samuel F. Barger, John E. Burrill, Darius O. Mills, Edwin D. Worcester, William L. Scott, Charles M. Reed, Rasselas Brown, John Newell, Jeptha H. Wade, John Dekoven) Grand Central depot

Lake J. P. & Son (John P. & John P. Lake jr.) 903 Third av.

Lake & Byrne (no inf.) 1107 Third av.

Lalance & Grosjean Mfg. Co. (Florian Grosjean, Pres.; Edwin W. Martin, Sec. Capital, $500,000. Directors: Florian Grosjean, John C. Milligan, J. Harry Smith, August J. Cordier, George L. Nichols, Julien P. Cordier, Edwin W. Martin) 19 Cliff

Lalanne & Aguals (dissolved) 57 E. 9th

Lalla Rookh Pattern Co. (Ltd.) (Theodore A. Liebler jr. Pres.; John J. G. C. Schmidt, Sec.; John A. J. Maas, Treas.; further inf. unattainable) 76 Park pl.

Lally & Durkin (Michael Lally & James Durkin) 290 Front

Lamakin Brothers (Carlo & Frank & Louis Lamalda) 124 Mulberry & 402 E. 119th

Lamanna Brothers (Alfonso & Felix Lamanna) 320 E. 9th

Lamarche's H.. Sons (Henry J. & Matthew J. Lamarche) 53 John

Lamb C. W. & Son (Charles W. & Edwin L. Lamb) 237 E. 117th

Lamb J. & R. (Joseph & Richard) 59 Carmine & 53 Downing

Lamb & Bell (Richard Lamb & Alexander Bell) 1 B'way

Lamb & Griesbach (Robert Lamb & Albert Griesbach) 85 Franklin

Lamb & Petty (Gilbert D. Lamb & Robert D. Petty) 5 Beekman

Lamb & Rich (Hugh Lamb & Charles A. Rich) 205 B'way

Lambard & Co. (Francis P. Lambard, no Co.) 32 Gold

Lambden Joseph & Son (Joseph & Eugene Lambden) 26½ E. 42d

Lambeck H. W. & Son (Herman W. & Henry W. Lambeck) 75 First av.

Lambert P. W. & Co. (Peter W. & Julius C. Lambert) 46 Howard

Lambert Brothers (August V. & Henry V. & Robert Lambert) 608 Third av.

Lambert & Lacquet (dissolved) 222 Wooster

Lamline's U., Son (dissolved) 421 Hudson

Lamontagne E. & Sons (Edward & Ernest C. & Rene L. & Maurice Lamontagne) 53 Beaver

Lamontagne, Clarke & Co. (Edward Lamontagne jr. Norman Clarke & Wallace B. Smith) 44 B'way

La Mothe Mfg. Co. (William W. Kirby, Pres.; Edward L. Cushman, Sec. Capital, $1,000,000. Directors: W. C. Moore, Robert M. Cushman, William W. Kirby, Edward L. Cushman, C. F. Dittler) 60 Liberty

Lamp, Baker & Co. (Alexander Lamp, George W. Baker & John M. Rapp) 1557 B'way

Lamson Cons. Store Service Co. (Frank M. Ames, Pres.; William S. Lamson, Treas. Directors: Frank M. Ames, William S. Lamson, John Shepard, Frank W. Fitts, Oakes A. Ames, James F. Almy, B. W. Currier, A. J. Lane, E. Q. Kenehy) 23 E. 14th

Lamson John S. & Brother (Edwin Lamson, only) 77 Maiden la.

Lamson Roger & Co. (Roger Lamson & Frederick W. Flint) 108 Franklin

Lancaster Caloric Engine Co. (James H. Lancaster, Pres.; Miles A. Stafford, Treas.; Nugent Robinson, Sec. Capital, $50,000; further inf. refused) 171 B'way

Lancaster Comb Co. (Franklin P. Shumway jr. propr.) 51 Lispenard

Lancaster Dredging & Excavating Co. (James H. Lancaster, propr.) 171 B'way

Lancaster Gas Engine Co. (James H. Lancaster, Pres.; Miles A. Stafford, Treas.; Nugent Robinson, Sec. Capital, $50,000; further inf. refused) 171 B'way

Lancaster Hydraulic Wedge Co. (James H. Lancaster, Pres.; Willard P. Ward, Treas.; Joseph H. Bramwell, Sec. Capital, $100,000; further inf. refused) 171 B'way

Lancaster Mfg. Co. (James H. Lancaster, Pres.; Miles A. Stafford, Treas.; Nugent Robinson, Sec. Capital, $50,000; further inf. refused) 171 B'way

Lancaster Petroleum Engine Co. (James H. Lancaster, Pres.; Miles A. Stafford, Treas.; Nugent Robinson, Sec. Capital, $100,000; further inf. refused) 171 B'way

Lancaster Rock & Ore Crusher Co. (James H. Lancaster, propr.) 171 B'way

Lancaster R. A. & Co. (Robert A. Lancaster, no Co.) 10 Wall

Lancaster's Hydraulic Coal Wedge Co. (James H. Lancaster, Pres.; Willard P. Ward, Treas.; Joseph H. Bramwell, Sec. Capital, $100,000; further inf. refused) 171 B'way

Lancet Publishing Co. (Henry McRichard, Pres.; J. H. Butler, Sec. Capital, $30,000. Trustees: Henry McRichard, J. H. Butler) 540 Pearl

Land & Goldstein (dissolved) 56 Ridge

Land & River Improvement Co. (Francis H. Weeks, Pres.; Henry W. Deforest, Sec. Capital, $750,000. Directors: Francis H. Weeks, William E. Strong, William P. Stevenson, George S. Baxter, James B. Williams) 120 B'way

Land & Security Investment Co. (James K. O. Sherwood, Pres.; Alfred C. Chapin, Sec.; further inf. refused) 192 B'way

Landaner, Kalm & Streng (Julius Landauer, Maurice Kalm & Lewis J. Streng) 412 E. 64th

Landgraff H. A. & Co. (Henry A. Landgraff, no Co.) 176 B'way

Landman & Bernheimer (Meyer A. Bernheimer, only) 177 Pearl

Landman & Son (Solomon & Jacob P. Landman) 354 Third av.

Landon Charles G. & Co. (Charles G. Landon & Theodore D. Howell) 62 Broome

Landray & Krone (dissolved) 817 B'way

Landru Silk Co. (Edward G. Landru, Pres.; Francis D. Peabody, Sec.; Frederick A. Von Bernuth, Treas. Capital, $30,000. Directors: Edward G. Landru, Frederick A. Von Bernuth, Francis D. Peabody) 62 Greene & 430 W. 14th

Landwermann & Peterson (Frank Landwermann & Severin W. Peterson) 845 Sixth av.

Lane Charles W. & Co. (Charles W. & Richard A. Lane) 163 B'way

Lane George W. & Co. (Morris Woodruff & Thomas A. Phelan, only) 93 Front

Lane C. & Co. (dissolved) 145 Eighth av.

Lane J. H. & Co. (J. Henry & James W. Lane) 110 Worth

Lane & Clifford (Michael J. Lane & James Clifford) 205 Front

Lane & McLaughlin (dissolved) 215 Park row

Lane's Nathan, Sons (George W. & Edward A. & Frederick H. Lane) 126 Pearl

Lang Mfg. Co. (no inf.) 30 Dey

Lang Brothers (dissolved) 342 Grand

Lang & Co. (Sour) (Peter & Charles W. Lang) 30 Moore

Lang & Co. (shoes) (David Lang, Co. refused) 343 Grand

CINCINNATI, BALTIMORE, PHILADELPHIA, | **SNOW, CHURCH & CO.** CORRESPONDENTS EVERYWHERE. | **NEW YORK, BOSTON, CHICAGO, LOUISVILLE.**

LAN 166 **LAT**

Lang & Co. (smiths) (Charles Lang & Louis Gattineau) 397 First av.

Langan M. P. & Co. (Michael P. Langan, no Co.) 426 Second av.

Langan Brothers (Hugh & Andrew Langan) 184 W. 38th

Langan & Brother (Thomas A. & Michael J. Langan) 59 Park pl.

Langbein Brothers & Langbein (George F. & J. C. Julius & Leonard J. Langbein) 258 B'way

Langdon & Armstrong (dissolved) 868 B'way

Langdon & Granger Brewing Co. (Ltd.) (Septimus W. Granger, Pres.; Thomas B. Langdon, Sec. Capital, $165,000. Directors: Septimus W. Granger, Thomas B. Langdon, August Finck, T. G. McCarthy, A. W. Miller) 408 E. 14th

Langdon, Batchellor & Co. (Charles H. Langdon, George C. Batchellor, Frank I. Perry & George C. Miller) 345 B'way

Lange George & Son (Anne Lange, only) 227 E. 22d

Lange Brothers (Carl Lange, only) 84 Gansevoort

Lange & Blakeslee (Henry Lange & Seldon Blakeslee) 114 Broad

Lange & Trillich (Louis Lauge & Adam Trillich) 57 Willett

Langen Brothers (Michael H. & Cord F. Langen) 731 G'wich

Langenhop & Siebold (dissolved) 816 Fifth

Langer Dischinger (Charles Langer & Louis A. Dischinger) 420 E. 15th

Langer & Kimmel (dissolved) 179 Stanton

Langfeld & Cohen (Louis L. Langfeld & Henry M. Cohen) 120 Walker

Langfelder A. & Sons (Alois & Louis & Adolph Langfelder) 4 Montgomery

Langill & Darling (Cranmer C. Langill & Clarence M. Darling) 10 E. 14th

Langley W. C. & Co. (William C. & William H. Langley, Charles C. Goodrich & William H. Book) 78 Worth & 15 Thomas

Langley, Michaelis & Toplitz (dissolved) 51 Greene

Langsam & Beck (dissolved) 121 Spring

Langsdorf S. & Co. (Sigmund Langsdorf & Sanford Wolf) 414 B'way

Langstadter & Co. (Benjamin Langstadter, no Co.) 79 Franklin

Langtry Gold Paint Co. (Friedberg Brothers, proprs.) 29 Murray & 36 Warren

Langwasser H. P. & Brothers (Henry P. & William C. & Adam Langwasser) 214 W. Houston

Langworthy & Brown (William R. Langworthy & Frank R. Brown) 88 South

Laning File Co. (Laning L. Ferris, Pres.; William L. Ferris, Sec. Capital, $5,000; further inf. unattainable) 58 Pearl

Lanman & Kemp (Edward Kemp & George Massey; —special partner, George Kemp, $300,000; terminates 31st Dec. 1890) 68 William & 69 Maiden la.

Lanneau J. B. & Co. (Jefferson B. Lanneau & J. Edwin Dodge) 172 Chambers

Lanphear & Haff (dissolved) 12 Fulton fish mkt

Lanson & Edgar (dissolved) 161 W. 29th

Lapham Edwin N. & Co. (Edwin N. & Arden B. & Walter S. Lapham) 9 Ferry

Lapham D. W. & Co. (Daniel W. Lapham, no Co.) 102 Nassau

Lapham H. G. & Co. (John J. & Lewis H. Lapham, George A. Vail & estate of Henry G. Lapham) 26 Ferry

Lapidus Brothers (Jacob L. & Herman Lapidus) 39 Mercer

Laplante & Pause (dissolved) 45 Exchange pl.

La Plata Mining & Smelting Co. (Thomas P. Fowler, Pres.; William F. Dunning, Sec. Capital, $2,000,000, Trustees: Thomas P. Fowler, William F. Dunning) 67 Wall

Lapper R. W. & Co. (Richard W. Lapper & Alfred G. Butcher) 51 Warren

Lappin Drake Shoe Co. (Henry F. Taintor, Pres.; Winfield S. Dehart, Sec.; Thomas Milburn, Treas. Capital, $1,200,000. Directors: Henry F. Taintor, Winfield S. Dehart, Thomas Milburn, Harry O. Darwin, Andrew B. Rogers jr. Malcolm W. Niven, Joseph D. Gallagher) 45 B'way

Lapsley Howard & Co. (Howard Lapsley & David S. Willard) 79 B'way & 9 New

Lapsley & Gallup (David Lapsley & Howard Gallup) 30 Broad & 1180 B'way

Larcey K. & E. (Catharine & Ellen) 60 W. 36th

Larchan & Hechinger (dissolved) 628 Sixth

La Rica Gold Mining Co. (no inf.) 62 B'way

Laridon Remi & Co. (Remi Laridon, no Co.) 223 W. 40th

Larkin E. & M. (Eleanor E. & Margaret J.) 373 E. 10th

Larkin M. & Son (Michael & James J. Larkin) 519 E. 16th

Larkin Brothers (Matthew & Daniel Larkin) 287 Seventh av.

Larned & Warren (William Z. Larned & Ira D. Warren) 170 B'way

Laroche & Fletcher (William T. Laroche & Thomas A. Fletcher) 67 W. 54th

La Roza & Co. (John H. La Roza, Orris E. Thayer & John F. Nelson) 41 Dey

Larrabee E. J. & Co. (Edward J. Larrabee & William G. & Charles H. Thomas) 427 W. 15th & 423 W. 16th

Larter, Elcox & Co. (Frederick H. Larter, Ann Elcox, William H. Jones & Theodore M. Woodland) 41 Maiden la.

L'Artiste Publishing Co. (Charles H. Williamson, Pres.; Theodore D. Rich, Sec. Capital, $5,000. Directors: Charles H. Williamson, William I. Farrell, Theodore D. Rich, James A. Rogers, M. Lee Ross) 7 Warren

Lary's Express Co. (William Barbour, Pres.; William S. Cooke, Sec.; Seymour M. Lary, Treas. Capital, $30,000. Directors: William Barbour, Seymour M. Lary, Garrett A. Hobart, Robert S. Hughes) 108 Chambers, 45 Church, 319 Canal & 56 Beekman

Lascalls D. & Co. (dissolved) 4 Stone

Las Casas Gold Mining Co. (Lee R. Shryock, Pres.; Dominique F. Verdenal, Sec. Capital, $500,000. Directors: Alexander Westphal, James B. Clews, Lee R. Shryock, Henry Clay Lookwood, Joseph Treat) 45 B'way

Lascolies A. S. & Co. (Alfred S. Lascolies, Elliott A. de Pass & Joseph L. Myers) 108 Broad & 20 Water

Lasher John K. & Brother (John K. & William M. Lasher) 147 Roade

Lasker A. & Son (Abraham & Edwin M. Lasker) 415 Pearl

Lasker Brothers (Moses & Aaron Lasker) 227 Pearl

Lasker & Bernstein (Gustav Lasker & Charles Bernstein) 183 William

Lasky & Levy (Philip Lasky & Max M. Levy) 101 Bleecker

Lasorovich & Rubin (no inf.) r 105 Wooster

Lasser Brothers (Jacob & Elias Lasser) 80 Ludlow

Latermann B. & Son (dissolved) 66 Nassau

Latham, Alexander & Co. (John C. Latham jr. & Henry E. Alexander, no Co.) 16 Wall

Lathrop Co. (S. Park Lathrop, Pres.; D. Nichols Lathrop, Sec.; Albert A. Miller, Treas. Capital, $10,000. Directors: S. Park & D. Nichols Lathrop, Albert A. Miller) 80 John

WATER METERS, GAS ENGINES, FOR PUMPING AND POWER. | **NATIONAL METER CO. 252 Broadway, N. Y.**

LAT 167 LAX

Lathrop J. & Co. (Joshua & Joshua Lathrop jr.) 19 Whitehall
Lathrop, Smith & Oliphant (Levi C. Lathrop, Oscar B. Smith & James H. Oliphant) 35 Broad
Lattemann J. J., Shoe Mfg. Co., (inf. unattainable) 96 Reade
Lattimore & Dougherty (John Lattimore & Patrick Dougherty) 142 Monroe
Lau J. H. & Co. (Jacob L. & Louis Lau) 75 Chambers
Laushheimer J. & Co. (Jacob Lauchheimer & Isaac Harris) 1659 Second av.
Laue Brothers (liquors) (Henry & Arp Laue) 262 Seventh av. & 748 Tenth av.
Laue Brothers (stables) (Charles & William Laue) 188 Division
Laue Brothers (trucks) (Henry & Albert Laue) 36 Beaver
Lauer & Goodwin (Edward Lauer & Moses H. Goodwin) 2 Seventh av.
Laufer A. & Co. (Abraham & Max Laufer, David F. Meyer & Henry R. Wechsler) 512 B'way & 58 Crosby
Lauferty Joseph & Son (Joseph & David Lauferty) 54 Leonard
Lauferty & Marx (dissolved) 188 W. Houston
Laun & Salle (John Laun & Joseph Salle) 30 W. 12th
Launder & Macdonald (William Launder & James Macdonald) 116 E. 14th
Lauppe & Lawlor (dissolved) 902 Fifth
Laurel Hill Chemical Works (G. H. Nichols & Co., proprs.) 68 William
Lanten Edward A. & Co. (Edward A. Lanten & William Hennings) 48 University pl. & 26 E. 10th
Lautz Brothers & Co. (no inf.) 402 G'wich
Laux E. & J. (Edward & Joseph) 136 Eighth av.
Lavalle Wallace & Co. (Wallace Lavalle, no Co.) 963 Tenth av.
Lavanoux & Underhill (Edward Lavanoux & William H. Underhill) 639 B'way
Lavelle O. & Son (Owen & William B. Lavelle) 120 Pearl
Laventhall J. & Co. (Jacob Laventhall & Francis Dilson) 63 Reade
Lavery John & Co. (John Lavery & John A. Brophy) 162 B'way
Law John & Co. (John Law & John G. McCowan) 1679 B'way
Law Telephone Co. (William A. Childs, Pres.; George F. Durant, Sec.; Capital, $400,000. Directors: William A. Childs, George F. Durant, John H. Emerick) 85 John
Law Telephone System of the Metropolitan Telephone & Telegraph Co. (Metropolitan Telephone & Telegraph Co., proprs.) 18 Cortlandt
Law A. & Son (Alexander & George Law) 45 W. 20th
Law & Boyd (John Law & David Boyd) 68 E. B'way
Law & Cleary (Thomas W. Law & William E. Cleary) 72 Mangin
Law & Trade Printing Co. (Mark M. Pomeroy, Pres.; George Levison, Sec.; Capital, $10,000. Directors: Mark M. Pomeroy, Henry F. Clinton, George Levison) 249 William & 9 New Chambers
Law & Turner (S. Howard Law & William W. Turner) Tenth av. n W. 157th
Lawall & Searles (Edmund D. Lawall & Arthur C. Searles) 124 Av. C
Lawles S. L. & J. H. (Silas L. & Joseph H.) 243 Centre
Lawless M. & Sons (Michael & John H. & Robert Lawless) 92 Pine
Lawrence B., Stationery Co. (Adolphus S. Solomons, Pres.; Albert Asher, Sec.; Benjamin Lawrence, Treas.; Capital, $10,000. Directors: Adolphus S. Solomons, Albert Asher, Benjamin Lawrence) 75 John
Lawrence Cement Co. (Warren Ackerman, Pres.; Thomas A. Smith, Sec.; Capital, $300,000. Directors: Warren Ackerman, John R. Platt, George S. Coutant, John A. Stewart) 67 William
Lawrence Curry Comb Co. (John D. Lawrence, Pres.; William C. Lawrence, Sec.; Capital, $12,000. Directors: John D. & William C. Lawrence) 204 E. 43d
Lawrence Cyrus J. & Sons (Cyrus J. & Richard H. & Henry C. Lawrence) 81 Broad
Lawrence Railway Brake Co. (James I. Raymond, Pres.; John M. Shedd, Sec.; James Davidson, Treas.; Capital, $100,000. Trustees: James I. Raymond, James Davidson, John M. Shedd) 16 Wall
Lawrence Rope Works (Charles W. Cooper, Pres.; George C. Cooper, Sec.; Capital, $9,000. Trustees: Charles W. & George C. Cooper, Edward F. Bedell) 160 Front
Lawrence E. N. & J. B. jr. (dissolved) 35 Liberty
Lawrence J. S. & W. M. (John S. & William M.) 51 Liberty
Lawrence S. & Co. (Sidney & Edward Lawrence) 2 W. 14th
Lawrence & Co. (Amory A. Lawrence, Alfred Ray, Henry S. Howe, & Frederick W. Haynes) 113 Duane & 24 Thomas
Lawrence & Mattoon (Josiah B. Lawrence & Samuel J. Mattoon) 1449 B'way
Lawrence & Smith (Frederick N. Lawrence & Andrew W. Smith) 30 Broad
Lawrence & Waehner (Frank R. Lawrence & Louis C. Waehner) 120 B'way
Lawrence, Frazier & Co. (Charles F. Lawrence, Charles Frazier & Henry G. Marshall) 63 Nassau
Lawrence, Giles & Co. (George P. Lawrence & John C. Giles, no Co.) 11 S. William & 59 Stone
Lawrence, Son & Gerrish (Chester B. Lawrence & William L Gerrish jr. only) 134 Pearl, 221 South & 755 Water
Lawrence, Taylor & Co. (Henry E. Lawrence, Franklin E. Taylor, Courtland D. Moss, William A. Taylor & Joseph Lawrence) 314 B'way
Lawrenceville Cement Co. (Sophia V. Bluhm, Pres.; William N. Hoag, Sec.; Capital, $40,000. Directors: Sophia V. Bluhm, Frank M. Hoag, Albert C. Hall, Edward Kearny) 115 B'way
Lawshe & Co. (Lewis H. & Jacob R. Lawshe) 280 Pearl
Lawson M. F. & Son (Manning F. & A. Franklin Lawson) 601 Hudson & 181 Christopher
Lawson W. S. & Co. (William Shelden Lawson, Harry A. Day & Bennet H. Preston) 49 Exchange pl. 945 B'way & 175 Fifth av.
Lawson Brothers (Robert Lawson, only) 55 White
Lawson & Van Winkle (Samuel Lawson & Henry Van Winkle) 11 Maiden la.
Lawson, Wilson & Co. (David & William Lawson & Andrew Wilson) 610 W. 46th
Lawton C. & N. D. (Cyrus & Newbury D.) 40 Wall
Lawton's G. B., Sons (George B. jr. & Nelson A. Lawton) 23 Tenth av.
Lawyers' Title Ins. Co. (Edwin W. Coggeshall, Pres.; William P. Dixon, Sec.; John Duer, Treas. Capital, $1,000,000. Directors: Edwin W. Coggeshall, Henry Day, William P. Dixon, John Duer, Henry E. Howland, John T. Lockman, J. Lawrence Marcellus, David B. Ogden, John H. Riker, Charles E. Strong, Herbert B. Turner, James M. Varnum, John Webber) 120 B'way
Lax & Co. (no inf.) 160 Orchard

EXCELSIOR BIRD FOOD. | The recognized standard. The most reliable for your Canary. Use no other. Insist upon getting it.
Packed only by **G. ROSENSTEIN & CO.**, 373 Washington Street, New York.

Lay, Clarke & Co. (Jonathan W. Lay, Kanaye Nagasawa & Ray P. Clarke) 62 Vesey

Layton B. C. & Son (Richardson C. & Charles H. Layton) 29 Burling sl.

Lazar & Marcus (dissolved) 66 Eldridge

Lazard Freres (Alexandre & Elie & Simon Lazard, Alexandre Weill, David Cahn, Eugene Mehler & Eugene Arnstein) 10 Wall

Lazarus Lessa & Son (Lessa & Adolph Lazarus) 111 Sheriff

Lazarus L. & Co. (Levi Lazarus & Samuel L. Israel) 101 W. 14th

Lazarus Brothers (Max & Gustav & Louis Lazarus & Ludwig A. Gutmann) 17 Lispenard

Lazarus' I. Sons (Edward Lazarus, only) 15 Lispenard

Lazell, Dalley & Co. (Lewis T. Lazell, Henry Dalley jr. Alfred U. Andras, Francis R. Wardle & Charles H. Tompkins;—special partner, Lucina K. Witmerding, *Islip, N. Y.*, $150,000; terminates 31st Dec. 1892) 99 Maiden la.

Lazzari & Barton (John B. Lazzari & Horace W. Barton) Woodlawn

Leach, Shewell & Sanborn (Orlando Leach, Thomas R. Shewell & Benjamin H. Sanborn) 16 Astor pl.

Leadville Cons. Mining Co. (Peter A. Hegeman, Pres.; Charles A. Cameron, Sec. Capital, $4,000,000. Directors: Stephen B. Elkins, Peter A. Hegeman, Charles A. Cameron, James Hedges, Thomas Moore jr.) 1 B'way

Leaf Tobacco Board of Trade (Edgar M. Crawford, Pres.; William Vigelius, Treas.; Charles L. Holt, Sec.) 175 Pearl

Leaman W. & A. (Walter L. & Alfred V.) 17 William

Leaman & Kerr (William S. Leaman & Howard D. Kerr) 105 West

Leamy & Co. (Patrick Leamy, no Co.) 904 Third av.

Leask George & Co. (George Leask & Julian W. Robbins) 35 Wall

Leask & Co. (George Leask, Julian W. Robbins & Henry S. Warner) 35 Wall

Leather Manufacturers' National Bank (John T. Willets, Pres.; Isaac H. Walker, Cashier; Noel B. Sanborn, Notary. Capital $600,000. Directors: John T. Willets, William H. Macy jr. William M. Kingsland, William Rockefeller, John A. Tucker, Joseph Agostini, Ambrose C. Kingsland, N. F Palmer) 29 Wall

Leavens, Thompson & McIlrath (Frederick Leavens, John H. Thompson & James McIlrath) 525 B'way

Leavitt George A. & Co. (Eugene O'Connor, only) 789 B'way

Leavitt C. K. & Co. (Cecil K. Leavitt & Daniel R. Gillie jr.) 1805 Third av.

Leavitt C. W. & Co. (Charles W. Leavitt, no Co.) 171 B'way

Leavitt & Keith (John B. Leavitt & Boudinot Keith) 111 B'way

Leavitt & Leavitt (Humphrey H. & Edwin R. Leavitt) 280 B'way

Leavitt & Mitchell Brothers (James T. Leavitt & John F. D. & Ernest Mitchell) 74 Leonard

Leavy & Kaufmann (Joseph Leavy & Abraham Kaufmann) 39 E. 4th

Leaycraft & Co. (Charles R. Leaycraft & George S. McCulloh) 142 Pearl & 108 Water

Lebanon Mining Co. (inoperative) 92 Elizabeth

Lebarbier & Brewster (Charles B. Lebarbier & John T. M. Brewster) 35 D'way

Lebel & Fink (dissolved) 2 College pl.

Leber & Bernhard (Edward F. Leber & Albert Bernhard) 5 William & 3 S. William

Lebes Sponge Co. (not inc.) (Junius B. Raboteau, Aaron Moses, Demetrius N. Lebess & John E. Lcousi) 87 Maiden la.

Lebeuf & DeGrandmont (Eugene Lebeuf jr. & Jules DeGrandmont jr.) 16 Howard

Lebihan Charles & Co. (refused) 1e Barclay

Le Boulllier Brothers (drygds.) (George Le Boulllier, only) 48 E. 14th & 847 B'way

Le Boutillier Brothers (drygds.) (John & Charles Le Boutillier) 50 W. 23d & 39 W. 22d

Le Boutilier & Co. (Thomas Le Boutillier, no Co.) 2 Maiden la.

Lebowski S. & Co. (Samuel Lebowski & Max Applebone) 497 Eighth av.

Lebrun N. & Sons (Napoleon & Pierre L. & Michel M. Lebrun) 24 Park pl.

Leclanche Battery Co. (Frank Roosevelt. Pres.; Horatio J. Brewer, Sec. Capital, $5,000; further inf. refused) 149 W. 18th

Leclanché Medical Bureau (refused) 41 Union sq. W.

Le Compte & Brunet (Oliver Le Compte & Hippolyte Brunet) 1126 Lex. av.

Lecount H. M. & W. (Henry M. & William) 32 Cotton Ex.

Lederer Henry A. & Co. (no inf.) 37 College pl.

Lederer S. & B. (Sigmund L. & Benedict) 202 B'way

Lederhos Brothers (Philip & Carl Lederhos) 155 William

Lederle & Co. (Joseph Lederle & Lewis Oberlein) 196 B'way

Lederman Joseph & Sons (Moses J. & Nathan J. & estate of Joseph Lederman) 140 Maiden la.

Lederman & Co. (Samuel Lederman, Co. refused) 20 Whitehall

Lediard & Co. (Charles Lediard, no Co.) 79 Pearl

Ledoux & Co. (Albert R. & Augustus D. Ledoux) 10 Cedar

Lee James & Co. (William E. & John E. Leech & John M. Blake, only) 72 Pine

Lee & Co. (W. Creighton & Charles H. Lee & Robert J. Hutton) 20 Ferry

Lee & Lee (Benjamin F. & William H. L. Lee) 20 Nassau

Lee, Tweedy & Co. (William H. Lee, John A. Tweedy, Charles N. Lee, Henry D. Sanger, James Halliday & Frederick H. Lee) 86 Worth & 9 Thomas

Lee, Typond & Co. (K. Pahn Lee, Yip Typond & Chung Sbang) 350 Hudson

Lee, Yeury & Watts (dissolved) 95 Prince

Leech J. W. & Co. (John W. Leech, no Co.) 70 Wall

Leech & Co. (Robert D. Leech, no Co.) 144 Centre

Leeds Forge Co. (Ltd.) (no inf.) 45 B'way

Leeds F. A. & Co. (Frank A. Leeds & Henry Colley) 529 B'way

Leeds & Morse (Charles C. Leeds & Howard H. Morse) 120 B'way

Leeming Thomas & Co. (Thomas Leeming, no Co.) 55 Park pl.

Leerburger S. & Co. (no inf.) 1050 Second av.

Lees Samuel & Co. (Samuel Lees, no Co.) 63 B'way

Leffel James & Co. (John W. Bookwalter, only) 110 Liberty

Lefferts Marshall & Co. (Marshall Lefferts & Herman E. Dunn) 84 Cliff & 455 Cherry

Lefferts & Co. (Leffort Lefferts, Co. refused) 18 John

Lefko & Eichner (dissolved) 209 E. B'way

Lefkowits & Grossman (dissolved) 1485 First av.

Legal Aid & Protective Assn. (Leonard D. Gumpert, Pres.; Columbus Gottschalk, Sec.) 264 B'way

Legal Protective Assn. of Cigar Manufacturers (Edward Heyman, Pres.; James Brussel, Treas.; Morris S. Wise, Sec.) 52 Exchange pl.

Leggat Brothers (Andrew R. & Richard J. Leggat) 63 Reade & 81 Chambers

IDEN & CO., MANUFACTURERS OF
University Place, 9th to 10th Sts., N. Y. | **GAS FIXTURES AND ELECTROLIERS**

Leggett Francis H. & Co. (Francis H. Leggett, Albert H. Jones & Lewis Wallace) 126 Franklin & 106 W. D'way

Leggett William A. & Co. (William A. Leggett & Peter McCallum) 210 Franklin

Leggett A. W. & F. W. (Abraham W. & Frederick W.) 151 Chambers

Leggett & Brother (E. Howard & Clinton H. Leggett) 301 Pearl

Leggo Brothers & Co. (Thomas A. & Edward & Henry F. Leggo) 44 Vesey

Lehigh Coal & Navigation Co. (Joseph S. Harris, Pres.; Solomon Shepherd, Treas. Capital, $13,799,250. Directors: Joseph S. Harris, Francis C. Yarnall, Edward W. Clark, Francis R. Cope, Fisher Hazard, Charles Parrish, James M. Willcox, Edward Lewis, T. Charlton Henry, Samuel Dixon, Edward B. Leisenring, Abram S. Hewitt) 26 D'way

Lehigh Valley Portland Cement Co. (inoperative) 60 B'way

Lehigh Valley R. R. Co. (Elisha P. Wilbur, Pres.; John R. Fanshawe, Sec.; William C. Alderson, Treas. Directors: Charles Hartshorne, William L. Conyngham, Ario Pardee, William A. Ingham, Robert H. Sayre, James L Blakeslee. John R. Fell, Robert A. Lambertin, John B. Garrett, Charles O. Skeer, William Brockie, Calvin Pardee, Elisha P. Wilbur, John R. Fanshawe, William C. Alderson) 6 & 235 B'way & Pier 2 N. R.

Lehigh Valley & Wabash Despatch (Lehigh Valley R. R. Co. proprs.) 235 B'way & Pier 2 N. R.

Lehigh & Hudson River Railway Co. (Grinnell Burt, Pres.; Daniel B. Halstead, Sec.; John Sayor, Treas. Capital, $1,340,000. Directors: Joseph S. Harris, Francis C. Yarnall, Edward W. Clark, E. Lewis, John S. Martin, William C. Sheldon, George W. Sanford, J. R. Maxwell, Austin Corbin, George F. Baker, Edwin D. Adams, Garret A. Hobart) 171 B'way

Lehigh & Wilkesbarre Coal Co. (J. Rogers Maxwell, Pres.; George S. Jones, Sec. Capital, $10,000,000. Directors: J. Rogers Maxwell, George F. Baker, Charles Parrish, Edward D. Adams, Benjamin Williamson, Henry Graves, James A. Garland) 119 Liberty

Lehigh & Wyoming Coal Co. (Ferral C. Dininny jr. propr.) 1 B'way & Boulevard n W. 81st

Lehmaier & Brother (Louis A. Lehmaier, only) 88 Fulton

Lehmaier & Co. (Ludwig Lehmaier & Sigmund Herzog) 23 Greene

Lehmaier & Williams (James S. Lehmaier & William P. Williams) 132 Nassau

Lehmaier, Schwartz & Co. (Martin H. Lehmaier, Mayer M. Schwartz & Albert Siebel) 85 Bleecker

Lehman J. & M. (Joseph & Martin) 447 B'way

Lehman Brothers (brokers) (Emanuel & Mayer E. & Meyer H. & Sigmund M. & Philip Lehman) 40 Exchange pl. & 551 D'way

Lehman Brothers (heaters) (Mitchell & Albert Lehman) 131 Bowery

Lehman & Clark (I. Lehman & John P. Clark) 596 B'way

Lehmann Charles & Co. (Charles & J. S. Lehmann) 87 College pl.

Lehmann & Arnheim (Charles Lehmann, only) 216 Sixth

Lehmann & Frankel (Oscar L. Lehmann & Eugene I. Frankel) 248 E. 30th

Lehmann & Frey (Max Lehmann & Joseph Frey) 1022 Av. A

Lehmann & Passholz (Charles Lehmann & George J. Passholz) 186 Lewis

Lehmann & Platt (Jacob S. Lehmann & Samuel Platt) 315 Church

Lehmann, Requa & Co. (dissolved) 7 Murray

Lehn & Fink (Frederick W. Fink, Charles Eberhardt & Albert Plaut;—special partner, Henry Merz, $40,000; terminates 1st May, 1893) 128 William

Lehr & Locks (no inf.) 37 John

Leibold John & Son (John & George Leibold) 197 Prince

Leibundgut E. & Co. (Edward Leibundgut & Albertus Bielenberg) 10 Old sl.

Leicht Brothers (dissolved) 643 Eighth av.

Leik & Koch (dissolved) 519 E. 19th

Leipuner & Silverstein (dissolved) 71 Attorney

Leland S. C. & Co. (Sara C. & Juanita K. Leland) 56 W. 34th

Leland, Whitney & Co. (Amory Leland, James M. Whitney, Frank S. Jordan & Joseph P. Bickerton) 47 Worth

Lellis, Skahan & Co. (Daniel P. Lellis, James Skahan & Matthew H. Murray) Jerome av. n Diabrow

Lemaitre & L'Eplattenier jr. (Alexander Lemaitre & Virgil L'Eplattenier jr.) 146 S. 5th av.

Leman G. W. & Brother (George W. & Edwin Leman) 51 Fulton

Lemcke & Doscher (Albert W. Lemcke & John Doscher) 204 Fulton

Lemken William & Fahrenholtz (William Lemken & Henry Fahrenholtz) 2406 Second av.

Lemlein P. & Co. (Philip Lemlein & Richard E. Sause) 217 Third av.

Lemmermann F. & Co. (Frederick Lemmermann & Henry F. Lohmann) 392 E. 4th

Lemmermann F. & M. (Frederick & Henry) 2 Fulton

Lemon E. J. & Son (Emanuel J. & Joseph E. Lemon) 470 Sixth av.

Lemoyne & Son (dissolved) 49 Exchange pl.

Lenair Co. (Edward Lenair, propr.) 2268 Seventh av.

Lenane P. & Brother (Thomas Lenane, only) 807 West

Lenehan & Dowley (John J. Lenehan & Francis D. Dowley) 160 B'way

Leng's John S., Son & Co. (Charles W. Long & James B. Pratt; special partner, Mary S. Long, W. New Brighton, S. I., $5,000; terminates 1st Feb. 1891) 4 Fletcher

Lengemann & Burns (dissolved) 85 Walker

Lenihan & Milliken (Daniel Lenihan & James Milliken) 183 Canal

Lenk Wine Co. (inf. unattainable) 25 William

Lenk & Co. (Herman D. Lenk & John B. Haemmerlein) 131 Chambers

Lennon James & Son (James & James Lennon jr.) 215 Centre

Lenox Hill Bank (Lee Wolff, Pres.; William H. Mellins, Cashier. Capital, $100,000. Directors: Lee Wolff, Conrad N. Jordan, William H. Mellins, David A. De Lima, E. Gorgoza, Benjamin Russak) 1248 Third av.

Lenox Hill Beef Co. (inf. unattainable) 1408 Second av.

Lent & Braman (William H. Lent & Samuel L. Braman) 520 B'way

Lenz & Breuer (Oscar Lenz & Hubert L. Breuer) 18 Bond

Lenz & Smith (dissolved) 838 W. 43th & 446 W. 54th

Leo Arnold & Co. (Arnold Leo, no Co.) 85 Broad

Leo & Coan (Newman N. Leo & Henry Coan) 525 Grand

Leon & Rosenberg (no inf.) 1920 Third av.

Leonard Charles T. & Brother (Charles T. & Warren A. Leonard) 245 W. 125th & ft. E. 130th

Leonard R. W. & Co. (dissolved) 7 Wall

Leonard T. & Son (Terence & Vincent L. Leonard) 718 Eighth av.

TYPEWRITING DONE BY THE TROW CITY DIRECTORY CO., 11 University Place.

LEO   170   LEV

Leonard & Anderson (Charles H. Leonard & Frederick V. Anderson) 191 Duane
Leonard & Byrnes (William H. Leonard & Jeremiah J. Byrnes) 198 Bowery
Leonard & Clune (Daniel Leonard & Daniel Clune) 163 E. 32d
Leonard & Ellis (Theodore M. Leonard & Wilbur D. Ellis) 157 Chambers
Leonard & Hughes (Owen Leonard & Thomas C. Hughes) 180 G'wich av.
Leonard & McCoy (Charles H. Leonard & John H. McCoy) 118 Liberty
Leonard & Moody (George H. Leonard & Horace Moody) 5 Cotton Ex.
Leonard, Jackson & Fowler (Henry W. Leonard, Benjamin C. Jackson & Robert L. Fowler) 126 B'way
Leonhard F. W. & Co. (Frederick W. Leonhard & Frederick W. Deltering) 24 Walker
Leonori Frank R. & Co. (Frank R. Leonori:—special partner, J. Howard Cowperthwait, B'klyn, N. Y., $5,000; terminates 1st Jan. 1892) 76 Pine
Leopold James M. & Co. (James M. & Alfred M. Leopold) 84 B'way
Leopold I. & Sons (Samuel & Simon & Abraham Leopold, only) 10 Park pl.
Leopold Brothers & Co. (no inf.) 216 Church
Leroy Augusta C. & Co. (dissolved) 4½ Barclay
Leroy Shot & Lead Mfg. Co. (Oscar B. Schmidt, Pres.; Charles de Rham jr. Sec.; August Hahn, Treas. Capital, $100,000. Directors: Oscar E. Schmidt, Edward A. Leroy, Charles de Rham jr.) 261 Water, 1343 B'way & 212 E. 125th
Leschhorn & Riegelmann (Frederick Leschhorn & Simon H. Riegelmann) 21 Howard
Lesem, Mayer & Dazian (Solomon J. Lesem, William W. Mayer & Philip Dazian) 74 Walker
Lesher, Whitman & Co. (Stephen R. Lesher, Nathaniel Whitman, George H. Dunham & Arthur L. Lesher) 504 B'way & 46 Crosby
Leslie Brothers (James S. & Frank J. Leslie) 483 B. 152d
Leslie & Co. (no inf.) r. 43 Centre
Leslie's Frank, Publishing House (Frank Leslie, propr.) 110 Fifth av.
Lespinasse L. & Co. (dissolved) 50 Vestry
Lespinasse & Co. (George S. Lespinasse, no Co.) 181 B'way
Lessels C. & M. R. (Charles & Morris R.) 257 W. 19th
Lessels Brothers (George W. & Edgar A. Lessels) 201 Sixth av.
Lesser J. S. & Co. (Joseph S. & Morris Lesser) 27 Walker
Lesser Brothers (Tobias & Israel & Simon Lesser) 531 B'way
Lesser & Baruch (dissolved) 53 Lispenard
Lesser & Goldsmith (Nathan Lesser & Adolph Goldsmith) 444 Broome
Lester George & Co. (George Lester & William Gaynor) 88 Park pl.
Lester Milk Co. (not inc.) (Amos W. Cramer & German L. Coffin) 1537 B'way
Lester D. B. & H. M. (David B. & Henry M.) 581 B'way & 152 Mercer
Lester, Cary & Co. (Joseph H. Lester & Roscoe G. Cary, no Co.) 95 Wall
Lester's Andrew, Sons (James F. & Charles S. & William O. Lester) 581 Madison av.
Lestrade Brothers (James W. & Francis W. Lestrade) 195 Duane
Lethbridge & Cornwell (George Lethbridge, George R. Cornwell & Frank R. & Edgar E. Lethbridge) 2 Cotton Ex.
Lethbridge & Davidge (Robert P. Lethbridge & William H. Davidge) 1 Cotton Ex.

Letson & Hashagen (Peter R. Letson & John F. Hashagen) 281 Church
Levene & Co. (Harry & Solomon Levens) 53 Franklin
Levensohn & Spector (Isidor Levensohn & Joseph Spector) 44 Canal
Leventhal & Ackerman (Marx Leventhal & Harris Ackerman) 120 Division
Leventhal & Son (Martin & Benjamin Leventhal) 120 Crosby
Leverich C. D. & Co. (Charles D. Leverich & Walter H. Clarke) 48 Wall
Levey Frederick H. & Co. (Frederick H. Levey, Noah R. Hart, Charles E. Newton & Louis Theyson) 59 Beekman
Levi Emil S. & Co. (Emil S. & Henlein Levi & Julius Sondheimer) 58 White
Levi Jacob & Co. (Jacob & Moses Levi) 191 Washn.
Levi Brothers (Isaac & Joseph Levi & Edward C. Blum) 19 Greene
Levi & Co. (no inf.) 203 E. 97th
Levi & Mayor (Louis Levi, only) 47 Greene
Levi, Wechsler & Co. (Lewis Levi, Abram F. Sterne, Albert D. Wechsler & Mangold H. Eilenbogen;—special partner, Benjamin Wechsler, $50,000; terminates, 1st Jan. 1892) 521 B'way
Leviberg & Co. (Jacob Leviberg, Co. refused) 252 Pearl
Levin M. & Co. (Moses & Samuel Levin) 10 Suffolk
Levinger & Rothenberg (Benjamin Levinger & Henry Rothenberg) 41 Fulton & 820 Bowery
Levins & Hanigan (John P. Levins & David F. Hanigan) 1645 Ninth av.
Levinsky & Samuelson (Daniel Levinsky & Jacob Samuelson) 60 Division
Levinson & Rosenthal (no inf.) 26 Willett
Levis Henry & Co. (Henry Levis, no Co.) 10 Wall
Levison I. & Co. (Isidor Levison & Louis Hirsch) 52 W. Houston
Levison Brothers & Co. Bernhard & Benno Levison jr. no Co.) 286 Church
Levy Bernard & Co. (Bernard & Isaac I. Levy) 408 B'way
Levy Herman & Co. (Herman & Arthur Levy) 205 Church
Levy Joseph & Son (Joseph & Daniel Levy) 378 Eighth av.
Levy Louis & Brother (Louis & Benjamin Levy) 1721 First av.
Levy Robert & Co. (Robert Levy & Fanny Bindskopf) 632 B'way
Levy A. & Brother (Abraham & Louis Levy) 612 B'way & 150 Crosby
Levy A. & J. (Abraham & Jacob) 625 B'way & 192 Mercer
Levy A. & S. (August & Simon) 22 Walker
Levy A. & S. & Co. (August & Simon Levy, Meyer Weinberg & William Weissager) 22 Walker
Levy B. & Co. (Barnet Levy & Sarah Shapiro) 178 Grand
Levy D. & Son (David & George Levy) 169 Water
Levy D. & Sons (David & Michael D. & Henry J. & Morris M. Levy) 519 B'way
Levy E. & Co. (Emanuel Levy, Co. refused) 305 Mulberry
Levy G. & M. (Gustavus & Mitchel) 132 Nassau
Levy H. & Brother (Harris & Nathan Levy) 175 E. B'way
Levy H. & Son (clothing) (Harris & Abraham Levy) 41 E. B'way
Levy H. & Son (drygds) (no inf.) 180 Division
Levy H. H. & Co. (Herrman H. Levy & George Beck) 40 Walker

THE CALIGRAPH WRITING MACHINE,
HARTFORD, CONN.

LEV　　　　171　　　　LIB

Levy H. L. & Brother (Herman L. & Aaron Levy) 19 Mercer
Levy H. R. & Brother (Henry R. & Alfred Levy) 1 W. 3d
Levy L. & Co. (Lazarus Levy & David U. Herrmann) 70 D'way & 15 New
Levy M. & Brother (Morris & Adolph Levy) 155 Water
Levy M. R. & Co. (Morris R. Levy & Benjamin Van Veen) 27 Wooster
Levy P. & J. (Philip & John) 79 Cortlandt
Levy S. & Co. (cases) (Siegfried & Gottlieb Levy) 95 Liberty
Levy S. & Co. (toys) (Simon Levy, Elias Wolf & Carl Bloedel) 522 D'way
Levy S. & Son (cigars) (Solomon & Louis & Charles Levy) 229 E. 120th
Levy S. & Son (quilters) (Samuel & Meyer Levy) 300 Canal
Levy Brothers (cigars) (Armand M. & Sigismund Levy) 214 Av. C
Levy Brothers (clothing) (Nathan Levy, only) 4 G'wich & 5 Battery pl.
Levy Brothers (toygds.) (no inf.) 2437 Eighth av.
Levy Brothers (frames) (Caspar & Louis Levy) 665 Eighth av.
Levy Brothers (meat) (Herman & Abraham Levy) 208 E. 59th
Levy Brothers (meat) (Leon & Moise & Joseph Levy) 353 First av. 865 Second av. & 370 Third av.
Levy Brothers (meat) (Nathan Levy, only) 1572 First av.
Levy Brothers (ribbons) (Ernest & Herman & Abraham Levy) 71 Greene & 345 W. 37th
Levy & Abmhams (Samuel Levy & Morris Abrahams) 448 Broome
Levy & Cook (dissolved) 615 Hudson
Levy & Goodman (Joseph Levy & Sarah Goodman) 28 Orchard
Levy & Horwitz (Isaac Levy & Abraham Horwitz) 218 Sixth av. & 28 Gt. Jones
Levy & Katzman (Solomon Levy & Charles Katzman) 132 Duane
Levy & Lewis (Berthold Levy & Sigmund & Aaron Lewis) 50 Stone & 68 Pearl
Levy & Levy (Louis & Julius Levy) 51 Chambers
Levy & Loeb (Leopold Levy & Simon Loeb) 703 B'wny
Levy & Meyer (Lehman Levy & Charles Meyer) 414 E. 105th
Levy & Meyers (no inf.) 29 Bond
Levy & Miskend (dissolved) 40 Walker
Levy & Rabinowitz (Herman Levy & Abraham Rabinowitz) 21 W. 3d
Levy & Wertheimer (Bernard Levy & Joseph Wertheimer) 60 White
Levy Brothers & Co. (Julius & Augustus H. Levy; —special partner, estate of Adolph Levy, $101,000; terminates 31st Dec, 1891) 612 D'way & 150 Crosby
Levy Brothers & Pincus (Morris & Charles C. Levy & Charles Pincus) 814 B'way
Levy, Dreyfus & Co. (Louis W. Levy & Edward Dreyfus, no Co.) 11 Malden la.
Levy's Henry, Son (David M. Levy) 47 E. Houston
Lewando's French Dyeing & Cleansing Establishment (refused) 2 W. 14th, 280 Fifth av. & 731 Sixth av.
Lewenthal M. & D. (no inf.) 1002 Third av.
Lewin Brothers (Herman & Charles S. Lewin) 205 Hudson
Lewinson A. & Co. (Albert & Herman & William Lewinson) 26 E. Houston
Lewinson A. & Son (dissolved) 2 Bond

Lewis August & Co. (August & Alphonso & Eugene Lewis & William S. Kahnweiler) 149 Greene
Lewis Charles & Brothers (Charles & Jacob & Martin M. & Henry A. Lewis) 313 Church
Lewis David W. & Co. (David W. Lewis & William H. Forker) 177 Chambers
Lewis Isaac & Sons (Isaac & Joseph D. & Henry Lewis) 182 Worth
Lewis H. & W. H. (Henry & Walter H.) 50 Worth
Lewis J. & Son (Henry & Rosa Lewis, only) 20 Lispenard
Lewis J. H. & Son (John H. & John H. Lewis jr.) 1329 D'way
Lewis S. M. & Co. (Sylvanus M. Lewis, no Co.) 5 Malden la.
Lewis S. W. & Co. (Isaac L. V. & John J. Lewis, only) 24 South
Lewis 'Brothers (eatings) (George & Samuel Lewis) 2482 Second av.
Lewis Brothers (jewelers) (Charles E. F. & Wright F. Lewis jr.) 41 Malden la.
Lewis & Bodine (Joseph Lewis & William A. Bodine) 87 West
Lewis & Cohen (Hyman Lewis & Barnet Cohen) 116 Division
Lewis & Co. (brokers) (William G. Lewis & John E. Huntoon) 11 W. 25th
Lewis & Co. (real estate) (William & H. Henry Lewis) 28 Dey
Lewis & Co. (shades) (Emily R. Lewis, no Co.) 2 E. 14th
Lewis & Co. (whitegds.) (Thomas W. Lewis, Co. refused) 1894 Bathgate av.
Lewin & Conger (Richard V. Lewis & Henry C. Conger) 1338 B'way & 601 Sixth av.
Lewis & Edman (Frank Lewis & Morris L. Edman) 1 Elizabeth
Lewis & Harris (Lewis Lewis & Thomas W. Harris) 7 Warren
Lewis & Holder (Thomas C. Lewis & Robert E. Holder) 718 Tremont av.
Lewis & Jones (John J. Lewis & Thomas Jones) 2 W. 14th & 133 W. 17th
Lewis Brothers & Co. (dissolved) 86 Worth & 7 Thomas
Lewis, Kaiser & Luthy (Frederick W. Lewis, David Kaiser & Adolph Luthy) 35 Ann
Lewis, Wessel & Leward (Frederick Wessel & James Leward, only) 41 Malden la.
Lewisohn Importing & Trading Co. (Ltd.) (Leonard Lewisohn, Pres.; Philip Lewisohn, Treas.; Albert Lewisohn, Sec. Capital, $150,000. Directors: Leonard & Philip & Albert Lewisohn) 154 S. 5th av.
Lewisohn Brothers (Leonard & Adolph & Philip Lewisohn) 81 Fulton
Lewisohn & Co. (Raphael & Leon Lewisohn) 41 Malden la. & 217 Mercer
Lewy Brothers (Berthold & Julius Lewy) 140 Nassau
Lexow R. G. & Co. (Rudolph G. & Charles K. Lexow) 906 Third av.
Lexow & Haldane (Clarence Lexow & William H. Haldane) 48 Exchange pl.
Lexow & Leo (Charles K. Lexow & Leopold Leo) 146 D'way
Leyror & Co. (refused) 2917 & 2374 Third av.
L'Hommedieu S. Y. & Co. (Sylvester Y. L'Hommedieu & Reginald A. Lawrence) 65 Reade & 83 Chambers
Libby & Ryker (Abraham B. Ryker, only) 625 B'way & 102 Mercer
Libby H. J. & Co. (Harrison J. & Augustus F. Libby) 55 White
Libby & Scott Brothers (James L. & Henry M. Libby, Walter E. & Edward W. Scott jr.) 120 B'way

SPECIAL ATTENTION PAID TO THIS CLASS OF WORK } BANKERS' & BROKERS' CIRCULARS DELIVERED { THE TROW CITY DIRECTORY CO. 11 University Place.

LIB 172 **LIN**

Liberman Brothers (Jacob & Julius & Charles Liberman) 558 B'way

Libermann & Schulman (Pincus Liberman & Harris W. Schulman) 70 E. D'way

Liberty Ins. Co. (George A. Morrison, Pres.; Philip La Tourette, Sec. Capital, $500,000. Directors: George A. Morrison, Horace J. Fairchild, Samuel R. Weed, Julian T. Davies, Elijah R. Kennedy, John Claflin, James McCreery, W. John W. Aitken, George F. Victor, Otto K. Krause, John Herriman, Olin G. Walbridge, Stephen R. Lesher, John Sloane, Eugene Higgins, Edward D. Adams, Louis Fitzgerald, T. W. Evans, John A. McCall, Joseph F. Knapp, John R. Inman, Marcellus Hartley, Edward M. Field, Edward Holbrook, Hubert L. Judd, Gustave A. Jahn, Charles W. Gould, Eduardo Gogorza, James Stokes, Thomas Birkin, Oliver Ames) 120 B'way

Liberty Knitting Co. (Mossbacher & Myros, proprs.) 310 Church

Liberty Machine Works (Bryant Godwin, Pres.; Charles H. Martini, Treas.; Frederick Vanwyck, Sec. Capital. $55,000. Directors: Bryant Godwin, Charles H. Martini, Frederick Vanwyck) 54 Frankfort

Liberty Novelty Co. (R. S. Trischet & Son, proprs.) 145 Elm

Liberty Silk Works (H. A. Vanliew & Co. proprs.) 1 Greene & 548 W. 57th

Libman S. & Co. (dissolved) 207 Bowery

Libman Joseph & Co. (Joseph Libmann & Adolph Mintzer) 191 8, 5th av.

Lichtblau Brothers (dissolved) 7 Clinton

Lichtenberg & Frank (dissolved) 122 Lewis

Lichtenberger P. & Brother (Paul & Anton Lichtenberger) 33 Av. A

Lichtenstein A., Son & Co. (Abraham & Solomon Lichtenstein, no Co.) 309 E. 55th

Lichtenstein Isaac & Son (dissolved) 58 Grand

Licht nstein H. & Sons (Henry & David & Max & Benjamin Lichtenstein) 107 Greene

Lichtenstein J. & Sons (Joanna & Abraham & David H. & Isaac & Jacob H. Lichtenstein) 265 Grand

Lichtenstein S. & Co. (Seamen & Seamen Lichtenstein jr. & Lawrence O'Brien) 85 Barclay

Lichtenstein Brothers (Julius & Bernhard Lichtenstein) 117 Maiden la.

Lichtenstein & Lyons (Henry Lichtenstein & Benjamin Lyons) 376 B'way

Lichtenstein Brothers Co. (Reuben Lindheim, Pres.; Solomon B. Lichenstein, Sec.; Siegmund Brussel, Treas. Capital, $220,000. Directors: Reuben Lindheim, Solomon B. Lichtenstein, Siegmund Brussel, William J. Brown, B. Lichtenstein, A. Brussel, Michael Greenspecht) E. 32d & First av.

Lichtwitz & Bueschen (Frances Lichtwitz & Anthony W. Bueschen) 809 Ninth av.

Lidgerwood Mfg. Co. (William V. V. Lidgerwood, Pres.; John H. Lidgerwood, Treas., Walter L. Pierce, Sec. Capital, $80,000. Directors: William V. V. & John H. Lidgerwood, Walter L. Pierce) 96 Liberty

Liebenroth, Vonnau & Co. (Iwan & Alwin Vonnau & Herman Schleicher, only) 48 Franklin

Lieber D. & Co. (David Lieber & Florean Hendricks) 17 S. William

Lieber & Dreyfous (George Lieber & Henry Dreyfous) 122 Front

Lieberknecht H. & Co. (Henry Lieberknecht & William H. Bickelhaupt) 38 Crosby

Liebig Laboratory & Chemical Works Co. (inf. unattainable) 36 Murray

Liebig & Rückert (no inf.) 286 Lenox av.

Liebler A., Bottling Co. (John J. Schmitt, Pres.; Anton Liebler, Sec. Capital, $150,000. Directors: John J. Schmitt, Michael A. Breid,

Anton Liebler, Peter Koch, William J. G. Yuengling) 402 W. 126th

Liebler & Maass (Theodore A. Liebler jr. & John A. J. Maass) 76 Park pl.

Liebmann & Butler (Joseph C. Butler & John Solari, only) 98 Pearl & 58 Stone

Lienau M. & Co. (Michael Lienau & Henry Eggers) 2 Jones la.

Liepmann Brothers (Richard & Paul Liepmann) 12 Greene

Lies George P. & Co. (George P. Lies & Emil Soldenberg) 1610 Av. A

Liescgang Joseph E. & Co. (Joseph E. & Benjamin Liescgang) 50 South

Liesenbein Brothers (William & Nicholas Liesenbein) 234 E. 42d

Life Union (Horace Moody, Pres.; Ralph Marden, Sec. Directors: Horace Moody, William D. Barron, Ralph Marden, V. B. Chamberlain, Douw H. Fonda, E. Wright Nelson, Joseph T. Baldwin. W. Jenks Merritz, Smith T. Woolworth, William F. Walker, William H. Law, Franklin Edwards, George D. Whoedon, J. J. Cooper) 284 B'way

Life & Accident Ins. Corporation (no inf.) 132 Nassau

Light & Force Co. (inoperative) 44 B'way

Light & Leather (William J. Light & Thomas Leather) E. 107th n First av.

Lightbody John G. & Co. (J. Lewis Leib, only) 24 Beekman & 540 W. 33d

Lights & Brother (Charles & William Lights) 507 E. 17th

Ligienger George & Son (dissolved) 765 & 801 Ninth av.

Lilienthal Brothers (Theodore M. & Albert Lilienthal) 5 Water

Lilliputian Perfume Co. (Clifford M. De Mott, propr.) 39 Barclay

Lilly J. C. & Co. (John C. Lilly & John Guilford) 1542 Ninth av.

Lincks John & Co. (John & Louis Lincks) 525 W. 19th

Lincoln National Bank (Thomas L. James, Pres.; William T. Cornell, Cashier; A. Lansing Baird, Notary. Capital, $300,000. Directors: Thomas L. James, Alfred Van Santvoord, William R. Grace, Noah Davis, Frederick Kuhne, Matthew C. D. Borden, H. Walter Webb, Charles C. Clarke, John Stratton, Samuel Barton) 82 E. 42d

Lincoln Safe Deposit Co. (Thomas L. James, Pres.; John R. Van Wormer, Sec. Capital, $500,000. Trustees: Thomas L. James, William R. Grace, Alfred Van Santvoord, Noah Davis, Frederick Kuhne, Matthew C. D. Borden, Frederick W. Vanderbilt, William Seward Webb, H. Walter Webb, William D. Sloane, Harvey P. Farrington) 82 E. 42d

Lincoln F. W. & Co. (Frederick W. Lincoln & Robert M. Barber) 52 John

Lincoln, Bacon & Co. (James D. Lincoln, Harland G. Bacon & Daniel O. Scofield) 41 Maiden la.

Lineroute Walton Mfg. Co. (Albert S. Swords, Pres.; Franklin Miller, Treas.; William P. Mitchell, Sec. Capital, $225,000. Directors: Albert S. Swords, Schuyler Merritt, Joseph A. Dean, John L. Riker, Frederick Beck, Brent Good, Franklin Miller, N. R. Hart, Timothy H. Porter) 7 W. 28th

Linde Frederick C. & Co. (Frederick C. Linde & Frederick W. Conklin :—special partner, Colson C. Hamilton ; further inf. refused) Beach e Varick & 173 & 182 Pearl

Linde F. C., Hamilton & Co. (Frederick C. Linde & Frederick W. Conklin :—special partner, Colson C. Hamilton ; further inf. refused) 162 Pearl & 408 E. 53d

Lindeman J. & Co. (Julius Lindeman & Julian Brummer) 24 Cath. sl.

FOR THE BEST CO-PARTNERSHIP IN THE BEST CORPORATION SEE PAGE F IN BACK OF BOOK

LIN   173   LIV

Lindeman & Sons (dissolved) 146 Fifth av.
Lindemann O. & Co. (Otto Lindemann & Charles T. Worms) 81 Beekman
Lindenborn D. & Co. (David Lindenborn, no Co.) 4 W. 22d
Lindenfelsen & Cotthaus (Stephen Lindenfelsen & Richard C. Cotthaus) 36½ Macdougal
Lindenkohl & Oeltze (dissolved) 516 Fifth
Lindenstein & Co. (Simon M. Lindenstein & Benjamin Stern) 4 Loew av. W. Washn. mkt
Linder & Brothers (dissolved) 256 Av. B
Linderman G. B. & Co. (refused) 1 B'way
Lindh & Teden (Charles J. Lindh & Frederick Teden) 11 Vandewater
Lindner, Eddy & Clauss (Frank H. Lindner, Charles Eddy & Christian Clauss) 66 Centre
Lindo Brothers (Abraham & Isaac Lindo) 1205 B'way
Lindon & Bannin (Luke J. Lindon & Michael E. Bannin) 97 Spring
Lindsay A. W., Type Foundry (Alexander W. Lindsay, Pres.; Charles W. Tarbell. Sec. Capital, $15,000. Trustees: Alexander W. Lindsay, Charles W. Tarbell, Flora S. Lindsay) 70 Park pl.
Lindsay Type Foundry (not inc.) (Robert Lindsay & Burr Dauohy) 75 Fulton
Lindsay & Allen (Henry E. Lindsay & William R. Allen) 299 Eighth av.
Lingemann, Hoffman & Co. (John A. Lingemann, George Hoffman & Christian Dautermann) 195 Chrystie
Link G. L. & G. H. (George L. & G. Henry) 127 Christopher
Link-Belt Engineering Co. (William D. Ewart, Pres.; Edward H. Burr, Sec.; S. Howard Smith, Treas. Capital, $200,000. Directors: William D. Ewart, James M. Dodge, Edward M. Burr, S. Howard Smith) 49 Dey
Link-Belt Machinery Co. (no inf.) 49 Dey
Linneman Brothers (Louis & George & Ferdinand Linneman) 201 Chambers & 193 Reade
Linspar Decorating Co. (Milton J. Hardy, Pres.; J. Walter Righter, Sec. Capital, $100,000. Directors: Milton J. Hardy, J. Walter Righter) 45 B'way
Lion Andrew & Son (Andrew & David Lion) 36 Av. B
Lion Mfg. Co. (Lion & Dryfoos, proprs.) 43 Walker
Lion Silk Assn. (Gustave Hurliman, Pres.; further inf. unattainable) 92 Grand
Lion & Dryfoos (Nathan Lion & Emil Dryfoos) 43 Walker
Lipman & Peniston (dissolved) 83 Beaver
Lipman & Son (Isaac & Solomon Lipman) 1426 Second av.
Lippe & Co. (Charles Lippe & Charles Fishel) 110 Bowery
Lippman J. & Co. (Julius Lippman & Samuel Ullmann) 133 Seventh av.
Lippmann L. & Sons (Leopold & Jacob & Henry Lippmann) 557 B'way & 128 Mercer
Lippmann W. & L. (Wolf & Louis) 391 Eighth av.
Lippmann, Hilborn & Co. (Gustav Lippmann, Gustav Hilborn & George Lippmann) 515 B'way & 84 Mercer
Lipsker & Munk (Jacob Lipsker & David Munk) 115 Nassau
Liscomb W. H. & Co. (William H. Liscomb, no Co.) 240 Washn.
Lisa Brothers (John F. & Charles A. Lisa) 344 W. 41st & 227 W. 31st
Lissa Henry & Co. (Henry Lissa, no Co.) 598 B'way & 168 Mercer
Lissauer & Sondheim (Max J. Lissauer & Lewis H. Sondheim) 12 Maiden la.

Lissberger L. & Co. (Lazarus Lissberger & Bernhard Schutz) 40 Cliff
Lisso Morris & Son (Morris & Henry M. Lisso) 93 Grand
List & Lennon (Alexander List & Thomas Lennon) 507 W. 14th
Lister's Agricultural Chemical Works (Edwin Lister, Pres.; Edward Lancaster, Sec. Capital, $600,000. Directors: Edwin Lister, E. C. Hay, Edward Lancaster, John Kehoe, P. H. Martin, William Selby) 159 Front & ft. W. 38th
Literary Publishing Co. (James T. Wiggins, Pres.; L. L. Levey, Sec. Capital, $25,000. Directors: James T. Wiggins, L. L. Levey, F. B. Forster) 32 Broad
Lithauer's L., Sons (Theodore & Lehman Lithauer) 676 B'way
Lithographic Patent Zinc Plate Co. (inf. unattainable) 98 William & 490 Cherry
Lithold Mfg. Co. (Julius Levine, Pres.; James H. Hoffman, Sec.; Silas L. Kenyon, Treas. Capital, $200,000; further inf. unattainable) 52 Howard
Lithotype Printing Co. (Albert G. Bushnell, propr.) 111 Nassau
Litofuge Mfg. Co. (Frederick N. Blanc, Pres.; Frederick W. Hadfield, Sec.; further inf. unattainable) 53 Cedar
Littauer L. & Son (Louis & Benjamin Littauer) 1493 Third av.
Littauer Brothers (Lucius N. & Eugene Littauer) 450 B'way
Littell A. C. & Co. (Amos C. Littell, Conrad H. Abelman & William B. Yale) 260 Washn.
Littell E. B. & Co. (Elias B. & Theodore S. & John N. Littell) 124 Warren
Little Chief Mining Co. (Thomas Fitbladdo, Pres.; Edward Earle, Sec. Capital, $10,000,000. Trustees: Thomas Fitbladdo, Edward Earle, Remsen L. Brower, E. C. Kimboll) 45 B'way
Little Falls Gas Light Co. (William Henry White, Pres.; Valentine S. Watrous, Sec. Capital, $100,000. Directors: William Henry White, Valentine S. Watrous) 30 Pine
Little John H. & Co. (John H. Little, no Co.) 5 W. 14th
Little Pittsburgh Cons. Mining Co. (inoperative) 120 B'way
Little J. J. & Co. (Joseph J. Little, W. Jennings Demorest & George C. Travis) 10 Astor pl.
Little & Hamilton (E. Knox Little & Walter S. Hamilton) 336 W. 125th
Little & O'Connor (Willard P. Little & Michael J. O'Connor) 28 W. 23d
Littlefield & Co. (James W. Littlefield & William L. Ross) 144 Reade
Littlewood C. L. & Co. (Charles L. Littlewood:— special partner, James M. Bloomfield, Yonkers, N. Y. $2,000; terminates 1st Jan. 1894) 33 John
Litzinger Brothers (Charles jr. & Emile A. Litzinger) 267 Bowery
Live Stock Car Equipment Co. (Charles Matthews, Pres.; Peter B. Matthews, Treas.; Charles J. Wells, Sec. Capital, $250,000. Directors: Charles Matthews, Matthew Taylor, Hugh Baines, Peter B. Matthews, Charles J. Wells, B. A. Hegeman jr., James McAlley, William R. Potts) 15 Broad
Livermore & Enders (Edwin R. Livermore & Martin Enders) 119 Broad
Liverpool Clothing Co. (Henry P. Ansorge, propr.) 60 Bowery
Liverpool & London Clothing Co. (Julius Crager, propr.) 24 Bowery
Livesey & Son (James & James Livesey jr.) 62 Centre
Livingston Mining & Mfg. Co. (George Bell, Pres.; James H. Lancaster, Treas.; Nugent Robin-

son, Sec. Capital, $1,000,000; further inf. unattainable) 171 B'way
Livingston Morris & Co. (Frederick & Felix Livingston & Warren A. Jacobson, only) 121 Liberty, 493 & 589 B'way & 444 Broome
Livingston Nail Co. (S. Otis Livingston, propr.) 104 Reade
Livingston W. & F. (William S. & Francis A. & William S. Livingston jr.) 391 G'wich
Livingston Brothers (Isaac & Louis & William Livingston) 28 Lispenard & 63 Baxter
Livingston & Olcott (Robert A. Livingston & J. Van Vechten Olcott) 4 Warren
Llado Francisco & Co. (William J. Farrell, only) 132 Maiden la.
Lloyd John C. & Co. (John C. Lloyd, no Co.) 99 Front
Lloyd John W. & Co. (dissolved) 1730 Ninth av.
Lloyd Thomas J. & Son (Thomas J. & Thomas J. Lloyd jr.) 813 Broome
Lloyd William T. & Co. (William T. & William R. Lloyd) 317 B'way
Lloyd & McKean (Joseph P. Lloyd & William C. McKean) 31 Nassau
Lloyd, Finlay & Co. (William H. Lloyd, Frederick W. Finlay & Robert H. Turle) 352 Produce Ex.
Lloyd, Finlay & Coster (dissolved) 24 State
Lloyds Plate Glass Ins. Co. (James G. Deemer, Pres.; William T. Woods, Sec. Capital, $100,000. Directors: James G. Deemer, Thomas W. Strong, James S. Oakley, Charles Jones, John H. Seed, Daniel B. Halstead, John J. Drake, Thomas S. Thorp, George M. Olcott, Samuel A. Warner, Henry Coffin, William D. Chase, Benjamin J. Sturges, William A. Nash, Frederick A. Guild, Henry B. Hall) 63 William
Lobdell J. H. & Co. (refused) 12 Cliff
Lobenstein & Koesur (Emanuel Lobenstein & Ignatz Koeser) 1230 Third av.
Lobenthal M. & L. (Michael & Levi) 407 B'way & 68 Mercer
Lobsitz & Powell (dissolved) 85 Murray
Loch & Granau (no inf.) 159 Ludlow
Locher & Demott (George H. Locher & Jacob J. Demott) 264 Canal
Lock-Nut Bolt & Iron Co. (James B. McKinney, Pres.; Edward C. Smith, Sec. Capital, $100,000. Directors: James B. McKinney, Edward C. Smith, L. M. Didwell) 79 Cedar
Lock-Shank Button Co. (George P. Bradford, Pres.; Avery G. Wheeler, Sec. Capital, $75,000; further inf. unattainable) 30 Warren
Locke J. B. & Potts (Thomas Potts & David Henesey, only) 61 Franklin
Locke J. H. & Co. (Joseph H. Locke & Joseph McMahon) 414 Produce Ex.
Locklin F. P. & Brother (Francis P. & Peter H. Locklin) 208 Canal
Locks H. & S. (dissolved) 369 Eighth av.
Lockwood Chemical Co. (Ltd.) (William Lockwood, Pres.; Charles G. Sentis, Sec.; William S. Lockwood, Treas. Capital, $20,000. Directors: William & William S. & J. Lockwood, Charles G. & S. L. Sentis) 276 Pearl
Lockwood Howard & Co. (Howard Lockwood & William P. Hamilton) 126 Duane
Lockwood A. C. & Co. (no inf.) 36 E. 43d
Lockwood C. B. & Co. (Calvin D. Lockwood & Fitch J. Stranahan) 361 Produce Ex.
Lockwood F. M. & Co. (Frederick M. & Frederick R. Lockwood) 8 Exchange ct.
Lockwood G. & Co. (dissolved) 175 Fifth av.
Lockwood & Coombes (dissolved) 275 Fifth av.
Lockwood & Geery (Henry F. Lockwood & Isaac J. Geery) 165 Front

Lockwood & Hill (Luke A. Lockwood & John L. Hill) 59 Liberty
Lockwood & Holly (Frederick W. Lockwood & John I. Holly) 81 New
Lockwood & Lowe (Frederick F. Lockwood & James M. Lowe) 460 Produce Ex.
Lockwood Brothers & Holly (dissolved) 81 New
Lodi Chemical Co. (inf. unattainable) 38 Platt
Lodemes & Rappe (dissolved) 378 W. 12th
Loeb Herman & Co. (Herman A. Loeb, only) 16 B'way
Loeb A. & H. (Aaron & Herman) 24 Prince
Loeb Brothers (Aaron & David & Herman Loeb) 238 Av. A & 153 Av. C
Loeb & Berliner (Paul H. Loeb & George Berliner) 34 Walker
Loeb & Brother (Heineman & Marcus Loeb) 529 B'way
Loeb & Co. (Morris Loeb, no Co.) 90 Warren
Loeb & Francis (Leo Loeb & Hubert Francis) 21 Spruce
Loeb & Hoffmann (Emil Loeb & Ignatz Hoffmann) 124 G'wich & 107 Trinity pl.
Loeb & Schoenfeld (David & Max Schoenfeld, only) 26 Franklin
Loeb & Waldheimer (Leopold Loeb, Philip Waldheimer & Julius R. Loeb) 407 B'way & 68 Mercer
Loebel & Gerber (Florian Loebel & Sigmund Gerber) 34 Bond
Loeber Brothers (Charles H. Loeber, only) 111 Nassau
Loebie Brothers (Frederick C. & Gottlob E. Loebie) 65 Grand
Loeffel Brothers (Andrew & Louis & Charles Loeffel) 78 Roosevelt
Loeffel & Stadecker (Joseph Loeffel & Frederick Stadecker) 14 W. Houston
Loehr's Henry, Sons (George & John Loehr) 429 W. 55th
Loesser H. & Co. (Henry Loesser, Co. refused) 885 First av.
Loesser & Boenneken (dissolved) r 381 Broome
Loew & Schaffner (Louis A. Loew & Charles E. Schaffner) 934 Eighth av.
Loewenberg's J., Sons (Edward Loewenberg, only) 112 Bowery
Loewensohn & Co. (Solomon Loewensohn & Gustave Kallski) 26 G'wich
Loewenstein M. & Brother (Max & Alexander Loewenstein) 23 Lispenard
Loewenstein Brothers (Saul & Louis Loewenstein) 180 Greene
Loewenstein & Co. (Morris Loewenstein & Emile Bissas) 1709 Ninth av.
Loewenstein & Keminer (Robert Loewenstein & George Kemmer) 12 Desbrosses
Loewenstein & Marcus (Charles Lowenstein & George Marcus) 99 Nassau
Loewenstine J. H. & Brother (dissolved) 41 Greene & 461 G'wich
Loewenthal Charles & Co. (Charles Loewenthal; —special partners, Heilbut, Symons & Co., London & Liverpool, Eng., $100,000; terminates 1st Jan., 1891) 67 Pine
Loewenthal Jacob & Sons (Jacob & Adolph & Simon J. & Emil M. Loewenthal) 54 White
Loewenthal Julius & Co. (Julius & Bendix Loewenthal & Salig Rosenbaum) 38 Mercer
Loewenthal J. & Co. (Jacob Loewenthal & Anne Russak) 715 B'way
Loewenthal L. & Son (Leonard & Marcus Loewenthal) 36 Leonard
Loewenthal P. & S. (Perry & Samuel) 146 Water
Loewenthal S. & Son (Max Loewenthal, only) 115 Clinton & 749 Sixth av.

THADDEUS DAVIDS CO., WRITING INKS, SEALING WAX,
MAKE THE BEST MUCILAGE.

LOE 175 LOP

Loewenthal & Morganstern (Rudolph A. Loewenthal & Albert G. Morganstern) 132 Nassau

Loewenthal & Seligman (Louis Loewenthal & Lena Seligman) 317 E. 58th

Loewthal & Silvermann (dissolved) 327 Bowery

Loewer's V., Gambrinus Brewing Co. (Valentine Loewer, Pres.; George Loewer, Sec.; Charles J. G. Hall, Treas. Capital, $100,000. Trustees: Valentine Loewer, Charles J. G. Hall, Uriah W. Tompkins) 525 W. 41st

Loewns L. & Co. (Leopold Loewns, no Co.) 4 Gt. Jones

Loewy L. & Brother (Leopold & Joseph Loewy) 50 Lispenard

Logan & Patterson (dissolved) 222 Produce Ex.

Logan & Son (Hugh & John J. Logan) 3030 Third av.

Logan, Cowl & Co. (Frank G. Logan, Clarkson Cowl & Frank K. Dunn) 205 Produce Ex.

Logeling G. & Son (Guillaume & Charles W. Logeling) 239 E. 57th

Lehman J. & F. (John D. & J. Frederick) 245 South & 479 Water

Lohman & Co. (Henry J. Lohman & J. F. Farley) 141 Charles

Lohmann & Co. (William Lohmann, Co. refused) 1234 Third av.

Lohrke Otto E. & Co. (Otto E. Lohrke & William F. Callaghan) 219 Produce Ex.

Lohse & Borger (Henry Lohse & Ahrend J. Borger) 50 Ann

Loizeaux Brothers (Paul J. & Timothy O. Loizeaux) 63 Fourth av.

Lombard Investment Co. (Benjamin Lombard jr. Pres.; William A. Lombard, Sec.; Lysander D. Skinner, Treas. Capital & Surplus, $1,650,000. Directors: Benjamin jr. & James L. & Lewis & William A. Lombard, William McGeorge jr. Joseph Jacobs jr, Isaac P. T. Edmands, John D. W. Joy, John J. Currier, Gilbert L. Streeter, Irving Wood, Lysander D. Skinner, K. Harris, J. T. Cockran, George Burnham, William B. Bement, George Philler, George M. Troutman, Charles H. Pine, Albert L. Fessenden, Thomas N. McCarter, W. E. Swentzel) 150 B'way

London Clothing Co. (Simon Shapiro, propr.) 54 & 100 Bowery

London Harness Agency (Martin & Martin, proprs.) 235 Fifth av.

London Mfg. Co. (Jacob Rothschild, propr.) 66 W. 23d

London Needle Co. (Julius T. Rosenheimer, Pres.; Benjamin F. Rosenheimer, Sec. Capital, $2,500. Directors: Julius T. & Benjamin F. Rosenheimer) 539 E. 116th

London Rubber Clothing Mfg. Co. (Frank & Sonneborn, proprs.) 425 B'way

London Supply Co. (Freeman Hiscox, propr.) 853 B'way

London Suspender Co. (J. Yalovitz & Brother, proprs.) 4 Walker

London Tailoring Co. (Jacob Harris, propr.) 12 Fourth av.

London Toilet Bazar Co. (Anthony P. Couture, Pres.; George H. Cassidy, Sec. Capital, $100,000. Directors: Anthony P. Couture, Isabel & George H. Cassidy) 88 W. 23d

London L. & J. (Louis & Jacob) ft. E. 44th

London & Brother (Louis & Albert London) 159 Division & 74 Ridge

London & Liverpool Clothing Co. (Isidor Rosenheim & Co. proprs.) 85 Bowery

London & N.Y. Scientific Dressmaking & Millinery Co. (Reid & Co. proprs.) 57 W. 125th

Lonergan Brothers (James & Daniel Lonergan) 105 Franklin & 120 Mercer

Long Acre Pharmacy (George W. Holmes, propr.) 1491 B'way

Long Beach Hotel & Cottage Co. (Ltd.) (Henry Graves, Pres.; Frank McDonough, Sec.; William G. Wheeler, Treas. Capital, $400,000. Directors: Austin Corbin, Henry W. Maxwell, Frederick W. Dunton, James D. Campbell, John R. Maxwell, Henry Graves, William G. Wheeler) 192 B'way

Long Distance Telephone Co. (dissolved) 53 B'way

L. I. Bituminous Rock Paving Co. (inf. unattainable) 45 B'way

L. I. Button Co. (Arthur P. Fowler, propr.) 417 Broome

L. I. Embroidering Co. (H. Solomon & Son, proprs.) 90 Walker

L. I. Express Co. (L. I. R. R. Co, proprs.) ft. James st. ft. E. 34th, 653, 652 & 1313 B'way, 142 West, 296 Canal, 11 E. 14th & 62 W. 125th

L. I. Improvement Co. (Ltd.) (Samuel L. Parrish, Pres.; Frank McDonough, Sec.; William G. Wheeler, Treas. Capital, $478,000. Directors: Austin Corbin, George Maxwell, Frank K. Pendleton, Henry W. Maxwell, Samuel L. Parrish, William G. Wheeler) 192 B'way

L. I. Ins. Co. (inf. unattainable) 172 B'way

L. I. Jockey Club (inf. unattainable) 66 Wall

L. I. R. R. Co. (Austin Corbin, Pres.; Elmur B. Hinsdale, Sec.; Henry Graves, Treas. Capital, $10,000,000. Directors: John R. Maxwell, Alfred Sully, Frederick W. Dunton, James D. Campbell, Henry W. Maxwell, James G. K. Duer, William G. Wheeler, W. B. Kendall, Edward Tuck, J. P. Townsend, Austin Corbin, Elmur D. Hinsdale, Henry Graves) 192 B'way

Long John & Co. (John Long, no Co.) 210 E. 57th

Long S. S. & Brother (Samuel S. & Isaac S. Long, William Martin & John A. Kunkul) 450 W. 14th & 62 Dey

Long & Heppner (William G. Long & George W. Heppner) 539 E. 84th

Long & Markert (dissolved) 2394 Third av.

Long & Weeks (Michael F. Long & Charles E. Weeks) 236 Eighth av.

Longinotte James & Co (dissolved) 219 Spring

Longman & Martinez (Walter Longman & Aristides Martinez) 207 Pearl

Longman's R., Sons (Samuel & Charles Longman) 8 John

Longo G. & Co. (Giovanni Longo & Giovanni Patani) 292 Washn.

Loning & Stock (William K. Loning & Jens F. Stock) 1416 Third av.

Loomis Electric Mfg. Co. (John C. Howe, Pres.; George W. Dickerman, Sec.; Francis E. Southard, Treas. Capital, $100,000. Trustees: John C. Howe, George W. Dickerman, Charles C. Southard, R. H. Parker, Francis E. Southard, Benjamin Dickerman, Charles M. Lyman) 18 B'way

Loomis E. P. & Co. (Edward P. Loomis & Thomas A. Watson) 95 Barclay

Loonam's Peter, Sons (dissolved) 105 E. 31st

Loonie & Parker (Dennis Loonie & Eugene Parker) 115 E. 59th

Loos Mfg. Co. (August Loos, propr.) 26 Frankfort

Loos C. & Co. (Christian Loos, no Co.) 228 W. 46th

Loos L. & H. (Louis & Henry) 206 E. 50th

Loos' John A., Sons (John & Charles Loos) 481 Third av.

Lopes Calixto & Co. (Calixto & Manuel & Eugene Lopez) 8 Cedar

Lopez Habana Cigar Co. (not inc.) (Francisco Lopez & Matthew Bird) 105 Maiden ln.

Lopez B. & Co. (Boniface Lopez & Francisco Suarez) 184 Water

Lopez V. & Co. (Virgil Lopez, no Co.) 42 Pearl

COMPILED WITH ACCURACY AND DESPATCH. } **CLASSIFIED BUSINESS LISTS.** { THE TROW CITY DIRECTORY CO. 11 University Place.

LOP 176 LOW

Lopez & Gonzalez (dissolved) 105 Maiden la.
Lorch Louis & Son (Louis & Felix Lorch) 734 Second av.
Lord Haynes & Co. (John Anderson & John H. Lord, only) 187 Duane
Lord & Austin (Frank J. Lord, John C. Austin & Farley Clark) 18 B'way
Lord & McLean (Perez G. Lord & Joseph S. McLean) 174 Pearl
Lord & Taylor (Samuel Lord jr. & Edward P. Hatch, only) 901 D'way & 255 Grand
Lord, Day & Lord (Henry Day, George De Forest & Daniel & Franklin D. Lord & George Lord Day) 120 B'way
Lorentzen Brothers (Edward & George Lorentzen) 970 Tenth av.
Lorenz & Co. (no inf.) 102 William
Lorillard Refrigerator Co. (George R. Wight & Co. proprs.) 1168 B'way
Lorsch Albert & Co. (Albert Lorsch & Alfred Krower) 87 Maiden la.
Lorsch & Vonschuller (Isaac D. Lorsch & Charles S. Vonschuller) 94 E. 14th
Loschinger Brothers (Anthony & John Loschinger) 647 Tenth av.
Losee Brothers (dissolved) 175 W. 48th
Losee & Dunker (Ira & Albert Losee & Edward F. Weekes, only) 97 Pine
Losi & Coarl (Louis Losi & Louis Coarl) 361 W. 59th
Loss Warren H. & Co. (Warren H. Loss & Edward B. Crane) 45 B'way
Loth Joseph & Co (Joseph & Bernard & Henry A. Loth) 63 Greene & Tenth av. c W. 150th
Lothrop & Marsh (Frederick O. Lothrop & Benjamin F. Marsh) 16 Courtles sl.
Louchelm James & Co. (dissolved) 112 Pearl
Loucks Cornelius & Co. (Cornelius Loucks & Daniel L. Hallock) 23 Sixth av.
Loud H. W. & Co. (Edward H. & John H. Loud, only) 23 South
Louderback & Parker Wire Co. (Albert B. Parker, Pres.; William S. Louderback, Sec.; further inf. unattainable) 171 B'way
Louderback & Stout (dissolved) 47 Lispenard
Loudon & Johnson (J. Carlisle Loudon & J. Demarest Johnson) 181 Chambers
Lough G. F. & Co. (George F. & B. St. George Lough & Robert H. Burrows) 119 Produce Ex.
Loughran W. & P. (William & Patrick F.) 290 E. 24th
Louis Samuel & Son (Samuel & Charles H. Louis) 258 Canal
Louise & Co. (John Bruce Thompson, only) 204 Fifth av.
Louisiana Western R. R. Co. (Collis P. Huntington, Pres.; Isaac E. Gates, Sec. Capital, $3,360,000. Directors: Collis P. Huntington, Isaac E. Gates, Frank H. Davis, Horace E. Garth, Alexander C. Hutchinson) 23 Broad
Louisiana, Arkansas & Missouri R. R. Co. (Harlow M. Hoyt, Pres.; Lewis Coon, Sec.; Charles R. Kimball, Treas. Capital, $6,200,000. Directors: Harlow M. Hoyt, Lewis Coon, Charles O. Thompson, William R. Thomas, Logan H. Roots, N. H. Myers, T. H. Jackson, O. M. Norman, B. H. Mess) 58 William
Louisville & Nashville R. R. Co. (Eckstein Norton, Pres.; John K. Ellis, Sec.; William W. Thompson, Treas. Capital $34,100,100. Directors: August Belmont jr. John A. Carter, Joseph A. Horsey, John H. Inman, Arnold Marcus, William Mertens, Eckstein Norton, John D. Probst, Thomas Rutter, J. S. Rogers, John D. Taggart, Edmund Smith, Jacob Schiff) 52 Exchange pl.
Louisville, New Albany & Chicago Railway Co. (William L. Breyfogle, Pres. Capital, $6,000,-

000. Directors: William L. Breyfogle, S. Nenstadt, Hiram W. Hunt, Samuel Castleman, George L. Hutchings, James L. Breese, Charles H. Ludington, Isaac S. Winstandley, John B. Hughes, John. B. Reynolds, George F. Postlethwaite) 51 Nassau
Lounsbery & Co. (Richard P. Lounsbery & Henry J. Macdonald) 15 Broad
Louvre Glove Co. (Capital, $10,000; farther inf. unattainable) no address
Love J. & Co. (Joseph Love & Munroe Crane) ft. W. 40th
Love W. & G. W. (William & George W.) 141 Elm
Lovejoy Co. (James H. Ferguson, Pres.; Michael J. Creegan, Sec. Capital, $75,000. Directors: James H. Ferguson, Michael J. Creegan, R. M. Ferguson) 45 Rose
Lovejoy John F. & Co. (John F. Lovejoy & Charles R. Bates) 102 Chambers
Loveland W. & H. (William R. & Henry P.) 87 West
Lovell Frank F. & Co. (Frank F. & Caroline F. Lovell) 142 Worth
Lovell John W., Co. (John W. Lovell, Pres.; Charles E. Lange, Sec.; farther inf. unattainable) 150 Worth
Lovell Mfg. Co. (Charles W. Lovell, Pres.; Caroline F. Lovell, Sec. Capital, $5,000. Trustees: Charles W. & Caroline F. & Joseph B. Lovell) 142 Worth
Lovell A. & Co. (Aaron Lovell, Henry R. Parry & William S. M. Silber) 3 E. 14th
Lovell F. H. & Co. (Frank H. & Orville D. Lovell) 235 Pearl & 119 John
Low Joseph T. & Co. (Joseph T. Low, Charles M. Bebee & John L. Salter) 65 Worth
Low Moor Iron Co. of Va. (John Means, Pres.; H. M. Bell, Sec.; Edward A. Low, Treas. Capital, $600,000. Directors: John Means, Edward A. Low, H. M. Bell. John F. & A. S. Winslow, A. A. Low, Edward H. R. & Frank Lyman, Archer Anderson) 31 Burling sl.
Low A. & A. (Alexander B. & Archibald) 103 W. 83d
Low A. A. & Brothers (dissolved) 31 Burling sl.
Low H. P. & Co. (Frank A. Lowe & Samuel B. Low, only) 342 Produce Ex.
Low's Exchange (Edwin H. Low, propr.) 947 B'way
Lowdon & Rutherford (William L. Lowdon jr. & Archibald Rutherford) 1645 B'way & 778 Seventh av.
Lowe & Brother (Isaac N. & James A. Lowe) 203 W. 12th
Lowe & Granville (James H. Lowe & Bovil G. Granville) 166 Mercer
Lowenbein's A., Sons (David & Morris Lowenbein) 88 W. 23d
Lowenberg & Bruenn (Adolph S. Lowenberg & Nathaniel Bruenn) 438 Broome
Lowengard & Stern (Otto Lowengard & George W. Stern) 44 Exchange pl.
Lowensohn S. & Co. (Simon Lowensohn & Isidor Byk) 294 Grand & 674 Third av.
Lowenstein B. & Brother (Benjamin & Moses Lowenstein) 4 Desbrosses
Lowenstein J. & Co. (Joseph Lowenstein, no Co.) 52 Howard
Lowenthal Mfg. Co. (Isaac M. Sloman, propr.) 292 Church
Lowenthal & Lowenstein (Ferdinand Lowenthal & Henry Lowenstein) 4 First av.
Lowerre & Co. (Charles H. & Thomas H. Lowerre jr.) 511 B'way & 83 Mercer
Lowndes H. T. & S. C. (Henry T. & Samuel C.) 211 Washn. mkt
Lowrey J. S. & Co. (Edward G. Dickson, John M. Campbell & James R. Kaiser, only) 66 Mercer
Lowrey, Stone & Auerbach (Grosvenor P. Lowrey,

| SPECIAL ATTENTION PAID TO THIS CLASS OF WORK | BANKERS' & BROKERS' CIRCULARS DELIVERED | THE TROW CITY DIRECTORY CO. 11 University Place. |

LOW 177 LYN

Charles Francis Stone, Joseph S. Auerbach & Richard W. Stevenson) 15 Broad

Lowry Robert C. & Co. (Robert C. Lowry, no Co.) 28 State

Lowther & Brother (George & Charles Lowther) 104 W. 11th, 32 E. 59th, 500 Sixth av., 203 E. 30th & ft. E. 32d

Lowy & Co. (Max & B. Lowy) 90 Warren

Lozano, Pendas & Co. (Fanatino Lozano, Ysidro Pendas & Miguel Alvarez) 209 Pearl

Lozier J. L. & Co. (dissolved) 4 Bond

Lubbert Brothers (John & John H. Lubbert) 216 Grand

Lubelsky Reuben & Son (Reuben & Jacob Lubelsky) 74 Mott

Lubert & Allen (Morris Lubert & Harris Allen) 47 Bleecker

Lubetkin Brothers (Max & Nathan Lubetkin) 14 Front

Lublin & Esty (Alfred W. Lublin & G. Frederick Esty) 66 Beaver

Lucas Charley & Co. (Charley Lucas, no Co.) 520 B'way

Lucas A. H. & Co. (Alexander H. Lucas & John S. Rossoll) 111 B'way

Lucas Brothers (Michael & James Lucas) 2236 Third av.

Luce A. J. & Co. (Alfred J. Luce, no Co.) 80 Whitehall

Luchesi & Klein (Joseph Luchesi & Robert Klein) 124 Baxter

Luchs Brothers (Adelaide & Jacob N. Luchs, only) 187 Greene

Lucky Cuss Mining Co. (A. Francis Southerland, Pres. Capital, $100,000. Trustees: A. Francis Southerland, James E. Reynolds; further inf. unattainable) 17 New

Ludder & Ziegler (dissolved) 127 Av. D

Ludeke & Co. (Ernest & Adolph Ludeke) 23 John

Ludemann A. & M. (August & Herman) 16 E. 18th

Ludlow E. H. & Co. (Morris & Edward M. Wilkins & Albert M. Arneberg, only) 47 Liberty & 500 Fifth av.

Ludlow, Day & Co. (Samuel H. Ludlow & George Day, no Co.) 54 W. 31st

Ludorff & Nacke (Albert Ludorff & Herman Nacke) 508 W. 58th

Ludovici & Heizenroeder (Charles E. Ludovici & Frederick C. Heizenroeder) r 118 Wooster

Ludovici's Portraits (August Bendinger, propr.) 254 Fifth av.

Ludwig Edward & Co. (dissolved) 212 E. 111th

Ludwig Brothers (boxes) (Louis C. & Frederick Ludwig) r 557 E. 151st

Ludwig Brothers (drygds.) (Bernhard J. & Isidor & Morris J. Ludwig) 38 W. 14th & 37 W. 18th

Ludwig & Rohland (Robert Ludwig & Richard Rohland) 318 B'way;

Lueckel, Unger & Co. (August Lueckel, William Unger & Henry Heininger) 310 B'way

Luehrs Brothers (John & Henry Luehrs) 937 Sixth av.

Luft & Brecht (Louis Luft & Gottlob C. Brecht) 641 E. 11th

Lugar's George C., Son (Henry P. Lugar) 435 E. Houston

Lugar's J. G., Son & Co. (Frank Lugar, only) 302 Fourth av.

Luhmann & Helmke (Henry D. Luhmann & Henry Helmke) 383 Alexander av.

Luhrman M. G. & Co. (Martin G. Luhrman, no Co.) 200 Washn. mkt

Luhrs A. & Co. (Adolph & Frederick Luhrs & Frederick J. Harra) 424 Third av.

Luhrs & Ilse (dissolved) 2364 Eighth av.

Lummis & Parsons (Charles A. Lummis & Samuel H. Parsons) 3 Broad

Lungren Incandescent Gas Light Co. (inf. unattainable) 26 West

Lunn's W. B., Sons (Richard B. & Charles J. B. Lunn) 267 Washn

Luqueer R. S. & Co. (Francis T. jr. & Robert S. & John J. T. & Louis H. Luqueer) 67 Murray

Luscia B. & Co. (Bartelomeo Loscia, no Co.) 55 Park

Lusk Richard F. & Son (Richard E. & J. Earll Lusk) 97 Liberty

Lusk & Cavanagh (Robert J. Lusk & Thomas Cavanagh) 253 South

Lusk & Gaffney (dissolved) Boulevard n W. 148th

Lustberg H. & Son (Harris & Morris Lustberg) 45 Lispenard

Lustgarten & Perps (dissolved) 91 W. 3d

Lustig Brothers (Philip H. & David L. Lustig) 50 Bleecker

Lustral Oil Co. (Eugene B. Sanger, Pres.; Alfred E. Foster, Sec.; Charles H. Madden, Treas. Capital, $125,000. Trustees: Eugene B. Sanger, Charles H. Madden, Alfred E. Foster, Horace C. Sanger, W. L. Matthews) 154 Maiden la.

Luth John F. & Co. (John F. Luth, Henry Ottens & Otto Wieters) 141 Av. A

Luth & Schluter (Julius A. Luth & Frederick Schluter) 255 First av.

Luther William H. & Son (William H. & Frederick D. Luther) 200 B'way

Lutheran Cemetery (Jacob A. Geissenhainer, Pres.; Frederick W. Geissenhainer, Treas.; further inf. unattainable) 263 B'way

Lutheran Emigrant House Assn. (E. Christian Korner, Pres.; William Kauff, Sec.; William A. Schmittheimer, Treas.) 26 State

Lutye & Grim (William N. Lutye & Lowry B. Grim) 4 East

Lutz Charles & Co. (Charles Lutz & Frederick Goemel) 155 First av.

Lutz John & Son (John & Charles F. Lutz) 41 Mercer

Lutz C. A. & Co. (Charles A. Lutz, no Co.) 167 Third av.

Lutz & Movius (dissolved) 15 Warren

Lutz & Oetjen (Frederick Lutz & Herman Oetjen) 331 Washn.

Lutz & Sauer (William Lutz & Ernst A. Sauer) 113 Fulton

Luxenberg & Vidal (Jonas Luxenberg & Felix A. Vidal) 69 Centre

Luyties Brothers (Gerhard & Henry E. G. Luyties) 1 Wall & 673 B'way

Lyall J. & W. (James & William) 549 W. 23d

Lyceum (N. Y. Theatre Co. proprs.) 191 Fulton & 314 Fourth av.

Lydecker & Co. (dissolved) 36 Ann

Lyford & Knobloch (Charles W. Lyford & Henry Knobloch) 612 B'way & 148 Crosby

Lykens Valley R.R. & Coal Co. (William A. Nash, Pres.; Frederick A. Platz, Treas. Capital, $600,000. Directors: William A. Nash, Frederick A. & Isaac H. Platz, Edward Dunham, John W. Hoffman, George P. Lawrence, De Witt C. Falls) 13 William

Lyman T. C. & Co. (Thomas C. Lyman & Henry L. Groesman;—special partners, William Brown, *Flatbush, L. I.* $133,333.33 & Jeanette G. Brown, *B'klyn, N. Y.* $100,000; terminates 1st May 1891) 420 W. 38th

Lynam William J. & Sons (William J. & Benjamin J. & Thomas E. Lynam) 385 B'way

Lynch B. & P. (Bernard & Patrick J.) 901 Third av.

Lynch Brothers (hats) (inf. unattainable) 227 S. 5th av.

Lynch Brothers (liquors) (dissolved) 1921 Third av.

TYPEWRITING DONE BY THE TROW CITY DIRECTORY CO., 11 University Place.

LYN 178 McC

Lynch & Co. (John H. & George W. Lynch) 16 Fulton fish mkt
Lynch & Nevins (Philip Lynch & Thomas A. Nevins) 315 E. 45th
Lynch, Cole & Meehan (William L. Cole & Thomas F. Meehan, only) 19 Warren
Lynn John & Co. (John & Sarah E. Lynn) 769 B'way
Lyon Amasa & Co. (Amasa Lyon, Pres.; Herman E. Nicolay, Sec.; Thomas Breslin, Treas. Capital, $900,000. Directors: Amasa Lyon, Thomas & James H. Breslin, Bernard C. Lyon, Herman E. Nicolay) 684 B'way
Lyon John H. & Co. (John H. Lyon & Philip M. Knight) 19 Reade & 95 Park
Lyon John W. & Sons (Hannah A. & Oliver A. & John W. Lyon jr. only) 69 E. 125th
Lyon Mfg. Co. (P. H. Drake & Co. proprs.) 59 Fifth av.
Lyon William H. & Co. (dissolved) 486 B'way
Lyon J. B. & Co. (Jeremiah B. Lyon & Arthur Miller) 280 Washn.
Lyon J. W. & Co. (James W. Lyon, no Co.) 253 Front
Lyon Brothers (fruit) (Leroy M. & Jeremiah B. Lyon:—special partner, William Lillis, $15,000; terminates 31st Dec. 1891) 96 Barclay
Lyon Brothers (furs) (Edmond R. & Gerald Lyon) 100 Prince
Lyon & Co. (Edward Steinbrugge & Ludovic Pagenstecher, only) 4 Bowling gr.
Lyon & Smith (Edward P. Lyon & Percival C. Smith) 84 Nassau
Lyon Brothers & Co. (dissolved) 96 Barclay
Lyons Armored Hose Co. (James Lyons, propr.) 6 Ferry
Lyons Julius J. & A. (Julius J. & Alfred) 140 Nassau
Lyons E. J. & Brothers (dissolved) 142 Liberty
Lyons Brothers (ice) (Louis & Oscar Lyons) 342 E. 106th
Lyons Brothers (liquors) (Patrick J. & William J. Lyons & Thomas Hamilton) 792 Eighth av.
Lyons Brothers (liquors) (William H. & Thomas E. Lyons) 822 Second av.
Lyons & Besnard (Robert S. Besnard, only) 28 South
Lyons & Campbell Ranch & Cattle Co. (John C. Barron, Pres.; Lester M. Clark, Sec.; William W. Skiddy, Treas. Capital, $1,500,000; farther inf. unattainable) 83 B'way
Lyons & Co. (John & Thomas Lyons) 648 Eighth av.

M

McAdam Robert & Sons (Robert & George G. & John C. McAdam) 88 Warren
McAdam & McAdam (Lucine & George H. & Graham McAdam) 171 B'way
McAdams & Cartwright (John McAdams & Robert F. Cartwright) 57 Elm
McAdams & Duane (dissolved) 224 E. B'way, 47 Chrystie & 213 Division
McAllister John & Brother (John J. & Thomas H. McAllister) 27 Cherry
McAllister T. H. (Thomas H. & Caldwell W. McAllister) 49 Nassau
McAlpin D. H. & Co. (David H. & Edwin A. McAlpin) 150 Av. D
McAmbley C. F. & Co. (no inf.) 80 Wall
McAnarney John & Co. (John McAnarney & H. St. George Offutt) 58 Trinity pl.
McAnneny & Co. (Michael F. McAnneny, James R. Clements & Charles Ostertag) 9 Carmine
McAnulty E. & Son (Edward & Edward F. McAnulty) 509 Hudson

McArdle John F. & Co. (John F. & Henry & Peter A. McArdle) 31 N. Moore
McArthur J. & Co. (Joseph McArthur, no Co.) 181 Reade
McAuley & Montgomery (Elizabeth McAuley & Margaret Montgomery) 585 Eighth av.
McAuliffe & Gabay (Timothy McAuliffe & Henry G. Gabay) 892 Third av.
McBride James & Co. (James McBride, Co. refused) 2423 Third av.
McBride T. & Son (dissolved) 144 Elm & 55 Greene
McBride W. T. & Co. (dissolved) 45 B'way
McBride & Co. (Henry McBride & Charles F. Droste) 74 Warren
McBride & Stafford (John A. McBride & Arthur F. Stafford) 19 Coenties sl.
McCabe J. & Brother (John & James McCabe) 454 W. 35th
McCabe Brothers (builders) (Bryan C. & Peter & Lawrence McCabe) 1620 B'way
McCabe Brothers (liquors) (Michael & Matthew McCabe) 538 Hudson
McCabe & Co. (Rosanna & James W. McCabe & Jeremiah J. Deady) 215 Pearl
McCafferty William & Co. (William McCafferty & William H. Page) 825 Third av.
McCafferty & Buckley (Robert McCafferty & Richard W. Buckley) 894 Park av.
McCafferty & Co. (Hugh F. McCafferty & Charles J. Frost) 78 Church
McCafferty & Donovan (dissolved) 76 Church
McCafferty & Holton (Robert E. McCafferty & Morris L. Holton) 155 William
McCaffery Brothers (William & James McCaffery) 1883 Third av.
McCaffrey W. H. & J. J. (William H. & John J.) 261 W. 27th
McCain Samuel & Son (Samuel & James S. McCain) 15 Spruce
McCaldin Brothers (James & Joseph McCaldin) 79 Broad
McCall James & Co. (Laura S. McCall, only) 46 E. 14th
McCall & Arnold (Edward E. McCall & William C. Arnold) 88 Park row
McCallum John & Co. (Lee McCallum & Walter Macdonald, only) 420 Washn.
McCalmont Oil Co. (David Kirk, Pres.; Theodore E. Tack, Sec. Capital, $500,000. Directors: David Kirk, A. H. Tack, George W. Dilworth, Frank & Theodore E. Tack, J. L. Davidson) 18 B'way
McCann Edward A. & Co. (Edward A. McCann & Henry W. Bischoff) 184 Reade
McCann M. T. & B. (Margaret T. & Bella) 343 Fifth av.
McCann & Co. (no inf.) 486 G'wich
McCarey Thomas F. & Co. (dissolved) r 126 William
McCarroll William & Co. (William & James R. T. McCarroll:—special partner, John Ennis, B'klyn, N. Y., $15,000; terminates 31st Dec. 1890) 16 Spruce
McCarthy John & Sons (John & John J. & Eugene & David McCarthy) 609 First av.
McCarthy D. J. & Co. (dissolved) 137 Washn. mkt.
McCarthy & Davis (John McCarthy & Joseph L. Davis) 128 Front
McCarthy, Lawrence & Buckley (John Henry McCarthy, Malcolm R. Lawrence & Charles G. Buckley) 49 Chambers
McCarty J. C. & Co. (John C. McCarty, William H. Littell & Tyree P. Burke) 97 Chambers & 81 Reade
McCarty & Brady (Matthew McCarty & Lawrence Brady) 544 W. 41st

THE CALIGRAPH WRITING MACHINE,
HARTFORD, CONN.

McCarty & Co. (Barclay E. V. McCarty:—special partner, Elina Mead, Keyport, N. J., $5,000; terminates 15th Jan., 1891) 525 B'way

McCaskie G. T. & J. (George T. & John) 32 John

McCaslin Machine Co. (Charles W. Hunt, Pres.; John Allen, Sec.; George M. Luther, Treas. Capital, $20,000. Directors: Charles W. Hunt, George M. Luther, John Allen, Charles C. King) 45 B'way

McCauley & McGuire (James McCauley & John J. McGuire) 179 Hudson

McChesney & Co. (Peter McChesney, no Co.) 533 W. 22d & 326 Pearl

McClain Brothers (Damon H. & Benjamin H. McClain) 169 Spring

McClain & Talbot (Daniel W. McClain & Frederick Talbot) 110 Worth

McClave E. W. & Co. (Edmund W. McClave & William A. Parke) 18 B'way

McCloskey Henry & F. A. (Henry & Francis A.) 102 D'way

McCloskey J. & J. A. (John & James A.) 392 Ninth av.

McCloskey M. & A. (Mary & Anne C.) 114 E. 52.1

McCloskey & Anderson (Thomas McCloskey & Walter A. Anderson) 24 State

McCollam & Parr (Henry McCollam, only) 44 Eldridge

McConnell Edward & Co. (Edward & Edward McConnell jr.) 121 Franklin

McConnell J. & J. (John & James) 60 Sheriff

McConnell Brothers (Terence & Patrick McConnell) 100 Eighth av.

McConnell & Grimshaw (Andrew McConnell & William C. Grimshaw) 620 Madison av.

McConnell & Moran (John J. McConnell & James Moran) 65 Suffolk

McConvill John & Co. (John McCann, only) 12 Walker

McCooey Brothers (Arthur & Owen McCooey) 370 Third av.

McCormick Peter & Sons (Peter & Benjamin W. & James. J. & Edward L. McCormick) 39 Duane & 89 R. 52d

McCormick W. G. & Co. (William G. McCormick, Edward M. Switzer, Nelson C. Chapman & Irving H. Waggoner) 44 B'way

McCormick & Hubbs (John McCormick & Manly R. Hubbs) 250 Washn.

McCosker & Molloy (David McCosker & George J. Molloy) 36 Walker

McCotter Samuel G. & Co. (Samuel G. McCotter & Samuel M. Moneypenny) 32 Cedar

McCoun & Lee (dissolved) 315 Church

McCoun & Strasburg (Frederick H. McCoun & Gilbert J. Strasburg) 315 Church

McCoy J. & Co. (John McCoy & Charles W. Dowers) 184 W. Houston

McCoy J. D. & Co. (Josiah B. McCoy, Monroe Green & Ernest Napier) 5 Thompson

McCoy Brothers (cigars) (Frank & Edward McCoy) 118½ Dowery

McCoy Brothers (shoers) (Thomas & William J. McCoy) 511 E. 19th

McCoy & Co. (Frank McCoy & Amasa H. Scoville) 190 Av. C

McCoy & Sanders (Joseph F. McCoy & Walter Sanders) 26 Warren

McCoy & Wildman (J. Cresap McCoy & Henry G. Wildman) 663 D'way & 5 E. 42d

McCracken R. J. & W. H. (Robert J. & William H.) 1750 W. Farms rd.

McCracken W. V. & Co. (William V. McCracken, Co. refused) 40 Wall

McCrea & Ryan (John McCrea & Michael Ryan) 108½ Broad

McCreery James & Co. (James & J. Crawford McCreery & Thomas Rosevear) 801 D'way

McCreery & Prendergast (William L. McCreery & Patrick Prendergast) 966 Sixth av.

McCreery's John, Son (Robert McCreery) 65 Broad

McCroden John & Co. (John McCroden, no Co.) 23 West & 58 Washn.

McCrorken Brothers (Francis & Owen McCrorken) 97 & 524 Ninth & 184 Seventh av.

McCue Brothers (Charles S. Hill, only) 52 New

McCue & Dalton (Patrick F. McCue & John J. Dalton) r 59 Ann

McCulloch & Co. (James W. McCulloch & Asa B. Gardiner jr.) 68 Water

McCullow & Sturm (Charles F. McCullow & William F. Sturm) 82 Nassau

McCurdy & Warden (John McCurdy & Jacob S. Warden) 276 West

McCurrach James & Brother (James & George McCurrach) 569 B'way

McCutcheon James & Co. (James McCutcheon & James M. Speers) 64 W. 23d

McCutcheon R. H. & Co. (Robert H. McCutcheon & Angust Crosius) 227 Canal

McDermott & Callanan (Francis McDermott & William H. Callanan) 526 W. 38th

McDermott & Duffield (Walter McDermott & Patrick W. Duffield) 2 Wall & 526 W. 16th

McDermott & Howard (John McDermott, William J. Howard & Michael F. McDermott) 180 William

McDermott & Johnson (no inf.) 2148 Third av.

McDermott & Smith (dissolved) 1069 Ninth av.

McDonagh William & Co. (William McDonagh & John Lynch) 180 Front

McDonald Willis & Co. (Willis McDonald, William E. Dormitzer & Stephen A. Powell) 89 Gold

McDonald C. E. & Co. (Curran E. & Frederick McDonald) 47 B'way

McDonald & Clyne (Thomas McDonald & Edward F. Clyne) 67 Nassau

McDonald & Co. (liquors) (William McDonald, no Co.) 3453 Third av.

McDonald & Co. (lithographers) (no inf.) 71 Park pl.

McDonald & Kilduff (dissolved) 427 E. 61st

McDonald & Stewart (Charles McDonald & Perea M. Stewart) 103 W. 52d

McDonnald Joseph & Co. (Joseph McDonnald, no Co.) 586 W. 28th

McDonnell M. & Son (Michael & James McDonnell) r 195 Mott

McDonnell P. & A. (Peter & Alexander) 98 Washn.

McDonough & McTeague (dissolved) 2239 Second av.

McDougall & Potter (Henry McDougall & Roger Potter) 606 W. 65th

McDougall & Sprague (dissolved) 97 Wall

McDowell Garment Drafting Machine Co. (Albert McDowell, Pres.; William McDowell, Treas. Capital, $15,000. Directors: Albert & William & Charles E. McDowell) 6 W. 14th

McDowell M. E. & Co. (Ltd) (consolidated with Blackwell's Durham Co-operative Tobacco Co.) 102 Chambers

McDowell P. & Co. (Peter McDowell & George Stark) 478 E. 130th

McDowell, Pierce & Co. (Joseph T. McDowell, Charles Pierce & George A. McDowell) 270 Washn. & 109 Warren

McDuffee & Emerson (Charles H. McDuffee & James O. Emerson) 44 College pl.

McKilfatrick J. B. & Sons (John B. & J. Morgan & William H. McElfatrick) 1193 B'way

| SPECIAL ATTENTION PAID TO THIS CLASS OF WORK | BANKERS' & BROKERS' CIRCULARS DELIVERED | THE TROW CITY DIRECTORY CO. 11 University Place. |

McE 180 McK

McElroy John & Co. (John & Edward McElroy) Manhattan mkt
McElroy & Son (William & Thomas H. McElroy) Brooklinc n Marion av.
McElroy, Duffy & Co. (John McElroy, Bernard Duffy & Patrick Sheehan) Manhattan mkt
McElwee Mfg. Co. (William J. Hendrick, Pres.; Don A. Gaylord, Sec.; James G. McElwee, Treas.; Capital, $200,000. Directors: Robert B. Cotter, William J. Hendrick, Don A. Gaylord, James G. McElwee) 507 W. 35th
McEnerny & Hilton (Mary McEnerny & John Hilton) r 112 Cedar
McEntee Philip & Co. (James & Bernard McEntee, only) 189 West
McEntee & Lawlor (James D. McEntee & James S. Lawlor) 1631 Ninth av. & Morris Dock
McEntegart & Sullivan (James McEntegart & Christopher J. Sullivan) 660 Eleventh av. & 817 Ninth av.
McEntyre P. B. & Son (Patrick B. & George B. McEntyre) 229 W. 86th
McEwan Mfg. Co. (no inf.) 140 Baxter
McEwan & McEwan (George J. & Thomas McEwan jr.) 120 B'way
McEwen C. C., Co. (Clarence C. McEwen, Pres.; G. E. McEwen, Treas.; Daniel Van Dewater, Sec. Capital, $25,000. Directors: Clarence C. & G. E. McEwen, Martin Fleischer) 9 W. 14th
McFadden S. & Co. (Sarah A. McFadden & Levi Hitchcock) 193 Hudson
McFaddin H. G. & Co. (Harrison G. McFaddin & Arthur N. White) 38 Warren
McFarland Brothers (George & Walter McFarland) r 261 W. 25th
McFarland & Coyle (Stephen McFarland & John Coyle) 803 Bowery
McFaul & Seddon (William H. McFaul & George D. Seddon) 558 W. 34th
McGarry & Wallace (Thomas McGarry & Robert Wallace) 61 Roosevelt & 205 Franklin
McGay Brothers (Charles S. & Frank D. McGay) 814 Third av. & 421 E. 59th
McGibbon & Co. (William C. McGibbon, Charles H. Allcock & James B. Lord) 913 B'way & 145 Fifth av.
McGillick Brothers (Joseph & William McGillick) 471 & 1289 Third av. & 500 & 2480 Second av.
McGinn James & Brother (James & John P. McGinn) 121 W. 24th
McGinn John & Edward F. (dissolved) 144 Sullivan
McGinness H. F. & Co. (dissolved) 680 Sixth av.
McGirr & Stevens (George McGirr & John W. Stevens) 152 South
McGloin Brothers (Michael & John McGloin) 2089 First av.
McGoey & King (dissolved) 19 B'way
McGovern James & Co. (James McGovern & Lemuel C. Benedict) 2 Nassau
McGovern J. P. & Brother (Joseph P. & Philip A. McGovern) 29 W. Houston
McGowan P. & Son (Peter & Patrick McGowan) 204 E. 81st
McGowan Brothers (dissolved) 1069 Third av.
McGrath Thomas J. & Co. (dissolved) 188 Park row
McGrath E. & E. (no inf.) 151 E. 81st
McGrath & Co. (Mary A. McGrath & James Gilloon) 138 Canal
McGreevey & Mock (Henry McGreevey & William Mock) 18 John
McGregor Mfg. Co. (not inc.) (Lewis B. McGregor & Roderick B. Mitchell jr.) 98 Cliff
McGrury T. & J. (Thomas & John) 344 Fourth av
McGuinness E. & Co. (Edward McGuinness & Daniel E. Reilly) 360 E. 76th
McGuire P. & T. (Patrick & Thomas J.) 195 Mercer
McGuire & Dowling (dissolved) 2165 Second av.
McGuire & McKenna (Thomas McGuire & John McKenna) 460 W. 57th
McGuire & Mullan (dissolved) 521 Canal
McGuire & Sloane (Samuel K. McGuire & William Sloane) 151 W. 28th
McGunigle Thomas & Son (Thomas & Thomas McGunigle jr.) 92 Gold
McGunnigle Patrick & Son (Patrick J. & Matthew F. McGunnigle) 506 Sixth av.
McHale & Rohde (Frank McHale & William Rohde) 9 Cortlandt
McHugh Joseph P. & Co. (Joseph P. McHugh & James Slater) 3 W. 42d
McHugh & Dwyer (Patrick A. McHugh & Joseph P. Dwyer) 75 Av. D
McIlhargy's John, Sons (Charles A. & Thomas F. & Joseph I. & Malcolm A. McIlhargy) 414 G'wich
McIlroy & Emmet (John McIlroy & Herman Le Roy Emmet) 3d Cortlandt
McIlvain & Davis (Robert B. McIlvain & Joseph W. Davis) r 210 E. 19th
McIlvaine & Baldwin (James W. McIlvaine & Elizabeth Baldwin) 37 Nassau
McIntosh & Heydrich (Alexander McIntosh & Alfred Heydrich) 17 Murray
McIntosh & Yule (Donald McIntosh & John Yule) 809 Sixth av.
McIntyre Ewen & Son (Ewen & Ewen McIntyre jr.) 874 B'way & 992 Sixth av.
McIntyre & Embary (Byron F. McIntyre, only) 99 N. Moore
McIntyre & Reardon (Edmund H. McIntyre & Dennis Reardon) 115 West
McIntyre & Wardwell (Thomas A. McIntyre & Henry L. Wardwell) 212 Produce Ex.
McJilton & Co. (William E. McJilton, no Co.) 17 Thompson
McKay Stewart & Son (dissolved) 124 Clinton mkt
McKay & Dix (Lauchlan McKay & Charles B. Dix) 46 South
McKee M. M. & Co. (Moses M. McKee & Arthur W. Burt) 251 W. 105th
McKee & Harrington (Joseph McKee & Charles F. Harrington) 173 Grand
McKeever Drothers (John & Alexander McKeever) 93 Vesey, 386 West, 15 Carmine & 207 Sixth av.
McKelvey & Christie (John McKelvey & Daniel P. Christie) 426 W. 25th
McKenna James J. & Brother (James J. McKenna, only) 424 E. 23d
McKenna Brothers (Peter F. & Michael J. & Owen E. McKenna) 1602 First av.
McKenzie A. & M. (Angus & Malcolm) 122 Front'
McKenzie & Kaneen (Isabelin McKenzie & John A. Kaneen) 207 E. 23d
McKenzie & McPherson (John McKenzie & Duncan McPherson) 52 E. 41st
McKeon J. F. & Brother (John F. & Stephen J. McKeon) 184 E. 64th
McKeon Brothers (Patrick F. & Michael J. McKeon) 2108 & 2312 Third av.
McKeon & Buckley (James F. McKeon & Michael Buckley) 1829 Third av.
McKeon & Gunther (John McKeon & Henry C. Gunther) 960 Eighth av.
McKeon & McCann (Felix J. McKeon & Joseph McCann) 802 W. 33d
McKeon & McNally (dissolved) 531 Eighth av.
McKeon & Roche (Charles McKeon & Cornelius Roche) 1897 Third av.

MERCHANTS EXCHANGE NAT. BANK OF THE CITY OF N. Y.
SOLICITS YOUR ACCOUNT. 257 Broadway.
PHINEAS C. LOUNSBURY, President   ALLEN S. APGAR, Cashier.

McKesson & Robbins (John McKesson jr. Herbert D. Robbins, William Hall Wickham, George C. McKesson & William L. Vennard) 91 Fulton

McKibben & Co. (George C. McKibben, no Co.) 41 Park row

McKibbin George & Co. (George McKibbin, Co. refused) 84 S. 5th av.

McKillop, Walker & Co. (Richard H. Walker & estate of John McKillop, no Co.) 335 B'way

McKim Brothers & Co. (Haslett & John A. McKim, no Co.) 18 Wall

McKim, Mead & White (Charles F. McKim, William R. Mead & Stanford White) 57 B'way

McKinlay & Semple (Warren F. McKinlay & Edward M. Semple) 32 Warren

McKnight Edward & Son (Edward & John McKnight) 2137 Third av.

McKnight William & Co. (William McKnight & Christopher W. O'Brien) 333 Washn. mkt

McKone & Wells (Joseph F. McKone & Edwin C. Wells) 1602 Third av.

McLanahan & Co. (no inf.) 165 E. 69th

McLaren & Co. (Duncan McLaren jr. & Augustus Dellinger) 323 Canal

McLarney & Co. (Frank J. McLarney & William H. Mackinney) 2434 Eighth av.

McLaughlin A. W. & Co. (Arthur W. & Frank W. McLaughlin) 146 B'way

McLaughlin B. & D. (Bernard & Daniel) r 140 Ludlow

McLaughlin & Bergin (dissolved) 132 Park row

McLaughlin & Co. (Thomas P. McLaughlin, John Gallagher & Michael J. Kennedy) 346 E. 81st

McLaughlin & Gleason (John A. McLaughlin & Stephen Gleason)62 Spring

McLean Andrew & Co. (Andrew & George McLean) 46 Wooster

McLean Benjamin & Co. (Frank E. Tyler, only) 29 Peck sl.

McLean Brothers (no inf.) 7 B'way

McLean & Morrison (John H. McLean & Daniel L. Morrison) 43 E. 92d

McLean's D. W., Sons (George W. McLean, only) 37 South

McLeod David & Son (Anne & D. Adrian McLeod, only) 9 Stone

McLeod J. B. & Co. (dissolved) 1461 Ninth av.

McLeod Brothers (dissolved) 1222 Tenth av.

McLeod & Weir (Charles McLeod & Alexander Weir) 45 Crosby

McLewee F. & Son (Frederick & Frederick C. McLewee) 25 Waverley pl.

McLoughlin Brothers (plumbers) (John B. & Henry J. McLoughlin) 260 E. 57th

McLoughlin Brothers (publishers) (John McLoughlin, only) 623 B'way

McMahon Brothers (James & John McMahon) 186 Chambers

McMahon & Handley (Dennis McMahon & Theodore W. Handley) 243 B'way

McMahon, Vanderhoef & Co. (dissolved) 175 Greene

McMann T. R. & Brother (Thomas R. & Henry W. McMann) 56 Gold

McManus J. F. & Co. (Catharine A. McManus, only) 1307 Washn. av.

McManus' Charles, Sons (James V. & John A. & Edward McManus) 21 Park row & ft. E. 14th

McMaster & Dolan (John D. McMaster & Patrick Dolan) Jackson av. n Columbine

McMicken J. A. & Co. (James A. McMicken & John G. McMickin) 3 Broad

McMillan & Jameson (John McMillan & Hunter Jameson) 400 W. 17th

McMillan & McVaugh (dissolved) 236 Church

McMillan's W. H., Son (Lewis A. McMillan) 113 South

McMonegal & Eckerson (Morgan D. Monegal & J. Reuben Eckerson) 1634 Ninth av.

McMulkin Francis & Co. (Francis McMulkin & Charles D. Hovey) 27 Lawton av. W. Washn. mkt

McMullen Thomas & Co. (Thomas McMullen & Thomas Day) 44 Beaver & 412 W. 16th

McMurray R. T. & W. H. (Robert T. & William H.) 9 Dey

McMurray & Co. (real estate) (dissolved) 361 W. 24th

McMurray & Co. (stationers) (James G. McMurray & Jane Emden) 408 Fourth av.

McMurray & Legallee (dissolved) 13 West

McMurtry John & Co. (John & Logan McMurtry & Alfred M. Smith) 277 Eighth av.

McNab & Belden (dissolved) 29 Hubert

McNab & Harlin Mfg. Co. (John Harlin, Pres.; Arthur L. Merriam, Sec.; Edward Fifield, Treas. Capital, $150,000. Directors: John Harlin, Arthur L. Merriam, Edward Fifield, James McClain, John O'Keefe) 50 John

McNamara Thomas & Son (Thomas & John McNamara) 529 Pearl

McNamara Brothers (Michael & Thomas F. McNamara) 64 Fulton

McNamee Richard & Co. (Richard McNamee & James G. Gardiner) 234 B'way

McNamee J. & C. (dissolved) 32 Nassau

McNaught & Co. (James McNaught, no Co.) 107 Walker

McNaughten & Co. (William jr. & John McNaughten) 29 Broad

McNay & Nicholls (dissolved) 31 W. 35th

McNeal Pipe & Foundry Co. (Alexander H. McNeal, Pres.; L. L. Sturges, Sec.; Theodore Sturges, Treas. Capital, $350,000. Directors: Alexander H. McNeal, Benjamin G. Clarke, Percy R. Pyne, Samuel Thomas, Theodore Sturges) 52 Wall

McNeil J. S. & Co. (John S. McNeil & Laura F. Turner) 926 Sixth av.

McNear & Demera (Samuel A. McNear & Moses Demera) 56 Grand & 266 G'wich

McNulty & Kneeland (Albert McNulty, A. C. Kneeland & Dennis F. Driscoll) 111 B'way

McPartlan Brothers (James & Patrick McPartlan) 1491 Av. A

McPartland & O'Flaherty (Stephen McPartland & Edward O'Flaherty) 629 Eighth av.

McPherson D. & Co. (Daniel McPherson & Henry C. Seymour) 54 College pl.

McQuade & Markus (Bernard McQuade & Samuel Markus) 1057 First av.

McQuaid G. E. Publishing Co. (George E. McQuaid, propr.) 150 Nassau

McShane William & Co. (dissolved) 625 Sixth av.

McShane & Co. (plumbers' matls.) (Julian J. G. McShane & George S. Rodgers) 625 Sixth av.

McShane & Co. (wood) (Patrick McShane, Co. refused) 189 King

McShane & McKown (Hugh McShane & David E. McKown) 283 Morris av.

McSherry Brothers (John & Patrick McSherry) 460 W. 40th

McSorley John A. & Son (John A. & Charles V. McSorley) 42 Pine

McSwegan Francis & Sons (Francis & Frank jr. & Harvey McSwegnn) 1 N. Y. & B'klyn bridge

McTear Flax Felt Mfg. Co. (not inc.) (inf. unattainable) 292 Pearl

McWilliams Printing Co. (Charles McWilliams, Pres.; John J. Macauly, Sec.; James McWilliams, Treas. Capital, $35,000. Directors: Charles McWilliams, John J. Macauly, James McWilliams) 51 Elm

**SNOW, CHURCH & CO.,
265 & 267 BROADWAY.**

COLLECTIONS IN ALL PARTS OF THE WORLD.
T. C. Campbell and Arthur Murphy, *Counsel.*
TELEPHONE, 785 MURRAY.

McWilliams Brothers (Charles & Daniel & Frank McWilliams) 1 B'way
McWilliams & Burloe (Frank McWilliams & William J. Burloe) 1 B'way
Maas Samuel & Brother (Samuel & Martin Maas) 107 Second
Maas William & Co, (William Maas & Moritz Blum) 870 B'way & 2424 First av.
Maas A. W. & Co. (Abraham W. Maas & Abraham S. Rascovar) 110 Mercer
Maas & Blom (dissolved) 97 Division
Maas & Waldstein (Adolphus H. Maas & Martin R. Waldstein) 44 Trinity pl, & 81 G'wich
Maas, Blum & Co. (William Maas & Moritz Blum, no Co.) 870 B'way & 2424 First av.
Maas S. & Co. (Selig Maass, Samuel P. Hyman, Max Maass & Theodore Meyer) 477 Broome
Maass & Foucart (William Maass & Charles A. Foucart) 87 Desbrosses
Mabb T. W. & Co. (William H. Mabb, only) 8 South
Mabie, Todd & Bard (George W. & John H. Mabie, Henry H. Todd & Jonathan S. Bard) 198 B'way & 52 Grove
Macandrew & Forbes (Robert Macandrew & David Forbes) 55 Water
Macbeth James & Co. (James Macbeth, no Co.) 128 Maiden la.
Macdonald E. & J, (Mary Ellen & Josephine) 84 W. 25th
Macdonald & Hearn (dissolved) 205 E. 108th
Mace John & Son (John & William H. Mace) 403 Washn
Mace L. H. & Co. (Levi H. Mace & Frederick S. & John L. Gwyer) 111 E. Houston & E. 130th n Harlem r
Macfarland & Murray (dissolved) 308 W. 15th
Macfarlane James & Son, (James & Thomas J. Macfarlane) 1539 B'way
Macfarlane William & Co. (no. inf.) 55 Mercer
Macfarlane's A., Sons (John A. & William B. Macfarlane) 72 University pl,
Macgowan & Slipper (Robert W. Macgowan, only) 80 Beekman
Macgregor & Donaldson (dissolved) 150 W. 26th
Macgregor & Douglas (Susan A. Macgregor & Amy Douglas) 300 W. 42d
Macgregor & Jones (John T. Macgregor & Percy V. Jones) 19 Union sq. W.
Macheret & Butler (Mary A. Macharet & Catharine & Martina L. Butler) 34 E. 23d
Mack Drug Co. (Julius J. Mack, Pres.; Jacob Rosenthal, Sec.; Joseph Koshland, Treas.; Capital, $100,000. Directors: Julius J. Mack, Jacob Rosenthal, Joseph Koshland) 80 Reade
Mack D. & Co. (David Mack & Henry Delmel) 150 S. 5th av.
Mack & Lowis (dissolved) 120 B'way
Mack & Steinberg (Arthur J. Mack & Morris A. Steinberg) 659 B'way
Mackay John & Son (John & John W. Mackay) 27 William
Mackay A. G, & Co. (no inf.) 26 Reade
Mackenzie Storage & Mfg. Co, (Ltd.) (inf. unattainable) 88 Eleventh av.
Mackenzie W. & J. (dissolved) 56 W. 30th
Mackenzie & Douglas (dissolved) 120 Lincoln av.
Mackenzie, Chase & Co. (Charles W. Chase & John Morrison, only) 92 Warren
Mackey & Small (William D. Mackey & Cyrus K. Small) 97 Front
Mackin Brothers (Henry & James Mackin) 448 W. 17th
Mackinaw Refrigerator Co. (Francis T. Witte Hardware Co. proprs.) 106 Chambers

Mackinney, Smith & Co. (dissolved) 59 Maiden la.
Mackinnon J. A., Machinery Co. (John A. Mackinnon, Pres.; John A. Mackinnon jr., Sec.; Capital, $200,000. Directors: Arthur & John A. Mackinnon, Matthew Wiard) 22 Warren
Mackintosh, Green & Co. (William H. Mackintosh, Henry A. Green, Charles H. Wheeler, Lewis M. Taft & William J. & Henry P. McKenney) 59 Leonard
Macklin N. J. & Co. (Nicholas J. & John Macklin) 46 Broad
Maclay & Davies (Isaac W. Maclay & William E. Davies) 120 B'way
Maclay & Forrest (Moses R. & Archibald M. Maclay & Michael M. Forrest) 102 Chambers
Maclay, Davies & Co. (Isaac W. Maclay & William E. Davies, no Co.) 120 B'way
Macken R. B. & Co. (Robert B. Mackes & Charles F. Hinternhoff) 457 Broome
Macleod Donald W. & Co. (Donald W. Macleod & Justus H. Hosse) 293 Church
Macnaughtan's William, Sons (Ramsay & James & Allan Macunaughtan) 170 S. 5th av.
Macray & Brother (Francis B. & Robert J. Macray) 558 W. 43d
Macready R. & Co. (Robert & Robert A. & William H. Macready) 59 Cotton Ex.
Macready & Smith (Joseph E. Macready & John Smith) Av. A. n E. 67th
Macullar, Parker & Co. (no inf.) 19 Beekman
Macy F. A. & Co. (Frederick A. & Frederick D. Macy) 413 B'way
Macy R. H. & Co. (Charles B. Webster & Isidor & Nathan Straus, only) 200 Sixth av. & 60 W. 14th
Macy & Dunham (Isaac A. Macy & Harrison G. O. Dunham; —special partner, Robert McD. Kirkland, *Morristown, N. J.*, $40,000; terminates 30th June, 1891) 66½ Pine
Macy & Jenkins (Francis & William B. Jenkins, only) 67 Liberty
Macy's Josiah, Sons (Francis H. & William H. Macy 2d & Edwin S. Neal) 101 Front & 366 South
Madalene & Co.(Sarah M.Cogan,only) 827 Fifth av.
Madden Brothers (John & William Madden) 840 E. 122d
Maddock & Steel (refused) 46 Park pl.
Madison Avenue Depository & Exchange for Woman's Work (Mrs. Hooper C. Vanvorst, Pres.; Mrs. H. O. Armour, Treas,; Mrs. J. T. Williams, Sec.) 628 Madison av.
Madison Square Bank (W. Wetmore Cryder, Pres.; Lewis Thompson, Cashier; Robert McGill, Notary. Capital $200,000. Directors: W. Wetmore & Duncan Cryder, Hector DeCastro, Charles C. Delmonico, Edward S. Stokes) 202 Fifth av.
Madison Square Garden Co. (Hiram Hitchcock, Pres.; William A. Hafiez, Sec.; Thomas W. Pearsall, Treas. Capital, $1,500,000. Directors: Hiram Hitchcock, J. Pierpont Morgan, Charles Lanier, Adolf Ladenburg, Darius O. Mills, Frank K. Sturgis, Herman Oelrichs, Thomas W. Pearsall, William F. Wharton, Harry I. Nicholas, Henry H. Hollister) 10 W. 23d
Madison C. F. & Co. (Charles F. & Gerritt W. Madison) 187 B'way
Maerlender Brothers (dissolved) 589 B'way
Magee Lumber Co. (dissolved) 234 West
Magee H. F. & Co. (refused) 234 West
Magee W. T. & Co. (William T. & Hubert F. Magee) 70 Wall
Magen Bernard & Brothers (Bernard & Nathan & Jacob Magen) 476 & 570 Grand
Magerhans & Brokaw (Adolph W. Magerhans & Daniel DeW. Brokaw) 19 John

WATER METERS, GAS ENGINES, | **NATIONAL METER CO.**
FOR PUMPING AND POWER. | 252 Broadway, N. Y.

MAG 183 MAM

Magic Introduction Co. (Inf. unattainable) 41 Park row
Magic Ruffle Mfg. Co. (no inf.) 202 Church
Magill Brothers (Elmer E. & Harry N. W. Magill) 141 Eighth
Maginn & Davis (Charles Maginn & George C. Davis) 47 University pl.
Magna & Tiemann (C. Henry Magna & Carl G. Tiemann) 188 Ninth av.
Magneto Electric Machine Co. (Inf. unattainable) 102 Chambers
Magnolia Anti-Friction Metal Co. (Charles B. Miller, Pres.; George E. Miller, Sec. Capital, $100,000. Directors: Charles B. Miller, S. Victor Constant, George E. Miller) 74 Cortlandt
Magnolia House Cleaning Co. (W. L. Eaton & Brother, propr.) 109 W. 10th
Magnolia Land & Improvement Co. (inf. unattainable) 245 W. 20th
Magnus Joseph & Brother (Joseph & Louis Magnus) 1245 Third av.
Magnus E. & L. (no inf.) 524 Eighth av.
Magnus S. & Co. (Samuel Magnus & Frederick Hildebrandt) 275 Pearl
Magor John & Son (John & William A. Magor) 408 Produce Ex.
Magovern & Thompson Brothers (John P. Magovern, Edward W. & Frank S. Thompson & William Magovern) 126 Duane
Magovern & York (Edward E. Magovern & Herbert W. York) 22 Cortlandt
Magrath & O'Brien (Thomas Magrath & Thomas O'Brien) r 74 Irving pl.
Magrino Daniel & Brother (Daniel & Joseph Magrino) 478 Canal
Maguire Brothers (eatingh.) (Thomas & Sarah Maguire only) 226 Bleecker
Maguire Brothers (hames) (Frank E. & John J. Maguire) r 205 E. 22d & 208 E. 28d
Maguire & Rogers (Frank I. Maguire & Nathaniel P. Rogers jr.) 19 Whitehall
Maguire & Son (dissolved) r 205 E. 22d
Maher & Schmidt (Edward Maher & John Schmidt jr.) 41 Bowery
Mahlond Brothers (no inf.) 460 Fourth av.
Mahler Edward I. & Co. (dissolved) 104 Greene & 615 W. 52d
Mahler P. & Sons (Pius & William P. & Louis P. Mahler) 302 Pearl
Mahler Brothers (Samuel & Louis Mahler) 505 Sixth av.
Mahler & Edler (no inf.) 263 E. 89th
Mahler, Bohme & Co. (Edward I. Mahler, Reinhard Bohme & Adolph Oberste Lehn) 104 Greene & 615 W. 52d
Mahn Charles & Co. (Charles Mahn & George W. Nagel) 1568 First av.
Mahn & Hanpersberger (John P. Mahn & John Happersberger) 510 Second av.
Mahnken & Schmackenberg (John Mahnken & John Schmackenberg) 901 Park av.
Mahon & McGivney (dissolved) 894 First av.
Mahoney & Watson (Timothy Mahoney & Horatio Watson) 1215 Second av.
Mahony Daniel J. & Co. (dissolved) 330 Seventh av.
Mahony James & Son (James & Frank Mahony) 245 B'way
Mahony Brothers (builders) (Michael J. & Daniel F. Mahony) 52 New Bowery
Mahony Brothers (painters) (Thomas Mahony, only) 124 Leonard
Mahony & Dwyer (dissolved) 235 Fifth av.
Mahony & Westermayer (Daniel P. Mahony & Arthur J. Westermayer) 132 Nassau

Mahr Casper & Co. (Casper Mahr & Jacob Hoehn jr.) 263 Washn.
Mahr John C. & Sons (John C. & Henry J. & Julius D. Mahr) 299 Washn.
Mahr Brothers (Charles & John C. Mahr jr.) 1203 Third av.
Maibrunn H. & Son (Henry & Morris L. Maibrunn) 72 G'wich av.
Maicas & Co. (Anthony R. Maicas, no Co.) 104 John
Maid of the Mist Silver Mining Co. (John Stanton, Pres.; Louis Fitzgerald, Treas. Capital, $35,000. Trustees: John Stanton, Louis Fitzgerald, Charlton T. Lewis, W. A. Street, Samuel L. Smith) 120 B'way
Mail Printing Assn. (Inf. unattainable) 26 Park row
Mailler & Quereau (William H. Mailler, Welding Ring & estate of Abram Quereau) 51 Stone
Mainhart & Lowe (Frank E. Mainhart & William R. Lowe) 288 W. 125th & 2282 Seventh av.
Maisch & Schoubner (John E. Maisch & Herman Scheubner) 207 E. 111th
Maitland, Phelps & Co. (George Coppell, Thomas Maitland & Gerald L. Hoyt, only) 24 Exchange pl.
Majewski & Ahearn (Anton Majewski & Jeremiah C. Ahearn) 45 Goerck
Malcolm & Taylor (Samuel L. Malcolm & Sutherland G. Taylor) 1548 Ninth av.
Malcomson & Co. (Henry T. Malcomson, Edward Bridgden & John McNevon) 686 B'way
Mall Henry T. & Co. (Henry W. T. & Charles & Pierre Mall) 329 B'way
Milkmus & Brahe (dissolved) 69 Dey
Mallard's F. Sons (William & Frederick T. & Stephen F. Mallard) 489 G'wich. 6 Little W. 12th & 12 & 71 Gansevoort
Mallet & Co. (refused) 6 S. William
Mallett Peter & Co. (Peter Mallett & Edward B. Bartlett) 19 Old sl.
Mallon P. & Co. (Patrick Mallon & Hiram Becannon) 2001 Third av.
Mallon Brothers (Thomas J. & John J. & Charles J. Mallon) 26 Graud & 515 W. 51st
Mallory Steamship Lines (C. H. Mallory & Co., propra.) Pier 20 E. R.
Mallory C. H. & Co. (Charles H. Mallory, Elihu Spicer & Charles & Henry R. & Robert Mallory) Pier 20 E. R.
Mallory M. H. & Co. (Marshall H. & George B. Mallory) 47 Lafayette pl.
Mallory P. J. & Co. (P. Judson Mallory, no Co.) 78 Broad
Malloy Brothers (Joseph H. & Luke F. Malloy) 217 Park row
Malone Frank & Co. (Frank Malone, Alexander List & Thomas Lennon) 537 W. 14th & 540 W. 15th
Malone Brothers (John A. & Francis J. Malone) 603 Hudson
Malone & Scanlan (Edward P. Malone & Michael J. Scanlan) 91 Ninth av.
Maloney & Norton (Francis J. Maloney & James F. Norton) 824 Hudson
Maltby, Bayne & Marshall (Anson Maltby, Howard R. Bayne & Fielding L. Marshall) 46 Wall
Maltby, Ellis & Albertson (George E. Maltby, Wesley Ellis & Nicholas S. Albertson) 354 G'wich
Maltby, Henley & Co. (Douglass F. & Julius Maltby & William I. Henley) 20 Warren
Maitine Mfg. Co. (Timothy L. Woodruff, Pres.; Vincent W. Chapman, Sec.; Rodney A. Ward, Treas. Capital, $100,000. Directors: Timothy L. Woodruff, Vincent W. Chapman, Rodney A. Ward, Lucius H. Biglow) 19 Warren
Mamlock M. & Son (Meyer & Albert Mamlock) 827 B'way

EXCELSIOR BIRD FOOD. The recognized standard. The most reliable for your Canary. Use no other. Insist upon getting it. Packed only by C. ROSENSTEIN & CO., 373 Washington Street, New York.

Mamlock & Green (dissolved) 640 B'way
Mammelsdorff Brothers & Co. (Edward & Theodore & Jacob & August Mammelsdorff) 109 Grand
Man A. P. & W. (Albon P. & William & Henry H. Man) 56 Wall & 59 Pine
Man & Protheroe (Alrick H. Man & Charles C. Protheroe) 56 Wall
Manchester Water Co. (William Henry White, Pres.; Henry B. Owen, Sec; Clement A. White, Treas. Capital, $100,000. Directors: William Henry & Clement A. White, Harry B. Owen) 30 Pine
Manchester & Philbrick (George N. Manchester & William N. Philbrick) ft. E. 51st & 1407 Third av.
Mandel A. G. & Co. (Adolphus G. Mandel, no Co.) 251 Front
Mandel & Wallach (Adolph Mandel & Heyman Wallach) dealers in paraffine wax, 156 Rivington
Mandelbaum G. & Co. (Gustav Mandelbaum, no Co.) 112 Chambers
Mandell K. & Co. (Kaufman Mandell, no Co.) 26 Howard
Mandeville H. & Son (Henry & Henry C. Mandeville) 247 W. 47th
Mandoville & Co. (no inf.) 196 B'way
Mandle D. & Co, (David & Max Mandle & Herman Reise) 52 Hewitt av. W. Washn, mkt
Mangam D. D. & Co. (Daniel D. & William L. & Daniel D. Mangam jr.) 92 Broad
Mangam & Ackerman (John W, Mangam & Jacob D. Ackerman) Pier 28 (old) N. R.
Mangam & Co. (Sylvester S, & William P. Mangam) 2363 Second av.
Mangam's W. D., Son (Edgar D. Mangam) 442 Produce Ex.
Mangan Brothers (John F. & Joseph J. Mangan) 672 Eleventh av.
Mangels William H. & Co. (William H. Mangels & Martin Jung) 27 Howard
Mangini & Barbieri (John Mangini & Andrew Darbieri) 26 Roosevelt
Mangles P & Co. (Powell Mangles & Robert Paterson) 94 Park row & 4 Chambers
Manhatta Steam Laundry (Alexander McGill, propr.) 1666 B'way
Manhattan Agency (Thomas R. Hawes, Pres.; Theresa Abrahams, Sec.; Marion K. Hawes, Treas. further inf. refused) 59 W. 30th
Manhattan Art Co. (Enos T. Throop, Pres.; George E. Throop, Sec. Capital, $30,000. Directors: Enos T. & George E. & F. H. Throop) 150 Nassau
Manhattan Beach Co. (Austin Corbin, Pres.; Frank McDonough, Sec.; William G. Wheeler, Treas. Capital, $4,000,000. Directors: John R. Maxwell, Charles L. Flint, Henry W. Maxwell, Frederick W. Dunton, James D. Campbell, Austin Corbin, William G. Wheeler) 192 B'way
Manhattan Beach Improvement Co. (Ltd.) (Austin Corbin, Pres.; Frank McDonough, Sec.; William G. Wheeler, Treas. Capital, $1,000,000. Directors: John R. Maxwell, John R. Upham, James D. Campbell, Edward R. Reynolds, Henry Graves, Charles L. Flint, Henry W. Maxwell, Frederick W. Dunton, Thomas F. Ward, Edwin H. Atkins, Austin Corbin, William G. Wheeler, Frank McDonough) 192 B'way
Manhattan Beef Co. (Joseph Gaines, propr.) 1890 Second av.
Manhattan Beef Co. (Thomas Woods, propr.) 2269 Tenth av.
Manhattan Beef Co. (Ltd.) (Thomas H. Wheeler, Pres.; Charles M. Webber, Sec.; Welter H. Wheeler, Treas.; further inf. refused) Manhattan mkt

Manhattan Bindery (Samuel J. Brown & Co. proprs.) 19 College pl.
Manhattan Brass Co. (James H. White, Pres.; Harry B. White, Sec.; Jonathan R. Crane, Treas. Capital, $200,000. Trustees: James H. White, Jonathan H. Crane, J. A. & E. H. Hayden, John Longhran, William A. Spealght, Henry Seibert) 338 E. 28th
Manhattan Brass Foundry & Machine Works (John Powers, propr.) 428 E. 10th
Manhattan Bridge Building Co. (no inf.) 115 B'way
Manhattan Building & Investment Co.(Ltd.) (Ferdinand H. Mela, Pres.; Samson Simon, Treas.; Henry Weil, Sec. Capital, $50,000. Directors: Ferdinand H. Mela, Samson Simon, Henry Weil, Maurice E, Strauss, Christian G. Norman) 529 B'way
Manhattan City Cigar Co. (Henry Hartig, propr.) 54 Bond
Manhattan Cloak & Suit Co. (Einstein, Finn & Waxelbaum, proprs.) 548 B'way & 82 Crosby
Manhattan Cloth Sponging & Refinishing Works (John W. Flock & Son, proprs.) 199 Centre
Manhattan Coal Co. (inf. unattainable) 261 B'way
Manhattan Commercial Agency (James H. Giles, propr.) 42 Tribune bldg
Manhattan Co. (Dewitt C. Hays, Pres.; Joseph T. Baldwin, Cashier; Hanson C. Gibson, Notary. Capital, $2,050,000. Directors: George W. Smith, William H. Swan, John W. Harper, James Talcott, Matthew C. D. Borden, Edgar S. Auchincloss, John S. Kennedy, Henry K. McHarg, John Sloane, Dewitt C. Hays, James M. McLean) 40 Wall
Manhattan Conservatory of Music (William Aschenbrenner, propr.) 11 E. 42d
Manhattan Dairy Co. (James W. Curley, propr.) 1981 Second av.
Manhattan Electric Light Co, (Ltd.) (Charles L. Bernheim, Pres.; Abram C, Bernheim, Sec.; L. Levy, Treas. Capital, $1,000,000. Directors: Charles L. & Abram C. Bernheim, L. Levy, A. Herrmann, Charles Sternbach) E. 50th c Av. B
Manhattan Electrical Supply Co. (John J. Gorman, Pres.; Henry T. Johnson, Sec. Capital, $10,000. Trustees: John J. Gorman, Henry T. Johnson, Patrick B. Kane) 26 Church
Manhattan Feather Duster Co. (Alexander G. Inness, propr.) 981 G'wich
Manhattan Felt Mills (T. New Mfg. Co. proprs.) 32 John
Manhattan Fire Brick & Enameled Clay Retort Works (Adam Weber, propr.) 639 E. 15th & 259 Av. C
Manhattan Glue Works (J. L. & J. Toch, proprs.) 85 Pearl
Manhattan Hardwood Lumber Co. (dissolved) 102 Chambers
Manhattan Hat Co. (August Kahn, propr.) 235 Eighth av.
Manhattan House Cleaning Bureau (James E. Garner, propr.) 148 W. 20th
Manhattan Iron Works (Bruno Schubert, propr.) 843 W. 44th
Manhattan Iron Works Co, (dissolved) 89 Wall & ft. W. 146d
Manhattan Jewelry Co. (Jacob Metzler, Pres.; Max Springer, Sec.; Albert Blum, Treas. Capital, $8,000. Directors: Jacob Metzler, Albert Blum, Max Springer) 481 B'way
Manhattan Laundry Co. (Wallach & Cohen, proprs.) 208 W. 23d
Manhattan Leather Works (Ziegel, Bisman & Co. proprs.) 178 William
Manhattan Life Ins. Co. (James M. McLean, Pres.; Henry Y. Wemple, Sec. Capital, $100,000. Directors: James M. McLean, Edward Schell, John T. Terry, Abram Dubois, Henry Van Schaick, Ambrose C. Kingsland, James Stokes,

IDEN & CO., MANUFACTURERS OF **GAS FIXTURES AND ELECTROLIERS**
University Place, 9th to 10th Sts., N. Y.

Olin G. Walbridge, David H. McAlpin, W. J. Valentine, Edward A. Walton, George W. Quintard, Leon Blum, C. Norwood, John W. Hunter, P. Van Zandt Lane, Jacob Naylor, Edward King, John H. Watson, James E. Yentinan, N. K. Masten, Spencer H. Smith, Henry D. Stokes, George H. McLean, Philip Bissinger, Artemas H. Holmes, James A. Garland, Frederick Billings, Henry B. Peirce, Emil F. Del Bondio, William H. Oakley, Robert S. Green, Jacob L. Halsey, Arthur Leary, Cornelius D. Wood, Dewitt C. Hays) 156 B'way

Manhattan Lighterage & Transp. Co. (George S. Dearborn, Pres.; John Muir, Sec. Capital, $150,000. Directors: George S. Dearborn, John Muir, E. Hawley, W. Sutton, E. M. Pardee) 104 Wall

Manhattan Lithographing Co. (Eberhard Faber, Pres.; Frederick S. Osborn, Sec. Capital, $10,000. Directors: Eberhard & Lothar W. Faber, Frederick G. Osborn, Harrison G. McFaddin, Herman Brasunlich) 10 Reade

Manhattan Machine & Novelty Co. (Daniel C. Oyster, Pres.; Horace Little, Sec. Capital, $300,000. Directors: Daniel C. Oyster, William H. Randel, Walter Carroll Low, Daniel J. Noyes) 62 Cedar

Manhattan Mfg. Co. (inoperative) 115 B'way

Manhattan Medicine Co. (John F. Henry, Pres.; L. D. Henry, Sec.; Henry E. Bowen, Treas. Capital, $2,000; further inf. unattainable) 24 College pl.

Manhattan Mills (I. & W. & U. Danenberg, proprs.) 83 Water

Manhattan Molding Co. (Capital, $10,000; further inf. unattainable) no address

Manhattan Mutual Co-operative Savings & Loan Assn. (Herbert M. Lloyd, Pres.; Frank S. Parmelee, Sec.; Samuel J. Holmes, Treas.) 47 B'way

Manhattan Mutual Fire Ins. Co. (Charles H. Spencer, Pres.; John W. Fitzgerald, Sec. Directors: Charles H. Spencer, J. S. Wyman, B. F. Nelson, R. G. Evans, E. S. Wheeler, A. P. Conlior, E. M. Mable, G. I. Whitehead, W. G. Wallace, D. S. Wagner, John W. Fitzgerald, J. J. Gilbert, C. O. Howard, W. F. Keefer) 111 B'way

Manhattan News Agency (Lawrence Kelly, propr.) 110 E. 125th

Manhattan Oil Co. (Philip M. Millspaugh, Pres.; John A. Clussman, Sec.; James B. Carpenter, Treas. Capital, $200,000. Directors: Philip M. Millspaugh, John A. Clussman, James B. Carpenter, Thornton N. Motley) 51 Front & 423 E. 112th

Manhattan Opera Glass Supply Co. (Sigmund Lorsch, Pres.; Adolph W. Magerhans, Sec.; Karl Thalmann, Treas. Capital, $500,000. Directors: Sigmund Lorsch, Adolph W. Magerhans, Karl Thalmann, James W. Patterson, John C. Day, George Holmes, Henry Dreyfus) 45 B'way

Manhattan Oracle Co. (inf. unattainable) 203 B'way

Manhattan Packing Co. (refused) 42 Pearl

Manhattan Pants Mfg. Co. (Rebecca Levy, propr.) 36 E. Houston

Manhattan Pie Baking Co. (John Steingester, Pres.; Henry F. Quast, Sec. Capital, $25,000. Directors: John Steingester, Henry F. Quast, Charles Book) 5 Cannon & 540 Grand

Manhattan Printing & Publishing Co. (John McGuire, Pres.; Edward V. Gambier, Sec. Capital, $6,000. Trustees: John McGuire, Edward V. Gambier, Nathaniel J. Lane) 12 Frankfort

Manhattan Quilting & Mfg. Co. (Asahel G. Darwin, Pres.; David H. Coles, Sec.; James C. Bench, Treas. Capital, $200,000. Directors: Asahel G. Darwin, David H. Coles, James C. Bench, John L. Coles, Henry W. Guernsey) 45 B'way

Manhattan Railway Advertising Co. (inf. unattainable) 85 Murray

Manhattan Railway Co. (Jay Gould, Pres.; Daniel W. McWilliams, Sec. Capital, $20,000,000. Directors: Jay Gould, Robert M. Callaway, Russell Sage, Samuel Sloan, Sidney Dillon, George J. Gould, J. Pierpont Morgan, John H. Hall, Cyrus W. Field, Edwin Gould, Chester W. Chapin, Simon Wormser, Stephen V. White) 71 B'way

Manhattan Railway News Co. (inf. unattainable) 85 Murray

Manhattan Real Estate Assn. (Samuel D. Babcock, Pres.; George P. Slade, Treas. Capital, $750,000 ; further inf. unattainable) 110 Leonard

Manhattan Real Estate Co. (Walter R. Lord, Pres. Paul Campaignac jr. Sec.; Israel Joseph, Treas. Directors: Walter R. Lord, Paul Campaignac jr. Israel Joseph, Joseph Abbott, Lyman C. Chapin) 55 Liberty

Manhattan Repair Works (John S. Voltok, propr.) 58 Ann

Manhattan Ribbon Co. (not inc.) (Isidor Weil & M. Belvin) 491 B'way

Manhattan Safe Deposit & Storage Co. (William H. Appleton, Pres.; John J. Pulleyn, Sec. Capital, $200,000. Trustees: William H. Appleton, George L. White, Cornelius N. Bliss, Walter H. Lewis, Charles S. Smith, Edward Martin, Henry Tuck, Archibald H. Welch, Theodore M. Ives, Arthur J. Lockwood, William T. Booth, William J. Westcott) 340 B'way

Manhattan Savings Institution (Edward Schell, Pres.; Robert S. Hayward, Sec. Trustees: Edward Schell, James M. McLean, Robert G. Remsen, Henry M. Taber, John H. Watson, Benjamin L. Swan jr, P. Van Zandt Lane, William J. Valentine, Henry J. Bowen, Dewitt C. Hays, Edward King, Henry B. Stokes, Edward A. Walton, George Bleglow, John D. Jones, George H. McLean, Frederick Billings) 644 B'way

Manhattan Shade Cloth Co. (William W. Fosche jr. propr.) 456 Broome & ft. E. 185th

Manhattan Shoe Co. (William B. Rice, Pres.; George S. Perry, Sec.; E. Parker Pond, Treas. Capital, $10,000. Directors: William B. Rice, George S. Perry, E. Parker Pond, George M. & H. L. Rice) 181 Duane

Manhattan Shoe Mfg. & Repairing Co. (James L. Lederer, propr.) 782 & 1002 Third av.

Manhattan Sign Co. (Rudolph Karwiese, propr.) 122 Liberty

Manhattan Steam Hair Picking & Renovating Works (John Meyer, propr.) 528 Eleventh av.

Manhattan Storage & Warehouse Co. (Lawrence Wells, Pres; Adrian Iselin jr. Sec. Capital, $715,000. Trustees: Adrian Iselin, Addison Cammack, Adrian Iselin jr. William Jay, Lawrence Wells) Lex. av. c E 42d

Manhattan Stove Works (Eugene Munsell & Co. proprs.) 218 Water

Manhattan Telegraph Co. (William De Groot, Pres.; Elisha J. Denison, Sec. Capital, $150,000 ; further inf. refused) 194 Water

Manhattan Telephone Co. (dissolved) 26 Church

Manhattan Therapeutic Co. (Walter B. Wills, Pres.; George M. Robertson, Sec. Capital, $50,000. Trustees: Walter B. Wills, George M. Robertson, Edward M. Jones, Charles W. Hooks) 85 Murray

Manhattan Tool Co. (Louis P. Valiquet, propr.) 142 Fulton

Manhattan Trading Co. (not inc.; further inf. unattainable) 13 B'way

Manhattan Transp. Co. (Ltd.) (inf. unattainable) 1 B'way

Manhattan Trust Co. (Francis O. French, Pres.; Charles W. Haskins, Sec.; Amos T. French, Treas. Capital, $1,000,000. Directors: Fran-

MAN 186 MAP

cls O. French, Richard J. Cross, H. L. Higginson, August Belmont jr. Edmund D. Randolph, C. C. Baldwin, Charles F. Tag, Henry Field, Henry W. Cannon, John R. Ford, T. J. Coolidge jr. James O. Sheldon, Albert S. Rosenbaum, Samuel R. Shipley, Richard T. Wilson, John I. Waterbury, Eckstein Norton, Hugh O. Northcote) 10 Wall *(see adv. in back)*

Manhattan Type Foundry (Bryant Godwin, Pres.; Frederick Van Wyck, Sec.; Charles H. Martini, Treas. Capital $50,000. Directors: Bryant Godwin, Frederick Van Wyck, Charles H. Martini) 199 William

Manhattan Type Writing Co. (not inc.) (Margaret S. Powers & Anna L. Hall) 5 Beekman

Manhattan Umbrella Store (Hugh Sprott, propr.) 344 W. 42d

Manhattan Wagon & Truck Works (Francis Wagner, propr.) 323 E. 29th

Manhattan Wall Paper Co. (not inc.) (Lucien Baer, David Kraemer & Charles D. Hexter) 617 W. 39th

Manhattan Watch Co. (Arthur O. Jennings, Pres.; Philip B. Jennings, Sec.; Trenor L. Park, Treas. Capital, $180,000. Directors: Arthur O. Jennings, Trenor L. Park; further inf. unattainable) 234 B'way & 159 Monroe

Manhattan Watch & Jewelry Co. (Ludwig Hess, propr.) 64 John

Manhattan Wire Works (John C. Kleemann, propr.) 206 E. 29th

Manhattan Worsted Mills (Prentiss & Butler, proprs.) W. 130th n Eleventh av.

Manhattan & Empire Print Works (Worthen & Aldrich, proprs.) 25 N. Moore

Manheimer S. & J. (Simon & Joseph) 542 Pearl

Manhelms' Misfit Clothing Co. (Henry Manheims, propr.) 129 Third av.

Manifold Book Co. (John W. Collins, Pres., Herman F. Lee, Sec. Capital, $100,000. Directors: John W. Collins, Herman F. Lee, J. B. Brutine, J. Platt Rogers, James L. O'Connor) 26 Reade & 58 Maiden la.

Manisof & Deutsch (Simon Manisof & Samuel Deutsch) 4½ Bleecker

Mann Car Improvement Co. (Ellis B. Edwards, Pres.; S. H. Hitchcock, Sec.; Lawrence J. Maher, Treas. Trustees: Ellis B. Edwards, S. H. Hitchcock, Lawrence J. Maher, Wood D. Loudoun, Joel B. Erhardt) 15 Broad

Mann Charles & Co. (Charles Mann & Herman Haendle) 2348 Third av.

Mann Louis & Co. (Louis & Ignatz Mann) 64 Nassau

Mann C. A. & Co. (Calvin A. Mann & William D. Carter) 43 Murray

Mann Brothers (Joseph H. & Samuel Mann) 32 E. B'way

Mann & Jackson (Charles H. Mann, Courtlandt S. Benedict & Henry R. Jackson) 771 B'way

Mann & Schuhmann (dissolved) 149 Ridge

Manne & Silberlust (Solomon J. Manne & Joseph Silberlust) 59 Bleecker

Manneck Mfg. Co. (T. Dwight Williams, Pres.; Jacob D. Otis, Sec. Capital, $2,500. Directors: T. Dwight Williams, Jacob D. Otis) 169 Bleecker

Manneck's H., Son (dissolved) 95 Chambers

Mannes Henry & Sons (Henry & Isaac H. & Aaron H. Mannes) 499 Eighth av.

Mannheim William & Co. (William C. H. & J. Richard Mannheim, only) 70 Warren

Mannheimer & Lauferty (Anton Mannheimer & David A. Lauferty) 456 B'way

Manning Edward & Co. (Edward Manning & Samuel A. Echols) 82 Vesey

Manning A. C. & Co. (Alfred C. & James S. Manning) 18 Vesey

Manning & Krausse (dissolved) 88 Nassau

Manning & Schmohl (Thomas H. Manning & John P. Schmohl) 144 Varick

Manning & Squier (William C. & Stuart C. & Charles B. & Edwin M. Squier, only) 111 Liberty

Manning, Maxwell & Moore (Henry S. Manning, Eugene L. Maxwell & Charles A. Moore) 111 Liberty

Manovill & Werther (dissolved) 47 Bond

Manress & Boyle (Joaquin Mauress & George W. Boyle) 1024 Third av.

Manress & Diaz (Joaquin Manress & Bruno Diaz jr.) 32 Platt

Manress, Ramirez & Co. (dissolved) 32 Platt

Mansbach Brothers (Abraham H. & Louis H. Mansbach) 425 B'way

Mansell & Blume (dissolved) 71 William

Mansingson & Co. (inf. unattainable) 813 B'way

Manson Daniel & Co. (Daniel Manson & George R. Brown) 12 Maiden la.

Manson & Perlman (Levi S. Manson & Louis H. Perlman) 5 Beekman

Mantel G. & J. J. Nuss (dissolved) Spring pl. c Fulton av.

Manthey & Paulsen (Rudolph Manthey & Martin Paulsen) 26 Desbrosses

Manufacturers' Advertising Bureau & Press Agency (Benjamin R. Western, propr.) 111 Liberty

Manufacturers' Distributing Co. (Wilbur F. Brown, propr.) 106 Greene

Manufacturers' Fire Equipment Co. (David P. W. McMullen, Pres.; Frederick C. Albrecht, Sec. Capital, $100,000. Directors: David P. W. McMullen, George A. Stanton, Edward C. Anderson, Frederick C. Albrecht) 155 B'way

Manufacturers' Gazette Publishing Co. (no inf.) 187 B'way

Manufacturers' Knit Goods Co. (not inc.) (George W. Potter, Edward H. Olift & William H. Sheip) 47 Leonard

Manufacturers' & Builders' Fire Ins. Co. (Edward V. Loew, Pres., J. Jay Nestell, Sec. Capital, $200,000. Directors: Edward V. Loew, John Inglis, Michael Coleman, Henry Schumacher, Alfred G. Nason, Thomas Goadby, Frederick W. Loew, J. Jay Nestell, Rudolph Wyman, Jacob Lorillard, William Burns, William L. Loew, George W. Quintard, Henry Steers) 152 B'way

Manufacturing Investment Co. (William C. Whitney, Pres.; Daniel S. Lamont, Sec. Capital, $750,000. Directors: William C. Whitney, Oliver H. Payne, Daniel S. Lamont, H. McK. Twombly, J. Pierpont Morgan, George G. Haven, Frederick Frelinghuysen, Samuel D. Babcock, Don M. Dickinson) 15 Broad

Manwaring D. W. (David W. & William M. Manwaring) 248 Water

Manzanita Gold Mining Co. (William W. Gibbs, Pres. Robert A. C. Smith, Sec. Capital, $1,000,000. Directors: William W. Gibbs, Charles P. Robinson, Robert A. C. Smith. Edward L. Bartlett, Frederick T. Parsons) 40 Wall

Mapes Formula & Peruvian Guano Co. (P. Van-Zandt Lane, Pres.; Edward V. Z. Lane, Treas.; Capital, $100,000. Trustees: P. Van Zandt Lane, Charles V. Mapes, Francis T. L. & Edward V. Z. Lane, Charles H. Mapes) 158 Front

Mapes H. C. & Co. (Henry C. & John S. Mapes) 59 Liberty & 1066 Boston rd.

Mapes & Kelly (John A. Mapes & James R. Kelly) 200 B'way

Mapes & Rudd (Daniel S. Mapes & David L. Rudd) 94 Greene

Maple Grove Cemetery (William S. Cogswell, Pres.; Charles S. Goodwin, Sec.; John P. Morris, Treas. Trustees: William S. Cogswell, John P. Morris, Charles S. Goodwin, John H. Sutphin, Jay H. Van Norden, Ferris S. Thompson) 1273 D'way

Marble, Mason & Canfield (Edward M. Marble, Robert Mason & William W. Canfield) 160 B'way

Marbury & Fox (Francis F. Marbury & Charles Fox) 8 Broad

Marcellus & Cubberley (H. Wilson Marcellus & Nelson S. Cubberley) 1334 Ninth av. & 185 W. 104th

March John P. & Co. (John P. & John F. March) 109 Water

March P. S. & Son (Peter S. & Egbert G. March) 91 Water

March & Smith (Clement March & Sidney J. Smith) 45 William

Marchal & Smith Piano & Organ Co. (Robert W. Smith, Pres.; George L'Hommedieu, Sec.; Capital, $1,000. Directors: Robert W. Smith, George L'Hommedieu, Orlando Smith) 235 E. 21st

Marchand Institute (dissolved) 10 W. 4th

Marcial & Co. (Francis Spies, only) 36 B'way

Marco J. & Sons (John & Benjamin B. & Julius L. Marco) 416 E. 122d

Marco Brothers (Manuel E. Marco, only) 2 W. 125th

Marcotte L. & Co. (Fanny R. Herzog, Pres.; Frederick S. Walt, Sec.; Charles R. Ecklin, Treas. Capital, $150,000. Directors: Fanny R. & Louis Herzog, Frederick S. Walt) 298 Fifth av. & 153 W. 23d

Marcus A. J. & Co. (Alfred J. Marcus & Martin & Albert & William Frank) 30 Ferry

Marcus Brothers (Joseph S. & Nathan Marcus) 97 Canal

Marcus & Schwab (Martin Marcus & Leo Schwab) 785 B'way

Marcus, Leibowitz & Lazar (Copel Marcus, Aaron Leibowitz & Abraham Lazar) 66 Eldridge

Marcy Cigar Co. (not inc.) (Moss Samuel & Moss Bloaveron) 32 Bond

Marcy Stove Repair Co. (Caesar, Denis & Houser, propra.) 63 Beekman

Marcy & White (Erastus E. Marcy & William H. White) 353 Fifth av.

Marden Engraving Co. (Stephen J. Marden, propr.) 84 Park row

Mardin & Whelan (Frank M. & George I. Mardin & John T. Whelan) 907 D'way

Marga & Jouard (Emile & Marie Marga & Felicie Jouard) 500 Park av.

Margraf C. & Son (Conrad & George Margraf) 308 E. Houston

Mariani & Co. (Angelo Mariani & Julius N. Jaros) 52 W. 15th

Marietta & North Georgia Railway Co. (Lenox Smith, V. Pres.; H. M. Hammett, Sec.; J. B. Glover, Treas. Capital, $1,421,425. Directors: Lenox Smith, W. G. Oakman, Elisha Thayer, A. A. Arthur, E. E. Malcolm, E. G. Pierce, A. L. Hartridge, R. J. Lowry, J. B. Glover, H. M. Hammett, J. W. Patton) 19 William

Marine Co. (inoperative) 44 B'way

Marine Journal Co. (Samuel Samuels, Pres.; George L. Norton, Sec; further inf. refused) 132 Nassau

Marine Railway Co. (Austin Corbin, Pres.; Frank McDonough, Sec.; William G. Wheeler, Treas. Capital, $50,000. Directors: Austin Corbin, John R. & Henry W. Maxwell, John B. Upham, Frederick W. Dunton, Charles L. Flint, Gilman S. Moulton) 192 B'way

Marini Brothers (dissolved) 191 Spring

Marini & Scarneo (dissolved) 2182 Second av,

Marinoni Press (Henry R. Drowne, Pres.; F. H. Clarke, Sec. Directors: Henry R. Drowne,

F. H. Clarke, C. P. Noyes, John Winner jr, F. Walsh) 540 Pearl

Marion Steam Shovel Co. (no inf.) 52 B'way

Mariposa Land & Mining Co. (inf. unattainable) 40 D'way

Maris John M. & Co. (Henry J. & Theodore Maris & John Franklin, only) 26 College pl.

Maritime Assn. of the Port of N. Y. (Radcliffe Baldwin, Pres.; William H. Van Brunt, Sec.; Henry Stadlmair, Treas.) 14 Beaver

Maritime Co. (Ltd.) (Capital, $125,000 ; further inf. unattainable) no address

Maritime Exchange (Radcliffe Baldwin, Pres.; William H. Van Brunt, Sec.; Henry Stadlmair, Treas.) 14 Beaver

Markart Joseph & Brother (dissolved) 106 Pitt

Markel Brothers (Jacob L. & Gerson Markel) 94 Canal

Market & Fulton National Bank (Robert Bayles, Pres.; Alexander Gilbert, Cashier ; Thomas Hinwood, Notary. Capital, $750,000. Directors: Benjamin H. Howell, Henry Lyles jr. George B. Whitfield, Robert Bayles, George M. Alcott, Richard P. Merritt, John T. Willets, Alexander Gilbert, Henry W. Banks, W. Irving Clark, James L. Morgan jr. Frederick W. Devoe, John Abendroth) 83 Fulton

Markewitz & Son (Edward J. Markewitz, only) 656 D'way

Markowitz & Bass (dissolved) 1471 Ninth av.

Marks Adjustable Folding Chair Co. (Ltd.) (Frank R. Marks, Pres.; Nathaniel D. Harmon, Sec. Capital, $12,000 ; further inf. unattainable) 936 B'way & 403 E. 23d

Marks Automatic Car Coupler Co. (no inf.) 146 B'way

Marks David & Sons (David & Marcus M. & Frederick W. Marks) 889 B'way

Marks Samuel M. & Jules Meyer, 37 Old sl

Marks Selim & Son (Selim & Barnett Marks) 185 E. 55th

Marks Transfer Machine Co. (Capital, $250,000 ; further inf. unattainable) no address

Marks G. & Co. (Gabriel Marks & Philip Schwed) 20 Lispenard

Marks L. & E. (Louis & Elias) 149 Attorney

Marks L. & Sons (Levi & Charles & Marcus Marks) 788 B'way

Marks M. A. & Co. (Marcus A. Marks & Elias Wolf) 473 B'way

Marks M. B. & L. A. (Morris B. & Louis A.) 25 White

Marks Brothers (caps) (Marcus Marks & Eugene Arnheim, only) 121 Greene

Marks Brothers (clothing) (Michael & Nathan Marks) 5 Gt. Jones

Marks Brothers (stationers) (Marcus & Henry Marks) 190 Orchard

Marks & Co. (Lewis W. Marks, no Co.) 718 B'way

Marks & Cunningham (dissolved) 12 Spruce

Marks & Levy (Elias Marks & Israel W. Levy) 470 Grand & 250 Bowery

Marks & Levy Brothers (dissolved) 470 Grand & 250 Bowery

Marks & Norman (Woolf D. Marks & S. P. Norman) 25 W. 30th

Marks & Shine (dissolved) 186 Fourth av,

Marks & Stiebel (Harris Marks & Wolf Stiebel) 126 Attorney

Marks & Terry (Montague L. Marks & Henry T. Terry) 280 B'way

Marks & Wolf (Nathan Marks & William Wolf) 202 Bowery

Marks, Cunningham & Co. (Max J. Marks, Bernard C. Caningham & Ferdinand Greenebaum) 12 Spruce

Markt & Co. (Gustav Vintschger & Albert Pulvermann, only) 148 Worth

SPECIAL ATTENTION PAID TO THIS CLASS OF WORK } BANKERS' & BROKERS' CIRCULARS DELIVERED { THE TROW CITY DIRECTORY CO. 11 University Place.

Markus & Rosenstock (Henry Markus & Bernhard Rosenstock) 39 Nassau
Marlow & Co. (Matthew Marlow & Edward Harris) 68 John
Marlow & Neuser (dissolved) 725 D'way
Marquand & Parmly (Henry Marquand, Ebenezer K. Sibley & Duncan D. Parmly) 160 D'way
Marquardt H. & Co. (Hans Triest & Minna Marquardt, only) 21 S. William
Marquardt & Philippi (dissolved) 24 Prince
Marquette & Mecke (Hiram Marquette & John Mecke) 25 William
Marquette, Houghton & Ontonagon R. R. Co. (James McMillan, Pres.; Louis M. Schwan, Sec.; William A. C. Ewen, Treas. Capital, $5,657,126. Directors: James McMillan, Calvin S. Brice, H. McMillan, John W. Sterling, Samuel Thomas, George I. Seney, John G. Moore, Thomas W. Pearsall, Edward Tuck) 10 Wall
Marquis & Hahn (Alfred Marquis & Henry Hahn) 74 Fulton
Marr Construction Co. (consolidated with N. Am. Construction Co.) 171 D'way
Marrey & Co. (dissolved) ft. W. 52d
Marschall, Spellman & Co. (August Marschall, Emanuel L. Spellman & Justus Oesterlein) 5 N. Y. & B'klyn bridge
Marsching J. & Co. (John Marsching & Bernhard F. Drakenfeld) 27 Park pl.
Marsden-Andrews Co. (dissolved) 15 Cortlandt
Marsh Mantel & Heating Co. (Riverius Marsh, Pres.; James S. Zerbe, Sec.; Ira S. Elkins, Treas. Capital, $100,000. Directors: Riverius Marsh, Ira S. Elkins, R. H. Doxtater, Peter G. Polhemus, James S. Zerbe) 293 B'way
Marsh W. E. & Co. (William E. Marsh & Charles R. Palmer) 32 Wall
Marsh, White & Co. (John H. Fort, only) 25 Whitehall
Marshall & Collyer (Alfred Marshall & Robert S. Collyer) 18 D'way
Marshall & Walter (John W. Marshall & John W. Walter) 61 New
Marston Remedy Co. (refused) 19 Park pl.
Marston William H. & Brother (William H. & Charles B. Marston) 15 Broad
Marston & Hyman (Howard T. Marston & Samuel F. Hyman) 25 Chambers
Marston & Son (William H. & Frank H. Marston) 76 Beaver
Martha Washington Creamery Buttered Flour Co. of the U. S. (Ltd.) (E. A. Grossbeck, Pres.; Emil Rieser, Sec. Capital, $10,000 ; further inf. unattainable) 7 Murray
Martha Washington Flour Co. (John H. Cheever, Pres.; Joseph H. Strange, Sec. Capital, $25,000. Directors: Charles B. Caldwell, John R. Wright, George P. Tangeman, John H. Cheever, Joseph H. Strange) 875 Hudson
Marthaler & Cosine (Joseph Marthaler & Oscar W. Cosine) 218 W. 57th
Martin Anti-Fire Car Heater Co. (no inf.) 140 Nassau
Martin Jeremiah N. & Son (no inf.) 427 E. 58th
Martin John & Son (John & Charles J. Martin) 534 Third av.
Martin John S. & Co. (John S. & William V. Martin & Charles M. Vail) 168 Chambers & 209 G'wich
Martin Process & Chemical Co. (Henry W. Hayden, receiver) 48 Wall
Martin Reune & Sons (Reune & Noel B. & Ferrier J. Martin) 114 Worth
Martin Thomas & Co. (estate of Thomas Martin & James W. Vannek) 548 W. 46th
Martin E. H. & Co. (Edward H. & Robert H. Martin) 103 Pearl

Martin F. E. & Co. (Frank F. Martin, Robert E. Sedgwick & H. Southworth Pratt) 26 Pine & 132 Park av.
Martin G. W. & Brother (George W. & Elbert H. Martin) 5 Harrison
Martin R. W. F. & Co. (dissolved) 60 Pine
Martin T. & Brother (Thomas & William Martin) 9 Thomas
Martin W. C. & Co. (Theodore H. Martin, only) 102 Barclay
Martin & Breckinridge (Rufus Martin & David C. Breckinridge) 15 Broad
Martin & Broadhurst (Joseph W. Martin & William Broadhurst jr.) 105 Pearl
Martin & Brother (C. Grayson & W. Clarence Martin) 10 Wall
Martin & Campbell (Andrew Martin & Henry Campbell) 47 Vesey
Martin & Co. (eating h.) (dissolved) 530 Sixth av.
Martin & Co. (meat) (Wilbur F. & George W. & Joshua S. Martin) 144 West
Martin & Daly (dissolved) 2769 Third av.
Martin & Davis (dissolved) 35 Second av.
Martin & Devlin (dissolved) 632 E. 150th
Martin & Dreyer (Charles Martin & Henry H. Dreyer) 1003 Ninth av. & 400 W. 40th
Martin & Fagan (Isabella Martin & Patrick Fagan) 165 & 168 W. 53d
Martin & Fay (Frank B. Martin & John E. Fay) 109 Water
Martin & Flaherty (James G. Martin & John Flaherty) 1 Jones la.
Martin & Gass (Margaret Martin & Anne Gass) 132 E. 15th
Martin & Martin (John M. & George Martin) 235 Fifth av.
Martin & Runyon (Augustus F. R. Martin & Enos Runyon) 100 B'way
Martin & Smith (Isaac P. Martin, Aaron Pennington Whitehead, Michael W. Divine, Richard Stacpoole, John Duer, George A. Strong & Welcome S. Jarvis, only; 50 Wall
Martin & White (John C. Martin & Charles H. White) 2530 Eighth av. 1660 Tenth av. & 136 Alexander av.
Martin, Cook & Lipser (Max Martin, John A. Cook & Samuel L. Lipser) 155 S. 5th av. & 73 Wooster
Martin, Lawrie & Co. (Henry Martin & George P. Lawrie, no Co.) 40 White
Martin's J. M, C., Sons (James M. C. & Samuel F. Martin) 107 Fulton
Martine & Co. (Franklin Martine, no Co.) 94 Reade
Martineau & Pardee (dissolved) 10 Union sq. E.
Martinez R. & Co. (Rafael Martinez, no Co.) 226 E. 9th
Martines & Aberasturi (Lino Martinez & Leoncio Aberasturi) 192 Pearl
Martinka & Co. (Francis J. & Anton Martinka) 403 Sixth av.
Martins & Son (Martin & Eugene Martins) 17 E. 16th
Martire & Padula (dissolved) 345 Broome
Marty John & Son (John & Werner Marty) 7 Av. A
Marvel Mfg. Co. (M. Rosenberg & Co. proprs.) 77 Bowery
Marvin Safe Co. (Willis B. Marvin, Pres.; Wright D. Pownall, Sec. Capital, $60,000. Trustees: Willis D. Marvin, Frank S. Pownall, Robert M. Huntting) 90 S. 5th av. & 265 B'way
Marvin & Tolhurst (Marie B. A. Marvin & Mercy Tolhurst) 922 Sixth av.
Marwede & Buck (John Marwede & George Buck) 813 Canal

FOR THE BEST CO-PARTNERSHIP IN THE BEST CORPORATION SEE PAGE F IN BACK OF BOOK

Marx George E. & Co. (George E. Marx & Moses Block) 771 Tenth av.
Marx Kossuth, Jewelry Co. (Ltd.) (Samuel H. Fluk, Pres.; Simon Sichel, Sec.; Samuel Eichberg, Treas. Capital, $50,000. Directors: Samuel H. Fink, Simon Sichel, Samuel Eichberg) 39 Maiden la.
Marx Max & Co. (Max Marx, no Co.) 195 Pearl
Marx William & Co. (Samuel Marx & Adolph & Ignatz Kempner, only) 489 B'way
Marx H. M. & Son (Henry M. & Henry Marx & James Rothschild) 153 Greene & 50 W. Houston
Marx L. & Son (Lehman & Samuel Marx) 195 Seventh
Marx Brothers (Isaac & Gerard Marx) 85 Av. B
Marx & Co. (Ludwig Marx, no Co. (50 Exchange pl.
Marx & Neuberger (Bertha Marx & Caroline Neuberger) 1591 First av.
Marx & Rawolle (Frederick Marx & Frederick Rawolle) 163 William
Marx & Son (Marcus & Ernest Marx) 314 Church
Marx & Weis (David Marx & Moses Weis) 180 B'way
Marx's P., Son (George D. Marx) 412 E. 13th
Marxen & Co. (dissolved) 48 Pearl
Maryland Coal Co. (Henry Loveridge, Pres.; Henry B. Nedham, Sec. Capital, $4,400,000. Directors: George L. Kingsland, Ludlow Patton, Frank T. Robinson, Henry Loveridge, Daniel S. Appleton, Henry Janes, George P. Bangs, John E. Knapp, Nicholas Rath, John G. Wendel) 35 B'way
Maryland Meter & Mfg. Co. (Dickey, Tansley & Co. propra.) 766 B'wny
Maryland & Delaware Ship Canal Co. (inf. unattainable) 35 B'way
Mashin Daniel & Co. (dissolved) 192 E. 4th
Masini Antonio & Co. (no inf.) 379 Water
Mason George C. & Co. (George C. Mason, Alfred Muchmore & John Raymond) 19 Hudson & 180 Reade
Mason John S. & Co. (Ichabod T. & Thomas & Henry K. S. Williams, only) 340 Eleventh av.
Mason John W. & Co. (John W. Mason, Charles H. Blake & George B. Sterling) 52 Dey
Mason E. T. & Co. (Edmund T. & Henry J. Mason) 71 Franklin
Mason J. W. & Co. (Joel W. Mason, John Dawson, Frank Chichester & John T. Smith) 375 Pearl, 394 Madison & 237 Monroe
Mason W. B. & Co. (William B. Mason & William C. Salmon) 232 G'wich
Mason Brothers (Charles B. & Stephen H. Mason jr.) 74 E. 78th, 274 Mercer & 1174 Ninth av.
Mason & Bell (Marcus Mason & Jefferson D. Bell) 345 Produce Ex.
Mason & Co. (Owen R. & William M. Mason) 320 Madison av.
Mason & Hanson (Arthur L. Mason & David N. Hanson jr.) 79 Spring
Mason & Quigley (Thomas Mason & Michael Quigley) 16 South
Mason & Ranch (Joseph Mason & Henry Rauch) 62 Centre
Mason & Raynor (dissolved) 147 E. 130th
Mason & Smith (T. Henry Mason & William H. Smith) 52 B'way
Mason, Chapin & Co. (Earl Philip Mason, William P. Chapin, Samuel L. Peck & Edward E. Arnold) 58 Pine
Masonic Guild & Mutual Benefit Ass'n. (Robert Black, Pres.; Z. Francis Barnes, Sec. Directors: Robert Black, John H. Bonnington, Cyrus O. Hubbell, Samuel W. Strickland, Adolphus D. Pape, Benjamin T. Lynch, Andrew D. Martin, Frederick Heeg, J. Edward Colpe, Jared Timpson, Marcus S. Moss, Z. Francis Barnes) 243 B'way

Masonic Publishing Co. (Catharine M. Barker, propr.) 63 Bleecker
Massachusetts & Southern Construction Co. (Azariah B. Harris, Pres.; William G. McIntyre, Sec. Capital, $250,000; further inf. refused) 45 B'way
Massau & Hanley (dissolved) 5 W. B'way
Massey S. J. & A. G. (no inf.) 756 B'way
Masson & Charron (Julien Masson & Emile L. Charron) 195 Bleecker
Mast J. B., Co. (refused) 111 Mercer
Mast M. J. & Son (dissolved) 825 Washn.
Masten & Nichols (Arthur H. Masten & George L. Nichols jr.) 145 B'way
Master Car Builders Ass'n. (Ross Kells, Pres.; William G. Pomeroy. Sec.; Calvin A. Smith, Treas.) 113 Liberty
Master Stevedores' Ass'n. (George W. Tucker, Pres.; Arthur M. Smith, Sec.; Thomas Rose, Treas.) 81 South
Masterson & Neary (Andrew Masterson & Edward Neary) ft. E. 82d
Masullo J. & Son (Joseph & Januro Masullo) 66 Spring
Matchett James J. & Co. (James J. Matchett, no Co.) 43 Cortlandt
Matchless Lighting Co. (George K. Cooke, propr.) 132 Reade
Material Men's Mercantile Ass'n. (Ltd.) (Irving M. Avery, Pres.; further inf. refused) 154 Nassau
Mather J. C. & Co. (John C. Mather & Donald H. Matheson) 20 Lispenard
Mather & Wentworth (Charles E. Mather & John W. Wentworth) 16 Maiden la.
Mather's George, Sons (Ralph N. Porlee & estate of S. Talmage Mather, only) 60 John
Mathesius & Vallosio (William Mathesius & Joseph Vallosio) 1300 B'way
Matheson William J. & Co. (William J. Matheson, no Co.) 178 Front
Matheson & Ferres (William E. Matheson & Allan J. Ferres) 120 B'way
Mathews James & Son (James & William J. Mathews) 506 E. 19th & 172 E. 110th
Mathews O. & Son (Owen & Allen L. Mathews) 23 Howard
Mathews Brothers (no inf.) 29 Bedford
Mathews, Blum & Vaughan (John Mathews, Joseph A. Blum & Charles D. Vaughan) 83 Leonard
Mathewson J. B. & Co. (Charles H. S. Hubbard, Henry A. Monroe & Charles H. Cooke, only) 20 Maiden la.
Mathowson & Keane (Rollin Mathewson & David Keane) 146 B'way
Mathey Brothers, Mathez & Co. (John L. & August S. Mathey, Fritz H. Mathez & Charles H. Meylan) 16 Maiden la.
Mathias H. & Sons (Jacob & Samuel Mathias, only) 28 Peck sl.
Mathie Soeurs (Amelia & Frances Mathie) 122 Park av.
Mathlen & Gerz (estate of Auguste N. Mathlen & William P. Gerz) 1267 B'way
Mathushek & Son (Victor Hugo Mathushek, only) 313 W. 125th
Matler Henry & Co. (Henry Matler, John Rogers, Mark Finley & Robert & Alexander S. Matler) 17 White
Mattcawan Mfg. Co. (Charles R. Henderson, Pres.; Norman Henderson, Sec. Capital, $150,000. Trustees: Charles R. Henderson, Willard H. Mase, Norman Henderson) 789 B'way
Mattern Brothers (Gustave & Jacob Mattern) 125 W. 28th

TYPEWRITING DONE BY THE TROW CITY DIRECTORY CO., 11 University Place.

MAT 190 MEA

Mattes E. & Son (Max Mattes, only) 138 Wooster
Mattfeld & Claire (no inf.) 324 E. 77th
Matthews Decorative Glass Co. (George Matthews, Pres.; James S. Ferguson, Sec.; John H. Matthews, Treas. Capital, $75,000. Directors: George Matthews, James H. Ferguson, John H. Matthews) 328 E. 20th
Matthews John, The Firm of (George & John H. Matthews) 449 First av.
Matthews & Co. (bags) (James E. Matthews, no Co.) 168 Church
Matthews & Co. (sauce) (dissolved) 138 Reade
Matthews & Hays (John D. Matthews & Simon Hays) 108 W. 82d
Matthews & Pierson (James C. Matthews & Frank A. Pierson) 1180 B'way
Matthews & Rofkar (James W. Matthews & John Rofkar) 192 B'way
Matthews & Smith (James Matthews & Frank E. Smith) 91 Cortlandt
Matthews, Underhill & Co. (John C. B. Matthews & Henry M. Underhill, no Co.) 197 Chambers
Matthiessen F. O. & Wiechers Sugar Refining Co. (Francis O. Matthiessen, Pres.; Henry E. Niss, Sec.; John J. Jurgensen, Treas.; further inf. refused) 106 Wall
Mattson Rubber Co. (Henry Lemmermann, Pres.; John Behrens, Treas. Capital, $75,000. Trustees; Henry Lemmermann, John Behrens, E. H. Hines) 3 College pl.
Matty M. & Co, (Charles & Marie Matty) 335 E. 77th
Mauger & Avory (Nicholas Mauger & Charles F. Avory) 105 Reade
Maul Hugo & Co. (Hugo Maul & Frederick Laudenberger) 10 Bond
Maurer Henry & Son (Henry & Henry A. Maurer) 420 E. 23d
Maurer Brothers (dissolved) 2228 Eighth av.
Maurer & Miller (Charles Maurer & Martin Miller) 18 Fulton mkt
Mauriao & Bishop (Eugene A. Mauriao & Sydney Bishop) 38 Broad
Mauthe & Brother (Conrad & John J. Mauthe) 506 & 642 Eleventh av.
Mautner J. & L. (Julius & Louis) 94 Bond
Maverick & Wissinger (Brewster Maverick & Jacob G. Wissinger) 176 Fulton
Maxcy Brothers (Thomas F. & David Maxcy) 506 E. 14th
Maxfield J. B. & Co. (Joseph B. Maxfield, no Co.) 75 Park pl.
Maxfield & Todd (John F. Maxfield & Herbert W. Todd) 101 Park pl.
Maxheimer & Beresford (John H. Maxheimer & George C. Beresford) 3 Maiden la.
Maxwell Crawford & Son (dissolved) 822 South & 403 Front
Maxwell & Dempsey (Robert C. Maxwell & John M. Dempsey) 277 Cherry
Maxwell & Graves (J. Rogers Maxwell, Henry Graves & Henry W. Maxwell) 192 B'way
Maxwell & Mansfield (dissolved) 186 Bowery
Maxwell & Radford (dissolved) 224 Grand
May John & Brother (John & Otto May) 230 First av.
May A. S. & Co. (Albert S. & Frieda May) 13 Walker
May J. A. & Brother (Julius A. & Edward May) Vandam c G'wich
May Brothers (refused) 47 Murray
May & Grover (E. Hinsdale May & Ernest Grover) 835 B'way
May & Higgins (John May & Hugh Higgins) 48 Av. D

Mayer Charles & Co. (Charles & Albert Mayer) 41 Dey
Mayer Charles F. & Co. (Charles F. Mayer & John Oehler) 515 Ninth av.
Mayer Henry & Co. (Henry & Albert Mayer) 88 Prince
Mayer John V. & Co. (John V. Mayer & Henry A. Maeltzer) 100 Second
Mayer Otto G. & Co. (Otto G. Mayer & William Jox) 9 Bridge
Mayer Robert & Co. (Louis V. Hengstler & Joseph A. Kapp, only) 50 Barclay
Mayer Theobald & Son (Theobald & Theobald P. Mayer) 209 First av.
Mayer A. & Co. (Abraham Mayer, Joseph W. Wenk & Emil L. Mayer) 29 Walker
Mayer M. & A. (Mary & Amelia) 250 E. 50th
Mayer M. & B. (dissolved) 23 Thompson av. W. Washn. mkt
Mayer M. & C. (Max W. & Charles) 892 B'way
Mayer M. & S. (Matilda & Sophia) 815 B. 49th
Mayer Brothers (clothing) (Solomon & Ferdinand Mayer) 268 & 284 Bowery
Mayer Brothers (shades) (Abraham Mayer, only) 204 & 206 W. 23d
Mayer & Coppock (Henry Mayer & Samuel Coppook) 16 G'wich
Mayer & Stern (dissolved) 358 Canal
Mayer & Way (Joseph Mayer & Edward G. Way) 52 W. 23d
Mayer Brothers & Co. (Carl & Simon & William Mayer) 60 Wall
Mayer, Feld & Co. (Jacob Mayer, I. August Feld & Henry Dexheimer) 11 Lawrence
Mayor, Strouse & Co. (Saly I. Mayor, Abraham Strouse & Max Adler) 412 B'way
Mayer's Joseph, Sons (Gerson Mayer, only) 193 Pearl
Mayers & Brother (dissolved) 615 B'way
Mayerson & Simon (Abraham I. Mayerson & Moses Simon) 12 Elizabeth
Mayfield Milk & Cream Co. (Dennis & Austin, propr.) 759 Third av.
Mayhew & Carrington (Alfred P. Mayhew & Charles L. Carrington) 100 B'way
Maynard Effingham & Co. (Effingham Maynard & Everett Yeaw) 771 B'way
Maynard F. S. & Co. (Francis S. Maynard & John R. Stevens) 210 Washn.
Mayo & Watson (dissolved) 40 W. B'way
Mayor, Lane & Co. (George Lane, Pres.; Louis F. Merian, Sec.; Victor A. Harder, Treas. Capital, $30,000. Trustees: George Lane, Louis F. Merian, Victor A. Harder) 119 Walker, 44 Mott & 161 E. 54th
Maywood Brown Stone Co. (R. McDonald Reynolds, Pres. ; Miner D. Randall, Sec. ; Perrin H. Sumner, Treas. Capital, $2,000,000. Directors: S. E. & R. McDonald Reynolds, Miner D. & J. Sturges Randall, Arthur E. & Perrin H. Sumner) 198 B'way
Mazapil Copper Co. (dissolved) 71 B'way
Mazoyer L. & Co. (dissolved) 348 Fourth av. & 240 E. 70th
Mazzeo Brothers (Joseph & Dominick Mazzeo) 256 W. 15th
Mazzetti Louis F. (Sophia A. Mazzetti, only) 44 W. 125th, 867 Sixth av. & 1217 Ninth av.
Mead Edwin & Ralph jr. & Co. (Edwin & Ralph jr. & Alfred P. Mead) 18 Coenties sl. & 36 Front
Mead Frederick & Co. (Frederick Mead, James Voorhis & Frederick Mead jr.) 138 Pearl & 104 Water
Mead Titus & Co. (Titus & Ivon T. Mead & Thomas J. Rielly) 51 Wall
Mead A. E. & Co. (dissolved) 200 W. 34th

THADDEUS DAVIDS CO., WRITING INKS, SEALING WAX, MUCILAGE.
MAKE THE BEST

MEA 191 MEL

Mead C. L. & Son (Charles L. & C. Henry Mead) 103 R. 125th & 2495 Eighth av.
Mead F. W. & Co. (George E. Mead, only) 28 Liberty
Mead H. V. & Co. (Henry V. Mead, Louis P. Van Riper & William H. Smith) 422 Eighth av.
Mead I. F. & Co. (Isaac F. Mead & Thomas H. Curtis) 66, 841 & 1181 B'way & 19 New
Mead N. R. & Son (dissolved) 25 E. 17th
Mead Brothers (William & Henry Mead) 980 Sixth av.
Mead & Barry (Michael J. Mead & Charles Barry) 28 E. 20th
Mead & Mulligan (dissolved) 500 Pearl
Mead & Rossman (George H. Mead & Jonas A. Rossman) 477 Fourth av.
Mead, Mason & Co. (Charles & Charles E. Mead & William G. & William M. Mason) 820 Madison av.
Mead's G. & H., Sons (Halsey & George H. Mead) 97 Pine
Meader William & Co. (William Meader & Herman Scholl) 152 William
Meagher J. & E. (James A. & Edward P.) 427 Tenth av. & 682 W. 34th
Meagher N. & Brother (Nicholas & C. Walter Meagher) 484 Tenth av. & 396 Eleventh av.
Meagher S. F. & Co. (Stephen F. Meagher & Maurice H. Baumgarten) 24 White
Meagher Brothers (refused) 241 Canal
Meath T. & Co. (Thomas Meath & James McGarrigle) 165 Greene
Mccabe Charles P. & Son (Henry H. & Orlando S. Mccabe, only) 291 Washn.
Mechanical Invention Co. (Ltd.) (Frank G. Johnson, Pres.; Frank R. Johnson, Sec.; William T. B. Milliken, Treas. Capital, $15,000. Directors: Frank G. & Frank R. Johnson, William T. B. Milliken, Charles Ruston, I. Newton Williams) 287 D'way
Mechanical Publishing & Engineers Supply Co. (Edwin A. Hayes, propr.) 203 West
Mechanics' Ice Co. (L. H. Adams & Co. proprs.) 234 E. 121st
Mechanics' National Bank (Horace E. Garth, Pres.; William Sharp jr, Cashier; William Q. Riddle, Notary. Capital, $2,000,000. Directors: Henry F. Spaulding, Henry E. Nesmith, Alexander E. Orr, William B. Kendall, Charles H. Isham, Lowell Lincoln, Henry Hentz, Eckstein Norton, Charles M. Pratt, Henry Talmadge, Thomas Miller, John Sinclair, William Sharp jr.) 87 Wall
Mechanics' & Traders' Bank (Meyer Thalmessinger, Pres.; Fernando Baltes, Cashier; Thomas J. McKee, Notary. Capital, $200,000. Surplus, $200,000. Directors: Meyer Thalmessinger, George W. Roosevelt, Thomas E. Tripler, G. Schwab, Thomas J. McKee, Leo Schleslnger, Nathan Peck, Samuel Cohn, Edward Illhon, Isaac D. Einstein, Carl Callmann, James W. Clark jr. John P. O'Brien, Kaufman Mandell, John N. Hayward, Isaiah Josephi, Joseph A. Wooley, Joshua Piza, Ignatz Boskowitz, Fernando Baltes) 486 B'way
Mechanics' & Traders' Exchange (Samuel I. Acken, Pres.; Henry W. Redfield, Sec.; Edmund A. Vaughan, Treas.) 14 Vesey
Mecke & Co. (Edward & Herman Mecke) 55 Ferry
Mecklem Brothers (William Mecklem, only) 287 G'wich
Medford Fancy Goods Co. (Isidor Bremer, Pres.; Capital, $40,000; further inf. refused) 44 Duane
Medical Monthly Publishing Co. (Frederick C. Heppenheimer, Pres.; Charles Kahler, Sec. Capital, $5,000. Directors: Frederick C. Heppenheimer, Charles Kahler, Frederick W. Holls) 120 B'way
Medico-Legal Journal Assn. (William G. Davies,

Pres.; George Lawyer, Sec.; Clark Bell, Treas. Capital, $2,000. Directors: William G. Davies, Clark Bell, George Lawyer, David McAdam, Richard B. Kimball) 57 B'way
Medico-Legal Soc. (Clark Bell, Pres.; Albert Bach, Sec.; Lucy M. Hall, Treas.) 57 B'way
Medley & Clements (Antonio Medley & Leopold Clements) 140 Seventh av.
Medina J. A. (Joaquin A. Medina :—special partner, Pablo Gonzales, Merida, Mex., $20,000 ; terminates 20th Feb. 1892) 104 John
Medlicott Morgan Co. (James C. Cooley, Pres.; Henry J. Straukamp, Sec.; Henry M. Morgan, Treas. Capital, $15,000. Trustees: James C. Cooley, Henry J. Straukamp, William B. Medlicott) 113 Duane
Medole John & Son (John & George J. Medole) 23 Vandewater
Mee Kee & Co. (Quan Yue & Tam Tong, only) 49 Bayard
Mee D. & Co. (dissolved) 120 Liberty
Meehan F. & H. (dissolved) 555 First av.
Meehan & Co. (dissolved) 75 Gold
Meehan & Dugan (dissolved) 254 Tenth
Meehan & Schramm (Patrick C. Meehan & Arnold H. E. Schramm) 95 Front
Meehan & Wilson (Thomas Meehan & James Wilson) 298 Bowery
Meeker & Carter (Frederick W. Meeker & James W. Carter) 205 B'way
Meeker & Co. (Elizabeth J. Smith, only) 346 Sixth av.
Meeker, Payne & Co. (Caroline H. Meeker, William G. Payne, Joseph E. Brister & Jesse L. Eddy) 1 B'way
Meeks W. F. & Co. (William F. & Samuel A. Meeks) 0 Murray
Meenan & Duff (Daniel Meenan & Patrick F. Duff) 670 Third av.
Meerbott William & Son (dissolved) 59 Nassau
Megros, Portier, Groso & Co. (dissolved) 85 Grand
Megros, Portier, Magny & Co. (Louis Megros, Henry Portier & estate of Georges Magny, Co. refused) 457 Broome
Mehaffey & Phillips (William H. Mehaffey & Charles H. Phillips) 437 D'way
Mehl John & Co. (John & John jr. & Henry & Emil F. H. Mohl) 282 B'way
Mehlen's Family Oil Co. (Ltd.) (refused) 60 B'way
Mehlich & Ruckert (William H. Mehlich & Wendelin Ruckert) 21 Park row
Mehlin Paul G. & Sons (Paul G. & Henry P. Mehlin, only) 461 W. 40th
Mehlman Brothers (Frederick J. Mehlman, only) 276 Sixth av.
Mehrtens Brothers (Herman & Henry Mehrtens) 531 E. 185th
Mei Lee Wa & Co. (Wong He Chong & Wong Quong Chong, only) 10 Bowery
Meier George & Co. (George Meier, Arnold Uhlfelder & Samuel J. Landauer) 185 William
Meierdiercks J. A. & Sons (John A. & John jr. & Charles Meierdiercks) 710 Water
Meincke & Schliemann (Gustav Meincke & Peter Schliemann) 982 First av.
Meiners & Schnette (Gustav Meiners & Henry Schnette) 709 Eighth av.
Meinhold & Heineman (Henry Meinhold & Henry Heineman) 55 Warren
Meinken E. A. & Co. (dissolved) 1065 First av.
Meirowitz & Altman (Ignatz Meirowitz & Samuel Altman) 370 E. Houston
Meissner, Ackermann & Co. (Charles F. L. Meissner & Charles F. Ackermann, no Co.) 27 Beaver
Meldowny John V. & Son (John V. Meldowny jr. only) 68 South

Melick J. W. & Co. (John W. Melick & Franklin J. Minck) 199 Duane

Meliff Brothers (Patrick & James Meliff) 1617 B'way

Mellen Brothers (John L. & Peter Millen) 114½ Bowery

Mellen & Kirby (Nathan C. Mellen & Henry P. Kirby) 55 B'way

Mellen, Westell & Kirby (dissolved) 55 B'way

Mellinger Brothers (no inf.) r 159 Attorney

Melrose Hat Co. (Isaac Rummelsburg, propr.) 2925 Third av.

Meltzner Brothers (Joseph & Benso Meltzner) 593 B'way

Melville Hat Mfg. Co. (not Inc.) (Abijah H. Topping, Edwin Maynard, Samuel Raymond & Frank Comstock) 677 B'way

Melvin & Fuller (no inf.) 229 B'way

Memory Co. (John A. Shedd, propr.) 4 W. 14th

Memphis & Charleston R.R. Co. (Charles M. McGhee, Pres.; Louis M. Schwan, Sec. Capital, $5,312,725. Directors: Charles M. McGhee, Calvin S. Brice, Samuel Thomas, Samuel Shethar, John T. Martin, John G. Moore, B. H. R. Lyman, Napoleon Hill, Addison White, Henry S. Chamberlain, J. C. Neely) 10 Wall

Memphis, Little Rock & Indian Territory R.R. Co. (Gustave A. J. Milair, Pres.; Frank F. Smith, Sec. Capital, $8,000,000. Directors: Gustave A. J. Milair, Benjamin B. Orr, James F. Fagan, John J. Sumter, Frank F. Smith) 6 Wall

Mena & Ronda (A. P. de Mena & Nicolas Ronda) 1126 Ninth av.

Menahan John & Co. (Henry S. Cross, only) 147 Mulberry

Mende Alexander P. & Co. (Alexander P. Mende, no Co.) 108 Broad

Mendel M. W. & Brother (Marx W. Mendel, only) 17 Bowery

Mendel Brothers (clothing) (Herman & Andrew Mendel) 13 E. 4th

Mendel Brothers (men's furng.) (Moses I. & Pynckney Mendel) 212 Grand

Mendel & Tompkins (Samuel Mendel & George V. Tompkins) 26 Darling al.

Mendels E. S. jr. & Co. (Emanuel S. Mendels, only) 80 B'way

Mendelsohn A. & Co. (Abraham & Jacob Mendelsohn) 1435 First av.

Mendelsohn & Co. (Moses & Sigmund Mendelsohn) 18 White

Mendelson Brothers (Solomon & Jonas & Henry Mendelson) 93 Grand

Mendes D. De S. & Co. (D. De Sola & Leonard P. Mendes) 49 Maiden la.

Mendes E. A. & Co. (Emanuel A. Mendes & Edward McCrea) 69 Pearl

Mendy J. & Co. (dissolved) 250 G'wich

Menendez José & Co. (José Menendez & Claudio F. Doffiarry) 171 Pearl

Menendez Jose Ma & Co. (Jose Ma Menendez—special partner, Pedro R. Gayo, $10,000; terminates 31st Jan. 1891) 222 Pearl

Menendez & Rodriguez (Joaquin Menendez & Jose Rodriguez) 5 Cedar

Mengel & Co. (dissolved) 319 Canal, 117 W. B'way, 97 Mercer & 86 Wooster

Menke, Brassel & Co. (John Menke, William Brassel & Henry Gutmann) 47 Greene

Menlo Park Ceramic Works (Jeremiah T. Smith, propr.) 11 Pine

Mente & Clause (Albert Mante & Albert Clause) 26 Maiden la.

Mentges & Burmeister (Frederick P. Mentges & Christian Burmeister) 78 Rutgers

Menton Brothers (dissolved) 551 W. 51st

Menut E. B. & Co. (Edouard B. Menut:—special partner, G. Hilton Scribner, *Yonkers, N. Y.*, $20,000; terminates, 11th June, 1891) 29 Ferry

Menzel William & Son (Hugo Menzel, only) 16 Exchange pl.

Mercadante & Freschi (Ignacio B. Mercadante & George Freschi) 69, 96 & 340 Bowery

Mercantile Benefit Assn. (Joseph W. Congdon, Pres.; Ira W. Steward, Sec. Directors: Winfield S. Gilmore, William Wills, S. Ellis Briggs, John W. Jacobus, Alonzo Alford, Henry Rosenheim, Alburn R. Krum, Joseph Gates, Alfred W. Duxbury, Gardner F. Badger) 319 B'way

Mercantile Cloak Co. (not inc.) (Isaac S. & Ralph Flaut & Samuel Kahn) 394 B'way

Mercantile Co-operative Bank (Stephen W. Fullerton, Pres.; Edward B. Walker jr. Sec.; Charles H. Spencer, Treas. Directors: Stephen W. Fullerton, H. C. Alleman, Eugene S. Eunson, Edward B. Walker jr. Charles H. Spencer, Grant B. Taylor, L. G. Gadd) 37 Wall

Mercantile Credit League (Harris & Harper, attorneys) 280 B'way

Mercantile Fire Ins. Co. (in liquidation) 10 Wall

Mercantile Library Assn. (T. S. Rumney, Pres.; Augustus Wetmore jr. Sec.; Whittlesey D. Searls, Treas. Directors: Charles H. Patrick, Charles Wager Hull, Alexander M. Eagleson, Frederick A. Sandland, James Magee, John Byers, J. L. Graham, M. E. Townsend) 67 & 426 Fifth av. & 33 Liberty

Mercantile Mutual Accident Soc. (dissolved) 234 B'way

Mercantile National Bank (William P. St. John, Pres.; Frederick B. Schonck, Cashier; Thomas S. Vanvolkenburgh, Notary. Capital, $1,000,000. Directors: Charles T. Barney, William C. Browning, Charles L. Colby, George W. Grossman, Henry T. Kneeland, Emanuel Lehman, Seth M. Milliken, George H. Sargent, Charles M. Vail, Isaac Wallach, James M. Wentz, Francis H. N. Whiting, Richard H. Williams, Frederick B. Schenck, William P. St. John) 191 B'way

Mercantile Photograph & Photo Engraving Co. (Elizabeth A. Blauvelt, propr.) 63 Duane

Mercantile Press (no inf.) 44 Gold

Mercantile Printing & Stationery Co. (William Scott, propr.) 709 B'way

Mercantile Purchasing Co. (Samuel Davidson, propr.) 30 Maiden la.

Mercantile Safe Deposit Co. (Lyman Rhoades, Pres.; Elmer M. Billings, Sec.; George Bosauwen, Treas. Capital, $300,000. Trustees: Henry B. Hyde, Henry A. Hurlbut, Lyman Rhoades, Henry S. Terbell, George W. Phillips, D. F. Randolph, Louis Fitzgerald) 120 B'way

Mercantile Trust Co. (Louis Fitzgerald, Pres.; Henry C. Deming, Sec. Capital, $2,000,000. Trustees: Louis Fitzgerald, John T. Terry, Henry B. Hyde, Edward L. Montgomery, Henry A. Hurlbut, Henry G. Marquand, Russell Sage, Henry M. Alexander, Sidney Dillon, Norvin Green, John W. Hunter, Henry Day, J. Hampden Robb, Austin Corbin, Richard Irvin jr. Thomas T. Eckert, Edward F. Winslow, Thomas Maitland, Brayton Ives, Whitelaw Reid, Frederick L. Ames, James Stokes, James W. Alexander, George L. Rives, A. L. Dennis, Marcellus Hartley, B. F. Randolph, John J. McCook, Elbert B. Monroe, Edward A. Quintard, William H. Slocum, William L. Strong, Charles Coudert, Henry C. Deming, William P. Thompson, William H. Crocker) 120 B'way

Mercantile & Insurance Agency (Havilah D. McBurney, Pres.; Marinus P. Melby, Sec. Capital, $25,000) 291 B'way

Mercer Mining Co. (William H. Whiton, Pres.; Augustus S. Whiton, Sec. Capital, $300,000.

MER 193 MER

Trustees: Augustus S. Whiton, Henry A. Sherrill, William H. Whiton) 115 B'way
Mercer William S. & Co. (dissolved) 96 B'way
Mercer J. P. & Brother (no inf.) r 129 W. 25th
Merchant S. L., Co. (Stephen L. Merchant, propr.) 15 State
Merchant Steel Assn. (James W. Brown, Chairman; L. Cryder Lea, Sec.) 15 Cortlandt
Merchant & Co. (met ds) (Clarke & Harry W. Merchant) 9 Burling sl
Merchant & Co. (pat. meds.) (William J. Merchant & Isaac F. Mead) 118 Pearl
Merchants' Assn. of N. Y. (John Reed Smith, Pres.; Francis B. Thurber, Treas.; Charles Burkhalter, Sec. Capital, $20,000. Directors: John Reed Smith, Frank Sittig, Robert A. Powers, Francis B. Thurber, Charles Burkhalter, Robert B. Davis) 5 Harrison
Merchants' Casualty Ins. Assn. (George J. Medole, Pres.; L. C. York, Sec. Directors: Aaron Brinkerhoff, William D. Barron, L. C. York, F. A. Winans, William J. Groo, John R. Pawling, Henry T. Boyle, F. Williams, Charles L. Coon, George J. Medole, F. R. Huntington) 21 Park row
Merchants' Commercial Credit Assn. (Henry B. Kinghorn, propr.) 32 Warren & 102 Chambers
Merchants' Construction Co. (William C. Joy, Pres.; Samuel J. Burrell, Sec.; further inf. refused) 54 Broad
Merchants' Despatch Transp. Co. (James C. Fargo, Pres.; Francis F. Flagg, Sec. Capital, $5,000,000. Directors: James C. Fargo, Francis F. Flagg, William K. Vanderbilt, Chauncey M. Depew, Charles C. Clarke, Horace J. Hayden, Theodore M. Pomeroy, Charles Fargo) 335 B'way, 119 Front & 1 Beaver
Merchants' Exchange National Bank (Phineas C. Lounsbury, Pres.; Allen S. Apgar, Cashier; Jonathan Marshall, Notary. Capital, $600,000. Directors: Robert Seaman, Jesse W. Powers, Joseph Thomason, Allen S. Apgar, Alfred M. Hoyt, Phineas C. Lounsbury, James G. Powers, Alfred J. Taylor, E. Christian Körner, Lucius H. Biglow, John H. Hanan, Isaac G. Johnson, Timothy L. Woodruff, Lyman Brown) 257 B'way (see top lines)
Merchants' Ins. Co. (John H. Morris, Pres.; Isaac S. Mettler, Sec. Capital, $200,000. Directors: John F. Papke, James L. Wise, John Watson, E. Christian Korner, John T. Wilson, William Mustace, Albert N. & J. Romaine Brown, William Morrison, George W. Powers, Jonas Stremmell, Thomas E. Ostrander) 115 B'way
Merchants' Lighterage Co. (Andrew J. Wight, Pres.; Jesse Benton, Treas.; James S. Wight, Sec.; further inf. refused) 20 South
Merchants' Line (S. C. Evans & Co., proprs.) 36 South & Pier 10 E. R.
Merchants' Line (W. R. Grace & Co., proprs.) 1 Hanover sq. & Pier 13 E. R.
Merchants' National Bank (Jacob D. Vermilye, Pres.; Cornelius V. Banta, Cashier; James G. Baldwin, Notary. Capital, $2,000,000. Directors: Jacob D. Vermilye, John A. Stewart, Henry Sheldon, Hugh Auchincloss, Elbert A. Brinckerhoff, Charles S. Smith, David Dows, Jacob Wendell, Henry Hilton, William G. Vermilye, Gustav H. Schwab) 42 Wall
Merchants' Print Works (Wellington & Johnson, proprs.) 415 W. 14th
Merchants' Real Es ate Co. (Jacob Wendell, Pres.; Gordon Wendell, Treas.; further inf. refused) 61 Worth
Merchants' Sample Card Co. (refused) 25 Howard
Merchants' Steam Laundry (Julius & Joseph G. Wallach, proprs.) 753 Sixth av. & 154 E. 67th
Merchants' Steamboat Co. (Charles H. Throckmorton, Sec.; James S. Throckmorton, Treas.; further inf. unattainable) Pier 24 (new) N. R.

Merchants' Stencil Works (John N. Burns, propr.) 281 G'wich
Merchants' Towel Supply Co. (Burns & Knapp, proprs.) 126 Chambers
Merchants' Transp. Co. (Horatio N. Holt, propr.) 1 B'way
Merchants' Union Collection Agency (Max Bayersdorfer, Pres.; Henry Seldner, Sec.; Christian Schaefer, Treas. Directors: Max Bayersdorfer, Henry Seldner, Christian Schaefer) 620 B'way
Merchants' Warehouse Co. (dissolved) 63 Beaver & 50 Jay
Merchants' & Manufacturers' Law & Collecting Agency (Henry C. Banks, Pres.; Arthur A. Anderson, Sec., Henry G. Conklin, Treas. Capital, $10,000. Directors: James T. Williamson, William Shrady, Walter W. Livingston, Howard E. Sinclair, Elwood Montague, Paul C. Archer) 194 B'way
Merchants' & Tanners' Line (Hunt & Donaldson, proprs.) Pier 24 (new) N. R.
Merck E. (Wilhelm & J. H. E. & E. A. & Carl & W. Merck & Theodore Weicker) 73 William
Mergenthaler Printing Co. (Lemon G. Hine, Pres.; Frederick J. Warburton, Treas.; Daniel O. McEwen, Sec. Capital, $1,000,000. Trustees: Samuel M Bryan, J. O. Clephane, John Dunbar, Sulicon Hutchins, Lemon G. Hine, Ogden Mills, Daniel C. McEwen, William H. Smith, Frederick J. Warburton) 154 Nassau
Mergenthaler & Co. (John N. Mergenthaler & Morris Schlossheimer) 122 Park row
Mergentime J. H. & Co. (James H. Mergentime & William Lamm) 168 Chambers
Meriden Britannia Co. (Horace C. Wilcox, Pres.; George H. Wilcox, Sec.; George R. Curtis, Treas. Capital, $1,100,000. Directors: Horace C. Wilcox, Isaac C. Lewis, W. W. Lyman, George R. Curtis, D. B. Hamilton, Charles L. Mitchell, George Rockwell, George H. Wilcox, George M. Curtis) 46 E. 14th
Merkel H. & C. (Henry & Conrad) 65 W. 37th
Merkel & Kupfer (Louis J. Merkel & Otto Kupfer) 19 Whitehall
Merkle F. O. & Co. (Frederick O. Merkle & John T. Richards) 20 Exchange pl.
Merklen Brothers (Valentine & Martin & Michael & Benjamin & Ignace & Xavier Merklen) 300 Third
Merle & Co. (Henry J. Merle & William L. Andree) 71 Wall
Merrell Brothers (William H. & Augustus M. Merrell) 32 E. 14th
Merriam Edward J. (firm) (dissolved) 156 William
Merriam J. S. & Son (John S. & William H. Marriam) 113 E. 84th
Merrill Charles E. & Co. (Charles E. & Edwin C. Merrill) 743 B'way
Merrill & Co. (William Merrill, no Co.) 90 Varick
Merrill & Rogers (Payson Merrill, Noah C. Rogers & Donald B. Toucey) 111 B'way
Merrill & Wehrle Charcoal Co. (Warren M. Merrill, Pres.; Frederick J. Wehrle, Sec. Capital, $30,000; further inf. refused) 549 W. 25th
Morrill's Robert, Sons (William G. & George W. Merrill) 179 Water
Merritt Dr. Charles & Sons (Charles & John P. & Charles G. Merritt) 29 W. 42d
Merritt Mfg. Co. (Carlos C. Alden, Sec.; further inf. unattainable) 59 William
Merritt & Conway (Roland Merritt, & William L. Conway) 1602 W. Farms rd.
Morritt & Ronaldson (William H. Merritt & Thomas Ronaldson) 81 Front
Merritt & Ryan (Frederick R. Merritt & Frank E. Ryan) 624 Eighth av.
Merritt, Osborn & Moore (James C. Merritt, J.

13

TYPEWRITING DONE BY THE TROW CITY DIRECTORY CO., 11 University Place.

MER 194 MET

Kelsey Osborn & Hugh Moore) 320 B'way & 92 Jacob
Merritt's Wrecking Organization (not inc.) (Israel J. & Israel J. Merritt jr.) 49 Wall
Merry John & Co. (John & George E. Merry) 589 W. 15th & 84 Eleventh av.
Marselos P. & Co. (Marselos P. Marselos & Isaac I. Myers, only) 76 Dey
Mersereau W. T. & Co. (William T. Mersereau, George W. Holt & Frank D. Mersereau) 321 B'way & 39 Union sq. W.
Mertens F. W. & Sons (Frederick W. & Frederick W. jr. & Robert E. Mertens) 446 E. 75th
Merwin & Co. (The) (Edward P. Merwin, Pres.; Berkeley R. Merwin, Sec. Capital, $250,000. Directors: Edward P. & Berkeley R. Merwin, Jonathan M. Bishop) 240 Fifth av.
Merwin, Hulbert & Co. (Milan & William A. Hulbert, only) 26 W. 23d
Meryweather & Scott (no inf.) 98 Chambers
Merz George & Son (George & Andrew Merz) 69 Av. B
Merz Louis & Co. (dissolved) 41 Ann
Merz R. & A. (Rose & Anna) 49 W. 125th
Merzbach & Wade (Henry Merzbach & Richard A. Wade) 322 D'wey & 528 Eighth av.
Mesam & Nedwick (dissolved) 80 Fourth av.
Meserole J. S. & Co. (Darwin J. & estate of Jeremiah S. Meserole) 16 Broad
Meserole & Co. (inf. unattainable) 26 Church
Meshel & Jamjachky (dissolved) 51 Bleecker
Messambria Mineral & Timber Co. (inf. unattainable) 150 B'way
Messenger T. H. & Co. (Thomas H. Messenger & Sidney Larremore) 151 Maiden la.
Messer Louis & Co. (Louis Messer & William F. Schlosser) 174 Worth
Messner & Freienstein (Jacob Messner & John Freienstein) 813 Eighth av. & 2394 Third av.
Metal Novelty Co. (Robert Snelder, propr.) 102 Fulton
Metal Stamping Co. (John Watters, Pres.; Jacob Bauer, Sec.; John F. Galvin, Treas. Capital, $25,000. Directors: John Watters, John F. Galvin, Jacob Bauer, Robert Loercher) 329 E. 26th
Metal Tip Wick Co. (Charles S. Terrett, Pres.; William H. Griffing, Sec.; Edward B. Griffing, Treas.; further inf. refused) 70 Cortlandt
Metal & Glass Etching Co. (inf. unattainable) 150 B'way
Metallithic Paving Co. (H. Victor Gause, Pres.; Henry B. B. Stapler, Sec.; George W. Hall, Treas. Capital, $30,000. Directors: H. Victor Gause, George W. Hall, J. Taylor Gause, Benjamin G. Haun, Warner Jenkins, William Tomlinson, Henry B. D. Stapler) 115 B'way
Metallic Burial Case Co. (Scott Tremains, receiver) 260 B'way
Metallic Cap Mfg. Co. (Henry S. Chapman, Pres.; Frank K. Brewster, Sec. Capital, $10,000. Directors: Henry S. Chapman, Frank K. Brewster) 85 B'way
Metallic Construction Co. (no inf.) E. 91st n Av. A
Metallic Sign Cleaning Co. (A. C. Todd, propr.) 712 B'way
Metcalf B. F. & Co. (Benjamin F. Metcalf, no Co.) 190 Front
Metcalf J. B. & Co. (James B. Metcalf, Rensselaer H. Bissell:—special partner, Brayton Ives, $100,000; terminates 1st May, 1891) 8 Broad
Metcalf & Co. (Benjamin F. Metcalf, no Co.) 91 Maiden la.
Metcalf & McCleery (Henry B. Metcalf & William McCleery) 346 Canal
Metcalfe H. T. & Sons (Henry T. & George & Charles Metcalfe) 145 B'way

Meteor Despatch Co. (no inf.) 855 B'way
Methodist Book Concern (Hunt & Eaton, agents) 150 Fifth av.
Methodist Book Concern Employees Co-operative Building & Loan Assn. (inf. unattainable) 52 Union sq. E.
Methodist Episcopal Cemetery (Charles Meytrott, Pres.; Charles Boetger, Sec.; Frederick Hanschildt, Treas. Capital, $25,000. Trustees: Charles Meytrott, Charles Boetger, Frederick Hanschildt, George C. Stehl, John Meytrott, Adam & Sebastian Weiffenbach) 456 E. Houston
Metropole Mfg. Co. (Danenbaum Brothers, proprs.) 72 W. 23d
Metropolis Tin Ware Co. (Simon E. Marum, Pres.; William T. Stewart, Sec. Capital, $25,000. Directors: Simon E. Marum, William T. Stewart, Ralph Danziger) 58 Beekman
Metropolitan Addressing & Mailing Co. (H. D. & E. VanAuken, proprs.) 35 Frankfort
Metropolitan Agency (William D. True, propr.) 685 B'way
Metropolitan Automatic Refrigerating Co. (dissolved) 165 W. 23d & 530 West
Metropolitan Board of Fire Ins. Brokers (Robert C. Rathbone, Pres.; J. Q. Aymar Williamson, Sec.; John H. Rieger, Treas.) 43 Cedar
Metropolitan Building & Loan Assn. (F. J. Butler, Pres.; D. Griffin, Treas.; James C. Dillon, Sec.) 412 Grand
Metropolitan Burglar Alarm Co. (William R. Alling, Pres.; Henry Hayes, Treas. Capital, $50,000. Directors: William R. Alling, D. Untermeyer, James C. Aikin, Henry Hayes, O. F. Homer, Joseph Herzog, Ludwig Nissen) 6 Maiden la.
Metropolitan Cigar Factory (S. Jacoby & Co. proprs.) R. E. 52d
Metropolitan Cloak & Jersey Co. (George Schoen & Co. proprs.) 128 W. B'way
Metropolitan Clothing House (Mayer Brothers, proprs.) 268 & 264 Bowery
Metropolitan Co. (William ap Rees, propr.) 376 Bowery
Metropolitan Conservatory of Music (Groene & Hawley, proprs.) 91 E. 14th
Metropolitan Crosstown Railway Co. (Andres B. Stone, Pres.; Julian A. Hawks, Sec.; Herman L. Kingsbury, Treas. Capital, $300,000. Directors: Andres B. Stone, Charles A. Winch, Warren A. Decker, William Carroll, Alfred Heyn, Herman S. Mendelson, Herman L. Kingsbury) 81 B'way
Metropolitan Dye Works (Charles H. Weigle, propr.) 9 Chrystie, 1500 & 2000 Third av. 140 E. 49th, 734 Eighth av. & Bronx o Samuel
Metropolitan Electric Service Co. (Charles H. Ropes, Pres.; Samuel J. Bailey, Sec. Capital, $100,000. Trustees: Charles H. Ropes, Edwin P. Goodwin, Samuel J. Bailey) 150 B'way & 575 Madison av.
Metropolitan Electric Signal Co. (Charles L. Browne, Pres.; A. Livingston Norman, Sec.; George W. Hart, Treas. Capital, $1,500,000. Directors: Charles L. Browne, Franklin Lynch, George W. Hart, J. Henry Brown, Halcyon M. Close) 45 B'way
Metropolitan Elevated R. R. Co. (Jay Gould, Pres.; Daniel W. McWilliams, Sec. Capital, $6,500,000. Directors: Jay Gould, Robert M. Gallaway, Russell Sage, Samuel Sloan, Sidney Dillon, George J. Gould, J. Pierpont Morgan, John H. Hall, Cyrus W. Field, Edwin Gould, Chester W. Chapin, Simon Wormser, Stephen V. White) 71 B'way
Metropolitan Embossing Works (David Leitner, propr.) 207 Bowery
Metropolitan Embroidering Co. (Samuel A. Caro, propr.) 356 Canal
Metropolitan Exhibition Co. (John B. Day, Pres.

Capital, $7,000. Trustees: John B. Day, Charles T. Dillingham, George F. Duysters) 121 Maiden la.

Metropolitan Ferry Co. (Harry B. Hollins, Pres.; Edward S. Knapp, Sec. Capital, $1,500,000. Directors: Harry B. Hollins, Edward S. Knapp, James T. Woodward, Charles C. Edey, Isaac L. Rice, E. Lehman, N. Biljur) ft. James sl. & ft. E. 34th

Metropolitan Foreign Claim Agency (David J. Cotter, propr.) 685 B'way

Metropolitan Gas Stove Works (Abraham L. Bogart, propr.) 22 Union Sq. E.

Metropolitan Hardware Co. (Robert W. Pryor, Pres.; William J. La Roche, Sec. Capital, $100,000. Directors: Robert W. Pryor, William J. La Roche) 82 Vesey & 76 Church

Metropolitan Hat Mfg. Co. (William S. Kallscher, propr.) 211 Hudson

Metropolitan Improvement Co. (Ltd.) (Adrian Iselin jr. Pres.; Alfred Roosevelt, Sec. Capital, $250,000. Directors: Adrian Iselin jr. Alfred & James A. Roosevelt, Edmund C. Stanton, Auguste Richard) 32 Pine

Metropolitan Iron Works (Julius Benedict, propr.) 549 W. 55th

Metropolitan Job Printing Office (not inc.) (Robert F. Gillin, Joseph H. Tooker, Philip Dillon & Timothy Hayes) 38 Vesey

Metropolitan Laundry (Leopold Stern, propr.) 363 Sixth av.

Metropolitan Leather Chair Works (inf. unattainable) 109 Suffolk

Metropolitan Letter Book Co. (Henry J. Janton, propr) 103 Beekman

Metropolitan Life Ins. Co. (Joseph F. Knapp, Pres.; John R. Hegeman, Sec. Capital, $500,000. Directors: Joseph F. Knapp, Thomas L. James, William Henry Arnoux, Silas B. Dutcher, Enoch L. Fancher, John M. Crane, James L. Stewart, Emery M. Van Tassel, D. O. Ripley, Eli Beard, Hector Toulmin, John R. Hegeman) 32 Park pl.

Metropolitan Loan Co. (Frey & Forgotston, proprs.) 104 E. 125th

Metropolitan Machine Oil Co. (Bernhard Brilles, propr.) 56 Thomas

Metropolitan Mfg. Co. (Ross C. Browning, Pres.; Lyman A. Mills, Sec.; Moses W. Terrill, Treas. Capital, $12,000. Directors: Ross C. Browning, Lyman A. Mills, Moses W. Terrill) 32 Cortlandt, 353 Second av. 229 E. 59th & 1562 First av.

Metropolitan Milk & Cream Co. (Richard W. Macomber, Pres ; Frank B. Wells, Sec. Capital, $10,000. Directors: Richard W. Macomber, Frank B. Wells, Spencer H. Horton, Charles E. Davison, John L. Dye) 185 Sixth av. & 95 Eighth av.

Metropolitan National Bank (in liquidation) 2 Wall

Metropolitan Oil Co. (not inc.) (Marcus J. Stuart & Daniel W. Brigham) 180 Maiden la.

Metropolitan Opera House Co. (Ltd.) (James A. Roosevelt, Pres.; Luther Kountze, Treas.; Edmund C. Stanton, Sec. Capital, $1,295,000. Directors: James A. Roosevelt, George H. Warren, Luther Kountze, George G. Haven, William K. Vanderbilt, William H. Tillinghast, Adrian Iselin, Robert Goelet, Edward Cooper, Henry G. Marquand, George N. Curtis, George P. Wetmore) Seventh av. c W. 39th

Metropolitan Opera Programme Co. (dissolved) 112 Fifth av.

Metropolitan Perfumery Works (Bernhard Brilles, propr,) 56 Thomas

Metropolitan Phonograph Co. (Charles A. Cheever, Pres.; F. Gottschalk, Sec.; Andrew L. Taylor, Treas. Capital, $1,000,000. Trustees: Charles A. Cheever, John L. Martin, Andrew L. Taylor, F. Gottschalk, J. B. Metcalf, Noah Davis, J. S. Auerbach, Jesse Young, J. J. Gunther) 257 Fifth av.

Metropolitan Picture Frame & Art Novelty Co. (Louis Marx, propr.) 217 Canal

Metropolitan Pipe Works (F. J. Kaldenburg, Co. proprs.) 219 E. 33d, 125 Fulton & 6 Astor h.

Metropolitan Plate Glass Ins. Co. (Henry Hartenu, Pres.; Eugene H. Winslow, Sec. Capital, $100,000. Directors: Henry Hartenu, Cyrus B. Davenport, George G. Reynolds, Rufus Litchfield, Joseph S. Spinney, Theodore E. Smith, Felix Campbell, Charles Kellogg, Samuel H. Cornell, Alfred C. Barnes, James M. Leavitt, Matthew P. Robbins, Daniel D. Whitney, Charles T. Corwin, Calvin E. Pratt, Thomas D. Carman, Robert Porterfield, Clement Lockitt, Forter Pettit, Peter Wyckoff, James L. Brumley, John H. Rieger) 56 Liberty

Metropolitan Printing & Publishing Co. (Herbert W. Greene. Pres.; Charles B. Hawley, Sec.; Frederick W. Nostrand, Treas.; further inf. unattainable) 21 E. 14th

Metropolitan R. R. Advertising Co. (no inf.) 10 E 14th

Metropolitan Real Estate Co. (Charles E. Smith, Pres.; Henry C. Craig. Treas.; Lyman Nichols. Sec. Capital, $100,000. Directors : Charles E. Smith, D. M. Bright, Henry C. Craig, Lyman Nichols, H. D. Logan, T. D. Pease) 11 Wall

Metropolitan Rubber Co. (Charles A. Place, Pres.; William B. Dowse, Sec.; Abner J. Tower, Treas. Capital, $125,000. Directors : Charles A. Place, William B. Dowse, Abner J. Tower) 549 B'way

Metropolitan Savings Bank (S. Warren Snoden, Pres.; George N. Conklin, Sec. Directors: Waldo Hutchins, S. Warren Snedon, George N. Conklin, William Burrell, Augustus S. Hutchins, Andrew L. Taylor, John S. Spencer, William Sherer, Charles H. Adams, J. B. Currey, William H. Riblet, Henry Spratley, William F. Raynor, William D. Maxwell) 8 Third av.

Metropolitan Shoe Mfg. & Repairing Co. (Charles Koch, propr.) 457 Sixth av.

Metropolitan Sign Co. (Arnold Perlmann, propr.) 146 Centre

Metropolitan Steam Laundry Co. (Byron Alger, propr.) 222 E. 34th

Metropolitan Storage Warehouse & Van Co. (Ltd.) (inf. unattainable) 202 Mercer & 1485 B'way

Metropolitan Telephone & Telegraph Co. (Charles F. Cutler, Pres.; John H. Cahill, Sec.; William R. Driver, Treas. Capital, $2,000,000 ; further inf. unattainable) 18 Cortlandt

Metropolitan Toilet Co. (Capital, $3,000 ; further inf. unattainable) no address

Metropolitan Toilet Supply Co. (Seymour Samuels, propr.) 72 University pl.

Metropolitan Trust Co. (Thomas Hillhouse, Pres.; Beverley Chew, Sec. Capital, $1,000,000. Trustees: A. Gracie King, Darius O. Mills, Frederick D. Tappen, Morris K. Jesup, John T. Terry, Walter T. Hatch, Collis P. Huntington, Bradley Martin, Dudley Olcoct, Heber R. Bishop, George A. Hardin, J. Howard King, Joseph Ogden, Henry B. Plant, Edward B. Judson, Phineas Prouty, Thomas Hillhouse, William A. Slater, John W. Ellis, W. H. Tillinghast, Robert Hoe, W. Y. Mortimer) 37 Wall

Metropolitan Unitype Printing Co. (dissolved) 63 B'way

Metropolitan Watch Co. (Henry F. Atkinson. Pres.; Harry D. Kingsley, Sec. Capital, $900,000. Trustees: W. H. Chamberlin, Henry F. Atkinson, G. Benson, Harry D. Kingsley, G. Landsman) 80 E. 14th

Metropolitan Wine, Liquor & Tea Co. (refused) 121 Av. A & 421 Seventh av.

Metropolitan Wire Nail Mfg. Co. (dissolved) 312 E. 22d

Metz Albert & Co. (Albert & Albert E. Metz) 60 John

COMPILED WITH ACCURACY AND DESPATCH } **CLASSIFIED BUSINESS LISTS.** { THE TROW CITY DIRECTORY CO. 11 University Place.

MET   196   MEY

Metz R. R. & Co. (Harriet R. & Elias P. Metz) 50 W. 23d

Metz & Meyer (Nathan Metz & Nathan Meyer) 12 Mercer

Metzger Louis & Co. (Louis Metzger & Samuel Schiff) 621 D'way & 188 Mercer

Metzger Martin & Co. (Martin & Otto L. Metzger) 5 Maiden la.

Metzger J. & Co. (Julius Metzger, Paul Mutschler & Albert Bauer) 80 B'way

Metzger L. & Co. (Leo Metzger & James Traub) 1057 Lex. av.

Metzger Brothers (Felix & Abraham Metzger) 1044 Second av.

Metzger & Co. (dissolved) 176 B'way

Metzsterer & Levy (David Metzger & Solomon Levy) 602 W. 40th

Metzger & Schiff (dissolved) 70 Mercer

Meuer S. & Co. (Samuel Meuer & Rachel Goldberg) 56 Bleecker

Mexican Central Telegraph & Telephone Co. (George W. Ballou, Pres.; John J. McGinty, Sec.; John W. Weed, Treas. Capital, $450,000. Directors: George W. Ballou, Charles O. Morris, John W. Weed, John D. Sargent, John J. McGinty) 7 Nassau

Mexican International R. R. Co. (Collis P. Huntington, Pres.; James S. Mackie, Sec.; Frank H. Davis, Treas. Capital, $11,895,500. Directors: Collis P. Huntington, Charles Crocker, Lynde Harrison, Edward L. Plumb, Richard T. Colburn, Edward H. Pardee, Edward St. John) 15 Broad

Mexican National Coal, Timber & Iron Co. (Hanson A. Risley, V. Pres; Charles W. Drake, Treas.; John E. Lundstrom, Sec. Capital, $1,000,000. Directors: William A. Bell, Thomas J. Fisher, Hanson A. Risley, John E. Lundstrom) 32 Nassau

Mexican National Construction Co. (William J. Palmer, Pres.; William W. Nevin, Sec.; Walter Hinchman, Treas. Capital, $7,000,000. Directors: William J. Palmer, Walter Hinchman, William W. Nevin, Henry Amy, Henry Morton, Joseph D. Potts, John H. Small, George Foster Peabody, James Sullivan, D. C. Dodge, Santiago C. Lohse, Manuel Ortega y Reyes, Francisco Noranjo) 32 Nassau

Mexican National R. R. Co. (William G. Raoul, Pres.; Gabriel Morton, Treas.; Andrew Anderson jr. Soc. Capital, $68,350,000. Directors: William G. Raoul, Eckstein Norton, Josiah A. Horsey, Charles C. Beaman, George Coppell, Lloyd Aspinwall, Emilio Velasco, Manuel Saavedra, George F. Peabody, William J. Palmer, James Sullivan, Manuel V. Conde, Justo Sierra) 6 Wall

Mexican Northern Telegraph & Telephone Co. (John W. Weed, Pres.; John J. McGinty, Sec.; Winthrop Pond, Treas. Capital, $200,000. Directors: John W. Weed, Winthrop Pond, William T. Patterson, Robert Colgate, John J. McGinty) 7 Nassau

Mexican Pacific Coast Railway Co. (James S. Negley, Pres.; Morris Cooper, Sec. Directors: James S. Negley, H. M. Munsell, J. H. Rice, Edmund Green, Alonzo B. Cornell, Frank Hopson, Morris Cooper, R. F. Ritchie) 40 Wall

Mexican Telegraph Co. (James A. Scrymser, Pres.; James R. Beard, Sec.; Samuel C. Blackwell, Treas. Capital, $1,500,000. Directors: John E. Alexandre, Edgar S. Auchincloss, Edmund L. Baylies, William G. Hamilton, Charles H. Marshall, J. Pierpont Morgan, Percy R. Pyne, W. Emlen Roosevelt, James A. Scrymser) 87 Wall

Mexican Telephone Co. (inf. unattainable) 68½ Pine

Mexican Tin Mining Co. (inf. unattainable) 60 B'way

Mexican Trust & Investment Co. (James S. Negley, Pres.; Francis A. Bates, Sec. Capital, $3,900,000. Directors: James S. Negley, Edmund Green, Robert G. Ingersoll, E D. Woodruff, M. C. Jewell, Francis A. Bates, Alfred Clarke, Alonzo B. Cornell, J. P. Jones, Preston B. Plumb, Thomas Ewing, Orson Adams, Henry W. Blair, James A. Waymire) 40 Wall

Mexican City Improvement Co. (Bernard Beinecke, Pres.; William H. McCabe, Sec.; Stephen D. Hatch, Treas. Capital, $3,000,000. Directors: Bernard Beinecke, Salvador Malo, Carlos A. de Medina, William H. Hope, Stephen D. Hatch, James W. Elgar, Orestes Cleveland, Manuel A. Kursheedt, Joseph L. Stickney, A. G. Mills, William H. McCabe) 115 D'way

Meyen Charles & Co. (Charles Mayne, only) 154 Nassau

Meyen & Stock (Hans H. Meyen & Bernhard Stock) 660 First av.

Meyer Anton & Son (Anton & Dorothea Meyer, only) 392 Bowery

Meyer Frederick & Co. (Frederick Meyer & Adolf Lehmann) 207 Centre

Meyer H. C. Mfg. Co. (James Conity, Pres. Capital, $30,000. Trustees: James Conity, Henry C. Meyer) no address

Meyer Henry (Fanny J. & Edward H. Meyer, only) 87 Walker

Meyer Henry & Co. (dissolved) 429 First av.

Meyer Henry & Son (Henry & Charles Meyer) 81 E. D'way

Meyer Henry L. & Son (Henry L. & Adolph H. Meyer) 25 John

Meyer Hugo & Co. (Hugo & Felix Meyer ;—special partners, Nathan Falk, Hamburg, Germany, $25,000, & Ferdinand Hoilborn & Bernhard Nathau, Bradford, Eng., each $7,500 ; terminates 31st Dec. 1892) 42 Greene

Meyer Isaac & Co. (Isaac Meyer & Max Mendelsohn) 258 Pearl

Meyer John H. & Co. (John H. Meyer & Bernard Kruse) 319 Third av.

Meyer Siegmund T. & Son (Siegmund T. & Arthur L. Meyer) 7 D'way

Meyer William & Co. (dissolved) 518 Tenth av.

Meyer A. J. H. & Co. (dissolved) 980 Tenth av.

Meyer F. W. & Co. (Frederick W. Meyer & Joseph Hailer) 820 Washn.

Meyer G. A. & E. (George A. & Edwin O.) 80 Cliff

Meyer H. & Co. (Henry & Barthold Meyer) 322 G'wich

Meyer H. & F. (Henry Meyer, only) 408 First av.

Meyer H. & R. (dissolved) 1602 Second av. 1435 Third av. & 553 Madison

Meyer J. & Co. (dissolved) 477 Broome

Meyer J. & F. Katz (Joanna Meyer & Frieda Katz) 181 Clinton

Meyer J. H. & Co. (John H. & Herman B. Meyer) 2 South, 4 Washn. & 3 West

Meyer L. & E. (Louis & Ernst) 109 E. 86th

Meyer O. & Co. (J. F. Otto Mayer, only) 104 Broad

Meyer V. & A. & Co. (Victor & Adolph & Solomon Meyer) 17 William

Meyer Brothers (drugs) (Charles & Frank Meyer) 1210 Third av.

Meyer Brothers (grocers) (August & John & Louis M yer) 177 Elm

Meyer Brothers (grocers) (Frederick & John Meyer) 224 Second av. & 215 Ninth av.

Meyer Brothers (meat) (Frederick & Meyer Meyer) 5 First av.

Meyer Brothers (shoes) (Morris & Bernard Meyer) 197 G'wich

Meyer Brothers (stationers) (William jr. & Benjamin F. & George C. Meyer) 871 Third av.

Meyer & Arendes (Andrew Meyer & John Arendes) 402 E. 25th

Meyer & Breyer (Matthew C. Meyer & Lawrence B. Breyer) 186 Mulberry

Meyer & Co. (canes) (no inf.) 26 Beekman
Meyer & Co. (frames) (dissolved) 36 W. 14th
Meyer & Dickinson (dissolved) 85 Greene
Meyer & Dotzauer (Charles Meyer & Peter Dotzauer) 10 Second av.
Meyer & Jacobson (Charles Meyer & Jens C. Jacobson) 227 E. 80th
Meyer & Kessler (Henry Meyer & Hugo Kessler) 61 Frankfort
Meyer & Kleine (John F. Meyer & August F. Kleine) 259 Fourth av.
Meyer & Koch (Frederick Meyer & John Koch) 75 Third av.
Meyer & Kuhn (Francis Meyer & Daniel Kuhn) 329 E. 25th
Meyer & Landwehr (Rudolph Meyer & Henry Landwehr) 1435 Third av.
Meyer & Lange (Julian H. Meyer & Hugo V. Lange) 344 G'wich
Meyer & Legenhausen (Charles Meyer & Henry Legenhausen) 422 W. 48th
Meyer & Mendelsohn (Max Meyer & Samuel Mendelsohn) 244 Pearl
Meyer & Niemann (dissolved) 275 Washn.
Meyer & Reppert (Marie Meyer & Anna Reppert) 158 Third av.
Meyer & Rodewald (Nicholas Meyer & Charles Rodewald) 1533 First av.
Meyer & Schmedes (Henry L. Meyer & Otto F. Schmedes) 81 Broad
Meyer & Stern (Samuel Meyer & Aaron Stern) 87 Av. C
Meyer & Stock (dissolved) 1526 Av. A
Meyer & Thues (dissolved) 75 W. 125th
Meyer & Wiegand (Julius Meyer & Nicholas Wiegand) 93 Essex
Meyer, Ebeling & Co. (Charles H. & Henry L. Meyer & Carl Ebeling jr.) 85 Greene
Meyer, Heine & Co. (William Meyer, Sigmund B. Heine, David Aaron & Ferdinand Porsch) 46 White
Meyer, Moore & Co. (dissolved) 33 S. William & 35 Stone
Meyer's A., Sons (Henry & Albert Meyer) 114 William
Meyer's Henry, Sons (John H. & Henry Meyer) 4 Washn. & 69 Broad
Meyer's Philip P., Son (Oscar Meyer) 220 Centre
Meyer-Sniffen Co. (Ltd.) (William Bunting jr. Treas. Capital, $100,000; further inf. refused) 48 Cliff
Meyerdierks Brothers (Frederick & Henry Meyerdierks) 905 First av. & 1178 Second av.
Meyerholz & Blum (Dederich Meyerholz & Henry Blum) 77 Third av.
Meyers Alexander & Son (Alexander & Sanderson Meyers) r 15½ Sullivan
Meyers George & Son (George & Morris E. Meyers) 99 Norfolk
Meyers Louis & Son (Louis & Edwin L. Meyers) 890 B'way
Meyers J. C. & Co. (dissolved) 27 Bond
Meyers M. & Son (Meyer & Abraham R. Meyers) 5 Grace sq. W. Washn. mkt & E. 45th c First av.
Meyers Brothers (Jacob & George H. Meyers;—special partner, Henry Meyers, $20,000; terminates 31st Dec. 1890) 377 & 406 B'way
Meyn & Schutt (William Meyn & Arnold Schutt) 305 West
Meyrowitz Brothers (Emil B. Meyrowitz, only) 295 Fourth av. & r 295 E. 22d
Mica Mfg. Co. (John O'Neill, propr.) 117 John
Mica Roofing Co. (William H. H. Childs, propr.) 73 Maiden la.

Michael James R., Mfg. Co. (dissolved) 63 Chambers
Michael L. & Co. (Louis Michael & Louis Phelps) 540 B'way & 78 Crosby
Michaelis E. & Son (Edward & Emil M. Michaelis) 139 Bowery
Michaelis L. & J. (Leopold & Julius) 14 Cedar
Michaelis M. & Son (Moses & Harry M. Michaelis) 81 Murray
Michaelis & Lindeman (Nathan Michaelis & Edward Lindeman) 302 B'way
Michaelis & Rohman (Jacob Michaelis & Max S. Rohman—special partner, Nathan Michaelis, $20,000; terminates 1st May, 1891) 14 W. 23d
Michaelis & Zincke (dissolved) 23 E. 14th
Michaelson Philip & Son (Philip & Joseph L. Michaelson) 99 Av. C
Michaelson & Rubenstein (dissolved) 100 Norfolk
Michaelson & Schonholtz (dissolved) 462 E. Houston
Michales J., Son & Co. (William H. Michales & Edwin T. Frankton) 40 Commerce
Michel M. & E. (dissolved) 80 W. Houston
Michel S. & Sobel (Simon Michel & Frederick Sobel) 475 B'way & 46 Mercer
Michel & Hartmann (Joseph L. Michel & Charles Hartmann) 64 John
Michel & Link (Andrew Michel jr. & John Link) 212 First av.
Micheletti D. & Son (no. inf.) 93 Park
Michelot J. & Co. (John Michelot & Isaac H. Burns) 42 New
Michels Barthold & Son (Barthold & Herman F. A. Michels) 180 Washn. mkt
Michels & Heydacker (dissolved) r 134 W. 26th
Michelson I. & Co. (Isidor Michelson & Myer D. Cohn) 3 Malden la.
Michigan Central R. R. Co. (Henry B. Ledyard, Pres.; Edwin D. Worcester, Sec.; Henry Pratt, Treas. Capital, $18,738,204. Directors: Cornelius Vanderbilt, Chairman; William K. Vanderbilt, Henry B. Ledyard, Edwin D. Worcester, Samuel F. Barger, Chauncey M. Depew, Ashley Pond, William L. Scott, John V. Farwell) Grand Central depot
Michigan Condensed Milk Co. (James M. Turner, Pres.; Hart A. Farrand, Sec. Capital, $100,000. Directors: James M. Turner, Hart A. Farrand, A. W. Wright, Birt F. Parsons) 17 Hudson
Michigan Congress Water Co. (dissolved) 16 Warren
Micolino M. & Co. (Matthew Micolino, no Co.) 97 Washn. mkt & 426 W. 37th
Micro-Audiphone Co. (Frank M. Blodgett, propr.) 1286 B'way
Microphone Carbon Battery Co. (Joseph G. Noyes, Pres.; Henry Mesler, Sec.; Frank J. Stevens, Treas. Capital, $25,000. Directors: Joseph G. Noyes, Frank E. Morgan, Frank J. Stevens, Henry Mesler) 112 Liberty
Middle States Inspection Bureau (J. Montgomery Hare, Chairman; J. W. Barley, Treas.) 67 Wall
Middleditch Livingston & Co. (Livingston & Thomas J. Middleditch) 26 Cortlandt
Middleton W. E. & Co. (refused) 280 B'way
Middleton & Brother (Reuben S. & John D. Middleton) 10 Maiden la.
Middleton & Co. (John N. B. & Clifford L. Middleton & Donald B. L. Lee) 60 New
Middleton, Carman & Co. (William H. Middleton, only) 70 Fulton mkt & 215 Front
Midland Mining Co. (James C. Hartt, Pres.; Robert Courtney, Sec. Capital, $1,500,000. Trustees: James C. Hartt, Jesse V. A. Craighead, Robert Courtney) 21 Cortlandt

Midler Harris & Co. (Harris Midler & Joseph Friedman) 79 Bayard

Miehling Charles & Edward, 140 Nassau

Mielcke & Peters (William R. H. Mielcke & John Peters) 41 Little W. 12th

Mignault & Prichard (dissolved) 1 W. 3d

Mike & Starr Gold & Silver Mining Co. (Charles H. Tompkins, Pres.; Foster B. Gilbert, Sec. Capital, $1,000,000. Directors: Charles H. Tompkins, Foster B. Gilbert, Richard Pancoast, Thomas M. Blanhard) 15 Cortlandt

Miles William A. & Co. (William A. Miles, Pres.; James W. Taylor, Treas.; Charles J. Hawkins, Sec.; further inf. unattainable) 55 Chrystie

Miles R. M. & Co. (Robert M. Miles & Antonio del Solar) 45 B'way

Miles & Helfer (William Miles jr. & Charles A. Helfer) 242 Monroe

Miles & Holman (Sweeting Miles, only) 55 West

Miles Brothers & Co. (Alfred S. & William H. Miles jr. no Co.) 102 Fulton

Milhau's J., Son (Edward L. Milhau) 183 B'way

Milius E. & Brother (Edward & Samuel Milius) 107 Franklin

Milius, Shire & Co. (Leopold Milius, Jacob Shire & Samuel Hesse) 6 Gt. Jones

Milk Exchange (Ltd.) (William A. Wright, Pres.; John W. Tayntor, Sec. Capital, $10,000. Directors: William A. Wright, Milton L. Sanford, D. W. Borry, John W. Tayntor, John Lobman, Joseph Laemmle, Charles H. C. Beakes, Casper Flicken, Frederick H. Beach, Thomas O. Smith, James Cusick, E. D. Pierson, John P. Wierk) 6 Harrison

Millar George W. & Co. (George W. Millar & William D. May) 64 Duane

Millard T. C. & Co. (Thomas C. Millard & Thomas R. Duncan) 137 Greene

Millard & Avery (Charles Millard & George W. Avery) 1267 B'way

Millen E. & Co. (Edmund Millen & Thomas W. Aikenhead) 113 Greene

Millen L. R. & Co. (Loring R. Millen & Lemuel Johnson) 16 Beaver

Miller Charles & Son (Charles & Charles W. Miller) 60 Nassau

Miller Edward & Co. (Edward Miller, Pres.; Edward Miller jr. Treas. Capital, $250,000. Directors: Edward Miller, O. B. Arnold, I. C. Lewis, F. W. Ives, George W. Lyon, J. L. Billard, Edward Miller jr.) 19 College pl.

Miller Eyeless Pick Co. (no inf.) 438 B'way

Miller Fire Extinguisher Co. (William K. Thorne, Pres.; Edward D. Butler, Sec. Capital $500,000. Directors: William K. Thorne D. B. Carroll, Edward D. Butler) 5 Dey

Miller Frank & Sons (Edwin A. & James L. & Frank C. & Frank B. Miller, only) 849 W. 26th

Miller Louis & Son (Louis & Louis Miller jr.) 436 E. 58th

Miller Mrs. G. B. & Co. Tobacco Mfy. (refused) 97 Columbia

Miller Nathan & Son (Nathan & Alfred Miller) 326 Canal

Miller Thomas & Sons (Thomas L. & George F. & James W. Miller, only) 1151 B'way & 70 W. 23d

Miller Walter T. & Co. (Walter T. & Samuel W. Miller) 123 Pearl

Miller William & Son (William & John T. Miller) 114 Water

Miller A. B. & Co. (Abram B. Miller & George F. Kohler) 88 Pearl

Miller H. C. & Sons (Henry C. & Louis P. & Emil H. & Henry C. Miller jr.) 393 Madison

Miller H. S. & Co. (Horace S. Miller & Alfred Lister) 184 Water

Miller I. & Co. (Isaac Miller, no Co.) 1600 Third av.

Miller L. & Sons (Leopold & Abraham & Frank Miller) 149 Chambers & 131 Reade

Miller L. B. & Son (Lester B. & Merritt B. Miller) 145 Reade

Miller P. & Son (Peter & Joseph E. Miller) 273 Division

Miller R. & Son (Robert & John Miller) 643 Eighth av.

Miller S. B. & Co. (Samuel B. & Clarence G. Miller) 7 Fulton fish mkt

Miller W. H. & J. E. (William H. & Joseph E.) 304 Bleecker

Miller W. W. & Brother (William W. & Pierre V. C. Miller) 18 B'way

Miller Brothers (brokers) (Ephraim & William H. Miller) 145 B'way

Miller Brothers (drugs) (Theodore & Edward Miller) 703 Tenth av.

Miller Brothers (furs) (Charles & Julius Miller) 54 Mercer

Miller Brothers (grocers) (David & Louis Miller) 140 Mott

Miller Brothers (liquors) (Charles F. & Frederick Miller) 113 Allen

Miller Brothers (opticians) (Frank & Louis & William Miller) 1319 B'way

Miller Brothers (pencilers) (Richard H. & Frank M. Miller) 419 E. 61st

Miller & Adams (Agnes S. Miller & Charles Adams) 15 Broad

Miller & Brewer (Charles A. Miller & Charles P. Brewer) 83 Maiden la.

Miller & Brother (Daniel & Marquis Miller) 577 B'way & 148 Mercer

Miller & Bruns (dissolved) 330 Bowery

Miller & Clauson (Charles W. Miller & Charles S. Clauson:—special partner, Henry Clauson jr.; terminates 31st Oct. 1894; further inf. refused) 227 E. 120th

Miller & Coates (George C. Miller, Robert M. Kelly & Franklin Miller, only) 279 Pearl

Miller & Co. (Stephen & Peter & Joseph J. Miller) 21 Centre

Miller & Doubleday (Charles A. Miller & S. Ward Doubleday) 44 Wall

Miller & Evans (Anna E. Miller & Norman H. Evans) 67 Prince

Miller & Flinn (Ebon Miller & Fitz Allen Flinn) 32 Beekman

Miller & Foeller (Anthony Miller & Charles Foeller) West c Gansevoort

Miller & Haffen (William F. Miller & Valentine Haffen) 939 E. 149th

Miller & Herrnstorf (dissolved) 173 E. 4th

Miller & Houghton (Elijah A. Houghton & William Watson, only) 22 South

Miller & Huber (Edward L. Miller & Frederick T. Huber:—special partner. Henry J. Robinson, $50,000 ; terminates 1st May 1890) 15 Water & 16 Front

Miller & Loechner (Peter Miller & George Loechner) 162 William

Miller & McLean (Laurence W. Miller & Robert McLean) 90 Pine

Miller & Phillips (Isaac L. Miller & John Phillips) 20 Nassau

Miller & Reismann (William S. Miller & Charles Reismann) 314 Centre & 146 Baxter

Miller & Savage (George W. Miller & Edward S. Savage) 146 B'way

Miller & Simonson (Howard R. Miller & Stephen D. Simonson) 61 Liberty

Miller & Son (William & Charles W. B. Miller) 434 B'way

Miller & Stabler (Henry Miller & Walter Stabler) 31 Nassau & 1167 Ninth av.

WATER METERS, GAS ENGINES, | NATIONAL METER CO.
FOR PUMPING AND POWER. | **252 Broadway, N. Y.**

MIL 199 MIR

Miller & Vanvalen (William A. Miller & Joseph R. Vanvalen) 284 South & 14 Vesey

Miller & Vanwinkle (William H. Miller, Nathaniel H. Vanwinkle & Edgar L. Miller) 102 Walker

Miller & Vaughan (William H. Miller jr. & Henry E. Vaughan) 145 B'way

Miller & Wells (Charles E. Miller & Mansing C. Wells) 32 Nassau

Miller & Williams (Hiram K. Miller & Ezekiel C. Williams) 306 Washn. & 203 Duane

Miller Brothers & Co. (James W. & Isaac M. Miller, only) 37 Union sq. W.

Miller, Ball & Co. (John E. Miller, Archibald H. Bull & Henry T. Knowlton) 48 South

Millur, Case & Clausen (dissolved) 237 E. 129th

Miller, Kastor & Co. (Albert W. W. Miller, Adolph Kastor & Amos C. Greenleaf) 32 Greene

Miller, Metcalf & Parkin (dissolved) 480 Pearl

Mille, Peckham & Dixon (George M. Miller, Wheeler H. Peckham. William P. Dixon & Hoffman Miller) 29 Wall

Millers Falls Co. (Henry L. Pratt, Pres.; George E. Rogers, Sec.; Levi J. Gunn, Treas. Capital, $200,000. Directors: Henry L. Pratt, Levi J. Gunn, George A. Arms, Chester C. Conant, Edward E. Lyman. D. B. Abercrombie, John L. Varick, Edward P. Stoughton, George E. Rogers) 93 Reade

Millard N. & Co. (Nelson Millard & Theron J. Paine) 168 Duane

Milligan & Higgins Glue Co. (Thomas Higgins, Pres.; William H. Vreeland, Sec.; William F. Nisbet, Treas. Capital, $25,000. Directors: Thomas Higgins, William H. Vreeland, William F. Nisbet) 222 Front

Milliken Brothers (Edward F. & Foster Milliken) 55 Liberty

Milliken & Cortles (James F. Milliken & Harry Cortles) 1162 B'way

Millinery Building & Loan Assn. (William H. Carpenter, Pres.; E. Frank Haven, Sec.; Joseph H. Patterson, Treas. Trustees: James Magee, Henry A. Meriotte, Max Mindhelm, Louis A. Myers, B. A. Duffhues, W. H. Morrill, John Nieles, Charles A. Coates, Isaac L. Rodberg, Alexander H. Tomkins, Eugene W. Moch, W. H. Anderson) 686 B'way

Millot Brothers (Theophilus & James Millot) 105 Bleecker

Mills Stephen H. & Co. (Stephen H. Mills, John L. Merrill & Roswell Mills) 107 South

Mills William & Son (Thomas B. Mills, only) 7 Warren

Mills D. T. & Co. (Dexter T. Mills & Erasmus C. Gaffield) 80 Pearl

Mills Brothers (dissolved) 216 Mulberry

Mills & Coleman (Mary A. Mills & George B. Coleman) 189 Grand

Mills & Co. (Abraham Mills, no Co.) 19 William

Mills & Everett (Albert D. Mills & Elijah Everett) 106 Warren

Mills & Ford (dissolved) 83 Pine

Mills & Gibb (Philo L. Mills, John Gibb & William T. Evans) 462 B'way

Mills & Relyea (Silas R. Mills & John Relyea) 168 Chambers

Mills, Robeson & Smith (George H. Mills, William P. Robeson & Albert H. Smith) 90 B'way

Mills' B., Sons (Augustus R. & Mortimer Mills) 52 South

Millward & Co. (James Millward & William P. Richardson) 80 West

Milmine, Bodman & Co. (George Milmine, Edward C. Bodman & William M. Cooper) 401 Produce Ex.

Milne A. & Co. (Alexander Milne & Luther Little) 1 B'way

Milne J. G. & Co. (James G. Milne, no Co.) 59 Dey

Milo Cons. Mining & Smelting Co. (A. Foster Higgins, Pres.; William Trotter, Sec. Capital, $100,000. Trustees: A. Foster Higgins, Theodore V. A. Trotter, Uache McK. Whitlock, William Trotter) 49 Wall

Mimbres Cons. Mining Co. (Thomas F. Mason, Pres.; W. Hart Smith, Sec. Capital, $100,000. Trustees: James D. Hague, Thomas F. Mason, W. Hart Smith) 52 B'way

Minaldi A. & Co. (Antonio Minaldi, no Co.) 24 State

Minard Brothers (James H. & William E. Minard) 271 W. 87th

Minas Nuevas Mining Co. (inoperative) 46 Exchange pl.

Minas Prietas Mining Co. (James J. Higginson, Pres.; William N. Olmstead, Sec. Capital, $1,000,000; further inf. refused) 18 Wall

Minder & Dreyer (John Minder & John Dreyer) 104 Washn. mkt

Miner Brothers (dissolved) 2484 Eighth av.

Miner & Canary (Harry C. Miner & Thomas Canary) 312 Eighth av.

Mineralized Rubber Co. (George P. Dodge, Pres.; Ove Von Gedde, Sec. Capital, $40,000. Trustees: George P. Dodge, Ove Von Gedde, L. P. Dodge) 16 Cliff

Miners' Oil Co. (Joseph A. Bixome, propr.) 43 Front

Miners' Oil & Supply Co. (Ltd.) (inoperative) 189 Pearl

Minerva Publishing Co. (Telemaque T. Timayenis, Pres.; Demetrius Jannopoulo, Sec. Capital, $10,000. Directors: Telemaque T. Timayonis, Demetrius Jannopoulo) 10 W. 23d

Minette & Co. (Joseph H. Coxe & Alfred J. E. Knight, only) 60 Pearl

Minford L. W. & Co (Lewis W. Minford & Charles M. Bull) 104 Wall

Mingey & Brewster (Edward Mingey & Nestor H. Brewster) 72 Grand

Mining Record Printing & Publishing Co. (Alexander R. Chisolm, Pres.; Albert D. Wagner, Sec. Capital, $50,000. Directors: Alexander R. Chisolm, Albert D. Wagner, Ellsworth M. Eastwood) 61 B'way

Minis P. H. & Co. (Philip H. Minis, no Co.) 54 B'way & 19 New

Minisman I. & Brother (Israel & Michael Minisman) 73 Baxter

Minners C. & H. (Charles & Henry) 75 W. 96th

Minnesota Iron Co. (Jay C. Morse, Pres.; Charles P. Coffin, Sec.; Alexander J. Paterson, Treas. Capital, $20,000,000. Directors: Jay C. Morse, Marshall Field, P. H. Kelly, Henry Siebert. H. M. Flagler, Darius O. Mills, H. H. Porter, Benjamin Brewster, Roswell P. Flower, George C. Stone, Heber R. Bishop, D. H. Lee, D. H. Bacon) 15 Broad

Minnigerode & Co., (Jennie C, Minnigerode & John E. Franks) 40 B'way

Minot, Hooper & Co. (Stephen W. Marston, Nathan Hobart, George H. Minot, James R. Hooper & John W. T. Nichols) 53 Leonard

Minton & Smith (Harlan P. Minton & William H. Smith) 35 Centre mkt

Mintz Michael & Co., (no inf.) 136 Canal

Minzesheimer Charles & Co. (Charles Minzesheimer, Abraham Rosenfeld, Charles L. Davis, Frederick H. Cohn, Edward Sallinger, Leon Klopman & Clarence C. Minzesheimer) 14 Wall & 847 & 1111 B'way

Minzesheimer Moses & Sons (Moses & Benjamin & Milton Minzesheimer) 626 Madison av.

Miranda F. & Co. (Froilan Miranda & Juan Campano) 222 Pearl

Mirick & Co. (no inf.) 520 W. 43d

Mirrielees W. L. & Co. (refused) 804 B'way

EXCELSIOR BIRD FOOD. The recognized standard. The most reliable for your Canary. Use no other. Insist upon getting it. Packed only by C. ROSENSTEIN & CO., 373 Washington Street, New York.

MIS　　　　200　　　　MOL

Mischler Brothers (Ferdinand & August Mischler) 417 W. 26th

Miskend S. H. & Co. (Solomon H. Miskend & Benjamin Sachs) 94 Division

Misses' Cloak Co. (Meyers Brothers, proprs.) 377 & 406 B'way

Mississippi Mineral Springs Co. (Andres B. Stone, Pres.; Lyndon H. Stevens, Sec. Capital, $100,000. Directors: Louis H. Scott, Lyndon H. Stevens, Andres B. Stone, John M. Young, C. B. Smith) 15 Broad

Missouri Pacific Railway Co. (Jay Gould, Pres.; Amos H. Colof, Sec. Capital, $30,000,000. Directors: Jay Gould, Sidney Dillon, Samuel Sloan, Russell Sage, R. S. Hayes, Thomas T. Eckert, Amos L. Hopkins, George J. Gould, Frederick L. Ames, George J. Forrest, Henry G. Marquand, C. S. Greeley, S. H. H. Clark) 195 & 391 B'way

Missouri, Kansas & Texas Railway Co. (R. V. Martinsen, Pres.; J. de Neufville, Treas.; Henry B. Henson. Sec. Capital, $46,405,000. Directors: E. Ellery Anderson, R. V. Martinsen, Henry K. Enos, H. R. Baltzer, J. de Neufville, William Bond, Simon Sterne, Maynard C. Eyre, William Dowd, Lee Clark Parsons, Benjamin P. McDonald, H. C. Cross, John Hancock, James C. Thompson) 44 B'way

Mitchell John J., Co. (John J. Mitchell, Pres.; John J. Mitchell jr, Sec. Capital, $50,000; further inf. unattainable) 830 B'way

Mitchell Vance Co. (William E. Curtis, Sec. Capital, $250,000, Trustees; Samuel B. H. Vance, William E. Curtis, G. Pierrepont Davis, Louis D. Griggs, Frederick A. Mason, Frederick P. Wilcox, William H. Davol, E. Berry Peets) 836 B'way & Tenth av. c W. 24th

Mitchell William & Son (William & William A. Mitchell) 1 Desbrosses

Mitchell E. P. & Co. (Walter H. Mitchell, only) 64 Wall

Mitchell J. & Co. (John Mitchell, Co. refused) 143 E. 41st

Mitchell L. A. & Co. (Louis A. Mitchell & Joseph Chauvin) 15 Centre

Mitchell P. & D. (Peter & David) 135 B'way

Mitchell P. R. & Co. (Pierson R. Mitchell, Lewis T. Launey, Gustavus A. Willey & Harvey W. Hall) 13 Elizabeth

Mitchell R. G. & Co. (Roland G. Mitchell, no Co.) 141 Water & 330 South

Mitchell & Boyeson (David A. Mitchell & Frank Boyeson) 149 Eleventh av.

Mitchell & Co. (William J. & William F. & John W. Mitchell) 255 W. 42d

Mitchell & McMein (John Mitchell & George R. McMein) 113 Hudson

Mitchell & Miller (John A. Mitchell & Andrew Miller) 28 W. 23d

Mitchell & Mitchell (lawyers) (Edward & William & John Murray Mitchell) 45 Wall

Mitchell & Mitchell (real estate) (William H. & Henry S. Mitchell) 84 Church

Mitchell & Picard (Isaac Mitchell & Samuel Picard) 626 B'way & 158 Crosby

Mitchell, Kinsler & Southgate (Rebecca B. Mitchell, Francis Kinsler & Richard H. Southgate) 226 Fifth av.

Mittelmark M. & Bondor (no inf.) 68 Clinton

Mittnacht Eagle Safe Mfg. Co. (not inc.) (estate of George M. Mittnacht, Jacob A. Mittnacht, Trustee) 24 Spring

Mix G. I. & Co. (Walter L. C. Glenney, only) 82 Chambers

Mobile & Birmingham R. R. Co. (Thomas G. Bush, Pres.; Louis M. Schwan, Sec.; William A. C. Ewon, Treas. Capital, $8,000,000. Directors: Edward R. Bacon, John Greenough, Thomas M. Logan, George S. Scott, Edward Lauterbach, Calvin S. Brice, John G. Moore,

E. R. Chapman, Thomas G. Bush, D. T. Parker, George F. Stone) 10 Wall

Mobile & Dauphin Island R. R. & Harbor Co. (Robert Sewell, Pres.; Daniel G. Gillette, Treas.; William A. Wolff, Sec. Capital, $3,000,000. Directors: Robert & William J. Sewell, H. Austill, Walter R. Gillette, Frederick J. Winston, William Rasquin jr, Henry S. Van Duzer, Daniel G. Gillette) 32 Nassau

Mobile & Ohio R. R. Co. (James C. Clarke, Pres.; Henry Tacon, Sec. Capital, $10,000,000 Directors: Adrian Iselin jr. H. B. Plant, A. H. Stevens, Sidney Shepard, R. K. Dow, J. H. Fay, James C. Clarke, F. D. Trappen, John Paton, T. G. Bush, E. L. Russell, W. J. Hearin, W. Butler Duncan) 11 Pine

Moch E. & Co. (Eugene W. Moch, Martin Frank & Samuel Geismar) 173 Mercer

Model Dress-Steel & Bustle Co. (John B. Goodbody, propr.) 74 Grand

Modemann G. H. & C. (dissolved) 255 Sixth av. & 502 Third av.

Modry L. & Co. (Ignatz Modry & Louis Frankenstein) 40 Lispenard

Moe Ira W. & Co. (Ira W. & Zoradia M. Moe) 9 South

Moe N. R. & Co. (Nathaniel R. & Ira W. Moe) 9 South

Moehl & Rathjen (Charles Moehl & August Rathjen) 104 Water

Moeller H. D. & J. (Henry D. & John) 1485 B'way & 617 Seventh av.

Moeller & Litzaner (Edward Moeller & Ludwig Littauer;—special partner, Frederick Moeller, $14,000; terminates 1st July, 1892) 109 Mercer

Moen's Asphaltic Cement Co. (Eleazar S. Vaughan, Pres.; Jerome W. Vaughan, Sec. Capital, $90,000 Directors: Eleazar S. & Jerome W. & Frederick A. & Edmund A. Vaughan) 108 Maiden la.

Moessner Thomas F. & J. H. Knickerbocker (dissolved) 317 B'way

Moffat David & Co. (William L. & Fraser M. Moffat, only) 5 Jacob

Moffat Frank D. & Co. (Frank D. Moffat & Joseph D. Donald) 81 Fulton

Moffat & Co. (Thomas H. & Margaret J. Moffatt) 484 & 924 Sixth av.

Moffitt-West Drug Co. (John S. Moffitt, Pres.; C. H. West, Sec. Capital, $250,000; further inf. refused) 18 Gold

Mogey W. & D. (William & David) 420 W. 27th

Mohl F. W. & Co. (Frederick W. Mohl & Walter L. Smith) 109 Greene

Mohlman J. H. & Co. (John H. Mohlman & Dederick Schmidt) 339 G'wich

Mohr F. & Co. (Frederick Mohr, no Co.) 50 Elizabeth

Mohr, Hanemann & Co. (William Mohr & Henry W. Hanemann, no Co.) 27 Cotton Ex.

Molesworth W. & Co. (William H. Bowlsby, propr.) 254 B'way

Molinari & Son (Giuseppe & Giuseppe Molinari jr.) 153 Elizabeth

Mollan & Vorrath (dissolved) 87 E. 110th & 1121 Park av.

Moller Christian & Son (Christian & William Moller) 14 E. 13th

Moller O. W. & Son (Charles W. & Alexus O. Moller) 86 S. William

Moller & Co. (George H. Moller, no Co.) 11 Pine

Mollenson Brothers (K. E. Molleson, only) 18 Beekman

Molloy Joseph & Sons (Joseph & Bernard J. & James J. Molloy) 310 W. 25th

Molloy Brothers (Thomas & John M. Molloy) 110 W. 14th

Maloney Salt Co. (George Quackenbush, Pres.; Thomas H. O'Neill, Sec. Capital, $5,000,

IDEN & CO., University Place, 9th to 10th Sts., N.Y. | **MANUFACTURERS OF GAS FIXTURES AND ELECTROLIERS**

MOL   201   MOO

Directors: George Quackenbush & Thomas H. & Henry O'Neill) 72 Greene
Moloney & Co. (Patrick H. Moloney, no Co.) 482 Third av.
Moloney & O'Donnell (Cornelius Moloney & Joseph O'Donnell) 259 South
Mommer E. & Co. (Ewald Mommer, Jesse T. Higgins & Otto Welpmann) 98 Grand
Momper's Frederick, Son (Joseph N. Momper) 217 Centre
Monaghan & Co. (Patrick H. Monaghan & Francis Forster) 66 W. 53d
Monarch Palace Car Co. (Henry K. Baker, Pres.; Clarence J. Gray, Sec. Capital, $500,000. Directors: Henry K. Baker, Damon N. Coats, Clarence J. Gray) 45 B'way
Moncrieff & Leake (dissolved) 321 Washn.
Monds & Ryan (James Monds & James Ryan) 55 W. 16th
Mones & Co. (Jose P. & Pedro J. Mones) 85 Front
Monheimer J. & Co. (Jonas Monheimer & Joseph Zenn) 206 Pearl
Monheimer Brothers (Jonas H. & Marcus H. Monheimer) 707 B'way
Monitor Automatic Scale Co. (Adolph Zinn, Pres.; Max Kayser, Sec. Capital, $50,000. Directors: Adolph Zinn, Max Kayser, Charles A. Lieb, H. L. & E. Einstein) 63 Prince
Monjo Louis jr. & Co. (Louis Monjo jr. no Co.) 19 Whitehall
Monk & Gillies (George Monk & William Gillies) 239 W. 19th & r 92 Eighth av.
Monks John & Son (John & John M. Monks) 130 Water
Monmouth Park Assn. (Andrew J. Cassatt, Pres.; Henry G. Crickmore, Sec.; David D. Withers, Treas.) 60 Madison av.
Monné R. & Brothers (Ramon & Evaristo & Peter Monné) 108 Duane
Monnis & Moehring (Eugene L. Monnis & Paul Moehring) 1686 Third av.
Monopol Tobacco Works (Joseph Huppmann jr. Pres.; J. O'Tard, Sec.; Carl P. Dietz, Treas.; further inf. unattainable) 112 Second av.
Monsky M. & Son (Morris & Jacob I. Monsky) 22 Essex & 191 E. B'way
Montagne & Fuller (Frank L. Montagne & Egbert C. Fuller) 156 William & 41 Beekman
Montal G. & Co. (George Montal & Joseph Barrera) 90 W. Houston
Montanye W. H. & Co. (William H. & George E. & Lewis F. Montanye) 66 Barclay
Montauk Gas Coal Co. (Charles G. Cornell, Pres.; Joseph P. Quin, Sec.; John C. Provost, Treas. Capital, $2,500,000. Directors: Charles G. Cornell, John White, Joseph P. Quin, John C. Provost, Samuel E. Johnson, Samuel M. Mills, Jonathan O. Fowler) 19 Whitehall
Montauk Steamboat Co. (Ltd.) (George C. Gibbs, Pres.; Robert J. Clyde, Sec.; George W. Hall, Treas. Capital, $100,000. Directors: George C. Gibbs, George H. Smith, George W. Hall, Robert J. Clyde, Henry A. Bourne, Charles A. Pierson) 107 South
Montelac Park (The) (Capital, $600,000; further inf. unattainable) no address
Montell F. T. & Son (Frank M. & John B. Montell, only) 53 Pine
Monterey & Mexican Gulf R. R. Co. (Geronimo Trevino, Pres.; Victor A. Wilder, Sec. Capital, $100,000. Directors: Geronimo Trevino, Victor A. Wilder, Thomas S. Bullock, John J. Fisher, Emeterio de la Garza, Joseph A. Robertson, Frank Rudd, Francisco Olivares, Nicolos Regules) 40 Wall
Montgomery James & John R. & Co. (John R. & Henry B. Montgomery & Elmile M. Gillet, only) 127 Water
Montgomery James & Sons (James & Charles W. & Alfred K. Montgomery) 164 Lincoln av.

Montgomery Richard M. & Co. (Richard M. Montgomery, Frank S. Thomas & Edward W. Stevens) 152 Front
Montgomery William M. & Co. (William M. & Robert Montgomery) ft. W. 40th
Montgomery C. A. & Co. (Charles A. Montgomery, no Co.) 7 Murray
Montgomery & Bray (no inf.) 9 Chambers
Montgomery & Co. (George W. Montgomery & George W. Church) 195 Fulton
Montgomery & Pattison (William Montgomery & Henry J. Pattison) 253 W. 18th
Monti & Hudon (Frederick E. Monti & Demetrius Hudon) 2063 Seventh av.
Moody & Bracken (Edwin A. Moody & William R. Bracken:—special partner, Leon R. S. De Agreda, $4,000; terminates 1st Aug. 1891) 639 Sixth av.
Moon & Lanphear (dissolved) 2 Fulton fish mkt
Mooney D. & Son (Nicholas Mooney, only) 95 G'wich & 12 Stone
Mooney H. & F. (Henry & Frederick) 101 Mercer
Mooney H. R. & Co. (Henrietta R. Mooney, no Co.) 50 Lispenard
Mooney P. L. & Co. (dissolved) 834 B'way
Mooney W. H. & Co. (William H. Mooney, no Co.) 170 Greene
Mooney & Boland (James Mooney & John Boland) 132 B'way
Mooney & Connor (Bernard Mooney & John F. Connor) 130 W. 99th
Mooney & O'Sullivan (Daniel Mooney & Thomas J. O'Sullivan) 229 Hudson
Mooney's George, Son (Joseph T. Mooney) 246 E. 23d
Moore John & Son (John & Jeremiah Moore) 578 G'wich
Moore John E. & Co. (John E. Moore, no Co.) Castle Garden
Moore John M. & Co. (no inf.) 1390 B'way
Moore Robert & Co. (Robert & Clement Moore) 29 William
Moore A. & C. A. (Albert & Charles A.) 158 W. 19th
Moore B. F. & Son (Benjamin F. & Benjamin F. Moore jr.) 71 Nassau
Moore F. E. & Co. (Frank E. Moore, Co, refused) 18 Chambers
Moore G. E. & Co. (dissolved) 115 Pearl
Moore I. & C. & Co. (William M. & Silas C. Force, & William B. Fisher, only) 142 Pearl & 108 Water
Moore J. H. & Co. (James H. Moore & William H. Cummings) 41 Broad
Moore J. W. Leduc & Co. (John W. & Henry R. Moore, Alexander S. & Janvier Le Duc) 335 Produce Ex.
Moore S. H. & Co. (Stuart H. Moore & Frank M. Lupton) 27 Park pl. & 24 Murray
Moore W. D. & Co. (Frederick L. Moore & Frank Curtis, only) 66 Exchange pl.
Moore Brothers (Erastus D. & John L. Moore) 108 Liberty
Moore & Barnes Mfg. Co. (George T. Moore, Pres.; Ralph G. Barnes, Sec. Capital, $16,200. Directors: George T. Moore, Ralph G. Barnes, Edwin H. Hastings) 112 Chambers
Moore & Braden (dissolved) 146 B'way
Moore & Co. (canned gds) (Francis A. & Hampden Moore) 150 W. 28th
Moore & Co. (furniture) (Elric L. Moore, no Co.) 42 Elizabeth
Moore & Co. (printers) (William Moore, no Co.) 619 B'way
Moore & Horton (Albert V. Moore & John T. Horton) 11 Maiden la.
Moore & Kibler (dissolved) 820 B'way

CIRCULARS ADDRESSED TO ANY TRADE IN THE U. S. { Facilities
PROMPT, CAREFUL WORK } THE TROW CITY DIRECTORY CO., { Unequalled.
AT MODERATE PRICES. } 11 University Place.

MOO 202 MOR

Moore & McLaughlin (Thomas Moore & John McLaughlin) 346 E, 81st
Moore & Moore (Andrew J. & Anson B. Moore) 21 Beekman
Moore & Pyne (J. Frank Moore & Walter F. Pyne) 67 W. 23d
Moore & Schley (John C. Moore, Grant B. Schley, William H. Duff & Elverton R. Chapman) 29 Broad & 72 Wall
Moore & Sinnott (Andrew M. Moore & Joseph F. Sinnott) 52 Broad
Moore & Wallace (Thomas S. Moore & Jackson Wallace) 102 B'way
Moore & Warren (Thomas J. Moore & Edmond A. Warren) 67 John
Moore's John, Son (Thomas M. Moore) 193 Front
Moorhead R. L. & Co. (Robert L. Moorhead & Edgar L. Logee) 202 B'way
Moorhouse & Co. (Stephen Moorhouse & James Harrison) 66 Gansevoort
Moos & Co. (Isidor Moos, no Co.) 31 S. William
Moran Bottling Co. (Isaac A. Moran, Pres.; William H. Merriam, Sec. Capital, $15,000. Directors: Lucien Knapp, William H. Merriam, Isaac A. Moran, Philip Ebling, Marcius C. Moran, William Ebling, Frederick W Kalbfleisch) 119 E. 124th
Moran Daniel A. & Co (Daniel A. & Michael T. Moran) 27 Pine
Moran A. & Co. (Adam Moran & David Ryan) 284 E. B'way
Moran Brothers (bankers) (Charles & D. Comyn & Amedeo D. Moran) 69 William
Moran Brothers (stone) Francis N. & Nathan L. Moran) 333 E. 93d
Moran & Armstrong (Owen Moran & Lancelot W. Armstrong) 1128 First av.
Moran & Saunderson) John Moran & William G. Saunderson) 53 Wooster
Moran & Williams (Charles A. Moran & Stephen G. Williams) 46 B'way
Moran, Goff & Co. (James H. Moran, Charles A. Goff & John W. Cooke) 1168 Ninth av.
Morand Chemical Co. (in liquidation) 32 Burling sl.
Morant & Heydnoker (Ferdinand Morant & Victor Heydacker) r 134 W. 20th
Mordecai A. L. & Sons (Allen L. & Benjamin jr. & R. E. Lee Mordecai) 62 Liberty
More & Nicoll (Edwin More & Augustus W. Nicoll) 7 Warren
More & Ostrander (inf. unattainable) 117 Nassau
Morehead & Ogden (Franklin C. Morehead & John R. Ogden) 48 Exchange pl.
Moreno Valley Gold Gravel Mining Co. (James E. Bloomer, Pres.; George H. Atwood, Sec. Capital, $300,000. Trustees: James E. Bloomer, George H. Atwood, W. S. Gilmore, William Sharpley, Edward D. Harson) 229 B'way
Moreno & Lopez (Antonio Moreno & Jose Lopez) 4 E. 14th
Moreno & Martinez (dissolved) 111 B'way & 45 William
Morewood George B. & Co. (George B. & Henry F. & John R. & George B. Morewood jr.) 121 Front
Morewood & Co. (William M. Carson & William H. Lefferts, only) 71 South
Morey Brothers (Frank & George C. Morey) 1907 Second av.
Morgan Charles H. & Co. (dissolved) 22 Beaver
Morgan Iron Works (George E. Weed, Pres.; James Mooney, Sec.; Stephen W. Roach, Treas. Capital, 40,000. Directors: George E. Weed, Stephen W. Roach, William Rowland) 814 E. 9th. (see adv. back cover)
Morgan James K. & Co. (James K. Morgan, Augustus H. Schmittmann & Henry S, Morgan) 83 Dey

Morgan James L. & Co. (James L. Morgan, John M. Goetuhlus, Edward L. Kalbfleisch & James L. Morgan jr.) 47 Fulton
Morgan A. C. & Co. (Alexander C. Morgan, no Co.) 35 William
Morgan E. D. & Co. (John T. Terry & Solon Humphreys, only) 54 Exchange pl.
Morgan M. & Son (Michael & Joseph P. Morgan) 1301 Third av.
Morgan T. & J. (Thomas & John) 53 Bleecker
Morgan T. C. & Co. (Thomas C. Morgan, no Co.) 32 Platt
Morgan Brothers (William F. & Obadiah A. Morgan) ft. W. 10th
Morgan & Allen (James C. Allen, only) 59 John
Morgan & Bartlet (Henry K. Morgan & Henry P. Bartlet) 41 Wall
Morgan & Brother (Patrick & Francis Morgan) 242 W. 47th
Morgan & Co. (shoes) (dissolved) 34 E. 14th
Morgan & Co. (watches) (no inf.) 37 College pl.
Morgan & Cornell (William M. Morgan & Stephen E. Cornell) 42 Hudson & 213 Duane
Morgan & Ives (Rollin M. Morgan & Eugene S. Ives) 187 B'way
Morgan & Walker (Dankson T. Morgan & Alfred L. Walker) 140 Nassau
Morgan & Worthington (Charles N. Morgan & Robert H. Worthington) 69 Wall
Morgan, Selwin & Co. (no inf.) 53 Franklin
Morgan's Enoch. Sons Co. (George F. Morgan, Pres.; Edward W. Francis, Treas.; H. Fleming Handy, Sec. Capital, $200,000. Trustees: George F. Morgan, Henry D. Dupee, John H. Giffin jr. A. J. Akin, A. J. Morgan) 483 West
Morgan's Louisiana & Texas R. R. & S. S. Co. (Alexander C. Hutchinson, Pres.; John B. Richardson, Sec. Capital, $5,000,000. Directors : Collis P. Huntington, Alexander C. Hutchinson, J. G. Schriever, John B. Richardson, Julius Kruttachnitt) 28 Broad & Piers 25 & 27 (new) N. R.
Morgenroth & Brother (Julius & Jacob Morgenroth) 267 Rivington
Morgenstern H. & Son (dissolved) 1610 Second av.
Morgenstern & Co. (Ernst Morgenstern & Frederick G. Kahler) 58 Thomas
Morhous & Co. (Burgess F. Morhous, Co. refused) 31 W. Houston
Morisan, Allen & Co. (Samuel L. Morison, Pres.; John P. Gillis, Sec.; Vanderbilt Allen, Treas. Capital, $100,000. Directors : Samuel L. Morison, John P. Gillis, Vanderbilt Allen) 145 B'way
Mork & Romberg (Moses S. Mork & Henry J. Romberg) 147 Greene
Mornen & Flynn (no inf.) 2859 Eighth av.
Morning Journal Assn. (Albert Pulitzer, Pres.; Gilbert K. Riker, Sec.; Frank B. Robinson, Treas.; further inf. refused) 102 Nassau
Morning Star Cons. Mining Co. (Watson B. Dickerman, Pres.; Henry K. McHarg, Sec. Capital, $1,000,000. Trustees: Watson B. Dickerman, W. Gayer Dominick, George D. Greer, A. H. Porter, Henry K. McHarg, George G. Nevers, George F. Dominick) 53 B'way
Morningstar Charles & Co. (Joseph Morningstar & Edward Woldenbach, only) 48 Park pl. & 536 W. 14th
Morrell J. B. & Co. (Joseph B. Morrell & Frederick M. McWilliams :—special partners, Murray Whiting & Daniel J. Lynch, B'klyn, N. Y., each $10,000 ; terminates 1st Nov.1893) 75 Front
Morrell & Lubeck (Nicholas W. Morrell & George W. Lubeck) 251 E. 52d
Morrill George H. & Co. (George H. & George H. Morrill jr. Edmund J. Shattuck & Frank T. Morrill) 21 Vandewater

THE CALIGRAPH WRITING MACHINE,
HARTFORD, CONN.

Morris Enropean & Am. Express Co. (Ltd.) (Louis W. Morris, Pres.; William J. Morris, Sec.; Frank Kronfeld, Treas. Capital, $50,000. Directors: Louis W. Morris, William O. Hempstead, Abraham B. de Frece, Frank Kronfeld, William J. Morris) 18 B'way

Morris Joseph A. & Co. (Joseph A. Morris & Charles Hyams) 93 Prince

Morris Lewis & Co. (Lewis & Frank T. Morris) 17 Cedar

Morris Mfg. Co. (not Inc.; further inf. refused) 103 Gold

Morris Nelson & Co. (Nelson & Edward Morris & Frank E. Vogel) Manhattan mkt

Morris Theodore W. & Co. (Theodore W. Morris, no Co.) 442 Canal

Morris A. & V, (Abraham & Victor) 66 Hester

Morris C. E. & Son (Edward Morris, only) 15 Cedar

Morris L. W. & Son (dissolved) 18 B'way

Morris M. P. & Brother (no inf.) 346 W. 42d

Morris Brothers (Abram & Jacob M. Morris) 277 Church

Morris & Appelbaum (dissolved) 153 Centre

Morris & Batt (Charles S. Morris & Simon Batt) 76 Duane

Morris & Blum (no inf.) 29 Bond

Morris & Cahill (Patrick Morris & Thomas Cahill) 504 E. 81st

Morris & Combs (dissolved) 801 W. 29th

Morris & Co. (clothing) (dissolved) 450 Broome

Morris & Co. (fish) (dissolved) ft. Dockman

Morris & Cumings Dredging Co. (Joseph Cumings, Pres.; James M. Cumings, Treas. Capital, $125,000; further inf. refused) 45 Duane

Morris & Dinkin (no inf.) 100 W. 125th

Morris & Goldman (Isaac Morris & Samuel Goldman) 21 Orchard

Morris & Haddock (Charles H. Morris & Robert J. Haddock) 487 Seventh av.

Morris & Iskiwitch (no inf.) 32 Desbrosses

Morris & Keane (William E. Morris & J. Oliver Keane) 132 Nassau

Morris & Saloman (Charles Morris & Radgoski Saloman) 714 B'way

Morris & Steele (Fordham & Henry Lewis Morris & John A. K. Steele) 16 Exchange pl.

Morris & Stilwell (Charles B. Morris & William M. Stilwell) Twelfth av. c W. 131st

Morris & Williamson (dissolved) 24 State

Morris, Davis & Saloman (dissolved) 714 B'way

Morris, Marks & Wolf (dissolved) 202 Bowery

Morris, Wheeler & Co. (inf. unattainable) 28 Reade

Morrismin Beef Co. (G. F. & E. C. Swift, proprs.) 518 Willis av.

Morrison J. L., Co. (James L. Morrison, propr.) 21 Centre

Morrison John G. & Co. (John G. Morrison & William M. Whitney) 23 Cedar

Morrison Mfg. Co. (John H. Morrison, Pres. Capital, $10,000; further inf. unattainable) 24 Park pl. & 19 Barclay

Morrison J. & J. (James jr. & John) 547 W. 50th

Morrison & Kennedy (Lewis J. Morrison & John C. Kennedy) 44 B'way & 47 New

Morrison & Mott (James Morrison & Charles E. Mott) 359 W. 52d

Morrison & Wheaton (dissolved) 36 E. 48d

Morrison, Horriman & Co. (dissolved) 503 B'way & 70 Mercer

Morrissey M. J. & Son (Michael J. & William Morrissey) 107 Trinity pl.

Morrissey & Moffatt (Julia Morrissey & Agatha Moffatt) 129 Fifth av.

Morrow Gold Mining Co. (of Va.) (John A. Kunkel, Pres.; William Martin, Sec. Capital, $9,000. Directors: Robert N. Avery, John A. Kunkel, William Martin) 82 Dey

Morrow Shoe Mfg. Co. (Cornelius Morrow, Pres.; George T. Morrow jr. Sec. Capital, $80,000; further inf. unattainable) 41 Warren

Morse Musical String Co. (no inf.) 435 Seventh av.

Morse Frank E. Co. (Frank E. Morse, Pres.; Deforest O. Wilsey, Sec. Capital, $25,000. Directors: Frank E. Morse, Benjamin H. Belknap, Deforest O. Wilsey) 7 Coenties sl.

Morse S. E. & G. L. (Sidney E. & G. Livingston) 140 Nassau

Morse & Co. (Harry F. & Charles W. & estate of Benjamin W. Morse) 78 Broad

Morse & Marshall (Charles E. Morse & Charles P. H. Marshall) 27 Lex. av.

Morse & Rogers (Daniel P. Morse :—special partner, Chester O. Corbin, *Webster, Mass.*, $50,000 ; terminates 31st Dec. 1892) 134 Duane

Morse, Haynes & Wensley (Waldo G. Morse, David A. Haynes & Robert L. Wensley) 111 B'way

Morstatt & Son (George W. & William Morstatt) 227 W. 29th

Mortgage Investment Co. (Charles R. Otis, Pres.; Matthew H. Ellis, Sec.; Sidney E. Morse, Treas. Capital, $50,000. Directors: Charles R. Otis, G. Livingston & Sidney E. Morse, Matthew H. Ellis, William S. Eno, Adam C. Ellis) 140 Nassau

Mortgage Loan Co. (dissolved) 146 B'way

Mortimer George & Co. (George Mortimer & Thomas B. Moore) 359 Canal

Mortimer & McKenna (William Mortimer & Patrick H. McKenna) 778 Sixth av.

Mortimer & Wisner (Henry C. Mortimer & William T. Wisner) 141 Pearl

Morton Heel Stiffener Co. (William H. Quinn, propr.) 99 Chambers

Morton Thomas (Andrew A. Bremner & William H. Harris, executors) 65 Elizabeth

Morton Thomas & Co. (Thomas Morton, no Co.) 202 B'way

Morton D. G. & Co. (David G. Morton & John Seablom) 78 Cortlandt

Morton & Bathe (James M. Morton & John Bathe) 931 Sixth av.

Morton & Chesley (Francis F. Morton & William F. Chesley) 18 B'way

Morton Brothers & Co. (William L. & Thomas Morton & David Brown) ft. W. 54th

Morton, Bliss & Co. (Levi P. Morton, George Bliss, Richard J. Cross & George T. Bliss) 28 Nassau

Morton, Wright & Co. (dissolved) 29 Park row

Mosaic Tile Co. (Frederick A. Reichard, propr.) 15 Platt

Mosbacher & Co. (Samuel Mosbacher & Sigmund Hersfelder) 105 Water

Moscato & Bryant (no inf.) 48 B'way

Moschcowitz Brothers (no inf.) 10 E. 22d

Moschcowitz & Co. (dissolved) 281 Second

Mosel & Rehme (William Mosel & Charles Rehme) 269 Third av. & 165 E. 32d

Moseley Iron Bridge & Roof Co. (John S. McClure, Pres.; John H. McClure, Sec. Capital, $50,000. Directors: John S. & John H. McClure) 6 Dey

Moseley G. S. & Co. (George S. Moseley & James McArdle) 785 Washn.

Moseley & Moody (William F. Moseley & Preston R. Moody) 82 Walker

Mosoman C. M. & Brother (Charles M. & Edgar W. Mosoman) 125 Chambers

Moser Charles & Co. (Charles Moser & Frederick Renner) 75 Maiden la.

Moser John & Son (dissolved) 63 E. Houston & 624 E. 13th

SPECIAL ATTENTION PAID TO THIS CLASS OF WORK. **BANKERS' & BROKERS' CIRCULARS DELIVERED** THE TROW CITY DIRECTORY CO. 11 University Place.

MOS   204   MUL

Moser & Heidenheimer Malting Co. (Herman B. Scharmann, Pres.; Charles Heidenheimer, Sec.; John M. Moser, Treas. Capital, $300,000. Directors: Herman B. Scharmann, Charles Heidenheimer, John Moser) 13 Stone & 726 E. 11th

Moses Bernard J. & Co. (Bernard J. & Joseph Moses) 917 Third av.

Moses M. H. & Co. (Moses H. Moses & Henry M. Herrman) 79 Vesey

Moses & Mendelsohn (dissolved) 668 B'way

Moses, Sohn & Oppenheimer (Julius Moses, Henry S. Sohn & Ferdinand Oppenheimer) 589 B'way

Mosher & Damon (refused) 4 College pl.

Moskowits & Berkowits (dissolved) 246 Canal

Moskowitz I. & S. (dissolved) 267 Second

Mosle Brothers (George Mosle & Adolf Pavenstedt, only) r 52 Exchange pl.

Mosler Safe Co. (Moses Mosler, propr.) 7 Wash. pl.

Mosler, Bowen & Co. (dissolved) 787 B'way

Moss Engraving Co. (John C. Moss, Pres.; James E. Rumsey, Sec.; Mary A. Moss, Treas. Capital, $50,000. Directors: John C. & Mary A. Moss, James E. Rumsey, Robert B. Moss, Henry A. Jackson) 535 Pearl

Moss J. & Co. (Joseph & Rebecca Moss) 524 B'way

Moss J. A. & Co. (John A. Moss & Emil Sorgenfrei) 245 First av.

Moss & Graham (Arthur J. Moss & John Graham) 139 Elm

Moss, Goldstone & Co. (Harry E. Moss, Nathan L. Goldstone & Louis Jerkowski) 652 B'way

Mossbacher & Myres (Michael Mossbacher & Max M. Myres) 310 Church

Mossop & Engelsen (Anthony Mossop & Peter A. Engelsen) 210 E. 17th

Mothner S. & I. (Samuel & Isaac) 432 Broome

Motley Thornton N. & Co. (Thornton N. Motley, Jabez C. Gilbert & James M. Motley) 48 John

Mott Haven Canal Docks (William E. Rider, Pres.; Francis J. Rider, Sec. Capital, $50,000. Directors: William E. & Francis J. Rider) 18 Park row

Mott J. L., Iron Works (Jordan L. Mott, Pres.; John Reid, Sec. Capital, $80,000. Trustees: Jordan L. Mott, Mary J. Vandoren, John Reid) 88 Beekman, 147 W. 25th & 2411 Third av.

Mott S. R. & J. C. (Samuel R. Mott, Pres.; Frederick G. Mott, Sec.; John C. Mott, Treas. Capital, $100,000. Directors: Samuel R. & Frederick G. & John C. Mott) 118 Warren

Mott & Ross (Samuel C. Mott & Henry C. Ross) 121 W. 23d

Mott & Sands (John A. Mott & Daniel H. Sands) 56 Barclay

Motto M. & P. (Michael & Pasquale) 51 Crosby

Mould, Burr & Co. (dissolved) 45 B'way

Moulton Francis D. & Co. (William A. Hazard & Emma C. & Franklin W. Moulton, only) 127 Water

Moulton & Lynn (no inf.) 2 W. 14th

Moulton & Poling (Francis J. Moulton & Samuel Poling) Pier 23 E. R.

Mt. Desert Paving Co. (Ltd.) (Dennis W. Moran, Pres.; Robert P. Beecher, Sec. Capital, $50,000. Directors: Dennis W. Moran, Robert P. Beecher, Cyrus J. Hall, Michael Giblin, Michael McGrath) 41 Park row

Mt. Hope Cemetery Assn. (Frank B. Lawrence, Pres.; Henry A. Taylor, Sec.; Edward M. L. Ehlers, Treas.) 71 W. 23d

Mt. Morris Bank (Joseph M. De Veau, Pres.; Thomas W. Robinson, Cashier; George H. Livermore, Notary. Capital, $100,000. Directors: Joseph M. De Veau, Christopher C. Baldwin, George B. Robinson, Benjamin Russak, Lebbeus H. Rogers, David L. Evans, Cyrus O. Hubbell, Jesse G. Keys, Thomas W. Robinson, Heman Clark, Levi P. Morton) 85 E. 125th

Mt. Morris Bank Safe Deposit Vaults (Mt. Morris Bank, proprs.) 81 E. 125th

Mt. Morris Beef Co. (Isaac Brown, propr.) 2201 Second av.

Mt. Morris Electric Light Co. (Edward May, Pres.; Harry Sanderson, Sec.; Julius A. May, Treas. Capital, $500,000. Directors: Edward May, John Hills, Harry Sanderson, William M. Middleton, Julius A. May, William Hills, William Foster) 96 Vandam & 2265 Eighth av.

Mt. Morris Safe Deposit Co. (dissolved) 83 E. 125th

Mt. Neboh Cemetery Assn. (Meyer Stern, Pres.; Louis Gotthold, Sec.; Lewis Sternbach, Treas. Capital, $180,000. Trustees: Meyer Stern, Louis Gotthold, Benjamin Russak, Lewis Sternbach, Morris Tuska, Julius Bien, Philip Cowen, Daniel Herrman, Herbert A. Kingsbary) 7 Wash. pl.

Mt. Olivet Cemetery (James M. Waterbury, V. Pres.; Jarvis C. Howard, Sec.; John S. Ellis, Treas.; farther inf. unattainable) 182 Front & 54 E. 23d

Mt. Pleasant Mining Co. (James D. Hague, Pres.; William N. Olmsted, Sec. Capital, $150,000. Directors: James D. Hague, Henry Day, Charles G. White, Livingston Gibson, William N. Olmsted, John J. Crane) 18 Wall

Mount Brothers (Frank R. & William P. & Joseph E. Mount) 2281 Eighth av.

Mountain City Industrial Co. (of Col. & New Mexico) (William S. Tisdale, Pres.; Edward O. Ball, Sec.; H. Grandville Corning. Treas. Capital, $250,000; further inf. unattainable) 31 B'way

Mouquin Restaurant & Wine Co. (Ltd.) (Henry Mouquin, Pres.; John L. Mouquin, Sec.; Joseph Fallert, Treas. Capital, $80,000. Directors: Henry & John L. Mouquin, Joseph Fallert) 20 Ann, 149 Fulton & 438 Sixth av.

Movius J. & Son (Joseph & August Movius) 15 Warren

Mowe W. R. & R. H. Goffe jr. (William R. Mowe & Robert H. Goffe jr.) 88 Wall

Moyer & Orlieb (dissolved) 108 William

Moynahan J. & Co. (Jeremiah & Nora & Catharine Moynahan) 1398 Third av.

Moynahan Brothers (Timothy Moynahan, only) 189 Fulton mkt

Mudgett A. & Co. (Alvah Mudgett, no Co.) 89 South

Mudgett J. W. & Co. (John W. Mudgett, no Co.) 155 B'way

Mueller Brothers (William jr. & Herman Mueller) 198 Water

Muench & Kesner (dissolved) 90 White

Muhl & Brecht (Jacob Muhl & Louis Brecht) 32 Clinton

Muhlhauser S. & Son (Susannah & Henry Muhlhauser) 57 Clinton

Muir, Hawley & Mayo Co. (John Muir, Pres.; Arthur B. Ray, Sec.; Edward A. Hawley, Treas. Capital, $100,000. Directors: John Muir, Edward S. Mayo, Edward A. Hawley) 343 B'way

Muir's James, Sons & Co. (James & John & James F. & John F. Muir) 27 E. 20th

Mulcare Brothers (Andrew & Patrick Mulcare) 120 Elm

Mulford & Bonnet (dissolved) 21 Maiden la.

Mulford Brothers & Co. (James H. Mulford, only) 26 Cedar

Mulford, Cary & Conklin (Benjamin H. Cary & Eugene H. Conklin, only) 84 Spruce

Mülhens & Kropff (Ferdinand Mülhens & William Kropff) 47 Murray

Mulholland & Grady (dissolved) 116 W. 28th

Mulholland & Hickcox (William Heartt, Charles J. Stelle & John R. & James R. Knowlton jr. only) 81 Exchange pl.

FOR THE BEST CO-PARTNERSHIP IN THE BEST CORPORATION SEE PAGE F IN BACK OF BOOK

Mull W. D. & Co, (no inf.) 617½ Tenth av.
Mullancy James & Son (James & James A. Mullaney) 204 E. 28d
Mullanney T. J. & Co. (Thomas J. Mullaney & Max Rosenberg) 250 Canal & 96 Walker
Mullen G. Allen & Co. (no inf.) 198 B'way
Mullen J. & Co. (James Mullen & David Ryan) 371 Pearl
Mullen Brothers (Thomas J. & Patrick F. & Jeremiah Mullen) 2832 & 2396 Third av.
Mullen & Mallotnon (dissolved) 214 Centre
Muller Adrian H. & Son (William F. Redmond, Louis Mosler & Peter F. Meyer, only) 1 Pine
Muller Ernst & Co, (Ernst Muller & William Luhmann) 59 Beaver
Muller George & Co. (George & Valentine H. Muller) 25 E. 61st
Muller Henry (Henry & Henry J. Muller) 116 Prince
Muller Joseph & Son (Joseph & George Muller) 214 Stanton
Muller Thomas & Son (Thomas & William Muller) 278 Av. B
Muller Valentine H. & Co. (dissolved) 717 B'way
Muller A. & Co. (Arthur Muller & William H. Haecker) 27 New Chambers
Muller G. H. & Co. (Candace J. Muller, only) 783 B'way
Müller H. L. & Co. (dissolved) 88 Greene
Muller J. & Son (dissolved) 815 Eighth av. & 551 Tenth av.
Muller M. & Son (Mario Muller, only) 164 Essex
Muller Brothers (bakers) (Herman H. & John D. Muller) 320 Monroe
Müller Brothers (grocers) (dissolved) 122 St. Mark's pl.
Muller Brothers (grocers) (Henry & Charles H. Muller) 208 E. 104th
Muller Brothers (grocers) (William & Frederick Muller) 1471 Lex. av.
Muller Brothers (umbrellas) George & Charles Muller) 498 Broome
Muller & Brother (William Muller, only) 759 Tenth av.
Muller & Buttner (Peter G. Muller & Julius W. Buttner) 88 South
Muller & Co. (Henry Muller, no Co.) 4 Gold
Müller & Dittes (Adam Muller & John Dittes) 230 Third
Muller & Fink (dissolved) 111 Nassau
Muller & Harris (dissolved) 409 Third av.
Muller & Krone (John H. Muller & George W. Krone) 254 G'wich
Muller & Ringen (G. Henry Muller & Peter Ringen) 1270 Third av.
Müller & Schmidt (Ernst Müller & Peter Schmidt) 352 W. 38th
Müller & Wetzel (Valentine Möller & John Wetzel) 510 W. 56th
Muller & Wood (Cuno Muller & Samuel Wood) 781 Seventh av.
Muller, Chandler & Sweetser (William L. Muller, Sumner C. Chandler & William A. Sweetser) 280 B'way
Müller, Galinski & Vogel (John A. Müller, Oscar Galinski & Henry Vogel) 107 Beekman
Muller, Luchsinger & Co. (John Muller & Jacques Luchsinger, no Co.) 69 Duane
Muller, Schall & Co. (Frederick Muller, William Schäll jr. & Carl Muller) 54 Wall
Muller's Jr., Son (Louis Muller) 551 Tenth av. & 815 Eighth av.
Muller's Nicholas, Sons (Herman J. Muller, only) 117 Chambers
Mulligan Brothers (John & Bernard Mulligan) 422 Eighth av.

Mullin & Danta (dissolved) 206 E. 111th
Mulrane & Long (Patrick Mulrane & William Long) 906 Sixth av.
Mulry Thomas & Son (Thomas & Thomas M. Mulry) 301 W. 12th & 10 Perry
Mulvany P. & T. (Patrick J. & Thomas) 211 E. 85th
Mulvihill & Costello (James Mulvihill & Bridget Costello) 4 Bowery
Mumby A. H. & Son (Albert H. & Charles H. Mumby) 125 Pearl
Mumford Mining Co. (Cairn-Cross Downey, Pres.; Henry M. Duncan, Sec. Capital, $18,000. Trustees: Cairn-Cross Downey, Henry M. Duncan) no address
Mumford E. H. & Son (Egbert H. & Louis E. Mumford) 182 Thompson
Mumford & Bushnell (Thomas J. Mumford & Frank Bushnell) 165 B'way
Munch & Rübencamp (Henry M. Munch & George Rubencamp) 202 E. 40th
Muncie Pulp Co, (Henry Blackman, Pres.; S. H. Tacy, Sec.; Gustav L. Jaeger, Treas. Capital, $250,000. Trustees: Henry Blackman, Gustav L. Jaeger, Frank Norris) 136 Mulberry
Mundt Charles & Sons (Charles & Otto & Charles Mundt jr.) 90 Walker
Mundt & Creter (dissolved) 90 Walker
Munger L. A., Publishing Co. (Louis A. Munger, propr.) 80 Nassau & 53 Liberty
Munger, Thomas & Co. (A. Mauger & Abraham Thomas, no Co.) 150 B'way
Munich Co. [Ltd.] (Maunsell Van Rensselaer jr. Pres.; Henry R. Hoyt, Sec. Capital, $25,000. Directors: James E. Grannis, Henry R. Hoyt, Maunsell Van Rensselaer jr. Solomon Ranger) 267 W. 17th
Munn S., Son & Co, (A. Godwin Munn jr. & George W. Cummings, only) 122 Pearl
Munn & Co. (Orson D. Munn & Alfred E. Beach) 361 B'way
Munn & Jenkins (Alexander Munn & James E. Jenkins) 9 Bowling gr.
Manos Manuel jr. (firm) (in liquidation) 108 Water
Munos & Espriella (Jose Ma Munos & Justo R. de la Espriella) 61 Liberty
Munro & Baldwin (John R. Munro & Charles M. Baldwin) 98 Maiden la.
Munroe John & Co. (John & Henry W. Munroe, Edward Kern & Edgar Lockwood) 82 Nassau (see adv. front cover)
Munroe & Wyckoff (Benjamin F. Munroe & Peter B. Wyckoff) 61 B'way
Munroe's William Otis, Son & Co. (William E. & Matilda L. Munroe & Charles J. Mortimer) 645 Sixth av.
Muns & Terrel (dissolved) 41 Water
Munsell Eugene & Co. (Eugene Munsell, Lewis W. Kingsley & Franklin Brooks) 218 Water
Munsell & Co. (William W. Munsell & William L. Conley) 206 B'way
Munsey Frank A. & Co. (Frank A. Munsey, Pres.; Richard H. Titherington, Sec. Capital, $100,000. Trustees: Frank A. Munsey, Richard H. Titherington, Charles E. Bushmore) 81 Warren
Munstermann John F. W. & Son (dissolved) 225 Ninth av.
Munzer Alfred & Co. (Alfred Munzer & Jacob Mayers) 615 B'way
Murchie Horace D. & Co. (Horace B. & James Murchie) 82 Wall
Murchison & Co, (Kenneth M. Murchison & William F. Sorey) 74 Wall
Murdoch & McKnight (no inf.) 42 W. 23d
Murdoch & Ogle (no inf.) 1786 Tenth av.
Murdock R. O. & Co. (dissolved) 104 John

TYPEWRITING DONE BY THE TROW CITY DIRECTORY CO., 11 University Place.

MUR 206 MUT

Murley Lawrence & Co. (Lawrence & Christina Murley) 334 Washn. mkt
Murphy Alexander & Co. (John F. Klumpp, Joseph B. Bartleman, John E. Heywood & Edmund J. Snydor, only) 48 Exchange pl.
Murphy William T. & Co. (William T. Murphy, no Co.) 96 John & 19 Platt
Murphy J. C. & Co. (Jeremiah C. Murphy, no Co.) 7 South
Murphy M. & Son (Michael R. & William F. Murphy) 173 W. Houston
Murphy T. J. & Co. (Thomas J. Murphy, no Co.) 1667 Third av.
Murphy Brothers (builders) (no inf.) 504 W. 53d
Murphy Brothers (carpenters) (refused) 72 E. 85th
Murphy Brothers (stable) (Michael & Patrick Murphy) 156 E. 90th
Murphy & Barry (Patrick Murphy & William Barry) 79 Fulton mkt
Murphy & Co. (hats) (John & James E. & Charles P. Murphy) 118 Bowery & 2350 Third av.
Murphy & Co. (jewelers) (Charles C. & Frank D. Murphy) 196 B'way
Murphy & Co. (meat) (Edward Murphy & Herman Heinemann) 619 W. 40th
Murphy & Harbourne (James Murphy & James J. Harbourne) 161 Bowery
Murphy & Jones (Joseph Murphy & James Jones) 1908 Third av.
Murphy & McCarthy (Patrick Murphy, only) 90 Warren
Murphy & McCormack (James W. Murphy & Michael McCormack) 185 Pearl
Murphy & Norton (dissolved) 6 South
Murphy & Taylor (Elton M. Murphy & Frances Taylor) 238 E. 24th
Murphy, Lloyd & Boyd (Starr J. Murphy, Herbert M. Lloyd & Robert M. Boyd jr.) 111 B'way
Murphy's D., Son (William H. Murphy) 65 Fulton
Murray Hill Bank (William A. Darling, Pres.; Albert H. Gale, Cashier; Thomas Darling, Notary. Capital, $100,000. Directors: William A. Darling, Henry Clausen, Rufus M. Silvers, John Weber, James Carney, Bernard Metzger, Ferdinand T. Hopkins, Charles H. Willson, Philip Diehl, John Burlinson, Robert O. N. Ford, Charles H. Helmburg, Albert H. Gale) 760 Third av.
Murray Hill Beef Co. (G. F. & E. C. Swift, proprs.) 430 E. 31st
Murray Hill Employment Agency (James Foye, propr.) 114 E. 41st
Murray Hill Publishing Co. (Edward B. Foote, Pres.; Edward B. Foote jr. Sec.; Louis Cohn, Treas. Capital, $20,000. Directors: Edward B. & Edward B. Foote jr. Louis Cohn) 129 E. 28th
Murray John & Co. (no inf.) 841 E. Houston
Murray Printing Co. (Louis Cohn, propr.) 147 E. 23d
Murray C. E. & Co. (Catharine E. Murray & John J. Collier) 42 Water
Murray F. J. & Co. (Francis J. Murray & James H. May) 249 Washn. mkt
Murray H. & H. (Henry Murray, only) 608 W. 42d & First av. c E. 111th
Murray J. F. & Co. (dissolved) 1686 B'way
Murray J. P. & E. J. (Joseph P. & Edward J.) 2030 Third av.
Murray Brothers (no inf.) 495 E. 135th
Murray & Birge (Edward F. Marray & John T. Birge) 19 Coenties sl. & Pier 6 E. R.
Murray & Callahan (John Murray & John H. Callahan) 415 W. 42d
Murray & Co. (cotton gds.) (dissolved) 212 Church
Murray & Co. (trucks) (Joseph Murray & John Cloughen) 602 E. 16th & 207 Av. C

Murray & Drury (Minos H. Murray & Hugh J. Drury) 5 Beekman
Murray & Early (dissolved) 170 Varick
Murray & Edwards (Edward Murray & John D. Edwards) 737 Ninth av.
Murray & Hill (James Murray & Robert Hill) 439 W. 42d
Murray & Reid (John Murray & Jeremiah Reid) 29 South
Murray & Schoen (James J. Murray & Julius Schoen) 113 W. B'way
Murray & Stoll (Samuel Murray & Albert Stoll) 683 Sixth av.
Murray, Droking & Frost (A. Murray, Henry C. Droking & Charles A. Frost) 212 Church
Murray, Lebar & Kennard (Robert I. Murray, Frank Lebar & William Kennard) 409 B'way
Murray's Charles, Son (Patrick C. Murray) 64 New Chambers & 72 Roosevelt
Murray's Line (Murray & Birge, proprs.) 19 Coenties sl. & Pier 6 E. R.
Murrill & Murlo (dissolved) 115 Third av.
Murtagh Charles E. & Co. (Charles E. Murtagh & John A. McCarthy) 309 Rivington
Muschel & Miller (Max Muschel & Louis Miller) 3 Wooster
Muser Brothers (Frederick W. & Richard & Curt Muser) 467 Broome
Musgrave & Co. (dissolved) 29 Pine
Music Hall Co. (Ltd.) (Morris Reno, Pres.; Frederick W. Holls, Sec.; Stephen M. Knevals, Treas. Capital, $600,000. Directors: John W. Aitken, Andrew Carnegie, Walter J. Damrosch, Frederick W. Holls, Stephen M. & Sherman W. Knevals, Morris Reno, William B. Tuthill, John J. Wilson) 210 W. 57th
Music Supply Assn. (inf. unattainable) 83 Fifth av.
Musical Instrument Mfg. Co. (Adolph Cohn, propr.) 342 Bowery
Musical Monthly Publishing Co. (Hewitt & Hosier, proprs.) 19 E. 14th
Muskat & Lipman (no inf.) 392 Second av.
Musliner Joseph & Co. (Moses & Isaac Musliner & Isaiah Friesner, only) 100 Gold & 319 E. Houston
Mussgiller Brothers (Frederick C. & George P. Mussgiller) 203 Duane
Muth & Son (John A. & Charles A. Muth) 130 W. 23d
Mutual Benefit Exchange for Women's Work (not inc.) (Hester Wilson Dart & Sarah Louise Howell) 184 W. 22d
Mutual Benefit Ice Co. (John Mulford, Pres.; Provost S. Haines, Sec. Capital, $250,000. Directors: Augustus C. Bechstein, Elias T. Hopkins, John C. Shaw, John Mulford, Provost S. Haines, John N. Lewis, Samuel McMillan, Miles Hughes, Elias Van Benschoten) 202 W. 43d, ft. Little W, 112th, ft. Stanton, ft. Beekman, ft. W, 132d, 420 W. 14th & 539 W, 40th
Mutual Benefit Life Assn. of America (Edward Henry Kent, Pres.; Theodore C. Landmesser, Sec. Directors: Rufus D. Bullock, Charles B. Bostwick, Zachariah Dederick, James Crissy Peabody, James S. Millard, Brewster Maverick, William H. Whiton, Edward Henry Kent, James E. Ostrander, Sidney H. Stuart, William L. Gardner, Horatio C. King, Moses Mehrbach) 111 E. 42d
Mutual Co. (William E. Ferguson, Pres.; Edward M. Timmins, Sec. Capital, $500,000. Directors: William E. Ferguson, Edward M. Timmins) 137 Produce Ex.
Mutual District Messenger Co. (Ltd.) (Marcellus Hartley, Pres.; William W. Hder, Sec.; Albert Blackburne, Treas. Capital, $7,500. Directors: Thomas M. Foote, Clark B. Hotchkiss, Marcellus Hartley, Anson Phelps Stokes, Albert Blackburne, William E. D. Stokes,

THADDEUS DAVIDS CO., WRITING INKS, SEALING WAX, MUCILAGE.
MAKE THE BEST

MUT 207 NAE

Thomas E. Stillman, William H. Wickham, Edmund W. Corlies, James A. Hewlett, William W. Rider) 29 Murray & 33 Warren

Mutual District Telegraph Co. (Marcellus Hartley, Pres.; William W. Rider, Sec.; Albert Blackburne, Treas. Capital, $300,000. Directors: Thomas M. Foote, Clark D. Hotchkiss, Marcellus Hartley, Anson Phelps Stokes, Albert Blackburne, Thomas E. Stillman, Edmund W. Corlies, James A. Hewlett, William W. Rider) 29 Murray & 33 Warren

Mutual Electric Construction Co. (no inf.) 152 B'way

Mutual Electric Mfg. Co. (Theodore E. Otis, Pres. Capital, $1,000,000. Trustees: Theodore E. Otis, Richard Arnold, Charles T. Carret) no address

Mutual Express (Bell & Kimball, proprs.) 8 Old sl.

Mutual Fire Ins. Co. (Philander B. Armstrong, Pres.; Joseph C. Halls, Sec. Directors: Philander B. Armstrong, Oscar R. Meyer, Joseph Fox, John Dickson, Anton F. Treescher, Otto Von Hoin, Aaron Carter, Emil Calman, William E. Lowe, Rudolph A. Loewenthal, Charles S. Braisted, J. W. Mack, Jacob H. Loewenstine, William Eggert, James Jourdan, Frederick A. Von Bernuth, David Calman, Samson Lachman, Nathan D. Bill, J. Spencer Turner, F. Forsch) 155 B'way

Mutual Furniture Co. (Thomas Kelly, propr.) 263 Sixth av. & 104 W. 17th

Mutual Life Ins. Co. (Richard A. McCurdy, Pres.; Frederic Cromwell, Treas.; William J. Easton, Sec. Trustees: Samuel Esprouls, Lucius Robinson, Samuel D. Babcock, George S. Coe, Richard A. McCurdy, James C. Holden, Hermann C. von Post, Alexander H. Rice, Lewis May, Oliver Harriman, Henry W. Smith, Robert Olyphant, George F. Baker, Joseph Thompson, Frederic Cromwell, Julien T. Davies, Robert Sewell, S. Van Rensselaer Cruger, Charles R. Henderson, George Bliss, Rufus W. Peckham, J. Hobart Herrick, William P. Dixon, Robert A. Grannies, Nicholas C. Miller, Henry H. Rogers, John W. Auchincloss, Theodore Morford, William Babcock, Preston D. Plumb, William D. Washburn, Stuyvesant Fish, Augustus D. Julliard, Charles E. Miller, James W. Husted) 32 Nassau (see adv. front cover.)

Mutual Protective Co. (James O'Neill, propr.) 323 B'way

Mutual Real Estate Co. (Augustus H. Levy, Pres.; Abraham Levy, Sec.; Julius Levy, Treas. Capital, $500,000. Directors: Augustus H. & Abraham & Julius & Louis & Moses S. Levy) 612 B'way

Mutual Reserve Fund Life Assn. (Edward B. Harper, Pres.; Frederick T. Braman, Sec.; Henry J. Reinmund, Treas. Directors: Edward B. Harper, O. D. Baldwin, Newell W. Bloss, Henry J. Reinmund, Samuel A. Robinson, Charles R. Bissell, John J. Acker, James W. Bowden, Anthony N. Brady, Samuel W. Wray, Frederick T. Braman, Thomas P. Baldwin) Potter bldg.

Mutual Savings & Distribution Fund Assn. (John H. Durland, Pres.; John P. Anderson, Sec.; Richard H. Taylor, Treas. Directors: John P. Anderson, John H. Durland, Harrison Johnson, Frederick W. Carl, W. W. Granger, Richard H. Taylor, R. A. Baggage, Lyman Taylor) 20 W. 14th

Mutual Steam Laundry Co. (Curry & Smyer, proprs.) 401 E. 23d

Mutual Trust Co. (William H. Guion, Pres.; John F. Langan, Sec. Capital, $50,000. Directors: William H. Guion, Orin C. Frost, John F. Langan, William McMahon, John Weaver, Quinton Corwine, Rudolph Allen, Jonas H. French, Benjamin F. Butler, Frederick S. Helser, James Boyce jr. Louis Guion, Willis A. Darnes, Philip H. Driggs) 115 B'way

Mutual Union Telegraph Co. (dissolved) 195 B'way

Mutual Watch Co. (Thomas F. Costello, Pres.; William Sohmer, Sec. Capital, $10,000. Directors: Julius Schwartzkopf, Marie Costello, Julia Sohmer) 196 B'way

Mycenian Marble Co. (Elbridge Walcott, Pres.; Stoddart W. Pollard, Sec.; Oscar Yenni, Treas. Capital, $500,000. Directors: Elbridge Walcott, Stoddart W. Pollard, Oscar Yenni, Henry S. Vanderbilt, George W. Dresser) 284 & 320 Pearl

Myer & Feig (Isaac Myer & Ralph Feig) 217 E. Houston & 55 Av. A

Myers Charles & Brother (Charles & Louis Myers) 27 Greene

Myers Fred J. & Vanburen (Frederic J. Myers & Edward M. Vanburen) 80 Cedar

Myers Lawrence & Co. (Robert G. Larsson & Lawrence Myers:—special partners, Angelo L. & Julien L. Myers, each $30,000; terminates 31st Dec. 1890) 35 S. William

Myers Sanitary Depot (Andrew G. Myers, Pres.; E. T. Griffin, Sec. Capital, $20,000. Directors: Andrew G. Myers, Lucien Knapp, E. T. Griffin) 80 Beekman

Myers Theodore W. & Co. (Theodore W. & Edward H. Myers & Fordyce D. Barker) 45 New & 44 B'way

Myers D. & O. (Brinkerhoff & Oscar) 16 Beekman

Myers E. & Co. (I. Harby Moses & Elijah Myers) 436 Produce Ex.

Myers P. V. & Co. (Philip V. Myers, no Co.) 26 White

Myers S. F. & Co. (Samuel F. & Marcus A. Myers & Simon Blumauer) 50 Maiden la.

Myers Brothers (Jacob & Phineas D. Myers) 85 John

Myers & Barry (dissolved) 123 Roosevelt

Myers & Clark (John L. Myers & James T. Clark) 1293 B'way

Myers & Co. (Charles A. Myers & Samuel Solifrey) 63 Reade

Myers & Gordon (David Myers & George A. Gordon) 82 Gold

Myers & Heineman (Herman Myers & Nathan Heineman) 435 B'way

Myers & Hern Shoe Co. (Michael Myers, Pres.; William F. Hern, Sec.; Henry Hern, Treas. Capital, $25,000. Directors: Michael Myers & William F. & Henry Hern) 63 Reade

Myers & Nuneviller (no inf.) 101 W. 21st

Myers & Underhill (Mason Myers & Benjamin T. Underhill) 65 Dey

Myers & Vonpreif (William H. Myers & Adolph Vonpreif) 213 Grand

Myers, Rutherfurd & Co. (John A. & Walter Rutherfurd & Gouverneur W. Morris, only) 58 Wall

Myers' Excursion & Navigation Co. (Robert Haddon, Pres.; John L. Gwyer, Sec.; Frederick S. Gwyer, Treas. Directors: Robert Haddon, John L. & Frederick S. Gwyer) 371 West

Myres J. M. & Brother (Julius M. & Albert M. Myres) 102 Franklin

Myres & Wallach (Rudolph M. Myres & Moses Wallach) 597 B'way & 170 Mercer

N

N. & B. Cleaning Co. (Charles W. Newkirk, Pres.; Palmer Brown, Sec. Capital, $2,500; further inf. unattainable) 1483 B'way & 617 Seventh av.

Nackenhorst & Winter (dissolved) 173 Chambers

Naegele Watch & Jewelry Co. (Eugene Naegele, Pres.; Henry B. Apple. Treas. Capital, $100,000. Directors: Eugene Naegele, Arthur J. Foote, Henry B. Apple, Henry C. Haines, John Price) 268 B'way

COMPILED WITH ACCURACY AND DISPATCH } **CLASSIFIED BUSINESS LISTS.** { THE TROW CITY DIRECTORY CO. 11 University Place.

NAE 208 NAT

Naething Brothers (Charles F. & Herman E. Naething) 118 Fulton, 19 Lispenard & 360 Canal

Nagel Brothers (dissolved) 91 Barclay, 31 Hudson & 313 Canal

Nagel & Werner (Charles Nagel & George Werner) 62 Duane

Nagelsmith & Rothschild (Nathan D. Nagelsmith & Samuel Rothschild) 314 Church

Nagle & Keating (dissolved) 13 New Bowery

Nahm & Loughrey (Julius Nahm & Charles Loughrey) 28 Union sq. W.

Nail Brothers (John B. & Edward Nail) 461 Sixth av.

Nail T. J. & Co, (Thomas J. Nail & Myron H. Cavanagh) 178½ & 365 Bowery

Naphtha Renovating, Steam Carpet Shaking & Dyeing Works (estate of George P. Bryant, propr.) 716 B'way, 358 Av. A & 2084 Seventh av.

Napier Alexander D. & Co. (Alexander D. Napier, Thomas Hiller & Harkort Napier) 526 B'way

Napier Brothers (Charles & Joshua W. Napier) 438 B'way

Nash S. P. & J. McL. (Stephen P. & John McL. Nash & Charles L. Jones) 67 Wall

Nash & Brush (Charles W. Nash & George S. Brush) 16 Park pl.

Nash & Kendall (George W. Nash & John A. Kendall) 31 Pearl, 20 Bridge & 271 South

Nash & Williams (dissolved) 460 Sixth av.

Nash, Whiton & Co, (James H. Nash. Sylvester G. Whiton & Timothy L. Woodruff;—special partner, Lucius H. Biglow, $30,000; terminates 1st Feb., 1896) 120 Warren

Nason E., Co. (Joseph W. Kay, Pres.; Frederick L. Degener jr. Sec.; Edwin F. Nason, Treas. Capital, $2,500. Directors: Joseph W. Kay, Edwin F. Nason, Frederick L. Degener jr.) 21 Ann

Nason Mfg. Co. (Carleton W. Nason, Pres.; Samuel Greason, Treas. Capital, $25,000. Directors: Carleton W. Nason, Samuel Greason, Franklin Darracott) 71 Beekman

Nass Jacob & Co. (Jacob Nass & Samuel Goldfarb) 243 Delancey

Nassau Bank (Francis M. Harris, Pres.; William H. Rogers, Cashier; Raphael M. Matteson, Notary. Capital, $500,000. Directors: Francis M. Harris, James C. Doll jr. Charles G. Harmer, Thomas B. Hidden, Enos Richardson, Augustine Smith) 9 Beekman

Nassau Bank Safe Deposit Vaults (Nassau Bank, propr.) 9 Beekman

Nassau Coffee Co. (Ltd.) (Hasbrouck Bartow, Pres.; Charles Lange jr, Sec. Capital, $10,000. Directors: Walter J. Peck, Hasbrouck Bartow, Charles Lange jr. John M. Miner, P. J. Seuring) 82 Water

Nassau Ferry Co. (James M. Waterbury, Pres.; Samuel C. Ellis, Sec. Capital, $150,000. Directors: D. D. Withers, Anthony V. Winans, John S. Ellis, Robert Center, James M. Waterbury) 132 Front & ft. E. Houston

Nassau Fire Ins. Co. (William T. Lane, Pres.; Thomas M. Harris, Sec. Capital, $200,000. Directors: A. L. Low, John T. Martin, John W. Hunter, John French, James A. H. Bell, Silas Ludlam, Thomas Stratton, Foster Pettit, John J. Vanderbilt, L. M. Sheldon, Henry D. Polhemus, William T. Lane, Rufus Litchfield, Elias Lewis jr. H. Zabriskie, Daniel Underhill) 179 B'way

Nassau Mfg. Co. (refused) 140 Nassau

Nassau News Co. (Ferdinand Greenebaum, propr.) 13 Spruce

Nassau Shoe Co. (Capital, $10,000; further inf. unattainable) no address

Nassau Stamp Works (John H. Vancourt, propr.) 58 Fulton

Nassau Sulphur Works (Beggs & Still, proprs.) 143 Maiden la.

Nassau Trading Co. (Ltd.) (Thomas T. Barr, Pres.; James P. Holland, Sec.; Thomas M. Barr, Treas.; further inf. refused) 107 & 125 Front

Natches, Red River & Texas R. R. Co. (Hugh Porter, Pres.; William H. Murphy, Sec. Capital, $2,250,000. Directors: Hugh Porter, George W. Debevoise, Charles H. Stone, William H. Murphy, Hiram R. Steele, R. F. Learned, Louis Doth) 11 Pine

Nathan Mfg. Co. (Max Nathan, Pres.; Jacob W. Mack, Sec. Capital, $300,000. Trustees: Max Nathan, William Toothe, Jacob W. Mack) 102 Liberty & ft. E. 106th

Nathan P. & Co. (Pincus Nathan, Henry Morris & Albert Sklarek) 87 Bowery & 65 Chrystie

Nathan S. J., Son & Co. (Solomon J. & Isaac Nathan & Lewis J. Reinhelmer) 554 B'way & 92 Crosby

Nathan Brothers (cigars) (Julius & David Nathan) 1765 Ninth av.

Nathan Brothers (clothing) (Moses & Henry & George W. & Solomon & Robert A. Nathan) 519 B'way & 92 Mercer

Nathan Brothers (meat) (Ernest A. & Albert Nathan) Highbridge rd. c Kingsbridge rd.

Nathan Brothers (printers) (Augustus & Paul Nathan) 140 W. 23d

Nathan & Barnett (Samuel H. & Caroline Nathan & Lawrence C. Barnett) 102 Barclay

Nathan & Co. (Benjamin Nathan, no Co.) 533 B'way

Nathan & Sondheim (Harold Nathan & Leopold Sondheim) 60 B'way

Nathan & Wight (Henry C. Nathan & George R. Wight) 139 W. B'way

National Academy of Design (Daniel Huntington, Pres.; Horace W. Robbins, Sec.; Alfred Jones, Treas.) 63 E. 23d

National Accident Soc. (Joshua L. Barton, Pres.; Joseph I. Barnum, Sec.; James C. Brower, Treas. Directors: Joshua L. Barton, Benjamin C. Wetmore, John W. Harman, John S. Williamson, James C. Brower, Stephen W. Collins, Jacob Oberholser, Joseph I. Barnum, Victor E. Wetmore) 280 B'way

National Advertising Co. (Herman L. Ensign, Pres.; George A. Kellogg, Sec. Capital, $75,000. Directors: Herman L. Ensign, George A. Kellogg, Willard D. Stevens) 2 Tribune bldg.

National Alliance (Harvey M. Munsell, Pres.; Abel C. Hunt, Sec. Directors: Orson & Charles K. Adams, John Lebonbillier, Benjamin F. Tracy, Henry Lylburn, Harvey M. Munsell, Thomas C. Long, R. Delevan Wondruff, Henry R. Simmons, Abel C. Hunt, H. G. Lyttle, J. S. Byington) 5 Beekman

National Am. Business Exchange (Inf. unattainable) P. O. Box 2986

National Autographic Register Co. (Erastus Wiman, Pres.; Alfred P. Boller, Treas.; James C. Shoup, Sec. Capital, $1,000,000. Directors: Erastus Wiman, Alfred P. Boller, James C. Shoup, C. Benninghofen, Joseph Swift, H. K. Knapp, Samuel Shoup, H. P. Potter) 293 B'way

National Automatic Fire Alarm Co. (Frank E. Morgan, Pres.; Joseph W. Frost, Sec. Capital, $100,000. Directors: Frank E. Morgan, James W. Husted, J. Gillet Noyes, Charles A. Tinker, Garrie S. Pearsall, George V. B. & Joseph W. Frost) 317 B'way

National Automatic Transfer Co. (James C. Shoup, Pres.; Lucius O. Robertson, Sec. Capital, $500,000. Directors: James C. Shoup, Lucius O. Robertson, John Franklin Clark) 293 B'way

National Baking Co. (Anne Miller, propr.) 121 W. 100th

SPECIAL ATTENTION PAID TO THIS CLASS OF WORK. } **BANKERS' & BROKERS' CIRCULARS DELIVERED** { **THE TROW CITY DIRECTORY CO. 11 University Place.**

NAT — 209 — NAT

National Baking Co. (Bernard D. Coyle. propr.) 712 Third av.
National Baking Co. (George W. Kimmo, propr.) 942 Tenth av.
National Baking Co. (Jacob Rodenbach, propr.) 750 Ninth av.
National Baking Co. (James Fay, propr.) 650 Second av.
National Baking Co. (James Wixted, propr.) 1462 Second av.
National Baking Co. (John D. Hennessy, propr.) 196 Grand
National Baking Co. (John Ryan, propr.) 279 Av. A
National Baking Co. (Mary Gombert, propr.) 504 First av.
National Baking Co. (Matthew T. Lindsay, propr.) 770 Tenth av.
National Baking Co. (Patrick B. Burns, propr.) 460 Second av.
National Baking Co. (Patrick Walsh, propr.) 659 Tenth av.
National Baking Co. (Peter J. Stumpf, propr.) 3375 Third av.
National Baking Co. (Valentine Blaesser, propr.) 2750 Third av.
National Baking Co. (William F. Naegele, propr.) 2687 Eighth av.
National Bank Note Co. (consolidated with Am. Bank Note Co.) 86 Trinity pl.
National Bank of Commerce (Richard King, Pres.; William W. Sherman, Cashier; William A. Duer, Notary. Capital, $5,000,000. Directors: Richard King, A. A. Low, J. Pierpont Morgan, William Libbey, Frederick Sturges, Charles Lanier, Charles H. Russell jr. A. L. Dennis, Alexander E. Orr, John S. Kennedy) 29 Nassau
National Bank of Deposit (Lewis E. Ransom, Pres.; Frank L. Brown, Cashier; Henry L. Gilbert, Notary. Capital, $300,000. Directors: John H. Gilbert, George W. Hoagland, Gustavus A. Jahn, Alfred C. Mintram, Sinclair Myers, E. S. Ormsby, David B. Powell, Andrew Simonds, Augustus K. Sloan, Charles F. Sanborn, Leopold Stern, Thomas B. Sloan, Noah C. Rogers, Lewis E. Ransom, H. B. Moore) 55 Liberty
National Bank of the Republic (John Jay Knox, Pres.; Eugene H. Pullen, Cashier; Noel B. Sanborn, Notary. Capital, $1,500,000. Directors: George B. Carhart, Sumner R. Stone, Oliver S. Carter, David H. McAlpin, Wallace C. Andrews, George E. Simpson, John Jay Knox, Charles R. Flint, A. H. Wilder, James S. Warren, William H. Tillinghast, William Barbour) 2 Wall
National Barrow & Truck Co. (Joseph V. Annin, Pres.; Edward F. Cole, Sec. Directors: Joseph & Joseph V. Annin, Edward F. & Edward H. Cole) 52 Fulton
National Benefit Soc. (Henry K. Shackleford, Pres.; William Abbott. Sec.; David E Smith, Treas. Directors: Henry K. Shackleford, David B. Smith, A. J. Perry, Louis P. Levy, J. F. Hotchkiss, J. G. Kearney, William A. Timpson, George O. Foster, William Abbott) 187 B'way
National Blank Book Co. (Henry S. Dewey, Pres.; Frank B. Towne, Sec. Capital, $150,000. Directors: Henry S. Dewey, J. W. Towne, Martin B. Klopp, Alfred J. Taylor, William Whiting) 76 Duane
National Board of Fire Underwriters (Daniel A Heald, Pres.; Robert B. Beath, Sec.; Frederick W. Arnold, Treas.) 156 B'way
National Board of Marine Underwriters (Thomas C. Hand, Pres.; J. Raymond Smith, Sec.; James Lawson, Treas.) 25 William
National Brass & Wire Works (William Lathers, propr.) 14 Second av.

National Broadway Bank (Francis A. Palmer, Pres.; Arthur T. J. Rice, Cashier, Richard B. Kelly. Notary. Capital, $1,000,000. Directors: Francis A. Palmer, Francis P. Furnald, Henry L. Hoguet, John Lawrence, Hudson Hoagland, Henry O. Havemeyer, George L. Whitman, George F. Gantz, James T. Swift, Samuel A. Sawyer, Arthur T. J. Rice, Andrew Mills, Joel E. Fisher, John F. Talmage, David S. Walton, James Talcott, George C. Clarke) 237 B'way
National Butchers' & Drovers' Bank (Gurdon G. Brinckerhoff, Pres.; William H. Chase, Cashier; James Otis Hoyt, Notary. Capital, $300,000. Directors: George W. Quintard, John C. Chamberlain, Henry Silberhorn, John B. Cotte, Langstaff N. Crow, Gurdon G. Brinckerhoff, William H. Chase, John Wilkin, John A. Delaney jr.) 124 Bowery
National Button Works (Kessler & Co. proprs.) 16 Howard
National Cable Railway Co. (Joseph Britton, Pres.; James W. Towne, Treas.; Charles R. Parsons, Sec. Capital, $2,500,000. Directors: Joseph Britton, Frank W. Wilson, Alfred Peckham, James W. Towne, Edward Lyman Short, George Maynard, Martin B. Klopp, William C. Davis, Charles R. Parsons) 140 Nassau
National Calcium Light Co. (William Gullery, propr.) 187 Mulberry
National Car Spring Co. (Richard Vose, Pres.; Benjamin Atha, Treas.; John C. N. Gulbert, Sec. Capital, $200,000. Directors: Benjamin Atha, James Lancey, Henry G. Atha, Richard Vose, John S. Silver) 115 B'way
National Car & Locomotive Assn (Robert M. Van Arsdale, propr.) 140 Nassau
National Card Co. (Robert H. McCutcheon, Pres.; August Crudus, Sec.; J. C. McCutcheon, Treas. Directors: Robert H. & J. C. McCutcheon, August Crosius, Samuel J. Murray, Henry C. Carmer) 297 Canal
National Carpet Cleaning Works (Robert N. Blackhall, propr.) 884 Third av.
National Chemical Co. (Henry S. Firman, Pres.; Daniel C. Hood, Sec.; William H. De Hart, Treas.; further inf. unattainable) 115 B'way
National Citizens' Bank (William H Oakley, Pres.; David C. Tiebout, Cashier; Robert Owen, Notary. Capital, $600,000. Directors: William H. Oakley, James McLean, William J. Valentine, Edward Schell, Pearson Halstead, Elkan Naumburg, Robert Irwin, Stephen R. Lesher, Thomas J. Davis, Edward L. Merrifield, Charles H. Tonney, Ewald Fleitmann, Charles H. Wheeler) 461 B'way
National City Bank (Percy R. Pyne, Pres.; David Palmer, Cashier; Hanson C. Gibson, Notary. Capital, $1,000,000. Directors: Percy R. Pyne, Henry Parish, Samuel Sloan, William Walter Phelps, Benjamin Dunning, Roswell G. Rolston, Lawrence Turnure, George W. Campbell, Cleveland H. Dodge) 52 Wall
National Collecting Agency (David B. Hotzel, propr.) 38 Park row
National Collection & Commercial Agency (Charles D. Holmes, propr.) 38 Park row
National Conduit Mfg. Co. (Caleb H. Jackson, Pres.; James P. McQuaide, Sec. Capital, $250,000. Directors: Caleb H. Jackson, James F. McQuaide, Edward S. Perot, Paul D. Cravath, George L. Wiley) 18 Cortlandt
National Conservatory of Music of America (refused) 128 E. 17th
National Cordage Co. (James M. Waterbury, Pres.; Caleb P. Marsh, Sec. Elisha M. Fulton, Treas.; further inf. refused) 132 Front
National Cotton Oil Co. (inf. unattainable) 45 B'way
National Curing Tube Co. (Henry C. Green, Pres.; Andrew Lomon, Sec.; Andrew Ruehl, Treas. Capital, $25,000. Directors: Henry C. Green, Andrew Ruehl, John J. & George Bailey) 151 E. 114th

14

TYPEWRITING DONE BY THE TROW CITY DIRECTORY CO., 11 University Place.

NAT 210 NAT

National Drill & Compressor Co. (Gilbert H. McKibbin, Pres.; Henry L. Jones, Sec. Capital, $5,000. Directors: Gilbert H. McKibbin, Henry L. Jones, James R. Steers jr.) 84 S. 5th av.

National Electric Light Assn. (Allan V. Garrett, Sec.) 18 Cortlandt

National Electric Machine Co. (John Q. Preble, Pres.; James G. Bennett, Sec.; Frederick J. Lancaster, Treas. Capital, $20,000. Directors; John Q. & Walter E. Preble, Frederick J. Lancaster, B. S. Bennett) 60 Murray

National Electric Protector Co. (Herman Stutzer jr. Pres.; Edward C. Halsey, Sec. Capital, $500,000. Trustees: Herman Stutzer jr., Edward C. Halsey, E. C. Bridgman) 18 B'way

National Electric Service Co. (inf. unattainable) 76 Fifth av.

National Enquiry System of the Sugar Manufacturers of the U. S. (Edward Heyman, Pres.; Morris S. Wise, Sec.; James Brussel, Treas.) 52 Exchange pl.

National Express Co. (Johnston Livingston, Pres.; Robert C. Livingston, Sec.; Locke W. Winchester, Treas. Capital, $500,000. Directors; Johnston & Robert C Livingston, Locke W. Winchester, James C. Fargo, Theodore M. Pomeroy, Ebenezer H. Virgil) 145 D'way

National Fine Art Foundry (Maurice J. Power, propr.) 237 B'way & 218 E. 25th

National Fire Ins. Co. (Henry T. Drowne, Pres.; John H. Kattenstroth, Sec. Capital, $200,000. Directors: Charles F. Southmayd, Henry T. Drowne, Charles Watrous, William G. Ward, Henry E. Nesmith, Warren Ackerman, James M. Thorburn, Joseph Park, John Watson, John A. Stewart jr. George A. Barker, Robert S. Holt, Thomas W. Thorne) 85 Pine

National Furniture Assn. (A. S. Talcott, Pres.; Marshall D. Talcott, Sec.) 150 Canal

National Galvanic Battery Co. (inf. unattainable) 18 Cortlandt

National Gas Improvement Co. (Winfield S. Chamberlin, Pres.; Alexander M. Sutherland, Sec. Capital, $1,000,000; further inf. refused) 115 B'way

National Heat & Power Co. (Daniel H. Hastings, Pres.; James M. West, Sec.; James A. Beaver, Treas. Capital, $5,000,000. Directors: Daniel H. Hastings, Alfred Sully, Robert H. Coleman, James A. Beaver, James M. West, James L. Hastings, John S. Smith, O. L. Jones, A. R. Ledoux) 40 Wall

National Heating Co. (Theodore N. Vail, Pres.; Delmore Elwell, Sec. Capital, $1,750,000. Directors: Theodore N. Vail, G. H. Wynkoop, Nathan Guilford, James Thompson, Samuel M. Bryan, William K. Prall, O. E. Madden, Edgar T. Wells, Asbhel Green) 44 B'way

National Horse Show Assn. of America (Ltd.) (Cornelius Fellowes, Pres.; James T. Hyde, Sec.; Henry H. Hollister, Treas. Capital, $70,000. Directors: Cornelius Fellowes, Henry H. Hollister, William F. Wharton, Henry I. Nicholas, Frank K. Sturgis, G. Peabody Wetmore, Frederic Bronson, Francis T. Underhill, Lawrence Kip, James T. Hyde, John G. Heckscher, Henry W. T. Mali, Thomas Hitchcock jr.) 80 Broad

National Ice Co. (William De Groot, Pres.; Alfred Nelson, Sec. Capital, $250,000. Directors: William De Groot, John W. Mason, Smith Fancher, Clarence T. Sanford, William N. Bavier, Frank Burns, George H. Macy, Alfred Nelson) 100 E. 40th, ft. E. 11th & ft. E. 114th

National Ice Machine Co. (Edward N. Dickerson, Pres.; Anthony Gref, Sec. Capital $350,000. Directors: Edward N. Dickerson, Julius J. Suckert, Henry J. Davison, Anthony Gref, Stephen F. Byrnes, Henry E. Barr) 5 Beekman

National Improvement Co. (Charles H. Harman, Pres.; William W. Flannagan, Treas.; Dallas Flannagan, Sec. Capital, $50,000. Directors: Charles H. Harman, William W. Flannagan, Orson Adams, William Brookfield, Jefferson M. Levy) 52 Nassau

National Iron Fence Co. (Francis B. Spinola, Pres.; Onesimus P. Shaffer, Sec. Capital, $25,000. Francis B. Spinola, Wallace C. Andrews, Onesimus P. Shaffer, Charles & James Carpenter) 2 Cortlandt

National Iron Works (William E. Kelly, propr.) 18 Cortlandt

National Key Holder Ins. Co. (inf. unattainable) 111 B'way

National Lead Trust (William P. Thompson, Pres.; F. W. Rockwell, Sec.) 1 B'way

National Lloyds (Charles C. Leary, manager) 61 William

National Machine Co. (William M. House, Pres.; Edward O. House, Sec.; George H. Sutton, Treas. Capital, $75,000. Directors: William M. House, Shepard Tappen, Edward O. House, George H. Sutton) 885 B'way & 151 W. 29th

National Meter Co. (John C. Kelley, Pres.; David H. Gildersleeve, Sec.; John I. Holly, Treas. Capital, $200,000. Directors: John C. Kelley, Eugene Pitou, John I. Holly, George Lawrence, David H. Gildersleeve) 252 B'way (see top lines)

National Mutual Building & Loan Assn. (Charles B. Peet, Pres.; George R. Sutherland, Sec.; James R. Pitcher. Trans. Directors: Charles B. Peet, Joseph J. Little, J. Edward Simmons, George R. Sutherland, Edward J. Peet, William B. Smith, James B. Pitcher) 205 B'way

National News Co. (Thomas F. Cormick, Treas.; further inf. unattainable) 81 Beekman

National Oil Works & Mill Supply Co. (John S. Snedeker, Pres.; William A. Skinkle, Sec. Capital, $100,000. Trustees: John S. Snedeker, William A. Skinkle, George C. Crum, Moses R. Gildersleeve, George C. Rodwell) 59 Front

National Park Bank (V. Mumford Moore, Pres.; George S. Hickok, Cashier; Thomas B. Clifford, Notary. Capital, $2,000,000. Directors: Arthur Leary, Eugene Kelly, Ebenezer K. Wright, Francis H. Leggett, Joseph T. & V. Mumford Moore, Stuyvesant Fish, George S. Hart, James H. Parker, Charles Sternbach, Charles Scribner, Edward C. Hoyt, Edward E. Poor, W. Rockhill Potts, David L. Wallace) 216 B'way (see auto. in back)

National Photographic View Co. (Long & Heppner, propr.) 339 E. 34th

National Phototype Co. (refused) 16 Reade

National Pie Baking Co. (Muller Brothers, proprs.) 520 Monroe

National Press Co. (Marshman W. Hazolt, Pres.; William W. Hallock, Sec.; Henry B. Spood, Treas. Capital, $80,000. Directors: Marshman W. Hazen, William W. Hallock, W. N. Valls) 54 Warren

National Press Intelligence Co. (William F. G. Shanks, Pres.; John T. de Bell, Sec.; Lynn H. Shanks, Treas. Capital, $30,000. Directors: William F. G. Shanks, John T. de Bell, Lynn H. Shanks, James H. Knowle, W. R. Shanks) 26 Church

National Printers' Materials Co. (Thomas F. Donnelly, Pres.; George C. Moon, Treas. Capital, $25,000. Directors: Thomas F. Donnelly, George C. Moon) 279 Front

National Printing Telegraph Co. (dissolved) 171 B'way

National Progress Bunching Machine Co. (August Roessler, Pres.; Adolph C. Schutz, Sec. Capital, $300,000. Directors: August Roessler, Adolph C. Schutz, Louis Ettlinger, William J. Brown, Adolph Brussel, Adolph Lewyn, Nicholas H. Bornfeldt) 1290 Second av.

National Provident Union (Edward O. Bragdon, Pres.; John L. Kendall, Sec.; William H. De Hart, Treas.) 124 Front

THE CALIGRAPH WRITING MACHINE,
HARTFORD, CONN.

NAT 211 NEG

National Publishing Co. (John A. Taylor, propr.) 47 B'way

National Railway Publication Co. (William H. Woulverton, Pres.; Edmund Allen, Sec.; Egbert T. Sees, Treas.; further inf. refused) 46 Bond

National Remedy Co. (refused) 17 Laight

National Rifle Assn. of Am. (George W. Wingate, Pres.; John S. Shepherd, Sec.; Leslie C. Bruce, Treas.) 5 Beekman

National Sewerage & Sewage Utilization Co. (W. Scott West, Pres.; George S. Drew jr. Sec.; Jacob L. Kennedy, Treas. Capital, $3,600,000. Directors: W. Scott West, George W. Delano, Jacob L. Kennedy, Walter S. Church, Gracie S. Roberts, John W. Smith, J. S. Hackett, James McCausland, William H. Pancoast, John J. Doory, Samuel G. DeCourency, Louis M. Simpson) 280 B'way

National Sheet Metal Roofing Co. (Charles B. Cooper, Pres.; Willard F. Wallace, Sec. Capital, $120,000. Directors: Charles B. Cooper, Willard F. Wallace, John J. Hammond, James M. Wade, Henry W. Buttorff, jr. M. Sharpe, J M. Eubanks) 516 E. 20th

National Shoe & Leather Bank (John M. Crane, Pres.; William D. Vanvleck, Cashier; Edward J. Anthony, Notary. Capital, $500,000. Directors: John M. Crane, George L. Pease, Thomas Russell, Theodore M. Ives, William Sulzbacher, Joseph F. Knapp, Abraham Bussing, Joseph S. Stout, Alonzo Slote, Thomas Porter, Moritz Josephthal) 271 B'way

National Silver Co. (inf. unattainable) 79 Nassau

National Stamp & Novelty Co. (dissolved) 58 John

National Stave & Cooperage Stock Co. (no inf.) 401 W. 14th

National Stove Co. (John B. Thomas, Pres.; further inf. unattainable) 244 Water

National Temperance Soc. & Publication House (Theodore L. Cuyler, Pres.; John N. Stearns, Sec.; William D. Porter, Treas. Managers: Theodore L. Cuyler, Albert G. Lawson, B. J. Warner, Matthew H. Pogson, Henry B. Metcalf, A. A. Robbins, W. C. Steele, Henry M. Lester, J. A. Bogardus, D. C. Biddy, T. L. Poolson, Peter Carter, John N. Stearns, James Black, E. H. Clapp, J. O. Peck, James S. Chadwick, C. L. Wells, William T. Sabine, Louis Wagner, S. L. Parsons, I. Simmons, Joshua L. Baily, Norman W. Dodge, John Ellis, Halsey Moore, R. A. Sinclair, T. A. Brouwer, Clinton B. Fisk, John D. Slayback) 58 Reade

National Transit Co. (Clement A. Griscom, Pres.; John Bushnell, Sec.; George W. Colton, Treas. Capital, $25,455,200. Directors: Clement A. Griscom, William Rockefeller, John D. Archbold, Henry H. Rogers, Joseph D. Potts, Henry M. Flagler, Benjamin Brewster) 26 B'way

National Trucking & Forwarding Co. (not inc.) (Enoch Harris & Michael Shelley) 13 B'way

National Vulcan Burner Co. (no inf.) 132 Nassau

National Vulcanite Co. (George W. Quintard, Pres.; Lyndon H. Stevens, Sec. Capital, $1,000,000. Directors: George W. Quintard, Alexander H. Shepherd, James H. Breslin, Louis H. Scott, Edgar W. A. Jorgenson, Andrew B. Stone, Lyndon H. Stevens, John C. New, Matthew Taylor, Samuel Elliott, James S. Green, E. P. Alexander, H. E. Craig) 15 Broad

National Water Purifying Co. (William M. Deutsch, Pres.; Theodore F. Miller, Treas.; John C. Symons, Sec. Capital, $800,000. Directors: William M. Deutsch, Charles O. Worthington, Theodore F. Miller, Albert R. Leeds, John C. Symons) 145 B'way

National Water Tube Boiler Co. (William E. Kelly, propr.) 18 Cortlandt

National Water Works Co. (Giles E. Taintor, Pres.; Robert M. Weems, Sec. Capital, $3,000,000. Trustees: Giles E. Taintor, Leonidas M. Lawson, Robert M. Weems, Gaston D. L'Huilier, George E. Simpson, Henry B. Bowers, Alfred Ray) 102 B'way

National Water Works Investment Co. (Charles C. Pomeroy, Pres.; William J. Curtis, Sec.; Valentine P. Snyder, Treas. Capital, $500,000. Directors: George F. Baker, Archer N. Martin, Harris C. Fahnestock, E. W. Clark, Charles C. Pomeroy, F. M. Colston, Theodore C. Waterbury) 34½ Pine

National Weighing Machine Co. (John Q. Preble, Pres.; James G. Bennett, Sec.; Frederick J. Lancaster, Treas. Capital, $20,000. Directors: John Q. & Walter E. Preble, Frederick J. Lancaster, Bellop S. Bennett) 60 Murray

National Wood Co. (no inf.) 30 Cortlandt

National Wood Mfg. Co. (Boynton & Vanwinkle, props.) 129 Fifth av. & 151 Eleventh av.

Natural Dam Pulp Co. (John Q. Preble, Pres.; Theodore W. Bayand, Treas.; Cornelius R. Dimond jr. Sec. Capital, $250,000. Directors: John Q. Preble, Theodore W. Bayand, Cornelius R. Dimond jr. Walter E. Preble, Gustave F. Perrenoud) 60 New

Naugatuck Valley Steamboat Co. (no inf.) Pier 39 E. R.

Naumann & Co. (Arthur Naumann & Henry J. Ruesor) 444 Broome

Naumburg S. & Co. (dissolved) 127 Roosevelt

Naumburg, Kraus, Lauer & Co. (Elkan Naumburg, William Kraus, Emanuel Lauer & Max Naumburg) 650 B'way & 294 Mercer

Nauss A. & Co. (Adam Nauss, no Co.) 98 Rivington

Nauss Brothers (Wendelin J. & Charles E. Nauss, 67 Second av. & 2176 Third av.; Wendelin J. Nauss & Adolph Schnabel, only, 1538 Second av.)

Nauss Brothers & Co. (Wendelin J. & Charles E. Nauss & Charles Hubachek) 73 Delancey & 2201 Third av.

Nautical Publishing Co. (inf. unattainable) 24 State

Nawrath C. W. & Co. (Charles W. Nawrath, no Co.) 876 Canal

Nawrath J. P. & Co. (John P. Nawrath, no Co.) 2 Lispenard

Naylor & Co. (Edward Ascherson, Alexander S. Hay, Frederick L. Lehmann, J. Mitchell Clark, Ludwig Dreier & Arthur Holland, only) 45 Wall

Naylor & Felter (Charles H. Naylor & Walter Felter jr.) 97 Chambers & 81 Reade

Neal Walter W. & Herbert J. (dissolved) 9 Prince

Neal's John, Sons (Ambrose O. & Arthur H. Neal) 226 Grand

Neale & Dixon (Francis M. Neale & Edmund W. A. Dixon) 58 W. 30th

Neumann & Hass (no inf.) 1 B'way

Neary & Co. (George F. Neary & Frank Vaughan) 11 Vandewater

Nebraska Distilling Co. (no inf.) 80 Pearl

Nechamcus & Brother (Peter & Michael Nechamcus) 60 Bayard

Neck N. & Co. Nicholas Neck & Celina Schwarz) 1895 First av.

Needham R. P. & Son (Charles A. Needham, only) 145 E. 23d

Neely William & Co. (William & William T. F. Neely) 108 Duane

Neergaard Pharmacy (Olmstead & Weyh, proprs.) 936 Sixth av.

Nesson & Woodward (Robert D. Nesson & John W. Woodward) 81 Wooster

Neftel & Oothout (Knight Neftel & E. Austin Oothout) 41 Liberty

Negaunee Concentrating Co. (Henry Seibert, Pres.; William de L. Benedict, Sec.; Elias C. Benedict, Treas. Capital, $350,000. Directors:

Henry Seibert, William de L. & Elias C. Benedict, B. Haskell, George C. Wetmore, R. S. Middleton) 29 Broad

Negus T. S. & J. D. (Thomas S. & John D.) 140 Water

Neher & Carpenter (Philip H. Neher & James H. Carpenter) 170 B'way

Nehrbas A. & Son (Anton & Charles Nehrbas) 184 William

Neidlinger Brothers (William & Philip Neidlinger) 27 Beekman

Neidlinger, Schmidt & Co. (Adam Neidlinger, Henry W. Schmidt, Charles A. Stadler & George F. Neidlinger) 466 E. 17th & ft E. 64th

Neiwerth & Brother (no inf.) r 256 Delancey

Neike & Gatjen (John Neike & Charles F. Gatjen) 95 Broad

Nellis A. C. & Co. (Arthur C. Nellis, Co. refused) 62 Cortlandt

Nelson Mortgage Co. (no inf.) 32 Liberty

Nelson F. O. & Co. (dissolved) 58 Wall & Custom h.

Nelson & Co. (Adolph Nelson, no Co.) 13 Cortlandt

Nelson & Finkel (Charles Nelson & Edwin Finkel) 489 E. 10th

Nelson & Hayward (dissolved) 13 Cortlandt

Nelson & Heuberger (John Nelson jr. & William Heuberger) 96 Sixth av.

Nelson & Liftchild (Gustav Nelson & James Liftchild) 415 Washn. mkt

Nelson & Sanderson (John Nelson & Samuel Sanderson) 368 Grand

Nelson & Thompson (Frederick O. Nelson & Edwin K. Thompson) 58 Wall & 80 Laight

Noppel Brothers (Jacob L. & Emil Noppel) 409 & 420 Third av.

Norssheimer E. August & Co. (E. August & Louis Norssheimer) 21 Molden la.

Neri & Chiesa (Nicholas Neri & Antonio Chiesa) 70 W. Houston

Nesbitt George F. & Co. (James White, Edmund P. Martin & Frederick A. Harter, only) 167 Pearl & 77 Pine

Nesmith & Sons (Henry E. & Henry R. Nesmith jr. only) 2d South

Nesslage, Colgate & Co. (John H. H. Nesslage, M. Starr Colgate & Edward H. Fuller) 29 Wall

Nettleton & Mills (Charles Nettleton & Charles Edgar Mills) 115 B'way

Netzel & Frambach (Ferdinand F. Netzel & Peter Frambach) 27 Union sq. W.

Neubeck August & Co. (August Neubeck, no Co.) 111 Nassau

Nenberger & Finn (dissolved) 428 B'way

Neubirk M. & Brother (Meyer & Ephraim Neubirk) 433 Broome

Neuburger L. & H. & Co. (Louis & Herman & Isidor Neuburger) 10 Greene

Neuburger M. & Co. (foyods.) (Meyer Neuburger & Joseph Rosenberg) 372 B'way

Neuburger M. & Co. (tobacco) (Moses & David M. Neuburger) 172 Water

Neudorfer & Osnowitz (Simon Neudorfer & Jacob Osnowitz) 58 W. B'way

Neufeld J. & Brother (dissolved) 50 Canal

Neufeld & Schlesinger (Harris Neufeld & Emil Schlesinger) 168 Greene

Neufeld J. & Co. (Joseph Neufeld & Herman Epstein) 177 Monroe

Neugass Brothers (Moritz & William Neugass) 127 Grand

Neugass Brothers & Blum (Leopold & Henry Neugass & Samuel Blum) 110 Grand

Neuhaus Brothers (Isaac H. & Charles H. Neuhaus) 979 Second av.

Neuman Louis E. & Co. (Louis E. Neuman & John H. Poggenburg) 534 Pearl

Neuman & Co. (Daniel Neuman, no Co.) 263 Fifth av.

Neuman & Gross (dissolved) 326 Canal

Neuman & Janson (dissolved) 555 W. 14th

Neumann F. & Co. (Ferdinand Neumann, no Co.) 51 Murray

Neumann D. & Co. (Gustav Bornheim & Clemens Heltemeyer, only) 76 Duane

Neumann Brothers (bkbinders) (Charles G. & Ferdinand N. Neumann) 76 E. 9th

Neumann Brothers (eatingh.) (Henry & Herman Neumann) 387 Canal & 49 W. B'way

Neumann Brothers (real estate) (William & Louis Neumann) 118 W. 19th

Neumann & Bachr (Joseph Neumann & Herman Baehr) 99 Spring

Neumann & Co. (Julius Neumann & Frank E. Mitzenwei) 2018 Third av.

Neumann & Herman (August W. Neumann & Herman C. Herman) 241 Water

Neumann & Luniak (dissolved) 37 College pl.

Neumark & Gross (Julius Neumark & Louis N. Gross) 125 Broad

Neumoegen & Co. (Berthold Neumoegen & Charles McNulty) 40 Exchange pl.

Neumuller & Schaefer (Frans Neumuller & Andreas F. Schaefer) 4 Union sq. E.

Neus Brothers (John & Henry Neus) 161 Eleventh av.

Neuss, Hesslein & Co. (Edward Neuss & Samuel A. Hesslein, no Co.) 20 White

Neustadt & Co. (Emile D. & Otto Neustadt & Henry Katz) 358 Produce Ex.

Neustaedter P. & Co. (refused) 161 Pearl

Never Rip Jersey Co. (no inf.) 496 Cherry

Neville R. & Co. (Richard Neville & Walter G. Walsh) 170 E. 113th

Nevin M. W. & Son (Matthias W. & William W. Nevin) 79 William

Nevins James & Sons (dissolved) 615 W. 49th

Nevins & Haviland (John H. C. Nevins & Edgar F. Haviland) 400 B'way

New T., Mfg. Co. (Tobias New, Pres.; Clarence H. New, Sec. Capital, $200,000. Directors: Tobias & Clarence H. New) 82 John & 540 E. 20th

New Am. Electrical Arc Light Co. (John W. Hinkley, Pres.; Abraham J. Vandeventer, Sec.; Charles E. West, Treas.; further inf. unattainable) 18 Cortlandt

New Brunswick, Amboy & N. Y. Steamboat Co. (Joseph Cornell, Pres.; George M. Lewis, Sec. Capital, $80,000. Directors: Joseph Cornell, George H. Janeway, John B. Osbourn, Luther Adams, McRee Swift) Pier 22 (old) N. R.

New Central Coal Co. of Maryland (Henry S. Little, Pres.; Malcolm Baxter jr. Sec.; Octavius D. Baldwin, Treas. Capital, $5,000,000. Directors: Henry S. Little, Rufus Blodgett, Octavius D. Baldwin, David G. Legget, Malcolm Baxter jr. H. H. Bunnell, Edward C. Homans, Edwin R. Livermore, Eugene D. Hawkins, Jose A. Del Valle, William S. Jacques) 1 B'way

New Champion Press Co. (August Olmesdahl, propr.) r 41 Centre

New Church Board of Publication (Richard A. Lewis, Pres.; Francis J. Worcester, Sec.; Mordaunt Bodine, Treas.) 20 Cooper Union

New Cure Co. (Walter Wolcott, propr.) 6 City Hall pl.

N. E. Biscuit Works (dissolved) 57 Gansevoort

N. E. Car Spring Co. (F. J. Kaldenberg Co., proprs.) 215 E. 33d

N. E. Electric Storage Co. (inoperative) 44 B'way

MERCHANTS EXCHANGE NAT. BANK OF THE CITY OF N. Y.
SOLICITS YOUR ACCOUNT. **257 Broadway.**
PHINEAS C. LOUNSBURY, President.   ALLEN S. APGAR, Cashier.

N. E. Gas Improvement Co. (inf. unattainable) 11 Pine

N. E. Gold & Silver Mining Co. (Leigh R. Hoyt, Pres.; Capital, $815,000. Directors: Leigh R. Hoyt, Frederick Nichols; further inf. unattainable) no address

N. E. Monument Co. (Charles B. Canfield, propr.) 1321 B'way

N. E. Piano Co. of N. Y. (Thomas F. Scanlan, Pres.; George E. Kimborly, Sec.; Walter A. Kimborly, Treas.; further inf. unattainable) 98 Fifth av.

N. E. Terminal Co. (Charles B. Tedcastle, Pres.; Andrew J. Porter, Sec.; Mead F. Stone, Treas.; Capital, $200,000. Directors: Charles B. Tedcastle, Mead E. Stone, Sidney Starbuck) 36 Wall, 261 South & Piers 45 & 49 E. R.

N. E. Whalebone Mfg. Co. (Sarah Seligman, propr.) 80 Duane

N. E. & Southwestern R. R. Co. (no inf.) 1 B'way

New Era Gas Co. (no inf.) 19 B'way

New Era Publishing Co. (Charles Constantine, propr.) 15 Vandewater

New Furniture Co. (Sarah C. Turner, propr.) 220 W. 14th

New Gansevoort Market Beef Co. (Isaac Rosenbaum, propr.) 189 Varick

New Haven Copper Co. (Thomas L. James, Pres.; Cornelius W. James, Sec.; Capital, $200,000. Directors: Thomas L. & Cornelius W. James, Franklin Farrel, Lewis A. Camp, George A. James) 294 Pearl

New Haven Steamboat Co. (Chester W. Chapin, Pres.; Richard Peck, Sec.; William Scott, Treas. Capital, $300,000. Directors: Chester W. Chapin, James A. Ingerill, Richard Peck) Pier 25 E. R.

New Home Sewing Machine Co. (Allen Schenck, Pres.; John W. Wheeler, Sec.; Capital $500,000. Directors: Allen Schenck, John W. Wheeler, William L. Grout) 28 Union sq. E.

New Iberia Salt Co. (J. Lowber Welsh, Pres.; Gottlob Haussmann, Sec.; Capital, $200,000. Directors: J. Lowber Welsh, A. Marens, William Toel, S. E. Nash, G. Reusens, H. Sommerholl) 70 Broad

N. J. Accumulator & Traction Co. (dissolved) 171 B'way

N. J. Construction Co. (Joshua L. Chamberlain, Pres.; Edward B. Crane, Sec.; William S. Carman, Treas. Capital, $2,000,000. Directors: Joshua L. Chamberlain, Edward B. Crane, William H. Ward, Henry H. Boody, R. N. Gere) 45 B'way

N. J. Ice Line (dissolved) 120 B'way

N. J. Junction R. R. Co. (Chauncey M. Depew, Pres.; Edward V. W. Rossiter, Sec.; Capital, $100,000. Directors: Cornelius & William K. Vanderbilt, Chauncey M. Depew, Charles O. Clarke, Horace J. Hayden, J. Pierpont Morgan, Ashbel Green, Joseph P. Ord, A. Q. Garretson, James B. Vredenburgh, Edward A. Walton, Thomas L. James, William W. Green) Grand Central depot & 5 Vanderbilt av.

N. J. Lighterage Co. (dissolved) 97 Water

N. J. Mfg. Co. (Frederick N. Goddard, Pres.; Charles Radcliffe, Sec. Capital, $30,000. Directors: Frederick N. Goddard, Charles Radcliffe) 385 B'way

N. J. Silk Co. (Gross & Wise, proprs.) 528 B'way

N. J. Southern Railway Co. (J. Rogers Maxwell, Pres.; Samuel Knox, Sec.; John W. Watson, Treas. Directors: J. Rogers Maxwell, Austin Corbin, Edward D. Adams, George F. Baker, Harris C. Fahnestock, Henry W. Maxwell, Henry Graves) 119 Liberty & Pier 8 N. R.

N. J. State Archer Gas Fuel Co. (Frederick Boone, Pres.; Carroll Spring, Sec.; Robert H. McPherson, Treas. Capital, $1,200,000. Directors: Frederick Boone, Carroll Spring, Robert H. McPherson, John B. Archer, Charles H. Knight, Robinson Gill) 45 B'way

N. J. Steamboat Co. (William W. Everett, Pres.; George S. Riggs, Sec.; Jacob Hays, Treas. Capital, $2,000,000. Directors: William W. Everett, John Englis jr., Jacob Hays, Charles M. Englis, Joseph J. O'Donohue, Henry B. Norton) Pier 41 (old) N. R.

N. J. Steel & Iron Co. (Edward Cooper, Pres.; Edwin F. Bedell, Sec.; Frederick J. Slade, Treas. Capital, $47,200. Directors: Edward Cooper, Frederick J. Slade, Edwin F. Bedell, James Hall, Augustus F. Childs) 17 Burling sl.

N. J. Sussex Stone Co. (dissolved) 64 College pl.

N. J. Title & Abstract Co. (Joseph F. Randolph, Pres.; John W. Heck, Sec.; John Ganich, Treas. Capital, $100,000. Directors: Samuel A. Besson, William Brinkerhoff, Frederick G. Burnham, Henry V. Condict, William C. Cudlipp, James S. Erwin, John Ganich, James A. Gurnlon, John Griffin, John W. Heck, John A. McGrath, Edward H. Murphy, Joseph F. Randolph, George L. Record, Edward Russ) 120 B'way

N. J. Zinc & Iron Co. (Benjamin G. Clarke, Pres.; Theodore Sturges, Sec. Capital, $3,040,000. Directors: Benjamin G. Clarke, Percy R. Pyne, John L. Riker, Arthur B. Graves, Andrew Ressoner, Edwin F. Hatfield, Theodore Sturges,) 52 Wall & 61 Maiden la.

N. J. & Perth Amboy Electric Light Co. (no inf.) 18 Cortlandt

N. J. & San Domingo City Bridge Co. (inf. unattainable) 19 Whitehall

New Mausoleum Co. (James S. Macooy, Pres.; Charles A. Harvey, Sec.; Charles R. Treat, Treas. Capital, $10,000,000. Directors: James S. Macooy, Charles A. Harvey, Charles R. Treat, James G. Batterson, W. Wetmore Cryder, Theodore Weston, P. T. Finch, Samuel C. Pomeroy, H. J. Kimball, Charles I. Pardee) 3 W. 25th

New Paper Box Co. (John Kienle, propr.) 215 Canal

New River Mineral Co. (George H. Seeley, Pres.; John T. Pearson, Sec. Capital, $500,000. Directors: Joshua Hendricks, Jordan L. Mott, George H. Seeley, Edwin Einstein, James M. Thorburn) 49 Cliff

New River Mining Co. (A. L. Maxwell, Pres.; Levi S. Tenney, Sec. Capital, $150,000. Directors: A. L. Maxwell, C. A. Raht, William M. Prichard, H. Cazenove Jones, Levi S. Tenney, A. G. Richey. Joseph M. Gazzam) 7 Nassau

New South Mining & Improvement Co. (Thomas L. Rosser, Pres.; William G. McIntyre, Sec., further inf. refused) 45 B'way

New World Travel Co. (George Leviaon, Sec. Capital, $10,000; further inf. unattainable) 120 & 553 B'way

N. Y. Academy of Anthropology (Edward C. Mann, Pres.; Henry G. Hanchett, Sec.; M. L. Holbrook, Treas. Trustees: Edward P. Thwing, L. Bennet, M. L. Holbrook, William G. Anderson, Henry S. Drayton, George F. Bread) 28 W. 9th

N. Y. Academy of Medicine (Alfred L. Loomis, Pres.; Arthur M. Jacobus, Sec.; Orlando B. Douglass, Treas.) 12 W. 31st

N. Y. Academy of Sciences (John S. Newberry, Pres.; Henry Dudley, Treas.; Thomas L. Casey, Sec.) 41 E. 49th

N. Y. Accident Ins. Co. (Clinton B. Fisk, Pres.; Charles T. Hopper, Sec. Directors: Clinton B. Fisk, William W. & Charles T. Hopper, Charles W. McMurran, David C. Inglis, John B. Watkins, W. L. Dowling, George W. Schooley, T. Dewitt Hasbrouck) 96 B'way

N. Y. Address Co. (Ltd.) (George H. Adams, Pres.; Charles G. Adams, Sec. Capital, $1,000. Directors: George H. Adams, John W. Crawford, Charles G. Adams, William H. Hendrickson) 50 Beekman

N. Y. Adjustment Co. (George W. Gilbert, Pres.; Walter R. Gilbert, Sec. Capital, $5,000; further inf. unattainable) 31 Pine

CINCINNATI, BALTIMORE, PHILADELPHIA, | **SNOW, CHURCH & CO.** CORRESPONDENTS EVERYWHERE. | NEW YORK, BOSTON, CHICAGO, LOUISVILLE.

NEW 214 NEW

N. Y. Advertising Agency (Ltd.) (Frank S. Edminster, Pres.; Adam Menet, Sec.; Herbert L. Bridgman, Treas. Capital $30,000. Directors: Frank S. Edminster, Adam Menel, H. A. Bridgman, Robert Bowne) 6 Wall

N. Y. Advertising Sign Co. (Arthur F. Allen, propr.) 6 & 14 Park pl.

N. Y. Air Pump Co. (dissolved) 705 B'way

N. Y. Amusement Co. (Ltd.) (Alfred Reichelt, Pres.; William T. Gieselberg, Sec.; Frederick Knenncke, Treas.; further inf. unattainable) 115 W. 23d & 110 W. 24th

N. Y. Anderson Pressed Brick Co. (James C. Anderson, Pres.; John C. Cushman, Sec.; George F. Kreischer, Treas. Capital, $500,000. Directors: James C. Anderson, George F. Kreischer, John C. Cushman, S. R. Bingham, Charles C. Kreischer, Elisha Gray, F. D. Everett, John & Louis Weber) 132 Mangin

N. Y. Arcade Railway Co. (Melville C. Smith, Pres.; Eugene W. Austin, Sec.; George S. Coe, Treas. Capital, $25,000,000. Directors: George S. Coe, Charles P. Daly, James F. Pierce, Morris S. Miller, Melville C. Smith, George W. Lyon, Edward A. Abbott, James Milliken, James E. Granniss, James Jordan, Frederic P. Olcott, James Fassler) 115 B'way

N. Y. Architectural Terra Cotta Co. (Walter Geer, Pres.; Herman L. Matz, Sec.; J. Maas Schermerhorn jr. Treas. Capital, $250,000. Directors: Walter & Asahel C. Geer, J. Maas Schermerhorn jr. Orlando B. Potter, Herman L. Matz) 316 Potter bldg.

N. Y. Art Brass Co. (Emil Biselius, propr.) 84 W. 8d

N. Y. Artistic Portrait Co. (Wilson & Brown, proprs.) 100 Maiden la.

N. Y. Artists' Union (Charles B. Dickinson, Pres.; George F. Dickinson, Sec.; further inf. unattainable) 10 E. 14th

N. Y. Associated Press (David M. Stone & Whitelaw Reid, proprs.) 195 B'way

N. Y. Balance Dock Co. (William F. Buckley, Pres.; William H. Galon, Sec. Capital, $250,000. Directors: William F. Buckley, William H. Webb, William H. Galon, William H. Gebhard, Richard H. L. Townsend) 8 Broad

N. Y. Ball Club (inf. unattainable) 121 Maiden la.

N. Y. Bank Note Co. (Russell Sage, Pres.; George P. Sheldon, Sec.; George H. Kendall, Treas. Capital, $1,000,000. Directors: Russell Sage, George J. Gould, William R. Grace, George P. Sheldon, Alfred M. Hoyt, N. S. Hill, Richard A. McCurdy, Robert Sewell, James F. Pierce, George H. Kendall, C. H. Crosby) B'way

N. Y. Baptist Education Soc. (Samuel Colgate, Pres.; H. S. Lloyd, Sec.) 41 Park row

N. Y. Base Ball Bulletin Co. (Edwin A. Grozier, Pres.; Henry Melville, Sec.; Frederic A. Duneka, Treas. Capital, $50,000. Trustees: Frederic A. Duneka, Edwin A. Grozier, Henry Melville) 32 Park row

N. Y. Base Ball Club (John B. Day, Pres.; Charles T. Dillingham, Treas. Directors: John B. Day, Charles T. Dillingham, Walter S. Appleton) 121 Maiden la.

N. Y. Base Ball Club (Ltd.) (Cornelius Van Cott, Pres.; Frank B. Robinson, Sec. Capital, $20,000. Directors: Edwin A. McAlpin, Frank B. Robinson, E. B. Talcott, Cornelius Van Cott, William Ewing, Timothy J. Keefe) Eighth av. o W. 157th

N. Y. Beef Co. (Gunther & Kahn, proprs.) 1860 & 1995 Third av.

N. Y. Beef Co. (Henry Rubsam, propr.) 153 E. Houston

N. Y. Beef Co. (Isaac Rothschild, propr.) 2507 Eighth av.

N. Y. Beef Co. (Louis J. Kahn & Co. proprs.) 2318 Third av.

N. Y. Beef Co. (Ltd.) (Thomas M. Wheeler, Pres.; C. M. Webber, Sec.; Walter H. Wheeler, Treas.; further inf. unattainable) 102 Gansevoort

N. Y. Belting & Packing Co. (Pauline A. Durant, Pres.; John H. Cheever, Treas. Capital, $1,000,000. Directors: Pauline A. Durant, John H. & Charles A. Cheever, F. Cazenove Jones, John D. Cheever) 15 Park row

N. Y. Bible Soc. (Henry D. Nicoll, Pres., Robert Carter jr. Sec.; Daniel J. Holden, Treas.) 66 Bible h.

N. Y. Bible & Common Prayer Book Soc. (Henry C. Potter, Pres.; Edwin S. Gorham, Sec.; James Pott, Treas.) 14 Astor pl.

N. Y. Bicycle Co. (not inc.) (Charles & Charles M. & Lewis M. Irving) 4 E. 60th

N. Y. Biscuit Co. (*see too later*) 157 Duane

N. Y. Blank Book Co. (Am. News Co. proprs.) 29 Beekman

N. Y. Block Co. (C. F. Batt, Pres.; J. A. K. Steele, Sec.; W. W. Dashiell, Treas. Capital, $25,000. Directors: C. F. Batt, J. A. K. Steele, F. A. Smith, E. H. Morse, W. W. Dashiell) 41 Centre

N. Y. Board of Fire Underwriters (George M. Coit, Pres.; William W. Henshaw, Sec.; William M. St. John, Treas.) 32 Nassau

N. Y. Board of Trade & Transportation (Ambrose Snow, Pres.; Darwin R. James Sec.; Frank O. Herring, Treas.) 55 Liberty

N. Y. Boat Oar Co. (Frank D. Wilsey, Pres.; Frank C. Cintterbuch, Sec. Capital, $12,500. Directors: Frank D. Wilsey, Frank C. Cintterbuch, Otterson D. Wilson, Jay F. Wilsey, William A. Arnold) 69 West

N. Y. Book Depository (Emanuel Glasser, Pres., Leonard Knopf, Sec.; Ernest A. Brickwedel, Treas. Capital, $20,000. Directors: Emanuel Glasser, Leonard Koepf, Ernest A. Brickwedel, Jacob Salathe, James Kurtz) 14 Clinton pl.

N. Y. Bottle Co. (S. & E. Weinlander, proprs.) 80 Clinton

N. N. Bottle Stopper Co. (Charles A. Post, Pres.; Charles A. Post, Sec. Capital, $5,000. Directors: George B. & Charles A. Post) 15 Cortlandt

N. Y. Bottlers' Supplies Mfg. Co. (Ltd.) (Jacob Merserean, propr.) 78 Warren

N. Y. Bottling Co. (Rayner & Steele, proprs.) 160 S. 5th av.

N. Y. Bowery Fire Ins. Co. (John A. Delaney jr. Pres.; Charles A. Blanvelt, Sec. Capital, $200,000. Directors: Charles C. Pinckney, John B. Cotte, William P. Woodcock 2d, Thompson Pinckney, John C. Chamberlain, Henry Silberhorn, William P. Woodcock, John G. Wendel, John A. Delaney jr. John Wilkin, Gordon G. Brinckerhoff, F. Frederic Gunther, Helmnth Kranich, Charles A. Blanvelt, Henry D. Pye) 141 B'way & 124 Bowery

N. Y. Braid Co. (not inc.) (Joseph Haberman, William Mundi & Richard Cohn) 101 Thompson

N. Y. Brass Co. (William M. Thatcher, Pres.; D. Kellogg Baker, Treas.; William B. Froeligh, Sec. Capital, $150,000; further inf. unattainable) 37 W. 14th

N. Y. Brass Furniture Co. (W. T. Merserean & Co. proprs.) 321 B'way & 39 Union sq. W.

N. Y. Brass & Wire Works Co. (Kopankiewicz & Dabrowski, proprs.) 177 Grand

N. Y. Brokers' & Freighters' Exchange (no inf.) 1 B'way

N. Y. Buffet Co. (inf. unattainable) 167 B'way

N. Y. Building-Loan Banking Co. (Joseph Roberts, Pres.; Winslow E. Busby, Sec.; Paul O. Wiedemann, Treas. Directors: Joshua C. Purdy, Charles Wendell, Edward Busby, G. W. Crossman, William E. Roberts, Paul O. Wiedemann, Richard E. Townsend, Winslow E. Busby, Joseph Roberts) 12 E. 15th

N. Y. Building Plan Co. (inf. unattainable) 62 Cedar

N. Y. Burial Co. (Frederick H. Ernst, Pres.; Ed-

WATER METERS, GAS ENGINES, | **NATIONAL METER CO.**
FOR PUMPING AND POWER. | 252 Broadway, N. Y.

NEW 215 NEW

ward Grimm, Sec.; William Vonglahn, Treas. Directors: Frederick H. Ernst, Andrew Gerndt, William Vouglahn, Emil Lachmann, Martin Lehersen, Edward Grimm, William Dressler) 351 Broome

N. Y. Butchers' Calf Skin Ass'n. (Ltd.) (George Thomson, Pres.; Moses Sanders, Sec.; Jacob Ringkleb, Treas. Capital, $25,000. Directors: George Thomson, Moses Sanders, Jacob Ringkleb, Arthur Bloch, Felix Haas, Edward F. O'Neil, Moses Hellmann, Julius Dietz jr. A. W. Schneider, Herman Hellmann, Herman Apman) 403 E. 45th

N. Y. Button Works (Swartz & Elias, propr's.) 254 Canal

N.Y. Cab Co. (Ltd.) (James G. K. Lawrence, Pres.; Peter T. Barlow, Sec.; William T. Ryerson, Treas. Capital, $500,000. Directors: James G. K. Lawrence, Peter T. Barlow, William T. Ryerson, Frederic Bronson, George P Wetmore, William Jay, Ira & Walter W. Brown) 21 E. 12th, 110 W. 33d, 523 Fifth av, 3 W. 45th, 221 W. 53d & 5 E. 58th

N. Y. Cable Railway Co. (William S. Williams, Pres.; Charles E. Gildersleeve, Sec.; Samuel F. Pierson, Treas. Capital, $2,000,000. Directors: William S. Williams, Charles P. Shaw, Samuel F. Pierson, Joshua B. Shaw, Charles E. Gildersleeve, John Irving, Augustine Snow, A. G. Rogers, R. N. Hazard) 90 B'way

N. Y. Cable Railway Construction Co. (inoperative) 170 B'way

N. Y. Café Co. (Ltd.) (dissolved) 231 B'way

N. Y. Calcium Light Co. (Caffrey, Murray & Wilson, propr's.) 410 Bleecker

N. Y. Car Wheel Works (Patrick H. Griffin, Pres.; S. H. Jones, Sec. Directors: Patrick H. & T. H. Griffin) 115 B'way

N. Y. Carbon Works (Albert Storer, Pres.; Henry Miller jr. Sec.; further inf. unattainable) 16 Cortlandt

N. Y. Carbon & Transfer Paper Co. (L. Wesley Frost, Pres.; Herman F. Lee, Sec. Capital, $100,000. Directors: L. Wesley Frost, Herman F. Lee) 53 Maiden la.

N. Y. Carpet Lining Co. (George Dodson, Pres.; William H. Pomeroy, Sec.; John Constable, Treas. Capital, $6,000; further inf. unattainable) 308 E. 95th

N. Y. Carriage Co. (Peake & Butler, propr's.) 213 Grand

N. Y. Catholic Protectory (Henry L. Hoguet, Pres.; Richard H. Clarke, Sec.; Eugene Kelly, Treas.) 415 Broome

N. Y. Cement Co. (Thomas Miller, Pres.; Thomas Miller jr. Sec. Directors: Thomas & Thomas Miller jr., William A. Cumming, John Miller) 16 Cortlandt

N. Y. Central Lighterage Co. (Gibson L. Douglass, manager; further inf. unattainable) 1 Beaver, Pier 5, E. R. & ft. W. 63d

N. Y. Central & Hudson River R. R. Co. (Chauncey M. Depew, Pres.; Edwin D. Worcester, Sec.; Edward V. W. Rossiter, Treas. Capital, $89,428,300. Directors: Cornelius & William K. & Frederick W. Vanderbilt, Chauncey M. Depew, Charles C. Clarke, Horace J. Hayden, Samuel F. Barger, J. Pierpont Morgan, Cyrus W. Field, William Bliss, Erastus Corning, George C. Duell, Sherman S. Jewett) Grand Central depot

N. Y. Chair Co. (Romaine Van Riper, propr.) 486 Canal

N. Y. Chapter of the Am. Institute of Architects (Emlen T. Littell, Pres.; Alfred J. Blour, Sec.) 18 B'way

N. Y. Chemical Mfg. Co. (William H. Weeks, Pres.; further inf. unattainable) 3 E. 4th

N. Y. Chemical Works (Henry M. Anthony, Pres.; Charles F. Sullivan, Sec.; further inf. unattainable) 102 Reade & 524 W. 16th

N. Y. City Drug Mills (Gregory & Jennings, propr's.) 403 Cherry

N. Y. City Ice Co. (Albert D. Winch, Pres.; Gilbert Seaman, Sec. Capital, $250,000. Directors: Albert D. Winch, Gilbert Seaman, John A. Kemp, Abel M. Parker, William M. Kemp, Moses Huntoon) 409 W. 19th

N. Y. City News Bureau (Newton Digoney, propr.) 11 Park row & 11 Ann

N. Y. City Oil Co. (Edward G. Kelley, propr.) 167 Maiden la.

N. Y. City Press Ass'n. (not inc.) (Mary E. O'Rourke, Raymond E. Dodge & Henderson D. Owen) 115 Nassau

N. Y. City Purchasing Co. (A. L. Dunlevey & Co, propr's.) 71 South

N. Y. City Savings & Loan Ass'n. (inf. unattainable) no address

N. Y. City Soap Co. (Albert Higgons, propr.) 146 Reade

N. Y. City Suburban Surface R. R. Co. (Franklin Edson, Pres.; James L. Wells, Sec.; Hugh N. Camp, Treas. Capital, $500,000. Directors: Franklin Edson, Hugh N. Camp, Henry W. T. Mali, Daniel D. Conover, Richard Kelly, Maximilian Fleischman, J. P. Balter) 55 Liberty

N. Y. City Transfer & Harlem Despatch Express (Bernard Biglin, propr.) 508 Wash'n. 78 E. 125th, 8 Hudson & 704 E. 131th

N. Y. City & Westchester Railway Co. (inf. unattainable) 15 Cortlandt

N. Y. Clearing House (William A. Camp, manager) 14 Pine

N. Y. Coal Tar Chemical Co. (Isaac D. Fletcher, Pres.; Edward H. Kidder, Sec.; Thomas W. Weeks Treas. Capital, $275,000. Directors: Isaac D. Fletcher, Edward H. Kidder, Thomas W. Weeks) 10 Warren

N. Y. Coin & Stamp Co. (not inc.) (David Proskay & Harlan P. Smith) 583 B'way

N. Y. Collar & Cuff Laundry Co. (Gardner & Vail, propr's.) 778 & 100 B'way

N. Y. College of Dentistry (William T. Laroche, V.-Pres.; Fanouil D. Weisse, Sec.; Alexander W. Stein, Treas.) 245 E. 23d

N. Y. College of Electricity, Telegraphy & Typewriting (Henry Greer, propr.) 122 E. 26th

N. Y. College of Magnetics (Frank G. Welch, Pres.; Edwin D. Babbitt, Sec. Trustees: M. L. Holbrook, S. H. Brown, Albert Day, J. W. Currier, L. Wesley Frost) 50 Union sq. E.

N. Y. College of Music (Everett P. Wheeler, Pres.; Latham G. Reed, Sec.; Otto Rother, Treas. Capital, $50,000. Trustees: Herman Lambert, Morris Cooper, Otto Rother, Latham G. Reed, Walter Damrosch, Alexander Lambert, Frank Fowler, Emil Gramm) 163 E. 70th

N. Y. College of Music

163 E. 70th Street.

EVERETT P. WHEELER, President.
ALEXANDER LAMBERT, Director.

N. Y. College of Veterinary Surgeons (inf. unattainable) 382 E. 27th

N. Y. Collegiate Institute for Girls (Alfred C. Roe, propr.) 233 Lenox av.

N. Y. Colophonite Co. (John H. Piper, Pres.; George E. Baker, Sec.; further inf. unattainable) 64 College pl.

N. Y. Commercial Co. (Ltd.) (George A. Alden, Pres.; Adelbert H. Alden, Sec.; Charles B. Flint, Treas. Capital, $600,000; further inf. unattainable) 140 Pearl

N. Y. Commercial Co. (of Alaska) (Ltd.) (Capital,

PROTECTION For Family, Home, Store, Factory, etc., by using only the "VULCAN" BRAND OF SAFETY MATCHES. Headquarters, 373 Washington Street, New York.

NEW 216 NEW

$1,000,000. Directors: William B. Pope, Thaddeus D. Bradford, William T. Davis, John H. Drege, Henry S. Tibbey; further inf. unattainable) no address

N. Y. Concert Co. (Ltd.) (Rudolph Aronson, Pres.; William J. Finch jr. Sec.; Albert Aronson, Treas. Capital, $200,000. Directors: Rudolph Aronson, Austin Corbin, H. S. Mendelsohn, R. R. Stuyvesant, John H. Nesbit, Sanford Bernheimer, William J. Finch jr. Francis H. Kimball, Albert Aronson) 1410 B'way

N. Y. Condensed Milk Co. (John G. Borden, Pres.; William J. Rogers, Sec.; further inf. unattainable) 71 Hudson, 227 E. 34th & 306 E. 117th

N. Y. Couditor-Vorein (Gustave Thomas, Pres.; Henry Quilling, Sec.; Herman Marquardt, Treas. Capital, $3,000. Trustees; Louis Becker, John Forster) 169 E. Houston

N. Y. Confection Co. (Joseph Elsworth, Pres.; Sylvester Pope, Sec. Capital, $9,000. Directors: Joseph Elsworth, Samuel J. Everitt, Sylvester Pope) 76 Varick

N. Y. Conservatory of Music (Sextus N. Griswold, Pres.; Clemence Raoux, Sec.; further inf. refused) 5 E. 14th

N. Y. Consolidated Card Co. (Solomon L. Cohen, Pres.; Isaac Levy, Sec.; Stanley A. Cohen, Treas. Directors: Solomon L. Cohen, Isaac Levy, Stanley A. Cohen) 226 W. 14th

N. Y. Contract Co. (Julius Lipman, Pres.; Moses Kind, Sec. Capital, $100,000. Directors: Julius Lipman, George C. Scofield, James A. Bruen, Moses Kind, Henry Lipman) 206 B'way

N. Y. Cotton Exchange (James H. Parker, Pres.; Samuel T. Hubbard jr. sec.; Walter T. Miller, Treas.) William c Beaver

N. Y. County National Bank (Francis L. Leland, Pres.; William H. Jennison, Cashier; Lewis L. Pierce, Notary. Capital, $200,000. Directors: Francis L. Leland, Joseph Park, John M. Tilford, Daniel T. Hong, Charles B. Webster, Isidor Straus, S. F. Jayne) 79 Eighth av.

N. Y. County Safe Deposit Vaults (N. Y. County National Bank, proprs.) 79 Eighth av.

N. Y. Crayon Co. (inf. unattainable) 32 Church

N. Y. Crayon Portrait Co. (Alois Weiss, propr.) 65 E. 4th

N. Y. Cremation Soc. (Richard W. G. Welling, Pres.; Theodore Berendsohn, Sec.; Daniel W. Craig, Treas. Directors: Richard W. G. Welling, William J. Flagg. James Chaskel, Daniel W. Craig, M. R. Spazzalt, Sigmund & Theodore Berendsohn) 140 Nassau

N. Y. Cylinder Boring Co. (George McVay, propr.) 40 John

N. Y. Daily Bulletin Assn. (William Dodsworth, Pres.; Alfred W. Dodsworth, Sec.; John W. Dodsworth, Treas.; further inf. unattainable) 32 B'way

N. Y. Development Co. (Capital, $30,000 ; further inf. unattainable) no address

N. Y. Diet Kitchen Assn. (Mrs. Abby Hopper Gibbons,' Pres.; Mrs. George W. White, Sec.; Mrs. James. D. Smillie, Treas.) 187 Centre, 722 Sixth, 99 Varick & 378 W. 36th

N. Y. Dispatch Publishing Co. (William H. Duckworth, Pres.; Nelson A. Farrand, Sec.; John N. Drake, Treas. Capital, $125,000. Directors: William H. Duckworth, Nelson A. Farrand, John N. Drake) 11 Frankfort

N. Y. District Railway Co. (Sherburne B. Eaton, Pres.; David Paton, Sec.; J. Coleman Drayton, Treas. Capital, $36,000,000. Directors: J. Coleman Drayton, William A. Street, Rowland R. Hazard, David Paton, William Barclay Parsons jr. Calvin Goddard, Looke W. Winchester, George B. Post, Sherburne B. Eaton, David R. Hazard, Richard W. Stevenson, Elisha Dyer, Robert W. Blackwell) 120 B'way

N. Y. Door Plate Co. (not inc.) (Gilbert B. Wright & J. S. Glen Edwards) 16 Ann

N. Y. Dress Steel Co. (Louis Kortz, propr.) 215 Sixth av.

N. Y. Driving Club (inf. unattainable) E. 165th n Sheridan av.

N. Y. Dyewood Extract & Chemical Co. (Joseph C. Baldwin, Pres.; William M. Baldwin, Sec. Capital, $250,000. Directors: Joseph C. Baldwin, John G. Steenken, Henry Steers, William M. Baldwin, John L. Riker) 55 Beekman

N. Y. Economic Gas Light & Fuel Co. (Henry Bradstreet, Pres.; Charles S. Carnaghan, Sec.; Thomas S. Smith, Treas. Capital, $250,000 ; further inf. unattainable) 115 B'way

N. Y. Economical Printing Co. (Thomas R. Hopkins, Pres.; Walter T. Chatterley, Sec.; further inf. unattainable) 24 Vesey

N. Y. Egg Co. (dissolved) 470 Grand

N. Y. Elbow Co. (Shoch & Kraft, proprs.) 18 Cliff

N. Y. Electric Lines Co. (Charles J. Warren, Pres.; George L. Weed, Sec. Capital, $5,000,000. Directors : Charles J. Warren, George L. Weed, Edward Barr, Ferdinand Cook, Charles Riley, Jesse Larrabee, Bainbridge Henkley, George M. Riley, James S. White, William F. Wagner, Daniel W. Schoonmaker, Johnson S. Carey) 11 Gold

N. Y. Electric Mail Box Co. (Adolph Wimpfheimer, Pres.; Albert F. Hochstadter, Sec.; Charles H. Parsons, Treas. Capital, $50,000 ; further inf. unattainable) 451 G'wich

N. Y. Elevated R. R. Co. (consolidated with Manhattan Railway Co.) 71 B'way

N. Y. Embroidering & Mfg. Co. (Tobias & Schneitlacher, proprs.) 385 Broome

N. Y. Emery Wheel Co. (Belcher Brothers & Co. proprs.) 92 Chambers

N. Y. Enamel Paint Co. (Sylvester J. Miller, Pres.; Sylvester M. Neville, Sec. Capital, $500,000. Directors: Sylvester J. & F. B. Miller, Sylvester M. Neville, S. Tilghman, V. Klein, G. Rowland) 240 Pearl

N. Y. Engineering Co. (inf. unattainable) 18 Cortlandt

N. Y. Engraving & Printing Co. (Alexander R. Hart, Pres.; Charles M. Cooper, Sec. Capital, $50,000. Directors: Alexander R. Hart, Julius C. Vonarx, Charles M. Cooper) 320 Pearl

N. Y. Equipment Co. (James Irvine, Pres.; William V. Carolin, Sec. Capital, $100,000. Directors: James Irvine, George B. F. Cooper. William V. Carolin, L. V. Walkley, Charles Muller) 10 Wall

N. Y. Equitable Ins. Co. (in liquidation) 58 Wall

N. Y. Exchange for Woman's Work (Mary L. Choate, Pres.; Jeannette M. Thurber, Sec.; Isabella G. Paton, Treas.) 329 Fifth av.

N. Y. Export Timber Co. (Thomas T. C. Brewster, Pres.; Henry W. Clements, Sec.; Edward Morton, Treas. Capital, $50.000. Directors : Thomas T. C. Brewster, Edward Morton, Henry R. Campbell, Thomas Wood, Henry W. Clements) 85 B'way

N. Y. Family Medicine Co. (Charles F. Hanson, propr.) 81 Catharine

N. Y. Feed Co. (John B. Smith, Pres.; Isaac L. Smith, Sec. Capital, $500,000. Directors: F. W. Weiserbock, A. C. Fransdoll, John B. & Isaac L. Smith) 2 Nassau & 214 E. 99th

N. Y. Fifth Wheel Co. (Caleb R. Turner, Pres. ; Frank J. Smith, Sec. Capital, $150,000. Directors : Caleb R. Turner, Thomas Evans, Frank J. Smith) 45 Grand

N. Y. Fire Ins. Co. (Daniel Underhill, Pres. ; Augustus Colson, Sec. Capital, $200,000. Directors: Daniel Underhill, Samuel C. Harriot, John E. Andrew, William Haxtun, Joseph A. Dreyfous, James C. Gulick, James T. Wright, James C. Holden, A. H. Cardozo, Claiborne Ferris, John N. Quirk, Hewlett Scudder, Augustus Colson) 72 Wall

IDEN & CO., | **MANUFACTURERS OF**
University Place, 9th to 10th Sts., N. Y. | **GAS FIXTURES AND ELECTROLIERS**

NEW   217   NEW

N. Y. Fire Proof Paint Co. (inf. unattainable) 65 William

N. Y. Floating Dry Dock Co. (George Briggs, Pres.; Andrew A. Bremner, Sec. Capital, $750,000; further inf. unattainable) 254 South & Pier 42 E. R.

N. Y. Floating Elevator Assn. (not Inc.) (Edward J. Rawson, James Veitch & Louis M. Lent) 310 Produce Ex.

N. Y. Freestone Quarrying Co. (Frederick T. Parson, Pres.; Henry E. Parson, Sec.; Capital, $125,000. Directors: Frederick T. & Henry E. Parson, Henry A. Richardson, Samuel A. Harriman, Charles N. Finch) 48 Maiden la.

N. Y. Fresh Tripe Co. (Henry C. Derby, Pres.; Frank P. Bugbee, Sec.; Herbert Derby, Treas. Capital, $40,000. Directors: Henry C. & Herbert Derby, James P. Robertson, Frank P. Bugbee & Alonzo M. Robertson) 626 W. 30th

N. Y. Fruit & Produce Auction Co. (Ltd.) (no inf.) 60 Park pl.

N. Y. Furniture Board of Trade (Theodore Hofstatter jr. Pres.; Frederick A. Burnham, Sec.) 150 Canal

N. Y. Furniture Co. (Edward R. Jeffcott, Pres.; James E. Reed, Treas. Capital, $20,000. Directors: Edward R. Jeffcott, James E. Reed, Lewis B. Jeffcott) 120 W. 14th

N. Y. Furniture Supply Co. (Foster, Merriam & Co. proprs.) 225 Canal

N. Y. Gas Fixture Co. (W. H. Hayden Miller, Pres.; Henry O. Schmidt, Sec. further inf. unattainable) 20 Warren

N. Y. Gazette Co. (David M. Gazlay, Pres.; Andrew A. Bibby, Sec. Capital, $50,000. Directors: David M. Gazlay, Andrew A. Bibby) 24 Dockman

N. Y. Gorman Conservatory of Music (Louis G. Parina, Pres.; Charles T. Clarke, Sec. Trustees; Stephen T. Gordon, Adolph Bader, Adolph T. Weber, Andrew Billings, Henry D. Richmond, Francis C. Campbell, Henry D. Wallen, Frederick A. Hilton, Frederick T. Jefferson, Joseph G. Moore, Frederick Antholz, John McGill) 7 W. 42d

N. Y. Glass Co. (Robert Gemmell, Pres.; G. Osgood Andrews, Sec.; S. Bryan Kneass, Treas. Capital, $40,000. Directors: Robert Gemmell, G. Osgood Andrews, S. Bryan & Strickland Kneass, D. C. Andrews) 100 S. 5th av.

N. Y. Glass Enameling Co. (not Inc.) (George W. Wastie & George W. Gullett) 7 G'wich av.

N. Y. Grape Sugar Co. (Thomas C. Platt, Pres.; William C. Sheldon, Treas.; Alfred C. Harrison, Sec. Capital, $1,100,000. Trustees: Thomas C. Platt, William C. Sheldon, Theodore A. Havemeyer, Alfred C. Harrison) 49 B'way

N. Y. Guaranty & Indemnity Co. (in liquidation) 52 B'way

N. Y. Hand Stamp Co. (Conrad Konig, propr.) 97 Murray

N. Y. Harbor Tow Boat Co. (Lewis Pulver, Pres.; J. Gordon Emmons, Sec.; Charles E. Evarts, Treas. Capital, $45,000. Directors: Lewis Pulver, J. Gordon Emmons, Charles E. Evarts, Edwin R. Kirk, John E. Moore, Thomas C. & Edwin M. Millard) 305 West

N. Y. Hay Co. (William M. Williams. Pres.; Kelson H. Cleminshaw, Sec. Capital, $25,000. Trustees: William M. Williams, Nelson H. Cleminshaw, Charles Philip Eaton) 187 West

N. Y. Hay Exchange (Edward A. Dillenbeck, Pres.; Thomas Fonda, Sec.; John Kerwin, Treas.) 601 W. 3d

N. Y. Health Agency (Theodore H. Babcock, propr.) 285 B'way

N. Y. Hollow Ware Co. (not Inc.) (Robert S. Willauson, William B. Donahey & Ellie G. Potter) 18 & 9 Cliff

N. Y. Horse Manure Co. (Henry Van Brunt, Pres.; Bernard Naughton jr. Sec.; Bernard M. Shan-

lev, Treas.; further inf. unattainable) ft. W. 44th & ft. E. 39th

N. Y. House Cleaning Bureau (William Greene, propr.) 113 Sixth av.

N. Y. Ice Exchange (inf. unattainable) 269 Eighth av.

N. Y. Ice & Cold Storage Co. (Frederick W. Wolf, Pres.; Edwin C. Donnell, Sec. Capital, $250,000. Directors: Frederick W. Wolf, Frederick W. Mesick, Edwin C. Donnell) 207 Fulton

N. Y. Improved Real Estate Co. (Samuel L. Parrish, Pres.; Casimir Tag, Sec.; Francis K. Pendleton, Treas. Capital, $600,000. Trustees; Samuel L. Parrish, Howland Davis, Casimir Tag, Francis K. Pendleton, Charles F. & Albert Tag) 44 B'way

N. Y. Indoor Cuspadore Co (inf. unattainable) 334 Pearl

N. Y. Inland Commercial Guaranty Co. (Ltd.) (John S. Morton, Pres.; Everett D. Barlow, Treas.; S. M. Hayward, Sec. Directors: John S. Morton, Everett D. Barlow, S. M. Hayward) 206 B'way

N. Y. Insulated Wire Co. (Clermont H. Wilcox, Pres.; R. Eccleston Gallaher, Sec.; Abner J. Tower, Treas. Capital, $500,000. Directors: Clermont H. Wilcox, Charles A. Place, Abner J. Tower, William B. Dowse, R. Eccleston Gallaher) 649 B'way

N. Y. Insulating Paint Co. (George N. Gardiner, Pres.; James W. Eaton, Treas. Capital, $50,000. Directors: George N. Gardiner, James W. Eaton, Joseph A. Reilly, George W. Piper, Thomas Pickering) 53 South

N. Y. Iron Roofing & Corrugating Co. (Henry M. Warren, Pres.; Lewis Moss, Sec. Capital, $25,000. Directors: Henry M. Warren, Lewis Moss, Frederick L, Warren) 115 B'way

N. Y. Iron Shoe Card Co. (John M. Fuchs. Pres.; Julius C. F. Lang, Sec. Capital, $10,000. Trustees: John M. Fuchs, Julius C. F. Lang, Clemens R. Jacobi) 20 Warren

N. Y. Iron Works (Horace Theall, propr.) 67 Bethune

N. Y. Iron & Glass Co. (dissolved) 261 B'way

N. Y. Jewelers' Assn. (Frederick S. Douglas, Pres.; Andrew E. Pritchard, Sec.; Henry E. Ide, Treas.) 146 B'way

N. Y. Jewelers' Board of Trade (Edward J. Scofield, Pres.; Herbert M. Condit, Sec.; David Keller, Treas.) 41 Maiden la.

N. Y. Jockey Club (H. DeConrcey Forbes, Pres.; Theodore H. Keck, Sec.; Charles E. Coddington, Treas.) 945 B'way

N. Y. Labor News Co. (Benjamin J. Gretch, manager) 25 E. 4th

N. Y. Land Improvement Co. (Samuel L. Parrish, Pres.; Casimir Tag, Sec.; Francis K. Pendleton, Treas. Capital, $600,000. Trustees: Samuel L. Parrish, Francis K. Pendleton, Casimir & Charles F. Tag, James C. Parrish) 44 B'way

N. Y. Laundry Works (Henry C. Smith, propr.) 28 Dey

N. Y. Law Publishing Co. (Anson G. McCook, Pres.; David S. Owen, Sec.; John M. Bowers, Treas. Capital, $100,000. Directors: Anson G. McCook, David S. Owen, John M. & William C. Bowers) 303 B'way

N. Y. Lead Seal & Press Co. (William Fullerton, Pres.; William F. Moore, Sec.; William C. McIntire, Treas. Directors: William Fullerton, William F. Moore, William C. McIntire, Frederick W. Brooks) 40 Wall

N. Y. Leather Belting Co. (Loring A. Robertson, Pres.; William G. Hoople, Treas. Capital, $65,000. Directors: Loring A. Robertson, William G. Hoople) 84 Gold

N. Y. Life Ins. Co. (William H. Beers, Pres. Trustees; William H. Appleton, William H. Beers, William A. Booth, Henry Bowers, John

TYPEWRITING DONE BY THE TROW CITY DIRECTORY CO., 11 University Place.

Claflin, Robert B. Collins, Alexander Studwell, Walter H. Lewis, Edward Martin, Richard Muser, C. C. Baldwin, John N. Stearns, William L. Strong, W. F. Buckley, Henry Tuck, Archibald H. Welch, Loomis L. White, Henry C. Mortimer, Edward N. Gibbs) 346 B'way *(see adv. on front cover, head lines & page P in back)*

N. Y. Life Ins. Credit Co. (Ltd.) (William P. Chase, Sec.; R. Earle Smith, Treas. Capital, $100,000; further inf. unattainable) 74 Cortlandt

N. Y. Life Ins. & Trust Co. (Henry Parish, Pres.; Joseph R. Kearny, Sec. Capital, $1,000,000. Trustees: John Taylor Johnson, James P. Kernochan, William C Schermerhorn, Robert Goelet, William E. Dodge, Charles E. Strong, Francis R. Rives, S. Van Rensselaer Cruger, Charles G. Thompson, Robert Winthrop, Henry Parish, James A. Roosevelt, Frederick W. Stevens, George A. Robbins, Stuyvesant Fish, Ludlow Thomas, Charles F. Southmayd, Rutherfurd Stuyvesant, William W. Astor, Wilson G. Hunt, James M. Brown, Edmund L. Baylies) 52 Wall

N. Y. Lighterage & Transp. Co. (Harrison B. Moore, Pres.; Joseph Wills, Sec.; Harrison B. Moore jr. Treas. Capital, $100,000. Directors: Harrison B. & Harrison B. Moore jr. W. L. G. Wilbee, John Taylor, H. Stanley Goodwin, James Donnelly) 6 B'way

N. Y. Limited (Cornelius Van Cott, Pres.; Edward B. Talcott, Sec. Capital, $20,000. Directors: Cornelius Van Cott, Edwin A. McAlpin, Edward B. Talcott, John Montgomery Ward, William Ewing) Eighth av. c W. 157th

N. Y. Litho Co. (inf. unattainable) 17 Ann

N. Y. Loan Co. (Alexander Henry, propr.) 178 Sixth av.

N. Y. Loan Office (Leopold Hecht, propr.) 329 Ninth av.

N. Y. Loan & Improvement Co. (Henry F. Dimock, V. Pres., Daniel S. Lamont, Sec. Capital, $1,000,000. Directors: Charles T. Barney, James J. Belden, A. M. Dillings, Henry F. Dimock, Daniel S. Lamont, Arthur Leary, John J. McCook, Oliver H. Payne, William C. Whitney) 15 Broad

N. Y. Lubricating Co. (Charles H. Kuske, Pres.; E. Porter Mason, Sec.; George H. Moore, Treas. Capital, $10,000. Trustees: Charles H. Kuske, George H. Moore, Horace E. Merrill) 221 Front

N. Y. Lumber Drying Co. (James H. Osgood, receiver) 301 Eleventh av.

N. Y. Lumber & Wood Working Co. (Wallace C. Andrews, Pres.; Lewis Coon, Sec.; Onesimus P. Shaffer, Treas. Capital, $200,000. Directors: Wallace C. Andrews, George F. Smith, Onesimus P. Shaffer, Lewis Coon, H. G. Lyon) 178 B'way & 526 E. 134th

N. Y. Lye Co. (Eliza N. Hall, propr.) 91 Wall & 549 W. 22d

N. Y. Machinery Depot (Charles Place, propr.) 16 N. Y. & D'klyn bridge

N. Y. Mfg. Co. (Ltd.) (dissolved) 55 Pine

N. Y. Mfg. Concern (Gay Brothers & Co., proprs.) 54 Reade

N. Y. Mfg. & Pavement Co. (no inf.) 15 Broad

N. Y. Marine Underwriters (not inc.) (Chubb & Son, Attorneys) 77 Beaver

N. Y. Maritime Register Publishing Co. (Ltd.) (John R. Smith, Pres.; William F. Smith, Sec.; Arthur Bender, Treas. Capital, $90,000. Directors: John R. & William F. Smith, Arthur Bender) 91 Maiden la.

N. Y. Mastic Works (Edwin E. Wootton, propr.) 85 B'way & 602 E. 20th

N. Y. Mat & Duster Mfg. Co. (Morris Schleissner, propr.) 402 B'way

N. Y. Memorial Co. (E. S. & F. C. Bettelheim, proprs.) 22 Ann

N. Y. Mercantile Exchange, (James H. Snyder,

Pres.; F. N Barrett, Sec.; Daniel B. Halstead, Treas.) 6 Harrison

N. Y. Metal Exchange (Tallmadge Delafield, Pres., Edward J. Shriver, Sec.; Carl Mayer, Treas.) 234 Pearl

N. Y. Metallurgical Works (Eugene N. Riotte propr.) 104 Washn.

N. Y. Milk & Cream Co. (Stone & Beyer proprs.) 484 Sixth av. & 2310 Eighth av.

N. Y. Millwright & Machine Co. (not inc.) (Charles F. & F. Hugo Lang) 507 W. 50th

N. Y. Music Electrotyping Co. (Gunther & Co., proprs.) 63 Duane

N. Y. Music Publishing Co. (Ltd.) (John M. Lander, Pres.; J. Malisch, Sec.; Charles W. Wernig, Treas. Capital, $5,000. Directors: John M. Lander, J. Malisch, Charles W. Wernig, Charles Boswald, Leopold Fuenkenstein) 9 E. 14th

N. Y. Musical Institute (Louis Zadora, Pres.; Joseph F. Dalbee, Sec. Directors: Louis Zadora, Titus D'Ernesti, Joseph F. Dalbee) 253 E. 72d

N. Y. Mutual Gas Light Co. (John P. Kennedy, Pres.; William C. Besson, Sec. Capital, $3,500,000. Directors: Cornelius Vanderbilt, John P. Kennedy, Charles C. & Arthur Leary, John B. Ford, William K. Vanderbilt, R. L. Crawford, Charles H. Kerner, Joseph S. Stout, Robert M. Galloway, Joseph Harker, E. S. T. Kennedy, Samuel Thorne, Louis de Beblan, George W. Hall, Lawrence Wells) 36 Union sq. E. & ft, E 11th

N. Y. Mutual Ins. Co. (Theophylact B. Bleecker, jr. Pres.; Edward Laruque, Sec. Directors: Arthur Leary, Henry Meyer, Edward H. R. Lyman, Francis Hathaway, Theophylact B. Bleecker jr. George Mosle, R. D. Perry, W. Irving Clark, Stephen W. Carey, John H. Earl, L. Bayard Smith, Henry C. Hulbert, Charles C. Leary, Jacob S. Wetmore, Richard Irvin jr. Hermon C. Von Post, John W. Wilson, Louis de Beblan) 61 William

N. Y. Mutual Savings & Loan Assn, (Edward V. Loew, Pres.; Chester Huntington, Sec.; George L. Hutchings, Treas. Directors: Edward V. Loew, Thomas V. Johnson, E. C. Dillingham, Chester Huntington, George L. Hutchings, O. D. Baldwin, Smith M. Wool. Smith T. Woolworth, J. G. Butler jr.) 55 Liberty

N. Y. Mutual Telegraph Co. (John G. Moore, Pres.; Charles F. Peck, Sec.; George H. Holt, Treas. Capital, $2,500,000. Directors: John G. Moore, Charles F. Peck, George H. Holt, George F. Baker, George W. Ballou, George S. Scott, Jay & George J. Gould. Russell Sage, Harris C. Fahnestock, Grant B. Schley) 195 B'way

N. Y. National Building & Loan Assn. (Benjamin F. Moore, Pres.; Wilber C. Marsh, Sec.; Joseph W. Blood, Treas. Directors: Benjamin F. Moore, Wilber C. Marsh, Joseph W. Blood, Gifford W. Sayre, William F. Thompson, 50 B'way

N. Y. National Exchange Bank (Daniel B. Halstead, Pres.; Cornelius B. Outcalt, Cashier; John L. Brower, Notary. Capital, $300,000. Directors: William J. Merrill, William H. Albro, Henry A. Blyth, Daniel B. Halstead, John Guth, Alexander T. Vannest, J. W. Rosenstein, Jacob H. Vanderbilt, John H. Seed) 136 Chambers

N. Y. Navigation School (Richard J. Bennington, propr.) 26 Burling sl.

N. Y. News Assn. (no inf.) 44 E. 76th

N. Y. News Co. (Henry Dexter, Pres.; Charles K. Willmer, Sec.; John W Rhoades, Treas.; further inf. unattainable) 20 Beekman

N. Y. News Publishing Co. (Benjamin Wood, Sec. Capital, $30,000; further inf. unattainable) 25 Park row

N. Y. Newspaper Union (James H. Beals jr. Pres.; Frank G. Bryson, Sec. Capital, $30,000; further inf. unattainable) 184 Leonard

THE CALIGRAPH WRITING MACHINE,
HARTFORD, CONN.

NEW 219 NEW

N. Y. Nickel Plating & Mfg. Co. (George F. Dodge, Pres.; Mary F. Dodge, Sec. Capital, $25,000. Directors: George F. & Mary F. Dodge) 227 W. 29th

N. Y. Novelty Advertising Co. (Thomas J. Fay, propr.) 197 W. 60th

N. Y. Novelty Co. (G. Schwab & Brothers, proprs.) 41 Greene

N. Y. O. K. Model Baking Co. (Christian G. Friedmann, Pres.; Herman Wellbrock, Treas. Capital, $50,000. Directors: Christian G. Friedmann, Herman Wellbrook) 23 Jackson

N. Y. Observer Co. (Wondell Prime, Pres.; Charles A. Stoddard, Sec. Directors: Wondell Prime, Charles A. Stoddard, Edward D. G. Prime) 38 Park row

N. Y. Oil Cabinet Co. (Albina E. Goodspeed, propr.) r 160 Cherry

N. Y. Ore Milling & Testing Works (McDermott & Duffield, proprs.) 2 Wall & 526 W. 16th

N. Y. Packing Co. (Ltd.) (Inf. unattainable) 196 Fulton

N. Y. Packing & Provision Co. (Daniel J. Lavery, propr.) 577 Tenth av.

N. Y. Pants Co. (William L. Farrell, propr.) 62 Bowery

N. Y. Paper Box Co. (Hug & Boscowitz, proprs.) 55 Day

N. Y. Paper Clothing Co. (Charles G. Barrett, Pres.; George Palen, Sec.; further inf. refused) 200 Pearl

N. Y. Patent Safety Gate Co. (J. Edward Weld, Pres.; David B. Hart, Sec. Capital, $75,000. Directors: J. Edward Weld, P. L. Meyer, David B. Hart) 44 B'way

N. Y. Pattern, Machine & Die Co. (John S. Ebert, Pres.; John H. Ebert, Sec.; Jacob Veith, Treas. Capital, $11,500. Directors: John S. Ebert, Carl Franck, John H. Ebert, Jacob Veith) 442 Water

N. Y. Pharmacal Ass'n. (John Carnrick, Pres.; Hamlin J. Andrus, Sec.; John E. Andrus, Treas. Capital, $50,000. Directors: John Carnrick, Hamlin J. & John E. Andrus) 6 Harrison

N. Y. Phonograph Co. (John P. Haines, Pres.; Richard Townley Haines, Sec. Capital, $1,250,000. Trustees: John P. & Richard Townley Haines, John D. Cheever, Noah Davis, William Fahnestock, W. Seward Webb, John L. Martin) 257 Fifth av.

N. Y. Phosphate Co. (Marcus Jenkins, Pres.; Edward N. Jackson, Sec.; A. Frank Stafford, Treas. Capital, $40,000. Directors: Marcus Jenkins, Edward N. Jackson, A. Frank Stafford) 194 Warren

N. Y. Photo-Electrotype Co. (Harry C. Jones, propr.) 92 Fifth av.

N. Y. Photo-Etching Co. (Lyman C. Hershey, propr.) 63 Duane

N. Y. Piano Forte Key Co. (not inc.) (Charles Hagen, John Euefer, Jacob Heinrich & Sebastian Roefer) 440 W. 41st

N. Y. Pie Baking Co. (William Thompson, Pres.; John F. Fullwood jr. Sec.; James Dowling, Treas. Capital, $150,000. Directors: William & William Thompson jr. John H. Meyer, James Blake, James Dowling, F. Michel, Matthew Demle, H. W. Schwoder, John F. Fullwood jr.) 82 Sullivan

N. Y. Pipe Mfg. Co. (Caleb H. Jackson, Pres.; James P. McQuaide, Sec. Capital, $100,000. Directors: Caleb H. Jackson, James P. McQuaide, Edward S. Perot, Thomas F. Goodrich, Samson Perot) 18 Cortlandt

N. Y. Plating Works (Kilian & Meyer, proprs.) 389 Broome

N. Y. Pneumatic Cigar Rolling Co. (Frank McCoy, Pres.; John R. Williams, Sec. Capital, $30,000. Directors: Frank McCoy, Myer Foster, Louis Haas, Joseph J. Powell,

John R. Williams, Isaac Bijur, William Hodgson) 102 Chambers

N. Y. Popular Publishing Co. (dissolved) 87 Bond

N. Y. Poultry Exchange (Robert Colgate, Pres.; Gustave R. Reynaud, Treas.) 68 William

N. Y. Press Co. (Ltd.) (inf. unattainable) 38 Park row

N. Y. Printing Co. (not inc.) (William S. Rossiter & Edward H. Hall) 118 Nassau

N. Y. Produce Exchange (Charles C. Burke, Pres.; Thomas F. White, Sec.; Edward C. Rice, Treas.) B'way c Beaver

N. Y. Produce Exchange Bank (Forrest H. Parker, Pres.; William A. Sherman, Cashier; Frederick K. Burckott, Notary. Capital, $1,000,000. Directors: Alexander E. Orr, Herman O. Armour, Samuel Jacoby, Alexander Munn, Jabez A. Bostwick, Edmund S. Whitman, Richard H. Laimbeer, Munroe Crane, Henry W. O. Edye, Forrest H. Parker, William H. Wallace, Augustus C. Bochstein) 2 B'way

N. Y. Produce Exchange Safe Deposit & Storage Co. (James McGee, Pres.; William H. Pearson, Sec.; Edwin R. Livermore, Treas. Capital, $150,000. Trustees: Franklin Edson, George F. Gregory, Alfred M. Hoyt, Samuel Jacoby, Daniel A. Lindley, Edwin R. Livermore, James McGee, Alexander E. Orr, Gustav H. Schwab, Forrest H. Parker, E. M. Van Tassel, William A. Pullman, Richard H. Laimbeer) Whitehall c Stone

N. Y. Progress Bunching Machine Co. (Adolph Brussel, Pres.; Adolph C. Schutz, Sec. Capital, $200,000. Directors: Adolph Brussel, Adolph C. Schutz, Sigmund Jacoby, Louis Ettlinger, William J Brown, Adolph Lowyn, Sigismund Lovy) 1230 Second av.

N. Y. Quinine & Chemical Works (Ltd.) (Herbert D. Robbins, Pres.; John L. Kirkland, Sec. Capital, $294,000; further inf. unattainable) 114 William

N. Y. Quotation Co. (Albert B. Chandler, Pres.; George W. Casper, Sec. Capital, $500,000. Directors: Albert B. Chandler, George W. Casper, John O. Stevens, Edward C. Platt, George G. Ward, Charles E. Merritt, T. L. Cuyler jr. John H. Emerick) 18 B'way

N. Y. Railway Press & Seal Co. (dissolved) 45 B'way

N. Y. Railway Publishing Co. (no inf.) 18 Cortlandt

N. Y. Railway Supply Co. (Ltd.) (Neil Macdonald, Pres.; Victor A. Wilder, Treas. Capital, $100,000. Directors: Neil Macdonald, Victor A. Wilder, William T. Pratt, Mariner A. Wilder) 40 Wall

N. Y. Railway & Steamship Advertising Co. (J. Buckley, Pres.; H. B. Jagoe, Sec. Capital, $12,000. Trustees: J. & Charles G. Buckley, John E. Wyman, Milton C. Roach, C. P. Craig, H. B. Jagoe, Samuel Carpenter) 30 Union sq. E.

N. Y. Real Estate Ass'n. (Samuel D. Babcock, Pres.; George F. Slade, Treas. Capital, $1,000,000; further inf. unattainable) 110 Leonard

N. Y. Real Estate & Building Improvement Co. (Ferdinand Fish, Pres.; Joseph C. Davis, Sec.; George W. Lithgow, Treas. Capital, $100,000. Trustees: Ferdinand Fish, William Hamilton, George W. Lithgow, Frederick M. Littlefield, Joseph C. Davis, Thomas Dimond, Charles T. Galloway) 149 B'way

N. Y. Refining Co. (dissolved) 151 Maiden la.

N. Y Refrigerating Construction Co. (George M. Hard, Pres.; Frank A. Bochmann, Treas.; George M. Brooks, Sec. Directors: George M. Hard, Frank A. Bochmann, George M. Brooks, Ferdinand E. Conde, Edwin A. Cruikshank, Robert Gantz, John Glass Jr. Conrad N. Jordan, Frederick J. Remor) 530 West

N. Y. Refrigerating Warehouse Co. (George H. Shaffer, Pres.; Ansel K. Powell, Sec.; William

SPECIAL ATTENTION PAID TO THIS CLASS OF WORK. } **BANKERS' & BROKERS' CIRCULARS DELIVERED** { THE TROW CITY DIRECTORY CO. 11 University Place.

NEW 220 NEW

R. Place. Treas. Capital, $0,000. Directors: George H. & Jacob Shaffer, Ansel K. Powell, William H. Place) 107 Murray

N. Y. Renovating & Waterproofing Co. (James L. McNamee, propr.) 61 W. 54th

N. Y. Roll Wrapping Paper Co. (Woolworth & Graham, proprs.) 154 Nassau & 31 Rose

N. Y. Roofing Co. (Edward H. Kidder, Pres.; Henry G. Homer, Sec.; Charles L. Pitts, Treas. Capital, $50,100. Directors: Edward H. Kidder, Charles L. Pitts, Michael F. Wynne, Owen McBreen) 437 E. 23d, 10 Warren & 445 Pleasant av.

N. Y. Rubber Co. (William H. Acken, Pres.; Rufus A. Brown, Sec. Capital, $300,000. Directors: William H. Acken, John P. Rider, Benjamin F. Lee, Olin O. Walbridge, Richard Butler, George D. Ripley, Henry G. Wolcott) 84 Reade

N. Y. Rubber Matrix Co. (Hendrickson & Bartel, proprs.) 93 Cliff

N. Y. Safety Steam Power Co. (Amos G. Nichols, Pres.; F. J. Thomas, Sec.; Henry Clay Nichols, Treas. Capital, $60,000. Directors: Amos G. & Henry Clay Nichols, F. J. Thomas, U. O. Orms) 30 Cortlandt

N. Y. Sail Making Co (Mark Shaw, Pres.; William W. Simpson, Sec. Capital, $20,000. Directors: Mark Shaw, William W. Simpson; further inf. unattainable) 27 Coenties al.

N. Y. Sample Card Co. (Abraham Vehon, propr.) 127 Elm

N. Y. Sand & Facing Co. (Anne Bell, propr.) 273 Cherry

N. Y. Sanitary Supply Co. (J. Hurtin King, Pres.; John A. Beuermann, Sec.; John J. Parsons, Treas. Capital, $175,000. Directors: J. Hurtin King, R. Schirmer, John J. Parsons, D F. Watson, A. G. Bailey, John A. Beuermann, E. J. Tram, Samuel Pickford, John Lamont) 59 Maiden la.

N. Y. Sarven Wheel Co. (Royer Wheel Co. proprs.) 101 Bowery

N. Y. Sash, Door & Blind Co. (George B. Christman, propr.) 1210 Second av.

N. Y. Savings Bank (Stephen W. Jones, Pres.; Cornelius W. Brinckerhoff, Sec.; Frederick Hughson, Treas. Trustees: Rufus H. Wood, Frederick Hughson, Richard H. Bull, Edward M. Voorhees, John Webber, Stephen W. Jones, William H. Jackson, Archibald M. Pentz, Ewen McIntyre, Andrew J. Campbell, Peter A. Welch, John McMurtry, Isaac Hendrix) 81 Eighth av.

N. Y. School Book Clearing House (Henry T. Clauder, Pres.; William D. Harison, Sec. Capital, $25,000. Trustees: Henry T. Clauder, William D. Harison, M. S. Gates) 65 Duane

N. Y. School of Training for Massage (Edwin T. Osbaldeston, propr.) 721 Sixth av.

N. Y. Security & Trust Co. (Charles S. Fairchild, Pres.; John L. Lamson, Sec. Capital, $1,000,- 000. Trustees: Charles S. Fairchild, William H. Appleton, William L. Strong, William F. Buckley, William A. Booth, William H. Tillinghast, William H. Beers, William L. Scott, O. C. Baldwin, Stuart G. Nelson, M. C. D. Borden, Loomis L. White, James J. Hill, Hudson Hoagland, Roswell P. Flower, James Stillman. A. Decker, John King, E. N. Gibbs, William T. Booth, Edward Uhl, Daniel S. Lamont, August Koenitze, S. T. Hanser, M. H. Folger, John Z. McCullough) 46 Wall

N. Y. Segar Manufacturers' Assn. (Isidor Frey, Pres.; Leopold Kaufmann, Treas.; Morris S. Wise, Sec.) 52 Exchange pl.

N. Y. Shellac Co. (George A. Alden & Co. proprs.) 229 Pearl

N. Y. Sign Co. (O'Connell Brothers, proprs.) 153 Fulton & 45 Liberty

N. Y. Silicate Book Slate Co. (Edward Coles, Pres.; John B. Coles, Sec. Capital, $50,000. Directors: Edward & John B. & Francis & Edward O. Coles) 35 Vesey

N. Y. Silicate Co. (Harvey N. Wood, Pres.; William A. Wood, Sec. Capital, $100,000. Directors: Harvey N. & Jarvis & William A. Wood, E. C. Hancock, Pierre de P. Ricketts) 40 B'way

N. Y. Silk Conditioning Works (Briton Richardson, Pres.; James Morris, Sec. Capital, $10,- 000. Directors: Briton Richardson, Robert J. Hoguet, Itioichiro Arai, Harper Sagendorf, James Morris) 12 Wooster

N. Y. Silk Dyeing Works (John Heidenreich, propr.) 423 W. 53d

N. Y. Silver Plate Co. (George A. Higgins, propr.) 20 Warren

N. Y. Smelting & Refining Co. (Bernhard Schutz, Pres.; Lazarus Lissberger, Sec. Capital, $70,- 000; further inf. unattainable) 506 West & 46 Cliff

N. Y. Soap Works (Rosenblatt & Co. proprs.) 441 Water

N. Y. Soap & Chemical Co. (Richard F. M. Chase, propr.) 237 B'way

N. Y. Society Review Publishing Co. (Inf. unattainable) 154 Fifth av.

N. Y. Solar Thermohme Co. (Edwin D. Babbitt, Pres.; L. Wesley Frost, Sec.; further inf. unattainable) 80 Union sq. E.

N. Y. Solid-Circle Gas Light Co. (no inf.) 152 B'way

N. Y. Sportsman (Lorenzo C. Underhill, Pres. Capital, $20,000; further inf. unattainable) 48 Murray

N. Y. Standard Directory Co. (Orimal C. Hatch, Pres.; Michael C. Gross, Sec. Capital, $25,- 000. Directors: Orimal C. Hatch, Michael C. Gross, S. S. Vanderhoef) 92 Gold

N. Y. Standard Watch Co. (Adam Dutenhofer, Pres.; James M. Hallowes, Sec. Capital, $400,000. Trustees: Adam Dutenhofer, William C. Roberts, James M. Hallowes, B. Spicer, R. D. Smith, Edward D. Hicks, Edward E. Quick) 13 John

N. Y. State Brewers' & Maltsters' Ass'n. (Cornelius H. Evans, Pres.; Gaius Thomann, Sec.; William Hoffmann, Treas.) 2 Irving pl.

N. Y. State Colonization Soc. (Charles T. Geyer, Treas.) 19 William

N. Y. State Private Detective Agency (William G. Irving, propr.) 141 B'way

N. Y. Steam Co. (Wallace C. Andrews, Pres.; Lewis Coon, Sec.; Onesimus P. Shaffer, Treas. Capital, $7,500,000. Directors: Wallace C. Andrews, Lewis Coon, Onesimus P. Shaffer, Charles M. Day, F. H. Prentiss) 173 B'way & 35 E. 58th

N. Y. Steam Fitting Co. (George F. Hall, propr.) 211 Centre

N. Y. Steam Laundry Co. (Mary E. Sloan, propr.) 230 E. 37th

N. Y. Steam Paste & Sizing Co. (Samuel Weil, propr.) 106 Franklin

N. Y. Steam Power Co. (John Mulford, Pres.; Archibald T. Moore, Sec.; John L. Cameron, Treas. Capital, $100,000. Directors: John Mulford, Archibald T. Moore, John L. Cameron, Rowland F. Hill, John C. Shaw) 58 Ann

N. Y. Steam Wire Works (Hopkins & Co. proprs.) 90 W. B'way & 20 Harrison

N. Y. Steamship & Hotel Supply Co. (Robert S. Beston, Pres.; Saruco S. Leon, Sec.; George A. Beston, Treas. Capital, $10,000. Directors: Robert S. Beston, Saruco S. Leon, George A. Beston) 243 G'wich;

N. Y. Steel Mat Co. (John F. Bonn, Pres.; Frederick Bonn, Treas.; Henry Pattberg, Sec. Capital, $100,000. Directors: John H. Bonn, Henry Pattberg, Frederick Bonn, William C. Spelman, Rudolph F. Rabe) 234 B'way

N. Y. Stencil Works (Eugene L. Tarbox, Pres.;

FOR THE BEST CO-PARTNERSHIP IN THE BEST CORPORATION SEE PAGE F IN BACK OF BOOK

NEW 221 NEW

Henry L. Tarbox, Sec.; Perry Van Alstyne, Treas. Capital, $80,000. Trustees: Eugene L. & Jerome L. & Henry L. Tarbox) 100 Nassau

N. Y. Stock Exchange (William L. Bull, Pres.; George W. Ely, Sec.; Dewitt C. Hays, Treas.) 13 Wall & 10 Broad

N. Y. Stock Exchange Building Co. (Donald MacKay, Pres.; Edwin S. Coles, Sec.; Daniel M. Walbridge, Treas.; further inf. unattainable) 10 Broad

N. Y. Stock Exchange Safe Deposit Co. (Donald Mac Kay, Pres.; Edwin S. Coles, Sec.; Daniel M. Wulbridge, Treas.; further inf. unattainable) 10 Broad

N. Y. Straw Works (Frederick E. Platt, propr.) 82 Bond

N. Y. Sunday School Assn. (Ralph Wells, Pres.; Frank Dickerson, Sec.; John S. Dussing, Treas.) 304 Fourth av.

N. Y. Tack Co. (James S. Barron & Co, proprs.) 2 Hudson & 141 Chambers

N. Y. Tag & Label Mfg. Co. (William B. Steiner, propr.) 431 Broome

N. Y. Tartar Co. (Joseph C. Hoagland, Pres.; William M. Hoagland, Sec.; Benjamin G. Templeton, Treas. Capital, $80,000. Directors: Joseph C. & Raymond & William M. Hoagland, Benjamin G. Templeton) 63 William

N. Y. Tea & Portrait Co. (Jacob Zinn & S. Tenner proprs.) 201 Fifth

N. Y. Theatre Co. (Brent Good, Pres.; George M. Hard, Treas.; Stephen R. Pinckney, Sec. Capital, $110,000. Directors: Brent Good, Pringle Mitchell, Stephen R. Pinckney, George M. Hard, Joseph Hutchinson) 191 Fulton & 314 Fourth av.

N. Y. Thermostatic Fire Alarm Co. (William H. Stevens, Pres.; Roswell D. Burchard, Sec.; J. Gillet Noyes, Treas. Capital, $300,000. Directors: William H. Stevens, Frank E. Morgan, J. Gillet Noyes. J. W. Frost, Charles A. Tinker, James W. Husted, George V. D. Frost, F. J. Stevens, Arthur C. Thomson) 338 B'way

N. Y. Times Assn. (inf. unattainable) 41 Park row

N. Y. Tobacco Machine Co. (H. A. Forrest & Co, proprs.) 104 John

N. Y. Tooth Co. (Frederick W. White, propr.) 224 Sixth av.

N. Y. Transfer Co. (William H. Woolverton, Pres. Capital, $400,000. Managers: William G. Stetson, William Thompson, Charles E. Pugh, James P. Scott, Stephen Little, George H. Hoyt, Samuel Carpenter) 849, 944 & 1823 B'way, 737 Sixth av., 521 Seventh av., Grand Central depot, ft. Desbrosses, ft. Liberty, ft. Cortlandt, 1170 Ninth av., 184 E. 125th & 364 W. 125th

N. Y. Underground Railway Co. (Edward Lauterbach, Pres.; Louis H. Hallmann, Sec.; Calvin Goddard, Treas. Capital, $10,000,000. Directors: Origen Vandenburgh, Edward Lauterbach, Henry D. Sedgwick, Richard Irvin jr. Jonathan H. Crane, John H. Davis, Henry Clews, William C. Behrens, David H. Bates, John D. Cheever, C. Francis Bates, Douglas Alexander, James M. Waterbury) 120 B'way

N. Y. Underground Telegraph Co. (D. Morgan Hildreth Jr. Pres.; William E. Findley, Sec.; George R. Thompson, Treas. Capital, $50,000; further inf. unattainable) 45 B'way

N. Y. Underwriters' Agency (Alexander Stoddart, agent; 82 Nassau

N. Y. Wagon Co. (refused) 589 Hudson

N. Y. Wall Paper Co. (Ltd.) (Lucian C. Warner, Pres.; Harris H. Hayden, Treas.; Henry M. Cowles, Sec. Capital, $200,000. Directors: Lucien C. Warner, Harris H. Hayden, Henry M. Cowles, Henry A. Smith, H. P. Cowles) 500 W. 42d

N. Y. Wall Paper & Fresco Cleaning Co. (Whitlock & Dovale, proprs.) 10 E. 14th

N. Y. Warehouse & Security Co. (Frederick Sturges, Pres.; Samuel C. Knapp, Sec. Capital $1,000,000. Directors: Frederick Sturges, Isaac B. Crane, Edmund W. Corlies, Benjamin G. Arnold, Theodore Gilman, William H. Galon, Christopher M. Bell) 74 Wall

N. Y. Warehousing Co. (James P. Wallace, Pres.; Charles K. Wallace, Sec. Capital, $200,000. Directors: James P. Wallace, William W. Wickes, William H. Wallace, William W. Rossiter, Charles K. Wallace) 52 B'way

N. Y. Watch Repairing Co. (Benedict & Drower, proprs.) 219 Sixth av.

N. Y. Wax Engraving Co, (W. H. & H. Fountney, proprs.) 26 Frankfort

N. Y. Weather Strip Co. (Charles R. Vincent, Pres.; further inf. unattainable) 368 Sixth av.

N. Y. Weekly Digest Co. (no inf.) 19 Park pl.

N. Y. Wire Nail Co. (Isaiah Kaufmann, propr.) 12 First

N. Y. Wood Cnt Co. (Tomay & Heinly, proprs.) 7 Murray

N. Y. World Building & Loan Assn. (Henry Martin, Pres.; William H. Lanahan, Treas.; Charles Wright, Sec. Directors: John T. Lanagan, T. Y. Crafts, William Hawkey, E. C. Tuttle, J. W. Shiffer, Darius Minshull, James Collins, J. T. Drew, F. E. Fitch) 31 Park row

N. Y. Woven Label Mfg. Co. (George H. Friedhof & Son, proprs.) 262 Canal

N. Y. Woven Wire Mattress Co. (James B. Ryan, propr.) 304 Hudson

N. Y. Yacht Agency (refused) 31 Broad

N. Y. & Amsterdam Carpet Co. (Carroll Brothers, proprs.) 264 Canal

N. Y. & Baltimore Coffee Polishing Co. (inf. unattainable) 126 Front

N. Y. & Bangor S. S. Line (inf. unattainable) 81 South

N. Y. & Bermudes Co. (William H. Thomas, Pres.; A. Howard Carner, Sec.; Thomas H. Thomas, Treas. Capital, $1,000,000. Directors: William H. Thomas, A. Howard Carner, Thomas H. Thomas, Nathaniel S. W. Vanderhoef, Melvin Stephens) 55 Beaver

N. Y. & Boston Baked Bean Co. (Adolphus C. Horbscher, propr.) 86 Jackson

N. Y. & Boston Despatch Express Co. (Henry O. Sherburne, Pres.; John C. Paige, Sec.; Charles W. Sherburne, Treas. Capital, $100,000; further inf. unattainable) 304 Canal, 57 Liepenard, 45 Church & 840 B'way

N. Y. & Boston Express Line (N. Y., New Haven & Hartford R. R. Co., proprs.) Grand Central depot

N. Y. & Boston Rapid Transit Co. (inf. unattainable) 15 Broad

N. Y. & B'klyn Electric Co. (Thomas Wilson, propr.) 174 Centre

N. Y. & B'klyn Ice Co. (John T. Welch, Pres.; Henry W. Wilcox, Sec. Capital, $10,000; further inf. unattainable) 385 Front

N. Y. & B'klyn Suburban Investment Co. (Herbert H. Walker, Pres.; George E. Hagerman, Sec. Capital, $100,000. Directors: Herbert H. Walker, George E. Hagerman, George Weaver) 146 B'way

N. Y. & B'klyn Transfer Co. (Ltd.) (Capital, $6,000; further inf. unattainable) no address

N. Y. & Buffalo Transp. Co. (David Taylor & Co. proprs.) 14 South

N. Y. & Charleston Warehouse & Steam Navigation Co. (in liquidation) 63 William

N. Y. & Chicago Chemical Co. (Preston C. Houston, Pres.; Henry Stubbendorff, Sec. Capital, $50,000. Directors: Preston C. Houston, Henry Stubbendorff. Walter H. Clark, William F. Johnson) 96 Maiden la.

N. Y. & China Tea Co. (M. H. Moses & Co. proprs.) 79 Vesey

CIRCULARS ADDRESSED TO ANY TRADE IN THE U. S. { Facilities
PROMPT, CAREFUL WORK } THE TROW CITY DIRECTORY CO., { Unequalled
AT MODERATE PRICES. }   11 University Place.

NEW   222   NEW

N. Y. & China Tea Co. (Minnie T. Egan, propr.) 1562 First av.

N. Y. & China Tea & Coffee Co. (James Carroll, propr.) 604 Second av. & 766 Tenth av.

N. Y. & College Point Ferry Co. (Matthew Coleman, Pres.; Frederick Eder, Sec. Directors: Matthew Coleman, Frederick Eder, Michael F. Coleman) ft. E. 99th

N. Y. & Conn. Air Line Railway Co. (dissolved) 15 Broad

N. Y. & Cuba Mall S. S. Co. (Henry P. Booth, Pres.; William H. T. Hughes, Sec. Capital, $2,500,000. Directors: Henry P. Booth, James E. Ward, William E. T. Hughes, George E. Weed, A. Vanderbilt) 113 Wall & Pier 16 E. R.

N. Y. & Greenwood Lake Railway Co. (Abram S. Hewitt, Pres.; Augustus R. Macdonough, Sec.; Tappan Bowne, Treas. Capital, $100,000. Directors; Abram S. Hewitt, John King, Cortlandt Parker, Edward Cooper, John G. McCullough, Samuel M. Felton jr. Theodore M. Etting, Augustus R. Macdonough, Andrew Donaldson) 21 Cortlandt

N. Y. & Harlem R. R. Co. (Cornelius Vanderbilt, Pres.; Edward V. W. Rossiter, Sec. Capital, $10,000,000. Directors: Cornelius & William K. & Frederick W. Vanderbilt, Samuel F. Barger, John D. Dutcher, Chauncey M. Depew, John B. Burrill, William H. Leonard, Charles C. Clarke, Robert Schell, Francis P. Freeman, Samuel D. Babcock, Alfred Van Santvoord) Grand Central depot & 433 Fourth av.

N. Y. & Harlem Window Shade Co. (Enos B. Smith, propr.) 2418 Second av.

N. Y. & Honduras Rosario Mining Co. (H. G. B. Fisher, Pres.; Samuel Jacoby, Trens. Capital, $1,500,000. Directors: H. G. B. Fisher, Samuel Jacoby, William F. Fluhrer, John C. Dore, John J. Marvin, William F. Buckley, William H. Power, J. Lathrop, M. Abenheim) 16 B'way

N. Y. & Hudson Steamboat Co. (William H. Traver, Pres.; Milton Martin, Sec. Capital, $75,000. Directors: William H. Traver, William J. Hughes, William A. Harder jr. George H. Power, L. Woolfe, Alexander Reed jr. E. A. Chase, D. M. Hamilton, F. H. Sutherland) Pier 32 (old) N. R.

N. Y. & Inland Commercial Guaranty Co. (Ltd.) (inf. unattainable) 206 B'way

N. Y. & Lake Champlain Transp. Co. (Robert H. Cook, Pres.; Edward P. Newcomb, Sec, Capital, $45,000. Directors: Robert H. Cook, Edward P. Newcomb, Frederick W. Stark) 33 Coenties sl.

N. Y. & Long Branch R. R. Co. (George F. Baker, Pres.; Samuel Knox, Sec.; John W. Watson, Treas. Capital, $2,000,000. Directors : J. Rogers Maxwell, George F. Baker, Benjamin Williamson, J. S. Harris, Edward D. Adams, James A. Garland, Lewis B. Brown, Henry Graves, Henry W. Maxwell, Charles Lanier, Harris C. Fahnestock) 120 Liberty

N. Y. & L. I. Bridge Co. (inf. unattainable) 340 Third av.

N. Y. & L. I. R. R. Co. (James D. Leary, Pres. Directors: James D. Leary, Thomas Rutter, O. W. Barnes; further inf. unattainable) 45 Exchange pl.

N. Y. & L. I. Telegraph Co. (John W. Roloson, Pres.; Charles Shirley, Sec. Capital, $5,000. Directors : Charles Shirley, John W. Roloson, Simon E. Ostrom, Thomas F. Jennings) 51 William

N. Y. & Maine Granite Paving Block Co. (John Peirce, Pres.; John Boardman jr. Sec.; Henry S. Lanpher, Treas. Capital, $38,000. further inf. unattainable) 5 Beekman

N. Y. & Mobile S. S. Co. (inoperative) 12 B'way

N. Y. & Morrisania Window Shade Co. (Abraham Bennett, propr.) 2797 Third av.

N. Y. & N. E. Seed Co. (dissolved) 29 Fulton

N. Y. & N. E. Telephone Co. (John L. Bullard, Pres.; Theodore I. Wilson, Sec. Capital, $500,000. Directors : John L. Bullard, Henry M. & Benjamin P. Wheeler, Eugene M. Sanger, Charles R. Braine, Louis F. Whitin, Louis B. & T. Irving Wilson, Charles T. Parker) 19 B'way

N. Y. & New Haven Automatic Sprinkler Co. (John Simmons, Pres.; Charles H. Simmons, Sec.; Victor A. Harder, Treas. Capital, $100,000. Directors : John & Charles H. Simmons, Victor A. Harder, Orrin C. Frost) 105 B'way

N. Y. & N. J. Globe Gas Light Co. (Ltd.) (William L. Elkins, Pres.; Charles K. Robinson, Sec.; William L. Elkins, jr. Treas. Capital, $50,000. Directors : William L. Elkins, Martin Maloney, William L. Elkins jr.) 115 B'way

N. Y. & N. J. Power Co. (J. Coleman Drayton, Pres.; T. J. Edmondson, Sec.; R. L. Edwards, Treas. Directors : J. Coleman Drayton, D. D. Withers, Samuel W. Boocock, Chester H. Davis. Joseph Larocque, Robert Dooley, T. G. McCullough, F. Cooper Clarke) 30 Broad

N. Y. & N. J. Telephons Co. (Charles F. Cutler, Pres.; Joel C. Clark, Sec. Capital, $2,400,000. Directors : Charles F Cutler, Joel C. Clark, William D. Sargent, Alexander Cameron, Theodore N. Vial, Morris F. Tyler, Joseph P. Davis, Samuel Klots, Hugh Kinnard) 16 Cortlandt

N. Y. & Northern Land Improvement Co. (Daniel S. Lamont, Pres.; Sherman Evarts, Sec. Capital, $50,000. Trustees : Henry Dimock, Daniel S. Lamont, Sherman Evarts) 15 Broad

N. Y. & Northern Railway Co. (Richard S. Hayes, Pres.; George G. Haven, Sec. Capital, $9,000,000. Directors : Charles T. Barney, J. J. Belden, A. M. Billings, Thomas Denny, Henry F. Dimock, Robert M. Galloway, George G. Haven, Richard S. Hayes, William Mertens, Oliver H. Payne, George W. Smith, William C. Whitney, George Coppell) 32 Nassau

N. Y. & Norwalk, Steamboat Co. (John E. Hoffmire, Pres.; George H. Frew, Sec. Capital, $30,000. Directors : John E. Hoffmire, John Englis jr. Edward S. Knapp, C. S. Englis, Andrew Patterson, John Harvey, George H. Frew) 116 South & Pier 23 E. R.

N. Y. & Ohio Railway Co. (Benjamin F. Holmes, Pres.; further inf. unattainable) 45 B'way

N. Y. & Pa. Telephone & Telegraph Co. (Charles F. Cutler, Pres.; Joel C. Clark, Sec. Capital, $1,0.0,000. Directors : Charles F. Cutler, Joel C. Clark, W. N. Estabrook, Henry L. Storke, C. A. Nichols, John E. Hudson, D. B. Parker) 16 Cortlandt

N. Y. & Perry Coal & Iron Co. (George A. Blood, Pres.; S. William Blood, Sec.; Frank P. Perkins, Treas. Capital, $3,000,000. Directors : George A. Blood, Frank P. Perkins, George K. Sistare, S. William Blood) 52 B'way

N. Y. & Phila. Coal & Stone Transp, Co. (Horace T. Caswell, Pres.; Walter J. Ford, Sec. Capital, $50,000. Directors : Horace T. Caswell, Asa Bigelow Kellogg, Herbert M. Caswell, W. F. Wolfe, Howard C. Bogardus) 85 Stewart bldg

N. Y. & Portland Express Co. (Robert M. Lott, propr.) 98 Wooster

N. Y. & Rockaway Beach Railway Co. (Austin Corbin, Pres.; Patrick H. Cassidy, Sec.; Henry Graves, Treas. Capital, $1,000,000. Directors : John R. Maxwell, Stephen A. Caldwell, Henry W. Maxwell, John Stralzton, William G. Wheeler, Frederick W. Dunton, Thomas F. Ward, Edwin H. Atkins, Willis T. Wild, James K. O. Sherwood, Edward H. Graves, Austin Corbin, Henry Graves) 192 B'way

N. Y. & Rome Line (William B. Walsh, propr.) 111 Broad & Pier 3 E. R.

THADDEUS DAVIDS CO., WRITING INKS, SEALING WAX, MUCILAGE.
MAKE THE BEST

N. Y. & Rosendale Cement Co. (Hamilton B. Tompkins, Pres.; Hiram Snyder, Sec. Capital, $50,000. further inf. unattainable) 229 B'way

N. Y. & Rossmore Laundry (Joseph A. Blanchard, propr.) 1368 B'way

N. Y. & Rudolstadt Pottery Co. (Isidor Straus, Pres. Capital, $100,000. Directors: Isidor Straus, Emanuel Eising, John F. Hillman, Edgar Gathers; further inf. unattainable) 42 Warren

N. Y. & San Domingo S. S. Line (William P. Clyde & Co. proprs.) 5 Bowling gr. & Pier 15 E. R.

N. Y. & Santo Domingo Lumber & Mining Co. (Henry L. Bean, Pres.; James E. Coleman, Sec. Capital, $750,000. Directors: Henry L. Bean, James E. Coleman, Charles E. Wilson, William H. Bibby, L. W. Haus) 32 Liberty

N. Y. & Santo Domingo Rock Salt Improvement Co. (Henry L. Bean, Pres.; James E. Coleman, Sec. Capital, $1,000,000. Directors: Henry L. Bean, G. G. Ward, James E. Coleman, Horatio C. King, William H. Bibby, S. W. Hals) 32 Liberty

N. Y. & Saugerties Transp. Co. (H. D. Laflin, Pres.; B. M. Freligh, Sec.; J. M. Boies, Treas. Capital, $25,000. Directors: J. M. Boies, H. D. Laflin, B. M. & E. Q. Freligh) Pier 35 (old) N. R.

N. Y. & Sea Beach Railway Co. (Albon P. Man, Pres.; Airick H. Man, Sec. Capital, $500,000. Directors: Albon P. Man, George Peabody Wetmore, John Barker, Airick H. Man, L. G. Lathrop, Benjamin B. Lawrence, William O. Platt) 59 Wall

N. Y. & Sing Sing Freight & Passenger Line (Jonks Brothers, proprs.) Pier 24 (new) N. R.

N. Y. & S. B'klyn Ferry & Steam Transp. Co. (John W. Ainbrose, Pres.; Francis H. Bergen, Sec.; William A. Stephens, Treas. Capital, $100,000. Directors: W. Bayard Cutting, Joseph Richardson, Tunis G. Bergen, Frank K. Hain, William A. Stephens, Edward T. Hunt, William Cruikshank, Richard M. Hoe, J. A. Murray, Jonathan K. Gapen) Pier 2 E. R.

N. Y. & S. Carolina S. S. Co. (William P. Clyde & Co. proprs.) 5 Bowling gr. & Pier 29 E. R.

N. Y. & Southern Lumber Co. (James Austin, Pres.; Peter J. Hughes, Sec. Capital, $10,000. Trustees: Thomas E. Kavanagh, Peter J. Hughes, James Austin, John Delclinar, August Junger) 16 Beaver

N. Y. & Suburban Co-operative Building & Loan Assn. (Elijah D. Clark, Pres.; Joseph Gill jr. Sec.; William J. Palmer, Treas. Directors: Louis Borg, Joseph Patzel, George T. Adams, William H. O'Dwyer, Patrick Martin, Evander Childs, Henry R. Fox, Lewis Harding, M. A. Brummer, Charles Curtis, John McCarron, Theodore B. Barringer, James Lee, A. Margolies) 110 E. 125th

N. Y. & Suburban Land & Improvement Co. (In-operative) 45 B'way

N. Y. & Texas Freight Traffic Assn. (dissolved) 280 B'way

N. Y. & Texas S. S. Co. (C. H. Mallory & Co. proprs.) Pier 20 E. R.

N. Y. & Wakefield Co-operative Building & Loan Assn. (Max Parpart, Pres.; J. G. Clegg, Sec.; John G. Folsom, Treas.) 150 E. 125th

N. Y. & Westchester Clothing Co. (Isaac Levy, propr.) 2714 Third av.

N. Y. & Wilmington S. S. Co. (William P. Clyde & Co. proprs.) 5 Bowling gr. & Pier 29 E. R.

N. Y. & Yucatan S. S. Co. (refused) 37 South

N. Y., Boston, Albany & Schnectady R. R. Co. (no inf.) 45 B'way

N. Y., Bridgeport & Eastern Railway Co. (H. R. Parrott, Pres.; Thomas N. Browne, Sec.; George E. Spare, Treas. Capital, $6,000,000.

Directors: H. R. Parrott, George S. Forbush, Thomas N. Browne, James D. Mowry, C. B. Coolidge, George R. Cowles, E. K. Lockwood, A. L. Whiton, George E. Spare, Charles D. Ingersoll, William Rouch, W. W. Douglas, C. B. Adams) 15 Broad

N. Y., B'klyn & Manhattan Beach Railway Co. (William G. Wheeler, Pres.; Frank McDonough, Sec. Capital, $1,000,000. Directors: William G. Wheeler, Frank McDonough, William J. Kelly, Frederick W. Danton, Charles L. Flint, Edward E. Sprague, John R. Maxwell, Henry Graves, Henry W. Maxwell, J. H. Atkins, Thomas F. Ward, Gilman S. Moulton, James K. O. Sherwood) 192 B'way

N. Y., Charleston & Florida Line (William P. Clyde & Co. proprs.) 5 Bowling gr. & Pier 29 E. R.

N. Y., Chicago & St. Louis R. R. Co. (Daniel W. Caldwell, Pres.; Allyn Cox, Sec. Capital, $30,000,000. Directors: William K. & Cornelius & Frederick W. Vanderbilt, H. McK. Twombly, John S. Kennedy, James A. Roosevelt, Frederic P. Olcott, Chauncey M. Depew, Allyn Cox, Daniel W. Caldwell, Joptha H. Wade, Charles M. Reed, Frank A. Missner) Grand Central depot

N. Y., Conn. & Eastern R. R. Co. (Charles D. Ingersoll, V.-Pres.; Thomas N. Browne, Sec.; Cornelius V. Sidell, Treas. Capital, $4,000,000. Directors: Charles D. Ingersoll, Cornelius V. Sidell, Thomas N. Browne, George M. Hard, James D. Mowry, George S. Forbush, W. W. Douglas, L. E. Chittendon, F. W. Ford, Frank S. Collins, John C. Sidell, James S. Leods, William M. Thayer) 15 Broad

N. Y., Lackawanna & Western R. R. (Samuel Sloan, Pres.; Frederick F. Chambers, Sec. Capital, $10,000,000. Directors: Samuel Sloan, John I. Blair, Percy R. Pyne, George Bliss, Russell Sage, Henry D. Polhemus, Eugene Higgins, Sidney Dillon William F. Hallstead, William R. Storrs, Frederick F. Gibbens, Edgar S. Auchincloss, Moses T. Pyne) 26 Exchange pl.

N. Y., Lake Erie & Western R. R. Baggage Express (N. Y., Lake Erie & Western R. R. Co. proprs.) 21 Cortlandt, ft. Chambers & 401 & 713 & 987 B'way

N. Y., Lake Erie & Western R. R. Co. (John King, Pres.; Augustus R. McDonough, Sec.; Edward White, Treas. Capital, $46,550,900. Directors: Josiah Belden, Henry H. Cook, Samuel M. Felton jr. William N. Gilchrist, James J. Goodwin, Morris K. Jesup, John King, William Libbey, John G. McCullough, Ogden Mills, Courtlandt Parker, George W. Quintard, M. F. Reynolds, William L. Strong, J. Lowber Welsh, William A. Wheelock, William Whitewright) 21 Cortlandt

N. Y., Maine & New Brunswick S. S. Co. (Thomas M. Bartlett, Pres.; further inf. refused) 17 William

N. Y., New Haven & Hartford R. R. Co. (Charles P. Clark, Pres.; William D. Bishop jr. Sec.; William L. Squire. Treas. Capital, $18,500,000. Directors: George N. Miller, Wilson G. Hunt, E. B. Trowbridge, William D. Bishop, Nathaniel Wheeler, Henry C. Robinson, Edward M. Reed, Leverett Brainard, Charles P. Clark, Joseph Park, Chauncey M. Depew, Henry S. Lee, William Rockefeller) Grand Central depot

N. Y., Ontario & Western Railway Co. (Thomas P. Fowler, Pres.; Richard D. Rickard, Sec. Capital, $58,113,082. Directors: Thomas P. Fowler, Joseph Price, Francis R. Culbert, John Greenough, Richard Irvin, Julien L. Myers, William H. Paulding, Harry Pearson, Charles J. Rosell, Albert S. Roe, Eben K. Sibley, Charles S. Whelen, Samuel Barton) 16 Exchange pl. & 322 B'way

N. Y., Susquehanna & Western R. R. Co. (Simon Borg, Pres.; John P. Rafferty, Sec.; R. C. Shimeall, Treas. Capital, $21,000,000. Directors: Simon Borg, Stephen V. White

COMPILED WITH ACCURACY AND DESPATCH } **CLASSIFIED BUSINESS LISTS.** { THE TROW CITY DIRECTORY CO. 11 University Place.

NEW 224 NIA

Charles Minzesheimer, Henry Marks, Henry Sanford, Robert K. Dow, Charles Siedler, John I. Blair, Garret A. Hobart, Alfred Sully, James M. Hartshorne, Horatio S. Pierce) 15 Cortlandt & Pier 16 N. R.

N. Y., West Shore & Buffalo Railway Co. (Consolidated with West Shore R. R.) Grand Central depot

New Yorker Handels-Zeitung Co. (Moritz Meyer, Pres.; Emil A. Norton, Sec.; further inf. unattainable) 72 Pine

New Yorker Staats-Zeitung Corporation (Oswald Ottendorfer, Pres.; Paul Loeser, Sec.; Edward Uhl, Treas. Capital, $25,000. Directors: Oswald Ottendorfer, Edward Uhl, Paul Loeser, Emma Schalk, Andrew H. Green) Tryon row

New Yorker Zeitung Publishing & Printing Co. (William Mayer, Pres.; Joseph Merwitz, Sec.; Charles B. Wolffram, Treas. Capital, $70,000. Trustees: William Mayer, Charles D. Wolffram) 7 Frankfort

Newark Embroidering Works (Herman Bornemann, propr.) 86 Walker

Newark Fancy Goods Mfg. Co. (inf. unattainable) 531 B'way

Newark Lamp Black Co. (not inc.) (John Rogers & Charles Calman) 299 Pearl

Newark Leather Belting Co. (Conrad F. Katsch, Sec.; Joseph Meier, Treas.; further inf. unattainable) 82 Ferry

Newark Spring Horse Shoe Co. (H. M. Clark, Pres.; George F. Ross, Sec. Capital, $12,500. Trustees: H. M. Clark, George F. Ross) no address

Newark & N. Y. R. R. Co. (Central R. R. Co. of N. J. proprs.) 119 Liberty & Pier 15 N. R.

Newberger & Perry (dissolved) 77 Mott

Newberry L. & M. (dissolved) 326 W. 49th

Newborg D. L. & Son (David L. & Joseph L. Newborg) 541 B'way & 112 Mercer

Newborg, Rosenberg & Co. (Joseph & Moses Newborg, Leopold B. Rosenberg & Mulvin Gutman) 620 B'way & 154 Crosby

Newboror Sons (dissolved) 315 Church

Newburg & Uthoff (no inf.) 7 W. 14th

Newburgh Orrel Coal Co. (inf. unattainable) 1 B'way

Newburgh Street Railway Co. (Antonio Rasines, Pres.; William Moores, Sec. Capital, $40,000. Directors: Antonio Rasines, William Moores, C. W. Dayton, George Silver, Arthur L. Meyer, John M. & John S. McWilliam) 45 Pine

Newburg, Dutchess & Conn. R. R. Co. (John S. Schultze, Pres.; William A. Wells, Sec. Capital, $1,087,450. Directors: John S. Schultze, William S. Eno, William N. Sayre, H. B. Willits, Samuel I. Wright, Albert Emans, R. G. Coffin, George Potter, Charles L. Kimball, R. C. Van Wyck, Labbeus B. Ward, William Lummis, N. T. Pian) 59 Wall

Newby & Evans (Alfred J. Newby & John Evans) E. 136th n 8. Boulevard

Newcomb Mfg. Co. (Theodore Newcomb, Pres.; Edward I. Hyde, Sec. Capital, $30,000. Directors: Theodore & C. E. Newcomb, Edward I. Hyde) 16 Thomas

Newcomb & Owen (Edward W. Newcomb & Walter G. Owen) 63 W. 36th

Newcombe I. B. & Co. (Isaac B. Newcombe & Camille Weidenfeld) 54 Wall

Newcome & Traver (dissolved) 171 B'way

Newcorn J. S. & Brother (Maurice S. Newcorn, only) 124 Park row

Newell Universal Mill Co. (Henry J. Chapin, Pres.; Louis H. Blackman, Sec. Capital, $400,000; further inf. refused) 23 Bethune

Newell D. C. & Sons (Darius C. & George H. & Darius E. Newell) Eleventh av. c. W. 19th

Newgnas L. & Co. (Lewis Newgnas & Joseph L. Rolling) 131 Maiden la.

Newhall Henry B., Co. (Henry B. Newhall, Pres.; Charles L. Phipps, Sec. Capital, $100,000; further inf. unattainable) 105 Chambers

Newhall Ship Chandlery Co. (Henry B. Newhall, Pres.; John W. Bancroft, Sec.; Charles L. Phipps, Treas. Capital, $6,000. Trustees: Henry B. Newhall, Charles L. Phipps, John W. Bancroft) 105 Chambers

Newhall & Fitzpatrick (Richard W. Newhall & James D. Fitzpatrick) 52 B'way

Newick S. J. & Co. (Samuel J. Newick & Stephen L. Morgan) 66 Fulton

Nowlin & Lindsley (dissolved) 130 Front

Newman Henry & Co. (Henry Newman, August Millus, Uriah J. Hecht, Seymour S. Guggenheimer & Sanford Simons) 630 B'way & 100 Crosby

Newman A. & Co. (Abraham Newman & Theodore Hacker) 42 Walker

Newman C. O. & Co. (dissolved) 244 Fulton

Newman G. & Co. (dissolved) 130 Second av.

Newman I. & Sons (Isaac & Abraham L. & Jacob J. Newman) 405 B'way

Newman L. & Sons (dissolved) r 114 Cannon

Newman Brothers (ice) (Charles & John H. Newman) 551 W. 27th

Newman Brothers (tailors) (Jonas & Leopold Newman) 416 E. 86th

Newman & Capron (Allen G. Newman & Jacob Capron) 167 W. 29th

Newman & Co. (awnings) (Hiram E. Newman & Andrew I. Brush) 300 E. B'way

Newman & Co. (photographs) (dissolved) 188 Essex

Newman & Kinkele (Frank V. Newman & Robert A. Klukole) 12 Barclay

Newman & Silverstein (Morris Newman & Joseph Silverstein) 596 B'way & 129 Crosby

Newmann Brothers (Abraham & Henry & Marks & Mark A. Newmann) 126 Greene

Newmann & Bennolt (Moses Newmann & George H. Bennett) 37 Clinton pl.

Newport Laundry (Carl Engel, propr.) 915 Sixth av.

Newport News & Mississippi Valley Co. (Collis P. Huntington, Pres.; Isaac E. Gates, Sec. Capital, $50,000,000. Directors: Collis P. Huntington, Isaac E. Gates, Edward H. Pardee, Richard T. Colburn, Frank H. Davis, Edward St. John, A. N. Hawley) 23 Broad

Newton Bottle Stopper & Britannia Co. (Stephen S. Newton, Pres.; William R. Baird, Sec. Capital, $150,000. Trustees: Stephen S. Newton, William S. Haniord, Charles H. Lawton, William R. Baird) 40 College pl.

Newton Copper Type Co. (Thomas N. Rooker, Pres.; Cuthbert J. Orchard, Sec. Capital, $100,000. Directors: John Cook jr. Thomas N. Rooker, Cuthbert J. & Robert R. & Alfred S. Orchard) 14 Frankfort

Newton Eye Water Co. (Henry S. Griggs, propr.) 211 Water

Newton H. & Co. (Edward Newton & Robert T. Lewis) 27 E. 15th

Newton & Howell (John Newton & Elias Howell) 645 Third av.

Newton & Shipman (James W. Newton & Orlando E. Shipman) 83 John

Newton's E. Sons (Franklin D. Newton, only) 371 Pearl

Newwitter & Rosenheim (Morris J. Newwitter & David Rosenheim) 513 B'way

Niagara Beef Co. (Henry Wormser, propr.) 401 E. 83d

Niagara Falls Power Co. (refused) 15 Broad

Niagara Fire Ins. Co. (Peter Notman, Pres.; West Pollock, Sec. Capital, $500,000. Directors:

SPECIAL ATTENTION PAID TO THIS CLASS OF WORK	BANKERS' & BROKERS' CIRCULARS DELIVERED	THE TROW CITY DIRECTORY CO. 11 University Place.
NIA	225	NIR

David Stewart, J. Taylor Johnston, William H. Wisner, Edward L. Hedden, James R. Taylor, Peter Notman, James W. Elwell, Thomas G. Ritch, Thomas F. Goodrich, William B. Tefft, Austin Corbin, J. Herbert Johnston, George A. Halsey, Charles B. Farwell, Dumont Clarke) 185 B'way

Niagara Mining Coal Co. (Rudolph V. Martinsen, Pres.; Henri M. Suermondt, Sec.; Cornelius C. Cuyler, Treas. Capital, $1,000,000. Trustees: Rudolph V. Martinsen, Henry M. Huydecoper, John R. Plumbdeau, Cornelius C. Cuyler, James L. De Fremery) 44 B'way

Niagara Mixer Mfg. Co. (Charles Hornbostel, propr.) 33 Dey

Nicaragua Canal Construction Co. (Warner Miller, Pres.; John W. Miller, Sec.; Edward Holbrook, Treas. Directors: Warner Miller, Francis A. Stout, Horace L. Hotchkiss, John W. Miller, Frederick Billings, C. Ridgeley Goodwin, Hiram Hitchcock, Alfred C. Cheney, J. P. O'Shaughnessy, Henry C. Taylor, Charles F. Daly, Allen F. Hedges, Alexander T. Mason, R. A. Lancaster) 44 Wall

Nicaragua Trading Co. (John A. Handren, Pres.; Orson Adams, Sec. Capital, $50,000. Directors: John A. Handren, Orson Adams, C. L. Buckl, John A. Horn) 18 B'way

Nichol, Stanley, & Brown (dissolved) 37 Walker

Nicholas James & Co. (James Nicholas & James H. Lancaster) 171 B'way

Nicholas H. I. & Co. (Henry I. & John S. Nicholas & Marcus Mayer) 11 Wall

Nicholls & Co. (Nicoll Nicholls, no Co.) 70 Crosby

Nichols George W. & Co. (George W. & Archibald B. & Harry Nichols & Francisco Perez) 128 Chambers

Nichols Harvester Co. (John H. Boynton, Pres.; Robert S. Walker, Sec. Capital, $40,000. Directors: John H. Boynton, M. L. Nichols, William Foster jr. Robert S. Walker, George B. Satterlee) 28 Beaver

Nichols Henry T. & Co. (Frank W. & Margaret M. Nichols, only) 68 Broad

Nichols J. J., Mfg. Co. (Jacob J. Nichols, Pres.; Sidney B. Clark, Sec.; Henry M. Haviland, Treas. Capital, $75,000. Directors: Jacob J. Nichols, Sidney B. Clark, Henry M. Haviland, George Dusenbury jr, Andrew F. Bode) 20 Barclay

Nichols Samuel & Son (Samuel & Charles H. Nichols) 66 W. 3d

Nichols A. S. & Co. (Adelbert S. & Grant L. Nichols) 15 W. 27th & 109 E. 128th

Nichols G. D. & Co. (George D. Nichols, no Co.) 25 E. 14th

Nichols G. H. & Co. (George H. & William H. Nichols) 68 William

Nichols J. R. & Co. (James R. & Charles Nichols) 70 B'way

Nichols W. S. & Co. (William S. Nichols & William L. Jenkins jr.) 85 Broad

Nichols Brothers (Henry T. & Amasa H. Nichols) 142 Reade

Nichols & Bacon (John A. Nichols & Alexander S. Bacon) 71 D'way

Nichols, Hine & Moul (John B. Nichols, Edward A. Hine & Charles H Moul) 144 Greene

Nichols, Panli & Hunt (Jasper Nichols, George Panli & Charles B. Hunt) 419 Fourth av. & 1186 Ninth av.

Nichols' Sillick, Son (Richard M. Nichols) 47 South

Nicholson John & Co. (John Nicholson & William C. Taggard) 152 Canal

Nicholson M. T. & Son (Meadows T. & Joshua C. Nicholson) 4 Hanover

Nicholson & Duval (dissolved) 778 Seventh av.

Nicholson & Galloway (Miriam Nicholson & Charles T. Galloway) 648 Hudson

Nickel-in-Cigar Co. (Charles Schendel & Co. 15

proprs.) 72 B'way, 62 Fulton, 116 Nassau & 322 Canal

Nickerson Frank & Co. (no inf.) ft. E. 37th & ft. E. 60th

Nickerson A. C. & Co. (Andrew C. & Alvah C. Nickerson) 31 B'way

Nickerson J. & Son (Joshua Nickerson, only) 24 State

Nickerson P. W. & Co. (Prince W. & Charles W. Nickerson) 634 W. 30th

Nicklas & Deion (John Nicklas & John Deion) 1507 Ninth av.

Nickles James & Co. (dissolved) 120 Worth

Nicoll & Ohle (Edward L. Nicoll & August C. Ohle) 167 S. 5th av.

Nicoll & Roy (Charles H. Nicoll & John H. Roy) 16 Dey

Niebrugge & Day (Frank B. Niebrugge & Charles H. Day) 121 Pearl

Niederstadt E. & Co. (Edward Niederstadt, no Co.) 172 Reade

Niemann & Wulp (George Niemann & Theodore Wulp) 44 G'wich

Nienaber Brothers (dissolved) W. 14th c Thirteenth av.

Nier & Lincke (Rudolph Nier & August Lincke) 50 Av. A

Niess J. & Son (Joseph & Leonard J. Niess) 485 Sixth av.

Niesterman & Novei (dissolved) 41 Lex. av.

Nieuwland Edward J. & Co. (Edward J. & Edward J. Nieuwland jr.) Tenth av. n W. 157th

Nightingale Floor Co. (Albert T. Kelley, Pres.; Charles B. Goring, Sec. Capital, $200,000. Directors: Albert T. Kelley, Charles B. Gorlug, Robert B. Nunan) 372 W. 33d

Nightingale Printing & Publishing Co. (refused) 13 W. 42d

Nightingale W. H. & H. Benneche (William H. Nightingale & Herman Benneche) 27 E. Houston

Nightingale Brothers (Joseph & John Nightingale) 84 Greene

Nigro S. & Son (Sylvester & Francis Nigro) 189 Elizabeth

Niles Tool Works (Alexander Gordon, Pres.; Robert C. McKinney, Sec. Capital, $500,000; farther inf. unattainable) 68 Liberty

Niles L. H. & Co. (Lucien H. & Philip B. Niles) 80 Broad

Nill & Klumpp (Courad Nill & Charles Klumpp) 402 Pleasant av.

Nilson A. & Co. (Adolph Nilson & Frederick P. James) 472 W. 46d

Nilson Co. (Eric Nilson, propr.) 184 Hester

Nineteenth Ward Bank (Samuel H. Rathbone, Pres.; James B. Story, Cashier; Louis H. Holloway, Notary. Capital, $100,000. Directors: Martin B. Brown, Richard A. Cunningham, Myer Hellman, John P. Kane, A. Bigelow Kellogg, Joseph J. Kittel, Julien L. Myers, Samuel H. & Robert C. Rathbone, George P. & Richard K. Sheldon, James B. Story) 963 Third av.

Ninth Avenue R. R. Co. (George Law, Pres.; James Affleck, Sec. Capital, $800,000. Directors: George Law, Paul N. Spofford, Otis W. Randall, Edward St. J. Hays, Joseph H. Godwin, Jacob Hays, G. Granville Wright, Stephen H. Herriman, William Ravenscyn, James & Joseph G. Affleck) 814 Ninth av.

Ninth National Bank (John T. Hill, Pres.; Hiram H. Nazro, Cashier; John H. V. Arnold, Notary. Capital, $750,000. Directors: John T. Hill, Hiram H. Nazro, C. Henry Garden, Haskell A. Searle, Albert C. Hall, William E. Tefft, Solomon M. Swartz, John H. Coon, Augustus T. Libbey) 407 B'way

Nirrnheim & Palmedo (Eugene Nirrnheim & D. Petri Palmedo) 14 Dey

TYPEWRITING DONE BY THE TROW CITY DIRECTORY CO., 11 University Place.

NIS 226 NOR

Nissen Ludwig & Co. (Ludwig Nissen & Alexander C. Chase) 16 John
Nitschke Brothers (Gustave & Emil Nitschke) 7 W. 27th
Niven D. MacM. & Co. (Daniel MacM. Niven, Pres.; Charles H. Lediard, Sec.; Malcolm W. Niven, Treas. Capital, $100,000. Directors: Daniel MacM. & Malcolm W. & Alexander S. Niven, Charles H. Lediard) 1 B'way
Nix John & Co. (John & John W. & George W. & Frank W. Nix) 281 Washn.
Nixon & Co. (Kate M. H. Nixon, no Co.) 62 Dey
Noakes James Orin & Co. (James Orin Noakes, Pres.; Conrad A. Mayer, Sec. Capital, $30,000. Directors; James Orin Noakes, Conrad A. Mayer, Thomas D. Warner) 216 E. 9th
Noble & Ferguson (Clarence M. Noble & James W. Ferguson) 140 B'way
Noble & Ganss (James Noble & Frederick Ganss) 1267 Ninth av.
Noble & Mestre (Henry G. S. Noble & Alfred Mestre) 15 Broad
Noble & O'Donnell (Frederick H. Noble & James A. O'Donnell) 280 Sixth av.
Noble & Severin (William C. Noble & Herman Severin) 118 E. 13th
Noe H. M. & Co. (Henry M. Noe & John C. Shields) 881 Hudson & 36 Ninth av.
Noe Brothers (dissolved) 339 W. 37th
Noe's James H., Son (William Noe) 275 G'wich
Noel & Sons (Auguste & Auguste jr. & Leon Noel) 449 W. 14th
Nolen & Boardman (Albert V. Nolen & John Boardman jr.) 5 Beckman
Nolen & Shute (Harry C. Nolen & John C. Shute) 227 Washn.
Noll Augustus & Co. (Augustus Noll & Charles L. Eichtz) 12 E. 16th
Nolte Brothers (Louis & Frank & Frederick Nolte) 400 Canal
Nolting & Bennett (August Nolting & Peter Bennett) 2 Cuenties sl.
Non-Magnetic Watch Co. (David Ward, Pres.; Charles P. Bruch, Sec.; Ezra T. Gilliland, Treas. Capital, $600,000. Trustees: David Ward, E. W. Struss, W. S. Ward, A. C. Smith) 177 B'wny
Nonnenbacher & Co. (Bertha Nonnenbacher & August Sieberg) 102 Mulberry
Nonotuck Pocket Book Co. (Bernard Lipshytz, propr.) 74 Franklin
Noonan D. & Son (David & Dennis J. Noonan) 7 Coenties sl.
Noonan & Graham (Michael Noonan & James Graham) 141 Eighth
Noonan & Michael (Andrew A. Noonan & Charles E. Michael) 141 Maiden la.
Nopper & Hornock (Andrew Nopper & Philip C. Hornock) 406 E. 6th
Norcross Regulator Co. (Alfred Gorham, propr.) 9 Murray
Norcross Brothers (James A. & Orlando W. Norcross) 43 W. 125th
Norden A. & Co. (Adolph Norden, no Co.) r 52 Exchange pl.
Norden Brothers (William & Henry E. Norden) 2059 & 2159 Seventh av.
Norden & Co. (dissolved) 61 Nassau
Nordenbrook & Zahner (dissolved) 854 Tenth av.
Nordenholt & Kirnan (Claus Nordenholt & John Kirnan) 23 Old sl.
Nordenschild J. & Co. (Joseph Nordenschild, no Co.) 205 Seventh av.
Nordheim & Co. (Moses Nordheim & Louis Mindheim) 22 Union sq. E.
Nordinger & Schmid (no inf.) 184 Essex

Nordlinger Henry & Co. (Henry Nordlinger, Sigmund Hirsch & Edwin H. Nordlinger) 8 Harrison
Nordlinger E. & E. (Emil S. & Edward) 41 Harrison
Nordt & Heppding (J. Charles Nordt & Gotzfried Heppding) 17 Maiden la.
Norman Brothers (Frederick H. & Alfred J. Norman) 201 E. 56th
Norman & O'Brien (Frank Norman & James O'Brien) 23 South
Normandale Lumber Co. (Norman W. Dodge, Pres.; Allen N. Sexton, Sec. Capital, $150,000. Directors: Norman W. Dodge, Allen N. Sexton, John C. Forsyth, Robert H. Wilkinson, Joseph Hilton) 81 New
Normandie Skirt Co. (I. Barnstein & Co. proprs.) 442 B'way & 36 Howard
Norris Brothers (dissolved) 664 Hudson & 432 W. 19th
Norris & Borchert (Wallace Norris & Oscar Borchert) 211 E. 23d
Norris & Murphy (dissolved) 35 Tenth av.
Norris & Williams (John Norris & John C. Williams) 79 W. 9th
Norris & Zabriskie (James N. Norris & Jacob G. Zabriskie) 53 Loew av. W. Washn. rnkt
Norris, Leonard & Pigot (Maurice A. Norris, William B. Leonard & Edward N. Pigot) 720 B'way
North C. F. & Co. (Charles F. North, Co. refused) 150 B'way
North, Ward & Wagstaff (Thomas M. North, J. Langdon Ward & Alfred Wagstaff) 120 B'way
N. Am. Beef Co. (Julius Leok, propr.) 1998 Second av.
N. Am. Dredging & Improvement Co. (D. C. Howell, Pres.; Nathaniel S. Bailey, Sec.; F. C. Munvel, Treas. Capital, $300,000; further inf. unattainable) 45 B'way
N. Am. Electric Co. (inf. unattainable) 14 Ann
N. Am. Exchange Co. (Ltd.) (Joseph Richardson, Pres.; Thomas J. Hand, Sec. Capital, $20,000. Directors: Joseph Richardson, John W. Young, Thomas L. Shurd, Thomas J. Hand, Newton S. Pinney, Curtis R. Boan, Royal M. Bassett) 57 B'way
N. Am. Iron Works (Jordan L. Mott, Pres.; Max Goebel, Sec.; Jordan L. Mott jr. Treas. Capital, $50,000. Directors: Jordan L. & Jordan L. Mott jr, John Reid) 88 Beckman
N. Am. Machinery Co. (John W. Newbery, Pres.; John Frankenhofner, Sec. Capital, $500,000. Trustees: John W. Newbery, John Frankenhelmer, Abraham I. Elkus, L. E. Salmon, Elias Asiel, Sigmund Jacoby, Alexander Cameron, D. J. Brehm, Edward Lauterbach) 120 B'way
N. Am. McLaline Co. (John C. Campbell, Pres.; Charles E. Tracy, Sec. Capital, $150,000. Trustees; John C. Campbell, Francis Gordon Brown, Charles E. Tracy) 35 Bleecker
N. Am. Phonograph Co. (Jesse H. Lippincott, Pres.; George H. Fitzwilson, Sec.; John Robinson, Treas. Capital, $10,000,000. Directors: Jesse H. Lippincott, George H. Fitzwilson, John Robinson, Thomas R. Lombard, George S. Evans, Charles A. De Witt, Charles A. Washburn) 160 B'way (see adv. in back)
N. Am. Publishing Co. (Lloyd S. Bryce, propr.) 3 E. 14th
N. Am. Railway Improvement Co. (G. Creighton Webb, Pres.; Edwin D. Worcester jr. Sec. Capital, $60,000. Trustees: G. Creighton Webb, George P. Erhard, Thorndike Saunders, Edwin D. Worcester jr.) 170 B'way
N. Am. Underground Telegraph & Electric Co. (Lewis May, Pres.; George R. Thompson, Sec. Percival Farquhar, Treas. Capital, $5,000,000. Directors: Lewis May, Percival Farquhar, Edward V. Loew, William H. Johnstone, D. Morgan Hildreth jr.) 45 B'way

THE CALIGRAPH WRITING MACHINE,
HARTFORD, CONN.

N. Carolina Lumber Co. (Harold H. Fries, Pres.; N. Macrae Robinson, Sec. Capital, $100,000; Directors: Harold H. Fries, N. Macrae Robinson) 92 Reade

North N. Y. Co-operative Building & Loan Assn. (Inf. unattainable) 2561 B'way

North N. Y. Lighting Co. (Henry D. Fuller, Pres.; John J. Moore, Sec. Capital, $150,000. Directors: Jordan L. Mott jr, Henry D. Fuller, John J. Moore) Ridor av. c E. 149th

North River Bank (Edward B. Gedney, Pres.; Frank R. Ingersoll, Cashier; Millard R. Jones, Notary. Capital, $240,000. Directors: Joseph Brokaw, John R. Greason, James L. Wise, Nicholas C. Miller, Edward L. Hedden, William E. Tefft, Aaron Close, Charles C. Worthington, John H. Starin, Millard R. Jones, Edward E. Gedney, David B. Paige) 187 G'wich

North River Beef Co. (J. Heidelburger & Brother, proprs.) 502 Hudson

North River Blue Stone Co. (Peter E. Van Riper, Pres.; Louis E. Bliss, Sec.; Edward F. Robinson, Treas. Capital, $50,000. Trustees: Peter E. Van Riper, Edward F. Robinson, Charles W. Kirby) 187 B'way

North River Coal & Wharf Co. (Charles J. Langdon, Pres.; Clarence D. Delany, Sec.; John C. Graves, Treas. Capital, $500,000. Directors: Charles J. Langdon, George J. Magee, M. H. Arnot, Austin Lathrop, John Donaldson, David B. Duncan, William Brinkerhoff) 1 B'way

North River Ice Co. (William E. Hotchins, Pres.; Frederick H. Crum, Sec. Capital, $450,000. Directors: John J. Lagrave, Peter R. Warner, John C. Tucker, Jay L. Adams, Waldo Hutchins, Joshua Jones, Edward H. Van Winkle, William E. Hutchins, William Darrow, Lawrence M. Van Wart, John M. Knox, Albert Bogert jr. James M. Thorburn, Hampton A. Coursen, William J. Haddock, James B. Mingay, William P. Douglas, John Crolins, Theophilus A. Brouwer, Leonard Warner, Samuel W. Johnson, William R. Bowne, John M. Knox jr, William W. Seymour, David M. Morrison, William M. V. Hoffmann, George N. Conklin, Frederick H. Crum, Henry Spratley) 175 B'way

North River Kiln Drying Co. (Behr Brothers & Co. proprs.) 298 Eleventh av.

North River Safe Deposit Vaults (Dilmon F. Renne, Manager) 187 G'wich (see advt. in back)

North River Savings Bank (William B. Stafford, Pres.; William D. Krug, Sec. Trustees: Albert Mathews, Gustavus Levy, William B. Stafford, Alanson Cary, William Wade, Samuel D. Styles, Hudson Hoagland, Benjamin F. Mills, Frank Tilford, Edward A. Newell, Henry V. Parsell, Henry De Peyster, Adolph H. Fischer, Joseph C. Baldwin, James W. Edgar) 474 Eighth av.

North River Steamboat Co. (James H. Blauvelt, Pres.; W. Dewitt Barclay, Sec. Capital, $50,000. Directors: James H. Blauvelt, Denton Fowler, James E. Morris, Clarence Lexow, George M. Hard, W. Dewitt Barclay, F. Eugene Pitman, Ira M. Hedges) 192 B'way & Pier 34 (old) N. R.

North River Sugar Refining Co. (In liquidation) 52 William

North Shore Co. (no inf.) 51 Nassau

North Third Av. & Fleetwood Park R. R. Co. (Capital, $100,000; further inf. unattainable) no address

N. & E. R. Railway Co. (Aaron Raymond, Pres.; Nathaniel S. Smith, Treas.; Douglas Alexander, Sec. Directors: Aaron Raymond, Michael J. Dady, Nathaniel S. Smith, O. W. Child, Stewart McDougall, Alexander Hudnut, A. J. Hutchinson, W. H. Delany, Ira K. Perego, Rowland E. Hazard, Homer A. Nelson, William G. Smith, David Banks) 115 B'way

N. & E. R. Steamboat Co. (Elizabeth Wright, Pres.; Gilbert A. Wright, Sec.; Moses G. Wright, Treas. Capital, $135,000. Directors: Elizabeth Wright, Marietta Benedict, Simon & Moses G. & Gilbert A. Wright) 466 S. Boulevard & Pier 82 (new) E. R.

N. & E. R. Terminal Railway Co. (Inoperative) 146 B'way

North & South Am. Construction Co. (Inf. unattainable) 1 B'way

Northern Boatmen's Assn. (George W. Hunt, Pres.; William Guindon, Sec. Trustees: George W. Hunt, Thomas J. Smith, William Guindon, A. Bristol, D. G. Case) 23 South

Northern Chief Mining Co. (Charles E. Gross, Pres.; J. W. Kirk, Sec. Capital, $2,000,000; further inf. unattainable) 75 Murray

Northern Eagle Publishing Co. (Ltd.) (Peter E. Tarpey, Pres.; James S. Lundy, Sec. Capital, $5,000. Directors: Peter E. & Michael Tarpey, John Raleigh, James S. Lundy) 2420 Third av.

Northern Gas Light Co. (Charles W. Bathgate, Pres.; John S. Bush, Sec. Capital, $125,000. Directors: Charles W. Bathgate, John S. Bush, William R. Beal, James M. Cummings, John P. Munn, Charles C. Lery, John G. Davis, William W. & Bartow W. Van Voorhis jr.) 1845 Vanderbilt av. W.

Northern Light Oil Co. (Charles W. Burton, Pres. Capital, $200,000. Trustees: Charles W. Burton, George W. Wight, Charles H. Burton) 12 B'way

Northern Pacific Express Co. (Inf. unattainable) 63 B'way

Northern Pacific R. R. Co. (Thomas F. Oakes, Pres.; George H. Earl, Asst. Sec.; George S. Baxter, Treas. Capital, $66,172,577.91. Directors: William L. Bull, Charles T. Barney, Charles B. Wright, Thomas F. Oakes, Charles L. Colby, Colgate Hoyt, Henry Villard, George Austin Morrison, James B. Haggin, Charles H. Leland, James B. Williams, Charles C. Beaman, Roswell G. Rolston) 35 Wall

Northern R. R. of N. J. (J. Hull Browning, Pres.; Orville A. Boorbach, Sec. Capital, $1,000,000. Directors: J. Hull Browning, Orville A. Boorbach, William C. Browning, Henry G. Marquand, Lansing Zabriskie, John W. McCullough, Elias H. Slason, Franklin W. Hopkins) 187 West & Pier 20 (new) N. R.

Northern S. S. Co. (no inf.) 93 Wall

Northrop C. S. & Co. (Charles S. Northrop & John H. Wheeler) 2 W. 14th

Northrop & Curry (Theodore F. Northrop & James S. Curry) 720 B'way

Northup J. M. & W. B. (James M. & William B.) ft. Franklin

Northwestern Masonic Aid Assn. (Daniel J. Avery, Pres.; James A. Stoddard, Sec.; Amos Grannis, Treas.) 7 Murray

Norton Can Co. (Edwin Norton, Pres.; Oliver Norton, Sec.; Frank Bartlett, Treas. Directors: Edwin A. & Oliver W. & L. A. Norton, S. A. Ginna, J. C. Milligan, L. B. Moore, Frank Bartlett) 284 Pearl

Norton Ex. & Co. (Eckstein Norton, no Co.) 50 Exchange pl.

Norton John & Son (John & Edward N. Norton) 90 Wall & Pier 13 E. R.

Norton Naval Construction & Shipbuilding Co. (Francis L. Norton, Pres.; J. Roberts Job, Sec.; Lemuel K. McKinsey, Treas. Capital, $750,000. Directors: Francis L. Norton, J. Hugh Peters, Neil McDonald, Chester C. Munroe, Lemuel K. McKinsey) 18 B'way

Norton Thomas & Co. (Thomas & Gerrit Norton) 490 G'wich

Norton E. & G. (Eugene & George) 6 South

Norton H. Z. & E. D. (dissolved) 1833 Park av.

Norton & Christman (George F. Norton & Charles A. Christman) 160 Eleventh av.

Norton, Weyl & Bevan (T. Frank Norton & George E. Weyl, only) 99 Front

SPECIAL ATTENTION PAID TO THIS CLASS OF WORK	BANKERS' & BROKERS' CIRCULARS DELIVERED	THE TROW CITY DIRECTORY CO. 11 University Place.
NOR	228	OBR

Norwalk Lock Co. (Edward Beard Pres.; David E. Distrow, Sec. Capital, $235,000 ; further inf. unattainable.) 82 Chambers

Norwegian Wood Pulp Co. (Ltd.) (Frederick Bertsch, Pres.; John L. McCabe, Sec. Capital, $15,000.; further inf. refused) 41 Broad

Norwich Line (Norwich & N. Y. Transp. Co. propra.) Pier 40 (old) N. R.

Norwich Nickel & Brass Works (William A. Aiken, propr.) 702 B'way

Norwood & Coggeshall (Carlisle Norwood jr. & Edwin W. Coggeshall) 140 Nassau

Norz B. & D. (Benjamin & David) 2718 Third av.

Nostrand & Clyne (John I. Nostrand & Frank E. Clyne) 17 William

Nostrand & Co. (Elbert B. Nostrand & Nevin W. Butler) 41 Fulton

Nostrand's Thomas C., Sons (William H. & John Nostrand) 186 South

Notin & Deutsch (Claudius Notin & Louis Deutsch) 127 Grand & 313 Av. A

Notin & Molseet (dissolved) 156 W. 24th

Nottingham Iron & Land Co. (Frederic H. Wilkins, Pres.; Luther E. Riddle, Sec. Capital, $500,000. Directors: Frederic H. Wilkins, George A. Boynton, Henry O. Miller, Charles D. Morrison, E. M. Lewis, Luther E. Riddle, Frederick Grube, E. R. Dickinson, Lewis German) 47 B'way

Nourse Charles & Co. (Charles H. Nourse, only) 37 Walker

Novelty Drum Package Co. (Ephraim A. Schwarzenberg, Pres.; John T. Larkin, Sec. Capital, $5,000. Directors: Ephraim A. Schwarzenberg, John T. Larkin) 336 G'wich

Novelty Embroidering Co. (G. & W. J. Ranch, propra.) 1 Walker

Novelty Fountain Pen Co., (dissolved) 419 B'way

Novelty Mfg. Co. (Grinberg & Schana, propra.) 32 Malden la.

Novelty Printing Works (Rose Redolsheimer, propr.) 408 Broome

Nowacke & Co. (dissolved) 104 Centre

Nowell & Presby (Samuel J. Nowell & William A. Presby) 20 White

Newell & Schermerhorn (no inf.) 84 W. 57th

Noxon Brothers (Charles H. & Willis B. & John F. Noxon) 5 Beekman

Noyes J. M. & Co. (Charles F. Noyes, only) 58 Exchange pl.

Noyes B. A. & D. J. (Samuel A. & Daniel J.) 62 Cedar

Noyes, Smith & Co. (Howard M. Giles, Elbridge G. Brown & Robert M. Ongle:—special partner, Isaac P. Smith, $25,000.; terminates 31st December, 1890) 63 Leonard

Nucase & Wagenbrenner (no inf.) 348 E. 11th

Nuffer & Lippe (dissolved) 51 Marion

Nugent J. S. & Co. (John S. Nugent & John F. Romig) 16 Reade

Nugent & Kelly (Catherine Nugent & Anne A. Kelly) 430 W. 27th

Nugent & Son (Charles F. & James Nugent) 617 Seventh av. & 314 E. 11th

Nuhn & Strohsecker (Michael Nuhn & August Strohsecker) 227 Sixth

Nuls & Bayer (Henry Nuls & Joseph Bayer) 1581 First av.

" No. 80 Madison Avenue " (apartment house) (Frank T. Robinson, Pres.; Henry W. Hayden, Treas. Capital, $175,000. Directors: Frank T. Robinson, Henry W. Hayden, Hiram Duryea) 80 Madison av.

" No. 121 Madison Avenue " (apartment house) (John S. Ellis, Pres.; Jarvis C. Howard, Sec. Capital, $350,000. Trustees: John S. Ellis, John K. Pruyn, Grosvenor P. Lowrey, William F. Wadsworth, Jarvis C. Howard, Allen Hay,

Joseph S. Auerbach, Mason Young, Andrew G. Myers) 121 Madison av. & 132 Front

Nurse E. F. & Co. (Edward F. Nurse & Alphonso L. Aderton) 341 Hudson

Nusbaum S. & Co. (dissolved) 545 B'way & 116 Mercer

Nusbaum & Co. (dissolved) 94 Prince

Nusbaum & Oppenheimer (Simon Nusbaum & Frederick Oppenheimer) 94 Prince

Nussbickel J. & Co. (Jacob Nussbickel, no Co.) Ogden av. c Jerome av.

Nutting T. B. jr. (Thomas B. Nutting jr. & Joseph W. Thompson) 187 B'way

O

O. K. Cutlery & Mfg. Co. (P. Tenney Gates, Pres.; Frank W. Gates, Sec. Capital, $10,000. Trustees: P. Tenney & Frank W. & D. B. Gates) 59 Dey

Oak Point & Bowery Bay Steamboat Co. (G. A. & M. G. Wright, propra.) ft. E. 130th & Pier 22 E. R.

Oakes Mfg. Co. (Francis J. Oakes, propr.) 98 Pearl & 58 Stone

Oakes & Alden (Thomas J. Alden, only) 516 W. 21st

Oakley Soap & Perfumery Co. (John A. Oakley, Pres.; Alfred P. Babcock, Sec. Capital, $25,000. Directors: John A. Oakley, Alfred P. Babcock, E. M. Oakley) 122 Duane

Oakley & Keating (John M. Oakley & John Keating) 40 Cortlandt

Oakley & Sachs (Charles P. Oakley & Herman Sachs) 1 Vesey

Oakley & Smith (Whitson Oakley & George Smith) 150 E. 24th

Oakley's Gilbert, Sons (Gilbert jr. & Thomas O. & John B. H. Oakley) 184 Duane

Oates Thomas & Co. (Thomas Oates, Co. refused) 224 E. 104th

Obbard A. E. & Co. (Arthur E. Obbard & Edward F. Hornick) 209½ Pearl

Oberhauser & Co. (Frederick Oberhauser & I. Henry Blanchard) 40 W. B'way

Oberly & Newell (John L. Oberly & Herbert C. Newell) 550 Pearl

Obermayer & Layng (Charles Obermayer & George R. Layng) 16 Malden la.

Oberndorf & Frank (Julius Oberndorf & Emil J. Frank) 114 Franklin

Oberst & Blum (John Oberst & John C. Blum) 478 G'wich

Obertreis & Morris (dissolved) 548 Hudson

O'Brien John J. & Son (John J. & Daniel F. O'Brien) 397 Fourth av.

O'Brien Maurice & Son (Maurice & Joseph L. O'Brien) 812 B'way

O'Brien William & John (John O'Brien, only) 58 Wall

O'Brien C. W. & T. F. (Christopher W. & Thomas F.) 18 Washn. mkt

O'Brien L. G. & Co. (Lawrence G. & Matthew D. O'Brien) 52 E. 13th

O'Brien M. & Son (Michael & Edward J. O'Brien) 209 Washn.

O'Brien W. K. & Brother (William K. & James A. O'Brien) 53 Third av.

O'Brien Brothers (carpenters) (dissolved) 207 E. 25th

O'Brien Brothers (stone) (Henry & Thomas F. & Joseph O'Brien) 49 South

O'Brien & Clark (John O'Brien & Heman Clark) 40 Wall & 35 Hancock pl.

O'Brien & Co. (no inf.) 160 Greene

O'Brien & Daughter (no inf.) 11 Chatham sq.

MERCHANTS EXCHANGE NAT. BANK OF THE CITY OF N. Y.
SOLICITS YOUR ACCOUNT. **257 Broadway.**
PHINEAS C. LOUNSBURY, President.   ALLEN S. APGAR, Cashier.

OBR 229 OGD

O'Brien & Lavelle (Daniel J. O'Brien & Patrick S. Lavelle) 164 Clinton
O'Brien & McKnight (dissolved) 327 Washn. mkt
O'Brien & Ryder (Joseph W. O'Brien & Patrick J. Ryder) 184 Spring
O'Brien & Whiting (Henry S. O'Brien & Kenneth D. Whiting) 59 Liberty
Obrig Camera Co. (A. Clinton Wilmerding, propr.) 152 B'way
Obrig Charles E. & Co. (Charles E. Obrig & Aquila B. Rich) 35 Broad
Occidental Oil Co. (Robert B. Brown, Pres.; Charles C. Fuller, Sec.; further inf. refused) 14 Whitehall
Ocean Bay Soc. (no inf.) 115 B'way
Ocean Navigation & Pier Co. (inf. unattainable) 65 South
Oceanic Tea Co. (Martin J. Glynn & Co. proprs.) 79 Catharine
Ochs M. B. & Sons (Martin B. & Bernard & David Ochs) 58 Walker & 282 E. Houston
O'Connell Nicholas & Son (Nicholas & Eugene O'Connell) 1461 First av.
O'Connell Brothers (grocers) (Bernard & Thomas O'Connell) 2251 Seventh av.
O'Connell Brothers (signs) (John & William O'Connell) 153 Fulton & 45 Liberty
O'Connell & Clark (dissolved) 82 New Chambers
O'Connell & McMurray (Dennis O'Connell & William McMurray) 349 Water
O'Connell, Tighe & Co. (John W. O'Connell, John J. Tighe & Joseph G. Moonan) 283 Hudson
O'Connor James & Son (James & Francis J. O'Connor) 50 Roosevelt
O'Connor Richard & Son (Richard & Richard O'Connor jr.) 569 E. 135th
O'Connor M. & E. (Maurice P. & Edward) 715 Water
O'Connor M. & Sons (Mary & Patrick & Jeremiah O'Connor) 39 Ann
O'Connor T. & J. (Thomas & Jeremiah) 6 Water
O'Connor Brothers (liquors) (Jeremiah & Martin O'Connor) 22 Counties sl.
O'Connor Brothers (liquors) (John & Michael & Timothy O'Connor) 808 Second av.
O'Connor Brothers (liquors) (Patrick & William O'Connor) 897 Third av. & 970 Eighth av.
O'Connor & Blank (dissolved) 527 Fifth av.
O'Connor & Co. (John O'Connor & George R. Macey) 97 S. 5th av.
O'Connor & Dyer (dissolved) 18 E. 114th
O'Connor & Elliott (Thomas D. O'Connor & William Elliott) 16 Exchange pl.
Ode & Gerbereaux (Adolph Ode & Denis F. Gerbereaux) 131 S. 5th av.
O'Dell Daniel & Co. (Daniel O'Dell & E. Bayard Halstead;—special partner, Timothy C. Eastman, $100,000; terminates 30th April, 1891) 68 B'way
Odell J. H. & C. S. (John H. & Caleb S.) 407 W. 42d
Odell & Co. (refused) 117 W. 42d
Odendahl & Lehner (Martin J. P. Odendahl & Frank J. Lahner) 115 Third
Odenheimer & Zimmern (Joseph Odenheimer & Henry B. Zimmern) 89 Nassau
Odiorne Frank H. & Co. (Frank H. & George F. Odiorne) 25 Whitehall
Odiorne & Co. (Ida E. Odiorne & Sylvester Swain) 28 White
O'Donnell N. & H. (Neil & Hugh) 678 Water
O'Donnell & Co. (Charles O'Donnell, no Co.) 78 Vesey
O'Donnell & Isaacs (dissolved) 78 Vesey
O'Donnell & Treanor (Nicholas O'Donnell & Joseph H. Treanor) 513 W. 51st

O'Donoghue & Co. (Hugh &, William & Dennis O'Donoghue) 91 Grand
O'Donohue's Sons (John B. & John V. & Charles A. O'Donohue) 98 Front
O'Donohue's Joseph J., Sons (Joseph J. jr. & Thomas J. O'Donohue) 101 Front
O'Dougherty P. & Sons (Patrick & Francis C. & Daniel M. O'Dougherty) 34 Walker & 309 Church
Oechsle Brothers (Franz & Robert Oechsle) r 80 Eldridge
Oehler & Leunig (John F. Oehler & Carl W. Leunig) 374 Pearl
Oelbermann E. & Co. (dissolved) 57 Greene & 65 Worth
Oelbermann, Dommerich & Co. (Emil Oelbermann & Louis F. Dommerich:—special partners, Christopher Andreae, *Muelheim, Prussia*, & Leopold Schoeller, *Dueren, Prussia*, each $25,000; further inf. unattainable) 57 Greene & 65 Worth
Oelrichs & Co. (Herman C. Von Post, Gustave H. & Herman C. Schwab & Herman Oelrichs) 2 Bowling gr.
Oelschlaeger Brothers (Oswald Oelschlaeger, only) 88 Fulton
Oest C. & H. (Christian & John H. Oest, only) 48 Jackson
Oestreicher & Mayer (Benjamin Oestreicher & Herman Meyer) 166 S. 5th av.
Oestricher George F. & Co. (George F. Oestricher & John Lambert) 369 Washn.
Oetjen John H. & A. (John H. & Albert) 547 E. 84th
Oetjen & Tietjen (dissolved) 205 E. 47th
Oettinger Brothers (Adolph & Emanuel Oettinger) 151 Chambers
O'Farrell D. & Co. (Daniel O'Farrell & John J. Herbert) 408 Eighth av.
Offenbach & Marx (Joseph Offenbach & Stephen Marx) 51 Exchange pl.
Offenheiser & Co. (Godfrey Offenheiser & John W. Morgan) 92 Park pl.
Office Publishing Co. (David Williams, Pres.; Anson O. Kittredge, Treas. Capital, $8,000. Directors: David Williams, Anson O. Kittredge) 66 Duane
Office Toilet Supply Co. (John E. Griffiths, propr.) 9 Murray
Offutt & Co. (H. St. George Offutt & Theodore R. Varick) 58 Trinity pl.
Ogden Alfred & Son (Alfred & George B. Ogden) 41 Wall
Ogden A. B. & Son (Alfred B. & Samuel B. Ogden) 1061 Madison av.
Ogden A. H. & Co. (Arthur H. Ogden & Thomas R. Gascoigne) 58 Wall
Ogden C. S. & Co. (Charles S. Ogden & David J. Hogg) 59 Ferry & 676 E. 150th
Ogden E. H. & Co. (E. Hudson Ogden & Abner P. Bigelow) ft. W. 22d
Ogden J. W. & Co. (Joseph W. & E. Hudson Ogden & William E. Magie) 120 B'way
Ogden & Clark (Henry Ogden & C. Stacy Clark) 11 Pine & 240 Fourth av.
Ogden & Co. (express) (Thomas F. Ogden, Cornelius L. Gilmore & Amanda S. Ogden) 23 & 45 Church, 1 Lispenard, 8 Old sl. 3 & 31 Hudson, 2 Walker, 55 Reade, 56 Beekman, 313 Canal & 60 W. Houston
Ogden & Co. (mahogany) (John B. Hunting & Charles A. Melgs, only) 411 Washn.
Ogden & Katzenmayer (William B. Ogden & Richard Katzenmayer) 83 Liberty
Ogden & Wallace (Charles W. Ogden & Theodore C. Wallace) 65 Elm
Ogden, Beekman & Ogden (Thomas L. Ogden, Henry B. Beekman & David B. Ogden) 111 B'way

SNOW, CHURCH & CO.,
265 & 267 BROADWAY.

COLLECTIONS IN ALL PARTS OF THE WORLD.
T. C. Campbell and Arthur Murphy, *Counsel*.
TELEPHONE, 736 MURRAY.

OGD 230 ONG

Ogden's Express Co. (Ogden & Co. proprs.) 23 & 45 Church, 1 Lispenard, 8 Old sl. 3 & 31 Hudson, 2 Walker, 85 Reade, 66 Beekman, 318 Canal & 60 W. Houston

Ogdensburg Transit Co. (Orson Breed, Agent) 6 Coenties al.

Ogilvie & Stephen (William Ogilvie & Alexander Stephen) 103 W. 95th

O'Grady James & Sons (James & Joseph & Thomas H. O'Grady) 590 Ninth av.

O'Grady & Co. (David O'Grady & Peter Daulton) 946 Third av.

O'Grady & Gorman (Robert O'Grady & John J. Gorman) 486 Washn. mkt

O'Halloran Brothers (John & William O'Halloran) 127 W. 17th & 163 W. 15th

O'Halloran & Co. (Dennis W. O'Halloran, no Co.) 761 Sixth av.

O'Hara J. & Brother (James & John O'Hara) 308 & 860 Third av.

Ohio Roll Paper Co. (no inf.) 24 Stone

Ohio Southern R. R. Co. (Alfred Sully, Pres.; Wilberforce Sully, Sec.; Henry Graves, Treas. Capital, $5,840,000. Directors: John R. Maxwell, Austin Corbin, Dumont Clarke, Robert K. Dow, Amos Whiteley, H. S. Willett, H. L. Chapman, H. M. Weakley, Alfred Sully, Henry Graves) 192 B'way

Ohio & Western Coal & Iron Co. (inf. unattainable) 44 B'way

Ohio, Indiana & Western Railway Co. (Austin Corbin, Pres.; Frederick W. Dunton, Treas.; James D. Campbell, Sec. Capital, $10,000,000. Directors: Charles E. Henderson, John A. Glover, William Beckwith, Charles W. Fairbanks, John B. Mann, Edwin L. Stewart, Austin Corbin) 192 B'way

Ohlandt & Schmeelcke (Charles H. Ohlandt & Henry Schmeelcke) 2011 Second av.

Ohlrich & Oest (William Ohlrich & William Oest) 1133 First av.

Ohlrich & Voltmer (dissolved) 1133 First av.

Ohly, Schmidt & Co. (Louis M. Ohly & Herman W. Schmidt:—special partner, William Krumor, $25,000; terminates 1st April, 1894) 88 Warren

Ohmels P. M. & Co. (Peter M. Ohmels, no Co.) 146 Fulton, 538 G'wich & 519 Washn.

Ohmstadt Charles & Co. (Charles Ohmstadt & John Riefe) 952 Third av.

Ohry O. & Son (Charles & Charles Ohry jr.) 189 E. 4th

Oil Seeds Pressing Co. (Henry M. Pierson, Pres.; Mansfield B. Snevily, Sec. Capital, $50,000. Directors: Henry M. Pierson, Mausfield B. Snevily, Howard R. Burk, Oscar Frisbie, James Alexander) 27 Water

Oil, Paint & Drug Publishing Co. (William O. Allison, Pres.; William D. Templeton, Sec.; Franklin H. Tinker, Treas. Capital, $150,000. Directors: William O. Allison, Charles T. Root, Franklin H. Tinker) 73 William

O'Keefe & Shigley (John O'Keefe & William H. Shigley) 253 G'wich

O'Keeffe & Fitzpatrick (John J. O'Keeffe & David M. Fitzpatrick) 33 Ferry

O'Keenan Electric Mfg. Co. (dissolved) 45 B'way

Okonite Co. (Charles A. Cheever, Pres.; H. Durant Cheever, Sec.; Willard L. Candee, Treas. Capital, $1,000,000. Directors: H. Durant & Charles A. Cheever, Willard L. Candee, F. Cassenove Jones, Edward Simpson) 15 Park row

Olancho Syndicate (Luther E. Shinn, Pres.; Henry A. Kirkham, Sec. Capital, $300,000. Directors: Luther E. Shinn, Sheppard Homans, William Wilson, Stephen W. Fullerton, C. Robinson Griggs, Sidney DeKay, William F. Johnson) 120 B'way

Olcott & Co. (Richard M. Olcott, no Co.) 77 William

Olcott & Deal (Horatio L. Olcott & Edgar Deal) 40 Broad

Olcott, Mestre & Gonzalez (Emmet R. Olcott & Antonio C. Gonzales, only) 35 B'way

Old Dominion Land Co. (Calvin B. Orcutt, Pres.; Edward St. John, Sec.; Isaac E. Gates, Treas. Capital, $2,000,000. Directors: Collis P. Huntington, A. A. Low, Calvin D. Orcutt, Frederick Meisaner, Isaac E. Gates) 22 Broad & 1 B'way

Old Dominion S. S. Co. (John M. Robinson, Pres.; William L. Guillauden, Sec. Capital, $1,250,000. Directors: John M. Robinson, William H. Stanford, F. J. Kimball, Collis P. Huntington, C. P. Fischer, Mordaunt Boding, Charles C. Stockley, John W. Cansey, William Rowland) 235 West & Pier 26 (new) N. R.

Old Original Carpet Cleaning Co. (Albert Bowser, propr.) 916 Second av.

Old Regular Line (John Norton & Son, propr.s.) 90 Wall & Pier 18 E. R.

Old Staten Island Dyeing Establishment (James T. Young, Pres.; Henry C. Blake, Treas. Capital, $200,000. Trustees: James T. Young, J. Davis Tileston, Henry C. Blake, Crowell Hadden, Edward L. Kalbfleisch) 98 Duane, 679 B'way, 610 Sixth av. 1474 Third av. & 248 W. 125th

Ohlach J. & Co. (dissolved) 521 B'way

Olena & Craig (Theophilus Olena & Frank E. Craig) 46 Vesey

Olenick M. L. & Co. (Moses L. Olenick & Jacob Matlawsky) 54 Lispenard

Oliano & Capozre (dissolved) 76 E. 116th

Olin & Co. (Edwin R. Olin & William D. Lowden, 956 Third av. Edwin R. Olin & Edward Longton, 1405 Third av.)

Olin, Rives & Montgomery (Stephen H. Olin, George L. Rives & John H. Montgomery) 32 Nassau

Oliphant Mfg. Co. (inf. unattainable) 112 Liberty

Oliver George & Co. (George Oliver & Wesley F. Smith) 34 Lawton av. W. Washn. mkt

Oliver Richard & Bloomfield (Richard Oliver & James M. Bloomfield) 28 John

Oliver & Co. (Ebenezer Oliver, no Co.) 124 E. 125th

Olivit Brothers (George W. & Ambrose Olivit, & Josiah P. Cowper) 335 Washn.

Ollesheimer Tucodore & Brothers (Henry & Julius Ollesheimer, only) 54 Walker

Olliffe William M. (Maric MacLean, only) 6 Bowery

Olmstead & Weyh (Frederick Olmstead & Robert G. Weyh) 936 Sixth av.

Olmsted Henry & Son (Henry & George B. Olmsted) 78 Nassau

Oltmanns Brothers (Frederick & Andrew Oltmanns) 1071 Third av.

Olwell James & Co. (James Olwell, John E. McWhorter, Joseph F. Carrigan & Marcus J. McLoughlin) 181 West

Onderdonk N. & D. (Nicholas & Daniel) 22 W. 3d

Onderdonk W. M. & Co. (William M. Onderdonk & Charles V. Moore) 1 Beaver

One Hundred & Twenty-Fifth St. & Tenth Av. Cable Road (see Third Av. R. R. Co.) Tenth av. & W. 129th

O'Neil B. & F. (dissolved) 578 Ninth av.

O'Neil & Bevier (dissolved) 2817 & 2874 Third av.

O'Neil & Co. (John O'Neil & S. Gibson) 666 First av.

O'Neill F. & Co. (Francis O'Neill & Alfred J. O'Keeffe) 940 Third av. & 735 Sixth av.

O'Neill H. & Co. (Hugh O'Neill, no Co.) 829 Sixth av.

O'Nicll & Byrne (dissolved) 45 Cherry

O'Niell & Quackenbush (Henry & Thomas H. O'Niell & George Quackenbush) 72 Greene

Ongley Electric Register & Safety Signal System (inf. unattainable) 1 B'way

WATER METERS, GAS ENGINES, | NATIONAL METER CO.
FOR PUMPING AND POWER. | 252 Broadway, N. Y.

OPA   231   ORR

Opaline Mfg. Co. (Frank Rich, propr.) 96 Maiden la.

Open Board Clearing House (Ltd.) (no inf.) 46 Broad

Open Board of Brokers (refused) 46 Broad

Openhym William & Sons (William & Adolph & Joseph & Emile Openhym) 42 Greene

Opier Mfg. Co. (Minnie Opier, propr.) 7 Clinton pl.

Oppenheim Marx & Co. (Marx & Emil Oppenheim & Henry Rothschild) 469 B'way

Oppenheim Samuel & Co. (Samuel Oppenheim & David May) 80 Greene

Oppenheim E. L. & Co. (Edward L. Oppenheim & Walter Delmar) 4 Exchange ct.

Oppenheim & Isaac (Emma Oppenhalm & Alfred Isaac) 66 Grand

Oppenheim & Schilling (dissolved) 503 E. 19th

Oppenheim, Collins & Co. (Albert D. & Charles J. Oppenheim, only) 154 Greene

Oppenheimer Henry E. & Co. (Henry E. & Milton E. Oppenheimer) 47 Maiden la.

Oppenheimer Max & Co. (Max Oppenheimer & Henry Rosenholm) 110 W. 42d

Oppenheimer H. Z. & H. (Harry Z. & Herman jr.) 46 Maiden la.

Oppenheimer M. & Co. (refused) 180 Mercer

Oppenheimer S. & Co. (Sigmund & Julius Oppenheimer, Oscar Aberle & Gustave Freund) 90 Pearl

Oppenheimer S. & Levy (Simon Oppenheimer, Robert I. Levy & Nathan Morganstern) 471 B'way

Oppenheimer & Co. (dissolved) r 138 Attorney

Oppenheimer & Hirsch (Marcus Oppenheimer & Julius Hirsch) 40 Beaver

Oppenheimer, Bonnem & Co. (Herman Oppenheimer & Abraham Bonnem, no Co.) 400 B'way

Oppenheimer Brothers & Veith (Seligman & August Oppenheimer & Henry F. & Gustave F. Veith) 35 Maiden la.

Oppits William & Son (William & William Oppits jr.) 9 E. 17th

Oppszinsky & Silverstein (dissolved) 158 Greene

Oracle Co. (inf. unattainable) 298 B'way

Orange Co. Milk Assn. (Richard Decker, Pres.; William B. Conklin, Sec. Capital, $100,000. Directors: Richard Decker, William D. & George Conklin) 185 W. 24th

Orange & Sullivan County Milk Assn. (Anna Kling, propr.) 27 Vestry

Oregon Development Co. (refused) 45 William

Oregon Improvement Co. (Elijah Smith, Pres.; W. T. Wallace, Sec.; Prosper W. Smith, Treas. Capital, $5,000,000. Directors: Elijah Smith, James H. Benedict, Stephen H. Thayer, Prosper W. Smith, Frederick L. Ames, Henry Failing, Cicero H. Lewis, Joseph Simon, William S. Ladd, Cyrus A. Dolph, C. J. Smith) 15 Broad

Oregon Iron Works (James R. Floyd & Sons, proprs.) 530 W. 20th

Oregon Pacific R. R. Co. (T. Egenton Hogg, Pres.; Norman S. Bentley, Asst. Sec. Capital, $18,000,000. Directors: John I. Blair, Osgood Welsh, Norman S. Bentley, Jacob Halsted, H. C. Atwood, George S. Coe, R. G. Hazard, Peace Dale, George S. Brown, William M. Hoag, T. Egenton Hogg, Wallis Nash, B. W. Wilson, Thomas Graham, Zehhin Job, G. R. Farra, T. E. Cauthorn, D. R. Job, E. A. Abbey, John Harris, A. Hackleman) 45 William

Oregon Railway & Navigation Co. (Edmund Smith, Pres.; Theodore Wygant, Sec.; Prosper W. Smith, Treas. Capital, $24,000,000. Directors: Charles B. Fosdick, V. Mumford Moore, Francis O. French, Henry R. Reed, Edmund Smith, William P. St. John, Henry W. Corbett, Henry Failing, William S. Ladd, Cicero H. Lewis, William Mackintosh, John McCraken) 15 Broad

Oregon Short Line Railway Co. (dissolved) 40 Wall

Oregon & Transcontinental Co. (Henry Villard, Pres.; Trollus H. Tyndale, Sec.; Edward Edes, Treas. Capital, $40,000,000. Directors: Henry Villard, Charles L. Colby, Colgate Hoyt, C. A. Spofford, Paul Schultze, Charles B. Bellinger, Joseph Simon, Charles H. Prescott, Alexander D. Chariton, M. G. Hall, T. H. Bartlett, S. G. Fulton, Joseph S. Decker, Charles H. Ropes, Hector H. Tyndale, E. H. Abbot, George H. Williams) 15 Broad

O'Reilly H. & Co. (Hugh O'Reilly, Patrick Skelly & estate of Patrick Fogarty) 300 Hudson & 263 W. Houston

O'Reilly T. & Brothers (Thomas & John O'Reilly, only) 33 & 763 Second av.

O'Reilly Brothers (Cornelius & Thomas J. & Michael J. O'Reilly) 123 E. 44th

O'Reilly, Skelly & Fogarty (Hugh O'Reilly, Patrick Skelly & estate of Patrick A. Fogarty) 400 W. 14th & 208 W. 19th

O'Reilly's Express Co. (James A. O'Reilly, propr.) 302 W. 55th & 348 W. 50th

O'Reilly's Miles, Son & Co. (Charles M. & Peter W. & Miles O'Reilly) 246 Front

Orford Copper Co. (Robert M. Thompson, Pres.; I. W. Clarke, Sec. Capital, $250,000. Directors: Robert M. Thompson, I. W. & E. B. Clarke, Austin A. Wheelock) 87 Wall

Orient Chemical Co. (D. Etienne, propr.) 49 E. Houston

Orient Mutual Ins. Co. (in liquidation) 41 Wall

Oriental Bank (Clinton W. Starkey, Pres.; Nelson G. Ayres, Cashier.; Joseph E. Kehoe, Notary. Capital, $300,000. Directors: Clinton W. Starkey, Charles F. Goodhue, Stephen R. Halsey, Edward Wood, Charles H. Bailey, August W. Weismann, Thomas K. Lees, Daniel D. Youmans, Robert C. Fisher) 122 Bowery

Oriental Carpet Co. (Jacob Schnitzer, propr.) 1 Cedar

Oriental Cigar Co. (Louis Stern jr. propr.) 70 Pine

Oriental Mfg. Co. (Rosenblatt & Co. proprs.) 441 Water

Oriental Mills (Lange & Trillich, proprs.) 57 Willett

Oriental & Occidental Tea Co. (Ltd.) (Edward A. Willard, Pres.; William G. Wilson, Sec.; Lyman R. Greene, Treas. Capital, $100,000. Directors: Edward A. Willard, William G. Wilson, Lyman R. Greene, Richard M. Montgomery, C. E. Bigelow) 31 Burling st.

Origet A. & Co. (Arthur Origet, Robert S. Ridgely & Camille Manen) 29 W. 23d & 3 W. 24th

Original Am. Tea Co. (Robert Wells, propr.) 43 Vesey

Ormiston & Dorsett (Thomas S. Ormiston & R. Clarence Dorsett) 7 Nassau

Ormsby S. C. & S. K. (Sidney C. & Senter H.) 35 Wall

Ornamental Glass & Button Works (Leo Popper & Sons, proprs.) 65 Grand

Ornamental Iron Works (A. B. & W. T. Westervelt, proprs.) 102 Chambers

Oro Bella Mining Co. (Isaac T. Stoddard, Pres.; Charles H. Briggs, Sec. Capital, $600,000. Directors: George S. Frink, Richard S. Barnes, William T. Parks, J. P. Haynes, D. R. Sonic, Charles H. Briggs, Isaac T. Stoddard, Charles A. Darr, William R. Stevens) 160 B'way

O'Rourke & Lennox (Frank O'Rourke & Thomas W. Lennox) 553 W. 39th

O'Rourke & Tracy (dissolved) 1840 Ninth av.

Orr Allen & Co. (Allen Orr & John F. Eggert) 83 Frankfort

EXCELSIOR BIRD FOOD. The recognized standard. The most reliable for your Canary. Use no other. Insist upon getting it.
Packed only by C. ROSENSTEIN & CO., 373 Washington Street, New York.

Orr Brothers (George & William Orr) ft. E. 62d
Orrs & Co. (William & Alexander M. & Frederick W. & S. Alexander Orr) 182 Nassau
Orselli & Bernardoni (dissolved) 90 Park
Orsor & Anderson (Esther J. Orsor & Margaret A. Anderson) 53 B'way
Ortgies & Co. (John Ortgies & Robert Somerville;—special partner, Samuel P. Avery jr. $10,000; terminates 1st May, 1893) 366 Fifth av.
Orton F. M. & Co. (Frank M. Orton, no Co.) 668 First av.
Orvis Brothers & Co. (Charles E. & Edwin W. Orvis & Roland M. Smythe) 44 B'way
Osborn John, Son & Co. (Francis Pares & Charles Spencer & William & Robert Arthur Osborn:— special partner, Mary C. Osborn, B'klyn, N.Y. $100,000; terminates 1st Jan. 1893) 45 Beaver
Osborn Mfg. Co. (Benjamin A. Drayton, Pres.; Harry W. Lawrence, Sec.; Alvan Drayton, Treas. Capital, $25,000. Directors: Benjamin A. Drayton, Harry W. Lawrence, Alvan Drayton) 79 Bleecker
Osborn A. H. & W. E. (Albert H. & William E.) 206 B'way
Osborn & Bailey (Bryon Osborn & James Bailey) 1929 Washn. av.
Osborn & Broderick (William B. Osborn & William Broderick) 28 W. B'way
Osborn & Lindsley (Edward M. Osborn & Charles A. Lindsley) 97 Water
Osborn & Wilson (Albert E. Osborn & Frank W. Wilson) 37 Warren & 239 Front
Osborne Brothers (liquors) (dissolved) 19 E. 42d
Osborne Brothers (mers.) (Thomas Osborne, Frederick Klorber & Peter Van der Willigen, only) 441 Produce Ex.
Osborne & Burke (Elias S. Orborne & Lemuel L. Burke) 60 Barclay
Osborne & McBride (Thomas W. Osborne & George A. McBride) 150 B'way
Osenkop O. H. & Co. (Otto H. Osenkop, no Co.) 27 Greene
Oshinsky, Liberman & Co. (Joseph Oshinsky, Isaac Liberman & David Levy) 11 White
Osmer H. & Co. (Herman & John Osmer) 121 Av. C
Osmundson H. & Co. (Hans Osmundson, no Co.) 109 Broad
Osoldson & Lebkuecher (Niels Osoldson & Arthur E. Lebkuecher) 40 Spruce
Osswalt & Schmults (Otto Osswalt & John H. Schmults) 1317 First av.
Osterman F. & Son (Ascher Osterman, only) 1148 Third av.
Ostermoor H. D. & Son (Henry A. Ostermoor, only) 85 B'way & 11 Trinity pl.
Ostertag Brothers (Ernest L. & Frank R. Ostertag) 89 Centre
Osterweis Brothers (David & Max Osterweis) 517 Sixth av.
Ostheimer Brothers (Alfred J. & William J. & George R. Ostheimer) 406 B'way
Osthoff's F. V., Son (John B. Osthoff) 458 Sixth av.
Ostman C. R. & Co. (dissolved) 167 Third av.
Ostrander W. R. & Co. (John B. Peck, only) 25 Ann
Ostrander & Bruen (no inf.) 77 Varick
Ostrander & Loomis Land & Live Stock Co. (Welton D. Ostrander, Pres.; Frederick L. Oniver, Sec.; John A. Loomis, Treas. Capital, $220,000. Directors: Welton B. Ostrander, John A. Loomis, Samuel N. Bacon, Benjamin Arnold, Charles F. Brown, Edward P. Dates, Chester H. Loomis) 146 B'way
Ostrov Brothers (David & Harry Ostrov) 408 Broome

O'Sullivan Eugene & Co. (Eugene & James O'Sullivan) 96 Wall
Oswald F. & Sons (Fidelius & John Oswald, only) 1106 Second av.
Oswego Mfg. Co. (Thomas H. Wheeler, Pres; William T. Wardwell, Sec.; Paul Babcock jr. Treas.; further inf. unattainable) 26 B'way
Osyor M. & Brother (William H. & Martin Osyor jr.) 368 Broome
Otheman, Dyer & Southwick (Francis. W. Otheman, Edward T. Dyer & Francis H. Southwick) 22 White
Otis Bed Co. (Daniel C. Otis, propr.) 204 W. 23d
Otis Iron & Steel Co. (dissolved) 280 B'way
Otis & Gorsline (Ira L. Otis & Henry L. Gorsline) 484 E. 138th
Otis Brothers & Co. (Norton P. Otis, Pres.; Abraham G. Mills, Sec.; William D. Baldwin, Treas. Capital, $600,000. Directors: Norton P. Otis, William D. Baldwin, Abraham G. Mills) 38 Park row
Otten F. & Co. (dissolved) 270 Stanton
Otten & Flagge (Charles Otten & Henry A. Flagge) 1194 Ninth av.
Ottenberg I. & H. N. (Isaac & Henry N.) 155 South
Ottenberg S. & Brothers (Simon & Herman & Henry Ottenberg) 305 E. 2d
Ottenheimer Brothers (Salomon & Julius & Charles Ottenheimer) 446 B'way
Otterstedt Brothers (dissolved) 67 Hudson
Ottinger & Brother (Marx & Moses Ottinger) 137 D'way
Ottmann J. Lithographing Co. (William Ottmann, Pres.; Adolph Schwarzmann, Treas.; further inf. refused) 39 E. Houston
Ottmann William & Co. (William & Charles Louis & Philip Ottmann) 81 Fulton mkt & 210 Front
Ottmann & Metz (Leonard Ottmann & William F. Metz) 725 First av.
Otto Morris & Son (Morris & Samuel Otto) 248 Broome
Otto Robert & Co. (dissolved) 149 Church
Otto F. G. & Sons (Ferdinand G. & Gustav & Albert Otto) 42 E. 23d
Otto & Hillmann (Gustav A. Otto & John Hillmann) 152 Church
Oudin & Oakley (Lucien Oudin & Ralph Oakley) 79 Cedar
Our Age Publishing Co. (not inc.; further inf. unattainable) 18 R. 42d
Outerbridge A. Emilius & Co. (A. Emilius & Adolphus J. Outerbridge) 51 B'way & Pier 47 (new) N. R.
Outing Co. (Ltd.) (James H. Worman, Pres.; E. P. Worman, Sec.; George J. Schviffl, Treas. Capital, $100,000. Directors: James H. & E. P. Worman, E. B. Davis, George J. Schviffl, Louis B. Schram) 239 Fifth av.
Outwater & Felter (Edwin Outwater & Jacob A. Felter) 428 W. 25th
Overbagh C. E. & Co. (Charles E. & Frank A. Overbagh) 265 B'way
Overin & Markert (Henry C. Overin & Anton Markert jr.) 143 E. 30th, 1542 B'way, 2 W. 39th, 50 E. 41st & 122 W. 54th
Overton Charles C. & Co. (Charles C. Overton & Michael J. McGrath) 164 Maiden la.
Overton & Co. (Edwin A. & T. Chalmers Overton) 20 Exchange pl. & 65 Beaver
Overton & Hawkins (Charles C. Overton & Asor O. Hawkins) 165 Maiden la.
Ovington Brothers (Edward J. & Edward J. jr. & Theodore T. & Charles K. Ovington) 330 Fifth av.
Owen Electric Belt & Appliance Co. (inf. unattainable) 626 B'way

IDEN & CO., University Place, 9th to 10th Sts., N.Y. | MANUFACTURERS OF **GAS FIXTURES AND ELECTROLIERS**

OWE 233 PAL

Owen Thomas J. & Co. (Francis T. & Emily K. Owen & Charles A. Gilberg, only) 65 South

Owen G. & S. & Co. (George Owen, James P. Snow & Charles E. Westcott, only) 3 Maiden la.

Owen, Gray & Sturges (Edward L. Owen, Joseph H. Gray & Frank D. Sturges) 71 Wall

Owens H. & Brother (Hugh & Arthur Owens) 400 Eleventh av.

Owens J. D. & Co. (John D. Owens & James W. McCoy) 67 Barclay

Owens & Co. (James E. & Richard K. Owens) 160 E. 45th, ft. E. 47th & 575 Madison av.

Owens & Phillips (William W. Owens jr. & John B. Phillips) 32 Liberty

Oxford Gold Mining Co. (Emerson Coleman, Pres.; Frank F. Randolph, Sec. Capital, $125,000. Directors: Emerson Coleman, Edward Tuck, Charles Morris, John C. Coleman, John J. Gould, F. F. Randolph) 45 B'way

Oxford Publishing Co. (no inf.) 31 W. 13th

Oxley, Giddings & Enos (Charles F. Oxley, Silas M. Giddings & Alanson T. Enos) 224 Canal & 118 Walker

Ozokerite Mining Co. (Jacob Wallace, Pres.; Charles H. Burkley, Sec. Capital, $1,250,000 ; further inf. unattainable) 280 B'way

Ozono Disinfectant Co. (refused) 105 Broad

Ozone Park Land Co. (John S. Cain, Pres.; William P. Harvey, Sec. Capital, $100,000. Trustees: John S. Cain, William P. Harvey, Augustus S. & Louis C. Whiton, Charles Bell) 115 B'way

P

Pabor George & Co. (no inf.) 131 E. 120th

Pabst Theodore & Co. (Theodore Pabst, no Co.) 26 Barclay

Pace J. B., Tobacco Co. (Julius Ehrmann, Pres.; Solomon Oberfelder. Sec. Capital, $150,000. Trustees: Ernest & Julius Ehrmann, Charles Scholle) 98 William

Pach Brothers (Gustavus W. & Oscar & Gotthelf Pach) 185 B'way

Pacharzewsky & Jacobowsky (dissolved) 34 W. Houston

Pachtmann & Moelich (Herman R. Pachtmann & Charles F. Moelich) 308 Canal

Pacific Bank (Hart B. Brundrett, Pres.; Samuel C. Merwin, Cashier. Capital, $422,700. Directors: Charles L. Tiffany, Henry Weil, Thomas B. Kerr, Hart B. Brundrett, Olin G. Walbridge, Lewis M. Hornthal, Alexander D. Napier, John F. Degoner, Charles H. Steinway, Joseph M. Valentine, George A. Hearn, William H. Beadleston, Robert Buck) 470 B'way

Pacific Construction Co. (T. Egenton Hogg, Pres.; further inf. refused) 45 William

Pacific Fire Ins. Co. (Frank T. Stinson, Pres.; George Jeremiah, Sec. Capital, $200,000. Directors: Allan Hay, Loring P. Hawes, Robert Buck, Harmon Blauvelt, William W. Wickes, George H. Moller, A. W. White, Henry Silberhorn, John Morton, Hart B. Brundrett, Leonard Jacob, William H. Beadleston, Henry J. Robinson, Albert Crane, John B. Snook, Francisco Bianchi, John J. Williams, Frank T. Stinson) 173 & 470 B'way

Pacific Improvement Co. (J. R. Strobridge, Pres.; Frank S. Douty, Sec. Capital, $5,000,000. Directors: J. H. Strobridge, Arthur Brown, C. E. Green, Frank S. Douty, W. E. Brown) 2 Broad

Pacific Mail S. S. Co. (George J. Gould, Pres.; William H. Lane, Sec.; Joseph Helfen. Treas. Capital, $20,000,000. Directors: Jay Gould, Sidney Dillon, Russell Sage, Collis P. Huntington, Henry Hart, William Remsen, Edward Lauterbach, George J. Gould) 195 B'way

Pacific Mutual Ins. Co. (Jacob R. Telfair, receiver) 58 Wall

Packard Sea King Caboose Co. (refused) 39 South

Packard & Co. (dissolved) 39 South

Packard & James (Mitchell N. Packard, Darwin R. & John W. & William H. H. James & Robert G. Thomas) 123 Maiden la.

Packer Mfg. Co. (Edward A. Olds, propr.) 100 Fulton

Packer E. A. & Co. (Elisha A. Packer & Hugh N. Hartwell) 1 B'way

Packer & Son (James W. & James W. Packer jr.) 139 West

Packert & Lewis (Frederick F. Packert & Frank Lewis) 187 Spring

Paddock & Fowler (Benjamin C. Paddock & Charles Fowler) 4 Bridge

Padlock Button Co. (John H. Leonhard, Pres.; Robert E. Vanhovenberg, Sec.; Alfred A. Vanhovenberg, Treas. Capital, $5,000. Directors: John H. Leonhard, Robert E. & Alfred A. Vanhovenberg) 304 B'way

Paducah & Mt. Vernon Railway Co. (inf. unattainable) 120 B'way

Paepke & Tellkampf (Herman G. Paepke & George T. Tellkampf) 213 Sixth av.

Page John R. & Son (John B. & Bartlett B. Page) 102 Park pl.

Page William H. & Co. (William H. Page, Co. refused) 1451 First av.

Page S. W. & Co. (dissolved) 508 Pearl

Page & McMillin (George Shepard Page & Emerson McMillin) 66 Wall

Page & Taft (William D. Page & Henry W. Taft) 45 William

Page, Dennis & Co. (William C. Page, only) 325 B'way

Pagenstecher & Co. (dissolved) 18 Beaver

Paget & Kintner (Leonard Paget & Charles J. Kintner) 45 B'way

Paige David R. & Co. (David R. Paige & John J. Ridgway) 45 B'way

Paige, Carey & Co. (John R. Paige, Dominick M. Carey & Albert T. Paige) 45 B'way

Paillard M. J. & Co. (Alfred E. & George A. Paillard, only) 680 B'way

Paine Uptown Business College (Henry W. Remington, propr.) 107 W. 84th

Paisley Building & Loan Assn. (William J. Snyder, Pres.; Carl A. Sautter, Sec.; Russell J. W. Snyder, Treas. Directors: Oscar Fansner, E. A. Froeman, Vespera M. Freeman, Russell J. W. Snyder, James Hay, C. R. F. Topham, William J. Snyder, S. Maduro, M. D. Senior, N. P. Todd, Carl A. Sautter, Robert Easdale) 100 Duane

Pakenham & Dowling (John Pakenham & Edwin J. Dowling) 12 Spruce

Palace Ribbon Mfg. Co. (William Reichman, propr.) 71 Franklin & 440 Canal

Palacio Celestino & Co. (Ferdinand Hirsch, only) 2 Burling sl.

Palais Royal (Rosa Lisner, propr.) 4 E. 14th

Palen W. W. & Co. (William W. Palen & J. E. Fitzgerald) 290 Fifth av.

Palen, Nelson & Co. (William Palen & Richard Nelson, no Co.) 87 Gold

Palermo Mica Co. (George F. Breed, Pres.; Edwin S. Larcher, Sec.; Frank M. Larchar, Treas. Directors: George F. Breed, Edwin S. & Frank M. Larchar) 27 Peck sl.

Palette Art Co. (Francis Koehsel, propr.) 283 Fourth av.

Palisade Stone Co. (inf. unattainable) 72 William

Palisades R. R. Co. (William S. Opdyke, Pres.; William O. Allison, Sec.; George S. Coe, Treas. Capital, $250,000. Directors: William S. Opdyke, William O. Allison, George S. Coe, William E. Bond) 15 Broad

CIRCULARS ADDRESSED TO ANY TRADE IN THE U. S. { Facilities
PROMPT, CAREFUL WORK } THE TROW CITY DIRECTORY CO., { Unequalled.
AT MODERATE PRICES. } 11 University Place.

PAL 234 PAR

Pall Mall Electric Assn. (George A. Scott, propr.) 842 B'way

Palliser, Palliser & Co. (Charles Palliser, only) 24 E. 42d

Palm, Fechteler & Co. (Charles Palm. Caspar Fechteler & Paul E. Vacquorel) 9 W. 13th

Palme & Co. (Julius Palme, no Co.) 33 Barclay

Palmenberg's J. R., Sons (Raymond P. & William F. & Emil T. Palmenberg) 406 Broome

Palmer Albert, Co. (Albert Palmer, Pres.; Albert W. Palmer, Sec.; Stephen A. Palmer, Treas. Capital, $100,000; farther inf. refused) 222 Fulton

Palmer Galvanic Bed Co., (Ltd.) (Frederick A. Palmer, Pres.; farther inf. refused) 261 E. 9th

Palmer George G. & Son (George G. & George O. Palmer) 10 Ninth av.

Palmer Mfg. Co. (no inf.) 290 Pearl

Palmer F. C. & Co. (Frederick C. & Ella Palmer & Adelaide S. Corning) 221 Alexander av.

Palmer H. H. & Co. (Harvey H. & Frederick E. Palmer) 43 Harrison

Palmer J. & Co. (John Palmer & L. Adolph Zadig) 29 Av. D & 2240 Third av.

Palmer L. S. & Co. (Lorenzo S. Palmer & George W. Bryant) 2617 Third av.

Palmer N. F. jr. & Co. (Nicholas F. Palmer, George W. Quintard & William Bromley) 740 E. 12th & 735 E. 11th

Palmer Brothers (John D. & Clarence Palmer) 74 Chambers

Palmer & Boothby (dissolved) 280 B'way

Palmer & Burger (J. Culbert Palmer & Clarence L. Burger) 165 B'way

Palmer & Capron (John S. Palmer & Charles S. Capron) 29 Maiden la.

Palmer & Co. (James Palmer, no Co.) 77 Fulton

Palmer & Embury (Theodore J. Palmer & Peter A. Embury) 20 E. 18th & 9 Gouvernour st.

Palmer & Hughes (Sarah A. L. Palmer & George Hughes) 64 Bible h.

Palmer & Mead (Chester W. Palmer & Arthur W. Mead) 883 Sixth av.

Palmer & Sibell (dissolved) 104 Duane

Palmer's J. F., Son (James A. Palmer) 47 University pl.

Panama R. R. Co. (John Newton, Pres.; Ernest L. Oppenheim, Sec. Capital, $7,000,000. Directors; John Newton, Julius W. Adams, Samuel R. Probasco, Charles Coudert, David A. de Lima, L. de Bebian, Gustav Amsinck, Ernest L. Oppenheim, Robert A. Chesebrough, E. A. Drake, Richard W. Thompson) 15 Broad

Panama Star & Herald & La Estrella de Panama Co. (Ltd.) (Francis Spies, Pres.; Henry A. Thomas, Sec.; John F. Boyd, Treas. Capital, $25,000. Directors; Francis Spies, Henry A. Thomas, John F. & Frederick & Samuel Boyd) 36 B'way

Panama Trading & Development Co. (Henry E. Pearce, Pres.; Lawrence H. Redmond, Sec. Capital, $100,000. Trustees; Henry E. Pearce, Lawrence H. Redmond, Clarence Creighton, George H. Simpson) 16 Beaver

Pancoast & Rogers (Richard Pancoast & Archibald Rogers) 28 Platt & 15 Gold

Panne H. E. & Co. (Henry E. Panne, Co. refused) 160 E. 118th

Panse Loom Co. (not Inc.) (Frederick W. Panse, George J. Braitmayer & John G. Gnadt) 178 Grand

Panse & Gnadt (Frederick W. Panse & John G. Gnadt) 178 Grand

Panthorapean Co. (Bradley S. Osbon, propr.) 184 South

Panzer S. & H. (Sophia C. & Henricks) 166 Seventh

Pape & Brother (William & Henry Pape) 1812 Park av.

Pape & Deyo (Charles Pape & Walter C. Deyo) 861 Washn.

Papenhausen & Co. (dissolved) 1935 Third av.

Papenhausen & Kreienberg (Frederick Papenhausen & William Kreienberg) 1682 Ninth av.

Papillou F. & E. Wiet (Felix Papillou & Eugene Wiet) 189 Wooster

Pappenheimer M. & Co. (Max Pappenheimer & Jacob Newman) 43 Broad

Paquet & Co. (no inf.) 41 W. 4th

Para Transp. & Trading Co. (refused) 19 Broad

Paragon Mfg. Co. (not inc.) (Seward E. & Clarence H. Bowman, Joseph Baker & William K. Squires) 247 W. 125th

Paragon Shear Co. (Fuller Brothers, proprs.) 32 Chambers

Parallel Ruler Co. (N. S. Phelps, Pres.; J. B Seeley, Treas.; farther inf. unattainable) 834 D'way

Pardee & Gleeson (Michael Pardee & John Gleeson) 204 E. 28th

Pardo Q. & Co. (Carlos & Rafael Pardo) 81 E. 17th

Pardo, Velasco & Co. (George Pardo, F. Perez de Velasco & Jacobo S. Lobo) 61 William

Parent J. & Co. (Julius Parent & Blanche Leroux) 75 Christopher

Paris, Allen & Co. (Marshall J. & George H. Allen, Frank S. Stevens, Edson Bradley & Augustus S. Pyatt, only) 51 B'way

Parisian Laundry (not Inc.) (Marie & Josephine & Jane Chaudoir) 1655 D'way

Parisian Mfg. Co. (Paul Dart, propr.) 835 B'way & 171 Macdougal

Parisio G. & Co. (dissolved) 246 Washn.

Park Fire Ins. Co. (William Jaffray, Pres; William Valentine, Sec. Capital, $200,000. Directors; William Jaffray, Edward Scholl, Mahlon Apgar, Arthur L. Lory, Thomas Gardiner, Francois P. Furnald, Everett P. Wheeler, H. H. Haight, John B. Emory, James H. Hercy, Mordaunt Bodine) 166 B'way

Park M. & R. A. (Margaret & Rebecca A.) 247 W. 36th

Park W. F., Co. (W. F. Park & B. W. Buxton, proprs.) 43 Elm

Park W. F. & B. W. Buxton (William F. Park & Benjamin W. Buxton) 43 Elm

Park & Tilford (Joseph Park, John M. Tilford & Charles Park) 917 B'way, 120 & 658 Sixth av. & 754 Fifth av.

Park, Bell & Co. (William T. Park & James A. Bell, no Co.) 21 Warren

Parke William A. & Co. (William A. Parke & Edmund W. McClave) 18 B'way

Parker J. H. & Brother (John H. & Charles Parker) 1409 Lex. av.

Parker J. R. & Co. (John R. Parker & Christopher J. Conlon) 28 South

Parker J. W. & Co. (John W. Parker, James E. Stafford & James W. Edgett) 56 New

Parker & McIntyre (James F. Parker & John McIntyre) 200 Produce Ex.

Parker & Townsend (no inf.) 52 B'way

Parker & Vanbuskirk (Cortlandt Parker jr. & Dewitt Vanbuskirk) 135 B'way

Parker, Behringer & Co. (dissolved) 96 Centre

Parker, Stearns & Sutton (Russell Parker, James H. Stearns & Benjamin F. Sutton) 229 South & 451 Water

Parker, Wilder & Co. (Earn Farnsworth, Benjamin Phipps, William H. Sherman, James Streat, Marshall Shepard & William H. Wilder, only) 63 Leonard

Parkin William B. & Co. (William B. Parkin & William H. Boyd) 421 Eighth av.

Parkinson Morris B. & Oscar F. Smith 29 W 26th

THE CALIGRAPH WRITING MACHINE,
HARTFORD, CONN.

Parks & Campbell (dissolved) 61 Tenth av.

Parmele & Eccleston (Edward A. Parmele & John B. Eccleston) 1 B'way

Parmelin A. & Co. (refused) 1a Barclay

Farraga Brothers (Rafael R. & C. Frederic Farraga) 54 William

Parrish & Conklin (Francis E. Parrish & S. Louise Conklin) 329 Fifth av.

Parrish & Pendleton (Samuel L. Parrish & Francis K. Pendleton) 44 B'way

Parsells E. W. & Co. (Edward W. Parsells & John J. Bannan) 15 Cortlandt

Parshall William V. & Son (William V. & William V. Parshall jr.) 295 Mott

Parson A. T. & Co. (Alfred T. & Frederick T. Parson) 35 Liberty

Parson F. T. & Co. (dissolved) 48 Maiden la. & 35 Liberty

Parsons Block, Switch & Frog Co. (Edward N. Dickerson, Pres.; Henry T. Lowndes, Sec. Capital, $1,000,000. Directors: Edward N. Dickerson, Henry T. Lowndes, Henry F. Parsons, John J. Staples, John Cornwell, James Kay, Charles Francis) 45 B'way

Parsons Charles & Co. (Charles & Charles Parsons jr.) 96 B'way

Parsons Charles & Sons (Charles H. Parsons, only) 252 Washn.

Parsons Charles H. & Co. (Charles H. Parsons & J. Walter Thompson) 292 B'way

Parsons C. S. & Sons (Clement S. jr. & John H. & Henry C. & Edward Parsons) 19 Warren

Parsons S. L. & Son (Charles S. & estate of Samuel L. Parsons) 189 B'way

Parsons W. H. & Co. (William H. & William H. Parsons jr. & George F. Hicks) 4 Warren

Parsons & Daracs (William H. Parsons & George Barnes) 60 South

Parsons & Petit (Schuyler L. Parsons, only) 186 Pearl

Parsons, Harris & Co. (refused) 73 Park row

Parsons, Scarlett & Co. (Truman Parsons, James Scarlett & Adolph W. Wallander) 398 Fifth av.

Partlin & Co. (John G. Partlin, no Co.) 7 & 32 Little West 12h

Partridge H. M. & Son (Henry M. & Charles R. Partridge) Eleventh av. c W. 20th

Pasca Luciano & Co. (Luciano Pasca, no Co.) 2162 First av.

Pascal & Nacht (Sigmund Pascal & Isaac Nacht) 378 Eighth av.

Pasco & Palmer (George E. Pasco & George W. Palmer) 1293 B'way

Pascocello Brothers (Antonio & Charles Pascocello) 76 Sixth av.

Pascueco & Adelheimo (Peter Pascueco & James Adelheimo) 302 W. 25th

Paskuss J. & Co. (Jacob Paskuss & Mannic Frank) 98 Gold

Passaic Chemical Co. (Walter Edwards, Pres.; Wheeler De F. Edwards, Sec.; Florian Alexander, Treas. Capital, $180,000. Directors: Walter & Wheeler De F. Edwards, Florian Alexander) 254 Pearl

Passaic Print Works (James L. Morgan jr. Pres.; George P. Slade, Treas. Capital, $300,000; further inf. unattainable) 110 Leonard

Passaic Rolling Mill Co. (Watts Cooke, Pres.; Albert C. Fairchild, Sec.; William O. Fayerweather, Treas. Capital, $200,000. Directors: Watts Cooke, William O. Fayerweather, John S. & Frederick W. & John K. Cooke) 45 B'way

Passaic Zinc Co. (William R. Brown, Pres.; Charles B. Squier, Sec. Directors: William C. & Stuart C. & Charles B. Squier & William R. & William S. Brown) 111 Liberty

Passavant & Co. (Friedericke S. Passavant, George W. Sutton, Gustav Kotzenberg, William Sandhagen & Anton & Heinrich Meyer) 320 Church

Passe H. & Son (Henry & Frederick G. Passe) 2815 Second av.

Pasteur Filter Co. (Ltd.) (dissolved) 5 D'way

Pate William & Co. (William & Albert H. Pate) 148 William

Pate & Robb (William C. Pate & Alexander Robb) 76 Cedar

Patent Cereals Co. (George W. Pier, Acting Pres. Capital, $400,000. Directors: George W. Pier, Frederick Licht, Publius V. Rogers, John M. Crouse, J. H. Licht, Frederick Gilbert) 45 Pearl

Patent Cloth Sponging & Refinishing Co. (John H. Sanford, Pres.; Thomas L. Cornell, Treas.; further inf. unattainable) 146 Wooster

Patent Development Co. (William P. Ward, Pres.; Henry D. Norris, Sec.; Robert H. Thompson, Treas. Capital, $250,000. Directors: William P. Ward, Robert H. Thompson, Henry D. Norris) 59 Fifth av.

Patent Metallic Weather Strip Co. (C. R. Vincent & Co. proprs.) 74 W. 23d

Patent Sign Co. (Max Meyer, propr.) 1250 First av.

Patent Water & Gas Pipe Co. (James L. Davis, Pres.; Uriah H. Hazard, Sec.; Melvin Stephens, Treas. Capital, $50,000. Directors: James L. Davis, Uriah H. Hazard, Anson P. Stephens, Frank E. Idell) 41 Dey

Patents Investment & Mfg. Co. (James H. Lancaster, propr.) 171 B'way

Paterson Ribbon Co. (George F. Kuett, Pres.; William T. P. Hollingsworth, Sec. Capital, $125,000. Directors: George F. Kuett, William T. P. Hollingsworth) 119 Spring

Paterson, Downing & Co. (Robert W. Paterson & Edmund S. Nash, only) 104 Front

Paton Granitic Stone Co. (no inf.) 156 W. 125th

Paton John & Co. (John Paton, Cornelius C. Cuyler & Benjamin Graham—special partner, Morris K. Jesup, $250,000; terminates 1st May 1890) 52 William

Pattberg Lewis & Brothers (Lewis Pattberg, Pres.; Philip Pattberg, Sec. Capital, $175,000. Directors: Lewis & Hilarius & Philip Pattberg) 550 B'way

Patten John, Mfg. Co. (Louis Engelhorn, Pres.; J. Einathan Smith, Sec.; John M. Forbes, Treas. Capital, $1,000,000. Directors: Louis Engelhorn, Frederick G. Moyer, John M. Forbes, John Patten, Henry Vulbrecht, Adolph Nordes, Joseph Glatz) 15 Broad

Patterson C. Venton, Publishing Co. (William R. Harper, Pres.; Watson J. Mosier, Sec.; C. Venton Patterson, Treas. Capital, $60,000. Trustees: William R. Harper, Watson J. Mosier, C. Venton Patterson, John R. Anderson) 28 Cooper Union

Patterson George B. & Son (George B. & Samuel S. Patterson) 174 Canal

Patterson John & Co. (John & Andrew & James H. Patterson) 25 W. 26th

Patterson C. & Son (Chauncey & Clarence B. Patterson) 71 Wall

Patterson S. W. & Co. (Samuel W. & John Patterson) 916½ Ninth av.

Patterson W. & W. A. (William & William A.) 187 Washn.

Patterson W. S. & Co. (dissolved) 226 Produce Ex.

Patterson W. S. & Preston (dissolved) 216 Produce Ex.

Patterson Brothers (hardware) (Edgar C. Patterson, Pres.; Denis Nunan, Sec.; David J. Tingley, Treas. Capital, $50,000. Directors: Edgar C. & Henry A. Patterson, Minot C. Kellogg, David J. Tingley, Denis Nunan, Edward Stagg, Robert N. Brundage, Millard F. Griffiths) 27 Park row

PAT 236 PEC

Patterson Brothers (wool) (James C. & William A. Patterson) 184 Duane

Patterson & Greenough (Albert M. Patterson & William Greenough) 41 Worth

Patterson & Purdy (Charles W. Purdy, only) 158 William

Patterson, Bevins & Plowright (Tunis H. Patterson, Silus H. Bevins & Charles Plowright) 355 Fourth av.

Patterson, Gottfried & Hunter (Ld.) (Henry T. Patterson, Pres.; William H. Jackson, Sec.; Robert J. Hunter, Treas. Capital, $50,000. Directors: Henry T. Patterson, Frederick Gottfried, Robert J. Hunter, William H. Jackson, Daniel Morrell, C. S. Shepard) 148 Centre

Patteson Thomas A. & Son (Thomas A. & Edward 11 Patteson) 186 Pearl

Patteson W. M. & Co. (William M. & Henry B. Patteson) 67 Exchange pl.

Patton Alexander & Son (Alexander & George F. Patton) 218 Canal

Patton William L. & Co. (William L. Patton & Henry L. Saltonstall) 6 Wall

Patarei F. & Co. (Frederick Patarel, no Co.) 56 Duane

Patzowsky & Co. (Richard & Charles Patzowsky) 133 William & 511 W. 33d

Paul Brothers (Gustave J. & Frank M. Paul) 229 E. 120th

Paulding J. P. & Co. (James P. Paulding & J. Dimon Smith) 24 New

Paull J. A. & Co. (John A. & Herman G. Paull) 10 S. William

Pauls Brothers (Albert & August Pauls) 88 Chambers

Paulson Frederick & Co. (Frederick Paulson, no Co.) 19 Old sl.

Paulsen & Walter (Jacob F. Paulsen & Martin Walter) 704 Tremont av.

Pavonia Ferry Co. (Cortlandt Parker, Pres.; Augustus R. Macdonough, Sec.; Edward White, Treas. Capital, $100,000. Directors: Cortlandt Parker, Augustae R. Macdonough, John King, Lansing Zabriskie, Robert E. Stockton) 21 Cortlandt, ft. Chambers & ft. W. 23d

Payne B. W. & Sons (Benjamin N. & David W. Payne, only) 45 Dey

Payne O. N. & E. T. (Oliver N. & Edward T.) 115 Nassau

Payne S. H. & Son (Shepard H. & Clarence E. Payne) 9 Burling sl.

Payne & Dehnert (Anne Payne & Minnie Dehnert) 29 Catharine

Payne & Westover (Thomas P. Payne & John H. Westover) 96 B'way

Paynter W. R. & Brothers (William R. & David & A. Lincoln Paynter) 210 Fulton

Pazourek A. & I. (Antonia & Ida) 73 Sheriff

Peabody A. & Co. (Adolph & Michael Peabody) 182 B'way

Peabody & Co. (brokers) (Stephen & Richard A. Peabody) 46 Exchange pl.

Peabody & Co. (real estate) (Arthur J. Peabody & Alexander L. Morton) 79 Cedar

Peabody & Stearns (Robert S. Peabody & John G. Stearns) 45 B'way

Peabody, Baker & Peabody (Charles A. Peabody, Fisher A. Baker & Charles A. Peabody jr.) 2 Wall

Peace River Phosphate Co. (Morris F. Knudson, Pres.; Henry Moritz, Sec.; Robert W. Paterson, Treas. Capital, $1,000,000. Directors: Morris F. Knudson, Robert W. Paterson, John T. Wilson, George W. Scott, Micajah T. Singleton, Elisha F. Hurt, William D. Hill) 154 Front

Peace, Miller & Co. (Richard & Adam Peace & John Miller) 39 South

Peacock T. R. & Son (Thomas R. & Thomas J. P. Peacock) 55 Liberty

Peake & Butler (A. D. Peake & C. E. Butler) 213 Grand

Pearce J. E. & Co. (James E. Pearce & Anselme Lanson) 126 W. 19th

Pearce W. H. & Co (William H. Pearce & John P. Beirne) 242 W. 50th

Pearce & Jones (Frederick Pearce & James Jones) 79 John

Pearce, Kursh & Co. (Thomas D. Pearce, Frank Kursh & F. Stephen Feraille) 857 B'way

Pearl & Co. (Dyer Pearl, no Co.) 7 Nassau

Pearlmau M. & J. Uttal (no inf.) 599 B'way

Pearsall T. W. & Co. (Thomas W. Pearsall & James B. & T. Truxton Houston;—special partner, Edwin Thorne, Millbrook, N. Y. $200,000; terminates 31st May, 1890) 15 Broad

Pearce A. F. & Co. (Augustus F. Pearce & Samuel Derickson) 16 W. 4th

Pearce & Thornton (George A. Pearce & George F. Thornton jr.) 51 W. 125th

Pearson & Emmott (James Pearson & John M. Emmott) 104 Reade

Pearson & Madden (George W. Pearson & Thomas H. Madden) 1672 Park av.

Pearson & Warren (dissolved) 537 First av.

Pearson, Crocker & Co. (Charles J. Pearson & Otis D. Crocker, no Co.) 120 B'way

Peary & Clark (George H. Peary & Garrett D. Clark) 2263 Seventh av.

Peavy J. & Brothers (Jacob & Isaac & Louis H. Peavy) 546 B'way & 62 Crosby

Peck Charles E. & W. F. (Charles E. & Wallace F.) 56 William

Peck Charles M. & Co. (Charles M. & Herman M. Peck & William S. Banta) 38 Pine

Peck Henry A. & Co. (Henry A. & William L. Peck) 666 First av. & Pier 61 E. R.

Peck T. & M. (dissolved) 1614 First av.

Peck & Coster (no inf.) 7 Exchange ct.

Peck & Field (Edward S. Peck & Frank Harvey Field) 265 B'way

Peck & Fursman (George Peck & George W. Fursman) 345 Grand

Peck & Hauchhaus (Samuel W. Peck & William Hauchhaus) 691 B'way & 254 Mercer

Peck & Mason (dissolved) 2 Wall

Peck & Snyder (Andrew Peck & Washington I. Snyder) 126 Nassau

Peck Brothers & Co. (Henry F. Peck, Pres.; Oliver D. Peck, Sec.; John M. Peck, Treas. Capital, $300,000. Directors: Henry F. & Oliver D. & John M. Peck, Arad T. Foster, L. L. Camp) 47 Cliff

Peck, Fursman & Lloyd (dissolved) 345 Grand

Peck, Martin & Co. (Joshua S. & Nathan Peck & Robert O. Martin) ft. W. 30th, 358 West, ft. E. 48th, ft. E. 80th, ft. W. 66th & ft. E. 137th

Peck, Stow & Wilcox Co. (Enos R. Stow, Pres.; Stephen D. Neal, Sec.; Stephen Walkley, Treas. Capital, $1,500,000. Directors: Enos E. Stow, Webster H. Walkley, R. T. Goldsmith, J. B. Savage, Samuel H. Wilcox, S. H. Sessions, Marcellus B. Willcox, A. R. Treadwell, Stephen D. Neal, Frederick Willcox, Stephen Walkley) 27 Chambers & 5 Reade

Peck, Winterbottom & Peck (dissolved) 230 Hudson

Peckham Paper Car Wheel Co. (inf. unattainable) 239 B'way

Peckham Street Car Wheel & Axle Co. (see too lates) 239 B'way

Peckham & Tyler (William G. Peckham, Eliphalet W. Tyler, Charles A. B. Pratt & Edward A. Hibbard) 111 B'way

FOR THE BEST CO-PARTNERSHIP IN THE BEST CORPORATION SEE PAGE F IN BACK OF BOOK

Peckham, Little & Co. (George E. Peckham & Henry T. Little, no Co.) 106 Duane

Peconic Park Improvement Co. (no inf.) 32 Beaver

Peddie T. B. & Co. (George B. Jenkinson & estate of Thomas D. Peddie) 77 Chambers

Pedersen & Milmaster (Thomas P. Pedersen & Charles L. Milmaster) 265 Bleecker

Pedersen & Buhl (inf. unattainable) 806 W. 23d

Pedro Segundo, Am. Telegraph & Cable Co. (refused) 44 B'way

Peebles & Thompson (Victoria A. Peebles & Anna K. Thompson) 32 E. 57th

Peek & Son (David T. & George W. Peek) 210 W. 47th

Peek & Velsor (Joseph A. Velsor, only) 9 Gold

Peekskill Stove Works (Cornelius C. Lent, Pres.; Charles D. Shepard, Sec.; Edwin B. Lent, Treas. Directors: Cornelius C. & Edwin B. Lent, Charles D. Shepard, Robert B. Keeler) 12 Peck sl.

Peel & Motz Co. (William B. Peel, Pres.; Anton Motz, Sec. Capital, $25,000. Directors: Robert C. Ludd, William B. Peel, Anton Motz) 104 W. 42d & 315 E. 22d

Peene Brothers (John G. & George & Joseph Peene jr.) Pier 24 (new) N. R.

Peerless Metal Co. (dissolved) 194 Front

Peerless Portable Oven Co. (no. inf.) 220 William

Peerless Punch & Shear Co. (Henry Adams jr. Pres.; Thomas B. Alton, Sec. Capital, $100,000. Directors: Henry Adams jr. Thomas D. Alton & Peter W. Rankin) 529 B'way

Peerless Rubber Co. (William B. Brook & Co. propRs.) 47 Murray

Peerless Rubber Mfg. Co. (Edward L. Perry, Pres.; William G. Winans, Sec. Capital, $75,000. Directors: Edward L. Perry, William G. Winans, John H. Deming) 84 Murray

Peers W. S. & Brother (Walter S. & George P. Peers) 16 Cedar

Peet, Smith & Murray (George J. Peet, William Bro Smith & David Murray) 330 B'way

Peeters & Rombauts (Peter J. Peeters & John F. Rombauts) 54 University pl.

Peirson O. L. & Co. (Charles L. Peirson & J. Brooks Fenno jr.) 16 Exchange pl.

Peiser C. & J. (John Peiser, only) 409 Eighth av.

Pejko J. & S. Vazzilik (John Pejko & Stephen Vazzilik) 190 Third

Pelgram & Meyers (Herman & Alfred Schiffer, only) 58 Greene

Pelham Hod Elevating Co. (M. A. Pelham, Pres.; John E. Eustis, Sec.; Alphonso E. Pelham, Treas. Capital, $50,000. Directors: M. A. Pelham, John E. Eustis, Alphonso E. Pelham) 410 W. 26th

Pelham Park R. R. Co. (William B. Lamberton, Pres.; Eliphalet N. Anable, Sec. Capital, $50,000. Directors: William R. Lamberton, Henry D. Carey, Eliphalet N. Anable, Howard N. Potter, Sherman T. Poll, Inglis Stuart, Ethan W. Waterhouse) 16 Exchange pl.

Pelican & Dives Mining Co. (dissolved) 195 B'way

Pell Brothers (John C. & Joshua S. Pell) 12 Ann

Pell, Wallack & Co. (Charles E. Wallack & William M. Kildnff, only) 47 Liberty

Poll-Hazard Fire Extinguisher Co. (William Fuller Tufts, Pres.; Edward R. Powers, Sec. Capital, $100,000. Directors: William Fuller Tufts, Henry C. Stetson, James G. Terbell, Herbert Hazard, Edward R. Powers) 47 Liberty

Pellacani M. & F. Miserocchi (dissolved) 213 E. 13th

Pellegrini A. & Co. (Anacleto & Louis Pellegrini) 119 Park row

Pelletier James B. & Co. (James B. Pelletier, no Co.) 109 Fourth av.

Pellithero Nicolo & Co. (Nicolo Pellithero & Antonio Briganto) 200 Elizabeth

Pelle & Co. (David Clarkson & Norton B. Wood, only) 138 Pearl

Peloubet A. H. & Co. (A Howard Peloubet & James L. Tobin) 86 Barclay

Pelton & Poucher (Gay R. Pelton & George W. Poucher) 165 B'way

Pelz M. & Co. (Morris & Julius Pelz) 237 Canal

Pemberton Clifford jr. & Co. (Clifford jr. & John C. Pemberton) 135 B'way

Pence & Snider Iron Development Co. (dissolved) 42 New

Pencoyd Bridge & Construction Co. (A. & P. Roberts & Co. propRs.) 85 B'way

Pendleton & Co. (Samuel H. & Arthur T. Pendleton) 456 Produce Ex.

Pendleton & Tredwell (James Pendleton & Edgar A. Tredwell) 41 Park row

Pendleton, Carver & Nichols (Benjamin F. Pendleton, Benjamin F. Carver & Wilfred V. Nichols) 38 South

Peniston & Tunison (dissolved) 144 Pearl

Pennell Mfg. Co. (Thomas Taylor, Pres.; Charles G. Colville, Sec. Capital, $10,000. Directors: Thomas Taylor, John W. Pennell, Charles G. Colville) 211 Centre

Penner & Bumb (Frederick Penner & Jacob Bumb) 502 E. 19th

Pennewill D. & Co. (dissolved) 33 Jay

Pennsylvania Coal Co. (Edwin H. Mead, Pres.; William E. Street, Sec. Capital, $5,000,000. Directors: Edwin H. Mead, Samuel Thorne, William H. Webb, A. S. Hurlbutt, George W. Quintard, Joseph Ogden, John B. Platt, George G. Williams, Walton Ferguson) 1 B'way

Pennsylvania Co. (inoperative) 44 B'way

Pennsylvania R. R., Delaware & Raritan Canal Division (Daniel C. Chase, manager) 120 Broad

Pennsylvania R. R. Co. (George B. Roberts, Pres.; John C. Sims jr. Sec.; Robert W. Smith, Treas.; further (inf. unattainable) 2 Beaver, 1 Astor h. 435, 849 & 944 B'way

Pennsylvania R. R. Co. (in Maryland) (consolidated with George's Creek & Cumberland R. R. Co.) 35 B'way

Pennsylvania & Ohio Railway Co. (inf. unattainable) 42 New

Pennsylvania & Western R. R. Co. (dissolved) 187 B'way

Pennsylvania, Lehigh & Eastern R. R. Co. (Samuel F. Pierson, Pres.; Silas W. Neuberger, Sec. Capital, $10,000,000. Directors: Samuel F. Pierson, Silas W. Neuberger, Simon P. Woolverton, J. W. Fellows, Elias Lowenstein, Jacob Neuberger, E. P. Darling) 111 B'way

Pennsylvania, Poughkeepsie & Boston R. R. Co. (William W. Gibbs, Pres.; Morris R. Bockius, Sec. Capital, $1,750,000. Directors: William W. Gibbs, Morris R. Bockius, James W. Husted, Georgu W. Murray, Arthur E. Newbold, William T. Carter, John C. Stanton) 25 B'way

Penrhyn Slate Co. (Perry P. Williams, Pres.; Edward Willis, Sec.; Louis E. Lefferts, Treas. Capital, $70,000. Directors: Perry P. Williams, Edward Willis, Louis E. Lefferts. J. August Lieman, Stephen G. Williams, Archibald M. Pentz, A. M. Underhill) 101 E. 17th

Pensel & Co. (dissolved) 6 University pl.

Pentermann Henry & Co. (Henry Pentermann & Aaron Morris) 45 Ninth av.

Pentz E. C. & Son (Enoch C. & Enoch C. Pentz jr.) 2 Gouverneur la.

Penzel G. L. & Brother (Gustav L. & Gustav F. & Frederick C. & Louis G. Penzel) 368 Bowery

People's Bank (Scott Foster, Pres.; William Milne, Cashier; Christian Zabriskie, Notary. Capital, $200,000. Directors: John A. C. Gray,

TYPEWRITING DONE BY THE TROW CITY DIRECTORY CO., 11 University Place.

PEO   238   PER

Ichabod T. Williams, James E. Hedges, Robert Maclay, Charles T. Van Santvoord, Adolph Wimpfheimer, Theodore W. Morris, Scott Foster, William Milne) 395 Canal

People's Express Co. (dissolved) 117 John

People's Fire Ins. Co. (Frederick V. Price, Pres.; Alexander C. Milne, Sec. Capital, $200,000. Directors: William Moir, Cornelius Stephens, Henry David, Albert Mann, James E. Hedges, Frederick V. Price, Joseph H. Wood, John A. C. Gray, Scott Foster, Albert T. Stephens, Henry Demarest, Alexander C. Milne, Hiram V. V. Braman) 895 Canal & 168 B'way

People's Legal Aid Soc. (Ignacio T. Roves, Pres.; Edward Pouti, Sec.) 132 Nassau

People's Line Steamers (N. J. Steamboat Co. propre.) Pier 41 (old) N. R.

People's Rapid Transit Co. (Gilbert L. Morse, Pres.; William M. Riley, Sec.; Cornelius V. Sidell, Treas. Capital, $500,000. Directors: Gilbert L. Morse, William M. Riley, Cornelius V. Sidell, Sidney E. Morse, James M. Townsend, John H. Rice, Lucius E. Chittenden, Nicholas C. Miller, Job Abbott, Rufus Delafield, William S. Church jr. James M. Townsend jr. Horace H. Chittenden) 150 B'way

People's Stove Works (Southard, Robertson & Co. propre.) 21 Peck sl.

People's Street Railway Co. (of Scranton, Pa.) Lathrop R. Bacon, Pres.; Horace B. Hand, Sec. Capital, $400,000. Directors: W. W. Sherman, Lathrop R. Bacon, C. Weidenfeld, O. T. Sutton, C. H. Minton, J. A. Davis, W. J. Jessup) 54 Wall

People's Street Railway & Electric Light & Power Co. (of St. Joseph, Mo.) (Lathrop R. Bacon, Pres.; Arthur J. Moulton, Sec. Capital, $600,- 000. Directors: Lathrop R. Bacon, Arthur J. Moulton, William M. Harriman, C. Weidenfeld, I. B. Newcombe, S. E. Palmer, Joseph A. Corby, Charles A. Shoup, Thomas F. Van Natta, W. T. Van Brunt) 54 Wall

Peoria & Bureau Valley R R Co. (James R. Cowing, Pres.; J. F. Phillips, Sec.; William A. Nash, Treas. Capital, $1,500,000. Directors: David Dows, Josiah M. Fiske, Frederick A. Platt, William A. Nash, James R. Cowing, Richard M. Hoe, J. F. Phillips) 18 William

Peoria & Pekin Union Railway Co. (Amos L. Hopkins, Pres.; H. K. Pinkney, Sec. Capital, $2,000,000. Directors: Amos L. Hopkins, Solon Humphreys, Ossian D. Ashley, Henry Graves, Heman Clark, Jay Gould, Austin Corbin, D. J. Mackey, Henry W. Maxwell, W. D. Ewing, James F. How, John T. Terry) 195 B'way

Peoria, Decatur & Evansville R. R. Co. (D. J. Mackey, Pres.; W. J. Lewis, Sec. Capital, $8,400,000. Directors: H. J. Nicholas, J. H. Mooney, J. M. De Vean, Heman Clark, Arnold Kummer, D. J. Mackey, William Heilman, Christopher C. Baldwin) 7 Nassau

Peper Brothers (candy) (George J. & Charles Peper) 489 Pearl

Peper Brothers (liquors) (Frederick & John H. Peper) 1715 Ninth av.

Peper & Ohlhaver (Frederick H. Peper & Charles Ohlhaver) 87 E. 110th

Peram D. & Co. (dissolved) 301 Third av.

Pereu Brothers (Ladislao Perus, only) 124 E. 14th

Perego Ira & Co. (Ira & Ira K. & Arthur W. Perego) 126 Fulton & 87 Nassau

Pereira & Co. (Isaac B. Pereira, no Co.) 16 Platt

Perez-Triana & Co. (Santiago Perez-Triana:—special partners, L. Pombo & Brothers, *Bogota, Colombia* & Koppel & Schloss, *Bucaramanga, Colombia*; further int. refused) 16 Beaver

Perfect Block Pavement Co. (Martin V. B. Steinmetz, Pres.; Charles H. Gardner, Sec. Capital, $500,000. Directors: Martin V. B. Steinmetz, Charles H. Gardner, Charles R. Clarke) 137 B'way

Perfection Playing Card Co. (not inc.) (Edward Stern & Charles Ditzman) 332 B'way

Perfection Portrait Co. (Ullman & Co. propre.) 847 B'way

Perial Brothers (John & Romano & Victor Perini) 141 Prince

Periodical Printing Co. (Henry E. Melville, propr.) 25 Beekman

Perkins Dennis & Co. (Henry O. & George D. Perkins, only) 125 Pearl

Perkins John J. & Co. (John J. Perkins & Hugh Nelson) 749 Sixth av.

Perkins Thomas jr. & Co. (Thomas Perkins jr. & Matthew J. Richards) 110 Pearl

Perkins F. E. & Brother (Frederick E. & Willard C. Perkins) 405 South & 435 Front

Perkins & Co. (James D. Perkins & Frank Seaverns) 229 Produce Ex.

Perkins & Mott (James P. Perkins & Lawrence S. Mott) 115 B'way

Perkins & Welsh (Benjamin Perkins & Osgood Welsh) 41 Wall

Perkins, Goodwin & Co. (George F. Perkins, Edward Goodwin, Frank Squier & J. Frederick Ackerman) 68 Duane

Pernaux & Co. (Eleanor M. Blaupain, Charles A. Shuman & John Lewall, only) 6 E. 17th

Peroxide Silicate Co. (in liquidation) 422 West

Perpente & Clarke (Albert J. Perpente & Henry S. Clarke) 132 Park av.

Perri Henry & Co. (Henry Perri & Francesco Biociuppi) 148 Leonard

Perrin Grenville & Co. (Grenville Perrin:—special partners, William Schlesinger, *N. Y.* & Adolf Schlesinger, *London, Eng.*, each $12,- 500; terminates 30th April, 1891) 458 Produce Ex.

Perrin, Payson & Co. (Raymond S. Perrin, Pres.; Horace E. Payson, Sec. Capital, $50,000; further inf. refused) 68 & 75 Little W. 12th

Perris & Browne (Henry H. & Arthur E. & Norman W. Browne, only) 55 Liberty

Perry Edward & Co. (Edward Perry, no Co.) 69 Wall

Perry Lloyd & Co. (dissolved) 194 B'way

Perry Stove Co. (Nathan B. Perry, Pres.; John T. Perry, Sec. Capital, $500,000. Trustees: Nathan B. & John T. & Willard E. Perry, George W. Hobbs, E. R. Perry, George W. Packard, Arthur A. Thompson) 74 Beekman

Perry Vincent & Co. (Vincent Perry & James R. Kendrick) 12 Union sq. E.

Perry W. B. & Son (William B. & William M. Perry) Manhattan mkt & 808 Washn.

Perry Brothers (dissolved) 84 Elm

Perry & Alger (William Perry & Cyrus D. Alger) 19 South

Perry & Collins (Carolina Perry & Eliza Collins) 55 W. 21st

Perry & Co. (engravers) (Charles C. Perry & August O. Christensen) 141 Fulton

Perry & Co. (real estate) (no inf.) 1584 Ninth av.

Perry & Ryer (Edward W. Perry, John C. Ryer, Edward T. Coons & G. Frederick Esty) 65 Beaver & 20 Exchange pl.

Perseverance Soap Works (John T. Stanley, propr.) 525 W. 15th

Persian Glass Enameling Co. (Amedee H. De Caranza, propr.) 446 Canal

Persian Rug & Carpet Co. (Louis Ettlinger, Pres.; Robert Stunix, Sec. Capital, $30,000. Trustees: Louis Ettlinger, Robert Stunix, Theodore Schumacher, Adam Bollentin, Gustav J. Poznanski) 340 W. 40th

Person & Co. (dissolved) 126 Fifth av.

Perth Amboy Terra Cotta Co. (Edward J. Hall jr. Pres.; George P. Putnam, Sec. Capital, $250,000. Directors: Edward J. jr. & Will-

THADDEUS DAVIDS CO., WRITING INKS, SEALING WAX, MUCILAGE.
MAKE THE BEST

- lam C. Hall, George P. Putnam, Oswald Spier) 18 Cortlandt
- Perth Amboy Towing Line (Lehigh Valley R. R. Co. propr.) 1 B'way & 14 South
- Pertsch F. & W. (Frederick F. & William A.) 124 Baxter & 50 Sheriff
- Petchell & Lawrence (Clement T. Petchell & Ernest M. Lawrence) 52 Broad
- Peter Cooper's Glue Factory (Edward Cooper, Pres.; George C. Cooper, Sec.; Abram S. Hewitt, Treas. Directors: Edward & George C. Cooper, Abram S. Hewitt) 18 Burling sl.
- Peter J. Jacob & Son (J. Jacob & Frederick Peter) 583 Ninth av.
- Peters William R. & Co. (William R. Peters & George Parker) 58 William
- Peters H. & Brother (Henry C. & William Peters) 1429 First av.
- Peters J. G. & W. H. (John G. & William H.) 142 W. 66th
- Peters B. G. & Co. (Robert G. Peters & Elspeth S. Stephen) 43 Harrison
- Peters W. A. & Co. (William A. Peters, no Co.) 39 Nassau
- Peters & Calhoun Co. (G. Willis Peters, Pres.; Clarence Peters, Sec.; John L. Dodge, Treas. Capital, $100,000. Directors: John L. Dodge, G. Willis & George & Clarence Peters, John L. Dodge) 33 Warren
- Peters & Heins (John F. Peters & Frederick Heins) 1081 Av. B
- Peters & Hyer (Philip Peters & Henry Hyer jr.) 873 Washn.
- Peters & Moreland (John Peters & Henry A. Moreland) 8 Spruce
- Peters, Schenck & Co. (Charles G. Peters & J. Frederic Schenck; — special partner, Charles F. Wetmore, $50,000; terminates 31st Dec. 1890) 55 B'way
- Petersburg Granite Quarrying Co. (William E. Dibble, Pres.; Egerton Brown, Sec.; James O. Bowdish, Treas. Capital, $75,000. Directors: William E. Dibbell, George A. & Egerton Brown, James O. Bowdish, James Abbott) 32 Wall
- Petersen C. & Son (Christian & James H. Petersen) 19 Clinton pl.
- Petersen E. & F. (Ernst A. & Frederick J.) 1310 Second av.
- Petersen & Schussler (Herman Petersen, only) 210 Third av.
- Peterson Charles & Co. (Charles Peterson, John V. Quackenbush & Clinton Beckwith) 247 W. 125th
- Peterson Brothers (Edwin G. & Wendell L. Peterson) 161 W. 13th
- Peterson & Royce (Richard N. Peterson & estate of George W. Royce) 160 B'way
- Peterson Brothers (dissolved) 845 Sixth av.
- Petra Crusta Matt Co. (Ltd.) (dissolved) 1078 Ninth av.
- Petri & Pels (George Petri & Louis F. Pels) 73 Park row
- Petry Frank & Son (Frank & John J. Petry) 889 Tenth av.
- Petry F. H. & Co. (dissolved) 55 Beaver
- Petry & Hauck (Peter H. Petry & Edward J. Hauck) 55 Beaver
- Petry & Tighe (Charles F. Petry & James C. Tighe) 1780 Tenth av.
- Petry & Wainright (Frank A. Petry & David Wainright) 1432 B'way
- Pettengill S. M. & Co. (dissolved) 38 Park row
- Pettit Chemical Co. (William Pettit, propr.) 256 Front
- Pettit & Co. (Foster & Stephen B. Pettit) 136 Water

- Pettit & Reed (Mortlock Pettit & Charles Reed) 229 Fulton
- Pettus & Curtis (James T. Pettus & David C. Curtis) 234 Fifth av.
- Petty & Bostwick (dissolved) 86 New
- Peuchot A. & Co. (Alfred Peuchot, no Co.) 529 B'way
- Peyrous Brothers (Noel P. & Edward E. Peyrous) 695 Third av.
- Peyser Henry M. & Co. (Henry M. & John F. Peyser) 183 Grand
- Peyser J. & Son (Julius & Isaac M. Peyser) 2 E. 4th, 123 Grand & 102 Second
- Peyser & Riley (dissolved) 846 First av.
- Pezold H. & A. (Hugo & Arthur) 143 Franklin
- Pfeifer Charles & Co. (dissolved) 10 Old sl.
- Pfeiffer & Brother (Samuel & Jacob Pfeiffer) 96 Cannon
- Pfeiffer & Knapp (dissolved) 323 Sixth av.
- Pfeiffer & Lavanburg (Isaac Pfeiffer & Frederick L. Lavanburg) 165 William
- Pfister F. J. & Co. (Frank J. Pfister & Louis F. & Victor J. Grunbacher) 71 University pl.
- Pfister & Groth (dissolved) 143 Ludlow
- Pitzner, Leudesdorff & Co. (William M. Pitzner, Julius Leudesdorff, August Arnold, Lucas Kehrer & Arnd Softye) 12 Jacob
- Pfizer Charles & Co. (Charles Pfizer, Charles F. Erhart & Behrend H. Huttmann) 81 Maiden la.
- Pflaum & Kampier (Jacob Pflaum & Joseph Kampier) 222 Third
- Pfleging & Schabel (Carl Pfleging & Albert Schabel) 1043 Third av.
- Pforsheimer, Keller & Co. (dissolved) 24 John
- Pfuller Charles & Son (William C. Pfuller, only) r 12 Columbia
- Pharmaceutical Publishing Co. (Moritz Wolfram, propr.) 104 John
- Pharmaceutical Record Co. (P. W. Bedford, Pres.; Richard B. Williams, Sec. Capital, $15,000. Trustees: P. W. Bedford, Richard B. Williams, John S. King) 66 Duane
- Phelan Billiard Ball Co. (M. E. Newhall, Pres.; Ann A. Phelan, Sec. Capital, $1,000. Directors: M. E. Newhall, Ann A. Phelan) 114 Fulton
- Phelan E. F. & Co. (Edwin F. Phelan ;— special partner, John C. Runkle *Paris, France*, $50,000; terminates 31st Dec. 1892) 57 & 125 Front
- Phelan & Co. (John Phelan & Edward J. Moss) 2197 Seventh av.
- Phelan & Duval (James J. Phelan & George Duval) 23 S. William
- Phelps Frame & Easel Co. (George W. Phelps, propr.) 216 Sixth av.
- Phelps & Dingie (Lucius J. Phelps & Samuel K. Dingle) 115 B'way
- Phelps Brothers & Co. (George A. & Frank & Charles H. & Howard Phelps & Albert A. Guild) 31 B'way
- Phelps, Dodge & Co. (William E. Dodge, D. Willis James, Joseph Van Vleck, James McLean & Cleveland H. Dodge, only) 11 Cliff & 315 West
- Phenix Ins. Co. (George P. Sheldon, Pres.; Philander Shaw, Sec. Capital, $1,000,000. Directors: George P. Sheldon, Arthur B. Graves, Edwin F. Knowlton, Albion K. Bolan, George W. Bergen, Augustus Studwell, Edwin T. Rice, William P. Beale, Charles Phelps, William H. Wallace, William J. Logan, John H. Latham, David B. Powell, Felix Campbell, William H. Male, Samuel F. Howard, John Cartledge, George M. Hard, George Ingraham, Charles W. Bregn, Henry B. Southwell, William A. Hammond) 195 B'way, 65 Wall, 131 Fourth av. & 526 Willis av.
- Phenix National Bank (Eugene Dutilh, Pres.; Alfred M. Bull, Cashier; Charles F. Streight-

opf, Notary. Capital, $1,000,000. Directors: Eugene Dutilh, Charles P. Hemenway, Daniel G. Bacon, Jonathan Thorne, John H. Pool, George L. Nichols, Clarence W. Goold, Henry R. Kunhardt, Alfred M. Bull, John C. Milligan, William H. Male, Josiah Lombard, William H. H. Moore, Pierson G. Dodd) 49 Wall

Phila. Smelting & Refining Co. of Pueblo, Col. (M. Guggenheim's Sons, proprs.) 2 Wall

Phila. & N. Y. Line (W. P. Clyde & Co. proprs.) 5 Bowling gr. & Pier 34 E. R.

Phila. & Reading R. R. Co. (Austin Corbin, Pres.; William R. Taylor, Sec.; William A. Church, Treas. Capital, $39,480,361.78. Directors: A. J. Antelo, Samuel B. Shipley, Thomas Cochran, George de B. Keim, Stephen A. Caldwell, George F. Baer) 192 B'way

Philipp, Phelps & Hovey (Moritz B. Philipp, Myron H. Phelps & James A. Hovey) 5 Beckman

Philippe E. & J. Ryan (Eugene Philippe & John Ryan) 423 Second av.

Philips Tobacco Co. (Charles S. Philips, propr.) 188 Pearl

Phillips & Berliner (Morris Philips & Abram Berliner) 111 Av. D

Phillips J. F., Advertising Co. (James P. Logan, Sec.; John F. Phillips, Treas. Capital, $15,000. Directors: James P. Logan, John F. Phillips) 29 Park row

Phillips Morris & Co. (Morris Phillips, no Co.) 240 B'way & 22 Spruce

Phillips Petroleum Co. (Charles W. Barton, Pres.; Russell C. Root, Sec. Capital, $2,500,000. Trustees: Charles W. Barton, Russell C. Root, Paul Worth, E. A. Packer, D. W. Robinson) 12 B'way

Phillips Publishing Co. (Philip Phillips, propr.) 50 Bible h.

Phillips A. L. & Co. (Asher L. Phillips & Louis Lamy) 500 Broome

Phillips L. & Brother (Leo & Henry Phillips) 405 Broome

Phillips L. J. & I. (Lewis J. & estate of Isaac Phillips & Samuel Goldsticker) 149 B'way & 1174 Ninth av.

Phillips M. & Son (no inf.) 1 Orchard

Phillips M. B., Jones & Co. (Milton B. Phillips & David S. & Albert G. Jones) 17 Whitehall

Phillips W. & Co. (Wolfe & Louisa Phillips) 61 Nassau

Phillips Brothers (Evan M. & John Phillips) 87 Pearl

Phillips & Avery (Edgar J. Phillips & Frank M. Avery) 154 Nassau

Phillips & Cannon (Henry C. Phillips & Nathaniel B. Cannon) r. E. 138th

Phillips & Cooney (Thomas Phillips & Peter J. Cooney) r 501 E. 144th

Phillips & Ferguson (John B. Phillips & Thomas Ferguson) 46 Beekman

Phillips & Hook (George W. Phillips & George T. Hook) 259 W. 27th

Phillips & Meyer (Jacob L. Phillips & Harrison D. Meyer) 93 Franklin & 18 Desbrosses

Phillips & Mower (Charles A. Phillips & John L. Mower) 92 Nassau

Phillips & Wells (Joseph Phillips & Charles A. Wells) 154 Nassau

Phillips, Henry & Co. (James J. Phillips, Edward M. Henry & William J. Phillips) 164 West

Phillips' J. B., Son (Alfred B. Phillips) 35 Front

Phipps J. L. & Co. (William W. & Charles N. P. & Frederick H. Phipps & Ernest W. Landon, only) 66 Wall

Phœnix Bottling Co. (H. Clausen & Son Brewing Co., proprs.) 838 Second av. & 31 Broad

Phœnix Card & Paper Co. (Sartor Brothers Co., proprs.) 47 Beekman

Phœnix Construction Co. (Theodore N. Vail, Pres.; John H. Cahill, Sec. Capital, $200,000. Directors: Theodore N. Vail, John H. Cahill, Leonard F. Beckwith) 18 Cortlandt & 290 West

Phœnix Electric Light & Power Co. (Capital, $500,000 ; further inf. unattainable) no address

Phœnix Furniture Co. (James W. Converse, Pres.; Robert W. Merrill, Sec. Capital. $500,000. Directors: James W. Converse, Frank Smith, Robert W. Merrill, Joseph H. Martin, O. G. Swensberg, D. W. Kendall, W. D. Talford) 177 Canal

Phœnix Loan & Trust Co. (dissolved) 53 B'way

Phœnix Mining Co. (Albion G. Bradstreet, Pres.; Henry G. Romaine, Sec.; Henry E. Wallace, Treas. Capital $500,000. Directors: Albion G. Bradstreet, Charles I. Hardy, Henry E. Wallace, S. W. Curtis, George F. Chamberlain) 35 Pine

Phœnix Novelty Co. (Morris Schleissner, propr.) 402 B'way

Phœnix Photo Enameling Co. (W. H. Nightingale & H. Bennecke, proprs.) 27 E. Houston

Phœnix Plaster Mills (Henry H. Wotherspoon, propr.) 429 W. 13th

Phœnix Powder Mfg. Co. (William H. Taylor, Pres.; George S. Van Wickle, Sec. Capital, $132,000. Directors: William H. Taylor, F. Lasllo Kellogg, John Claffey, Nathan Kellogg, Augustus S. Van Wickle) 280 B'way

Phœnix Print Works (Hartman & Wilcox, proprs.) 51 Leonard

Phœnix Printing House (Horatio B. Elkins, propr.) 15 Vandewater

Phœnix Railway Supply Co. (inf. unattainable) 15 Cortlandt

Photo-Copying Co. (Charles Douffer, propr.) 4 New Chambers

Photo-Electrotype Engraving Co. (Joseph E. Rhodes, Pres.; Joseph Cherry, Sec. Capital, $30,000. Directors: Joseph E. Rhodes, Joseph Cherry, Annie A. Rhodes) 9 New Chambers

Photo-Engraving Co. (John Hastings, Pres.; Charles S. Lawrence, Sec. Capital, $20,000. Directors: John Hastings, Joseph Tripp, Charles S. Lawrence) 87 Park pl.

Photo-Etching Co. (refused) 19 Beekman

Photo-Gravure Co. (inf. unattainable) 187 W. 23d

Photo-Plate Engraving Co. (George H. Bull & Co. proprs.) 31 Beekman

Photo-Printing & Mfg. Co. (John Loeber, propr.) 59 Beekman

Photo-Type Co. (Ignatz Oesterreicher, propr.) 76 Beekman

Photographic Times Publishing Assn. (Scovill & Adams Co. proprs.) 423 Broome

Phyfe James W. & Co. (James W. & James Phyfe & Leon J. Louis) 123 Front

Physicians' Protective Bureau (no inf.) 45 College pl.

Physicians' Supply Mfg. Co. (Howard Campbell, Pres.; Samuel Campbell, Sec. Capital, $10,000. Directors: Howard & Samuel Campbell, Daniel Messmore) 140 Nassau

Pianophone Co. (Frederick M. Hill, Pres.; Charles E. Mielke, Sec.; John Q. Preble. Treas. Capital, $150,000. Directors: John Q. Preble, Henry Wellington, Frederick M. Hill, Charles E. Mielke) 462 Cherry

Piasecki & Weinberg (Max Piasecki & Philip Weinberg) 149 Prince

Picaut Brothers (dissolved) 46 Bleecker

Pick A. R. & Co. (Alfred R. Pick & Albert Levi) 29 Broad

Pickard & Gordon (Frederick W. Pickard & George G. Gordon) 59 Gold

Picken & Carlisle (Samuel S. Picken & William S. Carlisle) 77 Warren

Picken & Lilly (William H. Picken & Harry Lilly) 1441 Third av.

Pickering M. F. & Co. (McLaurin F. & McLaurin J. Pickering) 84 Broad

Pickering T. R. & Co. (dissolved) 10 Dey

Pickhardt William & Kuttroff (William Pickhardt & Adolph Kuttroff:—special partners, The Badische Aniline & Soda Fabrick, *Manheim, Germany*, $150,000; terminates 31st Dec. 1894) 96 Liberty

Pickhardt J. F. C. & Co. (John F. C. & Christina Pickhardt) 848 Lenox av.

Picot & Co. (Marie & Louis Peguiron, only) 38 E. 19th

Pictet Artificial Ice Co. (Ltd.) (Robert Whitehill, Pres.; William C. Durain, Sec.; Henry Dexter, Treas. Capital, $500,000; further inf. unattainable) 21 Cortlandt

Pictorial Associated Press (Charles F. Larzelere, Pres.; J. Lawson Powers, Sec. Capital, $25,000; further inf. unattainable) 86 Centre

Pictorial Weeklies Co. (John A. Mitchell, Pres.; James S. Metcalfe, Sec.; Andrew Miller, Treas. Capital, $100,000. Directors: John A. Mitchell, James S. Metcalfe, Andrew Miller, D. R. Davenport) 28 W. 23d

Pidcock J. N. & Sons (James N. & John F. & James N. Pidcock jr.) 312 W. 60th

Pidcock & Kentana (James N. Pidcock jr. & William H. Kentana) 6 Thompson av. W. Washn. mkt

Piebes Brothers (Louis F. & Charles H. Piebes) 306 G'wich

Piedmont Cattle Co. (Henry S. Van Beuren, Pres.; Dewitt C. Bates, Sec.; Wells H. Bates, Treas. Capital, $1,500,000. Directors: Henry S. Van Beuren, Charles H. Dillingham, Dewitt C. & Wells H. Bates, J. J. Dimock) 11 Wall

Piedmont Coal & Land Co. (Winfield S. Chamberlain, Pres.; James D. Henderson, Sec. Capital, $550,000; further inf. refused) 115 B'way

Piedmont Electric Illuminating Co. (Charles H. Harmon, Pres.; William W. Goodrich, Sec.; William W. Flannagan, Treas. Capital, $70,000. Trustees: Charles H. Harmon, William W. Flannagan, Orson Adams, Jefferson M. Levy, J. P. Bell, J. H. Lewis, Clinton Dewitt) 32 Nassau

Pieper F. & Sons (dissolved) 227 Grand

Pieper Brothers (Alfred & Frederick Pieper) Anthony av. c E. 174th

Pieper & Heineck (dissolved) 1 Av. A

Pieper's L., Son (Louis F. Pieper) 2005 Third av.

Pier Brothers (George W. Pier, only) 45 Pearl

Pierce Artesian & Oil Well Supply Co. (Charles D. Pierce, propr.) 80 Beaver & 127 Pearl

Pierce Iron Works (Charles D. Pierce, propr.) 80 Beaver & 127 Pearl

Pierce Robert & Co. (Robert Pierce, no Co.) 53 Lafayette pl.

Pierce F. O. & Co. (Frederick O. Pierce, no Co.) 170 Fulton

Pierce & Sons (James & Scott S. & Chace B. Pierce) 2418 Eighth av.

Pierce & Thomas (Frank M. Pierce & Robert M. Thomas) 42 Cortlandt

Piercy H. C. & Z. T. (Henry C. & Zachary T.) 207 & 227 Thompson

Piercy's Express Co. (not Inc.) (Henry Clay & Zachariah T. Piercy, C. C. Smith & George Lahr jr.) 23 Astor pl, 62 W. 125th & 65 W. 131st

Pierra F. G. & Co. (Fidel G. Pierra & Luis Veranes) 81 New

Pierson & Arthur (Henry B. Pierson & George A. Arthur) 406 B'way

Pierson & Co. (Henry L. jr. & J. Frederick Pierson) 24 West

Piesbach & Strahan (dissolved) 337 E. 93d

Pietschmann Ch. F. & Sons (dissolved) 91 Chambers

Pike & Banks (James Pike & William T. Banks) 98 Park pl.

Pike's Benjamin, Son (Daniel Pike) 12 E. 23d

Pike's Joseph, Son (dissolved) 96 Park pl.

Pilger Brothers (barbers) (dissolved) 206 West

Pilger Brothers (milk) (John & Philip Pilger) 507 Bergen av.

Piller & Kovach (Joseph Piller & John Kovach) 219 E. 59th

Pillow Inhaler Co. (dissolved) 30 E. 14th

Pilzer & Sprits (Bernhard Pilzer & Simon Sprits) 420 Fira av.

Pinard J. B. & Sons (Charles & John A. & Narcissus Pinard, only) 6 E. 15th

Pinckney H. F. A. & Co. (Henry F. A. Pinckney, no Co.) 204 West

Pine Creek Railway Co. (Henry Sherwood, Pres.; Edward V. W. Rossiter, Sec. Capital, $1,000,000.; Directors: William K. & Cornelius Vanderbilt, Chauncey M. Depew, H. McK. Twombly, George J. Magee, William Howell, E. G. Schieffelin, Walter Sherwood, Jefferson Harrison, Jerome B. Niles, Anton Hardt, John W. Bailey) Grand Central depot

Pine, Twiggs & Co. (William E. Tine, Henry L. Twiggs, Henry C. Simonsson & Charles C. Perpall) 2 Gouverneur la.

Pinga & Pinner (Julius B. Pinga & Leo Pinner) 884 B'way

Pinkerton R. A. & W. A. (Robert A. & William A.) 66 Exchange pl.

Pinkerton's National Detective Agency (R. A. & W. A. Pinkerton. proprs.) 66 Exchange pl.

Pinkussohn J. S. & Brothers (Jeremiah S. & Jacob & Samuel Pinkussohn) 1039 Third av.

Pinnell, May & Co. (dissolved) 1½ Maiden la.

Pinney & Johnson (Charles K. Johnson, only) 195 Fulton

Pinney & Sterling (George M. Pinney jr. & Willis R. Sterling) 55 Liberty

Pinover A. & Co. (Alexander & Samuel Pinover) 25 Ann

Pinto John & Austalo Matera, 36 Spring

Pinto F. E. & Sons (Francis E. & Francis B. jr. & William A. Pinto) 459 Produce Ex.

Pintsch Compressing Co. (Edwin M. Bulkley, Pres.; Frederick W. Tappenbeck, Sec.; William R. Thomas, Treas. Capital, $500,000. Directors: Edwin M. Bulkley, Arthur W. Soper, Wallace C. Andrews, Henry R. Wolcott, Elbert H. Monroe, Benjamin R. Sullivan, Frederick W. Tappenbeck) 160 B'way

Pioneer Cash & Credit Co. (J. Rauth & Co., proprs.) 284 Eighth av.

Pioneer Fresh Egg Supply Co. (no inf.) 44 Murray

Pioneer Line (R. W. Cameron & Co., proprs.) 23 S. William & Pier 9 E. R.

Piper F. W. & Co. (Frederick W. Piper, no Co.) 57 B'way & 23 Trinity pl.

Piper, Doremus & Co. (C. William Meinecke, only) 125 Pearl

Pippey B. Y. & Co. (Benjamin Y. & William F. Pippey) 45 Leonard

Pirson & Renwick (Robert L. Pirsson & Edward B. Renwick) 19 Park pl. & 16 Murray

Pisarra & Luzzi (Vincent T. Pisarra & Constantine Luzzi) 205 Division

Piser & Harris (Abraham Piser & Jacob Harris) 182 Bowery

Pitcher F. W. & Co. (Frederick W. Pitcher & William L. McKinney) 184 Eighth av.

Pitman & Black (Will R. Pitman & John Black) 115 Worth

TYPEWRITING DONE BY THE TROW CITY DIRECTORY CO., 11 University Place.

Piton Eugene & Co. (Eugene Piton & D. Edmund Dealy) 15 State
Pitt William R., Iron Works (William R. Pitt, propr.) 83 Reade
Pitt & Scott's Foreign Express (Pitt & Scott, proprs.) 85 B'way
Pitt, Darnum & Glidden (Malcom R. Pitt, R. Duke Barnum & Robert G. Glidden) 158 Reade
Pittsburgh & Western Railway Co. (Henry W. Oliver, Pres.; Howard D. Campbell, Sec. Capital, $12,000,000. Directors; Henry W. Oliver, John W. Chalfant, James L. Callery, M. K. Moorhead, William Scople, Anthony J. Thomas, Solon Humphreys, Charles H. Coster, Samuel Spencer) 3 Broad
Pittsburgh, Marion & Chicago Railway Co. (John I. Holly, Pres.; R. W. Taylor, Sec.; Henry M. Curtis, Treas. Capital, 7,500,000. Directors: John I. Holly, B. Y. Frost, Henry Day, Walter S. Gurnee, Frederick Meissner, Charles Stadler, J. F. Mansfield, J. E. Umbstaetter, J. H. Wallace, N. B. Billingsley, W. M. Hostetter, James Chartiers) 81 New
Pittsburgh, Shenango & Lake Erie R.R. Co. (no inf.) 50 B'way
Piza, Nephews & Co. (Joshua & Joshua S. Piza, Joshua J. Lindo & Elias L. Maduro) 18 B'way
Place & McGuinness (Warren Place & Joseph McGuinness) 96 & 289 Water & 119 Maiden la.
Plain Talk Publishing Co. (William J. Myers, Pres.; George H. Richmond, Sec. Directors: William J. Myers, George H. Richmond, William A. O. Paul, Eugene Van Schaick, Frank Myers) 5 Beekman
Planet Mills (Buchanan & Lyall, proprs.) 101 Wall
Plant & Owen (dissolved) 222 Washn.
Plante H. P. & Brother (Holland P. & Falconbridge Plante) 62 Greene
Planten H. & Son (John R. Planten, only) 224 William
Plastic Slate Roofing Co. (Edward Vanorden & Co. propr.) 110 John
Plate Brothers (dissolved) 241 E. 80th
Plath Charles & Son (Charles & Clemens L. Plath) 190 Canal
Platky Adolph & Co. (Adolph Platky, no Co.) 83 Mercer
Platt Oliver & Brother (Oliver S. & Charles R. Platt) 85 Frankfort
Platt & Bowers (James N. Platt, John M. Bowers & B. Aymar Sands) 54 William
Platt & Eaton Wagon Co. (dissolved) 225 Greene
Platt & Washburn Refining Co. (Charles W. Burton, Pres.; John E. Burns, Sec.; George S. Richards, Treas. Capital, $100,000. Directors: Charles W. Burton, George S. Richards, George A. Keeney, Robert O. Benson, William H. Palmer) 248 Front
Platt & Woodward (Charles B. Platt, Robert B. Woodward & Charles Hathaway) 26 Pine
Platte J. & Co. (Joseph & Catharine Platte) 571 Courtlandt av.
Plaut Leopold & Co. (Leopold Plaut, no Co.) 496 Cherry
Plaut Brothers (Joseph D. & Hugo H. Plaut) 6 Thomas
Pleasants & Woodworth (dissolved) 61 W. Houston
Plonsky & Simon (Ezekiel Plonsky & Morris Simon) 512 B'way & 58 Crosby
Ploog & Schliemann (Matilda Ploog & Henry Schliemann) 1618 Third av.
Plum James R. & Gale (James R. Plum & Frank A. Gale) 42 Spruce
Plumb & Evers (Dederick Plumb & Christian Evers) 311 Fourth av.
Plumbers' Material Protective Assn. (Edward A. Le Roy, Pres.; Edward W. Lowe, Sec.; Benjamin C. Smith, Treas.) 46 Cliff

Plume & Atwood Mfg. Co. (Burr Tucker, Pres.; Lewis J. Atwood, Sec.; David S. Plume, Treas. Capital, $400,000. Directors: Burr Tucker, David S. Plume, Lewis J. Atwood, R. C. Lewis, Aaron Thomas, E. M. Burrall, B. H Sweeyze) 18 Murray
Plummer John F. & Co. (John F. & Albert T. Plummer & William S. Darling) 345 B'way
Plummer J. S. & Co. (Jerome S. Plummer & Charles S. Burr) 159 Mercer
Plummer M. & Co. (Myrick Plummer & Isaac M. Cook) 161 William
Plummer & Wilson (Jesse J. Plummer & James E. Wilson) 1500 Ninth av.
Plump Brothers (dissolved) 807 Spring
Plunkett Brothers (Patrick & John & Thomas Plunkett) 279 Mott
Plunkett & Lathrope (Charles Plunkett & Frederick Lathrope) 492 Water
Plutus Mining & Smelting Co. (Henry Rosener, Pres.; Dominique F. Verdenal, Sec. Capital, $2,000,000. Trustees: Henry Rosener, George Laing, Louis Rosenfeld, A. B. Chandler, Dominique F. Verdenal) 45 B'way
Plymouth Coal Co. (John C. Haddock, propr.) 1 B'way
Plymouth Cons. Gold Mining Co. (Warner Van Norden, Pres.; Harry W. Lazelle, Sec. Capital, $5,000,000. Directors: Warner Van Norden, H. T. Bronson, A. Hayward, W. S. Hobart, W. N. Cromwell, P. W. Bedford) 120 B'way
Plympton Nathaniel (firm) (dissolved) 428 B'way
Pneumatic Cabinet Co. (no inf.) 280 B'way
Pneumatic Dynamite Gun Co. (Spencer D. Schuyler, Pres.; George R. Williamson, Sec.; Richard Irvin jr. Treas. Capital, $1,100,000. Directors: Spencer D. Schuyler, George R. Williamson, Richard Irvin jr. Alexander K. Leith, Daniel W. McWilliams, John B. Yale) 71 B'way
Pneumatic Pulverizer Co. (Lyman F. Holman, Pres. Capital, $200,000. Trustees: F. A. Luckenbach, Samuel B. Thorp, Lyman F. Holman) 4 Stone
Pneumatic Steering Gear & Mfg. Co. (James E. Hodges, Pres.; Charles D. Brown, Sec.; Joseph G. Walcott, Treas. Capital, $700,000. Directors: James E. Hodges, Charles E. Francis, Joseph C. Walcott, George M. Walker, Charles E. Crocey, Horace Cunningham, H. W. Weeks, W. J. Moud) 32 Pine
Pocantico Water Works Co. (Joseph M. Low, Pres.; Charles Howden Smith, Treas. Capital, $500,000. Directors: Joseph M. Low, Charles Howden Smith, A. N. Martin, John S. Ellis, J. H. Foster, J. S. Suydam, Charles M. Kimball, Thomas J. Lawrence) 32 Liberty
Pocasset Coal Co. (dissolved) 1 B'way
Podeyn & Greiner (Henry M. F. Podeyn & Charles F. Greiner) 223 Grand
Poetsch-Sooysmith Freezing Co. (William Sooysmith, Pres.; Edward L. Abbott, Sec.; Charles Sooysmith, Treas. Capital, $400,000. Directors: William & Charles Sooysmith, Edward L. Abbott) 2 Nassau
Poggenburg H. F. & Brother (Henry F. & William H. Poggenburg) 155 B'way
Poggenburg & Schouw (dissolved) 21 B'way
Pohalski A. L. & Co. (Abraham L. Pohalski, no Co.) 87 Nassau
Pohalski P. & Co. (Pincus & David Pohalski) 17 Warren
Pohs A. & Son (Adolph & Joseph Pohs) 42 Nassau
Poillon C. & R. (Richard & James O. Poillon, only) 224 South & 450 Water
Poillon & Staples (John E. Poillon, only) E. 146th c Railroad av.
Poker & Malzman (dissolved) 69 Chrystie & 55 Suffolk

Pokorny & Winkler (Frank Pokorny & Charles Winkler) 333 E. 60th

Poland Spring Water Depot (Hiram Ricker & Sons, proprs.) 164 Nassau

Polatzek, Warnstadt & Co. (Szigo Polatzek, Albert A. Warnstadt & Adolph P. Loveman) 500 Broome

Polhamus & Dolan (Charlotte A. Polhamus & Margaret A. Dolan) 949 B'way & 179 Fifth av.

Politziner & Frank (dissolved) 62 Division

Pollack W. L. & Co. (William L. & William G. Pollack) 4 John

Pollard R. T. & Co. (Reuben T. Pollard, Zebulon R. Hyde & James H. Denehy) 54 Broad

Pollard & Moss (dissolved) 37 Barclay & 42 Park pl.

Pollard, Pettus & Co. (dissolved) 54 Broad

Polley George H. & Co. (George H. & Thomas W. Polley) 18 W. 23d

Pollock & Co. (Dennis Pollock, no Co.) r 440 W. 38th

Pollock, Levy & Milan (Solomon M. Pollock, Emil Levy & Morris Milan) 32 Greene

Pole Express & Van Co. (Krahmer Brothers, proprs.) 178 E. 105th

Polytechnical News Co. (Francis M. F. Cazin, Pres.; H. Cazin, Sec.; M. E. Cazin, Treas.; further inf. refused) 7 Pearl

Pomares & Cushman (Marino Pomares & Edward G. Cushman) 86 B'way

Pomeroy Mfg. Co. (Pomeroy & Hall, proprs.) 177 Grand

Pomeroy Pharmaceutical Co. (Cyrus Pyle, Pres.; Howard C. Pyle, Sec.; Wellesley W. Gage, Treas. Capital, $100,000. Trustees: Howard C. & Cyrus Pyle, Wellesley W. Gage) 88 Warren

Pomeroy-Truss Co. (Daniel Pomeroy, Pres.; Charles R. Dean, Sec. Capital, $50,000. Directors: Daniel Pomeroy, Charles R. Dean, Mary E. Pomeroy) 765 B'way

Pomeroy & Fischer (Joseph Pomeroy & Frederick Fischer) 30 Frankfort

Pomeroy & Hall (Benjamin H. Pomeroy & James Hall) 177 Grand

Pomroy Brothers (Henry K. & H. Arthur Pomroy) 39 Broad

Pomroy & Gambell (Mary A. Pomroy & Walter J. Gambell) 7 Mott

Pond Electric Signal Co. (Charles N. Talbot, Pres.; William P. Stevenson, Sec. Capital, $300,000. Trustees: Charles N. Talbot, Robert L. Belknap, William P. Stevenson, Charles T. Barney) 115 B'way

Pond William A. & Co. (estate of William A. Pond, only) 25 Union sq. W.

Pond & Smith (Theodore P. Pond & John E. Smith) 256 Washn.

Pond's Extract Co. (Léon H. Hurtt, Pres.; Edward O. Stanley, Treas. Capital, $100,000. Directors: E. D. Palmer, Leon H. & Francis D. Hurtt, Edward O. Stanley) 76 Fifth av.

Pondir & Co. (John Pondir & Augustus Nathan) 25 Wall

Pons Emilio & Co. (Emilio Pons, Candido A. Martines-Ybor & William Kling) 89 Water

Pontiac, Oxford & Northern R. R. Co. (George W. Debevoise, Pres.; William H. Murphy, Sec.; Hugh Porter, Treas. Capital, $1,000,000. Directors; George W. Debevoise, William H. Murphy, Hugh Porter, James Houston, August C. Baldwin, Frank H. Carroll, Charles H. Stone) 11 Pine

Pontier C. E. & Co. (Charles E. & Mary A. Pontier) 151 Spring

Pontifex Refrigerating & Ice Making Machine Mfg. Co. (Robert Hewitt, Pres.; Henry J. W. S. Cooke, Sec. Capital, $600,000. Directors: Robert Hewitt, Pierre P. Keller, Henry J. W. S. Cooke, W. Nelson Cromwell, A. A. Dame) 518 West

Pool Charles A. & Co. (dissolved) 1 Beaver & Pier 5 E. R.

Pool John H. & Macy (John H. Pool & William H. Macy jr.) 76 Broad

Poole George E. & H. Co. (dissolved) 51 E. 41st & 13 E. 53d

Poor H. V. & H. W. (Henry V. & Henry W.) 70 Wall

Poor & Duffy (Walter S. Poor & James King Duffy) 47 Liberty

Poor & Greenough (Henry W. Poor, John Greenough & George E. Porter) 36 Wall

Pootoo F. & Co, (dissolved) 38 Broad

Pope C. H. & Co. (Charles H. Pope, George B. Earle & Arthur T. Doyle) 64 W. B'way

Pope & Kile (John H. Pope & Henry Kile) 87 Barclay

Pope & Stevens (Walter B. Stevens, only) 114 Chambers

Pope, Edgcoumb & Terry (dissolved) 11 Wall

Pope's Gevert, Son & Co. (George Pope & John H. Tangemann) 180 Washn.

Pope's Thomas J., Sons & Co. (James E. jr. & Harry S. Pope & Charles C. Thomas) 202 Pearl

Popham & Co. (Lewis C. Popham, Co. refused) 16 E. 23d, 1 B'way & ft. E. 86th

Popham & Sedgwick (Alexander F. Popham & John Sedgwick) 208 W. 125th & E. 135th n Madison av.

Popkin & Marks (Abraham Popkin & Abraham Marks) 476 B'way

Popp Compressed Air & Electric Power Co. (Elisha Dyer 3d, Pres.; Albert Strauss, Sec. Capital, $1,000,000. Directors: Elisha Dyer 3d, Eugene Seligman, Albert Strauss, George Hyatt, E. D. Phillips, E. Thalman, E. Cartebach) 15 Broad

Popper Leo & Sons (Leo & Edwin S. & Caleb F. Popper) 55 Grand

Porawski & Rist (M. T. Porawski & G. A. Rist) 207 E. 12d

Porous Plaster Co. (George A. Brandreth, Pres.; Ralph Brandreth, Sec. Directors: George A. & Ralph & Franklin Brandreth) 274 Canal

Port Aransas Co. (E. H. Ropes, Pres.; Charles E. Miller, Sec. Capital, $5,000,000. Directors: E. H. Ropes, Charles E. Miller, H. B. Chamberlain, William V. Carolin) 10 Wall

Port Chester & Rye Beach Street R. R. Co. (Frank H. Skeele, Pres.; James H. Moran, Sec.; V. A. Kreppa, Treas. Capital, $50,000. Directors: Frank H. Skeele, V. A. Kreppa, James H. Moran, Daniel G. Thompson, O. D. Newton, A. H. Farrar, John W. Lounsbury) 15 Cortlandt

Port Chester, White Plains & Tarrytown Street Railway Co. (Jacob M. Schuyler, Sec. Capital, $125,000. Directors: James H. Moran, John M. Digney, V. A. Kreppa, Frank H. Skeele, Jacob M. Schuyler, James E. Miller, James M. Nelson) 15 Cortlandt

Port Morris Land & Improvement Co. (William Reynolds Brown, Pres.; William Smith Brown, Sec. Capital, $600,000. Directors; Charles D. Dickey, William C. Squier, Lewis B. & William Smith & William Reynolds Brown) 140 B'way

Portable House Building & Mfg. Co. (Daniel T. Atwood, Pres.; A. Dalton Atwood, Sec. Capital, $300,000; further inf. unattainable) 335 B'way

Porter Electric Messenger Co. (George A. Kelly, Pres.; Murray Corrington, Sec. Capital, $200,000. Trustees: George A. Kelly, Solomon Hanford, Murray Corrington, George J. Schermerhorn, Henry B. Lyle) 35 William

Porter John G. & Co. (dissolved) 405 Pearl

COMPILED WITH ACCURACY AND DESPATCH. } **CLASSIFIED BUSINESS LISTS.** { THE TROW CITY DIRECTORY CO. 11 University Place.

POR   244   POW

Porter Teletype Co. (Anthony N. Brady, Pres.; Albert L. Judson, Sec. Capital, $300,000. Directors: Anthony N. Brady, Patrick T. Wall, Albert L. Judson, E. V. Foote, William D. Garrison, Thomas B. Casey) 30 Union sq. E.

Porter Thomas E. & Co. (Thomas E. Porter & James H. Francis) 143 Chambers

Porter William J. & Son (William J. & William J. Porter jr.) 120 Lincoln av.

Porter & Co. (David F. Porter, no Co.) 77 E. 125th

Porter & Kilvert (Anthony B. Porter & Thomas Kilvert) 154 Nassau

Porter & Flyer (George S. Porter & Charles Whiting Flyer) 95 Liberty

Porter Brothers & Co. (Thomas & Nathan T. Porter, Henry C. Robinson, Frank H. Tooker, Joseph L. Porter, Anthony D. Schroeder & Ernest E. Weiskotten) 78 Worth & 15 Thomas

Porter's A. D., Sons (William R. & Charles A. Porter) 1125 B'way

Porter's William, Sons (William Porter jr. only) 271 Pearl

Porterfield & Derivers (Charles B. Porterfield & William J. Derivers) 19 William

Porth & Davies (dissolved) 397 West

Portland Cement Stone Co. (Frederick W. Lawrence propr.) 18 Exchange pl.

Portland, Vancouver & Northern Railway (no inf.) 45 B'way

Portsmouth Street Railway Co. (Charles B. Peck, Pres. Capital, $50,000. Directors: Charles B. Peck, W. M. Stewart, Arthur E. Bateman, C. C. Pearson, C. E. Coon) 87 B'way

Posner S. I. & Brother (Solomon I. & Samuel I. Posner) 508 Sixth av.

Posner & Hein (dissolved) 55 Grand

Post Building Co. (Charles A. Post, Pres.; George B. Post, Sec. Capital, $575,000. Trustees: Charles A. & George D. Post, J. Langdon Ward) 10 Exchange pl.

Post Percheron Horse Assn. (John Arbuckle, Pres.; James N. Jarvis, Sec.; Horace K. Thurber, Treas. Directors: John Arbuckle, Horace K. Thurber, Charles Arbuckle, Leander Waterbury, James N. Jarvis, Morton E. Post, William H. Force) 136 Front

Post A. J. & Son (George W. & Franklin H. Post, only) 261 B'way

Post E. L. & Co. (Ezra L. Post & George C. Waldo) 10 Peck sl.

Post L. D. & Co. (Lyman D. Post, no Co.) 21 Centre

Post & Flagg (George B. Post jr., W. Allston Flagg & Augustus L. Revere) 44 B'way

Post & McCord (Andrew J. Post & William H. McCord) 102 B'way

Post, Martin & Co. (Henry A. V. Post, Archer N. Martin & Charles C. Pomeroy) 34½ Pine

Postage Stamp Service Machine Co. (Francis L. Wellman, Pres.; Benjamin B. Odell jr. Sec. Capital, $300,000. Directors: Francis L. Wellman, Benjamin B. Odell jr, Hans S. Beattie, Gilbert M. Spier jr.) 1 B'way

Postal Express Co. (Ltd.) (inf. unattainable) 59 William

Postal Telegraph Cable Co. (Albert B. Chandler, Pres.; John O. Stevens, Sec.; Edward C. Platt, Treas. Capital, $5,000,000. Directors: George S. Coe, Richard V. Dey, William H. Barker, Albert B. Chandler, Edward C. Platt, Hector de Castro, George G. Ward, John O. Stevens) 1 B'way

Postel Brothers (Herman N. & Henry A. Postel) 32 First av.

Postley & Bertine (Thomas Postley & Josiah H. Bertine) 81 Fulton

Postley & Johnson (dissolved) 90 Ann

Potsdamer, Lion & Moyer (David T. Potsdamer, Simeon M. Lion & William K. Moyer) 6 Bond

Pott James & Co. (James Pott, Edwin S. Gorham & James Pott jr.) 14 Astor pl.

Potter Gilbert & Co. (Gilbert Potter;—special partner, George H. Watson, Groton, Ct., $50,000; terminates 4th Feb. 1893) 164 Front

Potter A. E. & Co. (dissolved) 150 Beekman

Potter C. jr. & Co. (Charles Potter jr. Horace W. Fish & Joseph M. Titsworth) 12 Spruce

Potter E. C. & Co. (Edward C. Potter & Charles M. Oelrichs;—special partner, Theodore A. Havemeyer; $100,000; terminates 11th Nov. 1890) 36 Wall

Potter F. W. & Co. (Franklin W. Potter & Edward E. Tucker) 325 Washn.

Potter Brothers (dissolved) 32 Liberty

Potter & Brother (Frederick G. & E. Clifford Potter) 126 B'way & 1354 Ninth av.

Potter & Buffinton (Isaac M. Potter & John M. Buffinton) 176 B'way

Potter & Cochrane (William E. Potter & William Cochrane) 45 Front

Potter & Crandall (Luther H. Potter & Harlan Crandall) 18 Liberty

Potter & Johnson (Frederick Potter & John Q. A. Johnson) 38 Park row

Potter & Locke (Charles E. Potter & William H. Locke) 87 Warren

Potter & Potter (Isaac B. & Charles F. Potter) 38 Park row

Potter, Linsley & Pearson (Lewis J. Potter, John M. Linsley & Edwin S. Pearson) 144 Duane

Potter-Compton Electric Co. (no inf.) 385 B'way

Pottier, Stymus & Co. (Adrian A. Pottier, Pres.; William P. Stymus, Sec.; Frank R. Pentz, Treas. Capital, $100,000. Directors: Adrian A. Pottier, William P. Stymus jr, Frank R. Pentz, B. Maybeck) 877 Lex. av.

Potts Frederic A. & Co. (William R. Potts, Nelson J. Gates, George S. Rockwell, George M. Weld, Charles R. Oliver, Edward Lawrence & estate of Frederic A. Potts) 26 B'way

Potts Brothers (James & Thomas Potts) 48 Duane

Poughkeepsie Bridge Co. (John S. Wilson, Pres.; William B. Carlile, Sec. Capital, $5,000,000. Directors: John S. Wilson, Henry C. Seixas, Henry McCormick, Arthur Brook, William W. Gibbs, Henry C. Gibson, Charles Henry Hart, Joseph F. Sinnott, Charlemagne Tower jr. George A. Fletcher, W. Van Benthuysen, Julius H. Appleton, John I. Platt) 115 B'way

Poughkeepsie Transp. Co. (John H. Brinckerhoff, Pres.; Abraham V. V. Haight, Sec. Capital, $100,000. Directors: John H. Brinckerhoff, Abraham V. V. Haight, Frank B. Lown) Pier 34 (new) N. R.

Poughkeepsie & Connecticut R. R. Co. (dissolved) 115 B'way

Poulson & Eger (Niles Poulson, Michael Eger & B. Edward J. Eils) 216 W. 23d

Pountney W. H. & H. (William H. & Henry) 26 Frankfort

Pouquet E. & Co. (Ernest Pouquet & Henry Pfeiffer) 62 E. 14th

Powe George W. & Co. (George W. Powe & Peter Wood) 66 South

Powell Mary, Steamboat Co. (inf. unattainable) Pier 39 (old) N. R.

Powell Brothers (Alexander B. & Ansel K. Powell) 99 Barclay

Powell & Bennett (Robert S. Powell & Eugene L. Bennett;—special partner, Frank Ross, Quebec, Can., $20,000; terminates 9th Nov. 1892) 121 Pearl

Powell & Campbell (Leander T. Powell & Robert Campbell) 122 Duane

Powell & Lockwood (William N. Powell & F. Crosby Lockwood) 112 Chambers

MERCHANTS EXCHANGE NAT. BANK OF THE CITY OF N. Y.
SOLICITS YOUR ACCOUNT. **237 Broadway.**
PHINEAS C. LOUNSBURY, President.   ALLEN S. APGAR, Cashier.

POW 245 PRE

Powell & Maccaffil (dissolved) 125 Pearl
Powell, Brother & Co. (David B. & Gideon N. Powell & Enoch R. Tuthill) 130 Duane
Powell, Smith & Co. (Joseph Powell, George J. Smith & Henry J. Luce) 1230 Second av.
Powell's Chemical Co. (Louis Beer, propr.) 78 Broad
Powell's Express Co. (Richard Powell, propr.) 95 Watts
Powell's John, Son & Co. (Mary A. & Robert S. Powell & Amos Grinnell) 8 Fulton fish m'kt
Power Brothers (Patrick H. & Robert Power) 1764 B'way
Power, Son & Co. (Edward & Edward J. Power & Frederick Weber) 76 Broad
Powers James G. & Co. (James G. & Robert A. Powers & Allen B. Potter) 99 Murray
Powers John B. & Son (John B. & John C. & Walter E. Powers) 101 Chambers
Powers D. & Son (Daniel & John V. Powers) 215 W. Houston
Powers D. & Sons (Deborah & Albert K. & Nathaniel B. Powers) 465 Wash'n.
Powers M. F. & Son (Michael F. & Thomas W. Powers) 102 Water
Powers & Lee (Edmund W. Powers & Thomas H. Lee) 45 William
Powers & Weightman (William Weightman, only) 56 Maiden la. & 25 Liberty
Powerville Felt Roofing Co. (Ltd.) (Joseph A. Smith, Pres.; Charles E. Lockwood, Sec.; Francis J. Palmer, Treas. Capital, $100,000. Directors: Joseph A. Smith, Charles E. Lockwood, Francis J. Palmer, Howard Ayres, Warren D. Fields) 100 Maiden la.
Practical Publishing Co. (not inc.) (Arthur G. M. & Robert F. Ashley) 21 Park row
Prager Charles & Brother (Charles & George B. Prager) 8 Maiden la.
Prager S. L. & Co. (Sigmund L. Prager, no Co.) 123 Mercer
Prager Brothers (Benjamin & William Prager) 417 Seventh av.
Prange Peter & Brothers (no inf.) 410 Cherry
Pratt Charles & Co. (Charles & Charles M. & Horace A. & Frederick B. Pratt) 26 B'way
Pratt Charles D., Co. (dissolved) 83 Chambers
Pratt George W. & Co. (George W. Pratt & Ira Goddard) 14 John
Pratt James T. & Co. (James T. Pratt & Willis Dodge;—special partner, Charles Pratt, *F'klyn, N. Y.,* $12,000; terminates 1st Jan. 1894) 53 Fulton
Pratt Mfg. Co. (inf. unattainable) 26 B'way
Pratt A. E. & Co. (Albert E. Pratt, no Co.) 178 Park row
Pratt J. W. & Son (James W. Pratt, only) 75 Fulton
Pratt & Armitage (no inf.) 86 Leonard
Pratt & Farmer (George P. Farmer, only) 353 B'way
Pratt & Hamann (Robert H. Pratt & Julius Hamann) 512 W. 36th
Pratt & Lambert (Charles M. Pratt, Pres.; Henry S. Lambert, Sec. Capital, $60,000. Directors: Charles M. & Alfred W. Pratt, Henry S. Lambert) 5 Dutch & 47 John
Pratt & Molleson (Charles E. Pratt & George K. Molleson) 50 B'way
Prawdzicki Paul & Scelor (dissolved) 80 Pine
Pray T. T. & Co. (Thomas T. Pray & Treadwell B. Kellum) 157 Cedar
Pray, Small & Co. (no inf.) 104 Duane
Prentor P. M. & Co. (dissolved) 359 Pearl
Preble J. Q. & Co. (T. S. Bassford, assignee) 280 B'way
Preferred Mutual Accident Ass'n. (Henry L. Coe,

Pres.; Kimball C. Atwood, Sec.; John L. Childs, Treas. Directors: Phineas C. Lounsbury, Henry N. Whitney, Allen S. Apgar, Charles D. Spencer, Henry L. Coe, Kimball C. Atwood, John L. Childs, Charles F. Ketcham, William Westlake) 257 B'way
Preiss William & Co. (dissolved) 154 Ludlow
Preiss Brothers (Edward & Louis Preiss) 44 Av. A
Prelle Brothers (William F. J. & Bernard W. Prelle) 454 G'wich & 22 Desbrosses
Premium Mustard Mills (Ferdinand Wolff, propr.) 158 W. 27th
Prendergast L. & M. (no inf.) 811 W. 21st
Prentice Brown Stone Co. (Frederic Prentice, Pres.; George H. Barr, Sec. Capital, $1,250,000. Directors: Edwin Ellis, Frederic Prentice, E. A. Shores, George H. Barr, Luther C. Voorhees) 44 B'way
Prentice James & Son (Charles F. & estate of James Prentice) 178 B'way
Prentice H. & Co. (dissolved) 64 & 74 D'way
Prentice Brothers (Henry & N. Sartell Prentice) 64 B'way
Prentiss Calendar & Time Co. (Leonard W. Sweet, Pres.; Henry S. Prentiss, Sec.; George E. Fahys, Treas. Capital, $100,000. Directors: Lewis A. Parsons, Joseph Fahys, George W. Shiebler, George M. Bacon, Henry F. Cook, George E. Fahys, Joseph B. Bowden, Paul Morse Richards, Joseph L. Porter, Leonard W. Sweet, Henry S. Prentiss) 40 Maiden la.
Prentiss George H. & Co. (George H. & William D. Prentiss, William W. Walsh & La Fayette Olney jr.) 87 William
Prentiss Tool & Supply Co. (Henry G. Marshall, Pres.; Albert Frazier, Sec. Capital, $25,000. Directors: Charles Frazier, Henry G. Marshall, David Mitchell) 115 Liberty
Prentiss Vise Co. (John E. Mulford, Pres.; Edwin H. Mulford, Sec. Capital, $50,000. Directors: John E. & Edwin H. Mulford, Mortimer G. Lewis, William S. Morrow) 21 Dey
Prentiss C. C. & S. F. (Charles C. & Samuel F.) 57 B'way
Prentiss & Butler (Frederick C. Prentiss & George H. H. Butler) W. 130th n Eleventh av.
Prescott & Arizona Central Railway Co. (Thomas S. Bullock, Pres.; William M. Kelley, Sec.; William E. Hazeltine, Treas. Capital, $1,200,000. Directors: Henry C. Nutt, George O. Manchester, E. T. Smith, Thomas S. Bullock, William C. & William E. Hazeltine, William M. Kelley, Thomas J. Butler, Levi Bashford) 40 Wall
Presdee & Moore (Homer W. Presdee & Archibald T. Moore) 58 Ann & 1475 Ninth av.
Present & Co. (David & estate of Julius Present) 654 B'way
Preservaline Mfg. Co. (Emil C. Calm, Pres.; Charles E. Calm, Sec. Capital, $50,000. Directors: Emil C. & Charles E. Calm, William W. Whiteman) 23 Cedar
Press Engraving Co. (William J. Carlton, propr.) 86 Centre
Press Publishing Co. (Joseph Pulitzer, Pres.; J. Angus Shaw, Treas. Trustees: Joseph Pulitzer, William L. Davis, Melville C. Day) 32 Park row
Pressey, Haviland & Co. (Andrew Pressey, Howard Haviland & Henry R. Brigham) 18 Counties al.
Pressler & Reich (dissolved) no address
Preston W. R. & Co. (William R. & William D. & George R. Preston) 54 Broad
Preston W. W. & Co. (Wilson W. & Luther E. Preston) 247 B'way
Pretzfeld & Co. (William & Simon Pretzfeld) 165 Water
Preusser & Looram (Richard E. Preusser & Matthew M. Looram;—special partner, Lucian

SNOW, CHURCH & CO. — ESTABLISHED 1874.

PRE   246   PRU

C. Appleby, $15,000; terminates 6th Dec. 1890) 56 B'way
Prevear & Gleason (Herbert P. Prevear & William C. Gleason) 402 B'way
Price Barnett L. & Co, (Barnett L. & Barnett L. Price) 23 Gt. Jones
Price J. A., Express Co. (James A. Price, propr.) Alexander av. n E. 142d, 91 Barclay, 60 Dey & 163 Reade
Price William E. & Co. (William E. Price & John H. Carl) 514 First av.
Price & Carl (Mortimer W. Price & John H. Carl) 512 First av.
Price & Steuart (Benjamin Price & James L. & Arthur Steuart) 29 Wall
Price Brothers & Co. (Edward A. & Theodore H. Price & John E. Douglass) 112 Fulton
Priest J. & Son (Joseph & George W. & Frank W. Priest) r 190 Hester
Prime R. E. & A. J. & Burns (Ralph E. & Alanson J. Prime & Arthur J Burns) 140 Nassau
Prince Henry & Co. (dissolved) 27 W. Houston
Prince F. A. & Co. (Frederick A. Prince, no Co.) 419 B'way
Prince R. & Son (Rachel & Harry D. Prince) 165 Mercer
Prince & Stolpe (Leonard K. Prince & Hugo Stolpe) 330 Seventh av.
Prince & Whitely (James Whitely, Thomas H. Bolmer, H. Cruger Oakley, & Maynard C. Eyre, only) 64 B'way & 19 New
Prince's Metallic Paint Co. (John S. Davenport, Pres.; David Prince, Sec. Capital, $1,000. Directors: John S. Davenport, David Prince) 71 Maiden la.
Princess of Wales Co. (Austin Kelley, Pres. Capital, $10,000; further inf. unattainable) 458 B'way
Princeton Co. (inoperative) 748 B'way
Principe & Co. (dissolved) 15 Marion
Pringle & Gondran (James W. Pringle & Adolph L. Gondran) 140 Liberty
Prior Brothers (Robert J. & George B. Prior) 125 E. 129th, 504 S. Boulevard & W. 126th c Boulevard
Pritchard & McGourkey (Emilio Pritchard & Samuel D. McGourkey) 433 Produce Ex.
Proben Charles A. & Son (Charles A. & John A. Proben) 192 Second av. & 152 Eldridge
Probst Frederick & Co. (Adolph Victor:—special partner, Carl Wilhelm Volckmann, Bederkesa, Germany, $75,000; terminates 31st Dec. 1893) 51 Broad
Probst J. D. & Co. (John D. Probst, Gustav J. Wetzlar & Paul Mayer) 50 Exchange pl.
Proctor & Turner (Frederick F. Proctor & Philip T. Turner) 189 W. 23d
Proctor, Hunt & Haskell (no inf.) 7 Ferry
Prodgers William & Son (William & George W. Prodgers) 264 W. 25th
Produce Exchange Grain Elevating Assn. (no inf.) 12 Bridge
Producers' Cons. Land & Petroleum Co. (Joseph Bushnell, Pres.; Henry C. Crane, Sec.; Joel F. Freeman, Treas. Capital, $1,000,000. Directors: Joseph Bushnell, Henry C. Crane, Joel F. Freeman, George H. Vilas, Daniel O'Day) 26 B'way
Producers' Milk Co. (Charles E. Emmons, propr.) 903 Sixth av.
Progress Publishing Co. (no inf.) 202 W. 125th
Progress Watch Case Co. (Charles H. Pinnell, Pres.; Jules P. May, Sec. Capital, $35,000. Directors: Charles H. Pinnell, Jules P. May, John Geiger, Edward Muller) 1½ Maiden la.
Progressive Age Publishing Co. (Ernest C. Brown, Pres.; further inf. unattainable) 18 B'way

Progressive Credit Clothing Co. (Anna Feinberg, propr.) 112 W. 14th
Progressive Shoe Co. (Michael Finnegan, propr.) 104 Duane
Propach Brothers (Henry & William Propach) 779 B'way
Prosch Mfg. Co. (Cyrus Prosch, Pres.; David L. Haskell, Sec. Capital, $4,000. Trustees: Cyrus Prosch, David L. Haskell, George C. Kobbe) 389 Broome
Prosnitz & Greenebaum (Daniel Prosnitz & Asor Greenebaum) 64 Lispenard
Prosnitz & Kraus (William Prosnitz & Julius C. & Joseph Kraus) 1827 Av. A
Prosser Thomas & Son (Thomas & Richard & William H. & Thomas Prosser jr.) 15 Gold
Protective Employment Assn. (dissolved) 1384 B'way
Protective Employment Bureau (William H. Prosser, propr.) 1334 B'way & 597 Sixth av.
Protective Life Assurance Soc. (William H. Voorhees, Pres.; William C. Davis, Sec.; Adolphus Smedberg, Treas. Directors: William H. Voorhees, Adolphus Smedberg, Rufus Hatch, Alexander McDonald, Harry Wilber, Norman Freeman, Russell O. Johnson, A. W. Foster, John T. Salter, Eugene F. Vacheron, William C. Davis) 44 B'way
Protective Live Stock Mutual Benefit Soc. (inf. unattainable) 111 B'way
Protective Ventilator Co. (James E. Hummel, propr.) 158 Fulton
Protin Brothers (Albert P. & Gaston L. Protin) 179 Wooster
Proudfoot & Co. (Lewis & Orince Proudfoot) 109 W. 36th
Prousite Mining Co. (dissolved) 81 B'way
Provenzano & Sciortino (dissolved) 19 Whitehall
Providence Line (Providence & Stonington S. S. Co. propr.) Piers 29 (old) & 86 (new) N. R.
Providence Mfg. Jewelry Co. (Joseph Herzog, propr.) 176 B'way
Providence & Stonington S. S. Co. (Jacob W. Miller, Pres.; Edward P. Taft, Sec.; Wilbur F. Herbert, Treas. Capital, $1,500,000. Directors: George M. & Jacob W. Miller, Samuel D. Babcock, Amos N. Beckwith, J. L. Riker, B. F. Vaughn, Edward P. Taft, G. G. Haven, Henry Howard) Pier 36 (new) N. R.
Provident Fund Soc. (Adolphus N. Lockwood, Pres.; William W. Dodge, Sec.; Joseph Perlam, Treas. Directors: Adolphus N. Lockwood, William W. Dodge, Joseph Perlam, John D. Taylor, Francis E. Dodge, Victor Shaller, Henry A. Jones, Cyrus Pyle, G. K. Smith) 250 B'way
Provident Homestead Co. (dissolved) 45 B'way
Provident Savings Life Assurance Soc. (Sheppard Homans, Pres.; William E. Stevens, Sec. Capital, $100,000. Directors: Abraham Avery, Stephen G. Clarke, Alonzo B. Cornell, John O. Heald, Sheppard Homans, J. B. Houston, Theodore F. Miller, Joseph H. & Samuel Parsons, G. S. Plumley, James H. Saville, William Stanley, William E. Stevens, Edward C. Homans, Heywood C. Broun) 120 B'way
Provincial Dry Dock Co. (George Edgett, Pres.; David E. Taylor, Sec. Capital, $100,000; further inf. unattainable) 66 New
Prudential Fire Assn. (George L. Dale, Pres.; Abraham P. M. Roome, Sec. Capital, $200,000. Directors: John Claflin, William H. Lee, Joseph T. Low, George F. Victor, Julius Hammerslough, William T. Ryle, Henry Newman, Francis O. Lloyd, Adolph Herrmann, Henry Gittermann, Samuel Inslee, Frederick W. Devoe, Adolph Wimpfheimer, Daniel S. Appleton, William Barbour, Francis R. Upton, George W. Davis, John Russita, Simon Goldenberg, Abraham P. M. Roome, Henry Abegg.

**WATER METERS, GAS ENGINES, | NATIONAL METER CO.
FOR PUMPING AND POWER. | 252 Broadway, N. Y.**

PRU 247 QUE

J. Crawford McCreery, Eberhard Faber, John D. Cutter, George L. Dale) 173 B'way

Prudential Ins. Co. (John F. Dryden, Pres.; Edward S. Johnson, Sec.; Henry J. Yates, Treas. Capital, $125,000. Directors: John F. Dryden, Leslie D. Ward, Horace Alling, Henry J. Yates, Edgar B. Ward, Edward S. Johnson, Charles G. Campbell, Elias S. Ward, Theodore C. E. Blanchard, Aaron Carter jr. Alfred A. Reeves, James Perry, S. A. Keeney) 224 Centre

Prudential League (Gustave Berg, Pres.; George Gunther, Sec.; Isaac J. Cahen, Treas. Capital, $51,000. Directors: Gustave Berg, George Gunther, Isaac J. Cahen, F. Beyer) 24 Park pl. & 19 Barclay

Pryor & Hartshorne (dissolved) 154 Maiden la.

Pryor S, Morris & Co. (S. Morris Pryor, no Co.) 51 B'way

Public Debt Adjustment Co. (Edward B. Wesley, Pres.; William McMichael, Sec. Capital, $250,000. Directors: Edward B. Wesley, Alonzo B. Cornell, Robert B. Roosevelt, Noah Davis, George M. Hard, Charles F. Huntington, Samuel Jacoby, William McMichael, John R. Planten, John D. Vermeule, Sanford Steele, W. S. Williams, George W. Van Sielen, G. Van Nostrand, Jenkins Van Schaick, K. R. Wilson) 18 Wall

Public Grain & Stock Exchange (Ltd.) (Charles H. Platt, Pres.; Alfred F. Hovey, Sec. Capital, $100,000 ; further inf. refused) 18 B'way

Publishers' Commercial Union (J. G. Orr, Pres.; Frank B. White, Sec.; L F. Dunwiddie. Treas. Capital, $10,000. Directors: J. G. Orr, H. F. Bliss, I. F. Dunwiddie, Frank B. White) 245 B'way

Publishers' & Booksellers' Protective Assn. (no inf.) 132 Nassau

Publishers' Printing Co. (Joseph Gantz, Pres.; John W. Lieb, Sec.; Isidor Furst, Treas. Capital, $50,000. Directors: Joseph Gantz, John W. Lieb, Isidor Furst) 80 W. 13th

Puerto Cabello Contracting Co. (George S. Field, Pres.; Nathaniel Haven, Sec. Directors: George S. Field, George S. Morison, John Bogart ; further inf. refused) 1 B'way

Puffer & Hope (dissolved) 66 Beckman

Pugsley & Chapman (Van Allen Pugsley & Girard F. Chapman) 8 Liberty

Pull Hard Pantaloon Mfg. Co. (Bernstein & Jacobs, propr.) 127 Division

Pulling & Ford (John T. Pulling & Ernest W. Ford) 123 Produce Ex.

Pulling's A. C., Sons (dissolved) 6 Broome

Pullman John & Co. (Samuel C. Pullman & Robert G. Davisson, only) 12 White

Pullman's Palace Car Co. (George M. Pullman, Pres.; Alfred S. Weinsheimer, Sec. Capital, $20,000,000. Directors: George M. Pullman, Marshall Field, J. W. Doane, Norman Williams, O. S. A. Sprague, Henry C. Hulbert, Henry R. Reed) 15 Broad

Pulsion Telephone Co. (Stephen W. Fullerton, Pres.; Henry A. Kirkham, Sec. Capital, $1,000,000. Directors: Stephen W. Fullerton, William Wilson, Luther E. Shinn, Sidney DeKay, William S. Johnson, H. W. Ladd, T. King) 120 B'way

Pulsometer Steam Pump Co. (Augustus H. W. Johnson, Pres.; Gardnier F. Badger, Sec. Capital, $25,000. Directors : Augustus H. W. & William F. & Joseph F. Johnson, Gardnier F. Badger, Burbank Roberts) 120 Liberty

Pulver Peter & Sons (Peter & William H. & Robert E. Pulver) 214 Franklin

Pulver & Vanauken (dissolved) 18 E. 14th

Punchard George & Son (George & George M. C. Punchard) 203 Spring

Punchard H. & Son (Henry & Henry Punchard jr.) 55 New Chambers & 23 Oak

Pund Brothers (Joseph & Clemens Pund) 648 Courtlandt av.

Punderford & Co. (James A. Punderford & Francisco A. Perozo) 33 Pine

Pupke, Walter & Co. (Eberhard L. Pupke, Henry Walter & Henry J. Bruner) 11 Wall

Purdon & Wiggin (Augustus Wiggin & Clarence W. Goold, only) 93 Front

Purdy E. H., Mfg. Co. (Ltd.) (Duncan, Phyfe, Pres.; Albert R. Searles, Sec. Capital, $60,000. Directors : Duncan Phyfe, Albert R. Searles, Granville M. Drummond, L. Phyfe, F. Hefter) 46 W. 13th

Purdy J. K. & B. F. (Joshua K. & Benjamin F.) 25 Beaver

Purdy J. S. & Sons (James S. & James & William Purdy) 1588, 1990, 2195 & 2920 Third av.

Purdy W. M. & J. H. (William M. & John H.) 140 Nassau

Purdy & Arnold (A. Delmont Purdy & Charles H. Arnold) 51 Broad

Purdy & Huntington Co. (Ltd.) (dissolved) 44 Beaver

Purdy & McLaughlin (Ambrose R. Purdy & James W. McLaughlin) 230 B'way

Purdy & Shannon (Charles E. Purdy & Caroline S. Shannon) 659 Fifth av.

Puritan Laundry (Union C. Finch, propr.) 372 Eighth av.

Purnell, Hagaman & Co. (James E. Purnell, Theodore Hagaman & William S. Wallace) 104 & 320 B'way, 4 College pl, & 200 Water

Purrington & Shannon (William A. Purrington & Richard C. Shannon) 63 Wall

Pursell Mfg. Co. (Pinckney Amarr, Pres.; Dela M. Farnham, Sec. Capital, $60,000. Directors: Pinckney Amarr, Dela M. Farnham, John H. Ives, John W. Salter, Frank J. Walsh) 910 B'way, 893 Sixth av. & 46 E. 42d

Purton & Fair (Henry J. Purton & Richard Fair) 25 William

Purviance W. E. & Co. (William E. & William T. Purviance) 69 Gansevoort

Purvin & Myers (William Purvin & Samuel H. Myers) 37 Walker

Pusey & Co. (Emma L. Pusey & Johnson M. Trozell) 1898 B'way

Pustau C. v. & Co. (Carl von Pustau & Otto Schneider) 134 Pearl & 100 Water

Pustet Frederick & Co. (Frederick Pustet, Alois Diepenbrock & Erwin Steinbach) 52 Barclay

Putnam County Ice Co. (inoperative) 15 Exchange pl.

Putnam H. W. & Co. (Harry W. Putnam & Edward N. Furleigh) 28 Dey

Putnam's G. P., Sons (George H. & John B. & Irving & Victorine H. Putnam ;—special partner, Walter Howe, $26,000 ; terminates 31st Jan. 1892) 27 W. 23d & 8 W. 24th

Putney & Bishop (William B. Putney & James L. Bishop) 115 B'way

Pyle James & Sons (James & James T. & William S. Pyle) 436 G'wich

Q

Qua & Wray (Thomas Qua & Joseph Wray) 165 W. 25th

Quackenboss & Eadie (dissolved) 59 Wall

Quackenbush, Townsend & Co. (Abraham & Charles E. Quackenbush & William H. Townsend) 65 Chambers & 67 Reade

Quackinbush B. F. & Co. (Benjamin F. & David Quackinbush) 703 G'wich

Quaintance W. B. & J. E. (William B. & John E.) 104 Franklin

Queen Frank, Publishing Co. (Ltd.) (refused) 68 Centre

PROTECTION For Family, Home, Store, Factory, etc., by using only the "VULCAN" BRAND OF SAFETY MATCHES. Headquarters, 373 Washington Street, New York.

QUE 248 RAI

Queen Knitting Mills (Stern & Steinman, proprs.) 204 E. 43d

Queens County Water Co. (Richard V. W. Du Bois, Pres.; Frank Keck, Sec. Capital, $50,000. Directors: Richard V. W. & Abram Du Bois, Frank Keck, Henry F. Butler) 120 B'way

Querling J. & W. (John & John W. Querling, only) 544 Hudson

Quesada F, & L. (Flora & Leopoldina) 60 Lex. av.

Quick E. B. & Brother (Elias B. & Emerson W. Quick) 818 Fifth

Quicksilver Mining Co. (David Mahany, Pres.; Frederick N. Lawrence, Treas.; Mortimer M. Weed, Sec. Capital, $10,000,000. Directors: David Mahany, George W. Butts jr. James D. Smith, Edward Brandon, Samuel W. Doocock, Charles Fries, Frederick N. Lawrence, Sheppard Gandy, Frank K. Sturgis, George G. Haven, Joseph Milbank) 20 Nassau

Quigley Furniture Co. (William D. Quigley, Pres.; Jay C. Smith, Treas.; George H. Lynch, Sec. Capital, $120,000. Directors: William B. Quigley, Jay C. Smith, George H. Lynch, Frederick T. Proctor, Melvin Bancroft) 4 W. 14th

Quigley M. & Co. (dissolved) 389 Av. A

Quimby J. L. & Co. (John L. Quimby:—special partner, Edward C. Hong, $1,500; terminates 15th Feb. 1891) 194 Front

Quimby W. F. & Co. (W. Frederick Quimby & Edward R. Dimick) 291 B'way

Quincey Charles E. & Co. (Charles E. Quincey & Addison R. McCanless) 70 D'way & 15 New

Quincy John W. & Co. (John E. Thompson & A. Digby Bonnell, only) 93 William

Quincy Mining Co. (Thomas F. Mason, Pres.; William Rogers Todd. Sec. Capital, $1,250,000. Directors: Thomas F. Mason, Morris H. Smith, John Brown, Edwin Rice, Samuel B. Harris) 52 D'way

Quinlan & O'Keefe (William Quinlan & John J. O'Keefe) 25 Chambers

Quinlin L. G. & Co. (Leonard G. Quinlin & A. Frank Beales) 11 New & 72 D'way

Quinn Thomas S. & Sons (Thomas S. & John J. & Thomas S. Quinn jr.) 501 W. 40th

Quinn W. H. & Co. (William H. Quinn, no Co.) 99 Chambers

Quinn & Fuller (Mary A. Quinn & Mary J. Fuller) 10 E. 14th

Quinn & Hall (Thomas S. Quinn & Benjamin J. Hall) 60 South

Quintard Iron Works (N. F. Palmer jr. & Co., proprs.) 740 E. 12th & 735 E. 11th

Quintini Brothers (Donato Quintini & Peter Bensaldi, only) 70 Thompson

Quirolo & Roussean (Felix Quirolo & John Roussena) 117 Prince

Quong Hong Luong & Co. (refused) 5 Mott

Quong Lan Wah & Co. (Lun Wah & Far Quong) 32 Mott

R

R. & R. Chemical Co. (Rosenheim & Rosenfield, proprs.) 81 G'wich & 44 Trinity pl.

Raabe Henry & Sons (Henry & Herman Raabe, only) 321 W. 64th

Raabe Henry F. & Co. (Henry F. Raabe & Alexander O. Bergen) 29 Second

Rab & Oswald (Charles Rab & Herman Oswald) 421 B'way

Rabe & Keller (Rudolph F. Rabe & Ferdinand W. Keller) 243 D'way

Rabiner & Bernstein (Abraham J. Rabiner & Bessie Bernstein) 299 Henry

Rablitte C. L. & Co. (Charles L. Rablitte, no Co.) 437 B'way

Rackett & Brother (Edward E. Rackett, only) 52 South

Radam William, Microbe Killer Co. (George W. Kirk, Pres.; Louis Goodman, Sec. Capital, $200,000. Directors: Louis Goodman, Julius Sands, George W. Kirk) 56 Sixth av. & 1361 B'way

Radde William & Son (Matilda Kaufmann, only) 26 Beekman

Rademacher & Maxwell (William H. Rademacher & Henry W. Maxwell) 484 D'way

Rader G. W. & Co. (Gustavus W. Rader & Michael Schmitt) 609 W. 51st & 606 W. 52d

Rader L. B. & Co. (Louis B. Rader & Albert N. Camp) 246 W. 125th

Radix Mfg. Co. (no inf.) 39 Old sl.

Radley & Greenough (Frank X. Radley & Frederick A. Greenough) 281 Fifth av. & 502 E. 74th

Radtke, Lauckner & Co. (Gustavus A. Radtke & Bernard Lauckner, no Co.) 6 E. 18th

Radway & Co. (John S. Radway, Pres.; William D. Reid, Sec.; further inf. unattainable) 32 Warren & 102 Chambers

Rafalsky Brothers (Henry & Mark Rafalsky) 140 W. 23d

Raftery & Brown (John Raftery & William S. Brown) 60 Thomas

Rahaim Joseph & Brothers (Joseph & Thomas & David Rahaim) 68 Washn.

Railroad Brake, Switch, Signal & Safety Gate Co. (George V. Hann, Pres.; A. Hamilton Renvey, Sec.; Amend Schlehenried, Treas. Capital, $100,000. Directors: George V. Hann, John Hahn, A. Hamilton Renvey, Amend Schlehenried, Edmund M. Moffett) 102 Chambers

Railroad Equipment Co. (Clarence H. Clark, Pres.; George W. Dennison, Sec.; Henry A. V. Post, Treas. Capital, $1,500,000. Directors: Charles H. Clark, Henry A. V. Post, William B. Isham, Archer N. Martin, Charles C. Pomeroy) 84¾ Pine

Railroad Gazette (William H. Boardman, Pres. Capital, $200,000. Directors: William M. Boardman, James H. Bailey, S. Wright Dunning) 71 B'way

R. R. Signal Lamp & Lantern Co. (Armour & Osterhoudt, proprs.) 100 Beekman

Railroad Topics Co. (George R. Fitch, Pres.; Alexander D. Penfold, Treas.; Charles D. Galvin, Sec. Trustees: George R. Fitch, Alexander D. Penfold, Charles D. Galvin) 35 Frankfort

Railway Age Publishing Co. (Elisha H. Talbott, Pres.; William H. Shuey, Sec. Capital, $100,000. Directors: Elisha H. Talbott, William H. Shuey, Horace R. Hobart) 45 B'way

Railway Cab Electric Signal Co. (no inf.) 42 B'way

Railway Directory Publishing Co. (Raymond L. Donnell, Pres.; Edwin C. Donnell, Sec.; Charles D. Marsh, Treas. Capital, $15,000. Directors: Raymond L. & Edwin C. Donnell, Charles D. Marsh) 18 Cortlandt

Railway Electric Car Lighting Co. (William Bracken, Pres.; Henry R. Waite, Sec. Capital, $500,000. Directors: William Bracken, Henry G. Morris, Henry R. Waite, Henry Weston, A. H. Bauer) 120 B'way

Railway Map & Publishing Co. (Edward C. Dridgman, propr.) 84 Warren

Railway Safety Appliance Co. (Thorndike Saunders, Pres.; Edwin D. Worcester jr. Sec. Capital, $300,000. Directors: Thorndike Saunders, G. Creighton Webb, Edwin D. Worcester jr. John T. Salter, James F. Dwight) 170 B'way

Railway & Bankers' Engraving & Lithographing Co. (Lee R. Shryock, Pres.; Ernst Bartro, Sec. Capital, $1,000. Directors: Lee R. Shryock, Ernst Bartro) 45 B'way

Raiman & Ackerman (William H. Raiman & David R. Ackerman) 200 E. 29th

Raisbeck Electrotype Co. (John E. Raisbeck,

IDEN & CO., University Place, 9th to 10th Sts., N. Y. | **MANUFACTURERS OF GAS FIXTURES AND ELECTROLIERS**

Pres.; James Raisbeck, Sec. Capital, $2,000. Trustees: John E. & James Raisbeck) 24 Vandewater
Raives & Helperin (dissolved) 91 White
Ralli P. C. & Co. (Pandia C. Ralli & Richard Walford) 125 Pearl
Ralli Brothers (Pandelli Y. Pachiri & Theodore P. Ralli, only) 15 Old sl. & 115 Pearl
Ralli & Searle (Pandia C. Ralli & Charles Searle) 125 Pearl
Ramapo Iron Works (William B. Wilkins, Pres.; Robert J. Davidson, Sec.; George Church, Treas. Capital, $125,000. Directors: William B. Wilkins, George Church, Robert J. Davidson, William W. & Frederick W. Snow) 115 B'way
Ramel A. (Daniel & Emile A. Ramel & Daniel Daime, only) 88 Duane
Ramel, Conley Iron & Steel Co. (Emile Ramel, Pres.; John B. Monnot, Sec.; Edmond Huerstel, Treas. Capital, $500,000. Directors: Emile Ramel, John B. Monnot, Edmond Huerstel, John E. Dullwinkel, Gustave Huerstel) 200 B'way
Ramsdell Homer, Transp. Co. (Homer Ramsdell, Pres.; Homer S. Ramsdell, Sec.; James A. P. Ramsdell, Treas. Capital, $200,000. Directors: Homer & James A. P. & Homer S. & H. P. Ramsdell) Pier 24 (new) N. R.
Ramsdell Realty Co. (Capital, $500,000. Directors: James A. P. & Homer S. & H. P. Ramsdell; further inf. unattainable) Pier 24 (new) N. R.
Ramsgate Robert H. & Co. (Robert H. Ramsgate & Solomon Blog) 10 Maiden la.
Ramsperger H. G. & Co. (Herman G. Ramsperger, no Co.) 160 Pearl
Rand Drill Co. (Addison C. Rand, Pres.; Jasper R. Rand, Treas. Capital, $250,000. Directors: Addison C. & Jasper R. Rand, Joel Goldthwaite, Edward Greene) 23 Park pl.
Rand Brothers (Thomas D. & John H. & George W. Rand) 1404 B'way
Randall M. M. & Co. (Margaret M. & Harry Randall) 294 B'way
Randall R. A. & Son (Roswell A. & William H. Randall) 902 Sixth av.
Randall & Goodenough (Richard N. Randall & Frank L. Goodenough) 90 Chambers
Randall & Streck (dissolved) 92 W. 26th
Randall & Wierum (Charles K. Randall & Otto C. Wierum) 50 Exchange pl.
Randall's Theatrical Bureau (William W. Randall, propr.) 1145 B'way
Randebrock E. & Co. (Ernest Randebrock, no Co.) 61 New
Randel, Baremore & Billings (Henry Randel, Pres.; Chester Billings, Sec.; further inf. refused) 58 Nassau & 20 Maiden la.
Randell L. W. & Co. (Lydia W. Randell & Walter J. Ward) 558 Third av. & 554 Eighth av.
Randolph Anson D. F. & Co. (Anson D. F. & Arthur D. F. Randolph) 38 W. 23d
Randolph Edmund & Charles, 7 Nassau
Randolph Shafting Trust (John J. Vail, Pres.; Peter Milne, Sec.; further inf. refused) 280 B'way
Randolph Spindle Co. (dissolved) 22 Jacob
Randolph West Virginia Boom Co. (dissolved) 1 D'way
Randolph T. E. F. & Co, (Thompson E. F. Randolph, Thomas Hegeman, Eugene W. Paige & Charles A. Peck) 106 West
Randolph Brothers (in liquidation) 111 B'way
Randolph & Silva (Frederick E. F. Randolph & Theodore V. Silva) 2258 Third av.
Randolph, Condict & Black (Joseph F. Randolph, Henry V. Condict & Charles C. Black) 120 B'way

Ranhofer Brothers (Louis & John Ranhofer) 722 Sixth
Rankin John C. jr. (John C. Rankin jr.:—Special partner, E. Wells Sackett, $50,000; terminates 30th April, 1893) 34 Cortlandt
Rannenberg Brothers (Henry W. & William H. Rannenberg) 16 Exchange pl.
Ransom & Co. (William H. Ransom, Co. refused) 94 Centre
Rapid Addressing Machine Co. (Frank D. Belknap, Pres.; Robert Dun Douglass, Sec. Capital, $10,000. Directors: Frank D. Belknap, Robert Dun Douglass, Erastus Wiman, Arthur J. King, William Safford) 314 B'way
Rapid Copyist Co. (Amelia M. Dana, propr.) 58 Exchange pl.
Rapid Duplicating & Copying Machine Co. (inoperative) 84 Warren
Rapid Transit Cable Co. (Cornelius Tiers, Pres.; Heyward H. McAllister, Sec. Capital, $100,000. Directors: Cornelius Tiers, Andrew Bryson jr. Heywood H. McAllister, Robert M. Gallaway, R. Duncan Harris, Robert I. Sloan, Robert M. Miles, Alexander H. Tiers, John H. Pendleton, Thomas L. Snead, Thomas Swinyard) 1 Beaver
Rapid Transit & Bridge Construction Co. (Henry Keene, Pres.; Charles Lyman, Sec.; Marshall G. Moore, Treas. Capital, $3,000,000. Directors: Henry Keene, Charles Lyman, Marshall G. Moore, Casimir Tag, Henry W. Edye, Frank Sizerr, James Sinter, Alfred F. Walcott, R. W. V. Parker) 15 Broad
Rapp F. B. & Co. (Frank B. & John W. Rapp) 1000 Park av.
Rapp & Johnson Lumber Co. (Charles G. Rapp, Pres.; James C. Johnson, Sec.; Benjamin P. Johnson, Treas. Capital, $50,000. Directors: Charles G. Rapp, Benjamin P. & James C. Johnson) ft. E. 125th
Rapp, Loeser & Co. (Herman Rapp, John F. Loeser & August Roggenbrodt) 196 B'way
Rapp's J. H. Son & Co. (John H. Rapp & George Pieper) 53 Tompkins
Rappahannock Gold Mining Co. (John A. Macpherson, Pres.; Louis F. Bauersfeld, Sec. Capital, $250,000. Directors: John A. Macpherson, Louis F. Bauersfeld, George Thomson, William Hoffmann) 60 B'way
Rappard A. & Co. (Auguste Rappard, no Co.) 87 Greene
Raritan Hollow & Porous Brick Co. (Edward Keasbey, Pres.; Henry M. Keasbey, Sec. Capital, $110,000. Directors: Edward & Anthony Q. & Henry M. Keasbey) 115 B'way
Rasenberger C. & Son (Charles & Henry Rasenberger) 106 Chambers
Raskin & Abramson (dissolved) 119 Division
Rasmussen & Weise (Hans O. Rasmussen & Adolph Weise) Rider av. n E. 138th
Ratel & Liegeois (dissolved) 87 Crosby
Rath Nicholas & Co. (Nicholas & Matthew Rath) 30 S. William
Rath Brothers (Asmus & Frederick Rath) 222 G'wich
Rathbone Oil Tract Co. (David Thomson, Pres.; Allen L. Purves, Sec. Capital, $5,000,000. Directors: David Thomson, Allan L. Purves) 52 Wall
Rathbone A. H. & Co. (Aaron H. Rathbone, Fredcric W. Satterlee & Cleveland D. Fisher) 71 Wall
Rathbone R. C. & Son (Robert C. & R. Bleecker Rathbone) 187 B'way
Rathbone & Hefner (no inf.) 24 State
Rathborne C. L. & Co. (Charles L. Rathborne & Cord Meyer jr.:—special partner, Christopher C. Baldwin, $75,000; terminates 31st Dec. 1890) 11 Wall

CIRCULARS ADDRESSED TO ANY TRADE IN THE U. S. { Facilities
PROMPT, CAREFUL WORK } **THE TROW CITY DIRECTORY CO.,** { Unequalled.
AT MODERATE PRICES.   11 University Place.

RAT 250 RED

Rathbon J. P. & Co. (Jason F. Rathbun & Marshall Woodward) 40 Vesey
Rathbun W. L. & Co. (William L. Rathbun, no Co.) 232 Fulton
Rathgeber A. & H. (Adam & Henry) 36 Thompson av. W., Washn. mkt
Rathgeber F. & J. (Frank jr. & John) 273 Elizabeth
Rathkamp Brothers (dissolved) 84 W. B'way
Rathkamp & Grunwald (August Rathkamp & Frederick Grunwald) 84 W. B'way
Rathyen Brothers (Henry C. & Herman Rathyen) 367 Cherry
Ratkowsky R. & Brother (Harris & Aaron S. Ratkowsky) 104 E. B'way
Ratkowsky & Cohen (dissolved) 94 E. B'way
Rattan & Cane Co. (Foppes & Partisch, propra.) 20 Vesey
Ratz Henry & Brother (Henry & George Ratz jr.) 1223 Washn. av.
Rau Emanuel, Mfg. Co. (R. Mac'ay Bull, Pres.; Gerard M. Barretto, Sec. Capital, $1,000 ; further inf. refused) 51 Liberty
Rau Max L. & Sons (Max L. & Marcus & William Rau) 71 Leonard
Rauch D. & Co. (David Rauch & Charles Frommann) 131 Av. D
Rauch G. & W. J. (George & William J.) 1 Walker
Rauch H. & Son (Henry & Moses H. Rauch) 24 Av. B
Rauch Brothers (Ferdinand & Moses Rauch) 521 B'way
Rauh John & Son (John & John M. Rauh) 167 Alexander av.
Rauscher & Wielandt (Christian Rauscher & William Wielandt) 117 Prince
Rauth J. & Co. (Jacob Rauth & Charles Aaron) 284 Eighth av.
Raven & Co. (Henry S. Raven, Frederick Moyer & William Cross) 102 B'way
Ravenswood Art Glass Works (Emanuel Bergman, Pres.; Hugo S. Mack, Sec. Capital, $50,000. Directors: Emanuel Bergman, Simon & Hugo S. & Henry S. Mack, Henry Worms) 59 Park pl.
Rawak & Co. (Henry Rawak, no Co.) 534 B'way
Rawitzer S. & Co. (Simon & Herman Rawitzer) 138 Duane
Rawson H. B. & Co. (Horace B. & George S. Rawson) 45 South
Ray Mfg. Co. (no inf.) 62 Liberty
Ray C. H. & Co., (Conrad H. Ray & William S. Mowray jr.) 50 B'way
Ray J. & D. Repole (Jeremiah Ray & Daniel Repole) 44 Thompson
Ray, Hardy & Co. (dissolved) 50 B'way
Raymond A. & Co. (Aaron & Augustus Raymond) 129 Fulton & 254 B'way
Raymond C. P. & Co. (Charles P. & Robert M. Raymond & Frederick D. Dalzell) 70 South
Raymond F. C. & Co. (Frederick C. Raymond, no Co.) 5 Mercer
Raymond & Co. (hats) (dissolved) 80 Nassau
Raymond & Co. (mns. insts.) (dissolved) 254 W. 35th
Raymond & May (William F. Raymond & Joseph May jr.) 1175 Third av.
Raymond & Ryan (Charles E. Raymond & James F. Ryan) 2281 Third av.
Rayner & Steele (George W. Rayner & John R. Steele) 150 S. 5th av. & 7 Macdougal
Raynolds C. T. & Co. (Thomas B. Hidden, Edward L. Molineux & Edward H. Raynolds, only) 106 Fulton
Raynor George B. & Co. (George B. Raynor & Hiram R. Smith) 129 Broad

Raynor & Martin (William P. Raynor & William I. Martin) 115 William & 59 John
Razzetti Brothers (Joseph & Caesar Razzetti) 145 S. 5th av.
Rea Thomas H. & Co. (dissolved) 552 B'way
Reach A. J. & Co. (no inf.) 296 B'way
Read Fertilizer Co. (Isaac Read, Pres.; Clement Read, Treas. Capital, $230,000. Trustees: Isaac & Abram C. & Clement Read) 86 Wall
Read J. Parker, Co. (Henry E. Chapman, Pres.; John D. Brooks, Sec.; Charles H. Vibbard, Treas. Capital, $15,000. Directors: Henry E. Chapman, John D. Brooks, Charles H. Vibbard, Charles H. Tyrrell) 19 Barclay & 24 Park pl.
Read C. H. & Co. (Cassius H. Read & Edward S. Stokes) 1111 & 50 B'way & 7 Beaver
Read & Shelton (no inf.) 35 Frankfort
Ready Food Co. (Ltd.) (August Vonderburg, propr.) 329 G'wich
Reaglon & Son (Isaac V. & Clarence C. Reaglon) 12 Jacob
Real Estate Exchange & Auction Room (Ltd.) (George H. Scott, Pres.; Isaac Fromme, Sec.; George R. Read, Treas. Capital, $500,000. Directors: Hermann H. Cammann. George H. Scott, Richard V. Harnett, Myer S. Isaacs, Cornelius W. Luyster, J. Romaine Brown. Ira D. Warren, Isaac Fromme, George R. Read, Jere Johnson jr. Philip A. Smyth, Richard Deeves, Charles A. Schermerhorn) 66 Liberty
Real Estate Investment Co. (not inc.) (Henry G. Harris, Isaac J. Culling & Charles H. Woodhull) 260 B'way
Real Estate Roofing Co. (inf. unattainable) 169 Front
Reamer, Turner & Co. (Abraham Reamer, William E. Turner & Abraham Reamer jr.) 112 Front
Reardon J. A. & Son (John A. & Andrew A. Reardon) 107 W. 49th
Reardon & Morley (Jeremiah Reardon & Jeremiah Morley) 320 E. 26th
Recamier Mfg. Co. (Harriet Hubbard Ayer, Pres.; J. E. Eustis, Sec.; George D. Bentiys, Treas.; further inf. unattainable) 395 Fifth av.
Rechenberg William H. E. (William H. E. Rechenberg;—special partner, Mathilde D. Rechenberg, $10,000; terminates 14th Jan. 1891) 10 Desbrosses
Rechten & Rohrs (dissolved) 192 & 198 Hester
Reck Brothers (no inf.) 413 G'wich
Recknagel & Co. (Carl L. & Gustav A. Recknagel) 74 Cortlandt
Reckalek Brothers (William & Frederick Reckalek) 2632 Second av.
Red Bird Cons. Mining Co. (Henry Bradstreet, Pres.; N. Dana Whipple, Sec. Capital, $500,000. Directors: Henry Bradstreet, George H. Torres, Frank B. Whitfield, N. Dana Whipple) 115 D'way
Red Chief Gold Mining Co. (Charles Roblee, Pres.; Cornelius H. Webster jr, Sec.; Edward K. Kattell, Treas. Capital, $1,000,000. Directors: Charles Roblee, G. T. Rogers, J. B. Landfield, W. L. Griswold, Cornelius H. Webster jr. A. E. Baxter, D. B. Goodell, L. J. Lewis) 280 B'way
Red D Line of Steamships (Boulton, Bliss & Dallett, propra.) 71 Wall & Pier 50 E. R.
Red Sulphur Springs Water Co. (inf. unattainable) 590 Seventh av.
Reddaway F. & Co. (Frank Reddaway, no Co.) 52 New
Redding & Co. (Moses W. Redding, no Co.) 731 B'way
Redemption Mining & Milling Co. (Francis K. Pendleton, Pres.; Samuel L. Parrish, Sec. Capital, $2,000,000. Directors: Francis K. Pendleton, Samuel L. Parrish) 44 B'way

THE CALIGRAPH WRITING MACHINE,
HARTFORD, CONN.

Redfield & Lydecker (dissolved) 120 B'way

Redfield & Redfield (Amasa A. & Robert L. Redfield) 120 B'way

Redington & Mayer (Lyman W. Redington & Alexander U. Mayer) 250 B'way

Redlich William F. & Co. (William F. Redlich & Emil Schimpff) 332 Washn.

Redmayne Gas Stove Co. (refused) 39 Dey

Redmond & Co. (Edward Redmond, no Co.) 210 Washn. mkt

Redmond & Sheehy (Dennis Redmond & Patrick J. Sheehy) 142 Third av. & 612 Sixth av.

Redmond's James, Son (John L. Redmond) 380 Spring

Redner & Howe (John J. Redner & James P. Howe) 136 E. 42d

Reeber's J. Sons (George A. & William C. Reeber) ft. E. 107th

Reed Charles C. & Co. (Charles C. Reed, no Co.) 112 E. 14th

Reed Glass Co. (Emma A. Reed, propr.) 65 Warren

Reed Isaac B. & Co. (Isaac B. Reed & William T. A. Hart) 112 E. 13th

Reed Isaac H. & Co. (James B. Turner, only) 5 State

Reed Novelty Works (Edward D. St. George, propr.) 239 Centre

Reed F. & Son (Frederick & Franklin C. Reed) 2040 Seventh av.

Reed F. A. & Co. (Frank A. Reed, no Co.) 25 Ann

Reed J. P. & Co. (dissolved) 239 Centre

Reed Brothers (Arthur L. & Frederic P. Reed) 52 Warren

Reed & Auerbacher (William A. Reed & Louis H. Auerbacher) 220 Bowery

Reed & Bassett (Charles A. Reed & William B. Bassett) 353 B'way

Reed & Carnrick. (John Carnrick, Pres.; George W. Carnrick, Sec.; Allen Chamberlin, Treas. Capital, $400,000. Directors: John & George W. Carnrick, Allen Chamberlin, Richard S. Newcombe, Meyer & Henry Feuchtwanger) 447 G'wich

Reed & Flagg (Josiah H. Reed & William H. Flagg) 11 Pine

Reed & Herzog (Thomas Reed jr. & Alfred M. Herzog) 30 Broad

Reed & Hurlbut (Josiah H. Reed & Horace A. Hurlbut) 11 Pine

Reed & Keller (Henry F. Reed & Samuel Keller) 122 W. 25th

Reed & Powell Transp. Co. (inf. unattainable) Pier 33 (old) N. R.

Reed & Roosevelt (dissolved) 46 Exchange pl.

Reed, Hall & Hewlett (Frederick P. Read, Henry J. Hall & George B. Hewlett) 20 Platt

Rees & Rees (William Ap & Howell C. Rees) 307 Fourth av. & 232 E. 49th

Rees' Hans, Sons (Norman I. & Frank Rees) 17 Ferry

Reese Alexander & Co. (Alexander Reese & Henry Illexelzer) 104 Second av.

Reese S. W. & Co. (Samuel W. Reese & Christian H. Hanson) 73 Cortlandt & 29 Church

Reese & Hagen (Henry A. Reese & Henry Hagen) 334 Washn.

Reese & Mandler (Henry Reese & John Mandler) 311 Av. B

Reeve, Osborn & Co. (dissolved) 97 Water

Reeves Robert C. Co. (Robert C. Reeves, Pres.; Samuel C. B. Heiss, Sec.; Capital, $10,000. Directors: Robert C. Reeves, Samuel C. B. Heiss, Alice Reeves) 165 Water

Reeves S. H. & Co. (William E. & Caroline &

Anna J. & Lucretia M. Reeves, only) 380 Hudson

Reeves & Todd (Alfred G. Reeves & Ambrose G. Todd) 55 Liberty

Refeld Brothers (John B. Refeld, only) 126 Av. C

Refined Food Co. (Fillmore Moore, Pres.; Alexander H. Moore, Sec. Capital, $20,000. Trustees: Fillmore Moore, Adrian H. Joline) 9 E. 17th

Regan Brothers (James Regan, only) 2057 Seventh av.

Regan & Higgins (F. A. Regan & Jeremiah O. Higgins) 50 E. 59th

Regan & Hoagland (dissolved) 219 E. 120th

Regenburg & Co. (Julius Regenburg, Co. refused) 25 Whitehall

Regenhard, Shevill & Co. (Herman Regenhard, James B. O. Shevill & Frederick C. Cassel:— special partner, Randolph N. Bowlby, Boston, Mass., $5,000; terminates 1st July, 1892) 46 Dey

Rehm & Co. (Carl Rehm & George E. Koch) 157 Fulton

Rehmann R. & Co. (no inf.) 1076 Second av.

Rehorn & Son (dissolved) 2058 First av.

Reich & Linn (dissolved) 957 Third av.

Reich & Livesey (dissolved) 115 B'way

Reichard & Co. (Gustav Reichard, Co.refused) 226 Fifth av.

Reichardt F. Alfred & Co. (F. Alfred Reichardt, no Co.) 1328 B'way

Reichardt Fritz & Co. (dissolved) 20 Dey

Reichart & Blume (Francis X. Reichart & D. Hugo Blume) 354 E. 54th

Reiche Charles & Brother (Herman Reiche, only) 96 Park row

Reicher W. & Co. (William Delcher & Joseph Zablocki) 97 Stanton

Reichert & Co. (Emma K. Reichert & Frederick Kiefer) 221 Mercer, 84 N. Moore & 135 W. 26th

Reichhelm F. P. & Co. (Edward P. Reichhelm & Charles A. Leibman) 80 Nassau

Reid James & Co. (James J. Reid, only) 57 Broad

Reid John & Son (dissolved) 233 B'way

Reid M. J. & Co. (Mary J. Reid, no Co.) 277 Lenox av.

Reid Brothers (liquors) (James & Joseph Reid) 257 W. 29th

Reid Brothers (paints) (George & Walter Reid) 1472 Third av.

Reid & Alexander (dissolved) 816 Sixth av.

Reid & Barry (Peter Reid & William I. Barry) 108 Worth

Reid & Brennan (Robert W. Reid & Edward P. Brennan) 233 B'way

Reid & Co. (refused) 57 W. 125th

Reid & Mills (dissolved) 120 B'way

Reiff & Rosenhain (Charles Reiff & Jacob Rosenhain) 930 Second av.

Reilay & Ballard (Charles B. Reilay & Nathan Ballard) 216 Franklin

Reiley & Co. (dissolved) 381 Canal

Reilley T. F. & Son (Terence F. & Richard S. Reilley jr.) 416 W. 42d

Reilley Brothers (Terence F. & Richard S. Reilley) 418 W. 42d

Reilly Grate Bar Co. (Salamander Grate Bar Co. proprs.) 110 Liberty

Reilly D. J. & Co. (Oscar J. Maigne & estate of Dennis J. Reilly) 224 Pearl

Reilly T. & Co. (Thomas Reilly, no Co.) 18 Bond

Reilly Brothers (harness) (Patrick & Jeremiah Reilly) 2464 Third av.

Reilly Brothers (ice) (Edward & John & Peter & Michael Reilly) 441 E. 119th

Reilly & Donohue (John J. Reilly & Patrick Donohue) 4 E. 59th

Reilly & Guy (Patrick F. Reilly & William T. Guy) 82 Whitehall & 66 Pearl

Reilly & Neems (inf. unattainable) 268 W. 34th

Reilly & Ware (John Reilly & Frederick A. Ware) 263 B'way

Reimann & Co. (Rudolph Reimann & Julius Badarsky) 694 Ninth av.

Reimer & Gohres (dissolved) 854 Fifth

Reimherr & Co. (George Reimherr, no Co.) 351 Pearl

Reincke & Shafer (Paul F. Reincke & George T. Shafer) 48 Delancey

Reiners Brothers (Dedcrick & Henry & John M. Meiners) 101 W. 21st

Reinhard Brothers (Henry F. & George W. Reinhard) 165 B'way

Reinhardt George N. & Co. (George N. & John G. Reinhardt & Charles F. Kleiu) 697 E. 162d & 3602 Third av.

Reinhardt Brothers (bakers) (dissolved) 181 E. Houston

Reinhardt Brothers (drygds.) (Henry & Aaron Reinhardt) 105 Av. B

Reinheimer B. & Son (Benjamin & Henry Reinheimer) 1346 First av.

Reinheimer Brothers (Herman & Louis Reinheimer) 74 E. Houston

Reinking V. J. & Co, (dissolved) 417 E. 9th

Reintans R. A. & Co. (Reinhold A. Reintans & William Fiedler) 82 Third av.

Reis Robert & Co. (Robert Reis, Pres.; Alphonse E. Voss, Sec.; Abraham Silverstine, Treas. Capital, $15,000. Directors: Robert Reis, Alphonse E. Voss, Abraham Silverstine) 520 B'way

Reis & Newman (Leopold Reis & Abraham Newman) 177 Lewis

Reisert A. & F. Orth (Anthony Reisert & Frederick Orth) 181 Prince & 122 Sullivan

Reiset Frederic & Co. (Frederic Reiset, Gustav A. Washer & Henri Barbelet) 78 Hudson

Reisman Brothers (Elias & Louis Reisman) 202 Stanton

Reismann & Wolf (Gustav Reismann & Theodore Wolf) 192 Front

Reiss E. & Co. (no inf.) 141 Attorney

Reiss & Brady (Solomon Reiss, Siegmund Brady & Baruch Wolff) 260 Washn.

Reiss & Waldeck (Henry M. Reiss & Henry Waldeck) 87 Cortlandt

Reiss & Zimmermann (Marcus Reiss & Samuel Zimmermann) 104 E. Houston

Reisser George & Co. (George Reisser & Frederick Dreyer) 75 Washn. mkt

Reitlinger A. H. & Co. (Alexander H. Reitlinger, no Co.) 41 Spruce

Reitman & Mayer (Albert Reitman & Joseph Mayer) 303 E. Houston

Reitmayr Frank & Co. (dissolved) 530 Courtlandt av

Reliable Printing & Blank Book Mfg. Co. (Philip Ascher, Pres.; John J. Connelly, Sec.; Eugene C. Patterson, Treas. Capital, $75,000. Directors: Philip Ascher, John J. Connelly, Eugene C. Patterson) 17 Rose

Relief Mfg. Co. (inf. unattainable) 57 B'way

Rembrandt House (John Elderkin, Pres.; Ehrick K. Rossiter, Treas.; William Sartain, Sec. Capital, $96,000; further inf. refused) 152 W. 57th

Remington Standard Typewriter (Wyckoff, Seamans & Benedict, propra.) 327 B'way

Remington H. H. & Co, (Henry H. Remington & Franklin F. Friedman) 60 B'way

Remsen & Parsons (Daniel S. Remsen & Frank H. Parsons) 69 Wall

Remy, Schmidt & Pleissner (William E. Remy, Fedor Schmidt & Guido Pleissner 43 White

Renard & Co. (Charles F. Renard & Ferdinand F. Francke) 684 B'way

Renauld & Niederstadt (H. L. Charles Renauld & Albert K. K. & Edward Niederstadt) 58 Water

Rendle Co. (Ltd.) (inf. unattainable) 2 Wall

Rendrock Powder Co. (Jasper R. Rand, Pres.; Addison C. Rand, Treas. Directors: Jasper R. & Addison C. Rand, Nathan W. Horton, Silas R. Divine) 22 Park pl.

Renn L. & Son (Ludwig & Jules J. Renn) 758 B'way

Renner Brothers (Cornelius & Charles Renner) 129 Waverley pl.

Renulson & Brown (James C. Renuison & Alexander S. Brown) 38 Dover

Rent Guarantee Co. (William A. Fowler & Co., proprs.) 540 Grand

Renton H. S. & Paul A. (dissolved) 103 E. 14th

Rentz & Lange (dissolved) 163 Fourth av.

Renwick, Aspinwall & Russell (James Renwick, J. Lawrence Aspinwall, William H. Russell & William W. Renwick) 71 B'way

Reporter Printing Co. (Am. Mercantile & Collection Assn. proprs.) 284 B'way & 7 Barclay

Ropper & Rosenschein (Henry F. Ropper & Hyman Rosenschein) 60 Essex

Requa J. M. & Co. (James M. Requa, no Co.) 18 B'way

Requa & Lewis (Samuel Requa & Albert Lewis) Pier 34 (old) N. R.

Roshower J. & Co. (Joseph Roshower & August Heck) 70 Spring

Ressel & Son (John & Emil Ressel) 75 First av.

Restaurant Furniture Co. (Edward R. Biehler, propr.) 180 Wooster

Restorff & Bettmann (Theodore G. Restorff & William Bettmann) 70 Pine

Resumption Mining & Smelting Co. (Charles H. Tompkins, Pres.; William V. Carr, Sec. Capital, $500,000. Directors, N. F. Hurcomb, Charles H. Tompkins, Lewis F. Hostelmann, William A. Kirkland, William V. Carr) 15 Cortlandt

Retail Coal Exchange (Thomas Thedford, Pres.; Jeremiah Pangborn jr. Sec.; John H. Frank Treas.) 305 W. 23d

Retail Dealers' Protective Assn. (Jesse Platt, Pres.; John T. Weeks. Sec.; George I. Wichman, Treas.; further inf. refused) 39 Union sq. W.

Retail Grocers' Publishing Co. (Henry H. Ritterbusch, Pres.; Henry Goldberger, Sec.; Charles F. Bussing, Treas. Capital, $10,000. Directors: John Rylers, Henry Goldberger, John F. Blohm, Michael Hahn, Herman H. Becker, Charles F. Bussing, C. A. Mettler, J. H. Ahrens, Henry H. Ritterbusch, H. H. M. Bruninga, J. Laubenberger, B. Ottmer) 213 E. 23d

Retail Ice Exchange (inf. unattainable) 260 Eighth av.

Retsof Mining Co. (William Foster jr, Pres.; Robert S. Walker, Treas. Capital, $3,600,000 ; further inf. refused) 146 B'way

Rottagliata L. & G. (Louis & George) 173 Worth

Rettig Philip & Sons (Philip & Philip jr. & Peter Rettig) 239 E. 28th

Reuhenstone H. & Son (Hyman & Isaac Reubenstone) 109 William

Routerdahl & Wilmot (Olof Routerdahl & Isidor B. Wilmot) 1244 B'way

Review Publishing Co. (Sheppard Knapp, Pres.; Edward H. Bailey, Sec. Capital, $25,000. Directors: Sheppard Knapp, Edward H. Bailey, William Berri, William A. Harris) 335 B'way

Rewald & Weber (dissolved) 35 Hester

**FOR THE BEST CO-PARTNERSHIP IN THE BEST
CORPORATION SEE PAGE F IN BACK OF BOOK**

Rexford Brothers (William M. Rexford, only) 29 Broad
Reyes & Pressinger (dissolved) 111 B'way
Reynard & Co. (Henry Reynard, Co. refused) 248 E. 117th
Reynders John & Co. (John & Charles Reynders) 308 Fourth av. & 814 E. 22d
Reynes Brothers & Co. (Antonio & Jaime Reynes, no Co.) 46 Exchange pl.
Reynolds Card Mfg. Co. (George P. Schinzel jr, Pres.; Robert Schinzel, Treas. Capital, $20,000. Directors: George P. jr. & Robert Schinzel) 60 Duane & 466 Cherry
Reynolds James E. & Co. (James E. Reynolds & George W. Morgan jr.) 70 Thomas & 443 W. 15th
Reynolds A. L. & J. J. (Alvah L. & John J.) 808 G'wich
Reynolds J. E. & Co. (James E. Reynolds, no Co.) 17 New & 68 D'way
Reynolds M. & Co. (Martin Reynolds & Philip F. Donohue) 25 Centre
Reynolds Brothers (Bryant C. & Jesse Reynolds) 117 John, 2406 Third av. & Vanderbilt av. W. n Kingsbridge rd.
Reynolds & Chambers (Christopher H. Reynolds & Andrew Z. Chambers) 141 Pearl
Reynolds & Co. (dissolved) 222 W. 51st
Reynolds & Darcy (Robert W. Reynolds & Philip J. Darcy) 59 W. 27th
Reynolds & Harrison (Clinton G. Reynolds & Robert L. Harrison) 59 Wall
Reynolds & Hunter (William H. Reynolds & Thomas Irving Hunter) 46 Dockman
Reynolds & Myers (Edward B. Reynolds & Evert Myers) 486 B'way
Reynolds & Nichols (dissolved) 2384 Eighth av.
Reynolds, Welch & Co. (John H. Reynolds, James Donaldson & Ellis G. Welch) 55 B'way
Reynolds' H. M., Sons (Edward J. & Michael J. Reynolds) 222 W. 51st
Rheinfrank John & Co. (John Rheinfrank & Henry Ganzenmuller) 865 Third & ft E. 14th
Rhode Island Locomotive Works (Charles Felix Mason, Pres.; Arthur Livingston Mason, Sec.; William P. Chapin, Treas. Capital, $500,000. Directors: William P. Chapin, Charles Felix & Carl Philip & Arthur Livingston Mason) 58 Pine
Rhodes Benjamin N. & Co. (dissolved) 96 Front
Rhodes Bradford & Co. (Bradford & Robert J. Rhodes) 76 William
Rhodes George H. & Co. (George H. Rhodes & Frank Woodward) 101 Pearl & 64 Stone
Rhoner Frank & Co. (Frank Rhoner, no Co.) 440 E. 23d & 487 E. 22d
Rhule & Thomas (John W. Rhule & Evan R. Thomas) 150 Nassau
Rice E., Mfg. Co. (not Inc.) (Emanuel Rice & Henry Flesch) 405 Broome
Rice Musical String Co. (George P. Nelson, Pres.; Thomas Nelson, Treas. Capital, $30,000; further inf. refused) 161 W. 29th
Rice William B & Co. (William B. Rice & T. Warren Welter) 2282 Third av.
Rice L. H. & Co. (Lewis H. Rice & Moses Seligman) 40 Walker
Rice S. W. & Co. (Solomon W. & Edward R. Brock, only) 51 Dey
Rice Brothers (Merritt H. & William B. Rice) 86 Park pl.
Rice & Bijur (dissolved) 32 Nassau
Rice & Brother (Bernard & Ignatius Rice) 474 B'way & 186 Grand
Rice & Davis (Albert C. Rice & Abraham Davis) 151 Third av.
Rice & McCoy (dissolved) 206 Hester

Rice & Thompson (Edwin T. Rice & Frank Thompson) 50 Liberty
Rice Brothers & Tiffany (A. Wheelock & Frederick B. Rice & D. E. Tiffany) 148 Duane
Rice, Duval & Luckey (Harry Rice, Lawrence Duval & Robert Luckey) 231 B'way
Rice, Quinby & Co. (Edward C. Rice, Franklin Quinby & Edward Bailey) 114 Produce Ex.
Rich Aquila, Paint & Color Co. (Aquila Rich, Pres.; Edward C. Winter, Sec. Capital, $100,000. Directors: Aquila Rich, Edward C. Winter, A. E. Lincoln, N. D. Lent) 84 William
Rich E. C., Co. (Ltd.) (Edwin T. Holmes, Pres.; Eleazer C. Rich, Sec. Capital, $25,000; further inf. unattainable) 166 Franklin
Rich Hill Electric Placer Co. (Wells H. Bates, Pres.; Samuel D. Hayward, Sec.; Sterling F. Hayward, Treas. Capital, $12,000,000. Directors: Wells H. & Dewitt C. Bates, Samuel D. & Sterling F. Hayward, S. E. Edmunds) 11 Wall
Rich William A., Shoe Co. (Ltd.) (In liquidation) 104 Duane
Rich C. E. & Co. (Carlos E. Rich & Gustav J. Reno) 40 Walker
Rich D. & Co. (David & Alfred J. Rich) 31 Park pl.
Rich H. S. & Co. (Henry S. Rich, Smith P. Fowler & J. Frank Nickerson) 206 B'way
Rich & Harris (Isaac B. Rich & William Harris) 1207 B'way
Rich & Manheimer (Charles M. Rich & Morris Manheimer) 81 Grand
Rich & Son (dissolved) 124 W. Houston
Richard C. B. & Co. (Oscar L. Richard & Emil L. Boas, only) 61 B'way & 30 Platt
Richard J. & Son (John & J. Frank Richard) 4 Park pl.
Richards Daniel W. & Co. (Daniel W. Richards & Morton B. Smith) 92 Mangin & 68 Wall
Richards E. Ira & Co. (E. Ira & Lucy M. Richards) 200 D'way
Richards A. S. & Co. (Abiathar Richards, only) 61 Reade
Richards J. J. & Co. (James J. Richards & Warren Springstoed) 278 W. 25th
Richards J. J. & J. M. (James J. & James M.) 104 B'way
Richards & Arnold (John M. Richards & Albert W. Arnold) 59 Fifth av.
Richards & Brown (J. Tredwell Richards & Alfred S. Brown) 58 William
Richards & Co. (apparatus) (Leonard Richards, no Co.) 41 Barclay
Richards & Co. (patents) (William B. Richards, no Co.) 88 B'way
Richards & Heald (George & Dickinson W. Richards & John O. Heald) 62 Wall
Richards & Sause (Benjamin Richards & Edmond J. Sause jr.) 53 Liberty
Richardson Enos & Co. (Enos & Frank H. Richardson) 23 Maiden la.
Richardson J. Smith & Co. (J. Smith Richardson & Daniel R. Blackford) 29 Thompson av. W. Washn. mkt
Richardson A. M. & Co. (Alvin M. & James W. Richardson) 106 W. 42d
Richardson B. & Son (Briton & Driton H. Richardson) 48 Mercer
Richardson J. W. & Co. (George H. Richardson & Aldridge B. Gardiner, only) 196 D'way
Richardson P. C. & Co. (Parker C. Richardson & Theodore F. Stanford) 60 Warren
Richardson & Boynton Co. (Henry T. Richardson, Pres.; Frederick B. Richardson, Sec.; Dwight S. Richardson, Treas. Capital, $250,000. Directors: Henry T. & Augustus F. & Dwight S. & Frederick B. Richardson) 232 Water

TYPEWRITING DONE BY THE TROW CITY DIRECTORY CO., 11 University Place.

Richardson & Co. (Joseph N. Richardson, no Co.) 243 Canal
Richardson & Foos (George Patterson, only) 112 Fourth av.
Richardson & Heney (George H. Richardson & John S. Heney) 204 Spring
Richardson & Morgan Co. (Tallmadge Baker, Pres.; Alonzo R. Morgan, Treas. Edward V. Baker, Sec. Capital, $75,000. Directors: Frederick Ayer, Tallmadge & Edward V. Baker, Jeremiah J. Richardson, Alonzo R. Morgan) 92 Beekman
Richdale & Perry (James C. Richdale & Charles G. Perry) 804 G'wich
Richman & Mayers (Jacob Richman & James Mayers) 62 E. B'way
Richman, Schmidt & Wolf (Daniel W. Richman, Sigmund A. Schmidt & Arthur D. Wolf) 393 B'way
Richmond (The) (apartment house) (inf. unattainable) 20 Nassau
Richmond Union Passenger Railway Co. (no inf.) 63 Wall
Richmond Brothers (Edward B. & Frederick H. Richmond) 132 Greene
Richmond & Alleghany R. R. Co. (inf. unattainable) 2 Wall
Richmond & Co. (Harry S. Richmond & Frank C. Mott) 127 Fifth av.
Richmond & Creed (dissolved) 649 Hudson
Richmond & Danville R. R. Co. (John H. Inman, Pres.; Richard Brooke, Sec.; John W. Hall, Treas. Capital, $3,000,000. Directors: George S. Scott, Calvin S. Brice, H. C. Fahnestock, John A. Rutherford, J. C. Maben, Samuel Thomas, John G. Moore, John C. Calhoun, Charles M. McGhee, John H. Hall, John S. Barbour, Samuel M. Inman) 2 Wall
Richmond & Fischer (Louis Richmond & Harris M. Fischer) 48 Mercer
Richmond & West Point Terminal Railway & Warehouse Co. (John H. Inman, Pres.; further inf. refused) 2 Wall
Richtberg & Schmidt (Ferdinand Richtberg & Charles Schmidt) 779 Second av.
Richter Electric Construction Co. (Charles Richter Pres.; A. G. Gray, Sec.; Hiram L. White, Treas.; further inf. unattainable) 20 Cortlandt
Richter H. F., Publishing Co. (Herman F. Richter, propr.) 50 Union sq. E.
Richter Simon & Co. (no inf.) r 252 Delancey
Richter C. H. & Co. (Charles H. Richter, Ferdinand Neurohr & Gustavo Knaper) 7 Pine
Richter & Gerth (dissolved) 885 B'way
Richter's H., Sons (Bruno & Daniel & Max Richter) 502 D'way & 48 Crosby
Richters & Stein (dissolved) no address
Rickard & Co. (dissolved) 35 Little W. 12th
Rickard & Hewitt (Alexander Rickard & Frank R. Hewitt) 104 John
Rickard & Hubbe (Luke W. Rickard & Martin Hubbe) 24 State
Ricker Hiram & Sons (Edward F. & Alvin B. & Hiram W. Ricker, only) 164 Nassau
Ricker & Lawrence (dissolved) 875 Hudson & 28 Ninth av.
Ricketts F. M., Co. (dissolved) 18 Cortlandt
Ridabock & Co. (Henry G. Ridabock, no Co.) 141 Grand
Ridder A. F. & Co. (dissolved) 114 Washn. mkt
Riddle Mfg. Co. (refused) 538 W. 23d
Rider Engine Co. (William M. Sayer, Pres.; Henry Sinsabaugh, Sec. Capital, $90,000. Trustees: William Murray Sayer, Henry Sinsabaugh, Richard S. & William Murray Sayer jr.) 37 Dey

Ridgely & Co. (William F. Ridgely & M. Philip Emden) 76 Worth
Ridgewood Ice Co. (John Clark, Pres.; Edwin H. Close, Sec. Directors: John & William J. Clark, Edwin H. Close, James H. Cousans, Grove P. Jenks) ft. Rutgers, ft. Third, ft. E. 53d, ft. E. 79th & ft. W. 24th
Ridgewood Re-Distilling Co. (Leopold Blaier, Pres.; Jacob P. Balter, Treas. Capital, $25,000 ; further inf. refused) 701 Washn.
Ridgway J. W. & C. W. (James W. & Charles W.) 45 B'way
Ridgway & Griffin (no inf.) 43 Leonard
Ridley Edward & Sons (Edward A. & Arthur J. Ridley, only) 315 & 289 Grand
Ridley & Co. (Helen E. Aitken & Edwin D. Bensel, only) 139 Chambers
Rieder G. & J. Haag (George Rieder & Jacob Haag) 132 Second
Rieger & Cooke (John H. Rieger & Theodore R. Cooks) 71 Liberty
Rieger & Klussmann (Hugo Rieger & Herman Klussmann) 2938 Tenth av.
Rieger's Christian, Sons (Christian jr. & Charles & Edward Rieger) 559 E. 144th
Riehl & Conghlin (Julius Riehl & Michael Coughlin) 1253 Ninth av.
Riehle & Steinberger (dissolved) 300 Monroe
Rieken & Hopkins (Henry Rieken & Jesse L. Hopkins) 112 William
Rieken & Luerssen (Henry Rieken & Frederick W. Luerssen) 99 Sixth av.
Riemer J. & Son (John & Theodore Riemer) 154 Orchard
Rieper F. & W. Urban (Frederick Rieper & William Urban) 69 Av. A
Rieper Brothers (Henry & Jacob Rieper) 1120 Ninth av.
Rieper & Schmoelk (Henry Rieper & William N. Schmoelk) 93 Varick
Ries Brothers (John F. & Herman H. Ries) 138 First av.
Ries & Janssen (dissolved) 22 Rivington
Riesenburger Alexander & Co. (dissolved) 317 Canal
Riessner & Co. (dissolved) 406 Pearl
Riester & Schmidt (Joseph Riester & Gottlieb A. Schmidt) 1861 Lex. av.
Riesthal A. de & Co. (Alphonse & Gustave E. de Riesthal) 55 Murray & 200 South
Rieth J. F. & Co. (Joseph F. & George Rieth) 267 Third av.
Rigall George & Co. (no inf.) r 220 William
Rigall & Sons (Peter & Charles B. & Robert Rigali) 26 W. 13th
Rigerone D. & T. Chieffo (Dominick Rigerone & Thomas Chieffo) 234 Division
Riggs George (George C. Riggs & George W. MacCutcheon) 99 Franklin
Rigney Thomas & Co. (Thomas Rigney & Galatian F. Harmon) 121 Pearl
Riker William B. & Son (William D. & William H. Riker) 553 Sixth av. 585 Washn. & 87 Clarkson
Riker J. L. & D. S. (John L. & Daniel S. & William J. & John J. Riker) 45 Cedar
Riker & Son (E. Stanton & Nathan W. Riker) 966 Sixth av. & 49 Liberty
Riker & Stonenll (Clarence B. Riker & Frank S. Stonaall) 101 Park pl.
Riker & Walsh (dissolved) 20 Chambers
Riley W. H. & Co. (William H. Riley, no Co.) 21 Mercer
Riley & Crosby (no inf.) 1804 Park av.
Riley, French & Heffron (William H. Riley, George H. French & Frederick D. Heffron) 176 B'way

THADDEUS DAVIDS CO., **WRITING INKS, SEALING WAX,**
MAKE THE BEST **MUCILAGE.**

RIL 255 ROB

Riley-Osborn Mfg. Co. (John M. Riley, Pres.; Joseph K. Osborn, Sec.; Gabriel Schwab, Treas. Capital, $300,000. Directors: John M. Riley, Joseph K. Osborn, Gabriel Schwab) 529 B'way & 41 Greene

Rilling & Schock (Charles F. Rilling & Gustave Schock) 530 W. 29th

Rindskopf & Barbier (Charles S. Rindskopf & Albert L. Barbier) 628 B'way & 100 Crosby

Rindskopf & Schwab (no inf.) 417 Broome

Rinehart E. & Son (Egbert & Jesse T. Rinehart) 254 W. 23d

Ringgold Hypatia Co. (inf. unattainable) 142 W. 23d

Ringler George & Co. (Frederick A. Ringler, Pres.; John C. Boettner, Treas.; John C. Orth, Sec. Capital, $600,000. Directors: William G. Ringler, John C. Boettner, Christian Hackmeister, Frederick Orth, Frederick A. Ringler) 212 E. 92d

Ringler F. A. & Co. (Frederick A. & Justin Ringler) 21 Barclay & 26 Park pl.

Rinn & Co. (dissolved) 66 S. 5th av.

Rintein August & Son (August & Anthony J. Rintein) 88 Cortlandt

Rio Grande Western Railway Co. (William J. Palmer, Pres.; Charles W. Drake, Treas. Capital, $15,000,000. Directors: William J. Palmer, Frederic P. Olcott, James C. Parrish, Charles J. Canda, J. Kennedy Tod, George Foster Peabody, Joseph D. Potts, Bartholdi Schlesinger, D. C. Dodge) 32 Nassau

Riordan & Cunningham (dissolved) 615 E. 18th

Ripley George D. & Co. (George D. & Horace Ripley) 240 Pearl

Ripley George H., Co. (inoperative) 254 B'way

Ripley & Co. (George D. Ripley, no Co.) 66 B'way

Rippe & Wilkens (Frederick Rippe & Christian Wilkens) 236 G'wich

Risley Chas. F., Co. (inf. unattainable) 62 Cortlandt

Rist & Maxwell (Frederick C. Rist & John H. Maxwell) 466 Cherry

Ritch Thomas & Son (Thomas & William T. Ritch) 14 Vesey & 408 Front

Ritchie George B. & Co. (George B. Ritchie:— special partners, John B. Cumming & Co. London, Eng., $10,000; terminates 31st Dec. 1890) 57 Ferry

Ritchie J. W. & Co. (John W. Ritchie, no Co.) 414 Seventh av.

Ritt & Steinborg (dissolved) 10 Rutgers pl.

Ritter Brothers (Marcus & Louis Ritter) 743 E. 9th

Ritterman M. I. & Co. (Morris L. Ritterman & David B. Kraemer) 102 W. 126th

River & Rail Electric Light Co. (George L. Wright, Pres.; Frank F. Randolph, Sec. Capital, $1,000,000. Directors: George L. Wright, Albon Man, Stilson Hutchins, Simeon B. Chittenden, Frank F. Randolph, Myron H. Phelps, Henry E. Tremain, William Main, Frederick W. Holls) 45 B'way

Riverside Bank (Floyd Clarkson, Pres.; Henry C. Copeland, Cashier. Capital, $1,000,000. Directors: John J. Clancy, J. Edward Simmons, William Rankin, John Mulford, Frank A. Bochmann, Max Ams, Charles N. Taintor, James H. Hume, Daniel Seymour, John Reisenweber, Floyd Clarkson, Augustus F. Holly, Alexander Brown jr. George R. Lansing) 962 Eighth av.

Riverside Bridge & Iron Works (inf. unattainable) 18 B'way

Riverside Instalment Clothing Co. (Joseph Jandernal, propr.) 350 W. 16th

Riverside Pharmacy Co. (Capital, $5,000; further inf. unattainable) no address

Riverside Soap Co. (Garret A. Hobart, Pres.; Albert A. Wilcox, Sec. Capital, $10,000. Directors: Garret A. Hobart, George Law, Albert A. Wilcox) 20 Platt

Riverside & Fort Lee Ferry Co. (John S. McWilliam, Pres.; William Moores, Sec. Capital, $150,000. Directors: Antonio Haslnes, James B. Paulding, Charles Place, William Moores, John M. & John S. McWilliam) 45 Pine

Riz Robert & Thomas, 430 W. 58th

Rizzolo & Co. (dissolved) 55 Crosby

Roach E. H. & Co. (E. H. Roach, Co. refused) 52 New

Roach & Guthorn (George P. Roach & Joseph Guthorn) 305 Bowery

Roane Brothers (James H. & George B. Roane) 392 Spring & 126 Tenth av.

Robartes & Son (Frank W. jr. & estate of Frank W. Robartes) 5 Dey

Robb & Morrison (John M. Robb & James Morrison) 647 W. 50th

Robbins George B. & Co. (George B. Robbins & Henry W. Bell) 9 Bleecker & 2477 Third av.

Robbins A. & M. (Milton Robbins, only) 108 Fulton mkt & 217 Front

Robbins Brothers (Frank W. & Arthur J. Robbins) 81 Centre

Robbins & Appleton (Royal & Royal E. Robbins, Daniel F. Appleton, Ezra C. Fitch & Francis R. Appleton) 5 Bond & 10 John

Roberson W. H. & Co. (William H. & William C. Roberson) 197 West

Robert J. Eugene & Co. (dissolved) 30 Maiden la.

Robert's A. A., Sons (Samuel & Henry Robert) 576 Second av. & 192 First av.

Roberts George I. & Brothers (George I. & Edwin H. & M. Elmer Roberts) 471 Fourth av.

Roberts A. F. & Co. (Addison F. Roberts, Henry M. Requa & Clarence F. Moulton) 24 State

Roberts Brothers (eating.) (Roderick E. & George F. Roberts) 579 First av.

Roberts Brothers (grain) (W. Lea Roberts, only) 425 Produce Ex.

Roberts Brothers (stevedores) (John J. & James C. & Charles F. Roberts) 87 South

Roberts & Bevan (Robert Roberts & John Bevan) 22 Christopher

Roberts & Bokee (Martin Roberts & Alfred W. Bokee) 144 Front

Roberts & Collin (George H. Roberts jr. & N. Park Collin) 11 Front

Roberts & Co. (florists) (Robert Roberts & Leopold Zimmermann) 1166 Ninth av.

Roberts & Co. (real estate) (B. J. Roberts, no Co.) 2056 Seventh av.

Roberts & Co. (shoes) (Herbert A. Roberts & Della C. Rich) 16 Bible h.

Roberts & Cook (dissolved) 25 Park pl.

Roberts & King (John C. Roberts & John F. H. King jr.) 29 South & Pier 11 E. R.

Roberts & Merkel (dissolved) 400 Tenth av.

Roberts & Morris (dissolved) 11 West

Roberts & Priestley (Thomas Roberts & Samuel R. Priestley) 11 West

Roberts & Scofield (dissolved) 74 B'way

Roberts, Cushman & Co. (Richard S. & Nathan B. & Edward Roberts, only) 175 Greene

Roberts-Drevoort Electric Co. (Ltd.) (Edmund Tweedy, Pres.; Bernhard T. Vetterlein, Sec.; Samuel B. Lawrence, Treas. Capital, $250,000. Directors: Edmund Tweedy, Isaiah L. Roberts, Samuel B. Lawrence, Bernhard T. Vetterlein, S. C. Barnum, Henry L. Drevoort, A. W. Burchard, G. R. Tweedy, C. H. Merritt) 206 B'way & 287 Fifth av.

Robertson Henry M. & Co. (Henry M. Robertson & George T. Sinclair) 319 B'way

Robertson Lawrence D. & Son (dissolved) 7 Barclay

Robertson Walter & Co. (Walter Robertson & Charles D. Harrod) 450 G'wich
Robertson E. R. & Co. (Edwin R. Robertson, no Co.) 26 Cotton Ex.
Robertson L. F. & Sons (Julius Robertson, only) 29 Spruce
Robertson & Co. (bkbinders) (Andrew Robertson, no Co.) 205 Water
Robertson & Co. (printers) (dissolved) 52 Dey
Robertson & Hoople (Loring A. Robertson & William G. Hoople) 84 Gold
Robertson & James (Joseph L. Robertson & Charles E. James) 7 Nassau
Robertson & Kaufman (Albert Robertson & Jacob Kaufman) 545 B'way & 116 Mercer
Robertson & Smethurst (John J. Robertson & William R. Smethurst) 165 W. B'way
Robertson & Wallace (Alexander J. Robertson & John M. Wallace) 52 Dey
Robertsons & Harmon (Arthur R. & Roderick Robertson & Frank D. Harmon) 32 Park pl.
Robins & Foy (John V. Robins & Augustus Foy) 52 John
Robins & Wright (George H. Robins & John P. Wright) 146 Front
Robinson Cons. Mining Co. (John Jay White, Pres.; Frank C. Poucher, Sec. Capital, $10,-000,000. Directors: John Jay White, Frank C. Poucher, Arthur E. White, A. J. Robinson) 45 B'way
Robinson Frederick S. & Co. (Frederick S. Robinson & Louis Contencin) 126 Pearl
Robinson Jeremiah P. & Co. (Jeremiah P. Robinson, Mark W. Maclay, Louis H. Leonard & William A. Lentilhon) 14 Coenties sl.
Robinson John & Co. (John Robinson & Andrew J. & Thomas M. Armstrong) 46 Murray
Robinson John & Son (John & Frederick J. Robinson) 1000 Third av.
Robinson John H. & Co. (John H. Robinson & George H. Thorp) 48 Harrison
Robinson Tooth Crown College (Charles L. Robinson, propr.) 61 W. 43d
Robinson William & Co. (William Robinson & Elbridge C. Sewall) 64 E. 125th
Robinson William P. D. & Co. (William P. D. Robinson & Robert A. Andrews) 257 W. 42d
Robinson M. & Co. (Morris Robinson & Gerson & Tobias Krakower) 132 E. B'way
Robinson R. W. & Son (Frederick M. Robinson, David W. Kent & Charles B. Litzell, only) 184 G'wich
Robinson S. B. & Co. (Seth B. Robinson, no Co.) 48 Howard
Robinson T. M. & Co. (Thomas M. Robinson & Robert J. Johnson) 195 Pearl
Robinson W. G. & Co. (William G. Robinson, no Co.) 19 New & 64 B'way
Robinson W. H. & Co. (William H. Robinson & W. A. Goodenough) 1557 Ninth av.
Robinson & Booth (George W. Robinson & Theodore F. Booth) 91 Wall
Robinson & Co. (Joseph D. & Edwin T. Robinson) 290 Washn.
Robinson & Hamm (dissolved) 1459 Third av.
Robinson & Meade (dissolved) 275 Pearl
Robinson & Parmele (dissolved) 1 B'way
Robinson & Roe (William A. Robinson & Alfred J. Roe) 54 W. 14th
Robinson & Shackelton (James A. Robinson & Oscar O. Shackelton) 71 Worth
Robinson & Wallace (Andrew J. Robinson & Edward H. Wallace) 129 E. 23d
Robinson & Woolworth (William G. Robinson & James G. B. Woolworth) 1667 B'way & 240 Third av.
Robinson, Haydon & Co. (Frank T. Robinson & James C. Haydon, no Co.) 1 B'way
Robinson, Scribner & Bright (E. Randolph Robinson, John M. Scribner & Osborn E. Bright) 150 B'way
Robinson, Shackelton & Cooley (dissolved) 57 Worth
Robitzek G. & Brothers (Gustave & Emil & Edward Robitzek) Rider av. n E. 136th & 843 E. 161st
Rocciolo Joseph & Co. (no inf.) 1866 Third av.
Roch & Harrington (refused) 132 E. 40th
Rochat C. G. & Co. (Charles G. Rochat & Pierre T. Joly) 20 Maiden la.
Roche David & Co. (Honora Roche & John T. Hannon, only) E. 80th u Av. A
Roche E. & Co. (Edward Roche, no Co.) 65 Thomas
Rochester Brewing Co. (no inf.) 125 Hudson
Rochester Canal Line Co. (William B. Walsh, propr.) 111 Broad & Pier 3 E. R.
Rochester Lamp Co. (Charles S. Upton, Pres.; Matthew W. Hawes, Sec. Capital, $100,000. Directors: Charles S. & D. F. Upton, Matthew W. Hawes) 25 Warren & 1201 B'way
Rochester Transp. Co. (dissolved) 111 Broad
Rockaway Steeplechase Assn. (dissolved) 40 Broad
Rockbottom Clothing Mfg. Co. (Charles I. R. Mestin, propr.) 300 Canal
Rockey & Baltzly (Walter S. Rockey & Albert R. Baltzly) 501 Eighth av.
Rockfellow & Shepard (William H. Rockfellow & Benjamin Shepard) 70 Worth
Rockland Cemetery (Andres D. Stone, Pres.; William H. Whiton, Sec.) 185 B'way
Rockland County Milk Assn. (Henry Y. Canfield, propr.) 411 Seventh av.
Rockwell Charles & Co. (Charles Rockwell & William H. Bolander) Pier 50 E. R.
Rockwell Charles H. & Co. (Charles H. Rockwell & E. L. McElroy) 417 Pearl
Rockwell J. S. & Co. (John T. Rockwell, only) 195 William
Rockwell & Co. (Herbert G. & Arthur C. Rockwell) 2480 Third av.
Rockwell & Pearson (William Rockwell & Charles J. Pearson) 120 B'way
Rockwood Solar Printing Co. (not inc.) (J. Angustus Randel & George H. Rockwood) 17 Union sq. W.
Rockwood & Co. (William E. Rockwood & Wallace T. Jones) 470 Cherry
Roddy & Maher (William Roddy & John T. F. Maher) 169 First av.
Rode Frederick (Frederick Rode:—special partner, Milton Knapp, $20,000; terminates 30th April, 1891) 249 Fifth av.
Rode & Brand (Edward Rode & Charles Brand) 10 Barclay
Rodenburg John & Son (John & John Rodenburg jr.) 525 W. 42d
Rodgers & Farrell (John C. Rodgers & Edward J. Farrell) 247 W. 125th
Rodgers & Randolph (Robertson Rodgers & William F. Randolph) 30 Broad
Rodgers, Shanly & Co. (John C. Rodgers, Edward Shanly & Edward J. Farrell) 24; W. 125th
Rodier & Fitzgerald (Louis B. Rodier & Michael J. Fitzgerald) 206 Pearl
Rodman & Cogswell (Thomas H. Rodman & William S. Cogswell) 59 Liberty
Rodney & Osyor (James W. Rodney & Martin Osyor) 388 Broome
Rodrigue C. W. & Sister (Charlotte W. & L. Withers Rodrigue) 3371 Third av.
Rodriguez A. C. & Co. (Andrew C. Rodriguez & Joaquin M. Pons) 5 Beekman
Rodriguez & Garcia (Salvador Rodriguez & Francisco Garcia) 24 Gold

SPECIAL ATTENTION PAID TO THIS CLASS OF WORK } **BANKERS' & BROKERS' CIRCULARS DELIVERED** { THE TROW CITY DIRECTORY CO. 11 University Place.

ROE   257   ROM

Roe Justus & Sons (Justus & Howard & Austin Roe) 40 Cortlandt

Roe & Cuddeback (Jemima C. Roe & Joseph Cuddeback) 194 Varick

Roe & Jessup (James D. Roe & Josephine Jessup; —special partner, Gilbert W. Roe, *Oshkosh, Wis.*, $10,000; terminates 1st May, 1892) 243 B'way

Roe & Macklin (Alfred Roe & John J. Macklin) 156 B'way

Roebuck & Co. (Thomas G. Roebuck, no Co.) 89 Broad

Roeder Brothers (George & John Roeder) 167 Ninth av.

Roeder & Bernard (Simon M. Roeder & William Bernard) 25 Chambers

Roeder & Briesen (Frank V. Briesen, only) 82 Nassau

Roemer Brewing Co. (inf. unattainable) 355 W. 44th

Roemer Peter & Sons (Peter & William A. & George P. Roemer) Woodlawn

Roes & Elfers (Frederick J. Roes & Henry Elfers) 94 Av. D

Roessel Louis & Co. (Louis & Carl A. Roessel) 462 Broome

Roessler & Hasslacher Chemical Co. (Jacob Hasslacher, Pres.; William A. Hamann, Sec. Capital, $150,000. Directors: Jacob Hasslacher, Franz Roessler, A. Andra, J. K. Creevey) 75 Pine

Roeth Frederick & Son (Frederick & Louis Roeth) 222 E. 59th

Roethlisberger & Gerber (Robert Roethlisberger & John Gerber) 147 Chambers & 129 Reade

Roettger & Wobbekind (Julius Roettger & August Wobbekind) 38 Antigers pl.

Roetting & Beckmann (Frederick Roetting & Peter Beckmann) 427 Sixth av.

Roff B. B. & Son (Bela B. & Henry R. Roff) 811 Seventh av.

Rofrano & Carosselli (Michael Rofrano & Alberico Carosselli) 18 Roosevelt

Rogan J. H. & Co. (James H. Rogan & Michael J. Hanrahan) 846 Sixth av.

Rogers Automatic Safety Lock Attachment Co. (In liquidation) 59 Wall

Rogers Charles E. & Co. (Charles E. & Winfield S. Rogers) 108 Wall

Rogers Charles P. & Co. (Charles P. Rogers & George M. Burt) 248 Sixth av.

Rogers Locomotive & Machine Works (inf. unattainable) 44 Exchange pl.

Rogers Manifold & Carbon Paper Co. (Lebbeus H. Rogers, Pres.; Hiram D. Rogers, Treas.; Hiram D. Rogers jr. Sec. Capital, $50,000. Directors: Alexander B. Fernald, Lebbeus H. & Hiram D. & Hiram D. Rogers jr.) 75 Maiden la.

Rogers Thomas & Co. (Thomas Rogers & James A. Hammond) 208 W. 40th & 51 W. 30th

Rogers C. B. & H. B. (Caroline B. & Helen B.) 220 W. 88th

Rogers C. H. & Co. (Charles H. & Caroline L. Rogers) 32 W. 125th

Rogers H. D. & Co. (Hiram D. Rogers, no Co.) 75 Maiden la.

Rogers H. M. & Co. (Herbert M. & Albert M. & Henry C. Rogers) 11 Fulton fish mkt & 207 Front

Rogers J. F. & Co. (John F. Rogers, no Co.) 107 Liberty

Rogers & Carroll (Henry W. Rogers & J. Howell Carroll) 45 B'way

Rogers & Co. (lampblack) (dissolved) 299 Pearl

Rogers & Co. (mers.) (no inf.) 128 B'way

Rogers & Gould (Edward L. Rogers & William S. Gould :—special partner, Charles T. Barney, $25,000; terminates 30th April, 1890) 7 Wall

Rogers & Livingston (H. Livingston Rogers & Henry B. Livingston) 48 Exchange pl.

Rogers & Pyatt (Andrew D. Rogers jr. & Runyon Pyatt) 80 Maiden la.

Rogers & Sherwood (William C. Rogers & Lamberson Sherwood) 21 Barclay

Rogers, Peet & Co. (William R. H. Martin & Frank R. Chambers, only) 258, 560 & 1260 B'way

Rogers, Smith & Co. (Meriden Britannia Co. proprs.) 46 E. 14th

Rogers' A., Sons [(estate of Francis T. Rogers, only) 281 Bleecker

Rogers' T. P., Son (Theodore H. Rogers) 60 Gansevoort

Roggen & Eisenstein (Nathan Roggen & Toba Eisenstein) 43 E. B'way

Rohbeck Brothers (no inf.) 149 E. 14th

Rohde & Nowak (Henry Rohde & Michael Nowak) 157½ Stanton

Rohe & Brother (Florian & Charles Rohe) 266 W. 33d, 547 W. 35th, 588 W. 86th, 534 W. 37th & 344 Produce Ex.

Rohman S. & Co. (Samuel Rohman, no Co.) 147 Wooster

Rohtman & Warshawsky (Jacob Rohtman & Louis Warshawsky) r 87 Ridge

Rokohl Brothers (Herman L. & Gustav W. Rokohl) 359 E. 20th

Rolffes & Co. (John F. Rolffes, no Co.) 85 Spring

Röker August & Sons (August & Winfried & Herman & Joseph S. Röker) 126 W. 24th

Rollins Gold & Silver Mining Co. (Charles Siedler, Pres.; Addison F. Andrews, Sec.; Robert Sherwood, Treas. Capital, $5,000,000. Trustees: Charles Siedler, Addison F. Andrews, Robert Sherwood, Joseph M. Marshall, Edward M. Rogers, Isaac Freese, J. V. B. Lewis, H. McK. Twombly, T. H. Potter) 201 B'way

Rollins C. N. & Co. (Charles N. Rollins, no Co.) 256 Washn.

Rollins J. & R. (James & James H. & Robert S. Rollins) 467 Second av.

Rollins & Co. (Gustavus A. & Edward A. Rollins) 16 Broad

Rolston & Bass (William H. Rolston, W. Alexander Bass, jr. & Edwin S. Hooley) 20 Broad

Romain Brothers (Samuel W. & Stephen M. Romain) 538 W. 125th

Romaine George W. & Co. (George W. Romaine, Co. refused) 60 B'way

Romaine & Co. (Benjamin F. & Louis T. & Girard Romaine) 84 Beaver & ft. E. 4th

Romaine's Peter, Son (Ira D. Romaine) 13 Thirteenth av. W. Washn. mkt

Roman Charles H. & Co. (Charles H. Romain & Alfred Hahn) 447 B'way

Romano D. & G. Dipersia (no inf.) 118 Thompson

Rome City Street Railway Co. (Antonio Rusines, Pres.; William Moores, Sec. Capital, $50,-000. Directors: Antonio Rasines, William Moores, C. W. Dayton, Arthur L. Meyer, John M. & John S. McWilliam) 45 Pine

Rome, Watertown & Ogdensburg R. R. Co. (Charles Parsons, Pres.; Joseph A. Lawyer, Sec. Capital, $10,000,000. Directors: Charles Parsons, Clarence S. Day, William Lummis, John S. Farlow, William M. White, J. F. Maynard, Edwin & George Parsons, Walter Ferguson, John Thorn, J. M. Crouse, Charles Parsons jr. John Q. A. Johnson) 96 B'way

Romer & Tremper (Jane Romer & Jacob H. Tremper) Pier 84 (old) N. R.

Romer & Tremper Steamboat Co. (Romer & Tremper, proprs.) Pier 84 (old) N. R.

17

TYPEWRITING DONE BY THE TROW CITY DIRECTORY CO., 11 University Place.

Romeyn Charles W. & Co. (Charles W. Romeyn & Arthur J. Stover) 206 B'way
Romm Brothers (Hyman & Louis Romm) r 72 Hester
Ronalds & Co. (Pierre L. jr. & Reginald Ronalds) 54 Cliff
Rondout Steamboat Co. (Romer & Tremper, proprs.) Pier 34 (old) N. R.
Ronk H. W. & Co. (Hezekiah W. Ronk, Co. refused) 683 Hudson
Roome Electric Protective Co. (Henry C. Roome, Pres.; further inf. unattainable) 32 Liberty
Rooms William P. & Co. (William P. Roome, James B. Weir jr. & Willard N. Banks) 90 Front
Roome & Co. (Mary Roome, Francis Many & James J. Duffy) 462 W. 18th
Rooms & Roome (Claudius M. & W. Harris Roome) 16 Broad
Rooney C. J. & Co. (Cornelius J. Rooney, no Co.) 229 B'way
Rooney M. J. & Co. (Michael J. Rooney & George Harlen) 1329 B'way
Rooney & Dean (no inf.) 1766 Third av.
Roos August & Sons (Charles & Frederick W. Roos, only) 232 W. 27th
Roos Louis & Co. (Louis Roos & Simon Schiff) 129 Av. A
Roosevelt & Boughton (Nicholas L. Roosevelt & William De L. Boughton) 44 Pine
Roosevelt & Esteve (Ltd.) (Samuel M. Roosevelt, Pres.; Francis Cambreleng, Sec.; Robert M. C. Graham, Treas. Capital, $250,000. Directors: Samuel M. Roosevelt, Francis Cambreleng, Robert M. C. Graham, Raymond Esteve, Montgomery R. Schuyler) 55 Beaver
Roosevelt & Schuyler (Samuel M. Roosevelt & Montgomery R. Schuyler) 55 Beaver
Roosevelt & Son (James A. & Alfred & W. Emlen Roosevelt) 32 Pine
Root & Childs (G. Wells Root & Harris C. Childs) 84 Leonard
Root & Clarke (Elihu Root, Samuel B. Clarke & Joseph Kunzmann) 32 Nassau
Root & Tinker (Charles T. Root & Franklin H. Tinker) 78 Walker
Ropes R. W. & Co. (Reuben W. & Ripley Ropes) 73 Pearl
Ropes W. & Co. (mers.) (William H. & Joseph S. Ropes, Charles H. Trask & William H. Ropes jr.) 74 Wall
Ropes W. & Co. (refused) 47 Leonard
Rorke Edward & Co. (Edward jr. & James Rorke, only) 40 Barclay
Roscoe & Caldwell (Elbert O. Roscoe & Arthur P. Caldwell) 97 Pine
Rose Leopold & Co. (no inf.) 79 Mercer
Rose Mfg. Co. (extracts) (Charles L. F. Rose, propr.) 17 S. William
Rose Mfg. Co. (gas fixtures) (not Inc.) (Edwin L. Rose & W. Stammer Brown) 219 W. 125th
Rose D. E. & Co. (Daniel E. Rose & Matthias Lachenbruch) 18 Fulton
Rose F. & Co. (Frederick Rose & Bernhard Josephson) 158 Chambers
Rose T. M. & Son (Thomas M. & James W. Rose) 8 Christopher
Rose Brothers (dissolved) 536 W. 14th
Rose & Beck (Albert Rose & Samuel Beck) 161 Christopher & 775 & 847 Tenth av.
Rose & Bonnet (A. Middleton Rose & Pierre Bonnet) 853 B'way
Rose & Brockhaus (dissolved) 259 W. 29th
Rose & Co. (frames) (Isaac A. Rose:—special partner, James F. Sutton, $2,000 ; terminates 1st May, 1892) 335 Fourth av. & 229 E. 34th

Rose & Co. (tailors) (B. Mitchel Hart, only) 180 Nassau
Rose & Howard (dissolved) 46 Marion
Rose & Lipschitz (Jacob Rose & Ignatz Lipschitz) 153 Eighth av.
Rose & Putzel (William R. Rose & Gibson Putzel) 330 B'way
Rose & Quail (James F. Rose & J. Henry Quail) 40 South
Rose & Settle (dissolved) 121½ Division
Rose & Stone (Charles F. Rose & Howard C. Stone) 111 B'way
Rose, McAlpin & Co. (George L. Rose, George L. & William McAlpin & Martin Dennis) 97 Reade
Rosecrans & Weymann (Thomas Rosecrans & William G. Weymann) 1-16 E. 16th
Roselle Land & Improvement Co. (James Moore, Pres.; Aaron D. Hope, Sec.; Hiram P. Baldwin, Treas. Directors: Aaron D. Hope, James Moore, Samuel Knox, P. Sanford Ross, Hiram P. Baldwin, John R. Moore, John Mason Knox) 121 Liberty
Roseman & Levy (Abram Roseman & Max G. Levy) 41 Maiden la.
Rosen Harris & Son (Harris & Frank E. Rosen) 70 & 83 Hester
Rosen & Brother (Marcus & Jacob S. Rosen) 20 E. B'way
Rosenbaum Carl & Co. (Carl Rosenbaum, no Co.) 305 Canal & 47 Howard
Rosenbaum Morris & Co. (Morris Rosenbaum & David Sawyer) 518 Canal
Rosenbaum A. S. & Co. (Albert S. Rosenbaum, no Co.) 165 Water
Rosenbaum J. A. & Co. (John A. & John H. Rosenbaum) 310 Washn.
Rosenbaum L. & Son (Leon & Herman Rosenbaum) 11 Forsyth
Rosenberg I. & H. (Isabella & Henrietta) 92 Orchard
Rosenberg M. & Co. (Moses Rosenberg & Lotus D. Cohn) 77 Bowery
Rosenberg S. & Co. (Siegfried & Herman Rosenberg) 515 B'way & 84 Mercer
Rosenberg Brothers (Jacob Rosenberg, only) 152 Fulton
Rosenberg & Baker (Louis Rosenberg & Ismar Baker) 9 Gt. Jones
Rosenberg & Horn (dissolved) 712 B'way
Rosenberg & Jacobson (Adam Rosenberg & Isaac W. Jacobson) 230 B'way
Rosenberg & Krause (William Rosenberg & Jacob Krause) 430 Broome
Rosenberg & Reibstein (Hyman Rosenberg & Emil Reibstein) 135 E. B'way
Rosenberg, Kalmus & Co. (Israel M. Rosenberg, Philip Kalmus & Harris Rosenberg) 385 Canal
Rosenberger H. & Son (dissolved) 1795 Ninth av.
Rosenberger & Co. (Albert Rosenberger & Isaac Gutmann) 178 Park row
Rosenberger & Gutmann (dissolved) 89 Division
Rosenblatt & Co. (Simon M. & Samuel Rosenblatt) 411 Water
Rosenblieth & Katz (Jacob Rosenblieth & Isaac Katz) 89 Clinton
Rosenbohm B. & Co. (Bohlke Rosenbohm & Philip Schlosser) 311 Washn.
Rosendorf & Co. (Daniel & William Rosendorf) 47 Walker
Rosendorff M. & Sons (Morris & Louis J. & Isaac Rosendorff) 277 Grand
Rosenfeld Louis & Co. (bronze powders) (Louis & Leo Rosenfeld) 70 Park pl.
Rosenfeld Louis & Co. (mers.) (Louis Rosenfeld, no Co.) 64 Stone & 101 Pearl
Rosenfeld H. A. & Co. (Herman A. Rosenfeld,

William J. Redpath, Isaac Strauss & Morris Levy) 97 Bleecker
Rosenfeld Brothers (Samuel & Jacob Rosenfeld) 367 E. Houston
Rosenfeld & Jonas (Julius S. Rosenfeld & William Jonas) 120 Walker
Rosenfield Brothers (Samuel & David Rosenfield) 594 Second av. & 1704 Lex. av.
Rosenham Brothers (Louis K. & Elias A. Rosenham) 1165 Fulton
Rosenham & Co. (James P. Rosenham, no Co.) 349 W. 68th
Rosenheim Leider & Co. (Isidor Rosenheim & Isaac S. Mack) 86 Bowery
Rosenheim & Rosenfield (Max Rosenheim & Alfred S. Rosenfield) 81 G'wich & 44 Trinity pl.
Rosenheim's E., Son (Louis Rosenheim) 24 Walker
Roseno Brothers (Louis & Daniel & John Roseno) 345 Canal
Rosenquest Charles F. & Co. (Charles F. & J. Wesley Rosenquest) 107 W. 14th
Rosenshine Brothers (Aaron & George & Max Rosenshine) 529 B'way
Rosenstein Isaac & Co. (Isaac Rosenstein & Herman Hessel) 23 White
Rosenstein A. & Son (Albert & Julius Rosenstein) 264 Bleecker
Rosenstein C. & Co. (Clara Rosenstein, no Co.) 373 Washn. (*see head lines*)
Rosenstein S. & Co. (Samuel Rosenstein & Meyer Lemmon) 554 B'way & 92 Crosby
Rosenstein Brothers (Julius W. & Leo Rosenstein) 317 G'wich
Rosenstock C. & Co. (Carl & Philip Rosenstock) 102 Spring
Rosenstock & Cohn (Max Rosenstock & Leopold Cohn) 10 Wooster
Rosenswike & Golden (dissolved) 164 Park row
Rosenthal Charles & Co. (Charles Rosenthal & Joseph Freeman) 90 Wall
Rosenthal A. S. & Co. (Abraham S. Rosenthal, Samson Fried & Jonas Hoenigsberger) 469 Broome
Rosenthal F. & Son (Ferdinand & Simon Rosenthal) 80 Bleecker
Rosenthal G. & Son (Gustav & Joseph Rosenthal) 326 Church
Rosenthal H. & Brother (Henry & Maurice Rosenthal) 120 Chambers & 50 Warren
Rosenthal H. & Co. (no inf.) 36 Beekman
Rosenthal H. & Son (Henry & Emanuel C. Rosenthal) 10 Wooster
Rosenthal H. B. & Co. (Henry B. Rosenthal & Tobias Levien) 699 B'way
Rosenthal L. & Son (Isaac & Max Rosenthal) 85 Franklin
Rosenthal J. & Co. (Jesse & Samuel Rosenthal) 412 B'way
Rosenthal S. & Son (Simon Rosenthal, only) 61 Crosby
Rosenthal Brothers (cigars) (Charles & Abraham Rosenthal) 351 E. 73d
Rosenthal Brothers (drygds.) (John & Moses Rosenthal) 2 Av. C
Rosenthal Brothers (ruffles) (Max & Herman Rosenthal) 48 Greene
Rosenthal & Bloom (Herman Rosenthal & Jacob Bloom) 7 Sixth av.
Rosenthal & Co. (Isidor Rosenthal, no Co.) 520 B'way
Rosenthal & Gordon (Louis Rosenthal & Michael Gordon) 106 Franklin
Rosenthal & Kean (Michael Rosenthal & Samuel Kean) 125 Mercer
Rosenthal & Krolimann (William Rosenthal & William Krolimann) 26 William

Rosenthal & Zeisler (Nathan Rosenthal & Louis Zeisler) 223 Second
Rosentreter G. & L. (Louis H. Rosentreter, only) 934 University pl.
Rosenwald E. & Brother (Edward & Isaac & Henry & Sigmund Rosenwald) 145 Water
Rosenweig & Aronson (dissolved) 97 Norfolk
Rosevelt & Griffiths (George W. Rosevelt & Rowland W. Griffiths) 267 South & 605 Water
Rosevelt & McDonald (Henry J. Rosevelt & John W. McDonald) 52 & 268 South
Rosinsky Brothers (J. Meyer & Moritz J. Rosinsky) 62 E. B'way
Roslyn Heights Improvement Co. (inf. unattainabl) 280 B'way
Rosofsky & Luboff (Philip Rosofsky & Jacob Luboff) 129 E. B'way
Ross John & Co. (John Ross, no Co.) 107 Reade
Ross C. G. & Co. (Charles G. Ross & Delancey W. Pervell) 56 Leonard
Ross W. & Co. (Walter Ross, no Co.) 107 Prince
Ross W. A. & Brother (William A. Ross, only) 56 Pine
Ross & Bennett (Charles R. Ross & William H. Bennett) 118 Cedar
Ross & Fuller Assn. (not inc.) (William K. Ross & Joseph A. & William K. Fuller) 32 Chambers
Ross & Keany (William G. Ross, Patrick F. Keany & William F. Hull) 64 Water
Ross & Marvin (Alexander W. Ross & Charles R. Marvin jr.) 53 B'way
Ross & Millong (Duncan Ross & Frank Millang) 1168 B'way
Ross & Wronker (Samuel Ross & Solomon Wronker) 689 B'way
Rossbach J. H. & Brothers (Jacob & Leopold Rossbach, only) 27 Ferry & 2 Jacob
Rossheim & Co. (Henrietta & Ella Rossheim) 56 Thomas
Rossin S. & Sons (Morris Rossin, only) 173 Water
Rossiter & Skidmore (William W. Rossiter & Charles H. Skidmore :—special partner, William W. Wickes, *Elym, N. Y.*, $25,000; terminates 30th April 1891) 156 Franklin
Rossiter & Wright (Ehrick K. Rossiter & Frank A. Wright) 47 Liberty
Rosenagel & Kommer (dissolved) 5 Water
Rotary Sewing Machine Co. (Joseph L. Follett, Pres.; William E. Beames, Sec. Capital, $500,000. Directors: Joseph L. Follett, Ira M. Hedges, William R. Beams, Robert B. Cantrell, Frederick W. Christern) 150 Nassau
Rotchford M. & Son (Henry & William Rotchford) 420 Cherry
Roth J. & H. (Jacob & Henry) 149 Av. C
Roth Brothers (dissolved) 2904 Third av.
Roth & Berkowitz (Henry Roth & Joseph Berkowitz) 197 Delancey
Roth & Brother (Charles Roth, only) 246 Av. A
Roth & Goldschmidt (Emile H. Roth & Julius Goldschmidt) 16 Walker
Roth's John, Son (Louis Roth) 393 Seventh av. & 524 Sixth av.
Rothbarth Martin & Co. (Martin & Adolf Rothbarth) 76 Broad
Rothbarth & Sons (David & Max Rothbarth, only) 35 Pearl
Rothe & Lips (Herman H. Rothe & Herman Lips) 175 William
Rothfeld, Stern & Co. (Solomon Rothfeld, Jacob H. Stern & Sigmund Ruthfeld) 818 B'way & 84 Mercer
Rothkopf S. & Son (Salomon & Henry Rothkopf) 477 B'way
Rothschild V. Henry & Co. (V. Henry Rothschild & Isaac Dreyfus) 43 Leonard

CIRCULARS ADDRESSED TO ANY TRADE IN THE U. S. **Facilities**
PROMPT, CAREFUL WORK **THE TROW CITY DIRECTORY CO.** Unequalled.
AT MODERATE PRICES. **11 University Place.**

ROT 260 RUG

Rothschild S. & Brother (Simon & Frank Rothschild) 820 Canal & 51 Howard
Rothschild S. & Co. (Simon Rothschild & Joseph Stodola) 180 First av.
Rothschild S. F. & A. (Simon F. & Alfred) 440 B'way
Rothschild Brothers (Louis & James Rothschild) 51 Nassau
Rothschild & Hoff (Henry V. Rothschild & Samuel Hoff) 140 Nassau
Rothschild & Kahn (Seligman Rothschild & William Kahn) 543½ Sixth
Rothschild & May (dissolved) 577 B'way
Rothschild & Ulmann (dissolved) 41 Maiden la.
Rothschild Brothers & Co. (Ludwig & Edward & Charles A. Rothschild, Jacob L. Holden & Samuel H. Cragg) 428 B'way
Rothschild, Hoff & Bostwick (dissolved) 140 Nassau
Rothschild, May & Co. (Simon Rothschild, Laura A. May & Isaac Dobriner) 640 B'way
Rothschild's M., Sons (Simon & Alexander Rothschild) 326 Church
Rothstein's H., Sons (Louis & Abraham Rothstein) 171 Mercer
Rotman & Malcolm (James E. Rotman & Leroy Malcolm) 244 Fulton
Rottenberg Blank Book Co. (Frances Rottenberg, propr.) 308 Second
Rotterdam Line (Netherlands Am. Steam Navigation Co. proprs.) 89 B'way
Rottiger L. & J. (Louisa & Joanna) 451½ W. 46d
Rottmann John F. & Sons (John F. & Henry D. & Herman H. & Anna E. C. Rottmann) 549 W. 46th
Roumage C. C. & Co. (Camille C. & Victor E. Roumage) 10 Broad
Rountree & Co. (Robert H. & Willie D. & Albert L. Rountree) 4 Cotton Ex.
Rourke B. & Co. (refused) 503 Tenth av.
Rouse & Goldowsky (dissolved) 1527 Lex. av.
Rousseau's Electrical Works (David Rousseau, propr.) 810 Mott av.
Roussel & Hicks (Henry C. Hicks & Frederick C. Terry, only) 71 D'way
Roux & Co. (Alexander J. Roux, no Co.) 182 Fifth av.
Rovics & Friedman (dissolved) 1396 Second av.
Row Charles H. & Co. (Charles H. Row & Joseph S. Blanco).7 Battery pl.
Rowan & Wilcox (Samuel Rowan & Robert M. Wilcox) 46 E. 14th
Rowe Edwin & Co. (Edwin Rowe, no Co.) 403 Produce Ex.
Rowe Regulator Co. (L. Leroy Rowe, propr.) 99 Beekman
Rowe & Brother.(Edward V. & Claude D. Rowe) 500 B'way & 134 Crosby
Rowell George P. & Co. (George P. Rowell, Charles N. Kent & Oscar G. Mosse) 10 Spruce
Rowell & Hone (dissolved):22 Pine
Rowland James & Co. (James Rowland & Walter Burt) 65 Warren
Rowland John & Sons (John & Charles H. & Ralph W. & John Rowland jr.) 168 Greene
Rowland & Co. (brokers) (dissolved) 171 B'way
Rowland & Co. (flour) (Samuel Rowland, no Co.) 47 Water
Rown Tea Co. (Siegfried Rown, propr.) 312 Spring
Rown S. & Co. (dissolved) 312 Spring
Rown Brothers (Sigmund Rown, only) 53 Catharine
Rowtrees & Munstuk (dissolved) 82 E. 12th
Rowold Brothers (dissolved) 562 Second av.
Roworth Mfg. Co. (Joseph G. Roworth jr. Pres.; John C. Harvey, Treas. Capital, $10,000.

Directors: Joseph G. Roworth jr. John C. & Charles E. Harvey) 854 Pearl
Roworth's William, Sons Mfg. Co. (Joseph G. Roworth jr. Pres.; M. M. D. Roworth, Sec. Capital, $75,000. Directors: Joseph G. jr. M. M. D. & M. M. Roworth) 854 Pearl
Roy W. H. & Co. (William H. Roy & Thomas H. Graham) 118 Nassau
Roy & Anthony (dissolved) 308 Produce Ex.
Royal Baking Powder Co. (Joseph C. Hoagland, Pres.; Alfred R. Porter jr. Sec.; William M. Hoagland, Treas. Capital, $160,000. Directors: Joseph C. & Raymond & William M. Hoagland) 106 Wall
Royal Hungarian Wine Co. (Sigismund B. Wortmann, Pres.; Julius Engel, Sec. Capital, $10,000. Directors: Sigismund B. Wortmann, Julius Engel, Bernhard Heller) 60 Broad
Royal Laundry (Catharine M. Gannon, propr.) 1486½ B'way
Royal Lead Co. (inf. unattainable) 455 Produce Ex.
Royal Rubber Co. (Frederick M. Shepard, Pres.; Joseph A. Minott, Sec. Directors: Frederick M. Shepard, Joseph A. Minott; further inf. unattainable) 487 B'way
Royal Silk Mfg. Co. (Ferdinand Straus, propr.) 4 Stone
Rozea Brothers (no inf.) 154 Nassau
Rozinsky & Tally (Samuel Rozinsky & Hyman Tally) 4 Montgomery
Rubber Clothing Co. (Frederick M. Shepard, Pres.; Joseph A. Minott, Sec. Directors: Frederick M. Shepard, Joseph A. Minott; further inf. unattainable) 487 B'way
Rubenoff Brothers (Israel & Simon Rubenoff) 300 Broome
Rubenowitz & Romansky (no inf.) 54 Forsyth
Rubens Brothers (dissolved) 104 Greene
Rubenstein & Sammet (Jacob Rubenstein & Joel Sammet) 76 E. B'way
Rubin Brothers (dissolved) 80 Orchard
Rubin & Levin (no inf.) 79 Mercer
Rubinat Co. (Legrand L. Benedict, Pres.; James W. Tappin, Sec. Capital, $75,000. Trustees: Legrand L. Benedict, James W. Tappin, Ernest Groesbeck) 80 Broad
Rubino Brothers (William H. A. & Joseph C. Rubino) 158 Ludlow
Rubino & Schwars (dissolved) 216 Rivington
Ruby Jewel Mining & Milling Co. (Jerome E. Morse, Pres.; Joseph H. Morse, Sec. Capital, $1,000,000. Directors: Jerome E. & Joseph H. Morse) 230 B'way
Ruckel & Hendel (John H. Ruckel & estate of Jacob Hendel).59 Barclay
Rudd & Hunt (Robert S. Rudd & James M. Hunt) 31 Pine
Ruddiman A. S. & W. (Alexander S. & William) 371 Walton av.
Rudinger J. & Co. (Julius Rudinger & Jacob Basch) 10 Lispenard
Rudisch Co. (Phineas Rudisch, Pres.; Julius Goldman, Sec. Capital, $5,000. Trustees: Phineas Rudisch, Julius Goldman, Julius Radisch) 317 G'wich & 125 Warren
Rudkin's William, Sons (dissolved) 74 William
Rudloff John & Brother (John & Jacob Rudloff) 494 W. 52d
Ruehl & Merkel (Andrew Ruehl & Charles C. Merkel) 646 Sixth av.
Ruehl & Son (no inf.) 171 Eldridge
Ruffner & Mackey (dissolved) 101 Park pl.
Rugen Henry & Co. (Henry & Catharine Rugen) 40 South
Rugen & Wolfers (Henry F. Rugen & Max Wolfers) 61 Goerck

MERCHANTS EXCHANGE NAT. BANK OF THE CITY OF N. Y.
SOLICITS YOUR ACCOUNT. **287 Broadway.**
PHINEAS C. LOUNSBURY, President.   ALLEN S. APGAR, Cashier.

RUG 261 RYE

Ruger Theodore & Co. (Theodore Ruger & Claus Steengrafe) 68 New

Ruger Brothers (dissolved) 24 Stone

Rugge H. L. & F. (Henry L. & Frederick) 1238 Second av.

Ruggiero F. & Brother (Francisco & Raphael Ruggiero) 72 Vesey & ft. E. 110th

Ruhe H. & Co. (Herman Ruhe & Henry Carstens) 2856 Hoffman

Ruhe & Redling (Francis H. Ruhe & August Redling) 165 West & 202 Chambers

Ruhl John & Co. (John Ruhl & Charles E. Mutalg) 179 Grand

Ruhlman Philip & Co. (Philip & Edward Ruhlman) 261 Wash'n.

Ruland & Whiting (Manly A. Ruland & William H. Whiting) 5 Beekman

Rulon H. E. & Co. (dissolved) 104 Fulton

Rumbold George W. & Son (George W. & G. Walter Rumbold) 411 Canal

Rummel & Wetzstein (Frank Rommel & Max Wetzstein) 548 Tenth av.

Rump Emil & Co. (Emil Rump & Frederick W. Lotz) 22 S. William

Runkel Charles F. & Co. (Charles F. Runkel & Howard Munn) 378 Seventh av.

Runkel Brothers (Louis & Herman Runkel & Adhemar Fleux) 445 W. 30th

Runkle, Smith & Co. (Daniel Runkle, Pres.; Henry G. Runkle, Sec. Capital, $450,000. Directors: Daniel Runkle, Robert A. C. Smith, Henry G. & Michael Runkle, Elias R. Pope) 40 Wall

Runne Brothers (Frederick & Dederick Runne) 353 Broome & 63 Walker

Rupp Michael & Co. (Richard M. Rupp & Jesse P. Sutton, only) 30 South

Rural New Yorker (not Inc.) (Lawson Valentine & Edgar H. Libby) 34 Park row

Ruschmeyer H. & Co. (Herman & William Ruschmeyer) 1245 Third av.

Ruschmeyer Brothers (John & Herman Ruschmeyer) 1714 Third av.

Rusher & Fagan (William J. Rusher & John L. Fagan) 24 Old sl.

Rushforth Feed Water Heater Co. (Inf. unattainable) 61 B'way

Rushmore J. F. & Co. (J. Frederick Rushmore, no Co.) 67 William

Rushmore L. E. & Co. (dissolved) 208 E. 14th

Rushmore & Finch (Lewis E. Rushmore & Walter L. Finch) 208 E. 14th

Russ & Brand (dissolved) 19 Whitehall

Russ & Heppenheimer (Edward Russ & William C. Heppenheimer) 229 B'way

Russell Embroidering Co. (Alfred Russell, propr.) 161 E. 86th

Russell Henry & Nathan & Day (dissolved) 42 Barclay

Russell Thomas (Thomas & Robert W. Russell) 24 New Chambers

Russell Thomas & Co. (Thomas Russell & Robert W. Ferguson) 442 B'way & 36 Howard

Russell J. W. & Co. (James W. Russell & Emile Dauphinot) 294 Pearl

Russell R. H. & Son (Robert H. & Robert H. Russell jr.) 33 Rose

Russell W. I. & Co. (William I. Russell, no Co.) 2 Barling sl.

Russell Brothers (Theodore Russell & Michael McMunn, only) 17 Rose

Russell & Co. (Robert S. Russell & George S. Brophy) 107 Water

Russell & Co. (of China) (represented by John M. Forbes) 60 Wall

Russell & Erwin Mfg. Co. (Henry E. Russell, Pres.; Henry E. Russell jr. Sec.; Mahlon J. Woodruff, Treas. Capital, $1,000,000. Directors: Henry E. Russell, Mahlon J. Woodruff, Henry E. Russell jr. James E. Terry, William G. Smythe, J. Andrew Pickett, George R. Post) 45 Chambers

Russell & Hoar (dissolved) 1347 B'way

Russell, Dennison & Latting (Leslie W. & Charles H. Russell, James A. Dennison. Charles P. Latting & Welton C. Percy) 32 Nassau

Russell, Harrison & Co. (dissolved) 3 S. William

Russell, Lewis & Co. (John H. Russell, Orlando C. Lewis & Samuel Louis) 130 Fulton

Russian Hair Felt Co. (S. Stroock & Co. proprs.) 62 Walker

Russian-Am. Tea Co. (R. Klapper & B. Goodson, proprs.) 156 E. B'way

Russmann & Galland (Albert Russmann & Henry Galland) 464 Broome

Rustic Mfg. & Construction Co. (James M. Pinckney, Pres.; Eugene A. Pinckney, Sec.; further inf. unattainable) 29 Fulton

Ruter & Meyer (Henry Ruter & Henry F. Meyer) 122 Chrystie

Rutgers Fire Ins. Co. (Edward B. Fellows, Pres.; Joseph F. Hanford, Sec. Capital, $200,000. Directors: Edward B. Fellows, Oliver W. Woodford, David H. McAlpin, William Peet, Jacob Miller, John Ash, James L. Stewart, Edgar M. Crawford, David Mahany, Seth P. Squire, William R. Foster, Thomas H. Brown, Stephen C. Barnum, John Eadie, William C. Dewey, George Williamson, Thomas H. Dolan, Henry Silberhorn, Oscar Purdy, Joseph Haight jr.) 200 Park row, 58 Wall & 1205 B'way

Ruther & Burfeindt (dissolved) 1162 First av.

Rutherford & Barclay (Henry Rutherford & Charles Barclay) 77 Maiden la.

Rutherford L. & W. (Lewis M. jr. & Winthrop) 51 Liberty

Rutter Robert & Son (Robert & Horace L. Rutter) 116 E. 14th

Rutter William & Co. (William P. Rutter, only) 32 Spruce

Rutter & Gross (J. Louis Gross jr. only) 49 Exchange pl.

Rutzler & Blake (in liquidation) 178 Centre

Ryan John & Son (John & John Ryan jr.) 576 G'wich, 209 W. Houston & 132 Mercer

Ryan J. L. & J. P. (Joseph L. & John P.) 171 B'way

Ryan K. & M. (Catharine E. & Mary A.) 1643 Av. B

Ryan M. A. & Brothers (Matthew A. & Patrick J. & Nicholas W. Ryan) 210 E. 88th

Ryan T. J. & E. (Timothy J. & Edward) 343 B'way

Ryan & Cooper (Thomas Ryan & James T. Cooper) 611 Hudson

Ryan & Devaney (Daniel Ryan & John J. Devaney) 778 Sixth av.

Ryan & Halsch (dissolved) 681 Ninth av.

Ryan & Hodge (dissolved) 576 Grand

Ryan & Parsons (dissolved) 753 Sixth av.

Ryan & Rawnsley (Patrick Ryan & Rawden Rawnsley) 338 E. 64th

Ryan & Thompson (James H. Ryan & Duncan Thompson) 103 Lewis

Ryan & Vogt (William J. Ryan & William Vogt) 1017 First av.

Ryan Brothers & McGowan (dissolved) 171 B'way

Ryan's William, Sons (dissolved) 28 Worth

Ryder Chauncey C. & Co. (Chauncey C. Ryder & T. Milton Lamberson) 97 Water

Ryder & Corley (Nicholas Ryder & Thomas J. Corley) 175 W. 46th

Ryer J. B. & Co. (James B. Ryer & Thomas F. J. Tynan) 167 Canal

CINCINNATI, BALTIMORE, PHILADELPHIA, | **SNOW, CHURCH & CO.** CORRESPONDENTS EVERYWHERE. | NEW YORK, BOSTON, CHICAGO, LOUISVILLE.

Ryer & Berrian (Alfred L. Ryer & Frank M. Berrian) 351 Sixth av.
Ryle William & Co. (William T. & Arthur Ryle & Boetius Murphy:—special partners, Mary R. Ryle, *Paterson, N. J.*, & Charles Danforth, *each* $250,000; terminates 15th Jan. 1900) 54 Howard
Rynd Farm Oil Co. (C. W. Burton, Pres. Capital, $500,000. Trustees: Charles H. Burton, George W. Wright, C. W. Burton; further inf. unattainable) no address
Ryon Stationery Co. (H. C. Ryon & Co., propra.) 55 Walker
Ryon H. C. & Co. (Henry C. & Harry P. Ryon) 55 Walker

S

S, O. Corset Co. (Moses S. Rosenback, propr.) 855 B'way
Sabatier & Thoron (Ernest Sabatier & Casimir Thoron) 23 S. William
Sabiston & Williams (Colin J. Sabiston & Thomas Williams) 1971 Ninth av.
Sachs Adolph & Co. (dissolved) 337 E. 75th
Sachs Martin & Co. (no inf.) 42 Walker
Sachs Philip & M. Tabac (no inf.) 31 Norfolk
Sachs L. & Brother (Louis & Samuel Sachs) 26 W. Houston
Sachs & Davis (Isaac Sachs & Abraham Davis) 51 Forsyth
Sachs, Gellin & Co. (dissolved) 337 E. 75th
Sackett George W. & Co. (dissolved) 53 Wall
Sackett James H. & Co. (James H. Sackett & Samuel B. Bossey) 102 Cedar
Sackett & Bennett (Henry W. Sackett & Charles G. Bennett) 154 Nassau
Sackett & Fiske Stationery Co. (George W. Sackett, Pres.; Charles P. Sackett, Treas.; Edgar A. Fiske, Sec. Capital, $15,000. Trustees: George W. Kenyon, George W. & Charles P. Sackett) 141 B'way
Sackett & Wilhelms Lithographing Co. (Charles Wilhelms, Pres.; Thomas Randall, Sec.; Robert L. Sackett, Treas. Capital, $140,000. Trustees: Charles Wilhelms, Robert L. Sackett, George W. Kenyon) 110 Fifth av.
Sackett, Lang, Reed & McKewan (Guernsey Sackett, Frank C. Lang, Charles A. Reed & James D. McKewan) 31 Park row
Sackmann's H. E., Sons (dissolved) 39 Centre
Sacks & Brother (Gustave M. L. & Henry M. Sacks) 163 Greene
Sadler J. F. & Co. (Jerome F. & Louis L. Sadler & Rufus F. Lindsay) 623 W. 40th
Sadler & Bauersfeld (Jerome F. Sadler & Louis F. Bauersfeld) 60 B'way
Sadlier D. & J. & Co. (Julia A. & James F. Sadlier, only) 83 Barclay
Sadokiersky Jacob & Son (dissolved) 104 Suffolk
Saet & Brodsky (Joseph Saet & David Brodsky) 222 South
Safe Deposit Co. of N. Y. (Francis M. Jencks, Pres.; George H. Vose, Sec. Capital, $300,000. Directors: Sidney Dillon, Joseph I. Bicknell, Joseph T. Low, Aaron D. Hope, John F. Halsted, John L. Brewster, William H. Hollister, Peter B. Wyckoff, Isaac P. Martin, Warren D. Sage, Francis M. Jencks, Charles T. Barney, Daniel F. Appleton) 146 B'way
Safety Car Heating & Lighting Co. (Arthur W. Soper, Pres.; Benjamin R. Stillman, Sec.; William R. Thomas, Treas. Capital, $1,000,000. Directors: Arthur W. Soper, S. C. Blodgett, J. J. Sloanm, Ebenezer K. Sibley, Robert Andrews, Sidney Dillon, Thomas Rutter, Edward Lauterbach, William Barbour, Wallace C. Andrews, William P. Shinn, S. M. Dodd, Frederick Kühns) 160 B'way
Safety Electric Construction Co, (J. Murray Mitchell, Pres.; Emil A. July, Sec. Capital, $100,000. Directors: J. Murray Mitchell, Emil A. July, William M. Berrien) 45 Wall
Safety Electric Power Co. (J. Murray Mitchell, Pres.; Henry S. Iselin, Sec.; William R. Crowell, Treas. Capital, $600,000. Directors: J. Murray Mitchell, Henry S. Iselin, Gordon Macdonald) 45 Wall
Safety Electric Railway & Power Co. (J. Murray Mitchell, Pres.; Emil A. July, Sec.; Karrick Riggs, Treas. Capital, $600,000; further inf. unattainable) 45 Wall
Safety Elevator Co. (William D. Andrews, Pres.; George H. Andrews, Sec. Capital, $100,000. Trustees: William D. & George H. Andrews) 233 B'way
Safety Insulated Wire & Cable Co. (Horace K. Thurber, Pres.; Edward A. Moen, Sec. Capital, $250,000. Directors: Horace K. Thurber, Henry E. Hawley, Edward A. Moen) 234 W. 29th
Safety Pocket-Book Co. (inf. unattainable) 758 B'way
Safety Valve Publishing Co. (refused) 55 Liberty
Saffery & Schofield (no inf.) 1300 B'way
Safran B. & Brother (Bernhard & Max Safran) 355 E. Houston
Sage & Vaughan (dissolved) 42 Broad
Sage & Wilkins (David Sage & Mark Wilkins) Ackerman n Riverdale av.
Sahlein D. A. & Co. (David A. & Maurice D. Sahlein) 149 Greene
Sahm & Mahr (dissolved) 947 Third av.
Sahrbeck & Martin (Peter W. Sahrbeck & Charles R. Martin) 271 Washn. & 107 Warren
Saidler William jr. & Brother (William jr. & Thomas Saidler) 429 W. 17th
St. Clair Charles & Co. (Charles St. Clair, no Co.) 275 W. 23d
St. Crispin Cut Sole Co. (Forest Delaney & Son, propra.) 14 N. Y. & B'klyn bridge
St. Denis & Home Cons. Laundry Co. (Harris & Kingsley, propra.) 42 University pl.
St. James Laundry (Isaac C. Simonson, propr.) 1007 Sixth av.
St. Joe Painting & Decorating Co. (James B. Burke, propr.) 2056 Seventh av.
St. John City Railway Co. (John F. Zebley, Pres.; Austin Gallagher, Sec.; further inf. unattainable) 3 Broad
St. John Brothers (Cortlandt & Theodore St. John) 17 Cedar
St. John & Co. (no inf.) 42 E. 20th
St. John, Kirkham & Co. (Jesse St. John, Angustus Kirkham & estate of Adolphus F. Carter) 134 Grand
St. Joseph Lead Co. (J. Wyman Jones, Pres.; Hugh N. Camp, Sec. Capital, $1,500,000. Directors: J. Wyman Jones, Hugh N. Camp, Charles B. Parsons, William H. Harris, Russell H. Hoadley, J. H. Crane, Firman Desloge, Lewis F. Whitin, Frederick E. Camp) 55 Liberty
St. Joseph Loan & Trust Co. (no inf.) 55 Liberty
St. Kevin Mining Co. (inf. unattainable) 25 Beaver
St. Lawrence Marble Co. (John Benham, Pres.; Anstin Stevens, Sec. Capital, $250,000. Directors: John Benham, Anstin Stevens, John W. Griswold, Milo M. & Milo M. Bolding jr. J. L. Woodward, Henry D. Fuller) 115 B'way
St. Louis Southern R. R. Co. (Ephraim C. Dawes, Pres.; Charles H. Bosworth, Sec.; John E. McGettigan. Treas. Capital, $500,000. Directors: Charles W. Fairbanks, S. M. Dodd, Ephraim C. Dawes, Charles H. Bosworth, J. M. Richard, S. T. Bush, F. W. Macy) 16 Broad
St. Louis & San Francisco Railway Co. (Edward F. Winslow, Pres.; Thomas W. Lillie. Sec. Capital, $30,000,000. Directors: William F. Buckley, George Coppell, Walter L. Frost, I. E.

WATER METERS, GAS ENGINES, | NATIONAL METER CO.
FOR PUMPING AND POWER. | 252 Broadway, N. Y.

SAI 263 SAM

Gates, George J. Gould, Bryce Gray, Collis P. Huntington, John O'Day, Horace Porter, John Paton, Jesse Seligman, Russell Sage, Edward F. Winslow) 15 Broad

St. Louis, Alton & Terre Haute R. R. Co. (George W. Parker, Pres.; Edward F. Leonard, Sec. Capital, $4,768,400. Directors: W. Bayard Cutting, George F. Peabody, William A. Read, Edward H. Litchfield, Schuyler L. Parsons, F. K. Youngblood, Eli Wiley, William K. Murphy, James A. Eads, Henry K. Bench, Levi Davis, George W. Parker, Edward Abend) 16 Broad

St. Louis, Arkansas, & Texas Railway Co. (S. W. Fordyce, Pres.; Edwin Gould, Sec.; G. K. Warner, Treas. Capital, $16,251,000. Directors: S. W. Foydyce, Edwin Gould, G. K. Warner, R. C. Kerens, J. W. Phillips, W. F. Homan, J. C. Reiff, H. G. Allis, V. D. Wilkins, W. M. Senter, S. A. Bemis, C. M. Seley, George Clark, James Garrity, William Bohan, Thomas Randolph) 195 B'way

St. Louis, Des Moines & Northern Railway Co. (dissolved) 1 B'way

St. Louis, Iron Mountain & Southern Railway Co. (Jay Gould, Pres.; Arnos H. Calef, Sec. Capital, $26,000,000. Directors: Jay Gould, R. S. Hayes, Russell Sage, Amos L. Hopkins, Samuel Shethar, John T. Terry, George J. Gould, Duncan D. Parmly, Henry Whelen, Rufus J. Lackland, S. H. H. Clark, George W. Allen, Logan H. Roots) 195 B'way

St. Louis, New Orleans & Ocean Canal & Transp. Co. (Chester C. Munroe, Pres.; Nathaniel S. Bailey, Sec. Capital, $1,000,000. Directors: Chester C. Munroe, Albert C. Janin, Nathaniel S. Bailey, A. Raymond, John A. Blair) 1 B'way

St. Nicholas Bank (Arthur R. Graves, Pres.; William J. Gardner, Cashier; William Tharp, Notary. Capital, $500,000. Directors: Arthur B. Graves, Henry F. Hitch, Joseph H. Parsons, John Straiton, William H. Akin, William J. Gardner, Joseph W. Ogden, George P. Sheldon, Gustav K. Kissel) 193 B'way

St. Paul & Duluth R. R. Co. (Richard S. Hayes, Pres.; Philip S. Harris, Sec. Capital, $9,500,000. Directors: Thomas Denny, K. W. Peet, William H. Fisher, Samuel Smith jr. Alexander H. Stevens, Walter C. Tuckerman, Richard B. Dodson, Richard S. Hayes, Clarence S. Day) 32 Nassau

St. Paul, Minneapolis & Manitoba Railway Co. (James J. Hill, Pres.; Edward T. Nichols, Treas. Capital, $20,000,000. Directors: James J. Hill, George Stephen, Donald A. Smith, Henry D. & William Minot jr. George Bliss, John W. Sterling) 40 Wall

St. Paul's Bookbindery (John L. Rile, propr.) 195 Fulton

Saitta James, Son & Co. (James & Peter Saitta & N. Fugazzi) 15 State

Saitta S. & Co. (Simone & Joseph & Placido Saitta) 24 State

Sala J. & Co. (Juan Sala & Cosme Batlle) 24 State

Saladino A. & Co. (dissolved) 369 Broome & 122 Bleecker

Salamander Grate Bar Co. (Augustus C. Walbridge, Pres.; John B. Hegeman, Sec.; further inf. unattainable) 110 Liberty

Salamander Works (William Pollon, Pres.; Cornelius Pollon, Sec. Capital, $100,000 ; further inf. unattainable) 63 Bethune

Salberg I. & Co. (dissolved) 252 W. 39th

Salisbury & Travers (Charles H. Salisbury & Irvin D. Travers) 305 W. 128th

Salisbury & Vanwagenen (dissolved) 159 Duane

Sallade & Loveland (Charles H. Sallade & William F. Loveland) 109 John

Salmon Charles A. & Co. (Charles A. Salmon & Jose A. Gutierrez) 75 Pine

Salmon Hamilton H. & Co. (Hamilton H. Salmon & Richard Brandt) 136 Pearl

Salmon River Paper Co. (dissolved) 140 Nassau

Salomon Gustav & Brothers (Gustav & Salomon Salomon, only) 133 Malden la.

Salomon L. A. & Brother (Louis A. & Charles Salomon) 216 Pearl

Salomon M. & E. Tobacco Co. (Emanuel Salomon, Pres.; John W. Schmidt, Sec.; Henry Adler, Treas. Capital, $50,000. Directors: Emanuel Salomon, Henry Adler, John W. Schmidt) 65 Malden la.

Salomon Brothers (Siegfried & August Salomon) 127 Roosevelt

Salomon & Gutman (Samuel Salomon & Bernhard Gutman) 494 B'way

Salomon & Phillips (Bernard J. Salomon & S. Phillips Mendel, only) 33 Spruce

Salomon, Dulon & Sutro (Edward Salomon, Rudolf Dulon & Theodore Sutro) 115 B'way

Salomon's B., Sons (Samuel & Morris Salomon) 175 W. 46th & 511 Park av.

Salomon's Simon, Sons (David E. & Charles W. Salomon) 428 E. Houston

Salter B. & Co. (Benjamin Salter & George Alexander) 462 Washn. mkt

Salter M. & Co. (dissolved) 401 Washn. mkt

Salter Brothers (Richard J. & Charles G. Salter) 60 Reade

Saltman & Degenhardt (Charles Saltman jr. & Henry Degenhardt) 604 Eleventh av.

Saltsburg Coal Co. (B. K. Jamison, Pres.; J. H. Kershow, Treas.; further inf. unattainable) 1 B'way

Saltzsieler F. W. & Co. (Frederick W. Saltzsieder & William Kropp) 884 Sixth av.

Salutaris Co. (James W. Inches, Pres.; Charles M. McGowan, Sec. Capital, $100,000. Directors: James W. Inches, Charles M. McGowan) 45 B'way

Salvin & Co. (Paul Salvin, Co. refused) 164 Park row

Salvini & Jais (dissolved) 393 Grand

Salzer & Wolf (Leopold Salzer & Frank Wolf) 271 Canal

Sam Mayer & Co. (Mayer & Jacob Sam, 2259 Third av. Mayer & Charles & Jacob Sam, 24 W. 125th)

Samck & Son (Alexander Samek, only) 882 B'way

Samelson J. & Co. (Joseph Samelson & John Panli) 84 Greene

Sammis G. R. & Co. (George R. Sammis, no Co.) 414 Fourth av.

Sammis P. P. & Co. (dissolved) 414 Fourth av.

Sammons Store Stool Co. (inoperative) 205 Canal

Samper S. & Co. (Silvestre & Rafael Samper) 93 Wall

Sampers H. P. & Co. (Henry P. Sampers & Leon Monnier) 19 Barclay

Sampson Alden & Sons (Edward C. & Henry & Elijah P. Sampson, only) 58 Reade

Sampson O. H. & Co. (Oscar H. & Charles E. Sampson, Joseph Sargent & Eugenie H. Sampson) 57 Leonard

Sampter M., Sons & Co. (Michael & Morris & Arnold Sampter & Sigmont Simon) 15 E. 4th

Sampter & Bloomfield (Rudolph Sampter & Charles S. Bloomfield) 320 B'way

Samson & Goodwin (Daniel T. Samson & Sylvester Goodwin) 97 Market

Samter M. L. & Co. (Martin L. & Bernard M. Samter) 416 B'way

Samuels Lehman & Son (Lehman & Samuel Samuels) ft. E. 44th

Samuels Simon & Son (Simon & Henry Samuels) 94 Baxter

Samuels D. M. & Co. (dissolved) 4 Bond

Samuels J. & Brother (Julius & Isaac Samuels) 58 E. Houston

EXCELSIOR BIRD FOOD. The recognized standard. The most reliable for your Canary. Use no other. Insist upon getting it. Packed only by C. ROSENSTEIN & CO., 373 Washington Street, New York.

Samuels M. & Co. (Mark Samuels & Levi Abrahams) 164 Mott

Samuels Brothers (Abraham & Peter Samuels) 114 E. B'way

Samuels & Cohn (Samuel Samuels & Harry L. Cohn) 153 Chambers

Samuels & Friedman (Julius Samuels & Jacob Friedman) 635 B'way

Samuels & Isaacs (Julius Samuels & Jechinovsky Isaacs) 436 B'way

Samuels, Lyon & Co. (Jacob J. Samuels, Charles Lyon & Isaac Samuels) 25 E. Houston & 137 Crosby

San Antonio & Aransas Pass Railway Co. (Uriah Lott, Pres.; Reagan Houston, Sec.; Arthur Hanel, Treas. Capital, $5,000,000. Directors: Uriah Lott, Reagan Houston, William Heureman, George W. Brackenridge, Albert C. Schryver, Benjamin F. Yoakum, Arthur Hanel, Herman D. Kampmann, Henry Elmendorf, Eric P. Swenson) 45 & 353 B'way

San Diego Gas & Electric Light Co. of N. J. (Carmon R. Hetfield, Pres.; William H. Miller, Sec. Capital, $750,000. Directors: Carmon R. Hotfield, Frederick F. Durkee, E. S. Babcock, Gordon Macdonald, John D. Spreckels, William H. Miller, Benjamin F. Sherman) 120 B'way

San Juan Chief Mining Co. (Asahel G. Darwin, Pres.; Malcolm W. Niven, Sec.; James C. Beach, Treas. Capital, $500,000. Directors: Asahel G. Darwin, James C. Beach, Malcolm W. Niven, Samuel H. Beach, James L. Hill) 45 B'way

San Juan Smelting & Mining Co. (Henry Amy, Pres.; Joseph A. Davidson, Sec. Capital, $2,000,000. Directors: Henry Amy, George Foster Peabody, Theodore F. H. Meyer, Edwin M. Bulkley, Charles G. Miller) 16 Broad

San Martin Mining Co. (James L. Carnaghan, Pres.; Henry Bradstreet, Sec. Capital, $1,500,000; further inf. unattainable) 1 B'way

San Miguel Gold Placers Co. (Benjamin F. Butler, Pres.; Joseph Torrey, Sec.; James Gilfillan, Treas. Capital, $3,000,000. Directors: Benjamin F. Butler, Charles E. Parker, James Gilfillan, Joseph Torrey) 41 Wall

San Sebastian Gold Mining Co. (Charles A. Doten, Pres.; Cornelius I. Blauvelt, Sec.; Dudley S. Steele, Treas. Capital, $1,600,000. Directors: Charles A. Doten, Dudley S. Steele, Charles Stewart, Charles Cushman, Ludwig Drier, E. C. Wells, C. M. Ward, George W. Brown) 145 B'way

San Vicente Cattle Co. (Alexander Guan, Pres.; Lester M. Clark, Sec.; John C. Barron, Treas.; further inf. unattainable) 35 B'way

Sanborn George H. & Sons (Herman L. & George E. Sanborn, only) 69 Beekman

Sanborn Map & Publishing Co. (Ltd.) (dissolved) 115 B'way

Sanborn & Rose Mfg. Co. (Daniel S. Sanborn, Pres.; Garrett F. Rose, Treas. Capital, $20,000. Trustees: Daniel S. Sanborn, Garrett F. & Dennis F. Rose) 479 B'way

Sanborn-Perris Map Co. (Ltd.) (refused) 115 B'way

Sanchez & Haya (Serafin Sanchez & Ygnacio Haya) 81 Pearl

Sand & Koenig (Frederick Sand & Moses Koenig) ft. E. 55th

Sanday & Shepherd (Samuel Sanday & Joseph Shepherd) 304 Produce Ex.

Sander & Henshel (dissolved) 65 Reade

Sanders Edward & Co. (Frances & Joanna Sanders, only) 212 B'way

Sanders Leather Co. (no inf.) 126 Chambers

Sanders Mfg. Co. (Eliza Sanders, Pres.; Herman Schloss, Sec.; Louis Sanders, Treas. Capital, $10,000. Directors: Eliza & Louis Sanders, Herman Schloss) 85 Walker

Sanders B. & N. (Benjamin & Nathan) 151 Bowery

Sanders Brothers (dissolved) 368 Ninth av.

Sanders, Wagner & Auerbach (Lewis Sanders, Louis A. Wagner & Meyer Auerbach) 5 Beekman

Sanders' Theodore, Sons (Solomon & Moses Sanders) 502 First av.

Sanderson & Son (Richard & Harold A. Sanderson) 22 State & Pier 54 (new) N. R.

Sandford & Klatte (J. G. William Klatte, only) 78 Broad

Sandford, Ayres & Co. (dissolved) 75 Dey

Sands Alfred B. & Son (Alfred B. & Ernest P. Sands) 164 Beekman

Sands Samuel S. & Co. (Samuel S. Sands, W. Henry Reese & Charles E. Sands) 10 Wall & 9 Pine

Sands Brothers (Redman & Louis Sands) 6 Reade

Sands & Depeyster (Andrew H. Sands & Henry Depeyster) 51 Pine

Sandy Hill Quarry Co. (John H. Drake, Pres.; Nathaniel F. Jones, Sec. Capital, $50,000. Trustees: John H. Drake, William D. Stratton, Alfred P. Boller, Edward Kelly, Nathaniel F. Jones) 71 B'way

Sandy Hook, Quarantine & City Island Telegraph Co. (Radcliffe Baldwin, Pres.; Francis W. Houghton, Sec.; Albert H. Brown, Treas. Capital, $40,000. Directors: Radcliffe Baldwin, Charles P. Sumner, Charles A. Pool, Daniel Barnes, Albert H. Brown) 14 Beaver

Sanford F. E. & Co. (Pierson E. & Lansing H. & Milton L. Sanford) 135 & 138 W. 26th

Sanford S. & Sons (Stephen & John & William C. Sanford) 869 B'way

Sanford S. T. W. & Sons (Drurie S. Sanford, Pres.; Horatio S. Sanford, Sec.; Clarence T. Sanford, Treas. Capital, $500,000. Directors: Drurie S. & Clarence T. & Horatio S. Sanford) 231 B'way

Sanford & Cook (Edward F. Sanford:—special partner, Ferdinand H. Cook. Sag Harbor, N. Y., $12,000; terminates 28th Jan. 1892) 14 John

Sanford & Robinson (Samuel B. Sanford & George S. Robinson) 69 Mercer

Sang Chong & Co. (Sang Chong & Lee Num) 28 Mott

Sanger Brothers (Isaac & Philip & Alexander Sanger) 127 W. B'way

Sanger & Davis (William Cary Sanger & Gherardi Davis) 52 Wall

Sanger & Wells (dissolved) 86 Front

Sanitaline Mfg. Co. (dissolved) 13 Spruce

Sanitary & Fertilizer Co. (Julius Hirshfeld, V. Pres.; Frank M. Miller, Sec. Capital, $2,000,000. Directors: Julius Hirshfeld, Frank M. Miller, Oscar D. McClellan, William O. Jacquette) 60 B'way

Sanna, Pesataro & Jacolucci (Carmine Sanna, Francesco Pesataro & Giuseppe Jacolucci) 71 Thompson

Sans Souci Twine Mills (Henry Gade, propr.) 349 Broome

Santa Clara Lumber Co. (George E. Dodge, Pres.; Frederick D. Soper, Sec. Capital, $400,000. Directors: George E. Dodge, Titus B. & Ferris J. Meigs, John Hurd, Charles L. Hotchkiss, Henry Patton, Frederick D. Soper) 72 Wall

Santa Lucia Mining & Milling Co. (no inf.) 1 B'way

Santee Construction Co. (A. Ames Howlett, Pres.; Oliver M. Chace, Sec. Directors: A. Ames Howlett, Oliver M. Chace, John Harlin, John B. Silver) 115 B'way

Santo Domingo Central R. R. Co. (Horatio C. King, Pres.; James E. Coleman, Sec.; Philip P. Harris, Treas. Capital, $2,000,000. Direc-

IDEN & CO., University Place, 9th to 10th Sts., N.Y. | **MANUFACTURERS OF GAS FIXTURES AND ELECTROLIERS**

SAN 265 SCH

tors: Horatio C. King, Henry L. Bean, George G. Ward, Henry W. Alden, James E. Coleman, William H. Bibby, Chester C. Munroe, Milton Griswold) 32 Liberty

Sanxay J. F. & Co. (Joseph F. Sanxay, no Co.) 104 Fulton

Saqui & Ducker (John Saqui & George M. Ducker) 54 E. 12th

Sar-Alvarez & Co. (dissolved) 4 Stone

Saramacca Development Co. (inoperative) 102 B'way

Sarasohn & Son (Kassyel H. & Ezekiel Sarasohn) 185 & 211 E. B'way

Saratoga Express Co. (Michael Casey, propr.) 877 Sixth av.

Saratoga Lafayette Spouting Spring (Francisco Lavandeyra, propr.) 697 B'way

Saratoga Natural Liquefied Carbonic Acid Gas Works (Francisco Lavandeyra, propr.) 697 B'way

Saratoga Vichy Spring Co. (Roswell A. Roberts, Pres.; A. Godwin Munn jr. Sec. Capital, $50,000. Directors: Roswell A. Roberts, Louis W. James, A. Godwin Munn jr. George H. Tuttle, Levi C. Lathrop, Robert M. Brace, Simon August) 122 Pearl

Sardy, Coles & Co. (John L. Sardy & J. Bard Rogers, only) 96 Maiden la.

Sargent Mfg. Co. (George F. Sargent, Pres.; Hugh Park Sec.; John L. Murray, Treas. Capital, $100,000. Directors: George F. Sargent, Mollie Fancher, Thomas Hume, John L. Murray, Hugh Park, Louis Kenitz, John J. Howden) 814 B'way & 157 Eleventh av.

Sargent & Brothers (George W. & William H. Sargent) 34 Platt

Sargent & Co. (George H. & Joseph B. Sargent) 37 Chambers & 18 Reade

Sarner H. & Son (Heyman & Julius Sarner) 916 & 1420 Third av.

Sarre & Le Lacheur (John Sarre & John I. Le Lacheur) 43 W. 29th

Sartirano & Co. (Augustus Sartirano & William Ryan) 352 Eighth av. & 116 Gansevoort

Sartor Brothers & Co. (Joseph F. Sartor, Joseph M. Ryan & Charles Lane, only) 47 Beekman

Sartorius A. & Co. (August Sartorius, Louis Reuscho & Otto Schmiedicke) 29 Barclay

Sartorius & Co. (Otto Sartorius, Henry F. Gierisch & Moses Bijur) 171 Pearl

Sasse J. & L. (dissolved) 1838 Park av.

Sasserath K. & Brother (Kaufman & Simon Sasserath) 1487 & 1730 Ninth av.

Satinas Mfg. Co. (I. Samuels, propr.) 335 B'way

Satteries John & Co. (dissolved) Kingsbridge rd. n W. 224th

Satteries & Smith (Edward R. Satteries & L. Jaquelin Smith) 36 Cedar

Satteries, Bostwick & Martin (Livingston Satteries, Charles B. Bostwick & L. Kingsley Martin) 55 Cedar

Satterthwaite & Platt (Clayton Platt & Nicholas W. S. Catlin, only) 16 Exchange pl. & 16 Beaver

Sattler Brothers (George & Henry Sattler) 602 E. 16th

Saubiac D. & Son (Bernard & Ernest Saubiac) 28 Union sq. E.

Sauer J. P. & Co. (Joseph P. Sauer & Frederick H. Schacht) 343 Washn.

Sauer & Burrowes (Emil M. Sauer & William A. Burrowes) 3 Hanover

Sauer & Lange (George W. Sauer & Harold C. Lange) 1 Chambers

Sauer & Schmitz (Anthony Sauer jr. & Henry J. Schmitz) 9 W. B'way

Saugerties Blank Book Co. (Howard Gillespy, receiver) 10 Thomas

Saulpaugh's M. J., Sons (James M. & William L. Saulpaugh) 704 E. 12th & 180 Lewis

Saulson Designing Co. (Joseph Samelson, propr.) 173 Grand

Saunders Mfg. Co. (Charles Saunders, propr.) 7 Murray

Saunders E. A. & Co. (Edmund A. Saunders & Thomas F. Pollard) 25 West

Saunders, Webb & Worcester (Thorndike Saunders, G. Creighton Webb & Edwin D. Worcester jr.) 170 B'way

Saunderson & Co. (William S. Saunderson & Charles G. Adams) 194 Water & 256 Pearl

Sauter L. & Co. (Lorenz Sauter & Robert Stahl) 1 Maiden la.

Savarese A. & Co. (dissolved) 501 Pearl

Savery's John, Son & Co. (William E. Savery, George W. Mason & George W. Vanschaack) 97 Beekman

Saville B. L. (Leah M. Saville, only) 11 Platt

Savin F. W. & Co. (Frank W. Savin & J. Arthur Dramwell) 67 Exchange pl. & 26 New

Savin & Vanderhoof (dissolved) 26 New

Sawtooth Milling & Mining Co. (Ludlow Paton, Pres.; Francis H. Weeks, Sec. Capital, $100,000. Trustees: Ludlow Paton, Robert Lenox Belknap, Francis H. Weeks) 120 B'way

Sawyer John M. & Son (John M. & John M. Sawyer jr.) 85 South

Sawyer & Getty (Merritt E. Sawyer & Robert P. Getty jr.) 206 B'way

Sawyer & Gilman (Henry F. Sawyer & Charles W. Gilman) 163 Mercer

Sawyer & McCormack (Frank S. Sawyer & Edward A. McCormack) 185 Pearl

Sawyer, Manning & Co. (Joseph & Joseph D. Sawyer, John B. Manning & Thomas F. Patterson) 86 Franklin

Sawyer, Wallace & Co. (Samuel A. Sawyer, David L. Wallace & Thomas Miller) 18 B'way

Sawyer-Man Electric Co. (George Westinghouse jr. Pres.; George H. Lowrey, Sec.; Caleb H. Barney, Treas. Capital, $128,000. Directors: George Westinghouse jr. H. M. Byllesby, C. H. Jackson, John Caldwell, Hugh R. Garden) 510 W. 23d

Saxe & Robertson (George G. Saxe & James H. Robertson) 331 B'way

Saxton James & Sons (James & Bernard F. & James J. Saxton) 32 B'way

Sayer & Co. (William M. jr. & Richard S. Bayer) 87 Dey

Sayre A. J. & Co. (Andrew J. & Gabriel H. Sayre) 130 Fulton mkt

Sazarac Jules & Co. (Jules Sazarac, no Co.) 97 Water

Scammell Brothers (J. Walter & Frederick B. & Joseph H. Scammell) 29 Beaver

Scandinavian & Finlanders' Emigrant Co. (Ltd.) (Gustaf A. Gronlund, Pres.; Gustaf G. Wikander, Treas.; David W. Johanson, Sec. Capital, $10,000. Directors: Gustaf A. Gronlund, George Drown, Gustaf Pihlman, David W. Johanson, John Erickson) 24 State

Scanlan J. & M. & P. (James & Michael & Patrick) 613 W. 40th & 14 Thompson av. W. Washn. mkt

Scanlon & Drake (Terence P. Scanlon & Edmund F. Drake) 54 Grand

Scarborough W. A. & Co. (William A. Scarborough, no Co.) 141 Reade

Scarborough & Morris (Edward W. Scarborough & William F. Morris) 28 Beekman

Schaaf & Mack (Charles Schaaf & Philip Mack jr.) 43 Park

Schachne Louis & Brother (Louis & Siegfried Schachne) 60 Walker

Schachno & Oppenheim (no inf.) 5 Orchard

TYPEWRITING DONE BY THE TROW CITY DIRECTORY CO., 11 University Place.

Schachtel M. & G. (Michael jr. & George) 158 Seventh av. & 244 W. 16th
Schade Brothers (William & George Schade) 106 Third av.
Schaefer Henry & Son (Henry & Henry C. Schaefer) 95 W. Houston
Schaefer Philip & Son (Philip & Louis Schaefer) 530 W. 57th
Schaefer F. & M., Brewing Co. (Edward C. Schaefer, Pres.; Rudolph J. Schaefer, Sec.; George G. Schaefer, Treas. Capital, $650,000. Directors: Edward C. & Emil & George G. & Rudolph J. & Frederick & Max Schaefer) 112 E. 51st
Schaefer H. & F. (Henry & Frederick) 370 Seventh av.
Schaefer & Egenberger (Robert Schaefer & Edward Egenberger) 60 Nassau
Schaefer & Schneider (dissolved) 1563 First av.
Schaefer & Vonasten (no inf.) 365 Lenox av.
Schaefer & Weber (Louis F. Schaefer & John Weber jr.) 142 Fulton
Schaeffer Frank & Sons (Frank & Joseph F. & Edward S. Schaeffler) 408 E. 48th
Schaeffler Joseph & Son (Joseph & Joseph Schaeffler jr.) 98 E. 4th
Schafer J. & Brothers (Jacob & Michael & Nathan Schafer) 183 Broome & 154 Delancey
Schafer Brothers (Samuel M. & Simon Schafer) 41 Wall
Schaffer & Budenberg Building Co. (Ludolf Portong, Pres.; Albert L. Portong, Sec.; Percival Knauth, Treas. Capital, $40,000. Directors: Ludolf & Albert L. Portong, Percival Knauth) 40 John
Schaffer & Carroll (dissolved) 359 Third av.
Schaffner Brothers (George & Gustav F. Schaffner) 488 Second av.
Schaidner & Saul (dissolved) 186 E. 124th
Schalk Emil & Co. (dissolved) 50 New
Schall & Co. (Wilhelmina Schall & Martin Keppler) 61 Barclay
Schanning F. & Co. (Frederick Schanning, Joseph Lublin & Maria L. Estey) 195 Greene
Schappert A. & Son (Anton & William Schappert) 195 Lincoln av.
Schappert Brothers (dissolved) 1809 Second av.
Scharlach Louis & Co. (Louis A. & Herman Scharlach & Emil Delemos) 391 Grand
Scharies Brothers (Philip & Max B. Scharies) 24 W. 23d
Schastey George A. & Co. (George A. Schastey, no Co.) 1683 B'way
Schastey & Diesel (Frank C. Schastey & August W. Diesel) 215 Forsyth
Schattman J. & H. & Co. (Jacob & Hyman Schattman & Charles C. Tobias) 577 B'way
Schattman Brothers (Morris & Julius Schattman) 9 E. 4th
Schatzmann & Steiniger (Benjamin Schatzmann & Philip Stainiger) 1370 First av.
Schaul & Borck (Julius Schaul & Max Borck) 527 B'way & 108 Mercer
Schaumann G. & Co. (Gustav Schaumann, no Co.) 87 Spruce
Schaumburger N. & C. (Nathan & Charles) 2066 Third av.
Schaus William (Herman Schaus & Augustus W. Conover, only) 204 Fifth av.
Schawel James & Co. (James & Rosalie Schawel) 29 John
Scherer & Gross (Matthew Gross, only) 148 Baxter
Schefer, Schramm & Vogel (Carl Schefer, William Schramm & Herman Vogel:—special partner, Edward Luckemeyer, Paris, France, $350,000; terminates 31st Dec, 1891) 476 Broome

Schefers V. & Co. (Valentine Schefers & Paul Kauffmann) 1242 B'way
Scheftel Brothers (Adolph Scheftel, only) 31 Spruce
Scheiber J. & H. (John J. & Henry) 1176 Second av.
Scheidecker Charles & Co. (Charles Scheidecker & Henry Gonder) W. 170th n Tenth av.
Scheidel & Co. (dissolved) 314 W. 44th
Scheidig John & Co. (Frederick Scheidig, only) 43 Malden la.
Scheinberg L. & C. & Co. (no inf.) 97 Spring
Scheitlin Edward & Co. (Edward Scheitlin & Armin Hartmann) 75 Leonard
Scheland Brothers (Ernest F. W. & August F. W. Scheland) 350 Tenth av.
Schell & Hogan (Frank H. Schell & Thomas Hogan) 835 B'way
Schellings C. J. & Co. (Cornelius J. Schellings & Egbert Witterdink) 116 Pearl
Schenck J. H. & Co. (no inf.) 252 B'way
Schenck W. K. & Co. (William K. Schenck & Frederick Woodcock) 1591 B'way
Schenck & Punnett (N. Pendleton Schenck & James Punnett) 94 Liberty
Schendel Charles & Co. (Charles Schendel & Michael Deutsch) 72 B'way, 63 Fulton, 116 Nassau & 332 Canal
Schenectady Gas Light Co. (William Henry White, Pres.; Clement A. White, Sec.; John McEnroe, Treas. Capital, $200,000. Directors: William Henry & Clement A. White, John McEnroe, Charles Stanford) 30 Pine
Schenk & Schlichte (George Schenk & Arnold W. Schlichte) 93 Sixth av.
Schenkein H. & Sons (Hyman & Morris & Benjamin Schenkein) 88 John
Schepflin C. & Co. (Christian Schepflin & Edward Winter) 318 B'way
Scherck & Co. (Nathan L. Scherck & Frank Blanchy) 37 Beaver
Scherer P. & Co. (Paul & Pauline Fanny Scherer & Charles Moebus) 11 Barclay
Scherf Louis J. & Co. (Louis J. Scherf & Henry J. Ulfers) 40 Crosby
Schering & Glatz (Joseph Glatz & estate of Hugo Schering) 56 Malden la.
Schermerhorn J. W. & Co. (George M. Kendall, only) 3 E. 14th
Scherrer Brothers (William & George & Peter Scherrer) 937 First av.
Scherwinsky & Harrison (Max Scherwinsky & Meyer Harrison) 91 Division
Scheuer A. & Co. (dissolved) 6 E. 125th
Scheuer J. & S. (Julius & Samuel) 329 E. Houston
Scheuer S. & Son (Simon & Max & Ralph & Isaac Scheuer) 60 Leonard
Scheuer Brothers (umbrs.) (Henry & Nathan & Max Scheuer) 342 Canal
Scheuer Brothers (flowers) (Jonas & Charles Scheuer) 631 B'way
Scheuer Brothers (leather) (dissolved) 961 Second av.
Scheuer & Brother (Isaac & Herman & Charles Scheuer) 359 B'way
Scheuer & Rothschild (Simon Scheuer & Marks Rothschild) 107 Duane
Scheuer & Steinberg (dissolved) 186 Pearl
Scheuer, Bloom & Simon (Charles Scheuer, Jacob N. Bloom & Alexander B. Simon) 699 B'way
Schey & Co. (Simon Schey & Simon Herz) 15 Walker
Scheyer Herrmann S. & Co. (Herrmann S. Scheyer, no Co.) 178 Canal
Scheyer & Son (Emanuel Scheyer, only) 280 Bowery

Schick & Walter (Carl Schick & August Walter) 126 Ludlow
Schickel William & Co. (William Schickel, Isaac E. Ditmars & Fredrick P. Dinkelberg) 346 B'way
Schichlor O. H. & Co. (Otto H. Schiebler & John Kempf) 289 Bowery
Schieffelin W. H. & Co. (William H. Schieffelin, William N. Clark, William S. Merserenu, William L. Brower, William J. Schieffelin & Henry S. Clark:—special partners, Samuel B. Schieffelin, N. Y. & Sidney A. Schieffelin, Geneva, N. Y. each $50,000; terminates 31st Dec. 1894) 170 William & 402 Front
Schiele Lewis & Co. (Lewis Schiele & Seligman Gutman) 390 B'way
Schieren Charles A. & Co. (Charles A. Schieren & Frederick A. M. Burrell) 47 Ferry & 76 Cliff
Schierenbeck A. & Co. (Ahrend Schierenbeck & Frederick D. Herrmann) 135 Maiden la.
Schierenbeck & Vonelm (Frederick Schierenbeck, only) 402 E. 48th
Schiff Mac & Co. (Mac Schiff, no Co.) 397 B'way
Schiff Mfg. Co. (Solomon H. Schiff, Pres.; Moritz Schiff, Sec. Capital, $10,000. Directors: Solomon H. Schiff, Samuel Solinger, Felix Schiff) 1 Greene & 607 W. 30th
Schiff M. & Son (Meyer & Bernhard Schiff) 1196 Third av.
Schiff & Bodenheimer (Henry Schiff & Max Bodenheimer) 100 Franklin
Schiff & Co. (Charles J. Schiff & Philip Krakor) 20 W. 3d
Schiffer Henry & Co. (Henry Schiffer, L. Fred. Olt & Theodore E. Zocher) 159 E. 88th
Schiffman & Weinstein (no inf.) 126 Attorney
Schildknecht J. & C. Riecker (dissolved) 28 Stanton
Schile H. & Sons (Henry J. & Romeo H. & Erwin D. Schile) 285 Bowery
Schilling A. & Co. (August Schilling & George F. & John H. Volkmann) 5 Worth
Schilling Brothers (William A. & Christian Schilling) 14 First av.
Schilling & Maurer (Peter Schilling & Herman Maurer) 49 Eldridge
Schilling, Stollwerck & Co. (August Schilling, Peter & Hulnrich & Ludwig & Karl Stollwerck & George F. & John H. Volkmann) 5 Worth
Schillinger Fire-Proof Cement & Asphalt Co. (John J. Schillinger, Pres.; Theodore Schillinger, Sec. Capital, $100,000. Directors: John J. & Theodore & Gustave & Henry Schillinger) 413 E. 91st
Schimper William & Co. (William Schimper, Robert R. Detacher & John R. Mahlstedt) 587 Hudson
Schimpf John & Son (John & John Schimpf jr.) 62 John
Schimpf Brothers (dissolved) Tenth av. n W. 160th
Schindler Brothers (Philip A. & Anthony J. Schindler) 26 Beekman
Schindler & Co. (John S. Schindler, Robert D. Hopkins, Isaac H. Francis & William T. Brigham) 1179 B'way
Schinkowsky Brothers (David & Julius Schinkowsky) r 15 Leonard
Schirmer Charles F. & Son (Charles F. & Charles J. Schirmer) 181 Third av.
Schittenholm G. & W. (George & William) 196 Elizabeth
Schlaeppi Brothers (Ulrich & Andrew Schlaeppi) 136 Bleecker
Schlageter & Meyer (Matthias Schlageter & Bernard Meyer) 1072 Tenth av.
Schleich C. F. & Dietrich (Charles F. Schleich & Louis Dietrich) 36 Maiden la.
Schlesier F. H. W. & Son (Frederick H. W. & Frederick E. J. Schlesier) 250 Eighth av.

Schlesinger Charles & Sons (Charles & Elias D. Schlesinger, only) 94 Liberty
Schlesinger John & Sons (dissolved) 145 Elm
Schlesinger Leo & Co. (Leo & Abraham Schlesinger) 129 Crosby
Schlesinger A. & Son (agents) (Abraham & Samuel Schlesinger) 350 E. Houston
Schlesinger & Roth (dissolved) 350 E. Houston
Schlesinger A. & Son (tailors) (Abraham & Baldwin Schlesinger) 88 E. Houston
Schlesinger F. G. & Sons (Frederick G. & Frederick S. & Charles T. Schlesinger) 52 Exchange pl.
Schlesinger M. & Co. (designers) (no inf.) 218 Fulton
Schlesinger M. & Co. (neckwear) (Max Schlesinger & Emile Lux) 426 Broome
Schlesinger Brothers (cigars) (Morris & Henry Schlesinger) 401 Madison
Schlesinger Brothers (ore) (William & Adolph Schlesinger) 45 Wall
Schlesinger & Postman (dissolved) 90 Wooster
Schlesinger's John, Sons (Siegfried & Alexander Schlesinger) 145 Elm
Schley Frederick & Co. (Frederick Schley & Jacob Young) 118 Nassau
Schleyer Brothers (no inf.) 225 W. 27th
Schlichting & Rendsburg (Emil Schlichting & Wolff E. Rendsburg) 12 Vesey
Schlobohm & Sturtz (Otto H. Schlobohm & Henry N. Sturtz) 118 W. 10th & 1676 Ninth av.
Schloesser Philip & Co. (Philip & Henry Schloesser) 424 Eighth av.
Schloesser & McManus (Charles A. Schloesser & Hugh McManus) 806 E. 77th
Schloss William & Co. (William Schloss & Caroline Zeimer) 619 B'way
Schloss E. & Co. (Gustave B. Schloss & Moses M. Lindenstein, only) 879 Pearl & 153 Goerck
Schloss N. J. & Co. (Nathan J. & Henry J. Schloss & Joseph H. Louis) 653 B'way
Schloss Brothers (Philip & Gustave & Alexander P. Schloss) 836 B'way
Schloss & Katz (Harry Schloss & Alfred E. Katz: —special partners, Isidor Gartner & Isaac Friedenholt, each $5,000; terminates 31st Jan. 1892) 70 Wooster
Schloss & Sons (William J. & Henry W. & Meyer W. Schloss) 15 Mercer
Schlosser & Co. (Leopold V. Schlosser, no Co.) 71 New
Schlosser & Gerken (Abraham Schlosser & Henry H. Gerken) 773 Tenth av.
Schlueter & Bartholdi (Ferdinand Schlueter & George W. Bartholdi) 751 B'way
Schlusing G. F. & Co. (Gustav F. & Herman F. Schlusing) 1199 Third av.
Schmeckenbecher's M., Sons (George & John G. Schmeckenbecher) 355 E. 58th
Schmeidler L. & Sons (Leopold & Henry Schmeidler, only) 38 Lispenard
Schmelz John & Co. (John Schmelz & Louis Becker) 17 Dey
Schmelzle Frederick & Co. (Frederick Schmelzle & Henry T. Steinhauer) 458 Canal
Schmelzle & Mount (George Schmelzle & Joseph E. Mount) 205 South
Schmenger John P. & Co. (dissolved) 130 Third av.
Schmerbach Brothers (dissolved) 65 Grand
Schmersahl & Wittpenn (Frederick L. Schmersahl & Louis Wittpenn) 214 West
Schmickl F. & Co. (Franz Schmickl & James Bryson) 63 Chambers & 65 Reade
Schmickl M. & Schmidt (Matthias Schmickl & Ferdinand Schmidt) 28 Warren

SCH 268 SCH

Schmidt Charles & Son (ganges) (Charles & Charles Schmidt jr.) r 41 Centre
Schmidt Charles & Son (wagons) (Charles & Albert Schmidt) 9 Norfolk
Schmidt Charles D. & Co. (Charles D. Schmidt & Louis Lichtenstein) 741 E. 9th
Schmidt Charles F. & Peters (Charles F. Schmidt & Carl Otto Peters) 24 Beaver
Schmidt E., Mfg. Co. (E. Schmidt, propr.) 232 Sixth
Schmidt Henry & Co. (dissolved) 388 Canal
Schmidt Henry & Son (Henry & Gustave Schmidt) 247 Centre
Schmidt Henry G. & Co. (Emil Cuntz, only) 38 Beaver
Schmidt A. & Son (Anthony & William H. Schmidt) 347 Fifth av.
Schmidt F. & Son (dissolved) 28 Carmine
Schmidt G. & L. (Gustave & Ludwig) 216 Centre
Schmidt G. W. & Brother (no inf.) 146 Essex
Schmidt K. & Co. (Konrad Schmidt & Henry Lohrburger) 44 College pl.
Schmidt P. H. & Son (Philip H. & W. Charles Schmidt) 1311 B'way
Schmidt Brothers (Charles & Otto Schmidt) 2411 Second av.
Schmidt & Co. (hammers) (David H. Schmidt, William F. Gerlach & John Eckel) 814 E. 22d
Schmidt & Co. (lithographers) (David Schmidt & George Schmitt) 9 New Chambers
Schmidt & Co. (mech. engs.) (dissolved) 21 Centre
Schmidt & Co. (patterns) (John J. G. C. Schmidt, no Co.) 75 Park pl.
Schmidt & Putterer (dissolved) 70 First
Schmidt & Hamerle (Charles Schmidt & Michael Hamerle) St. Nicholas av. n W. 157th
Schmidt & Heithoff (Charles Schmidt & Herman Heithoff) 1480 Second av.
Schmidt & Meier (Charles Schmidt & Franz Meier) 185 Prince
Schmidt & Selle (Louis Schmidt & Alfred Selle) 51 Beaver
Schmidt, Muller & Schweitzer (Hugo Schmidt, John Muller & August Schweitzer) r 122 Elizabeth
Schmieder L. E. & Co. (Louis E. Schmieder, no Co.) 62 Worth
Schmitt George & Brother (George & Frederick Schmitt) 246 E. 46th
Schmitt C. J. & Co. (Charles J. Schmitt, no Co.) 42 Bloomfield, W. Washn. mkt
Schmitt Brothers (Louis & Philip & George Schmitt) 34 W. 20th
Schmitt & Haas (Conrad R. Schmitt & George Haas) 13 Chambers
Schmitt & Scheuermann (dissolved) 745 Tenth av.
Schmitt & Schwanenfluegel (George Schmitt & Louis Von Schwanenfluegel) 400 E. 57th
Schmitz Henry & Son (dissolved) 506 Pearl
Schmolze & Hildenbrand (Frederick Schmolze & Otto Hildenbrand) 16 Vandewater
Schmolze & Welfenbach (dissolved) 68 Fulton
Schmuckler Brothers (Mark & Simon Schmuckler) 604 B'way
Schmults Brothers (August F. & Ernst H. Schmults) 82 Church
Schnabel Brothers (Richard A. Schnabel & Auguste F. Montant, only) 73 Worth
Schnakenberg Brothers (Richard & Charles Schnakenberg) 1491 Third av. & 2430 Eighth av.
Schnapmann G. & J. (Gustava & Justina) 405 Grand
Schnarr & Delius (Lorenz Schnarr & Henry W. Delius) 115 Worth

Schnatz & Massoth (George J. Schnatz & Charles Massoth) 49 Sheriff
Schnaufer Mrs. H. & Sons (Christiana & John H. & George A. Schnaufer) Daly av. c Poms
Schneer B. & Co. (Benjamin Schneer & Isidor Smith) 615 D'way
Schneider Daniel & Son (Daniel & Christopher Schneider) 85 Av. D
Schneider Peter & Co. (Henry Fehrabend & John P. Harman, only) 182 B'way
Schneider C. & Co. (Charles Schneider & Benjamin F. Corell) 496 West
Schneider C. J. & Brother (Charles J. & Adolph Schneider) 6 Burling sl.
Schneider J. G. & Co. (John G. Schneider, no Co.) 767 D'way
Schneider L. & Sons (Louis & Louis jr. & William Schneider) 746 Ninth av.
Schneider Brothers (Anton & Frederick Schneider) 17 Bond
Schneider & Chassenud (Louis H. Schneider & Jasper B. Chassenud) 287 B'way
Schneider & Hertor (Ernst E. W. Schneider & Henry Hertor) 48 Bible h.
Schneider & Schramm (Louis Schneider & Charles B. Schramm) 490 Eighth av.
Schneider, Campbell & Co. (Charles Schneider, James R. Mack & Joseph H. Olcutt, only) 7 Union sq. W., 20 E. 15th & 627 W. 23d
Schneider's Peter, Sons & Co. (Otto Schneider Francis M. Jaeger & John H. Knoeppel, only) 165 Canal
Schneler A. & Co. (dissolved) 80 Hester
Schnell, Metzger & Co. (dissolved) 30 B'way
Schnittman & Jacobson (Philip Schnittman & Jacob Jacobson) 138 Division
Schnitzler & Co. (Ignatz & Bernhard Schnitzler) 630 B'way & 14 Second av.
Schnoter T. & H. (Theresa & Henrietta) 515 Sixth av.
Schnurmacher Brothers (Samuel & Marcus & Albert & Joseph & Lippmann Schnurmacher) 1214 & 1491 First av. & 335 E. 54th
Schoellkopf, Hartford & Maclagan (Ltd.) (Jacob F. Schoellkopf, Pres.; George Maclagan, Sec. Capital, $25,000. Directors: Jacob F. Schoellkopf, James Hartford, George Maclagan, Jacob F. jr. & Hugo Schoellkopf) 3 Cedar
Schoen George & Co. (George Schoen & Robert L. Stix) 129 W. B'way
Schoen S. & Son (Simon & Louis Schoen) 72½ Essex
Schoen & Co. (dissolved) 287 Centre
Schoen & Loewenthal (Daniel Loewenthal, only) 287 E. 4th
Schoenfeld Louis & A. Harris (Louis Schoenfeld & Adolph Harris) 18 G'wich
Schoenfeld S. & Co. (Simon Schoenfeld & Frederica Goldstein) 264 Canal
Schoenmann & Rumpf (William Schoenmann & John W. Rumpf) 146 Elm
Schoenrock & Kessler (Ferdinand Schoenrock & Carl E. Kessler) 58 Av. D. & 623 Second av.
Schoenthal Max (Max Schoenthal:—special partner, Henry Dergelsheimer, *Furth Bavaria, Germany*, $50,000; terminates 15th July, 1892) 31 Pearl
Schoff, Fairchild & Co. (Arno H. Schoff, George M. Fairchild jr. & Frederick L. Holmquist) 41 Worth
Schofield William H. & Sons (William H. & Albert B Schofield, only) 170 B'way
Scholes Brothers (dissolved) 585 Hudson, 281 First av. & 370 Ninth av.
Scholle Brothers (William & Jacob Scholle) 31 Broad
Scholtz & Mechow (dissolved) 526 Canal

FOR THE BEST CO-PARTNERSHIP IN THE BEST CORPORATION SEE PAGE F IN BACK OF BOOK

Scholtz, Sanchez & Co. (Carlos A. Scholtz & Jose A Sanchez, no Co.) 24 State

Schoeneberger Brothers (Adolph & Frederick Schoueberger) 20 Jackson

School News Co. (Capital $5,000; further inf. unattainable) no address

Schoolhouse Charles & Son (Charles & Lewis Schoolhouse) 40 Walker

Schoonmaker L. E. & Co. (Lucas E. & Hiram Schoonmaker) 28 Warren & 98 Chambers

Schoonmaker Brothers (refused) 220 Grand

Schoonmaker & Bainbridge (Frank S. Bainbridge, only) 142 Maiden la.

Schorenstone Frères (Henri & Jacques Schorenstens) 158 Mercer & 140 Wooster

Schorling Brothers (Victor & George Schorling) 299 Seventh av.

Schorsch & Son (Meyer & Isaac Schorsch) 6 Av. D

Schott Brothers (Charles & Conrad Schott) 384 B'way

Schott & Franke (Charles A. Schott & Frederick R. Franke) 262 Washn.

Schott & Pulsford Mfg. Co. (Capital, $50,000; further inf. unattainable) no address

Schoverling H. & Co. (Herman Schoverling & Otto Martens) 18 Burling sl.

Schoverling, Daly & Gales (Augustus Schoverling, Charles Daly & Joseph Gales) 302 B'way & 84 Duane

Schrade & Priester (George Schrade & Charles Priester) 92 White

Schrader A. & Son (Augustus & George Schrader) 32 Rose

Schrader & Blohm (no inf.) 182 Chrystie

Schrader & Vondohren (dissolved) 316 Washn.

Schradzki H. & M. (Henry & Michael) 1958 Third av.

Schramm & Diberthuler (dissolved) 49 Ridge

Schrecke & Riestadt (Richard Schrecke & Henry Riestadt) 170 Bowery

Schreiber & Co. (no inf.) 79 Stanton

Schreiber, Pollatchek & Son (Ludwig Schreiber & Max & Morris Pollatchek) 40 B'way

Schrenkeisen M. & H. (Martin & Henry G.) 23 Elizabeth & 180 Monroe

Schroder G. & Son (dissolved) 191 Canal

Schroder Brothers (Frederick & Frank Schroder) 637 First av.

Schroder & Feldmann (Herman H. Schroder & John D. Fehlmann) 984 Tenth av.

Schroeder Julius & Co. (Julius Schroeder & Frederick J. Kall) 6 Leight

Schroeder William & Co. (William Schroeder & Co. Crefeld, Germany, George C. & Otto Andreae jr. & Fritz Hill) 73 Mercer

Schroeder G. & Co. (Gilliat Schroeder & Frank Holme Wiggin) 36 Cotton Ex.

Schroeder H. & Son (painters) (Henry & William Schroeder) 451 E. 83d

Schroeder H. & Son (tailors) (Henry & Charles F. Schroeder) 326 Sixth av.

Schroeder Brothers (Henry & Claus H. Schroeder) 32 Gansevoort

Schroeder & Bon (Frederick A. & Edwin A. Schroeder, Isidor M. Bon & William J. Hazlewood) 178 Water

Schroeder & Goldberger (Caroline Schroeder & Henry Goldberger) 911 Third av. & 983 Second av.

Schroeder & Kahrs (dissolved) 1602 Third av.

Schroeder & Masing (Frank H. Schroeder & Gustav Masing) 187 Bowery

Schroeder & Wenner (William A. Schroeder & Louis Wenner) 117 Barrow

Schubert H. & Co. (Aaron & William Schubart, only) 100 Water

Schubert Piano Co. (Peter Duffy, Pres.; Thomas Marty, Sec.; Margaret A. Duffy, Treas. Capital, $3,000. Directors: Peter Duffy, Henry Harty, Margaret A. Duffy) E. 134th n Alexander av.

Schubert & Co. (Constantine Schubert, Co. refused) 326 Pearl

Schubert C. & Co. (dissolved) 326 Pearl & 12 First

Schuberth Edward & Co. (Juergen F. H. Meyer, only) 23 Union sq. W.

Schuchman & Kehr (Christian Schuchman & Caspar Kehr) 805 E. 80th

Schuerer & Lammer (Joseph Schuerer & Henry Lammer) 206 Waverley pl.

Schuh F. & Son (Frederick & Charles Schuh) 2446 Third av.

Schulang P. & Co. (Philip Schulang & Adolph Hochstim) 508 Broome

Schuldenfrei & Fishel (Solomon Schuldenfrei & Samuel J. Fishel) 89 Mercer

Schuler Brothers (Frank & Otto Schuler) 959 Tenth av.

Schuler & Wibel (Frederick P. M. Schuler & William Wibel) 1011 Third av.

Schulhof Firearm Mfg. Co. (Benjamin F. Dospassos, Pres.; Joseph J. Schmidt, Sec. Capital, $750,000. Trustees: Joseph K. McCammon, Benjamin F. Dospassos, Charles C. Shelton, William G. Davis, Joseph J. Schmidt) 15 Broad

Schulhof Brothers (Sigmund & Max Schulhof) 90 Second

Schulhof Sisters (Sophia & Mary & Caroline Schulhof) 158 E. 56th

Schuller Frederick & Son (Frederick & Octave Schuller) 132 Thompson

Schuller & Saulpaugh (dissolved) 656 B'way

Schult's D. H. Sons (William H. & John M. Schult) 601 Third av.

Schulte & Gerberding (dissolved) 115 Stanton

Schulte & Werner (no inf.) 225 Grand

Schultheis & Gebhardt (Adam Schultheis & Henry Gebhardt) 370 B'way

Schultz Joseph & Co. (Joseph Schukz & Ferdinand Oppenheimer) 110 Mercer

Schultz E. & R. (Eldor A. L. & Ernest R. J.) 83 S. William & 35 Stone

Schultz M. & Brother (Michael jr. & Edward Schultz) 152 E. Houston

Schultz Brothers (Otto J. & C. Gustav A. Schultz) 320 Sixth av.

Schultz & Co. (gold leaf) (Nicholas & Henry Schultze) 25 St. Mark's pl.

Schultz & Co. (soap) (Robert D. Schultz & John Hoge) 164 Franklin

Schultz & Gerstel (dissolved) r 18 Clinton

Schultz & Hoyt (Norman Schultz & Joseph B. Hoyt) 111 Cliff

Schultz, Innes & Co. (James H. Percival, Edward W. Richardson, Louis H. Schultz & John A. Innes) 111 Cliff & 20 Vandewater

Schultze Emil & Co. (Emil Schultze & Edmand de Brackeleer) 36 Denver

Schultze W. L. & Co. (William L. & Charles A. Schultze) 619 Sixth av.

Schulz & Ruckgaber (Carl Goepel & Max Ruckgaber jr.:—special partners, Friedrich G. Schulz, Stuttgart, Germany, $100,000 & Max Ruckgaber, B'klyn, N. Y., $250,000; terminates 1st Jan, 1894) 29 William

Schulze & Coors (Ida Schulze & Henry Coors) 182 Park row

Schulze-Berge & Koechl (Paul Schulze-Berge & Victor Koechl) 186 Front

Schumacher Edward & Co. (Edward Schumacher, Carl Muller & Frederick W. Quass) 53 Greene

Schumacher Henry & Son (Henry & Henry J. Schumacher) 851 Eighth

Schumacher C. & Co. (Charles Schumacher, George Reitze & Charles Stern) 42 Exchange pl.
Schumacher H. & G. (Henry & George) 438 West
Schumacher & Co. (William Schumacher & John Miller) 793 Third av.
Schumacher & Ettlinger (Theodore Schumacher & Louis Ettlinger) 34 Bleecker
Schuman & Pidgeon (Arthur E. Schuman & James J. Pidgeon) 84 Murray
Schumann Charles W. & Sons (Charles W. & Charles W. jr. & George H. Schumann) 800 D'way & 27 E. 17th
Schumann Herman & Co. (Herman Schumann & Henry Stern) 384 Canal
Schumann W. F. & Co. (William Schumann & Henry Kanenbley, only) 286 Washn.
Schupak & Co. (no inf.) 186 Clinton
Schureman M. F. & Co. (Melancthon F. Schureman & Charles S. Bartlett) First av. c E. 100th
Schuster Brothers (George & William Schuster) 11 Av. A
Schutte H. & Co. (Herman Schutte & John F. Buell) 105 Broad
Schutz Brothers & Dieth (A. Henry & Julius Schutz & Henry Dieth) 426 D'way
Schuyler G. L. & Co. (Walter G. & James B. Schuyler, only) First av. c E. 98th
Schuyler P. C. & Co. (Schuyler Miller, only) 93 Wall
Schuyler's Detective Agency (Frank D. Schuyler, propr.) 190 D'way
Schwaab & Landau (Louis Schwaab & Samuel Landau) 300 E. 72d
Schwab C. & Co. (Caroline Schwab, no Co.) 81 Greene
Schwab G. & Brothers (Gabriel & Nathan & Abraham & Lee L. Schwab) 41 Greene
Schwab S. M. jr. & Co. (Samuel M. jr. & Noah Schwab) 73 Worth
Schwab & Co. (no inf.) 9 Second av.
Schwab & Frankenhauser (Leah Schwab & William Frankenhauser) 42 Bond
Schwab's Moritz, Son (Emil Schwab) 96 Eighth av.
Schwager & Shine (Emil Schwager & Michael Shine) 188 Fourth av.
Schwalb & Page (Robert Schwalb & Frank C. Page) 73 Christopher
Schwalbe William H. & Co. (William H. Schwalbe, no Co.) 21 Park row
Schwanhauser & Muller (Ernest Schwanhauser & Arthur H. Muller) 87 Beaver
Schwannecke A. F. & Co. (Albert F. Schwannecke & Arthur L. Meyer) 1068 Madison av.
Schwarm & Aufenanger (Charles Schwarm & William Aufenanger) 58 Fulton
Schwarm & Prange (dissolved) 58 Fulton
Schwarting & Schrader (John Schwarting & Frederick Schrader) 313 E. 35th
Schwartz J. & Co. (Jacob Schwartz & Anton Wolzel) 171 First av.
Schwartz R. & Co. (no inf.) 229 Grand
Schwartz S. & Son (Sophia & Samuel Schwartz jr.) 72 William
Schwartz Brothers (liquors) (Simon & Marcus Schwartz) 148 E. 42d
Schwartz Brothers (meat) (Joseph Schwartz, only) 111½ First av.
Schwartz & Blum (no inf.) 101 Mangin
Schwartz & Brother (Albert G. Schwartz, only) 416½ Sixth av.
Schwartz & Colby (no inf.) 844 Sixth av.
Schwartz & Co. (David & Charles Schwartz) 619 D'way

Schwartz & Feldtman (Samuel Schwartz & Abraham Feldtman) 125 Columbia
Schwartz & Rubinstein (dissolved) r 35 Pitt
Schwartz & Stoll (Jacob Schwartz & Harris Stoll) 108 E. D'way
Schwartz & Wedde (Franz Schwartz & Albert Wedde) 40 Stone
Schwarz Benjamin & Sons (Emil & Louis Schwarz, only) 45 Pearl
Schwarz L. & Co. (Louis Schwarz, no Co.) 144 Grand
Schwarz S. & Brother (Simon & Joseph Schwarz) 149 Spring
Schwarz Brothers (cigars) (Julius & Adolph Schwarz) 255 G'wich
Schwarz Brothers (meat) (Moritz A. & Louis A. Schwarz) 384 Cherry
Schwarz Brothers (meat) (William H. & Franz A. Schwarz) 2540 Eighth av. & 1001 Tenth av.
Schwarz & Gerhardt (August Schwarz & Adolph Gerhardt) 348 E. 115th
Schwarze Julius & Co. (Julius Schwarze & Oscar Dietzel) 176 Prince
Schwarzenbach, Huber & Co. (refused) 472 Broome
Schwarzenberg & Schneider (John Schwarzenberg & Henry Schneider) 60 Barclay
Schwarzkopf Dan & Co. (Daniel & Benjamin Schwarzkopf) 607 Eighth av. & 2230 Third av.
Schwarzkopf L. & Co. (Leopold Schwarzkopf & Francis Marks) 1387 Av. A
Schwarzkopf & Ellinger (Morris Schwarzkopf & Simon Ellinger) 173 Lewis
Schwarzkopf & Oppenheimer (Edward Schwarzkopf & Meyer Oppenheimer) 53 Av. A
Schwarzschild & Sulzberger (Joseph Schwarzschild, Ferdinand Sulzberger, Joseph & Samuel Weil & Frederick Joseph) 800 First av. 187 Washn. & 9 Grace av. W. Washn. mkt
Schwarzschild & Sulzberger Refrigerating Co. (Ltd.) (Joseph Schwarzschild, Pres.; Samuel Schwarzschild, Sec.; Ferdinand Sulzberger, Treas. Capital, $300,000; further inf. unattainable) 9 Grace av. W. Washn. mkt & 806 First av.
Schwarzwaelder William & Co. (William & William O. Schwarzwaelder) 250 Pearl
Schwarzwalder J. & Sons (Henry & Elizabeth Schwarzwalder & Ernest H. Horb, only) 637 W. 51st
Schweers F. & H. (Frederick & Herman) 240 South
Schwegler Brothers (William & Charles Schwegler) 1443 Third av.
Schweinburg Philip & Co. (Philip Schweinburg, no Co.) 61 Walker
Schweitzer H. & A. (dissolved) 776 Second av.
Schweitzer Brothers (Henry J. & Eugene Schweitzer) 87 Crosby
Schweitzer & Diemer (Bernard J. Schweitzer & Julius J. Diemer) 84 W. D'way
Schweizer Jules E. & Co. (Jules E. & Alfred Schweizer) 353 Produce Ex.
Schwencke O. L. (firm) (refused) 38 Bleecker
Schwerin & Jacobs (Bernhard Schwerin & Harry C. Jacobs) 670 D'way
Schwieder & Moll (Herman Schwieder & Conrad Moll) 350 E. 48d
Schwiers & Helferich (dissolved) 332 W. 37th, 314 W. 39th & 605 W. 48th
Schwietering H. H. & Co. (Herman H. Schwietering, Alpheus P. Ralph & Louis Wurster:— special partner, William Scheldt, Kestwig, Germany, $100,000; terminates 31st Dec. 1892) 100 Grand
Sciarrone & Co. (dissolved) 43 Fulton
Scientific Publishing Co. (Richard P. Rothwell, Pres.; Sophia Braeunlich, Sec. Capital,

THADDEUS DAVIDS CO., WRITING INKS, SEALING WAX, MUCILAGE.
MAKE THE BEST

SCI 271 SEA

$100,000. Directors: Richard P. Rothwell, Sophia Braeunlich, F. J. Pratt) 27 Park pl.

Scioto Valley & N. E. R. R. Co. (John Byrne, Pres.; William H. Whitney, Sec.; L. C. Newsom, Treas. Capital, $5,000,000. Directors: John Byrne, Camille Weldeufeld, Frank Sullivan Smith, Collis P. Huntington, William Moneypenny, L. C. Newsom, Charles Parrott P. W. Huntington, W. W. Franklin) 54 Wall

Scofield John H. & Co. (John Hocker Scofield & Augustus H. W. Johnson) 74 B'way

Scofield Brothers (Louis F. & Edward H. Scofield) B'way n Kingsbridge rd.

Scofield & Gray (John C. Scofield & George Gray) 82 Franklin

Scontoni Brothers (Thomas & James Scontoni) 86 Nassau

Scoria Block & Tile Co. (inf. unattainable) 40 B'way

Scoria Mfg. Co. (inf. unattainable) 49 B'way

Scott Alfred & Co. (Alfred Scott & George B. Class) 11 Frankfort

Scott Archibald & Sons (Archibald & Walter E. & Archibald T. Scott) 545 W. 21st, ft. E. 19th & ft. W. 23d

Scott J. W., Co. (Ltd.) (J. Walter Scott, Pres.; Charles P. Scott, Sec. Capital, $20,000. Directors: J. Walter & Charles P. Scott, Charles W. Gregory, William T. Calloway, Charles H. Bechtol) 163 Fulton

Scott John R. & Co. (John R. Scott, no Co.) 67 Broad

Scott Leonard, Publication Co. (Samuel P. Ferree, propr.) 29 Park row

Scott Stamp & Coin Co. (Ltd.) (Henry Collin, Pres.; Henry L. Calman, Sec. Capital, $30,000. Directors: Henry Collin, Henry L. & Gustave D. & David & Charles Calman) 12 E. 23d & 155 B'way

Scott Thomas & Co. (Thomas Scott, Norman T. Pease & Edward A. Anderson;—special partner, Camden C. Dike, B'klyn, N. Y., $50,000; terminates 1st May, 1890) 120 Duane

Scott Walter & Co. (Walter & Albert E. Scott) 272 W. 125th

Scott William B. (William B. Scott;—special partner, Isaac Buchanan, $1,000; terminates 1st Aug. 1894) 407 Fifth av.

Scott J. & W. (John & William) 509 W. 87th, ft. W. 84th & E. 135th n Madison av.

Scott J. T. & Co. (James T. & Samuel C. Scott) 4 Maiden la.

Scott N. & P. (Niels S. & Paul S.) 446 Canal

Scott T. & Son (Theodore & Julius Scott) 1262 Third av.

Scott Brothers (James & Edward W. & George W. Scott) 78 Franklin

Scott & Bowne (Alfred B. Scott & Samuel W. Bowne) 132 S. 5th av.

Scott & Coleman (Alexander J. Scott & Franklin Coleman) 95 Wall & Pier 38½ E. R.

Scott & Co. (dressmkrs.) (Josephine Scott, Co. refused) 101 W. 45th

Scott & Co. (ice) (John & William & Robert Scott) 509 W. 37th, ft. W. 84th & E. 135th n Madison av.

Scott & Malleson (William H. Scott jr. & Henry H. Malleson) 80 Whitehall

Scott & May (Andrew Scott & John May) 15 Spruce

Scott & Myers (George H. Scott & Sinclair Myers) 146 B'way

Scott & Newman (George D. Scott & Patrick Newman) 161 Ninth av.

Scott & Pearson (Charles B. Scott & Eugene Pearson) 260 Front

Scott & Reynolds (Louisa Scott & Lillian Reynolds) 50 W. 22d

Scott, Alexander & Talbot (William A. Scott,

James A. Alexander & John M. Talbot) 45 William

Scott's William, Son & Co. (John F. & William S. Scott, Caldwell R. Blakeman & George W. Vanderhoef) 111 Wall

Scovill Mfg. Co. (Frederick J. Kingsbury, Pres.; Mark L. Sperry, Sec.; Chauncey P. Goss, Treas. Capital, $400,000. Directors: Frederick J. Kingsbury, Chauncey P. Goss, Mark L. Sperry, Douglas F. Maltby, W. Irving Adams) 423 Broome & 205 Elizabeth

Scovill & Adams Co. (W. Irving Adams, Pres.; Harry Littlejohn, Sec. Capital, $200,000. Directors: W. Irving Adams, Harry Littlejohn, Frederick J. Kingsbury, Chauncey P. Goss, Mark L. Sperry, Henry W. Scovill, William E. Curtis) 423 Broome

Scoville A. H. & Co. (Amasa H. Scoville & Frank McCoy) 170 Water

Scowcroft & Schoonmaker (Edward T. Scowcroft & Paul Schoonmaker) Boulevard n W. 94th

Scranton Suburban Railway Co. (Arthur J. Moulton, Pres.; Horace E. Hand, Sec. Capital, $200,000. Directors: Arthur J. Moulton, J. B. Newcombe, W. H. Thomas, J. J. Dimock, W. Jessup) 54 Wall

Screw Dock Co. (Chester W. Chapin, Pres.; Alfred C. Chapin, Sec.; Theodore K. Hazard, Treas. Capital, $150,000. Directors: Chester W. & Alfred C. Chapin, Theodore K. Hazard) Pier 30½ E. R.

Scribner & Wolford (Charles & Arthur H. Scribner, only) 743 B'way

Scribner's Charles, Sons (Charles & Arthur H. Scribner) 743 B'way

Scriven J. A. & Co. (Jeremiah A. Scriven & Lemuel M. Baldwin) 16 E. 15th

Scudder S. V. & F. P. (no inl.) 4 Cedar

Scully & Devitt (John S. Scully & Martin Devitt) 3 Battery pl. & Castle Garden

Scully & Moran (John H. Scully & James W. Moran) ft. E. 104th

Seaboard Lumber Co. (Erastus H. Barnes, Pres.; Horace C. Burrows, Sec. Capital, $200,000. Directors: Erastus H. Barnes, Henry D. Haven, Horace C. Burrows, Josiah Lombard, Marshall Ayres) 12 B'way

Seaboard National Bank (William A. Pullman, Pres.; Stuart G. Nelson, Cashier; Charles H. Symmes, Notary. Capital, $500,000. Directors: William A. Pullman, Joseph Seep, Daniel O'Day, Henry M. Curtis, Samuel G. Bayne, T. Wistar Brown, Lewis H. Smith, William A. Ross, Henry Allen, Samuel T. Hubbard jr. Stuart G. Nelson) 18 B'way

Seabury & Johnson (contractors) (dissolved) 19 Cortlandt

Seabury & Johnson (plasters) (George J. Seabury, Pres.; Robert J. Seabury, Sec.; John M. Peters, Treas. Capital, $100,000. Trustees: George J. Seabury, John M. Peters, Robert J. Seabury) 21 Platt

Seagrist F. W. jr. & Co. (Francis W. Seagrist jr. & Byron W. Greene jr.) 302 Av. D

Seaich Joseph & Son (William H. Seaich, only) 44 & 50 E. 32d

Seale Charles & Co. (Charles Seale & Edward Bruce) 860 B'way

Seale & Bruce (dissolved) 860 B'way

Seals D. & Co. (Samuel H. Seals, Oscar & Oscar M. Lyon, only) 62 Water

Seaman John H. & Co. (John H. Seaman & John H. Miller) ft. Horatio

Seaman Lloyd I. & Co. (Lloyd I. Seaman & James H. Snyder) 313 Washn.

Seaman R. F. & Co. (Robert F. Seaman & Louisa H. McKeon) 38 Burling sl.

Seaman T. & Walter C. (Treadwell & Walter C.) 343 E. 125th

Seaman & Conger (James A. Seaman, Clarence B. Conger & James A. Lynch) 45 B'way

Seamen's Bank for Savings (William C. Sturges, Pres.; Daniel Barnes, Cashier; John H. Boynton, Sec.; Silvanus F. Jenkins, Treas. Trustees: William C. Sturges, William A. Booth, E. H. R. Lyman, Horace Gray, John H. Boynton, George Briggs, Ambrose Snow, Emerson Coleman, James R. Taylor, William H. H. Moore, James A. Howlett, Charles H. Trask, William De Groot, George H. Macy, John D. Wing, Vernon H. Brown, Frederick Sturges, J. W. Frothingham, George C. Magoun) 76 Wall

Searing United Mfg. Co. (Theodore W. Searing, propr.) 118 Lincoln av.

Searle, Dalley & Co. (Haskell A. Searle, Granville F. Dalley & Edwin V. Mitchell) 600 B'way & 184 Crosby

Searles, Shorey & Co. (dissolved) 16 E. 15th

Sears Commercial Co. (Ltd.) (Richard F. Sears, Pres.; Alberto Falcon, Sec. Directors: Richard F. Sears, William R. Grace, Alberto Falcon) 1 Hanover sq.

Sears & Howell (Benjamin C. Sears & James B. & Joseph E. Howell) 446 W. 19th

Seashore Electric Railway Co. (Frank W. Child Pres.; William P. Stevenson, Sec. Capital, $200,000. Directors: Frank W. Child, William P. Stevenson, Daniel S. Thompson, Francis H. Weeks, A. J. Hutchinson, Hugh S. Kiumouth, Edward M. Fielder) 115 B'way

Seattle Coal & Iron Co. (refused) 2 Wall & 35 William

Seattle & Eastern Construction Co. (Franklin M. Jones, Pres.; John Craig, Sec.; A. S. Dunham, Treas. Capital, $1,000,000. Trustees: Franklin M. Jones, Angus Mackintosh, Richard H. Talcott, John Craig, John H. Bryant) 35 William

Seattle, Lake Shore & Eastern Railway Co. (James R. McDonald, Pres.; A. S. Dunham, Sec. Capital, $15,000,000. Directors: William M. Akin, John F. Alexander, A. S. Dunham, Thomas M. Logan, J. D. Pace, John Leary, Joseph A. Jamison, James R. McDonald, Jacob Furth, Morton S. Paton, George G. Lyon, Frank H. Osgood, John H. Bryant) 35 William

Seaver Warehousing Co. (F. Mortimer Seaver, Pres.; William Moores, Treas.; further inf. unattainable) 3 Bridge

Seavey, Foster & Bowman (Joseph W. C. Seavey, Frederick A. Foster, John A. Bowman, Henry Frost, Simeon W. Clapp & George C. Oakes) 441 B'way

Sebastian Mfg. Co. (Charles A. Stadler, Pres.; William Hoffmann, Treas. Capital, $50,000. Directors: Charles A. Stadler, William Hoffmann, Adolph G. Hupfel, Henry M. Haar) 223 E. 43d

Seckel M. & Co. (Moritz Seckel, George C. Hensel & Frederick Ellerbrook) 15 Mercer

Seckendorf A. & Son (dissolved) 1228 Second av.

Seckendorf & Co. (dissolved) 11 Bond

Seckendorf, Korn & Co. (Maurice Seckendorf, Henry Korn & Henry Stodeker) 26 E. Houston

Seckendorf, Ulrop & Young (Abraham Seckendorf, Nicholas H. Ulrop & Willard F. Young) 1228 Second av.

Second Avenue R. R. Co. (George S. Hart, Pres.; John B. Underhill, Sec.; Henry B. Dorrance, Treas. Capital, $1,862,000. Directors: George S. Hart, M. M. White, Moses Mehrbach, Charles Brenneman, Edward C. Smith, Samuel Knox, Noah C. Rogers, Charles F. Cox, Richard A. Anthony. William E. Peck, James L. Dreese, Payson Merrill, Augustus S. Hutchins) Second av. c E. 97th

Second National Bank (George Montague, Pres.; Joseph S. Case, Cashier; Henry B. Gibbons, Notary. Capital, $300,000. Directors: Amos R. Eno, Henry A. Hurlbut, Alfred B. Darling, John L. Riker, William C. Brewster, William P. St. John, George Montague, Charles B. Fosdick, George Sherman, Welcome G. Hitchcock) 100 Fifth av.

Second National Gold Mining Co. (inoperative) 56 Wall

Secor Marine Propeller Co. (Edgar S. Hicks, Pres.; John A. Secor, Sec. Capital, $10,000,000. Directors: Edgar S. Hicks, John A. Secor, Richard Poillon, William Schwarswelder, Stephen E. Mills, William J. March, Andrew J. Disney) 60 Wall

Secor Self-Leveling Berth Co. (inoperative) 120 B'way

Security Electric Signal Co. (Edward C. Cockey, Pres.; Thomas T. Eckert jr. Sec. Capital, $25,000; further inf. unattainable) 8 Day

Security Loan, Real Estate & Storage Co. (Herman Wronkow, Pres.; Griffin Tompkins, Sec. Capital, $250,000; further inf. unattainable) 23 Union sq. W.

Security Mutual Benefit Soc. (R. Carman Combes, Pres.; William D. Chandler, Sec. Directors: Rowland N. Hazard, R. Carman Combes, Edward A. Quintard, Henry C. Robinson, Andrew L. Soulard, John Stralton, William D. Snow, William B. Fuller, Henry B. Pierce, Elijah D. Wheeler) 238 B'way

Seddon & Rice (Charles A. Seddon & Adolph B. Rice) 206 B'way

Sedgman & Best (William J. Sedgman & J. Frank Best) 2558 Eighth av.

Seditzky P. & Co. (dissolved) 117 Wooster

See A. & Son (Amos L. & Edgar G. See) 519 W. 54th

See A. W. & Co. (Abram W. See, Edward A. Peirce, Edward J. Fagan, J. Otis Cox & John H. Walker) 1286 B'way

See & Conover (George See & Allen Conover) 210 W. 49th

See, Johnson & Depew (Abraham S. See, George T. Johnson & R. Henry Depew) 60 Liberty

Seebeck Brothers (John H. & Charles & Ernest Seebeck) 41 Beekman

Seed & Denby (John H. Seed & Isaac Denby) 83 Reade

Seeger & Guernsey Co. (Charles L. Seeger, Pres.; Frederic R. Guernsey, Sec.; George A. Dounce, Treas. Capital, $150,000. Trustees: Charles L. Seeger, Frederick R. Guernsey, George A. Dounce, H. B. Fullerton, William T. Seeger) 7 Bowling gr.

Seekamp Brothers (Herman & John Seckamp) 142 Liberty & 67 Gouverneur

Seekamp & Meyarhols (dissolved) 255 First av.

Seeley Mfg. Co. (no inf.) 45 B'way

Seeley Brothers (George H. & Nathan Seeley & James H. Taylor) 32 Burling sl.

Seeley & Schuckle (dissolved) 840 B'way

Seelig Brothers (Charles & Henry & Herman & William Seelig) 293 & 297 Bowery

Seelig & Taylor (Adolph Seelig & John H. Taylor) 10 Second av.

Seely & Griffen (dissolved) 56 Market

Seely & Holland (John A. Seely & James M. Holland) 14 Cortlandt

Seely & Lewthwaite (Charles Seely & Thomas H. Lewthwaite) 130 Worth

Seely's G. B., Son (Frank Seely) 319 W. 15th

Seeman Brothers (Joseph & Siegel W. Seeman) 339 G'wich

Seeman Brothers & Doremus (dissolved) 339 G'wich

Seemeyer & Fischer (Ernst Seemeyer & August Fischer) 985 First av.

Seer A. S., Theatrical Printing Co. (refused) 19 E. 17th

Seery & Conlon (Peter Seery & Thomas Conlon) 678 Third av.

Segal & Adelson (Israel Segal & Simon Adelson) 55 Ludlow

SPECIAL ATTENTION PAID TO THIS CLASS OF WORK } BANKERS' & BROKERS' CIRCULARS DELIVERED { THE TROW CITY DIRECTORY CO. 11 University Place.

Segall & Harris (Joseph Segall & Abraham Harris) 594 B'way & 124 Crosby
Seggermann Henry (Martha G. & Frederick K. & Victor A. Seggermann, only) 121 Front
Seggermann Brothers (Frederick K. & Victor A. Seggermann) 121 Front
Sehlbach E. & Co. (Ernst Sehlbach, William Diestal & Dawson Miles) 46 Cedar
Selb & Starke (George A. Selb & Otto E. Starke) 1197 Railroad av.
Seibel Brothers (Philip & Frederick Seibel) 496 Seventh av.
Seibert Henry & Brother Co. (Henry Seibert, Pres.; Jacob Lowenhaupt, Sec.; Robert T. Seibert, Treas. Capital, $100,000. Directors: Henry & Charles & Robert T. Seibert, Jacob Lowenhaupt, George E. Tooker) 12 Warren
Seidenberg & Co. (Joseph Seidenberg, no Co.) 327 E. 63d & 2298 Third av.
Seidenberg & Stiefel (Joseph Seidenberg & Adolph Stiefel) 413 E. 91st
Seidl J. & F. Martinek (Jacob Seidl & Frank Martinek) 963 Second av.
Seiferd Brothers (Louis & Joseph & Charles Seiferd) 214 E. 86th
Sekosky Brothers (Marx & Isaac Sekosky) 231 Park row & 63 New Bowery
Selchow & Righter (Elisha G. Selchow & John H. Righter) 41 John
Selden & Co. (Bolling Selden & Charles Poe) 287 B'way
Self Generating Electric Light & Power Co. (Inf. unattainable) 26 Lafayette pl.
Selig M. & Son (Moses & Max Selig) 86 First av.
Selig & Son (Isaac & Moses Selig) 358 & 827 Hudson & 102 Delancey
Seligman J. & W. & Co. (James & Jesse Seligman, only) 21 Broad
Seligman & Seligman (Theodore & Eugene & George W. Seligman) 15 Broad
Seligman & Sons (L. Guy & Louis G. Seligman) 84 Howard
Seligmann Brothers (Albert & Charles Seligmann) 248 Fulton
Seligmann & Hahn (David Seligmann & Isaac Hahn) 150 E. 24th
Seligsberg Joseph (Abraham Seligsberg, only) 174 Front
Seligsberg & Co. (Abraham Seligsberg & Theodore Hollman) 19 New & 66 B'way
Selleck & Son (no inf.) 34 W. 29th
Sellers John & Sons (John & William B. Sellers, only) 17 Dey
Sellner A. & Co. (Agustus Sellner & Aaron Wollholm) 511 B'way
Selma Water Co. (William Henry White, Pres.; Samuel W. John, Sec.; J. Ensign Fuller, Treas. Capital, $100,000. Directors: William Henry White, J. Ensign Fuller, Samuel W. John) 80 Pine
Selonick S. & Sons (Simon & Max & Edward Selonick) 101 Mercer
Semel J. H. & Co. (Jacob H. Semel & Louis Ettinger) 403 B'way
Semel Brothers (Louis J. & George Semel) 49 Walker
Semmer Philip, Glass Co. (Ltd.) (John P. Semmer, Pres.; George P. Brock, Sec.; Paul I. Clarke, Treas. Capital, $40,000. Directors: John P. Semmer, George P. Brock, Paul I. Clarke, Thomas McKie, Philip Semmer) 14 Desbrosses
Semon John G. & Co. (James L. Semon, only) 149 W. 30th
Sence L. & Son (Leonard & Victor Sence) 130 Bleecker

Sender & Mayer (Elias Sender & Bernhard Mayer) 26 Rivington
Senftenberg Brothers & Co. (Leopold & Adolph Senftenberg & Isidor & Gustav Mohringer) 57 Walker
Senger Martin & Sons (Martin & Jacob & Martin Senger jr.) 732 Ninth av. & 339 W. 52d
Senior E. M. & Son (Edward M. & Clarence W. Senior) 1139 Ninth av. 625 Madison av. & 1269 B'way
Senior M. D. (Mendes D. Senior;—special partner, Aaron B. Gomes (Casseres, Mandeville, W. I. $10,000 ; terminates 1st July, 1890) 19 Whitehall
Senior H. & Co. (Henry Senior, Co. refused) 10 Spruce
Senior & Fogerty (John W. Senior & James J. Fogerty) 58 Maiden la.
Senk & Prohal (Charles Senk & Vincenc Prchal) 305 Fifth
Sergeant Brothers (William R. & Joseph R. Sergeant) 182 Nassau
Serrand & Boulanger (dissolved) 169 Seventh av.
Serrell Silk Reeling Co. (Henry W. Munroe, Pres.; Charles Lyman, Sec. Capital $86,000. Trustees: Henry W. Munroe, Charles Lyman, Philip Walker) 16 Broad
Serrell A. T. & Son (Alfred T. & Alfred W. Serrell) Eleventh av. c W. 58th
Seton & Wissmann (Alfred Seton jr. & Francis de R. Wissmann) 79 Cedar & 1142 B'way
Settle Brothers & Co. (Edward & Alfred & J. Arthur Settle) 159 Greene
Sets J. R. & Co. (John R. Sets, Louis Dannemann, August Broltinger & Theodore Golden) ft. E. 79th
Sets & Bianchi (John H. Sets & Louis Bianchi) Woodlawn
Seventh National Bank (Gardiner Sherman, Pres.; John D. W. Grady, Cashier; Thomas Hinwood, Notary. Capital,$800,000. Directors: James Hall, Frank H. Lovell, Harry B. Hollins, William H. Pulsifer, Henry R. Beekman, W. C. Whittingham, Henry A. Rogers, H. Duncan Wood, Gardiner Sherman, John D. Crimmins, Harry I. Nicholas, Frederick Edey) 184 B'way
Seventy-third Street Building Co. (inoperative) 272 W. 125th
Severin Enameling Co. (dissolved) 297 Bowery
Sewall C. H. & Co. (Charles H. & William H. Sewall) 17 B'way
Seward James A. & Co. (James A. Seward, no Co.) 6 E. 20th
Seward & Son (dissolved) 60 Jeff. mkt.
Seward & Tourtellot (James B. Seward & James E. Tourtellot) 71 Franklin
Seward, Dacosta & Guthrie (Clarence A. Seward, Charles M. Dacosta, William D. Guthrie & Victor Morawetz) 29 Nassau
Sewell & Pierce (Robert Sewell & James F. Pierce) 34 Nassau
Sexton & Stodeker (William Sexton & Henry Stadeker) 1292 B'way
Sexton Brothers & Washburn (Augustus W. & William L. Sexton & George W. Washburn) 41 & 100 Maiden la.
Seymour Charles A. & Co. (Charles A. Seymour, Co., refused) 184 Park av.
Seymour Henry, Cutlery Co. (Henry Seymour, Pres.; Robert H. Seymour, Sec. Capital, $25,000. Directors: Henry & Robert H. & George M. Seymour) 84 Chambers
Seymour James H. & Co. (James H. Seymour, no Co.) 159 Chambers
Seymour Paper Co. (Charles E. O'Hara, Pres. Capital, $450,000. Directors: Charles E. O'Hara, Charles A. Nichols, Andrew Outerson, William P. Raynor, Charles E. O'Hara jr.) 45 John

TYPEWRITING DONE BY THE TROW CITY DIRECTORY CO., 11 University Place.

Seymour & McDougall (Saprina Seymour & Howard McDougall) 74 Tenth av.
Seymour & Noe (Egbert Seymour & James H. Noe) 176 Chambers
Sgobel & Day (Paul Sgobel & Horace W. Day) 24 State
Shackell & Clauss (Francis Shackell & William F. Clauss) 828 Third av.
Shaen H. B. & Co. (dissolved) 466 Broome
Shafer I. Calvin, Co. (Ltd.) (William Thompson, Pres.; Albert Dovell, Sec. Capital, $65,000. Directors: William Thompson, Albert Dovell, Samuel S. Missl, W. D. Applegate) 86 Cortlandt
Shafer & Douglas (Joseph H. Shafer & Frederick S. Douglas) 8 Maiden la.
Shafer & Gottgetreu (Luther Shafer & Henry Gottgetreu) 291 B'way
Shaffer George H. & Co. (George H. Shaffer, no Co.) ft. Perry
Shaffer & Burt (Chauncey Shaffer & Warren S. Burt) 99 Nassau
Shahir & Marona (dissolved) 73 Wash.
Shaller & Knowles (Russell H. Shaller & William P. Knowles) 33 Warren
Shalgian & Simidian (Peter Shalgian & Mihran Simidian) 100 Centre
Shallcross G. W. & Co. (dissolved) 113 Warren
Shanahan James M. & Co. (John J. Shanahan, only) 267 Bowery
Shand T. Y. & Co. (Thomas & William Harper & Thomas Y. Shand;—special partner, John Marchbing, $5,000; terminates 9th Oct. 1894) 230 B'way
Shannon & Williams (Joseph W. Shannon & Frederick Williams) 1441 B'way
Shannon, Miller & Crane (Livingston A. Shannon, Walsingham A. Miller, Harold L. Crane, David Pearson jr. & Richard Magee) 46 Maiden la.
Shants & Strong (Mary C. Shants & William B. Strong) 831 B'way
Shaped Seamless Stocking Co. (E. Karelsen's Sons, proprs.) 111 Franklin & E. 107th n First av.
Shapiro M. & Co. (no inf.) 74 Wooster
Shapiro & Moretsky (Frank Shapiro & Daniel Moretsky) 8 Mott
Sharbel Mansour & Co. (Mansour & Joseph Sharbel) 57 Wash.
Sharkey & Tyler (Michael Sharkey & Rodney Tyler) 1646 B'way
Sharp & Burke (Anna Sharp & Catharine A. Burke) 410 Lex. av.
Sharp & Sons (George B. Sharp; further inf. refused) 13 Baxter
Sharp, Alleman & Hill (Isaac S. Sharp, Silas H. Allemann & Charles E. Hill) 206 B'way
Sharp, Cox & Urie Co. (not inc.) (Warner A. Sharp, John W. Cox & Addison Urie) 33 Jay
Sharp, Taylor & Perkins (John Sharp, Edwin M. Taylor & John I. Perkins) 375 Wash. & 16 Jay
Sharpe W. W. & Co. (William W. Sharpe & George L. J. Norman) 21 Park row
Sharpe & Co. (Robert J. Sharpe, no Co.) 27 South
Shattuck & Binger (Warren S. Shattuck & Gustav Binger) 90 Spruce
Shaver Corporation (H. H. Warner, Pres.; J. L. Luckey, Sec. Capital, $100,000. Directors; H. H. Warner, George F. Shaver, George Condit, Roderick H. Smith, J. L. Luckey) 207 B'way & 7d Cortlandt
Shaver Telephone Co. (dissolved) 35 Wall
Shaw Alexander D. & Co. (Alexander D. Shaw, no Co.) 68 Broad
Shaw Daniel A. & Co. (Daniel A. Shaw & Michael J. Daun;—special partner, Ira Bursley, $20,000; terminates 1st May, 1893) 90 Pine

Shaw J. G., Blank Book Co. (James M. Ham, Pres.; Harry D. D. Ripley, Sec. Capital, $30,000; further inf. refused) 261 Canal
Shaw James M. & Co. (William A. & James K. Shaw only) 25 Duane & 108 Park row
Shaw John M. & Co. (John M. Shaw, no Co.) 54 New
Shaw Mfg. Co. (inf. unattainable) 171 B'way
Shaw & Co. (publishers) (James Shaw & William G. Cameron) 498 Third av.
Shaw & Co. (real estate) (A. Frank Shaw & Frederick A. Phillips) 61 W. 125th
Shaw & Marsh (Frederick Shaw & James B. Marsh) 70 Murray, 160 Maiden la. & 250 Canal
Shaw & Morss (dissolved) 18 Cortlandt
Shaw & Thomas (dissolved) 74 Warren
Shaw's Frederick J., Sons (Frederick W. & William J. Shaw) 118 W. 39th
Shea John & Co. (John Shea & Timothy J. Sullivan) 163¼ Wash.
Shea D. & J. (dissolved) 17 South
Shea J. & Son (Jeremiah & John Shea) 2584 Third av.
Shea P. & Son (Patrick & John J. Shea) 59 Grace av. W. Wash. mkt
Shea Brothers (Robert F. & Samuel Shea) 652 W. 39th
Shea & Hull (dissolved) 2220 Third av.
Shearman & Sterling (Thomas G. Shearman, John W. Starling & John A. Garver) 45 William
Shedlinsky, Shweitzer & Co. (Harris Shedlinsky & Julius & Isidor Shweitzer) 550 B'way & 56 Rutgers
Sheehan M. H. & Co. (Michael H. Sheehan & Mary J. Larkin) 99 Sixth av.
Sheehy Brothers (Patrick & Edward C. Sheehy) 422 E. 82d
Sheehy & Son (John & Ambrose T. Sheehy) 99 E. 130th
Sheer & Shumsky (Louis Sheer & Morris Shumsky) 1 Pike
Sheer & Solnick (Morris Sheer & Louis Solnick) 26 Eldridge
Sheet Metal Machine Co. (Edward Small, Pres.; Samuel M. Hitchcock, Sec.; Walton Ferguson, Treas. Capital $1,000,000; further inf. unattainable) 79 Cedar & 13 Doyers
Sheffield Steel Works (inf. unattainable) 377 Broome
Sheffield T. A. & Co. (Theodore A. Sheffield & Walter E. Field:—special partner, Thomas T. Barr, B'klyn, N. Y., $50,000; terminates 31st Dec. 1890) 92 Front
Sheffield & Balestier (Frederick Sheffield & Wolcott Balestier) 80 Beekman
Sheldon Henry & Co. (Henry Sheldon, G. Theodore Duckwitz & Charles F. & Alexander J. Sheldon) 109 Front
Sheldon Mfg. Co. (William C. Bucklin, Pres.; Edwin Thorne, Sec. Capital, $150,000. Directors: William C. Bucklin, Edwin Thorne, Landon Ketchum) 18 W. 23d
Sheldon William C. & Co. (William C. & George B. & William C. Sheldon jr. & William S. P. Prentice) 4 Wall
Sheldon G. W. & Co. (George W. Sheldon & Henry W. Ackhoff) 1 Beaver
Sheldon J. D. & Co. (Augustus & Clarence D. Sheldon, only) 119 Chambers
Sheldon N. & Co. (Nicholas Sheldon, Co. refused) 154 Chambers
Sheldon & Co. (Isaac E. & Alexander E. & William D. Sheldon) 734 B'way
Shelter Island Park (Thomas H. Wood, Pres.; Henry K. Motley, Sec. Capital, $150,000. Trustees: Erastus F. Carpenter, Virgil S.

Pond, Thomas H. Wood, Henry C. Morse, Francisco Bianchi, Henry K. Motley, William H. Carty) 579 B'way

Shanandoah Land & Anthracite Coal Co. (Anastasius Nicholas, Pres.; Charles Cook, Sec. Capital, $2,500,000. Trustees: Anastaline Nicholas, Earn F. Raymond, Charles A. Jackson, W. McCarty Little) 35 Pine

Shenfield & Levy (Leo Shenfield & Moe M. Levy) 96 Spring

Shepard Lecture Bureau (Shepard & Co. proprs.) 685 B'way

Shepard A. T. & Co. (Augustus T. Shepard, no Co.) 188 Chambers

Shepard C. D. & Co. (Charles D. Shepard, no Co.) 1241 B'way

Shepard & Co. (Thomas Shepard & L. V. Williams) 685 B'way

Shepard & Dudley (Sumner F. & Frederick A. Dudley, only) 150 William

Shepard & Osborne (William H. Shepard & James W. Osborne) 10 Wall

Shepherd J. A. & Son (James A. & Henry F. Shephard) 99 Market

Shepherd & Atwater (Thomas S. Shepherd & Theron S. Atwater) 39 Nassau

Shepperd J. T. & Son (John T. & Alston L. Shepperd) 46 Centre

Sherer Brothers (John A. Sherer, only) 122 Front

Sherick & Turk (Mark Sherick & Samuel Turk) 95 Bleecker

Sheridan E. & M. (Ellen & Mary) 231 E. 32d

Sheridan G. K. & Co. (Greenleaf K. Sheridan & William T. Richmond) 68 Thomas

Sheridan J. & L. (James & Lawrence) r 482 Pearl

Sheridan J. W. & Co. (James W. Sheridan, no Co.) 317 E. 93d

Sheridan T. W. & C. B. (Theodore W. & Charles B.) 25 Centre & 6 Reade

Sheridan Brothers (liquors) (John & Robert Sheridan) 574 Grand

Sheridan Brothers (meat) (dissolved) 58 Carmine

Sheridan, Potter & Co. (dissolved) 44 B'way

Sherman George W. & Co. (George W. Sherman & James T. Boyle) 91 Duane

Sherman Publishing Co. (Sherman & La Bree, proprs.) 294 B'way

Sherman William P. & Co. (William P. Sherman, no Co.) 946 B'way

Sherman M. & Son (Max & Isaac Sherman) 29 Grand

Sherman & Fearing (Arthur G. Sherman & William S. Fearing) 100 Chambers

Sherman & La Bree (Jacob A. Sherman & Benjamin La Bree) 294 B'way

Sherman & McHugh (Charles H. Sherman & Anthony J. McHugh) 11 E. 42d

Sherman, Cecil & Co. (John T. Sherman, Frank F. Cecil, Aaron L. Reid jr. & Robert T. Sherman) 54 Leonard

Sherwin-Williams Co. (Henry A. Sherwin, Pres.; William H. Hogarth, Sec.; Sereno P. Fenn, Treas. Capital, $400,000. Directors: Henry A. Sherwin, William H. Hogarth, Sereno P. Fenn, E. P. Williams, J. F. Weare) 178 Fulton

Sherwood John & Co. (John Sherwood, no Co.) 97 Pearl & 60 Stone

SHERWOOD PARK LAND ASSN. (Frederick W. Patterson, Pres.; Anthony H. Swasey, Treas.; J. W. Thompson, Sec. Executive Committee: Frederick W. Patterson, William S. Watson, Anthony H. Swasey, J. W. Thompson, Scott R. Sherwood) 140 Nassau

Sherwood A. G. & Co. (Abraham G. Sherwood & John S. Brown) 47 Lafayette pl.

Sherwood J. C. & Co. (dissolved) 368 South

Sherwood Brothers (William & Daniel Sherwood) 170 E. 62d

Sherwood & Waldron (James D. Sherwood & Walter H. Waldron) 1076 Third av.

Shidlovsky M. & Brother (Morris & Isaac Shidlovsky) 17 Catharine

Shields & Brown Co. (Henry W. Johns, Pres.; Frederick E. Brown, Sec.; James H. Shields, Treas. Capital, $25,000. Directors: Henry W. Johns, Frederick E. Brown, James H. Shields) 143 Worth

Shields & Keegan (dissolved) 127 Ninth av. & 144 Tenth av.

Shields & Vanderhoof (no inf.) 1594 Ninth av.

Shier D. A. & Co. (dissolved) no address

Shliansky M. L. & Son (Moses L. & Max Shliansky) 128 E. B'way

Shimer R. B. & Co. (Robert B. & Harry C. Shimer) 300 Washn.

Shine & Hart (Michael R. Shine & Thomas J. Hart) 1272 B'way

Shinnecock Inn & Cottage Co. (Ltd.) (Henry W. Maxwell, Pres.; William G. Wheeler, Sec. Capital, $25,000. Directors: Wager Swayne, Samuel L. Parrish, William L. Hoyt, Henry W. Maxwell, William G. Wheeler) 192 B'way

Shipkoff & Co. (Karl F. & Theodore K. & Peter K. Shipkoff) 9 Burling sl.

Shipman & Co. (John Underwood & Co., proprs.) 30 Vesey

Shipman, Barlow, Larocque & Choate (dissolved) 35 William

Shipman, Larocque & Choate (William D. Shipman, Joseph Larocque, William G. Choate, Solomon Hanford & Charles C. Marshall) 35 William

Shipman's Asa L. Sons (James D. & Edward L. Shipman) 10 Murray

Shipsey & Co. (refused) 1249 B'way

Shirley Mfg. Co. (C. A. Edgarton & Son, proprs.) 99 Franklin

Shlanowsky Brothers (Isaac & Bernhard Shlanowsky) 95 Division

Shoaff T. B. & Co. (Thomas B. Shoaff, Frank W. Pond, Lorenzo Duncan & Walter H. Judson) 935 B'way

Shoch & Kraft (Frederick L. Shoch & Charles H. Kraft) 18 Cliff

Shoe & Leather Reporter (refused) 17 Spruce

Shoenfeld & Lustig (dissolved) 20 Av. C

Shoninger, Moses & Co. (Bernard J. Shoninger, Aaron H. Moses & Charles Shoninger) 430 B'way

Shonk John J. & Son (dissolved) 1 B'way

Shook & Everard (Sheridan Shook & James Everard) 673 Washn.

Shookovsky & Abramsky (dissolved) 122 Elizabeth

Short William G. & Co. (Lydia M. Short & Gilbert C. Arrowsmith, only) 27 Warren

Shortland Brothers & Co. (Stephen F. & Thomas S. & T. Francis Shortland, William C. Parker, Thomas Mathews, Alonzo Aldrich & Ezra J. B. Southworth) 106 Wall

Shostak & Greenslein (no inf.) 229 W. 35th

Shotwell & Burrall (Hugh W. Shotwell & George E. Burrall) 25 Whitehall

Shoyer D. W. & Co. (Daniel W. & William L. Shoyer) 416 B'way

Shrady J. & W. (Jacob & William) 194 B'way

Shreve & Adams (George H. Shreve & Ambrose R. Adams) 66 Leonard

Shreveport Water Works Co. (William Yorke At Lee, Pres.; Whiting G. Snow, Sec. Capital, $250,000. Trustees: William Yorke At Lee, Whitney Conant, William J. Curtis, Whiting G. Snow, B. B. McCutchen) 2 Wall

SPECIAL ATTENTION PAID TO THIS CLASS OF WORK. } BANKERS' & BROKERS' CIRCULARS DELIVERED { THE TROW CITY DIRECTORY CO. 11 University Place.

SHR 276 SIM

Shrier Brothers & Co. (Morris & Henry Shrier & Nathan Lemlein) 656 B'way.
Shrimpton Alfred & Sons (Ltd.) (Alfred A. Wright, Pres.; John W. Wright, Sec. Capital, $60,000. Directors: Alfred A. & John W. & David E. & Anna L. Wright) 273 Church
Shriver T. & Co. (Walter Shriver, only) 838 E. 55th & 21 Park row
Shriver & Co. (Walter H. C. Shriver, no Co.) 27 Union sq. W.
Shuler-Shutz & Co. (Louis P. Shuler-Shutz & W. Eaton Levin) 294 Church
Shulman & Son (Yetta & Charles H. Shulman) 67 & 89 Canal
Shumway Albert & Son (Albert & Albert Shumway jr.) 598 B'way & 106 Mercer
Sibell & Miller (E. Gardner Sibell & Charles E. Miller) 149 B'way
Sibley & Chapin (Clarence C. Sibley & John J. Chapin) 602 W. 2d
Siccardi & Whelan (dissolved) 28 Grand
Sichel Moses & Co. (Moses Sichel & Abraham & Samuel Holzinger) 35 Av. C
Sicilian Asphalt Paving Co. (Howard Carroll, Pres.; Charles S. Chamberlin, Sec.; George C. Clausen, Treas. Capital, $250,000. Directors: Howard Carroll, George C. Clausen, Charles S. Chamberlin, Henry Duke, Henry W. Schmidt, William C. Egerton, A. J. Dittenhoefer, Julius Simon, John S. Taylor) 41 Park row
Sidenberg G. & Co. (Gustavus & Henry & Richard Sidenborg) 49 Mercer & 186 Mulbery
Siebert Brothers (John & Joseph Siebert) 155 Essex
Siebrecht & Wadley (Henry A. Siebrecht & Albert Wadley) 409 Fifth av.
Siedenburg Reinhard & Co. (Reinhard Sledenburg & Frank G. Speck) 16 Exchange pl.
Siegel A. & Sons (Abraham & Jacob D. & August & Charles Siegel) 1266 B'way
Siegel Brothers (Benjamin & Gerson Siegel) 65 Wooster & 165 S. 5th av.
Siegel & Co. (Gabriel & Julius E. & Julius A. Siegel & Julius B. Ikelheimer) 1842 Third av.
Siegman Brothers (Michael & Alfred & Henry & Richard Siegman) 870 B'way
Siegrist Brothers (Jacob & William Siegrist) 287 Canal
Sielke & Birkenstock (Leo Sielke & John Birkenstock) 841 W. 50th
Siemer Brothers (Frederick jr. & John W. Siemer) 118 Canal
Siemers Brothers (Frederick C. & John J. Siemers) 58 Thomas
Siems & Gatje (Christopher Siems & John H. Gatje) 35 & 39. Washn.
Sierichs Henry & Co. (Henry Sierichs & Herman Hoffmann) 150 Elizabeth
Siessenbyttle H. & Co. (dissolved) 661 Second av.
Silberberg L. & Co. (Louis Silberberg & Jacob Meyer) 61 Stanton
Silberberg Brothers (Siegfried & Max & David Silberberg) 81 Wooster & 167 S. 5th av.
Silberberg & Siegman (Benjamin Silberberg & Moses Siegman) 475 B'way
Silberhorn Brothers (Charles T. Silberhorn, only) 94 Chrystie
Silberman H. & Son (Harris & Samuel J. Silberman) 79 Canal
Silberman J. & Brother (Jacob & Morris Silberman) 94 Greene
Silberman & Joseph (Levi Silberman & Abraham Joseph) 1 Wall
Silbermann J. & Co. (Jacob & Arthur Silbermann) 35 Mercer & 456 Tenth av.
Silbermann & Markus (Louis Silbermann & Emil Markus) 399 E. 72d

Silberstaedter & Pollak (dissolved) 315 Canal
Silberstein D. & Son (David & Isaac J. Silberstein) 10 Sixth av.
Silberstein M. & Son (no inf.) 113 Mercer
Silberstein & Desbohlaw (dissolved) 259 Canal
Silk Assn. of America (Frank W. Cheney, Pres.; Briton Richardson, Sec.; Louis Franke, Treas.) 70 Grand
Silk L. & Co. (Louisa & Joseph Silk) 875 G'wich
Silkworth's Brother & Co. (dissolved) 414 Fourth av.
Sillcocks Brothers (James & Charles W. H. Sillcocks) 9 Thomas
Sillock Brothers (W. Frederick & John S. Sillock) 297 B'way
Sillock & Co. (Wilhelmina F. Sillock & Ernest L. Wals) 98 Fulton
Silsbe & Son (John N. & Edward F. Silsbe) 209 Sixth av.
Silva George & Co. (George Silva & Georges Blumenfeld) 142 Greene
Silva & Draffin (Thomas Silva & George T. Draffin) 101 Mercer & 130 W. 105th
Silver Brush & Novelty Co. (no inf.) 502 B'way
Silver Cigar Co. (F. Silver & Co., proprs.) 207 E. 101st
Silver Inlet Cons. Mining & Lands Co. (inoperative) 52 B'way
Silver King Shirt Co. (T. Lasell Jacobs, propr.) 590 B'way
Silver Queen Mining Co. (inf. unattainable) 52 B'way
Silver Springs, Ocala & Gulf R. R. Co. (Thomas C. Hoge, Pres.; Robert B. Upham, Sec. Capital, $1,500,000. Directors: Thomas C. Hoge, J. Baxter Upham, James T. Van Rensselaer, James G. Gardiner, R. F. Taylor, E. W. Agnew, Alexander C. Quarrier) 56 Wall
Silver State Cons. Mining Co. (Herman W. Huising, Pres.; Henry Bradstreet, Sec. Capital, $2,000,000; further inf. unattainable) 115 B'way
Silver G. & D. (George & David) 76 Reade
Silver H. N. & Co. (Howard N. Silver, no Co.) 1505 Ninth av.
Silver P. & Co. (Philip Silver, no Co.) 217 E. 101st
Silver S. & M. (Simon & Marks) 90 Bayard
Silver & Co. (William H. Silver & John H. Ernst) 50 Warren
Silver & Woodward (dissolved) 1595 Ninth av.
Silverberg J. & Co. (Jacob & Sarah Silverberg) 400 Pearl
Silverberg & Uransky (Jacob Silverberg & Jacob Uransky) 21 Forsyth
Silverman Israel & Brother (dissolved) 140 E. B'way
Silverman H. M. & Co. (Robert H. Silverman & Philip Trautwein, only) 12 E. 18th
Silverstein Jacob & Co. (Jacob Silverstein, no Co.) 97 Baxter
Silverstein L. & Co. (dissolved) 112 Spring
Silverstone Brothers (Abraham & Moyer Silverstone) 283 Bowery
Silverthau M. & Co. (Max & Abraham Silverthau & Samuel Heilbronner) 1595 First av.
Simis A. & Son (Adolph Simis, only) 49 Church
Simmonds & Brown (Morris Simmonds & T. Allston Brown) 1441 B'way
Simmonds & Gildemeister (Alexander H. Simmonds & Arthur Hunt, only) 18 B'way
Simmonds & Newton (Herman Simmonds & John Newton) 103 Front
Simmons William H. & Co. (William H. Simmons & Lorenzo Hull) 234 W. 10th
Simmons W. A. & Co. (William A. & Charles P. & Howard F. Simmons) 280 B'way

MERCHANTS EXCHANGE NAT. BANK OF THE CITY OF N. Y.
SOLICITS YOUR ACCOUNT. **257 Broadway.**
PHINEAS C. LOUNSBURY, President.   ALLEN S. APGAR, Cashier.

Simmons & Mischo (Jacob Simmons & Hugo J. Mischo) 20 Bond
Simon Alfred L. & Co. (Alfred L. & Leo L. Simon) 634 B'way
Simon Charles & Son (Charles & Harry Simon) 484 B'way
Simon Edward & Brothers (Morris Schwerin & Edward Simon, only) 543 B'way & 114 Mercer
Simon John & Co. (John Simon, no Co.) 21 W. Houston
Simon A. & Son (bottles) (Abraham & Simon Simon) 268 Seventh
Simon A. & Son (liquors) (dissolved) 236 Rivington
Simon B. & Co. (Benjamin Simon, no Co.) 12 Bond
Simon H. & Co. (dissolved) 34 Jones
Simon J. R. & Co. (Jacques R. & Gustave F. & David E. & Harry G. & Samuel Simon jr.) 19 Greene
Simon L. & Co. (Louis & Jacob & Abraham Simon) 272 Canal
Simon M. & Sons (Marcus & August & Louis & Samuel Simon) 259 West & 91 W. Houston
Simon S. & Son (Solomon & Jacob Simon) 23 E. B'way
Simon S. & Sons (Solomon & Louis & Gustave Simon) 13 Third av.
Simon & Bennett (dissolved) 107 Hester
Simon & Kaufman (Charles Simon & Israel Kaufman) 622 W. 47th
Simon & Sass (dissolved) 94 E. B'way
Simon & Selden (Hyman Simon & Philip Selden) 112 Clinton
Simon & Silverstein (dissolved) 81 Bleecker
Simon & Weigert (dissolved) 683 B'way
Simon Brothers & Co (dissolved) 150 S. 5th av.
Simon Brothers & Samuel (Solomon & Philip Simon & Joseph Samuel) 150 S. 5th av.
Simonds J. A. (Jefferson A. Simonds:—special partners, George E. Buell, *Franklin, N. H.,* & James F. Osborne, *Tilton, N. H.* each $2,500; terminates 1st April, 1893) 582 E. 134th
Simonds Mfg. Co. (Richard S. T. Cissel, Pres.; Benjamin Darby, Sec.; Henry W. LeRoy, Treas. Capital, $154,000. Trustees: Richard S. T. Cissel, Benjamin Darby, Henry W. LeRoy, Edward C. Moffat, H. Granville Parkin) 50 Cliff
Simonds Soap Co, (Edward Schwacofer, Sec.; Ninian Stevenson, Treas. Capital, $75,000; further inf. refused) 523 W. 98th
Simonds F. W. & Son (Frederick W. & Henry A. Simonds) 18 S. William
Simons Henry F. & Co. (Henry F. Simons & Frederic G. Cunningham) 78 Warren
Simonson T. H. & Son (William H. Simonson, only) ft. E. 100th
Simonson & Weiss (Michaelis Simonson & Theodore Weiss) 467 B'way & 116 Grand
Simpson James & Co. (no inf.) 32 Mercer
Simpson Restaurant Co. (dissolved) 058 B'way
Simpson William & Co. (blocks) (William W. & James A. Simpson) 27 Coenties sl.
Simpson William & Co. (pawnbrokers) (William & estate of William Simpson sr.) 151 Bowery
Simpson William, Sons & Co. (William jr. & James Simpson, John U. Fraley & Lincoln Godfrey, only) 318 B'way
Simpson B. & Co. (Charles Johnson & Thomas D. Ormiston, only) 33 Murray
Simpson J. & Co. (John F. & Charles H. Simpson) 225 Park row & 62 New Bowery
Simpson J. E. & Co. (James E. & James E. jr. & Alfred H. & William E. Simpson) 35 B'way
Simpson R. & Co. (Robert Simpson, no Co.) 195 Bowery
Simpson Brothers (Edward & Montague Simpson) 315 Fifth av.
Simpson & Beers (Edward Simpson & Albert B. Beers) 58 William
Simpson & Co. (insts.) (George H. Simpson, no Co) 1265 Boston rd.
Simpson & Co. (printers) (Samuel W. Simpson & George F. Kick) 30 W. 14th
Simpson & Labarre (dissolved) 147 E. 23d
Simpson & Proddow (John B. Simpson jr. & Robert Proddow) 5 E. 14th
Simpson & Shaw (William Simpson jr. & Mark Shaw) 27 Coenties sl.
Simpson & Werner (Angel J. Simpson & Louis Werner) 181 B'way
Simpson, Clapp & Co. (Charles H. Ryan, Zeb Mayhew & Joseph C. Simpson, only) 129 Broad
Simpson, Crawford & Simpson (James Simpson & William Crawford, only) 307 Sixth av.
Simpson, Spence & Young (Ernest L. Simpson, Lewis H. Spence & William M. Young) 76 Broad
Simpson, Thacher & Barnum (John W. Simpson, Thomas Thacher, William M. Barnum & Philip G. Bartlett) 10 Wall
Simpson's Paint Remover Co. (John Simpson, propr.) 355 E. 58th
Sims-Edison Electric Torpedo Co. (Everett Frazar, Pres.; George W. Casper, Sec.; William M. Deen, Treas. Capital, $1,000,000. Trustees: Thomas A. Edison, Charles Batchelor, Gardiner C. Sims, Everett Frazar, William M. Deen, W. Scott Sims, Ambrose H. Snow, Hector De Castro, George W. Casper) 53 B'way
Simson, Greenebaum & Rosenthal (Louis M. Simson. Simon Greenebaum & Felix L. Rosenthal) 42 Greene
Sinclair James & Co. (James & John J. Sinclair) 418 E. 130th & ft. E. 30th
Sinclair John & Co. (John Sinclair & Charles D. Souter) 1 B'way
Sinclair N. B. & Co. (Napoleon B. Sinclair & Nicholas T. Newham) 45 South
Sinclair & Babson (Robert S. Sinclair & Arthur C. Babson) 16 Exchange pl.
Sinclair & Co. (Margaret A. Sinclair, no Co.) 183 William
Sinclair's H., Sons (James M. & Hector Sinclair jr.) 327 Seventh av.
Sinclaire Rectifying Machine Co. (Francis S. Sinclaire, Pres.; John B. Marston, Sec. Capital, $400,000; further inf. refused) 99 Maiden la.
Sindle & Hepner (Jules Sindle & Charles Hepner) 32 W. Houston
Sing Yuet & Co. (Sing Yuet, no Co.) 10 Chatham sq.
Singer Mfg. Co. (Frederick G. Bourne, Pres.; Charles A. Miller, Sec.; Edwin H. Bennett, Treas. Capital, $10,000,000. Directors: Frederick G. Bourne, William F. Proctor, Charles A. Miller, Edwin H. Bennett, Alfred Corning Clark, Hugh Oheyne) 34 Union sq. E.
Singer A. & Son (dissolved) 1600 Ninth av.
Singer J. & Son (Joseph & Sigmund Singer) 32 Hudson & 334 B'way
Singer & Co. (Moses Singer, no Co.) 205 Rivington
Singer & Ebner (dissolved) 47 B'way
Singer & Rothblatt (dissolved) 8 Market
Sinnit & Marino (dissolved) 1307 Third av.
Sinnock & Sherrill (William P. Sinnock & Horace D. Sherrill) 3 Maiden la.
Sinnot Amos J. & Co. (Amos J. Sinnot, Co. refused) 2051 First av.
Sinnott & Shannon (Matthew Sinnott & Michael Shannon) 30 Whitehall, 94 G'wich & 6 West
Sinram & Schmidt (George Sinram & William Schmidt) 132 Essex

**SNOW, CHURCH & CO.,
265 & 267 BROADWAY.**

COLLECTIONS IN ALL PARTS OF THE WORLD.
T. C. Campbell and Arthur Murphy, *Counsel*.
TELEPHONE, 785 MURRAY.

Sinsheimer J. & Sons (Joseph & Samuel W. & Mayer Sinsheimer) 169 Water
Sinsheimer R. & Son (Regina Sinsheimer, only) 3421 Third av.
Sinsheimer, Levenson & Co. (Leopold Sinsheimer & Louis & Max L. Levenson) 542 B'way & 83 Crosby
Sintef's F., Sons (Victor & Christopher & Joseph & Henry & Frank Sintef jr.) 9 Baxter
Sinteff & Klumpp (Michael Sinteff & John G. Klumpp) 13 Baxter
Sior & Treusch (Martin Sior & John Treusch) 447 W. 52d
Siphon Pump Co. (inf. unattainable) 6 City Hall pl.
Sire & Sons (Benjamin & Lawrence & Charles Sire) 163 B'way & 160 W. 38th
Sise, Gibson & Co. (dissolved) 118 Chambers
Sisenwain, Israel & Shaffer (no inf.) 139 Spring
Siskiyou Mining Co. (inoperative) 750 Third av.
Sistare's George K., Sons (William H. M. Sistare & Harold Clements, only) 16 Broad
Sivin & Lubitz (dissolved) 599 B'way & 172 Mercer
Sixth Avenue R. R. Co. (Frank Curtiss, Pres.; Henry S. Moore, Sec. Capital, $1,500,000. Directors: Frank Curtiss, William Y. Mortimer, Henry Demarest, Albert W. Green, Theodore E. Macy, Charles G. Landon, Samuel Thorne, Henry S. Moore, Frederic P. Olcott, Edward Weston, William Carpender, Alexander T. Van Nest, T. Brownell Burnham) 756 Sixth av.
Sixth Av. Steam Laundry Co. (Charles A. Gerlach, propr.) 452 Sixth av.
Sixth National Bank (Alexander H. Stevens, Pres.; Andrew E. Colson, Sec. Capital, $200,000. Directors: Alfred Roosevelt, Adrian Iselin jr. Alexander H. Stevens, Frederick D. Tappen, Charles G. Landon, Joseph Park, William J. Quinlan jr. Frederic W. Stevens, Lewis W. Parker, J. Romaine Brown, Charles W. Wetmore) 1282 B'way
Skerry A. T. & Co. (Amory T. & Amory T. Skerry jr.) 29 Greene
Skibik & Hirsch (Joseph Skibik & John Hirsch) 515 Third av.
Skiddy, Minford & Co. (Thomas Minford, Michael Callaghan, George G. Nevers & Thomas Minford jr. only) 101 Wall
Skidmore L. & William B. (dissolved) 98 Nassau
Skidmore & Co. (Jacob & Phineas B. Moyers, only) 85 John
Skidmore's Jeremiah, Sons (William L. McLane & Franklin H. Knower:—special partner, William L. Skidmore, $30,000; terminates 15th April, 1892) 7 Broad, 137 Fourth av. ft. E. 18th & ft. E. 35th
Skilton & Son (Julius A. & Harry L. Skilton) 31 B'way
Skinner William & Sons (dissolved) 506 B'way
Skinner & Nellis (Reuben Skinner & Edward J. Nellis) 1169 Ninth av.
Skinner, Bloom & Co. (William R. Skinner, Peter C. Bloom & Harold Strebeigh) 74 Cortlandt
Slack William & Sons (William & William E. & George A. Slack) 466 Cherry
Slade C. M. & Co. (Charles M. Slade & Joseph B. Martin) 99 Franklin
Slagelse Mfg. Co. (Gustave R. de Riesthal, Pres.; Alphonse de Riesthal, Sec.; Christian Pabst, Treas. Capital, $10,000. Directors: Gustave R. & Alphonse de Riesthal, Christian Pabst) 55 Murray
Slaght & Bailey (James E. Slaght & Andrew J. Bailey) 44 South
Slater Sidney P. & Co. (Sidney P. & Charles I. Slater) 58 Wall
Slater J. & J. (John & James) 1185 B'way
Slater J. P. & Brother (Joseph P. & Abraham M. Slater) 115 R. B'way

Slater S. & Sons (Horatio N. Slater, only) 44 Leonard
Slator T. & J. (Thomas & John) 23 Dey & 403 E. 114th
Slattery & Hanley (Matthew Slattery & Timothy Hanley) 11 Third av.
Slauson A. & Co. (Albert & Austin M. Slauson & Robert H. Moss) 89 Dey
Slawson Brothers (Daniel S. Slawson, Loton Horton, Isaac A. Vanbomel, Charles H. Cuddeback, Charles B. Carpenter, Edwin A. Young, Sayer J. Slawson, Jefferson D. Fuller, Isaac M. Elliott & Oscar Shute) 226 E. 46th, 1282 Tenth av. & 107 W. 127th
Slawson & Hobbs (George L. Slawson & Frederick G. Hobbs) 1906 Ninth av.
Slevin & Kelly (dissolved) 188 Bleecker
Slevin & Sheeran (James F. Slevin & Thomas Sheeran) 29 Oliver
Slimmon Robert & Co. (Robert Slimmon & Arthur J. Wilkinson) 12 College pl.
Sloan Mfg. Co. (not inc.) (Ella L. & Christina A. Sloan) 775 B'way
Sloane H. A. & Co. (dissolved) 153 E. 24th
Sloane W. & J. (John & William D. & Henry T. & Thomas C. Sloane, Walter W. Law, & Alvoni R. Allen, only) 884 B'way
Sloane's James, Sons (James & Theophilus & Franklin H. Sloane) 2063 Bronx
Slocovich & Co. (dissolved) 4 Stone
Slomka Solomon & Sons (Solomon & Max & Adolph Slomka) 43 Bowery
Slosson & Berdan (Edwin A. Slosson & Daniel W. Berdan) 35 Wall
Slosson & Riley (dissolved) 948 B'way
Slote Daniel & Co. (William A. Mauterstock, Frank Bowman & Sarah B. Slote, only) 119 William
Slote & Janes (Henry L. Slote & Jonathan Janes) 140 Nassau
Slotkin M. & Co. (dissolved) 189 Clinton
Slotkin, Chertoff & Praglin (Meyer Slotkin, Noah Chertoff & Julius Praglin) 189 Clinton
Slover & Tyler (Warren G. F. Slover & Owen Tyler) 47 South
Smack Robert & Co. (Robert Smack, no Co.) 237 Cherry & 502 Water
Small Hopes Cons. Mining Co. (Richard C. McCormick, Pres.; Charles A. Cameron, Sec. Capital, $5,000,000. Directors: Richard C. McCormick, Charles A. Cameron, Peter A. Hegemen, Thomas Moore jr. Frank Blankenhorn) 1 B'way
Small Brothers (George S. jr. & Charles T. Small) 60 B'way
Small & Noerdlinger (Elias Small & Isaac M. Noerdlinger) 37 Franklin
Small & Schrader (George S. Small & John C. Schrader) 245 B'way
Smallwood W. M. & Co. (William M. & Herman V. Smallwood) 56 Wall
Smart W. I. & Co. (dissolved) 39 Broad
Smart, Patterson & Rice (Theodore B. Smart, Joseph H. Patterson & Wilmot B. Rice) 518 B'way
Smeallie J. K. & Co. (John K. & James A. Smeallie) 402 B'way & 278 Ninth av.
Smillie Coupler Co. (George W. Smillie, propr.) 52 B'way
Smith Abram S. & Co. (Abram S. Smith & Edmund D. Robinson) 11 N. Y. & B'klyn bridge
Smith Albert & Son (Albert & John A. Smith) 479 Eleventh av.
Smith Alfred & Co. (Alfred Smith & James McMillen) 249 Washn. mkt
Smith Alfred H. & Co. (Alfred H. & Harrison B. Smith) 182 B'way
Smith Andrew J. & Charles 68 Dey

**WATER METERS, GAS ENGINES, | NATIONAL METER CO.
FOR PUMPING AND POWER.   252 Broadway, N. Y.**

SMI 279 **SMI**

SMITH AUGUSTINE & CO. (Augustine Smith, Robert H. Tillson, Edgar S. Ryder & George La Monte) 110 Nassau

Smith Bridge Co. (no inf.) 1193 B'way

Smith Charles & Son (Charles & Alfred C. R. Smith) 169 E. 84th

Smith E. Osborne & Co. (E. Osborne Smith, no Co.) 5 Beekman

Smith Edgar M. & Son (Edgar M. & Scudder Smith) 19 Chambers

Smith Edward & Co. (Alexander Maitland, Pres.; Andrew M. Bates, Sec.; Chester Huntington, Treas. Capital, $100,000 ; further inf. refused) 153 William

Smith Elliot & S. Sidney (Elliot & S. Sidney Smith) 59 Wall

Smith Emmet H. & Son (Emmet H. & Alfred L. Smith) 513 Grand

Smith Francis H. (F. Hopkinson Smith & James Symington) 16 Exchange pl.

Smith George & Son (George & Samuel Smith) 601 E. 144th

Smith George H. & Hicks (George H. Smith, George A. Hicks, Wilbur L. Molyneaux & Joseph L. White) 69 William

Smith George W. & Co. (George W. Smith & Charles F. Buxton) 215 Produce Ex.

Smith Havilah M. & Son (William C. Smith, only) 35 N. Moore

Smith Henry Milford & Son (L. Dinwiddie Smith, only) 1236 B'way

Smith Higbie & Co.(Charlotte A. & Orlando Smith, only) 65 Broad

Smith Hinsdale & Co. (Hinsdale & Edmond H. & Enos Smith) 125 Maiden la.

Smith J. Galt & Co. (J. Galt Smith & William B. Conrad) 44 White

Smith J. Lee & Co. (Orison B. & Jay L. & Sinclair Smith, only) 59 Frankfort & 21 Jacob

Smith J. M., Ornamental Glass Works (James M. Smith, propr.) 69 Charles

Smith J. O., Mfg. Co. (Alfred O. Smith, Pres.; Theodore V. Smith, Sec.; Herbert E. Smith, Treas. Capital, $30,000. Directors: Alfred O. & Theodore V. & Herbert E. Smith) 52 John

Smith J. Trumbull & Son (J. Trumbull & Thomas C. Smith) 40 Warren

Smith James & Son (James & Frank Smith) 1633 Ninth av.

Smith James P. & Co. (James P. & Henry L. Smith & John W. Eginton) 45 Park pl.

Smith James S. & Son (dissolved) 947 Sixth av.

Smith John A. & Brother (John A. & Landline Smith) 297 Washn.

Smith John E. & Son (John E. & Edward R. Smith) 70 Clinton mkt

Smith Jonas & Co. (Lewis S. Davis, only) 66 South

Smith Leonard K. & Co. (Leonard K. & Henry Albro Smith) 252 Canal

Smith Mfg. Co. (Smith & Manning, proprs.) 123 Fulton & 156 E. 125th

Smith Norman & Son (Norman & Frederick M. Smith) 52 South

Smith Portable Rail Saw Co. (James B. Kinney, Pres.; Edward C. Smith, Sec. Capital, $100,-000. Directors: James B. Kinney, Edward C. Smith, E. S. Peck) 79 Cedar

Smith R. Harmer & Sons (R. Harmer & Robert B. & Joseph R. Smith) 82 Beekman

Smith R. Penn & Co. (dissolved) 1 B'way

Smith Rest Fenner & Co. (Rest Fenner & Spencer C. Smith) 701 B'way & 20 Pell

Smith Rufus & Co. (Rufus Smith, no Co.) 36 Broad

Smith S. T., Co. (John R. Keatinge, propr.) 14 Park pl.

Smith Sidney E. (Sidney E. Smith :—special partner, John H. Hodgson, B'klyn, N. Y.; further inf. refused) 75 Fulton

Smith W. Cook & Co. (W. Cook Smith & Albert E. Hamilton) 75 Chambers

Smith Warren G. & Co. (Warren G. Smith, no Co.) 170 B'way

Smith William & Co. (William & David N. Smith) 33 Maiden la.

Smith William Alexander & Co. (William Alexander & Robert Hobart Smith) 70 B'way & 15 New

Smith William E. & Co. (William E. Smith & Jarvis L. Carter) 300 G'wich

Smith A. & Sons (August & George A. & Albert C. Smith) 114 Fulton

Smith B. & W. D. (William B. & Jacob W. Smith, only) 220 W. 29th

Smith B. H. & Co. (Bryan H. Smith, Duncan D. Chaplin & Cyrus P. Smith) 52 Worth

Smith B. J. & E. P. jr. (Bradish J. & Edwin P. jr.) 266 W. 23d

Smith D. & Son (Daniel & William J. Smith) 20 Coenties sl.

Smith E. D. & Brother (Ebenezer D. & Eli Smith) 16 Thomas

Smith E. W. & Co. (Edward W. Smith & John J. Carlock) 42 John

Smith F. B. & Horst (Frederick B. Smith & Gustav Horst) 96 Fulton

Smith F. C. & Co. (grocers) (Frederick C. Smith, Co. refused) 2143 Third av.

Smith F. C. & Co. (printers) (Frank C. Smith & A. Clarence Isaacs) 92 White

Smith F. H. & Co. (Melbourn P. Smith & Thomas M. Bartlett, only) 81 South

Smith F. V. & Co. (Francis V. Smith, no Co.) 520 E. 121st

Smith H. B. & W. P. (Henry B. & William P.) 74 B'way

Smith H. M. & Co. (Horace M. Smith, Horace R. Bateman, Chauncey N. Frazier & I. Augustus Noe) 83 Nassau

Smith I. N. & Co. (Isaac N. & Frederick H. Smith) 58 Centre

Smith J. A. & Co. (dissolved) 834 B'way

Smith J. B. & Co. (James B. Smith & Everett L. Brown) 359 Washn.

Smith J. B. & Son (John B. & Arthur E. Smith) 155 Maiden la.

Smith J. G. & Co. (John G. Smith & Edgar J. Mott) 83 Beekman

Smith J. W. & Son (John W. & Winfield S. Smith) 110 West

Smith M. & J. F. (Matthew & James F.) 96 Worth

Smith M. B. & Co. (Monroe B. Smith & Harry P. Henriques) 17 William

Smith R. & Co. (Robert Smith, no Co.) 500 Broome

Smith S. G. & Brother (Seymour G. & Chester M. Smith) 127 Water

Smith W. & C. (William Reed, William H. Walsh & Charles & estate of William Smith) 58 Liberty

Smith W. A. & Co. (Waightstill A. & John Y. Smith) 61 B'way

Smith W. C. & Co. (dissolved) 329 Washn.

Smith W. C. & Son (William C. & Charles E. Smith) 91 Liberty

Smith W. H. & Co. (William H. & Ursaline P. Smith) 28 Cedar

Smith W. O. & Co. (John M. Smith, only) 43 Exchange pl.

Smith Brothers (beer) (no inf.) 52 Vestry

Smith Brothers (candy) (no inf.) 85 E. 113th

EXCELSIOR BIRD FOOD. The recognized standard. The most reliable for your Canary. Use no other. Insist upon getting it. Packed only by **C. ROSENSTEIN & CO., 373 Washington Street, New York.**

Smith Brothers (fwdg.) (Francis H. & John J. & Thomas F. Smith) 21 Barclay & 315 Front
Smith Brothers (glass) (Henry T. & William C. & John H. Smith) E. 150th n Harlem r.
Smith Brothers (poultry) (Patrick J. Smith, only) 205 & 216 Washn. mkt
Smith & Angell (J. Henry Smith & Charles Angell) 22 Thomas
Smith & Barton (dissolved) 318 B'way
Smith & Bateman (James Smith & Robert S. Bateman) 977 Park av.
Smith & Bell (J. Boyce Smith & George S. Bell) 505 E. 70th
Smith & Bowman (Artemas B. Smith & Henry H. Bowman) 38 Park row
Smith & Brother (J. McIntyre & William V. Smith) 99 Nassau
Smith & Carman (William H. Smith & Thomas F. Carman) 117 W. B'way
Smith & Cole (James H. Smith & Parsells Cole) 17 Thirteenth av. W. Washn. mkt
Smith & Co. (Aaron Smith, no Co.) 48 Canal
Smith & Darling (James D. Smith & Sidney S. Darling) 573 Hudson
Smith & Dewson (Elliott Smith & George B. Dewson) 24 State
Smith & Dougherty (Duncan Smith & J. Hampden Dougherty) 7 Nassau
Smith & Dowling (George W. Smith & Walter W. Dowling) 2 Rector
Smith & Esterbrook (Marianna Smith & Bertha E. Esterbrook) 156 E. 56th
Smith & Farrow (dissolved) 464 W. 35th
Smith & Gannon (no inf.) 19 Whitehall
Smith & Griesel (Joseph A Smith & John H. Griesel) 34 Broad
Smith & Hadden (George S. Smith & Alexander M. Hadden) 58 E. 13th
Smith & Hardy (Henry C. Smith & Francis H. Hardy) 685 Sixth av.
Smith & Hatred (John Smith & William Hatred) 59 Maiden la.
Smith & Haverstick (dissolved) 640 Madison av.
Smith & Haysman (Francis J. Smith & Samuel W. Haysman) 302 Delancey
Smith & Heath (John Smith & Robert T. Heath) 428 E. 23d
Smith & Hessler (George J. Smith & Jacob Hessler) 80 John
Smith & Huckel (Michael Smith & Edward Huckel) First av. n E. 102d
Smith & Kaufmann (Augustus Smith & Julius Kaufmann) 79 Grand & 540 W. 132d
Smith & Knapp (Edward S. Smith & Bradford H. Knapp) 182 B'way
Smith & Lockwood (Henry C. Smith, only) 76 Beaver & 123 Pearl
Smith & Lowe (Charles S. Smith & Robert Lowe) 45 Ann
Smith & McCormack (Philip Smith & William H. McCormack) 378 Third av.
Smith & McKeever (John M. Smith & Timothy W. McKeever) 10 Peck sl.
Smith & McNeil (Thomas R. McNeil, only) 199 Washn. & 108 G'wich
Smith & Manning (Conklin Smith & Peter F. Manning) 123 Fulton & 156 E. 125th
Smith & Mentel (Samuel Smith & Joseph Mentel) 47 Canal
Smith & Miller (William Smith & Charles Miller) 441 W. 39th
Smith & Mohr (Edward M. Smith & Alonzo D. Mohr) 16 Beaver & 8 Old sl.
Smith & Nichols (Highie Smith & Seth Nichols) 148 Front

Smith & Parsons (Paschal R. Smith & Herbert Parsons) 45 B'way
Smith & Pound (Henry C. Smith & Edward D. Pound) 167 Eighth av.
Smith & Ripley (Joshua D. Ripley & estate of James N. Smith) 61 B'way
Smith & Roffler (Thomas Smith & William Roffler) 130 E. 86th
Smith & Rosenthal (Montague M. Smith & Max Rosenthal) 360 B'way
Smith & Sanford (Jay C. Smith & Oscar M. Sanford) 214 Church
Smith & Sayre Mfg. Co. (dissolved) 245 B'way
Smith & Scherr (Howard C. Smith & Emilius W. Scherr) 99 Franklin
Smith & Schipper (Pierre J. Smith & Charles & Gustav Schipper) 91 Wall
Smith & Schober (Florence Smith & Henrietta Schober) 287 B'way
Smith & Sills (G. Waldo Smith & John S. Sills) 752 Eighth av.
Smith & Stevens Mfg. Co. (William J. Hiss, Pres.; William P. Sandford, Sec. Capital, $111,000. Trustees: William J. Hiss, William P. Sandford, Benjamin M. Dennis) 83 Murray
Smith & Stoughton (no inf.) 133 Duane
Smith & Sturgess (Henry L. Smith & William D. Sturgess) 39 Maiden la.
Smith & Vosburgh (dissolved) 35 William
Smith & White (Albridge C. Smith & Henry White) 280 B'way
Smith, Bowman & Close (Artemas B. Smith, Henry H. Bowman & Halcyon M. Close) 38 Park row
Smith, Hogg & Gardner (John Hogg, Harrison Gardner, Ralph L. Cutter, Walter M. Smith, James Lockett & Stewart W. Smith) 115 Worth
Smith, Leonard & Co. (dissolved) 359 Washn.
Smith, Lyon & Field (William T. Smith, Judson A. Lyon & Richard C. Field) 139 Duane & 64 Thomas
Smith, McLagan & Co. (dissolved) 4 Stone
Smith, Worthington & Co. (Charles B. Smith & George Worthington, no Co.) 40 Warren
Smith's Carll, Son (Carll V. Smith) Pier 58 E. R.
Smith's Homœopathic Pharmacy (Henry M. Smith, Pres.; T. Franklin Smith, Sec. Capital, $75,000. Directors: Henry M. & T. Franklin Smith, H. J. Moorhouse) 130 W. 23d
Smith's Isaac, Son & Co. (James T. & Deming B. Smith) 928 B'way.
Smith's James, Son (William M. Smith) 816 Sixth av.
Smith's John, Son (Edward C. Smith) 146 Front
Smith's Mfg. Co. (Henry M. Smith, Pres. Capital, $10,000; further inf. refused) 130 W. 23d
Smith's W. B., Sons (Jefferson P. & Wallace B. Smith) 52 Coriears & Pier 54 E. R.
Smithers C. H. & Co. (Charles H. & John Smithers) 3 Broad
Smiths & Bender (John R. & William F. Smith & Arthur Bender) 91 Maiden la.
Smock & Bolles (dissolved) 240 B'way
Smullen & Dudley (Lawrence Smullen & James Dudley) 610 Forest av.
Smyth B. L. & Co. (Bernard L. & Sidney L. Smyth) 40 Exchange pl.
Smyth M. A. & Co. (Mary A. Smyth, no Co.) 128 E. 26th
Smyth & Ryan (Philip A. Smyth & William M. Ryan) 70 Liberty
Smyth & Schroeder (John W. Smyth & Jules Schroeder) 26½ E. 42d
Snackenborg L. O. & Co. (Lewis O. Snackenberg & Samuel Reeder) 98 Murray

IDEN & CO., MANUFACTURERS OF
University Place, 9th to 10th Sts., N. Y. **GAS FIXTURES AND ELECTROLIERS**

SNE 281 SON

Snedecor J. L. & Sons (Jordan L. & Abraham & Eliphalet Snedecor) 255 Washn. mkt
Snedeker & Boynton (Valentine Snedeker & James H. Boynton) 516 B'way
Snedeker & Morrow (John W. Snedeker & William S. Morrow) 19 Cortlandt
Snell Mfg. Co. (Emory L. Bates, Pres.; W. Kumbel Wilson, Sec. Capital, $60,000. Directors: Emory L. Bates, W. Kumbel & E. M. Wilson) 72 Reade
Snook John B. & Sons (John B. & James H. & Samuel B. & Thomas E. Snook & John W. Boylston) 12 Chambers
Snook & Halbe (Charles W. Snook & Charles H. Halbe) 30 Front
Snow H. H. & Son (Henry H. & Frederick M. Snow) 36 Fulton & 88 Park row
Snow & Burgess (Alfred D. Snow & Levi G. & Joseph S. Burgess) 66 South
Snow & Foulke (dissolved) 144 Duane
Snow, Bassett & Co. (Homer V. Snow, Edwin B. & Joseph P. Bassett & Walter H. Snow) 500 B'way & 68 Crosby
Snow, Church & Co. (Thomas C. Campbell, Pres.; Arthur Murphy, Sec. Capital, $40,000. Directors: Thomas C. Campbell, Arthur Murphy, E. K. Duvall) 265 B'way (see head lines)
Snow's U. S. Sample Express Co. (Ltd.) (Michael Snow, Pres.; Henry S. Snow, Sec.; Edward L. Snow, Treas.; further inf. unattainable) 418 Washn.
Snyder Frank & Son (Frank & Frank jr. & Henry Snyder) 184 Suffolk
Snyder William J. & Brother (William J. & Russell J, W. Snyder) 68 Murray
Snyder G. M. & Co. (George M. Snyder, Benjamin W. Rowe & William Magee) 210 Duane
Snyder N. H. & Brothers (Nicholas H. Snyder & Jacob & John Huber, only) 93 Washn. mkt
Snyder & Black (John V. & Henry V. D. Black, only) 93 William
Snyder & Rode (Frank Snyder & Julius T. Rode) 751 Ninth av.
Snyder & Wheeler (Joseph H. Snyder & Charles W. Wheeler) 132 Pearl
Sobel Elias & Brother (Elias & Philip Sobel) 185 G'wich
Social Register Assn. (Louis Keller, Pres.; Joseph J. Sullivan, Sec. Capital, $5,000 ; further inf. unattainable) 85 Liberty
Socialistic Co-operative Publishing Assn. (Christian Ludwig, Pres.; Herman Gottschalk, Treas. Capital, $10,000. Directors: Joseph Hildebrandt, Henry Hofmeister, John Nagel, Hugo Vogt, Emil Kirchner, Reinhard Meyer, Samuel Jacobson, Christian Ludwig) 184 William
Soc. Hygienique Alimentaire (Samuel C. Hickey, Pres.; David M. Mackaye, Sec. Capital, $140,000 ; further inf. unattainable) 1 Water
Soc. List Publishing Co. (Edward W. Miller, Pres.; Charles D. Miller, Sec. Capital, $10,000. Directors: Edward W. & Charles D. & Elizabeth A. Miller) 96 B'way
Soc. of Decorative Art (Catharine C. Hunt, Pres.; George C. Magoun, Treas.) 28 E. 21st
Soden Mineral Springs Co. (Ltd.) (James Pollitz, Pres.; Harry W. Elliott, Sec. Capital, $250,000 ; further inf. unattainable) 15 Cedar
Soder & Carpenter (dissolved) 580 Washn. & 62 Clarkson
Soder & Son (William & Christian H. Soder) 580 Washn. & 62 Clarkson
Sohl & Wiese (Christopher Sohl & Ernest Wiese) 201 W. 40th
Sohmer Lithographing & Printing Co. (refused) 2 Spring
Sohmer & Co. (Hugo Sohmer & Josef Kuder) 149 E. 14th

Sohn & Oppenheimer (dissolved) 688 B'way
Sohns Brothers (dissolved) 191 Tenth av.
Schval L. & A. Susman (dissolved) 406 E. 62d
Solid Fibre Collar & Cuff Co. (no inf.) 387 B'way
Solid Link Chain Mfg. Co. (Samuel W. Saxton, Pres.; further inf. refused) 51 John
Solidarity Watch & Jewelry Co. (not inc.) (E. V. Sands, E. F. Ganville, A. Nelison, J. F. Gordon) 35 Liberty
Solidity Iron Last Co. (inoperative) Produce Ex.
Solomon S., Distilling Co. (in liquidation) 444 G'wich
Solomon H. & Son (Hannah & Finck Solomon & Leopold S. Greenbaum) 90 Walker
Solomon J. & Son (Joseph & Max W. Solomon) 51 E. B'way
Solomon L. & Co. (Leopold Solomon & Arthur Eisig) 59 Grand
Solomon & Bruder (Morris D. Solomon & Abraham Brader) 120 Ridge
Solomon & Cohen (Abraham Solomon & Daniel Cohen) 9 Walker
Solomon, Kantrowitz & Esberg (Jacob P. Solomon, Joshua Kantrowitz & Moses Esberg) 335 B'way
Solomon's D. L. Sons (Solomon B. & Judah H. & Simeon B. Solomon & Daniel D. Earle) 99 Union sq. W.
Soltau Brothers (John & Charles & Francis Soltan) 874 Washn.
Somborn L. & Co. (Julius Somborn, only) 67 Broad
Sombrerete Mining Co. (Clarence King, Pres.; William N. Olmsted, Sec. Capital, $2,500,000. Trustees: James J. Higginson, Quincy A. Shaw, A. Agassiz, J. E. Knapp, George Bingden) 18 Wall
Somers, Lindleman & Co. (John E. Somers, William T. Lindeman & C. Frank Barrett) 261 Pearl
Somerset Distilling Co. (Maximilian Fleischmann, Pres.; Jacob P. Bailor, Treas. Capital, $25,000 ; further inf. refused) 701 Washn.
Somerset Ranch & Cattle Co. (inf. unattainable) 13 B'way
Sommer D. & H. H. (Berthold & Henry H.) 5 N. Moore
Sommer Brothers (Louis & William Sommer) 910 Sixth av.
Sommer & Weiner (George Sommer & Frank J. Weiner) 71 Washn.
Sommerich & Co. (Rosa & Milton S. Sommerich) 28 E. Houston
Sommers Isaac & Co. (Isaac Sommers, no Co.) 12 Vesey
Sommers & Davis (no inf.) 1128 Second av.
Sondheim Anton & Son (Anton & Julius Sondheim) 80 Nassau
Sondheim Brothers (Samuel S. & Henry P. Sondheim) 70 Broad
Sondheim, Alsberg & Co. (Meinhard Alsberg & Israel M. Schloss, only) 84 Maiden la.
Sons & Fleming Mfg. Co. (Ltd.) (Paul Babcock jr. Pres.; William D. Emerson, Treas. ; further inf. unattainable) 26 B'way
Sonius P. C. & Co. (Peter C. & James Sonius) 63 W. 44th
Sonn Julius & Brother (Julius & Herman Son) 8 Greene
Sonn Leopold & Brother (Leopold & Isaac Sonn) 144 Mulberry
Sonn Brothers (Hyman & Henry Sonn) 365 Washn. & 334 G'wich
Sonneborn J. P. & Co. (James P. Sonneborn & William H. McNickle) 92 Chambers
Sonneborn, Loew & Co. (Jonas Sonnsborn, Jacques Loew & Morton Sonneborn) 425 B'way & 7 Laight

Sonnenburg & Liebel (Frederick Sonnenburg & Adam Liebel) 624 Madison av.

Sonnenschein & Fuchs (Lisette Sonnenschein & Joseph Fuchs) 49 Wooster

Sonntag & Beyer (Paul Sonntag & Gustave Beyer) 498 B'way

Sonoma Wine & Brandy Co. (Benjamin Kittredge, propr.) 1 Front

Sons & Cunningham (Joseph Sons & Michael Cunningham) 208 E. 58th

Sontheimer & Greenthal (Benjamin Sontheimer & Joseph E. Greenthal) 61 Crosby

Sooysmith & Co. (Charles Sooysmith, Pres.; George M. Newcomer, Sec. Capital, $100,000. Directors: Charles Sooysmith, James R. Willard, George M. Newcomer) 2 Nassau

Soper Music Co. (Charles C. Hoarne, propr.) 87 College pl.

Soper W. R. & Co. (William R. Soper & B. Frederick Schroeder) 185 South

Soper & Co. (Elizabeth R. G. Soper, no Co.) 30 E. 14th

Sorenson & Quern (no inf.) 204 W. 64th

Sorgan & Co. (dissolved) 508 Pearl

South Brooklyn Galvanizing Works (George Thwaites & Co., propr.) 77 Front & 28 Old sl.

South Brooklyn R. R. & Terminal Co. (John W. Ambrose, Pres.; Francis H. Bergen, Sec.; W. Bayard Cutting, Treas. Capital, $500,000. Directors: John W. Ambrose, W. Bayard Cutting, Joseph Richardson, Edward T. Hunt, Frank K. Hain, Alfred L. Dennis, Clarence Stephens) Pier 2 E. R.

South Brunswick Terminal R. R. Co. (John I. Holly, Pres.; Edward P. Kennard, Sec.; John Sloane, Treas. Capital, $500,000. Directors: John I. Holly, Norman W. Dodge, John Sloane, Edward P. Kennard, Joseph Hilton, Warren A. Fuller, Joseph W. Woolfolk) 81 New

South Carolina Railway Co. (in liquidation) 68 William

South Ferry R. R. Co. (Charles E. Warren, Pres.; William J. Ramsey, Sec. Directors: Charles E. Warren, William J. Ramsey, Joseph J. Swan, Henry J. G. Merritt, George W. Horne, Henry A. & Henry A. Newell jr. Hiram W. Edes, Thomas P. Jones, Thomas A. Delaney, Oscar W. Heartt, S. Otis Livingston, Charles W. Russell) 761 Seventh av.

South Publishing Co. (Obadiah A. Clough, Pres.; M. R. Bacon, Sec. Capital, $100,000. Directors: Obadiah A. Clough, M. R. Bacon, Charles P. Granville, William H. Conklin) 76 Park pl.

South Side Improvement Co. (Henry A. V. Post, Pres.; George F. Crane, Sec. Capital, $5,000. Trustees: Henry A. V. Post, George C. Magoun, George F. Crane, Samuel T. Peters, Henry B. Hyde) 1 Nassau

South Western Coal & Improvement Co. (Colgate Hoyt, Pres.; Charles W. Wetmore, Sec.; further inf. refused) 36 Wall

South Western Land & Cattle Co. (dissolved) 737 B'way

South Yuba Water & Mining Co. (dissolved) 120 B'way

South & North American Lloyds (Whipple & Co. proprs.) 33 Liberty

Southard & Bohde (Greene M. Southard & Charles H. Bohde) ft. W. 11th

Southard & Co. (Charles C. & Francis R. Southard) 18 B'way

Southard, Robertson & Co. (William D. Southard, George W. Robertson & William Corry) 21 Peck sl. & 257 Water

Souther & Stedman (Charles Edward Souther & Ernest G. Stedman) 120 B'way

Southerland's J. P., Son (Sidney H. Southerland) 125 Maiden la.

Southern Bell Telephone & Telegraph Co. (John E. Hudson, Pres.; David I. Carson, Sec.; Roswell H. Rochester, Treas. Capital, $1,000,000. Directors: John Vanhorne, Norvin Green, James Merrihew, Charles F. Cutler, C. Jay French, John E. Hudson, Theodore N. Vail, Thomas T. Eckert, Joseph M. Brown, Joseph P. Davis) 195 B'way

Southern Colorado Mining Co. (Daniel W. Sisson, Pres.; Silas O. Brigham, Sec. Capital, $1,500,000. Directors: Daniel W. Sisson, Joseph Rodgers, Silas O. Brigham, W. Peterson, C. H. Brigham, W. H. Thomas, H. Libby) 110 Pearl

Southern Co. (of N. Y.) (Thomas A. Eddy, Pres.; Henry F. Crosby, Sec.; William J. Coombs, Treas. Capital, $6,500. Directors: Thomas A. Eddy, Henry F. Crosby, William J. Coombs) 78 South

Southern Development Co. (J. H. Strobridge, Pres.; Frank S. Douty, Sec. Capital, $5,000,000. Directors: J. H. Strobridge, Arthur & W. E. Brown, Frank S. Douty, C. E. Green) 23 Broad

Southern Express Co. (Henry B. Plant, Pres.; George H. Tilley, Sec.; further inf. unattainable) 12 W. 23d, 309 Canal & 684 B'way

Southern Improvement Co. (no inf.) 2 Wall

Southern Natural Gas & Oil Co. (Wallace C. Andrews, Pres.; Scoville C. Williams, Sec.; William S. Williams, Treas. Capital, $1,000,000. Directors: Wallace C. Andrews, Frederick Prentice, William S. & Scoville C. Williams) 44 B'way

Southern Pacific Co. (Leland Stanford, Pres.; Gerritt L. Lansing, Sec.; Timothy Hopkins, Treas. Capital, $150,000,000. Directors: Leland Stanford, A. N. Towne, Thomas E. Stillman, Charles F. Crocker, Edward H. Miller jr, Collis P. Huntington, Frank S. Douty, William E. Brown, Stephen T. Gage, Ariel Lathrop, Willard V. Huntington) 23 Broad

Southern Pacific R. R. Co. (Charles F. Crocker, Pres.; Joseph L. Willcutt, Sec.; Nicholas T. Smith, Treas. Capital, $90,000,000. Directors: Charles F. Crocker, Leland Stanford, Timothy Hopkins, Charles Mayne, Willard V. Huntington, Nicholas T. Smith, Joseph L. Willcutt, A. N. Towne) 23 Broad

Southern Pine Co. (Joseph Hilton, Pres.; Charles C. Southard, Sec.; Capital, $50,000. Directors: Joseph Hilton, Charles E. Southard, Loring R. Millen, Norman W. Dodge, Charles L. Buckl, John J. Cooney) 18 B'way

Southern States Electric Storage Co. (E. W. Carritt, Pres.; Hugh R. Parrish, Sec. Capital, $2,000,000. Trustees: E. W. Carritt, Hugh R. Parrish) 44 B'way

Southern States Land & Timber Co. (Ltd.) (Ernest Noll, Pres.; J. Hardy, Sec. Capital, $300,000. Directors: Ernest Noll, J. P. Richardson, P. K. Seddon, Hugh Bellas, B. F. Bosanquet, Charles L. Buckl, F. C. Brent) 18 B'way

Southern Transfer Co. (not inc.) (refused) 430½ Sixth av.

Southern & Western Air Line R. R. Co. (Samuel McD. Tate, Pres.; J. A. Claywell, Sec. Capital, $1,500,000; further inf. unattainable) 13 Park row

Southfield Branch R. R. Co. (A. W. Humphreys, Pres.; James M. Scofield, Sec.; further inf. refused) 45 William

Southington Cutlery Co. (Mortimer O. Ogden, Pres.; J. W. Gridley, Sec. Capital, $200,000. Directors: Mortimer O. Ogden, George Munson, Webster R. Walkley, R. A. Neal, J. P. Pratt, J. W. Gridley, E. J. Neal) 98 Chambers & 17 Warren

Southwick N. & Son (Walter Southwick, only) 149 Church

Southwick Brothers (Arthur Q. Southwick & Campbell Mortimer, only) 4 Cedar & 182 South

Souto B. & Co. (Baldomero Souto & Frederick A. Thompson) 138 Front

Souvenir Publishing Co. (Emma M. Brokovski, propr.) 53 Eighth av.

Souweine & Co. (Adolph Souweine & Mortimer H. Julian) 210 Canal

Sowden & Bloch (George H. Sowden & Joseph Bloch) 738 B'way & 47 Lafayette pl.

Spadone & Cabaret (Alfred A. Spadone & Paul E. Cabaret) 107 E. 13th

Spalding E. P. & Co. (Ely P. Spalding, no Co.) 17 William

Spangehl W. E. & Sons (William E. & Charles J. & Frederick A. & Louis W. Spangehl) 66 Duane

Spangenberg & Bishop (dissolved) 60 Liberty

Spanish Am. Light & Power Co. (Cons.) (Walter S. Johnston, Pres.; Robert A. C. Smith, Sec. Capital, $3,000,000. Directors: Walter S. Johnston, Robert A. C. Smith, Michael Chauncey, Daniel Runkle, Thomas J. Hayward, James E. Ward, John F. Gibbons) 40 Wall

Spanish Chamber of Commerce (Serafin Sanchez, Pres.; Charles O'Neill, Sec.; Juan Sabater, Treas.) 88 Wall

Spanner Michael & Son (Michael & Leopold F. Spanner) 61 Carmine

Sparks Mfg. Co. (Edward G. Sparks, Pres.; Frederick C. Bench, Sec. Capital, $5,000. Directors: Edward G. Sparks, Frederick C. Bench, C. A. Gilbert) 22 Burling al.

Sparks A. M. & Son (Alfred M. & Alfred A. Sparks) 12 Barclay

Sparmann & Stienen (dissolved) r 109 Seventh av. & 154 W. 17th

Sparr Brothers (Benjamin F. & Millard F. Sparr) 39 Nassau & 58 Liberty

Spath George & Son (George & Charles Spath) 1117 Washn. av.

Spaulding & Tewksbury (John F. Spaulding, James G. Tewksbury & Benjamin Spaulding) 7 N. Y. & B'klyn bridge

Spear Charles & Co. (Charles Spear jr. no Co.) 61 New

Spear & Hogan (Edwin C. Spear & James H. Hogan) 95 West

Spearing James J. & Son (James J. & Thomas F. Spearing) 801½ W. 116th & 54 W. 29th

Spears J. & W. C. (Joseph & William C.) 2281 Third av.

Special Despatch Agency (dissolved) 101 Potter bldg.

Spectator Co. (James H. Goodsell, Pres.; Arthur L. J. Smith, Sec.; Samuel Elliott, Treas. Capital, $200,000. Directors: James H. Goodsell, Arthur L. J. Smith, Samuel Elliott) 14 Cortlandt

Speed Stationery Co. (A. J. E. Speed, propr.) 26 Reade

Speed A. M. & Co. (A. M. Speed & Frederick G. Book) 52 Dey

Speer New Jersey Wine Co. (Alfred Speer, Pres.; William H. Speer, Sec. Capital, $200,000. Directors: Alfred & William H. Speer, David Campbell jr. Joseph T. & A. W. Speer) 28 College pl.

Speir Benjamin & Co. (Benjamin Speir & Joseph J. Cohn) 48 Maiden la.

Speir John & Son (John & George H. D. Speir) 18 Fletcher

Spektorsky A. & Son (Abraham & Hyman Spektorsky) 257 Canal

Spelman R. W. & Co. (Robert W. Spelman & Anne Fairchilds) 364 Third av.

Spelman Brothers (Timothy M. & William C. & William A. Spelman) 361 B'way

Spelman's P. H., Sons (Martin H. & William & Charles Spelman) 209 E. 19th

Spelterine Co. (John E. White, Pres.; Reginald P. Sherman, Sec. Capital, $100,000. Directors:

John E. White, Reginald P. & Frederick W. Sherman) 62 William

Spence Sky Dining Book Mfg. Co. (John T. M. Brewster, Pres.; Lucas P. Britt, Sec.; Payton Spence, Treas. Capital, $200,000. Directors: John T. M. Brewster, Lucas P. Britt, Payton Spence, Henry F. Cox, Amanda M. Spence) E, 163d c Fleetwood av.

Spence J. & Co. (Ernst Hutshenrider, only) 21 Clinton pl.

Spence Brothers (Andrew jr. & James W. Spence) 137 Reade

Spencer Edward E. & Co. (Edward E. Spencer, Edward F. Fanning & William C. Dutts) 84 Warren

Spencer Optical Mfg. Co. (James E. Spencer, Pres.; John S. Spencer, Sec. Capital, $100,000. Directors: James E. & John S. Spencer) 15 Maiden la.

Spencer William & Son (William T. Spencer, only) 16 S. William

Spencer C. E. & J. A. (Charles E. & John A.) 19 Hewitt av. W. Washn. mkt

Spencer & Co. (Alice F. Spencer & Charles L. C. Child) 183 G'wich

Spongler & Schwaner (Philip Spongler & Louis Schwaner) 1611 Ninth av. & 045 Tenth av.

Sprenoke & Wahlers (dissolved) 116 Gansevoort

Sperling Brothers (Albert F. & William Sperling) 354 Third av.

Sperling's E. M., Sons (Jacob E. & Louis & Pauline Sperling) 389 Broome

Sperry John, Mfg. Co. (Francis H. Elgar, Pres.; Reuben H. Sperry, Treas.; John Sperry, Sec. Capital, $10,000. Directors: Francis R. Elgar, Reuben H. & Kate A. Sperry) 332 Hudson

Sperry & Beale (Timothy S. Sperry, Joseph H. Beale & J. Henry & Charles D. Sperry) 88 White

Speyer Brothers (Meyer J. & Noah J. Speyer) 101 Bowery

Speyer & Co. (refused) 11 Broad

Spiegel Charles & Steiner (Charles Spiegel & Sigmund B. Steiner) 378 Pearl

Spiegel M. & Co. (Morris Spiegel, no Co.) 103 Broad

Spiegel Brothers (dissolved) 421 Seventh av.

Spiegel Sisters (Bertha & Amelia & Anna Spiegel) 327 E. 58th

Spiegel & Isenburger (dissolved) 378 Pearl

Spiegel & Prohs (Hyman Spiegel & Conrad Prohs) 64 Canal

Spiegel, Marckhoff & Co. (Charles F. L. Spiegel, George Marckhoff & Charles Vietze) 76 Murray

Spiegelberg L. & Sons (Levi & Charles S. & William Spiegelberg) 462 Broome

Spiehler Anthony & Son (Anthony & George J. Spiehler) 174 E. 119th

Spielmann & Co. (Charles Spielmann, Jeremiah Richards & Henry Spielmann) 85 Grand

Spiero & Fleck (Isaac Spiero & John W. Fleck) 190 Centre

Spies Brothers (John jr. & Jacob Spies) 1524 Third av.

Spies & Long (Henry H. Spies & John M. Long) 120 B'way

Spies Frederick & Son (Frederick & John C. Spies) 224 E. 42d

Spies Brothers (Carl F. & Julius Spies) 2 Bond

Spies & Co. (August Spies, no Co.) 172 Centre

Spietzler & Ankele (dissolved) 1602 Third av.

Spinell Michael & Brother (no inf.) 161 Elizabeth

Spinetto P. & Co. (Peter Spinetto, no Co.) r 535 Broome & 8 Watts

Spingarn E. & Co. (Elias & Samuel H. Spingarn) 5 Burling sl.

SPECIAL ATTENTION PAID TO THIS CLASS OF WORK } BANKERS' & BROKERS' CIRCULARS DELIVERED { THE TROW CITY DIRECTORY CO. 11 University Place.

SPI 284 STA

Spingarn Brothers (Henry D. & Louis Spingarn) 92 G'wich

Spink & Martin (Erwin I. Spink & Richard M. Martin) 38 Park row

Spinner Louis & Franz (dissolved) 157 Sixth av.

Spiral Weld Tube Co. (James C. Bayles, Pres.; William S. Church. Sec.; George C. Hallett, Treas. Capital, $350,000. Directors: James C. Bayles, David Bingham, George Burnham jr. William S. Church, George C. Hallett, William P. Prentice, John A. Price, Henry R. Towne, Samuel T. Wellman) 5 Beekman

Spirit of the Times (Elisha A. Buck, Pres.; John F. Buck, Sec.; Harry A. Buck, Treas. Capital, $30,000. Directors: Elisha A. & John F. & Harry A. Buck, Horace Russell, Elihu Root, Daniel G. Rollins) 101 Chambers

Spitz S. B. & Co. (Samuel B. Spitz & Saul Engel) 122 Greene

Spitz & Henschel (Albert Spitz & Kaufman Henschel) 172 Seventh av.

Spitz & Ungar (dissolved) 246 Canal

Spitzfaden H. & Co. (Henry Spitzfaden & Charles Deininger) 291 Dowery

Spitzner C. H. & Son (Charles H. & Charles H. Spitzner jr.) 128 Water

Spivey & Lawrence (Joseph Spivey & John J. Lawrence) 3480 Third av.

Splitdorf Wire Co. (Arthur O. Jennings, Pres.; J. Gillett Noyes, Treas.; P. B. Jennings, Sec. Capital, $10,000. Directors: Arthur O. & P. B. Jennings, J. Gillett Noyes, F. J. Stevens) 187 Cherry

Spofford Brothers (Paul N. & Joseph L. & E. Clarence Spofford) 81 B'way

Spohn Joseph & Son (Joseph & Andrew Spohn) 182 Eighth av.

Spokane Falls & Northern R. R. Co. (Horace K. Thurber, Pres.; Alfred C. Chaplin, Sec. Directors: Alfred C. Chaplin, J. K. O. Sherwood, Horace K. Thurber, Albert Allen, A. A. Newberry, Chester W. Chaplin, James Monahan) 192 B'way

Spooner Mfg. Co. (Ebenezer Spooner, Pres.; Edward A. Spooner, Sec.; George A. Whitman, Treas. Capital, $48,000. Directors: Ebenezer & Edward A. Spooner, George A. Whitman, Sarah C. Spooner, Walter B. Hatch) 253 W. 27th

Sporting Times Publishing Co. (John B. Day, Pres. Capital, $50,000. Trustees: John D. Day; further inf. refused) 73 Park row

Spott & Metz (Gottfried Spott & John Metz) 667 Elton av.

Sprague Electric Railway & Motor Co. (inf. unattainable) 16 Broad

Sprague & Rhodes (Irvin A. Sprague & Benjamin N. Rhodes) 97 Wall

Sprague & Terhune (Oliver C. Sprague & Abraham V. Terhune) 291 Monroe & 210 Centre

Spreckels Brothers (Charles & Frederick Spreckels) 307 Seventh av.

Spring Creek & Rockerville Water & Mining Co. (J. Irving Burns, Pres.; Thomas J. Temple, Sec. Capital, $150,000. Trustees: Thomas J. Temple, J. Irving Burns, William J. Russell, Robert Gair, Robert J. Dean, William D. Sammis) 5 Beekman

Spring Hill Poultry Yard (Thomas Longhran, propr.) W. 142d n Lenox av.

Spring M. & Haynes (William S. Haynes, only) 21 Loew av. W. Washn. mkt

Springer Lithographing Co. (John H. Springer, Pres.; H. Clay Miner jr. Sec. Capital, $50,000. Trustees: John H. Springer, H. Clay & H. Clay Miner jr, Asa R. Cassidy, Hugo Ziegfeld) 550 W. 23d

Springer Torsion Balance Co. (Alfred Springer, Pres.; Albert Fries, Treas. Capital, $1,000,000. Directors: Alfred Springer, Charles &

Gustave R. & Albert Fries, William Kent) 92 Reade

Springer R. & Co. (Jacob M. Springer & Maurice M. Kohner, only) 458 Broome

Springer & Co. (Max & Frederick E. Springer) 80 B'way

Springfield Gas Machines (Gilbert & Barker Mfg. Co. proprs.) 10 Dey

Springmeyer H. & Co. (Edward H. Springmeyer & Mary C. Knerth) 522 E. 119th

Springmeyer Brothers (Edward C. & William H. & George A. Springmeyer) 330 E. 77th

Springsted & Mockabee (George W. Springsted & John B. Mockabee) 106 W. 37th

Sprung & Cohn (Abraham Sprung & Max Cohn) 61 Sheriff

Spurr Charles W., Co. (Charles W. Spurr, Pres.; John L. Stephens, Sec. Capital, $75,000; further inf. unattainable) 465 E. 10th

Spuyten Duyvil & Port Morris R. R. Co. (Cornelius Vanderbilt, V.-Pres.; Edwin D. Worcester, Sec.; Charles C. Clarke, Treas. Capital, $999,000. Directors: Cornelius & William K. & Frederick W. Vanderbilt, Chauncey M. Depew, Charles C. Clarke, Horace J. Hayden, Samuel F. Barger, John B. Dutcher, John E. Burrill, William H. Leonard, Francis P. Freeman, Alfred Van Santvoord, Edwin D. Worcester) Grand Central depot

Squier & Whipple (Albert C. Squier & Nelson M. Whipple) 146 B'way

Squire H. N. & Sons (Horatio N. & Francis J. & George H. Squire) 16 John

Squires Brothers (Herbert W. & Flavius S. Squires) 1277 Ninth av. & 2256 Third av.

Staab O. P. & Co. (Charles P. Staab, no Co.) 108 Duane

Staats Pine Liniment Co. (George W. Campbell jr. Pres.; Henry N. Simmons, Sec.; further inf. unattainable) 58 Wall

Staats R. P. & J. H. (Robert P. & John H.) 85 B'way

Staats & Reuning (Frederick Staats & Henry Reuning) 1265 Ninth av.

Stabile Brothers (Gabriel & Rosario Stabile) 74 Mulberry

Stabler & Werner (Charles M. Stabler & Robert M. Werner) 41 Park row

Stachelberg M. & Co. (Michael & Charles O. & Edgar J. Stachelberg) 159 S. 5th av.

Stack R. & Co. (Richard Stack & Gustave Baumann) 244 Washn. mkt

Stackpole & Brother (William Stackpole, only) 41 Fulton

Stacy, Adams & Co. (William H. Stacy & Oliver D. Quimby, only) 142 Duane

Stadecker & Ensheimer (Leopold Stadecker & Jacob Ensheimer) 31 E. Houston

Stadie Charles & Son (no inf.) 2079 Second av.

Stadler Max & Co. (Henry M. & Emanuel M. Stadler:—special partner, Max Stadler, $75,000; terminates 1st May, 1890) 465 B'way & 621 Eighth av.

Staffa A. & Son (Antonio & Joseph Staffa) 111 & 121 Mulberry

Stafford Corset Co. (Benjamin F. Stafford, propr.) 255 Greene

Stafford's Ventilating Co. (James E. Vail jr. Pres.; Frank M. Demorest, Sec.; Frederick H. Smith jr. Treas. Capital, $50,000. Trustees: James E. Vail jr. Frederick H. Smith jr. Marshall B. Stafford, Frank M. Demorest) 69 Liberty

Stagg George T., Co. (no inf.) 19 S. William

Stahl John R. & Co. (dissolved) 529 B'way

Stahl Jacob jr. & Co. (Jacob jr. & Jacob Stahl) 3460 Third av.

Stahl C. & Son (Carl & Gustave Stahl) 579 Courtlandt av.

FOR THE BEST CO-PARTNERSHIP IN THE BEST CORPORATION SEE PAGE F IN BACK OF BOOK

STA 285 STA

Stahl Brothers (Hyman & Abraham M. Stahl) 91 Grand
Stahl & Jaeger (Charles Stahl & Gustave L. Jaeger) 136 Mulberry
Stahl & Murphy (dissolved) 836 Third av.
Stahlberg & Hansen (Frederick Stahlberg & Henry Hansen) 89 South
Stalb & Gaul (John G. Stalb & John Gaul) 22 Vesey
Stalhuth J. & Co. (no inf.) 54 Roosevelt
Stallman & Fulton (John H. Stallman & John Fulton jr.) 10 Gold
Stamford Mfg. Co. (William W. Skiddy, Pres.; Stephen E. Reed, Sec.; Arthur F. Bissell, Treas. Capital, $250,000. Directors: William W. Skiddy, Arthur F. Bissell, Stephen E. Reed) 157 Maiden la.
Standard Alkali & Gas Co. (Capital, $10,000. Trustees: Joseph Flannery, George W. Kuehnle, James D. Griswold; further inf. unattainable) 261 B'way
Standard Biscuit Co. (not inc.) (Frederick W. & James P. & William E. Brooker) 3493 Third av.
Standard Brush Co. (William C. Howard, Pres.; Edwin M. Felt, Sec. Capital, $12,000. Directors: Edwin M. Felt, William C. Howard) 400 Broome
Standard Car Coupling Co. (E. Clinton Clark, Pres.; Alfred P. Dennis, Sec. Capital, $100,000; further inf. unattainable) 45 B'way
Standard Cash Register Co. (John H. Derby, Pres.; William H. Wyeth, Sec.; George W. Evans, Treas. Capital, $100,000. Directors: John H. Derby, C. E. Howland, William H. Wyeth, George W. Evans, W. W. Wyeth) 30 E. 14th
Standard Collar Co. (James H. Hoffman, Pres.; Charles H. Montague, Sec.; Henry J. White, Treas. Capital, $6,000. Directors: James H. Hoffman, Eben Denton, Henry J. White, V. N. Taylor, Hinsdale Smith, Joseph A. Ward, William F. Moseley, E. E. Mack, Solomon Zeman, Julius Lovine, Charles H. Montague) 52 Howard
Standard Construction Co. (inf. unattainable) 284 Pearl
Standard Cotton Picking Machine Co. (inoperative) 192 B'way
Standard Disinfectant Co. (refused) 7 Warren
Standard Electric Light Co. (Daniel E. Colborn, Pres.; E. Augustus Abry, Sec.; further inf. unattainable) 211 Centre
Standard Explosives Co. (Ltd.) (dissolved) 239 B'way
Standard Fashion Co. (Frank Koewing, Pres.; James W. Comstock. Sec. Capital, $50,000. Directors: Frank Koewing, James W. Comstock, R. R. Donnelly, M. C. Holly) 59 W. 14th
Standard Feather Co. (John Vanderroest, Pres.; William Vanderroest, Sec. Capital, $15,000. Directors: John & William Vanderroest, Matthew W. Hawes) 52 W. Houston
Standard Fire Ins. Co. (William M. St. John, Pres.; Robert H. Meyers, Sec. Capital, $200,000. Directors: Samuel McLean, Henry Sheldon, Stephen Pritchard, James M. Thorburn, William M. St. John, Edward E. Eames, William Whitewright, Robert W. Stuart, Charles A. Townsend, Frederic Cromwell, James McLean, John T. Walker, Benjamin W. How, James C. Gulick, John L. Riker, Franklin Woodruff) 52 Wall
Standard Folding Bed Co. (William C. Ilsley, Pres.; Frederick Ansley, Sec.; Chester F. Doubleday, Treas. Capital, $100,000. Directors: James P. Hayes, Edwin S. Doubleday, William C. Ilsley, Frederick Ansley, Chester P. Doubleday) 36 W. 14th & 227 Front
Standard Gas Light Co. (Wallace C. Andrews, Pres.; Ferdinand McKelge, Sec.; Onesimus P. Shaffer, Treas. Capital, $10,000,000. Directors: Wallace C. Andrews, Jabez A. Bostwick, Lewis Coon, Onesimus P. Shaffer, H. P.

Brookman, H. H. Brockway, William G. Schenck, Francis B. Spinola, E. V. Cary) 2 Cortlandt
Standard Gine Co. (Bernhard Herzfelder, propr.) 15 Crosby
Standard Glue Works (Arthur S. Hoyt, propr.) 126 Chambers
Standard Rod Elevating Co. (Albert T. Hull, Sec. Capital, $10,000 ; further inf. refused) 317 E. 123d
Standard Homœopathic Globule Manufactory (Julius Koch, propr.) 174 Worth
Standard Index & Register Co. (Eli Baldwin, Pres.; Walter S. Baldwin, Sec. Capital, $100,000; further inf. unattainable) 136 Fulton
Standard Investment Co. (John C. Short, Pres.; Oscar H. Short, Sec. Capital, $500,000 ; further inf. unattainable) 96 B'way
Standard Iron Works (W. H. & J. J. McCaffrey, proprs.) 261 W. 27th
Standard Knitting Mill (Weil, Haskell & Co. proprs.) 458 B'way & 211 E. 33d
Standard Lead Pencil Co. (Henry Ropes, propr.) 82 Chambers
Standard Leather Nail Co. (refused) r 43 Centre
Standard Loan & Investment Co. (no inf.) 1285 B'way
Standard Mantel & Slate Works (inf. unattainable) 315 W. 125th
Standard Match Co. (T. & S. C. White, proprs.) 30 Burling sl.
Standard Metal Tie & Construction Co. (James H. Rodgers, Pres.; Alexander Molhado, Sec.; Nathan Barney, Treas. Capital, $1,000,000. Directors: James H. Rodgers, Alexander Molhado, Nathan Barney, William H. Spencer, Jacob J. Storer, Francis A. Bassler, Isaac S. McGlehan) 15 Cortlandt
Standard Mineral Co. (Charles M. DuPuy, Pres.; Frank E. Thompson, Treas.; William G. Eaton, Sec. Capital, $100,000. Directors: Charles M. DuPuy, Frank E. Thompson, Daniel H. Bacon, Herbert DuPuy, S. Blythe Rogers, Ira W. Shattuck) 153 Maiden la.
Standard Multiplex Telegraph Co. (inf. unattainable) 84 B'way
Standard Music Co. (J. Charles Grasmuk, propr.) 55 E. 4th
Standard Noiseless School Slate Co. (Scofield & Gray, proprs.) 82 Franklin
Standard Novelty Co. (Cushing C. Adams, Pres.; Henry M. Potter, Sec.; John P. Adams, Treas.; further inf. unattainable) 62 Water
Standard Oil Co. of N. Y. (William Rockefeller, Pres.; George H. Vilas, Sec.; Joel F. Freeman, Treas. Capital, $5,000,000. Directors: William Rockefeller, Charles Pratt, John D. Archbold, George H. Vilas, Wesley H. Tilford) 26 Broadway
Standard Oil Trust Co. (John D. Rockefeller, Pres.; Henry M. Flagler, Sec. Trustees: John D. Rockefeller, Charles Pratt, William Rockefeller, John D. Archbold, Henry M. Flagler, Henry H. Rogers, Wesley H. Tilford, J. H. Magee) 26 B'way
Standard Oiled Clothing Co. (not inc.) (Solomon Lorsch & Samuel H. & Henry Emanuel) 93 Spring & 529 B'way
Standard Paint Co. (Ralph L. Shainwald, Pres.; Felix Jellenik, Sec. Capital, $250,000. Directors: Ralph L. Shainwald, Leopold Peck, Max Drey, Charles Fischel, Felix Jellenik) 50 Maiden la.
Standard Pencil Co. (Albert Terry, Pres.; Anne R. Winfield, Sec.; Edwin Terry, Treas. Capital, $15,000. Directors: Albert & Edwin Terry, Anne R. Winfield) 8 Cornies sl.
Standard Perfumery Works (Bloomingdale & Levy, proprs.) 18 Mercer
Standard Press & Printing Co. (Wilbur E. Lewis, Pres.; Harold W. McManus, Sec. Capital,

TYPEWRITING DONE BY THE TROW CITY DIRECTORY CO., 11 University Place.

STA 286 STA

$25,000. Directors, Wilbur E. Lewis, Harold W. MacManus) 16 Beekman

Standard Pump Mfg. Co. (Francis J. Herron, Pres.; Robert Des Anges, Sec. Capital, $50,000. Directors: Francis J. Herron, Robert Des Anges, E. C. Hancock) 148 Elm

Standard Real Estate Co. (Howard MacNutt, propr.) 145 B'way

Standard Recorder Co. (Norvin Green, Pres.; John Gilmour, Sec. Capital, $500,000. Trustees: Norvin Green, Logan C. Murray, Thomas L. Watson, John C. Calhoun, John Jay Knox, Henry O. O'Neill, John Gilmour) 15 Broad

Standard Rubber Co. (Lena Levi, propr.) 177 Grand

Standard Scouring Mill Co. (no inf.) 102 Reade

Standard Shade Cloth Co. (dissolved) 115 Worth

Standard Soap Sions Co. (Nathaniel F. Potter, Pres. Capital, $15,000. Trustees: Nathaniel F. & Nathaniel F. Potter jr.) no address

Standard Spirit Co. (George W. Kidd, Pres.; further inf. unattainable) 35 Water

Standard Storage Warehouse (George A. Sohastey & Co. proprs.) 1681 B'way

Standard Suit Co. (Kadane & Levy, proprs.) 311 Church

Standard Thread Co. (L. Lincoln Hoffman, Pres.; Benjamin B. Hoffman, Sec.; Emil E. Hoffman, Treas. Capital, $10,000. Directors: L. Lincoln & Benjamin B. & Emil E. Hoffman) 52 Howard

Standard Varnish Works, D. Rosenberg & Sons (Herman Rosenberg, Pres.; Max Wolf, Sec. Capital, $400,000. Directors: Herman & Theodore Rosenberg, Max Wolf & Oscar & William Rosenberg) 207 Av. D

Standard Ventilating Co. (no inf.) 12 Cortlandt

Standard Watch Club Co. (Louis Harry, propr.) 140 Maiden la.

Standard White Lead Mfg. Co. (Richard W. How, Pres.; Henry T. McCann jr. Sec.; Edwin O. Moffat, Treas. Capital, $200,000; further inf. unattainable) 139 Front

Standard Window Sash Lift Co. (Lloyd D. Waddell, Pres.; William H. Hamilton, Sec. Capital, $24,000. Trustees: Lloyd D. Waddell, William S. Darling, William H. Hamilton) 171 B'way

Stanfield G. O. & Co. (George O. & Mark M. Stanfield) 28 E. 14th

Stanley Corrugated Fireproof Lathing Co. (James T. Hyde, Pres. Capital, $75,000. Trustees: James T. Hyde, James Stanley, Thomas Stent) 30 Broad

Stanley Rule & Level Co. (Charles L. Mead, Pres.; Frederick N. Stanley, Sec. Capital, $400,000 ; further inf. unattainable) 29 Chambers

Stanley J. & W. (John. J. & William F.) 66 Laight & 415 & 427 G'wich

Stanley Brothers (Stephen & Benjamin Stanley) 194 B'way

Stanley, Clarke & Smith (William Stanley, Stephen G. Clarke, Edwin B. Smith & Melvin Brown) 120 B'way

Stanley-Bradley Publishing Co. (James T. White, Pres.; Winant V. P. Bradley, Sec.; Robert O. Woodcock, Treas. Capital, $20,000. Directors; James T. White, Winant V. P. Bradley, Robert O. Woodcock, Edward J. Stanley) 771 B'way

Stannard & Tisbout (William T. Tisbout, only) 94 Wall

Stanton Brothers (Lucius M. & Thomas G. Stanton) 458 B'way

Stanton & Cole (no inf.) 73 Park pl.

Stanton & Co. (John E. Stanton, no Co.) 60 William

Stapleton's F., Sons (John P. & William H. Stapleton) 16 Pearl

Star Carpet Cleaning Works (Killan Brothers, proprs.) 157 W. 32d

Star Co. (William P. Sullivan, manager) 239 B'way

Star Co-operative Building & Loan Assn. (inf. unattainable) 258 B'way

Star Crockery Co. (J, Lauchheimer & Co. proprs.) 1669 Second av.

Star Engraving Co. (C. Harold Avery, propr.) 317 B'way

Star Exerciser Co. (Charles A. Kimball, propr.) 710 B'way

Star Feather Trimming Co. (inf. unattainable) 2 Wall

Star Fire Ins. Co. (in liquidation) 34 Nassau

Star Laundry (Benjamin Schneider, propr.) 984 Sixth av.

Star Lyceum Bureau (Alonzo Foster, propr.) 89 Tribune bldg.

Star Mfg. Co. (inf. unattainable) 58 E. 13th

Star Metal & Paper Stock Co. (Edward Abrahams, propr.) 50 Ann

Star Pants Co. (Michael Bach, propr.) 229 Park row

Star Perfumery Works (Rich & Manheimer, proprs.) 81 Grand

Star Photo-Engraving Co. (not inc.) (Thomas J. Roche & Andrew J. Russell) 110 Fifth av.

Star Printing Co. (Harris Bernstein, propr.) 186 Division

Star Roofing Co. (Matt Taylor, Pres.; Thomas Craig, Sec. Capital, $10,000. Directors: Matt Taylor, Thomas Craig, Adlei S. Hall, James McAliey, Ronald Taylor) 15 State

Star Union Line (Pennsylvania R. R. Co. proprs.) 2 Beaver, 76 Wall, 1 Astor h. & Piers 4 & 27 (new) N. R.

Starin Brothers (Frank & Louis Starin) 352 W. 59th, 928 Tenth av. & 161 Boulevard

Starin & Co. (Henry C. Schneider, only) 98 Park pl.

Starin's City, River & Harbor Transp. Co. (John H. Starin, Pres.; John Walsh, Sec.; James D. Spraker, Treas. Capital, $250,000; further inf. unattainable) Pier 18 N. R. & 106 Produce Ex.

Stark Isidor & Brothers (Isidor & Edward J. & Gustave Stark) 126 Bleecker

Stark Nut-Look Co. (no inf.) 280 B'way

Stark L. & Co. (Lazar & David Stark & M. Louis Ackermann) r 705 E. 9th

Stark M. & Co. (Morris & James H. Stark) 522 B'way

Stark W. F. & Co. (William F. Stark, Co. refused) 303 B'way

Stark Brothers (Godfrey J. Stark, only) 121 Manhattan

Stark & Staiger (John G. Stark & Frederick Staiger) 2321 Third av.

Starkman & Eichman (no inf.) 2036 Lex. av.

Starkweather & Co. (Edward W. Ashley & estate of George A. Starkweather jr.) 30 S. William

Starlight Brothers (Emanuel & Marks Starlight) 230 Pearl

Starling & Clayton (Samuel Starling & Thomas Clayton) 23 Warren

Starr Armory Machine Shop (Albert Schaper, propr.) 182 W. Houston

Starr Ira & Son (Ira & Alfred R. Starr) 104 E. 91st

Starr Knitting Works (Hyman Starr, propr.) 374 Canal

Starr Brothers (Nathan & Robert Starr) 127 Delancey

Starr & Ahern (Frederick Starr & John Ahern) 1699 Third av.

Starr & Ruggles (Peter Starr & Horace M. Ruggles) 120 B'way

State Gas Saving Co. (Benjamin T. Sealey, Pres.;

THADDEUS DAVIDS CO., WRITING INKS, SEALING WAX, MUCILAGE.
MAKE THE BEST

STA 287 STE

Benjamin H. Sealey, Sec. Capital, $25,000. Directors: Peter C. Adams, Benjamin T. & Benjamin H. Sealey) 169 B'way

State Safe Deposit Vault (Bank of the State of N. Y. proprs.) 35 William

State Trust Co. (Willis S. Paine, Pres.; John Q. Adams, Sec. Capital, $1,000,000. Trustees: Willis S. Paine, William A. Nash, William L. Trenholm, William B. Kendall, Walter S. Johnston, Joseph N. Hallock, Edwin A. McAlpin, William Mertens, Andrew Mills, George Foster Peabody, John D. Probst, George W. Quintard, Forrest H. Parker, Charles Scribner, William Steinway, Charles L. Tiffany, George W. White, Ebenezer K. Wright, William H. Van Kleeck, Henry H. Cook, Charles R. Flint, Frederick Kuhne, Henry Steers) 50 Wall

S. I. Amusement Co. (no inf.) 322 B'way

S. I. Dry Dock Storage & Improvement Co. (Chauncey Stillman, Pres.; Cornelius J. Bushnell, Sec. Capital, $2,000,000. Directors: Chauncey Stillman, James B. Metcalf, Cornelius S. & Cornelius J. Bushnell, Homer W. Nichols) 35 B'way

S. I. Dyeing Establishment (Old Staten Island Dyeing Establishment, proprs.) 98 Duane

S. I. Fancy Dyeing Establishment (Barrett, Nephews & Co. proprs.) 84 E. 14th, 12 John, 1199 B'way, 249 Hudson, 844 Sixth av. & 276 & 2320 Eighth av.

S. I. Land Co. (James B. Metcalf, Pres.; Cornelius J. Bushnell, Sec. Capital, $500,000. Directors: James B. Metcalf, Cornelius S. & Cornelius J. Bushnell) 35 B'way

S. I. Rapid Transit R. R. Co. (J. Frank Emmons, Pres.; William Koutgen, Sec.; William H. Ijams, Treas. Capital, $600,000. Directors: J. Frank Emmons, Erastus Wiman, O. S. Wood, Albert D. Boardman, James M. Davis, Charles Watrous, Orland Smith, Charles K. Lord, F. S. Gannon, A. C. Rose, Pierre H. Marshall, Thomas M. King, Charles F. Mayer) ft. Whitehall

S. I. Telephone Co. (Charles F. Cutler, Pres.; Joel C. Clark, Sec. Capital, $185,000. Directors, Charles F. Cutler, Charles A. Nichols, Joel C. Clark) 18 Cortlandt

Stationers' Board of Trade (George L. Pease, Pres.; William W. Davis, Sec.; Alexander Agar, Treas.) 97 Nassau

Statue of Liberty Mfg. Co. (Stephen S. Newton, propr.) 63 Murray

Staubsandt Eugene & Co. (Eugene & Robert F. Staubsandt) 122 Park av.

Staudinger R. & A. (Rudolph & August L.) 52 Water

Stead Boiler Mfg. Co. (no inf.) 149 B'way

Stead & Co. (William D. Stead & Frederick S. Myers) 312 E. 75th

Stead's Steam Carpet Cleaning Works (Stead & Co. proprs.) 312 E. 75th

Steadman Stationery Co. (George H. Steadman, Pres.; William B. Snyder, Sec.; Thomas Sloane, Treas. Capital, $30,000. Directors: George H. Steadman, William B. Snyder, Thomas Sloan) 97 Chambers

Stearns Fertilizer Co. (Benjamin F. Stearns, Pres.; Oscar R. Stearns, Sec. Capital, $200,000. Directors: Benjamin F. & Oscar R. Stearns, A. Wood) 133 Water

Stearns Herman & Co. (no inf.) 619 B'way

Stearns John N. & Co. (John N. & John N. Stearns jr. Charles W. Remick, John Scholes & Joseph T. Owings) 68 Greene & 213 E. 42d

Stearns Railway Improvement Co. (Oscar S. Stearns, Pres.; J. Sanford Potter, Sec; Dennis Nunan, Treas. Capital, $1,000,000; further inf. unattainable) 176 B'way

Stearns & Beale (Joel W. Stearns, William P. Beale & Sylvester E. Bergen) 155 Fulton

Stearns & Co. (Edward Stearns & George P. Squires) 91 Wall

Stearns & Curtis (James S. Stearns & William E. & F. Kingsbury Curtis) 68 William

Stearns & Spingarn (Benjamin Stearns & Solomon Spingarn) 585 B'way & 154 Mercer

Steck George & Co. (George Nembach, Pres.; Robert C. Kammerer, Sec. Capital, $100,000. Directors: George Nembach, Robert C. Kammerer, Frederick Dietz) 11 E. 14th & 520 W. 48th

Steck & Co. (Charles E. & Frederick G. Steck) 233 South

Steckler H. & Co. (dissolved) 1403 Second av.

Steckler & Steakler (Alfred & Charles Steckler) 47 Centre

Steel Rail Supply Co. (Montford P. Sayce, Pres.; George H. Humphreys, Treas; further inf. refused) 10 Wall

Steele George & Sons (dissolved) 2690 Third av.

Steele Brothers (Loraine & Louis Steele) 28 W. 4th

Steele & Costigan (Adam Steele & Edward R. Costigan) 228 W. 10th

Steele & Jamps (Alice H. Steele & Emma J. Jamps) 263 W. 38th

Steele & McDowell (James W. Steele & William H. McDowell) 704 & 1722 Ninth av.

Steen & Scotti (no inf.) 330 Eleventh av.

Steencken William & Christian 20 New Bowery

Steengrafe A. & Co. (Adolph Steengrafe, James de Estarre & Daniel Garvey) 230 South

Steers S. A. & M. E. (Susanna A. & Margaret E.) 153 W. 70th

Steers & Menke (Henry Steers & J. Frederick Menke) 29 Lawton av. W. Washn. mkt

Stefanini Brothers (no inf.) 431 W. 39th

Steffen & Co. (dissolved) 340 St. Nicholas av.

Steffen & Schuler (Herman Steffen & Frederick Schuler) 249 W. 124th

Stege & Behrman (George H. Stege & Henry Behrman) 259 Washn. & 689 Hudson,

Stager Julius (firm of) (dissolved) 712 B'way

Steglich & Baese (Julius Steglich & C. Otto Baese) 76 William

Stegmann & Rieper (John Stegmann & Henry Rieper) 731 Eleventh av,

Stegmann's C., Son & Co. (Conrad & George C. Stegmann) 246 Washn.

Steiger E. & Co. (Ernest Steiger, Pres.; Frederick Schack, Sec. Capital, $25,000. Directors: Ernest & B. Steiger, Frederick Schack) 25 Park pl.

Steigerwald I. & Sons (Isaac Steigerwald & Louis M. & David Kohnstamm, only) 223 First av.

Stein Abe & Co. (Abraham Stein & William H. Hildreth—special partners, Isaac F. T. Edmands, Boston, Mass., & Edwin S. Barrett, Concord, Mass., each $87,500; terminates 30th June, 1890) 97 Gold

Stein Julius & Co. (Julius Stein, Adolph Lewyn & Henry Bash) 507 B'way & 79 Mercer

Stein Mfg. Co. (Leo Stein, Pres.; Isaac A. Baum, Sec. Capital, $400,000. Directors: Leo & Jules Stein, Isaac A. Baum) 13 Bond

Stein J. & Co. (John Stein & Henry Eberheim) 165 Second

Stein S. & Co. (Solomon Stein, Co. refused) 694 B'way & 2086 Third av.

Stein Brothers (no inf.) 1568 Second av.

Stein & Brother (no inf.) Boulevard n W. 78th

Stein & Co. (Emanuel W. & Joseph W. & C. Stein) 377 Church

Stein & Freund (dissolved) 18 W. 4th

Stein & Heilbrun (Albert Stein & Adolph Heilbrun) 581 B'way & 152 Mercer

Stein & Hyman (Joachim Stein & Gerson Hyman) 68 E. 13th & 320 Fourth av.

COMPILED WITH ACCURACY AND DESPATCH. **CLASSIFIED BUSINESS LISTS.** THE TROW CITY DIRECTORY CO. 11 University Place.

STE 288 STE

Stein & Simon (Herman Stein & Monroe L. Simon) 211 Pearl
Stein, Bloch & Co. (Nathan Stein, Leo Bloch & Louis N. & Abram N. Stein) 658 B'way
Stein, Hirsh & Co. (William D. Stein & Morris Hirsh, no Co.) 65 Warren
Stein, Sexton & Co. (Emil E. Stein, Peter Sexton & Charles Ericson) 1207 Ninth av.
Steinberg B. & Co. (Bertha Steinberg, Kaufman Mandell & Herman M. Munzesheimer) 26 Howard
Steinberg I. & M. (Isaac & Marx) 214 E. 106th
Steinberg & Goldberg (no inf.) 10 Hester
Steinberg & Kuming (Meyer Steinberg & Jacob Kuming) 40 E. B'way
Steinberger L. & Co. (Louis Steinberger, Co. refused) 300 Monroe
Steinbuch F. & Sons (Frederick & Frederick jr. & Charles Steinbuch) 18 Platt
Steinbuch Brothers (Otto & Julius Steinbuch) 1640 Third av.
Steindler & Hahn (Isaac S. Steindler & Max Hahn) 2007 Third av. & 203 E. 118th
Steinecke & Farren (Samuel Steinecke & Edward R. Farren) 90 White
Steinecke & Kerr (Reinhold Steinecke;—special partners, Robert & William G. Kerr, Newport, R. I. jointly $25,000; terminates 31st Dec. 1890) 16 Seventh
Steiner Joseph & Brothers (Joseph & David Steiner, only) 91 Mercer
Steiner & Co. (Israel Steiner, no Co.) 388 Pearl
Steiner & Hirschfeld (Ignaco Steiner & Louis Hirschfeld) 56 E. 59th
Steiner & Kummer (Jacob Steiner jr. & John Kummer) 32 New Bowery
Steiner & Rosenthal (William Steiner & Isaac Rosenthal) 5 Murray
Steiner & Son (Mina & Edwin J. & Clarence S. Steiner) 515 B'way
Steiner, Kahn & Co. (Louis Steiner, Leopold Kahn & Isidor Blum) 561 B'way
Steinfeld S. & Co. (Solomon Steinfeld & Ferdinand Seligmann) 64 Lispenard
Steinfelder B. & Co. (dissolved) 588 B'way
Steinfelder & Rosenblatt (Samuel Steinfelder & Henry Rosenblatt) 604 B'way
Steingut & Co. (dissolved) 21 Second av.
Steinhardt A. & Brother (Abraham & Edward Steinhardt) 354 B'way
Steinhardt Brothers (dissolved) 619 Ninth av.
Steinhardt & Knittel (George Steinhardt & George F. Knittel) 133 Orchard
Steinhardt Brothers & Co. (Lewis & Morris & Henry Steinhardt) 315 Bowery
Steinhart, Adler & Co. (in liquidation) 384 B'way
Steinhart, Heidelberg & Co. (William Steinhart, Herman Heidelberg & Israel Steinhart) 384 B'way
Steinkamp Brothers (William H. & John H. Steinkamp) 863 Second av.
Steinle & Richmond (dissolved) 66 Nassau
Steinmann S. B. & Co. (Sigmund B. Steinmann, no Co.) 853 B'way
Steinmetz C. M. & Co. (Charles M. & George W. Steinmetz) 5 Beekman
Steinreich S. & Son (Simon & Joseph W. Steinreich) 39 Grace av. W. Washn. mkt
Steinthal M. & Co. (Martin Steinthal, no Co.) 139 W. B'way
Steinway & Sons (William Steinway, Pres.; Charles F. Tretbar, Sec. Capital, $1,500,000. Trustees; William & Charles H. & Frederick T. & George A. Steinway & Henry Ziegler) 109 E. 14th
Steinwender, Stoffregen & Co. (Julius Steinwender & Charles Stoffregen, no Co.) 130 Front

Steljes & Felter (John H. Steljes & John E. Felter) 1874 Third av.
Stelle W. H. & Co. (no inf.) 309 B'way
Stelzner & Miller (Charles Stelzner & Conrad Miller) 430 E. 76th
Stemme John & Co. (John & Henry Stemme) 18 Bowery
Stemmler T. W. & Co. (Theodore W. Stemmler, no Co.) 36 E. 14th
Stencil Co. (August F. Wiggers, propr.) 215 E. 59th
Stenographic Supply Co. (Capital, $10,000; further inf. unattainable) 5 Beekman
Stens & Beck (dissolved) no address
Stephani A. & Co. (William G. Moehring, only) 136 Cedar
Stephany Perfume Co. (August C. Neumer, Sec.; further inf. unattainable) 162 William
Stephens F. E. (Frank E. Stephens:—special partner, William S. Lines, Hartford, Ct., $10,000; terminates 31st Dec. 1891) 734 B'way
Stephens James & Son (James & Olin J. Stephens) 444 E. 158th & 200 W. 135th
Stephens A. T. & Co. (Albert T. Stephens, no Co.) 168 Water
Stephens H. H. & Brother (Hugh H. & William D. Stephens) 292 Tenth av.
Stephens & Bently (Richard W. Stephens & John Bently) 209 E. 85th
Stephenson John, Co. (Ltd.) (John Stephenson, Pres.; Leander M. Delamater, Sec.; Henry C. Valentine, Treas. Capital, $150,000. Directors: John Stephenson, Leander M. Delamater, Henry C. Valentine, Allen G. Newman, John J. Reid, John A. Tackaberry, Daniel W. Pugh, Stuart A. Stephenson, Charles B. Beckwith) 47 E. 27th
Stephenson F. W. & Co. (Francis W. Stephenson, David Ellis & Louis W. Ropes) 144 Greene
Stephenson & Greene (Robert S. Stephenson & Ernest Greene) 5 Beekman
Stereo-Relief Decorative Co. (Albert A. Drake, Pres.; Walter S. Wilson, Sec. Capital, $10,000. Directors: Albert A. Drake, Walter S. Wilson, Louis Enricht) 71 University pl.
Sterling Fire Ins. Co. (in liquidation) 167 B'way
Sterling Iron & Railway Co. (A. W. Humphreys, Pres.; James M. Scofield, Sec. Capital, $2,800,000; further inf. refused) 45 William
Sterling Laundry (Samuel T. Young, propr.) 80 W. 26th & 156 W. 23d
Sterling Lead & Zinc Co. (inf. unattainable) 52 B'way
Sterling Mfg. Co. (Ferdinand Groenebaum, Pres.; Albert Zimmerman, Sec. Capital, $50,000. Directors: Ferdinand Groenebaum, Albert Zimmerman) 12 Spruce
Sterling Mountain Railway Co. (A. W. Humphreys, Pres.; James M. Scofield, Sec. Capital, $50,000; further inf. unattainable) 45 William
Sterling H. M. & M. S. (Hannah M. & Margaret S.) 599 E. 140th
Sterling & Kingsbury (Samuel & George W. Sterling & Samuel D. Tillotson, only) 32 Jay
Stern Herman & Son (Herman & Charles Stern) 115 Columbia
Stern Leo & Brother (Leo & Emanual Stern) 69 Mercer
Stern A. & Co. (August Stern & Emanuel Salberg) 358 Canal
Stern B. & Co. (Betty & Daniel Stern & Henry Brandenstein) 64 Lispenard
Stern B. & Son (Louis & David & Michael Stern, only) 456 & 460 Grand
Stern C. & Co. (Charles Stern & David E. Mayer) 325 Church
Stern J. & Co. (dissolved) 22 Beaver
Stern J. & H. (Joseph & Henry) 534 B'way

Stern L. & Co. (shirts) (Louis & Zacharias Stern) 101 Franklin
Stern L. & Co. (soap) (dissolved) 75 Rutgers
Stern M. & Sons (Moses & Charles & Henry Stern) 1673 B'way
Stern S. & Brother (Simon S. & Isaac Stern) 532 B'way
Stern S. & M. & Co. (Solomon & Moses Stern, no Co.) 44 Lispenard
Stern Brothers (drygds.) (Isaac & Louis & Benjamin Stern & Herman A Flursoheim) 39 W. 23d & 23 W. 22d
Stern Brothers (meat) (Charles & Louis Stern) 61 Av. C
Stern & Co. (men's furng.) (Samuel & Louis S. & Leopold Stern) 580 B'way & 96 Crosby
Stern & Co. (printers) (A. Stern & S. Ungermach) 25 Ann
Stern & Glueckman (Joseph Stern & Adolph Glueckman) 30 E. Houston
Stern & Myers (Simon H. Stern, Nathaniel Myers & Herbert A. Kingsbury) 40 Wall
Stern & Rosenblatt (no inf.) 262 Broome
Stern & Saalberg (Julius Stern & Jacob Saalberg) 489 Eighth av.
Stern & Schloss (Aaron Stern & Joseph Schloss) 82 Howard
Stern & Son (M. & Edwin M. Stern) 636 B'way & 170 Crosby
Stern & Steinman (Isidor Stern & Siegfried Steinman) 204 E. 43d
Stern & Stern (dissolved) 19 Malden la.
Stern & Winstock (dissolved) 431 Broome
Stern Brothers & Co. (candy) (dissolved) 489 Eighth av.
Stern Brothers & Co. (jewelers) (Leopold & Isidor Stern, no Co.) 30 Malden la.
Stern, Falk & Co. (Hyman D. Stern, Ansel B. Falk & Henry Stern) 545 B'way & 116 Mercer
Stern, Leerburger & Stern (Julius Stern, George Leerburger & Emil Stern) 27 Greene
Stern, Rosenberg & Co. (Emanuel & Emily Stern & Meyer J. Rosenberg) 653 B'way
Sternau S. & Co. (Sigmund Sternau, no Co.) 180 Centre
Sternberg & Lowenhers (dissolved) 90 Walker
Sternberg & Son (Herman & Max Sternberg) 243 Bowery & 102 Norfolk
Sternberg & Unger (Moritz Sternberg & Joseph Unger) 234 E. 44th
Sternberger Louis & Co. (Louis & Julian Sternberger) 49 New
Sternberger M. & S. (Simon & estate of Mayer Sternberger) 96 Spring
Sternberger, Fuld & Sinn (Maurice M. Sternberger, Ludwig Fuld & Samuel Sinn) 52 Broad
Sternfeld Brothers & Co. (Adolph & Morris Sternfeld, no Co.) 125 Greene
Sternglanz J. & Co. (Jacob Sternglanz & Maurice H. Baumgarten) 24 White
Sternglanz & Loeb (no inf.) 23 Frankfort
Sterns Simon & Co. (Simon Sterns & Samuel Heidelsheimer) 19 White
Stetler F. M. & Co. (Frederick M. & George F. Stetler) 52 West & 84 Washn.
Stetler F. M. & Son (Frederick M. & Henry I. Stetler) 529 Washn.
Stetler & Engle (Frederick M. Stetler & Andrew S. Engle) 258 West
Stetson George W. & Co. (William W. & Bartow W. Van Voorhis jr.;—special partner, George W. Stetson, $10,000; terminates 31st Dec., 1892) 59 Wall
Stetthelmer J. & Co. (David & Marcus Bettman & estate of Joseph Stetthelmer) 18 B'way
Stetthelmer J. jr. & Co. (Charles J. & George Stetthelmer, only) 99 Greene

Stetthelmer & Bettman (David Bettman & estate of Joseph Stetzheimer) 18 D'way
Stettiner, Lambert & Co. (Louis Stettiner & Simon Lambert, no Co.) 26 Reade
Steuerwald & Moltz (Peter Steuerwald & Joseph Moltz) 119 Spring
Stevens D. T. & Son (Daniel T. & Morris D. Stevens) 108 Gold
Stevens M. H. & Co. (Martin H. & Elizabeth Stevens) Manhattan mkt
Stevens W. J. & Co. (William J. Stevens, Adolph G. Gutgsell & Frank P. Adams) 209½ D'way
Stevens & Benedict (Franklin H. Stevens & Charles H. Benedict) 20 Pearl & 65 Beach
Stevens & Freeman (Aaron J. Stevens & Edward M. Freeman) 145 D'way
Stevens & Larsen (dissolved) 64 Pearl
Stevens & Morris (Hugh L. C. Stevens & E. Walter Morris) 24 Cortlandt
Stevens & Roylance (Henry E. Stevens jr. & Edgar W. Roylance) 839 Eleventh av.
Stevens Brothers & Co. (Sydney G. & George C. Stevens, no Co.) 36 Pine
Stevens, Corwin & Co. (Daniel L. Stevens, Charles B. Corwin & Edward H. Coffey:—special partner, Clinton D. Davis, trustee, $45,000; terminates 1st April 1894) 140 Pearl
Stevens, Roylance & Co. (dissolved) 689 Eleventh av.
Stevens' Paint Specialty Co. (Francis T. Baker, Pres.; Alfred T. Stevens, Sec. Capital, $20,000. Directors: Francis T. Baker, Alfred T. & Helen A. Stevens) 17 East
Stevenson Robert & Son (Robert & Joseph Stevenson) Rider av. C. E. 136th
Stevenson A. & Son (Alexander & Frederick G. Stevenson) 24 E. 84th
Stevenson J. & Co. (dissolved) 38 Broad
Stevenson V. K. & Co. (Vernon K. Stevenson, no Co.) 106 B'way
Stevenson & Blew (Robert A. Stevenson & James B. Blew) 427 W. 14th
Stevenson & Tucker (William Stevenson & George W. Tucker) 42 South
Stevenson & Wood (dissolved) 15 Spruce
Stewart Ceramic Co. (Stewart & Co. proprs.) 812 Pearl & 540 W. 10th
Stewart Samuel & Co. (Samuel Stewart, no Co.) 610 Third av. 401 Fourth av. & ft. E. 28th
Stewart Theodore (Maximilian Cook, George H. A. Kohler & Eugene Hauck, only) 6 John & 8 Warren
Stewart E. & Son (Edwin & Merritt L. Stewart) 205 W. 24th
Stewart & Co. (pottery) (William D. & John Stewart) 512 Pearl & 540 W. 19th
Stewart & Co. (stable) (Peter & Charles Stewart) 137 W. 19th
Stewart & Co. (stamps) (Robert A. Stewart & George T. Holihan) 201 B'way
Stewart & Coyle (James Stewart & Patrick Coyle) 482 Eighth av.
Stewart & Parker (Henry Stewart & Frank S. Parker) 60 New
Stewart & Sheldon (John A. Stewart jr. & Edward W. Sheldon) 45 Wall
Stewart & Toll (Gardiner Stewart & Wilson H. Toll) 15 Jay
Stewart, Warren & Co. (John E. Stewart, William W. J. Warren, Abraham P. Haring & Jacob G. Ruhl) 29 Howard
Stich Brothers (Julius N. & Edward Stich) 17 E. 4th
Stickney & Shepard (Albert Stickney, Edward M. Shepard, Nelson S. Spencer & Samuel H. Ordway) 31 Nassau
Stickney, Conyngham & Co. (Joseph Stickney,

TYPEWRITING DONE BY THE TROW CITY DIRECTORY CO., 11 University Place.

Stiefel William L. Conyngham, Lemuel E. Wells, Daniel Edwards, George H. Bressette & Samuel Thaxter) 1 B'way

Stiefel J. K. & Co. (Jacob K. Stiefel, Edward E. Green & Adolph Meissel) 461 Broome

Stiefel & Adelsdorfer (Isaac Stiefel & David Adelsdorfer) 400 E. 44th

Stiefel, Sachs & Co. (Samuel Stiefel & Lippman & Samuel Sachs) 18 Walker

Stieglitz M. L. & Sons (Marcus L. & Louis Stieglitz, only) 47 Mercer

Stiehl G. H. & Co. (Gustav H. & Gustav H. Stiehl jr.) 104 Greene

Stiehl & Nissen (dissolved) 104 Greene

Stiehl's A. Sons (Henry & Philip Stiehl) 848 E. 23d

Stiene & Nothel (William Stiene & Henry Nothel) 204 South

Stier John & Son (John & John Stier jr.) 265 Elizabeth

Stietz Otto, N. Y. Glass Letter Co. (Charles Hellerson, Pres.; John A. Neville, Sec. Capital, $20,000. Trustees : Charles Hellerson, John A. Neville, William Schultz) 241 Centre

Stikeman & Co. (Henry W. Stikeman, David Shaw & Alfred H. Wapshare) 124 E. 14th

Stiles Galvanic Co. (inf. unattainable) 158 William

Stiles Thomas W. & Co. (Thomas W. Stiles & John T. Terry jr.) 130 Water

Stiles & Co. (Ltd.) (dissolved) 74 Walker

Stiles & Parker Press Co. (Dorcas A. Stiles, Pres.; E. S. Stiles, Sec.; Norman C. Stiles, Treas. Capital, $96,000. Directors : Dorcas A. & Norman C. Styles, D. R. Parker) 207 Centre

Still J. H. & Co. (Josiah H. & George M. Still) ft. W. 10th

Still J. H. & Son (George M. Still, only) 195 Third av.

Still & Yarrington (dissolved) ft. W. 10th

Stillgebauer & Brother (Gustave & Otto Stillgebauer) 719 Seventh av.

Stillman Remedies Co. (E. & M. Densmore, propra.) 356 W. 28th

Stillwell & Gladding (Charles M. Stillwell & Thomas S. Gladding) 55 Fulton

Stilwell Joseph B. & Co. (Joseph B. Stilwell & James J. Gallagher) 41 Beekman

Stilwell & Foster (dissolved) 111 Broad

Stilwell & Swain (Benjamin M. Stilwell, only) 11 Chambers

Stimpson R. B. & Son (Edwin B. Stimpson, only) 31 Spruce

Stimson & Williams (Frederick J. Stimson, William Pierrepont Williams & Ebenezer P. Johnson) 55 Liberty

Stine & Calman (Marcus Stine & David Calman) 30 Broad

Stiner Joseph & Co. (Joseph Stiner, no Co.) 36 & 71 Vesey & 196 Bowery

Stiner Max & Co. (Max Stiner & Samuel Munch) 180 Prince

Stiner Simon & Co. (Simon & Joseph Stiner) 857 Washn mkt

Stiner William H. & Son (William H. & Martin E. Stiner) 17 William

Stiner & Katzmann (Samuel Stiner & Adolph Katzmann) 44 Third av.

Stirn Brothers (Max & Leo Stirn) 413 E. 91st

Stirn & Lyon (Carl P. Stirn & Amos M. Lyon) 90 Park pl.

Stites D. H. & Son (Daniel H. & Daniel G. Stites) 51 Nassau

Stitt William J. & Co. (George Miller, George Sherrill, Thomas VanJoan & Oscar M. Miller, only) 156 Chambers

Stitz & Phillips (George S. & John H. Stitt & Charles Stewart Phillips) 113 Fulton

Stix & L'Allemand (Henry Stix & Ernest A. L'Allemand) 75 Fulton

Stock Quotation Telegraph Co. (William E. Hurst, Pres.; Eugene Durnin, Sec.; William H. Crawford. Treas. Capital, $1,000,000. Directors: William H. Hurst, Eugene Durnin, William H. Crawford, John J. Walsh, Adolph G. Hummel) 51 Cedar

Stock C. A. & Co. (Caspar A. Stock & Adolph Knobloch) 119 Wooster

Stockton & Co. (James M. Stonkton, no Co.) 58 Nsw

Stoddart C. G. & Co. (Curtis G. Stoddart, no Co.) 18 B'way

Stoddart & Hart (Thomas A. Stoddart & George William Hart jr.) 49 Chambers

Stodder Brothers (Samuel H. & Willie F. Stodder) 42 Dey

Stoecker & Gwalter (Adolph Stoecker & Henry L. Gwalter) 25 Mercer

Stoecker & Peters (John P. Stoecker & Eugene S. Peters) 2044 Seventh av.

Stoerger H. & A. (dissolved) 776 Second av.

Stoevesandt & Co. (Dederick & Herman & Henry Stoevesandt) 68 Murray

Stohlmann, Pfarre & Co. (Frederick A. Stohlmann, Edward Pfarre, Charles F. & George A. Stohlmann & Louis G. & Julius A. Pfarre) 107 E. 28th

Stokes Frederick A. & Brother (Frederick A. & Horace S. Stokes) 182 Fifth av.

Stokes Walter C. & Co. (Walter C. Stokes & John F. Thomson) 54 B'way & 501 Fifth av.

Stokes William A. & Co. (William A. Stokes, no Co.) 79 Reade

Stokes & Parrish Elevator Co. (inf. unattainable) 18 Cortlandt

Stokes & Thedford (Thomas Stokes & Thomas Thedford. ft. W. 29th. Thomas Stokes & Robert Thadford, ft. W. 55th)

Stoll & Ward (Frank Stoll & Sidney S. Ward) 98 S. 5th av.

Stolley & Strohsahl (Charles Stolley & William Strohsahl) 106 Trinity pl.

Stoltz J. W. & Co. (Julius W. & Jonas Stoltz) 227 Bowery

Stoltzenberg & Co. (Francis Stoltzenberg & Lambert A. J. Muller-Thym) 53 & 56.Barclay

Stols M. & Co. (Martin & Peter Stols jr. & Frederick A. Ringler) 21 Barclay & 26 Park pl.

Stolzenberg Brothers (Frederick & William Stolzenberg) 54 First av.

Stone Brick Co. (C. I. Walker, Pres.; H. E. Young, Sec. Directors: C. I. Walker, C. E. Miles, B. N. Gourdin, O. A. Chisolm, E. P. Jewey, A. F. Ravenel, H. E. Young) 174 Chambers

Stone Fred. & Co. (Frederick Stone, no Co.) 62 Gold

Stone John & Co. (refused) 457 Eighth av.

Stone Mary A. & Edmund, 215 Sixth av.

Stone Brothers (David & William Stone) 535 D'way

Stone & Beyer (Reuben R. Stone & Gustave E. Beyer) 434 Sixth av. & 2310 Eighth av.

Stone & Brick Waterproofing Co. (Henry M. Keasbey, Pres.; Rowland P. Keasbey, Sec.; further inf. unattainable) 115 B'way

Stone & Deforesta (George Stone & Margaret Deforesta) 843 Fifth av.

Stone & Ettinger (Elkan Stone & Isaac J. Ettinger) 494 B'way

Stone & Firth (John H. Stone & Louis W. Firth) 75 Spring

Stone & Gunther (Henry A. Stone & William H. Gunther) 101 W. 42d

Stone & Hart (no inf.) 2076 Seventh av.

Stone & Zellers (dissolved) 80 Laight

THE CALIGRAPH WRITING MACHINE,
HARTFORD, CONN.

Stone, Timlow & Co. (Albert H. Stone, William F. Timlow & Nathan S. Brennan) 105 Reade
Stoner Pneumatic Elevator Co. (Horace Little, Pres.; R. W. Milbank, Sec. Capital, $1,000,-000. Trustees: Horace & A. D. Little, R. W. Milbank, R. H. Miller) no address
Stonington Line (Providence & Stonington S. S. Co. proprs.) Pier 36 (New) N. R.
Storer S. L. & Co. (Samuel L. Storer, George H. Case & Kilburn Powers) 16 Fulton fish mkt & 226 Front
Storey & Tobin (no inf.) 2200 Second av.
Storey & Wilson (Edwin A. Storey & Lucius E. Wilson) 113 Sixth av.
Storm King Pants Co. (Ltd.) (inf. unattainable) 620 B'way
Story F. C. & Co. (Frank C. Story & Edward Russell) 120 D'way
Story R. G. & Co. (Rupert G. Story, no Co.) 110 Water
Story W. H. & Co. (Chauncey B. Hancock, Jacob H. Halsted & Thomas H. Story, only) 12 D'way
Story & Co. (Rowland & George H. Story) 522 & 548 Washn.
Story & Smith (dissolved) 60 Leonard
Story, Mapes & Co. (William E. Story & Abram W. Mapes, no Co.) 25 White
Stosch & Webor Mfg. Co. (no inf.) 719 Sixth
Stout Coal Co. (dissolved) 1 B'way
Stout Mfg. Co. (John R. Stout, Pres. Capital, $50,000. Trustees: John R. Stout, Elihu B. Baker, James O. Baird, John R. Mitchell) no address
Stout J. D. & Co. (James H. & Lewis A. Stout & Howard J. Runyon, only) 81 Warren
Stout W. & R. & Brother (Richard & George R. Stout, only) 87 Spruce
Stout & Co. (Joseph S. Stout & Randolph F. Purdy) 25 Broad
Stout & Thayer (Jacob Stout, Stephen H. Thayer & Ferdinand P. Pepin) 38 Broad
Stout, Spencer & Co. (William M. Stout, Frederick G. Spencer & William V. Stout) 308 G'wich
Stoutenborough X. (Xenophon Stoutenborough :—special partner, Chester B. Lawrence, B'klyn, N. Y., $10,000; terminates 8th March, 1893) 270 Pearl
Stover Alfred & Co. (dissolved) 55 Vesey
Stover Mfg. Co. (inf. unattainable) 55 Vesey
Stover, Myers & Vanburen (dissolved) 60 Cedar
Stow & Clayton (no inf.) 92 White
Stradtmann & Co. (dissolved) 91 Barclay
Strahmann John & Sons (John C. A. & Christian H. Strahmann, only) 1209 Lex. av.
Straiton & Storm (George Storm, Peter Miller & Henry Storm, only) 204 E. 27th
Straley, Hasbrouck & Schloeder (John A. Straley, Louis B. Hasbrouck & Nicholas Schloeder) 380 D'way
Strange & Brother (William T. A. Strange, only) 96 Prince
Strange, Kelly & Dennett (dissolved) 70 Greene
Stransky & Co. (Maurice & Jacob Stransky :—special partners, Edward Rothschild & Ephraim Arnstein, each $25,000; terminates 26th Sept. 1895) 182 E. 125th & 179 E. 124th
Strasburger Byron L. & Co. (Byron L. & Louis Strasburger) 31 Maiden la.
Strasburger Louis & Co. (Louis & Alvin L. & Mortimer L. Strasburger :—special partner, Charles Adler, $75,000; terminates 1st Jan. 1893) 16 Maiden la.
Strasburger E. & Co. (dissolved) 1357 B'way
Strascino Piano Co. (inf. unattainable) 90 Nassau

Stratton John F. & Son (John F. & Frank A. Stratton) 43 Walker
Stratton Separator Co. (E. Platt Stratton, Pres.; Henry L. Dogert, Sec. Capital, $15,000. Directors: E. Platt Stratton, Henry L. Dogert, Stephen Wilcox) 52 Cortlandt
Stratton J. C. & Co. (John C. & Byron F. Stratton) 112 Greene
Stratton & Ellingwood (Sidney V. Stratton & Francis L. Ellingwood) 57 B'way
Stratton & Hudson (Samuel H. Stratton & William M. Hudson) 36 Church
Straub Philip & Son (Philip & Philip Straub jr.) 92 E. 4th
Strauch Brothers (Peter D. & Albert T. & William E. Strauch) 26 Tenth av.
Straus Louis & Co. (no inf.) 15 William
Straus A. D. & Co. (Adolph D. Straus, Edward F. Eberstadt & Walter Dormitzer) 15 B'way
Straus L. & Sons (Lazarus & Isidor & Nathan & Oscar S. Straus & Lazarus Kohns) 42 Warren
Straus & Immen (Isaac Straus & Henry Immen) 161 E. 24th
Straus, Legg & Co. (George Legg, only) 109 Spring
Straus' H., Sons (dissolved) 22 Howard
Strauss Adolph & Co. (Adolph & Morris Strauss) 444 B'way & 10 Crosby
Strauss Charles T. & Brother (Charles T. & Gustavus E. Strauss) 424 D'way
Strauss Joseph H. & Co. (dissolved) 12 Desbrosses
Strauss M. & Son (dissolved) 508 B'way
Strauss Brothers (Charles L. & Adelbert A. T. Strauss) 633 Ninth av.
Strauss & Freeman (Isaac Strauss & William Freeman) 707 D'way
Strauss & Lipke (no inf.) r 128 Allen
Strauss & Ronan (Emanuel Strauss & Christopher C. Ronan) 506 E. 71st
Strauss Brothers & Co. (Ernest & Adolph & Julius Strauss) 110 Reade
Strauss, Kupfer & Co. (Joseph Strauss, Henry Kupfer & Julius H. Strauss) 471 Broome
Streat & Hellon (George Streat jr. & James S. Hellon) 35 E. 12th
Strebe Brothers (Henry F. & Charles E. Strebe) 2609 & 3223 Third av.
Street George O. & Sons (George O. & George W. & H. Louis Street) 15 John
Street Railway Trust Co. (in liquidation) 15 Broad
Street & Smith (George C. & Ormond G. Smith, only) 31 Rose
Streit Samuel & Co. (Samuel & Lewis A. Streit) 31 Liberty
Strens A. C. & Sons (Adolph C. & Robert & Charles C. Strens) 251 Grand
Strever Brothers (Monroe & Lewis B. Strever) 1484 & 1511 Second av.
Strich & Co. (Benjamin Strich, Co. refused) 585 Second av.
Stricker C. & Brother (Charles & Henry Stricker) 139 Stanton
Striffler C. & Co. (Christian Striffler & Emil Rudolph) 874 Ninth av.
Striker & Co. (William E. Striker & Thomas Adamson) 116 Gansevoort
Stringham J. & Son (dissolved) 1092 Park av.
Strippel & Son (Adam & John Strippel) 107 W. 29th
Stritch & Nolan (Thomas F. Stritch & Thomas J. Nolan) 14 Whitehall
Strittmatter Henry & Joseph, 150 Third av.
Strobel Philip & Sons (Philip & Herman C. & Emil & Otto F. Strobel) 59 & 82 Elizabeth
Strobel & Wilken Co. (Emil Strobel, Pres.; Edward H. Kruse, Sec. Capital, $250,000. Directors: Emil Strobel, George Wilken, Ed

ward H. Kruse, William R. Strobel & Henry Krucker) 501 B'way

Stroheim J. & Co. (Julius & Salo J. Stroheim) 209 Canal

Strohmeyer F. G. & Co. (Frederick G. Strohmeyer & Herman Arpe) 122 Water

Strohmeyer & Wyman (Henry A. Strohmeyer & N. Dwight Wyman) 216 William

Strong Locomotive Co. Asahel G. Darwin, Pres.; Malcolm W. Niven, Sec.; Henry F. Taintor, Treas. Capital, $1,200,000. Directors: Asahel G. Darwin, Henry G. Morris, Charles C. Worthington, George D. McCreary, George H. Myers, George S. Strong, A. B. Colt, Malcolm W. Niven) 45 B'way

Strong Pantaloon Mfg. Co. (Jacob A. Kohner, Pres.; Emanuel Finsterer, Treas. Capital, $50,000; further inf. unattainable) 542 B'way

Strong W. L. & Co. (William L. Strong, Spencer W. Coe, William B. Symmes, Frank L. Stott & Francis H. Cabot) 75 Worth

Strong Brothers (George W. & Frank L. Strong) 108 Canal

Strong & Brinsley (Philip C. Strong & Daniel J. Brinsley) 115 Fulton

Strong & Cadwalader (Charles E. Strong, John L. Cadwalader, George W. Wickersham & George F. Butterworth) 86 Wall

Strong & Mathewson (Theron G. Strong & Charles F. Mathewson) 45 William

Strong & Spear (Thomas S. Strong & Asa A. Spear) 80 Wall

Strong & Trowbridge (Henry H. Strong;—special partner, John J. Phelps, Englewood, N. J., $10,000; terminates 31st Dec. 1894) 24 State

Stroock S. & Co. (Louis S. & Mark E. Stroock, only) 62 Walker

Stroud & Co. (William L. & Edmund H. Stroud) 104 John

Strouse Joseph & Son (Joseph & Edward Strouse) 19 Whitehall

Strouse Morris & Co. (Morris Strouse & Ferdinand Meyer) 78 Reade

Strouse A. H. & Co. (Alexander H. Strouse & Adolph T. Scholle) 253 Church & 1615 Second av.

Strouse I. & Co. (dissolved) 440 B'way

Strouse L. K. & Co. (Lemen K. Strouse & Sophia A. Wilder) 95 Nassau

Struller, Meyer & Schumacher (Ricardo Struller, Luis A. Meyer & August Schumacher) 41 S. William

Struller, v. Pustan & Meyer (dissolved) 41 S. William

Struss & Koenig (Herman Struss & John H. Koenig) 1220 First av.

Struthers Joseph & Co. (Joseph Struthers & Eugene D. Bullinger) 24 New Chambers

Struve Brothers (Marcus & Paul J. Struve) 149, 974 & 1470 First av. 570 Second av. 1541 Av. A, 215 Av. B, 2011 Third av. & 202 E. 120th

Struve & Kuhl (Marcus Struve & Herman Kuhl) 214 First av.

Struvy Brothers (no inf.) 112 Third

Stuart William A. & Co. (William A. Stuart, no Co.) 205 Fifth av.

Stuart J. & J. & Co. (Joseph & Robert W. Stuart, only) 33 Nassau

Stuart M. J. & Co. (Mary J. Stuart & Daniel W. Brigham) 180 Maiden la.

Stuart, Bradford & Rockwell (Sanford Stuart, George Bradford & James R. Rockwell) 72 Murray

Studer & Le Tellier (Jacob Studer & Peter A. Le Tellier) 100½ W. 27th

Studio Publishing Co. (Clarence Cook, Pres.; Joseph J. Koch, Sec. Capital, $2,000; further inf. unattainable) 864 B'way

Studwell A. & Co. (Alexander & Henry A. & George S. & William J. Studwell) 154 Nassau

Studwell & Deveau (Augustus Studwell & Peter C. Deveau) 3 Hudson, 32 W. B'way & 101 Mercer

Studwell, Sanger & Co. (George H. Studwell & Eugene B. Sanger, no Co.) 32 Spruce

Stucck H. & Son (Henry & George Stucck) 265 Washn. mkt

Stucck & Boedecker (dissolved) 265 Washn. mkt

Stuetzer H. & Co. (Herman Stuetzer & Michael Fleckenstein) 39 Dey

Stuhl G. & J. (George & John) S. Boulevard c. E. 190th & 2545 Third av.

Stults & Bauer (Henry Stults & Frederick Bauer) 833 E. 31st

Stumpf Anthony & Co. (Anthony Stumpf & Charles D. Stourer) 27 Park pl. & 24 Murray

Stumpf Brothers (Louis & William Stumpf) 681 Fifth

Stumpp & Durr (Otto Stumpp & Gustave Durr) 68 Gansevoort

Stunz & Bock (Christian Stunz & John Bock) 1801 Ninth av.

Sturcke Richard & Co. (Richard Sturcke & John Wilshusen) 26 Harrison

Sturges D. J. & Son (dissolved) 55 Liberty

Sturges M. J. & G. W. (Macfarland J. & George W.) 205 Washn. mkt

Sturges & Roby (S. Perry Sturges & E. Willard Roby) 55 Liberty

Sturges & Wescott (Arthur D. Sturges & Eugene F. Wescott) 102 West

Sturm A. & J. Schleins (dissolved) 187 Elm

Sturm & Ackermann (Simon Sturm & Julius T. Ackermann) 43 Suffolk

Sturman B. & Son (Barnet & Raphael Sturman) 540 B'way

Sturmwald & Poppe (Raphael Sturmwald & Emil Poppe) 83 Wooster

Stursberg Hermann & Co. (Hermann Stursberg & Otto & Francis W. Randebrock) 81 New

Stursberg W. & Co. (William & Hermann Stursberg jr.:—special partner, Hermann Stursberg, $100,000; terminates 31st Dec. 1892) 69 Worth

Sturtevant Co. (George A. Sturtevant, propr.) 310 B'way

Sturz Brothers (Hugo & Arthur L. Sturz) 142 Lincoln av.

Stutzer Herman & Co. (Herman & Herman Stutzer jr.) 115 Produce Ex.

Stuyvesant Ins. Co. (George B. Rhoads, Pres.; Charles A. Carthwaite, Sec. Capital, $200,000. Directors: George B. Rhoads, Samuel P. Patterson, Adam W. Spies, A. Stewart Black, Dennis Hennessy, Samuel Weeks, Nathan A. Ohedsoy, Augustus T. Gillonder, William Ottmann, Michael Coleman, Benjamin Wright, Andrew Mills, Nelson G. Ayres, Robert B. Stuyvesant) 157 B'way

Stuyvesant Piano Co. (John W. Mason, Pres.; Charles B. Lawson, Sec.; S. Hubbard, Treas. Capital, $40,000. Directors: John W. Mason, William E. Wheelock, Charles B. Lawson, S. Lawson, A. D. Wheelock, R. P. Vidaut, R. F. Tilney) 204 E. 107th

Stuyvesant Safe Deposit Co. (William D. Maxwell, Pres.; William H. Harrison, Sec. Capital, $200,000. Directors: Robert Buck, Charles F. Goodhue, Edward Fuller, Henry Weill Charles E. Fleming, H. Blauvelt, John Lowry, Samuel T. Hubbard, W. D. Maxwell, Charles T. Ryan, John Corse, William H. Harrison) 1 Third av.

Styles & Cash (Samuel D. Styles & Alexander Cash) 77 Eighth av.

MERCHANTS EXCHANGE NAT. BANK OF THE CITY OF N. Y.
SOLICITS YOUR ACCOUNT. 257 Broadway.
PHINEAS C. LOUNSBURY, President.   ALLEN S. APGAR, Cashier.

Suan Henry F. & Brother (Henry F. & George M. Suan) 129 Broad
Sub-Silver Metal Co. (inf. unattainable) 156 B'way
Subterranean Conduction Co. (Chester C. Munroe, Pres.; Thomas W. Rae, Sec.; George N. McKibbin, Treas. Capital, $250,000. Directors: Chester C. Munroe, Thomas W. Rae, George N. McKibbin, Walter Thompson, Frederick H. Read) 32 Liberty
Suburban News Agency (no inf.) 73 Park row
Suburban Rapid Transit Co. (J. Hood Wright, Pres.; Lewis R. Pomeroy, Sec. Capital, $500,000; Directors: J. Hood Wright, J. Pierpont Morgan, Samuel Spencer, George Bliss, Charles Lanier, John H. Hall, Jay Gould, Cyrus W. Field, Russell Sage) 40 Wall
Suburban Street Railway Co. (inf. unattainable) 54 Wall
Suoblick J. D. & Co. (dissolved) 2 Stone
Sudbrink William & Co. (William Sudbrink, Co. refused) 348 E. 114th
Sudbury E. D. & Co. (Edward B. Sudbury, no Co.) 348 B'way
Sudhaus & Erienkotter (Herman Sudhaus & Charles Erienkotter) 74 Fulton
Suffolk County Water Co. (John Lockwood, Pres.; John C. Lockwood, Sec. Capital, $60,000. Directors: John & John C. & Frank S. Lockwood) 52 B'way
Suffolk Suspender Co. (Andrew Dow & Co. proprs.) 893 Canal
Suhr & Dierks (dissolved) 216 Mulberry
Suhrig A. & Brother (August & Henry C. Suhrig) 490 Seventh av.
Sullivan County R. R. Co. (inf. unattainable) 45 B'way
Sullivan Jeremiah & Co. (Jeremiah Sullivan, no Co.) 32 South
Sullivan Timber Co. (William A. S. Wheeler, Pres.; Thomas E. Jordan, Sec. Capital, $500,000. Directors: William A. S. Wheeler, Thomas E. Jordan, Martin H. Sullivan, John L. Macauly, Richard L. Campbell, J.W. Diack, S. R. Sanford) 24 Stone
Sullivan, E. & Co. (Elizabeth Sullivan, Emma Aufenanger & Catharine A. Kelly) 56 E. 10th
Sullivan J. & M. (Joseph L. & Michael E.) 2588 Third av.
Sullivan J. F. & Co. (Jeremiah F. Sullivan, no Co.) 271 D'way
Sullivan Brothers (grocers) (Dennis & Jeremiah Sullivan) 150 W. 17th
Sullivan Brothers (metal) (Robert D. & Marcus W. Sullivan) 254 South
Sullivan Brothers (painters) (Dennis L. & Thomas Sullivan) 221 E. 58th
Sullivan & Baker (Morris J. Sullivan & Joseph F. Baker) 40 W. 18th
Sullivan & Carey (Daniel Sullivan & Patrick Carey) B'way n W. 129th
Sullivan & Co. (dissolved) 345 Fifth av.
Sullivan & Cromwell (George H. Sullivan, William Nelson Cromwell & William J. Curtis) 45 Wall
Sullivan & Gorman (Maurice J. Sullivan & Thomas J. Gorman) 90 & 126 William
Sullivan & O'Brien (dissolved) 116 Centre
Sullivan & Pierson (dissolved) 61 Walker
Sullivan & Vaughan (Patrick Sullivan & John Vaughan) 122 Park row
Sullivan, Corrigan & Co. (Daniel F. Sullivan, William T. Corrigan & Cassel Cohen) 101 Spring
Sullivan, Drew & Co. (Thomas Sullivan, James Drew, John Dunphy & J. George Johnson) 600 B'way & 184 Crosby
Sullivan, Lowery & Co. (Timothy O. Sullivan & Francis Lowery, no Co.) 60 Dey & 12 Lawton av. W. Washn. mkt

Sullivan, Vail & Co. (Arthur T. Sullivan, Theodore F. Vail & Howard F. Randolph) 329 B'way
Sultzer J. B. & Co. (inf. unattainable) 52 W. 14th
Sulzbacher, Gitterman & Wedgles (William Sulzbacher & Henry Gitterman, only) 557 B'way & 138 Mercer
Summerfield J. B. & Co. (John B. Summerfield & Charles Schwecofer) 68 Wall
Sumner Charles P. & Co. (Charles P. Sumner & John S. Porter) 18 D'way
Sun Light Co. (L. C. Lewis, Pres; M. L. Andrews, Sec.; I. C. Reed, Treas. Capital, $5,000,000. Directors: L. C. Lewis, I. C. Reed, M. L. Andrews) 22 State
Sun Mutual Ins. Co. (John P. Paulison, receiver) 52 Wall
Sun Printing & Publishing Assn. (Charles A. Dana, Pres.; Charles S. Weyman, Sec. Capital, $350,000. Directors: Charles A. & Paul Dana, Thomas Hitchcock, Thomas B. Asten, Charles S. Weyman, Franklin Bartlett, William M. Laffan) 170 Nassau
Sun Type Writer Co. (Lee S. Burridge, propr.) 310 D'way
Sunday Courier Co. (refused) 132 Nassau
Sunderland Telephone Co. (John P. Sunderland, Pres.; William Sunderland, Sec. Capital, $650,000; further inf. unattainable) 39 D'way
Sunderland Telephone Co. of N. Y. (not inc.) (William Sunderland & James L. Armstrong) 39 D'way
Sundheimer Brothers (Ignatz & Max Sundheimer) 96 Greene
Sunnyside Island Ice Co. (Archibald Scott & Sons, proprs.) 545 W. 21st
Suppan W. H. & Co. (William H. & Charles) 83 Clinton
Surdos & Roos (dissolved) 226 E. 41st
Surety Contract Co. (Ltd.) (Richard J. Dodge, Pres.; Francis E. Dodge, Sec. Capital, $30,000; further inf. unattainable) 280 B'way
Surpless, Dunn & Adler (James Surpless, Robert M. Dunn & Benjamin S. Adler) 97 Chambers & 79 Reade
Suspension Car Truck Mfg. Co. (inf. unattainable) 11 Pine
Susadorff L. A. & Co. (Louis A. Susadorff, Ernesto Dezaldo & Rafael Padrajas) 4 Cedar
Sussex Blue Stone Co. (W. Irving Kent, Pres.; Allen W. Campbell, Sec.; further inf. unattainable) 58 Wall
Sussfeld, Lorsch & Co. (Louis Sussfeld & Sigmund Lorsch, no Co.) 13 Maiden la. & 81 Greene
Susskind J. & Co. (dissolved) 140 Canal
Sussman Brothers (Thomas & David Sussman) 208 Third av.
Sussner Charles A. & Co. (Charles A. Sussner & James J. Boylan) 868 G'wich
Sutherland Mfg. Co. (inf. unattainable) 178 Sixth av.
Sutherland, Innes & Co. (Samuel J. Sutherland & James Innes, no Co.) 29 Beaver
Sutphen & Myer (John S. Sutphen jr. & Charles R. Myer) 11 Desbrosses & 34 Vesey
Sutphen & Sutphen (William & Clinton Sutphen) 45 B'way
Sutro Tunnel Co. (no inf.) 115 B'way
Sutro Brothers Braid Co. (Ludwig Sutro, Pres.; Reinhard W. Strassberger, Sec. Capital, $100,000. Directors: Ludwig Sutro, Reinhard W. Strassberger, Theodore Tiedemann) 127 Spring & 404 W. 27th
Sutro & Newmark (Bernhard Newmark, only) 1899 Second av.
Sutro Brothers & Hirsch (Lionel & Richard Sutro & Robert B. Hirsch ;—special partner. Moriz Josephthal, $5,000 ; terminates 31st Dec. 1892) 91 Bleecker & 213 Mercer

SNOW, CHURCH & CO. {ESTABLISHED 1874.

SUT 294 SYR

Sutton & Co. (Effingham D. & Woodruff Sutton) 82 South & Pier 19 E. R.

Sutton & Co.'s Dispatch Line (Sutton & Co. proprs.) 82 South & Pier 19 E. R.

Sutton & Dunn (Walter T. Sutton & Robert M. Dunn) 15 Worth

Suzarte & Whitney (Eduardo Q. Suzarte & Thomas H. Whitney;—special partner, Lucy W. Whitney, *Stamford, Ct.*, $30,000; terminates 31st Dec. 1890) 51 New

Swan Incandescent Electric Light Co. (Edwin Einstein, Pres. ; Charles W. Spear, Sec. Capital, $800,000. Directors : Edwin Einstein, W. L. Strong, Felix Samson, Morris Fatman, D. L. Einstein, Charles W. Spear) 203 Elizabeth

Swan John & Co. (John Swan & George R. Love) 33 Fulton

Swan Publishing Co. (Frank M. Van Etten, propr.) 757 B'way

Swan Siskind & Son (Siskind & Simon I. Swan) 277 Church

Swan & Finch (Alden S. Swan & Charles N. Finch) 151 Maiden la.

Swan & Lewis (Gustavus Swan & John W. Lewis) 225 B'way

Swan & Son (John jr. & Harmonus Swan) 66 South

Swanson, Grierson & Co. (John Swanson, John Grierson & William S. Cairns) 40 Cotton Ex.

Swany A. Frank & Co. (A. Frank Swany, no Co.) 71 South

Swartwout F. G. & Co. (Frank G. Swartwout & Thomas W. Organ) 157 E. 125th & 247 W. 125th

Swarts M. E., Co. (inf. unattainable) 386 Sixth av. & 700 Eighth av.

Swartz H. & Son (Henry & Herman Swartz) 200 E. Houston

Swartz & Elias (Silas Swartz & Michael Elias) 254 Canal

Swartz & Goldstein (dissolved) 353 Canal

Swartz, Jerkowski & Co. (Solomon M. Swartz, Samuel Jerkowski & Lester J. Saul) 560 D'way & 98 Crosby

Sweeney W. H., Mfg. Co. (William H. Sweeney, Pres.; John J. Sweeney, Sec.; James Sweeney, Treas. Capital, $60,000. Directors: William H. & John J. & James Sweeney) 240 Water

Sweeney E. & Sons (Elizabeth & William A. & James J. Sweeney) 229 B'way

Sweeney J. & Barrett (Michael Barrett, only) 8 Dutch

Sweeney J. F. & J. J. (John F. & James J.) 41 Maiden la.

Sweeney Brothers (dissolved) 219 First av.

Sweeny Brothers (Edward J. & Frank M. Sweeny) 752 Ninth av.

Sweeny's D., Sons (Daniel & Charles D. & John H. Sweeny) 23 Duane

Sweany's Morgan J., Brother (no inf.) 100 Water

Sweet Edward & Co. (Frederic Van Lennep, Schuyler Quackenbush, A. Clifford Tower & William L. Bull, only) 33 Broad & 24 New

Sweet A. M. & Son (Abraham M. & Edwin A. Sweet) 4 Fulton

Sweet C. C. & Co. (Charles C. & William L. Sweet) 4 South

Sweet, Orr & Co. (Clinton W. Sweet, James Orr & Clayton E. Sweet) 115 Worth

Sweeten A. C. & Co. (Andrew C. Sweeten, no Co.) 103 Worth

Sweetser, Pembrook & Co. (George D. & J. Howard Sweetser, William A. Pembrook, Joseph H. Dumstad, George L. Putnam, Howard F. Sweetser, Theodore K. Pembrook & Frederick B. Dale) 376 B'way

Sweetwater Mining Co. (inoperative) 129 Pearl

Swenarton & Kaiser (Seaman A. Swenarton & Henry M. Kaiser) 104 Franklin

Swenson S. M. & Sons (Svante M. & Eric P. & S. Albin Swenson) 216 B'way

Swenson Brothers (Eric P. & S. Albin Swenson) 216 B'way

Swezey's N. T., Son & Co. (Christopher Swezey, no Co.) 170 South

Swift Charles N., Mfg. Co. (Charles N. Swift, Pres.; Gustave F. Perronoud, Sec.; Charles Swift, Treas. Capital, $50,000. Directors: Charles N. & Charles Swift, Gustave F. Perrenoud) 115 Chambers

Swift Co. (Magdalena Swift, propr.) 123 W. 30th

Swift James T. & Co. (James T. Swift, Douglas Hollister & Edwin R. Dillingham) 59 Worth

Swift Specific Co. (no inf.) 756 B'way

Swift, Billings & Co. (B. W. Swift & F. Swift Dillings, Co. refused) 142 Pearl & 108 Water

Swinton Brothers (Ralph W. E. & William Swinton jr.) 60 B'way

Swinton & Swinton (Herbert & Alfred Swinton) 838 B'way

Swiss Asphalte Rock Paving Co. (Edward Vanorden & Co. proprs.) 110 John

Swiss Publishing Co. (John Friederich, propr.) 116 Fulton

Switzer Joseph W. & Co. (Joseph W. & Mary A. Switzer) 21 Gold

Switzer & Miller (dissolved) 202 E. 84th

Switzer & Schussel (Frederick E. Switzer & E. Max Schussel) 48 Leonard

Swords & Dickson (Albert S. Swords & Joseph B. Dickson) 1 D'way

Sycamore Spring Water Co. (inf. unattainable) 11 Pine

Sykes S. & Co. (Helen & William F. & Edward S. & Charles Sykes, only) 8 Gt. Jones

Sykes & Street (Walter F. Sykes & Robert R. Street) 85 Water

Sykes & Wilson (Martha E. Sykes & Jane E. Wilson) 2107 Seventh av.

Sylvester Lewis, Son & Co. (Lewis & Alphonso L. Sylvester, no Co.) 130 Maiden la.

Sylvester, Bell & Co. (Horace C. Sylvester, Alexander P. Bell & David R. Standish) 503 B'way

Sylvester, Hilton & Co. (dissolved) 784 B'way

Sylvester, Levacher & Co. (Hyman Sylvester, John B. Levacher & Henry Zox) 170 Greene

Symmes & Donaldson (dissolved) 10 James sl.

Syndicate of Japanese Manufacturers (Ltd.) (Joseph R. Tillinghast, Pres.; John Proctor, Sec.; Martin P. Goller, Treas. Capital, $50,000. Directors: Joseph R. Tillinghast, Motomaro Sato, Martin P. Goller, John Proctor, Charles J. Smith) 428 B'way

Syndicate Trading Co. (A. Swan Brown, Pres.; James A. Swan, Treas. Directors: A. Swan Brown, James A. Swan, Walter Callender, Alexander Meldrum, A. M. Lindsay, F. S. Brown, A. B. Wallace, W. A. Denholm) 120 Franklin

Syndicate Watch Co. (Charles F. Brooks, Pres.; Albert Mellen Sec.; John H. Stoutenburgh, Treas. Capital, $50,000. Directors: Charles F. Brooks, John H. Stoutenburgh, Albert Mellen, John Dehrens, Philip Wood) 11 E. 14th

Sypher & Co. (Obadiah L. Sypher & Henry R. Treadwell) 860 B'way & 32 E. 18th

Syracuse & Oswego Line (William B. Walsh, propr.) 111 Broad & Pier 3 E. R.

Syracuse, Geneva & Corning R. R. Co. (George J. Magee, Pres.; Daniel Donch, Sec.; Edwin D. Worcester, Treas. Capital, $1,325,000. Directors: George J. Magee, Daniel Donch, Edwin D. Worcester, John Lang, Abram S. Stotboff, Austin Lathrop, Dwight W. Pardee, Chauncey M. Depew, Charles C. Clarke, Ed-

WATER METERS, GAS ENGINES, | **NATIONAL METER CO.**
FOR PUMPING AND POWER. | 252 Broadway, N. Y.

SYR 295 TAY

ward V. W. Rossiter, Samuel F. Barger, James Tillinghast) Grand Central depot

Syracuse, Ontario & N. Y. Railway Co. (Ashbel Green, Pres.; Edward V. W. Rossiter, Sec. Capital, $400,000. Directors: Albert Allen, Lawrence Depew, Edward V. W. Rossiter, Ashbel Green, Walter Katte, Herbert B. Kinney, James D. Layng, James W. Musson, Donald B. Toncey, William C. Taylor, William H. Sanford, Joseph P. Ord, Albert B. Taylor) Grand Central depot & 5 Vanderbilt av.

Szigethy Brothers (Timothy F. & Alexander & Stephen Szigethy) r 107 Rivington

Szuchar & Raab (Roman Szuchar & Hans Raab) 172 Essex

T

Taber Henry M. & Co. (Henry M. & William P. Taber) 141 Pearl

Taber & Co. (John R. Taber & Edward D. Thurston :—special partner, Augustus Taber, *Westchester, N. Y.*, $15,000 ; terminates 1st Dec. 1890) 714 Water & 412 Front

Taber & Delano (George H. Taber & George W. Delano) 255 W. 18th

Tablet & Ticket Co. (Henry Wilson, Pres.; Ernest D. Wilson, Sec. Capital, $25,000. Directors: Henry & Ernest D. Wilson) 260 Church

Tabor Mfg. Co. (Charles A. Moore, Pres.; Henry S. Manning, Sec. Capital, $300,000. Directors: Charles A. Moore, Henry S. Manning, Eugene L. Maxwell, Harris Tabor) 111 Liberty

Taft James H. & Co. (James K. & James H. jr. & Charles H. Taft & Alfred C. Mintram) 78 William

Taft Orray & Co. (dissolved) 11 E. 14th

Taft E. N. & T. M. (Enos N. & Theodore M.) 74 Wall

Taft Brothers (Francis H. & Alfred A. Taft) 44 Cedar

Tag Charles F. & Son (Charles F. & Casimir & Albert Tag) 29 Broad

Tag Peter & Son (Robert Tag, only) 107 Washn. mkt

Taller E. N. & W. H. & Co. (Edward N. & William H. Taller & Richard D. Baker) 45 White

Tailors' & Cutters' Exchange (Dittmar & Shelfer, proprs.) 758 B'way

Taintor & Holt (Giles E. Taintor, George H. Holt & Gaston D. L'Huillier) 11 Wall

Taintor Brothers & Co. (Charles N. Taintor, Edward L. Gates, Judah L. Taintor & J. Hunt Butler) 20 Astor pl.

Talbott Thomas, Mfg. Co. (dissolved) 109 Suffolk

Talbot Copying Co. (not inc.; further inf. refused) 213 E. 19th

Talbot & Forfar (Simeon H. Talbot & James Forfar) 35 Frankfort

Talbot & Phillips (Charles S. Phillips & Giraud Foster :—special partner, Charles de Rham jr. *Cold Spring, N. Y.*, $35,000 ; terminates 1st July, 1890) 1 B'way

Talcott & Co. (refused) 171 B'way

Talcott & Meyer (William Talcott & Charles Meyer jr.) 87 B'way

Tallmadge & Martin (Daniel W. Tallmadge & George G. Martin) 64 Broad

Tallman Automatic Car Brake Co. (Stephen P. Tallman, Pres.; David H. Jeffrey, Sec.; Seymour Hait, Treas. Capital, $2,000,000. Directors: Stephen P. Tallman, David H. Jeffrey, Seymour Hait) 171 B'way

Tallman & Co. (Alfred A. & Alfred A. Tallman jr.) 15 Bible h.

Tallon & Stadtfeld (Edward Tallon & Robert V. Stadtfeld) 207 E. 86th

Talmadge Henry & Co. (Henry & Henry P. Talmadge) 68 William

Talmage's Dan, Sons (John F. & Daniel & David Talmage) 115 Wall

Tams & Cromwell (J. Frederic Tams & Oliver E. Cromwell) 48 Exchange pl.

Tanenbaum I., Son & Co. (Moses Tanenbaum & Samuel L. Bear, only) 94 Liberty

Tanfani & Steudel (dissolved) 81 Walker

Tannahill W. T. (firm of) (refused) 68 Cotton Ex.

Tannenbaum L. & Co. (Lippman Tannenbaum, no Co.) 68 Nassau

Tapp E. W. & Son (Edward W. & Edward W. Tapp jr.) 15 Burling sl.

Tappan, McKillop & Co. (no inf.) 132 Nassau

Tappen & Mathers (George H. Tappen & Joseph W. Mathers) 175 B'way

Tappey L. C. & Co. (dissolved) 21 Spruce

Tapscott & Hibberd (William H. Hibberd, only) 24 Cliff

Tapscott Brothers & Co. (James & George L. Tapscott, no Co.) 83 South

Tarbox & Crandall (George W. Tarbox & John G. Crandall) 140 Reade

Tardio L. & Co. (Luigi Tardio & Angelo D. Girolamo) 2164 First av.

Tarlow & Baum (dissolved) 34 Walker

Tarlow & Hutshing (Jacob Tarlow & Berthold Hutshing) 34 Walker

Tarlton John J. & Co. (John J. Tarlton & Charles A. Swindell) 629 Hudson

Tarrant & Co. (refused) 278 G'wich

Tarrant & Gismond (George Tarrant & Lorenzo Gismond) 15 John

Tarrytown & Irvington Transp. Co. (Roqua & Lewis, proprs.) Pier 34 (old) N. R.

Tatham & Brothers (Henry B. & William P. & Benjamin & Charles Tatham) 82 Beekman

Taub R. & H. (Regina & Hermina) 250 E. 4th

Taurus Line (Miller, Bull & Co. proprs.) 48 South

Taussig G. F. & Co. (Gustave F. Taussig & John T. Vermett) 257 W. 27th

Taussig N. W. & Co. (Noah W. & Felix Taussig) 124 Front & 379 Washn.

Taussig Brothers (Oscar & Edwin F. Taussig) 2680 Third av.

Tax-Payers Protective Assn. (Jacob E. Bloom, Sec.; further inf. unattainable) 194 B'way

Taylor A. D., Mfg. Co. (Alva D. Taylor, propr.) 3 Hague

Taylor Charles R. & Co. (Charles R. Taylor, Co. refused) 92 Cotton Ex.

Taylor David & Co. (David Taylor & Thomas Millson) 14 South

Taylor Frederic & Co. (Frederic Taylor, Amory G. Hodges & John McGinnis jr.) 64 B'way

Taylor James H. & Co. (James H. Taylor & Charles J. Maguire) 91 Wall

Taylor John D. & Ellis (John D. Taylor & Lawrence E. Ellis) 246 Canal

Taylor John H. & Co. (John H. Taylor, no Co.) 81 Maiden la.

Taylor Matt. Paving Co. (Matt Taylor, Pres.; Ronald Taylor, Treas. Capital, $150,000. Directors: Matt & Ronald Taylor, William H. Shepard, Charles A. Porter) 15 State & 143 Horatio

Taylor S. T. (Curt Von Witzleben & James A. Blanchard, only) 980 B'way

Taylor William & Co. (no inf.) 104 Franklin

Taylor C. F. & H. L. (C. Fayette & Henry Ling Taylor) 201 W. 54th

Taylor F. M. & Co. (Finley M. & Basel E. Taylor) 74 E. 9th

Taylor H. E., Co. (refused) 163 Bowery

Taylor H. S. & Co. (Henry S. Taylor, no Co.) 229 Park row

EXCELSIOR BIRD FOOD. The recognized standard. The most reliable for your Canary. Use no other. Insist upon getting it. Packed only by **C. ROSENSTEIN & CO.**, 373 Washington Street, New York.

TAY   296   TEN

Taylor H. W. & Co. (Henry W. Taylor & Mary A. Kaler) 23 E. 20th
Taylor M. E. & Co. (dissolved) 332 Fifth av.
Taylor M. J. & Co. (Morton J. Taylor, no Co.) 84 Wooster
Taylor W. B. & Sons (William B. & William Edward & Frank B. Taylor) 738 Sixth av.
Taylor W. S. & Bloodgood jr. (William S. Taylor & William Bloodgood jr.) 6 Thomas
Taylor Brothers (bankers) (William L. & Irving K. Taylor) 3 Broad
Taylor Brothers (carpenters) (Warren S. & Clarence M. Taylor) 1628 B'way
Taylor Brothers (painters) (William A. & Edward W. Taylor) 104 Maiden la.
Taylor Brothers (pawnbrokers) (Henry & David C. Taylor) 59 Bowery
Taylor Brothers (wool) (John C. & James A. Taylor) 88 Reade
Taylor & Brother (George C. Taylor, only) 860 B'way
Taylor & Burck (Isaac O. Taylor & William Burck) 371 & 935 Eighth av.
Taylor & Co. (coffins) (Thomas M. & William F. & Frank R. Taylor) 163 Bowery, 131 Chrystie & 162 W. 56th
Taylor & Co. (painters) (Richard Taylor & Pierre B. Trainque) 117 W. 38th
Taylor & Co. (pictures) (dissolved) 1199 B'way
Taylor & Ferris (John A. Taylor, Morris P. Ferris & Charles F. Bishop) 111 B'way
Taylor & Littlewood (no inf.) 530 B'way
Taylor & Parker (Alfred Taylor & Frederick S. Parker) 88 Park row
Taylor & Pulsifer (no inf.) 115 W. End av,
Taylor & Seeley (Jerome Taylor & Edward S. Seeley) 138 Greene
Taylor & Son (jewelers) (John & Henry Taylor) 907 B'way
Taylor & Son (pianos) (Francis & John A. Taylor) 8 E. 18th
Taylor & Swart (dissolved) 425 Washn. mkt
Taylor & Tanbe (George Taylor & Henning G. Tanbe) 90 Wall
Taylor & Wallace (Thomas R. Taylor & Thomas P. Wallace) 157 Reade
Taylor & Wells (dissolved) 331 Washn.
Taylor, Cutter & Co. (Berthold M. Halmerdinger, propr.) 232 Bowery
Taylor-Plumas Mill & Mining Co. (Francis B. Forster, Pres.; Laurie L. Levey, Sec. Capital, $200,000. Directors: Francis B. Forster, Laurie L. Levey, Richard Hetzel, Henry W. Wilkins, A. Woelfel) 32 Broad
Tayntor C. E. & Co. (Charles E. & Emma J. Tayntor) 239 B'way
Teachers' Equitable Building-Loan Assn. (George Chase, Pres.; Reno R. Billington, Sec.; Jacob T. Boyle, Treas. Directors: George Chase, Reno R. Billington, Silas S. Packard, Isaac L. Hurlbut, J. S. Newberry, J. S. Babcock, Herbert E. Crisp) 120 B'way
Teachers' Publishing Co. (Edwin Shepard, Pres.; L. E. Litchfield, Sec.; Elijah E. Bemis, Treas. Capital, $5,000. Trustees: Edwin Shepard, Anson B. Guilford, Elijah E. Bemis) 6 Clinton pl.
Teasdale & Harrington (Charles E. Teasdale & John H. Harrington) 93 Elizabeth
Teator Brothers (Louis A. & William Teator) 487 & 2338 Third av. & 277 Av. B. & 197 Av. C
Teator & Wolcott (Harvey L. Teator & Egbert C. Wolcott) 282 Eighth av. & 402 Fourth av.
Tebbetts, Harrison & Robins (William C. Tebbetts, Charles F. Harrison & Edward B. Robins) 75 Worth
Techner & Frank (Charles Techner & Louis M. Frank) 404 B'way

Technics Publishing Co. (James H. Goodsell, Pres.; Clifford Thomson, Sec.; Samuel Elliott, Treas. Capital, $30,000. Directors: James H. Goodsell, Clifford Thomson, Samuel Elliott) 14 Cortlandt
Tedford & Stolt (no inf.) 176 Lewis
Teets A. & Co. (Albert Teets & John Wick) 605 Eighth av.
Teets J. W. & A. (Joseph W. & A. Alonzo) 505 Manhattan av.
Tefft, Weller & Co. (William E. & F. Griswold Tefft, George C. Clarke, John N. Beach & Morton D. Bogue, only) 326 B'way
Tegetmeier & Riepe (August Tegetmeier & Ignatz Riepe) 733 First av.
Teichman's Isaac, Sons (Louis M. & Joseph I. Teichman) 222 G'wich
Teichner & Happy (John Teichner & George W. Happy) 163 B'way
Tekulsky Brothers (John S. & Louis Tekulsky) 33 & 173 Monroe, 39 Oak & 568 Second av.
Telegraphers' Mutual Benefit Assn. (James Merrihew, Pres.; George W. E. Atkins, Treas.; Thomas E. Fleming, Sec.) 195 B'way
Telephone Directory Publishing Co. (Copeland & Clarke, propr.) 18 Cortlandt
Teleseme Electric Mfg. Co. (F. Benedict Herzog, Pres.; Philip Herzog, Sec. Capital, $75,000. Directors: F. Benedict & Philip Herzog) 30 Broad & 26 West
Telfer & Lane (R. Telfer & M. Lane) 104 Third av.
Tellado, Giberga & Co. (Jonquin Tellado, Benjamin Giberga & Eusebio Mayol) 118 Wall
Tembrook Brothers (no inf.) 26 G'wich av.
Temple T. J. & Co. (Thomas J. Temple & William D. Sammis) 155 B'way
Temple & Lockwood (Edward A. Temple & Arthur J. Lockwood) 12 Platt
Templeton & Co. (James A. Templeton & John E. Hutchinson) 36 Exchange pl.
Tenbroeck & Co. (Robert H. Tenbroeck, no Co.) 45 South
Teneick & Kent (Cornelius Teneick & John S. Kent) 1555 B'way
Ten Eyck & Parker (Herbert D. Ten Eyck & Harry J. Parker) 66 Pine
Teneyck & Remington (Sandford R. Teneyck & James H. Remington) 271 B'way
Tenner & Baum (Louis Tenner & Herman Baum) 150 B'way
Tenner & Co. (Julius Tenner, no Co.) 1646 Ninth av.
Tennessee Coal, Iron & R. R. Co. (Thomas C. Platt, Pres.; James Bowron, Sec. Capital, $10,000,000. Directors: Thomas C. Platt, Christopher C. Baldwin, Daniel S. Lamont, F. L. Lehmann, H. Duncan Wood, John C. Haskell, J. F. B. Jackson, William M. Duncan, Samuel Cowan, Sparrell Hill, James L. Gaines, Enoch Ensley, Napoleon Hill, H. G. Bond) 49 B'way
Tenney C. H. & Co. (Charles H. Tenney, no Co.) 612 B'way & 148 Crosby
Tenney & Dupee (Charles H. Tenney & George P. Dupee) 612 B'way & 150 Crosby
Tenney's (dissolved) 40 Beaver
Tennis Building Assn. (Francis H. Weeks, Pres.; Henry W. Deforest, Sec. Trustees: Francis H. Weeks, Henry W. Deforest, Lispenard Stewart, John N. Bowers, Herman S. Leroy, J. Herbert Johnston, William R. Stewart, Stanley Dwight) 212 W. 41st
Tension Envelope Co. (Abraham N. Emdin, propr.) 550 Pearl
Tenth & Twenty-Third St. Ferry Co. (Charles C. Edey, Pres.; Henry K. Knapp, Sec. Capital, $1,000,000. Directors: Charles C. Edey, Isaac L. Rice, Henry K. Knapp, M. B. Hollins, Emanuel Lehman, E. S. Knapp, Thomas Paton) ft. E. 10th & ft. E. 23d

IDEN & CO., University Place, 9th to 10th Sts., N. Y. | **MANUFACTURERS OF GAS FIXTURES AND ELECTROLIERS**

TER 297 THO

Terhune Henry & Son (Henry & William H. Terhune) 26 Murray

Terhune A. & Son (Albert & Albert H. Terhune) 965 & 2351 Eighth av.

Terhune & Robus (Samuel L. Terhune & Edward J. Robus) 723 Sixth av.

Terminal Warehouse Co. (William W. Rossiter, Pres.; Frank P. Rossiter, Sec. Capital, $50,000. Directors: William W. & Frank P. Rossiter, Frederic J. Middlebrook, Barent H. Lang) 77 Broad & 27 Front

Terpenning & Son (John L. & Irving R. Terpenning) 214 Fulton mkt

Terret N. L. & Son (Nathaniel L. & Nathaniel C. Terrel) 41 Water

Terrell & Travis (Theodore Terrell & Ira U. Travis) 17 Bond

Terrell & Vroom (Isaac M. Terrell & Henry S. Vroom) 368 Eighth av. & 261 W. 27th

Terrible Mining Co. (Richard P. Lounsbery, Pres. Capital, $125,000. Directors: Richard P. Lounsbery, A. B. Daylis, George G. Navers) 15 Broad

Terry Clock Co. (dissolved) 50 Maiden la.

Terry J. & Co. (John Terry, no Co.) 134 Pearl & 100 Water

Terry & Bayles (Edwin R. Terry & Joseph Bayles) 49 South

Terwilliger G. W. & P. (George W. & Pulaski) 477 Eighth av.

Terwilliger Brothers (no inf.) 1208 Third av.

Terwilliger & Peck (La Fevre Terwilliger & Charles P. B. Peck) 862 Second av.

Tesson & Co. (dissolved) 168 Pearl

Teuscher & Gernsheimer (Rudolph Gernsheimer, only) 104 Chambers

Towes E. H. & Co. (Elde H. Towes, no Co.) 357 G'wich

Tewksbury & Lynch (dissolved) 26 Coenties sl.

Texas Siftings Publishing Co. (Alexander E. Sweet, Pres.; J. Armory Knox, Treas.; A. Minor Griswold, Sec. Capital, $100,000; further inf. refused) 47 John

Texas & New Orleans R. R. Co. (Collis P. Huntington, Pres.; P. J. Huder, Treas.; E. M. Underhill, Sec. Capital, $5,000,000. Directors: Collis P. Huntington, Isaac E. Gates, Eber W. Cave, Charles C. Gibbs, Edward F. Hill, Thomas W. House, Julius Kruttschnitt) 23 Broad

Texas & Pacific Railway Co. (Jay Gould, Pres.; Charles E. Satterlee, Sec. Capital, $50,000,000. Directors: Jay Gould, Isaac J. Wistar, John N. Hutchinson, Russell Sage, George J. Gould, Amos L. Hopkins, Charles E. Satterlee, Silas H. H. Clark, Samuel Sloan, Charles M. McGhee, Thomas T. Eckert, Samuel Thomas, John T. Terry, Henry G. Marquand, E. B. Wheelock, Milton H. Smith) 195 B'way

Texas, Topolobampo & Pacific R. R. & Telegraph Co. (John H. Rice, Pres. Capital, $400,000; further inf. refused) 32 Nassau

Texas-Atlantic Seaboard Assn. (James F. Fuller, Chairman) 280 B'way

Thackray & Co. (Walter & Emma Thackray & Ravilo C. Hinman) 44 Exchange pl.

Thaden L. & A. (Louise & Augusta) 356 W. 48th

Thalheim J. & Co. (Julius Thalheim, no Co.) 99 Maiden la.

Thalheimer Brothers (Henry Thalheimer & David T. Klein) 28 Howard

Thalmessinger & Mendham (dissolved) 369 B'way

Thames Mfg. Co. (Inf. unattainable) 20 Cedar

Thatcher Furnace Co. (John M. Thatcher, Pres.; Edward Benedict, Sec.; Lewis M. Thatcher, Treas.; further inf. refused) 35 Peck sl.

Thatcher & Betts (dissolved) 264 Water

Thaxter & Denig (David W. Thaxter & John Denig) 584 Hudson

Thayer F. Porter & Son (F. Porter & Charles F. Thayer) 16 Warren

Thayer & Robinson (Frederick P. Thayer & John Beverley Robinson) 67 Liberty

Theall & Beam (John Theall & William H. Beam) 45 Wall

Theband Brothers (Edward V. & Paul L. & Frank F. Theband) 87 Broad

Thees John D. & Sons (John D. & Oscar D. & John D. Thees jr.) 74 W. 125th

Theis F. & Co. (dissolved) 22 Little W. 12th

Theis & Folz (August Theis & John Folz) 511 Fifth

Theis & Janssen (Peter Theis & Pierre Janssen) 337 E. 27th

Theis & Sleeth (Frederick Theis & John Sleeth) 29 Ninth av.

Theller A. & Son (Arnold & Cornell A. Theller) 30 Vesey

Theo R. & Co. (Raphael Theo & Helen Fourman) 22 W. 4th

Theodoro's Catering Co. (Lichtwitz & Boeschen, proprs.) 809 Ninth av.

Thibaut R. A. & Co. (inf. unattainable) 168 Pearl

Thie & Levy (Otto Thie & Charles M. Levy) 38 Maiden la.

Thiel M. & Son (Matthias & Louis Thiel) 1027 Second av.

Thiel's Detective Service (Gustav H. Thiel, propr.) 84 Nassau

Thilemann F. jr. & Co. (Frederick Thilemann jr. & Francis V. Smith) 520 E. 121st

Third National Bank (William A. Booth, Pres.; George L. Hutchings, Cashier; Eugene Delmar, Notary. Capital, $1,000,000. Directors: William A. Booth, John W. Sterling, Henry A. V. Post, John H. Watson. Caleb B. Knevals, Edward Scholl, Roswell P. Flower, John B. Woodward, Benjamin Griffen, William P. Anderson, Charles Rood, J. F. Chamberlin, Henry Buckhout) 26 Nassau

Thirkell & Macillie (Herbert F. Thirkell & Charles H. Macillie) 11 Wall

Thirty-fourth Street Ferry & Eleventh Av. R. R. Co. (Daniel D. Conover, Pres.; De Witt J. Apgar, Sec. Capital, $1,200,000. Directors: Daniel D. Conover, John S. Foster, G. M. Speir jr. P. Keenan, James Moran, Edward Selleck, De Witt J. Apgar) 45 William

Thirty-fourth Street R. R. Co. (William H. Page jr. Pres.; De Witt J. Apgar, Sec.; John H. Davis, Treas. Capital, $100,000. Directors: William H. Page jr. Daniel D. Conover, Jonathan H. Crane, John H. Davis, John S. Foster, P. Keenan, James Moran, Edward Selleck, De Witt J. Apgar) 45 William

Tholen Brothers (John & George Tholen) 174 Chambers

Thom John C., Mfg. Co. (John C. Thom, Pres.; Benjamin W. Burnet, Sec.; further inf. refused) 140 Maiden la. & 98 William

Thom & Bayley (William B. & Charles W. Thom, Horace S. Bayley & George A. Connor) 162 Greene

Thom & Fountain (dissolved) 180 Eleventh av.

Thom & Payne (Charles A. Thom & John H. Payne) 151 W. 29th

Thom & Wilson (Arthur M. Thom & James W. Wilson) 1207 B'way

Thoma Brothers (dissolved) 976 Eighth av.

Thomas E. M., Mfg. Co. (inf. unattainable) 9 Murray

Thomas Evan & Co. (Evan & Wethered B. Thomas) 426 Produce Ex.

Thomas Iron Co. (Benjamin G. Clarke, Pres.; John T. Knight, Sec.; further inf. unattainable) 59 Wall

Thomas William W. & Co. (William A. Osborne, William P. Thomas & Robert D. Kirk, only) 19 William

Thomas H. A. & Wylie (Henry A. Thomas & George A. Wylie) 130 W. 24th
Thomas L. P. jr. & Co. (dissolved) 565 First av.
Thomas W. H. & Brother (Samuel W. & William H. & Thomas H, Thomas) 25 Beaver
Thomas W. H. & Son (dissolved) 120 William
Thomas Brothers (Emile & Alfred J. Thomas) 50 Walker
Thomas & Boyd (Henry A. Thomas & John F. Boyd) 36 B'way
Thomas & Chambers (Theodore G. Thomas & P. Flewellon Chambers) 596 Lex. av.
Thomas & Co. (dissolved) 60 B'way
Thomas & Eckerson (William M. Thomas & John C. R. Eckerson) 35 W. 30th
Thomas & Fernald (Solomon Thomas & George H. Fernald) 49 South
Thomas & Harper (Charles N. Thomas & Thomas H. Harper) 87 Greene
Thomas & Odell (dissolved) 68 B'way & 17 New
Thomas & Post (William B. Thomas & Thomas B. Post) 106 Elm
Thomas & Prentice (Walter W. Thomas & George J. Prentice) 1347 B'way
Thomas & Studt (dissolved) 174 Pearl
Thommen's Albert, Sons (Albert jr. & Gustav & Emil Thommen) 462 Tenth av.
Thompson Charles F. & Co. (Charles F. Thompson, George W. Smalley & William H. Roston) 309 Spring
Thompson Henry G. & Sons (Henry G. & H. Grant & Arthur G. Thompson) 51 Leonard
Thompson James & Co. (linens) (James & Charles Thompson) 112 Franklin
Thompson James & Co. (twines) (James Thompson & Rosa D. Schoneman) 129 W. B'way
Thompson Joseph T. & Co. (Joseph T. Thompson & Samuel T. Cushing) 15 Broad
Thompson Lucas & Co. (Lucas Thompson & Adolphus Lecour) 40 Lispenard
Thompson Napoleon & Co. (Napoleon Thompson, Pres.; Christopher J. Clinton, Sec. Capital, $20,000; further inf. unattainable) 30 Gold
Thompson Richard, Co. (Richard Thompson, Pres.; Augustus T. Brook, Sec.; John M. Ryon, Treas.; further inf. unattainable) 103 Chambers
Thompson William & Bowers (William Thompson & Benjamin O. Bowers) 95 Front
Thompson A. L. & Co. (Albert L. Thompson & Stephen W. Goodwin) 511 W. 42d
Thompson D. C. & Co. (inf. unattainable) 1193 B'way
Thompson H. H. & Co. (Henry H. Thompson & Ardon K. Powell) 260 Canal
Thompson J. C. & Co. (Joseph C. Thompson, Co. refused) 9 Walker
Thompson R. N. & Co. (Robert N. Thompson, no Co.) 135 Front
Thompson & Bedford Co. (Ltd.) (Richard J. Thompson, Treas. Capital, $250,000; further inf. refused) 126 Pearl & 92 Water
Thompson & Bushnell (Richard Thompson & John S. Bushnell) 120 Liberty
Thompson & Co. (cloaks) (dissolved) 413 Broome
Thompson & Co. (jewelers) (Charles A. Thompson & Jay Milair) 141 B'way
Thompson & Davies (William Thompson & Richard H. Davies) 93 Wall
Thompson & Koss (Morris S. Thompson & Charles G. Koss) 140 Nassau
Thompson & Layley (dissolved) 28 E. 14th
Thompson & Mickens (John Thompson & William Mickens) 753 Seventh av.
Thompson & Son (David & Albert C. Thompson) 369 Lenox av.
Thompson & Steffens (dissolved) 545 G'wich

Thompson, Ackley & Kaufman (Daniel G. Thompson, J. Edward Ackley & Edward S. Kaufman) 95 Wall
Thompson, Culbert & Co. (dissolved) 39 B'way
Thompson, Moore & Co. (Joseph H. Thompson, D. Sackett Moore & Paul Calvi) 59 Front
Thompson, Reed & Co. (Walter Thompson, Frederick B. Reed, George K. McKibbin & George Thompson) 32 Liberty
Thompson's Samuel, Nephew (John W. Mason) 32 Gold
Thompson's Samuel, Nephew & Co. (John W. & William P. Mason & Joseph G. Webster) 142 Duane
Thoms William M. & Co. (William M. Thoms & Guido Hacker) 23 Union sq. W.
Thomsen & Co. (Christian de & H. Adelberto Thomsen) 87 Wall
Thomson Co. (inf. unattainable) 617 Madison av.
Thomson David & Co. (David Thomson, no Co.) 215 Water
Thomson John, Press Co. (John Thomson, Pres.; William Thomson, Sec.; Frederick A. Lovecraft, Treas. Capital, $50,000. Directors: John & William Thomson, Frederick A. Lovecraft) 5 Beekman
Thomson A. & W. (dissolved) 269 W. 4th
Thomson A. A. & Co. (Alexander A. & David & William A. Thomson & George W. Jaques) 213 Water
Thomson & Co. (James R. Thomson, no Co.) 55 Dey
Thomson & Foote (dissolved) 72 Cotton Ex.
Thone & Plumer (Frederick W. Thone & Henry Plumer) 52 Centre mkt
Thorburn George & Co. (George Thorburn & William W. Roe) 788 Water
Thorburn James M. & Co. (James M. Thorburn & Frederick W. Druggerhof) 15 John
Thorn J. S. & Co. (Joseph B. Thorn, only) 196 W. Houston
Thorn T. & W. & Co. (Thomas E. & William F. & John H. & William E. Thorn) Riverdale av. n B'way & Riverdale
Thorn T. H. & Co. (Thomas H. & Oscar Thorn) 524 Second av. 177 & 1013 Third av. & 1094 First av.
Thorn & Co. (Richard H. Thorn, no Co.) 35 Grace av. W. Washn. mkt
Thornall, Squires & Constant (Edward V. Thornall, James Duane Squires & S. Victor Constant) 120 B'way
Thorne J. & W. (Jonathan & William) 76 Gold
Thorne T. W. & Co. (Thomas W. & Newberry D. Thorne) 30 Broad
Thorne & Phipard (Maximilian L. Thomson & George R. Phipard, only) 52 Water
Thornton John & Co. (John Thornton, Henry Houghton & Harry W. Crouse) 345 B'way
Thornton Brothers (Charles H. & Edward A. Thornton) 915 Sixth av.
Thornton, Earle & Klendl (David Thornton, Charles M. Earle & Adolph Klendl) 38 Park row
Thornton's William, Sons (William M. & John P. & Hugh Thornton) E. 100th n Madison av.
Thoroughbred Dog Exchange (Percy C. Ohl, propr.) 50 D'way
Thorp Samuel S. & Co. (James D. Hopkins & Julia Thorp, only) 187 South
Thorp J. H. & Co. (James H. & W. Edwin Thorp) 429 Broome
Thorne Dr., Medicine Co. (Philip Thorpe, Pres.; Frederick W. Hurlbutt, Sec. Capital, $5.000. Directors: Philip Thorpe, Frederick W. Hurlbutt, Charles A. Dunn, J. A. Moody) 11 E. 14th

THE CALIGRAPH WRITING MACHINE,
HARTFORD, CONN.

Thorpe & Co. (Edward B. Thorpe & Harry Robinson) 80 Cortlandt

Thowless Aluminium Co. (inf. unattainable) 36 Park row

Thrift Publishing Co. (inf. unattainable) 207 B'way

Thumler & Co. (no inf.) 33 Chambers

Thurber, Whyland & Co. (Francis B. Thurber, Albert E. Wayland, William A. Paschall, Henry B. Kirkland, George B. Howard:—special partner, Horace K. Thurber, $500,-000; terminates 31st Jan., 1891) 116 Reade

Thurlow B. T. & Son (Belcher T. & Lewis E. Thurlow) 86 South

Thurmond Car Coupling Co. (Willie E. Ragan, Pres.; William D. Thurmond, Sec.; Allen S. Apgar, Treas. Capital, $1,000,000. Directors: Willis E. Ragan, William H. Thurmond, Alfred H. Colquitt, Mathew C. Butler, Thomas B. Gresham, Charles S. Whitman, John C. Calhoun, Henry Orth, Patrick Calhoun, William D. Thurmond, Allen S. Apgar, Timothy W. Getman) 45 B'way

Thurston L. V. & Co. (Louis V. Thurston, George R. Moore & Henry W. Bassett) 42 Lawton av. W. Washn. mkt

Tharston & Braidich (William R. Thurston jr. & Adolph F. Braidich) 130 William

Thwaites George & Co. (George Thwaites & William Nickel) 77 Front & 26 Old sl.

Tibbals Book Co. (Huldah F. Tibbals, Pres.; Marion H. Tibbals, Sec.; John A. J. Tibbals, Treas. Capital, $5,000. Directors: Huldah F. & Marion Tibbals, Robert I. Lomas jr.) 26 Warren

Tice Brothers (George S. & Walter J. Tice) 1 B'way

Tice & Jacobs (George W. Tice & Jacob Jacobs) 510 Pearl

Tice & Lynch (George W. Tice & Franklin Lynch) 84½ Pine

Tichborne & Melrose (James Tichborne & Benjamin F. Melrose) 1018 Third av.

Tichenor J. W. & Co. (James W. Tichenor, no Co.) 140 Reade

Tide Water Oil Co. (Samuel Q. Brown, Pres.; William S. Benson, Sec.; Alanson A. Sumner, Treas. Capital, $5,000,000. Directors: Samuel Q. Brown, David McKelvy, Alanson A. Sumner, Josiah Lombard, Robert D. Benson) 12 B'way

Tide Water Pipe Co. (Ltd.) (David McKelvy, Pres.; Robert E. Hopkins, Sec. Capital, $2,000,000. Directors: David McKelvy, Robert E. Hopkins, Robert D. Benson, Harris C. Fahnestock, Josiah G. Benton) 12 B'way

Tide Water Steel Works (no inf.) 40 B'way

Tie Kee & Co. (Tie Kee, no Co.) 26 Mott

Tiebout W. & J. (John Tiebout, only) 16 Chambers & 339 Stanton

Tiedemann Theodore & Brother (Theodore & Frederick Tiedemann) 35 Wooster

Tiedt & Markthaler (Louis W. Tiedt & Henry F. Markthaler) 270 Ninth av.

Tiemann George & Co. (Frederick A. Stohlmann, Edward Pfarre, Charles F. & George A. Stohlmann & Julius A. & Louis G. Pfarre, only) 107 Park row & 107 E. 28th

Tiemann D. F. & Co. (Daniel F. & Julius W. & Peter C. & William F. & Daniel F. Tiemann jr.) 16 Murray, 19 Park pl. & W. 129th c Twelfth av.

Tiemeyer & Ficken (John H. Tiemeyer & William Ficken) 1638 Second av.

Tienken & Co. (John Tienken & John H. Gerdes) 482 Broome

Tierney & Porter (John Mulholland, assignee) E 101st & Jerome av.

Tiers & Co. (Alexander H. & Cornelius Tiers) 1 Beaver

Tietzel E. & Co. (Ernest Tietzel, no Co.) 3 Hanover & 45 Mercer

Tiffany Chemical Co. (Walton C. Tiffany, Pres.; Charles O. Tiffany, Sec.; Francis P. Smith, Treas. Capital, $20,000. Directors: Walton C. & Charles O. Tiffany, Francis P. Smith) 21 Spruce

Tiffany Decorating Co. (Louis C. Tiffany, Pres.; Von Beck Canfield, Sec.; John C. Platt, Treas. Capital, $100,000. Directors: Louis C. Tiffany, Pringle Mitchell, John C. Platt, Von Beck Canfield, George Holmes) 335 Fourth av.

Tiffany Glass Co. (Louis C. Tiffany, Pres.; John L. Du Fais, Sec.; John Cheney Platt, Treas. Capital, $90,000. Directors: Louis C. Tiffany, Pringle Mitchell, John L. Du Fais, John Cheney Platt, Von Beck Canfield) 335 Fourth av.

Tiffany Joseph B. & Co. (Joseph B. Tiffany, Pres.; W. Stanley Camp, Sec.; Henry B. Kinghorn, Treas. Capital, $30,000. Directors: Joseph B. Tiffany, W. Stanley Camp, Henry B. Kinghorn) 12 E. 22d

Tiffany & Co. (Charles L. Tiffany, Pres.; Edward C. Moore, Sec. Capital, $2,400,000. Trustees: Charles L. Tiffany, Charles T. Cook, Edward C. Moore, Philip J. de Horrack, Louis C. Tiffany, Charles M. Moore, George P. Farsham) 15 Union sq. W. & 53 Prince

Tighe & Moonan (John J. Tighe & Joseph C. Moonan) 67 Gansevoort

Tilge George E. & Co. (George E. & J. Henry & Jesse A. Tilge) 100 Greene

Tilge Henry & Co. (J. Henry & Jesse A. Tilge, only) 106 Greene

Tilghman Elite Mfg. Co. (no inf.) 2237 Eighth av.

Tilghman, Rowland & Co. (Sidell Tilghman George Rowland, Frederick B. Tilghman & John T. Granger) 54 Exchange pl.

Tilley & Littlefield (James P. Tilley & Edgar Littlefield) ft. W. 15th

Tillmann & Hansgen (Ernest Hansgen, only) 91 Elizabeth

Tillotson & Kent (Gouverneur Tillotson & William & Edwin C. Kent) 59 Liberty

Tillotson's Newspaper Literature (Tillotson & Sons, proprs.) 5 Beekman

Tilton & Buck (Edward Tilton & Gurdon S. Buck) 55 Liberty

Tilton Edgar & Co. (dissolved) 294 Washn.

Tilton & Co. (William H. & Amos A. Tilton) 34 Harrison

Tim & Co. (Louis & Solomon Tim & Max Herman) 87 Franklin

Tim, Wallerstein & Co. (Louis & Solomon Tim, Edward Wallerstein & Max Herman) 87 Franklin

Time Publishing Co. (inf. unattainable) 227 B'way

Timme C. A. & Co. (Charles A. Timme & Horace Montague) 80 E. 14th

Timmer & Vossbrinok (Ernest Timmer & Henry Vossbrinck) 86 Dey

Timmermann & Sündermann (Frederick A. Timmermann & John H. Sündermann) 72 Rutgers

Timpe & Apffel (dissolved) 84 Centre mkt

Timpe & Co. (Theodore W. & Henry Timpe) 84 Centre mkt

Timpson & McDermott (Lewis G. Timpson & James H. McDermott) 320 B'way

Tin Edging Co. (S. Vandewater & Co. proprs.) 114 Hudson

Tin Plate Decorating Co. (Benjamin C. Mumford, Pres.; Henry L. Fenton, Sec.; George L. Nichols, Treas. Capital, $30,000; further inf. refused) 110 John

Tinagero J. F. & Co. (dissolved) 10 Old sl.

Tindall R. B. & Co. (dissolved) 103 Chambers

Tingue, House & Co. (William J. Tingue & Charles W. House, no Co.) 56 Reade

SPECIAL ATTENTION PAID TO THIS CLASS OF WORK. } **BANKERS' & BROKERS' CIRCULARS DELIVERED** { THE TROW CITY DIRECTORY CO. 11 University Place.

TIN 300 TON

Tinker & Weston (Henry C. Tinker, Rensselaer Weston & Francis L. Morrell) 2 Exchange ct. & 52 B'way

Tinsley Brothers (Francis B. & Gervase J. & Walter W. Tinsley) ft. E. 122d, 85 E. 120th & 3002 Third av.

Tip Sanitary Co. (Philip G. Hubert, Pres.; Gustave Frohman, Sec.; William J. Hoodless, Treas. Capital, $200,000. Directors: Philip G. Hubert, Gustave Frohman, William J. Hoodless, Lemuel Skidmore, Philip G. Hubert jr, August O. Hoddick, D. R. Riordan) 19 E. 28th

Tirrill Gas Machine Co. (Oakes Tirrill, propr.) 39 Dey

Tisdell & Whittelsey (Abner G. Tisdell & Elbert A. Whittelsey) 130 Fulton

Tissot & Schultz (John Tissot jr. & John L. Schultz) 212 Church

Title Guarantee & Trust Co. (John W. Murray, Pres.; Newell Martin, Sec.; Louis Windmuller, Treas. Capital, $1,000,000. Directors: John W. Murray, C. H. Kelsey, Louis Windmuller, Orlando D. Potter, William M. Ingraham, Emil Oelbermann, Martin Joost, Benjamin D. & John D. Hicks, Ellis D. Williams, William Trautwine, Henry C. Thompson, George G. Williams, Eugene Kelly, Alexander E. Orr, Hugo Wesendonck, Julien T. Davies, Willinm H. Male, Charles R. Henderson, Samuel T. Freeman, Charles Matlack, James D. Lynch, John T. Martin, John Jacob Astor jr. Henry L. Hoguet) 85 Liberty

Titsink & Elsing (Alfred G. Titsink & Henry Elsing) 382 Seventh av.

Titus H. E. & Co. (Henry E. Titus & J. Alvin Parshall) 8 Broad

Titus Brothers (Andrew R. & James L. Titus) 154 West

Titus & Dowling (William Q. Titus & Victor J. Dowling) 280 B'way

Titus, Wells & Willets (Samuel Titus, David F. Wells & Walter R. Willets) 133 Roosevelt

Tjarks & Fortenbacher (Tjark E. Tjarks & Emil Fortenbacher) 268 W. 37th

Tobacco Leaf Publishing Co. (Lorin Palmer, Pres.; Henry T. Duffield, Sec.; John G. Graff, Treas. Capital, $24,000. Directors: Lorin Palmer, Henry T. Duffield, John G. Graff) 105 Maiden la.

Toboy & Kirk (Harry G. & Salathiel H. Tobey & Edward C. Kirk) 8 Broad

Tobias C. & Co. (Christian Tobias, no Co.) 66 New

Tobias Brothers (Francis J. Tobias, only) 3 Chambers

Tobias & Schneittacher (Albert Tobias & Jacob Schneittacher) 385 Broome

Tobin M. J. & Co. (Michael J. Tobin, Frank Falk & Michael Green) 134 Park row

Tobin R. & Son (Richard H. & Joanna Tobin, only) 250 West

Toch J. B. & Co. (dissolved) 293 E. 10th

Toch J. L. & J. (Jacob L. & Joseph) 85 Pearl

Toch Brothers (Henry M, & Maximilian & Lucas Toch) 33 Bowery

Tod J. Kennedy & Co. (J. Kennedy Tod. Hugh O. Northcote & William Stewart Tod) 45 Wall

Todd Edward & Co. (Edward & Edward Todd jr. & Charles S. Freer) 44 E. 14th

Todd T. S. & Co. (Theodore S. & Augustus F. Todd) 67 William

Todd & Co. (plumbers) (Charles J. Todd, no Co.) 551 Courtlandt av.

Todd & Co. (plumbers) (George Todd, no Co.) 351 W. 59th

Todd & Co. (salt) (Theodore W. Todd, Alexander Spence, Perry C. Todd & Henry W. Palmer) 397 Eighth & 77 Front

Todd, Murphy & Co. (Albert U. Todd & William H. Oscanyan, only) 43 Leonard

Todd, Sullivan & Baldwin (Edward A. Todd. William T. Sullivan & Spencer S. Baldwin) 771 B'way

Tode Brothers (Adolph Tode, Oscar Wolff & John Wulling, only) 272 Bowery & 968 Third av.

Todt & Jordan (William Todt & Rudolph Jordan) 83 E. 18th

Toel & Wipperling (dissolved) 178 S. William

Tuffey Daniel & Co. (Daniel Tuffey, no Co.) 38 Hewitt av. W. Washn. mkt

Tolar & Hart (John R. Tolar & James H. Hart) 151 Front

Toledo, Ann Arbor & N. Michigan Railway Co. (James M. Ashley, Pres.; Benjamin F. Jervis, Treas.; Chauncey F. Cook, Sec. Capital, $5,300,000. Directors: James M. & Henry W. Ashley, John Cummings, T. W. Child, David Robinson jr. James M. Ashley jr. A.W. Wright, E. A. Todd, J. A. Fancher, S. Dean) 150 B'way

Toledo, St. Louis & Kansas City R. R. Co. (Samuel R. Callaway, Pres.; Isaac W. White, Sec. Capital, $11,250,000. Directors: James M. Quigley, Joseph S. Stout, Clinton W. Sweet, Robert G. Ingersoll, John C. Havemeyer, Samuel R. Callaway, Clarence Brown, Henry A. Neal, William H. Patton, Charles F. Tag, Samuel K. Wilson, Francis L. Russ, W. Howard Glider) 44 Wall

Toler Brothers (Henry P. & Hugh K. Toler) 7 Exchange ct.

Toler & Jenkins (Devereux Toler & Reginald W. Jenkins) 72 Beaver

Tolima Mining Co. (Henry Cummins, Pres.; William T. Black, Sec. Capital, $500,000. Directors: Henry Cummins, William T. Black, George W. N. Yost, John Cummins) 6 Wall

Tolk Brothers (dissolved) 39 Canal

Tolkamp & Dodman (Albert E. Tolkamp & Alfred C. Dodman) 269 Canal

Tomay & Heinly (Aloysius G. Tomay & John E. Heinly) 7 Murray

Tomes C. H. & Co. (Caroline H. Tomes & Thomas S. Phillips) 77 South

Tomford H. & Brother (no inf.) 226 E. 97th

Tomkins, McIndoe & Co. (Henry Tomkins & Peter W. & Walter J. McIndoe) 53 Lafayette pl.

Tommins & Adams (Francis J. P. Tommins & Walter Adams) 116 Chambers

Tompkins Lewis & Co. (Lewis Tompkins, no Co.) 636 B'way

Tompkins Mfg. Co. (Alfred H. Tompkins, Pres.; Stephen L. Purdy, Sec. Capital, $10,000; further inf. unattainable) 60 New

Tompkins Market Beef Co. (John Bohnet, propr.) Tomp. mkt

Tompkins D. D. & Son (States D. & estate of Daniel D. Tompkins) 155 Chambers

Tompkins J. B. & Co. (Joseph B. Tompkins & Frank L. Bell) 681 Ninth av.

Tompkins M. B. & Co. (Matthew B. Tompkins & Alonzo C. Smith) 26 Little W. 12th

Tompkins M. F. & Co. (Millard F. Tompkins & George R. Parker) 896 Eighth av.

Tompkins & Co. (William G. Tompkins, no Co.) 36 R. 19th & 8 R. 42d

Tompkins & Morrison (William A. Tompkins & Joseph G. Morrison) 84 B'way

Tomsuden & Jantzen (Henry Tomsuden & Ernst Jantzen) 616 Grand

Toner & McIver (dissolved) 930 Eighth av.

Tonjes Henry & Co. (Henry Tonjes & John H. Hachmann) 334 E. 31st

Tonjes Brothers (William & Dederick H. Tonjes) 1767 B'way

Tonk William & Brother (William & Charles J. Tonk) 26 Warren

FOR THE BEST CO-PARTNERSHIP IN THE BEST CORPORATION SEE PAGE IV IN BACK OF BOOK

Tonk & Co. (William & Charles J. & Max Tonk) 26 Warren

Tonsing & Heine (dissolved) 290 Third av.

Tooker & Gould (William T. Tooker, only) ft. E. 37th

Tooth Crown Co. (Herman E. Vanhorne, propr.) 444 Sixth av.

Toplitz L. & Co. (Lippman Toplitz & Herman Schwarz) 100 Greene

Topor P. H. & R. (Frank H. & Rozalana) 122 E. 11th

Topping William & Co. (William A. & Henry S. Topping) 7 White

Topping & Fox (Frederick & Joseph P. Topping & Walter H. Fox) 96 Chambers

Topping, Maynard & Hobron (Abijah H. Topping & Edwin Maynard, only) 677 B'way & 242 Mercer

Torock Louis & Co. (Louis Torock & Bernhard Cohn) 263 E. 4th

Torres J. & J. Forch (Joseph Torres & Joseph Forch) 402 E. 13th

Tostevin & Co. (estate of Rachel Tostevin, only) 50 Nassau

Tostevin's Peter, Sons (Henry M. & Peter L. P. Tostevin) 122 Bowery

Totans & Schmidt (Emma Totans & Max Schmidt) 89 Fulton

Totten Thomas & Co. (Thomas & Albert Totten) 196 B'way

Totten W. H. B. & Co. (William H. B. Totten, James Anderson & Charles L. Miner) 12 Harrison

Tower Copying Co. (E. Lilian Todd, propr.) 50 B'way

Tower Mfg. & Novelty Co. (Levi L. Tower, Pres.; Robert I. Lomas jr. Sec.; David A. Tower, Treas. Capital, $60,000; further inf. unattainable) 308 B'way

Tower & Lyon (John J. Tower & Polhemus Lyon) 95 Chambers & 77 Reade

Towers & Schultz (Frederick Towers & Henry Schultz) 43 W. 24th

Town & Co. (dissolved) 10 Union sq. E.

Townsend James R. & Co. (James R. Townsend & Lomax Littlejohn) 69 Pine

Townsend Thomas & Co. (no inf.) 210 Centre

Townsend W. A., Publishing Co. (William A. Townsend, Pres.; Charles W. Lane, Sec. Capital, $5,000. Directors: William A. & Catharine B. Townsend, Charles W. Lane) 153 B'way

Townsend F. R. & Co. (Frederick R. Townsend, William M. Richards jr. & Charles H. Wade) 78 Worth

Townsend & Edgett (James A. Townsend & George Edgett) 66 New

Townsend & Mahan (Henry P. Townsend & Joseph H. Mahan) 13 Chambers

Townsend & Montant (Alphonse Montant & C. Fred Richards, only) 81 Leonard

Townsend & Plumer (Volckert P. D. Townsend, only) 195 G'wich

Townsend & Washburn (Charles J. Townsend & Lansing C. Washburn;—special partner, John P. Townsend, $100,000; terminates 30th April, 1892) 6 Wall

Townsend & Whitaker (Everett Townsend & Charles Whitaker) 193 Mercer & 27 W. Houston

Townsend & Yale (Edward M. Townsend & Henry C. Yale) 345 B'way

Townsend, Dyett & Einstein (Randolph W. Townsend, Anthony R. Dyett & Benjamin F. Einstein) 247 B'way

Tracy & Russell (Edward Tracy, James R. Hogg & estate of James Russell) 71 G'wich av.

Tracy, Macfarland, Ivins, Boardman & Platt (Benjamin F. Tracy, William W. Macfarland, William M. Ivins, Albert B. Boardman, Frank H. Platt & William Parkin) 35 Wall

Trade Mark Ass'n. of Plug Tobacco Mfrs. (James T. Drummond, Pres.; Theodore E. Allen, Sec.; Charles H. Barkelew, Treas.) 16 B'way

Trade Promoting Co. (Barrows & Greene, proprs.) 41 Park row

Traders' & Travelers' Accident Co. (James E. Vail, Pres.; C. Stuart Somerville, Sec. Directors: F. N. Barrett, Daniel Birdsall, George E. Hamlin, John W. Jacobus, Frederick Jansen, G. G. Lansing, W. L. Saxton, W. C. Spelman, Benjamin W. West) 287 B'way

Traders' & Travelers' Union (dissolved) 287 B'way

Tradesmen's National Bank (James E. Granniss, Pres.; Oliver F. Berry, Cashier; Joseph N. Tuttle, Notary. Capital, $750,000. Directors: George Starr, Oliver F. Berry, James E. Granniss, Henry A. Smith, William M. Dean, Julius Kaufmann, Henry Campbell, Elliot L. Butler) 201 B'way

Tragesar John, Steam Copper Works (Augusta Tragesar, Pres.; William C. Tragesar, Sec. Capital, $60,000. Directors: Augusta & William C. & Albert F. Tragesar) 447 W. 46th & 35 Ferry

Trahan Noé & Co. (Noé & Emily E. Trahan) 176 B'way

Traitel Brothers (Benjamin D. & Bernard P. Traitel) 21 Malden la.

Tramonti Nicholas & Co. (no inf.) 182 Park row

Transatlantic Banking House (George Weber, propr.) 88 B'way

Transatlantic Express (Jacob Terkulle, propr.) 33 B'way

Transatlantic Independent Baggage Checking Co. (inf. unattainable) 5 Bowling gr.

Transferine Mfg. Co. (dissolved) 744 B'way

Trapp & Bussing (James Trapp & George & Edward O. Bussing) 544 E. 19th & 402 E. 65d

Trapp & Wingens (Nicholas E. Trapp & Ferdinand Wingens) 911 Second av. & 221 E. 107th

Trask Spencer & Co. (Spencer Trask, George Foster Peabody, Edwin M. Bulkley, Charles J. Peabody & Samuel C. Blodget jr.) 16 Broad

Trask Wayland & Co. (Wayland Trask & Theodore Baldwin) 19 Wall

Trask & Carmichael (Harry Trask & William N. Carmichael) 80 Centre

Trask's James W., Sons (Nathaniel W. & Charles W. Trask) 320 Produce Ex.

Traub & Co. (no inf.) 2467 Eighth av.

Traube & Co. (no inf.) 20 Harrison

Trautman & Co. (William Trautman, no Co.) r 120 W. 33d

Trautmann, Bailey & Blampey (Ralph Trautmann, Henry P. Bailey & George S. Blampey) 812 B'way

Travelers' Publishing Co. (James H. Breslin, Pres.; Washington L. Jaques, Sec. Capital, $100,000. Directors: James H. Breslin, D. S. Hammond, A. L. Ashman, P. T. Wall, W. D. Garrison, R. H. Brockway, James H. Rogers, Washington L. Jaques) 30 Union sq. E.

Traver J. P. & Co. (John P. Traver, no Co.) 7 Warren

Travers J. P. & Son (Adeline & Valentine A. Travers & Charles Hellerson, only) 46 Beekman

Travers Brothers (Francis C. & Vincent P. & Ambrose F. Travers) 107 Dunne, 16 Thomas & 52d & 556 W. 53d

Travis Eugene M. & Co. (Eugene M. & James M. Travis) 92 Barclay

Travis M. & Co. (Mabbitt Travis, no Co.) 212 Washn.

Traylor George M. & Co. (George M. Traylor, James T. Prince, Jeremiah B. Traylor & George W. White) 422 E. 63d

Treadwell & Carter (dissolved) Williamsbridge

TYPEWRITING DONE BY THE TROW CITY DIRECTORY CO., 11 University Place.

Treadwell & Co. (Henry & George H. Treadwell) 9 W. 3d
Treadwell & Harris Baking Co. (Ltd.) (Thomas B. Harris, Pres.; James S. Harris, Sec.; James T. Grady, Treas. Capital, $50,000. Directors: William E. Treadwell, Thomas R. & James S. Harris, James T. Grady, J. Morrison Champney) 244 Front & 265 & 299 Water
Treanor James J. & F. P. (James J. & Frank P.) 547 W. 45th
Treanor Brothers (Owen & Patrick Treanor) 372 Hudson
Trecartin & Turner (James W. Trecartin & Solon E. Turner) 27 South
Tredwell, Slote & Co. (Alanson Tredwell, Alonzo Slote & Alanson Tredwell jr.) 275 B'way
Treiss Brothers (Louis F. & Rudolph Treiss) 367 Grand
Trelease & Underhill (Francis A. Trelease & William J. & Elmer Underhill) 34 Jay
Tremain & Tyler (Henry E. Tremain & Mason W. Tyler) 146 B'way
Tremborg & Amandson (no inf.) 2473 Third av.
Tremont Building & Loan Assn. (Thomas C. Lewis, Pres.; Robert I. Lomas jr. Sec.; Louis S. Eickwort, Treas. Directors: Charles C. Kirkup, John M. Elting, William W. Osborn, James K. Price, Henry Lowenthal, Edwin Dodell, William H. Bogart, Michael M. McDermott, Alfred Vannostrand, Richard A. Turner, John A. Holder) 1687 Vanderbilt av. W.
Trench Charles S. & Co. (Charles S. Trench, no Co.) 54 Cliff
Trenton Iron Co. (Abram S. Hewitt, Pres.; James Hall, Treas.; Eagleton Hanson, Sec. Capital, $250,000. Directors: Abram S. Hewitt, James Hall, Eagleton Hanson, E. Gybbon Spilsbury) 17 Burling sl.
Trenton Rock Refining Co. (dissolved) 15 State
Trenton Terra Cotta Co. (dissolved) 60 Cortlandt
Treuhaft & Berger (Isidor Treuhaft & Gesa Berger) 70 Broome
Travett & Stopenhagen (dissolved) 2407 Eighth av.
Trevor William & Co. (William Trevor & James K. Middleton) 463 Broome
Tribble & McGann (William Tribble & Thomas McGann) 175 W. 48th
Tribune Assn. (Ogden Mills, Pres.; Thomas N. Rooker, Sec. Capital, $200,000. Trustees: Whitelaw Reid, Ogden Mills, William E. Dond, Frederick F. Ayer, Donald Nicholson, Philip A. Fitzpatrick, Thomas N. Rooker, Nathaniel Tuttle, George W. Graff) 154 Nassau
Trier S. & Son (Sellgman & Abraham S. Trier) 190 William
Trier Brothers (Edward & William Trier) 15 Maiden la.
Triest & Co. (Bernhard & Julius S. & Jesse E. Triest & Nathan Steinberger) 691 B'way
Trigge J. & Co. (John T. Trigge, only) 126 S. 5th av.
Trimble & Co. (Edward A. Trimble, no Co.) 202 Eleventh av.
Trinidad Asphalt Paving Co. (George Christall, Pres.; Lyndon H. Stevens, Sec.; James Greig, Treas. Capital, $300,000. Directors: George Christall, James Brand, Lyndon H. Stevens, Matthew Taylor, James Greig) 15 Broad
Trinidad-Heimann Insulated Wire Co. (Conrad N. Jordan, Pres.; James Dunne, Sec.; Eduardo Gogorza, Treas. Capital, $500,000. Directors: Conrad N. Jordan, Eduardo Gogorza, James Dunne, John R. Burdock, Adolph de Bary, Robert A. Jordan) 47 Liberty
Trinity Church Corporation (S. Van Rensselaer Cruger, comptroller) 187 Fulton
Triple Thermic Motor Co. (Inf. unattainable) 38 Park row

Tripler F. R. & Co. (Frederick R. Tripler :—special partner, John H. Hodgson, B'klyn, N. Y.; terminates 31st Dec. 1892) 527 B'way
Tripp S. V. & Co. (Smiten V. Tripp & Isaac C. Wickes) ft. W. 34th
Tripp & Kelly (dissolved) 26 Frankfort
Trischet B. S. & Son (R. Samuel & Albert W. Trischet) 145 Elm
Trisdorfer & Co. (Maurice Trisdorfer, no Co.) 56 Leonard
Trisdorfer & Lion (Isaac Trisdorfer & Emil Lion) 98 Bowery
Troescher A. & Co. (August Troescher, Anton Geiger & Charles G. Einfuehrer) 89 Nassau
Troja & Co. (Vincenzo Troja, no Co.) 2120 First av.
Troll Brothers (John & George Troll) 2091 Third av.
Tropical Ice Machine Co. (Francis B. Clark, Pres.; William J. Vail, Sec. Capital, $10,000. Directors: Francis B. & J. Shepherd Clark, William J. Vail) 178 B'way
Troup Charles A. & Co. (Charles A. & estate of William E. Tromp) 352 Washn.
Troutman & Co. (Henry & Sophia Troutman) 93 Bleecker
TROW CITY DIRECTORY CO. (Horace K. Thurber, Pres.; Robert W. Smith, Sec.; Edward Lange, Treas. Capital, $200,000. Directors: Horace K. Thurber, Robert W. Smith, Edward Lange, Henry Aplington, Albert E. Whyland) 11 University pl. (see head lines)
Trow Mutual Benefit Assn. (Robert J. Brown, Pres.; Alexander Parker, Treas.; Frank V. Hulse, Sec. Trustees: Andrew H. Mitchell, Jacob Doornbos, Henry E. Brown) 207 E. 12th
TROW'S PRINTING & BOOKBINDING CO. (Robert W. Smith, Pres.; Edward Lange, V.-Pres. & Treas.; Jacob Doornbos, Sec. Directors: Robert W. Smith, Edward & Charles E. Lange) 207 E. 12th
Trowbridge & Co. (dissolved) 52 Broad
Troxell & Hunt (dissolved) 24 State
Troy Laundry Machinery Co. (Ltd.) (Thomas S. Wiles, Pres.; Jacob H. Tenezyk, Sec.; Allen Conkling, Treas. Capital, $150,000. Directors: Thomas S. Wiles, Jacob H. Tenezyk, M. E. Wendell, George F. Dodge, Walter Bound, H. S. Wilcox) 44 Church & 32 Dey
Troy Brothers (Richard E. & Peter H. Troy) 420 Tenth av.
Truax & Crandall (Chauncey S. Truax & Elbert Crandall) 99 Nassau
True & Cotter (William D. True & David J. Cotter) 685 B'way
Trueheart & Well (Joseph Trueheart & David Well) 1464 First av.
Truesdell J. H. & Co. (John H. Truesdell, John E. Dusenbury, J. Willis Bingham, William H. Stiles, George E. Wheat, Frank D. McCloer & Frederick W. Briggs) 237 Eighth av.
Trujillo B., Co. (Dias Trujillo, propr.) 80 Front
Trujillo D. L. & Sons (Diego L. Trujillo, Remigio & Alfredo Lopez & Serapio Serpa, only) 119 Water & 90 Wall
Trundy & Bennett (Andrew S. Trundy & John H. Bennett) 49 South
Trunk Line Assn. (Charles W. Bullen, commissioner) 346 B'way
Trunk Brothers (John & Herman Trunk) 120 William
Truslow & Co. (James L. & James L. jr. & Frederick C. Truslow) 219 Pearl & 6 Platt
Truth Seeker Co. (refused) 28 Lafayette pl.
Tscheppe & Schur (Adolphus Tscheppe & Carl Schur) 1010 Third av. & 500 Park av.
Tubbs & Taylor (Clarence B. Tubbs & William M. Taylor) 5 Beekman
Tubby Josiah T. & Co. (Josiah T. Tubby :—special

THADDEUS DAVIDS CO., **WRITING INKS, SEALING WAX, MUCILAGE**
MAKE THE BEST

TUB 303 TWE

partner, Benjamin D. Hicks, *Old Westbury, N. Y.*, $150,000; terminates 31st Dec. 1890) 87 Gold

Tubular Barrow & Machine Co. (dissolved) 212 West

Tubular Despatch Co. (Sidney DeKay, Pres.; John F. Langan, Sec. Capital, $1,000,000. Trustees: Joel O. Stevens, Sidney DeKay, John F. Langan) 115 B'way

Tuch Brothers (Benjamin & Simon Tuch) 74 Grand

Tuchmann & Cohen (Leon Tuchmann & Koppel Cohen) 16 Walker

Tuck High & Co. (Tuck High, Co. refused) 19 Mott

Tuck Raphael & Sons (Raphael & Adolph & Gustav & Herman Tuck) 293 B'way

Tuckahoe Marble Co. (refused) 413 E. 29th

Tucker Cummings H. jr. & Brother (Cummings H. jr. & Francis C. Tucker) 126 Liberty

Tucker Electrical Construction Co. (inf. unattainable) 14 Whitehall

Tucker Letter & Document File Co. (Howard C. Condit, Pres.; A. Judson Clark, Sec.; Edmund P. Backus, Treas. Capital, $45,000. Directors: Howard C. Condit, William H. Tucker, Samuel M. Taylor, Edmund P. Backus, David D. Bragaw, George H. Hope, Andrew J. Woodworth) 12 Barclay

Tucker Brothers (Edwin & Stanton Tucker) 166 S. 5th av.

Tucker & Carter Cordage Co. (Caleb P. Marsh, Pres.; Edward M. Johnson, Sec.; John A. Tucker, Treas. Capital, $500,000. Directors: Caleb P. Marsh, John A. & R, C. & J. H. Tucker, Edward M. Johnson) 98 Pine

Tucker & Co. (brokers) (dissolved) 60 B'way

Tucker & Co. (stationers) (George D. Tucker & Justin Butterfield) 51 Nassau

Tucker & Connor (Selah Tucker & William E. Connor) 88 Thomas

Tucker & Schott (Eli A. Tucker & Robert J. Schott) 100 Fulton

Tufts William E. & Co. (William E. Tufts & Alexander B. Barry) 181 Pearl

Tufts L. C. & Co. (Louis C. Tufts & George E. Addison) 110 Elm & 84 Walker

Tuller & Hewins (Loren W. Tuller & Sheldon W. Hewins) 173 B'way

Tully Paint & Varnish Co. (John W. Tully, Pres. Capital, $1,000,000. Directors: John W. Tully, Michael McNally, Anthony Yeoman, John C. Tully; further inf. unattainable) no address

Tunison & Kidd (William F. Tunison & Frank E. Kidd) 77 Barclay

Tunley John, Co. (Ltd.) (Michaelis Simonson, Pres.; Theodore Weiss, Treas. Capital, $50,000. Directors: Michaelis Simonson, Theodore Weiss, John T. Tunley, William Taylor, Augustus Latz) 231 Sixth av.

Tupe D. W. & Co. (Dennis W. & Mary L. Tupe) 2239 Eighth av.

Tupper W. W. & Co. (William W. Tupper, George L. Smith & Jonas G. H. Tupper) 206 West

Tupper & Beattie (William V. Tupper & James H. Beattie) 116 Wall

Turgis J. & Co. (Louis Ellean & August Roche, only) 89 Barclay & 44 Park pl.

Türk Brothers (cigars) (Samuel & Nathan Türk) 238 Stanton

Turk Brothers (showmen) (William B. & Charles R. Turk) 418 W. 46th

Turkey Red Oil Mfg. Co. (William D. Faris, Pres.; Paul Sury, Sec. Capital, $25,000. Directors: C. Braker jr. William D. Faris, William King, Oscar Hoass, Paul Sury) 14 Dey

Turkish Medicine Co. (inf. unattainable) 304 B'way

Turkish Tablet Co. (Ltd.) (inf. unattainable) 10 E. 14th

Turi John & Sons (John & William J. & Joseph H. Turi) 534 W. 28th & ft. W. 27th

Turnbull George & Co. (George Turnbull, no Co.) 338 B'way

Turnbull William & Co. (dissolved) 57 Worth

Turnbull, Klein & Vonbernuth (in liquidation) 102 Greene

Turner Charles W. & Co. (Charles W. & William L. Turner) 36 Broad

Turner James & Son (James & Henry D. Turner) 514 W. 34th

Turner Will C. & Co. (dissolved) 120 B'way

Turner Will C. & Nitschke Brothers Publishing Co. (Will C. Turner, Pres.; J. F. Nitschke, Sec. Capital, $50,000; further inf. unattainable) 225 W. 23d

Turner C. J. & Son (Coll J. & Coll J. Turner jr.) 16 Broad

Turner P. W. & Co. (Phineas W. & Catharine E. Turner) 88 Prince

Turner Brothers (Joseph B. & John T. Turner) 122 Front

Turner & Timberman (Isaac W. Turner & William B. Timberman) 58, 90 & 183 Bowery

Turner, McClure & Rolston (Herbert B. Turner, David McClure & Louis B. Rolston) 20 Nassau

Turner, Manuel & Co. (Archibald Turner, Horace Manuel & Henry M, Oddie) 35 Wall

Turno Henry & Co. (Henry Turno & John Helmreich) 2291 Second av.

Turnure Lawrence & Co. (Lawrence Turnure, Percy R. Pyne jr. Lawrence Turnure jr. & Jose M. Andreini) 52 Wall

Turton's John, Sons (Edgar S. & John Turton) 133 Malden la.

Tuthill B. F. & Co. (Benjamin F. Tuthill, no Co.) 191 Duane

Tuthill Brothers (dissolved) 60 B'way

Tuttle F. W. & Co. (inf. unattainable) 180 S. 5th av.

Tuttle & Bailey Mfg. Co. (James S. Bailey, Pres.; Frederick W. Tuttle, Sec.; William Ogden, Treas. Capital, $200,000. Directors: James S. Bailey, William Ogden, Silas & Frederick W. Tuttle, Frank T. Bailey) 83 Beekman

Tuttle & Co. (Jason H. Tuttle, no Co.) 76 Nassau

Tuttle & Downing (Addison B. Tuttle & Valentine Downing) 171 B'way

Tuttle & Wakefield (George H. Tuttle & William A. Trunille, only) 66 Cotton Ex.

Tuttle, Goodell & Brooks (Ezra A. Tuttle, Edwin B. Goodell & George M. Brooks) 5 Beekman

Tuxedo Park Assn. (no inf.) 50 Liberty

Tweedy, White & Co. (Edmund Tweedy & William E. & William R. White jr.) 159 Greene

Twelfth Ward Bank (Edward P. Steers, Pres.; Isaac Anderson, Cashier; Thomas Crawford, Notary. Capital, $200,000. Directors: Enoch C. Bell, William N. Beers, Thomas Crawford, Charles W. Dayton, Rowland F. Hill, Thomas M. Kellar, James F. Paulding, Charles Place, Antonio Rasines, Frederick Roosevelt, David Rutsky, E. Wells Sackett, Edward P. Steers, Frank E. Towle, Andrew J. White) 153 E. 125th

Twelfth Ward Savings Bank (Antonio Rasines, Pres.; Arthur T. Timpson, Sec.; further inf. unattainable) 233 W. 125th

Twentieth Century Publishing Co. (Helen Weston, Pres.; Frederick C. Leubuscher, Sec. Capital, $30,000. Trustees: Frederick C. Leubuscher, Helen Weston, Hugh O. Pentecost) 4 Warren

Twenty-eighth & Twenty-ninth Sts. R. R. Co. (Jonathan H. Crane, Pres.; De Witt J. Apgar Sec.; John H. Davis, Treas. Capital, $500,000. Directors: Jonathan H. Crane, Daniel

COMPILED WITH ACCURACY AND DESPATCH. | **CLASSIFIED BUSINESS LISTS.** | THE TROW CITY DIRECTORY CO. 11 University Place.

TWE   304   UND

D. Conover, John H. Davis, P. Krenan, John S. Foster, Edward Sellock, De Witt J. Apgar) 45 William

Twenty-third St. District Railway Co. (Calvin Goddard, Pres.; Eugene H. Lewis, Sec. Capital, $4,000,000. Directors: Calvin Goddard, George P. Slade, Marvelle W. Cooper, George F. Seward, Eugene H. Lewis, Henry Lewis) 120 B'way

Twenty-third St. Railway Co. (Henry Sanford, Pres.; Thomas H. McLean, Sec.; Walter T. Hatch, Treas. Capital, $600,000. Directors: Henry Sanford, George N. Curtis, Walter T. Hatch, Theodore B. Starr, Charles Phelps, George H. Prentiss, John Downey, Elias Lewis jr. Solomon Mohrbach, T. B. Burnham, Stephen U. Cadwell, Samuel M. Smith, Albert S. Rosenbaum) 621 W. 23d

Twenty-third Ward Bank (Thomas Mackellar, Pres.; Charles W. Bogart, Cashier; Joseph O. Kern, Notary. Capital, $100,000. Directors: William R. Beal, John Haffen, David B. Sickels, Henry L. School, Samuel M. Purdy, Thomas Mackellar, James L. Wells, Brian G. Hughes, Frederick F. Nugent, George M. Mackellar, Charles W. Bogart) 2771 Third av.

Twist Pipe Co. (Capital, $15,000; further inf. unattainable) no address

Twisted Wire Box Strap Co. (Levi L. Gans, Pres.; Albert F. Hochstadter, Sec. Capital, $96,000. Directors: Levi L. Gans, Charles L. Bernheim, Clarence L. Gans, A. Smith) 451 G'wich

Two Fosters Brothers (refused) 605 Third av.

Tyler Batting & Warp Mfg. Co. (dissolved) 74 Franklin

Tyler & Co. (Henry C. Tyler, no Co.) 561 Tenth av.

Tyler & Finch (Corydon E. Tyler & George W. Finch; —special partner, Francis T. Robins, $30,000; terminates 30th April, 1892) 54 Cedar

Tyler, Myers & Co. (Charles C. Tyler, Matthew R. Myers & Carman Nichols) 74 Franklin

Tynberg's M. A., Son (Sieg Tynberg jr.) 137 B'way

Typewriter Exchange (Tudor C. Josselyn, propr.) 809 B'way

Typewriter Ribbon Co. (not inc.; further inf. unattainable) 186 Mercer

Typothetæ (William C. Martin, Pres.; William Charles Rogers, Sec.; William F. Hallenbeck, Treas.) 19 Park pl. & 16 Murray

Tyroler Brothers (Jacob S. & Herman A. Tyroler) 144 Clinton

Tyrrell J. F. & Co. (John F. Tyrrell, no Co.) 6 Harrison

Tysen & Totten (Edward P. Tysen & Joseph O. Totten) 24 Dey

Tyson & Brother (George L. & Charles W. Tyson) 571 Fifth av.

Tyson & Co. (George I. Tyson & George J. Bascom) 196, 225 & 671 Fifth av. 1133, 1186, 1200 & 1414 B'way, 112 & 121 Park av. & 462 Fourth av.

U

Ubl H. & Co. (Henry Uhl & Julius Ackerknecht) 45 Ann

Uhl & Ziegler (August Uhl & Ferdinand Ziegler) 139 Canal

Uhle & Wagner (no inf.) 1 Greene

Uhlig & Co. (Charles & H. Gustave Uhlig & William Büsing) 244 William

Uhlmann William & Co. (William Uhlmann & Hugo Kloesser) 69 Broad

Uhlmann S. & F. (Simon & Frederick & William Uhlmann) 69 Broad

Uhrig, Herman & Co. (John W. M. Uhrig, Israel Herman & Charles Meyer) 521 B'way

Uhry & Alloth (Charles L. Uhry & Henry A. Alloth) 194 B'way

Uibel & Barber (dissolved) 39 Vesey

Uihlein H. & Brother (Henry & Jacob Uihlein) 78 Lewis

Uinta Coal Co. (inf. unattainable) 29 William

Ulfelder Brothers (dissolved) 12 W. 4th

Ulan & Güldemeister (dissolved) 1422 B'way

Ullman A. & Brother (Ascher & Leopold Ullman) 844 Third av.

Ullman J. & Son (Jacob & Max J. Ullman) 19 Murray

Ullman L. & Co. (Leopold Ullman, Gabriel Mitchell & Jacob Goldberg) 269 Canal

Ullman & Co. (Nathan & Louis J. Ullman & Mark D. Stiles) 847 B'way

Ullmann L. & Co. (Louis Ullmann & Abram Schaap) 78 Walker

Ullmann Brothers (milk) (Robert R. & Meyer H. Ullmann) 345 E. 76th

Ullmann Brothers (shoes) (Max & Harry Ullmann) 87 Reade

Ullo & Ruebsamen (Lorenzo Ullo & Herman A. Ruebsamen) 96 Cotton Ex.

Ulrich J. & Co. (Jacob Ulrich, no Co.) 108 Liberty

Ulmann Bernhard & Co. (Bernhard & Ludwig Ulmann) 109 Grand & 189 S. 5th av.

Ulmar Brothers (Henry & Frederick & John Ulmar) 107 Seventh av. & 3105 Ninth av.

Ulmer Robert & Co. (dissolved) 35 Park row & 476 Canal

Ulrich George & Son (George & Henry Ulrich) 1592 Av. B

Ulster Lead Co. (John G. Steenken, Pres.; Frederick H. Borger, Sec.; Edward J. Brockett, Treas. Capital, $100,000; further inf. refused) 163 Front

Umbstaetter, Russell & Swift (Robert J. Umbstaetter, Leslie H. Russell & Charles F. Swift) 350 B'way

Umscheid & Strathman (no inf.) 33 W. 125th

Unadilla Valley Railway Co. (William D. Edwards, Pres.; R. Floyd Clarke, Sec.; Frederick L. Culver, Treas. Capital, $200,000. Directors: William D. Edwards, Russell H. Hoadley, Charles D. Ingersoll, Cornelius V. Sidell, Benjamin Wright, R. Floyd Clarke, Frederick L. Culver) 146 B'way

Underground Railway Construction Co. (J. Coleman Drayton, Pres.; Douglas Alexander, Sec.; Elisha Dyer, Treas. Directors: J. Coleman Drayton, Rowland B. Hazard, Elisha Dyer, Lloyd M. Mayer, William N. Amory, John C. Furman, Charles D. Orth, B. Davis Washburn, O. E. Tanchert) 120 B'way

Underhill A. M. & Co. (Andrew M. & Harvey I. Underhill) 35 B'way & Pier 38 (new) N. R.

Underhill F. M. & H. L. (Frances M. & H. Louisa) 43 Lafayette pl.

Underhill R. W. & Co. (dissolved) 110 Murray

Underhill & Scudder (Townsend Underhill & Hewlett Scudder) 8 Greene

Underhill, Clinch & Co. (Edgar Underhill, Alfred D. Clinch & William M. Glover) 94 Chambers

Underhill, Cornell & Brown (Thomas B. Underhill, Daniel L. Cornell & Frederick J. Brown) 746 B'way

Underhill, Jackson & Co. (Edward Underhill & Edwin M. & Robert G. Jackson) 197 Chambers

Underwood John & Co. (John T. & Frederick W. Underwood) 30 Vesey

Underwriter Printing & Publishing Co. (Henry R. Hayden, Pres.; Charles A. Jenny, Sec.; further inf. unattainable) 58 William

Underwriters' Protective Assn. (Charles C. Hine, Pres.; Charles G. Hine, Sec. Directors

SPECIAL ATTENTION PAID TO THIS CLASS OF WORK } BANKERS' & BROKERS' CIRCULARS DELIVERED { THE TROW CITY DIRECTORY CO. 11 University Place.

UND 305 UNI

Charles C. Hine, Walter S. Nichols, Thomas A. & Edward A. Hine) 137 D'way
Underwriters' Survey & Protection Bureau (Henry H. Dwight, propr.) 145 B'way
Unexcelled Fireworks Co. (Charles Crowell, Pres.; George W. Street, Sec.; Charles A. Johnson, Treas. Capital, $150,000. Directors: Charles Crowell, Charles A. Johnson, George W. Street) 9 Park pl.
Unexcelled Mfg. Co. (jerseys) (L. Loewenthal & Son, proprs.) 68 Leonard
Unexcelled Mfg. Co. (paper dusters) (inf. unattainable) 621 B'way
Unexcelled Paper Tube Co. (Richard F. Ware, propr.) 29 Rose
Unfricht & Co. (Adam & Adam Unfricht jr.) 69 First av.
Unfricht & Palm (dissolved) 69 First av.
Ungar Brothers (dissolved) 164 Attorney
Ungar & Barnkopf (Solomon Ungar & Lazarus Barnkopf) 61 Bleecker
Ungar & Simonsfeld (Morris Ungar & Gustave J. Simonsfeld) 240 Canal
Unger Emil & Co. (Emil Unger, Christel Gries & William Euler) 50 Park pl.
Unger Joseph & Brother (Joseph & Philip Unger) 807 Fifth
Unger Brothers (Eugene & Herman Unger) 192 B'way
Unger & Holahan (Edwin H. Unger & John E. Holahan) 121 Mercer
Unger & Mayer (dissolved) 55 Bleecker
Unger, Greenbaum & Co. (Solomon Unger, Joseph Greenbaum & David Lewin) 633 B'way
Unger, Smithers & Co. (Charles Unger, Francis S. Smithers, William Koch, George H. Schinzel, Charles Kollstede & Charles Diendonne) 55 William & 46 Pine
Ungrich L. & K. (Louis & Louis K. Ungrich, only) 260 W. 125th
Uniform Time Co. (dissolved) 45 B'way
Union Blue Stone Co. (Samuel D. Coykendall, Pres.; George Coykendall, Sec. Capital, $50,000. Directors: Samuel D. & George Coykendall, Samuel Onies) 280 B'way
Union Bottling Co. (Peter P. Krummeich, Pres.; Marcus C. Moran, Sec. Capital, $25,000. Directors: Peter P. Krummeich, John E. Planten, Marcus C. Moran) 240 W. 20th
Union Bridge Co. (not inc.) (George S. Field, Charles Macdonald Charles S. Maurice & Edmund Hayes) 1 D'way
Union Chemical Works (Louis Engelhorn, Pres.; Frederick G. Meyer, Sec. Capital, $100,000. Trustees: Louis Engelhorn, H. Volbrecht, Frederick G. Meyer, Victor Schaller, H. C. Hanser) 49 Cedar
Union Coal Co. (James Hoffernan & Co. proprs.) 212 South, 219 Grand & 418 Water
Union Dime Savings Institution (Silas B. Dutcher, Pres.; Charles E. Sprague, Sec., Gardner S. Chapin, Treas. Trustees: Aaron Close, Silas B. Dutcher, Gardner S. Chapin, William H. Locke, Charles E. Sprague, Charles H. Wheeler, Charles G. Dobbs, Warren M. Hosley, William A. Butler, Fred T. Locke, Henry C. Valentine, Channing M. Britzon, Floyd Clarkson, John McClave, James S. Herrman, Thomas B. Rand, Alfred C. Cheney, James H. Breslin, Alex. Brown jr. George N. Birdsall) 54 W. 32d
Union Dredging Co. (Chandler H. Loomis, Pres.; Clarence W. Francis, Sec.; Frederick W. Barker, Treas. Capital, $30,000. Directors: Chandler H. Loomis, Clarence W. Francis, Frederick W. Barker) 84 Pine
Union Electric Co. (John L. Somoff, propr.) 1 Ann
Union Embroidering Co. (Lewis C. Minster, propr.) 450 Broome

Union Enameling Co. (Charles Lehmann & Co. proprs.) 37 College pl.
Union Excelsior Lubricating Co. (Abraham Dreyfuss, propr.) 929 Front
Union Extract Works (J. H. Morgentime & Co. proprs.) 155 Chambers
Union Ferry Co. (James S. T. Stranahan, Pres.; Matthew Dunker, Sec. Capital, $1,000,000. Directors: Walter N. Degrauw, James S. T. Stranahan, Abiel A. Low, Bryan H. Smith, Ripley Ropes, Roswell Eldridge, William A. Perry, George C. White jr. Cornelius Zabriskie, William A. Hall, Walter N. Degrauw jr. Henry E. Pierrepont, Franklin E. Taylor, Alexander E. Orr, Felix Campbell) ft. Whitehall, ft. Wall, ft. Fulton & Pier 34 E. R.
Union Fire Alarm Co. (Peter N. Ramsey, Pres.) further inf. refused, 64 Cedar
Union Gas & Oil Stove Co. (Charles E. Meier, Pres.; James L. Sharp, Sec. Capital, $75,000. Directors: Charles E. Meier, Frederick Hildebrandt, James L. Sharp) 12 New Bowery, 398 & 400 Pearl & 34 Vandewater
Union Glove Co. (Louis C. Minster, propr.) 450 Broome
Union Granite Co. (John J. Cooney, Pres.; Joseph H. Eckstein, Sec. Capital, $80,000; further inf. refused) 168 Pearl
Union Heat & Light Co. (no inf.) 5 Beekman
Union Ice Co. (C. A. Winch & Co. proprs.) 523 W. 21st
Union Iron Works (P. Minturn Smith, Pres.; Charles Tremaine, Sec. Capital, $50,000. Directors: P. Minturn Smith, Charles Tremaine, Seymour N. Robinson) 45 D'way
Union Japanning & Decorating Works (George Danb & Son, proprs.) 102 Centre
Union Laundry (Charles E. Moore, propr.) 448 Sixth av.
Union Line (S. C. Evans & Co. proprs.) 86 South & Pier 10 E. R.
Union Mfg. Co. (cabinet mkrs.) (D. H. Hale, Pres.; further inf. unattainable) 38 Park row
Union Mfg. Co. (polish) (not inc.)(William A. Ball & Virgil N. Case) 267 B'way
Union Mercantile Agency (Henry White, Pres.; Edward J. Dickinson, Sec.; Joseph M. Williams, Treas. Capital, $10,000. Directors: Henry White, Edward J. Dickinson, Joseph M. Williams) 56 Wall
Union National Gas Saving Co. (refused) 744 B'way
Union News Co. (Am. News Co. proprs.) 13 Park pl.
Union Novelty Works (Nella B. Fuechsel, propr.) 487 D'way
Union Oil Works (J. Harris Noe, propr.) 154 Maiden la.
Union Pacific Tea Co. (Robert P. McBride, propr.) 79 Water, 80 Front, 19 Av. C, 210 Av. A, 12 First av. 1156 Second av. & 2886 Third av.
Union Paper Box Co. (inoperative) 99 Nassau & 430 W. 14th
Union Paper Co. (Charles A. Brooks, Pres.; Aaron R. Smith, Sec. Capital, $800,000. Trustees: Charles A. Brooks, Aaron R. Smith, Ebenezer B. Woodward, Robert I. Lomas jr. James Perry) 430 W. 14th
Union Paste & Sizing Co. (John S. Chase, propr.) 197 Chrystie
Union Pavement Co. (John B. Reynolds, Pres.; John F. Reynolds, Sec. Capital, $800,000. Directors: John B. Reynolds, George L. Hutchings, F. A. R. Baldwin, John H. Perine, John F. Reynolds, William L. Breyfogle, Ivan Prowatzain) 45 D'way
Union Pearl Works (S. L. & J. H. Lawles, proprs.) 241 Centre
Union Playing Card Co. (Bernard Dreyfuss, propr.) 79 Duane

20

TYPEWRITING DONE BY THE TROW CITY DIRECTORY CO., 11 University Place.

Union Press Exchange (William H. England, Pres.; Thomas C. Quinn, Treas.; Benjamin C. Stewart, Sec.) 118 Nassau

Union Print Works (William H. Locke, Pres.; William H. Locke jr. Sec. Capital, $120,000. Directors; William H. & William H. Locke jr.) 47 Leonard

Union Printing Co. (Capital, $30,000; further inf. refused) 15 Vandewater

Union Publishing House (David H. McConnell, Pres.; William T. Kightlinger, Sec. Capital, $10,000. Directors: David H. McConnell, William T. Kightlinger, Louis McCouncil) 126 Chambers

Union Saw Co. (no inf.) 64 Reade

Union School of Stenography & Typewriting (Mary F. Seymour, propr.) 120 & 280 B'way, 36 Park row & 467 W. 23d

Union Shoe Mfg. Co. (Fleming & Pierce, proprs.) 96 Duane

Union Sign & Banner Co. (George W. Warren, propr.) 2894 Third av.

Union Square Bank (Frederick Wagner, Pres.; Adam Fahs, Cashier; Rudolph P. Leube, Notary. Capital, $200,000. Directors: Edward Uhl, Henry Bischoff jr. Marvin S. Butzles, F. Henry Dugro, Samuel D. Folsom, John J. Gibbons, John G. Griesler, Charles Goelier, Paul Goepel, Henry Herrmann, Henry Iden, Paul Loeser, Wendelin J. Nauss, Jacob Ottmann, Louis C. Raegener, John Reilly, Charles Steckler, George A. Steinway, George H. Stonebridge jr. Edward J. H. Tamsen, Frederick Wagner, Adam Weber, Joseph Wiener, Herman Wunderlich) 8 Union sq. E.

Union Square Panorama Co. (Hector de Castro, Pres.; Edward Brandus, Treas. Capital, $200,000. Trustees: Hector de Castro, C. L. Willoughby, Edward Brandus, Paul Philippoteaux, C. Wheeler, M. Hecht, Peter T. Barlow) Fourth av. c B. 19th

Union Square Permanent Co-operative Building & Loan Assn. (William J. Worrell, Pres.; J. N. Munson, Sec.; C. R. Duffie jr. Treas.) 25 E. 14th

Union Square Printing Co. (dissolved) 36 E. 14th

Union Stamp Works (Manuel Daes, propr.) 34 Church

Union Steam Carpet Cleaning Works (Elizabeth Templa, propr.) 38 E. 19th

Union Stock Yard & Market Co (John B. Dutcher, Pres.; Akin T. Thomas, Sec. Capital, $200,000. Directors: John B. Dutcher, Timothy C. Eastman, Joseph Stern, Akin T. Thomas) ft. W. 61st

Union Stone Co. (dissolved) 36 John

Union Stove Works (Uriah Hill jr. Pres.; Peter B. Acker, Sec. Capital, $110,000. Directors: Uriah Hill jr. Reuben R. Finch, Peter B. Acker) 70 Beekman & 66 Gold

Union Straw Board Co. (no inf.) 280 B'way

Union Suspender Mfg. Co. (Adolph Bernstein, propr.) 100 Walker

Union Tank Line (inf. unattainable) 26 B'way

Union Teachers Agency (William D. Kerr, propr.) 16 Astor pl.

Union Tie Co. (Odiorne & Co. & H. Twitchell & Son, proprs.) 28 White

Union Toy Mfg. Co. (Benjamin F. England, propr.) 43 Fulton

Union Transfer & Storage Co. (W. McCarty Little, Pres.; John H. Jones, Treas. Capital, $40,000. Directors: W. McCarty Little, John H. Jones, Frederick E. Gilbert) 125 E. 22d

Union Trust Co. of N. Y. (Edward King, Pres.; Archibald O. Ronaldson, Sec. Capital, $1,000,000. Trustees: William Whitewright, Henry A. Kent, Edward King, E. B. Wesley, George C. Magoun, Edward Schell, William Alexander Duer, Cornelius Vanderbilt, Charles H. Leland, C. D. Wood, Chauncey M. Depew, James N. Platt, James H. Ogilvie, H. Van Rensselaer Kennedy, I. H. Frothingham, George A. Jarvis, Robert G. Remsen, A. A. Low, D. H. McAlpin, George B. Carhart, James T. Woodward, Ambrose C. Kingsland, G. G. Williams, R. T. Wilson, William F. Russell, James M. McLean, Amasa J. Parker, Samuel F. Barger, D. C. Hays, W. Emlen Roosevelt) 73 B'way

Union Tubing Co. (dissolved) 487 B'way

Union Tubing Co. (inf. unattainable) 18 Cortlandt

Union Upholstery & Trimming Co. (Hyman & Meyers, proprs.) 86 Worth & 504 W. 58th

Union Wall Paper Co. (Paul Gantert & Son, proprs.) 482 Third av.

Union White Lead Mfg. Co. (Reginald P. Rowe, Pres.; Edward J. Brockett, Sec. Capital, $100,000; further inf. refused) 163 Front

Union Wire Mattress Co. (David J. Powers. Pres.; William Hendley, Sec.; William D. Gibson, Treas. Capital, $100,000. Directors: David J. & Frank A. Powers, William D. Gibson, William Hendley) 8 W. 14th

Unique Carpet Cleaning & Renovating Works (Andrew M. Logan, propr.) 219 E. 51st

Unique Mfg. Co. (buttons) (Meyer D. Rothschild, Pres.; Lionel Sutro, Sec. Capital, $2,500. Directors: Meyer D. Rothschild, Lionel Sutro, Bedno Loewy) 130 S. 5th av.

Unique Mfg. Co. (toys) (Frank M. Oppenheim, propr.) 171 Suffolk

Unique Metal Novelty Co. (not inc.) (William & Adolph Marcus) 143 Centre

United Aid Soc. (Henry W. Van Cortlandt, Pres.; Louis A. Hill, Sec. Capital, $100,000; further inf. refused) 165 B'way

United Bottling Co. (Paul F. O'Neill, propr.) 185 Franklin

United Confectioners' Assn. (Ernst A. G. Intemann, Pres.; John Brummer, Sec.; Herman H. Maack, Treas. Capital, $27,000. Directors: Ernst A. G. Intemann, John Brummer, Herman F. Hoops, Charles Heins, John Reis, H. W. Hoops, Herman H. Maack, John F. Cordes, Frederick Lange, Jacob Hahn, J. G. C. Taddiken) 43 Jay

United Edison Mfg. Co. (J. Hobart Herrick, Pres.; Arnold Marcus, Sec. Capital, $1,000,000. Directors: Edward H. Johnson, Henry Villard, G. A. Spofford, Samuel Insull. C. E. Chinnock, J. Hood Wright, J. Hobart Herrick. Francis R. Upton, Charles H. Coster) 44 Wall & 65 Fifth av.

United Electric Light & Power Co. (Caleb H. Jackson, Pres.; Charles J. Marsh, Sec.; William H. Browne, Treas. Capital, $3,000,000. Directors: Caleb H. Jackson, Paul D. Cravath, William H. Browne, Charles J. Marsh) 59 Liberty

United Express & Van Co. (not inc.) (Christian Hess & Joseph I. Yetter) 2472 Third av.

United Foreign Express Co. (Henry H. Yard, Pres.; A. J. Hemphill, Sec. Capital, $100,000. Directors: Henry H. Yard, A. J. Hemphill, T. D. Richardson) 71 B'way

United Growers' Co. (not inc.) (Herman A. Curiel & Adolph jr. & Morris H. Woolner) 39 S. William & 26 Stone

United Ice Lines (Robert Harris, Pres.; James S. Thurston, Sec. Directors: Robert Harris, Thomas C. Platt, Joel B. Erhardt, Elihu Root, James S. Thurston, Henry W. de Forest, Frank W. Hawley) 120 B'way

United Life & Accident Ins. Assn. (Peter Bows, Pres.; J. Jay Pardee, Sec. Directors: Peter Bows, Leonard Paulson jr. Henry Campbell, Harry Wilber, Richard M. Waters, R. F. M. Chase, Joseph H. Tooker, Sparta Fritz, Thomas E. Crimmins) 44 B'way

United Lines Telegraph Co. (Edward S. Stokes, Pres.; Dwight Townsend, Sec. Capital, $8,000,000. Directors: Edward S. Stokes, J. Anderson, Dwight Townsend, Henry A. Tappin, Horace Stokes, J. Davidson, Isaac N. Baker, George H. Pell, Cassius H. Read) 1 B'way

United Mfg. Co. (Gustavus A. Goldsmith, Pres.; Silas L. Kenyon, Sec.; Julius Levine, Treas. Capital, $15,000. Directors: Gustavus A. Goldsmith, Julius Levine, James M. Hoffman) 52 Howard & 307 E. 53d

United Patent Co. (Alfred Poindexter, Pres.; J. Frank Supplee, Sec. Capital, $50,000. Directors: Alfred Poindexter, Henry Neustadter, J. Frank Supplee, David W. Thompson, Everett S. Tomlinson) 712 B'way

United Pipe Lines (inf. unattainable) 26 B'way

United Press (James W. Scott, Pres.; Charles R. Baldwin, Treas.; Walter P. Phillips, Sec. Capital, $20,000. Directors: Charles H. Taylor, James W. Scott, William L. Brown, William M. Laffan, Robert S. Davis, Arthur Jenkins, James E. Scripps, John H. Farrell, Samuel D. Lee, E. H. Butler, Charles R. Baldwin, William C. Bryant, Walter P. Phillips) 187 B'way

United Refiners' Export Oil Co. (Edward G. Cone, Pres.; Conrad H. Ruhl, Sec.; further inf. refused) 18 Beaver

United Service Publishing Co. (Frederick T. Wilson, Pres.; George F. Bingham, Sec. Capital, $50,000. Trustees: Frederick T. Wilson, George F. Bingham, E. M. Lewis, Henry Chauncey jr.) 1 B'way

U. S. Auxiliary Fire Alarm Co. (Robert Payne, Pres.; Howard P. Simmons, Sec.; William A. Simmons, Treas. Capital, $300,000. Directors: Robert Payne, Howard P. & William A. Simmons) 280 B'way

U. S. Axle Lubricator Co. (Louis Engelhorn, Pres.; William Arnold, Sec. Capital, $350,000. Directors: Louis Engelhorn, William Arnold, Charles Eglinger) 1541 B'way

U. S. Bottling Co. (Henry Freimuth, propr.) r 108 Delancey

U. S. Brake Co. (William T. Bothwell, Pres.; Harvey J. Ubert, Sec. Capital, $2,000,000. Directors: William T. Bothwell, Harvey J. Ubert, George W. Waite, E. O. Webb, A. R. Bolues) 111 B'way

U. S. Brewers' Academy (Anton Schwarz, Pres.; Max Schwarz, Sec.) 200 Worth

U. S. Brewers' Assn. (Thles J. Lefens, Pres.; Richard Katzenmayer, Sec.; Joseph Liebmann, Treas.) 2 Irving pl.

U. S. Brewing Co. (Ltd.) (Gottfried Krueger, Pres.; Isaac Danenberger, Sec.; further inf. unattainable) 44 Wall

U. S. Building & Loan Syndicate (John B. Altmann, Pres.; Nelson E. McCarn, Sec.; Charles H. Waring, Treas. Capital, $5,000,000. Directors: John B. Altmann, Edward P. Hovey, Nelson E. McCarn, William N. Ridge, W. Irving Baxter, Thomas P. Kilgore, Daniel A. Martin, Max Schaffer, Charles H. Waring) 152 B'way

U. S. Butter Extractor Co. (George Hoadly, Pres.; Simon B. Camacho, Sec.; George Taylor, Treas. Capital, $1,000,000; further inf. unattainable) 1 B'way

U. S. Carriage & Wagon Co. (Peter A. Cassidy, propr.) 795 Third av.

U. S. Cement Co. (William Allen Smith, Pres.; George F. Benton, Sec. Capital, $300,000. Directors: Walter C. Witherbee, William Allen Smith, George F. Benton, Joseph S. Auerbach, Lewis W. Francis) 60 B'way

U. S. Champion Gas Machine Co. (Jasper W. Carpenter, Pres. Capital, $75,000. Directors: Jasper W. Carpenter, Charles A. Fones, George W. Baremore, James D. Merritt; further inf. unattainable) no address

U. S. Cigar Rolling Table Co. (George M. Hard, Pres.; William L. Lyman, Sec. Capital, $200,000. Directors: William L. Lyman, George M. Hard, William Eggert, William D. Barclay, John R. Williams) 102 Chambers

U. S. Comb Co. (Fritz Achelis, Pres.; William W. Weitling, Sec.; Charles A. Hoyt, Treas. Capital, $400,000. Directors: Fritz Achelis, William W. Weitling, Charles A. Hoyt) 9 Mercer

U. S. Commercial Agency & Collecting Co. (William G. Jones, Pres.; Newton Q. Lucas, Sec. Capital, $25,000. Directors: William G. Jones, Newton C. Lucas, Joseph S. Jones, Abbie M. Baker) 280 B'way

U. S. Construction & Improvement Co. (inoperative) 45 B'way

U. S. Co-operative Watch & Jewelry Co. (John W. Sherwood, propr.) 58 Nassau

U. S. Costume & Embroidery Co. (William Schwind, propr.) 30 St. Mark's pl.

U. S. Cotton Harvester Co. (Owen T. Bugg, Pres. Capital, $1,000,000. Trustees: Owen T. Bugg, F. N. Ewe, G. A. Hammel, A. N. Hebre; further inf. unattainable) no address

U. S. Cotton Seed Cleaning Co. (E. Urquhart, Pres.; Robert F. Munro, Sec. Capital, $1,-500,000. Trustees: E. Urquhart, Robert F. Munro, P. Rand) 45 B'way

U. S. Cremation Co. (Ltd.) (John Townshend, Pres.; James K. Frothingham, Treas.; James B. Brown, Sec. Capital, $80,000. Directors: John Townshend, James K. Frothingham, James B. Brown, Andrew Carnegie, August Blumenthal, James Chaskel, C. W. C. Dreher, William J. Flagg, David Lewi, Robert Ormiston, Charles Putzel, Hugo Rothschild, Martin E. Waldstein) 140 Nassau

U. S. Dynamite Co. (Robert W. Warren, Pres.; Henry S. Deshon, Treas.; further inf. refused) 38 Platt

U. S. Dynamite Projectile Co. (Robert Sherwood, Pres.; William D. Horton, Sec. Capital, $2,-500,000. Directors: Robert Sherwood, John W. Blake, George B. & Frederick H. Snyder, William W. Horton) 44 B'way

U. S. Electric Lighting Co. (George W. Hebard, Pres.; Leonard E. Curtis, Sec. Capital, $1,-500,000. Trustees: George W. Hebard, Leonard Curtis, Marcellus Hartley, Henry Dey, P. Frederick Kobbe, Anson P. Stokes, Thomas H. Hubbard, W. T. Hatch) 120 B'way

U. S. Electric Railway Signal Co. (William B. Sterrett, Pres.; Oscar J. Cohn, Sec. Capital, $1,000,000. Directors: William B. Sterrett, Oscar J. Cohn, John H. Crook) 53 B'way

U. S. Electric Safety Co. (Byron W. Cohen, Pres.; Loron N. Downs, Sec.; Andrew J. Dam, Treas. Capital, $500,000. Directors: Byron W. Cohen, Loron N. Downs, Andrew J. Dam, David W. Bucklin, Edward Zimmerman) 853 B'way

U. S. Equitable Gas Co. (Charles F. Dieterich, Pres.; Arthur B. Proal, Sec.; Jacob Bertschmann, Treas. Capital, $1,200,000. Directors: Elias C. Benedict, Jacob Bertschmann, Henry J. Davison, Edward N. Dickerson, Charles F. Dieterich, Robert M. C. Graham, William H. Gebhard, Erasm J. Jerzmanowski, Augusta Richard, Charles F. & Casimir Tag) 45 B'way

U. S. Export Almanac Publishing Co. (Carl Schurz, Pres.; Alonzo Bell, Sec.; Joseph M. Senner, Treas. Capital, $10,000. Directors: Carl Schurz, Alonzo Bell, Joseph H. Senner, Karl Hutor, Bernard H. Gueterbock, John H. Poggenburg, Solomon Getzlar) 280 B'way

U. S. Express Co. (Thomas C. Platt, Pres.; Dan. F. Eells, Sec.; Theodore F. Wood, Treas. Capital, $10,000,000. Directors: Thomas C. Platt, Chauncey H. Crosby, Dan. P. Eells, George R. Blanchard, Russell A. Alger, Frank H. Platt) 49 B'way

U. S. Feather-Down Co. (Cyriac Du Brul, Pres.; Henry Gerken, Treas.; Benjamin C. Gerken, Sec. Capital, $35,000. Directors: Cyriac Du Brul, Henry & Benjamin C. Gerken) 1410 Av. A

U. S. Finance Co. (Frederick G. Corning. V, Pres.; Henry D. Weston, Sec.; John T. Sherman, Treas. Capital, $800,000. Directors: Frederick G. Corning, John T. Sherman, Douglass

CIRCULARS ADDRESSED TO ANY TRADE IN THE U. S. { Facilities
PROMPT, CAREFUL WORK } **THE TROW CITY DIRECTORY CO.,** { Unequalled
AT MODERATE PRICES. } **11 University Place.**

UNI 308 UNI

Green, John F. Plummer, John Firth, M. Roosevelt Schuyler, J. Seaver Page, Henry Weston) 35 Wall

U. S. Fire Ins. Co. (W. Wilson Underhill, Pres.; Walter H. Griffen, Sec. Capital, $250,000. Directors: Charles T. Cromwell, Henry S. Terbell, Robert Downs, William M. Bradford, William R. Thurston, William Kevan, William H. Jackson, W. Wilson Underhill, Augustus Taber, Charles O. Barrett, Edward C. Sampson, Charles H. Harbeck, William A. Cauldwell, Frederic DaP. Foster, Charles T. Corwin, Samuel M. Craft, Philip J. Sands, James W. Cromwell, James L. Morgan, John L. Riker, Edmund A. Hurry, Edward Merritt, Henry F. Crosby, Edwin A. Bradley, Edward G. Burgess, Paul Babcock jr. Edmund Penfold) 172 B'way

U. S. Foundry Co. (William A. Ross, Pres.; John G. Price, Sec.; John H. Carnes, Treas. Capital, $100,000. Directors: William A. Ross, John G. Price, John H. Carnes, Thomas M. Hart, John Lewis, James G. Delaplaine, Thomas J. Moore jr.) 58 Pine

U. S. Frame & Picture Co. (Julius H. Goldberg, propr.) 124 Wooster

U. S. Fuel Co. (Charles L. Cammann, Pres.; Gustav Frank, Sec.; further inf. unattainable) 12 Cortlandt

U. S. Gas Improving Co. (no inf.) 194 B'way

U. S. Guarantee Co. (Edward Rawlings, Pres.; Daniel J. Tompkins, Sec. Capital, $200,000. Directors: Henry W. Cannon. George Coppell, W. Butler Duncan, Charles M. Fry, W. J. Hancock, Morris K. Jesup, George J. Magee, Logan C. Murray, John Paton, Horace Porter, Russell Sage, George H. Scott, Philip D. Armour, Thomas L. Barrett, Calvin S. Brice, Sir Alexander T. Galt, R. M. Morsman, Asa P. Potter, Edward Rawlings, George M. Troutman, L. C. Weir) 111 B'way

U. S. Hydroleine Co. (Cornelius Oakley, Pres.; William Sulphen, Treas.; J. L. Chapin, Sec. Capital, $500,000. Directors: Philip V. Myers, Cornelius Oakley, William R. Cook) 45 B'way

U. S. Illuminating Co. (Caleb H. Jackson, Pres.; Joseph W. Hartley, Sec. Capital, $1,250,000. Directors: Caleb H. Jackson, Paul D. Cravath, James Stokes, Joseph W. Hartley, Duncan D. Parmly, George W. Hebard, George Westinghouse jr.) 59 Liberty

U. S. Incandescent Gas Lamp Co. (Albert R. Parker, Pres.; J. A. Browne, Sec.; William S. Louderback, Treas.; further inf. refused) 171 B'way

U. S. Incandescent Gas Light Co. (Chester C. Munroe, Pres.; John S. Wood, Sec.; Leo Levy, Treas. Capital, $1,000,000; further inf. unattainable) 7 Nassau

U. S. Land & Investment Co. (Daniel Macauley, Pres.; Charles A. Fenn, Sec. Capital, $2,500,000. Directors: Daniel Macauley, Walter S. Cowles, L. Bradford Prince, James C. Wetmore, Charles A. Fenn) 44 B'way

U. S. Lasting Machine Co. (William D. Stratton, Pres.; Patrick H. McNamee, Sec.; Nathaniel F. Jones, Treas. Capital, $500,000. Trustees: William D. Stratton, Nathaniel F. Jones, Isaac N. Forbes, Michael Donnelly, Patrick H. McNamee) 71 B'way

U. S. Law Assn. (James H. Remington, Pres.; Sandford R. Teneyck, Sec. Directors; James H. Remington, Sandford R. Teneyck) 271 B'way

U. S. Life Ins. Co. (George H. Burford, Pres.; Charles P. Fraleigh, Sec. Capital, $440,000. Directors: Clinton Gilbert, Henry W. Ford, Nathan F. Graves, Horace K. Thurber, Julius Catlin, Henry C. Hulbert, James R. Plum, George C. Williams, A. Wallach, Oliver P. Buell, Henry L. Clapp, E. Van Volkenburgh, Charles P. Fraleigh, John F. Munn, George H. Burford, Alfred S. Heidelbach, Alfred Wheelwright, Joseph M. Deveau, Francis Le-
land, E. H. Perkins jr. A. S. Frissell, John J. Tucker, D. H. Houghtaling, Thomas Russell, Orson D. Munn) 261 B'way & 15 Broad

U. S. Lighting & Ventilating Co. (dissolved) 24 W. 4th

U. S. Lloyds (A. Foster Higgins, James Farley Cox & John D. Barrett, attorneys) 50 Wall

U. S. Lyceum Bureau (Helen L. D. Potter, propr.) 10 E. 14th

U. S. Machine & Inventions Co. (Clement C. Clawson, Pres.; John C. Bouton, Sec. Capital, $50,000. Trustees: Clement C. Clawson, John C. Bouton, Albert E. Whyland, George B. Howard, Henry Aplington) 24 Hudson

U. S. Manufacturers' Export Co. (no inf.) 96 Maiden la.

U. S. Measuring Faucet Co. (Frank J. Tinkham, Pres.; J. G. Herman Lehmann, Sec.; Otto Fuhlrott, Treas. Capital, $100,000. Trustees: Frank J. Tinkham, J. G. Herman Lehmann, Otto Fuhlrott) 309 B'way

U. S. Medicine Co. (Clark W. Dunlop, Pres.; Gustavus H. Benermann, Sec.; further inf. refused) 12 Wash'n. pl.

U. S. Mercantile Protective Assn. (Douglas H. Lamb, Pres.; Tobias Samuels, Sec. Capital, $20,000. Directors: William H. & Samuel W. Kilvert, Douglas H. Lamb, Tobias Samuels) 154 Nassau

U. S. Mercantile Reporting Co. (Leonard S. Howard, Pres.; Lyman H. Howard, Sec. Capital, $100,000. Trustees: Leonard S. & Lyman H. Howard, Burrett W. Horton) 335 B'way

U. S. Mineral Wool Co. (Wallace C. Andrews, Pres.; Henry Franz, Sec.; Onesimus P. Shaffer, Treas. Capital, $200,000. Directors: Wallace C. Andrews, Henry Franz, Onesimus P. Shaffer, Lewis Coon) 173 B'way

U. S. Mortgage Co. (inoperative) 32 Nassau

U. S. Mutual Accident Assn. (Charles B. Peet, Pres.; James B. Pitcher, Sec.; Calvin T. Hazen, Treas. Directors: Charles B. Peet, Winsor B. French, James B. Pitcher, William B. Smith, Leopold Wormser, William Wade, William Gibson, James S. Leeds, E. S. Parker, John H. C. Nevius, George J. Peet) 320 B'way

U. S. National Bank (Logan C. Murray, Pres.; Evan G. Sherman, Cashier; John J. McAuliffe, Notary. Capital, $500,000. Directors: Logan C. Murray, Frederic P. Olcott, William F. Thompson, Thomas E. Stillman, Thomas W. Pearsall, James W. Alexander, Thomas H. Hubbard) 1 D'way

U. S. Net & Twine Co. (Charles M. Pratt, Pres.; William H. Wallace, Treas.; Alfred C. Bedford, Sec.; further inf. refused) 219 Fulton

U. S. Newspaper Advertising Agency (Manson & Perlman, proprs.) 5 Beekman

U. S. Ore Separating Co. (inoperative) 32 B'way

U. S. Photographic Supply Co. (Oscar L. Richard, Pres.; Emil L. Boas, Treas.; Arthur Schwarz, Sec. Capital, $25,000. Directors: Oscar L. Richard, Emil L. Boas, Arthur Schwarz, Edwin H. Richard, Francis Delmel) 9 E. 14th

U. S. Pianoforte Co. (dissolved) 428 Eleventh av. & 448 W. 34th

U. S. Pneumatic Co. (James G. Smith, Pres.; Charles K. Duell, Sec. Capital, $2,000,000. Directors: James G. Smith, Charles K. Duell, William W. Bevan, Frederick C. Ross) 171 D'way

U. S. Printing Co. (Henry A. Prast, Pres.; Henry A. Prast jr. Sec.; William W. Cowen, Treas. Capital, $80,000. Directors: Henry A. & Henry A. Prast jr. William W. Cowen) 114 Nassau

U. S. Quilting Mills (Michael Deutsch, propr.) 366 B'way

U. S. Rocking Grate-Bar Co. (no inf.) 74 Cortlandt

U. S. Rolling Stock Co. (Adolfo Hegewisch, Pres.; Thomas F. B. Parker, Sec.; Carl Benn, Treas.

MERCHANTS EXCHANGE NAT. BANK OF THE CITY OF N. Y.
SOLICITS YOUR ACCOUNT. 257 Broadway.
PHINEAS C. LOUNSBURY, President.   ALLEN S. APGAR, Cashier.

Capital, $5,000,000. Directors: Adolfo Hegewisch, George Place, Herman R. Beltzer, H. R. Duval, Cyrus D. Roys) 85 Wall

U. S. Sanitary Water Filter Co. (Wilmot & Co. proprs.) 182 South

U. S. Savings Bank (Constant A. Andrews, Pres.; George A. Middlebrook, Sec. Directors: Constant A. Andrews, Richard A. Anthony, Samuel Barton, Joseph B. Bloomingdale, Simon Borg, John D. Crimmins, Charles F. Cox, Richard H. Eggleston, Francis O. French, Frederic N. Goddard, George S. Hart, John Jardine, Homer Lee, Payson Merrill, George A. Middlebrook, Henry Newman, Louis E. Ransom, Noah C. Rogers, John M. Toncey, James S. Thurston, P. Henry Dugro, Hiram R. Ilomeyn, Walter Stanton) 214 E. 59th

U. S. Scoria Co. (inf. unattainable) 49 B'way

U. S. Scaled Postal Card Co. (Inoperative) 200 B'way

U. S. Standard Steamship Owners' Builders' & Underwriters' Assn. (Ltd.) (James F. Cox, Pres.; Herbert Appleton, Sec. Capital, $5,000. Directors: James F. Cox, Herbert Appleton, Sinclair Stuart, George E. Weed, John D. Barrett) 50 Wall

U. S. Steam & Street Railway Advertising Co. (Carleton & Kissam, proprs.) 41 Park row

U. S. Storage Warehouse (Peter A. Cassidy, propr.) 209 E. 40th

U. S. Supply Co. (Ltd.) (Charles A. Allen, Pres.; William Schwind jr. Sec.; Charles Plock, Treas. Capital, $100,000. Directors: Charles A. Allen, William & William Schwind jr. Charles Plock) 51 John

U. S. Surgical Supply Co. (A. J. Jacob, Pres.; John Cooper, Sec.; William B. Wiltbank, Treas. Capital, $100,000; further inf. unattainable) 1160 B'way

U. S. Suspender Co. (Joseph Lauferty & Son, proprs.) 54 Leonard

U. S. Traction Co. (Frank B. Koues, Pres.; Frank B. Spalding, Sec. Capital, $1,000,000. Directors, Frank B. Koues, George W. Delano, Albert B. Batchelder, George B. Perry, Frederick Allen, Frank Shepard, Frank B. Spalding) 99 Nassau

U. S. Trade Mark Assn. (Wright Duryea, Pres.; Francis Forbes, Sec.; further inf. refused) 137 B'way

U. S. Trading Co. (Alexander Simon jr. propr.) 539 B'way

U. S. Transfer & Exchange Assn. (Francis O. French, Pres.; C. H. Smith, Sec.; Amos T. French, Treas. Capital, $200,000. Directors: August Belmont jr. R. J. Cross, H. W. Cannon, John L. Cadwalader, Francis O. & Amos T. French, E. D. Randolph, John L. Waterbury, J. P. Adams, Wallace P. Groom, Conrad N. Jordan, Henry L. Higginson, Thomas Maitland) 10 Wall

U. S. Transp. Co. (Charles Stewart Schenck, Pres.; John Halls, Sec. Directors: John Halls, Charles Stewart Schenck, Joseph A. Cutler, W. J. Sullock, S. C. Schenck) 18 B'way

U. S. Trust Co. of N. Y. (John A. Stewart, Pres.; Henry L. Thornell, Sec. Capital, $2,000,000. Trustees: Wilson G. Hunt, Clinton Gilbert, Daniel D. Lord, Samuel Sloan, James Low, William Walter Phelps, D. Willis James, John A. Stewart, Henry E. Lawrence, Erastus Corning, John Harson Rhoades, Anson Phelps Stokes, George Henry Warren, George Bliss, William Libbey, John Crosby Brown, Edward Cooper, W. Bayard Cutting, Charles S. Smith, William Rockefeller, Alexander E. Orr, William H. Macy jr. William D. Sloan, Gustav H. Schwab, Frank Lyman, George F. Victor) 45 Wall (see advt. in back)

U. S. Ventilator Co. (Charles T. Murray, Pres.; Peter P. Pope, Sec. Capital, $25,000. Directors: Charles T. Murray, Peter P. Pope) 45 B'way

U. S. Volta Electric Battery Co. (refused) 58 Wall

U. S. Water Purifying Co. (George Muller, Pres.; N. C. Wooster, Sec.; further inf. unattainable) 10 Barclay

U. S. Water Supply Co. (William D. Andrews, Pres.; George H. Andrews, Sec. Capital, $50,000. Trustees: William D. & George H. Andrews) 233 B'way

U. S. Wenham Patent Gas Lamp Co. (dissolved) 18 W. 23d

U. S. Wood Vulcanizing Co. (Henry Steers, Pres.; William F. Holcomb, Sec. Capital, $8,000,000; further inf. refused) 327 Av. B

U. S. & Brazil Mail S. S. Co. (Horace K. Thurber, Pres.; John M. Lachlan, Sec. Capital, $1,000,000. Directors: Horace K. Thurber, Odilis P. Huntington, G. G. Williams, Charles M. Pratt, Charles B. Flint, William M. Ivins, Edward H. Ripley, E. B. Bartlett, H. C. Hulbert) 15 Broad (see advt. in back)

United Verde Copper Co. (James A. Macdonald, Pres.; Otis H. Kennedy, Sec. Capital, $3,000,000. Directors: James A. Macdonald, John L. Thomson, James Kitchen, James C. Savery, Alfred W. Montgomery, Lindsay Watson, Henry G. Atwater) 35 Wall

United Water Works Co. (Ltd.) (John W. Fairbanks, Pres.; Joseph W. Jackson, Sec.; Frederick H. Mills, Treas. Capital, $600,000. Directors: John W. Fairbanks, James S. Shepard, Charles A. Vialle, William A. Underwood, Charles W. Tidd, Clarence H. Venner, Francis Ware) 31 Pine

United Zylonite Co. (William L. Brown, Pres.; Charles H. Williams, Sec.; Frank S. Richardson, Treas. Capital, $500,000. Trustees: William L. Brown, S. Warren Ingalls, Edwin F. Ward, Charles A. Denny, George V. A. Congar) 361 B'way

Unity Publishing Co. (Alzire A. Chevafillier, propr.) 13 W. 42d

Universal Advertising Co. (Oscar J. Gude, propr.) 113 Sixth av.

Universal Arc Lamp Co. (William D. MacQueston, Pres.; John H. McClement, Sec. Capital, $100,000. Directors: William D. MacQuesten, O. J. Field, O. L. Edgar, Charles A. Noll, John H. McClement) 15 Cortlandt

Universal Automatic Lubricator Co. (Horace G. Wood, Pres.; Charles Benner, Sec. Capital, $1,000,000. Directors: Horace G. Wood, Charles Benner, John A. Wyman, William Talmestock) 18 B'way

Universal Buttonhole Attachment Co. (William E. Trull, Pres.; Warren H. Day, Sec. Capital, $50,000. Trustees: William E. Trull, Warren H. Day, Friend W. Smith) 17 E. 16th

Universal Card Index Co. (Eugene Fczandie, propr.) 8 William

Universal Cigar Factory (F. Frisch & Co. proprs.) Railroad av. n E. 157th

Universal Cigar Rolling Machine Co. (Gustav Falk, Pres.; Arnold Falk, Treas.; Frederick J. H. Attwood, Sec. Capital, $101,000. Directors: Gustav & Arnold Falk, Frederick J. H. Attwood, Carl Upmann, Leopold Wallach) 121 Water

Universal Comb Co. (David Lichtenstein, propr.) 18 Lispenard

Universal Crimper Co. (inf. unattainable) 16 Exchange pl.

Universal Fashion Co. (Herman H. Niemann, Pres.; Edward Lange. Treas. Directors: Herman H. Niemann, Edward Lange) 40 E. 12th

Universal Gas Lighting Co. (Loren N. Downs, Pres.; Harry T. Downs, Sec. Capital, $100,000. Directors: Loren N. & Harry T. Downs, Elias H. Peters) 853 B'way

Universal Information Exchange (William D. Myers, Pres.; Alvin B. Hallenbake, Sec. Capital, $20,000. Directors: William D. Myers, Alvin B. Hallenbake, Henrietta W. Myers) 28 Clinton pl.

CINCINNATI, BALTIMORE, PHILADELPHIA, | **SNOW, CHURCH & CO.** | NEW YORK, BOSTON, CHICAGO, LOUISVILLE.
CORRESPONDENTS EVERYWHERE.

UNI   310   VAN

Universal Introduction Co. (George A. Annable & Co. proprs.) 115 Warren

Universal Lasting Machine Co. (Louis Engelhorn, Pres.; F. Waldemar Ludovici, Sec.; J. Einathan Smith, Treas. Capital, $1,000,000. Directors: Louis Engelhorn, Adolph Norden, Henry E. Niese, Emil Von Destinon, John O. Donner, C. M. Oelrichs, John Patten) 15 Broad

Universal Lock Co. (Charles F. Frothingham, Pres.; George C. Thomas, Sec.; Alexander H. Do Haven, Treas. Capital, $500,000. Directors: Charles P. Frothingham, Alexander H. De Haven, George C. Thomas, John D. Slayback, Eugene C. Smith, F. D. Barker, Nelson J. Waterbury jr. James B. Wilson jr.) 50 Exchange pl.

Universal Press Co. (Merritt, Osborn & Moore, proprs.) 320 B'way & 22 Jacob

Universal Primary Battery Power & Light Co. (Capital, $50,000; further inf. unattainable) no address

Universal Rubber Co. (dissolved) 49 Rose

Universal Stair & Room Corner Co. (Daniel C. Hyde, propr.) 18 Cortlandt

Universal Stove Repair Co. (William Vanhouten, propr.) 305 Pearl

Universal Tea Co. (Edward Rafter, propr.) 2262 Second av.

University Grammar School (Hobby, Akin & Hendrickson, proprs.) 1478 D'way

University Piano & Organ Co. (Marshal & Smith Piano & Organ Co. proprs.) 285 E. 21st

University Publishing Co. (Edwin P. Whitmore, Pres.; Ezra D. Barker, Sec.; Edward D. Barker, Treas. Capital, $500,000. Directors: Edwin P. Whitmore, Edward A. Lawrence, Edward D. Barker, J. P. Gordon, Charles E. Stott, Gaylord Watson, Samuel T. Dauchy, J. W. Manson, Ezra D. Barker) 66 Duane

Unlandherr & Brother (dissolved) 339 E. 48th

Unz & Co. (Oscar Unz & John H. Z. Demarest) 12 B'way, 1 Bowling gr. & 27 Pearl

Upham H. H. & Co. (Henry H. Upham, John Tully & Louis I. Haber) 641 B'way

Upson, Singleton & Co. (John V. Singleton, Pres.; Charles M. Upson, Sec. Capital, $25,000. Directors: Charles M. & F. P. Upson, John V. Singleton) 185 Eighth av.

Uptegrove William E. & Brother (William E. & Jerome F. Uptegrove) 465 E. 10th & 510 E. 11th

Uptown Publishing Co. (dissolved) 258 W. 125th

Urbach & Bender (William Urbach & John Bender) 28 Av. A

Urbansky & Co. (Berthold Urbansky & Henry Schnitbels) 84 Vesey

Urner Publishing Co. (Benjamin Urner, Pres.; Frank G. Urner, Sec.; William C. Taber, Treas. Capital, $8,000. Directors: Benjamin & Frank G. Urner, William C. Taber, John Wilson, H. L. Peixotto) 70 Warren

Urwitz & Dykes (dissolved) 28 Canal

Utah Central Railway Co. (dissolved) 40 Wall & 287 B'way

Utica Belt Line Street R. R. Co. (Lathrop R. Bacon, Pres.; Charles W. Mather, Treas.; Edward Bushinger, Sec. Capital, $150,000. Directors: Lathrop R. Bacon, Arthur J. Moulton, I. B. Newcombe, William M. Harriman, John W. Boyle, Charles W. & Joshua Mather) 54 Wall

Utica & Unadilla R. R. Co. (Albert C. Couch, Pres.; Delos E. Culver, Treas. Capital, $300,000. Directors: Delos E. Culver, David T. Trundy, Henry L. Foote, Albert C. Couch, Everett M. Culver, Herman M. F. Randolph) 146 B'way

Utility Stove Cover Co. (inoperative) 54 William

Utley Brothers (Eugene O. & Perry B. Utley) 142 Eighth av.

V

Vaccheri M. T. & Co. (dissolved) 22 Ninth av.

Vacuum Oil Co. (Hiram B. Everest, Pres.; Frederick N. Beach, Sec.; Charles M. Everest, Treas. Capital, $25,000. Directors: Hiram B. & Charles M. Everest, F. N. Beach) 96 Water

Vaglica & Sciortino (Giovanni Vaglica & Pietro Sciortino) 19 Whitehall

Vagts J. & J. (John & Jacob) 235 Fulton

Vagts & Heitman (Frederick Vagts & John H. Heitman) 284 Boulevard

Vail George A. & Co. (George A. Vail & John J. & Lewis H. Lapham) 26 Ferry

Vail James E. jr. & Co. (dissolved) 62 White

Vail J. H. & Co. (J. Henry Vail & Frank P. Lennon) 21 Astor pl. & 142 Eighth

Valencia Mica Co. (Samuel Tickell, Pres.; Thomas S. Smith, Sec.; Henry Bradstreet, Treas. Capital, $150,000. Directors: Samuel Tickell, Henry Bradstreet, Thomas S. Smith, Charles S. Carnaghan, William P. Case) 115 B'way

Valenstein Brothers (Morris & Julius Valenstein) 74 Reade

Valenti & Priore (Orazio Valenti & Joseph Priore) 717 Sixth av.

Valentine Lawson, Co. (Lawson Valentine, Pres.; David S. Shanta, Sec.; Hadwin Houghton, Treas. Capital, $100,000. Trustees: Lawson Valentine, Nathan T. Pulsifer, Hadwin Houghton) 1712 B'way

Valentine E. R. & Brothers (dissolved) 173 West

Valentine E. R. & Co. (E. Russell Valentine, no Co.) 14 Little W. 12th

Valentine J. M. & Co. (Joseph M. & Alfred T. Valentine) 97 Franklin

Valentine N. & D. H. (Napoleon & D. Henry) 173 West

Valentine R. B. & Son (Robert B. Valentine, only) 156 B'way

Valentine Brothers (Lincoln Valentine, only) 345 Produce Ex.

Valentine & Co. (Henry C. Valentine, Pres.; Leland Fairbanks, Sec.; Charles B. Beckwith, Treas. Capital, $500,000. Trustees: Henry C. Valentine, Charles S. Homer jr. Charles E. Morrill) 245 B'way

Valentine & Flagler (Carlton C. Valentine & John W. Flagler) 99 Franklin

Valentine & Powers (William E. Valentine & Thomas Powers) 651 Hudson & 81 Gansevoort

Valentine & Rabinowitz (Moses M. Valentine & Jacob Rabinowitz) 118 Greene

Valentine's S., Sons (Samuel T. Valentine & Charles Griffen, only) 171 Cherry

Valfer S. & Co. (Solomon Valfer & Lazarus Well) 96 Nassau

Valinoto & Velege (Joseph Valinoto & Dennis Velege) 2 York

Valk S. J. & Brother (Susman J. & David W. Valk) 6 Harrison

Valleau Mfg. Co. (dissolved) 506 Broome

Vallentine & Co. (dissolved) 89 Nassau

Vallette Victor & Co. (Victor Vallette, Pres.; Oscar Mohle, Sec. Capital, $25,000. Directors: Victor Vallette, Oscar & Adolph Mohle) 58 Church

Valon Co. (Charles S. Northrop, propr.) 2 W. 14th

Vanallen's & Boughton (George W. & William H. Vanallen & C. Frank Boughton) r 59 Ann & 21 Rose

Vanalstyne & Co. (William & Andrew Vanalstyne) 4 Stone

Vanauken J. A. & Co. (James A. & Frank B. Vanauken, William Taylor & Harry C. Vanauken) 71 B'way

Vanaxte & Haaren (Frederick Vanaxte & Claus Haaren) 2423 Eighth av.

WATER METERS, GAS ENGINES, FOR PUMPING AND POWER.
NATIONAL METER CO.
252 Broadway, N. Y.

VAN 311 VAN

Vanbenschoten & Lassner (dissolved) 69 Nassau

Vanbergen, Matz & Co. (Theodore F. Matz, only) 180 Third

Vanbeuren A. & Co. (Alfred Vanbeuren, Samuel Pratt, Henry Munson & Michael Shine) 40 Rose & 162 E. 126th

Vanblankensteyn & Hennings (Henry F. L. Hennings :—special partner, George B. Goldschmidt, $20,000 ; terminates 1st July, 1891) 79 Grand

Vanblaricom & Bradley (Millard Vanblaricom & William S. Bradley) 11 Gansevoort

Vanboskerck L. J. & Co (Lucas J. & Cornelius Vanboskerck) 52 B'way

Vanboskerck & Wilson (Georgie C. Vanboskerck & Anna Wilson) 132 W. 21st

Vanbrimmer J. & Co. (Joshua Vanbrimmer, no Co.) 17 Park row

Vanbrunt & Bennett (Jay Vanbrunt & A. Graham Bennett) 871 Washn.

Vanburen A. & Co. (no inf.) 239 E. 127th

Vancamp & Brennan (John G. Vancamp & Patrick Brennan) 259 W. 14th

Vancampen O. W. & Son (Otto W. & Otto W. Vancampen jr.) 17 Jay

Vancampen Brothers & Co. (refused) 326 Pearl

Vancortlandt Park Land Improvement Co. (Joel B. Erhardt, Pres.; Wood D. Loudoun, Sec. Capital, $600,000. Trustees : Joel B. Erhardt, Guy R. Pelton, Augustus Van Cortlandt jr. John R. Voorhis, Howard Carroll, George H. Lowerre, Wood D. Loudoun) 15 Broad

Vancott G. & R. (Gabriel & Richard) 114 Clinton pl.

Vancott J. M. & A. H. (Joshua M. & Alexander H.) 45 William

Vancott & Terhune (Whitfield Vancott & William Terhune) 179 Wooster

Vandemark & Palmer (Henry S. Vandemark & William W. Palmer) 111 B'way

Vandenborg L. & Co. (Louis & Rosalie Vandenberg) 107 W. 40th

Vandenburg & Co. (Peter T. Vandenburg & Harry T. Finley) 19 Whitehall

Vandenhouten & Co (William F. Vandenhouten & John Harding) 45 Liberty & 256 Pearl

Vanderbeck & Brother (William H. & George W. Vanderbeck) 216 W. 37th

Vanderbilt & Hopkins (Edward W. Vanderbilt & Edward M. Hopkins) 120 Liberty

Vanderbilt & Reynolds (Oliver de G. Vanderbilt & Edward R. Reynolds) 7 Lispenard

Vanderburgh, Wells & Co. (Alexander Vanderburgh & Heber Wells, no Co.) 110 Fulton & 18 Dutch

Vanderhoef & Co. (Nathaniel S. W. & Harman B. Vanderhoef & Sherman B. Hall) 171 Greene

Vanderhoof & Co. (no inf.) 80 B'way

Vanderpoel, Cuming & Goodwin (James R. Cuming, Almon Goodwin, Augustus H. Vanderpoel, Delos McCurdy, Henry Thompson, John Yard, Richard W. Freedman & Charles V. Yates) 2 Wall

Vanderveer & Holmes Biscuit Co. (John R. Vanderveer, Pres.; Benjamin B. Vanderveer, Sec. Capital, $20,000. Directors : John R. & Benjamin B. Vanderveer & Louis C. Fuller) 396 Washn. 58 Vesey & 701 Elton av.

Vanderveer & Vanvliet (Frank F. Vanderveer & Purdy Vanvliet) 120 B'way

Vandesande Charles & Co. (Charles Vandesande, no Co.) 108 B'way

Vandewater S. & Co. (Eliza Vandewater, only) 114 Hudson

Vandien G. H. & Son (Garrett H. & John L. Vandien) 1040 Tenth av.

Vandolsen A. & Son (dissolved) 103 S. 5th av.

Vanduzer & Co. (Selah R. Vanduzer, no Co.) 35 Barclay & 40 Park pl.

Vanduzer & Taylor (Henry S. Vanduzer & Thomas F. Taylor) 31 Nassau

Vaudyck & Williams (William B. & Thomas B. Williams, only) 30 Broad

Vandyk James & Co. (no inf.) 103 Front

Van Emburgh & Atterbury (David B. Van Emburgh & John T. Atterbury :—special partner, Seth B. French. $150,000 ; terminates, 31st Dec. 1892) 17 Broad & 10 W. 23d

Van Gaasbeek & Arkell (Amos C. Van Gaasbeek & Bartlett Arkell) 935 B'way

Vangelder H. E. & Son (dissolved) 10 Maiden la.

Vangelder & Co. (John S. Vangelder & Charles P. Read) 16 W. 3d

Vanhoesen & Brother (Charles R. Vanhoesen, only) 57 South

Vanholten Brothers (August & William H. Vanholten) 231 Mulberry

Vanhorn F. S. & Co. (Frederick S. Vanhorn, no Co.) 54 Warren

Vanhorn & Ellison (Alfred Vanhorn & Guy R. P. Ellison) 113 Park av.

Vanhorn & Sowdon (Sarah W. Vanhorn & Augusta W. Sowdon) 304 Grand

Vanhorne & Jackson (John G. Vanhorne & Charles E. Jackson) 15 Cortlandt

Vanhorne, Griffen & Co. (Daniel A. Vanhorne, Benjamin Griffen & Charles W. Vanhorne) 133 Franklin

Vaningen E. H. & Co. (Edward H. Vaningen & David T. Leahy) 490 B'way

Vankoughnet Brothers (William R. Vankoughnot, only) 141 Reade

Vankuyck Henry & Son (dissolved) 237 Centre

Vanliew H. A. & Co. (Henry A. Vanliew :—special partners, Othniel Deforest, $20,000 & Charles A. Klots, B'klyn, N. Y., $5,000 ; terminates, 7th Nov. 1894) 1 Greene

Vanliew & Deforest (dissolved) 1 Greene

Vanloan J. & Co. (John & Zelah Vanloan) 21 E. 14th

Vanname Brothers (Peter & Jacob & William H. Vanname) ft. W. 10th

Vanness J, Newton & Co. (J. Newton Vanness, Alexander T. Vannest & Edward G. Jewett) 120 Chambers

Vannest A. R. & Co. (Alexander T. Vannest, J. Newton Vanness & Edward G. Jewett, only) 50 Warren

Vannett J. M. & Son (James M. & William P. Vannett) 652 Eighth av.

Vannostrand D., Co. (Edward N. Crane, Pres.; William H. Farrington, Sec. Capital, $50,-000. Trustees: Sarah A. Vannostrand, Edward D. Crane, William H. Farrington, Charles E. Spiers, Stephen G. Bogert, Charles Collins, Charles E. Wilson) 23 Murray & 27 Warren

Vannostrand Express Co. (Carman & Smith, proprs.) 117 John, 117 W. B'way, 81 Hudson & 290 & 313 Canal

Vannostrand H. & Co. (Henry D. Vannostrand & Hampton A. Coursen) 307 G'wich

Vanopstal & Co. (Andrew & John & Alfred Vanopstal) 408 Madison & 136 Chrystie

Vanorden Corset Co. (John M. Vanorden, propr.) 22 Clinton pl.

Vanorden Edward & Co. (Edward Vanorden, Co. refused) 110 John

Vanorden Brothers (Franklin C. Vanorden, only) ft. Perry

Vanpraag David J. & Co. (David J. Vanpraag & Arthur Doyo) 82 South

Vanpraag A. & Co. (Adolph Vanpraag & Thomas J. Savage) 18 Desbrosses

PROTECTION For Family, Home, Store, Factory, etc., by using only the "VULCAN" BRAND OF SAFETY MATCHES. Headquarters, 373 Washington Street, New York.

VAN 312 VER

Vanraden A. M. & Co. (Augustus M. Vanraden & John H. Knarr) 30 Spring
Vanriper Charles & Co. (Charles & Josiah P. Vanriper) 157 E. 126th
Vanrossem A. C. & Co. (Adriaan C. Vanrossem, no Co.) 4 Stone
Vansantvoord C. & Abraham (Cornelius & Abraham) 56 B'way
Vansantvoord & Hauff (John Vansantvoord & William Hauff) 41 Park row
Vansaun & Zeltner (Peter D. Vansaun & Joseph K. Zeltner) 14 John
Vanschaick & Co. (Jenkins Vanschaick, Augustus S. Gorham & Louis L. S. Clearman) 32 Broad
Vansingerlandt G. J. W. & Co. (no int.) 1124 Tenth av.
Vansyckle J. H. & Co. (dissolved) 80 John
Vantassel E. M. & Co. (Emery M. Vantassel & Charles B. Hillhouse) ft. W. 11th
Vantassel I. G. & Son (dissolved) 217 E. 122d
Vantassell & Kearney (Edward & Edward W. Kearney, only) 180 E. 13th
Vantine A. A. & Co. (James I. Raymond & Henry K. Bull jr. only) 879 B'way
Vantine A. C. & Co. (Albert C. Vantine & Paul Williams;—special partner, George E. Faile, $4,000; terminates 1st Jan. 1892) 77 Chambers
Vantine & Wehrman (Colin Vantine & Angust W. Wehrman) 37 Spring
Vanuxem L. C. & Co. (Louis C. Vanuxem & William L. More) 280 B'way
Van Valin & Co. (John H. Van Valin & M. O. Beekman) 32 Liberty
Vanvalkenburgh & Hall (Joseph D. Vanvalkenburgh jr. & William Hall) 71 Wall
Vanvalkenburgh & Ronk (Benjamin F. Vanvalkenburgh & Henry K. Ronk) 288 G'wich
Vanvilet D. M. & Co. (Deuse M. Vanvilet, no Co. 4 Stone
Vanvilet F. G. & I. N. (Frederick G. & Isaac N.) 402 Produce Ex.
Vanvolkenburgh P. & Co. (Edward & Thomas S. & estate of Philip Vanvolkenburgh) 62 Worth & 31 Thomas
Vauvorst E. & Co. (no inf.) 43 W. 28th
Vanvorst & Co. (George E. Vanvorst & Gilbert Plowman) 601 W. 33d
Vanwagoner & Williams Co. (Cornelius S. Vanwagoner, Pres.; Christian T. Stork, Sec.; William H. Williams, Treas. Capital, $50,000. Directors; Cornelius S. Vanwagoner, Christian T. Stork, William H. Williams) 82 Beekman
Vanwart & Rutherford (W. Irving Vanwart & Henry L. Rutherford) 79 Cedar
Vanwickle A. S. & Co. (Augustus S. Vanwickle & J. Wallace Morrell) 1 B'way
Vanwoert A. B. & Brother (Andrew B. & William A. Vanwoert) 9 Ninth av.
Vanwoert J. V. & Co. (John V. & Francis G. & James B. Vanwoert) 86 Ferry
Varian & O'Brien (Jacob Varian & John O'Brien) Av. A n E. 92d
Varian & Ward (Jacob Varian & Eugene Ward) 248 Bleecker
Varnum & Harison (James M. Varnum & Richard M. Harison) 81 Nassau
Vassar Burglar Alarm Mfg. Co. (John Simpson, Sec.; Louis A. Fellows, Treas. Capital, $90,000. Directors: John Simpson, Louis A. Fellows, Charles E. Corwin, Robert G. Vassar) 56 Warren
Vassar George & Son (George & George Vassar jr.) 133 Monroe
Vassar M. & Co. (James V. Harbottle & Oliver H. Booth, only) 455 G'wich
Vassilladas Brothers (dissolved) 58 Church

Vastolo Brothers (Lorenzo & Carmine Vastolo) 15 Rector
Vatable H. A. & Son (Emile & Jules & Augusto Vatable, only) 69 Water
Vatican Library Co. (dissolved) 12 Barclay
Vaughan F. S. & Sons (Eleazar S. & Jerome W. & Frederick A. & Edmund A. Vaughan) 108 Maiden la.
Vaughan T. & Co. (Thomas & Edward Vaughan) 42 W. 125th
Vaughn Automatic Machine Co. (Joseph M. Pray, Pres.; Anna H. Read, Sec. Capital, $100,000. Trustees: John W. Vaughn, Joseph M. Pray, Henry Read) 35 Liberty
Vause L. N. & Son (Lewis N. & William F. Vause) 781 B'way
Vaux & Co. (Calvert Vaux, Samuel Parsons jr., Downing Vaux & George K. Radford) 79 Bible h.
Vaux & Radford (Calvert Vaux & George Kent Radford) 76 Bible h.
Veole Bag & Package Co. (A. L. Case & Co. proprs.) 320 Wash'n.
Vedder & Budelman (Henry Budelman & estate of Henry N. Vedder) ft. W. 132d
Vedder & Harris (Albert C. Vedder & David B. Harris) 21 Fulton
Vega, Morton & Co. (Joseph A. Vega & Frank B. Morton, no Co.) 187 Pearl
Vehslage Brothers (J. Henry & John H. G. Vehslage) 69 Ninth av. & 72 N. Moore
Veil Brothers (J. Henry & Julius F. Veil) 116 Chambers
Veit, Son & Co. (Bernard Veit, Norman Sinauer, Maurice Veit & Albert Eiken) 629 B'way & 156 Crosby
Veith A. & H. (Albert & Hugo G.) 828 B'way & 190 Mercer
Venable & Heyman (George W. Venable & Moses J. Heyman) 22 Reade
Vendt M. & L. (Mary & Lucy) 184 E. 56th
Venner C. H. & Co. (Clarence H. Venner & William A. Underwood) 31 Pine
Verdcross V. & Co. (Vincent Verdcross & Anthony Licardo) 2076 Seventh av.
Verdier & Schultz (Gaston Verdier & Ernest Schultz) 480 B'way
Vermeule & Bien (Cornelius C. Vermeule & Joseph R. Bien) 71 B'way
Vermilya R. W. & C. H. (R. Willard & Charles H.) 1598 Ninth av.
Vermilye & Co. (James A. Trowbridge, Donald Mackay, Latham A. Fish, Frederick K. Trowbridge, George D. Mackay, William A. Read & Edwin D. Trowbridge, only) 16 Nassau
Vermont Marble Co. (Fletcher D. Proctor, Pres.; Fisher A. Baker, Sec.; Frank C. Partridge, Treas. Capital, $3,000,000. Directors: Fletcher D. Proctor, Francis B. Riggs, Frank C. Partridge, Adolphus Smedberg, Samuel A. Howard, Fisher A. Baker, Sidney W. Rowell, Thomas S. Williams, Edmund R. Morse) 35 Hancock pl.
Vermont Valley R. R. Co. (Azariah B. Harris, Pres.; James H. Williams, Treas. Capital, $1,000,000. Directors: Azariah B. Harris, Henry C. Robinson, Frederick Billings, Henry B. Folsom, Oscar Edwards, James H. Williams, Hugh Henry) 45 B'way
Vornam & Co. (Albert H. Varnam & Edward N. Bond) 34 New
Vernon S. E. & M. (Samuel E. & Miles) 69 Duane
Vernon Brothers & Co. (Thomas & George R. & T. Alfred Vernon) 67 Duane
Verplanck Brothers (dissolved) 92 Chambers
Verre Michel & Son (Michel & Frank Verre) 155 Elizabeth
Verrinder & Derbyshire (William Verrinder jr.

IDEN & CO., MANUFACTURERS OF
University Place, 9th to 10th Sts., N. Y. | **GAS FIXTURES AND ELECTROLIERS**

VER 313 VON

William H. Derbyshire & Arnold G. Verrinder) 1 & 17 Cooper Union

Vertical Tube Boiler Co. (Antonio Rasines, Pres.; Charles A. Mapes, Sec.; Thomas Crawford, Treas. Capital, $100,000. Directors: Antonio Rasines, Thomas Crawford, Richard Webber, Edward F. Steers, Charles W. Dayton, Theodore T. Barringer, Frederick A. Strang) 2225 Third av.

Vesey Ann A. & Catharine, 171 E. 62d

Vessel Owners' & Captains' National Assn. (James A. Vanbrunt, Pres.; Frederick F. Litchfield, Sec.; James H. Cox, Treas.) 17 William

Vessie & Bowers (David J. Vessie & William J. Bowers) 115 Broad

Vesta Oil Works (Albert K. Gregory, propr.) 184 Maiden la.

Veterinary Medicine Supply Co. (inoperative) 15 B'way

Veterinary Pharmaceutical Co. (not inc.) (Paul Weber & Mark L. Frey) 1330 Lex. av.

Vetter George F. & Sons (George F. & George F. jr. & Henry & Frederick Vetter) 309 Sixth av.

Vetter F. & Sons (Frank & Frank jr. & John Vetter) 402 & 502 E. 17th

Vetter J. C. & Co. (Joseph C. & Alexander F. Vetter) 214 E. 47th

Veysey & Veysey (William H. & Walter H. P. Veysey) 31 Nassau

Vicini J. B. & Co. (Juan B. Vicini & Santiago Porcella) 93 Wall

Vickers' Paxon, Sons (Thomas L. & Sumner P. Vickers) 180 Water

Victor Caloric Engine Co. (no. inf.) 5 Beekman

Victor Enameling Co. (no inf.) 96 Chambers

Victoria Mfg. Co. (Charles D. Thompson, Pres. Capital, $5,000. Trustees: Charles M. Wilcox; further inf. unattainable) no address

Vidoto & McDonald (no inf.) 2389 Third av.

Viebrook & Kampa (Jacob Viebrook & John Kampa) 84 Rector

Viele A. & Son (dissolved) 3 Hudson

Vienna Model Bakery (Louis Fleischmann, propr.) 766 B'way & Av. B, c E. 21st

Vienna Novelty Co. (Ferdinand Schloss, propr.) 217 Centre

Vierow V. & Co. (Victor Vierow & Victor E. Downer) 426 West

Victor Frederick & Achelis (George F. & Carl Victor & Thomas & John Achelis, only) 68 Leonard

Villard Freres & A. Mollnard (dissolved) 478 B'way

Vincent C. R. & Co. (engines) (Charles R. Vincent & Thomas C. Wood) 15 Cortlandt

Vincent C. R. & Co. (strips) (Charles R. Vincent, no Co.) 74 W. 22d

Vincent C. S. & W. F. (Charles S. & William F.) 41 Beekman

Vincent G. N. & Co. (Gibson N. Vincent & Harry Hawk) 465 Hudson & 779 Tenth av.

Vineta Paper Mills (Henry Gade, propr.) 349 Broome

Vinot & Twyeffort (dissolved) 253 Fifth av.

Virano & Co. (Frederick Virano, Co. refused) 1267 B'way

Virgil Practice Clavier Co. (E. M. Bowman, Pres; Almon K. Virgil, Treas.; Charles S. Virgil, Sec. Capital, $30,000. Directors: E. M. Bowman, Almon K. & Charles S. Virgil) 12 E. 17th

Virginia Buffalo Lithia Springs Co. (inoperative) 1 D'way

Virginia Gold Mining Co. (inoperative) 35 Liberty

Virginia Midland Railway Co. (Thomas M. Logan, Pres.; William H. Marbury, Sec. Capital, $6,000,000. Directors: George Parsons, Cal-

vin S. Brice, George F. Stone, Emanuel Lehman, John H. Inman, C. C. Holland, William H. Payne, James B. Pace, J. C. Mahen, J. A. Rutherford, George S. Scott, John McAnerny, John S. Barbour, C. M. Blackford, I. T. Lovell, E. D. Christian) 2 Wall

Virginia Mining & Improvement Co. (Azariah B. Harris, Pres.; William G. McIntyre, Sec.; further inf. unattainable) 45 D'way

Visitors' Exchange (Ltd.) (Capital, $25,000 ; further inf. unattainable) no address

Visual Synchroniam Co. (Thomas E. Waggaman, Pres.; Frederick C. Algeltinger, Sec.; Arthur W. Sherman, Treas. Capital, $6,000,000 ; further inf. unattainable) 21 W. 23d

Vita Co. (Henry M. Pierson, Pres.; Mansfield B. Snevily, Treas.; Charles E. Hubbard, Sec. Capital, $100,000. Directors: Henry M. Pierson, Mansfield B. Snevily, Charles E. Hubbard) 27 Water

Vix Jacob & Son (Jacob & George Vix) 620 Ninth av.

Voelcker Brothers (Conrad & Gustav Voelcker) 26 Spruce

Voelmy Brothers (Henry & Henry jr. & Albert Voelmy) r 418 W. 27th

Vogel F. & Co. (Frederick Vogel & John G. McCarthy) 84 Bowery & 220 E. 27th

Vogel Brothers (William & Heyman & Jacob & Louis Vogel) 607 B'way, 665 Eighth av. & 22 Av. A

Vogel & Brautigam (William H. Vogel & Henry Brautigam) 104 Park pl.

Vogel & Sons (Henry & William H."& Max H. Vogel) 796 & 2265 Third av.

Vogel & Whelan Cable Co. (Calvin Goddard, Pres.; Henry B. Hanford, Sec.; Orson G. McCall, Treas. Capital, $1,000,000. Directors: Calvin Goddard, Henry S. Van Duzer, Wendell Godwin, William G. Bumstead, Orson G. McCall, Charles Vogel) 45 D'way

Vogt Carl & Son (Carl & Charles Vogt jr.) 153 Canal

Vogt Charles & Co. (Charles & Charles B. Vogt) 182 Church

Vogt J. H. & Brother (John H. & George Vogt) 877 Hudson

Vogt Brothers (John & Charles Vogt) 104 William

Vogt & Doss (Frederick Dose, only) 43 Barclay

Voile & Wortley (refused) 151 Crosby

Voit Brothers (Selig & Meyer Voit) 107 Walker

Volokoning & Gerken (Charles G. C. Volokoning & Louis H. Gerken) 80 Old sl. & 1818 Av. B

Volckhausen C. L. & Co. (Charles L. Volckhausen, no Co.) 88 W. 3d

Volino & Son (Joseph & Peter Volino) 51 Crosby

Volkening & Co. (Bertha & Otto Volkening & Charles Plock) 228 E. 44th

Vollman Sponge Co. (not inc.) (Benjamin & Samuel & Morris Vollman) 93 William

Vollman & Gulke (Frederick Vollman & August W. Gulke) 821 G'wich

Volpe Francisco & Co. (Francisco Volpe & Michele Gallo) 56 Mulberry

Volz Brothers (Frank & Edward Volz) 820 Second av.

Volzing Christian & Son (Christian & Frederick Volzing & Otto H. Dage) 953 Third av.

Vomcleff & Co. (Robert Vomcleff & William Oppitz) 108 Duane

Vondannenberg C. & Co. (Carl Vondannenberg & Patrick A. Mahoney) 20 Vesey

Vondehsen & Bruse (dissolved) 21-19 Eighth av.

Vondestinen & Knoblauch (Emil Vondestinen & J. C. Charles Knoblauch) 86 Cotton Ex.

Vondohlen & Old (Theodore Vondohlen & Henry H. Old) 64 Mercer

Vonsiff G. & W. Vonscheele (dissolved) 347 G'wich

TYPEWRITING DONE BY THE TROW CITY DIRECTORY CO., 11 University Place.

VON　　　　　314　　　　　WAL

Vonglahn Brothers (Gustav T. Vonglahn, only) 781 Seventh av.
Vongraof Medical Co. (inf. unattainable) 3 Park row
Vonhagen Ferdinand & Co. (Ferdinand Vonhagen & Gustav Friedel) 120 Cedar
Vonhaus & Co. (Louise & Emma Vonhaus) 11 E. 14th
Vonhoffmann L. & Co. (Louis A. Vonhoffmann & William Mertens) 50 Wall
Vonlengerke & Detmold (Justus Vonlengerke & Ernst Detmold) 8 Murray
Von Minden & Eberth (Henry Von Minden & George Eberth) 125 Grand
Vono H. & Co. (Hans Vono & Thomas H. Werner) 21 Bond
Vonrunnen J. & H. (John & Henry) 1394 B'way
Vonsachs W. & Sons (Julius H. Vonsachs, only) 25 William
Vontwistern & Fischer (William Vontwistern & John H. Fischer) 649 W. 42d
Vonwieding & Tietjen (Christopher Vonwieding & Dederick Tietjen) 2325 First av.
Voorhies & Schults (dissolved) 184 Pearl & 100 Water
Voorhis & Vreeland (James H. Voorhis & Enoch H. Vreeland) 258 Washn.
Vorbach & Fuchs (dissolved) 283 E. 4th
Voss Brothers (no inf.) 54 Beaver
Voss & Stern (Philip Voss & Isaac Stern) 446 B'way
Vought & Williams (Isaac S. Vought & John O. Williams) 193 West
Vredenburgh & Brooks (Peter Vredenburgh & Nathan F. Penn, only) 104 Fifth av.
Vroman S. & Co. (Sanford & Peter Vroman) 601 W. 33d
Vulcan Oil Works (Joseph A. Bluxome, propr.) 49 Front
Vulcanized Fibre Co. (William Courtenay, Pres.; Frank Taylor, Sec. Capital, $211,000. Directors: William Courtenay, E. Bringhurst jr. J. Cummings Vail, W. W. Snow, Frederick Pierson, Joseph McDaniels) 14 Dey
Vyse & Vernam (Arthur F. Vyse & William S. Vernam) 60 B'way

W

Wabash R. R. Co. (Ossian D. Ashley, Pres.; John C. Ottesen, Sec.; James F. How, Treas. Capital, $52,000,000. Directors: Ossian D. Ashley, Edgar T. Wells, Thomas H. Hubbard, Henry K. McHarg, George J. Gould, Russell Sage, John T. Terry, James F. Joy, James F. How, Samuel C. Reynolds, Charles M. Hayes, Cyrus J. Lawrence, Sidney Dillon) 195 B'way
Wabash Western Railway Co. (dissolved) 195 B'way
Wachenheimer I. & Co. (dissolved) 687 Third av.
Wacheman & Pollak (Siegmund Wacheman & Felix G. Pollak) 9 Walker
Wacker & Kruegel (August Wacker & John K. Kruegel) 317 W. 40th
Waddell R. J. & Co. (Robert J. Waddell, no Co.) 52 Beekman
Waddell-Entz Electric Co. (Montgomery Waddell, Pres.; Jose A. Machado, Sec.; Justus B. Entz Treas. Capital, $100,000. Directors: Montgomery Waddell, Justus B. Entz, Jose A. Machado, Alfred A. Whitman, Ferdinand S. Entz) 50 B'way
Wade Button Co. (Wade & Curtis, proprs.) 207 Centre
Wade H. D. & Co. (William D. Wade, only) 117 Fulton
Wade & Curtis (George A. Wade & Herbert Curtis) 207 Centre

Wadsworth T. & H. Brothers (no inf.) 174 Franklin
Waentig, Solinger & Co. (Charles R. Waentig, Leopold Solinger & John W. Palmer) 112 Franklin
Wagar, Martin & Co. (Mortimer H. Wagar & James M. Martin, no Co.) 210 Produce Ex.
Wager & Acker (George W. Wager & Edward A. Acker) 287 B'way
Wagner Brush Co. (Irving Schmidt, propr.) 28 College pl.
Wagner George D. & Co. (dissolved) 134 Grand
Wagner Louis C. & Co. (Louis C. Wagner, no Co.) 79 Duane
Wagner Mfg. Co. (Philip Wagner, propr.) 712 B'way
Wagner Palace Car Co. (W. Seward Webb, Pres.; James D. Taylor, Sec.; further inf. unattainable) Vanderbilt av. c E. 44th
Wagner Philip & Co. (dissolved) 28 College pl.
Wagner H. & Co. (dissolved) 389 Bowery
Wagner Brothers (Isaac & Louis Wagner) 984 Third av.
Wagner & Co. (dissolved) 75 Murray
Wagner & Fountain (dissolved) 1622 B'way
Wagner & Lopard (dissolved) 1 Gt. Jones
Wagner & Sandford (Henry Wagner & Mark E. Sandford) 359 Bowery
Wagner, Kellam & Co. (Charles K. Wagner, Moses K. Kellam, Albert O. Allen & John F. Opdycke) 76 Murray
Wahlers & Cordes (Herman D. Wahlers & Charles H. Cordes) 56 West & 251 Church
Wait, Creighton & Morrison (Clarence Creighton & Cornelius Morrison, only) 87 Wall
Waite & Bartlett Mfg. Co. (Henry E. Waite, Pres.; Henry C. Beers, Sec. Capital, $10,000. Directors: Henry E. Waite, Samuel H. Bartlett, Henry C. Beers, Horatio J. Brewer, John Alexander Beall) 148 & 204 E. 23d
Waite, Thresher & Co. (William Waite & Henry G. Thresher, no Co.) 176 B'way
Waitzfelder & Seligman (Napoleon B. Waitzfelder & Adolph Seligman) 421 B'way
Wakeman John & Co. (John & Stephen H. Wakeman) 65 Broad
Wakeman & Campbell (Thaddeus B. Wakeman & Alfred B. Campbell) 98 Nassau
Walcott J. C. & Co. (Joseph C. Walcott, no Co.) 82 Pine
Wald & Serphos (Adolph Wald & Solomon N. Serphos) 733 B'way
Walde & Co. (dissolved) 311 Bowery
Walden C. C. & Co. (Charles C. Walden, no Co.) 29 Park row
Walden & Co. (Edward & Franklin & Lienau Walden) 41 Beaver
Waldheim Brothers (Henry & Nicholas Waldheim jr.) 34 W. 68th
Waldman, Burke & Ogden (dissolved) 117 Barrow
Waldron James T. & Co. (dissolved) 135 Duane
Waldron J. V. & Brother (Joseph V. & Charles F. Waldron) 54 Cliff
Waldron & Co. (dissolved) 1059 Third av.
Wales E. H. & Co. (dissolved) 74 B'way
Wales & Co. (Edward H. Wales, William L. Stow, George B. Parsons & William G. Read jr.) 74 B'way
Walfish L. & J. Rasmbow (Lazarus Walfish & Joseph Rasnbow) 126 Madison
Walker Electric Co. (Edwin Scott, Pres.; Lewis G. Tewksbury, Sec. Capital, $200,000. Directors: Edwin Scott, Lewis G. Tewksbury, George W. Walker, James M. Sigafus, E. A. Elliott, A. W. Goodell, Charles R. Truex) 50 B'way

THE CALIGRAPH WRITING MACHINE,
HARTFORD, CONN.

WAL 315 WAL

Walker George & Sons (George & William G. & Charles A. Walker) 656 Ninth av.
Walker James E. & Co. (Charles C. Skinner & Thaddeus Piza, only) 3 Burling sl.
Walker John & Son (no inf.) 1a Platt
Walker John T., Son & Co. (John T. & Joseph Walker & John W. Combs) 81 Pine & 87 Greene
Walker Joseph & Co. (no inf.) 104 Franklin
Walker Joseph & Sons (Joseph & Joseph jr. & E. Robbins Walker) 15 Broad
Walker Thomas & Co. (Thomas Walker, no Co.) 156 Greene
Walker F. R. & Son (Fernando R. & John H. Walker) 16 Reade
Walker Brothers (Calvin B. & Amos J. Walker) 85 B'way
Walker & Armstrong (Stuart S. Walker & John Armstrong) 1971 Third av.
Walker & Beman (dissolved) 255 W. 125th
Walker & Bresnan (Silliman R. Walker & Patrick H. Bresnan) 201 William
Walker & Co. (millinery) (refused) 237 Sixth av.
Walker & Co. (novelties) (Abram Walker, no Co.) 274 Grand
Walker & Co. (real estate) (Samuel Y. & D. M. Walker) 255 W. 125th
Walker & Coughlan (James Walker & Patrick Coughlan) 323 Av. A
Walker & Hockler (Sophia Walker & Wilhelmina Hockler) 557 Second av.
Walker & Hughes (William A. & Dexter H. Walker & Joseph C. Hughes) 63 Wall
Walker & Roon (William H. Walker & Patrick J. Roon) 110 Leroy
Walker & Thompson (dissolved) 145 E. 23d
Walker, Son & Co. (no inf.) 2002 Seventh av.
Walker's E., Son (James E. Walker) 20 Jacob
Walker's William C., Sons (William & John & James Walker) 209½ B'way
Walkinshaw & Voigt (Carl Voigt, John T. Hand & Augustus J. Rollé:—special partners, Henry Pastor, Aix-la-Chapelle, Germany, & Herman A. Lackemann, Bremen, Germany, each $62,-500; terminates 31st Dec. 1891) 83 Worth
Wall Street Bureau Associated Press (N. Y. City Press Assn. propr.) 57 B'way
Wall J. & Son (Jacob & John L. Wall) 838 Sixth av.
Wall's William, Sons (Frank T. & Eliza A. Wall, only) 118 Wall & 58 South
Wallace James & Son (James & Thomas F. Wallace) 384 Cherry
Wallace William H. & Co. (William H. Wallace, William Bispham & Edward O. Wallace) 181 Washn. & 12 Albany
Wallace F. B. & Co. (Morris H. Smith & Edward Linn, only) 56 Broad
Wallace Brothers (liquors) (Thomas J. & James F. Wallace) 86 Sixth av.
Wallace Brothers (mers.) (Isaac & David & William Wallace) 280 B'way
Wallace & Co. (William L. Wallace & Frank C. Swan) 31 Cortlandt
Wallace & Drake (James Wallace & James Drake) 1801 Third av.
Wallace & Keeney (Benjamin M. Wallace & Griswold I. Keeney) 10 Fulton fish mkt
Wallace & Sons (William Wallace, Pres.; John B. Wallace, Sec.; Thomas Wallace, Treas. Capital, $10,000. Directors: William & Thomas & John B. & William O. Wallace, Urinh T. Hungerford, Robert R. Wood, Charles H. Hayes) 29 Chambers
Wallace, Elliott & Co. (Edwin Wallace, Henry Elliott, John E. Jacobs & Clinton Elliott) 118 Duane

Wallace, Turner & Van Buren (David S. Wallace, Clifford G. Turner & Thomas B. Van Buren) 48 Mercer
Wallace's Trotting Register Co. (John H. Wallace, Pres.; Leslie E. Macleod, Sec.; Robert L. Wallace, Treas. Capital, $100,000. Trustees: John H. Wallace, Guy Miller, Albert E. Whyland, Henry C. Jewett, Charles D. Sibley, Leslie R. Macleod, J. C. Sibley, Charles Beekman, R. S. Veech, Samuel G. Boyle, S. H. Rundle, O. F. Emery, Norman J. Colman) 280 B'way
Wallach Julius & Joseph G. 753 Sixth av. & 154 E. 87th
Wallach Willy (Willy Wallach, Edgar S. Blackwell & William L. Martin) 281 B'way
Wallach Brothers (Meyer & Samuel & Jacob Wallach) 244 Dowery
Wallach & Cohen (Adolph Wallach & Alfred N. Cohen) 1108 Seventh av. 167 Third av. 408, 420, 731 & 749 Sixth av. 916 Ninth av. 203 W. 23d & 200 W. 14th
Wallach's A., Nephews (Leopold & Max Rosenberg, Samuel & Nathan Wallach & Sigmund M. & Louis Schiele) 5 Maiden la. & 72 Spring
Wallach's H., Sons (Isaac Wallach, Solomon Moses & Solomon Weill, only) 88 Thomas, 123 Duane & 94 Mott
Wallenhauer E. & G. Kuehn (dissolved) 1 Chambers
Wallenstein & Co. (dissolved) no address
Waller Robert jr. & Co. (Robert Waller jr. & Sidney H. Salomon) 48 Exchange pl.
Waller H. T. W. & Co. (dissolved) 50 B'way
Waller M. D. & Co. (dissolved) 350 Sixth av.
Waller W. & W. B. (William & William D.) 212 E. 9th
Walling & Henn (Elbert J. Walling & Louis G. Henn) 24 Fulton & 16 Fulton mkt
Wallis Sisters (Almira & Emily Wallis) 127 W. 24th
Wallkill Valley R. R. Co. (Ashbel Green, Pres.; Edward V. W. Rossiter, Sec. Capital, $330,-000. Directors: Ashbel Green, Charles H. Coster, Walter Katte, Herbert B. Kinney, James D. Layng, James W. Musson, Edward V. W. Rossiter, Lawrence Depew, Joseph P. Ord, William H. Sanford, Albert B. Taylor, Donald B. Toncey, William E. Taylor) Grand Central depot & 5 Vanderbilt av.
Walls & Vanriper (Peter Walls & Charles Vanriper) 167 E. 128th
Wallstein & Heinemann (no inf.) 500 Broome
Wallum & Crist (John Wallum & Frank Crist) 124 Elizabeth
Walnut Grove Water Storage Co. (Henry S. Van Beuren Pres.; Dewitt C. Bates, Sec. Capital, $12,000,000. Directors: Henry S. & Frederick T. Van Beuren, J. W. A. Davis, Dewitt C. & Wells H. Bates, Edward F. Brown, Edward R. Chadbourne, Charles H. Dillingham) 11 Wall
Walsh James & Son (James & Thomas J. Walsh) 5 Wall
Walsh James A. & Co. (James A. & James A. Walsh jr.) 116 & 118 Wall
Walsh M. & E. (Mary & Ella) 2252 Third av.
Walsh T. & A. (Thomas & Augustine) 114 Wall
Walsh Brothers (Richard H. & John J. Walsh) 16 W. 14th
Walsh & Campbell (dissolved) 61 Frankfort
Walsh & Co. (George Walsh, John J. Joyce & Eliza Walsh) 404 G'wich
Walsh & Floyd (James W. Walsh jr. & Nicoll Floyd jr.) 26 Broad
Walsh & O'Neill (James Walsh & Ann O'Neill) 145 W. 35th
Walsh & Powers (John F. Walsh & Robert C. Powers) 1194 Lex. av.
Walsh & Pye (dissolved) 109 W. Houston

SPECIAL ATTENTION PAID TO THIS CLASS OF WORK } **BANKERS' & BROKERS' CIRCULARS DELIVERED** { **THE TROW CITY DIRECTORY CO.** 11 University Place.

WAL   316   WAR

Walsh & Roville (Joseph Walsh & Richard J. Reville) 32d First av.

Walsh & Wertheim (James R. Walsh & Samuel J. Wertheim) 65 W. Houston

Walsh, Kirby & Co. (John J. Walsh, Ellen Kirby & David O'Brien) 618 W. 59th & 312 W. 60th

Walstrom E. de & Co (dissolved) 19 Whitehall

Walter Hub & Axle Co. (inoperative) 7 Murray

Walter John & Son (dissolved) 1616 Second av.

Walter H. R. & Co. (Herbert E. Walter & Ernest Anchor) 1295 Second av.

Walter Brothers (Charles F. & William G. Walter, 482 S. Boulevard; William G. & Winfield S. Walter, 577 S. Boulevard)

Walter & Call (no inf.) 355 Seventh av.

Walter & Co. (no inf.) 35 Liberty

Walter & Hillebrand (Anton Walter & Theodore Hillebrand) 164 E. Houston

Walter & Smith (Francis A. Walter & Charles Smith) 114 Maiden la.

Walter & Stearns (William H. Walter & James F. Stearns) 23 W. 23d

Walters L. M. & Co. (Luther M. Walters & David P. Durr) 347 B'way

Walters Brothers (Albert & Frank Walters) 512 Ninth av.

Walters & Buxton (dissolved) 69 Warren

Walters' Richard, Sons (Richard M. & Charles F. Walters) 1870 B'way

Waltham Watch Club Co. (—— Schneider, propr.) 10 E. 14th

Walther & Co. (Waldemar A. Walther, no Co.) 65 Duane

Walton Mfg. Co. (Joseph J. Walton, Pres; William H. Coolidge, Sec. Capital, $20,000; further inf. unattainable) 30 Church

Walton Oxygen Works (Alfred Walton, propr.) 280 Fourth av.

Walton D. S. & Co. (David S. Walton & George West) 182 Franklin

Walton J. D. & Co. (John D. & William T. Walton) 858 Eighth av.

Walton & West (David S. Walton & George West) 176 Fulton

Walworth C. A. & H. A. Spencer (dissolved) 108 E. 125th

Wals L. & Brother (Ludwig & Philip Wals) 1903 Tenth av.

Wamsley Philip & Co. (Philip & Philip G. Wamsley) 34 Greene

Wanier & Imgard (Frank Wanier, only) 1322 B'way & 101 W. 125th

Wannemacher Peter & Son (Peter & Louis Wannemacher) 296 Third

Wanner A. & Co. (dissolved) 36 W. 3d

Wanner & Heinrich (Joseph Wanner & Edward Heinrich) 69 W. Houston

Wanzor, Tobias & Co. (Moses G. Wanzor, George H. Tobias & George W. Oakley) 96 Wall

Ward Cons. Mining Co. (Watson B. Dickerman, Pres.; W. Gayer Dominick, Sec. Capital, $2,000,000. Trustees; Watson B. Dickerman, F. B. Nofsinger, George B. Greer, Bayard Dominick, George G. Nevers, A. H. Porter, Justin A. Edwards, W. Gayer Dominick, S. R. Leahor) 52 B'way

Ward Everett, Soap Co. (Everett Ward, propr.) 6 Harrison

Ward James E. & Co. (Henry P. Booth & William H. T. Hughes :—special porner, James E. Ward, Great Neck, N. Y., $200,000 ; terminates 31st Dec, 1894) 113 Wall & Pier 16 E. R.

Ward Mfg. Co. (Joseph A. Ward, Pres.; Charles H. Smyth, Sec. Capital, $1,000. Directors: Joseph A. Ward, Charles H. Smyth, Edward B. Lord) 52 Howard

Ward Owen & Sons (Owen & Peter J. & Francis D. & James P. Ward) 450 W. 39th

Ward Walworth & Co. (Walworth & Irving Ward) 104 B'way

Ward William H. & Co. (William H. Ward & Robert Ward Carroll) 68 Beekman

Ward A. H. & Co. (Augustus H. Ward & Nicholas J. Bishoprick) 89 Mercer

Ward E. & Co. (William D. Ward, only) 353 Grand

Ward E. & O. (Elizur & Orrin) 270 Washn.

Ward & Boswell (Matthew J. Ward & Eugene S. Boswell) 171 B'way

Ward & Co. (Charles R. Ward, no Co.) 154 Maiden la.

Ward & Doyle (John Ward & James Doyle) 49 Nassau & 301 E. 79th

Ward & Drummond (Samuel H. D. Ward & James L. Drummond) 711 B'way

Ward & Huntington (Josiah O. Ward & Wilbur Huntington) 87 South

Ward & Mangam (DeWitt C. Ward & Olliffe Mangam) 150 B'way

Ward & Olyphant (Robert & J. Kensett Olyphant, only) 21 Cortlandt & 412 Third

Ward's S. W. H., Sons (Joseph A. Ward, only) 52 Howard

Wardell Brothers (John J. & William H. Wardell) 321 Canal

Warden William & Sons (William & Ivie A. & William Warden jr.) 4 Stone

Wardwell Sewing Machine Co. (Clarence H. Serymser, Pres.; Henry Earle, Sec. Capital, $250,000. Trustees : Clarence H. Serymser, Henry Earle, F. M. Wells) 15 Cortlandt

Wardwell I. F. & C. S. (I. Franklin & Clolson S.) 36 W. 38th

Wardwell R, P. & Co. (Richard P. Wardwell & Henry S. Ferdon) 6 Harrison

Ware William & Sons (William & Richard & William T. & George H. Ware) 363 Produce Ex.

Warfords & Andrews (Benjamin H. & James P. Warford & William Andrews) 1 Beaver

Waring Hat Mfg. Co. (John T. Waring, Pres.; Arthur B. Waring, Sec.; further inf. unattainable) 612 B'way & 148 Crosby

Waring Mfg. Co. (John B. Waring, propr.) 15 State

Waring & Carley (dissolved) 51 Liberty

Waring & Hubbard (Joseph F. Waring & Alexander Hubbard) 24 Fourth av.

Waring & Stantial (Daniel H. Waring & John W. Stantial) 1390 Third av.

Warley Felix & Co. (Felix Warley, no Co.) 78 Cotton Ex.

Warner George P. & Co. (George P. Warner, Eugene M. Cole & John E. Whitaker) 66 Liberty

Warner A. L. & C. A. (Albion L. & Charles A.) 578 Washn.

Warner A. M. & Co. (Arion M. Warner & John T Caulfield) 40 Lispenard

Warner C. A. & Co. (Charles A. & Albion L. & Albion K. P. Warner) 33 W. 14th

Warner L. W. & Co. (Augustus H. Hall, Sec.; further inf. unattainable) 69 Murray

Warner Brothers (corsets) (Lucien C. & I. De Ver Warner) 359 B'way

Warner Brothers (Ice) (Lauren A. & John E. Warner) 412 E. 71st

Warner & Chaffee (no inf.) 253 E. 125th

Warner & Frayer (John DeWitt Warner & Eugene Frayer) 53 William

Warner & King (Robert S. Warner & William W. King) 404 Sixth av.

Warner & Wyman (Daniel W. Warner & Isaac Wyman) 18 South

Warnock & Co. (Samuel M. Warnock, no Co.) 304 Fifth av.

FOR THE BEST CO-PARTNERSHIP IN THE BEST CORPORATION SEE PAGE F IN BACK OF BOOK

Warren Chemical & Mfg. Co. (William R. Warren, Pres.; Joseph H. Hume, Sec. Capital, $100,000. Trustees: William R. Warren, William Burnham, Joseph H. Hume) 83 Fulton

Warren Iron Co. (John P. Jones, Pres.; John R. Bennett, Sec.; Joseph S. Moore, Treas. Capital, $200,000; further Inf. unattainable) 80 Broad

Warren Schuyler N. & Co. (Schuyler N. Warren, no. Co.) 61 Exchange pl.

Warren & Fowler (William S. Warren & James E. Fowler) 78 Varick

Warren & Rauth (Samuel J. Warren & Charles Rauth) 322 E. 115th

Warren & Stratton (Charles J. Warren & Amos D. Stratton) 5 South

Warren, Lange & Co. (James S. Warren, John M. Lange, George C. D. Brand, Fairman Warren & Edward F. Brand) 129 E. 42d

Warren, Wood & Co. (Henry M. Warren & Lester E. Wood, no Co.) 115 B'way

Warren-Scharf Asphalt Paving Co. (William R. Warren, Pres.; Henry R. Bradbury, Sec. Capital, $150,000. Trustees: William R. Warren, William Burnham, Joseph H. Hume) 83 Fulton

Warrin & Kniffin (George Warrin & Charles E. Kniffin) 49 Wooster

Warschawsky A. & Son (Abraham & Ephraim Warschawsky) 42 B'way

Warshauer J. & Greenberg (Jacob Warshauer & Jacob Greenberg) 7 Bowery

Washburn George & Co. (George Washburn, no Co.) 1974 Seventh av.

Washburn C. P. & Co. (Clark P. Washburn, no Co.) 96 Greene & 158 Spring

Washburn & Barnes (George W. Washburn & William H. Darms) 696 W. 80th

Washburn & Co. (Robert & Edgar Washburn) 626 W. 86th

Washburn & Moen Mfg. Co. (Philip L. Moen, Pres.; Charles F. Washburn, Sec. Capital, $1,500,000. Directors: Philip L. & Philip W. Moen, Charles F. & Charles G. Washburn) 16 Cliff & 241 Pearl

Washburne E. G. & Co. (Edward G. Washburne, no Co.) 46 Cortlandt

Washington Ammonia & Chemical Co. (dissolved) 245 B'way

Washington Brewery Co. (William Rasquin jr. Pres.; Robert Sewell, Treas.; C. V. V. Sewell, Sec. Capital, $200,000. Directors: William Rasquin jr. Monroe Crawford, Edward H. Carpenter, Frederick J. Winston, C. V. V. Sewell) 32 Nassau

Washington Bridge, Tremont & Westchester R. R. Co. (William H. Schott, Pres.; Henry B. Wesslman, Sec.; Charles V. Halley, Treas.; further Inf. unattainable) 187 B'way

Washington Building Co. (John Lindley, Pres.; Edward M. Field, Sec. Capital, $700,000. Directors: John Lindley, Edward M. Field, Daniel A. Lindley, George Waddington, Thomas E. Sulliman) 1 B'way

Washington Cemetery (Isaac Marx, Pres.; Samuel B. Hamburger, Sec.; Adolphus E. Karelsen, Treas. Trustees: Isaac Marx, Samuel B. Hamburger, Adolphus E. Karelsen, Joseph Grossmer, Salig Manilla, Adolph Crager) 201 B'way

Washington County R. R. Co. (Edward W. Sorrell, Pres.; William G. Ladd, Sec. Capital, $2,000,000; further Inf. refused) 38 Wall

Washington Express & Van Co. (William H. Hunt, propr.) 264 W. 124th

Washington Life Ins. Co. (William A. Brewer jr. Pres.; William Haxtun, Sec. Capital, $500,000. Directors: William A. Brewer jr. William Haxtun, Roland G. Mitchell, George N. Lawrence, Levi P. Morton, Abiel A. Low,

Morrill Trimble, Thomas Hope, James Thomson, Wilson G. Hunt, Charles H. Ludington, Robert Bowne, Francis Speir, Frederic R. Coudert, George Newbold, Benjamin Haxtun, Edwin H. Mead, Henry F. Hitch, Charles P. Britton, Benjamin W. McCready, David Thomson) 21 Cortlandt

Washington Market Beef Co. (Jacob L. Lissner, propr.) 278 First av.

Washington Market Sheep Co. (G. F. & E. C. Swift, proprs.) 20 West, W. Washn. mkt

Washington Steamboat Co. (Ltd.) (Robert G. Remsen, Pres.; Henry Remsen, Treas. Capital, $45,000; further Inf. refused) 115 B'way

Washington Trust Co. (David M. Morrison, Pres.; Francis H. Page, Sec. Capital, $500,000. Directors: Joseph F. Knapp, David M. Morrison, Henry H. Rodgers, Charles H. Russell, George H. Prentiss, Joel P. Freeman, L. T. Powell, George L. Pease, William H. Hall, George E. Hamlin, P. C. Lounsbury, Charles F. Clark, Theodore A. Havemeyer, Seth E. Thomas, Lucius K. Wilmerding, George A. Morrison, Joseph C. Baldwin) 280 B'way

Wasle & Co. (Simon Wasle & Anton Doll) 177 Hester

Wassermann Brothers (Jesse & Edward Wassermann) 54 Exchange pl. & 275 Church

Wasserstrom Brothers (no Inf.) 6 Av. B

Water Proof Collar Co. (no Inf.) 64 Reade

Water Waste Preventing Co. (Joseph W. Kay, Pres.; William Thompson, Sec.; Frederick A. Lovecraft, Treas. Capital, $1,000,000. Directors: Joseph W. Kay, Frederick A. Lovecraft, John Thompson, Ira M. Hodges, Frank Lambert) 5 Beekman

Waterbury Rubber Co. (William B. Fiske, Pres.; Alfred H. Howe, Sec.; George A. Howe, Treas. Capital, $100,000. Trustees: William B. Fiske, Alfred H. Howe, Joseph A. Couitaus, John Coon) 49 Warren

Waterbury L. & Co. (James M. Waterbury & Chauncey Marshall, only) 87 Pine & 132 Front

Waterbury S. & Son (Selleck & Zeno C. Waterbury) 37 Warren

Waterbury & Cox (Nelson J. & Nelson J. Waterbury jr. & Wilmot T. Cox) 82 Nassau

Waterbury & Force (William H. Force, Harry H. Lake, Isaac B. Rogers & Walter S. Force, only) 130 Front, 274 South & 344 West

Waterman L. E., Co. (Lewis E. Waterman, Pres.; Harriet J. Candee, Sec. Capital, $25,000. Trustees: Lewis E. Waterman, Harriet J. Candee, William I. Ferris) 155 B'way

Waterman & Lehmann (Charles H. Waterman & Emil A. Lehmann) 37 Maiden la.

Waters Horace & Co. (Horace Waters, Pres.; Samuel T. White, Sec.; T. Leeds Waters, Treas. Capital, $150,000. Directors: Horace & T. Leeds Waters, Samuel T. White) 134 Fifth av. & 844 E. 23d

Waters Paper Construction Co. (Charles H. Mullin, Pres.; Henry E. Irvine, Treas.; Homer W. Hedge, Sec. Capital, $200,000. Trustees: Charles H. Mullin, George A. Waters, Henry E. Irvine, Homer W. Hedge, Thomas Grimwood, W. Forno Scott, Clarence W. Waters) 115 B'way

Waters W. & Son (William & William E. Waters) 108 Fulton

Waters' John, Sons (John P. & Charles E. Waters) 12 John

Watertown Steam Blower Co. (Henry E. Parson, propr.) 48 Maiden la. & 85 Liberty

Watervliet Ice Co. (Tilley & Littlefield, proprs.) ft. W. 15th

Watjen, Toel & Co. (William Toel, only,) 70 Broad

Watkin F. W. & Co. (Frederick W. Watkin & Emile Longuemare) 4 Stone

CIRCULARS ADDRESSED TO ANY TRADE IN THE U. S. { Facilities
PROMPT, CAREFUL WORK } THE TROW CITY DIRECTORY CO., { Unequalled.
AT MODERATE PRICES. } 11 University Place.

WAT 318 WEE

Watkins, James Y. & Son (James Y. & William M. & Walter Watkins) 16 Catharine
Watkins F. H. & Co. (no inf.) 18 B'way
Watkins Brothers (William W. & Joseph & Charles Watkins) 610 Third av.
Watkins & Lewis (John W. Lewis, only) 67 W. 23d
Watling A. & Co. (Arthur Watling & Edwin B. Grove) 64½ University pl.
Watrous Walter W. & Co. (Walter W. Watrous, Charles H. Willson, Charles L. Adams, Jacob S. Curvalho & Allen W. Adams) 146 Pearl & 108 Water
Watson Egbert P. & Son (Egbert P. & Egbert P. Watson jr.) 150 Nassau
Watson J. C., Co. (Thomas A. McIntyre, Pres.; J. Curry Watson, Sec.; further inf. unattainable) E. 125th n Harlem r
Watson John W. (John W. Watson:—special partner, Ann E. Cawood, $10,000 ; terminates 31st Dec. 1691) 719 W. 38th
Watson H. B. & Co. (Henry B. & John H. Watson) 121 Front
Watson R. R, & Co. (Richard R. Watson, Pres.; L. F. Fetzer, Sec.; further inf. refused) 16 Reade
Watson W. B. & Co. (William B. Watson, no Co.) 595 Sixth av.
Watson Brother (George H. & Archibald A. Watson) 84 Broad
Watson & Blanpain (E. Frank Watson & Eleanor M. Blanpain) 6 E. 17th
Watson & Cody (Elizabeth J, Watson & Elizabeth M. Cody) 232 Sixth av,
Watson & Co. (George jr. & Edward H. & George D. Watson) 132 Nassau
Watson & Gibson (Thomas L. Watson & George R. Gibson) 55 B'way
Watson & Hagan (James Watson, Winston H. Hagan & Eugene A. Dike) 59 Wall
Watson & Karsch Mfg. Co. (John M. Karsch, Pres.; W. Morris Watson, Treas.; further inf. unattainable) 71 Bowery & 51 Chrystie
Watson & Pierce (John J. Watson & Leonard Pierce) 208 Duane
Watson & Stillman (Thomas H. Watson & Francis H. Stillman) 210 E. 43d
Watson, Bull & Co. (Austin H. Watson, John N. Bull & John I. Gisburne) 62 White
Watson's Musical-Conservatory (Anne A. Watson, propr.) 15 E. 14th
Watt & Johnstone (Charles Watt & Alexander Johnstone) 332 Produce Ex.
Watters & Loercher (John Watters & Robert Loercher) 106 Duane
Wattles' Alden, Son (Merrit Wattles) 108 Front
Wattson & Farr (John B. Wattson & John Farr) 140 Pearl & 108 Water
Waverly Refining Co. (Morris Hammerschlag, Pres.; Charles F. Teigeler, Sec, Capital, $100,000. Directors : Morris Hammerschlag, John C. Baetjer, Charles F. Teigeler, Nathan Hammerschlag, Joseph H. Rudiger) 50 Dey
Waxman Brothers & Rosman (Nahum & Jacob Waxman & Solomon Rosman) 57 Hester
Waydell & Co. (John H. & Frederic & Anderson Waydell) 21 Old sl.
Weathered's Thomas W., Sons (Charles B. & Edmund Weathered) 46 Marion
Weaver John G. jr. & Co. (John G. Weaver jr. & Frank M. Coleman) 39 E. 17th
Weaver C. A. & Co. (C. A. Weaver & John B, Ihl) 216 Fulton
Weaver S. J. & Co. (Stephen J. Weaver & Martin A. Mayer) 320 Canal & 6 Greene
Weaver Brothers (Eugene S. Weaver, only) 231 Grand

Weaver & Sterry (Ltd.) (George E. Sterry, Pres.; George E. Sterry jr. Sec.: William DeW. Sterry, Treas. Capital, $100,000. Directors : George E. & John A. & William DeW. & George E. Sterry jr.) 79 Pine & 166 Pearl
Webb James A. & Son (James A. Webb & Frederic M. Harrison, only) 165 Pearl
Webb John M. & Henry, 453 Produce Ex.
Webb A, P. & Co. (Arthur P. Webb & James O. Frain) 60 Cliff
Webb H. T. & Brother (Henry T. & Charles W. Webb) 83 Water
Webb J. & Sons (John J. & Julia & James T. Webb) 1284 Second av.
Webb & Mahen (Abraham Webb & Daniel Mahen) 187 Sixth av.
Webb & Prall (F. Edgerton Webb & John Howard Prall) 37 Wall & 32 E. 42d
Webb & Tree (Samuel Webb & Henry Tree) Riverdale av. n Ackerman
Webb's Adder Co. (Charles H. Webb, propr.) 58 Cedar
Weber Charles & Son (Charles & Charles Weber jr.) 234 Fulton
Weber Daniel & Son (no inf.) 1606 First av.
Weber J. & L. (John & Louis & Edward Weber) 212 E. 80th
Weber Brothers (dissolved) 666 & 694 Tenth av.
Weber & Brand (Charles H. Weber & William Brand) 27 Bond
Weber & Brocher (George Weber & Charles W. Brocher) 61 Suffolk & 132 Columbia
Weber & Bunke (William F. Weber & Ratje Bunke) Boulevard n W. 96th
Weber & Co. (barrels) (refused) 448 W. 13th
Weber & Co. (liquors) (Louis & Adam Weber) 141 Third av.
Weber & Dickson (dissolved) 1901 First av.
Weber & Drosser (Adam Weber & Hubert Drosser) 81 Bible b
Weber & Engel (William R. Weber & William Engel) 80 College pl.
Weber & Erskine (Frank A. Weber & Charles H. Erskine) 110 Reade
Weber & Phillips (John Weber & Henry Phillips) 522 W. 20th
Weber & Roeser (Charles F. Weber & John J. Roeser) 343 Eighth av.
Webster Charles L. & Co. (Samuel L. Clemens & Frederick J. Hall only) 3 E. 14th
Webster H., Co. (Horace Webster, Pres.; Frederick N. Lawrence, Sec. Capital, $100,000. Directors : Horace Webster, Frederick N. Lawrence, John W. Harway) 24 Monroe
Webster Hardware & Specialty Co. (G. Webster Peck, propr.) 59 Murray
Webster Loom Co. (inf. unattainable) 411 W. 51st
Webster R. G. & Son (Filsur G. & Frederick H. Webster) 14 Maiden la,
Webster & White (Adelbert A. Webster & Robert W. White jr.) 30 E. 14th
Weddigen Louis & Co, (Louis & August Weddigen & Abraham Sondera) 472 Broome
Weddle Whiting & Paint Works (William B. Weddle, propr.) 529 West
Wedemeyer & Pick (Herman Wedemeyer & Herman Pick) 227 Grand
Weed Joseph E. & Son (Joseph E. & William E. Weed) 35 Liberty
Weed & Brother (John & Henry F. Weed) 39 White
Weed & Kennedy (Samuel R. Weed & Elijah R, Kennedy) 50 Pine
Weed & Paul (Vitruvius E. Weed & Edward Paul) 117 John, 66 Beekman, 55 Reade, 1 Lispenard, 313 Canal & 206 Mercer

THADDEUS DAVIDS CO., WRITING INKS, SEALING WAX,
MAKE THE BEST MUCILAGE.

Weed, Riley & Co. (George L. Weed, Charles Riley & Henry F. Weed) 11 Gold
Weehawken Wharf Co. (Edward R. Dunham, Pres.; T. F. Hascall, Sec. Capital, $30,000. Trustees: Edward R. Dunham, John C. Scott, T. F. Hascall) 1 B'way
Week's Sport Co. (Caspar W. Whitney, Pres.; Charles D. Orth, Sec. Capital, $10,000. Directors: Caspar W. Whitney, Charles E. Clay, Charles D. Orth.) 9 E. 17th
Weekes J. W. & Co. (James W. Weekes, Charles Vanriper & George O. Edmunds) 78 Duane
Weekes Brothers (Arthur D. & Henry deForest & Frederic D. & John A. & John A. Weekes jr.) 58 Wall
Weekly Union Assn. (James W. O'Brien, Pres.; Joseph J. Marrin, Sec. Capital, $5,000. Trustees: James W. O'Brien, John F. Walsh, Joseph J. Marrin) 7 Barclay
Weeks Charles R. & Brother (Charles R. & Herbert A. Weeks) 74 Murray
Weeks Drug & Chemical Co. (no inf.) 115 Worth
Weeks S. H. & Co. (dissolved) 856 W. 11th
Weeks & Brother (William S. & Peter & Sanford E. Weeks) 74 Dey
Weeks & Campbell Co. (John B. Campbell, Pres.; Frederic T. Parsons, Sec. Capital, $50,000. Directors: John B. Campbell, Frederic T. Parsons, William E. Weeks) 51 Warren
Weeks & Co. (James & Edwin C. Weeks) 18 Wall
Weeks & Parr (Charles L. Weeks & Benjamin Parr) 4 State
Weems Electric Railway Co. (Julian J. Chilcim, Pres.; Alexander Brown, Treas.; William M. Pegram, Sec.; further inf. unattainable) 38 Park row
Weeser & Schmitt (dissolved) 206 B'way
Wehle Theodore & Co. (Theodore Wehle & Adam Ohlweiler) 32 Liberty
Wehmeyer & Miesner (Ernest Wehmeyer & Daniel Miesner) 2050 Third av.
Wehn Pavement Co. (inf. unattainable) 16 Exchange pl.
Wehncke & Co. (Ernst Wehncke, no Co.) 42 Beaver
Wehnes Brothers (Henry & Frederick Wehnes) 676 First av.
Weidemann Henry, Brewing Co. (dissolved) 8 Water
Weidmann & Co. (Lina & William F. Weidmann) 21 Warren
Weidner & Co. (William Weidner, Co. refused) 252 B'way
Weiffenbach C. & H. (Charles jr. & Henry) 196 E. Houston
Weigand & Carlier (Charles Weigand & Charles Carlier) 753 Sixth av.
Weigel & Schmidt (dissolved) 4 Walker
Weigelt & Petzel (Gustav Weigelt & Albert Petzel) 102 Second av.
Weigner & Kauder (Emanuel Weigner & Louis Kauder) 500 E. 73d
Weikert Brothers (John Weikert jr. only) 206 E. 12th
Wail Alphonse & Brother (Alphonse & Emile Weil) 51 Ferry
Weil Charles & Co. (dissolved) 279 B'way
Weil Emil & Co. (Emil Weil & Frank Wallach) 41 White
Weil Isidor & Co. (Isidor Weil & Isidor Rosenberger) 491 B'way
Weil Leopold & Brothers (Leopold & Isaac & Julius Weil) 121 Mercer
Weil Leopold & Co. (Leopold Weil & Julius Koch) 85 Malden la.
Weil A. J. & Co. (August J. Weil, James Edwards & Henry G. Weil) 86 Wall
Weil D. & M. (David & Moritz) 191 Mercer

Weil J. & Brothers (Jacob & Emanuel R. & Leopold Weil) 29 Spruce
Weil Brothers (drygds.) (Ralph & Isaac Weil) 105 Av. A
Weil Brothers (meat) (Jacob & Ralph Weil) 1504 Second av.
Weil & Co. (tobacco) (Julius Beer, only) 65 Pine
Weil & Co. (tobacco) (Leopold & Isidor Weil) 115 Malden la.
Weil & Heidelbach (Herman Weil & Albert Heidelbach;—special partner, Moses Heidelbach, $25,000; terminates 31st Dec. 1890) 21 White
Weil & Kornhauser (dissolved) 41 White
Weil & Livingston (Max Weil & Levi Livingston) 81 White
Weil & Schlaenger (Edward Weil & Bernhard Schlaenger) 20 Clinton
Weil, Haskell & Co. (August & Samuel Weil, William M. Haskell, Albert L. Cone & Frederick S. Haskell, 483 B'way. August & Samuel & Martin J. Weil, William M. & Frederick S. Haskell & Albert L. Cone, 211 E. 33d)
Weil's David, Sons (Henry & Maurice Weil) 14 Lispenard
Weilbacher Frank (Frank Weilbacher;—special partners, Isidor Gartner & Isaac Friedenheit, each $2,000; terminates 1st Feb. 1891) 560 W. 23d
Weill A. & H. (Alexander & Harry) 316 Church
Weill & Co. (Bertha Weill & Ferdinand Hecht) 2020 Third av.
Weille Julius & Co. (Alexander J. Dentourdeur & Abraham L. Coshland, only) 151 Mercer
Weiller, Strauss & Co. (Auguste Weiller, Jacob Strauss, Daniel Weiller & Harry Sachs) 857 B'way
Wellman, Andrews & Co. (Charles Wellman, Benjamin Andrews & Daniel C. Dalsheimer) 42 Walker
Weimar Brothers (Herman F. & Edward W. Weimar) Woodlawn
Weinberg Philip & Co. (Philip Weinberg & Louis Clark jr.) 647 B'way
Weinberg C. & Co. (Charles Weinberg, Alfred T. Loward & Abraham L. Newberger) 33 W. 23d
Weinberg H. & Son (Henry & Charles H. Weinberg) 229 First av.
Weinberg & Uhlfelder (Abraham Weinberg & Simon Uhlfelder) 318 Church
Weinfeld Brothers (dissolved) r 87 Ridge
Weingarten S. & Co. (Sindel Weingarten, no Co.) 235 Broome
Weingarten Brothers (Levi & David & Oscar Weingarten) 10 Walker
Weingartner J. & W. (John & William) 427 E. 53d
Weinlander S. & E. (Samson & Edward) 60 Clinton
Weinman J. & Co. (Jacob Weinman, Alexander Cable & Stuard Hirschman) 23 Walker
Weinman & Co. (Ernest Weinman & Max & Samuel M. Mainthow) 39 Walker
Weinschenk S. & Co. (Solomon Weinschenk & Isaac Hersberg) 36 Harrison
Weinstein I. & Co. (dissolved) 335 B'way
Weinstein & Co. (dissolved) r 122 Elizabeth
Weinstein & Levy (Simon Weinstein & Isaac Levy) 12 Ludlow
Weintraub M. & C. (dissolved) 11 Hester
Weir Ross W. & Co. (Ross W. Weir, no Co.) 60 Front
Weir & Hallett (John Weir & Charles S. Hallett) 220 Produce Ex.
Weir, Rogers & Co. (John Weir, Amos Rogers & Wyle T. Wilson) 45 B'way

Weis W. A. & F. A. (William A. & Frank A.) 2099 Third av.
Weis & Co. (Max Weis & Joseph Graf) 399 B'way & 69 Walker
Weisberger & Baum (dissolved) 228 E. 24th
Weisenberg & Putterman (Samuel Weisenberg & Louis Putterman) 568 Seventh av.
Weisensee John G. & Sons (John G. & George & August Weisensee) 237 W. 37th
Weisl Brothers (Bernhard & Sigmund L. Weisl) 368 B'way
Weismann & Muellenbach (Louis F. Weismann & Robert P. Mullenbach) 9 Bible h.
Weiss Adam & Son (August Weiss, only) 80 Chrystie
Weiss Albert A. & Co. (Albert A. Weiss, no Co.) 1 Chambers
Weiss Herman & Son (dissolved) 49 E. Houston
Weiss Jules C. & Co. (Jules C. Weiss & Andrew Sandahl) 23 W. 23d
Weiss Samuel & Son (Samuel & Mitchel Weiss) 97 Prince
Weiss A. & L. (Aaron & Lipman) 109 West & 65 South
Weiss D. & Co. (David & Philip Weiss) 63 Park row
Weiss H. & Co. (Henry & William Weiss) 100 Walker
Weiss J. & J. Kandel (dissolved) 149 Attorney
Weiss Brothers (Samuel & Nathan Weiss) 90 Walker & 294 Delancey
Weiss Brothers (cigars) (Ignats & Samuel Weiss) 69 Willett
Weiss & Berkovits (Jacob Weiss & Judah Berkovits) 270 Delancey
Weiss & Fairchild (Charles Weiss & George S. Fairchild) 487 Sixth av.
Weiss & Goodman (Adolph Weiss & Victor Goodman) 41 Suffolk
Weiss & Hagemeyer (Ernest J. Weiss & Charles F. Hagemeyer) 498 Third av.
Weiss & Heksch (Sigmund Weiss & Alfred Heksch) 300 Fifth
Weiss & Kandel (David Weiss & Joseph Kandel) 149 Attorney
Weiss & Klau Brothers (Paula Weiss & Nathan & Samuel Klau) 328 Grand
Weiss & Ottinger (Albert Weiss & George Ottinger) 282 First av.
Weitlauf & Pätzner (George Weitlauf & William E. Pätzner jr.) 108 First av.
Weitling Edward & Brother (Edward T. B. & William W. Weitling) 374 Grand
Welch E. N., Clock Co.'s. (E. N. Welch Mfg. Co. proprs.) 8 Warren
Welch Edgar & Co. (dissolved) 80 B'way
Welch James H. & Co. (James H. & Ambrose L. Welch) 214 Produce Ex.
Welch & Flynn (dissolved) 319 E. 59th
Welch & Lawson (Alonzo T. Welch & Samuel Lawson) 205 Centre
Welch & Miller (Robert Welch jr. only) 171 B'way
Welch, Fracker Co. (Arthur E. Welch, Pres.; Charles Edward Barns, Sec. Capital, $10,000. Directors: Willard Fracker, Charles Edward Barns, Arthur H. Welch) 87 Gt. Jones
Welch, Holme & Clark (Peter A. Welch, Moses E. Clark & Andrew M. Sherrill, only) 383 West
Welcker & Ries (William Welcker & Elias Ries) 60 Franklin
Weld, Stephen M. & Co. (Stephen M. Weld & Charles W. Ide) 25 Cotton Ex.
Weld, Colburn & Wickens (Dewit C. Weld, Nicholas A. Colburn & Martin H. Wickens) 593 B'way & 166 Mercer
Weldon John & William (dissolved) 956 E. 161st

Wellbrock J. H. & H. (Jurgen H. & Henry) 61 Vesey & 1 Hall pl.
Weller Samuel C. & Co. (Samuel C. Weller & William D. Rice) 2246 Third av.
Welles L. B. & Co. (dissolved) 14 Vandewater
Welles & Knight (Leonard R. Welles & Azariah L. Knight) 14 Vandewater
Welling Compressed Ivory Mfg. Co. (Ltd.) (dissolved) 251 Centre
Welling & Malcom (W. Brenton Welling & George I. Malcom) 51 Exchange pl.
Wellington Emery & Corundum Wheel Co. (Sheehy Brothers, proprs.) 428 E. 63d
Wellington Mfg. Co. (Henry Wellington, Pres.; Charles E. Mielke, Sec. Capital, $50,000. Directors: Henry Wellington, Charles E. Mielke) 468 Cherry
Wellington Scientific Vacuum Lamp Co. (dissolved) 468 Cherry
Wellington & Johnson (Aaron H. Wellington & Seth W. Johnson) 416 W. 14th
Wellman Carburated Mfg. Co. (inf. unattainable) 25 Warren
Wellman & Co. (George F. & Caryl M. Wellman) 7 Murray
Wellmann & Koeper (dissolved) 2345 First av.
Wells Engine Co. (Justin R. Wells, Pres.; Justin P. Wells, Sec. Capital, $500,000. Directors: Justin R. & Justin P. Wells, A. S. Davenport) 93 Liberty
Wells Rustless Iron Co. (William T. Wells, Pres.; Charles M. Davidson, Sec. Capital, $25,000. Directors: Charles M. Davidson, Charles L. Merritt, James S. C. Wells, Charles Stanford, William T. Wells) 21 Cliff
Wells Tea Co. (Robert Wells, propr.) 48 Vesey
Wells & Leavitt (dissolved) 48 University pl.
Wells, Fargo & Co. (Lloyd Tevis, Pres.; James Heron, Sec.; Henry B. Wadsworth, Treas. Capital, $6,250,000. Directors: Lloyd Tevis, Leland Stanford, William Norris, Charles Crocker, James C. Fargo, Oliver Eldridge, George E. Gray, C. F. Crocker, John J. Valentine) 63 B'way
Wellstood W. & Co. (William Wellstood, Charles C. Pierce & William Wellstood jr.) 44 Vesey
Wellwood Steam Carpet Cleaning Works (Joseph Wellwood, propr.) 502 W. 21st
Welsford & Cameron (dissolved) 109 Water
Welsh & Brother (Patrick H. Welsh, only) 97 Pearl & 60 Stone
Welsh & Dreyer (dissolved) 51 Little W. 12th
Welsh & Lea (Frank H. Welsh & George H. Lea) 96 Reade
Welsh's George W., Son (Samuel C. Welsh) 239 G'wich
Welt & Schwartzmann (dissolved) 97 Forsyth
Welte & Sons (Emil & Berthold & Michael Welte) 49 W. 20th
Welty & Woodrow (no inf.) 1199 B'way
Wemple Jay C., Co. (Alonzo E. Wemple, Pres.; William T. Hayward, Sec. Capital, $75,000. Trustees: Alonzo E. Wemple, William T. & John N. Hayward) 537 B'way & 108 Mercer
Wemple & Hutchinson (William R. Wemple & S. Lincoln Hutchinson) 59 Liberty
Wenck Perfumes Mfg. Co. (Wenck & Co. propra.) 36 W. 14th
Wenck & Co. (George J. Wenck & Regina Allers) 36 W. 14th
Wendehack E. & Son (Edward & Edmund Wendehack) 1272 Second av.
Wendell Jacob & Co. (Jacob Wendell, George P. Stockwell, Herman S. Bergen & Gordon Wendell) 61 North
Wendell, Fay & Co. (Mark R. Wendell, Sigourney W. Fay, John F. Praeger & Frank T. Wendell) 82 Worth

| SPECIAL ATTENTION PAID TO THIS CLASS OF WORK. | BANKERS' & BROKERS' CIRCULARS DELIVERED | THE TROW CITY DIRECTORY CO. 11 University Place. |

WEN 321 WES

Wendler, Gilligan & Barnes (dissolved) 74 Sixth av.

Wendt, Steinhauser & Co. (Frederick B. Wendt, Henry W. Steinhauser & Charles Ophuls) 23 Greene

Wenigmann & Engelberg (Ernest Wenigmann & William Engelberg) 119 Maiden la.

Wenman James F. & Co. (James F. Wenman & Abram Allen jr.) 113 Pearl

Wennels Brothers (Andrew & William Wennels) 12 Pell

Wenner's J., Sons (Charles & William Wenner) 612 W. 87th

Wenninger & Fresh (Frederick Wenninger & John Fresh) 775 Eleventh av.

Wenstrom Northern Electric Co. (Joseph B. De Lery, Pres.; Benjamin J. Sturges, Sec. Capital, $125,000. Directors: Joseph B. De Lery, Emil Henel, Benjamin J. Sturges, Benjamin Blum, C. S. Cowan) 5 Dey

Wentworth's Sons (Mitchell E. Wentworth, only) 111 Bowery

Wens & Co. (no inf.) 47 Gansevoort, W. Washn. mkt

Werfelman Brothers (George H. & Richard Werfelman) 286 Bowery

Werfelman & Harms (John Werfelman & Frederick Harms) 464 Fourth av.

Werner Henry (Henry Werner;—special partner, Charles Werner, $50,000; terminates 31st Dec. 1890) 108 Cliff

Worner Waldemar & Co. (Waldemar Werner & Rudolph Seiffert) 496 Tenth av.

Werner A. & Co. (August Werner, no Co.) 52 Warren

Werner S. & J. (Solomon & Julius) 515 B'way & 84 Mercer

Werner & New (John Werner & Abraham New) 649 B'way

Werner & Schuddekopf (Herman Werner & Richard Schuddekopf) 27 Delancey

Wernert N. & Co. (Nicholas Wernert, Co. refused) 81 Washn. mkt

Wernert & Zimmermann (Leon Wernert & C. Paul Zimmermann) 106 W. Houston

Wertheim B. & Son (Baruch & Solomon Wertheim) 100 Gold

Wertheim & Schiffer (dissolved) 1018 Second av.

Wertheimer L. & Co. (Louis Wertheimer & Joseph Cantor) 45 Barclay

Wertheimer L. & E. (Leopold Wertheimer & Joseph L. Hess, only) 131 Water

Wertheimer & Co. (Maurice Wertheimer & Jacob & Herman Steinberger) 502 B'way & 46 Crosby

Wertheimer & Delmel (Joseph Wertheimer & Henry Delmel) 159 S. 5th av.

Wescott Brothers (William F. jr. & Walter C. Wescott) 15 Platt

Wesel F., Mfg. Co. (Ferdinand Wesel, Pres.; Emil Stephany, Sec. Capital, $15,000. Directors: Ferdinand Wesel, Emil Stephany, J. Kissinger) 11 Spruce

Wesendonck, Lorenz & Co. (Walter Wesendonck, Leo Lorenz & Alwin Colth:—special partners, Otto Wesendonck, *Berlin, Prussia*, $75,000, & Hugo Wesendonck, *N. Y.*, $20,000; terminates 30th Nov. 1894) 251 Church & 69 Leonard

Weser Brothers (John A. Weser, only) 524 W. 43d & 103 W. 14th

Wesnage & Browne (Herbert H. Wesnage & William J. Browne) 120 Liberty

Wessel Concentrating Co. (Capital, $20,000; further inf. unattainable) no address

Wessel Metal Co. (dissolved) 521 W. 24th

Wessell Silver Co. (not Inc.) (Charles & Charles A. Wessell) 521 W. 24th

Wessell, Nickel & Gross (Otto Wessell, Adam Nickel & Rudolph Gross) 457 W. 45th

Wessels Co. (Gerhard Wessels, Pres.; Charles T. Wessels, Sec.; G. William Wessels, Treas. Capital, $50,000. Directors: Gerhard & Charles T. & Henry E. & G. William Wessels) 220 Washn.

Wessels G. & Co. (refused) 60 Front

West Brooklyn Land Improvement Co. (W. Frederick Snyder, Pres.; George A. Allin, Sec.; William A. Ingham, Treas. Capital, $150,000. Directors: W. Frederick Snyder, Percival Roberts, John M. Butler, John L. Kates, Jay Cooke, George A. Allin, M. McCormack, David A. Boody, William A. Ingham, C. E. Kelsey, H. B. Hubbard) 32 Liberty

West Coast Telephone Co. (Theodore N. Vail, Pres.; Henry L. Storke, Sec. Capital, $1,000,000. Directors: Theodore N. Vail, Henry L. Storke, Oscar E. Madden, E. L. Merrifield, William H. Woolverton, George W. Piper, E. W. Carritt, A. P. Sawyer, F. W. Jones) 18 Cortlandt

West End Building Co. (Directors: Charles T. Barney, Francis M. Jencks, William E. D. Stokes; further inf. refused) 84 B'way

West End Co-operative & Loan Assn. (R. M. Offord, Pres.; P. E. Dolan, Sec.; E. F. Carr, Treas. Directors: P. J. Carr, W. Z. Colwell, E. W. O'Hara, James M. McCauley, H. S. Harris, E. J. Atkinson, A. W. Schmitt, D. Sellers, W. G. Watt, Eli Smith, George Barron, C. W. Yeandle, M. Meehan, F. Hulberg) 77 W. 125th

West End Employment Bureau (Margaret Davis, propr.) 657 Sixth av.

West Florida & Alabama R. R. Co. (J. D. Pirrong, Pres.; J. H. Hamilton. Sec.; John Barr Glen, Treas. Capital, $1,000,000. Directors: J. D. Pirrong, Benjamin F. Howland, J. M. Withrow, J. H. Hamilton, John Barr Glen, J. McReynolds, C. M. Butterfield) 18 B'way

West India Co. (Stephen B. French, Pres.; Samuel Warren, Sec. Capital, $30,000. Directors: Stephen B. French, Daniel L. Gibbens, Samuel Warren, N. B. Price, F. Porter Thayer) 47 Broad

West India Improvement Co. (Capital, $500,000; further inf. unattainable) 25 Broad

West Jamaica Land Co. (Ltd.) (Frederick W. Dunton, Pres.; Frank McDonough, Sec.; William G. Wheeler, Treas. Capital, $500,000. Directors: James K. O. Sherwood, Thomas F. Ward, Frederick W. Dunton, Frank McDonough, William G. Wheeler) 102 B'way

West Milford Water Storage Co. (Henry C. Andrews, Pres.; John R. Bartlett, Sec. Capital, $500,000. Directors: Henry C. Andrews, John R. Bartlett, Whiting G. Snow, Garret A. Hobart, Thomas F. Hoxsey) 2 Wall

West Point Foundry Co. (Gouverneur Paulding, Pres.; T. N. Rhinelander, Sec.; Oscar Bunke, Treas. Capital, $50,000. Trustees: Frederick W. Rhinelander, Gouverneur Paulding, Frederick W. Rhinelander jr. Oscar Bunke, Colin Tolmie) 45 B'way

West Publishing Co. (refused) 13 W. 27th

West Shore R. R. (Chauncey M. Depew, Pres.; Edward V. W. Rossiter, Sec. Capital, $10,000,000. Directors: Cornelius & William K. & Frederick W. Vanderbilt, Chauncey M. Depew, Ahhbel Greene, J. Pierpont Morgan, Edward D. Adams, Charles C. Clarke, J. Hood Wright, Charles Lanier, Horace J. Hayden, C. Edward Tracy) Grand Central depot & 5 Vanderbilt av.

West Side Architectural Iron Works (Campbell & Vantassel, proprs.) 555 & 558 W. 33d

West Side Bank (John W. B. Dobler, Pres.; Theodore M. Bertine, Asst. Cashier ; Hulbert Peck, Notary. Capital, $200,000. Directors: John W. B. Dobler, John Mulford, Joseph Stern, T. C. Eastman, Mayer Eiseman, Samuel Mo-

21

TYPEWRITING DONE BY THE TROW CITY DIRECTORY CO., 11 University Place.

Milton, F. Beck, Frederick K. Keller, Christian F. Tietjen, Samuel D. Styles) 485 Eighth av.

West Side Beef Co. (John Bohnet, propr.) 22 Manhattan mkt

West Side Coal & Wood Co. (John J. Murdock, propr.) 148 W. 4th

West Side Electric Light and Power Co. (no inf.) 502 W. 53d

West Side Galvanising Works (John Merry & Co. proprs.) 34 Eleven'h av. & 539 W. 15th

West Side Instalment Co. (Emanuel Kolasky, propr.) 66 W. 15th

West Side Knitting Mills (Bartholomew F. Kenney, propr.) 445 W. 45th

West Side Savings Bank (Cornelius Van Cott, Pres.; John H. Hudson, Sec. Trustees: Daniel Bates, Clarence O. Bigelow, John J. Brogan, Patrick Brophy, Edward H. Coffin, Frederick A. Conkling, S. G. Cook, George B. Deane jr. Chileon B. Decker, Robert E. Deyo, J. H. Dorn, T. C. Finnell, George E. Horne, John W. Jacobus, Samuel M. Johnson, James Little, David McClure, William S. McCotter, Alexander H. McGarren, Frank M. Merriam, John J. Morris, Samuel C. Mott, John J. Murdock, D. E. O'Neil, David S. Paige, F. LeRoy Satteree, John S. Scully, Patrick Skelly, George Starr, Cornelius Van Cott, James J. Ward, Jacob S. Warden) 56 Sixth av.

West Side Sign Co. (William J. McAuliffe, propr.) 372 Eighth av.

West Side Tailoring Co. (John Stone & Co. proprs.) 457 Eighth av.

West Side Troy Laundry (Byron Alger, propr.) 38 Eighth av.

West Side Wire Works (Ulysses L. Washburn, propr.) 339 W. 52d

West Stockbridge R. R. Co. (William H. Starbuck, Pres.; Mead E. Stone, Sec. Capital, $20,000. Directors: William H. Starbuck, Mead E. Stone, John L. Macauley, James A. Bostwick, William H. Stevenson) 36 Wall

W. Va. Improvement Co. (Marcus Hulings, Pres.; John W. Snedeker, Sec. Capital, $1,000,000. Directors: Marcus Hulings, David Reynolds, John W. Snedeker, Willis J. Hulings, J. C. Stevenson, C. C. Lathrop, J. M. Payne, L. J. Jordon, J. W. Patton) 18 Cortlandt

West H. & Co. (Henry West, no Co.) 24 Jeff. mkt

West J. & Son (James J. & Alfred B. West) 462 Eighth av.

West J. D. & Co. (Joseph D. West, no Co.) 40 Cortlandt

West & Ingalls (William T. West & F. Abbot Ingalls) 61 Leonard

West & Melchers (Henry C. West, Alexander Melchers & Mortimer S. Bates) 126 Front

West, Pyke & Co. (John J. West, William C. M. Pyke & Allen Williams) 187 W. 125th

Westbay's John, Son (John F. Westbay) 174 W. 23d

Westbrook A., Co. (Percy L. Turner, Pres.; Julia Turner, Sec. Capital, $10,000. Directors: Percy L. & Julia Turner, Victor Schaller) 62 William

Westbrook & Mooney (dissolved) 7 Murray

Westchester Electric Co. (Robert Brown, Pres.; Sidney J. Everett, Sec.; Paul Bury, Treas. Capital, $50,000. Directors: Robert Brown, Sidney J. Everett, Paul Bury, Charles W. Price, Charles L. Rover) 14 Dey

Westchester Fire Ins. Co. (George R. Crawford, Pres.; John Q. Underhill, Sec.; Silas D. Gifford, Treas. Capital, $300,000. Directors: George R. Crawford, Samuel M. Purdy, Silas D. Gifford, Daniel D. Demarest, William H. Robertson, Henry Clement, William H. Van Every, John E. Marshall, Joseph B. Browster, William F. Bishop, Richard H. Burdsall, David W. Smith, George R. Cowles, Nicholas A. Colburn, Frederick E. Willits, John Lyon, John W. Lounsbury, Richard M. Bowne,

George W. L. Underhill, Morrell O. Brown, Thomas W. Thorne, Thomas R. Lowerre jr. (Jerd Martens, Edward M. Teall, John Q. Underhill) 27 Pine

Westchester Telephone Co. (Dexter A. Smith, Pres.; Charles F. Cutler, Sec.; further inf. unattainable) 16 Cortlandt

Westcott Express Co. (Robert E. Westcott, Pres.; Walter G. Eliot, Sec. Capital, $250,000. Directors: Robert E. Westcott, John H. Paul, Walter G. Eliot) 12 Park pl. 755 & 942 B'way, ft. Barclay, ft. Jay, 314 Canal, ft. Christopher, ft. W 42d, Grand Central depot, 1201 Ninth av. & 68 W. 125th

Westcott & Crouch (Henry A. Westcott & Leslie H. Crouch) 2084 Seventh av.

Westcott & Thornsson (James H. Westcott & L. Francis Thornsson jr.) 5 Dey & Eighth av. c W. 138th

Westerberg C. & Co. (Charles Westerberg & William W. Smith) 42 Loew av. W. Washn. mkt

Westerberg, Jefferson Co. (Thomas Jefferson, Pres.; John J. Jefferson, Sec. Capital, $100,000. Trustees: John J. & Susan & Thomas Jefferson) 540 W. 58th

Westerfield W. & Son (Eugene T. Westerfield, only) 177 Prince

Westerly Granite Co. (Ltd.) (William J. Squires, Pres.; Sassacus C. Sherwood, Sec. Capital, $25,000; further inf. unattainable) 10 W. 23d

Westerly Laundry (Matthew Quinn, propr.) 912 Sixth av.

Westermann B. & Co. (Ernest Lemcke & Oscar Buechner, only) 832 B'way

Westermann Brothers (August H. & Elbe D. Westermann) 1604 Third av.

Western Agency (Ltd.) (Charles W. D. Weber, Pres.; George von Skal, Sec.; Otto G. Mayer, Treas. Capital, $5,000. Directors: Charles W. B. Weber, Otto G. Mayer, George H. Tobias, William A. De Long, George von Skal) 19 William

Western Improvement Co. (Orlando W. Joslyn, Pres.; James B. Bach, Sec. Capital, $750,000. Directors: Orlando W. Joslyn, James B. Bach, John D. Slayback, A. Dunsano, J. Kirkham, H. L. Laughmar, George C. Thomas) 42 New

Western Land & Horse Co. (Ltd.) (Louis Gans, Pres.; Henry Klein, Treas.; Edward A. Meridian, Sec. Capital, $25,000. Directors: Louis Gans, Henry S. Bolce, Henry Klein, Edward A. Meridian, Isaac Oppenheimer) 28 Thomas

Western Land & Investment Co. (Ltd.) (Lewis A. Riley, Pres.; Henry A. Riley, Sec.; J. Howard Clapp, Treas. Capital, $100,000. Directors: Lewis A. Riley, A. M. Stewart, J. Howard Clapp, Henry A. Riley, William Libby, William A. Marr, Charles B. Beardsley, Gilbert C. Scott, Henry Camerden jr. Charles P. Ward, H. Edwards Rowland) 101 B'way

Western Loan & Securities Co. (Ltd.) (W. Lewis Boyle, Pres.; Arthur L. Tinker, Sec.; James McNeil, Treas. Capital, $500,000. Directors: W. Lewis Boyle, Arthur L. Tinker. J. F. Emmons, George R. Morse, James McNeil) 45 Wall

Western Loan & Trust Co. (Willard W. McDonald, Pres.; William L. Hulett, Sec.; Henry M. McDonald, Treas. Capital, $450,000. Directors: Willard W. & Henry M. McDonald, William I. Hulett, Charles G. Kidder) 2 Wall

Western National Bank (Conrad N. Jordan, Pres.; Ferdinand Blankenhorn, Cashier; William S. Mathews, Notary. Capital, $2,500,000. Directors: Conrad N. Jordan, Eduardo Gogorza, Francis O. Matthiessen, Benjamin Rusak, John E. Searles jr. Edward J. Berwind, Charles J. Canda, Marcellus Hartley, Ferdinand E. Canda, Henry W. Johns, William N. Coler jr. Sidney F. Tyler) 120 B'way (*See adv. in back*)

THE CALIGRAPH WRITING MACHINE,
HARTFORD, CONN.

Western Nevada Copper Co. (inoperative) 111 B'way

Western N. Y. & Pennsylvania R. R. Co. (Calvin H. Allen, Pres.; Joseph R. Trimble, Sec.; Franklin S. Buell, Treas. Capital, $30,000,-000. Directors: Calvin H. Allen, Samuel G. De Conway, Edward L. Owen, John D. Probst, Adolph Engler, Gustav E. Kissel, Edward T. Steel, Isaac N. Seligman, William Mertens, George E. Bartol, William T. Tiers, E. W. Clark jr. Pascal P. Pratt) 15 Broad

Western N. Carolina R. R. Co. (Alexander B. Andrews, Pres.; George P. Erwin, Sec. Capital, $8,000,000. Directors: Alexander B. Andrews, John A. Rutherford. J. H. Parker, W. E. Anderson. Calvin S. Brice, S. H. Wiley, J. E. Rankin, Frank Coxe, Walter J. Oakman) 2 Wall

Western Oil Refining Co. (William C. Dreyer, Pres.; William Pennington, Sec. Capital, $250,000. Directors: William C. Dreyer, William P. Robinson, Edward J. Palmer, William Pennington) 63 B'way

Western Stock Yards (inf. unattainable) ft. W. 40th

Western Union Tea Co. (Henry Morrow, propr.) 301 First av.

Western Union Telegraph Co. (Norvin Green, Pres.; Abijah R. Drewer, Sec.; Roswell H. Rochester, Treas. Capital, $86,200,000. Directors: Norvin Green, Thomas T. Eckert, John T. Terry, John Vanhorne, Jay Gould, Russell Sage, Alonzo B. Cornell, Sidney Dillon, Samuel Sloan, Robert C. Clowry, George J. & Edwin Gould, John G. Moore, Cyrus W. Field, Henry Weaver, Percy R. Pyne, Charles Lanier, Austin Corbin, J. Pierpont Morgan, Frederick L. Ames, John Hay, William D. Bishop, Collis P. Huntingdon, George B. Roberts, Sidney Shepard, Erastus Wiman, Chauncey M. Depew, James W. Clendenin, Henry M. Flager, William Waldorf Astor) 195 B'way

Western Wood-Working Co. (Wilson S. Dunn, Pres.; George W. Avery, Sec. Capital, $2,000. Directors: Wilson S. Dunn, George W. & Harry W. Avery) 46 Murray

Westervelt A. B. & W. T. (Adrian B. & Walter T. & Arthur S. Westervelt) 102 Chambers

Westervelt G. J. & Co. (Garret J. & James D. Westervelt) 170 West

Westervelt W. M. & Co. (William H. & Otto W. P. Westervelt & Carl F. Braun) 24 State

Westervelt & Demarest (William H. Westervelt & William E. Demarest) 202 Bleecker

Westfield Mfg. Co. (A. J. Hague & Co. proprs.) 74 Franklin

Westinghouse Electric Co. (George Westinghouse jr. Pres.; Asaph T. Rowand, Sec.; John Caldwell, Treas. Capital, $500,000. Directors: George Westinghouse jr. H. M. Byllseby, Robert Pitcairn, C. H. Jackson, John R. McGinley, Calvin Wells, Charles S. Pense, John Caldwell, Asaph T. Rowand) 120 B'way

Westinghouse Electric & Mfg. Co. (inf. unattainable) 32 Nassau

Westinghouse, Church, Kerr & Co. (Herman H. Westinghouse, William Lee Church, Walter C. Kerr & Isaac H. Davis) 17 Cortlandt

Westman Furnace Co. (John P. Jones, Pres.; Frederick L. Holmquist, Treas.; Gustave Stromberg, Sec. Capital, $125,000. Directors: John P. Jones, R. D. Harris, Frederick L. Holmquist, A. J. D. Wodemeyer, William B. Ellison, Gustaf M. Westman, A. O. Tate) 81 Broad

Westminster Laundry Co. (Emily Casey, propr.) 767 Sixth av.

Westmoreland Paper Co. (William H. Parsons, Pres.; Wilfred Barnes, Sec.; John P. Parsons, Treas. Capital, $100,000. Directors: William H. Parsons, George F. Hicks, Wilfred Barnes, William H. Parsons jr.) 4 Warren

Weston & Debillier (Frank S. Weston, Frederick & Henry Debillier & Harry M. Dyer) 60 New

Weston & Tuckerman (dissolved) 31 Broad

Westphal & Spiess (no inf.) 200 W. 14th

Westphal & Weinstein (Carl Westphal & Simon Weinstein) 215 E. 22d

Wetherbee & Fuller (Charles L. Wetherbee & Linus K. Fuller) 621 Fifth av.

Wetmore S. H., Co. (Stanley H. Wetmore, Pres.; Nathaniel Doyle, Sec. Frederick W. Cooper, Treas. Capital, $10,000. Directors: Stanley H. Wetmore, Charles M. Blackham, Frederick W. Cooper, A, C. Eggers) 242 Pearl

Wetmore' & Co. (Elias S. Wetmore, no Co.) 444 Broome

Wetmore & Jenner (Edmund Wetmore & William A. Jenner) 45 William

Wetmore & Wetmore (dissolved) 6 Wall

Wetter & Bluntschli (Edward Wetter & John Bluntschli) 61 Grand

Wetzel C. H. & Son (Charles H. & Charles F. Wetzel) 82 E. 14th

Wetzel & Stark (Richard E. F. Wetzel & Henry Stark) 181 Grand

Wetzler's Albert, Sons (refused) 90 Gold

Weydig Brothers (Charles & Julius Weydig) 415 Fifth

Weymann Brothers (August & Joseph Weymann) 841 Sixth

Weyrich & Maurer (Philip Weyrich & John E. Maurer) 200 W. 34th

Whalen & West (Frank T. Whalen & Joseph D. West) 40 Cortlandt

Whaley & Son (George & George Whaley jr.) 500 W. 50th

Whealen Brothers (James & Charles Whealen) 58 W. 24th & 3428 Third av.

Whant & Marks (dissolved) 157 William

Wheat & Pfisenmayer (Louis A. Wheat & Paul Pfisenmayer) 157 William

Wheatland Improvement Co. (George B. Smith, Pres.; Frank H. Brown, Sec.; Robert B. Getman, Treas. Capital, $150,000. Directors: George B. Smith, Frank H. Brown, Robert B. Getman, Edwin V. Machette, William H. D. Thomas) 111 B'way

Whedon C. A. & Co. (Charles A. & Charles C. Whedon) 132 Nassau

Wheeler A. H. (firm of) (dissolved) 6 Wall

Wheeler F. B., Co. (Frank B. Wheeler, Pres.; Robert H. Halstead, Treas.; Charles A. Woolsey, Sec. Capital, $150,000. Directors: Frank D. Wheeler, Robert H. Halstead, Charles A. Woolsey, Daniel B. Halstead, Alfred G. Peck, Henry C. Howell) 50 Pearl & 24 Stone

Wheeler Hayden W. & Co. (Hayden W. Wheeler & Hayden H. Butts) 2 Maiden la.

Wheeler W. B. & Co. (William B. Wheeler & Emile Guillaudeu(69 B'way & 561 Fifth av.

Wheeler & Co. (dissolved) 52 Broad & 50 New

Wheeler & Guck (George H. Wheeler & Arago J. Guck) 426 Pearl

Wheeler & Shiner (Charles W. Wheeler & Alexander W. Shiner) 614 B'way

Wheeler & Wilson Mfg. Co. (Nathaniel Wheeler, Pres.; Frederick H. Hurd, Sec. Capital, $1,-000,000. Directors: S. M. Buckingham, Nathaniel Wheeler, William H. Perry, A. S. Chase, James S. Elton, C. N. Wayland, Henry E. Russell, John W. Sterling, E. W. Shelton) 838 B'way

Wheeler, Cortis & Godkin (Everett P. Wheeler, Harold G. Cortis & Lawrence Godkin) 45 William

Wheeler, Kantor & Hays (Albert H. Wheeler, E. E. Kantor & Eugene D. Hays) 6 Wall

Wheeling & Lake Erie Railway Co. (Melanchton D. Woodford, Pres.; James M. Ham, Sec. Capital, $9,800,000. Directors: Melanchton D.

WHE 324 WHI

Woodford, S. C. Reynolds, George W. Davis, John G. Warwick, E. K. Sibley, John Greenough, Maunsell Van Rensselaer jr.) 40 Wall

Wheelock William E. & Co. (William E. Wheelock & Charles B. Lawson :—special partner, John W. Mason, B'klyn, N. Y., $40,000; terminates 1st May 1890) 23 E. 14th & 763 E. 149th

Wheelock J. W. & Co. (John W. Wheelock, no Co.) 152 Front

Wheelwright William D. & Co. (William D. Wheelwright & Charles R. Hewitt) 82 Wall

Wheelwright, Eldredge & Co. (John W. Wheelwright, Orris K. Eldredge, George Lewis & William A. Copeland :—special partner, John F. Anderson, Boston, Mass., $50,000; terminates 31st Dec. 1890) 61 Worth

Whelldon L. B. & Co. (Lewis B. Whelldon & Leonard A. Whitney) 41 Park row

Whelan & Riordan (James F. Whelan & William J. Riordan) 51 Mott

Whelpley & Whitehill (Albert O. Whelpley & Francis A. Whitehill) 21 Spruce

Whipple & Co. (Joseph L. Farraga & David F. Casey :—special partners. Frances A. Whipple & estate of Marie T. March, B'klyn, N. Y., each $5,000; terminates 20th Nov. 1890) 33 Liberty

Whitall, Tatum & Co. (James Whitall, Charles A. Tatum, John Mickle, Francis M. Underhill, John M. Whitall & J. Whitall Nicholson) 46 Barclay & 31 Jay

Whitcomb & Chapman (Joshua M. Whitcomb & Thomas C. Chapman) 9 Ferry

White C. C., Co. (Charles C. White Pres.; Clayton Slaughter, Sec.; William F. Kuntz, Treas. Capital, $10,000. Directors: Charles C. White, Clayton Slaughter, H. W. Mather) 87 Beekman

White Charles & Co. (Charles White, William F. Wilson & John King) ft. W. 40th

White Charles T. & Son (dissolved) 134 Pearl & 100 Water

White Granite Co. (Niles G. White, Pres.; James R. Dutton, Treas. Capital, $14,000. Directors: Niles G. White, Alfred Le Poidevin, Frank S. White) 547 W. 14th

White James F. & Co. (Bryce Gray, J. Martin White & Henry D. Cooper, only) 54 Worth

White James T. & Co. (James T. & Florence D. White) 771 B'way

White John E. & Co. (John E. White, no Co.) 82 William

White John J. & Co. (carpenters) (dissolved) 237 W. 80th

White John J. & Co. (plumbers) (dissolved) 159 E. 110th

White Lake Dairy Co. (Joshua E. A. Moore, propr.) 972 Eighth av.

White Lewis B. & Co. (dissolved) 145 Elm

White Loomis L. & Co. (Loomis L. White, William Viall Chapin & John O. Bartholomew) 40 Wall

White S. S., Dental Mfg. Co. (James W. White, Pres.; J. Clarence White, Sec.; Samuel T. Jones, Treas. Directors: James W. & Samuel S. White jr. Algernon K. Johnston, James M. Longacre, William H. Gilbert) 769 & 1280 B'way

White Star Line (Oceanic Steam Navigation Co. proprs.) 41 B'way & Pier 44 (new) N. R.

White Tar Co. (not inc.; further inf. refused) 125 Warren

White William A. & Sons (Augustus & Alfred L. White, only) 409 & 115 B'way

White A. W. & Co. (Arthur W. White & Emil Keller) 83 Beaver

White C. H. & Co. (Charles H. White, no Co.) 74 B'way

White J. M. & Co. (James M. White & Henry H. Johnson) 7 S. William & 68 Stone

White M. H. & Co. (dissolved) 47 Ann

White M. M. & Co. (Moores M. & Amos C. White) 531 W. 33d

White S. V. & Co. (Stephen V. White & Franklin W. Hopkins) 36 Wall

White T. & S. C. (Thomas White, only) 30 Burling sl.

White W. A. & A. M. (William A. & Alexander M. & Alfred T. White) 130 Water & 138 Greene

White W. A. & Son (Walter A. & Thaddeus White) 2050 Lex. av. & E. 130th c Lex. av.

White & Allen (J. Parker White & Frank Allen) 32 Gt. Jones

White & Anderson (Webster White & Stephan P. Anderson) 157 E. 125th

White & Co, (chandlers) (Ansel L. White, no Co.) 36 South

White & Co. (coal) (Sidney White, no Co.) Brook av. c E. 163d

White & Co. (publishers) (no inf.) 9 Murray

White & Gates Granite Co. (dissolved) 547 W. 14th & 14 Vesey

White & Hartshorne (Arthur E. White & J. Mott Hartshorne jr.) 4b B'way

White & Kerr (Peter White & Benjamin Kerr) 18 E. 27th

White & Levy (Samuel White & Israel N. Levy) 633 B'way

White & Oberfelder (Gustave White & Simon Oberfelder) 266 Canal

White & Raeder (W. Howard White & Henry Raeder) 76 Wall

White & Rider (dissolved) 104 Wall

White & Rusling (John G. White & George M. Rusling) 137 B'way

White & Sheldon (Charles T. & Norman White & Henry B. Sheldon jr.) 184 Pearl

White & Snow (Thomas White & Augustus M. Snow) 252 Third av.

White & Stratton (J. Lamont White & Byron P. Stratton) 83 Park row

White, Howard & Co. (Mary H. White & Margaret A. Howard, no Co.) 19 E. 34th

White, Howard & Major (George H. White, George D. Howard & Frank M. Major) 25 Union sq. W.

White, Morris & Co. (Leonard D. White, Louis E. Blackwell, Charles O. Morris jr. & Leonard D. White jr.) 102 B'way

White, Payson & Co. (Joseph H. White, Gilbert R. Payson & Francis D. Lecompte) 126 Duane & 40 Thomas

White, Post & Co. (Jefferson H. White, Hobart B. Post, Frank W. Pooler & William A. Root) 132 Duane

White, Potter & Paige Mfg. Co. (Gayton Ballard, Pres.; Stephen Ballard, Treas.; William H. Chandler, Sec. Directors: Gayton & Stephen Ballard & William H. Chandler) 18 E. 17th

White, Rider & Frost (Pendennis White, Laurence P. Rider, & William G. Frost) 15 Cortlandt

White, Vanglahn & Co. (Anna B. White, Edward C. Vanglahn & Anna B. Haulenbeek) 4 Catharine & 15 Chatham sq.

White's Dental Co. (Frederick W. White, propr.) 224 Sixth av.

White's Express Co. (M. & J. F. Smith, proprs.) 96 Worth

White's P., Sons (dissolved) 41 Peck sl.

White's Patent Lever Truss Co. (Nathaniel P. T. Finch, Pres; Nelson Y. Hull, Sec.; Charles A. Harvey, Treas. Capital, $25,000. Trustees: Nathaniel P. T. Finch, Nelson Y. Hull, Charles A. Harvey, J. L. VanNeste, Robert P. Rover) 20 E. 23d

Whitebreast Fuel Co. (John C. Osgood, Pres.;

MERCHANTS EXCHANGE NAT. BANK OF THE CITY OF N. Y.
SOLICITS YOUR ACCOUNT. 257 Broadway.
PHINEAS C. LOUNSBURY, President.   ALLEN S. APGAR, Cashier.

WHI   325   WID

Charles H. Parmelee, Treas. Capital, $2,000,-000. Directors: John C. Osgood, Paul Morton, William H. Mall, William F. Morgan, C. M. Schenck, William McNutt, George E. Prentiss, Charles H. Parmelee, David R. Stanford) 18 B'way

Whited D. W. & Co. (Daniel W. Whited & Henry Barclay) 168 E. 120th

Whitehead M. & Co. (Max Whitehead & Charles Simon) 327 Canal

Whitehead Brothers (Charles & John & Lydell & Van Loan Whitehead, Alfred J. Miller, & William H. Smith) 517 W. 15th

Whitehead & Lyon (Henry M. Whitehead & George W. Lyon) 47 B'way

Whitehead & Suydam (Gerrard Irving Whitehead & Charles C. Suydam) 206 B'way

Whitehead, Parker & Dexter (Charles F. Whitehead, James Parker & Stanley W. Dexter) 71 Wall

Whitehouse & Co. (George M. & J. Norman Whitehouse & Augustus V. Marckwald:—special partner. J. Henry Whitehouse, *Irvington, N. Y.*, $150,000; terminates 31st Dec. 1890) 25 Broad

Whitehouse, Smith & Co. (F. H. Whitehouse, S. P. Smith & Edward F. Underwood) 338 B'way

Whiteley, Spowers & Co. (Thomas C. Whitely, William H. Spowers & William R. Stewart) 20 West

Whiteside William & Co. (Anna & Joseph S. & William Whiteside) 105 Franklin

Whitin & Collins (Lewis F. Whitin & Clarence L. Collins) 112 Worth

Whiting Box Co. (Charles R. Whiting, propr.) 457 G'wich

Whiting Mfg. Co. (Charles R. Bulkley, Pres.; Frederick S. Salisbury, Treas. Capital, $300,000; further inf. refused) 31 Union sq. W. & 4 E. 4th

Whiting & Sons (Francis E. N. & Walter B. & Holland S. & Elliot B. Whiting) 427 W. 31st

Whitlaw Printing & Stationery Co. (James D. Whitlaw, Pres.; Edward Hebut, Sec.; Edwin H. Haines, Treas; further inf. unattainable) 7 W. B'way

Whitley & West (dissolved) 323 B'way

Whitlock & Dovale (Daniel G. Whitlock & Frank Dovale) 10 E. 14th

Whitlock & Simonds (Bache McE. Whitlock & Alexander B. Simonds) 51 Wall

Whitman Saddle Co. (Henry L. Duck, Pres.; William C. C. Mahlbach, Sec. Capital, $140,000; further inf. unattainable) 118 Chambers

Whitman Brothers (Edmund S. & Alfred Whitman) 302 Produce Ex.

Whitman & Farrell (Henry B. Whitman & William R. Farrell jr.) 302 Produce Ex.

Whitman & Fisher (Stephen Whitman & John Fisher) 19 Whitehall

Whitman & Phelps (George L. Whitman & Charles Phelps) 40 Leonard

Whitman, Creighton & Co. (Clarence Whitman, William Creighton & Charles L. Whitman) 39 Leonard

Whitmore George B. & Co. (George B. & Daniel W. Whitmore) 89 Warren

Whitmore W. R. & Co. (William R. Whitmore & John A. Gassner) 42 New

Whitney Charles M. & Co. (Charles M. Whitney & Edwin S. & Frank M. Larchar) 96 B'way

Whitney A. & W. E. (Abijah & Frank V. Whitney, only) 146 B'way

Whitney A. R. & Co. (Alfred R. Whitney & Daniel A. Nesbitt) 17 B'way

Whitney F. B. & Co. (Frank B. Whitney & Emma McCann) 413 W. 15th

Whitney F. E. & Co. (dissolved) 16 Murray

Whitney J. F. & Co. (Henry Buschman & Charles S. Whitney, only) 15 State

Whitney W. S. & Co. (Willis S. Whitney, no Co.) 115 Maiden la.

Whitney & Co. (drygds.) (James W. Whitney, no Co.) 41 Greene

Whitney & Co. (pianos) (Abijah & Frank V. Whitney) 2374 Third av.

Whitney & Kemmerer (William B. Whitney & Mahlon S. Kemmerer) 111 B'way

Whitney & Starr (Orville P. Whitney & James H. Starr) 232 West

Whitson J. H. & Son (John H. & Clarence R. Whitson) 144 E. 24th

Whittemore George & Co. (George Whittemore & George M. Jaques) 150 Canal & 49 W. B'way

Whittemore H. & Co. (Henry Whittemore & John L. Fraser) 58 William

Whittemore Brothers (Charles & Charles E. Whittemore) 570 B'way & 150 Mercer

Whittemore, Musgrave & Hill (Richard B. Whittemore, John G. Musgrave, T. Olney Hill & Samuel J. Harrison) 35 Broad

Whittier Elevator Co. (Charles R. Whittier, Pres.; John Cabot, Treas.; Robert A. McLean, Sec. Capital, $20,000. Directors: Charles R. Whittier, John Cabot, Robert A. McLean) 310 Eleventh av.

Whittier & Co. (Adea J. Whittier & William A. Drummond) 241 B'way

Whittle & Dowd (John H. Whittle & John F. Dowd) 184 E. 115th

Wholesale Drug Trade (James H. Goldey, Treas.) 4 Warren

Wholesale Grocers' Assn. (G. Waldo Smith, Pres.; John H. Mohlman, Treas.; Levi P. Lyon, Sec. Directors: Frederick C. Clark, August Koenig, W. B. A. Jurgens, Samuel J. Berry jr. E. G. Stoddard, Francis H. Leggett, Edwin H. Sayre) 6 Harrison

Wholesale Grocers' National Assn. (Richard Dymond, Pres.; William J. Seaver jr. Treas.; F. W. Inbusch, Sec.) 6 Harrison

Wholesale Liquor Dealers' Assn. (William G. Ross, Pres.; Ferdinand Boegler, Sec.; William A. Tyler, Treas. Trustees: William G. Ross, John Keresey, Justus Oosterlein, William A. Tyler, Ferdinand Boegler, Peter McQuade, James Loucheim, David M. Koehler, Max D. Stern, Louis Isanburger, George Duval, T. D. Parmele) 19 Whitehall

Whyard George W. & Co. (George W. Whyard & Edgar Patterson) 218 Fulton mkt & 22 Vesey

Whyland & Smith (Frank V. Whyland & Stanton M. Smith) 158 Cedar

Wiborn A. & Co. (Albin Wiborn & Charles England) 51 Elm

Wichelns F. & G. (George Wichelns, only) 343 Hudson

Wichmann Brothers (Charles J. & Frederick W. Wichmann) 209 Av. A

Wick Adam & Co. (Adam Wick & George Vix) 10 Front

Wicke William & Co. (William Wicke, August Rossler & Julius Brandes) 530 First av.

Wickham D. H. & Co. (Daniel H. & George S. Wickham & Samuel R. Turner) 94 Maiden la.

Wickliffe C. E. & Co. (inf. unattainable) 308 W. 38th

Wicks George W. & Son (George W. & George W. Wicks jr.) 174 Centre

Wickstead Umbrella Co. (Mary E. Wickstead, propr.) 68 Nassau & 47 John

Wickstead & Winsor (dissolved) 58 Nassau

Wictorowitz S. & Co. (Selig Wictorowitz & Max Halpern) 48 Bleecker

Widder George & Son (George & George Widder jr.) 511 W. 52d

Widmayer & Bothof (dissolved) 58 Bowery

SNOW, CHURCH & CO.,
265 & 267 BROADWAY.

COLLECTIONS IN ALL PARTS OF THE WORLD.
T. C. Campbell and Arthur Murphy, *Counsel.*
TELEPHONE, 735 MURRAY.

WID 326 WIL

Widmer & Singer (inf. unattainable) 139 Fifth av.

Wiebusch & Hilger (Ltd.) (Charles F. Wiebusch, Pres.; Rudolph Lienhart, Sec.; Walter M. Taussig, Treas. Capital, $250,000. Directors: Charles F. Wiebusch, Rudolph Lienhart, Walter M. Taussig, Ernst Hilger, Edward T. Smythe, Thomas J. Leary) 84 Chambers

Wiederer P. & Brother (Peter & Leonhard Wiederer) 521 B'way

Wiegard Brothers (Bernard & William Wiegard) 153 Av. A

Wichl & Widmann (Alfred Wichl & Eugene Widmann) 18 Beaver & 101 Chambers

Wielar & Chock (Joseph Wielar & Pincus Chock) 9 Gt. Jones

Wien S. V. & Co. (dissolved) 50 Bond

Wien, Hoguet & Co. (Samuel Von Wien & E. Hoguet, no Co.) 50 Bond

Wiener John & Co. (John Wiener & Benjamin S. Sugarman) r 17 John

Wiener Brothers (Max & Joseph Wiener) 484 B'way

Wienhold Joseph & Co. (Joseph Wienhold & William Walther) 24 John

Wierk John P. & Co. (John P. & William A. Wierk) 335 E. 47th

Wiese Brothers (Henry & Rudolph Wiese) 131 First av.

Wiesel J. & A. Knshes (Jacob Wiesel & Altar Knshes) 368 Grand

Wiesen Henry & Co. (Henry Wiesen & Christian Brinkmann) 352 E. 18th

Wiesenberger Brothers (David & William Wiesenberger) 1416 Second av.

Wigand Otto & Son (Otto & G. Adolph Wigand) 26 University pl.

Wigert C. R. & Co. (Carl R. Wigert & James Mellor) 4 Stone

Wigger J. J. & R. (dissolved) 1070 Tenth av.

Wigger & Swayze (Robert Wigger & Robert F. Swayze) 49 Lispenard

Wiggers & Froelick (Albert Wiggers & Louis W. Froelick) 60 Nassau

Wiggin's H. B., Sons (Joseph N. Wiggin, only) 124 Clinton pl.

Wiggins & Co. (Clinton G. Wiggins, Co. refused) 171 B'way

Wight Fire-Proofing Co. (Henry P. Day, Pres.; Peter B. Wight, Sec.; Thomas Ferguson, Treas. Capital, $100,000. Directors: Henry P. Day, Peter B. Wight, Thomas Ferguson) 604 W. 51st

Wight George R. & Co. (George R. Wight & Frank F. Basse) 1166 B'way

Wight J. S. & Co. (James S. & Andrew J. Wight) 20 South

Wight W. F. & Co. (dissolved) 72 B'way & 112 Park av.

Wight & Co. (Ltd.) (Charles J. Watson, Pres.; Maurice C. Dreshfield, Sec.; Charles K. Wight, Treas. Capital, $40,000. Directors: Charles J. Watson, Maurice C. Dreshfield, Charles K. Wight) 341 B'way

Wightman S. K. & F. B. (Sullivan K. & Frederick B.) 229 D'way

Wightman & Co. (engravers) (Frederick C. & Frederick T. Wightman) 87 William

Wightman & Co. (suits) (Richard jr. & Elizabeth Wightman) 108 Greene

Wilber J. J. & J. E. (John J. & John E.) 102 Nassau

Wilbern A. & H. (Albert H. & Henry H.) 431 E. Houston

Wilbur & Hastings (William M. Hastings & Charles C. Talcott, only) 40 Fulton

Wilckens Brothers (Doderick B. & Herman F. Wilckens) 939 Third av.

Wilcox W. J., Lard & Refining Co. (E. Urquhart, Pres.; G. Hunter Brown, Sec. Capital, $600,000. Directors: F. Urquhart, R. F. Munro, W. T. Wells) 59 Broad

Wilcox D. & Co. (Dutee Wilcox & Walter Gardiner) 123 B'way

Wilcox & Baird (dissolved) 64 B'way & 19 New

Wilcox & Durant (Clermont H. Wilcox & John L. Durant) 64 B'way & 19 New

Wilcox & Shelton (Ransom E. Wilcox & William A. Shelton) 245 W. 125th

Wilcox & White Organ Co. (Horace C. Wilcox, Pres.; James H. White, Sec. further inf. unattainable) 9 W. 14th

Wilcox, Adams & Macklin (Franklin A. Wilcox, George Bethuno Adams, James J. Macklin & Herbert Green) 69 Wall

Wilcox J. W., Sons (Myron L. & Charles F. Wilcox) 111 Front

Wild Joseph & Co. (Joseph Wild & John Cartledge) 82 Worth & 11 Thomas

Wilde James jr. & Co. (James Dewitt & Harriet B. & Robert L. Wilde, executors) 789 B'way

Wilde's Samuel, Sons (John Wilde, only) 13 Dutch & 110 Water

Wilder Leon & Son (Leon & Samuel Wilder) 86 B. B'way

Wilder W. P. & Co. (William P. Wilder & Theodore Vaanraden) 319 Washn.

Wilder, Wilder & Lynch (William R. Wilder & William J. Lynch, only) 140 Nassau

Wilds J. B. & H. P. (Judson B. & Howard Payson) 55 Liberty

Wildt E. A. & Co. (Edward A. Wildt, Co. refused) 83 Murray

Wile Julius, Brother & Co. (Julius & Isaac Wile & Louis Haas) 51 Murray

Wiley Franklin & Son (inf. unattainable) 42 New

Wiley John & Sons (John & Charles & William H. Wiley) 53 E. 10th

Wiley William H. & Co. (William H. Wiley & James C. Ross) 150 Reade

Wiley G. & S. (George & Sarah) 604 W. 39th & 491 Eleventh av.

Wiley S. W. & Co. (Samuel W. & Joseph Wiley) 353 G'wich

Wiley W. G. & Co. (William G. Wiley & Frederick L. Smith) 59 Wall

Wilhelm & Graef (Henry T. Wilhelm & Frederick E. Graef) 1143 B'way

Wilke & Schmitt (Frederick Wilke & Martin Schmitt) 915 Third av.

Wilkens William & Co. (Louis Wilkens, Herman Schoenjahn & William Wilkens) 217 Pearl

Wilkens J. & H. (John & Henry) 97 Monroe

Wilkens & Brother (William & Herman Wilkens) 209 Hester

Wilkens & Itkens (Peter Wilkens & August Itkens) 90 Cortlandt

Wilkes & Noyes (dissolved) 122 Duane

Wilkin Brothers (Sidney C. & Frank G. Wilkin) 29 Howard

Wilkinson P. & Co. (Frederick P. & Byron Wilkinson) 229 Washn.

Wilkinson & Co. (detectives) (James E. Wilkinson, no Co.) 162 B'way

Wilkinson & Co. (fertilizers) (William R. Wilkinson & Matthew & William Campbell) 59 William

Wilkinson Brothers & Co. (Thomas P. & William Wilkinson & William H. Leach) 72 Duane

Will & Moroney (Martin Will & Patrick Moroney) 121 West

Willamette Valley & Coast R. R. Co. (T. Egenton Hogg, Pres.; Norman S. Bentley, Asst. Sec. Capital, $18,000,000 ; further inf. unattainable) 45 William

WATER METERS, GAS ENGINES, | NATIONAL METER CO.
FOR PUMPING AND POWER. | **252 Broadway, N. Y.**

WIL 327 WIL

Willard John S. & Co. (John S. Willard, no Co.) 257 Canal

Willard Metal Co. (Samuel H. Willard, Pres.; William H. Hardy, Sec. Capital, $10,000. Directors: Samuel H. & Sarah L. & Emma L. Willard, William H. Hardy, Ettla E. Harkelew) 232 Canal & 115 Walker

Willard Mirror & Frame Mfg. Co. (inf. unattainable) 257 Canal

Willard E. A. & Co. (Edward A. Willard, Lyman D. Greene & Herbert Perry) 132 Front

Willard E. K. & Co. (Edward K. Willard, Co. refused) 80 & 1134 B'way & 740 Fifth av.

Willard & McKee (Henry P. Willard & George McKee) 21 Park pl.

Willcox A. O. & Son (Albert O. & Albert & William G. Willcox) 146 B'way

Willcox & Gibbs Sewing Machine Co. (George W. Carleton, Pres.; Jahial Parmly. Sec. Capital, $500,000. Trustees: George W. Carleton, Lucian Sharpe, Charles H. Willcox, Jahial Parmly, Robert W. Forbes, Orville W. Powers) 658 B'way

Wille A. Son (August & Charles H. Wille) 232 E. 125th

Willets Mfg. Co. (Joseph Willets, Pres.; Daniel Willets, Sec.; Edmund R. Willets, Treas. Capital, $50,000. Directors: Joseph & Daniel & Edmund R. Willets) 80 Barclay

Willets S. T. & Co. (Stephen T. Willets. Benjamin F. Bogart & Seth H. Allen) 353 Washn.

Willets & Co. (John T. & Robert R. & William H. & Howard Willets) 308 Pearl & 64 Cliff

Willett John A. & Co. (John A. Willett, Joseph S. Whitney & Thomas E. Lambly) 137 Reade

Willett W. J. & Co. (dissolved) 1102 Third av.

Willett & Gray (Wallace P. Willett & Alfred P. Gray) 91 Wall

Willett & Hamlen (dissolved) 91 Wall

Willey A. H. & Co. (Alfred H. Willey & William H. Ruffhead) 18 Park row

Willey & Johnston (James M. Willey & Samuel Johnston) 2 Liberty

Williams Benjamin F. & Co. (Benjamin F. Williams, Co. refused) ft. E. 101st

Williams Co. (Frances Goetz, propr.) 58 Lispenard

Williams David T. & Co. (David T. Williams & Frank V. Leeds) 238 Front

Williams Frank, Printing Co. (Frank Williams, Pres.; William R. Baird, Sec. Capital, $5,000. Directors: Frank Williams, William R. Baird, James T. Brown) 71 William

Williams Ichabod T. (Ichabod T. & Thomas & Henry K. S. Williams) 221 Eleventh av.

Williams John R., Co. (John R. Williams, Pres.; William L. Lyman, Sec. Capital, $100,000. Directors: John R. Williams, William L. Lyman, George M. Hard, William Eggert, Charles C. Gill) 102 Chambers

Williams Printing Co. (David Williams, Pres.; Richard R. Williams, Sec.; John S. King, Treas. Capital, $5,000. Trustees: David & Richard R. Williams, John S. King) 66 Duane

Williams Silk Mfg. Co. (Coleman G. W Illams, Pres.; Leonidas P. Williams, Treas. Capital, $12,500. Directors: Coleman G. & Leonidas P. Williams) 524 B'way & 204 E. 43d

Williams T., Co. (Ltd.) (Capital, $25,000 ; further inf. unattainable) no address

Williams B. A. & G. N. jr. (Benjamin A. & George N. jr.) Av. A & E. 68th

Williams D. M. & Co. (David M. & Sylvanus J. Williams) 2808 Third av. & 107 E. 125th

Williams E. C. & Co. (dissolved) 1 William

Williams F. G. & Brother (Edward G. & Henry V. Williams) 218 Fulton

Williams E. G. & Co. (refused) 9 Mercer

Williams F. & Co. (Frank Williams, Robert B. Hungerford & Sanford H. Weeks) 386 W. 11th & 601 W. 33d

Williams F. H. & Co. (Frank H. Williams, no Co.) 683 B'way

Williams H. E. & C. D. (Henry E. & Charles D.) 41 Spruce

Williams H. P. & Co. (Henry P. Williams, no Co.) 250 Canal & 98 Walker

Williams J. & W. (John & William) 353 W. 54th

Williams J. M. & Co. (John M. Williams, no Co.) 206 W. 125th

Williams R. & Son (Robert H. & Charles E. Williams) 175 Prince & r 26 Bedford

Williams R. C. & Co. (Roswell C. Williams, Frank Sittig & Edwin H. Sayre) 56 Hudson

Williams W. C. & Co. (no inf.) 97 Water

Williams Brothers (liquors) (Edward F. & James J. Williams) 2002 Third av.

Williams Brothers (posters) (Charles Williams, only) 202 William

Williams & Acker (Edward W Williams & John D. Acker) 69 Warren

Williams & Clark Fertilizer Co. (John T. Williams, Pres.; W. W. Green, Sec.; Henry L. Dudley, Treas. Capital, $100,000. Directors: John T. Williams, W. W. Green, Henry L. Dudley) 81 Fulton

Williams & Co. (agents) (John Williams, no Co.) 22 Cortlandt st.

Williams & Co. (grocers) (Lyndon O. Williams & Walter R. Stebbins) 1695 Madison av.

Williams & Co. (meat) (refused) 56 Fulton mkt

Williams & Guion (William H. Guion, receiver) 29 B'way

Williams & James (Samuel T. Williams & Charles F. James) 60 Barclay

Williams & Jones (Richard Williams & Edward Jones) r 151 E. 27th

Williams & Laporte (dissolved) 768 Third av.

Williams & Peters (Richard H. Williams & Samnel T. Peters) 1 B'way

Williams & Potter (Horace M. Williams & Frederick D. Potter) 15 Cortlandt

Williams & Prehn (Thomas Williams & George Prehn) 90 Cotton Ex.

Williams & Rankine (Richard Williams jr. & James Rankine) 19 Whitehall

Williams & Rickerson (Charles L. Rickerson, only) 64 Harrison

Williams & Stewart (John M. Williams & Charles Stewart) 501 Hudson

Williams & Terhune (Perry P. Williams & Abram B. Terhune) 4 B'way

Williams & Whitney (dissolved) 88 Fulton

Williams, Black & Co. (Richard P. & Francis S. Williams & Paul Schwarz, only) 1 William

Williams, Russell & Co. (Frank Williams, James C. Russell, Joseph D. Pickslay & Frederick P. Gordon) 105 Front

Williams, Stiger & Co. (Henry W. Williams, Oliver M. Stiger, Charles E. Lovett & Frank D. Otis) 20 College pl. & 65 Park pl.

Williams' Globe Wire Works (George A. Williams, propr.) 55 Fulton

Williams' John, Sons (dissolved) ft. E. 101st

Williams-French Fattening Poultry Co. (no inf.) 99 Barclay

Williamsburgh Brewing Co. (Ltd.) (Jacques A. Bernheimer, Pres.; Samuel M. Schafer Sec.; Martin R. Cook, Treas. Capital, $200,000. Directors: Jacques A. Bernheimer, Samuel M. Schafer, Martin R. Cook, Isaac & Simon Bernheimer, William Kramer) 144 Franklin & 4 Stone

Williamsburgh City Fire Ins. Co. (Marshall S. Driggs, Pres.; Frederick H. Way, Sec. Capital, $250,000. Directors: Samuel M. Meeker, William Marshall, Martin G. Johnson, John

EXCELSIOR BIRD FOOD. The recognized standard. The most reliable for your Canary. Use no other. Insist upon getting it. Packed only by **C. ROSENSTEIN & CO.**, 373 Washington Street, New York.

C. Debevoise, John Broach, James Rodwell, George E. Kitching, Henry W. Slocum, Moses May, Martin Joost, Adrian M. Suydam, Peter Wyckoff, John G. Jenkins, Chauncey Marshall, Steven P. Sturges, Silas W. Driggs, Henry W. Slocum jr, Joseph J. O'Donohue, Frederic L. Dubois, Marshall S. Driggs) 150 B'way & 100 Fourth av.

Williamson Extract Co. (Douw D. Williamson, propr.) 14 Day

Williamson James & Co. (Samuel A. S. Wilks, only) 63 Wall

Williamson Mfg. Co, (dissolved) 98 Duane

Williamson E. & M. (Eleanora Williamson & Margaret A. Greene, only) 1688 Third av.

Williamson G. V. & Co. (George V. Williamson, Co. refused) 903 Washn.

Williamson T. S. & Brother (Tennis S. & Reuben E. Williamson) 11 Lawton av. W. Washn. mkt

Williamson Brothers (dissolved) 903 Washn.

William on & Coletti (Charles Williamson & Emile Coletti) 201 B'way

Williamson & Co. (George H. Williamson, Co. refused) 98 Union sq. E.

Williamson & Reynolds (J. Schenck Williamson & John Reynolds) 7 Nassau

Williamson & Stowell (James Williamson & Charles S. Stowell) 10 Ninth av.

Williamson's A. J., Sons (dissolved) 11 Frankfort

Williamsport & Binghamton R. R. Co. (Francis M. Ward, Pres.; Charles F. Camp, Sec.; Ezra J. Sterling, Treas. Capital, $2,500,000. Directors: Joseph P. Noyes, A. P. Berthond, Ezra J. Sterling, E. R. Payne, Adgar Munson, William Gibson, Elias Dermer, John E. Dayton, Francis M. Ward, Charles Kilgore, Isaac O. Blight, Thomas E. Proctor, R. Carman Combes, John Ray Clark, James B. Weed) 111 B'way

Willich Theodore & Co. (Theodore Willich & William Muller) 159 William

Willimantic Silk Co. (no inf.) 69 Mercer

Willis W. F. & Co. (William F. Willis & estate of William H. Townsend) 729 B'way

Willis & Hunter (Henry C. Willis & Theodore F. Hunter) 83 Church

Williston & Knight Co. (Horatio G. Knight, Pres.; Horace L. Clark, Sec. Capital, $150,000. Directors: William H. Chapman, Frank P. Tenney, Bernard N. Farren, Horatio G. Knight, Horace L. Clark) 540 B'way & 78 Crosby

Willman-Cosenna Co. (dissolved) 60 Broad

Wills Henry T. & Co. (Henry T. Wills, no Co.) 24 State

Wills Brothers Co. (William Wills, Pres.; James Wills, Sec. Capital, $25,000. Directors: William & James Wills, Charles F. Wilday) 161 Chambers, 143 Reade, 395 G'wich & 62 Beach

Wills & Dyer (Stephen S. Wills & John N. Dyer) E. 92d n First av.

Wills & Hall (Frederick H. Wills, only) 24 Cotton Ex.

Wills & McCrae (John R. Wills & George T. McCrae) 32 Gansevoort

Wilson T. A., Optical Co. (Ltd.) (Gustave Walter, Pres.; Leopold M. Leberthon, Sec. Capital, $50,000. Directors: Gustave Walter, Leopold M. Leberthon, Theodore A. Wilson) 14 Maiden la.

Wilson & Redenberg (Hugh R. Wilson & Harry W. Redenberg) 111 B'way

Wilson, Adams & Co. (Charles H. Wilson, Charles L. & Allen W. Adams, Walter W. Watrous & Jacob S. Carvalho) 140 Pearl, ft. E. 42d & E. 138 n Mott av.

Willstatter & Stern (Max Willstatter & Joseph Stern) 496 Broome

Wilmer & Canfield (William N. Wilmer & George F. Canfield) 49 Wall

Wilmerding & Bisset (Lucius K. Wilmerding & Thomas B. Bisset) 78 Leonard

Wilmerding, Morris & Mitchell (John C. & J. Currie Wilmerding, John J. Morris, Cornelius B. Mitchell & John J. Morris jr.) 66 White

Wilmore J. A. & Co. (James A. & Arthur G. Wilmore & Walter W. Crawford) 43 Centre

Wilmore & Boyden (Elias W. Boyden, only) 647 Sixth av.

Wilmot & Co. (Inf. unattainable) 182 South

Wilmot & Gage (De Borden Wilmot & Wellesley W. Gage) 44 B'way

Wilmurt T. A. & Son (Thomas A. & Thomas A. Wilmurt jr.) 54 E. 13th

Wilmurt & Jarvis (Jefferson Wilmurt & Frank Jarvis) 269 E. 125th & 211 E. 100th

Wilsey O. J. & Co. (Otis J. Wilsey & Edward A. Dillenbeck) 601 W. 33d

Wilson Anti-Friction White Metal Co, (Inf. unattainable) 510 W. 32d

Wilson David & Son (David & James M. Wilson) 8 Spruce & 206 E. 120th

Wilson George & Son (George & James Wilson) 176 Third av.

Wilson Henry S. & Brother (Henry S. & John D. Wilson) 15 Broad

Wilson Jacob & Son (Jacob & Edward Wilson) 20 Cortlandt

Wilson James & Son (James & William J. Wilson) 54 E. 13th

Wilson John A. & Co. (John A. & Richard Wilson) 129 Broad

Wilson John C. & Co. (John C, Wilson & Charles W. Dreyer) 134 Greene

Wilson W. D., Printing Ink Co. (Ltd.) (George P. Rowell, Pres.; Charles N. Kent. Sec.; Oscar G. Mosos, Treas. Directors: George P. Rowell, Charles N. Kent, Oscar G. Moses, James H. Beals jr, Philip Carpenter, V. R. C. Giddings, Francis J. Schleicher, Daniel F. Barry, A. Frank Richardson) 140 William & 96 Fulton

Wilson William & Son (Samuel Wilson, only) 26 S. William

Wilson A. S. & Co. (Abraham S. Wilson & George Boyle) 3 E. 4th

Wilson D. H. & Co. (Henry A. & George L. Wilson, only) 78 Hudson

Wilson J. W. & Co. (John W. Wilson, Robert B. Lynch & Stephen A. Levy) 52 Front

Wilson O, C. & K. R. (Oliver C. & Kendrick R.) 59 West

Wilson P. K., Son & Co. (Peter K. & Samuel M. Wilson & Henry Gimpel) 451 B'way

Wilson R. T. & Co. (Richard T. Wilson, J. Marshall & William M. Johnston, Benjamin F. Wilson & Charles H. Rosher) 2 Exchange ct.

Wilson S. D. & Sons (Stephen D. & Charles H. Wilson, only) 200 Varick

Wilson S. H. & Co. (Samuel H. Wilson & William Mills) 19 White

Wilson Brothers (brass gds.) (John M. Wilson, only) 823 B'way

Wilson Brothers (cabinet mkrs.) (John & Alexander Wilson) 514 W. 24th

Wilson Brothers' Woodenware & Toy Co. (David W. Wilson, Pres.; Charles L. Wilson, Sec.; Isaac C. Wilson, Treas. Capital, $5,000; further inf. refused) 119 Chambers

Wilson & Baillie Mfg. Co. (Charles B. Johnson, Pres.; Ellis H. Baillie, Sec.; Frank B. Johnson, Treas. Directors: Charles B. Johnson, John J. Wilson, Frank B Johnson, Ellis H. Baillie) 40 B'way

Wilson & Brown (Thomas B. Wilson & Frank C. Brown) 100 Maiden la.

Wilson & Calder (dissolved) 473 B'way

IDEN & CO., University Place, 9th to 10th Sts., N.Y. | MANUFACTURERS OF **GAS FIXTURES AND ELECTROLIERS**

Wilson & Darnell (George W. Wilson & Henry Darnell) 120 B'way
Wilson & Griffin (Gilbert E. Wilson & John Griffin) 135 South
Wilson & Kellogg (Francis F. Wilson & John M. Kellogg) 629 Fifth av.
Wilson & Nattes (Kate A. Wilson & Antonio Nattes) 51 E. 11th
Wilson & Roake (James A. Wilson & John S. Roake) 261 Front & 536 Water
Wilson & Wallis (William G. Wilson, Hamilton Wallis, Walter C. Gilson & George E. Comey) 46 Wall
Wilson & Warren (dissolved) 1022 Lex. av.
Wilson & Welles (Theodore Wilson & Charles E. Welles) 74 B'way & 9 New
Wilson & Wheeler (dissolved) 129 Broad
Wilsonia Magnetic Appliance Co. (Wilsonia Magnetic Clothing Co. propr's.) 831 B'way
Wilsonia Magnetic Clothing Co. (Andrew B. Chalmers, Pres.; Frank M. Brooks, Sec.; Roderick Burt, Treas. Capital, $100,000. Directors: Andrew B. Chalmers, Rufus R. Goodell, Frank M. Brooks, Roderick Burt) 831 D'way
Wilts William & Co. (dissolved) 717 Courtlandt av.
Wimpfheimer Adolph & Co. (Adolph Wimpfheimer & Samuel Kuhle) 141 Greene
Wimpfheimer A. & Brother (Charles A. Wimpfheimer, only) 71 Greene
Winant George W. & Son (George W. & William F. Winant) 85 Ninth av.
Winant & Co. (James A. & William A. Winant) 75 Centre mkt
Winant & Phillips (William K. Winant & Ward Phillips) 58 William
Winch C. A. & Co. (Charles A. Winch, no Co.) 523 W. 21st
Winchester J. H. & Co. (James H. Winchester & Joseph C. Noyes) 135 Pearl
Winchester & Co. (Agnes E. Winchester & Henry A. Bartholomew) 162 William
Windhorst Brothers (John & Adolph Windhorst) 1496 First av.
Windmuller Louis & Roelker (Louis Windmuller & Alfred Roelker) 20 Reade
Windsor Manor (Duvivier & Co. propr's.) 49 Broad
Wing L. J., Co. (inf. unattainable) 80 John
Wing H. R. & Son (Herman R. Wing & Robert T. Brown, only) 21 Spruce
Wing & Evans (John D. & J. Morgan & L. Stuart Wing, only) 54 William
Wing & Lee (Luck Wing & Kouw P. Lee) 2810 Eighth av.
Wing & Son (Charles U. Wing, only) 245 B'way
Wing & Tuck (dissolved) 24 Oliver
Wing, Shoudy & Putnam (Henry T. Wing, Joseph A. Shoudy & Harrington Putnam) 46 William
Wingate & Cullen (George W. Wingate & Henry J. Cullen jr.) 20 Nassau
Wingendorf & Co. (dissolved) 297 First av.
Wingerter & Braun (dissolved) 182 Third
Wingfield & Taylor (George W. Wingfield & George W. Taylor) 140 Varick
Winklemeyer J. & Co. (Joseph Winklemeyer & Theodore Lutz) 464 Eleventh av.
Winne D. P. & Brother (no inf.) 337 E. 86th
Winne & Co. (no inf.) 17 South
Winship & Burr (Leonard A. Winship & James M. Durr) 346 Canal
Winslow Stewart & Co. (Stewart & Benedict S. Winslow) 81 B'way
Winslow, Lanier & Co. (Charles Lanier, Edward D. Adams, John Howard Latham, Edward Winslow. J. Frederick Chamberlin & James F. D. Lanier) 17 Nassau
Winslow, Whitlock & Co. (Francis D. Winslow,

C. Howard Whitlock & Richard M. Corwine) 36 New
Winter George, Brewing Co. (Jacob Hoffmann, Pres.; Henry Hoffmann, Sec.; William Hoffmann, Treas. Capital, $800,000. Directors: Jacob & William & Henry & Philip & George J. Hoffmann) 204 E. 55th
Winter & Goetz (Ferdinand Winter & Ferdinand Goetz) 156 William
Winter & Gloistein (George Winter & John H. Gloistein) 76 Grand
Winter & Schaumburg (Edward Winter & August F. Schaumburg) 99 Pearl & 62 Stone
Winter & Smillie (Henry P. Winter & Charles F. Smillie) 62 Wall
Winterborg & Co. (Abraham Winterberg, Co. refused) 148 Water
Winterbottom J. & Sons (James & Thomas W. Winterbottom, only) 194 Spring & 96 Sullivan
Winterbottom & Peck (William S. Winterbottom & John M. Peck) 289 Hudson
Winterle & Nebel (Max Winterle & Martin Nebel) 85 E. 4th
Winterroth & Co. (Emil J. Winterroth, no Co.) 17 E. 14th
Winters J. & Son (dissolved) 79 Cedar
Winterton & Wardell (dissolved) 95 Park pl.
Winthrop Robert & Co. (Robert Winthrop, Mark T. Cox & Robert Dudley Winthrop) 3 Broad
Winton & Harroun (no inf.) 190 Chambers
Wire Buckle Suspender Co. (Silvermann Brothers & Co. propr's.) 481 B'way
Wirsing & Walther (George Wirsing & John Walther) 25 Beekman
Wirth R. & Co. (inf. unattainable) 1730 B'way
Wirthe Brothers (Maurice & Walter & Rudolph Wirtha) 41 Walker
Wisansky Brothers (dissolved) 599 D'way
Wischebrink & Sauer (Herman Wischebrink & Theodore Sauer) 169 Stanton
Wise Luther & Co. (Luther Wise & Henry C. Perley) 300 Third av.
Wise C. & Co. (Colman Wise; further inf. unattainable) 250 B'way
Wise L. & C. (Leopold & Charles) 88 Reade
Wise Brothers (Leo H. & Edward H. Wise) 65 Leonard
Wise & Lichtenstein (Morris S. Wise & Solomon K. Lichtenstein) 52 Exchange pl.
Wisel A. & Co. (Adolph & Jacob & Morris Wisel) 26 Cliff
Wisner William H. & Co. (Henry G. & Charles Wisner, only) 45 Cotton Ex.
Wissemann Brothers (Conrad & Christopher Wissemann) 610 E. 11th
Wissmann & Fritz (dissolved) 90 Barclay
Wist & Hughes (Julius Wist & James H. Hughes) 84 Old sl.
Wiswall & Convis (Joseph P. Wiswall & Charles E. Convis) 6 Wall
Wiswall & O'Brien (Horatio D. Wiswall & John O'Brien) 3390 Third av.
Witbeck & Genung (Howard S. Witbeck & Abram P. Genung) 41 Liberty
Witbeck & Smith (Cornelius V. Witbeck & Henry R. Smith) 124 Prince & 169 Bleecker
Withers & Dickson (Frederick C. Withers & Walter Dickson) Bible h.
Withington Henry & Son (Henry & Richard W. Withington) 123 Pearl & 76 Beaver
Witkoski A. & R. (dissolved) 687 Eighth av.
Witmark Entertainment Bureau (M. Witmark & Sons, propr's.) 841 B'way
Witmark Simon & Son (dissolved) 370½ W. 29th
Witmark M. & Sons (Marcus & Isidor & Julius P. Witmark) 841 B'way

CIRCULARS ADDRESSED TO ANY TRADE IN THE U. S. { Facilities
PROMPT, CAREFUL WORK } THE TROW CITY DIRECTORY CO., { Unequalled.
AT MODERATE PRICES. } 11 University Place.

WIT   330   WOM

Witmark Brothers (Isidor & Jay Witmark) 402 W. 40th
Witmark & Hawkins (Isidor Witmark & Frederick D. Hawkins) 841 B'way
Witsch & Schmitt (Nicholas Witsch & Jacob Schmitt) 94 Bowery
Witt & Pursch (Julius Witt & Frank Pursch) 506 B'way
Witte Christoph & Co. (J. Adolph Witte, only) 76 Pine
Witte Francis T., Hardware Co. (Francis T. Witte, Pres.; Charles H. Biermann, Sec. Capital, $20,000. Directors: Francis T. Witte, Charles H. Biermann, Charles F. Wiebusch) 100 Chambers
Witte H. (George H. Witte, only) 41 Platt
Witte John G. & Brother (John G. & William Witte) 75 Chambers
Wittemann Lithographic Co. (Jacob F. Wittemann, Pres.; Edgar J. Eicke, Sec. Directors: Jacob F. Wittemann, Edgar J. Eicke) 158 William
Wittemann Brothers (Jacob F. Wittemann, only) 192 Fulton
Wittenstein & Marks (dissolved) 92 Canal
Witter & Kenyon (William C. Witter & William H. & Alan D. & Robert N. Kenyon) 38 Park row
Witthoff, Marsily & Co. (Charles Witthoff & Ferdinand A. Marsily, no Co.) 18 Beaver
Wittlich F. & A. (Frederick & Adolph) 1096 Third av.
Wittschen & Koster (Bernhard C. Wittschen & Herman Koster) 1438 Third av.
Wix Charles & Co. (Charles Wix & Jules Hashagen) 53 Dey
Wobse & Ihnen (dissolved) 28 Old sl.
Wobse & Selmers (Dederick Wobse & Herman Selmers) 506 S. Boulevard
Woehrle George & Son (George G. & Albert C. Woehrle) 2115 Third av.
Woehrle & Heuer (George W. Woehrle & Herman Heuer) 129 Division
Woelpper Brothers (Henry & George J. Woelpper) 145 Sullivan
Woeltje & Cutting (Charles H. Woeltje & Charles W. Cutting) 115 Pearl
Woerishoffer & Co. (Frederick G. Renner & Hans Sommerhoff, only) 50 Exchange pl.
Woest & Mencke (Charles W. Woest & Henry C. Mencke) 1896 Third av.
Wogram Frederick & Co. (dissolved) 176 Worth
Wohl & Branner (Samuel Wohl & Minnie Branner) 353 Canal
Wojcsik & Weber (dissolved) 243 Third
Wolf John G. & Co. (John G. Wolf, Co. refused) 102 Wooster
Wolf Joseph & Son (Joseph & Jacob Wolf) 452 Grand
Wolf Louis & Co. (Louis Wolf & Adolph Erichsohn) 438 Broome
Wolf Max & Co. (Max Wolf, no Co.) 264 E. B'way
Wolf William & Co. (dissolved) 145 Fulton
Wolf A. B. & Brother (Alexander B. & Joseph L. Wolf) 9 Gt. Jones
Wolf B. J. & Sons (no inf.) 708 B'way
Wolf E. & Sons (Elias Wolf, only) 1 Av. B
Wolf F. & J. C. (Frederick C. jr. & John C.) 1455 B'way
Wolf R. & A. (Henry & August) 92 Fulton
Wolf & Co. (cornice mkrs.) (John & George Wolf) 2182 Eighth av.
Wolf & Co. (tailors) (Rose Wolf & Rebecca Marks) 145 Fulton
Wolfe J. & Co. (Jacques & Virginia Wolfe) 669 First av.

Wolfe N. H. & Co. (inf. unattainable) 1 State
Wolfe's Udolpho, Son & Co. (Joel B. Wolfe, only) 9 Beaver
Wolfer & Guest (Jacob J. Wolfer & George H. Guest) ft. E. 97th
Wolff Baruch & Co. (Baruch & Kaufman Wolff) 259 Canal
Wolff Charles & Brother (Charles & Bernard Wolff) 62 W. 125th
Wolff Charles & Co. (Max Wolff:—special partner, Charles Wolff, $25,000; terminates 1st Jan. 1893) 405 B'way & 66 Mercer
Wolff Rudolph & Co. (Rudolph & Charles R. & Oscar R. Wolff) 44 Walker
Wolff William & Co. (William Wolff & Samuel M. Levy) 25 Howard
Wolff William & Son (William & Abraham Wolff) 239 E. 74th
Wolff K. & Co. (Herman & Louis Wolff) 497 B'way & 68 Mercer
Wolff R. H. & Co. (Ltd.) (Raphael H. Wolff, Pres.; Charles Weill, Sec.; Levi Bamberger, Treas. Capital, $400,000. Directors: Raphael H. Wolff, Levi Bamberger, Charles Weill, Ernest Bilhuber, Henry Diedel, Edwin Henes) 500 E. 118th
Wolff & Barry (Arnowitz Wolff & John F. Barry) 105 W. B'way
Wolff & Cohn (dissolved) 510 B'way
Wolff & Co. (hats) (Sarah Wolff & Louis Schoolherr) 126 Greene
Wolff & Co. (pictures) (Jacob Wolff, no Co.) 253 E. 10th
Wolff & Hodge (William Almon Wolff, J. Aspinwall Hodge jr, Frederick J. Winston & William Isaquin jr.) 84 Nassau
Wolff & Michelson (William Wolff & Adolph Michelson) 227 G'wich
Wolff & Roessing (Julius Wolff & Herman Roessing) 62 Front
Wolff & Seligsberg (Lee Wolff & Louis Seligsberg) 141 Pearl
Wolff & Sicherer (dissolved) 107 Wooster
Wolff's European Express (not inc.) (William S. Wolff & Marcus S. Friede) 47 B'way
Wolfsheim & Goldsmith (Louis Wolfsheim & Herman A. Goldsmith) 14 Malden ln.
Wolinski & Raymond (Jacob Wolinski & Joseph Raymond) 36 E. B'way
Wolk & Seff (Sigmund Wolk & Morris Seff) 90 Eldridge
Wolken & Berger (Henry Wolken & Louis M. Berger) 143 Broome
Woll Peter & Sons (Peter & Adolph & Peter jr. & Frederick Woll) 307 Pearl
Wollerman & Roeth (Charles T. Wollerman & John J. Roeth) 269 Canal
Wollner K. & Son (Koppleman & Henry Wollner) 65 Canal
Wollner M. L. & Co. (Moritz L. Wollner, no Co.) 86 Lispenard
Wollstein & Sulsberger (Minna Wollstein & Solomon Sulsberger) r 17 & 23 John
Wolter & Cordes (Herman H. Wolter & William Cordes) 198 Lex. av.
Wolters Peter & Co. (dissolved) 217 Bowery
Wolters, Hoberg & Co. (Herman Wolters, Christian Hoberg & Charles Beckman) 2181 Third av.
Woltmann, Keith & Co. (Emil Woltmann, George T. Keith, no Co.) 11 Wall
Women's Mutual Ins. & Accident Co. (Elizabeth B. Phelps, Pres.; Emily Taylor, Sec.; Margaret W. Holcombe, Treas. Directors: Elizabeth B. Phelps, Margaret W. Holcombe, Cornelia Kamping, Emily Taylor, Elizabeth Hardenburg, Elizabeth S. Robertson, Cathar-

THE CALIGRAPH WRITING MACHINE,
HARTFORD, CONN.

ine Garrick, Charlotte Mulligan, Mary F. Hoagland) 173 B'way

Wood Carpet Co. (William Hannam & Co, proprs.) 23 Union sq. W.

Wood George L. & Son (George L. & William D. Wood) 246 Pearl

Wood Gilbert & Son (Gilbert & Joseph Wood) 628 W. 30th

Wood H. Duncan & Co. (H. Duncan Wood, John P. Kelly & Walton C. Whittingham) 18 Wall & 8 Nassau

Wood James & William, 4 Stone

Wood Thomas H. & Co. (Thomas H. Wood, Henry K. Motley & Watts Gardner) 673 B'way

Wood Walter A., Mowing & Reaping Machine Co. (Walter A. Wood, Pres.; Charles M. Coultor, Sec.; Willard Gay, Treas. Capital, $2,500,000. Trustees: Walter A. Wood, William S. Nichols, William Tillinghast, James A. Eddy, William Gay, J. Wood Griswold, C. E. Dudley Tibbets) 12 Cortlandt

Wood Walter N. & Son (Walter N. & Frank A. Wood) 917 Sixth av.

Wood William & Co. (William H. S. & William C. Wood) 56 Lafayette pl.

Wood A. B. & Son (Augustus B. & D. Franklin Wood) 164 South

Wood A. H. & Co. (Arthur H. Wood & Anna C. Tasker) 2197 Second av.

Wood C. J. & Son (Caleb J. & Wescot A. Wood) 46 W. 36th

Wood F. R. & Son (Frederick R. & Clarence W. Wood) 219 W. 19th

Wood J. R. & Sons (John R. & Rawson L. & St. John Wood) 14 John

Wood M. Co. (Mary Wood, Co. refused) 88 Fifth av.

Wood & Chesebro (Israel B. Wood & Samuel Z. Chesebro) 150 Beekman

Wood & Co. (Squire & Marvin F. Wood) 325 B'way

Wood & Hughes (Henry Wood & Dixon G. Hughes) 16 John & 589 Hudson

Wood & Miller (Arthur E. Wood & James Miller) 2187 Seventh av.

Wood & Payson (Francis Payson, only) 64 Pine

Wood & Selick (Charles Wood & Charles H. Selick) 49 Jay

Wood & Tolmie (Robert Wood & Murric Tolmie) 208 W. 30th

Wood, Huestis & Co. (George C. Wood, Charles H. Huestis, Lyndon M. Swan & Edward H. Ladd jr.) 31 Pine

Wood, Nicbuhr & Co. (Fraley C. Nicbuhr, Henry Camerdon jr. & Henry R. Needham, only) 19 William

Wood-Brinkley Co. (dissolved) 1522 B'way

Wood-Mosaic Co. (Charles E. Rider, propr.) 315 Fifth av.

Woodbridge C. L. & Co. (Charles L. Woodbridge & Walter Hanford) 451 B'way & 28 Mercer

Woodbridge & Turner (J. Lester Woodbridge & William S. Turner) 74 Cortlandt

Woodburn W. C. & Co. (William C. Woodburn & Amos Morgan) 137 B'way

Woodbury Brothers (Oscar D. Woodbury, only) 200 Eleventh av.

Woodhaven Junction Land Co. (Joseph G. Briggs, Pres.; Charles G. Davison, Sec.; Louis C. Whiton, Treas. Capital, $50,000. Directors: Joseph G. Briggs, Charles G. Davison, Louis C. & Augustus S. Whiton, Charles Bell) 115 B'way

Woodhaven Water Supply Co. (Florian Grosjean, Pres.; Auguste J. Cordier, Sec.; Edwin W. Martin, Treas. Capital, $50,000. Directors: John C. Milligan, Florian Grosjean, Auguste J. Cordier, Edwin W. Martin) 19 Cliff

Woodhouse D. A., Mfg. Co. (Woodhouse, Forster, & Burchell, proprs.) 12 Barclay

Woodhouse & Forster (dissolved) 12 Barclay

Woodhouse & Stortz (John H. Woodhouse & Valentine Stortz) 76 Pine

Woodhouse, Forster & Burchell (Daniel A. Woodhouse, Thomas V. Forster & James J. Burchell) 12 Barclay

Woodhull N. D. & Co. (John W. Taynter, only) 20 N. Moore

Woodlawn Cemetery (William A. Booth, Pres.; James D. Smith, Sec.; Charles S. Smith, Treas. Trustees: William A. Booth, James D. Smith, Hugh N. Camp, George A. Peters, Sheppard Gandy, Charles S. Smith, William T. Booth, Sherman W. Knevals, Edward Schell, Caleb B. Knevals) 20 E. 23d

Woodlawn Improvement Assn. (George F. Gerrard, Pres.; William B. Short, Sec.; Myron C. Burton, Treas.) Woodlawn Heights

Woodley H. J. & Co. (Henry J. Woodley, no Co.) 208 Church

Woodman Joel H. & Co. (Joel H. Woodman, no Co.) 517 W. 30th

Woodman N. H. & Co. (Nathaniel H. Woodman, no Co.) 28 Water

Woodrow & Lewis (Sylvester A. Woodrow, Edward L. Lewis & Frederick Walker) 94 Pearl

Woodruff William T. & Co. (Hiram Woodruff, only) 97 William & Custom h.

Woodruff A. G. & Co. (Albert G. & Joseph M. Woodruff) 687 B'way & 250 Mercer

Woodruff A. J. & Co. (Anthony J. Woodruff, no Co.) 67 William

Woodruff F. & Co. (Franklin Woodruff & Frank W. Farnham) 202 Produce Ex.

Woodruff I. O. & Co. (Isaac Ogden Woodruff, no Co.) 88 Maiden la.

Woodruff R. W. & Co. (dissolved) 9 Little W. 12th

Woodruff & Co. (dissolved) 653 B'way

Woodruff, Conklin & Dayer (Aaron B. Woodruff, Lewis M. Conklin & Leonard Dayer) 161 Lewis

Woodruff's Amos, Sons (Valentine S. & Bayard T. Woodruff) 250 W. 40th

Woods James & Co. (James Woods & George Wright) 97 Water

Woods S. A., Machine Co. (Solomon A. Woods, Pres.; Elroy N. Heath, Treas. Capital, $300,000. Directors: Solomon A. & Frank F. Woods, Elroy N. Heath) 91 Liberty

Woods Brother (John F. & James J. Woods) 89 & 131 Washn. & 20 West

Woods & Blair (dissolved) 606 Hudson

Woods & Dreyfuss (Thomas Woods & Samuel Dreyfuss) 2284 First av.

Woods & Duff (Owen Woods & Dennis Duff) 375 First av, 295 Tenth av. & 470 Eleventh av.

Woods, Lowry & Co. (John Lowry & John W. Woolley;—special partner, James H. Woods, $50,000; terminates 1st Jan, 1891) 83 W. 23d

Woodward Steam Pump Co. (William Dauphin, propr.) 10 Reade

Woodward Willis & Co. (Willis & Frank W. Woodward) 842 B'way

Woodward & Buckley (John S. Woodward & Charles P. Buckley) 171 B'way

Woodward & Hoyt (Collin H. Wondward & John J. T. Hoyt) 51 W. 125th & 316 W. 144th

Woodward & Stillman (James & Charles Stillman & Simon J. Harding, only) 10 Exchange pl.

Woodward, Baldwin & Co. (William H. Baldwin jr. Elijah P. Smith & Rignal T. Woodward) 43 Worth

Woodward, Sherwood & Co. (Russell W. Woodward, Thorpe P. Sherwood & J. Q. Aymar Williamson) 168 B'way & 48 Cedar

Woodworth's C. F., Son & Co. (Frederick M. Wood-

SPECIAL ATTENTION PAID TO THIS CLASS OF WORK. } **BANKERS' & BROKERS' CIRCULARS DELIVERED** { THE TROW CITY DIRECTORY CO. 11 University Place.

WOO 332 WUE

worth & Charles F. Dewitt) 72 Dey & 111 Fulton mkt

Woog & Freeman (Jacob Woog & Benjamin Freeman) 616 B'way & 180 Crosby

Wooley & Co. (Adeline Wooley & William Grosback) 81 Fulton

Woolf Brothers (refused) 75 Nassau

Woolley M. & Co. (Michael Woolley & John Hughes) 50 Howitt av. W. Washn. mkt

Woolley & Moore Co. (Henry S. Woolley, Pres.; C. Arthur Baynon, Sec. Capital, $10,000. Directors: Henry S. Woolley, Henry Moore, C. Arthur Baynon) 80 Reade

Woolsey & Throckmorton (George C. Woolsey & Bogart R. Throckmorton) 20 Gansevoort

Woolworth & Graham (Calvin C. Woolworth & John S. Graham) 154 Nassau & 88 Rose

Worcester Corset Co. (David H. Fanning, Pres.; Frank W. Ruggles, Treas.; Charles B. Maynard, Sec.; further inf. unattainable) 425 B'way

Worden & Co. (Daniel T. Worden & Herman de Selding) 6 Wall

Work, O'Keeffe & Co. (no inf.) 52 B'way

Work, Strong & Co. (Frank Work, William E. Strong, George Wood & Frank K. Sturgis) 88 Broad

Workingman's Co-operative Assn. of the United Ins. League of N. Y. (Adolph O. Bothner, Pres.; Ernest A. Bastianelli, Sec.; John O'Shea, Treas. Directors: William B. Donahey, John O'Shea, Adolph O. Bothner, Frederick Marquard, Waldemar Dorfmann, William Schultze, Ernest A. Bastianelli, Frederick Stein) 50 Union sq. E.

Works H. S. & Co. (dissolved) 79 Chambers

World Beef Co. (not inc.) (Isabella Hauser, & Sigmund Gutfreund) 540 Second av.

World Building & Loan Assn. (Harry Martin, Pres.; Charles Wright, Sec.) 31 Park row

World Mfg. Co. (refused) 122 Nassau

World Purchasing Agency (refused) 151 E. 50th

World Tea Co. (Joseph Stiner & Co. proprs.) 86 Vesey

World Travel Co. (dissolved) 120 & 353 B'way

Worms Kaufman & Co. (Kaufman Worms & David Greenfield) 348 E. 23d

Worms A. & Co. (Abraham Worms & Simon Schwartzman) 314 E. 23d

Worms & Folger (Alexander Worms & John J. & John J. Folger jr.) 401 E. 45th

Wormser I. & S. (Isidor & Simon & Alexander J. & Isidor Wormser jr.) 15 Broad

Wormser Brothers (Moses & Adolph Wormser) 748 Third av.

Wormser & Simm (Leopold Wormser & Isaac A. Simm) 2298 Third av.

Wormser, Fellheimer & Co. (Salomon Wormser & August Fellheimer, no Co.) 853 B'way

Worrall & Co. (John W. Worrall, no Co.) 28 Elm

Worrell & Best (Charles G. Worrell & Edward C. Best) 1880 Third av.

Worth H. S. & Co. (Hiram S. Worth & William J. Cornell, 104 Reade

Worth & Huber (Edward M. Worth & George H. Huber) 106 E. 14th

Worthen & Aldrich (Moses E. Worthen & William P. Aldrich) ft. Jane & 25 N. Moore

Worthen & Co. (George S. B. Worthen & Benjamin F. White) 28 Moore

Worthington Co. (Margaret Worthington, Pres.; Richard Worthington, Sec.; Elizabeth Sproule, Treas. Capital, $20,000. Directors: Margaret Worthington, Elizabeth Sproule, John Hovendon) 747 B'way

Worthington Henry R. (William A. Perry & Charles C. Worthington, only) 145 B'way & 88 Liberty

Worthington Pumping Engine Co. (Charles C. Worthington, Pres.; T. W. Ridsdale, Sec.; Charles W. Potter, Treas. Capital, $200,000. Trustees: Charles C. Worthington, John H. Harris, T. W. Ridsdale, William A. Perry, J. G. Root) 145 B'way

Worthington, Smith & Co. (William R. Smith, only) 82 E. 17th

Wortmann S. B. & Co. (Sigismund B. Wortmann, no Co.) 1148 Second av.

Worzberger F. J. & Co. (Francis J. Worzberger & Jacob H. Durand) 244 Canal

Wotton Brothers (James A. jr. & William C. Wotton) 124 Greene

Wray & Pilsbury (Llewellyn A. Wray & Ernest R. Pilsbury) 287 B'way

Wrenks E. M. & J. F. (Eleanor M. & Judith F.) 87 E. 08th

Wrenks & Chubb (dissolved) 16 Exchange pl.

Wrenks & Loines (Charles F. Wrenks, Stephen Loines & Henry Wrenks) 16 Exchange pl.

Wrieden & Bellois (Martin Wrieden & William Bellois) 441 E. 81st

Wright C. L., Gravure Co. (Charles L. Wright, Pres.; Charlotte E. Wright, Sec. Capital, $5,000. Trustees: Charles L. & Charlotte E. Wright, Charles E. Reed) 48 Beekman

Wright Charles L. & Co. (Albert Kinkel, only) 81 B'way

Wright Garrett P. & Son (Garrett P. & Garrett P. Wright jr.) ft. Perry

Wright Lumber Co. (Capital, $15,000; further inf. unattainable) no address

Wright Peter & Sons (James A. Wright, Clement A. Griscom, Frank L. Neall, W. Redwood & James A. Wright jr. & Andrew M. Bye, only) 6 Dowling av.

Wright Silas F. & Co. (Silas F. & Frances L. Wright) 90 Chambers

Wright William J. jr. & Co. (William J. Wright jr. & Solomon Bloomfield) 265 Sixth av.

Wright F. H. & Co. (Francis H. & George H. Wright) 17 Lispenard

Wright G. A. & M. G. (Gilbert A. & Moses G.) ft. E. 180 & Pier 22 E. R.

Wright J. O. & Co. (James Osborne Wright & Robert Fridenberg) 84 E. 18th

Wright & Bauer (no inf.) 1125 Second av.

Wright & Co. (drygds.) (Earl B. & Alfred K. Wright) 826 W. 125th

Wright & Co. (tea) (Robert H. & Arthur D. F. Wright) 125 Front

Wright & Frost (Rebecca J. Wright & Margaret H. Frost) 78 Madison av.

Wright & Ginity (dissolved) 79 Nassau

Wright & Ryer (Henry B. Wright & Henry L. Ryer) 801 Eighth av.

Wright & Winsor (Thomas Wright & Washington Winsor) 190 Chambers

Wright & Young (William J. Wright & Thomas Young) 27 White

Wright Brothers & Co. (Joseph Wright, Charles S. Howe, George T. Moxey, Harris Pilson & estate of Edmund Wright) 450 B'way

Wright, Depew & Co. (Edgar Wright & Edward D. & Robert A. Depew) 108 Murray

Wrightington & Jackson (William B. Wrightington, only) 28 Liberty

Writers' Publishing Co. (Henry D. Newson, propr.) 21 University pl.

Writing Telegraph Co. (Brent Good, Pres.; Stephen R. Pinckney, Sec.; William B. Gump, Treas. Capital, $500,000. Trustees: Brent Good, Stephen R. Pinckney, William B. Gump) 87 Murray

Wuerth Gustav & Co. (Gustav Wuerth, no Co.) 46 Marion

FOR THE BEST CO-PARTNERSHIP IN THE BEST CORPORATION SEE PAGE F IN BACK OF BOOK

Wuers Brothers (Alexander & William Wuers jr.) 752 Eighth av.
Wulfers Brothers (John & Henry Wulfers) 72 University pl. & 10 E. Houston
Wulff W. & Co. (no inf.) 509 Second av.
Wulfhop John & Son (John & John Wulfhop jr.) 350 E. 106th
Wunderlich Herman & Co. (Herman Wunderlich, no Co.) 608 B'way
Wurfbain & Lugt (Leonard Wurfbain & Henry Lugt) 68 Water
Wurmser H. & L. (Herman & Leopold) 137 Mercer
Wurzburger & Hecht (Adolph Wurzburger & Myer Hecht) 605 B'way
Wurzburger, Goldsmith & Co. (Bernard Wurzbarger, Louis Goldsmith, Charles J. Hildesheim & Henry Goldsmith) 472 B'way & 36 Crosby
Wuterich C. & Co, (dissolved) 124 Baxter
Wyandance Brick & Terra-Cotta Co. (Levi J. Wing, Pres.; Daniel G. Harriman, Sec.; Moody B. Smith, Treas. Capital, $200,000. Directors; Henry H. Palmer, Moody B. Smith, Levi J. Wing, Daniel G. Harriman) 16 Murray & 19 Park pl.
Wyatt Chromatic Printing Co. (John McGinnis jr. Pres.; Frederic Taylor, Treas.; J. G. Case, Sec. Capital, $1,000,000. Directors: John McGinnis jr. Harry F. Wyatt, Frederic Taylor, J. G. Case, Sherburne B. Eaton, Samuel A. Walsh, Theodore Braine) 53 Cedar
Wyatt Mfg. Co. (dissolved) 50 W. Houston
Wyatt G. S. & Co. (George S. Wyatt & Leonard Wyeth jr.) 129 Warren
Wyatt & Trimble (William E. Wyatt & Walter Trimble) 160 B'way
Wyckoff, Seamans & Benedict (William O. Wyckoff, Clarence W. Seamans & Henry H. Benedict) 327 B'way
Wygand John & Co. (John Wygand & Louis Brass) 58 Park pl.
Wylie & Slocum (Edmund Wade Wylie & Ernest Foster Slocum) 252 B'way & 2 W. 14th
Wyman R. & Son (Rudolph & Isaac Wyman) 25 Chambers
Wyman Brothers (Maurice C. Wyman, only) 1374 B'way
Wyman & Cole (dissolved) 469 Sixth av.
Wyman & Lynch (no inf.) 177 E. 114th
Wyman & Phillips (A. Ross Wyman & Thomas Phillips) 20 Counties sl.
Wynen & Heesters (Peter Wynen & John C. Heesters) 125 Fourth av.
Wynkoop & Peasley (C. Evert Wynkoop & Charles W. Peasley) 19 Liberty
Wynkoop & Scott (dissolved) 18 Liberty
Wynkoop & Scudder (Gerardus H. Wynkoop & Charles D. Scudder) 7 W. 19th
Wynkoop, Andress & Co. (Henry M. Wynkoop, Judson C. Andress & Edward F. Davis) 10 Barclay
Wynkoop, Hallenbeck & Co. (Matthew B. Wynkoop, John J. & William E. & Harry C. Hallenbeck) 121 Fulton & 48 Ann
Wyoming Pacific Improvement Co. (inf. unattainable) 10 Wall
Wyoming Salt Co. (C. E. Faulkner, propr.) 205 Duane
Wysong J. J. & Co. (Otto J. & Hugo H. Boesaneck, Robert C. Seyd & Herman Broesel, only) 466 Broome

Y

Yalden, Brooks & Donnelly (James Yalden, William M. Brooks, George W. Donnelly & Louis Yalden) 11 Pine
Yale Fountain Pen Co. (Ferdinand S. Bartram, Pres.; Charles B. Bartram, Sec. Capital, $10,000. Directors: Ferdinand S. & Charles B. Bartram, E. M. Taylor) 125 William
Yale Publishing Co. (Ferdinand S. Bartram, Pres.; Charles B. Bartram, Treas. Capital, $3,000. Directors: Ferdinand S. & Charles B. Bartram, E. M. Taylor) 125 William
Yalovitz J. & Brother (Jacob & Samuel Yalovitz) 4 Walker
Yandell Charles R. & Co. (Charles R. Yandell, no Co.) 140 Fifth av. & 500 E. 18th
Yanser & Co. (Paul N. Yanser & George A. Dries) 16 Front
Yasinski Brothers (Casimir W. & Francis L. Yasinski) 2195½ Third av.
Yates J. & Co. (Jerome Yates, no Co.) 600 Sixth av.
Yates & Porterfield (Lorenzo D. Yates & Charles T. Geyer, only) 19 William
Yates, Wharton & Co. (Henry J. Yates, John & Charles A. Wharton & Robert Clark jr.) 180 Greene
Ybor V. Martinez & Co. (V. Martinez & Edward R. M. Ybor & Edward Manrara) 89 Water
Yellow Creek Coal Co. (Henry W. Ford, Pres. Capital, $100,000. Trustees: Henry W. Ford, J. W. Smith) 2 Wall
Yellowlees R. A. & Co. (Robert A. Yellowlee & Angustus Talbot) 4 Stone
Yeoman J. & Co. (Joseph Yeoman, no Co.) 110 Pearl
Yetter A. B. & Son (Andrew B. & William W. Yetter) 305 E. 61st & 908 Ninth av.
Yglesia J. & Co. (Josephine Yglesia, no Co.) 390 Bleecker
Yonkers Schuyler Electric Light Co. (Edward May, Pres.; Harry Sanderson, Sec.; Julius A. May, Treas. Capital, $100,000. Directors: Edward May, William L. Gerrish jr. James R. O'Blorne, Herman Liebert, Julius A. May, Hubert Cillis, James Williamson) 98 Vandam
York Safe & Lock Co, (dissolved) 122 Fulton
York & Swift (John A. York & William H. Swift) 805 E. 145th
Yorkville Beef Co. (G. F. & E. C. Swift, proprs.) 825 E. 86th
Yorkville Beef Co. (Louis Michel, propr.) 1509 Second av.
Yorston Brothers (no inf.) 23 Park row
Yost Charles A. & Co. (Charles A. & G. Andrew Yost) 600 B'way & 184 Crosby
Yost Writing Machine Co. (Phineas C. Lounsbury, Pres.; Allen S. Apgar, Sec. Capital, $500,000. Directors: Phineas C. Lounsbury, George W. N. Yost, Henry Cummins, George E. Lounsbury, Isaac G. Johnson, A. J. White, Allen S. Apgar) 6 Wall
Youlin & Davenport (dissolved) 96 B'way
Young Charles & Brother (Charles & George Young) 868 & 870 Park av.
Young Hearts Publishing Co. (no inf.) 82 Cedar
Young James K. & Co. (James K. Young & Francis Snyder) 316 Fifth
Young Robert B. & Co. (Robert B. Young & Sylvester F. Amerman) 42 Cortlandt
Young William (Anne Young & Nathaniel W. Keane, only) 21 Park row
Young William & Brother (William & Thomas M. Young) 1022 Third av. & 625 Madison av.
Young A. F. & Co. (Augustus F. Young, no Co.) 209 Duane
Young C. B. & W. B. (Charles B. & William B.) 1395 Third av.
Young E. & J. B. & Co. (Edwin & Edward R. Young & Frederick E. Hafely, only) 6 & 11 Cooper Union
Young J. M. & Co. (John M. & Thomas Young) 27 Murray

TYPEWRITING DONE BY THE TROW CITY DIRECTORY CO., 11 University Place.

YOU 334 ZIN

Young W. I. & Co. (William I. & Willard D. Young) 140 Reade
Young Brothers (hats) (Max L. & Boorne Young) 601 B'way
Young Brothers (liquors) (Richard & Henry G. Young) 230 W. 4th
Young Brothers (tailors) (Meyer E. Young, only) 423 Sixth av.
Young & Bryans (William J. Young & Andrew K. Bryans) 81 Reade
Young & Cowpland (dissolved) 24 Frankfort
Young & Elliott (dissolved) 56 Dey
Young & McLatchie (James Hamilton Young & William McLatchie) Railroad av. n E. 188th
Young & Macy (William G. Young & Walter F. Macy) 321½ W. 48th
Young & Nelson (Thomas S. Young, jr. & William S. Nelson) 46 Wall
Young & Rutherford (Eben Young & Thomas Rutherford) 441 B'way
Young & Stephenson (dissolved) 18 D'way
Young & Verplanck (William H. Young & William G. Verplanck) 36 Wall
Young & Wood (Robert L. Young & Samuel M. Wood) 115 D'way
Young-Brennan Crusher Co. (Gilbert G. Young, Pres.; Herbert S. Ogden, Sec. Capital, $200,000. Trustees; Gilbert G. Young, Robert H. Thomas, Herbert S. Ogden) 42 Cortlandt
Youngling H. W. & Co. (Henry W. Youngling, no Co.) 76 Nassau
Youngling & Ebmeyer (Louis Youngling & John C. Ebmeyer) 062 Sixth av.
Youngs William P. & Brothers (William P. & Charles A. & David L. Youngs) ft. Third & 434 E. 10th
Youngs & Cable (William H. W. Youngs & William A. Cable) 45 B'way
Younker L. M., Son & Co. (Lippman M. & Bernhard Younker, no Co.) 25 E. Houston
Yuba Gold Mining Co. (Richard P. Lounsbery, V. Pres. Capital, $250,000. Trustees; Richard P. Lounsbery, Willoughby Weston, Willard P. Ward) 15 Broad
Yuba Water Co. (William B. Leonard, Pres; Warner Vannorden, Treas. Capital, $2,000,000. Directors; William B. Leonard, Warner Vannorden, Henry H. Cook, William N. Cromwell, William Dowd, Edward C. Boardman, Clayton French, C. W. Funk, John D. Harris, George H. Earle jr. H. W. Lazelle) 120 B'way
Yucca Mining Co. (refused) 11 Cliff
Yuckman Brothers (Abraham & Jacob Yuckman) 543 Fifth
Yuengling D. G., jr. Brewing Co. (George M. Hard, Pres.; John Stralton, Sec.; John M. Moser, Treas. Capital, $2,000,000. Directors; George M. Hard, John Stralton, John M. Moser, S. K. Nester, D. G. Yuengling jr. Charles R. Bissell, Conrad N. Jordan) W. 128th & Tenth av.
Yung & Bauer (Frederick Yung & Frederick W. Bauer) 58 Third av.
Yung & Co. (Martin Yung & William L. Darmstadt) 798 Second av.
Yung, Willstatter & Stern (dissolved) 496 Broome
Yungel William W. & Brother (dissolved) 1917 Second av.
Yutte C. W. & Co. (Christian W. Yutte & William P. Hotmer) 454 D'way

Z

Zadek Brothers (Solomon & Jacob Zadek) 14 W. Houston
Zahn Jacob & Son (Jacob & John Zahn) 479 Pearl
Zahn & Meisner (George W. Zahn & William Meisner) 116 E. 14th
Zahner Brothers (Frederick & Gustav Zahner) 1715 Tenth av.
Zaidenberg H. & Co. (Herman Zaidenberg & Henry Rineberg) 137 Elm
Zaltzer & Sander (dissolved) 62 Essex
Zander Henry & Co. (dissolved) 16 G'wich
Zangheri & Gazzo (Joseph Zangheri & Virgilio R. Gazzo) 878 Sixth av.
Zapp & Pfnausch (dissolved) 211 Canal
Zaraus E. & Co. (Emilio Zaraus & Thomas W. Thompson) 110 Pearl
Zebley John F. & Co. (John F. Zebley, no Co.) 3 Broad
Zeiger & Spiro (dissolved) 216 Second
Zeimer S. & Feldstein (Samuel Zeimer & William Feldstein) 322 B'way & 150 Crosby
Zekind & Oestreicher (no inf.) 83 Division
Zelenko L. & J. Brothers (dissolved) 5 Elizabeth
Zelinka & Coblentz (no inf.) 303 E. 78th
Zellenka Philip & Son (Philip & Edward Zellenka) 37 Maiden la.
Zellmann & Kahzin (Herman Zollmann & Joseph Kahzin) 5 Canal
Zellner & Schwarz (Hugo Zollner & Ralph Schwarz) 645 B'way
Zeltner Henry (Henry & William H. & Charles H. Zeltner;—special partner, Frederick Folz, $25,000; terminates 1st Jan, 1893) Third av. c. E. 170th
Zeman & Schlesinger (Louis Zeman & Charles Schlesinger) 1460 D'way
Zendman Louis & Co. (dissolved) 280 Church
Zenn & Son (Joseph & Jacob Zenn) 10 John
Zenoni A. & Co. (dissolved) 143 Elm
Zephyr Rubber Mfg. Co. (Frederick Cox, propr.) 336 W. 40th
Zerbst Brothers (Gustav A. & Frederick H. M. Zerbst) 644 Eleventh av.
Zettler C. G. & D. (Charles G. & Bernhard) 207 Bowery
Ziegel, Eisman & Co. (Louis Ziegel, Max Eisman, & John Walter) 178 William
Ziegler S. & Son (Solomon & Caspar Ziegler) 637 Second av.
Zigler & Blum (no inf.) 5 Canal
Zigler & Mamlok (Ignatz Zigler & David Mamlok) 297 G'wich
Zimdars & Hunt (Adelaide O. Zimdars & John T. Hunt) 227 Mercer
Zimmer, Bolles & Dunkak (Edward Zimmer, James Bolles jr. & Henry Dunkak) 184 Reade
Zimmermann C. F. & Co. (Charles F. Zimmermann & W. Baring Wells) 88 Pine
Zimmermann F. E. & Co. (Franz E. Zimmermann, Gerhard Wunderle, August Schmit & Julius Steiber) 9 Daxter
Zimmermann J. & Brother (Joseph & Hyman Zimmermann) 400 Grand
Zimmermann & Fershay (Leopold Zimmermann & David F. S. Forshay) 11 Wall
Zimmermann & Rein (dissolved) 125 Grand
Zimmern Henry & Co. (Henry Zimmern & Michael J. Lambert) 87 Maiden la.
Zimmern & Abraham (Joseph Zimmern & Gustav Abraham) 2 Bond
Zinc Etching & Engraving Co. (Stevens & Morris, propra.) 34 Cortlandt
Zink C. & L. (Charles & Louis) 542 Courtlandt av.
Zink & Borgmann (Conrad Zink & Bernard Borgmann) 1831 Tenth av.
Zinn Charles & Co. (Felix & Carl Thurnauer, only) 188 Grand
Zinn Charles H. & Co. (Charles H. Zinn & George W. Albers) 94 Warren

THADDEUS DAVIDS CO., WRITING INKS, SEALING WAX, MUCILAGE. MAKE THE BEST

ZIN   335   ZWI

Zinn Jacob & S. Tonner (Jacob Zinn & Sigmund Tonner) 231 Fifth

Zinn's B. H., Sons (Louis A. & George F. Zinn) 190 E. 17th

Zins & Co. (Joanna Zins & Ellis Glaser) 355 Canal

Zinsmeister Brothers (inf. unattainable) West Farms

Zinsser William & Co. (William & August Zinsser) 197 William & 507 W. 58th

Zirkin & Kaufmann (Hyman Zirkin & Simon Kaufmann) 51 Bleecker

Ziskind Brothers (Hyman & Solomon Ziskind) 222 E. 26th

Zoeblsch C. A. & Sons (Charles A. & Clemence T. Zoebisch, only) 46 Maiden la. & 87 Liberty

Zubiller's H., Sons (Henry jr. & Paul P. Zubiller) 190 Stanton & 411 E. 84th

Zucca & Co. (Virginius Zucca & Cetterina Miniussi) 24 State

Zucker & Josephy (Samuel Zucker & William Josephy) 555 B'way & 126 Mercer

Zucker & Levett Chemical Co. (Alexander Levett, Pres.; Charles Loeb, Sec. Louis Levett, Treas. Capital, $30,000. Directors: Alexander & Louis Levett, Charles Loeb, Harry L. Hass) 40 Murray

Zuckercals Sisters (Amelia & Esther Zuckercals) 62 Orchard

Zulia Steam Navigation Co. (inf. unattainable) 67 Exchange pl.

Zundel B. W. & Co. (Robert W. Zundel & Aaron Isaacs) 51 Whitehall, 2 Fulton & 159 South

Zunner & Bernhold (George Zunner & Charles Bernhold) 456 Second av.

Zuricalday & Co. (Aquilino Zuricalday & George T. McKinney) 28 Beaver

Zwicker Brothers (Leopold & Emanuel Zwicker) 56 Attorney

NEW FIRMS, CORRECTIONS, &c., TOO LATE FOR INSERTION IN THEIR PROPER PLACE.

Am. Champagne Co. (Ltd.) (Charles E. Laidlaw, Pres.; Edward R. Grant, Sec. Capital, $500,000. Directors: Charles E. Laidlaw, Gustav H. & Herman C. Schwab, George W. Sessions) 62 Broad

Black Thomas & Son (Thomas & Robert W. Black) 448 Cherry

Blakeslee & Co. (Edward Holbrook, assignee) 216 Fifth av.

Brown O. E. & J. W. (O. Edward & J. Warren) 321 Canal

Brown G. F. & C. E. & Co. (dissolved) 821 Canal

Columbia Steel & Iron Co. (C. Yaeger, Pres.; E. M. Butz, Treas.; R. J. Butz, Sec. Capital, $450,000; further inf. unattainable) 81 Fulton

Co-operative News Co. (Henry Martin, propr.) 182 Park av. & Third av. c E. 120th

Crosson James J. & Co. (dissolved) 543 W. 22d

Electric Absorption Treatment Co. (Joseph J. Mackey, propr.) 258 B'way

Goldstein M. H. & Co. (dissolved) 75 Nassau

Grant, Quigley & Grant (William W. Grant, George V. Quigley & G. Chauncy Grant) 1169 Ninth av.

Halle & Stieglitz (Jacques S. Halle & Albert Stieglitz) 84 New

Hill Brothers (George M. & Hugh M. Hill) 154 W. 27th

Levy, Friend & House (Abraham Levy, Emanuel M. Friend & Frederick D. House) 26 Chambers

Meissner, Ackermann & Co. (Charles F. & Frederick T. Ackermann, only) 27 Beaver

Meyer William (Wilhelm P. G. & Dions & Louise & William L. Meyer) 626 W. 85th

Middleton & Seckendorf (Charles F. Middleton & Emanuel A. Seckendorf) 1228 Second av.

Moore John & Co. (John Moore, no Co.) 33 S. William & 25 Stone

N. Y. Biscuit Co. (William H. Moore, Pres.; J. A. McCormick, Sec.; George F. Johnson, Treas. Capital, $8,000,000; further inf. unattainable) 137 Duane

N. Y. Roof Stuffing Co. (Atkins & Durbrow, proprs.) 70 Wall

Obrig Charles E. & Co. (dissolved) 86 Broad

Peckham Street Car Wheel & Axle Co. (Edgar Peckham, Pres.; C. H. Duell, Sec.; E. C. Stark, Treas. Capital, $300,000. Directors: Edgar Peckham, E. C. Stark, C. D. Prescott, C. H. Duell, R. Lease) 250 B'way

Riverside Bridge & Iron Works (Charles O. Brown, Pres.; Gerrit Planten, Treas.; William G. A. Millar, Sec. Capital, $100,000. Directors: Charles O. Brown, Gerrit Planten, William G. A. Millar, Herman Sonntag) 18 B'way

Schlesinger John & Co. (John Schlesinger & Louis E. Wolff:—special partner, Adolph Platky. $2,000; terminates 17th March, 1895) 145 Elm

Serial Building Loan & Savings Institution (James Merrihew, Pres.; E. F. Howell, Sec.; Abijah R. Brewer, Treas.) 195 D'way

Siemens-Lungren Co. (inoperative) 2 Wall

COMPILED WITH ACCURACY AND DESPATCH } **CLASSIFIED BUSINESS LISTS.** { THE TROW CITY DIRECTORY CO. 11 University Place.

FOREIGN HOUSES AND THEIR REPRESENTATIVES
WITH
LOCATION OF HOME AND NEW YORK OFFICES.

ABT — AME

Name.	Home Office.	Agent or Representative.	New York Office.
Abt L. & Sons	Chicago, Ill.		75 Leonard
Acme Mills	Philadelphia, Pa.	Frederick C. Keely	58 Worth
Acme Silver Plate Co	Boston, Mass.	Vincent P. Tommins	116 Chambers
Acme Wood Fibre Co.	Buffalo, N. Y.	James Swanson	152 Front
Adam, Moldrum & Anderson.	Buffalo, N. Y.	Syndicate Trading Co.	120 Franklin
Adamant Mfg. Co	Syracuse, N. Y.	Thomas Barrington	99 Nassau
Adams Brothers	Norwalk, Conn.	Frederick V. Cole	96 Bleecker
Adams & Armstrong	Ft. Wayne, Ind.	Benjamin G. Glover	624 Broadway
Adams & Co	Pittsburgh, Pa.	Julius Wolff	55 Park pl.
Adams & Spitz	Boston, Mass		40 Thomas
Adger James & Co	Charleston, S. C	John M. Wilson	19 Whitehall
Adler David, Sons' Clothing Co.	Milwaukee, Wis.		75 Leonard
Adler L., Brothers & Co.	Rochester, N. Y.	Levi Adler	2 Bond
Adt Brothers	Forbach, Germany.	Carl Goerg	536 Broadway
Ærated Fuel Co.	Springfield, Mass.	William S. Collins	171 Broadway
Ætna Ins. Co.	Hartford, Conn.	Scott, Alexander & Talbot.	45 William
Ætna Life Ins. Co	Hartford, Conn.	Mumford & Bushnell	167 Broadway
Ætna Mills	Boston, Mass.	Morrell A. Smith	49 Leonard
Ætna Silk Co	Norfolk, Conn.	Walter H. Devore	546 Broadway
Agar, Cross & Co.	Glasgow, Scotland	Alexander Guild	56 Worth
Agnew E. W. & Co	Ocala, Fla.	Hibbert B. Masters	84 W. Broadway
Agricultural Fire Ins. Co	Watertown, N. Y.	C. Patterson & Son	71 Wall
Ajax Forge Co	Chicago, Ill.	Joseph R. Ellicott	115 Broadway
Akron Iron Co.	Akron, O.	Henry F. Holloway	121 Liberty
Alabama Midland Railway Co.	Montgomery, Ala.	Joseph W. Woolfolk	45 Wall
Alabama Terminal & Improvement Co.	Montgomery, Ala.	Joseph W. Woolfolk	45 Wall
Albany Brewing Co	Albany, N. Y.	Joseph M. Knap	365 West
Albany Dental Ass'n	Albany, N. Y.	Datus E. Rugg	291 Third av.
Albany Paper Collar Co	Albany, N. Y.	Standard Collar Co.	52 Howard
Albany Steam Trap	Albany, N. Y.	Peter Backus & Son	183 W. 25th
Albany Venetian Blind Co	Albany, N. Y.	William G. Orr	150 Broadway
Albion Carpet Mills	Philadelphia, Pa.	T. J. Keveney & Co.	528 Broadway
Albro S. & Co	Providence, R. I	Levi Stevens jr	170 Broadway
Alden Edwin, Co.	Cincinnati, O.	Edwin Alden	115 Nassau
Alden George A. & Co.	Boston, Mass.	Armstrong & McClintock	228 Pearl
Alexander Medicine Co	Elizabeth, N. J.	Elbert O. Stevens	195 Pearl
Alexander, Hoffman & Co.	San Francisco, Cal.	Charles Hoffman	27 Walker
Allegheny Bessemer Steel Co.	Pittsburgh, Pa	Francis G. Gorham	15 Broad
Allegheny & Clearfield Coal Co.	Altoona, Pa.	Charles J. Wittenberg	1 Broadway
Allen Fan Co.	E. Braintree, Mass.	C. E. Conover Co.	101 Franklin
Allen Fire Department Supply Co.	Providence, R. I.	James L. Bishop	r 59 Ann
Allen F. H. & Co.	Akron, O.	Frank H. Allen	19 Whitehall
Allen & Ginter	Richmond, Va.	George W. Augustin	28 Warren
Allen, Lane & Co.	Boston, Mass	Frank H. Syvett	49 Leonard
Allen-Bradley Co.	Frankfort, Ky.	Paris, Allen & Co.	51 Broadway
Allsopp Samuel & Sons (Ltd.)	Burton-on-Trent, Eng.	Edward & John Burke	24 S. William
Allyn & Bacon	Boston, Mass.	Baker & Taylor Co.	740 Broadway
Alma Button Co.	Baltimore, Md.	Milton Kerngood	695 Broadway
Alois & Doepke Co.	Cincinnati, O.	Frank H. Shevlin	56 Worth
Almy, Bigelow & Washburn.	Salem, Mass.	Syndicate Trading Co.	120 Franklin
Alosse, Dayral & Co.	London, Eng.	William B. Roe	66 W. 23d
Alsen's Portland Cement Works	Hamburg, Germany	Arthur C. Babson	16 Exchange pl.
Altman & Co	Buffalo, N. Y.		75 Leonard
Altmayer A. R. & Co	Savannah, Ga.	Aaron R. Altmayer	21 Wooster
Aluminum Brass & Bronze Co	Bridgeport, Conn.	Thomas L. Fowler	280 Broadway
Aluminum und Magnesium Fabrik.	Bremen, Germany	White & Sheldon	134 Pearl
Alyanakian K. M. & Co.	Constantinople, Turkey	Hovhannes S. Tavshanjian	252 Broadway
Ambach, Burgunder & Co	Baltimore, Md.	Max Ambach	96 Spring
Amborg File & Index Co.	Chicago, Ill.	William H. Naulty	69 Duane
Am. Baptist Publication Soc.	Philadelphia, Pa.	Thomas R. Jones	41 Park row
Am. Brake Co.	St. Louis, Mo.	John B. Gray	160 Broadway
Am. Bridge Works	Chicago, Ill.	William H. Price	10 Wall & 9 Pine
Am. Building Loan & Investment Soc.	Chicago, Ill.	Peter J. Tracy	13 Park row
Am. Central Ins. Co	St. Louis, Mo.	Vanvalkenburgh & Hall	71 Wall
Am. Curled Hair Co.	Pawtucket, R. I.	Lewisohn Importing & Trading Co. (Ltd.)	154 S. 5th av.
Am. Drying & Seasoning Co	Aiken, S. C.	William B. Watkins	145 Broadway
Am. Electrical Works	Providence, R. I.	Christie Ackerman	16 Cortlandt
Am. Enamel Co.	Providence, R. I.	Vanderbilt & Reynolds	7 Lispenard
Am. Fire Ins. Co.	Philadelphia, Pa.	Frame & Shade	206 Broadway

SPECIAL ATTENTION PAID TO THIS CLASS OF WORK	BANKERS' & BROKERS' CIRCULARS DELIVERED	THE TROW CITY DIRECTORY CO. 11 University Place.	
AME		337	APO

Name.	Home Office.	Agent or Representative.	New York Office.
Am. Fuse Co. (Ltd.)	Erie, Pa.	George B. Eddy	7 Murray
Am. Gas Co	Philadelphia, Pa.	W. & J. N. Carpender	42 Pine
Am. Gas Furnace Co	Jersey City, N. J.	E. P. Reichhelm & Co.	80 Nassau
Am. Glucose Co.	Buffalo, N. Y.	William S. Elliott	155 Reade
Am. Hosiery Co	New Britain, Conn.	James Talcott	108 Franklin
Am. Industrial Syndicate	London, Eng.	Page & McMillin	60 Wall
Am. Ins. Co	Boston, Mass.	Robert O. Glover	141 Broadway
Am. Ins. Co	Newark, N. J.	Benjamin T. Rhoads jr.	168 Broadway
Am. Investment Co	Emmetsburg, Ia.	Edwin S. Ormsby, Moury E. Simmons & Alvin L. Ormsby.	150 Nassau
Am. Investment & Guaranty Co. (Ltd.)	Kansas City, Mo.	Samuel R. MacLean	39 Broad
Am. Jewelry Mfg. Co	Newark, N. J.	Charles Smedley	17 Maiden la.
Am. Land Mortgage Guarantee & Debenture Trust Co. (Ltd.)	Kansas City, Mo.	Samuel R. MacLean	39 Broad
Am. Machine Co	Philadelphia, Pa.	John M. Graham & Co	118 Chambers
Am. Marble Co	Boston, Mass.	Henry E. Parson	85 Liberty
Am. Mills Co	Rockville, Conn.	Martin, Lawrie & Co.	46 White
Am. Mills Co	Waterbury, Conn.	George Maier	56 Leonard
Am. Percussion Cap Assn	Waterbury, Conn. & B'klyn, N. Y.	Walter Stillman	206 Broadway
Am. Plaster Board Co	San Francisco, Cal.	George W. Sessions	52 Broad
Am. Portrait Co	Chicago, Ill.	Simon Ettlinger	120 W. 23d
Am. Printing Co	Fall River, Mass	Bliss, Fabyan & Co.	32 Thomas
Am. Pure Paint Co.	Terre Haute, Ind.	William H. Schwalbe	21 Park row
Am. Railway Spring Co	Newark, N. J.	I. Cryder Lea	15 Cortlandt
Am. Rubber Co	Boston, Mass.	Washington E. Langley & Charles J. Osborn.	76 Reade & 177 Church
Am. Screw Co	Providence, R. I.	Underhill, Clinch & Co.	94 Chambers
Am. Shoe & Leather Trade Assn.	Philadelphia, Pa.	McKillop, Walker & Co.	335 Broadway
Am. Soapstone Finish Co	Chester Depot, Vt.	Smith & Dewson	24 State
Am. Square Co	Bridgeport, Conn.	Charles J. Healy	100 Chambers
Am. Straw Board Co	Chicago, Ill.	James F. Hayes	75 Duane
Am. Sunday-school Union	Philadelphia, Pa	J. Lindley Spicer	8 Bible b.
Am. Tack Co.	Fairhaven, Mass.	Sayres Hadley	116 Chambers
Am. Thread Co	Guttenberg, N. J.	Sigmund Singer	98 Spring
Am. Tube Works	Boston Mass.	William M. Bailey	20 Gold
Am. Waltham Watch Co.	Waltham, Mass.	Robbins & Appleton	5 Bond
Am. Water Gas Works Construction Co.	Philadelphia, Pa.	George F. Work	58 Broadway
Am. Whip Co.	Westfield, Mass.	William J. Cassard	30 Warren
Am. Wick Mfg. Co.	Troy, N. Y.	John Doud	26 Broadway
Am. Wood Paper Co	Providence, R. I.	Edward L. Embree	140 Nassau
Am. Workman's Life Assurance Soc.	Brooklyn, N. Y.	William E. Davis	338 Broadway
Am. Writing Machine Co	Hartford, Conn.	William C. Hardie	237 Broadway
Am. & Continental "Sanitas" Co. (Ltd.)	London, Eng.	Reginald C. Woodcock	640 W. 58th
Ames Iron Works	Oswego, N. Y.	Arthur L. Merriam	88 Cortlandt
Amos Oliver & Sons	Easton, Mass	Underhill, Clinch & Co.	94 Chambers
Amos Plow Co	Boston, Mass	Lowell A. Pratt	51 Beckman
Amory Mfg. Co	Manchester, N. H	John L. Bremer & Co.	62 Leonard
Anchor Line, Rail & Lake.	Philadelphia, Pa.	Horace S. Nichols	76 Wall & Pier 4 N. R.
Anchor Line S. S. Co	Glasgow, Scotland.	Henderson Bros.	7 Bowling gr. & Pier 41 (new) N. R.
Anderson Anderson & Anderson.	London, Eng.	William B. Roe	66 W. 23d
Anderson Preserving Co.	Camden, N. J.	George S. Millett	6 Harrison
Anderson Thomas & Co.	Louisville, Ky.	Henry A. Chamberlain	353 Canal
Anderson Wm. & Co.	Glasgow, Scotland.	John M. Anderson	120 Franklin
Anderson & Nelson Distilleries Co.	Louisville, Ky.	Clement Peppole	81 Broad
Anderson, DuPuy & Co.	Pittsburgh, Pa.	Henry J. Hopper	243 Broadway
Anderson, Moss & Sons.	La Crosse, Wis.		858 Broadway
Androscoggin Pulp Co.	Portland, Me.	James E. Hayes	75 Duane
Anglo-Am. Banking Co	Paris, France.	E. J. Mathews & Co.	2 Wall
Anglo-Am. Investment Co.	London, Eng.	William M. Deen	44 Wall
Anglo-Am. Mortgage & Trust Co.	Omaha, Neb	James N. Brown	83 Cedar
Anglo-Am. Provision Co.	Chicago, Ill.	Fowler Bros.	112 Produce Ex.
Anglo-Am. Telegraph Co.(Ltd.)	London, Eng.	Western Un. Tel. Co.	195 Broadway
Anglo-Mexican Mining Co. (Ltd.)	London, Eng.	William N. Olmsted	16 Wall
Anglo-Nevada Assurance Corporation.	San Francisco, Cal.	David L. Kirby	51 Cedar
Anglo-Swiss Condensed Milk Co.	Cham, Switzerland.	Ford, Rowell & Hone	39 Pine
		George F. Corbiere	82 Hudson
Angus Geo. & Co. (Ltd.)	Newcastle-on-Tyne, Eng.	Richard Anders	95 Gold
Ansonia Clock Co	Ansonia, Conn	Joseph Schwieser	11 Cliff & 11 Cortlandt
Anthracite Coal & Improvement Co.	Philadelphia, Pa.	Eaton N. Frisbie	1 Broadway
Apollinaris Co. (Ltd.)	London, Eng.	Charles Graef & Co.	32 Beaver

22

TYPEWRITING DONE BY THE TROW CITY DIRECTORY CO., 11 University Place.

ARB   338   BAL

Name.	Home Office.	Agent or Representative.	New York Office.
Arbuthnot, Stephenson & Co.	Pittsburgh, Pa.		95 Franklin
Arcade File Works	Sing Sing, N. Y.	C. F. Guyon & Co.	99 Reade
Aribeg Distillery Co.	Glasgow, Scotland.	Cnibert & Taylor	80 Broadway
Armenia Ins. Co.	Pittsburgh, Pa.	Ackerman, Deyo & Hilliard.	41 Pine
Armenian Trading Co.	Constantinople, Turkey.	Merant M. Kiretchjian	338 Broadway
Arminius Copper Mines Co.	Tolersville, Va.	William H. Adams.	71 Wall
Armitage & Cleland	Huddersfield, Eng.	Folkard & Lawrence.	432 Broome
Armour Canning Co.	Chicago, Ill.	Henry Raphael	182 Duane
Armour Glue Works	Chicago, Ill.	Frederick Willrath	182 Duane
Armour Packing Co.	Kansas City, Mo.	William H. Cragin / Abraham Moses.	406 Produce Ex., Manhattan mkt.
Armour & Co.	Chicago, Ill.	Thomas J. Connors	182 Duane, Manhattan mkt, & ft. E. 128th
Armstrong & Co.	Cambridge, Mass.	Charles E. Wample.	11 E. 17th
Armstrong, Cator & Co.	Baltimore, Md.	James Cator	96 Spring
Armstrong, Wilkins & Co.	Philadelphia, Pa.	Benjamin G. Glover	622 Broadway
Arnold S. J. & Co.	Rochester, N. Y.		214 Church
Arnold W. R. & Son	Providence, R. I.	Shepherd & Atwater	39 Nassau
Arnold & Co.	Lancaster, Pa.	Hugo Cabn & Co.	67 Murray
Arnold & Steere	Providence, R. I.	John M. Dayton	200 Broadway
Arnold, Abney & Co.	Charleston, W. Va.		38 Thomas
Art Lithographic Publishing Co.	Munich, Germany.	Samuel Garre	106 Duane
Art Stationery Co. of London.	London, Eng.	Walter Marshall	237 Fifth av.
Arthur Allen, Fletcher & Co.	Glasgow, Scotland.	George McConnel	319 Broadway
Arthur, Warren & Abbott	St. Paul, Minn.		50 Leonard
Asbestos Packing Co.	Boston, Mass.	E. S. Grealey & Co.	6 Dey
Ash Claudius & Sons.	London, Eng.	Charles A. Sykes.	30 E. 14th
Ashford W. & G.	Birmingham, Eng.	H. Roblitsek & Co.	486 Broadway
Ashton Valve Co.	Boston, Mass.	Charles H. Buckelew.	92 Liberty
Ashton & Co.	Manchester, Eng.	Folkard & Lawrence.	432 Broome
Assabet Mfg. Co.	Boston, Mass.	Lorenzo Maynard.	68 Worth
Astoria Silk Works	L. I. City, N. Y.		343 Broadway
Atchison, Topeka & Santa Fe R. R. Co.	Topeka, Kan.	Charles D. Simonson.	201 Broadway
Athol Silk Co.	Athol, Mass.	Daniel E. Adams	427 Broadway
Atkinson J. & E.	London, Eng.	F. R. Arnold & Co.	56 Murray
Atlantic Dynamite Co.	San Francisco, Cal.	Small & Schrader.	245 Broadway
Atlantic-Pacific R'y Tunnel Co.	Denver, Colo.	Mark M. Pomeroy	284 Broadway
Atlantic Rubber Co.	Elizabeth, N. J.	Walter S. Sinclair	133 William
Atlas Dredging Co.	Wilmington, Del.	William H. W. Morris.	121 Front
Atlas S. S. Co.	Liverpool, Eng.	Pim, Forwood & Co.	24 State & Pier 55 (new) N. R.
Atterbury & Co.	Pittsburgh, Pa.	William J. Snyder & Bro.	63 Murray
Atwood Machine Co.	Stonington, Conn.	Eugene Atwood.	68 Grand
Auburn Bolt & Nut Works.	Auburn, Pa.	George Damevel.	67 Reade
Auburn Mfg. Co.	Auburn, N. Y.	J. C. McCarty & Co.	97 Chambers & 81 Reade
Auerbach F. & Bro.	Salt Lake City, Utah	William Branner	7 Mercer
Aultman, Miller & Co.	Akron, O.	F. Porter Thayer	18 Warren
Aurora Watch Co.	Aurora, Ill.	Addison Conkling.	6 Malden la.
Austin Loan & Trust Co.	Austin, Tex.		66 Liberty
Austrian, Wise & Co.	Chicago, Ill.	Edwin O. Williams	75 Leonard
Automatic Bank Punch Co.	Louisville, Ky.		5 Beekman
Automatic Strength-testing Machines Co.	Hoboken, N. J.	John Chatillon & Sons.	89 Cliff
Avery Stamping Co.	Cleveland, O.	Hall & Kear	51 Cliff
Avery B. F. & Sons.	Louisville, Ky.	Leo Alexander.	63 Beekman
Ayala & Co.	Ay, France.	Emil Unger & Co.	50 Park pl.
Ayres Wm. & Sons.	Philadelphia, Pa.	David Barry	19 Thomas
Ayres L. S. & Co.	Indianapolis, Ind.	Norman T. Ayres.	56 Worth
Babcock John B. & Co.	Boston, Mass.	James E. Reardon	629 Broadway
Babcock Printing Press Mfg. Co.	New London, Conn.	Charles A. Collord	154 Nassau
Bachman Bros.	San Francisco, Cal.	Herman S. Bachman	68 Worth
Baer & Broiher	Vicksburg, Miss.		38 Thomas
Baer, Seasongood & Co.	St. Louis, Mo.		96 Franklin
Bagley John J. & Co.	Detroit, Mich.	John R. Sutten.	103 Beekman
Bailey John T. & Co.	Philadelphia, Pa.	Percy H. Brandage.	118 Chambers
Bailey Mfg. Co.	Hartford, Conn.	Henry C. Davison	81 Liberty
Bailey O. T. & Co.	Cincinnati, O.	Louis O. Ackley.	293 Broadway
Bally Joel J. & Co.	Philadelphia, Pa.		101 Franklin
Bally Joshua L. & Co.	Philadelphia, Pa.	Charles H. Brooks	19 Thomas
Bainbridge's Chas. T., Sons	Brooklyn, N. Y.	Henry C. Bainbridge.	21 Beekman
Baird David & Son	Louisville, Ky.	Loren W. True	622 Broadway
Baird Edward P. & Co.	Montreal, Canada.	Robert B. Baird	13 Park row
Baker, Colgate & Co.	Hiogo, Japan	Clinton G. Baker	124 Front
Baker A. T. & Co.	Philadelphia, Pa.	McClain & Talbot.	110 Worth
Baker & Hamilton	San Francisco, Cal.	Charles D. Graham	86 Wall
Baker & Vawter Co.	Chicago, Ill.	Henry B. Dado	270 Broadway
Bakewell & Mullins	Salem, O.	Julius T. Wagner	108 Chambers
Baldwin Mfg. Co.	Burlington, Vt.	Oscar A. Hauptner.	1213 Broadway
Baldwin A. & Co.	New Orleans, La.	W. R. Crossman & Bro.	77 Broad
Baldwin & Lamkin	Milford, Conn.	George Tonkin	102 Chambers

THE CALIGRAPH WRITING MACHINE,
HARTFORD, CONN.

BAL   339   BEL

Name.	Home Office.	Agent or Representative.	New York Office.
Baldwin, Lersch & Co.	Elyria, O.		84 W. B'way
Balfour, Williamson & Co.	Liverpool, Eng.	T. S. Hope Simpson	13 Cotton Ex.
Ball Wm. H. & Co.	Newark, N. J.	William H. Ball	15 John
Ballin & Ranshoff.	Denver, Colo.		355 Broadway
Ballou B. A. & Co.	Providence, R. I.	Cyrus C. Hicks	10 Maiden la.
Baltimore & Ohio R. R. Co.	Baltimore, Md.	Adelmorn C. Ross	415 Broadway
Daltzell & Ross.	Altoona, Pa.		378 Broadway
Bamberger S. & Brother.	St. Mary's, O.		512 Broadway
Bamberger, Bloom & Co.	Louisville, Ky.	Jacob F. & Levi Bamberger	115 Worth
Banco Internacionale Hipotecario de Mexico.	City of Mexico, Mex.	R. B. Hollins & Co.	18 Wall
Bank of British North America	London, Eng.	Harry Strikeman & Frederic Drownfield	52 Wall
Bank of California.	San Francisco, Cal.	Laidlaw & Co.	14 Wall
Dank of Montreal.	Montreal, Canada.	Walter Watson & Alexander Lang	59 Wall
Barber T. L, & Co.	S. Framingham, Mass.	Gotthold & Co.	561 Broadway
Barbour, Anderson & Lawson.	Glasgow, Scotland.	Innes R. Macpherson	480 Broadway
Baring Bros. & Co.	London, Eng.	Kidder, Peabody & Co.	1 Nassau
Barklie J. & A. & Co.	Larne, Ireland	Edward McConnell & Co.	121 Franklin
Barnard & Co.	Boston, Mass.	Frederick B. Harvie	245 Sixth av.
Barnegat Park Co.	Barnegat Park, N. J.	Marcus W. Conkling	40 Wall
Barnes Mfg. Co.	New Haven, Conn.	Harmon & Dixon	118 Chambers
Darnes Mfg. Co.	Paterson, N. J.	David A. Barnes	98 Spring
Barnes & Beyer.	Philadelphia, Pa.	George Drake Smith	86 Worth
Bates Bros.	Buffalo, N. Y.	Calvin F. Budd	34 Thomas
Barnett & Co.	Newark, N. J.	William A. E. Rowe	64 William
Barney Dumping Boat Co	Jersey City, N. J.	J. Wall Wilson	319 Broadway
Darney & Berry.	Springfield, Mass.	Pope & Stevens	114 Chambers
Barr Pumping Engine Co.	Philadelphia, Pa.	Cummings H. Tucker jr. & Bro.	126 Liberty
Barr William, Dry Goods Co.	St. Louis, Mo.	William Barr	335 Broadway
Barren Island Fertilizer & Oil Works	Barren Island, N. Y.	Moses Goodkind & Edwin Sternfels	173 Front
Barrow, Wade, Guthrie & Co.	London & Manchester, Eng.	Edward R. Sewell & James T. Anyon	120 Broadway
Barry John, Osthere & Co.	Kirkcaldy, Scotian'.	T. J. Keveney & Co.	329 Broadway
Bartel Adam H. & Co.	Richmond, Ind.		63 Leonard
Barth Samuel & Co.	Baltimore, Md.	Philip Straus & Daniel Buhre	36 Beaver
Bartlett, Hayward & Co.	Baltimore, Md.	Robert A. C. Smith	40 Wall
Barton & Guestier	Bordeaux, France.	B. Lamontagne & Sons.	53 Beaver
Baruch & Arnstein.	Knoxville, Tenn.	Hibbert D. Masters	84 W. B'way
Bassett Bros. & Co.	Providence, R. I.	Charles H. Anderson	198 Broadway
Batchelder & Lincoln.	Boston, Mass.	William W. Fay	104 Duane
Batchelor Bros.	Philadelphia, Pa.	James Evans	105 Nassau
Bates J. C, & Co.	Lake City, Fla.	J. C. Thompson & Co.	9 Walker
Bates Bros.	Athol, Mass.	James P. Bates	8 Thomas
Bates & Beaman.	Westboro, Mass.	Joseph S. Hart	36 E. Houston
Bauer Philip & Co	Hamburg, Germany	Henry Morrison jr.	19 Whitehall
Bauer Bros. & Co.	San Francisco, Cal.	William Brunner	7 Mercer
Baughman Bros.	Richmond, Va.	Oscar S. Grady	78 Warren
Baum Bros. & Stein.	Camden, S. C.		479 Broadway
Daum, Fischer & Co	Milwaukee, Wis.		501 Broadway
Baumgardener L. S. & Co.	Toledo, O.		91 Leonard
Baumgarten J. & Co.	San Francisco, Cal.		483 Broadway
Bausch & Lomb Optical Co.	Rochester, N. Y.	Henry Fincke.	46 Maiden la.
Baxter J. & L.	Philadelphia, Pa	Charles E. Wilmot.	92 Prince
Bay Line.	Baltimore, Md.	Howard V. Tompkins.	287 Broadway
Bayart-Parent Freres	Roubaix, France.	William H. Brown & Charles M. Stratton.	62 White
Dayer Chas. & Co.	London, Eng.	Gustav Kuinow.	638 Broadway
Dayley Hat Co.	Newburyport, Mass.	Charles H. Folsom.	187 Greene
Daylis Thos. & Co	Redditch, Eng.	John Dougan & Co.	354 Broadway
Beal, Higgins & Henderson.	Boston, Mass.		61 Leonard
Bean & Vail Bros.	Philadelphia, Pa.		335 Broadway
Bearse, Murphy & Co.	Portland, Me.		355 Broadway
Beattie Mfg. Co.	Little Falls, N. J.	Robert Beattie & Sons	85 White
Beatty A. J. & Sons	Boston, Mass	John K. Dobbs	60 Barclay
Beatty W. A. & Co.	Providence, R. I.	Frank T. Chapman	198 Broadway
Beaver Line	Montreal, Canada.	James Arkell & Co.	19 Whitehall
Beck A. & Sons.	Philadelphia, Pa.	A. C. Sweeten & Co.	198 Worth
Beck D. L. & Sons	San Francisco, Cal.	U. H. Dudley & Co.	4 Bridge
Behrend D. J. & Son	Washington, D. C.		48 Howard
Behrens Louis & Sons.	Manchester, Eng.	Walter E. & Ernest H. Dehrens.	35 Mercer
Beiermeister & Spicer.	Troy, N. Y.	James A. Miller jr.	758 Broadway
Belcher Bros. & Co.	Newark, N. J.	William H. Belcher	92 Chambers
Belding Refrigerator Co.	Belding, Mich.	Charles J. Hall	102 Meade
Belfast Warehouse Co. (Ltd.)	Belfast, Ireland.	Oliver Anketell	26 S. William
Bell Thomas & Co.	Lurgan & Belfast, Ireland	William H. Wardell	40 White
Bell Thos. & Sons.	Dundee, Scotland.	Alexander Logie.	56 Worth
Bell Bros.	Olean, N. Y.	Thomas S. Glover	376 Broadway
Bell's Henry H., Sons.	Milton, N. Y.	John Hamilton	33 Worth
Bellefonte Iron & Nail Co.	Bellefonte, Pa.	Thomas G. Boyle & Co.	45 Broadway

COMPILED WITH ACCURACY AND DESPATCH } **CLASSIFIED BUSINESS LISTS.** { THE TROW CITY DIRECTORY CO. 11 University Place.

BEL 340 BLO

Name.	Home Office.	Agent or Representative.	New York Office.
Bellot Lucien & Co............	Cognac, France....	Emil Schultze & Co.......	86 Beaver
Bell Line Railway Co........	Montgomery, Ala...	Joseph W. Woolfolk	45 Wall
Bement, Miles & Co..........	Philadelphia, Pa...	George Place	120 Broadway
Benedict Bros................	Baltimore, Md......	Max G. Boehm..........	58 Worth
Benedict & Burnham Mfg. Co.	Waterbury, Conn....	William A. Hungerford...	13 Murray
Benedict & Co................	Milwaukee, Wis.....		476 Broadway
Benedict M. & Co............	Dallas, Tex.........		15 White
Benfield & Milne Mfg. Co.....	Newark, N. J.......	Thomas Benfield........	87 Fulton
Benn Joseph & Sons..........	Bradford, Eng......	Joseph Inness..........	9 Walker
Bennett Wm. M. & Son........	Jackson, Mich......	Alexander Dobbin.......	112 Leonard
Bennington Knitting Co.......	Bennington, Vt.....	Abner S. Haight........	119 Franklin
Benton A. & Co...............	Cleveland, O........	Isaac Kuble & Co.......	90 Maiden la.
Bergasse H. & Co.............	Marseilles, France..	Emil Schultze & Co.....	36 Beaver
Berger Albert & Co...........	Lorraine, Switzerland	Alphonse Walter........	47 Maiden la.
Berger Lewis & Sons (Ltd.)...	London, Eng........	Haldane Haswell.......	97 Nassau
Berger & Wirth..............	Leipsic, Germany...	Paul Beisbarth.........	190 William
Bergner Frederick & Co......	Baltimore, Md......	Robert M. Ficker.......	505 Broadway
Bergner & Engel Brewing Co..	Philadelphia, Pa....	Alfred Liebenstein.....	55 Broad
Berkshire Life Ins. Co.......	Pittsfield, Mass.....	George W. English	271 Broadway
Beris & Co...................	Rio de Janeiro & Santos, Brazil }	Desire Dulin	87 Wall
Berlin Musical Instruments Mfg. Co. }	Berlin, Germany....	Paul Schaetzell	91 Chambers
Bernd J. D. & Co.............	Pittsburgh, Pa......		451 Broadway
Bernhard Geo. & Sons.........	Boston, Mass.......	George Bernhard	256 E. 91st
Bernheimer G. & Sons.........	Kansas City, Mo....		75 Leonard
Bernheimer S. & Son..........	Port Gibson, Miss...	K. Mandell & Co........	26 Howard
Berringer, Straus & West....	Eufaula, Ala........		589 Broadway
Berry Bros...................	Detroit, Mich.......	Alfred Hooper	252 Pearl
Bertail & Marlin Freres.......	Bordeaux, France...	Venable & Heyman.....	22 Reade
Berthon Boat Co. (Ltd.).......	Romsey, Hants, Eng.	Harry de B. Parsons....	35 Broadway
Bertin P. & L. Rigant........	Paris, France.......	Louis Rigant	66 W. 23d
Bortsch, Hans & Co...........	Philadelphia, Pa....	Philip Haus	309 Broadway
Berwind-White Coal Mining Co. }	Philadelphia, Pa....	Edward J. Berwind......	55 Broadway
Bethlehem Iron Co............	Bethlehem, Pa......	George A. Evans........	40 Wall
Bettmann B. & Co.............	Cincinnati, O.......		16 White
Bettmann, Bloom & Co........	Cincinnati, O.......		557 Broadway
Beveridge Brewing Co........	Newburgh, N. Y....	Patrick Comiskey.......	121 Warren
Beveridge Erskine & Co......	Dunfermline, Scotland	David Strachan	99 Franklin
Beyer & Nordlinger..........	St. Gall, Switzerland		401 Broadway
Bibb Mfg. Co.................	Macon, Ga..........	Isaac N. Hanson........	51 Leonard
Bibber, McMann & Co.........	Portland, Me.......	Loren W. True.........	622 Broadway
Bigelow Carpet Co...........	Boston, Mass.......	William B. Kendall	100 Worth
Bigelow Co...................	New Haven, Conn...	George S. Burnum & Frank L. Bigelow }	15 Cortlandt
Bigelow J. W. & Son..........	Litchfield, Conn....	F. R. Emmons & Bro....	21 Warren
Billings & Co................	Nottingham, Eng....	Stanley Billings.......	216 Church
Billings, Clapp & Co.........	Boston, Mass.......	George E. Callender....	85 Platt
Billings, Taylor & Co........	Cleveland, O........	William H'. King.......	16 Platt
Binet, Fils & Co..............	Reims, France......	Culbert & Taylor	30 Broadway
Bing S.......................	Paris, France.......	John Getz..............	220 Fifth Av.
Bingham John & Co..........	Liverpool, Eng......	David Bingham	121 Produce Ex.
Bingham William, Brothers & Co. }	Liverpool, Eng.....	William Bingham & Co...	119 Produce Ex.
Bingham Bros................	Liverpool, Eng......	David Bingham	121 Produce Ex.
Binghamton Oil Refining Co...	Binghamton, N. Y...	Byron Morgan	16 Destrosses
Bird J. A. & W. & Co.........	Boston, Mass.......	Frank M. Bartow.......	18 Cedar
Birge M. H. & Sons...........	Buffalo, N. Y.......	Joshua J. Goodrich.....	1155 Broadway
Birkin T. I. & Co.............	Nottingham, Eng....	Andrew B. Dick	29 Mercer
Birmingham Plane Mfg. Co ...	Birmingham, Conn..	Charles M. Hopkins....	64 Reade
Birnbaum B. & Son............	London, Eng........	G. Kuinow	658 Broadway
Birnie Paper Co..............	Springfield, Mass...	John F. Hitchcock......	297 Broadway
Bischoff & Rodatz............	Hamburg, Germany..	Henry E. Frankenberg..	70 Walker
Bishop, Hoyt & Co............	Citra, Fla..........	L. Jesse P. Bishop......	136 Reade
Bissell Carpet Sweeper Co	Grand Rapids, Mich.	Thomas W. Williams....	103 Chambers
Biswell Curling Iron Mfg. Co..	Chicago, Ill........	George Robins	47 Leonard
Bittner J. C. & Co............	Toledo, O...........	McCafferty & Holton....	105 William
Blabon Geo. W. & Co..........	Philadelphia, Pa....	Drevin & Clery........	110 Worth
Black D., Clonk Co............	Cleveland, O........		224 Church
Black Jas. & Co..............	Belfast, Ireland.....	Thomas Black	279 Church
Blackwell's Durham Co-operative Tobacco Co. }	Philadelphia, Pa....	Jay D. Bausher........	102 Chambers
Blake Geo. P. Mfg. Co........	Boston, Mass.......	George H. Stover	93 Liberty
Blake, Dowell & Helm........	Baltimore, Md......		585 Broadway
Blake, McFall & Co..........	Portland, Ore.......	James W. Towne.......	140 Nassau
Blake, Moffitt & Towne.......	San Francisco, Cal..	James W. Towne.......	140 Nassau
Blanchard, Booth & Hoff......	Columbus, Ga.......		376 Broadway
Blandon Rolling Mill Co. (Ltd.)	Blandon, Pa........	Frank L. Froment	112 John
Blankenburg R. & Co.........	Philadelphia, Pa....	Charles P. Watson.....	111 Franklin
Blankenship & Blake Co	Dallas, Tex.........	William G. Happy	56 Worth
Blass Gus & Co...............	Little Rock, Ark....	Gustav Blass	536 Broadway
Bliss R. Mfg. Co..............	Pawtucket, R. I.....	Willard & McKee	21 Park pl.
Bliss, Wilson & Co...........	Louisville, Ky......		364 Broadway
Bloch A. & Co................	Cincinnati, O.......		96 Franklin
Bloch Brothers...............	Clarksville, Tenn...		512 Broadway

MERCHANTS EXCHANGE NAT. BANK OF THE CITY OF N. Y.
SOLICITS YOUR ACCOUNT. **257 Broadway.**
PHINEAS C. LOUNSBURY, President.   ALLEN S. APGAR, Cashier.

BLO 341 BRI

Name.	Home Office.	Agent or Representative.	New York Office.
Block Elias & Sons	Cincinnati, O.	Emil Block	22 S. William
Blockhouse Coal Co. (Ltd.)	Cape Breton, N. S.	Belloni & Co.	87 South
Bloom Wm. & Co.	Boston, Mass.		260 Church
Bloomberg & Raphael	Brownsville, Tex. & Matamoras, Mex.	Aaron J. Bloomberg	56 Worth
Bloomsburg Iron Co.	Bloomsburg, Pa.	Strond & Co.	104 John
Bloosburg Coal Co.	Arnot, Pa.	Williams & Peters	1 Broadway
Blotchky Bros.	Des Moines, Ia.		9 White
Bluine Mfg. Co.	W. Acton, Mass.	Arthur D. Cochrane	884 Broadway
Blum Leon & H.	Galveston, Tex.	Hyman Blum	121 Duane & 88 Thomas
Blum Bros.	Chicago, Ill.		62 White
Blum Bros.	Louisville, Ky.		470 Broome
Blum L, Gerson & Co.	Paris, France	Laura Demacener	109 Prince
Blumenfeld & Fried.	Starkville, Miss.		479 Broadway
Blumenthal Bros. & Co.	Philadelphia, Pa.	Mack Latz	705 Broadway
Blun J. M. & Co.	Fairview, N. M.		18 Walker
Blundell, Spence & Co.	Hull, Eng.	Edward Hill's Son & Co.	27 Cedar
Boatman's Fire & Marine Ins. Co.	Pittsburgh, Pa.	Kirby & Dwight	81 Cedar
Bodwell Granite Co.	Rockland, Me.	John Peirce	7 Beekman
Boehringer C. F. & Soehne	Mannheim, Germany	Louis Engelhorn	49 Cedar
Boers & Co.	Palafrugell, Spain	Gabriel Boers	100 Maiden la.
Dogardus New Art Co.	Newark, N. J.	Charles C. Vanetten	7 Barclay
Bohm Bros. & Co.	Cincinnati, O.		313 Church
Boies Steel Wheel Co.	Scranton, Pa.	Coolbaugh, McMunn & Pomeroy	45 Broadway
Bolckow, Vaughan & Co. (Ltd.)	Middlesborough, Eng.	C. Lawrence Perkins	8 Cotton Ex.
Bolling R. E. & Co.	Montgomery, Ala.	Albert L. Crater	115 Worth
Bolster, Snow & Co.	Portland, Me.		55 White
Bondat Freres	Grenoble, France	Charles G. Landon & Co.	421 Broome
Bonner Mercantile Co.	Butte City, Mont.		224 Church
Bonner F. L. & Co.	Deer Lodge, Mont.		224 Church
Booth Steamship Co. (Ltd.)	Liverpool, Eng.	Booth & Co.	15 Frankfort
Bordeaux Line	Bordeaux, France	Funch, Edye & Co.	27 S. William
Borden Mining Co.	Frostburg, Md.	Borden & Lovell	70 West
Borgzinner Bros.	London, Eng.	Siegmund Borgzinner	52 William
Bortree Mfg. Co.	Jackson, Mich.	C. E. Conover Co.	101 Franklin
Bosant Pere & Fils	Bordeaux, France	August Ritz	48 Greene
Boston Belting Co.	Boston, Mass.	Benjamin F. Elson	100 Chambers
Boston Chair Mfg. Co.	Ashburnham, Mass.	Charles F. Griffith	295 Mott
Boston Clock Co	Boston, Mass.	William H. Atwater	6 Warren
Boston Dye Wood & Chemical Co.	Boston, Mass.	John H. Jones	159 Front
Boston Gossamer Rubber Co.	Boston, Mass.	Edward S. Simon	52 Leonard
Boston Improvement Co.	Boston, Mass.	John McGinnis & William H. Van Gulder	55 Broadway
Boston Rubber Shoe Co.	Boston, Mass.	Howard S. Randall	70 Reade & 112 Duane
Boston Terra Cotta Co.	Boston, Mass.	John C. Evatt	41 Park row
Boston Thread & Twine Co.	Boston, Mass.	Percy H. Brundage	116 Chambers
Boston Tow Boat Co.	Boston, Mass.	Frederick B. Dalzell	70 South
Boston & Lockport Block Co.	Boston, Mass.	Frank Baldwin	88 South
Boston & Montana Cons. Copper & Silver Mining Co.	Boston, Mass.	Lewisohn Bros.	61 Fulton
Bottomly F. L. & Co.	Manayunk, Pa.	Pitman & Black	116 Worth
Bouche Fils & Co.	Marseil-Sur-Ay, France	Paul Bouche	87 Beaver
Bouchard Pere & Fils	Beaune, France	George S. Nicholas	43 Beaver
Bourne, Graham & Foll	London, Eng.	Graham, Hinkley & Co.	9 S. William
Boussod, Valadon & Co.	Paris, France	Eugene W. Glaenzer	803 Fifth av.
Bowers Jas. & Co.	Newark, N. J.	Charles M. Adams	56 Worth
Bowker Fertilizer Co.	Boston, Mass.	Edwin M. Catz	29 Beaver
Boxwell John H. & Co.	Macaio, Brazil	Smith & Schipper	91 Wall
Boyd, Jones & Co.	Baltimore, Md.	William H. Jones	96 W. B'way
Boyd, White & Co.	Philadelphia, Pa.	W. Watson Martin	848 Broadway
Boyden & Co.	Chicago, Ill.	George H. Martin	850 Produce Ex.
Boyle Thos. G. & Co.	Pittsburgh, Pa.	Charles E. Pope.	45 Broadway
Boylston Ins. Co.	Boston, Mass	Frame & Shade.	206 Broadway
Bradford H. E. & Co.	Bennington, Vt.	Valentine & Flagler	99 Franklin
Bradley & Co.	Syracuse, N. Y.	Solomon B. Horton	63 Murray & 38 College pl.
Bradley & Pierson Mfg. Co.	Newark, N. J.	William W. Bradley	135 Duane
Brafman A. & Sons	Baltimore, Md.		86 Spring
Braman, Berry & Co.	Terre Haute, Ind.		87 Franklin
Brandeis J. L. & Sons.	Omaha, Neb.		491 Broadway
Brandenburg Freres	Bordeaux, France	Anthony Oschs	51 Warren
Brandt's Swiss Pill Co	Frankfort-on-Main, Germany	Adolph Schmidt	61 Park pl.
Brasch & Rothenstein	Berlin, Germany	R. F. Downing & Co.	20 Exchange pl.
Braselman J. A. & Co.	New Orleans, La.	Thomas A. Fulton	90 Walker
Bregaro & Co.	Ponce, Porto Rico	Enrique Bregaro	135 Pearl
Bremond John & Co.	Austin, Tex		71 Leonard
Brewer Bros.	Philadelphia, Pa.	Harmon & Dixon	118 Chambers
Brewer, Parker & Muse.	Brownwood, Tex.		50 Worth
Brice Bros	Pittsburgh, Pa.	William J. Snyder & Bro.	63 Murray
Bridgeport Dress Co.	Bridgeport, Conn.	Samuel Holmes	19 Murray

SNOW, CHURCH & CO. {ESTABLISHED 1874.

BRI 342 BUN

Name.	Home Office.	Agent or Representative.	New York Office.
Bridgeport Copper Co.	Bridgeport, Conn.		71 Wall
Bridgeport Forge Co.	Bridgeport, Conn.	Thomas H. Hallen	71 Wall
Bridgeport Gun Implement Co.	Bridgeport, Conn.	Hartley & Graham	17 Maiden la.
Bridgeport Steamboat Co.	Bridgeport, Conn.	John D. Hubbell	Pier 25 E. R.
Bridgeport Wood Finishing Co.	New Milford, Conn.	Granville M. Breinig	240 Pearl
Brigg John F. & Co.	Huddersfield, Eng.	Benjamin L. Brigg	437 Broadway
Brigg, Neumann & Co.	Bradford, Eng.	James D. Atherton	16 Mercer
Briggs Excursions	Hoboken, N. J.	Charles E. Peters	884 West
Briggs C. C. & Co.	Boston, Mass.	Charles H. Ditson & Co.	867 Broadway
Briggs & Co.	Manchester, Eng.	Joseph Walker	69 Leonard
Brigham, Hopkins & Co.	Baltimore, Md.	William P. Montague	685 Broadway
Bright J. C. & W. H.	Buffalo, N. Y.	Henry Godshall	56 Front
Brinkmann A. H. & Co.	Baltimore, Md.	Emil Ziegler	74 Franklin
Briscoes, Swepson & Co.	Knoxville, Tenn.		236 Church
Brisk & Jacobson	Mobile, Ala.		433 Broome
Bristol Brass & Clock Co.	Forestville, Conn.	George S. Brown	52 Warren
Bristol City Line	Bristol, Eng.	James Arkell & Co.	19 Whitehall
Bristol Mfg. Co.	Bristol, Conn.	H. Lee Mallory	128 Franklin
British Am. Assurance Co.	Toronto, Canada	John M. Whiton	32 Pine
British Mfg. Co.	Bridgeton, Scotland	S. Bacriein	351 Broadway
British & European Patent Agency	London, Eng.	Frederick W. Barker	252 Broadway
British & Foreign Marine Ins. Co. (Ltd.)	London & Liverpool, Eng.	L. Allyn Wright & Samuel P. Weir	Cotton Ex.
British & Foreign Freehold Mortgage Guarantee & Debenture Co. (Ltd.)	London, Eng.	Samuel R. MacLean	30 Broad
Brittain, Smith & Co.	St. Joseph, Mo.	Henry S. Hart	833 Broadway
Brizard Marie & Roger	Bordeaux, France	Theodore W. Slemmier	36 E. 14th
Broadhead Worsted Mills	Jamestown, N. Y.	Alvin J. Graffin	55 Worth
Broderick & Bascom Rope Co.	St. Louis, Mo.	Frank Baldwin	84 South
Brokaw Mfg. Co.	Newburg, N. Y.	Charles W. Haynes	56 Worth
Bromley John & Sons	Philadelphia, Pa.	T. B. Shonff & Co.	935 Broadway
Bromley Mfg. Co.	Philadelphia, Pa.	Wight & Co. (Ltd.)	341 Broadway
Bromschwig Henry & Co.	St. Louis, Mo.		540 Broadway
Bronson Supply Co.	Cleveland, O.	Hall & Near	51 Cliff
Bronx Co.	Bronxdale, N. Y.	Thomas Bolton jr.	115 Worth
Brook Jonas & Bros.	Huddersfield, Eng.	Philip H. Jonas	19 Thomas
Brooke Benj. & Co.	Philadelphia, Pa.	David H. M. Davis	5 Harrison
Brooke Joseph & Co.	Bradford & Huddersfield, Eng.		448 Broome
Brookfield Linen Co. (Ltd.)	Belfast, Ireland	David Carlisle	100 Franklin
Brooklyn Watch Case Co.	Brooklyn, N. Y.	Harlan S. Noyes	192 Broadway
Brooklyn Waterfront Warehouse & Dry Dock Co.	Brooklyn, N. Y.	George Davidson	29 South
Brooklyn Wire Nail Co.	Brooklyn, N. Y.	A. R. Whitney & Co.	17 Broadway
Brookmire J. H. & Co.	St. Louis, Mo.	George S. Adrian & Co.	90 Water
Brooks George & Sons	Philadelphia, Pa.	Walter M. Fairchild	348 Broadway
Brooks, Shoobridge & Co.	London, Eng.	Charles J. Stevens	7 Bowling gr.
Brouse & Co.	Akron, O.		876 Broadway
Brown Chas A. & Co.	Troy, N. Y.	Amos P. Dunn	56 Worth
Brown J. S., Hardware Co.	Galveston, Tex.	Charles O. Leconat	280 Broadway
Brown John & Son.	Glasgow, Scotland	William Robertson	119 Franklin
Brown John S. & Sons	Belfast, Ireland	George H. Billeck	118 Franklin
Brown R. S. & Co.	Fall River, Mass.		224 Church
Brown F. M. & Co.	New Haven, Conn.	Frank M. Brown	394 Broadway
Brown Bros. & Co.	Baltimore, Md.	John M. Hall	76 Franklin
Brown Bros. & Co.	San Francisco, Cal.	Ralph Brown	488 Broadway
Brown, Daughaday & Co.	St. Louis, Mo.	Thomas L. Rushmore	34 Thomas
Brown, Durrell & Co.	Boston, Mass.	John H. Howarth	744 Broadway
Brown, Thomson & Co.	Hartford, Conn.	Syndicate Trading Co.	120 Franklin
Brownfield Wm. & Sons	Coleridge, Eng.	Davison & Pitcairn	12 Barclay
Bruce Edward B. & Co.	Baltimore, Md.	Purdy & Arnold	51 Broad
Bruce S. R. & Co.	Mineola, Tex.	K. Mandell & Co.	22 Howard
Brush Electric Co.	Cleveland, O.	Samuel M. Hamill	35 Union sq. E.
Buchoy J. J. & Co.	Philadelphia, Pa.	Kennedy & Moon	55 Beaver
Buckbee J. C. & Co.	Chicago, Ill.	Baker & Taylor Co.	740 Broadway
Buckeye Engine Co.	Salem, O.	William L. Simpson	18 Cortlandt
Buckeye Glass Co.	Greensburg, Pa.	Thomas G. Edge	58 Barclay
Buckl L. & Co.	Ellaville, Fla.	Hibbert B. Masters	84 W. B'wy
Buckingham J. H. & Co.	London, Eng.	William B. Roe	68 W. 23d
Buckley W. W. & Co.	Jersey City, N. J.	William Warbrick	48 Cedar
Budd J. T. & Son	Monticello, Fla.	Hibbert B. Masters	84 W. B'way
Budgett Samuel & Son	London, Liverpool, & Bristol, Eng.	Walter F. Budgett	350 Produce Ex.
Budgett H. H. & S. & Co.	Bristol, Liverpool, & London, Eng.	John W. Nightingale	324 Produce Ex.
Budweiser Brewing Co. (Ltd.)	Brooklyn, N. Y.	J. S. & W. Brown	122 Produce Ex.
Buffalo Car Mfg. Co.	Buffalo, N. Y.	Chester Griswold	11 Pine
Buffalo German Ins. Co.	Buffalo, N. Y.	T. J. Temple & Co.	155 Broadway
Bufford's Sons Lithographing Co.	Boston, Mass.	George H. Davis	335 Broadway
Bugbee & Niles	N. Attleboro, Mass.	Frank H. Cutler	176 Broadway
Buhach Producing & Mfg. Co.	Stockton, Cal.	Thurston & Braidich	190 William
Building & Loan Assn	Aberdeen, S. Dak.	Munger, Thomas & Co.	150 Broadway
Bullene, Moore, Emery & Co.	Kansas City, Mo.	Hugh C. Nevins	51 Leonard
Bulow A. & Co.	London, Eng.	Clement W. Coombe	309 Broadway
Bunting's Samuel, Sons & Co.	Philadelphia, Pa.		81 White

WATER METERS, GAS ENGINES, | NATIONAL METER CO.
FOR PUMPING AND POWER. | **252 Broadway, N. Y.**

Name.	Home Office.	Agent or Representative.	New York Office.
Bureau of Press Clippings....	Chicago, Ill......	James A. Welch..........	39 Nassau
Burgos C. F. & Co............	Buenos Ayres, Argentine Rep.	M. Adrian King..........	35 Broadway
Burke Edward & John.......	Dublin, Ireland.....	John Burke.............	24 S. William
Burke & Co.................	Buffalo, N. Y......	Horace T. Austin.......	47 Broadway
Bürke & Co.................	St. Gall, Switzerland	Benjamin F. Robinson...	51 Leonard
Burke, Fitzsimons, Hone & Co.	Rochester, N. Y.....	——	115 Worth
Burleigh H. G. & Brother....	Whitehall, N. Y.....	Brackett W. Burleigh....	1 Broadway
Burlington, Cedar Rapids & Northern Railway Co.	Cedar Rapids, Ia....	Henry H. Hollister.....	42 New
Burnet Co..................	Trenton, N. J......	Benjamin W. Burnet.....	140 Maiden la.
Burnett Joseph & Co........	Boston, Mass.......	Cashman Bros...........	132 Reade
Burnham, Hanna, Munger & Co.	Kansas City, Mo....	Eugene F. Humphrey....	34 Thomas
Durnham, Stoepel & Co......	Detroit, Mich......	Eugene F. Humphrey....	34 Thomas
Burns William H. & Co......	Worcester, Mass....	John S. Baker & George M. Mowton	402 Broadway
Burns & Oates..............	London, Eng.......	Catholic Publication Soc. Co.	9 Barclay
Burns, Silver & Co..........	Bridgeport, Conn...	John S. Silver..........	115 Broadway
Burnshine Co...............	Chicago, Ill.......	Joseph Kelly...........	101 Pearl
Burroughs & Mountford Co...	Trenton, N. J......	Frank S. Warren........	46 Murray
Burroughs, Wellcome & Co...	London, Eng.......	Fairchild Bros. & Foster .	82 Fulton
Burrowes E. T. & Co........	Portland, Me.......	J. Parley Milliken.......	62 Warren
Burt Shirt Mfg. Co..........	Poughkeepsie, N. Y..	Lucius E. Burt.........	744 Broadway
Burt & Packard.............	Brockton, Mass.....	Allen F. Brett..........	126 Duane
Burton Brewing Co..........	Paterson, N. J.....	Bernard Katz..........	269 Ninth Av.
Busiel J. W. & Co...........	Laconia, N. H......	Shreve & Adams........	66 Leonard
Bushee A. & Co.............	Attleboro, Mass....	James E. Hills.........	237 Broadway
Butcher W. & S.............	Sheffield, Eng......	Francis Speir...........	136 Duane
Butterworth Edwin & Co....	Manchester, Eng....	James Pirnie..........	150 Nassau
Butzel Bros. & Co...........	Detroit, Mich......	——	54 White
Buyer & Reich..............	San Francisco, Cal..	Edward Buyer..........	74 Grand
Byers A. M. & Co...........	Pittsburgh, Pa.....	Edward F. Keating.....	14 Cliff
Byrne Bros. & Co...........	Passaic, N. J......	George C. Mercer......	51 Leonard
Bywater, Tanqueray & Co...	London, Eng.......	Arthur Hickey.........	17 Broadway
Cable Flax Mills............	Schaghticoke, N. Y..	Frank Carhart.........	113 Worth
Cahn Joseph & Co...........	Kansas City, Mo....	——	40 Thomas
Cahn E. & Co...............	Grenada, Miss.....	——	479 Broadway
Cahn Bros..................	Dallas, Tex........	——	40 Thomas
Cahn, Belt & Co's p.........	Baltimore, Md.....	Dexter B. Britton......	61 Park pl.
Cahn, Wampold & Co........	Chicago, Ill.......	Charles Cahn..........	52 Thomas
Caboone Geo. H. & Co......	Providence, R. I...	Jacob Solinger.........	176 Broadway
Caldwell & Peterson Mfg. Co.	Wheeling, W. Va....	B. Walker Peterson.....	97 Chambers
Caledonian Railway of Scotland	Glasgow, Scotland	Caesar A. Barattoni.....	862 Broadway
		Edwin M. Junkins.....	267 Broadway
California Associated Press...	San Francisco, Cal..	David H. Walker.......	11 Park row
California Dried Fruit Asn...	San Francisco, Cal..	Chapman & Meehan....	140 Franklin
California Ins. Co...........	San Francisco, Cal..	John M. Whiton.......	32 Pine
California Line.............	San Francisco, Cal..	Dearborn & Co........	104 Wall
California Water & Mining Co.	San Francisco, Cal..	Baxter Barker.........	47 Broadway
Callender, McAuslan & Troup.	Providence, R. I...	Syndicate Trading Co...	120 Franklin
Calvet J. & Co..............	Bordeaux, France...	Frederick de Bary & Co..	45 Warren
Cambria Iron Co............	Philadelphia, Pa....	Philip H. Fraser.......	16 Wall
Cambridge Roofing Co.......	Cambridge, O......	Holden & Cairns.......	35 Broadway
Camden Woollen Mills Co....	Camden, N. J......	Elliot Bigelow..........	47 Leonard
Cammell Chas. & Co. (Ltd.)...	Sheffield, Eng.....	Edmund Y. Jacobss.....	35 Park row
		Griswold & Gillott.....	5 Wall
Campbell Tile Co............	Stoke-on-Trent, Eng	T. Aspinwall & Son....	308 Fifth av.
Campbell, Achnach & Co.....	Glasgow, Scotland..	William Bell...........	10 Walker
Canada Atlantic Line........	Ottawa, Canada....	Frederick E. Goble.....	6 Counties L. & Pier 36 E. R.
Canada Southern Line.......	Rochester, N. Y....	Henry F. Lydecker.....	363 Broadway
Canadian Bank of Commerce..	Toronto, Canada...	Alexander Laird & William Gray	16 Exchange pl.
Canadian Pacific Railway Co..	Montreal, Canada..	Bank of Montreal	59 Wall
		Edward V. Skinner...	353 Broadway
Canal & Lake Steamboat Co...	Philadelphia, Pa....	Horace S. Nichols.....	76 Wall
Cannelton Coal Co..........	Cannelton, W. Va...	Calvin B. Orcutt.......	1 Broadway
Cannon & Byers............	Louisville, Ky.....	Henry Ide.............	530 Broadway
Canoe Cotton Mills..........	Valatie, N. Y......	George Copeland & Co...	134 Pearl
Canton Mfg. & Blanching Co..	Boston, Mass......	Jacob H. Sommer......	12 Laight
Cantrell & Cochrane........	Dublin, Ireland....	Edward & John Burke...	24 S. William
Caramin & Co..............	Thy-Le-Château, Belgium	Weir, Rogers & Co.....	45 Broadway
Cardeza, Gillams & Co.......	Philadelphia, Pa....	George Schoen	14 State
		William B. Barry.....	55 Beaver
Carenou & Tur.............	Zaragoza, Spain...	Emile Utard..........	15 Whitehall
Carey, Bayne & Smith.......	Baltimore, Md.....	George H. Bayne......	88 Leonard
Carlin & Fulton.............	Baltimore, Md.....	——	708 Broadway
Carlowitz & Co.............	Hong Kong, China..	Smith & Schipper.....	91 Wall
Carnegie Bros. & Co. (Ltd.)...	Pittsburgh, Pa.....	Charles H. Odell......	17 Broad
Carnegie, Phipps & Co. (Ltd.).	Pittsburgh, Pa.....	Herbert L. Waterman...	17 Broad
Carolan & Co...............	San Francisco, Cal..	Welsh & Lea..........	96 Reade
Carolina Oil & Creosote Co...	Wilmington, N. C...	Lamb & Bell..........	1 Broadway
Carr M. W. & Co............	Boston, Mass......	Louis B. Carr.........	419 Leonard
Carruth John G. & Co.......	Philadelphia, Pa....	Alexander H. Broadway..	61 Leonard

PROTECTION For Family, Home, Store, Factory, etc., by using only the "VULCAN" BRAND OF SAFETY MATCHES. Headquarters, 373 Washington Street, New York.

CAR 344 CHI

Name.	Home Office.	Agent or Representative.	New York Office.
Carslaw & Henderson (Ltd.)	Glasgow, Scotland	Anderson, Churchill & Co.	84 Leonard
Carslaw & Henderson of N. Y. (Ltd.)	Patchogue, L. I.	Anderson, Churchill & Co.	84 Leonard
Carson & Simpson	Philadelphia, Pa.	Charles Seifert & Edward J. Darcy	40 University pl.
Carson, Pirie & Co.	Chicago, Ill.	John T. Pirie	115 Worth
Carson, Pirie, Scott & Co.	Chicago, Ill.	John T. Pirie	115 Worth
Carstairs, McCall & Co.	Philadelphia, Pa.	Daniel H. Carstairs	1 State
Cartor White Lead Co.	Omaha, Neb.	Charles F. Coggeshall	5 Dutch
Carter Bros. & Co.	Louisville, Ky.	William A. Doan	115 Worth
Carter, Rice & Co.	Boston, Mass.	William B. Harwood	11 Murray
Cartwright Bros.	E. Liverpool, O.	Etienne Lebel	6 College pl.
Case, Lockwood & Brainard Co.	Hartford, Conn.	John F. Hitchcock	297 Broadway
Casics-Bourgeois	Cambrai, France.	Comptoirs Commerciaux Français	46 University pl.
Casper F. & Co.	New Orleans, La.	Morris Gonsenheim	18 Lispenard
Cassell & Co. (Ltd.)	London, Eng.	Oscar M. Dunham	106 Fourth av.
Castle Line	London, Eng.	Charles L. Morgan	70 South
Castle Wilmot & Co.	Rochester, N. Y.	A. G. Armstrong	8 E. 23d
Castleton Mfg. Co.	Castleton, N. Y.	Woolworth & Graham	154 Nassau
Castner & Curran	Philadelphia, Pa.	Henry C. Rogers	1 Broadway
Catasauqua Mfg. Co.	Catasauqua, Pa.	Elias T. Day	102 Broadway
Catherwood H. & H. W.	Philadelphia, Pa.	Samuel H. Burr	16 S. William
Cattle Ranch & Land Co. (Ltd.)	London, Eng.	Rufus Hatch & Co.	1 Broadway
Cauffmann, Dinkelspiel & Co.	Rochester, N. Y.		658 Broadway
Cauvin Hugues & Fils.	St. Quentin, France.	Comptoirs Commerciaux Français	46 University pl.
Cayuga Lake Ice Line	Rochester, N. Y.		41 Park row
Central Co.	Providence, R. I.	Robert J. Peterson	117 Duane & 34 Thomas
Central Expanded Metal Co.	Pittsburgh, Pa.	Jay K. Combs	85 Chambers & 67 Reade
Central Glass Co.	Boston, Mass.	Etienne Lebel	4 College pl.
Central Knitting Co.	Cleveland, O.	John Nathan	335 Broadway
Central Loan & Debenture Co.	Kansas City, Mo.	Thomas S. Knits	45 Wall
Central Loan & Land Co.	Emporia, Kans.	Alfred J. Taylor	257 Broadway
Central R. R. & Banking Co. of Ga.	Savannah, Ga.	William H. Rhett	317 Broadway
Central Vermont R. R. Co.	St. Albans, Vt.	Edward R. Coppins	317 Broadway
Central Vt. R. R. & Steamer Line	St. Albans, Vt.	Wyatt M. Bassett	Pier 36 (old) E. R.
Ceralins Mfg. Co.	Columbus, Ind.	Arthur Witzleben	3 State
Chadborn & Coldwell Mfg. Co.	Newburgh, N. Y.	John H. Graham & Co.	113 Chambers & 65 Reade
Chadwick Copying Book Co.	Lambertville, N. J.	Henry E. Pratt	60 Duane
Chadwick James & Bro.	Bolton, N. Y.	Frederick G. Payne	51 Walker
Challenge Iceberg Refrigerator Co.	Grand Haven, Mich.	Francis T. Witte Hardware Co.	106 Chambers
Challinor, Taylor & Co.	Tarentum, Pa.	John W. Burton	7 Barclay
Chambers & Co.	Philadelphia, Pa.	Victor R. Vaino	528 Broadway
Chambers Bro. & Co.	Philadelphia, Pa.	Montague & Fuller	41 Beekman
Champignaelle Charles & Emmanuel Vve.	Bar-Le-Duc, France.	Henry L. Bouche	857 Broadway
Champion Safety Sash Lock Co.	Cleveland, O.	Thomas Crane	92 Chambers
Chanut J. M. & Co.	Paris, France.	Jean M. Chanut	2 W. 14th & 1123 B'way
Chapin Hall Lumber Co.	Newark, N. J.	Charles Smith	409 Broadway
Chapin Mining Co.	Milwaukee, Wis.	William Schlesinger	45 Wall
Chaplin W. H. & Co.	London, Eng.	Venable & Huyman	22 Reade
Chapman Slate Co.	Chapman Quarries, Pa.	William Stoneback	502 West
Chapman Valve Mfg. Co.	Boston, Mass.	Pancoast & Rogers	23 Platt & 15 Gold
Chapman & Martin	Philadelphia, Pa.	Oswald J. Martin	69 Wall
Chappaqua Shoe Mfg. Co.	Chappaqua, N. Y.	Charles G. Hunt.	142 Duane
Chappell F. H. & Co.	New London, Conn.	Frank H. Chappell	1 Broadway
Charleston & Savannah R'y Co.	Charleston, S. C.	John D. Hashagen	261 Broadway
Charras & Co.	Nyons, Drome, France.	C. B. Richard & Co.	30 Platt
Chase Daniel E. & Co.	Boston, Mass.	George D. Bayand	62 New
Chase John & Sons	Webster, Mass.	B. H. Smith & Co.	54 Worth
Chautauqua Ice Co.	Rochester, N. Y.		41 Park row
Cheever G. W. & Co.	Providence, R. I.	Henry V. Lenau	176 Broadway
Chenery & Co.	Portland, Me.	Willis Chenery	375 Broadway
Cheney Henry, Hammer Co.	Little Falls, N. Y.	C. F. Guyon & Co.	99 Reade
Cheque Bank (Ltd.)	London, Eng.	Alfred Ray	2 Wall
Chesapeake Shirt Co.	Baltimore, Md.	George W. Naylor	79 Franklin
Chesapeake & Ohio Railway Co.	Cincinnati, O. Richmond, Va.	Charles R. Bishop & William Plummer	362 Broadway
Cheshire Watch Co.	Cheshire, Conn.	Leonard W. Sweet	40 Malden la.
Chesman Nelson & Co.	St. Louis, Mo.	Nelson Chesman	54 Beekman
Chicago Construction Co.	Chicago, Ill.	Herbert A. Shipman	5 Beekman
Chicago Credit Guide Co.	Chicago, Ill.	John Sherman Moulton	120 Broadway
Chicago Glycerine Co.	Chicago, Ill.	William H. Schwars	90 Maiden la.
Chicago Hardware Mfg. Co.	Chicago, Ill.	William K. Norris	290 Broadway
Chicago Horseman Newspaper Co.	Chicago, Ill.	Edward C. Walker	103 Potter bldg.
Chicago Newspaper Union	Chicago, Ill.	William J. Carlton & Patrick T. Barry	10 Spruce

IDEN & CO., **MANUFACTURERS OF**
University Place, 9th to 10th Sts., N. Y. | **GAS FIXTURES AND ELECTROLIERS**

CHI 345 COL

Name.	Home Office.	Agent or Representative.	New York Office.
Chicago Packing & Provision Co.	Chicago, Ill.	Charles H. Blanchford	351 Produce Ex.
Chicago Sewing Machine Co.	Chicago, Ill.	C. F. Guyon & Co.	90 Reade
Chicago Spring Butt Co.	Chicago, Ill.	Peter S. Wold	97 Chambers
Chicago Sugar Refining Co.	Chicago, Ill.	Joseph Bensel	101 Water
Chicago & Alton R. R. Co.	Chicago, Ill.	William J. Bogert	261 Broadway
Chicago & Atlantic Railway Co.	Chicago, Ill.	James H. Benedict	29 Broad
		Leonard H. Conant	15 Cortlandt
Chicago, Burlington & Northern R. R. Co.	St. Paul, Minn.	Edward J. Swords	817 Broadway
Chicago, Burlington & Quincy R. R. Co.	Chicago, Ill.	Edward J. Swords	817 Broadway
Chickies Iron Co.	Chickies, Pa.	Stroud & Co.	104 John
Childs Geo. F., Adjustable Chair Co.	Chicago, Ill.	Al G. Armstrong	8 E. 23d
China Mutual Ins. Co.	Boston, Mass.	Despard & Platt	16 Exchange pl.
Choate H. & Co.	Winona, Minn.		84 W. B'way
Christian Bros.	Minneapolis, Minn.	Andrew J. Toomey	17 Moore
Church A. M., Co.	Troy, N. Y.		376 Broadway
Church J., Co.	Cincinnati, O.	Avon F. Adams	19 E. 16th
Cincinnati Barb Wire Fence Co.	Cincinnati, O.	J. C. McCarty & Co.	97 Chambers & 81 Reade
Cincinnati Wire Co.	Cincinnati, O.	H. C. Mechling	81 Fulton
Cincinnati, New Orleans & Texas Pacific R'y Co.	Cincinnati, O.	William S. St. George	319 Broadway
Citizens Ins. Co.	Cincinnati, O.	Ackerman, Deyo & Hilliard	41 Pine
Citizens Ins. Co.	Pittsburgh, Pa.	T. J. Temple & Co.	155 Broadway
Citizens Ins. Co.	St. Louis, Mo.	Harold Herrick	64 Pine
Citizens Loan & Trust Co.	Kansas City, Mo.	Charles S. Butler	59 Broadway
Citroen Venve L. B. & Co.	Paris, France	Nathan Kauffmann	21 John
City of London Ins. Co.	London, Eng.	Charles M. Peck & Co.	33 Pine
Claflin George L. & Co.	Providence, R. I.	John D. Titsworth	71 William
Claflin, Larrabee & Co.	Boston, Mass.	John H. Hall	52 White
Clapperton William & Co.	Oldham, Eng.	Hughes Fawcett	25 White
Clark Mile-End Spool Cotton Co.	Harrison, N. J.	Thomas Russell & Co.	442 Broadway & 86 Howard
Clark L. & Sons	Coalisland, Ireland.	James & Smyth	325 Broadway
Clark B. G. & Co.	Rome, Ga.		115 Worth
Clark T. B. & Co.	Honesdale, Pa.	George C. Sterling	17 Murray
Clark W. G. & Co.	Attleboro, Mass.	Adolph L. Andlau	196 Broadway
Clark, Bunnett & Co. (Ltd.)	London, Eng.	Frank A. Howson	162 W. 27th
Clark's Cove Guano Co.	New Bedford, Mass.	George W. Kirke	181 Front
Clark-Neergaard Co.	Malone, N. Y.	C. Cooper Clark	140 Nassau
Clarke E. A. & Co.	Tampa, Fla.	Hibbert B. Masters	84 W. B'way
Clarke & Co.	Peoria, Ill.		84 W. B'way
Clarke & King	Troy, N. Y.	Thomas D. Clarke	815 Church
Clearfield Fire Brick Co.	Clearfield, Pa.	George Damerel	85 Chambers
Clerk Gas Engine Co.	Philadelphia, Pa.	George B. Edwards	142 Chambers
Clermont Knitting Co. (Ltd.)	Philadelphia, Pa.	Francis C. Brewster	86 Worth
Cleveland Faucet Co.	Cleveland, O.	Herman D. Borner	43 Centre
Cleveland Rolling Mill Co.	Cleveland, O.	Clarence Dickerson	34 Cliff
Cleveland Rubber Co.	Cleveland, O.	Benjamin L. Tomes	55 Warren
Cleveland Twist Drill Co.	Cleveland, O.	James D. Foot	101 Chambers
Cleveland, Cincinnati, Chicago & St. Louis R'y Co.	Cincinnati, O.	James D. Layng	5 Vanderbilt av.
Clicquot Ponsardin (Veuve)	Reims, France	Chas. F. Schmidt & Peters	24 Beaver
Cline Geo. S., Publishing House	Chicago, Ill.	Stella McRoberts	12 E. 10th
Clinton Wire Cloth Co.	Clinton, Mass.	George E. Howard	78 Beekman
Closeman & Co.	Bordeaux, France	Pardy & Arnold	51 Broad
Clough Corkscrew & Capsule Co.	Newark, N. J.	Clough & Maconnell	102 Nassau
Clydach Tin Plate Works	Clydach, Wales	Stroud & Co.	104 John
Coates Mfg. Co.	Worcester, Mass.	McCoy & Sandors	26 Warren
Coatesville Iron Works	Coatesville, Pa.	Henry J. Hopper	243 Broadway
Coats J. & P.	Paisley, Scotland	Auchincloss Bros.	47 White
Cobb Vulcanite Wire Co.	Wilmington, Del.	Robert J. Steen	45 Broadway
Coburn Whip Co.	Windsor, N. Y.	Charles N. Beckwith	90 Chambers
Cochran & Walsh	St. Paul, Minn.	Silas B. Walsh	18 Wall
Codding D. E. & Co.	N. Attleboro, Mass.	Edward A. Follett	176 Broadway
Cody A. & Co.	Brooklyn, N. Y.	Morton Penfield	80 E. 14th
Coes E. & Co.	St. Denis, France	Sykes & Street	65 Water
Cohen Julius & Co.	Athens, Ga.	Hibbert B. Masters	84 W. B'way
Cohen Michael & Son	Chicago, Ill.		586 Broadway
Cohen W. & Co.	San Francisco, Cal.	Theodore F. Stampf	115 Worth
Cohen Bros.	Jacksonville, Fla.	Samuel Cohen	83 Walker
Cohen Bros. & Co.	Milwaukee, Wis.		75 Leonard
Cohen, Davis & Co.	Portland, Ore.	Andrew A. Jones	81 Walker
Cohn H. C. & Co.	Rochester, N. Y.	Henry S. Cohn	658 Broadway
Cohn Bros.	Salt Lake City, Utah		470 Broome
Cohn & Co.	Buffalo, N. Y.		260 Church
Cohn Bros. & Co.	Cincinnati, O.		21 White
Cohoes Brewing Co.	Cohoes, N. Y.	Joseph Goetz	398 G'wich
Colburn A. & Co.	Philadelphia, Pa.	George S. Adams	127 Water
Coleman S. T., Darden & Co.	Macon, Ga.		115 Worth
Coles, Marshall & Co.	Newburgh, N. Y.	B. G. Coles & Co.	190 Forsyth
Colint, Wagner & Reiser	Calvert, Tex.	Heine & White	88 Walker
Collinsville Zinc Co.	Collinsville, Ill.	William Paulsen	10 Burling sl.
Colombia Coffee Co. (Ltd.)	Bogota, S. A.	Maurice Uribe	41 Fulton
Colonial Chemical Co.	Boston, Mass.	Stone, Timlow & Co.	105 Reade

Name	Home Office	Agent or Representative	New York Office
Colonial Mail Line S. S. Co	London, Eng	Charles L. Morgan	70 South
Colored Paper & Glue Mfg. Co.	Aschaffenburg, Germany	George Roeder	319 Broadway
Columbia Rubber Co	Boston, Mass	Walter S. Jones	338 Broadway
Columbia Rubber Works	Akron, O	S. Y. L'Hommedieu & Co	65 Reade & 63 Chambers
Columbia Silk Co	Paterson, N. J	Margaret Cameron	189 Sixth av.
Columbia Water Co	Columbia, Tenn	James Gambis	63 Wall
Columbus Borax Co	Columbus, Nev	Marcus A. Josephi	20 Cedar
Columbus Cons. Mining Co	San Francisco, Cal.	George H. Gill & Samuel P. Warren	31 Broadway
Columbus Store Service Co	Columbus, O	Alfred R. Cory	43 Elm
Columbus Watch Co	Columbus, O	James M. Morrow	41 Maiden la.
Colville David & Sons	Motherwell, Scotland	George B. Douglas	115 Broadway
Combination Roll & Rubber Co	Bloomfield, N. J	Stanley Grescen	38 Park row
Comins Geo. T., Co	Concord, N. H	Frederick Cowan	179 Canal
Commerce Ins. Co	Albany, N. Y	Roosevelt & Boughton	44 Pine
Commercial Express Line	Buffalo, N. Y	James D. Abranis	401 Broadway
Commercial Ins. Co.	San Francisco, Cal.	Ford, Rowell & Hone, David L. Kirby	33 Pine, 51 Cedar
Commercial Travelers Assn.	Syracuse, N. Y	Alexander G. Stewart	200 Broadway
Commercial Union Assurance Co. (Ltd.)	London, Eng	Charles Sewall	48 Pine, 100 Fourth av. & 108 W. 42d
Commonwealth Line	Philadelphia, Pa.	Roberts & King	23 South & Pier 11 E. R.
Compagnie Bordelaise de Navigation à Vapeur	Bordeaux, France	Finch, Edye & Co	27 S. William
Compagnie Générale Transatlantique	Paris, France	Augustin F. Forget	3 Bowling gr. & Pier 42 (now) N. R.
Compañía Transatlantica Española	Barcelona, Spain	J. M. Ceballos & Co	80 Wall & Pier 21 (old) N. R.
Compound Lumber Co	Chicago, Ill.	Colin M. Thompson	35 Wall
Comptoirs Commerciaux Français	Paris, France	L. Gustave Roch	46 University pl.
Concordia Fire Ins. Co	Milwaukee, Wis	Irving & Illnds.	161 Broadway
Conewago Iron Co	Middletown, Pa	Stroud & Co	104 John
Connecticut Fire Ins. Co	Hartford, Conn.	Scott, Alexander & Talbot.	45 William
Connecticut Indemnity Assn.	Waterbury, Conn	J. Herman Ashley	82 Liberty
Connecticut Mutual Life Ins. Co.	Hartford, Conn.	Philip S. Miller	1 Wall
Connelly & Shafer	Kingston, N. Y.	McIntyre & Reardon	115 West
Conrath & Liebsch	Steinschoenau, Bohemia	Hamburger & Co	416 Broome
Conshohocken Tube Co	Conshohocken, Pa.	Edward Barr Co. (Ltd.)	78 John
Consolidated Car-heating Co	Albany, N. Y	James T. Leighton	15 Cortlandt
Consolidated Ice Machine Co.	Chicago, Ill.	Joseph Koenigsberg	210 E. 54th
Consolidated Kansas City Smelting & Refining Co.	Kansas City, Mo.	Nathaniel Witherell	20 Nassau
Consolidated Safety Valve Co.	Bridgeport, Conn.	Charles A. Moore	111 Liberty
Consolidation Coal Co	Baltimore, Md.	Rossel & Hicks	71 Broadway
Continental Mills	Lewiston, Me	Clifford M. Bucknam	87 Worth
Converse Toy & Woodenware Co.	Winchendon, Mass.	Willard & McKee	21 Park pl.
Cook Thomas & Son	London, Eng	George Eade	951 & 1295 B'way
Cooke James W. & Co	Philadelphia, Pa.	James W. Cooke	214 Church
Cooke Locomotive & Machine Co.	Paterson, N. J	Henry A. Allen	45 Broadway
Cooke A. M. & Co	London, Eng	Daniel Feradike	16 W. 23d
Cookson & Co	Newcastle-on-Tyne, Eng.	Edward Hill's Son & Co	27 Cedar
Co-operative Wholesale Soc. (Ltd.)	Manchester, Eng.	John Gledhill & James M. Percival	422 Produce Ex.
Cops & Co	Philadelphia, Pa.		56 Worth
Copestake, Lindsay, Crampton & Co.	Nottingham, Eng.	Cornelius M. Kellock	98 Grand
Corbin Cabinet Lock Co	New Britain, Conn.	George H. Taylor	96 Murray
Corbin P. & F	New Britain, Conn.	William Bishop	96 Murray
Corliss Bros. & Co	Troy, N. Y	Wilbur F. Corliss	76 Franklin
Corry City Iron Works	Corry, Pa	Josiah C. Saxton	52 Broadway
Corticine Floor Covering Co	London, Eng.	Henry Beattell	109 Worth
Cortright Metal Roofing Co.	Philadelphia, Pa.	D. Lewis Grant	83 Cedar
Coryell Flint Paper Co	Williamsport, Pa.	C. F, Guyon & Co	99 Reade
Cosack & Co	Buffalo, N. Y	Joseph A. Berger	200 Broadway
Cossart, Gordon & Co	Madeira, Portugal	Culbert & Taylor	29 Broadway
Counselman Charles & Co	Chicago, Ill.	Thomas B. Counselman	15 Broad
Counselman & Day	Chicago, Ill.	Thomas B. Counselman	15 Broad
County Down Flax Spinning & Weaving Co. (Ltd.)	Belfast, Ireland	Charles E. Bycroft	91 Franklin
Couper Milling Co	Tarrytown, N. Y	John B. Couper	Manhattan mkt
Courtauld H., Co	London, Eng	Alexander D. Napier & Co.	526 Broadway
Coutarat & Bro	Paris, France	Emile Alfred Cornuel	97 Prince
Convertie B. & Bro	New Orleans, La	Theophilus Dubois	335 Broadway
Cowan, McClung & Co	Knoxville, Tenn		115 Worth
Cowdrey E. T., Co	Boston, Mass	Charles A. Adams	208 W. 15th
Cowperthwait & Co	Philadelphia, Pa	William H. Whitney	5 Clinton pl.
Cox Abram, Store Co	Philadelphia, Pa	Wilbur B. Wilkinson	250 Water
Cox P., Shoe Mfg. Co	Rochester, N. Y	James H. Thompson	78 Reade

THE CALIGRAPH WRITING MACHINE,
HARTFORD, CONN.

COX 347 DAV

Name.	Home Office.	Agent or Representative.	New York Office.
Cox Sons, Buckley & Co	London, Eng	A. Scariott Thomson	8 E. 15th
Coxe Bros. & Co	Philadelphia, Pa	Ezra R. Ely	190 Broadway
Cragin L L. & Co	Philadelphia, Pa	G. Clarke Huntington	77 Barclay
Craighead & Kintz	Ballard Vale, Mass	F. D. Tuck	38 Barclay & 38 Park pl.
Crandall Type Writer Co	Groton, N. Y	Reed & Bassett	853 Broadway
Crane Co	Chicago, Ill		40 Wall
Crane Elevator Co	Chicago, Ill	Frank B. Jones	40 Wall
Cranston Print Works Co	Cranston, R. I	Albert A. Williams	84 W. B'way
Cravon David & Co	Bradford, Eng	Eben Sugden	70 Worth
Crawford D. & Co	St. Louis, Mo	Lockland Ferguson	115 Worth
Cream City Furniture Co	Milwaukee, Wis	Frederick R. Morse	16 E. 15th
Crescent Mfg. Co	Cleveland, O	John Q. Maynard	12 Cortlandt
Crescent Steel Co	Pittsburgh, Pa	Philip H. Patriarche	480 Pearl
Crescent Watch Case Co	Brooklyn, N. Y	Robbins & Appleton	5 Bond
Croeson & Clearfield Coal & Coke Co.	Frugality, Pa	Charles J. Wittenbery	1 Broadway
Creston Water Co	Creston, Iowa	James Gamble	66 Wall
Crittenton C. M. & Son	Geneva, N. Y		550 Broadway
Crocker A. B. & Co	Boston, Mass	Edward H. Willis	62 Worth
Crocker J. & Son	Pawtucket, R. I	John F. Hitchcock	207 Broadway
Croft & Allen	Philadelphia, Pa	William M. Phelps	93 Murray
Cromble J. & J. (Ltd.)	Aberdeen, Scotland	John Leslie	55 Worth
Crooks Robert & Co	Liverpool, Eng	H. Fleming Crooks	64 John
Crosby Steam Gauge & Valve Co.	Boston, Mass	O. Chandler Wells & Charles A. Coutant	66 John
Crosland Geo. & Sons	Huddersfield, Eng	Hicks Bros	42 White
Crossley John & Sons (Ltd.)	Halifax, Eng	Henry Bentfall	100 Worth
Crouse & Brandegee	Utica, N. Y	William E. Stiles	80 Thomas
Crowell Thos. Y. & Co	Boston, Mass	William W. Wyman	13 Astor pl.
Cruse & Fils Frères	Bordeaux, France	Chas. F. Schmidt & Peters	24 Beaver
Crystal Plate Glass Co	St. Louis, Mo	Gilbert S. King	102 Chambers
Cuba Sponge Co	Havana, Cuba	Charles A. Salmon & Co	75 Pine
Cumberland Coal Co	Baltimore, Md	Stephen B. Elkins	1 Broadway
Cummings & Wexel	Attleboro, Mass	Charles M. Robbins	176 Broadway
Cummings, Matthews & Co	Orange Valley, N. J	William T. Everett	31 W. Houston
Cummins T. K. & Co	Boston, Mass	Thomas K. Cummins	74 Beaver
Cunard Steamship Co. (Ltd.)	Liverpool, Eng	Vernon H. Brown & Co	4 Bowling gr. & Pier 40 (new) N. R.
Cuniffe, Dobson & Co	Bordeaux, France	George S. Nicholas	43 Beaver
Cunningham C. G. & Co	Boston, Mass	Charles B. Stevens	54 Gold
Cunningham & Hinshaw	Liverpool, Eng	Danson Cunningham	26 Cotton Ex.
Cunningham, Curtiss & Welch	San Francisco, Cal	Edwin B. Curtiss	40 Chambers
Curds Publishing Co	Philadelphia, Pa	Winfield S. Niles	38 Park row
Curtis H. C. & Co	Troy, N. Y	Ralph A. Fry	685 Broadway
Curtis H. H. & Co	N. Attleboro, Mass	Charles E. Sandland	170 Broadway
Curtiss & Warren	Chicago, Ill	Lucienne I. Person	214 Church
Cutler Mfg. Co	Rochester, N. Y	J. Warren Cutler	45 Broadway
Cutter Silk Mfg. Co	Bethlehem, Pa	John D. Cutter & Co	44 E. 14th
Daggett & Clap	Attleboro, Mass	J. Parker Ford	41 Maiden la.
Dahl's Sulphate Pulp Co	Danzig, Germany	Herman Anderson	59 E. 10th
Dakota Farm Mortgage Co	Huron, S. Dak	W. N. Coler & Co	11 Pine
Dale & Davis	Trenton, N. J	John Nixon	6 College pl.
Dalsheimer S. & Co	New Orleans, La	Samuel Dalsheimer	51 Leonard
Dalton J., Mfg. Co	Norwich, Conn		529 Broadway
Dalton Shoe Co	Dalton, Mass	Charles B. Churchill	128 Duane
Dalton & Ingersoll	Boston, Mass	Oscar J. Saxe	64 Gold
Daly Mining Co	Salt Lake City, Utah	Lonnsbery & Co	16 Broad
Daly, Armstrong & Co	Augusta, Ga		49 Lispenard
Damkoehler's A. L., Wwe	Berlin, Germany	Clothar Boettcher	78 Greene
Dammann F. W. & B	Baltimore, Md	Ignatius M. Dammann	47 Leonard
Damon, Howe & Co	Leominster, Mass	Edgar A. Garbutt	390 Broadway
Dana, Tucker & Co	Boston, Mass	George J. Brown	89 Thomas
Daniels & Fisher	Denver, Colo	Norman T. Ayres	50 Worth
Daniels, Fisher & Smith	Leadville, Colo	Norman T. Ayres	56 Worth
Dannenberg & Doody	Macon, Ga		620 Broadway
Danville Nail & Mfg. Co	Danville, Pa	Borden & Lovell	70 West
Danziger & Brothers	Syracuse, N. Y		260 Church
Darling & Scholes	Buffalo, N. Y	Carl Wolff	713 Broadway
Darlington, Runk & Co	Philadelphia, Pa	Daniel Harding	658 Broadway
Dauphinot Père & Fils	Roubaix, France	Russmann & Galland	464 Broome
Daussa A. & Co	Catalonia, Spain	Augustine Dnussa	136 Maiden la.
Davenport & Fairbairn	Erie, Pa	Stroud & Co	104 John
Davidson B. & Co	Sioux Falls, S. Dak	David B. Heine	68 Walker
Davidson & Co	Belfast, Ireland	Robert B. Arthur	1496 Broadway
Davis Coal & Coke Co	Baltimore, Md	Stephen B. Elkins	1 Broadway
Davis James R. & Co	Detroit, Mich	John D. Titsworth	71 William
Davis Samuel C. & Co	St. Louis, Mo	John T. Davis	99 Franklin
Davis Sulphur Ore Co	Davis, Mass	Herbert J. Davis	45 Pine
Davis I. B. & Son	Hartford, Conn	Benjamin F. Kelley & Son	91 Liberty
Davis M. M. & Co	Petersburgh, Va	Michael M. Davis	260 Church
Davis S. & Sons	Kokomo, Ind		84 W. B'way
Davis & Samuels	Pittsburgh, Pa		11 White
Davis Brothers, Bergmann & Co.	San Francisco, Cal	Andrew A. Jones	81 Walker
Davis, Chambers Lead Co	Pittsburgh, Pa	William H. Paulding & Lyman B. Carhart	26 Burling sl.

SPECIAL ATTENTION PAID TO THIS CLASS OF WORK. **BANKERS' & BROKERS' CIRCULARS DELIVERED** THE TROW CITY DIRECTORY CO. 11 University Place.

DAV 348 DOO

Name.	Home Office.	Agent or Representative.	New York Office.
Davis, Drane & Co	Cumberland, Md		307 Canal
Davol Mfg. Co	Providence, R. I	Henry D. Titus	9 Thomas
Day J. H. & Co	Cincinnati, O	Edwin P. Jones	85 Murray
Dayton Last Works	Dayton, O	Robert T. Brown	21 Spruce
Dean, Chase & Co	Boston, Mass	Edward W. Dean	9 Thomas
Deane Steam Pump Co	Holyoke, Mass	Thomas Beards	72 Cortlandt
Debenham & Freebody	London, Eng	David G. Gardiner	68 W. 23d
Dehaven & Townsend	Philadelphia, Pa	Alexander H. Dehaven	40 Wall
Deinhard & Co	Coblenz, Germany	Emil Unger & Co	50 Park pl.
Delacamp & Co	Hiogo, Japan	Hugo O. Delacamp	106 Franklin
Delachapelle E. & Co	Ottawa, Ill	August Thiery	29 Murray
Delaney Forge & Iron Co	Buffalo, N. Y	Frank L. Froment	112 John
Delaplain L. S., Son & Co	Wheeling, W. Va		
Delaware Mutual Safety Ins. Co	Philadelphia, Pa	J. Raymond Smith	93 Franklin 75 Beaver
Delbeck & Co	Reims, France	E. Lamontagne & Sons	53 Beaver
Delinières R. & Cie	Limoges, France	F. W. Buning & Co	56 Murray
Delor A. & Co	Bordeaux, France	Purdy & Arnold	51 Broad
Delsarte Corset Co	Newark, N. J	Ida M. Row	142 W. 23d
Denholm & McKay	Worcester, Mass	Syndicate Trading Co	120 Franklin
Denny Brothers	London, Eng. & Zittau, Saxony	William Weidonkellar	76 Franklin
Denver Ins. Co	Denver, Colo	Hall & Henshaw	54 William
Denver Land & Security Co	Denver, Colo	John C. Avery	115 Broadway
Denver & Berkeley Park Rapid Transit Co.	Denver, Colo	John C. Avery	115 Broadway
Denver, Texas & Fort Worth R. R. Co.	Denver, Colo	John T. Granger	1 Broadway
Depasquale Fratelli & Co	Messina, Italy	Edward Hill's Son & Co	27 Cedar
Depper & Son	Louisville, Ky		705 Broadway
Derby Silver Co	Birmingham, Conn	Isaac W. Colefair	25 Maiden la. & 529 Broadway
Derby P. & Co	Gardner, Mass	George W. Cann	202 Canal
DeSilver Charles & Sons	Philadelphia, Pa	Baker & Taylor Co	740 Broadway
Des Moines Loan & Trust Co.	Des Moines, Iowa	Richard E. Carpenter	88 Park row
Detrick Calvin & Co	Stapleton, S. I	Calvin Detrick	47 Broadway
Detroit Breweries (Ltd.)	London, Eng	Robert Sewall	32 Nassau
Detroit Copper & Brass Rolling Mills	Detroit, Mich	Frank J. Daffner	259 Broadway
Detroit Fire & Marine Ins. Co.	Detroit, Mich	Harold Herrick	44 Pine
Detroit Radiator Co	Detroit, Mich	Williams & James	60 Barclay
Detroit, Grand Haven & Milwaukee Railway Co.	Detroit, Mich	Edward P. Beach	271 Broadway
Deutsch & Co	San Antonio, Tex		15 White
Devereux O. C. & Co	Providence, R. I	Orrin C. Devereux	102 Chambers
Devon Carpet Mills	Philadelphia, Pa	T. J. Keveney & Co	329 Broadway
Dewey Edward & Co	Boston, Mass	Augustus P. McGraw	10 Dey
Diamond Match Co	Chicago, Ill	George P. Johnson	187 Duane
Diamond Prospecting Co	Chicago, Ill	Charles H. Parmelee	18 Broadway
Diamond State Iron Co	Wilmington, Del	Charles G. Phillips	11 Pine
Dibble Mfg. Co	Trenton, N. J	William H. Jacobus, C. P. Guyon & Co.	99 Chambers 99 Reade
Dickerson & Co	Liverpool, Eng	Dickerson, Vandusen & Co	29 Cliff
Dickey W. J. & Sons	Baltimore, Md	Harry V. Powers	88 Leonard
Dickey, Tansley & Co	Baltimore, Md	William M. Crane & Co	756 Broadway
Dickinson Hard Rubber Co	Springfield, Mass	Newell Brothers Mfg. Co	25 Mercer
Dickinson Brothers & King	Chicago, Ill	Jerome A. King & Ira C. Hutchinson	24 State
Dickson Mfg. Co	Scranton, Pa	William H. Price	10 Wall & 9 Pine
Diebold Safe & Lock Co	Canton, O	William H. Butler	79 Duane
Dillingham & Co	Sheboygan, Wis	Wilson Brothers Woodenware & Toy Co.	119 Chambers
Dinkelspiel & Sons	San Francisco, Cal	Henry Dinkelspiel	34 Thomas
Direct States Line	Newcastle-on-Tyne, Eng.	John C. Seager	24 Stone
Direct U. S. Cable Co. (Ltd.)	London, Eng	James Brown	40 Broadway & 51 New
Disbrow & Barberie	Reading, Pa	Abraham V. Barberie	58 Warren
Disston Henry & Son	Philadelphia, Pa	John H. Graham & Co	113 Chambers
Dittenhoefer, Haas & Co	Portland, Ore	Isaac L. White	117 Duane
Ditteradorfer Felt Works	Ditteradorfer, Saxony	Louis Gehlert	204 E. 18th
Divas, Pomeroy & Stewart	Reading, Pa	Syndicate Trading Co	120 Franklin
Dobson W. E. & F	Nottingham, Eng	Thomas Wilson	44 White
Dodge & Co	Jersey City, N. J	Thomas Q. Gilson	16 Cortlandt
Doerr Philip & Sons	Philadelphia, Pa	McClain & Talbot	110 Worth
Doherty & Wadsworth	Paterson, N. J	Spielmann & Co	85 Grand
Dolan Thomas & Co	Philadelphia, Pa	Charles B. Gregory	51 Leonard
Dollfus, Dettwiller & Co	Mulhouse, Alsace	Louis Gehlert	204 E. 18th
Dolph A. M., Co	Cincinnati, O	Uriah T. Fackenthall	40 Cortlandt
Domecq Pedro & Co	Jerez, Spain	Calbert & Taylor	89 Broadway
Domestic Tapestry Co	Paterson, N. J	N. J. Wight & Co. (Ltd.)	341 Broadway
Don William & John & Co	Forfar & Dundee, Scotland	Anderson, Churchill & Co	84 Leonard
Donaldson Robert & Co	Madeira, Portugal	George S. Nicholas	43 Beaver
Donaldson William & Co	Minneapolis, Minn	Samuel Groocock	415 Broadway
Doob M. & Brother	Cincinnati, O	Moritz Doob	448 Broadway

FOR THE BEST CO-PARTNERSHIP IN THE BEST CORPORATION SEE PAGE F IN BACK OF BOOK

DOR   349   ELI

Name.	Home Office.	Agent or Representative.	New York Office.
Dormeuil Frères	Paris, France	Klaas Wijnstok	30 W. 23d
Dornan Brothers	Philadelphia, Pa	Harry A. Fitzgerald	86 Worth
Dorr Paint Co	San Francisco, Cal.	Guy C. Goss	18 Broadway
Doshin Silk Co	Yokohama, Japan	R. Arai	46 Howard
Dougherty D. H. & Co	Atlanta, Ga	Albert L. Crater	115 Worth
Douglas W. & B.	Middletown, Conn.	Henry M. Chase	87 John
Douglas Brothers & Co	Glasgow, Scotland	George B. Douglas	115 Broadway
Downie Boiler Incrustation Preventive Co.	San Francisco, Cal.	Delafield, McGovern & Co.	91 Hudson
Doyle & Co	Pittsburgh, Pa.	William J. Snyder & Bro.	63 Murray
Dresden Pottery Works	E. Liverpool, O.	Etienne Lebel	6 College pl.
Drewry & Co	Richmond, Va.		43 Worth
Dreyfus D. & Co	San Francisco, Cal.	Edward Frowenfeld	20 Desbrosses
Dreyfus S. G. & Co	Shreveport, La.	K. Mandell & Co.	26 Howard
Drucker & Whit	Wheeling, W. Va.		302 Broadway
Druid Felt Co	Baltimore, Md.	Robert M. Gilmour	52 John
Drysdale John & Joseph & Co.	London & Liverpool, Eng. & Buenos Ayres, Argentine Republic	John Dunn, Son & Co.	76 Wall
Duche T. M. & Sons	London, Eng.	Elfoim Reimann	101 Water
Duckworth, Turner & Co	Savannah, Ga.	E. P. Mitchell & Co.	64 Wall
Ducournau J. A. & Son	Natchitoches, La.	Theophilus Dubois	385 Broadway
Dueber Watch Case Mfg. Co.	Canton, O.	John W. Sherwood	178 Broadway
Dulary J. E. & Co	Cognac, France	George S. Nicholas	43 Beaver
Duminy & Co	Ay, France	Anthony Oechs	61 Warren
Dunbar, McMaster & Co.	Gilford, Ireland & Greenwich, N. Y.	Benjamin F. Howe	5 Walker
Duncan George & Sons	Pittsburgh, Pa.	Harry B. Duncan	Astor h.
Duncan James & Co	Dundee, Scotland	George D. Winter	89 Franklin
Dundee Water Power & Land Co.	Passaic, N. J.	Edmund Le B. Gardiner	56 Worth
Dunham Hosiery Co	Naugatuck, Conn.	Abner S. Haight	119 Franklin
Dunham E. H. & Co	Providence, R. I.	William Mount	200 Broadway
Dunham R. W. & Co	Chicago, Ill.	Rudolph Rodiger	58 New
Dunham, Carrigan & Hayden Co.	San Francisco, Cal.	Brace Hayden	107 Chambers
Dunham, Hotchkiss & Co	Brunswick, Ga.	Luther L. Hotchkiss	28 State
Dunkirk Engineering Co.	Dunkirk, N. Y.	Ernest W. Naylor	140 Broadway
Dunlap D. R., Mercantile Co	Mobile, Ala.	Hibbert B. Masters	84 W. B'way
Dunn W. G. & Co	Columbus, O.		224 Church
Dunnell Mfg. Co	Pawtucket, R. I.	T. Drew Dunnell	71 Leonard
Dupont E. I., De Nemours & Co.	Wilmington, Del.	Arthur Hyndman	87 Beaver
Duquesne Tube Works Co.	Pittsburgh, Pa.	Edward F. Keating	14 Cliff
Dutemple William R. & Co	Providence, R. I.	John Lamb	18 Cortlandt
Eagle Ins. Co	London, Eng.	Leaycraft & Co.	140 Pearl
Eagleson & Co	San Francisco, Cal.		107 Franklin
Earl W. D. & Co	Leominster, Mass.	Prevear & Gleason	402 Broadway
Earle & Prew	Providence, R. I.	N. Y. & Boston Despatch Express Co.	304 Canal
E. Hartford Mfg. Co	Burnside, Conn.	John F. Hitchcock	207 Broadway
E. N. Y. Boot, Shoe & Leather Mfg. Co.	Albany, N. Y.	Edgar P. Allyn	120 Duane
E. Trenton Pottery Co	Trenton, N. J.	John E. Heusaker	67 Barclay
Eastern Railway Co. of Minn.	St. Paul, Minn.	Edward T. Nichols	40 Wall
Eastman Freight Car Heater Co.	Boston, Mass.	Benjamin V. W. Owens	41 Park row
Easton & Kinkaid	Louisville, Ky.		86 Worth
Eaton Frederick & Co	Toledo, O.		224 Church
Eckel Brothers	Deidesheim, Germany	Charles H. Knoche	81 Broad
Eckert Brothers	Cincinnati, O.		63 Leonard
Eckman & Vetsburg	Savannah, Ga.	Samuel H. Eckman	117 Duane
Eckstein Gustave & Co	Savannah, Ga.		338 Broadway
Eddy Electric Mfg. Co.	Windsor, Conn.	Willis & Hunter	33 Church
Eddy George M. & Co	Brooklyn, N. Y.	John H. Graham & Co.	118 Chambers
Edison Phonograph Toy Mfg. Co.	Boston, Mass.	Edgar S. Allen	138 Fifth av.
Edson, Moore & Co	Detroit, Mich.	James S. Meredith	51 Leonard
Educational Publishing Co.	Boston, Mass.	George E. Bonis	6 Clinton pl.
Edwards B. & Co	Chicago, Ill.	Kent E. Edwards	63 Broadway
Egyptian Mfg. Co	Rahway, N. J.	Frederick E. Smith	132 Maiden la.
Ehrlich B. E. & Son	Elmira, N. Y.	Jacob Ehrlich	874 Broadway
Einstein & Co	Chicago, Ill.		86 Worth
Eiseman Henry & Co	Council Bluffs, Iowa		40 Thomas
Eiseman J. & Co.	Portsmouth, O.		601 Broadway
Eiseman L. & Brother	Portsmouth, O.		707 Broadway
Eisenstadt Brothers	Chicago, Ill.		73 Mercer
Elderkin-Taylor Co.	Rochester, N. Y.	Avery G. Wheeler	39 Warren
Eldredge Mfg. Co	Chicago, Ill.	Frank F. Green	39 Broad
Electrical Glass Corporation.	Boston, Mass.	James G. Pennycuick	57 Broadway
Electrical Publishing Co.	Chicago, Ill.	William H. Temple	5 Beekman
Eley Brothers (Ltd.)	London, Eng.	Alfred Field & Co.	98 Chambers
Elgin National Watch Co	Chicago, Ill.	Edmund J. Scofield	192 Broadway
Elinsberg & Hertz	Selma, Ala.		470 Broadway
Eliot Ins. Co	Boston, Mass.	Charles H. Post	195 Broadway
Elizabethport Car Wheel Co	Elizabethport, N. J.	Wo rall & Co.	28 Elm

TYPEWRITING DONE BY THE TROW CITY DIRECTORY CO., 11 University Place.

Name.	Home Office.	Agent or Representative.	New York Office.
Elizabethport Pulverising Works	Elizabethport, N. J.	William H. Rankin	91 Maiden la.
Elkus L. & Co	Sacramento, Cal		554 Broadway
Ellinger A. & Co	Chicago, Ill.	William B. Lawson	362 Broadway
Elliott Joseph & Sons	Sheffield, Eng.	Alfred Field & Co.	93 Chambers
Elliott George & Co	Ashford, Eng.	Samuel Druiff	38 Maiden la.
Elliott Machine Co	Newton, Mass.	Montague & Fuller	41 Beekman
Ellison John D. & Sons	Philadelphia, Pa.	Samuel W. Lambeth	59 Liepenard
Ellison & Harvey	Richmond, Va.	Sidney Barstow	704 Broadway
Ellithorpe Air-brake Co.	Chicago, Ill.	Albert C. Ellithorpe	74 Cortlandt
Elmendorf & Co.	San Antonio, Tex.	W. H. Croseman & Bro.	77 Broad
Elmira Iron & Steel Rolling Co.	Elmira, N. Y.	Henry H. Adams	145 Broadway
Elwell & Doty	Cleveland, O.	O. F. Guyon & Co.	99 Reade
Ely & Walker Dry Goods Co.	St. Louis, Mo.	Thomas J. Brew	84 Thomas
Ely, Collins & Hale	St. Louis, Mo.	Andrew J. McIntosh	66 W. 23d
Embossing Co	Albany, N. Y.	Edward C. Schoonmaker	104 Chambers
Emerson Piano Co	Boston, Mass.	E. P. Hawkins	92 Fifth av.
Emigh & Lolaloil	Troy, N. Y.	Mott Emigh	757 Broadway
Empire Gas & Electric Light Co. of Suffolk Co.	Huntington, N. Y.	George Olney	17 Broadway
Empire Knife Co.	Winsted, Conn.	McCoy & Sanders	26 Warren
Empire Laundry Machinery Co.	Boston, Mass.	William D. Porter	12 Cortlandt
Empire Line	Philadelphia, Pa.	William A. Jones	381 Broadway
Empire Loan & Trust Co	Hutchinson, Kan.	Orville B. Ackerly	71 Broadway
Empire Mills Co.	Doboy, Ga.	Samuel A. Stead	16 Beaver
Empire Oil Works	Reno, Pa.	Henry R. Angus	112 John
Empire State Ins. Co.	Rochester, N. Y.	Wood & Kennedy	50 Pine
Empire Transp. Co.	New Haven, Conn.	George B. Martin	1 Broadway
Empire & N. E. Transp. Co.	New Haven, Conn.	George B. Martin	1 Broadway
Employers' Liability Assurance Corporation (Ltd.)	London, Eng.	Kirby & Dwight	51 Cedar
Emrich I. & Co	Pforzheim, Germany	Isaac Schorsch	52 Maiden la.
Endel M. & Brother	Gainesville, Fla.		54 Walker
Engel Brothers	Gablonz, Bohemia.	Philip Phillipsen	353 Canal
Englehart, Winning, Daviscu Mercantile Co.	St. Joseph, Mo.	Leon Brocker	531 Broadway
Engicy, Wetherell & Co.	Chartley, Mass.	James B. Freeman	176 Broadway
English Bank of Rio da Janeiro (Ltd.)	London, Eng.	Charles M. Fry	46 Wall
English Bank of the River Plate (Ltd.)	London, Eng.	Charles M. Fry	46 Wall
English John & Co.	Feckenham, Eng.	Pratt & Farmer	258 Broadway
Enterprise Comb & Jewelry Co.	Philadelphia, Pa.	James D. Hall	176 Broadway
Enterprise Mfg. Co.	Philadelphia, Pa.	J. C. McCarty & Co.	97 Chambers
Epstein I. & Brother	Savannah, Ga.		89 Worth
Equitable Building & Loan Assn. of the U. S.	Los Angeles, Cal.	Hunter & Wisner	41 Park row
Equitable Fire & Marine Ins. Co.	Providence, R. I.	Hall & Henshaw	54 William
Equitable Trust & Investment Co.	Wichita, Kan.	Herbert G. Fowler	71 Broadway
Erie Basin Stores	Brooklyn, N. Y.	Estate of William Beard	5 Hanover
Erie Canal Line.	Albany, N. Y.	Sherman Petrie	14 South
Erie Despatch	Chicago, Ill.	Melville W. DeWolf	401 Broadway
Erie Elevator Co	Jersey City, N. J.	Annan & Hoyt	102 Produce Ex.
Erie Preserving Co	Buffalo, N. Y.	David W. Fenton	167 Maiden la.
Erie & Western Transp. Co.	Philadelphia, Pa.	Horace S. Nichols	76 Wall
Ernst Brothers	Uniontown, Ala.		15 White
Erskine William & Co.	Atlanta, Ga.		61 Franklin
Erwin D. P. & Co	Indianapolis, Ind		56 Worth
Erwin, Doisy & Co.	Cincinnati, O.		56 Worth
Esberg, Bachman & Co.	San Francisco, Cal.	Julius Ehrmann	98 William
Espenhain & Albrecht	Terre Haute, Ind.		355 Broadway
Espenhain & Bartels	Milwaukee, Wis.		355 Broadway
Essex Horse Nail Co	Essex, N. Y.	J. C. McCarty & Co.	97 Chambers
Essex Watch Case Co.	Newark, N. J.	Addison Conkling	6 Maiden la.
Estes & Lauriat	Boston, Mass.	Laurence Elkus	334 Broadway
Estey Mfg. Co	Owosso, Mich.	Romaine V. Vanriper	436 Canal
Eure, Farmr & Co	Norfolk, Va.	Farmr & Jones	132 Pearl
Eureka Folding Mat Co	Cranford, N. J.	Edward Bendle	1109 Broadway
Eureka Novelty Co	Newark, N. J.	Irwin S. Loewenthal	62 Cliff & 26 Howard
Eureka Salt Mfg. Co. (Ltd.)	Liverpool, Eng.	Charles F. Barger	6 Harrison
Eureka Silk Mfg. Co	Boston, Mass.	Seavey, Foster & Dowman	441 Broadway
Eureka Tempered Copper Co.	North East, Pa.	Ezekiel E. Chambers	16 Broadway
European Bond & Exchange Co.	Chicago, Ill	A. Zalay Zeisler	25 E. 14th
Eustis, Woodman & Co.	Lewiston, Me		101 Franklin
Evans D. C., Co.	Fort Worth, Tex.	Israel Goldberg	31 Thomas
Evans Thomas, Co.	Pittsburgh, Pa.	John H. Gorton & Harry M. Folker	39 Barclay
Evans William H. & Son	Baltimore, Md.	Robert F. Foster	832 Broadway
Everett & Post.	Chicago, Ill.	Henry F. Salyards	104 John
Ewart William & Son (Ltd.)	Belfast, Ireland	Richard H. Ewart	115 Franklin
Ewing, Son & Co	Belfast, Ireland	Alexander Guild	56 Worth
Excelsior Cutlery Co.	Northfield, Conn.	Ross & Fuller Assn.	39 Chambers
Excelsior Iron Works	Chicago, Ill.	Henry B. Murray	145 Broadway
Excelsior Race Track Co.	Chicago, Ill.	Simeon M. Jacobs	494 Broadway
Excelsior Umbrella Mfg. Co.	Boston, Mass.	William C. Minszek	441 Broadway
Exstein I. & Co.	Sherman, Tex.	L. Mandell & Co.	26 Howard

THADDEUS DAVIDS CO., **WRITING INKS,**
MAKE THE BEST **SEALING WAX,**
MUCILAGE.

EXS 351 FOO

Name.	Home Office.	Agent or Representative.	New York Office.
Exstein & Co.	Buffalo, N. Y.	——	538 Broadway
Fabre S. S. Line	Marseilles, France	Jacob Terkulle	83 Broadway
Fahy J. & Co	Rochester, N. Y.	Edward C. Raftery	199 Mercer
Fairbank Canning Co	Chicago, Ill	Louis H. Heymann	18 Jay
Fairbank N. K. & Co	Chicago, Ill	James B. McMahon	216 Produce Ex.
Fairfield Rubber Co	Fairfield, Conn.	George H. Meeker	95 W. B'way
Falck A. & Co	Hamburg, Germany	Adolph Falck	160 E. 125th
Falck & Co	Hamburg, Germany	Adolph Falck	39 Broadway
Fall River Line	Boston, Mass.	Borden & Lovell	70 West & Pier 28 (old) N. R.
Faller's Isaac, Sons & Co	Cincinnati, O.	——	892 Broadway
Falls Rivet Co	Cuyahoga Falls, O.	Akron Iron Co	122 Liberty
Famous Shoe & Clothing Co.	St. Louis, Mo.	——	650 Broadway
Fanning J. H. & Co	Providence, R. I	Benjamin Crandall	178 Broadway
Farbor H. J. & Co	Baltimore, Md.	Frederick M. Farber	36 White
Farcy & Oppenheim	Paris, France	Ottenheimer Brothers	446 Broadway
Farenbacher J. & Son	Baton Rouge, La.	J. Farenbacher	26 W. Houston
Farley & Hofman	Rochester, N. Y.	F. A. Brautigam & Co.	41 W. Broadway
Farmer C. H. & Co	Boston, Mass.	Charles H. Farmer	133 Wooster
Farmers' Fire Ins. Co.	York, Pa.	Harold Horrick	44 Pine
Farmville Lithia Spring Co. of Va.	Farmville, Va.	J. Weir Wiestling	21 E. 14th
Farnley Iron Co. (Ltd.)	Leeds, Eng	Meeker & Cartor	208 Broadway
Farwell J. V. & Co	Chicago, Ill	Boardman Burchard	115 Worth
Fay J. A. & Co	Cincinnati, O.	George Place	129 Broadway
Fechheimer M. & L. S. & Co.	Cincinnati, O.	——	518 Broadway
Feohheimer Brothers & Co.	Cincinnati, O.	——	79 Leonard
Feder, Silberberg & Co.	Cincinnati, O.	——	578 Broadway
Feldman & Beckman	Evansville, Ind.	——	261 Canal
Feigner F. W. & Son	Baltimore, Md.	John L. Woodfield	6 Harrison
Follman L. & Co	New Orleans, La.	Leon Follman	18 Lispenard
Follman & Grumbach	Galveston, Tex.	Morris Gonsonheim	18 Lispenard
Follman, Grumbach & Harris	Dallas, Tex	Morris Gonsenheim	18 Lispenard
Fellows & Co	Troy, N. Y.	George H. Atwood	612 Broadway
Fels & Co	Philadelphia, Pa.	Solomon Feis	338 Broadway
Felsenheld Brothers & Co.	Cleveland, O.	Emanuel Loeb	115 Worth
Felton & Son	Boston, Mass.	James Loncheim	816 Bowery
Fenallic & Despeaux	Paris, France	Spire Pitou	15 State
Fergusson & Mitchell	Melbourne, Australia	Joseph W. Oakman	68 Broadway
Ferrin Brothers Co.	Rochester, N. Y.	John McGill	112 Warren
Ferst's M., Sons & Co	Savannah, Ga.	Joseph Strauss	468 Broadway
Feuerheerd, May & Co	Oporto, Portugal	Emil Schultze & Co.	36 Beaver
Fidelity Mutual Life Assn	Philadelphia, Pa.	Samuel M. Davis	18 Park row
Fiedler, Meoldner & Co.	Boston, Mass.	——	32 Mercer
Field Marshall & Co.	Chicago, Ill	Robert B. Macpherson	104 Worth
Field A. & Sons	Taunton, Mass.	Albert Field	86 Chambers
Field, Benedict & Co	Chicago, Ill	Richard I. Field	305 Broadway
Field, Son & Co	London, Eng.	George S. Nicholas	43 Beaver
Fillebrown C. D. & Co.	Boston, Mass.	Frank G. Robinson	60 Leonard
Finch, Van Slyck & Co.	St. Paul, Minn.	William H. Van Slyck	51 Leonard
Finding Flint Glass Co	Findlay, O.	Julius Wolff	55 Park pl.
Finlay & Brunswig	New Orleans, La.	John A. Morton	13 Gold
Fire Assn	Philadelphia, Pa.	Charles M. Peck & Co.	83 Pine
Fire Ins. Co. of the County of Philadelphia.	Philadelphia, Pa.	Wood & Kennedy	50 Pine
Fireman's Fund Ins. Co.	San Francisco, Cal.	Charles M. Pook & Co.	83 Pine
Firemen's Fire Ins. Co.	Boston, Mass.	Frame & Shade	206 Broadway
Firemen's Ins. Co.	Baltimore, Md.	Alliance Ins. Assn.	52 Nassau
Firemen's Ins. Co.	Newark, N. J.	Benjamin T. Rhoades jr.	168 Broadway
Firmin & Sons (Ltd.)	London, Eng.	William B. Roe	66 W. 23d
First Japanese Mfg. & Trading Co.	Tokio, Japan	Hiromich Shugio	20 E. 18th
Firth Carpet Co.	Cornwall, N. Y.	Robert J. Hoguet & Co.	64 White
Firth Thomas & Sons (Ltd.)	Sheffield, Eng.	Jere Abbott & Co.	23 Cliff
Firth William, Sons & Co.	Bradford, Eng.	John Firth	513 Broadway
Firth, Booth & Co	London, Eng.	Thomas Perkins	96 Spring
Fischel D. G., Sons	Niemes, Austria.	Ignatz Strauss	428 Broome
Fisher William M. & Co.	Providence, R. I.	William F. McGown	175 Broadway
Fisher G. M. & Co.	Bradford, Pa	——	224 Church
Fisher M., Sons & Co.	Huddersfield, Eng. & Moutreal, Can.	James F. Longley & Arthur Ainley	734 Broadway
Fisher S. E. & Co.	N. Attleboro, Mass.	Clarence E. Settle	41 Maiden la.
Fisher & Randall (Ltd.)	Manchester, Eng	Joseph Cantor	122 Front
Fisher, Eaton & Co.	Toledo, O.	——	224 Church
Fisk D. B. & Co	Chicago, Ill	D. Milton Fisk	530 Broadway
Flagg Stanley G. & Co.	Philadelphia, Pa.	Edward F. Keating	14 Cliff
Flavell Brothers	Germantown, Pa.	William E. Crofts	269 Church
Fleisher S. B. & B W.	Philadelphia, Pa.	Langstadter & Co.	79 Franklin
Fleming A. B. & Co. (Ltd.)	Edinburgh, Scotland	Joseph L. Roberts	26 Beekman
Flershelm & Co	Nottingham, Eng.	William Robertson	119 Franklin
Fletcher Mfg. Co	Providence, R. I.	William B. Fletcher	18 Thomas
Fletcher Robert & Son	Stoneclough, Eng.	Henry F. Leidy	140 Nassau
Florence Iron River Co	Milwaukee, Wis.	William Schlesinger	45 Wall
Florence Mfg. Co	Florence, Mass.	George A. Wells	21 Greene
Folwell Brothers & Co	Philadelphia, Pa.	George Kerr	475 Broadway
Fong Lin & Co	Hong Kong, China.	Lai Nem	630 Broadway
Foote, Reed & Co	Cleveland, O.	Benjamin G. Glover	622 Broadway

COMPILED WITH ACCURACY AND DESPATCH. } **CLASSIFIED BUSINESS LISTS.** { THE TROW CITY DIRECTORY CO. 11 University Place.

FOR 352 GAN

Name.	Home Office.	Agent or Representative.	New York Office.
Forbes Lithograph Mfg. Co.	Boston, Mass.	Frederick T. Adler	1 W. 25th & 280 Broadway
Forbes & Wallace	Springfield, Mass.	Syndicate Trading Co.	120 Franklin
Forestor James & Co.	Dubuque, Iowa.		216 Church
Forester Thomas & Sons	Longton, Staffordshire, Eng.	W. & T. G. Forester	47 Murray
Forster Henry & Co.	Pernambuco, Brazil.	Allerton D. Hitch	112 Front
Fort Wayne Electric Co.	Fort Wayne, Ind.	Henry O. Adams	115 Broadway
Fort Worth Dry Goods Co.	Fort Worth, Tex.	Curtis A. Durling.	56 Worth
Fort Worth & Denver City Railway Co.	Fort Worth, Tex.	John T. Granger	1 Broadway
Foster F. A. & Co.	Boston, Mass.	Seth Sprague	51 Leonard
Foster & Post	E. Saginaw, Mich.		277 Church
Foster, Merriam & Co.	Meriden, Conn.	John R. Sutliff	225 Canal
Fostoria Glass Co.	Fostoria, O.	John Nixon	6 College pl.
Fowler George & Son	Kansas City, Mo.	George Morley	360 Produce Ex. & Manhattan mkt
Fowler Brothers (Ltd.)	Liverpool, Eng.	Fowler Brothers	112 Produce Ex.
Fownes Brothers & Co.	London, Eng.	Alexander D. Napier & Co.	626 Broadway
Fox Solid Pressed Steel Co.	Chicago, Ill.	Alexander J. Forbes-Leith	44 Wall
Fox A. & Brother	Corsicana, Tex.	Abraham L. Fox	52 Walker
Fraim Lock Works	Lancaster, Pa.	C. F. Guyon & Co.	99 Reade
Fraleigh, Coggins & Fraleigh	Madison, Fla.	J. C. Thompson & Co.	9 Walker
Frank A. B. & Co.	San Antonio, Tex.	Max Goldfrank	34 Thomas
Frank G. B. & Co.	San Antonio, Tex.		15 White
Frank J. & Co.	Tucson, Ariz.	K. Mandell & Co.	26 Howard
Frank Brothers	St. Louis, Mo.	August Frank	115 Worth
Frank & Co.	Savannah, Ga.	Edward C. Oppenheim.	117 Duane
Frank, Herrman & Co.	Boston, Mass.		505 Broadway
Frank, Wolf & Co.	Philadelphia, Pa.	Herman Wolf	690 Broadway
Frankel, Frank & Co.	Keokuk, Iowa		53 Greene
Frankenthal A. & Brother	St. Louis, Mo.		38 Thomas
Frankenthal, Freudenthal & Co.	Chicago, Ill.		40 Thomas
Frankford Steel Co.	Philadelphia, Pa.	Henry H. Mansfield.	52 Wall
Frankland Joseph & Co.	Nashville, Tenn.	Joseph Frankland	41 Greene
Franklin Co.	Charlestown, Mass.	Howard Brothers & Co.	19 Mercer
Franklin Fire Ins. Co.	Columbus, O.	Henry Honig & Son	170 Broadway
Franklin Fire Ins. Co.	Philadelphia, Pa.	Ford, Rowell & Hona.	35 Pine
Franklin Ins. Co.	Columbus, O.	Wend & Kennedy	56 Pine
Franklin Quarrying Co.	Franklin, N. J.	Walter J. Roberts	45 Broadway
Franklin E. I. & Co.	N. Attleboro, Mass.	William C. Parks	178 Broadway
Franklin M. & Brother	San Francisco, Cal.		14 Lispenard
Fraser & Chalmers	Chicago, Ill.	Walter McDermott	2 Wall
Frazar & Co. (of China)	Shanghai, China & Yokohama, Japan	Everett Frazar	124 Water
Freeman A. A. & Co.	Lacrosse, Wis.	Charles Haight & Co.	94 State
Freeman & Ruyter	River Falls, Wis.	Charles Haight & Co.	94 State
Freeport Notion Co.	Freeport, Ill.		50 Worth
Freiberg & Workum.	Cincinnati, O.	Leon Rheinstrom.	39 S. William
French A., Spring Co. (Ltd.)	Pittsburgh, Pa.	Charles B. Kaufman & Henry J. Gerlken	115 Broadway
French Atlantic Cable Co.	Paris, France	Stephen F. Austin	34 Broad
Freund, Bailor & Co.	Torino, Italy.	George S. Nicholas	43 Beaver
Freyhan Julius & Co.	Bayou Sara, La.	K. Mandell & Co.	26 Howard
Friedman & Loveman	Tuscaloosa, Ala.		224 Church
Friend Brothers Clothing Co.	Milwaukee, Wis.		21 White
Fries Alexander & Brothers	Cincinnati, O.	Charles Fries	92 Reade
Price & Schule	Cleveland, O.		84 W. B'way
Frisbie & Stansfield	Camden, N. Y.		108 Franklin
Frost George & Co.	Boston, Mass.	C. E. Conover Co.	101 Franklin
Frost Veneer Seating Co.	Sheboygan, Wis.	R. Van Dine	268 Canal
Frothingham T. G. & Co.	N. Attleboro, Mass.	Walter D. Cable	41 Maiden la.
Frowein Brothers & Co.	Elberfeld, Germany.	Pleitmann & Co.	480 Broome & 403 E. 91st
Frue Vanning Machine Co.	Detroit, Mich.	Walter McDermott	2 Wall
Fry J. S. & Sons.	Bristol & London, Eng.	Daniel Browne. Robert Duncan.	6 Harrison 18 College pl.
Fuess, Espenhain & Fisher.	Belleville, Ill.		355 Broadway
Fulcher H. C. & Co.	London, Eng.	Culbert & Taylor.	39 Broadway
Fulcher R. & A.	Newark, N. J.	Richard G. Williams.	17 W. Houston
Fuller & Warren Co.	Troy, N. Y.	Granville G. Halliott.	256 Water
Fulton George W. & Co.	Paterson, N. J.	Joseph Frank	341 Broadway
Furchgott H. & Co.	Denver, Colo.	Julius Brunner.	315 Broadway
Furland G. & Co.	Cognac, France.	Emil Schultze & Co.	38 Beaver
Gaddum H. T. & Co.	Manchester, Eng.	Alfred Taft	69 Mercer
Gage & Reynolds.	Monson, Mass.	William A. Miller.	818 Broadway
Gage Brothers & Co.	Chicago, Ill.	Arthur Decker.	530 Broadway
Gagelin, Delafon & Co.	Paris, France.	Fernand Oppenheim & George Mygatt	535 Broadway
Gair & Stroh	St. Louis, Mo.		85 Bleecker
Gaines W. A. & Co.	Frankfort, Ky.	Paris, Allen & Co.	51 Broadway
Gallet Julien & Co.	Chaux de Fonds, Switzerland	Charles Perrel.	1 Maiden la.
Gandy Belting Co.	Baltimore, Md.	Behringer & McCoy.	96 Centre
Gans & Klein	Helena, Mont.	Louis Gans.	28 Thomas

SPECIAL ATTENTION PAID TO THIS CLASS OF WORK. } BANKERS' & BROKERS' CIRCULARS DELIVERED { THE TROW CITY DIRECTORY CO. 11 University Place.

GAR 353 GOL

Name.	Home Office.	Agent or Representative.	New York Office.
Gardener T. O. & Co	Boston, Mass	Charles S. McFarland	51 Leonard
Gardiner T. J. & Co	Providence, R. I	Franklin W. Sackett	108 Broadway
Gardiner Governor Co	Quincy, Ill	Augustus F. McGraw	10 Dey
Gardner Mining Co	Robinson, Colo	Edward Earle	43 Broadway
Garity Brothers	Quincy, Mass	James Garity	19 W. 14th
Garlock Packing Co	Palmyra, N. Y	Caleb M. Peele	194 Water
Garratt E. D. & Co	Galveston, Tex	Theophilus Dubois	385 Broadway
Garritt & Bosch	Seymour, Conn	Harmon & Dixon	118 Chambers
Garson, Meyer & Co	Rochester, N. Y	Maurice N. Garson	807 Broadway
Gaselot Martinez & Co	Oporto, Portugal	George S. Nicholas	43 Beaver
Gaston Gas Coal Co	Baltimore, Md	James Boyce jr	45 Broadway
Gaston, Weston & Ladd	Torrington, Conn	Robert T. Ladd	46 Beekman
Gates Iron Works	Chicago, Ill	Clarence A. Burns	44 Dey
Gaudig G. & Blum	Leipzig, Germany	Alfred Braehmig	197 Greene
Gautier Steel Department, Cambria Iron Works	Johnstown, Pa	George V. Smith	104 Reade
Gawthrop H. & Co	Philadelphia, Pa	Charles W. Hays	1 Broadway
Gay & Parker Co	Boston, Mass	Horace C. Skinner	12 Broadway
Gebbie & Co	Philadelphia, Pa	Hhule & Thomas	150 Nassau
Gebhard & Co	Vohwinkle, Germany	Wernwag & Dawson	48 Leonard
Geiershofer Henry & Co	Cincinnati, O		75 Leonard
Geisler & Co	Avize, France	George S. Nicholas	43 Beaver
Gellen Henry & Co	L. I. City, N. Y	Henry J. Gellen	155 Maiden la.
Gendron Iron Wheel Co	Toledo, O	John W. Krueger	107 Chambers
General Ins. Co. of Dresden	Dresden, Germany	Jacob Bertschmann	18 Exchange pl.
Genesee Medicine Co	Rochester, N. Y	Bert M. Cole	685 Broadway
Genesee Oil Works	Buffalo, N. Y. & Perth Amboy, N.J. }	Henry Godshall	120 Maiden la.
Gennert & Steinke Mfg. Co	Berlin, Germany	Ernest G. Steinke	30 Bond
Georgia Midland & Gulf R. R.	Columbus, Ga	James E. Grannies	7 Nassau
German Bank of London (Ltd.)	London, Eng	Charles M. Fry	49 Wall
German Fire Ins. Co	Pittsburgh, Pa	Ackerman, Daye & Hilliard	41 Pine
Germania Brewing Co	Syracuse, N. Y	James M. Dall & Co	81 Broadway
Germann J. A. & Co	Plauen, Saxony & St. Gall, Switzerland }	William Borkowitz	56 Worth
Gernsbacher Joseph & Son	New Orleans, La	Curtis A. Darling	56 Worth
Gerst D. & Co	Louisville, Ky		855 Broadway
Gibbs George W. & Co	San Francisco, Cal	John P. Hardenbergh	146 Broadway
Gilbert George H., Mfg. Co	Ware & Gilbertville, Mass	A. Willard Kingman	68 Worth
Gilbert William L., Clock Co	Whitstead, Conn	George B. Owen	6 Murray
Gilbert W. K. & Co	Paris, France	William B. Gilbert	99 Franklin
Gilbert & Barker Mfg. Co	Springfield, Mass	William O. Clarke	10 Dey
Gilbertson W. & Co. (Ltd.)	Pontardulve, New S. Wales	Strond & Co	104 John
Gilchrist C. A. & Co	Boston, Mass	Alexander S. Merriam	419 Broadway
Giles Frank & Co	London, Eng	Frank Middlekoop	19 E. 16th
Gillespie Brothers & Co	London, Eng	William A. Griffin	41 Beaver
Gillinder & Sons	Philadelphia, Pa	Clarence E. Marter	50 Barclay
Gillott Joseph & Sons	Birmingham, Eng	Henry Hoe	91 John
Gilman Brothers	Boston, Mass	John D. Titsworth	71 William
Gilman's J. P., Sons	Haverhill, Mass	Patrick H. Malloy	181 Greene
Gilpin, Langdon & Co	Baltimore, Md	John D. Titsworth	71 William
Gimbel A. & Sons	Vincennes, Ind	Solomon M. Adler	385 Broadway
Gimbel Brothers	Milwaukee, Wis	Solomon M. Adler	385 Broadway
Gimbel & Co	Danville, Ill	Solomon M. Adler	385 Broadway
Gips F. & Brother	Albany, N. Y		45 Walker
Girard Fire Ins. Co	Philadelphia, Pa	Henry Honig & Son	170 Broadway
Gladding & Coombs Brothers	Providence, R. I	Franklin W. Sackett	108 Broadway
Glaenzer J. & Co	Paris, France	Leon J. Glaenser	80 Chambers
Glaser Brothers	St. Louis, Mo		21 White
Glasgo Thread Co	Worcester, Mass	Charles W. Briggs	236 Church
Glasgow Tube Works	Glasgow, Scotland	A. R. Whitney & Co	17 Broadway
Glass & O'Flaherty	Belfast, Ireland	James D. Smyth	325 Broadway
Glastonbury Knitting Co	Glastonbury, Conn	Scott Brothers	79 Franklin
Gledhill Lake & Co	Huddersfield, Eng	James B. Darris	107 Grand
Glen Mfg. Co	Boston, Mass	Albert B. Smith	154 Nassau
Glencoe Mfg. Co	Philadelphia, Pa	James P. Strecter	401 Broadway
Glenn Hugh & Co	Utica, N. Y	William Mackenzie	383 Broadway
Glenside Woolen Mills	Skaneateles Falls, N. Y.	Arnstaedt & Co	68 Greene
Globe Clock Co	Pittsfield, Mass	S. F. Myers & Co	50 Maiden la.
Globe Clothing House	New Britain, Conn		577 Broadway
Globe Co	Cincinnati, O	Brown, Green & Adams	40 Beaver
Globe Loan & Trust Co	Omaha, Neb	Charles H. Taylor	45 Broadway
Globe Mfg. Co	Palmyra, N. Y	Henry Johnson	44 Beekman
Globe Sulphite Boiler Co	Hartford, Conn	Charles A. Whedon	132 Nassau
Globe Woolen Co	Utica, N. Y	William W. Coffin	320 Broadway
Gloucester Mfg. Co	Philadelphia, Pa	Frank M. Wilson	59 Leonard
Gloucester Net & Twine Co	Boston, Mass	Stephen H. Mills & Co	107 South
Glover Thomas S. & Co	Warsaw, N. Y		316 Broadway
Glover H. B. & Co	Dubuque, Iowa		78 Worth
Glover & Willcomb	Boston, Mass	Francis S. Abell	5 White
Godshalk E. H., Co	Philadelphia, Pa	James A. Ryan	85 Worth
Goetter, Weil & Co	Montgomery, Ala	K. Mandell & Co	26 Howard
Goldberg Brothers	Milwaukee, Wis		40 Mercer
Goldfrank, Frank & Co	San Antonio, Tex	Max Goldfrank	54 Thomas

23

TYPEWRITING DONE BY THE TROW CITY DIRECTORY CO., 11 University Place.

Name.	Home Office.	Agent or Representative.	New York Office.
Goldman, Thurnauer & Co	Cincinnati, O		21 White
Goldsmith J & Son	Trinidad, Colo		447 Broadway
Goldsmith & Loewenberg	Portland, Ore	Philip Goldsmith	5 Bookman
Goldsmith Brothers & Co	Scranton, Pa		447 Broadway
Goldsmith, Kiaw & Co	Cincinnati, O		21 White
Goldsmith, Joseph, Feiss & Co	Cleveland, O		34 Thomas
Goldstein Louis & Sons	New Orleans, La	Nathan Goldstein	54 Worth
Goldstein & Migel	Waco, Tex		302 Broadway
Goldstein & Weinman	Albuquerque, N. M		505 Broadway
Goll & Frank Co. (Ltd.)	Milwaukee, Wis	John P. Enright	99 Franklin
Gondrand Frères	Milan, Italy	Alexander Oldrini	126 Pearl
Gonzalez, Byass & Co	London, Eng. & Jerez de la Frontera, Spain	Kessler, Behringer & Co	20 Beaver
Goodfellow R. S. & Co	Minneapolis, Minn		18 White
Goodman L. & Co	Terre Haute, Ind		637 Broadway
Goodman Brothers & Co	Philadelphia, Pa		260 Church
Goodman Brothers & Co	Richmond, Va	David S. Einstein	117 Duane
Goodrich B. F., Co	Akron, O	S. Y. L'Hommedieu & Co	65 Reade
Goodrich Hard Rubber Co	Akron, O	S. Y. L'Hommedieu & Co	65 Reade
Goodridge R. Read, Mfg. Co	Newport, R. I	R. Read Goodridge	214 Church
Goodstock Mfg. Co	Syracuse, N. Y	Lucius E. Burt	744 Broadway
Goodwin Gas Stove Meter Co	Philadelphia, Pa	George B. Edwards	142 Chambers
Goodyear Shoe Machinery Co	Boston, Mass	Charles T. Deforest	265 Broadway
Goodyear's M. R., Shoe Co	Naugatuck, Conn	Thomas M. Cressey	114 Duane
Goossens & Vanrossem	Rotterdam, Holland	A. Vanrossem & Co	4 Stone
Gordon & Co	London, Eng	E. Lamontagne & Sons	52 Beaver
Gore George P. & Co	Chicago, Ill	John Brown	50 Leonard
Gorham Mfg. Co	Providence, R. I	Edward Holbrook	889 Broadway & 9 Maiden la.
Gossage Charles & Co	Chicago, Ill	John T. Pirie	115 Worth
Gottschalk & Schram	Jersey City, N. J	John G. Schram	404 Broadway
Gould Commercial Co	Boston, Mass	Benjamin F. Vitt	72 William
Gould Coupler Co	Buffalo, N. Y	Charles A. Gould	120 Broadway
Gould S. W. & Co	N. Attleboro, Mass	William W. Middlebrook	10 Maiden la.
Goulds Mfg. Co	Seneca Falls, N. Y	Charles L. Zacharie	60 Barclay
Grabfield, Bickles & Co	Cincinnati, O		21 White
Grace J. W. & Co	San Francisco, Cal	W. R. Grace & Co	1 Hanover sq.
Grace & Co	Valparaiso, Chili	W. R. Grace & Co	1 Hanover sq.
Grace Brothers & Co	Lima, Peru	W. R. Grace & Co	1 Hanover sq.
Graeff, Wilcox & Co	Philadelphia, Pa	Henry C. Wells	1 Broadway
Graft J. A. & Co	Cincinnati, O	Henry M. Walker	101 Broadway
Graham J. C. & Co	Philadelphia, Pa	Joseph J. Morrison	858 Broadway
Grand Caymans Phosphate Co	Cayman, Jamaica, W. I.	Nathaniel B. Fowler	181 Pearl
Grand Trunk Railway Co	Montreal, Can	Edward P. Beach	271 Broadway
Grandy & Taylor	Norfolk, Va		426 Broome
Granies R. & Sons	Philadelphia, Pa	James G. Jenkins	8 Thomas
Grant G. W. & Son	Trenton, N. J		224 Church
Grasselli Chemical Co	Cleveland, O		71 Wall
Graves L. S. & Son	Rochester, N. Y	Frank M. Reynolds	94 Liberty
Gray F. P., Dry Goods Co	Little Rock, Ark	Theophilus Dubois	335 Broadway
Gray C. & Co	Augusta, Ga	Christopher Gray	75 Franklin
Gray C. & Son	Savannah, Ga	Christopher Gray	75 Franklin
Great Eastern Fast Freight Line	Detroit, Mich	William Townsend	429 Broadway & 98 Wall
Great Southern & Western Railway Co	Dublin, Ireland	Cæsar A. Barattoni	552 Broadway
Great Western Railway Co. of Canada	Montreal, Can	Edward P. Beach	271 Broadway
Great Western S. S. Co. (Ltd.)	Bristol, Eng	Charles L. Morgan	70 South & Pier 16 E. R.
Green Bay, Winona & St. Paul R. R. Co	Green Bay, Wis	Theodore Sturges	52 Wall
Green Edward & Sons	Wakefield, Eng	George H. Burpee	53 Broadway
Green L. E. & Son	St. Louis, Mo		573 Broadway
Green, Joyce & Co	Columbus, O	Albert W. Green	51 Leonard
Greenbank Alkali Co. (Ltd.)	St. Helens, Eng	Davis, Wolt & Co	55 Pine
Greene G. W. & Co	Brooklyn, N. Y	Herman Fredericks	402 Broadway
Greenebaum Alfred & Co	San Francisco, Cal	Edward M. Marum	396 B'wich
Greenebaum, Weil & Michels	San Francisco, Cal	Greenebaum & Co	27 Walker
Greenhood, Bohm & Co	Helena, Mont	Greenhood & Bohm	81 Walker
Greenmount Spinning Co	Dublin, Ireland	Ferguson, Weller & Co	102 Franklin
Greenaburg Glass Co	Greenaburg, Pa	Thomas G. Edge	58 Barclay
Greensfelder & Bettelheim	San Francisco, Cal		132 William
Greenupan & Co	Nashville, Tenn		66 Lispenard
Greenway Bottling Co	Syracuse, N. Y	James M. Bell & Co	31 Broadway
Greenway Brewing Co	Syracuse, N. Y	James M. Bell & Co	31 Broadway
Gribbon Edward & Sons	Belfast & Coleraine, Ireland	William Gribbon	41 White
Griel & Kohn	Selma, Ala		630 Broadway
Griffen, Smith & Co	Phoenixville, Pa	Harry G. Freese	63 Murray
Griffin Wheel & Foundry Co	Chicago, Ill	Joseph R. Ellicott	115 Broadway
Griggs S. C. & Co	Chicago, Ill	Baker & Taylor Co	740 Broadway
Grimes M. A., Dry Goods Co	Kansas City, Mo	Frederick Gwinn	51 Leonard
Grimond J. & A. D	Dundee, Scotland	William B. Cunningham	49 Chambers
Grimshaw Brothers	Paterson, N. J	Wendt, Steinhauser & Co	24 Greene

THE CALIGRAPH WRITING MACHINE,
HARTFORD, CONN.
GRI 355 HAR

Name.	Home Office.	Agent or Representative.	New York Office.
Grinbaum M. S. & Co	Honolulu, Hawaii	Greenebaum & Co	27 Walker
Grinnell Mfg. Co.	New Bedford, Mass	Grinnell Willis	41 Thomas
Griswoldville Mfg. Co.	Griswoldville, Mass.	Ethan D. Griswold	51 Leonard
Groat & Kissock	London, Eng	John Kissock	92 Wall
Gross, Strauss & Co	Worcester, Mass	—	470 Broome
Grossberger & Kurz	Nuremberg, Germany	Schwanhauser & Muller	37 Beaver
Grotjan, Mitchell & Co	Baltimore, Md	Henry A. Chamberlain	358 Canal
Grunsfeld, Lindheim & Co	Santa Fé, N. M	—	462 Broome
Guarantee Co. of North America	Montreal, Can	Daniel J. Tompkins	111 Broadway
Guaranty Investment Co.	Atchison, Kan	Henry A. Riley	191 Broadway
Guardian Assurance Co	London, Eng	Henry E. Bowers	50 Pine
Guckenheimer A. & Brothers.	Pittsburgh, Pa.	Adolph A. Solomon	21 Beaver
Guerin Vve & File	Lyons, France	Benjamin L. Loydler	101 Spring
Guggenheimer & Co.	Lynchburg, Va.	William G. Happy	56 Worth
Guhrauer, Kurt & Co	Paris, France	Frederick Gubrauer	3 E. 14th
Gulon S. S. Line	Liverpool, Eng.	A. M. Underhill & Co.	85 Broadway & Pier 38 (now) N. R.
Gulterman Brothers	St. Paul, Minn	—	561 Broadway
Gulf, Colorado & Santa Fé Railway	Galveston, Tex.	James N. Fuller	819 Broadway
Gundlach J. & Co.	San Francisco, Cal.	Charles Gundlach	52 Warren
Gunnison & Marvin.	Troy, N. Y.	Harry A. Clampett	8 Greene
Gunst, Wessel & Bockelmann.	Chemnitz, Germany	Benjamin F. Robinson	51 Leonard
Gurney Hot Water Heater Co.	Boston, Mass.	Milton H. Johnson	55 John
Gutman Joel & Co	Baltimore, Md	Thomas Walsh	828 Church
Gyrnos Tin Plate Co. (Ltd.).	Ystalyfera, S. Wales.	Stroud & Co.	104 John
Haas Brothers	San Francisco, Cal.	Kalman Haas	13 William
Haas & Oppenheimer	San Antonio, Tex.	—	8 W. 3d
Hadley Co.	Holyoke, Mass.	Frederick A. Nichols	53 Leonard
Haeniein H. & Co	Buffalo, N. Y.	—	54 White
Hagedorn J. J. & Co.	West Point, Ga.	—	479 Broadway
Haker W. & Hins	San Francisco, Cal.	Henry Ide.	530 Broadway
Hale J. M. & Co	Los Angeles, Cal.	Marshall Hale	51 Leonard
Hale & Kilburn Mfg. Co.	Philadelphia, Pa.	Owen W. Balcom	706 Broadway
Hale Brothers & Co	Sacramento, Cal	Prentis C. Hale.	51 Leonard
Half M. & Brother.	San Antonio, Tex.	—	115 Worth
Halff & Newbeoner Brothers	Houston, Tex.	K. Mandell & Co.	26 Howard
Hall Dudley & Co.	Boston, Mass.	Edward J. Hart.	132 Front
Hall Gardiner jr. & Co.	S. Wellington, Conn.	George F. Foster.	59 Walker
Hall Steam Pump Co.	Pittsburgh, Pa.	Edward J. Waring.	91 Liberty
Hall Thomas, Co	Jersey City, N. J.	Thomas Hall	858 Broadway
Hall William & Co	Jamestown, N. Y.	Charles A. Smith	407 Broadway
Hall & Garrison	Philadelphia, Pa	Henry C. Adams	280 Broadway
Hall & Jastrowitz	Greeley, Colo	—	705 Broadway
Hull, Elton & Co	Wallingford, Conn.	—	46 E. 14th
Hall's Safe & Lock Co	Cincinnati, O.	Edward W. Woolley	324 Broadway
Halle L., Sons	Cleveland, O.	—	560 Broadway
Hallet & Davis.	Boston, Mass	William F. Tway	85 Fifth av.
Hallett Franklin & Co.	Liverpool, Eng	John D. James	4 Stone
Hallowell Granite Works.	Hallowell, Me	John Peiroe	7 Beckman
Hallowell & Co.	Philadelphia, Pa.	A. W. Maas & Co	119 Mercer
Hamblin & Russell Mfg. Co.	Worcester, Mass	C. F. Guyon & Co. James A. Doughan	99 Reade 20 Cliff
Hamburg Am. Packet Co.	Hamburg, Germany.	Funch, Edge & Co. Richard J. Cortis.	27 S. William 37 Broadway
Hamburg-Bremen Fire Ins. Co.	Hamburg, Germany.	Francis O. Affeld & Hugo C. Duchenberger	22 Pine
Hamburger A. & Sons.	Los Angeles, Cal.	Curtis A. Darling	56 Worth
Hamburger Brothers & Co	Baltimore, Md	Achille Marx	751 Broadway
Hamerslough R. & Co	Trinidad, Colo	—	38 Walker
Hamilton W. H. & Co	Pittsburgh, Pa.	William J. Snyder & Brother	68 Murray
Hammacher & Delius	Hamburg, Germany	Louis E. Delius.	209 Bowery
Hammel L. & Co	Mobile, Ala	Leopold Frank.	56 Worth
Hampden Paint & Chemical Co.	Springfield, Mass.	T. M. Sharkey	274 Pearl
Hampden Watch Co	Canton, O	John W. Sherwood.	176 Broadway
Hampton J. W. jr. & Co	Philadelphia, Pa.	Frederic B. Vandegrift.	40 Exchange pl.
Hance & Co	Poughkeepsie, N. Y.	William H. Deforest.	9 Gt. Jones
Hance Brothers & White.	Philadelphia, Pa.	Edward W. Price.	17 Platt
Hancock John, Mutual Life Ins. Co.	Boston, Mass.	George R. Hill	28 Union sq. E.
Hancock C. C. & Co.	Philadelphia, Pa	John H. Boyce.	76 Franklin
Hancock & Co	Philadelphia, Pa.	Thomas B. Hamilton.	432 Produce Ex.
Hancock, Becker & Co	Providence, R. I.	Richard Robinson	196 Broadway
Hanifen John E. & Co	Philadelphia, Pa.	Bateson & Armstrong.	118 Franklin
Hannibal Bridge Co	Hannibal, Mo.	Alfred T. White.	130 Water
Hannibal & St. Joseph R. R. Co.	St. Joseph, Mo.	Edward J. Swords.	817 Broadway
Hannis Distilling Co	Hannisville, W.Va.	Theodore Bomeisler.	50 Beaver
Hano Samuel, Co	Boston, Mass.	Jacob L. Hano.	832 Broadway
Hanover Vulcanite Co	Hanover, Germany.	George Borgfeldt & Co.	425 Broome
Hansen Hop & Malt Co.	Milwaukee, Wis.	Adolph T. Boeeler.	3 State
Hard Brothers & Co	Oneida, N. Y.	Robert F. Denniston	120 W. B'way
Harden Hand Grenade Co	Chicago, Ill.	—	1 Broadway

CIRCULARS ADDRESSED TO ANY TRADE IN THE U. S. { Facilities
PROMPT, CAREFUL WORK } THE TROW CITY DIRECTORY CO., { Unequalled.
AT MODERATE PRICES. 11 University Place.

Name.	Home Office.	Agent or Representative.	New York Office.
Hardy George J. & Son	Brooklyn, N. Y.		5 Batavia
Hardy James North & Son	Manchester, Eng	Wright & Young	27 White
Hargadine, McKittrick & Co	St. Louis, Mo.		117 Worth
Hargreaves Mfg. Co	Detroit, Mich.	Frank A. Holmes	356 Broadway
Harlan & Hollingsworth Co	Wilmington, Del	George W. Hall	115 Broadway
Harper & Reynolds Co	Los Angeles, Cal.	Samuel G. Negus	42 College pl.
Harrington E., Son & Co	Philadelphia, Pa	John Q. Maynard	12 Cortlandt
Harrington & King Performing Co.	Chicago, Ill.	Joseph H. Drake	100 Beekman
Harris George S. & Sons	Philadelphia, Pa	Frank C. Jackson	335 Broadway
Harris Metal Wheel Co	Toledo, O	Charles L. Sherwood	63 Fulton
Harris L. & Co	St. Louis, Mo.		102 Franklin
Harris S. & Sons	Clinton, Mass	John H. Lephart	7 Mercer
Harrison Safety Boiler Works	Philadelphia, Pa	Frank E. Idell	41 Dey
Harrison Brothers & Howson	Sheffield, Eng	Henry A. Tilly	126 Chambers
Hart Henry C., Mfg. Co	Detroit, Mich	Henry D. Moore	9 Warren
Hart Brothers	Chicago, Ill.		88 Thomas
Hart & Co	Cleveland, O		96 Spring
Hartford Carpet Co	Hartford, Conn.	Roane Martin & Sons	114 Worth
Hartford Fire Ins. Co.	Hartford, Conn.	George M. Colt	158 Broadway
Hartford Life & Annuity Ins. Co.	Hartford, Conn.	George D. Harrison	189 Broadway
Hartford Steam Boiler Inspection & Ins. Co.	Hartford, Conn.	Theodore H. Babcock	285 Broadway
Hartford & N. Y. Transp. Co.	Hartford, Conn.	Simon G. Smith	Pier 24 E. R.
Hartley & Hanson	Philadelphia, Pa	Pittman & Black	115 Worth
Hartman Mfg. Co	Beaver Falls, Pa	Richard Thompson	92 Chambers
Harvey & Co	St. Johns, Newfoundland	Harvey & Outerbridge	305 Produce Ex.
Harwood Land Co	Jacksonville, Fla.	John H. Hubbell	817 Broadway
Harwood H. & Sons	Natick, Mass	Willard & McKee	21 Park pl.
Haskell Publishing Co	Boston, Mass	Edward D. Simpson	23 University pl.
Haskett B. L. & Co	Chicago, Ill.		84 W. B'way
Haskins & Clyde	Boston, Mass.	Schwartz & Wedde	40 Stone
Hastings & Co	Philadelphia, Pa	Edward W. Price	17 Platt
Hatch & Co	Cleveland, O		401 Broadway
Hatzfeld Philip & Co	Austin, Tex	Charles Rothschild	87 Walker
Hanok F. B. & Co	Yonkers, N. Y.		251 Canal
Havens, Geddes & Co	Terre Haute, Ind.	Walter L. Howell	56 Worth
Haverhill Paper Co	Boston, Mass.	Albert E. Smith	154 Nassau
Hawksworth, Wilson, Ellison & Co.	Sheffield, Eng.	Wetherell Brothers	115 Liberty
Hawley Brothers Hardware Co.	San Francisco, Cal.	Marcus C. Hawley	118 Chambers
Hawley Glass Co	Hawley, Pa	William F. Dorflinger	26 Murray
Hawley C. R. & Co	Bay City, Mich		376 Broadway
Haxall-Crenshaw Co	Richmond, Va	Crenshaw & Wisner	16 Exchange pl.
Hay J. & Sons	Easton, Pa		66 Leonard
Hayden Furniture Co	Rochester, N. Y.	L. Gridley Scranton	1286 Broadway
Hayden J. C. & Co	Janesville, Pa		1 Broadway
Haynes D. O. & Co	Philadelphia, Pa.	William B. Aitken	18 Liberty
Haynes N. B., Co	Chicago, Ill.		92 Prince
Hazard Mfg. Co	Wilkes Barre, Pa.	Thomas D. Conyngham	87 Liberty
Hearn & Braitsch	Providence, R. I.	John U. Russ	415 Broadway
Heath D. C. & Co	Boston, Mass.		16 Astor pl.
Heavenrich Brothers	Detroit, Mich		587 Broadway
Heavenrich Brothers & Co	E. Saginaw, Mich.		587 Broadway
Hecker Gottlieb & Sons	Chemnitz, Germany	Oscar Lang	115 Worth
Hedden C. M. & Co	Newark, N. J.	John P. Wallace	124 Greene
Heidelbach, Friedlander & Co	Cincinnati, O.	Moses Heidelbach	361 Broadway
Heidelberger & Co	Baltimore, Md.		694 Broadway
Heilbrun, Heldman & Co	Cincinnati, O.		75 Leonard
Hellgers F. W. & Co	London, Eng. & Calcutta, India	William B. Cooper jr.	71 Wall
Heiman M. & Co	Milwaukee, Wis.	Max Schiller	632 Broadway
Heine Safety Boiler Co	St. Louis, Mo.	Robert M. Huston	280 Broadway
Heine & Co	Leipzig, Germany.	George Lueders	218 Pearl
Heinemann Paul & Co	Yokohama & Hiogo, Japan	Paul Heinemann	112 Water
Heinz H. J. & Co	Pittsburgh, Pa.	William Hasker Co.	125 Hudson
Heisler Electric Light Co	St. Louis, Mo.	White & Rusling	187 Broadway
Held Brothers & Co	San Francisco, Cal.	Bernhard Held	581 Broadway
Heller M. & Sons	San Francisco, Cal.	William H. Stringer	48 Leonard
Heller & Katzenstein	Baltimore, Md		102 Franklin
Hellman L. & Co	Louisville, Ky.	David Levy	64 Beaver
Helme George W., Co	Helmetta, N. J.	J. Randolph Appleby	35 Pine
Hemingway & Co	London, Eng.	Harry Hemingway	90 Water
Hemingway's London Purple Co. (Ltd.)	London, Eng	Hemingway & Co.	90 Water
Heminway M. & Sons Silk Co.	Watertown, Conn.		76 Greene
Heminway & Bartlett Silk Co.	Watertown, Conn	William H. Brown	78 Franklin
Kempstead O. G. & Son	Philadelphia, Pa	R. F. Downing & Co.	20 Exchange pl.
Henkell & Co	Mainz, Germany	Charles Graef & Co.	32 Beaver
Henly's David, Sons	Philadelphia, Pa.	Henry B. Harwood	560 Broadway
Henry A. & S. & Co	Bradford, Eng.	Michael Mullen	96 Spring

MERCHANTS EXCHANGE NAT. BANK OF THE CITY OF N. Y.
SOLICITS YOUR ACCOUNT. **257 Broadway.**
PHINEAS C. LOUNSBURY, President   ALLEN S. APGAR, Cashier.

HEN   357   HOU

Name.	Home Office.	Agent or Representative.	New York Office.
Henzel, Colladay Co	Philadelphia, Pa	Augustus McKinney	886 Broadway & 105 Franklin
Heraty R. J. & Co	Philadelphia, Pa	E. Minor Payne	141 Front
Herfurth Brothers	Chemnitz, Saxony	Seward & Tourtellot	71 Franklin
Herman Brothers, Lindauer & Co.	Nashville, Tenn	—	328 Church
Hormann, Schmidt & Co	Pappenheim, Bavaria	Henry Fensterer	65 Warren
Herzog Charles & Co	Memphis, Tenn	—	30 Reade
Hess, Henle & Co	Louisville, Ky	—	38 Thomas
Hexter Brothers	Philadelphia, Pa	Henry Garrison	84 Bleecker
Heyman, Merz & Co	West Point, Ga	—	479 Broadway
Heymann & Alexander	Bradford, Eng	Bussmann & Galland	464 Broome
Heynemann & Co	San Francisco, Cal	Frederick P. Salomons	115 Worth
Heywood Boot & Shoe Co	Worcester, Mass	John N. Frazer	122 Duane
Hieber J. C. & Co	Utica, N. Y	—	214 Church
Higgins Charles M. & Co	Brooklyn, N. Y	Charles M. Higgins	5 Beekman
Higgins Charles S. & Co	Brooklyn, N.Y	Emott Seward	364 Broadway
Hildesheimer S. & Co. (Ltd.)	London, Eng	Lueckel, Unger & Co	810 Broadway
Hildesheimer & Faulkner	London, Eng	George C. Whitney	62 Duane
Hill R. W. Mfg. Co	Philadelphia, Pa	Stewart & Co	201 Broadway
Hill Clutch Works	Cleveland, O	Walter C. Wonham	18 Cortlandt
Hillebrand & Wolf	Philadelphia, Pa	Harmon & Dixon	118 Chambers
Hills Union Brewing Co. (Ltd.)	London, Eng	Robert Sewell	22 Nassau
Hills & Underwood	London, Eng	Purdy & Arnold	51 Broad
Hillsborough Linen Co. (Ltd.)	Hillsborough, Ireland	James D. Smyth	385 Broadway
Hillside Coal & Iron Co	Scranton, Pa	Augustus R. Macdonough	21 Cortlandt
Hinchliffe Brothers	Paterson, N. J	Cornelius A. King	68 Horatio
Hindley Walter H. & Co	London, Eng	Robert G. Winny	124 Front
Hinds O. L. Co	E. Highgate, Vt	Oscar L. Hinds	12 Walker
Hinz & Landt	San Francisco, Cal	Benjamin G. Glover	623 Broadway
Hirsch, Israel & Co	Charleston, S. C	—	050 Broadway
Hirschman K. & Son	Cincinnati, O	Henry Hirschman	319 Broadway
Hirschmann Brothers	Binghamton, N. Y	—	77 Wooster
Hirsh Abe & Brother	Philadelphia, Pa	Morris Vogel	891 Broadway
Hirsh, Elson & Co	Chicago, Ill	—	557 Broadway
Hirz, Zellweger & Co	Bale, Switzerland	Arnold Feldstein	67 Greene
Hislop, Porteous, Mitchell & Co.	Norwich, Conn	William Mackenzie	338 Broadway
History Co	San Francisco, Cal	Frank M. Derby	102 Chambers
Hoberg, Boot & Co	Terre Haute, Ind	Lewis D. Boot	56 Worth
Hobson Francis & Son	Sheffield, Eng	Charles Hugill	97 John
Hodges Frank F. & Co	Boston, Mass	Adon Smith jr	573 Broadway
Hodges H. & Co	Monson, Mass	—	611 Broadway
Hodgson Abraham & Sons	Liverpool, Eng	John H. Hodgson	22 Whitehall
Hoffheimer Brothers	Cincinnati, O	James Loscheim	315 Bowery
Hoggson & Pettis Mfg. Co	New Haven, Conn	W. F. Stark & Co	308 Broadway
Holland Mfg. Co	Willimantic, Conn	Henry Eldridge	551 Broadway
Holmes & Allan	Glasgow, Scotland	Robert Martin	45 White
Holmes & Edwards Silver Co	Bridgeport, Conn	Albert A. Clark	28 John
Holmes & Nichols	Boston, Mass	Charles P. Duffee	74 Pine
Holworthy & Co	Liverpool, Eng	Holworthy & Ellis	93 Wall
Holworthy, Ellis & Co	Santos, Brazil	Holworthy & Ellis	93 Wall
Holyoke Envelope Co	Holyoke, Mass	Frederick C. Atkins	8 Thomas
Holzheimer L. & Co	Elmira, N. Y	—	372 Broadway
Holzman Mfg. Co	Baltimore, Md	Leon C. Shoneman	468 Broome
Home Building & Loan Assn	Minneapolis, Minn	Charles G. Steele	42 New
Home Knowledge Assn	Chicago, Ill	Dederick J. Winkelman	20 E. 18th
Home Library Assn	Chicago, Ill	J. A. Hill & Co	44 E. 14th
Homestake Mining Co	San Francisco, Cal	Lounsbery & Co	Mills bldg
Homo & Co	Paris, France	Jacob H. Sommer	18 Laight
Honduras & Central Am. S. S. Co.	Glasgow, Scotland	Williams & Rankine	19 Whitehall
Honeyman & De Hart Co	Portland, Ore	William B. Fox & Brother	97 Chambers
Hong Kong & Shanghai Banking Corporation	Hong Kong, China	Alfred M. Townsend	50 Wall
Hood, Bonbright & Co	Philadelphia, Pa	Thomas G. Todd	74 Worth
Hook & Hastings Organ Co	Boston, Mass	William A. Braithwaite	145 E. 23d
Hooks Smelting Co	Philadelphia, Pa	William H. Price	10 Wall
Hoosic Tunnel Line	Chicago, Ill	J. Bolles Smith	368 Broadway
Hoosier Handle Co	Metamora, Ind	J. C. McCarty & Co	97 Chambers
Hoosier Mfg. Co	Fort Wayne, Ind	J. P. Evans	75 Franklin
Hooven, Owens & Rentschler Co.	Hamilton, O	William A. Hammett	18 Cortlandt
Hopedale Elastic Fabric Co	Hopedale, Mass	Lyman D. Brown	366 Broadway
Hopkins Weller, Drug Co	St. Louis, Mo	John D. Titsworth	71 William
Hopkins P. E. & Co	Tionesta, Pa	—	614 Broadway
Hopson & Chapin Mfg. Co	New London, Conn	—	172 Centre
Horne Joseph & Co	Pittsburgh, Pa	Henry D. Jewett	51 Leonard
Horner Brothers Carpet Co	Philadelphia, Pa	Melvin J. Bailey	108 Worth
Horse Owners' Mutual Indemnity Assn	Rochester, N. Y	William Wolf	29 Park row
Horstmann William H. & Sons	Philadelphia, Pa	Frederick Steeb	108 Grand
Horton, Angell & Co	Attleboro, Mass	James E. Hills	287 Broadway
Hoskins & Sewell	Birmingham, Eng	B. R. Barklow	16 & 21 E. 15th
Hotchkiss L. L. & Co	Bay City, Mich	Luther L. Hotchkiss	28 State
Hough W. S. jr. & Co	Providence, R. I	Charles A. Wilkinson	26 Maiden la.

CINCINNATI, BALTIMORE, PHILADELPHIA,	**SNOW, CHURCH & CO.** CORRESPONDENTS EVERYWHERE.		NEW YORK, BOSTON, CHICAGO, LOUISVILLE.
HOU		358	ITA

Name.	Home Office.	Agent or Representative.	New York Office.
Hough & Ford	Rochester, N. Y.	Frederick L. Grant	18½ Duane
Household Sewing Machine Co.	Providence, R. I.	Robert D. Andrews	9 E. 14th
Houseman, Donnally & Jones.	Grand Rapids, Mich.		645 Broadway
Houtman A. & Co	Schiedam, Holland	Samuel Streit & Co	31 Liberty
Hovey C. F. & Co	Boston, Mass.	Rufus L. Todd	20 Greene
Howard E., Watch & Clock Co.	Boston, Mass.	Ernest V. Clergue	41 Maiden la.
Howard Frank & Co	Atchison, Kan.		102 Franklin
Howard Strop Co	Charlestown, Mass.	Howard Brothers & Co.	119 Mercer
Howe, Brown & Co. (Ltd.)	Pittsburgh, Pa.	George B. Jewett	61 Fulton
Howell Charles H. & Co	Philadelphia, Pa.	John L. M. Allen	99 Maiden la.
Howell, Stein & Co	Philadelphia, Pa.	John H. Howarth	744 Broadway
Howland W. S. & Co	Denver, Colo.	Leon Brocker	581 Broadway
Hoyt Metal Co	St. Louis, Mo.	Addison L. Day	20 Cliff
Hoyt F. & Co	Philadelphia, Pa.	Walter H. Ruhe	325 Broadway
Huber Emile & Co	Sarreguemines, Germany	Schorestene Frères	153 Mercer
Huber & Holman Co	Lancaster, Pa.	Warren H. Erb	352 Canal
Huber, Stader & Co	St. Gall, Switzerland		291 Church
Hudson River Cement Co.	Kingston, N. Y.	Henry R. Brigham	18 Coenties sl.
Hudson River Chemical & Dye Wood Co.	Shady Side, N. J.	James L. Morgan & Co.	47 Fulton
Hudson River Pulp & Paper Co.	Palmer's Falls, N. Y.	Kennedy B. Fullerton	154 Nassau
Hudson Valley Knitting Co	Waterford, N. Y.	Scott Brothers	76 Franklin
Huebner K. & Sons.	Newark, N. J.	Julius Huebner	338 Broadway
Hughes, Son & Co.	London, Eng.	James H. Lancaster	171 Broadway
Hull George H. & Co	Louisville, Ky.	Jared M. B. Reis	71 Broadway
Hull E. R. & Co	Cleveland, O.		789 Broadway
Hultskamp & Zoon & Molyn	Rotterdam, Holland.	Anthony Orchs	51 Warren
Humphreyville Mfg. Co	Seymour, Conn.	Harmon & Dixon	119 Chambers
Hunt & Donaldson	Ellenville, N. Y.	Johnson Decker	Pier 24 (new) N. R.
Hunt & Winterbotham	Dursley, Gloucestershire, Eng.	William B. Ros.	60 W. 23d
Hunt, Roope, Teage & Co.	Oporto, Portugal	Kessler, Behringer & Co.	20 Beaver
Hunter, Benn & Co.	Mobile, Ala	Allan G. Sheriff	2 Stone
Huntington, Hopkins Co	San Francisco, Cal.	Charles Miller	20 Rende
Huntington, Norwalk & Bridgeport Steam Ferry Co.	Huntington, L. I.	William H. Hick	Pier 32 (new) N. R.
Hurlbut Paper Mfg. Co.	S. Lee, Mass.	John P. Hitchcock	297 Broadway
Huston Charles & Sons.	Coatesville, Pa.	Frank L. Froment	112 John
Hutchins S. & Co.	Providence, R. I.	William Wilkinson	178 Broadway
Hutchins Brothers Notion Co.	La Fayette, Ind.		63 Leonard
Hutchison & Huestis	Providence, R. I.	George W. Hutchison	196 Broadway
Hyams, Pauson & Co.	San Francisco, Cal.	William Hyams	594 Broadway
Hyatt School Slate Co. (Ltd.)	Bethlehem, Pa.	Henry T. Clauder	65 Duane
Hyman M. & Co	London, Eng.	G. Kuinow	658 Broadway
Hyman M. & Co	San Francisco, Cal.	Samuel Stiner	23 E. Houston
Hyman Brothers	San Francisco, Cal.	Michael Hyman	102 Chambers
Hyndman & Moore.	Philadelphia, Pa.	T. J. Kevency & Co.	329 Broadway
Ide & Haverstick Co	Philadelphia, Pa.	Dennis V. Bergen	161 Duane
Ikle Brothers	St. Gall, Switzerland	Charles Hoecknor	460 Broome
Imperial Brush Co	Philadelphia, Pa.	Alexander B. Hyer	595 Broadway
Imperial Chemical Co.	Philadelphia, Pa.	White & Sheldon	184 Pearl
Imperial Fire Ins. Co.	London, Eng.	Charles M. Peck	33 Pine
Imperial Tapestry Co.	Paterson, N. J.	William B. Smith	62 Worth
Impervious Package Co.	Keene, N. H.	James H. Sherwood	86 Park pl.
Indemnity Mutual Marine Assurance Co. (Ltd.)	London, Eng.	Henry Wreaks & Henry T. Pearse	70 Wall
India Mutual Ins. Co.	Boston, Mass	Currey & Whitney	16 Beaver
Inglis & Co.	Dunfermline, Scotland	Ira L. Bursley	62 White
Ingraham E., Clock Co.	Bristol, Conn.	Henry Terhune & Son	25 Murray
Ingram Brothers	London, Eng.	William H. Jones	110 Fifth av.
Inman & International S. S. Co. (Ltd.)	Liverpool, Eng.	Peter Wright & Sons	6 Bowling gr. & Pier 43 (new) N. R.
Ins. Co. of North Am.	Philadelphia, Pa.	Benoni Lockwood (fire), Satterthwaite & Platt (marine), William E. Hall (inland)	16 Exchange pl., 16 Exchange pl., 1st Beaver
Ins. Co. of the State of Pa.	Philadelphia, Pa.	Benoni Lockwood	16 Exchange pl.
Inter-State Freight Tariff Publishing Co.	Boston, Mass.	Abel C. Kenyon	293 Broadway
Inter-State Investment Co.	Kansas City, Mo.	Clarence L. Reid	15 Broad
International Canal Line	Montreal, Can.	George W. Hunt	23 South
International Dock & Warehouse Co.	St. Paul, Minn.	W. Lewis Boyle	45 Wall
International Navigation Co.	Philadelphia, Pa.	Peter Wright & Sons	6 Bowling gr.
International Pottery Co	Trenton, N. J.	Julius Wolff	59 Park pl. & 21 College pl.
Iowa Loan & Trust Co.	Des Moines, Iowa.	George M. Warner	30 State
Ireland Mfg. Co.	Cincinnati, O.	William H. Jacobus	90 Chambers
Irvin & Sellers	Liverpool, Eng.	Elijah M. Allen	114 Franklin
Irving John & Co.	New Brighton, S. I.	James K. Patterson	207 Church
Irwin-Phillips Co.	Keokuk, Iowa	Cyrus E. Phillips	61 Leonard
Isaacs' Max, Sons	Kansas City, Mo.	Bendet Isaacs	54 Walker
Ismay, Imrie & Co.	Liverpool, Eng.	J. Bruce Ismay	41 Broadway
Italian Line (Florio Rubbattino)	Rome, Italy.	Phelps Brothers & Co.	31 Broadway

WATER METERS, GAS ENGINES, FOR PUMPING AND POWER. | **NATIONAL METER CO. 252 Broadway, N. Y.**

IVE   359   **KAN**

Name.	Home Office.	Agent or Representative.	New York Office.
Ives H. B. & Co.	New Haven, Conn.	C. F. Guyon & Co.	98 Reade
Ivins, Dietz & Magee.	Philadelphia, Pa.	Patrick J. Donovan.	56 Worth
Jaccard Samuel et Fils.	Anderson, Scotland.	Hugo Frankfeld	18 State
Jackson I. & Brother	Pittsburgh, Pa.		689 Broadway
Jackson & Sharp Co.	Wilmington, Del.	Job H. Jackson	115 Broadway
Jacobs C. C., Cordage Co.	Cincinnati, O.	Joseph J. Duncan	338 Broadway
Jacobs Charles & Co.	San Francisco, Cal.	Morris Deutsch	227 E. 58th
Jacobs S., Bernheim & Co.	Galveston, Tex.		8 W. 3d
Jacobs & Co.	Denver, Colo.		512 Broadway
Jacobs & Isenberg	Wheeling, W. Va.		354 Broadway
Jacobs & Sachs.	Cincinnati, O.		260 Church
Jacoby M. & Co.	Nottingham, Eng.	H. L. Fesler & Co.	464 Broome
Jacoby Brothers.	Los Angeles, Cal.	Charles Jacoby	554 Broadway
Jacquot & Co.	Paris, France.	Rothschild Brothers & Co.	498 Broadway
Jaeger & Co.	Rutherford, N. J.	Henry G. Bell	96 Chambers
James A. & Co.	Colon, U. S. Columbia	Adolph James	549 Broadway
Jameson John & Son.	Dublin, Ireland.	Colbert & Taylor	30 Broadway
Jamestown Plush Mills.	Jamestown, N. Y.	Charles W. Griffin.	56 Worth
Jandt & Tompkins.	Sioux City, Iowa.	James O. Cleveland	84 W. B'way
Janeway & Carpenter	New Brunswick, N. J.	N. Bayard Nellson	20 E. 21st
Janis, Saunders & Co.	St. Louis, Mo.		102 Franklin
Janssen & Freyschlag.	Atchison, Kan.		68 Leonard
Jardine, Matheson & Co	Hong Kong, China.	George L. Montgomery.	76 Wall
Jarrow Chemical Co.	Newcastle-on-Tyne, Eng.	Edward Hill's Son & Co.	27 Cedar
Jarvis-Conklin Mortgage Trust Co.	Kansas City, Mo.	Thomas Clark Jr.	230 Broadway
Jay E. & S.	Grenoble, France	Walter Fletcher	84 Greene
Jefferson Iron Co.	Antwerp, N. Y.	Henry H. Adams / Frederick S. Salisbury	146 Broadway / 31 Union sq. W.
Jeffras N. A., Co.	Cincinnati, O.	Emanuel Loeb	115 Worth
Jennings & Griffin Mfg. Co.	Yalesville, Conn	C. F. Jennings & Co.	97 Chambers
Jensen Carl L., Co	Philadelphia. Pa	Herbert L. Ford	100 Maiden la.
Jersey City Galvanizing Co.	Jersey City, N. J.	C. Kruse	98 John
Jersey City Steel Co.	Jersey City, N. J.	Thomas C. Burrows	99 John
Jessop William & Sons (Ltd.).	Sheffield, Eng.	William F. Wagner	91 John
Jewell D. & Son	Brooklyn, N. Y.	Thomas F. Brown	4 Stone
Joachimsthal B. & Co.	Detroit, Mich.		53 Greene
Johnson Charles Eneu & Co.	Philadelphia, Pa.	Henry J. Weber	48 Rose
Johnson Co.	Johnstown, Pa.	Henry C. Evans	32 Nassau
Johnson Lawrence & Co.	Philadelphia, Pa.	Francis L. Byrne.	101 Water
Johnson R. R., Signal Co.	Rahway, N. J.	Charles R. Johnson.	146 Broadway
Johnson A. E. & Co.	St. Paul, Minn.	Max Straus.	5 Broadway
Johnson R. & Son	Madison, Ind.	Henry M. Anthony	100 Reade
Johnson Brothers	Hanley, Eng.	Edward Dutler	(3) Murray & 40 College pl.
Johnson & Forbes	Pensacola, Fla.	John W. White jr.	90 Walker
Johnston & Larimer Dry Goods Co.	Wichita, Kan.	Charles Walker	51 Leonard
Johnston, Crews & Co.	Charleston. S. C.		224 Church
Johnstone, Norman & Co.	London, Eng.	Charles R. Yandell.	140 Fifth av.
Joliet Steel Co.	Chicago. Ill.	Alexander J. Forbes-Leith	44 Wall
Jonap H. & Co.	Cincinnati, O.	Joseph Mayer	372 Broadway
Jones George A. & Co.	Bradford, Eng	Hicks Brothers.	42 White
Jones George V., Mfg. Co.	Boston, Mass	Edward G. Carter	81 Chambers
Jones George W., Distilling Co.	Brownsville, Pa.	Henry Pike jr.	39 Broad
Jones C. L. & Co	Boston, Mass.	George O. Stevens.	142 Reade
Jones W. C. & Co.	Sherman, Tex.		89 Worth
Jones & Laughlins (Ltd.).	Pittsburgh, Pa.	John F. Lovejoy & Co.	102 Chambers
Jones, Bailey & Furrar.	Manchester, Eng.	James & Smyth.	325 Broadway
Jones, Witter & Co.	Columbus, O.		87 Worth
Jorlemon A. & Co.	Newark, N. J.	D. S. Brush	17 Maiden la.
Jordan, Marsh & Co	Boston, Mass	James J. Smith	8 Greene
Joseph M. & Son	Fremont, O.		410 Broadway
Joseph Brothers.	Chicago, Ill.		44 White
Joseph Brothers & Davidson	Quincy, Ill.	Emanuel Loeb	115 Worth
Joske Brothers.	San Antonio, Tex.	Julius Joske	670 Broadway
Journu Frères, Kappelhoff & Co.	Bordeaux, France.	Charles Graef & Co.	32 Beaver
Joy, Langdon & Co.	Boston, Mass.	Woodbury Langdon.	108 Worth & 544 Pearl
Judge William & Brothers	Philadelphia, Pa.	William Simpson.	110 Worth
Judson Junius & Son	Rochester, N. Y.	Augustus P. McGraw	10 Dey
Jung & Simons.	Elberfeld, Germany.	Dieckerhoff, Raffloer & Co.	384 Broadway
Kahn & Co.	St. Joseph, Mo		512 Broadway
Kahn & Frieberg	Memphis, Tenn.	John W. White jr.	90 Walker
Kahn & Schloss.	Kansas City, Mo		512 Broadway
Kahn Brothers & Co.	Chicago, Ill.		48 Leonard
Kahn, Schoenbrnn & Co.	Chicago, Ill.		21 White
Kahn, Storm & Co.	Cincinnati, O.		75 Leonard
Kaiser John & Co.	Pittsburgh, Pa.		91 Franklin
Kalle & Co	Biebrich, Germany.	Charles Georgi	77 John
Kaminski H. & Co	Georgetown, S. C.	Hibbert B. Masters.	84 W. B'way
Kan Sai Trading Co.	Kioto, Japan.	Yesabro Wooyeno	456 Broadway

EXCELSIOR BIRD FOOD. The recognized standard. The most reliable for your Canary. Use no other. Insist upon getting it.
Packed only by C. ROSENSTEIN & CO., 373 Washington Street, New York.

Name.	Home Office.	Agent or Representative.	New York Office.
Kansas Investment Co	Topeka, Kan	Griswold & Gillett	8 Wall
Kansas Mortgage Co	Topeka, Kan	Jones & Fafle	187 Broadway
Kansas National Loan Co	Wichita, Kan	George F. Lewis	32 E. 42d
Kansas Trust & Banking Co	Atchison, Kan	Reuben M. Manley	115 Broadway
Katahdin Iron Works	Bangor, Me	Reginald Canning & Co	115 Broadway
Kato Mfg. Co	Jersey City, N. J	Arthur D. Giannini	56 Murray
Katz Henry & Co	Chicago, Ill	——	260 Church
Katz Brothers, Burton Drewing Co.	Paterson, N. J	Bernard Katz	282 Ninth av.
Katz & Barnett	New Orleans, La	Jacob Katz	81 Thomas
Katzensteiu E. & Co	Milwaukee, Wis	——	75 Leonard
Kaufer, Smithing & Co	Milwaukee, Wis	Henry A. Chamberlain	853 Canal
Kanfman S. & Sons	Pittsburgh, Pa	——	705 Broadway
Kaufman & Berliner	Tacoma, Wash	Max Toklas	481 Broadway
Kaufman & Isaac	New Orleans, La	Leopold Frank	86 Worth
Kaufman & Strauss	Louisville, Ky	——	443 Broadway
Kaufman Brothers & Co	Philadelphia, Pa	Richard F. Small	52 Franklin
Kaufmann I. & Co	Richmond, Va	Isaac Kaufmann	621 Broadway
Kaufmann J. & Brothers	Pittsburgh, Pa	——	560 Broadway
Kean S. A. & Co	Chicago, Ill	James E. Lewis	115 Broadway
Keely Motor Co	Philadelphia, Pa	Gulian Hook	85 Broadway
Keet & Rountree Mercantile Co.	Springfield, Mo	——	115 Worth
Keet, Rountree & Co	Springfield, Mo	——	115 Worth
Keim George DeB. & Co	Philadelphia, Pa	George De B. Keim	68 Leonard
Keim J. R. & Co	Philadelphia, Pa	C. E. Browne	713 Broadway
Keith Edson & Co	Chicago, Ill	——	96 Spring
Keller Dental Co	Fort Wayne, Ind	George A. Sanford	884 Broadway
Keller Piano Co	Bridgeport, Conn	Wintrroth & Co	17 E. 14th
Kellogg A. N., Newspaper Co	Chicago, Ill	Waverley W. Hallock	154 Nassau
Kellogg Charles P. & Co	Chicago, Ill	——	82 Leonard
Kelly George A. & Co	Pittsburgh, Pa	John D. Tibsworth	71 William
Kelly Thomas & Co	Boston, Mass	Peter E. Koville	86 White
Kelly & Jones Co	Greensburgh, Pa	John T. Kelly	75 John
Kendall R. W. & Co	Boston, Mass	James W. Aughitree	56 Worth
Kennedy & Murphy	Troy, N. Y	John Roarke	894 G'wich
Kensington Felt Co	City Mills, Mass	Hinman Brothers	359 Broadway
Kern Henry & Son	New Orleans, La	Morris Gonsenheim	18 Lispenard
Kerngood, Sloman & Rosenthal	E. Saginaw, Mich	——	681 Broadway
Kerr John E. & Co	Montego Bay, Jamaica	John E. Kerr jr	41 Beaver
Kerrison C. & E. L	Charleston, S. C	——	81 Franklin
Kester George B. & Co	Philadelphia, Pa	Daniel S. Downes	94 Front
Ketterlinus Printing House	Philadelphia, Pa	Joan F. Harfin	102 Chambers
Keveney Brothers & De Gan	Syracuse, N. Y	T. J. Keveney & Co	829 Broadway
Keystone Watch Case Co	Philadelphia, Pa	John L. Shepherd	12 Maiden la.
Killam Henry, Co	New Haven, Conn	John Murphy	1711 Broadway
Kimball Mfg. Co	Detroit, Mich	Rush S. Gilkeson	211 Pearl
Kimball C. J. & Son	Bennington, N. H	C. F. Guyon & Co	99 Reade
Kinane & Wren	Springfield, O	——	42 Lispenard
King Glass Co	Pittsburgh, Pa	——	58 Barclay
King Iron Bridge & Mfg. Co	Cleveland, O	Henry G. Clagstone	18 Broadway
King John & Son	Glasgow, Scotland	Innes R. Macpherson	456 Broadway
King John F., Mfg. Co	Augusta, Ga	William Fish jr. & Co	50 Leonard
King Julius, Optical Co	Cleveland, O	Leo Wormser	4 Maiden la.
King D. H. & Co	St. Louis, Mo	Benjamin G. Glover	622 Broadway
King H. W. & Co	Chicago, Ill	Browning, King & Co	408 Broome
Kingman E. D. & Co	Leominster, Mass	Edward B. Kingman	410 Broadway
Kirby, Beard & Co	Birmingham, Eng	Dieckerhoff, Raffoor & Co	854 Broadway
Kirby, Mowry & Co	Providence, R. I	Duncan K. Perrins	192 Broadway
Kirschbaum A. B. & Co	Philadelphia, Pa	Morris May	680 Broadway
Kirven J. A. & Co	Columbus, Ga	——	850 Broadway
Kiser M. C. & J. F. & Co	Atlanta, Ga	Walter L. Howell	66 Worth
Kistler, Lesh & Co	Boston, Mass	Francis M. Potter	101 Gold
Klaus J. & Co	Huntsville, Ala	——	637 Broadway
Klaus Brothers	Macon, Miss	——	657 Broadway
Klein Brothers	Chicago, Ill	——	872 Broadway
Klein & Rosenberg	Chicago, Ill	——	440 Broadway
Klein, Goodhart & Koch	Cleveland, O	——	76 Leonard
Kleine, Detmer & Co	Cincinnati, O	——	87 Greene
Kleinschmidt & Co	Lisbon, Portugal	Charles H. Knoche	81 Broad
Kleinwort, Sons & Co	London, Eng	Winter & Smillie	62 Wall
Klots & Dreyfoos	Baton Rouge, La	Morris Gonsenheim	18 Lispenard
Knabe William & Co., Mfg. Co	Baltimore, Md	Ferdinand Mayer	148 Fifth av.
Knappmann William & Co	Brooklyn, N. Y	Ellis P. Earle	71 Maiden la.
Knickerbocker Brass Co	Easton, Pa	McCafferty & Holton	165 William
Knight Investment Co	Wichita, Kan	G. D. Bruce Paton	1 Broadway
Knight A. C. & Co	Philadelphia, Pa	Vanderbilt & Reynolds	7 Lispenard
Knight B. B. & R	Providence, R. I	William E. Wall	69 Worth
Knight & Petch	London, Eng	William B. Roe	66 W. 23d
Knowles Steam Pump Works	Boston, Mass	George H. Stover	93 Liberty
Knox W. & J	Kilbirnie, Scotland	John Dougan & Co	864 Broadway
Kohlberg, Strauss & Frohman	San Francisco, Cal	Henry J. Sayers	529 Broadway
Kohler & Frohling	San Francisco, Cal	Herman Bohrmann	45 Broadway
Kohler & Vanbergen	San Francisco, Cal	Henry Vanbergen	42 Murray
Kohn Jacob & Josef	Vienna, Austria	Felix Kohn	10 W. 14th
Kohn Brothers	Chicago, Ill	St. Leger Palmer	205 Church
Kohn, Furchgott & Co	Jacksonville, Fla	Max Furchgott	385 Broadway
Kohrn & Widenfeld	Deadwood, S. Dak	——	650 Broadway

IDEN & CO., University Place, 9th to 10th Sts., N.Y. — MANUFACTURERS OF **GAS FIXTURES AND ELECTROLIERS**

KON 301 LEM

Name.	Home Office.	Agent or Representative.	New York Office.
Konig & Dwyer	New Orleans, La	Alexander J. Dwyer	21 Wooster
Kraft Brothers & Rosenberg	Wheeling, W. Va	—	21 White
Krakauer & Co	Vienna, Austria	Otto Schiffer	629 Broadway
Kramer Brothers	Scranton, Pa	—	689 Broadway
Kraus-Merkel Malting Co	Milwaukee, Wis	Louis J. Merkel & Otto Kupfer	19 Whitehall
Krupp Fried (firm of)	Essen, Germany	Thomas Prosser & Son	15 Gold
Kuehnert, Wachler & Neldner	Chemnitz, Germany	Henry Van Arsdale	115 Worth
Kuh, Nathan & Fisher	Chicago, Ill	—	2 White
Kuhn A. & Brother	Ogden, Utah	—	512 Broadway
Kyle J. & Co	Columbus, Ga	Albert L. Crater	115 Worth
Lackawanna Fast Freight Line	Buffalo, N. Y	Frank W. Smith	429 Broadway & 93 Wall
Lackawanna & Southwestern R. R. Co.	Angelica, N. Y	George D. Chapman	46 Wall
Ladd H. W. Co	Providence, R. I	William W. Marston	51 Leonard
Ladd Watch Case Co	Providence, R. I	James H. Bigelow	11 Maiden la.
Ladstatter & Sons	Vienna, Austria	John Monitzer	187 Greene
La Fayette Car Works	La Fayette, Ind	Reginald Canning	115 Broadway
Lafferty & Brother	Philadelphia, Pa	Pitman & Black	115 Worth
Lake Champlain Transp. Co	Whitehall, N. Y	Brackett W. Burleigh	1 Broadway
Lake Erie Iron Co	Cleveland, O	Josiah C. Saxton	52 Broadway
Lake Erie, Essex & Detroit River Railway Co.	Walkerville, Can	Raymond L. Ward	59 Broad
Lake Superior Ship Canal, Railway & Iron Co.	Lowell, Mass	Theodore M. Davis	41 Wall
Lake Superior Transit Co	Buffalo, N. Y	Horace S. Nichols	76 Wall
Lake L. & Brother	Baltimore, Md	Levin L. Lake	76 Franklin
Lalande A. A. & Co	Bordeaux, France	Emil Schultze & Co	36 Beaver
Lamaître & Ch. Pierre	Paris, France	Henry Berendt	47 Murray
Lamantia & Co	Palermo, Italy	Ignazio Lamantia-Salitz	16 State
Lambert & Clock	Dayton, O	William Lambert	99 Franklin
Lambert & Murphy	Bloomington, Ill	William Lambert	99 Franklin
Lambert Brothers & Miller	Paterson, N. J	Leslin, Neeser & Co	1 Greene
Lambertville Rubber Co	Lambertville, N. J	Goodyear Rubber Co	487 Broadway
Lamson & Goodnow Mfg. Co	Shelburne Falls, Mass.	William A. Willard	35 Chambers
Lancashire Ins. Co	Manchester, Eng	Edward Litchfield	40 Pine
Lancaster Caramel Co	Lancaster, Pa	Warren H. Erb	858 Canal
Lance Creek Cattle Co	Cheyenne, Wyoming Ter.	Charles F. Smillie	62 Wall
Landauer & Co	Milwaukee, Wis	Solomon Micholbacher	115 Worth
Landers, Frary & Clark	New Britain, Conn	Charles L. H. Clark	208 Broadway
Landon & Kent	Baltimore, Md	William M. Moore	15 Bond
Lane Mfg. Co	Waterbury, Conn	William C. Taylor	350 Canal
Lane Mills	New Orleans, La	Moses Weil	48 Leonard
Lane Brothers	Poughkeepsie, N. Y	John H. Graham & Co	113 Chambers
Langfeld Brothers & Co	Philadelphia, Pa	Jonas Langfeld	326 Broadway
Langfelder & Hammerschlag	Vienna, Austria	Hamburger & Co	416 Broome
Langley & Michaels Co	San Francisco, Cal	John D. Tibworth	71 William
Lansburgh & Brother	Washington, D. C	Henry Lansburgh	41 Greene
La Providence Iron Works Co.	Marchienne-Au-Pont, Belgium	Weir, Rogers & Co	45 Broadway
Larzelere William & Co	Philadelphia, Pa	Niebrugge & Day	121 Pearl
Lauberg J. W. & Sons	Lennep, Germany	William B. Roe	66 W. 23d
Lauteren C., Sohn	Mayence, Germany	Anthony Oechs	51 Warren
Lautier Fils	Grasse, France	{ F. R. Arnold & Co { George Lueders	56 Murray 218 Pearl
Lawton Brothers	Havana, Cuba	James M. Lawton	421 Produce Ex.
Lawyers' Co-operative Publishing Co.	Rochester, N. Y	Solon Briggs & Simeon N. Putnam	177 Broadway
Lazard C. & Co	New Orleans, La	Everett Lavendol	99 Franklin
Lazarus J. & Co	Cincinnati, O	—	58 Greene
Lazarus S., Sons & Co	Columbus, O	—	560 Broadway
Lazarus Brothers	Macon, Ga	—	8 W. 3d
Lazarus & Rosenfeld	London, Eng	Leopold Lehmann	60 Murray
Lazarus, Schwarz & Lipper	Philadelphia, Pa	Daniel Y. Bausher	416 Broadway
Leacock & Co	Madeira, Portugal	E. Lamontagne & Sons	51 Beaver
Leatheroid Mfg. Co	Kennebunk, Me	Andrew H. Teeple	36 Reade
Lebeck Brothers	Nashville, Tenn	—	57 Walker
Lecount Brothers	San Francisco, Cal	Thomas R. Lecount	225 Front
Lederer, Strauss & Co	Des Moines, Iowa	Leon Brocker	520 Broadway
Lee Hotel Fire Escape Co	Poughkeepsie, N. Y	David Proskey & Harlan P. Smith	683 Broadway
Lee's Boiler Compound Co	Muncie, Ind	Potchell & Lawrence	52 Broad
Leedon Thomas L. & Co	Philadelphia, Pa	Joseph B. Lord	115 Worth
Leeson J. R. & Co	Boston, Mass	John F. Bigelow & Edmund S. Hodges	295 Church
Leet & Knowlton	Rochester, Minn	—	80 Worth
Legler, Barlow & Co	Dayton, O	William H. Stiles	56 Thomas
Lehigh Valley Car Co	Stanton, Pa	Bernard R. Lehman	91 Liberty
Lehigh Valley Coal Co	Philadelphia, Pa	Louis R. Barrett	1 Broadway
Lehigh Zinc & Iron Co	Philadelphia, Pa	William Balbach	112 John
Lehman A. & Co	New Orleans, La	Herbert Dahlman	34 Thomas
Lehman I. & Brothers	Pittsburgh, Pa	—	680 Broadway
Leinkauf & Strauss	Mobile, Ala	—	59 Worth
Lemann B. & Brother	Donaldsville, La	Everett Lavendol	99 Franklin

TYPEWRITING DONE BY THE TROW CITY DIRECTORY CO., 11 University Place.

Name.	Home Office.	Agent or Representative.	New York Office.
Lemmon & Gale Dry Goods Co.	Memphis, Tenn.		375 Broadway
Lenox Shear Co	Brookfield, Conn	Fuller Brothers	33 Chambers
Leon & Metzger	Cincinnati, O		21 White
Leonard & Youngman	Albany, N. Y	Harry V. Youngman	1 Broadway
Leopold N. & Son	Ellenville, N. Y		512 Broadway
Le Page Co	Boston, Mass		95 Chambers
Lesem Isaac & Co	Quincy, Ill	William W. Marston	51 Leonard
Lesler, Frank & Co	Nashville, Tenn	Jacob Goldfarb	26 E. B'way
Lestienne, Labbe & Co	Roubaix, France	Walter Fletcher	84 Greene
Levi August & Co	Burlington, Iowa		83 Greene
Levi Brothers	Erie, Pa		40 Thomas
Levi Brothers	Philadelphia, Pa		630 Broadway
Levi & Isaacs	New Orleans, La		56 Worth
Levi, Wolf & Newburger	Louisville, Ky		587 Broadway
Levin Louis	Berlin, Germany	Gustav Kutnow	658 Broadway
Levis & Mohl	Springfield, Mo		96 Spring
Levy A. G. & Co	Mobile, Ala		433 Broome
Levy E. S. & Co	Galveston, Tex		670 Broadway
Levy J. D. & Co	Quincy, Ill		658 Broadway
Levy M. S. & Sons	Baltimore, Md	Patrick H. Malloy	131 Greene
Levy & Davis	Richmond, Va	Michael M. Davis	90 Franklin
Levy Frères, Ch. & M	Paris, France		82 Greene
Levy, Loeb & Co	New Orleans, La	Isaac Levy	117 Duane
Levy, Price & Co	Cincinnati, O		75 Leonard
Lewine Brothers	Waco, Tex		224 Church
Lewis O. J. & Co	St. Louis, Mo	John H. Hall	21 Walker
Lewis & Gregory	Columbus, Ga		114 Worth
Lexington Hydraulic & Mfg. Co.	Lexington, Ky	Charles G. Hildreth	45 Broadway
Libby, McNeill & Libby	Chicago, Ill	Henry M. Anthony	100 Reade
Liddell William & Co	Belfast, Ireland	James Girdwood	16 White
Liddle & Carter	Cedar Rapids, Iowa		87 Franklin
Liebenfrost Franz & Co	Vienna, Austria	Purdy & Arnold	51 Broad
Liebman & Schloss	Cincinnati, O		587 Broadway
Liebstadter B. & Co	Kansas City, Mo		604 Broadway
Liepold Brothers	Selma, Ala		8 W. 3d
Lightner M. C. & Co	Chicago, Ill	Arthur Vandyke	48 Broad
Lilienthal & Gassenheimer	Montgomery, Ala		650 Broadway
Lincoln Iron Works	Boonton, N. J	Elias T. Day	132 Broadway
Lindeke, Ladd & Co	St. Paul, Minn		51 Leonard
Lindekes, Warner & Schurmeier	St. Paul, Minn	Andrew Darr	51 Leonard
Linderman H. W. & Co. (Ltd.)	Buffalo, N. Y	Henry W. Linderman	111 Broadway
Linn & Scruggs	Decatur, Ill	Alexander Dobbin	112 Leonard
Lion Fire Ins. Co	London, Eng	Charles M. Peck & Co	33 Pine
Lipman S. & Co	Portland, Ore	Seymour S. Vankirk	46 Leonard
Lipman & Co	Dundee, Scotland	Ludwig A. Gutmann	30 Worth
Lipman, Wieger & Co	Sacramento, Cal	Seymour S. Vankirk	46 Leonard
Lipper M. W. & Co	Philadelphia, Pa	Paul Mende	80 Franklin
Lippincott J. B., Co	Philadelphia, Pa	Edward R. Felton	25 Bond
Lippincott, Son & Co	Philadelphia, Pa	Augustus H. Lockwood	107 Grand
Lippman Brothers	Anniston, Ala		705 Broadway
Lister & Co. (Ltd.)	Bradford, Eng	Thomas P. Latham	55 White
Little Giant Gold Mining Co	Black Hills, S. Dak	Charles K. Ellery	30 Broad
Little Rock & Fort Smith Railway Co.	St. Louis, Mo	William E. Hoyt	195 & 891 Broadway
Livermore & Knight	Providence, R. I	Richard D. Knight	333 Broadway
Liverpool & London & Globe Ins. Co.	Liverpool, Eng	Henry W. Eaton	45 William
Liviorato Brothers	Marseilles, France	Constantine D. Liviorato	91 Wall
Livingston M. & Son	South Bend, Ind		789 Broadway
Livingstone Woollen Mills	E. Greenwich, R. I	Howard E. McCoy	56 Worth
Loaiza W. & Co	San Francisco, Cal	Santiago Smithers	39 S. William
Lob's Charles, Sons	New Orleans, La		462 Broome
Lobe Moses & Sons	New Orleans, La		597 Broadway
Locke Johnson Mercantile Co.	San Francisco, Cal	Rossiter & Skidmore	150 Franklin
Lockwood Mfg. Co	S. Norwalk, Conn	C. F. Gayon & Co	90 Reade
Locose & L. Levic	Cronfestu, Belgium	Weir, Rogers & Co	45 Broadway
Lodge & Davis Machine Tool Co.	Cincinnati, O	William H. Harrison	64 Cortlandt
Loeb A. & Co	Meridian, Miss		479 Broadway
Loeb A. N. & Co	Stuttgart, Germany	Alfred N. Loeb	52 White
Loeb S. & Brother	Columbus, Miss		479 Broadway
Loeb & Louchheim	Philadelphia, Pa	Joseph A. Louchheim	661 Broadway
Loeb & Metzger	Cincinnati, O		21 White
Loeb, Hirsh & Co	La Fayette, Ind		435 Broadway
Loevenhart H. & L	Lexington, Ky		650 Broadway
Loewenstein L. & Co	Chicago, Ill		260 Church
Loewenstein Brothers	St. Louis, Mo		425 Broadway
Logan Silk Mills	Auburn, N. Y	Mathews, Binm & Vaughan	85 Leonard
Logan F. G. & Co	Chicago, Ill	Logan, Cowl & Co	205 Produce Ex.
Logan, Gregg & Co	Pittsburgh, Pa	William B. Fox & Brother	97 Chambers
London Assurance Corporation	London, Eng	George H. Marks (inland) Clement L. Despard (marine)	60 Wall / 56 Wall
London & Brazilian Bank (Ltd.)	London, Eng	J. Lawrence McKeever	71 Wall

THE CALIGRAPH WRITING MACHINE,
HARTFORD, CONN.
LON 363 McL

Name.	Home Office.	Agent or Representative.	New York Office.
London & County Financial Assn. (Ltd.)	London, Eng.	Townsend Percy	6 Wall
London & Lancashire Fire Ins. Co.	Liverpool, Eng.	Jeffrey Beaven	36 Nassau
London & N. Y. Investment Corporation (Ltd.)	London, Eng.	John Greenough	36 Wall
London & Northwestern Railway	London, Eng.	Cæsar A. Baratton	852 Broadway
London, Paris & Am. Bank (Ltd.)	London, Eng.	Lazard Frères	10 Wall
Londonderry Lithia Spring Water Co.	Nashua, N. H.	John W. Morris	323 Broadway
Long Branch Ocean Pier Co.	Long Branch, N. J.	Charles W. Held	58 Bowery
Long James, Brother & Co.	Philadelphia, Pa.	Joseph O. Martin	58 Leonard
Long John & Son	Braintree, Mass.	Richard W. Williams	78 Reade
Long & Allstatter	Hamilton, O.	Niles Tool Works	95 Liberty
Longmans, Green & Co	London, Eng.	Charles J. Mills	15 E. 16th
Lopowski S. & Brother	San Angelo & Abilene, Tex.		548 Broadway
Lord & Thomas	Chicago, Ill.	Frank H. Thomas	154 Nassau
Lorillard Brick Works Co.	Keyport, N. J.	Jacob Lorillard	65 South
Lorillard P. & Co.	Jersey City, N. J.	Frank G. Griswold	46 W. B'way
Lormine Mfg. Co.	Saylesville, R. I.	George E. Stedman	51 Leonard
Loth A. & Sons	St. Louis, Mo.		38 Thomas
Loth & Haas	Cincinnati, O.		355 Broadway
Louchheim Joseph & Co.	Philadelphia, Pa.	Isaac Steuerman	704 Broadway
Louchheim J. & Co.	Louisville, Ky.		658 Broadway
Louisville Underwriters	Louisville, Ky.	Carpinter & Baker	4 Hanover
Louisville, St. Louis & Texas Railway Co.	Louisville, Ky.	William V. McCrackon	40 Wall
Louatan J. & Bazanac	Bordeaux, France	Comptoirs Commercieaux Français	46 University pl.
Lovell Mfg. Co. (Ltd.)	Erie, Pa.	Henry A. Holzapfel	84 G'wich av.
Loveman D. B. & Co	Chattanooga, Tenn.		224 Church
Loveman, Joseph & Loeb	Birmingham, Ala.		587 Broadway
Low Moor Iron Co	Low Moor, Eng.	Edmund Y. Jacobus	38 Park row
Low Sampson, Maraton & Co.	London, Eng.	De Witt C. Lent	32 Park pl.
Lowell John A. & Co.	Boston, Mass.	V. Haurie-Emes.	10 W. 14th
Lowenhohm, Sineheimer & Kahn	Cincinnati, O.		21 White
Lowenstein B. & Brothers	Memphis, Tenn.	Isaac D. Marks	51 Leonard
Loweustein M. & Brother	Trenton, N. J.		598 Broadway
Loweuthal L. & Co	Evansville, Ind.		84 White
Lowman, Sons & Co	Cincinnati, O.		28 Greene
Lucas John & Co	Philadelphia, Pa.	William E. Lucas	69 Maiden la.
Luchting N. & Co.	Bremen, Germany.	R. F. Downing & Co.	20 Exchange pl.
Ludwig H. & Co	Providence, R. I.	Isaac Steinau	529 Broadway
Luther G. E. & Co	Providence, R. I.	Frank H. Dana	20 Maiden la.
Lyman & Allen	Burlington, Vt.		224 Church
Lyman, Knox & Co.	Montreal, Can.	John D. Titsworth	71 William
Lymansville Co.	Providence, R. I.	Brigham & Mann	61 Leonard
Lyons Silk & Tapestry Co.	Paterson, N. J.	W. G. Hitchcock & Co.	453 Broome
Lyons L. L. & Co	New Orleans, La.	John D. Titsworth	71 William
Lyons & Woods	Lurgan & Belfast, Ireland	Bulkley G. Robbins	51 Leonard
McAdam Quentin & Co	Utica, N. Y.		115 Worth
McAlpin George W., Co	Cincinnati, O.	E. Hinsdell May	835 Broadway
McCabe & Co	Rock Island, Ill.		633 Broadway
McCallum & Sloan	Philadelphia, Pa.	John Perry	108 Worth
McCarthy D. & Sons	Syracuse, N. Y.	John H. Long	58 Worth
McCaw, Stevenson & Orr	Belfast, Ireland	Henry H. Ross	58 Pine
McChesney & Fischer	Orange Valley, N. J.	Thos. J. Brereton	144 Greene
McClure Drug Co.	Fort Worth, Tex.	John A. Morton	13 Gold
McConway & Forley Co.	Pittsburgh, Pa.	Edward G. Aikman.	115 Broadway
McCord & Bradfield Furniture Co.	Grand Rapids, Mich.	James W. Wheelock	20 E. 18th
McCreery & Brother	Columbia, S. C.		224 Church
McCullough Iron Co.	Wilmington, Del.	McDaniel & Harvey Co.	284 Pearl
McCullough D. & Son	Louisville, Ky.		63 Leonard
McCutchen & Co.	Russellville, Ky.		705 Broadway
McDaniel & Harvey Co.	Philadelphia, Pa.	Francis Kelton	284 Pearl
McDonald R. H. Drug Co	Brooklyn, N. Y.	Frank S. Edminster	96 Broadway
McDonald R. L. & Co.	St. Joseph, Mo.	George Henderson	51 Leonard
McDonough & Co.	Savannah, Ga.	James C. Johnson	22 Beaver
McDougall Brothers	London, Eng.	F. Porter Thayer	16 Warren
McElwain J. F. & Co	Brookfield, Mass.		878 Broadway
McFadden Geo. H. & Brother	Philadelphia, Pa.	J. M. White & Co.	7 S. William
McGahan, Brown & Evans	Charleston, S. C		79 Spring
McGall Brothers	Orange Valley, N. J.	Edward H. Birmingham	187 Greene
McGillin F. M., Dry Goods Co.	Cleveland, O.	John A. Donahue	335 Broadway
McIntosh & Mygatt	Denver, Colo.	Francis L. Hine	96 Broadway
McKean, Eilers & Co.	Austin, Tex.	Charles Walker	51 Leonard
McKelvey G. M. & Co.	Youngstown, O.	John A. Donahue	335 Broadway
McLaughlin Brothers	Paterson, N. J.	Robert McLaughlin	513 Broadway
McLean Bros. & Rigg (Ltd.)	Melbourne, Sydney, Adelaide, Australia; & London, Eng.	Walter J. Travis	52 New

SPECIAL ATTENTION PAID TO THIS CLASS OF WORK. } BANKERS' & BROKERS' CIRCULARS DELIVERED { THE TROW CITY DIRECTORY CO. 11 University Place.

McN 364 MAS

Name.	Home Office.	Agent or Representative.	New York Office.
McNamara Dry Goods Co	Denver, Colo		503 Broadway
McNicol, Burton & Co	E. Liverpool, O	Julius Wolff	55 Park pl.
McNulty & Borches	Knoxville, Tenn		115 Worth
McPike & Fox	Atchison, Kan	John D. Titsworth	71 William
McTeer, Burger & Hood	Knoxville, Tenn		524 Broadway
Mabley & Carew	Cincinnati, O		104 Bleecker
Macarthur D. & Co	Glasgow, Scotland	Daniel Martin jr	130 Greene
Macauley Richard & Co	Detroit, Mich	Henry Ide	520 Broadway
Macdermott & Partridge	Philadelphia, Pa	Louis A. Croghan	105 Franklin
Macfarlane & Co	Mansfield Centre, Conn.	J. P. Cahen & Bro	24 Walker
Machpelah Cemetery Assn	New Durham, N. J	Alexander McNeill	804 W. 20th
MacIntosh Chas. & Co	Manchester, Eng	T. W. Stemmler & Co	36 E. 14th
Mack H. S. & Co	Milwaukee, Wis		75 Leonard
Mack J. J. & Co	San Francisco, Cal		80 Reade
Mack, Stadler & Co	Cincinnati, O		21 White
Mackeown, Dower, Ellis & Co	Philadelphia, Pa	Charles H. Rutherford	13 Gold
Mackey, Nisbet & Co	Evansville, Ind		258 Church
Macknight Flintic Stone Co		John W. Macknight	150 Broadway
Macmillan & Co	London, Eng	George E. Brett	112 Fourth av.
Maddock Thomas & Sons	Trenton, N. J	{ William W. Perrine { John Nixon	51 Cliff 6 College pl.
Maddux, Hobart & Co	Cincinnati, O	John A. Burke	1 Broadway
Magee Furnace Co	Boston, Mass	John Q. A. Butler	202 Water
Magee James F. & Co	Philadelphia, Pa	Edward W. Price	17 Platt
Magee Thos. H. & Co	Belfast, Ireland	James & Smyth	335 Broadway
Mahler, Kahn & Co	Milwaukee, Wis	R. Wallach's Sons	98 Thomas
Maillauderie Felix de la P. Germain	Beaune, France	Hartman, Goldsmith & Co	45 Warren
Maine S. S. Co	Portland, Me	Horatio Hall	Pier 38 E. R.
Maisham & Yeomans	Sheffield, Eng	David B. McIlwaine	97 Chambers
Mallinckrodt Chemical Works	St. Louis, Mo	Henry T. Jarrett	90 William
Mallory-Wheeler Co	New Haven, Conn	Henry C. Merrill	64 Reade
Malone Stone Co	Cleveland, O	Orlando Marine	86 Park row
Mandel Brothers	Chicago, Ill	Leon Mandel	107 Franklin
Mandell Brothers & Co	Albuquerque, New Mexico	K. Mandell & Co	26 Howard
Mandleberg J. & Co. (Ltd.)	Manchester, Eng	H. P. Plante & Bro	62 Greene
Manhattan Clothing Co	Norwich, Conn		479 Broadway
Manhattan Silver Plate Co	Lyons, N. Y	Albert A. Clark	25 John
Manheimer Brothers	St. Paul, Minn	Godfrey Manheimer	381 Broadway
Mann William, Co	Philadelphia, Pa	Theodore H. Bailey	88 Maiden la.
Mann J. & H. & Co	Baltimore, Md	Robert R. Bren	688 Broadway
Mannheim Ins. Co	Mannheim, Germany	Hugo Menzel	16 Exchange pl.
Manning, Bowman & Co	Meriden, Conn	Henry A. Manning	87 Beekman
Mansbach E. & Co	San Francisco, Cal	William Brunner	7 Mercer
Mansman Brothers	Pittsburgh, Pa		21 White
Manufacturers' Governor Co	Portland, Conn	Augustus P. McGraw	10 Dey
Manufacturers' Paper Co	Luzerne, N. Y	Kennedy B. Fullerton	154 Fulton
Manufacturers' Special Machine Co.	Danbury, Conn	Edward P. Hatch	557 Hudson
Manufacturers' & Merchants' Ins. Co.	Pittsburgh, Pa	Ackerman, Doyo & Hilliard	41 Pine
Marble & Shattuck Chair Co	Bedford, O	James W. Wheelock	20 E. 18th
March A. & Co	New Brunswick, N.J	Alexander Ross	335 Broadway
Marcus L. & Son	Buffalo, N. Y		260 Church
Marcus & Co	Wichita Falls, Tex	M. Marcus	403 Broadway
Marcy Fred. L. & Co	Providence, R. I	James Peacock	108 Broadway
Marey C. & Liger-Belair	Nuits, France	E. Lamontagne & Sons	53 Beaver
Marie, Brizard & Roger	Bordeaux, France	Hartman, Goldsmith & Co	45 Warren
Marine Ins. Co	St. Louis, Mo	Weed & Kennedy	50 Pine
Marine Ins. Co. (Ltd.)	London, Eng	Chubb & Son	77 Beaver
Marks C. S. & Co	Erie, Pa		589 Broadway
Marks M. H. & Co	Cincinnati, O		75 Leonard
Marks Bros. & Marks	Cincinnati, O		75 Leonard
Marks, Rothenberg & Co	Meridian, Miss	K. Mandell & Co	26 Howard
Marsh & Bigney	Attleboro, Mass	Max W. Potter	176 Broadway
Marsh & Harwood Chemical Works	Cleveland, O		71 Wall
Marshall Iron Co	Newport, Del	Frank L. Froment	112 John
Marshall J. & Ball	Newark, N. J	William B. Stiles	36 Thomas
Marshall & Driggs	Troy, N. Y	Frank H. Moore	18 E. 15th
Marshall & Co	Kearny, N. J	George A. Clark & Bro	400 Broadway
Martel Furnace Co	St. Ignace, Mich	Stroud & Co	104 John
Martin James & Co	Philadelphia, Pa	Edwin Martin	25 Franklin
Martin T. J. & Co	Philadelphia, Pa	Lieber & Dreyfous	122 Front
Martin & Powers	Richmond, Va		355 Broadway
Martin, Copeland & Co	Providence, R. I	William A. Copeland	9 Maiden la.
Martin, Wise & Fitzhugh	Paris, Tex	James D. Guest	55 Cotton Ex.
Martin-Brown Co	Fort Worth, Tex		117 Duane & 34 Thomas
Martini & Rossi	Turin, Italy	Culbert & Taylor	39 Broadway
Marx Luis, Blau & Co	Havana, Cuba	Louis Blun	166 Water
Marx & Haas	St. Louis, Mo	Felix B. Ruthenburg	719 Broadway
Maryland Union Coal Co	Baltimore, Md	James Boyce jr	45 Broadway
Mason & Hamlin Organ & Piano Co.	Boston, Mass	Edward P. Mason	46 E. 14th
Massachusetts Benefit Assn	Boston, Mass	George E. Curtis	86 Park row

FOR THE BEST CO-PARTNERSHIP IN THE BEST CORPORATION SEE PAGE F IN BACK OF BOOK

MAS 365 MEY

Name.	Home Office.	Agent or Representative.	New York Office.
Massachusetts Mutual Life Ins. Co.	Springfield, Mass.	Gilford Morse	243 Broadway
Massasoit Mfg. Co.	Fall River, Mass.	William H. Turner	86 Leonard
Massasoit Whip Co.	Westfield, Mass.	George Pirnie	47 Warren
Massey William, Brewing Co.	Philadelphia, Pa.	Walter Henly	14 State
Massman A. E., Bros. & Co.	Philadelphia, Pa.	Kuhlke & Blank	105 Broad
Matchless Metal Polish Co.	Chicago, Ill.	William B. Volger	53 William
Mather Electric Light Co.	Manchester, Conn.	Edward H. Dodge	35 Broadway
Mathews E. J. & Co.	Philadelphia, Pa.	Alfred Ray	2 Wall
Mathewson James & Son	Dunfermline, Scotland	Thomas K. Milliken	51 Leonard
Mathushek Piano Mfg. Co.	New Haven, Conn.	John W. French	50 Fifth av.
Matthai, Ingram & Co.	Baltimore, Md.	Lobelta & Powell	35 Murray
Matthews, Northrup & Co.	Buffalo, N. Y.	Charles E. Sickels	280 Broadway
Matthewson Angell & Co.	Parsons, Kan.	William H. Taylor	55 Liberty
Maxwell White Lead Co.	Chicago, Ill.	Thomas E. Sims	71 Broadway
May Shoe & Clothing Co.	Denver, Colo.	—	56 Worth
Mayell A. & Co.	Cleveland, O.	McCafferty & Holton	145 William
Mayer Chas. & Son.	San Francisco, Cal.	Theodore F. Stumpf	115 Worth
Mayer S. & Co.	Plattsmouth, Neb.	—	600 Broadway
Mayer Brothers	Lincoln, Neb.	—	650 Broadway
Mayer Brothers	Trenton, N. J.	Julius Wolff	55 Park pl.
Mayer & Co.	Munich, Germany.	Louis Trueg	124 W. 23d
Mayer, Engel & Co.	Chicago, Ill.	—	75 Leonard
Mayhew Silk Co.	Shelburne Falls, Mass.	Herbert H. Sanderson	32 Mercer
Mead's State Bank	York, Neb.	George G. Nichols & Schuyler N. Warren	51 Exchange pl.
Meade Geo. W. & Co.	San Francisco, Cal.	Rossiter & Skidmore	156 Franklin
Mechanics' Ins. Co.	Philadelphia, Pa.	Charles M. Peck & Co.	33 Pine
Meder J. J. & Co.	Amsterdam, Holland	Ferdinand Ruttmann	83 Liberty
Mediterranean & N. Y. S. S. Co. (Ltd.)	Liverpool, Eng.	Phelps Bros. & Co.	31 Broadway
Meier & Frank	Portland, Ore.	—	224 Church
Meigs, Hartley & Co.	Philadelphia, Pa.	Francis M. Hartley	57 Worth
Meinhard Bros. & Co.	Savannah, Ga.	Edward C. Oppenheimer	117 Duane & 34 Thomas
Mellert Foundry & Machine Co. (Ltd.)	Reading, Pa.	John Fox	160 Broadway
Mellor & Rittenhouse Co.	Philadelphia, Pa.	Charles H. Rutherford	12 Gold
Mendel Raphael & Son.	Hamburg, Germany.	Samuel Mendel	143 Division
Mendel & Co.	Chicago, Ill.	—	40 W. B'way
Menken J. S. & Co.	Memphis, Tenn.	John Isler	115 Worth
Mercantile Ins. Co.	Boston, Mass.	Robert O. Glover	141 Broadway
Mercantile Ins. Co.	Cleveland, O.	Alliance Ins. Assn.	32 Nassau
Merchants' Bank of Canada	Montreal, Can.	Henry Hague & John B. Harris jr.	61 Wall
Merchants' Ins. Co.	Newark, N. J.	Ogden & Katzenmayer	83 Liberty
Merchants' Ins. Co.	Providence, R. I.	Hall & Henshaw	54 William
Merchants' Transp. Co.	Trenton, N. J.	Horace B. Hitchcock	Pier 18 E. R.
Mercier's D., Sons	New Orleans, La.	—	126 Bleecker
Meriden Bronze Co.	Meriden, Conn.	Frank M. Randall	30 Park pl.
Meriden Cutlery Co.	Meriden, Conn.	James M. Gildersleeve	50 Chambers
Meriden Fire Ins. Co.	Meriden, Conn.	T. J. Temple & Co.	156 Broadway
Meriden Malleable Iron Co.	Meriden, Conn.	Frederick F. Clark	37 Barclay
Meriden Silver Plate Co.	Meriden, Conn.	Webster & White	30 E. 14th
Merrell William S., Chemical Co.	Cincinnati, O.	Charles A. Holmes	96 Maiden la.
Merriam H. W., Shoe Co.	Newton, N. J.	Francisco M. Chappell	122 Duane
Merrick Thread Co.	Holyoke, Mass.	Herbert F. Palmer	28 Thomas
Merriewold Park Co.	Merriewold Park, N. Y.	William D. Scott	132 Nassau
Merrimack Mfg. Co.	Boston, Mass.	Wheelwright, Eldredge & Co.	61 Worth
Merritt H. D. & Co.	N. Attleboro, Mass.	Albert H. Oakley	10 Maiden la.
Merritt Mfg. Co.	Springfield, Mass.	—	5 Cortlandt
Merry & Cunninghame	Glasgow, Scotland.	James Lee & Co.	72 Pine
Mersereau & Co.	Peoria, Ill.	—	22 Thomas
Mertens J. M. & Co.	Syracuse, N. Y.	William H. Silles	85 Thomas
Mers Capsule Co.	Detroit, Mich.	McCafferty & Holton	165 William
Metcalf Brothers	Council Bluffs, Iowa.	—	670 Broadway
Metropolitan S. S. Co.	Boston, Mass.	Henry F. Dimock	Pier 11 N. R.
Menmier, Kèrè & Fils	Voiron, France.	Comptoirs Commerciaux Français.	46 University pl.
Mexican Central R'y Co. (Ltd.)	Mexico City, Mex.	George W. Keeler	261 Broadway
Mexican Co. of London (Ltd.)	London, Eng.	Augustus A. Hayes & William J. Morton	11 Pine
Meyer Jacob & Bros.	Chicago, Ill.	—	355 Broadway
Meyer Jonas & Co.	Quincy, Ill.	—	670 Broadway
Meyer Julius & Sons	Richmond, Va.	—	392 Broadway
Meyer Max & Co.	Omaha, Neb.	—	120 Grand
Meyer Rubber Co.	New Brunswick, N.J.	James B. Ford	80 Reade
Meyer C. H. & Bros.	San Francisco, Cal.	Cauffman H. Mayer	96 Spring
Meyer M. & Co.	Athens, Ga.	—	54 Walker
Meyer Bros.	Demopolis, Ala.	—	15 White
Meyer Bros. Drug Co.	St. Louis, Mo.	Frederick G. Mayer	114 William
Meyer & Coblens	Bingen, Germany.	Venable & Heyman	22 Reade

CIRCULARS ADDRESSED TO ANY TRADE IN THE U. S. { Facilities
PROMPT, CAREFUL WORK } **THE TROW CITY DIRECTORY CO.,** { Unequalled.
AT MODERATE PRICES. } **11 University Place.**

MEY 366 MOR

Name.	Home Office.	Agent or Representative.	New York Office.
Meyers J. & Co.	Opelousas, La.	Everett Lavendol	09 Franklin
Michael Bros	Athens, Ga.	—	606 Broadway
Michaels, Stern & Co.	Rochester, N. Y.	Aaron J. Naumburg	609 Broadway
Michaelson J. & Co.	Bordeaux, France	Julius Wile, Brother & Co.	51 Murray
Michigan Radiator & Iron Mfg. Co.	Detroit, Mich.	Charles F. Gemert.	42 Dey
Michau Th. & Co.	Paris, France.	Thomas E. Harrison	460 Broome
Michell & Kimbel	Paris, France	Morris European & Am. Express Co. (Ltd.)	18 Broadway
Middlesex Banking Co.	Middletown, Conn.	William R. T. Johnston.	60 Broadway
Middlesex Co.	S. Amboy, N. J.	—	1 Broadway
Middleton & Co.	Yokohama, Japan.	John Middleton	60½ Pine
Middletown Plate Co.	Middletown, Conn.	John W. Johnson.	21 John
Midland Railway of England.	Derby, Eng.	Maurice H. Hurley	287 Broadway
Midwood Alfred H. & Co.	Manchester, Eng.	Healy & Co.	214 Church
Miles, Bancroft & Sheldon.	Columbus, O.	—	112 Leonard
Mill Creek Coal Co.	Mauch Chunk, Pa.	Warren Delano jr.	115 Broadway
Millar J. & R.	Paisley, Scotland	William Robertson	119 Franklin
Millard Mfg. Co.	Providence, R. I.	Ellis & Goltermann.	28 College pl.
Miller Daniel & Co	Baltimore, Md.	—	66 Leonard
Miller Jacob, Sons & Co.	Philadelphia, Pa.	Charles Miller	698 Broadway
Miller Mfg. Co.	Newark, N. J.	George M. Lynch.	1123 Broadway
Miller J. G. & Co.	Chicago, Ill.	—	260 Church
Miller Bros. Cutlery Co.	Meriden, Conn.	Isaac D. Hurlbutt	65 Duane
Miller, Dubrul & Peters Mfg. Co.	Cincinnati, O.	Henry C. Peters	413 E. 81st
Millhiser M. & Co.	Richmond, Va.	—	258 Church
Millie Iron Mining Co.	Iron Mountain, Mich.	Simon Dessau.	4 John
Milliken W. H. & Co.	Portland, Me.	—	79 Leonard
Mills Bros. & Co.	Boston, Mass.	Isaac B. Mills	19 Whitehall
Mills, Knight & Co.	Boston, Mass.	Legrand B. Woodruff	641 Broadway & 78 Bleecker
Milnesville Coal Co.	Milnesville, Pa.	A. S. Van Wickle & Co.	1 Broadway
Milton W. F. & Co.	Pittsfield, Mass.	Gustavus A. Morgenroth jr.	150 Maiden la.
Milward Henry & Sons.	Redditch, Eng.	George A. Clark & Brother.	400 Broadway
Milwaukee & Michigan Line.	Detroit, Mich.	William J. Jennings.	413 Broadway
Milwaukee & Northern R. R. Co.	Milwaukee, Wis.	Alfred M. Hoyt.	1 Broadway
Milwaukee, Lake Shore & Western R'y Co.	Milwaukee, Wis.	Frederick W. Rhinelander.	10 Wall
Mimnaugh J. L. & Co.	Columbia, S. C.	—	650 Broadway
Minetto Shade Cloth Co.	Oswego, N. Y.	Amos Gillette.	111 Franklin
Minneapolis Dry Goods Co.	Minneapolis, Minn.	Syndicate Trading Co.	120 Franklin
Minneapolis Union Railway Co.	St. Paul, Minn.	Edward T. Nichols.	40 Wall
Mississippi Glass Co.	St. Louis, Mo.	Gilbert S. King.	102 Chambers
Missoula Mercantile Co.	Missoula, Mont.	—	224 Church
Missouri Trust Co.	Sedalia, Mo.	George H. Warner.	30 State
Mitchell J. D. Co.	Corpus Christi, Tex.	Vincent W. Baldwin jr.	5 Dey
Mitchell W. H. & Co.	Detroit, Mich.	Alanson White jr.	552 Broadway
Miton Père & Fils.	Paris, France.	Comptoirs Commerciaux Français	46 University pl.
Mitting, Maclagan & Storme.	Park Ridge, N. J.	John W. H. Maclagan.	83 William
Moch, Berman & Co	Cincinnati, O.	—	21 White
Model Flint Glass Co.	Findlay, O.	Thomas G. Edge.	58 Barclay
Moet & Chandon.	Epernay, France.	Kessler, Behringer & Co.	20 Denver
Moffett, Hodgkins & Clarke.	Syracuse, N. Y.	John V. Clarke.	343¼ Pine
Mohr Bros.	Savannah, Ga.	—	48 Leonard
Mollison & Co.	Yokohama, Japan.	George Hamilton	91 Wall
Monida Woollen Mills	Philadelphia, Pa.	James P. Streeter.	401 Broadway
Montague W. W. & Co	San Francisco, Cal.	Henry B. Van Vleck	83 Fulton
Montana Central Railway Co.	Helena, Mont.	Edward T. Nichols.	40 Wall
Montana Coal & Coke Co.	Baltimore, Md.	Charles W. Hays.	1 Broadway
Montana Smelting Co.	Great Falls, Mont.	Walter S. Gurnee & Henry C. Cooper	7 Nassau
Montauk Construction Co.	Jersey City, N. J.	Samuel R. Bullock.	11 Wall
Montclair Water Co.	Montclair, N. J.	John R. Bartlett.	2 Wall
Montebello Alfred de & Co.	Château de Mareuil-sur-Ay, France	Leon Renault.	35 Nassau
Montessuy & Co.	Lyons, France.	W. G. Hitchcock & Co.	453 Broome
Montgomery, Tuscaloosa & Memphis Railway Co.	Montgomery, Ala.	Joseph W. Woolfalk.	43 Wall
Montour Iron & Steel Co.	Danville, Pa.	Milliken Brothers.	55 Liberty
Montrose Co.	Paris, France.	Rosenberg & Horn.	712 Broadway
Monument Mills	Housatonic, Mass.	Jere R. Ireland.	216 Church
Moody W. L. & Co.	Galveston, Tex.	William L. Moody	44 Wall
Moody & Jenkins.	Yonkers, N. Y.	Leonard & Moody.	5 Cotton Ex.
Mooney, Valentine & Goldsmith	Portland, Ore.	—	07 Franklin
Moore Wm. R. & Co.	Memphis, Tenn.	—	43 Worth
Moore R. L. & Co.	St. Croix, West Indies	Culbert & Taylor	89 Broadway
Moore W. T. & Co	Chicago, Ill.	Alexander Dobbin	112 Leonard
Moore & Beir.	Rochester, N. Y.	Isaac J. Beir.	702 Broadway
Moore, Morgan & Co.	La Fayette, Ind.	—	131 William
Moore, Weinberg & Co.	Belfast, Ireland.	Walter O. Portheim.	55 White
Moorhead-McGleane Co.	Pittsburgh, Pa.	William P. Loughry.	81 John
Morand A., Remond & Co.	Paris, France.	Emile Wirz.	74 W. 23d
Moret, Poeckes & Daumlin	Paris, France.	John W. Cockredge.	20 W. 23d
Morgan Crucible Co.	London, Eng.	Richards & Co.	41 Barclay

THADDEUS DAVIDS CO., WRITING INKS, SEALING WAX, MUCILAGE.
MAKE THE BEST

MOR 367 NAU

Name.	Home Office.	Agent or Representative.	New York Office.
Morgan Engineering Co	Alliance, O.	Niles Tool Works	96 Liberty
Morgan Envelope Co	Springfield, Mass.	John F. Hitchcock	297 Broadway
Morgan Furniture Co. (Ltd.)	Buffalo, N. Y.	Andrew J. McIntosh	55 W. 23d
Morgenthau, Bauland & Co.	Chicago, Ill.		52 Leonard
Morimura Bros	Tokio, Japan	Toyo Morimura	540 Broadway & 78 Crosby
Morley I. & M.	Nottingham, Eng.	Thomas Osborne	96 Grand
Morris & Co.	London, Eng.	Albert H. Davenport	932 Broadway
Morris & Lewis	Philadelphia, Pa.	A. Augustus Hyneman	87 Worth
Morrison A. S. & Bros.	Braintree, Mass.	Moses Appel	74 Franklin
Morrison, Plummer & Co.	Chicago, Ill.	John D. Titsworth	71 William
Morse, Williams & Co.	Philadelphia, Pa.	John Keir	108 Liberty
Morton Alexander & Co.	Darvel, Scotland	William Hunter	56 Worth
Moses D. & Co.	Lynchburg, Va.		876 Broadway
Moses L. & Co.	Louisville, Ky.		202 Church
Moses Bros.	Cleveland, O.		442 Broadway
Mosler Safe & Lock Co.	Cincinnati, O.	Moses Mosler	727 Broadway
Moulson Bros.	Sheffield, Eng.	Henry A. Tilly	126 Chambers
Moulton Mining Co	Butte City, Mont.	John T. Hamm	64 Broadway
Mt. Vernon Distillery Co.	Baltimore, Md.	Theodore Bomeisler	50 Beaver
Mt. Waldo Granite Works	Frankfort, Me.	John Peirce	7 Bookman
Mt. Washington Glass Co	New Bedford, Mass.	William H. Lum	46 Murray
Mower E. & Co.	Roxbury, Conn.	Ephraim Mower	82 Nassau
Muehling & Johnson	Philadelphia, Pa.	Smith & Scherr	119 Franklin
Muhr's H., Sons	Philadelphia, Pa.	Alfred M. Stevens	20 John
Muir Oil Co.	Warren, Pa.	Jedediah C. Paine	161 Front
Muir, Duckworth & Co.	London, Eng.	E. P. Mitchell & Co	64 Wall
Muir, Toward & Co.	Glasgow, Scotland	Alexander D. Napier & Co.	526 Broadway
Mulford H. K. & Co.	Philadelphia, Pa.	Henry K. Mulford	100 Maiden la.
Mumm G. H. & Co.	Reims, France	Frederick deBary & Co.	43 Warren
Muncie National Gas Land Improvement Co.	Muncie, Ind.	James M. Woods	45 Broadway
Muncie Rubber Co.	Muncie, Ind.	Charles T. Petchell	52 Broad
Munson Chas., Belting Co.	Chicago, Ill.	Emil Gatel	34 Dey
Munson & Co.	New Haven, Conn.	Morris T. Lynch	65 Murray
Muntz's Metal Co	Liverpool & Birmingham, Eng.	C. L. Peirson & Co.	16 Exchange pl.
Murdoch's Nephews	London, Eng.	William Miller	362 Broadway
Murphy & Brother	Springfield, O.		350 Broadway
Murphy & Stevenson	Belfast, Ireland	Anderson, Churchill & Co.	54 Leonard
Murphy, Grant & Co.	San Francisco, Cal.	Henry M. Murphy	86 Worth
Murphy, Hibben & Co	Indianapolis, Ind.	Henry S. Hart	836 Broadway
Mustin Thos. J., Knitting Co. (Ltd.)	Philadelphia, Pa.	Alexander Ross	335 Broadway
Muthmann Wm. & Son.	Elberfeld, Germany.	Hicks Brothers	42 White
Mutual Benefit Life Co	Hartford, Conn	Franklin Brown	229 Broadway
Mutual Benefit Life Ins. Co.	Newark, N. J.	L. Spencer Goble	137 Broadway
Mutual Oil Co.	Oil City, Pa.	Jedediah C. Paine	45 Broadway
Mutual Smelting & Mining Co.	Colville, Wyoming Ter.	Joseph S. Moore	30 Broad
Myers M. & Co.	Athens, Ga.		6 W. 3d
Myers Bros.	Terre Haute, Ind.		650 Broadway
Naef Brothers	Flawil, Switzerland.	Albert Deuble	59 Walker
Napheys George C. & Son	Philadelphia, Pa.	Charles W. Long	6 Harrison
Nashawannuck Mfg. Co.	E. Hampton, Mass.	Edward D. Candee	76 Worth
Nashua Iron & Steel Co.	Nashua, N. H	F. W. Jesup & Co	171 Broadway
Nashua Lock Co.	Nashua, N. H	C. F. Guyon & Co	99 Reade
Natchaug Silk Co	Willimantic, Conn	Henry G. Leask jr	540 Broadway
National Ammonia Co.	St. Louis, Mo.	Mallinckrodt Chemical Works	90 William
National Blank Book Co.	Holyoke, Mass.	Henry S. Dewey, Frank B. Towne	78 Duane
National Carpet Lining Co.	Boston, Mass	Walter Scott	60 White
National Cash Register Co.	Dayton, O.	John Crawford	1216 Broadway
National Chuck & Machine Co.	Mt. Vernon, N. Y.	John F. Lovejoy & Co	102 Chambers
National Despatch Fast Freight Line	Boston, Mass	Orson Bread	6 Counties sl.
National Enamel Co.	Pittsburgh, Pa.	White & Sheldon	184 Pearl
National India Rubber Co.	Bristol, R. I	Rubber Clothing Co.	487 Broadway
National Life Assn.	Hartford, Conn.	Alonzo S. Gear	13 Park row
National Life Ins. Co. of Vt.	Montpelier, Vt.	Joseph Wells	151 Broadway
National Line of Steamships	Liverpool, Eng.	Francis W. J. Hurst	27 State
National Mfg. Co.	Boston, Mass.	John Walsh	24 Cliff
National Mortgage & Debenture Co.	Boston, Mass.	Jones & Falls	137 Broadway
National Paper Bag Co.	Bridgeport, Pa.	Frank W. Felch	51 Leonard
National Pipe Bending Co.	New Haven, Conn.	Westinghouse, Church, Kerr & Co.	17 Cortlandt
National Shoe & Leather Exchange	Boston, Mass.	Eddy & Jones	320 Broadway
National Storage Co.	Jersey City, N. J.	Charles A. Sterling	55 Broadway
National Thread Co.	Mansfield Centre, Conn.	Isidor J. Dietz	107 Grand
National Tube Works Co	Boston, Mass.	S. A. Castle & Co.	50 Leonard
National Wire Mattress Co.	New Britain, Conn.	Edmund C. Converse	160 Broadway
Naulty John F. & Co.	Philadelphia, Pa	William L. Fielding	20 E. 14th
Naumkeag Steam Cotton Co.	Salem, Mass.	T. V. Kraft & Co.	4 Vesey
		John L. Bremer & Co.	62 Leonard

COMPILED WITH ACCURACY AND DESPATCH } **CLASSIFIED BUSINESS LISTS.** { THE TROW CITY DIRECTORY CO. 11 University Place.

Name.	Home Office.	Agent or Representative.	New York Office.
Naylor J. F. & Co	Baltimore, Md	Lawrence P. Naylor	79 Franklin
Naylor J. S. & Co	Wheeling, W. Va		101 Franklin
Naylor, Benzon & Co	London, Eng	Frederick L. Lehmann.. J. Mitchell Clark.... Ludwig Droier	45 Wall
Neal, Morse & Co	Boston, Mass	Samuel C. Ward	822 Broadway
Needham's D., Son	Chicago, Ill	Gaylord & Watson	278 Pearl
Neely William & Co	New Haven, Conn	Walter E. Malley	47 Leonard
Nelson Knitting Co	Rockford, Ill	Luceine J. Person	214 Church
Nelson Thomas & Sons	Edinburgh, Scotland	Gavin Houston	35 E. 17th
Nelson & Woolger	Huddersfield, Eng	M. B. Mellor	58 Worth
Nelson, Matter & Co	Grand Rapids, Mich	James W. Wheelock	22 E. 19th
Neptune Fire & Marine Ins. Co.	Boston, Mass	Wood & Kennedy	50 Pine
Ness James S. & Co	London, Eng	William H. Gillilan	58 Worth
Netherlands Am. Steam Navigation Co.	Rotterdam, Holland	G. H. Voorhoeve... William H. Vaudentoorn	89 Broadway 26 S. William
Netherlands Trading Soc	Amsterdam, Holland	Carter, Hawley & Co	54 Wall
Neuburger M. & C	Kreuznach, Germany	Abram Schoneman	1680 Third av.
Neuburger, Heiss & Co	San Francisco, Cal	Theodore F. Stumpf	118 Worth
Neuchatel Asphalte Co. (Ltd.)	London, Eng	Henry R. Bradbury	205 Broadway
Neumegen, Zacharias & Co	Weatherford, Tex	Samuel Neumegen	54 Walker
Neustadter Brothers	San Francisco, Cal. & Portland, Ore.	Henry Neustadter... Isaac Oppenheimer	23 Thomas
Nevada Bank of San Francisco	San Francisco, Cal	Edward C. Platt	62 Wall
Neverslip Horseshoe Co	Boston, Mass	Daniel K. Townsend	1586 Broadway
Nevins & Co	Boston, Mass	Henry C. Nevins	212 Church
New Bedford Copper Co	New Bedford, Mass	Stover & Tyler	47 South
New Bedford Line	Boston, Mass	Frank H. Forbes	Pier 39 E. R.
New Birmingham Iron & Land Co.	New Birmingham, Tex.	Henry H. Wibirt	47 Broadway
New Britain Knitting Co	New Britain, Conn	James Talcott	108 Franklin
New Coalisle Coal Co	Philadelphia, Pa	Richard H. Chipman	171 Broadway
N. E. Associated Press	Boston, Mass	Thomas H. O'Reilly	195 Broadway
N. E. Butt Co	Providence, R. I	C. F. Guyon & Co	99 Reade
N. E. Co-operative Boot & Shoe Co.	Lynn, Mass		279 Broadway
N. E. Despatch Co	Boston, Mass	Harry B. Pint	49 Broadway
N. E. Express Line	Boston, Mass	Joseph E. Martin	Grand Central depot
N. E. Furniture Co	Grand Rapids, Mich	Frederick R. Morse	16 E. 15th
N. E. Knitting Co	Winsted, Conn	Valentine & Flagler	90 Franklin
N. E. Loan & Trust Co	Des Moines, Iowa	Daniel O. Eshbaugh	160 Broadway
N. E. Mutual Accident Assn	Boston, Mass	James W. Stackpole	171 Broadway
N. E. Mutual Aid Soc	Boston, Mass	James W. Stackpole	171 Broadway
N. E. Mutual Life Ins. Co	Boston, Mass	Kenny & Ratcliffe	206 Broadway
N. E. Ship Building Co	Bath, Me	Guy C. Goss	18 Broadway
N. E. Steam Cooperage Co	Boston, Mass	Isaac B. Mills	19 Whitehall
N. E. Telephone & Telegraph Co.	Boston, Mass	John M. Cahill	18 Cortlandt
N. E. Transp. Co	New Haven, Conn	George B. Martin	1 Broadway
New Hampshire Fire Ins. Co	Manchester, N. H	T. J. Temple & Co	155 Broadway
New Haven Clock Co	New Haven, Conn	Frank J. Stevens	26 Murray
New Haven Web Co	New Haven, Conn	James B. Nay	72 Leonard
N. J. Car Spring & Rubber Co	Jersey City, N. J	Noyce C. Wooster... Edwin E. Stowell	10 Barclay 38 Church
N. J. Dry Dock & Transp. Co	Elizabethport, N. J	Thomas Drum	1 Broadway
N. J. Steam Laundry Co	Jersey City, N. J	John H. Cable	Pier 41 (old) N. R.
N. J. Thread Co	Newark, N. J	George S. Lings	448 Broome
N. J. & N. Y. R. R. Co	Hillsdale, N. J	Jacob D. Hasbrouck	Pier 20 (new) N. R.
New London & Northern R. R. Co.	New London, Conn	Wyatt M. Bassett	Pier 36 E. R.
New London & Norwich Line	Norwich, Conn		Pier 18 E. R.
New Mexico Mining Co	Santa Fe, N. Mex	Thomas Moore jr	1 Broadway
New Milford Hat Co	New Milford, Conn	John E. Bates	28 W. Houston
New Orleans Board of Underwriters	New Orleans, La	James Lawson	4 Hanover
N. Y. Locomotive Works	Rome, N. Y	Post, Martin & Co	34½ Pine
N. Y. Sand Blast Works	Philadelphia, Pa	Edmund H. Sentenne	132 Nassau
N. Y. Screw Top Works	Brooklyn, N. Y	Robert A. Colt	100 Chambers
N. Y. Silk Ribbon Mfg. Co	Paterson, N. J	Abegg, Daenlker & Co	92 Grand
N. Y. Slate Co	Bangor, Pa	Charles F. Brooks	71 Broad
N. Y. Star Spring Bed Bottom Mfg. Co.	Middletown, N. Y	William W. Harford	1652½ Broadway
N. Y. State Associated Press	Utica, N. Y	Stanley Schroff	195 Broadway
N. Y. Stone Contracting Co	Perth Amboy, N. J	John C. Goodridge jr	113 E. 25th
N. Y. Store	Madison, Wis	Solomon Michelbacher	116 Worth
N. Y. Store	Marshall, Mo	Joseph Mayer	372 Broadway
N. Y. Wood Fibre Co	Belvidere, N. J	Chapman & Meehan	140 Franklin
N. Y. Woven Hose Co	Trenton, N. J	S. Y. L'Hommedien & Co	65 Reade
N. Y. & Baltimore Transp. Line	Baltimore, Md	Harry C. Foster	Pier 7 N. R.
N. Y. & Montreal Transp. Co	Montreal, Can	N. R. Moe & Co	9 South
N. Y. & N. E. R. R. Co	Boston, Mass	Jabez A. Bostwick	36 Wall
N. Y., N. E. & Western Investment Co.	Chicago, Ill	Hugh Porter	11 Pine
N. Y., Phila. & Norfolk R. R. Co.	Philadelphia, Pa	Malcolm Townsend	Pier 28 (new) N. R.

SPECIAL ATTENTION PAID TO THIS CLASS OF WORK. } **BANKERS' & BROKERS' CIRCULARS DELIVERED** { THE TROW CITY DIRECTORY CO. 11 University Place.

NEW 369 **OCE**

Name.	Home Office.	Agents or Representatives.	New York Office.
N. Y., Providence & Boston R. R. Co.	Boston, Mass	Jacob W. Miller	Pier 36 (new) N. R.
Newark Fire Ins. Co	Newark, N. J.	Ogden & Katzenmayer	83 Liberty
Newark Paper Basket Co.	Newark, N. J.	Thomas W. Stephens	5 Beekman
Newark Specialty Co	Newark, N. J.	Morris J. Levy	650 Broadway
Newark & Rosendale Cement Co.	Newark, N. J.	Albert Delano	15 Cortlandt
Newberger & Strauss	Erie, Pa.		560 Broadway
Newburger A. & St. & Co.	Furth, Bavaria.	Anton Newburger	66 Warren
Newburger S. W. & Co	Louisville, Ky		21 White
Newburgh Hosochory	Newburgh, N. Y.	Chadwick Brothers	115 Worth
Newcomb, Endicott & Co.	Detroit, Mich.	Augustus B. Smith	338 Broadway
Newell Edgar A. & Co.	Ogdensburgh, N. Y.		111 William
Nowell Brothers Mfg. Co.	Springfield, Mass.	Albert W. Newell	25 Mercer
Newhall George M., Engineering Co. (Ltd.)	Philadelphia, Pa.	George M. Newhall	41 Wall
Nowhall's Sons & Co	San Francisco, Cal.	William D. McCarthy	32 Howard
Newman & Kalinbach	Nashville, Tenn.		705 Broadway
Newman & Levinson	San Francisco, Cal.	Louis N. Selig	9 Mercer
Newton George B. & Co	Philadelphia, Pa.	Thomas D. Uhler	1 Broadway
Newton Machine Co.	Boston, Mass.	Edwin Boose	29 Greene
Niagara Wood Paper Co	Niagara Falls, N. Y.	Henry M. Robertson & Co.	319 Broadway
Nicaragua Express Co.	Greytown, Nicaragua	Thomas W. Hubbard	45 Broadway
Nichol William & Co	Philadelphia, Pa.	Pitman & Black	115 Worth
Nickel Plate Line	Buffalo, N. Y.	Tunis B. Woolsey	363 Broadway
Nicolls W. J. & Co	Philadelphia, Pa.	John D. Henderson	35 Broadway
Nienaber, Son & Co	Cincinnati, O.		472 Broome
Niven & Co	Hoboken, N. J.	Frederick C. Marvin	5 E. 14th
No Name Hat Mfg. Co	Orange Valley, N. J.	Nathaniel B. Dey	546 Broadway
Nobles & Hoare	London, Eng.	Pomeroy & Fischer	30 Frankfort
Nonantum Worsted Co.	Boston, Mass.	Edwin Boose	29 Greene
Nonotuck Silk Co.	Florence, Mass.	Edwin W. Eaton	23 Greene
Norfolk & New Brunswick Hosiery Co.	New Brunswick, N. J.	John D. Ashwell	55 White
Norfolk & Western R. R. Co.	Roanoke, Va.	Thomas Pinckney	303 Broadway
Norris Carpet Mills	Philadelphia, Pa.	T. J. Keveney & Co.	329 Broadway
North & Judd Mfg. Co	New Britain, Conn.	Howard C. Noble	265 Broadway
N. Am. Construction Co	Pittsburgh, Pa.	Charles D. Doubleday	171 Broadway
N. Am. Ins. Co	Boston, Mass.	Ackerman, Deyo & Hilliard	41 Pine
N. Am. Mercantile Agency Co.	Meriden, Conn.	Emory J. Whitehead	206 Broadway
N. British & Mercantile Ins. Co.	London, Eng.	Samuel F. Blagden	54 William
N. Carolina Land & Immigration Bureau	Raleigh, N. C.	Nicholas W. Schenck	22 Dey
North German Lloyd S. S. Co.	Bremen, Germany.	Oelrichs & Co	2 Bowling gr.
North West Lumber Co	Mackinaw, Mich	Francis T. Witte Hardware Co.	106 Chambers
Northall-Laurie & Co	London, Eng.	Augustus A. Hayes, William J. Morton	11 Pine
Northampton Cutlery Co	Northampton, Mass.	Henry B. Titus jr	122 Chambers
Northern Assurance Co.	London, Eng.	George W. Babb jr	35 Pine
Northwestern Guaranty Loan Co.	Minneapolis, Minn.	Naher & Carpenter	170 Broadway
Northwestern Mining & Exchange Co.	Dagus Mines, Pa.	Williams & Peters	1 Broadway
Northwestern Mutual Life Ins. Co.	Milwaukee, Wis.	John L. D. Bristol	13 Park row
Northwestern Straw Works	Milwaukee, Wis.	Horace F. Clarke	581 Broadway
Norton Door-check & Spring Co.	Boston, Mass.	Horatio A. Berry	39 Dey
Norton Emery Wheel Co	Worcester, Mass	Estate of Frederick W. Gesswein.	39 John
Norton, Chapman & Co	Portland, Me.	Joseph S. Watson	19 Whitehall
Norton, Fessenden & Soule	Boston, Mass.	Robert B. Patterson	782 Broadway
Norwich Bleaching, Dyeing & Printing Co.	Norwich, Conn.	David L. Banning	96 Reade
Norwich Lock Mfg. Co.	Norwich, Conn.	Charles E. Whitney	96 Chambers
Norwich Union Fire Ins. Soc.	Norwich, Eng.	J. Montgomery Hare, James S. Carney	67 Wall, 417 Produce Ex.
Norwich & N. Y. Transp. Co	Norwich, Conn.	George W. Brady	Pier 40 (old) N. R.
Nova Scotia Central Railway Co.	Lunenburg, Nova Scotia.	Thomas G. Stearns	265 Broadway
Novello, Ewer & Co.	London, Eng.	Bernhard Bachur	21 E. 17th
Novelty Mfg. Co.	Waterbury, Conn.	Frank L. Brown	55 Walker
Noye John T., Mfg. Co	Buffalo, N. Y.	Albert Fisher	89 Liberty
Noyes William H. & Brother	Newburyport, Mass.	Samuel D. Thorp	8 Thomas
Nubian Iron Enamel Co	Chicago, Ill.	R. L. Cook & Co	77 Warren
Nugent R. & Brothers	St. Louis, Mo.	Frederick C. Lake	53 Leonard
Oakville Co.	Waterbury, Conn.	Charles F. Jones	48 Howard
Oberfelder I. & Co	Omaha, Neb		447 Broadway
Oberfelder & Co	Sidney, Neb	Simon Oberfelder	265 Canal
Oberndorf & Ullman	Selma, Ala		114 Franklin
O'Brien J. J. & Co	San Francisco, Cal.	John D. Desmond	460 Broome
Ocean Bathing Suit Co.	Brooklyn, N. Y.	D. Sachrach	402 Broadway
Ocean S. S. Co.	Savannah, Ga.	William H. Rhett, Richard L. Walker	317 Broadway, Pier 35 (new) N. R.

24

TYPEWRITING DONE BY THE TROW CITY DIRECTORY CO., 11 University Place.

Name.	Home Office.	Agent or Representative.	New York Office.
Oceanic Steam Navigation Co	Liverpool, Eng	J. Bruce Ismay	41 Broadway & Pier 45 (new) N. R.
O'Connor, Moffatt & Co	San Francisco, Cal	Jeremiah J. Callaghan & Michael B. Buckley	51 Leonard
O'Dwyer & Ward	Detroit, Mich	Loren W. True	822 Broadway
Oehm Charles & Son	Baltimore, Md		653 Broadway
Oehrle Brothers & Co	Philadelphia, Pa	Theodore Abbott	51 Leonard
Office Specialty Mfg. Co	Rochester, N. Y	Osmon J. Ramsdell	52 Reade
Oglesby, Tutwiller & Co	Lynchburg, Va	Curtis A. Darling	56 Worth
O'Hara Glass Co. (Ltd.)	Pittsburgh, Pa	George A. Lyon	16 Murray
Ohio Paper Co	Niles, Mich	Spaulding & Tewksbury	7 N. Y. & B'klyn bridge
Ohio & Mississippi R. R. Co	Cincinnati, O	Harry A. Wells	415 Broadway
Oil Well Supply Co. (Ltd.)	Pittsburgh, Pa	Edward H. Cole	82 Fulton
O'Keefe & Walsh	Nashville, Tenn		42 Lispenard
O'Keefe, Guide & Co	Vicksburg, Miss		670 Broadway
Olcott & De Friese	London, Eng	Emmet R. Olcott	35 Broadway
		Borden & Lovell	70 West & Pier 25 (old) N. R.
Old Colony Steamboat Co	Boston, Mass	Frank H. Forbes	Pier 39 E R.
Old Dominion Pickle Co	Baltimore, Md	Thomas Sturgis	45 & 1336 Broadway
Old Forge Coal Co. (Ltd.)	Pittston, Pa	Charles R. Vanname	1 Broadway
Old "76" Distilling Co	Newport, Ky	Loeb & Co	99 Warren
Oliver Iron & Steel Co	Pittsburgh. Pa	Henry B. Nowhall Co	106 Chambers
Olmstead F. C. & Co	Cedar Rapids, Iowa		650 Broadway
Olmsted Charles & Co	San Diego, Cal	Charles Olmsted	71 Park pl.
Olmsted Brothers	Saratoga Springs, N. Y.	John H. Howarth	744 Broadway
Olson S. E. & Co	Minneapolis, Minn	Curtis A. Darling	56 Worth
Ondows Paper Co	Greenwich, N. Y	George W. Hill	388 Pearl
Oneco Mfg. Co	New London, Conn	Frank Baldwin	33 South
Oneco Mfg. Co	Oneco, Conn	Abner S. Haight	119 Franklin
Oneida Community (Ltd.)	Kenwood, N. Y	Edwin Mackrille	6 Harrison
		Charles S. Joslyn	107 Grand
O'Neil & Dyas	Akron, O		42 Lispenard
O'Neill Richard & Co	Chicago, Ill	Joseph C. Chamberlain	358 Canal
Oneita Spring Co	Utica, N. Y	James M. Bell & Co	81 Broadway
Onslow Lumber Co	Jacksonville, N. C	Thomas A. McIntyre	212 Produce Ex.
Ontario Despatch	Oswego, N. Y	William M. Abbott	323 Broadway
Ontario Silver Mining Co	San Francisco, Cal	Lounsbery & Co	Mills bldg
Open Air Carpet Cleaning Co	Brooklyn, N. Y	Sheppard Knapp & Co	199 Sixth av.
Oppenheimer August, Co	St. Paul, Minn	Leon Drocker	520 Broadway
Oppenheimer D. & A	San Antonio, Tex		43 Leonard
Oppenheimer M. & Co	Pittsburgh, Pa		630 Broadway
Oppenheimer Frères	Paris, France	Laura Demaesener	109 Prince
Oppenheimer, Strauss & Co	Cincinnati, O		75 Leonard
Oregon Mfg. Co	Portland, Ore	Brown Brothers & Co	453 Broadway
Oregon Short Line & Utah Northern Railway Co.	Boston, Mass	James M. Ham	40 Wall
Orianna Mills	Philadelphia, Pa	T. J. Keveney & Co	390 Broadway
Orient Guano Mfg. Co	Orient, N. Y	Crenshaw & Wisner	16 Exchange pl.
Orient Ins. Co	Hartford, Conn	Ford, Rowell & Hone	33 Pine
Oriental Glass Co	Pittsburgh, Pa	Etienne Lebel	6 College pl.
Ormsby Land Co	Emmetsburg, Va	Edwin S. Ormsby & Henry E. Simmons	150 Nassau
Ornstein & Rice	Cincinnati, O		274 Church
Oro Flat Cons. Mining Co	Philadelphia, Pa		31 Broadway
Osborn, Solomon & Co	Dayton, O		610 Broadway
Osborne James & Co	Glasgow, Scotland	Osborne Brothers	444 Produce Ex.
Osborne & Cheeseman Co	Birmingham & Ansonia, Conn.	John B. Underwood	89 Barclay
		C. E. Conover Co	101 Franklin
Osborne & Klorboe	London, Eng	Frederick Klorboe & Peter Van der Willigen	444 Produce Ex.
Osceola Gravel Mining Co	Osceola, Nev	George W. Maynard	35 Broadway
Osgood Dredge Co	Albany, N. Y	Worth Osgood	3d Park row
Oskaloosa Water Co	Oskaloosa, Iowa	James Gamble	98 Wall
Ostby & Barton	Providence, R. I	Alfred Barton jr	176 Broadway
Oswego Indurated Fibre Co	Oswego, N. Y	Conlley & Hayes	173 Duane
Oswego Starch Factory	Oswego, N. Y	Edward Manning	146 Duane
Otard, Dupuy & Co	Cognac, France	Chas. F. Schmidt & Peters	24 Beaver
Otis Steel Co. (Ltd.)	Cleveland, O	William H. Fenner jr	580 Broadway
Ott-Brewer Co	Trenton, N. J	J. Quincy Walker	177 Broadway
Ottenheimer Brothers	Peoria, Ill		560 Broadway
Overstreet C. E. & Co	Louisville, Ky		67 Walker
Owen, Moore & Co	Portland, Me		106 Grand
Oxford Iron & Nail Co	Oxford, N. J	Theodore Sturges	52 Wall
		James S. Scranton	88 Washn.
Oxford Ochre Co	Sanda, Pa	Wallace Dunbar	94 Liberty
Pabst Brewing Co	Milwaukee, Wis	Charles F. Blancke	376 Washn.
Pacific Express Co	Omaha, Neb	U. S. Express Co	49 Broadway
Pacific Iron Works	San Francisco, Cal	Henry B. Murray	145 Broadway
Pacific Press Publishing Co	Oakland, Cal	Thomas A. Kilgore	43 Bond
Pacific Steam Navigation Co	Liverpool, Eng	J. Bruce Ismay	41 Broadway
Packers' & Provision Dealers' Ins. Co	Chicago, Ill	Alliance Ins. Assn	32 Nassau

THE CALIGRAPH WRITING MACHINE, HARTFORD, CONN.

Name.	Home Office.	Agent or Representative.	New York Office.
Page, Newell & Co	Boston, Mass	William H. Colbane	17 Broadway
Paige Car Wheel Co	Cleveland, O	Daniel M. Brady	115 Broadway
Pain James & Sons	London, Eng	Henry J. Pain	109 John
Pairpoint Mfg. Co	New Bedford, Mass.	William H. Tripp	20 Maiden la.
Paladini G. & Co	Milan, Italy	Ermenegildo Paladini	20 Greene
Palmer R. T., Co	New London, Conn.	Tyler R. Palmer	113 Worth
Palmer Brothers	New London, Conn.	Edward A. Palmer	86 Leonard
Palmer & Rey	San Francisco, Cal.	Sidney P. Palmer	154 Nassau
Palmetto Freight Line	Charleston, S. C.	David Carruthers & John D. Hashagen	261 Broadway
Pam Joseph & Co	Gablonz, Austria	Herman Aich	96 Spring
Panama Canal Co	Paris, France	Xavier Boyard	18 Broadway
Pancoast A. & Son	San Antonio, Tex		667 Broadway
Papenbrock & Co	Cincinnati, O		405 Broadway
Pardee A. & Co	Hazleton, Pa	William Mershon	1 Broadway
Pardee, Mills & Co	Peoria, Ill		18 Greene
Pardridge & Co	Chicago, Ill		40 W. B'way
Parfonry & Huvé Frs	Paris, France	Henry L. Bouché	657 Broadway
Paris Mfg. Co	S. Paris, Mo	Willard & McKee	31 Park pl.
Parisian Sauce Co	Paris, France	A. R. Gunn	100 Pearl
Park, Brother & Co. (Ltd.)	Pittsburgh, Pa	Charles X. Cordior	8 Cliff
Parke, Davis & Co	Detroit, Mich.	John Clay	60 Maiden la. & 218 Pearl
Parker Charles, Co	Meriden, Conn	Edward Bernard	97 Chambers
Parker & Co	Montreal, Can	George S. Lings	448 Broome
Parker Brothers	Meriden, Conn.	Edward Bernard	97 Chambers
Parsons Mfg. Co	Cohoes, N. Y	James E. Malone	260 Church
Partridge & Richardson	Philadelphia, Pa	Charles W. Sutcliffe	529 Broadway
Passaic Quarry Co	Avondale, N. J	Pierson & Renwick	19 Park pl.
Passaic Steam Laundry Co	Belleville, N. J	George F. Casebolt	877 Broadway
Passaic Woollen Co	Passaic, N. J	Jacob Basch	155 Duane
Patent Enamel Co. (Ltd.)	Birmingham, Eng	William P. Mitchell	7 Warren
Patent Shaft & Axletree Co. (Ltd.)	Wednesbury, Eng	Page, Newell & Co	17 Broadway
Paterson Iron Co	Paterson, N. J		64 College pl.
Patterson Alexander & Co	Glasgow, Scotland	Thomas K. Milliken	51 Leonard
Patterson William & Co	Liverpool, Eng	William S. Patterson	226 Produce Ex.
Payne W. G. & Co	Kingston, Pa	Meeker, Payne & Co	1 Broadway
Payson Mfg. Co	Chicago, Ill	Henry J. Drainard	97 Chambers
Payton & Kelley	Providence, R. I	H. Frank Payton	41 Maiden la.
Peabody Henry W. & Co	Boston, Mass	Henry C. Piper	38 New
Pearce F. T. & Co	Providence, R. I	George B. Angell	176 Broadway
Pears A. & F	London, Eng	Gaunt & Janvier	505 Canal
Pease J. F., Furnace Co	Syracuse, N. Y	Earl B. Chace & Co	208 Water
Pechoux & Benard	Paris, France	Henry L. Bouché	857 Broadway
Peck A. G. & Co	Cohoes, N. Y	C. F. Gayon & Co	96 Reade
Peck E. & Co	Cincinnati, O		102 Franklin
Peckham Mfg. Co	Coventry Centre, R. I.	James P. Streeter / Abner S. Haight	401 Broadway / 119 Franklin
Peerless Lead Glass Works	Pittsburgh, Pa	John B. Gordon & Harry M. Felker	39 Barclay
Peerless Plush Mfg. Co	Paterson, N. J	Jaeger & Timme	413 Broome
Pelpher Line	Harrisburg, Pa	John H. Starin	Pier 19 N. R.
Peirce & Bushnell Mfg. Co	New Bedford, Mass	Thomas P. Watkins	80 Gt. Jones
Penland S. M. & Co	Galveston, Tex	William R. Schwalbe	21 Park row
Penn Bridge Co	Beaver Falls, Pa	James W. Shipman	154 Nassau
Penn Chemical Works	Philadelphia, Pa	John H. Dusinberre	77 Warren
Penn G., Sons & Co	Danville, Va	Lichtenstein Brothers & Co	603 First av
Penn Gas Coal Co	Philadelphia, Pa	M. Briggs & Co	180 Water
Penn Hardware Co	Reading, Pa	Harmon & Dixon	115 Chambers
Penn Look Works	Philadelphia, Pa	William H. Jacobus	90 Chambers
Penn Mutual Life Ins. Co	Philadelphia, Pa	Ezra De Forest	13 Park row
Pennsylvania Fire Ins. Co	Philadelphia, Pa	Franc & Shade	206 Broadway
Pennsylvania Iron Works	Philadelphia, Pa	Martin Maloney	115 Broadway
Pennsylvania Life Ins. Co	Philadelphia, Pa	John A. Goulden	229 Broadway
Pennsylvania Oil Co. (Ltd.)	Philadelphia, Pa	Lewis J. Levick	7 Burling sl.
Pennsylvania Salt Mfg. Co	Philadelphia, Pa	Edward L. Embree	140 Nassau
Pennsylvania Steel Co	Philadelphia, Pa	Stephen W. Baldwin	2 Wall
Pennsylvania Woollen Co. (Ltd.)	Philadelphia, Pa	Roger N. Arms	21 White
People's Bridgeport & N. Y. Steamboat Line	Bridgeport, Conn	Charles L. Sneden	Pier 24 E. R.
People's Fire Ins. Co	Manchester, N. H	John M. Whiton	39 Pine
People's Ins. Co	Pittsburgh, Pa	Irving & Hinds	161 Broadway
People's Line Steamers	Jacksonville, Fla	John D. Hashagen	261 Broadway
People's Steamboat Co	Bridgeport, Conn	Charles L. Sneden	Pier 24 E. R.
Pepper James E. & Co	Lexington, Ky	Hart & Felbel	19 Broadway
Perfection Oil Tank Co	Syracuse, N. Y	Bernard F. J. Kiernan	180 Maiden la.
Pernod Fils	Couvet, Switzerland.	George S. Nicholas	43 Beaver
Petaluma Fruit Packing Co	San Francisco, Cal.	Henry M. Anthony	100 Reade
Pettinato Fratelli & Co	Catania, Italy	Michelangelo Pettinato	24 State
Pettingill & Co	Boston, Mass	Henry H. Douglass	71 Tribune bldg
Pettis & Co	Indianapolis, Ind	Alexander McIsaac	836 Broadway
Pettit H. L., Malting Co	Kenosha, Wis	Louis G. Bohmrich	19 Whitehall
Pfaelzer, Danbe & Cohn	Chicago, Ill		240 Church
Pfaff & Co	Paris, France	George Grill	96 Spring
Phelps & Bartholomew Co	Ansonia, Conn	F. Kroeber Clock Co	360 Broadway
Phila. Novelty Mfg. Co	Philadelphia, Pa	Cook, Valentine & Co	32 Howard
Phila. Steam Line	Philadelphia, Pa	Roberts & King	23 South

SPECIAL ATTENTION PAID TO THIS CLASS OF WORK. } BANKERS' & BROKERS' CIRCULARS DELIVERED { THE TROW CITY DIRECTORY CO. 11 University Place.

PHI 372 PRE

Name.	Home Office.	Agent or Representative.	New York Office.
Phila. & Reading Coal & Iron Co.	Philadelphia, Pa.	Frank M. Kelley	1 Broadway
Philipp J. & Co	Bradford, Eng.	John W. Stewart	487 Broome
Philips & Kunhardt	Lawrence, Mass.	F. Stanhope Philips	56 Worth
Phillips Charles H., Chemical Co.	Glenbrook, Conn.		77 Pine & 229 E. 24th
Phillips, Politzer & Co	London, Eng.	Sigmund Politzer	96 Spring
Phipps & Train	Newton Upper Falls, Mass.	William Ryle & Co.	54 Howard
Phœnix Assurance Co. of London	London, Eng.	Alexander D. Irving	67 Wall
Phœnix Bridge Co	Philadelphia, Pa.	Seymour P. Thomas	49 William
Phœnix Candle Co	Syracuse, N. Y.	Robert Lefferts	306 Fourth av.
Phœnix Glass Co	Pittsburgh, Pa.	Alexander H. Patterson	729 Broadway
		Frank J. Duffner	258 Broadway
Phœnix Horse Shoe Co	Poughkeepsie, N. Y.	Charles Miller	20 Reade
Phœnix Ins. Co	Hartford, Conn.	John R. McCoy	165 Broadway
Phœnix Iron Co	Philadelphia, Pa.	Milliken Brothers	55 Liberty
Phœnix Iron Works Co	Meadville, Pa.	John Dick	16 Dey
Phœnix Mutual Life Ins. Co.	Hartford, Conn.	Handford Liudsley	189 Broadway
Phœnix Packing & Rubber Co.	Tuckahoe, N. Y.	William B. Brook & Co.	47 Murray
Phœnix Paper Co	Pittsburgh, Pa.	John J. Bennett	258 Broadway
Picard P. & Co	Bordeaux, France.	Hartman, Goldsmith & Co.	45 Warren
Pickering Governor Co	Portland, Conn.	Augustus P. McGraw	10 Dey
Piedmont Lumber, Ranch & Mining Co.	Morganton, N. C.	John L. Martin	13 Park row
Piedmont & Cumberland Railway Co.	Baltimore, Md.	Stephen B. Elkins	1 Broadway
Pierce, Butler & Pierce Mfg. Co.	Syracuse, N. Y.	Samuel T. Williams	60 Barclay
Pilling & Madeley	Philadelphia, Pa.	Shreve & Adams	66 Leonard
Pillow, Hersey & Co	Montreal, Can.	Atkins & Durbrow	70 Wall
Pim Brothers & Co	Dublin, Ireland.	Ferguson, Weller & Co	103 Franklin
Pim, Forwood & Co	Liverpool, Eng.	Harold S. Forwood	24 State
Pine Charles S. & Co	Providence, R. I.	George A. Schoefer	196 Broadway
Pirie Alexander & Sons (Ltd.)	Aberdeen, Scotland.	John Hunter	23 Rose
Pitt & Scott	London, Eng.	John Matthews	35 Broadway
Pittsburgh Brass Co	Pittsburgh, Pa.		39 Barclay
Pittsburgh Bridge Co	Pittsburgh, Pa.	John C. Turk	31 Broadway
Pittsburgh Locomotive Works.	Pittsburgh, Pa.	Frank G. Dickson	115 Broadway
Pittsburgh Tube Co	Pittsburgh, Pa.	William P. Loughry	61 John
Pittsburgh, Fort Wayne & Chicago Railway	Pittsburgh, Pa.	Louis H. Meyer	31 Nassau
Pixley H. D. & Son	Utica, N. Y.	Henry S. Hart	333 Broadway
Plainville Stock Co	Plainville, Mass.	Caselus W. Seymour	176 Broadway
Plout & Isaac	Cincinnati, O		38 Thomas
Plant, Sibley & Co	Milwaukee, Wis.		75 Leonard
Plimpton Mfg. Co	Hartford, Conn.	Fairfax Brothers	312 Broadway
Plimpton, Fisk & Co	Boston, Mass.	George R. Fisk	330 Broadway
Plumb & Lewis Mfg. Co.	Grand Rapids, Mich.	Thomas W. Williams	108 Chambers
Plymouth Rock Pants Co	Boston, Mass.	William A. Brooks	279 Broadway
Plymouth Woollen Co	Plymouth, Mass.	Edwin C. Holton	771 Broadway
Pollack M. & Brother	Little Rock, Ark.		670 Broadway
Pollak Co	Montgomery, Ala.	George S. Virden	21 Wooster
Pollak & Simons	Milwaukee, Wis.		75 Leonard
Pollock J. & Co	Mobile, Ala.		48 Leonard
Pollock & Murphy	Quincy, Ill.		378 Broadway
Pommery & Greno	Reims, France	Charles Graef	32 Beaver
Pond Machine Tool Co	Plainfield, N. J.	Charles A. Moore	111 Liberty
Pond, West & Simons	Portchester, N. Y.	Marshall O. West	99 Franklin
Pope Mfg. Co	Boston, Mass.	Elliott Mason	12 Warren
Port Royal & Augusta Railway Co.	Augusta, Ga.	Charles B. Crowell	254 Broadway
Portage Iron Co. (Ltd.)	Duncansville, Pa.	A. R. Whitney & Co	17 Broadway
Portchester Transp. Co	Portchester, N. Y.	Edward F. Studwell	Pier 32 (new) E. R.
Porter Mfg. Co	Syracuse, N. Y.	Pierce & Thomas	42 Cortlandt
Porter & Coates	Philadelphia, Pa.	Henry Harrison	16 Astor pl.
Portheim & Co	Manchester, Eng.	Walter C. Portheim	55 White
Posen Edward & Co	Offenbach, Germany	Ludwig Maynz	523 Broadway
Potomac Paper Co	Cumberland, Md.	Charles Whedon	182 Nassau
Potter Edmund & Co	Manchester, Eng.	George McConnel	319 Broadway
Potter Lovell Co	Boston, Mass.	Edwin H. Corey	10 Wall
Potter & Snell	Deep River, Conn.	C. E. Conover Co.	101 Franklin
Potter & Wrightington	Boston, Mass.	William L. C. Potter	21 Harrison
Potter's Thomas, Sons & Co.	Philadelphia, Pa.	Henry A. Potter	35 Thomas
Pottstown Iron Co	Pottstown, Pa.	Milliken Brothers	55 Liberty
Poughkeepsie Iron Co	Poughkeepsie, N. Y.	Henri M. Braem	69 Wall
Powell Brothers	Philadelphia, Pa.	William Powell	18 Thomas
Powers Dry Goods Co	St. Paul, Minn.		101 Franklin
Powers Paper Co	Holyoke, Mass.	Joseph L. St. John	62 Duane
Prager Brothers	Portland, Ore.	William Prager	612 Broadway
Prang Educational Co	Boston, Mass.	Charles I. Webster	16 Astor pl.
Prang L. & Co	Boston, Mass.	Harry E. Brown	16 Astor pl.
Pranker Mfg. Co	Saugus, Mass.	Wilson K. Farrington	47 Leonard
Pratt, Hurst & Co	Nottingham, Eng.	John E. McCrea	318 Church
Pratt, Simmons & Co	St. Louis, Mo.		579 Broadway
Pray John H., Sons & Co.	Boston, Mass	Charles T. Hoogland & William L. Lundy	113 Worth
Press News Assn	San Francisco, Cal.	James B. Townsend	11 Park row

MERCHANTS EXCHANGE NAT. BANK OF THE CITY OF N. Y.
SOLICITS YOUR ACCOUNT. 257 Broadway.
PHINEAS C. LOUNSBURY, President.   ALLEN S. APGAR, Cashier.

PRE   373   REI

Name.	Home Office.	Agent or Representative.	New York Office.
Prevost & Cie..............	Paris, France......	Comptoirs Commerciaux Français	46 University pl.
Price Baking Powder Co...	Chicago, Ill.....	John Hollingsworth......	158 W. B'way
Price, Sherman & Co.....	Philadelphia, Pa...	George D. Colston......	32 Bond
Price, Welch & Co........	Baltimore, Md.....	Ernest M. Price.........	16 Exchange pl.
Priestley A. & Co........	Camden, N. J.....	Sullivan, Vail & Co.....	320 Broadway
Priestley B. & Co........	Bradford, Eng.....	W. G. Hitchcock & Co...	453 Broome
Prince Mfg. Co...........	Bowmans, Pa.....	David Prince...........	71 Maiden la.
Proby Walter & Co.......	Chicago, Ill.....	John A. Donahue.......	335 Broadway
Procter & Gamble........	Cincinnati, O.....	Henry M. Anthony.....	100 Reade
Providence Washington Ins. Co.	Providence, R. I...	Scott, Alexander & Talbot (fire)	45 William
		William H. McGee (marine).	30 Beaver
		George Lethbridge (inland marine).	2 Stone
Provident Chemical Works..	St. Louis, Mo.....	Franklin P. Gordon.....	140 Nassau
Provident Life & Trust Co..	Philadelphia, Pa...	Murray, Lobar & Kennard.	400 Broadway
Public Opinion Co........	Washington, D. C.	Albert H. Lewis........	141 Nassau
Puffer A. D. & Sons Mfg. Co.	Boston, Mass.....	Clark & Lyons..........	41 Centre
Pulaski F. & Co..........	Philadelphia, Pa...		589 Broadway
Pulaski M. H. & Co.......	St. Gall, Switzerland	Charles W. Israel.......	259 Church
Pulaski, Tillebaum & Co...	Decatur, Ala.....		549 Broadway
Pullar Robert & Sons......	Manchester, Eng...	James W. Mather.......	50 Worth
Pulverman Galvanic Co....	Cincinnati, O.....	William F. E. Burkhardt..	1104 Broadway
Purcell, Ladd & Co.......	Richmond, Va.....	John D. Titsworth......	71 William
Pursch & Wiener.........	San Francisco, Cal.	Samuel Pursch.........	119 Spring
Pusey & Jones Co.........	Wilmington, Del...	William B. Hoyt........	72 South
Putnam Carpet Co........	Philadelphia, Pa...	T. J. Kenney & Co......	320 Broadway
Putnam Machine Co.......	Fitchburg, Mass...	Prentiss Tool & Supply Co.	115 Liberty
Quaker City Dye Works....	Philadelphia, Pa...	R. F. Smith............	51 Leonard
Quaker Mill Co...........	Ravenna, O.......	Kirk D. Newell.........	5 Harrison
Quayle T. & Co...........	Providence, R. I...	Edward L. Bartlett.....	33 Maiden la.
Quebec S. S. Co...........	Quebec, Can......	A. Emilius Outerbridge & Co.	51 Broadway & Pier 47 (new) N. R.
Queen City Printing Ink Co.	Cincinnati, O.....	John Gresson..........	194 William
Queen Ins. Co............	Liverpool, Eng....	James A. Macdonald...	60 Wall
Queen & Crescent Route...	Cincinnati, O.....	William S. St. George...	310 Broadway
Quenardel & Co...........	Paris, France.....	Henry L. Bouché.......	887 Broadway
Querns Thomas D. & Co...	Philadelphia, Pa...	C. Wesley Wootton.....	99 Franklin
Quinn J. P., Dry Goods Co..	Little Rock, Ark...		601 Broadway
Raab R. M. & Brother.....	Burlington, Iowa...		707 Broadway
Raas E. & Co.............	San Francisco, Cal.	Theodore F. Stumpf....	115 Worth
Rachmann Brothers.......	Haida, Bohemia...	Henry W. Mattoni.....	59 Park pl.
Racine Wagon & Carriage Co.	Racine, Wis......	Elliot J. Smith.........	153 Spring
Railway Lighting & Heating Co	Philadelphia, Pa..	Coolbaugh, McMunn & Pomeroy	45 Broadway
Railway Register Mfg. Co.	Buffalo, N. Y.....	Edward Beadle........	1198 Broadway
Ramapo Wheel & Foundry Co.	Ramapo, N. Y.....	William W. Snow......	115 Broadway
Rand, McNally & Co......	Chicago, Ill.....	Caleb S. Hammond....	323 Broadway
Randolph Paper Box Co...	Richmond, Va.....	Theodore Willich & Co..	132 William
Raney & Bergen..........	Elmira, N. Y.....	Henry R. Adams.......	145 Broadway
Ranniger J. L. & Sons.....	Chemnitz, Germany.	Sohmayr & Delias......	115 Worth
Ransom C. S. & Co.......	Cleveland, O.....	C. S. Ransom..........	10 W. 23th
Rapid Transit Railway Co. of Mo.	St. Louis, Mo....	Samuel F. Scott.......	45 Wall
Raritan Woollen Mills.....	Raritan, N. J.....	David L. Einstein......	14 White
Rascher Map Publishing Co.	Chicago, Ill.....	William L. Niehorster..	30 Nassau
Rau Charles M. & Co......	Cincinnati, O.....		260 Church
Rauh Joseph & Co........	Pittsburg, Pa.....		512 Broadway
Rauh Brothers & Co.......	Pittsburgh, Pa....		512 Broadway
Ray Copper Co............	Riverside, Ariz....	Louis Zockendorf......	84 Thomas
Ray & Taylor Mfg. Co.....	Springfield, Mass..	Studdard Collar Co.....	52 Howard
Ray's Woollen Co.........	Franklin, Mass....	William L. Nichols.....	49 Worth
Read Carpet Co...........	Bridgeport, Conn..	David M. Read........	108 Worth
Read D. M., Co...........	Bridgeport, Conn..	David M. Read........	108 Worth
Read's Collection & Mercantile Agency	Boston, Mass.....	Consolidated Mercantile Agency	401 Broadway
Reading Fire Ins. Co......	Reading, Pa......	Harrold Herrick........	44 Pine
Reading Foundry Co. (Ltd.).	Reading, Pa......	John Fox..............	160 Broadway
Reading Hardware Co.....	Reading, Pa......	Naylor & Felter........	97 Chambers
Reading Iron Works.......	Philadelphia, Pa...	Pancoast & Rogers.....	28 Platt
Reakirt, Brother & Co.....	Philadelphia, Pa...	William R. McClellan...	76 Broad
Red Cross Line............	Liverpool, Eng....	Bowring & Archibald, Shipton Green.	16 Broadway 112 Pearl
Red Star Line.............	Antwerp, Belgium.	Peter Wright & Sons...	6 Bowling gr.
Redding Ink Co...........	Newark, N. J.....	Frank W. Gates........	39 Dey
Redfern John & Sons......	London, Eng. & Paris, France	Ernest A. Redfern......	210 Fifth av.
Reed & Barton............	Taunton, Mass....	Calvin P. Harris........	37 Union sq. W.
Reed & Peebles...........	Portsmouth, O....		354 Broadway
Reedy J. W., Elevator Mfg. Co.	Chicago, Ill.....	William H. Skerritt.....	31 Tenth av.
Regenstein J. & Co........	Atlanta, Ga......	Isaac C. Biesenthal.....	555 Broadway
Regester J. & Son.........	Baltimore, Md....	Charles Hoffman jr.....	55 Maiden la.
Regnier Jules & Co........	Dijon, France.....	Charles F. Schmidt & Peters	24 Beaver
Reich & Geiger...........	Albany, Ga.......		474 Broadway

SNOW, CHURCH & CO.,
265 & 267 BROADWAY.

COLLECTIONS IN ALL PARTS OF THE WORLD.
T. C. Campbell and Arthur Murphy, Counsel.
TELEPHONE, 788 MURRAY.

REI 374 ROC

Name.	Home Office.	Agent or Representative.	New York Office.
Reichenbach M. L. & Co	St. Gall, Switzerland	Isaac B. Moland	207 Church
Reid Andrew & Co	Dunfermline, Scotland	James Mawha	89 Franklin
Reifsnyder, Hibberd & Rutledge	Philadelphia, Pa	Allen Hibberd	81 White
Rein & Co	Malaga, Spain	Colbert & Tayler	89 Broadway
Reiss Brothers & Co	San Francisco, Cal.	Theodore F. Stumpf	115 Worth
Reliance Ins. Co	Philadelphia, Pa.	Charles M. Peck & Co	88 Pine
Remington Paper Co	Watertown, N.Y.	George P. Folts	41 Park row
Remington Brothers	Pittsburgh, Pa	Robert R. Remington	154 Nassau
Renauno Chemical Co	Wilmington, Del.	George F. Hamlin	239 Broadway
Renzicola V. S. & File	Messina, Italy	White & Sheldon	184 Pearl
Reuhl Moulding Mfg. Co	Cincinnati, O.	Julius Hertel	310 Broadway
Revere Copper Co	Boston, Mass.	Edward S. Atwood	242 South
Revere Rubber Co	Boston, Mass.	William Hillman	54 Reade
Reversible Collar Co	Boston, Mass.	Standard Collar Co	52 Howard
Rex Alfred C. & Co	Philadelphia, Pa.	G. L. Mix & Co.	82 Chambers
Reynolds Jewelry Co	Providence, R. I	Edward A. Follett	176 Broadway
Rheinstein F. & Co	Wilmington, N. C.		45 White
Rhode Island Horse Shoe Co.	Providence, R. I	Frank Durrie	80 Chambers
Rhode Island Tool Co	Providence, R. I	John F. Lovejoy	102 Chambers
Rice A. L. & Co	Wheeling, W. Va	Samuel M. Rice	621 Broadway
Rice J. H. & Friedman Co	Milwaukee, Wis.		102 Franklin
Rice, Born & Co	New Orleans, La	William B. Fox & Brother	97 Chambers
Rice, Friedman & Markwell	Milwaukee, Wis.		45 Leonard
Rice, Stix & Co	St. Louis, Mo.	Henry Rice	62 Franklin
Rich A. W. & Co	Milwaukee, Wis.		49 Mercer
Rich M. & Brother	Atlanta, Ga.		224 Church
Richards H. M. & Co	Boston, Mass.	Burton F. Reed	401 Broadway
Richards J	Aberdeen, Scotland	Ferguson, Weller & Co.	103 Franklin
Richards & Hartley Glass Co.	Tarentum, Pa.	Daniel R. Marshall	24 Park pl.
Richardson Drug Co	Omaha, Neb.	John A. Morton	13 Gold
Richardson Silk Co	Chicago, Ill.	Charles H. Keith	458 Broadway
Richardson H. M. & Co	Boston, Mass.	Willard & McKee	21 Park pl.
Richardson J. C. & Co	Jackson, Mich	Loren W. True	623 Broadway
Richardson J. N., Sons & Owden (Ltd.)	Belfast, Ireland	Samuel W. Richardson	84 Franklin
Richardson, Roberts, Byrne & Co.	St. Joseph, Mo.	William W. Marston	51 Leonard
Richardsons & Niven	Belfast & Lisburn, Ireland	Edward McConnell & Co.	121 Franklin
Richmond Cedar Works (Ltd.)	Richmond, Va	William C. Barker	86 Chambers
Richmond Granite Co	Richmond, Va	Hyman P. Dinawanger	140 Nassau
Richmond Paper Mfg. Co	Richmond, Va	Nathaniel H. Furness	123 Broadway
Richmond Standard Spike Co.	Richmond, Va	William H. Price	10 Wall
Richmond & Co	Providence, R. I.	Norman L. Richmond	175 Broadway
Richter F. Ad. & Co	Rudolstadt-Thuringia, Germany	Charles B. Druguiln	310 Broadway
Richter & Doetschmann	Tenafly, N. J.	E. P. Cooley	185 Duane
Rider, Wallis, Co	Dubuque, Iowa.	Joseph Carr	51 Leonard
Ridgway Refrigerator Mfg. Co. (Ltd.)	Philadelphia, Pa.		108 Church
Riegel John L. & Son	Hexelsville, N. J.	William B. Harwood	11 Murray
Riegelman M. & Co	Des Moines, Iowa.		601 Broadway
Riehle Brothers	Philadelphia, Pa.	William R. Cock	98 Liberty
Rieke C. H. & Sons	Paducah, Ky.		115 Worth
Rieusch Am Ende & Co	Manchester, Eng.	George McConnel	319 Broadway
Ries & Co	Chicago, Ill.		80 Franklin
Riley William D. & Co	Philadelphia, Pa.	William B. Riley	52 Leonard
Rindskopf, Stern, Lauer & Co.	Cincinnati, O.		21 White
Rio Grande Irrigation & Colonization Co.	Boston, Mass.	Smith & Parsons	45 Broadway
Rio Grande & Western Construction Co.	Denver, Colo.	Charles W. Drake	32 Nassau
Ripley & Co	Pittsburgh, Pa.	Etienne Lebel	6 College pl.
Ripley, Howland Mfg. Co	Boston, Mass.	Herbert L. Draper	17 Maiden la.
Risdon Iron Works	San Francisco, Cal.	Charles W. Whitney	63 Fulton
Ritchie R. J. & R., Co	Philadelphia, Pa	Robert J. Ritchie	110 Worth
Rittenhouse Mfg. Co	Passaic, N. J.	Edmund Le H. Gardiner	56 Worth
Ritter Philip, Conserve Co.	Philadelphia, Pa	Philip J. Ritter	346 Washn.
Riverside Iron Works	Wheeling, W. Va	A. R. Whitney & Co	17 Broadway
Roaring Spring Blank Book Co.	Roaring Spring, Pa.	George W. Cross	65 Duane
Roberts A. & P. & Co	Philadelphia, Pa.	Theodore Thomas / Frank L. Froment	85 Broadway / 112 John
Robin Jules & Co	Cognac, France.	E. Lamontagne & Sons	58 Beaver
Robinson J. T., Notion Co.	Omaha, Neb.		63 Leonard
Robinson J. M. & Co	Louisville, Ky		50 Worth
Robinson Brothers	Philadelphia, Pa.	Thomas Robb	27 Beckman
Robinson, Strauss & Co	St. Paul, Minn.	Alanson White jr	628 Broadway
Robinson, Zimmerman & Co.	Terre Haute, Ind.		34 Thomas
Robiteck H. & Co	Vienna, Austria.	Jason M. Bowen	466 Broadway
Robson, Block & Co	Memphis, Tenn.	Curtis A. Darling	56 Worth
Rochester German Fire Ins. Co.	Rochester, N. Y	Ogden & Katzenmayer	83 Liberty
Rochester Steel Mat Co	Rochester, N. Y	Henry Pattberg	74 Barclay
Rochester Tumbler Co	Pittsburgh, Pa.	John E. Gordon & Harry M. Felker	39 Barclay
Rock Mfg. Co	Rockville, Conn.	Benjamin R. Jacobs	86 Worth

WATER METERS, GAS ENGINES, | **NATIONAL METER CO.**
FOR PUMPING AND POWER. | 252 Broadway, N. Y.

ROO   375   RYL

Name.	Home Office.	Agent or Representative.	New York Office.
Rockford Watch Co.	Rockford, Ill.	Junius P. Drake	11 Maiden la.
Rodeffer Brothers	Bellaire, O.	Etienne Lobel	6 College pl.
Rodel & Fils Frères	Bordeaux, France	E. Lamontagne & Sons	53 Beaver
Rodgers Joseph & Sons (Ltd.)	Sheffield, Eng.	T. & W. Cletworthy	32 Chambers
Roe George & Co.	Dublin, Ireland	George S. Nichols	43 Beaver
Roebling's John A., Sons Co.	Trenton, N. J.	Henry L. Shippy	117 Liberty
Roederer Theophile & Co.	Reims, France	Ambrose I. Harrison	3 S. William
Rogers Silver Plate Co.	Danbury, Conn.	T. C. Webster	62 Reade
Rogers William, Mfg. Co.	Hartford, Conn.	Virgil P. Humason	80 Chambers
Rogers William & Son	Hartford, Conn.	Virgil P. Humason	80 Chambers
Rogers C. B. & Co.	Norwich, Conn.	Frederick E. Woodward	109 Liberty
Rogers H. B. & Co.	New Canaan, Conn.	Louis Hass	685 Broadway
Rogers & Brother	Waterbury, Conn.	George C. White	16 Cortlandt
Rollins John G. & Co. (Ltd.)	London, Eng.	John G. Rollins	4 Stone
Rollman & Sons	Cincinnati, O.	—	598 Broadway
Romer & Co.	Newark, N. J.	John H. Graham & Co.	113 Chambers
Ronemous & Co.	Baltimore, Md.	Robert Hartmann	6 Harrison
Ronehelm William & Brothers	Cincinnati, O.	—	21 White
Roos Brothers	San Francisco, Cal.	Adolph Roos	686 Broadway
Root & Co.	Fort Wayne, Ind.	Lewis B. Root	58 Worth
Root & McBride Brothers	Cleveland, O.	James J. Morris	51 Leonard
Roots P. H. & F. M., Co	Connersville, Ind.	Sylvanus S. Townsend	22 Cortlandt
Rosa L. J. & Co. (Ltd.)	San Gabriel, Cal.	Edward M. Marum	396 G'wich
Rose Brothers & Hartman	Lancaster, Pa.	John B. Applegate	82 Franklin
Rosenau, Crutchfield & Co.	Chattanooga, Tenn.	—	63 Leonard
Rosenbaum C. & Son	Fayette, Mo.	—	11 E. 4th
Rosenbaum L. & Sons.	Elmira, N. Y.	—	651 Broadway
Rosenbaum & Brother	Mt. Vernon, Mo.	—	512 Broadway
Rosenbaum & Co	Richmond, Va.	Morton Rosenbaum	117 Duane
Rosenbaum & Co	San Francisco, Cal.	Sigmund D. Rosenbaum	217 S. 5th av.
Rosenbaum & Speyer	Kalamazoo, Mich.	—	276 Broadway
Rosenberg & Blum	Rochester, N. Y.	Jacob S. Marks	695 Broadway
Rosenblatt & Brothers	Cleveland, O.	—	43 Leonard
Rosenburg, Happ & Siegel	Baltimore, Md.	Simon L. Frank	22 Spruce
Rosenbush L. & Co.	Columbus, Ind.	—	705 Broadway
Rosenfeld E. & Co.	Baltimore, Md.	Charles Schonfarber	698 Broadway
Rosenfeld, Smith Co.	Portland, Ore.	Henry Rosenfeld	117 Duane
Rosenfeld's John, Sons	San Francisco, Cal.	George Laing	39 Broadway
Rosenfeld Monroe & Co.	Detroit, Mich.	—	491 Broadway
Rosenfield J. & Co.	Galveston, Tex.	Max Katz	31 Thomas
Rosengarten & Sons	Philadelphia, Pa.	Charles H. Rutherford	12 Gold
Rosenheim L., Brother & Co.	Nashville, Tenn.	David Lyon	90 Walker
Rosenheim, Levis & Co.	St. Louis, Mo.	Abraham H. Rosenheim	96 Spring
Rosenshine M. & Brother	San Francisco, Cal.	Matthias Rosenshine	136 Water
Rosenthal Brothers	New Orleans, La.	—	21 White
Rosenwald & Weil	Chicago, Ill.	—	686 Broadway
Ross Heel Co	S. Easton, Mass.	Jesse Smith	221 Centre
Ross, Turner & Co.	Boston, Mass.	Percy H. Brundage	113 Chambers
Rosskam, Gemley & Co	Philadelphia, Pa.	Joseph Goetz	396 G'wich
Roth M. & Co.	Manayunk, Pa	Pitman & Black	113 Worth
Roth & Glick.	Cleveland, O.	—	21 Walker
Rothschild E. & Brothers	Chicago, Ill.	—	43 Leonard
Rothschild, Hays & Co.	Rochester, N. Y.	—	7 Bond
Rottmann, Strome & Co.	London, Eng.	William H. S. Lloyd	19 E. 21st
Rouff & Lehman.	New Orleans, La.	Everett Lavendol	99 Franklin
Roullet & Delamain.	Cognac, France.	Emil Unger & Co.	30 Park pl.
Routledge George & Sons (Ltd.)	London, Eng.	Joseph L. Blamire	9 Lafayette pl.
Rouvière Fils	Dijon, France.	Comptoirs Commerciaux Français	46 University pl.
Rouyer, Guillet & Co.	Cognac, France.	Culbert & Taylor	89 Broadway
Rowe W. H. & Son.	Troy, N. Y.	James R. Fleeman	76 Franklin
Rowland James & Co.	Philadelphia, Pa.	George Damerel.	85 Chambers
Roy Watch Case Co.	Brooklyn, N. Y.	Louis Degoll	8½ Maiden la.
Roy & Co.	W. Troy, N. Y.	Harmon & Dixon	115 Chambers
Royal Dutch West India Mail Service	Amsterdam, Holland	Kunhardt & Co.	32 Beaver
Royal Ins. Co	Liverpool, Eng.	Edward F. Beddall	50 Wall
Royal Mail Steam Packet Co.	London, Eng.	Sanderson & Son	24 State & Pier 54 (new) N. R.
Royce, Allen & Co.	Providence, R. I.	Frank J. Lightbody	419 Broadway
Royer Wheel Co.	Cincinnati, O.	Alexander V. Fraser	101 Bowery
Rubber Paint Co.	Cleveland, O.	Astley C. Jennings	154 Washn.
Rubel A. & Co.	Corinth, Miss.	—	48 Leonard
Rubel J. & Co.	Okolona, Miss.	—	479 Broadway
Rubel Brothers.	Chicago, Ill.	Ira L. Rubel	84 W. B'way
Ruddy Thread Co.	Worcester, Mass.	Hughes Fawcett	25 White
Rule & Greenloes	Glasgow, Scotland.	Wright & Young	27 White
Rule, Greenlees & McEwans.	Bradford, Eng.	Wright & Young	27 White
Rumford Chemical Works	Providence, R. I.	Henry M. Anthony	100 Reade
Rumsey & Chandler	Chicago, Ill.	Edward F. Nexsen	66 Broadway
Rumsey & Co. (Ltd.)	Boston, Mass.	Angus F. Compson	16 Dey
Russ, Cobb & Co.	Boston, Mass.	John H. Nichols	111 Greene
Russell J. & Co.	Turner's Falls, Mass.	Alexander McL. Rowland	37 Reade
Russell S. N. & C., Mfg. Co.	Pittsfield, Mass.	Franklin W. Russell	56 Worth
Russell & Birkett.	Penn Yan, N. Y.	Andrew J. Toomey	17 Moore
Russell & Morgan Printing Co.	Cincinnati, O.	Samuel Brunaugh	10 Spruce
Ryan John & Sons	Atlanta, Ga.	—	75 Franklin
Rylands & Sons (Ltd.)	Manchester, Eng.	Howard S. Jackson	319 Broadway

EXCELSIOR BIRD FOOD. The recognized standard. The most reliable for your Canary. Use no other. Insist upon getting it.
Packed only by C. ROSENSTEIN & CO., 373 Washington Street, New York.

Name.	Home Office.	Agent or Representative.	New York Office.
Ryttenberg J. & Sons	Sumter, S. C	Hibbert B. Masters	84 W. B'way
Sachs Brothers & Co	San Francisco, Cal.	Stiefel, Sachs & Co	18 Walker
Saddlery Hardware Mfg. Co.	Newark, N. J	Jacob F. Knorr	49 Murray
Sadler & Co.	San Francisco, Cal.	—	50 Leonard
Safety Hatch Door Co.	E. St. Louis, Ill.	Henry L Coe	12 Cortlandt & 57 Duane
Sage & Co	Boston, Mass.	Samuel L Arkush	153 Duane
St. Denis Dyestuff & Chemical Co.	Paris, France	Sykes & Street	65 Water
St. Louis Crystal Glass Co.	St. Louis, Germany	John Muller	69 Duane
St. Louis Stamping Co.	St. Louis, Mo.	Edward B. Brown	96 Beekman
St. Paul Fire & Marine Ins. Co.	St. Paul, Minn.	John M. Whiton	32 Pine
Salaman I. & Co	London, Eng	Henry Solomon	501 Broadway
Salem Wire Nail Co.	Salem, O	George H. Lamon	261 Broadway
Salin P., Fils ainé.	Bordeaux, France	Emil Schultze & Co.	35 Beaver
Salinger Brothers	Memphis, Tenn	—	49 White
Salinger Brothers	Oakland, Cal.	Charles E. Caspar.	26 Howard
Salter, Lewin & Co.	Philadelphia, Pa	John J. Cromwell	49 Warren
Salomon & Lumby.	Paris, France	Julius Eschwege	13 Mercer
Sampliner & Rich.	Pittsburgh, Pa.	—	476 Broadway
Sampson Herman & Leppoc	Bradford, Eng	Folkard & Lawrence.	482 Broome
San Gabriel Wine Co.	San Gabriel, Cal.	Marschall, Spellman & Co.	5 N. Y. & B'klyn bridge
Sanday Samuel & Co	Liverpool, Eng	Sanday & Shepherd.	304 Produce Ex.
Sandeman & Co.	Oporto, Portugal	B. Lamontagne & Sons	53 Beaver
Sandeman, Buck & Co.	Xeres, Spain	B. Lamontagne & Sons	53 Beaver
Sandeu Electric Co.	Chicago, Ill.	Albert T. Sanden.	819 Broadway
Sanderson A. & Sons.	London, Eng.	William H. S. Lloyd	19 E. 21st
Sandland, Capron & Co.	N. Attleboro, Mass.	James R. Palmer	176 Broadway
Sands Brothers	Aspen, Colo.	Bernard Sands	17 E. 4th
Sands Brothers	Helena, Mont.	Julius Sands	58 Worth
Sandvik Steel Works	Sandvik, Sweden.	Henry W. Belcher.	59 John
Sanford Mfg. Co.	Chicago, Ill	John F. Hitchcock.	207 Broadway
Sanford D. D. & Bartlett.	Watertown, N. Y.	Loren W. True.	632 Broadway
Sanitas Mfg. Co.	Boston, Mass.	C. G. Cunningham & Co.	54 Gold
Saranac Silk Mills	Philadelphia, Pa.	John Leonard.	348 Broadway
Saratoga Geyser Co	Saratoga, N. Y.	Charles J. Perry	166 Nassau
Sargent & Greenleaf	Rochester, N. Y	John M. Mossman.	101 Maiden la.
Saugatuck Mfg. Co.	Saugatuck, Conn.	Edward S. Wheeler jr.	82 Howard
Savage Fire Brick Co	Keystone Junction, Pa.	Thomas G. Boyle & Co.	45 Broadway
Savannah Fast Freight & Passenger Line	Savannah, Ga	William H. Rhett. Richard L. Walker	317 Broadway Pier 35 (new) N. R.
Savannah Line	Savannah, Ga	William H. Rhett. Richard L. Walker	317 Broadway Pier 35 (new) N. R.
Savannah, Florida & Western Railway Co.	Savannah, Ga.	John D. Hashagen	261 Broadway
Sawyer E. C., Soap Co.	Pittsburgh, Pa.	Metcalf & Co	91 Maiden la.
Sawyer Woollen Mills	Dover, N. H	Eleaser G. Lemon	58 Worth
Sax C. & Son	Ottumwa, Iowa.	—	13 E. 14th
Scarbrough & Hicks	Rockdale, Tex	Curtis A. Darling.	56 Worth
Scarth, Wilts & Co.	Bradford, Eng.	John F. Wilts	98 Greene
Schacht, Lemcke & Steiner	San Francisco, Cal.	Rosaiter & Skidmore.	156 Franklin
Schaefer Christopher F. & Co.	Richmond, Ind.	—	80 Franklin
Schaeffer & Kaufman	Liège, Belgium.	—	836 Broadway
Schaffer & Dudenberg	Buckau, Germany.	Ludolph Portong.	40 John
Schaghticoke Woolen Co	Schaghticoke, N. Y.	Forstmann & Co.	81 Worth
Scheffner A. & Sohn.	Elberfeld, Germany.	William B. Smith	62 Worth
Schellenberger E. L. & Sons	Manayunk, Pa	Pitman & Black.	115 Worth
Scheuerman & White	Griffin, Ga.	Joseph Mayer	372 Broadway
Scheuer M. & Brother	San Francisco, Cal.	—	392 Broadway
Schiff, Sommer & Co	Gainesville, Tex	—	48 Leonard
Schiffer H. & Brother,	Del Norte, Colo.	Herman Schiffer.	58 Greene
Schlesinger & Mayer.	Chicago, Ill.	Edward C. Stevens.	115 Worth
Schloss Brothers & Co.	Baltimore, Md	Samuel J. Rosenfeld	708 Broadway
Schloss Brothers & Co.	Detroit, Mich.	—	54 White
Schloss, Ochs & Co.	Chicago, Ill.	—	100 Grand
Schmachtenberg Brothers	Solingen, Germany.	William Schmachtenberg.	81 Warren
Schmitt H. H. & Co.	Brooklyn, N. Y.	James D. Hall	176 Broadway
Schnadig Simon & Co.	Frankfort, Germany	Moses Katzenstein	56 Worth
Schneider M., Brother & Co.	Sherman, Tex.	Abraham Schneider	39 Worth
Schofield George A. & Co.	Huddersfield, Eng.	Frederick Droom	529 Broadway
Schofield Joseph & Co.	L. I. City, N. Y.	Charles H. Crankshaw	418 Broadway
Schofield, Mason & Co	Philadelphia, Pa.	McClain & Talbot.	110 Worth
Schramm & Co	Maroim, Brazil.	Smith & Schipper.	91 Wall
Schramm, Stade & Co.	Dahia, Brazil.	Smith & Schipper.	91 Wall
Schulden Brothers	Solingen, Germany.	Oscar Schulden.	96 Spring
Schurz Johan N. & Co.	Coblenz, Germany.	Franke & Co.	1127 Broadway
Schuyler's Steam Towboat Line	Albany, N. Y.	Samuel Schuyler	15 South
Schuylkill & Lehigh Valley R. R. Co.	Philadelphia, Pa.	Eaton N. Frisbie.	1 Broadway
Schwab Clothing Co.	St. Louis, Mo.	—	90 Franklin
Schwab Samuel & Brother	St. Paul, Minn.	—	412 Broadway
Schwabacher Brothers	San Francisco, Cal.	Eugene Lippmann	117 Duane
Schwartz A. Sons	New Orleans, La.	Simon J. Schwartz.	56 Worth
Schwartz J. A. & Co	Philadelphia, Pa.	Luis M. Meyer.	529 Broadway
Schwartz & Graff	Philadelphia, Pa.	Carroll Brothers	264 Canal
Schweitzer & Co.	San Francisco, Cal.	Lee Goldsmith.	81 Walker

IDEN & CO., University Place, 9th to 10th Sts., N. Y. | **MANUFACTURERS OF GAS FIXTURES AND ELECTROLIERS**

Name.	Home Office.	Agent or Representative.	New York Office.
Scott James & Sons	Dundee, Scotland.	Edward R. Biddle...	73 Leonard
Scott Walter & Co	Plainfield, N. J	Albert L. Thomas...	145 Times bldg
Scott S. F. & T. A	St. Louis, Mo	Samuel F. Scott...	45 Wall
Scottish Union & National Ins. Co.	Edinburgh, Scotland	Ackerman, Doyo & Hilliard	41 Pine
Scranton Glass Co	Scranton, Pa	Marvin E. Doyo...	59 Murray
Scranton Jar & Stopper Co	Scranton, Pa	John S. Biesecker...	59 Murray
Scranton Steel Co	Scranton, Pa	Walter Scranton...	47 Broadway
Scruggs, Vandervoort & Barney Dry Goods Co.	St. Louis, Mo.	William L. Vandervoort...	8 Mercer
Sea Ins. Co. (Ltd.)	Liverpool, Eng.	Chubb & Son...	77 Beaver
Sea Island Chemical Co	Charleston, S. C	John M. Wilson...	19 Whitehall
Seabury Charles L. & Co	Nyack, N. Y.	William J. Parshw...	59 New
Seaman H.C. Parlor Frame Co.	Milwaukee, Wis.	Frederick R. Morse...	16 E. 15th
Seasongood, Menderson & Co.	Cincinnati, O		318 Church
Security Ins. Co	New Haven, Conn	Roosevelt & Boughton....	44 Pine
Security Trust Co	Nashua, N. H	Jedediah B. Ferry...	2 Wall
Sedgwick Loan & Investment Co.	Wichita, Kan.	William H. Lendrum...	96 Broadway
Seelig S. & Co	Helena, Ark.	K. Mandell & Co...	26 Howard
Seery Mfg. Co	Providence, R. I	Henry M. Rogers...	176 Broadway
Segelbaum Brothers	Minneapolis, Minn.		736 Broadway
Seibert Cylinder Oil Cup Co	Boston, Mass.	Max Nathan...	94 Liberty
Seidel & Hastings Co	Wilmington, Del.	William P. Hastings...	183 Christopher
Seitz Carl F. & Son	Newark, N. J	Carl F. Seitz...	150 Greene
Selbach Boehne	Uersig, Germany.	Schultze & Co...	30 Beaver
Selby, Moore & Colton	Coshocton, O.		84 W. B'way
Seliger & Newman	Baltimore, Md		61 Worth
Seligman J. R. & Co	Galveston, Tex.		408 Broome
Selling Brothers & Sinn	Detroit, Mich.		3 Thomas
Semon Charles & Co	Bradford, Eng.	Thomas Stewart...	96 Spring
Semper Idem Mills	Boston, Mass.	David J. Whitney...	47 Warren
Senate White Shirt Co	Mass.	Anderson & Price...	77 Franklin
Seydoux, Sieber & Co	Paris, France.	Charles G. Landon...	422 Broome
Seymour Mfg. Co	Seymour, Conn.	William S. Fearing...	100 Chambers
Shakman L. A. & Co	Milwaukee, Wis.		75 Leonard
Sharp Jonas & Son	Bradford, Eng	George M. B. Midge...	84 W. B'way
Sharp & Dohme	Baltimore, Md	Rieken & Hopkins...	112 William
Sharpless Brothers	Philadelphia, Pa	Alexander T. Lane...	402 Broadway
Shoble & Klemm	Philadelphia, Pa.	Peter McCartee...	79 Chambers
Sheffield J. B. & Son	Saugerties, N. Y.	William G. Killmer...	10 Thomas
Shelden Allan & Co	Detroit, Mich.	Charles H. Meade...	86 Worth
Shenandoah Valley R. R. Co.	Roanoke, Va.	Leigh J. Ellis...	303 Broadway
Shepard & Morse Lumber Co.	Boston, Mass.	Frederick W. Cole...	82 Wall
Shopard, Norwell & Co	Boston, Mass.	R. S. Todd...	41 Greene
Shepaug, Litchfield & Northern R. R. Co.	Litchfield, Conn.	George D. Chapman...	48 Wall
Sherman W. T. & Co	Providence, R. I.	Ezra S. Dodge...	176 Broadway
Sherwood Distilling Co	Baltimore, Md	Pringle & Gondran...	140 Liberty
Shillito John, & Co	Cincinnati, O		56 Worth
Shoninger B., Co	New Haven, Conn	Seymour H. Rosenburg...	60 Fifth av.
Short, Nerney & Co	Attleboro, Mass.	James H. Hillis...	237 Broadway
Shotter S. P., Co	Savannah, Ga.	J. F. Cooper Myers...	150 Front
Shoyer, Horner & Co	Chicago, Ill.		301 Broadway
Shreve, Crump & Low Co.	Boston, Mass	Henri O. Watson...	218 Fifth av.
Shriver, Bartlett & Co	Baltimore, Md	Walter L. McCorkle & James L. Stewart	29 Wall
Shufeldt Henry H. & Co	Chicago, Ill	James H. Bird...	21 Beaver
Schwartz A. & Sons	New Orleans, La	Simon J. Shwartz...	56 Worth
Sibley, Lindsay & Curr	Rochester, N. Y.	Syndicate Trading Co...	120 Franklin
Sideman, Lachman & Co	San Francisco, Cal.	Jacob Leviberg...	252 Pearl
Siedenbach & Dettelbach	Philadelphia, Pa.	Abraham Dettelbach...	601 Broadway
Siegel F. & Brothers	Chicago, Ill.	Emanuel Loeb...	115 Worth
Siemsen & Co	Hong Kong, China.	Delacamp & Co...	106 Franklin
Silber & Sidenberg	Milwaukee, Wis.		49 Mercer
Silberstein & Bondy	Duluth, Minn.		77 Wooster
Silsby Mfg. Co	Seneca Falls, N. Y.	Charles A. Allen...	81 John
Silva & Cosens	Oporto, Portugal.	Culbert & Taylor ... Venable & Hayman	39 Broadway / 22 Reade
Silver & Deming Mfg. Co.	Salem, O	Richard F. Day...	72 John
Silver, Burdette & Co	Boston, Mass.	Frank D. Beattys...	740 Broadway
Silverman & Opper	Chicago, Ill.		40 Thomas
Silverman Brothers & Co	Williamsport, Pa.	Henry Gutman...	481 Broadway
Simmons R. F. & Co	Attleboro Falls, Mass.	William A. Wightman...	41 Maiden la.
Simmons & Co	Providence, R. I.	Frank Fenstermaker...	150 Spring
Simon D. & Brother	Altoona, Pa.		312 Broadway
Simon H. T., Gregory & Co	St. Louis, Mo.	William A. Doan...	115 Worth
Simon L. & Co	Chicago, Ill.		260 Church
Simon R. & H	Union Hill, N. J.	Oclbermann, Dommerich & Co.	57 Greene
Simon S. & Co	Detroit, Mich.		389 Broadway
Simon Brothers	St. Louis, Mo		484 Broadway
Simon Brothers	Salt Lake City, Utah		501 Broadway
Simon & Frobein	Atlanta, Ga		479 Broadway
Simon, Israel & Co	Bradford, Eng	James Stern...	97 Prince
Simon, May & Co	Nottingham, Eng.	James D. Smyth...	335 Broadway
Simons, Brother & Co	Philadelphia, Pa.	Edwin S. Simons...	20 Maiden la.
Simons, Jacobs & Co	Glasgow, Scotland.	Charles Forster...	205 Duane

CIRCULARS ADDRESSED TO ANY TRADE IN THE U. S. { Facilities
Prompt, Careful Work | **THE TROW CITY DIRECTORY CO.,** { Unequalled.
at Moderate Prices. } **11 University Place.**

SIM   378   STA

Name.	Home Office.	Agent or Representative.	New York Office.
Simpson & McAllister	Philadelphia, Pa	William Simpson	110 Worth
Simpson, Hall, Miller & Co	Wallingford, Conn.	James A. Metcalf	80 University pl.
Singer J. E. & Co	Milwaukee, Wis		498 Broadway
Singer, Nimick & Co. (Ltd.)	Pittsburgh, Pa	Hogan & Son	248 Pearl
Singleton William & Co	Sheffield, Eng	David B. McIlwaine	97 Chambers
Skinner William, Mfg. Co	Holyoke, Mass.	William Skinner jr	508 Broadway
Skin or Brothers & Wright	Denver, Colo		571 Broadway
Slater Brothers	London, Eng	Daniel Foradike	16 W. 23d
Slater, Hillman & Co	Chicago, Ill	Leon Brocker	531 Broadway
Slocum, Lloyd & Orr	Pittsburgh, Pa	White & Sheldon	134 Pearl
Sloman's Robert M., Line	Hamburg, Germany.	Funch, Edye & Co	27 S. William
Smith Feed Water Heater & Purifier Co.	St. Louis, Mo	Charles E. Bleyer	41 Park row
Smith H. B., Co	Westfield, Mass.	Andrew Mercer	197 Centre
Smith Robert & Son	Stirling, Scotland	Folkard & Lawrence	462 Broome
Smith E. A. & Brothers, Morocco Mfg. Co.	Newark, N. J	Martin V. B. Smith	96 Reade
Smith G. Y. & Co	Kansas City, Mo	William C. Newbolt	87 Leonard
Smith M. E. & Co	Omaha, Neb	Henry S. Hart	336 Broadway
Smith T. & H. & Co	Edinburgh, Scotland	Francis J. Macnaughtan	20 Cedar
Smith T, L & Co	N. Attleboro, Mass.	John B. Haskin	16 Maiden la.
Smith Brothers	New Bedford, Mass.	William E. Smith	44 Murray
Smith & Egge Mfg. Co	Bridgeport, Conn.	{ William E. Trull { John J. Halpin.	17 E. 16th 92 Chambers
Smith & Griggs Mfg. Co	Waterbury, Conn	C. F. Conover Co	101 Franklin
Smith & Valle Co	Dayton, O	Moses M. Moore	112 Liberty
Smith & Wesson	Springfield, Mass.	Marcus W. Robinson	70 Chambers
Smith Brothers & Davis	Pittsburgh, Pa	James V. Davis	93 Liberty
Smith, Baker & Co	Yokahama, Japan.	Richard B. Smith	54 Wall
Smith, Gray & Co	Brooklyn, N. Y	Randolph & Silva	2253 Third av.
Smyth Book Sewing Machine Co.	Hartford, Conn.	Montague & Fuller	41 Beekman
Snook Glove Mfg. Co	Fayetteville, N. Y	Conrad J. Fisher	456 Broadway
Snow Charles W. & Co	Syracuse, N. Y	John D. Titsworth	71 William
Snow Flake Lime Co	Bowling Green, O	White & Sheldon	134 Pearl
Snyder C. B. & Co	Otter River, Mass.	George A. Frink	51 Leonard
Société Anonyme de Croix	Croix, France	Edward Hill's Son & Co	27 Cedar
Société Anonyme Steel Works	Marchienne-Au-Pont, Belgium	Weir, Rogers & Co	45 Broadway
Sockl & Nathan	London, Eng	Raymond Giesecke	65 Duane
Solidarity Watch Case Co	Brooklyn, N. Y	Simon Goldsmith	194 Broadway
Solomon A. Z. & Co	Denver, Colo		705 Broadway
Solomon B. & D	Wilmington, N. C.		479 Broadway
Somerset Mfg. Co	Raritan, N. J	David L. Einstein	14 White
Sommer J. J. & Co	N. Attleboro, Mass.	Jacob J. Sommer	196 Broadway
Sommers G. & Co	St. Paul, Minn		355 Broadway
Son Brothers & Co	San Francisco, Cal		30 Reade
Sonneborn Henry & Co	Baltimore, Md	Moses D. Frank	688 Broadway
Sonneborn Rubber Comb & Novelty Co.	Morrisville, Pa	Solomon S. Sonneborn	12 White
South Brooklyn Saw Mill Co	Brooklyn, N. Y	Samuel A. Skead	16 Beaver
South Florida R. R. Co	Sanford, Fla	John D. Hashagen	261 Broadway
South West Despatch	Toledo. O	George A. Eggleston	353 Broadway
Southbridge Printing Co	Southbridge, Mass	James L. Brown	70 Worth
Southern Cotton Oil Co	Philadelphia, Pa	Edward Flash jr	78 Broad
Southern Investment Co	Anniston, Ala	William C. Metcalf	45 Broadway
Southwark Scale Co	Philadelphia, Pa	C. F. Guyon & Co	99 Reade
Spa Spring Brick Co	Spa Spring Sta. N. J	F. E. Morse Co	7 Coenties sl.
Spalding A. G. & Brother	Chicago, Ill	Julian W. Curtiss	241 Broadway
Sparmann Furniture Co	Paterson, N. J	Edward B. Haines	r 109 Seventh av.
Spaulding & Merrick	Chicago, Ill	Weber & Erskins	110 Reade
Speciality Glass Co	E. Liverpool, O	Wm. J. Snyder & Brother	63 Murray
Specker Brothers & Co	Cincinnati, O		56 Worth
Speisberger M. & Son	Keokuk, Iowa		632 Broadway
Spencer Arms Co	Windsor, Conn	Joseph W. Frasier	290 Broadway
Spencer Charles & Co	Germantown, Pa	E. N. & W. M. Taller & Co	45 White
Sperry, Neal & Hyde	Syracuse, N. Y		56 Worth
Speyer Brothers	Wheeling, W. Va.		63 Leonard
Spitz, Landauer & Co	Chicago, Ill		76 Leonard
Spon E. & F. N	London, Eng	William Chamberlain	12 Cortlandt
Spot Cash Clothing Co	St. Louis, Mo		633 Broadway
Spratt's Patent (America)(Ltd.)	London, Eng	G. Gordon Cleather	245 E. 56th
Spring Garden Ins. Co	Philadelphia, Pa	Weed & Kennedy	50 Pine
Springfield Braid Co	Springfield, Mass.	Edward L. Coffey	96 Spring
Springfield Collar Co	Springfield, Mass.	Standard Collar Co	59 Howard
Springfield Fire & Marine Ins. Co.	Springfield, Mass.	Scott, Alexander & Talbot.	45 William
Springfield Perforated Paper Co.	Boston, Mass.	Frank M. Van Etten	767 Broadway
Squier George L., Mfg. Co	Buffalo, N. Y	Thomas Ryan	195 Water
Stadtlander & Co	Bremen, Germany	Petry & Hauck	55 Beaver
Stage Gold Mining Co	Black Hills, S. Dak	Charles K. Ellery	30 Broad
Stanard E. O., Milling Co	St. Louis, Mo	Nelson S. Munger	81 New
Standard Accident Ins. Co	Detroit, Mich	Edgar H. Bouton	190 Broadway
Standard Chemical Works	Cleveland, O	G. A. Schwarz	71 Wall
Standard Electric Co, of Vermont	Boston, Mass.	Albert E. Rich	254 Pearl
Standard Marine Ins. Co	Liverpool, Eng	John D. Barrett	50 Wall

THE CALIGRAPH WRITING MACHINE,
HARTFORD, CONN.

Name.	Home Office.	Agent or Representative.	New York Office.
Standard Rubber Co.	Boston, Mass.	Ralph W. Morrell	99 Franklin
Standard Sewing Machine Co.	Cleveland, O.	Augustus H. Tennis	26 Union sq. E.
Standard Shirt Co. (Ltd.)	Pottsville, Pa.		705 Broadway
Standard Steel Casting Co.	Thurlow, Pa.	Milliken Brothers	55 Liberty
Standard Thermometer Co.	Peabody, Mass.	Jay Torrey	18 Cortlandt
Standard Tool Co.	Cleveland, O.	Ross & Fuller Assn.	33 Chambers
Standard Underground Cable Co.	Pittsburgh, Pa.	George L. Wiley	18 Cortlandt
Stanley Works	New Britain, Conn.	Peter McCarter	79 Chambers
Staples Coal Co.	Taunton, Mass.	John G. Hannah	1 Broadway
Star Clothing Co.	Huntsville, Ala.		705 Broadway
Star Iron Tower Co.	Fort Wayne, Ind.	Henry C. Adams	115 Broadway
Star Lock Works	Philadelphia, Pa.	Harmon & Dixon	118 Chambers
Star Pin Co.	Birmingham, Conn.	S. A. Castle & Co.	60 Leonard
Star Rubber Co.	Trenton, N. J.	S. Y. L'Hommedieu & Co.	65 Reade
Star & Crescent Mills Co.	Philadelphia, Pa.	Edward Ball	86 Leonard
Starin Silk Fabric Co.	Fultonville, N. Y.	Aaron W. Michels	71 Franklin
State Mutual Life Assurance Co.	Worcester, Mass.	Charles W. Anderson	189 Broadway
State S. S. Co. (Ltd.)	Glasgow, Scotland	Austin Baldwin & Co.	53 Broadway
Staten Chemical Co.	Newcastle, Eng.	Frank Hill	32 Liberty
S. I. Flour Mills	Mariners' Harbor, N.Y.	Jacob S. Ott	347 Produce Ex.
Stauffer, Eshleman & Co.	New Orleans, La.	Thomas Chalmers	103 Chambers
Stavert, Zigomala & Co.	Bradford, Eng.		351 Broadway
Stead & Miller	Philadelphia, Pa.	David O. Kerbaugh	115 Worth
Stearns Frederick & Co.	Detroit, Mich.	Rush S. Gilkeson	211 Pearl
Stearns Mfg. Co.	Erie, Pa.	William Barnhurst	46 Cortlandt
Stearns E. C. & Co.	Syracuse, N. Y.	George B. Bonta	60 Chambers
Stecher Lithographic Co.	Rochester, N. Y.	Robert A. Carrick	21 Harrison
Steel Edward T. & Co.	Philadelphia, Pa.	Frank G. Taylor	52 Leonard
Steel & Co.	Dunfermline, Scotland	Healy & Co.	214 Church
Steele & Johnson Mfg. Co.	Waterbury, Conn.	Charles E. Bishop	35 Howard
Stolger & Co.	Herisau, Switzerland	William Robertson / Heinze, Lowry & Co.	119 Franklin / 81 Franklin
Stein D. & L.	Schlitigheim, Germany.	Hartman, Goldsmith & Co.	45 Warren
Stein & Koester	Mainz & Nuernberg, Germany	Hugo Reisinger	42 Beaver
Stein, Adler & Co.	Rochester, N. Y.		425 Broadway
Stein, Simon & Co.	San Francisco, Cal.	A. Jakobi & Co.	13 Walker
Steinberg & Brothers	Lawrence & Topeka, Kan.		616 Broadway
Steinberger & Kalisher	San Francisco, Cal.		502 Broadway
Stolzhart W. & I. & Co.	San Francisco, Cal.	Steinhart, Heidelberg & Co.	384 Broadway
Stephens & Co.	Riverton, Conn.	Virgil P. Humason	60 Chambers
Stephens & Condit Transp. Co.	Newark, N. J.	Henry F. Ayers	Pier 33 (old) N. R.
Sterling Coal Co.	Philadelphia, Pa.	Devenax Powel & Robert B. Baker	33 Broadway
Sterling Co.	Providence, R. I.	George W. Parks	176 Broadway
Sterling Emery Wheel Co.	W. Sterling, Mass.	Levi Best	17 Dey
Stern Charles & Co.	Athens, Ga.		650 Broadway
Stern H. jr. & Brother	Milwaukee, Wis.		15 White
Stern I. & Co.	Rochester, N. Y.		21 White
Stern J. & Sons	Quincy, Ill.	Joseph Stern	513 Broadway
Stern Brothers	Aberdeen, Miss.		595 Broadway
Stern & Goodman	Starkville, Miss.		595 Broadway
Stern, Loeb & Co.	Los Angeles, Cal.	Greenebaum & Co.	27 Walker
Stern, Mayer & Co.	Cincinnati, O.		21 White
Sternberger S. & Co.	Philadelphia, Pa.	August Hanff	677 Broadway
Sterns Paper Co.	Holyoke, Mass.	J. Almquist	60 Duane
Stetson John B. & Co.	Philadelphia, Pa.	Nathaniel D. Day	546 Broadway
Stevenson & Longwill	San Francisco, Cal.		63 White
Stevenson & Peckham	Topeka, Kan.		25 Thomas
Stewart Chemical Co.	St. Louis, Mo.	Matthew J. Dogert	290 Pearl
Stewart Robert & Sons.	Lisburn, Ireland.	Hughes Fawcett	25 White
Stewart W. G. & Son	Easton, Pa.		78 Worth
Stiefel & Cohen	Baltimore, Md	Joseph W. Taylor	89 Franklin
Stitt S. B. & Co.	Camden, N. J.	J. Elliot Bigelow	47 Leonard
Stix Louis & Co.	Cincinnati, O.	Louis Stix	361 Broadway
Stix, Krouse & Co.	Cincinnati, O.		21 White
Stoddart J. M., Co	Philadelphia, Pa.	Philip J. Fleming & Co.	69 University pl.
Stokes, Thompson & Co.	Philadelphia, Pa.	William F. Taliaferro	51 Leonard
Stone Charles D. & Co.	Chicago, Ill.	R. F. Downing & Co.	20 Exchange pl.
Stone Edward, Spring Co.	Poughkeepsie, N. Y.	John H. Graham & Co.	113 Chambers
Stone & Downer	Boston, Mass.	R. F. Downing & Co.	20 Exchange pl.
Stonometz Printers' Machinery Co.	Millbury, Mass.	Walter G. Bennett	160 Nassau
Storm & Hill	Chicago, Ill.	John H. Bradbury	51 Leonard
Stoughton Rubber Co.	Boston, Mass.	William D. Clark	335 Broadway
Straus Isaac S. & Co.	Cincinnati, O.		102 Franklin
Straus & Levy	San Francisco, Cal.	Sander Pelser	14 Lispenard
Strauss Levi & Co	San Francisco, Cal.	Nathan Strauss	58 W. B'way
Strauss S. & Co.	St. Louis, Mo.		573 Broadway
Strauss Brothers	Richmond, Va.		376 Broadway
Strauss & Joseph	Newark, N. J.		362 Canal
Strauss Brothers & Miller	Cleveland, O.		376 Broadway

SPECIAL ATTENTION PAID TO THIS CLASS OF WORK. } BANKERS' & BROKERS' CIRCULARS DELIVERED { THE TROW CITY DIRECTORY CO. 11 University Place.

STR 380 THO

Name.	Home Office.	Agent or Representative.	New York Office.
Strauss, Glaser & Co	Chicago, Ill.	—	690 Broadway
Strauss, Goodman, Yondorf & Co.	Chicago, Ill.	—	75 Leonard
Strauss, Ullman & Guthman	Chicago, Ill.	—	260 Church
Strawbridge & Clothier	Philadelphia, Pa.	William K. Warnock	56 Worth
Strobridge Lithographing Co.	Cincinnati, O.	Albert A. Stewart	1155 Broadway
Strong & Carroll	Boston, Mass.	Orlando N. Dana	84 Reade
Strong, Lee & Co.	Detroit, Mich.	—	56 Worth
Strontia Mineral Spring Co.	Baltimore, Md.	Charles H. Gillispie	21 Murray
Strouse & Brothers	Evansville, Ind.	—	650 Broadway
Strouse, Moore & Beirs	Rochester, N. Y.	—	557 Broadway
Strouss, Drom & Co.	Chicago, Ill.	Louis Eisendrath	24 White
Stuart & Corss	Pittsburgh, Pa.	F. W. Corse	38 Worth
Stuart-Peterson Co.	Philadelphia, Pa.	Lobsitz & Powell	85 Murray
Studebaker Brothers Mfg. Co.	South Bend, Ind.	Josiah F. Dny	81 Murray
Sturtevant Mill Co.	Boston, Mass.	Amini W. Young	140 Maiden la.
Subscription News Co	Chicago, Ill.	Willard F. Smith	47 Dey
Suffolk Mfg. Co.	Boston, Mass.	Andrew Dow & Co.	393 Canal
Sulphur Mines Co	Richmond, Va.	Crenshaw & Wisner	16 Exchange pl.
Sullivan, Powell & Co.	London, Eng.	Drummond & Fiske	94 State
Sumner S. S. Co.	Liverpool, Eng.	Charles P. Sumner & Co.	18 Broadway
Sun Fire Office	London, Eng.	John J. Gulis	54 Pine
Sun Kwong On & Co.	Hong Kong, China.	Sun Kwong On	84 Mott
Sun Mutual Ins. Co.	New Orleans, La.	T. J. Temple & Co.	155 Broadway
Sunnyside Distilling Co.	Cincinnati, O.	—	33 Broadway
Superior Gas Light & Fuel Co.	Hoboken, N. J.	Adam R. Schatz	164 E. 55th
Susquehanna Water Power & Paper Co.	Conowingo, Md.	William B. Dillon	85 Park row
Sussex Shoe Co	Newton, N. J.	Henry Kurz	122 Duane
Sutcliffe T. & Co.	Bradford, Eng.	James W. Mather	56 Worth
Sutherland & Edwards.	Paterson, N. J.	Joseph J. Duncan	838 Broadway
Sutphen C. Edgar, Co.	Newark, N. J.	C. Edgar Sutphen	75 Greene
Sutton & Co.	London, Eng.	R. F. Downing & Co.	20 Exchange pl.
Syracuse Brass Co.	Syracuse, N. Y.	Alden S. Swan & Edmund Blunt	41 Park row
Syracuse Tube Co.	Syracuse, N. Y.	Charles M. Woods	136 Centre
Swain Brothers	Philadelphia, Pa.	Wilfred Johnson	1 Broadway
Swann & Whitehead	Trenton, N. J.	Oliver C. Holmes	12 Barclay
Swanson, Cairns & Co.	Liverpool, Eng.	John Grierson	40 Cotton Ex.
Swanton Suspender Co.	Swanton, Vt.	Robert S. Capen	705 Broadway
Sweet, Fletcher & Co.	Providence, R. I.	Fayette N. Vaslet	200 Broadway
Sweetser, Caldwell & Co.	Evansville, Ind.	—	78 Franklin
Swift G. F. & Co.	Chicago, Ill.	Stephen W. Mahon	105 Barclay
Switzer, Newittor & Co.	Vicksburg, Miss.	—	518 Broadway
Switzerland Marine Ins. Co. of Zurich	Zurich, Switzerland.	Jacob Bertschmann	18 Exchange pl.
Taber Charles & Co.	New Bedford, Mass.	John R. Curtis	26 Bond
Taber H. C. & Co.	Norwalk, O.	—	84 W. B'way
Tallassee Falls Mfg. Co.	Montgomery, Ala.	Moses Well	46 Leonard
Tampier L. & Co.	Bordeaux, France.	Emil Ungor & Co.	50 Park pl.
Tancride Frères	Paris, France.	Sykes & Street	95 Water
Tanqueray C. & Co.	London, Eng.	Culbert & Taylor	39 Broadway
Tarlton E. G. & Co.	Mobile, Ala.	J. C. Thompson & Co.	9 Walker
Tarr & Wonson.	Gloucester, Mass.	J. C. Giffing & Son	25 South
Tate, Muller & Co.	Baltimore, Md.	Frederick C. Kirchhoff & Frederick Wilkins	107 Produce Ex.
Taunton Copper Mfg. Co.	Taunton, Mass.	Francis W. Doane	292 South
Taylor Brewing & Malting Co.	Albany, N. Y.	John T. Long	644 W. 34th
Taylor Iron Works.	Highbridge, N. J.	Samuel Raber	91 Liberty
Taylor William, Son & Co.	Cleveland, O.	—	375 Broadway
Taylor & Bramley.	Chicopee Falls, Mass.	H. Lee Mallory	121 Franklin
Taylor & Co.	Cleburne, Tex.	Curtis A. Darling	56 Worth
Taylor & Riggs.	Covington, Ky.	—	412 Broadway
Technical Chemical Co.	Newark, N. J.	Henry T. Jarrett	9 C William
Telegraphic Time Co	Providence, R. I.	Frank C. Spooner	55 Cedar
Tennant C., Sons & Co.	London, Eng.	James Lee & Co.	72 Pine
Tennant Charles & Co.	Glasgow, Scotland.	James Lee & Co.	72 Pine
Tennant Charles & Partners.	Newcastle-on-Tyne, Eng.	James Lee & Co.	72 Pine
Tennant & Co.	Liverpool, Eng.	James Lee & Co.	72 Pine
Tennis O. H. & Co.	Chicago, Ill.	—	476 Broome
Terre Haute Distilling Co.	Terre Haute, Ind.	William P. Blaney	81 Broad
Tetley Joseph & Co.	London, Eng.	Wright & Young	27 White
Teutonia Ins. Co.	New Orleans, La.	Ford, Rowell & Hone	83 Pine
Texas Co-operative Assn.	Galveston, Tex.	James M. Callaway	84 Thomas
Texas Loan Agency	Corsicana, Tex.	Abram S. Underhill & L. Whitney Searls	100 Broadway
Texas Trading Co.	Lampasas, Tex	William G. Happy	56 Worth
Thames Tow Boat Co.	New London, Conn.	Frank H. Chappell	1 Broadway
Thames & Mersey Marine Ins. Co. (Ltd.)	Liverpool, Eng.	Angus J. Macdonald	09 Wall
Thatcher H. C. & Co.	Boston, Mass.	Robert F. Perkins	72 Reade
Thaxton & Watkins.	Richmond, Va.	—	83 Leonard
Thayer Henry & Co.	Cambridgeport, Mass.	Walter Adams & Co.	105 William
Thingvalla S. S. Co.	Copenhagen, Denmark	Funch, Edye & Co. / Lorentz C. Petersen	27 S. William / 28 State
Thomas Seth, Clock Co.	Thomaston, Conn.	Seth E. Thomas	20 Murray

FOR THE BEST CO-PARTNERSHIP IN THE BEST CORPORATION SEE PAGE F IN BACK OF BOOK

THO 381 UNI

Name.	Home Office.	Agent or Representative.	New York Office.
Thomas A. A. & Co	Hiogo, Japan	William A. Avis & Co	91 Front
Thomas W. H. & Son	Louisville, Ky	George D. Royston	32 S. William
Thompson Mfg. Co	Cleveland, O	H. C. Mechling	81 Fulton
Thompson W. Baxter & Co	Baltimore, Md	George W. Sinar	51 Leonard
Thompson William & P	Dublin, Ireland	Schuyler L. Mackie	24 Denver
Thompson N. D., Publishing Co.	St. Louis, Mo	J. P. Thomas	787 Broadway
Thompson & Riley	Pine Bluff, Ark		650 Broadway
Thompson, Stewart & Co	Cincinnati, O	Henry Ide	630 Broadway
Thomson-Houston Electric Co	Boston, Mass	Curtis & Dean	115 Broadway
Thonet Brothers	Vienna, Austria	Albert E. Stiassny	836 Broadway
Thorndike Mfg. Co	Lowell, Mass	Bartlett C. Merrill	62 White
Thornlicbank Co. (Ltd.)	Manchester, Eng	James W. Mather	56 Worth
Thornton E. B. & Co	Providence, R. I	Rhodes G. Tucker	200 Broadway
Thornton & Co	Bradford, Eng	W. G. Hitchcock & Co	453 Broome
Thorp Disinfectant & Mfg. Co.	Plainfield, N. J	John Daisiel	658 Broadway
Thorp & Adams Mfg. Co	Boston, Mass	Frank W. Baffny	91 Duane
Ticonderoga Pulp & Paper Co.	Ticonderoga, N. Y	George D. Hanford	50 Duane
Tiffany Brothers	Bennington, Vt	Valentine & Flagler	99 Franklin
Tiffin Glass Co	Tiffin, O	Etienne Lebel	8 College pl.
Tillotson & Sons	London, Eng	W. Philip Robinson	5 Beekman
Timothy & Mets	Chattanooga, Tenn		42 Lispenard
Tingue Mfg. Co	Seymour, Conn	Tingue, House & Co	56 Reade
Tokias & Kaufman	Seattle, Washn	Max Tokias	483 Broadway
Tokins, Singerman & Co	Seattle, Washn	Max Tokias	483 Broadway
Toledo, Saginaw & Muskegon Railway Co.	Toledo, O	Edward P. Beach	271 Broadway
Tootal, Broadhurst, Lee & Co. (Ltd.)	Manchester & Bradford, Eng.	George T. Hill	47 Leonard
Tootle, Hosea & Co	St. Joseph, Mo	Henry S. Hart	338 Broadway
Toplitz Robert L. & Co	San Francisco, Cal	Emil Toplitz	180 Prince
Toplitz F. & Co	San Francisco, Cal	Fabian Toplitz	11 E. Houston
Torrey J. R., Razor Co	Worcester, Mass	Elliou W. Langley	97 Chambers
Torrey Roller Bushing Works	Bath, Me	Thomas L. Simpson	94 John
Torrey J. R. & Co	Worcester, Mass	Elliott W. Langley	97 Chambers
Tourell F. & Co	Cognac, France	Emil Unger & Co	50 Park pl.
Towanda Coal Co	Scranton, Pa	Edward White	21 Cortlandt
Townsend, Grace & Co	Baltimore, Md	George W. Leach	588 Broadway
Townsend, Wyatt & Young	St. Joseph, Mo	Milo W. Wilder	12 White
Tracy Mfg. Co	Worcester, Mass	Dwight C. Tracy	46 Murray
Traders' Despatch	Buffalo, N. Y	Franklin C. Hovey	225 Broadway
Train, Smith & Co	Boston, Mass	James N. Wallis	86 Beekman
Trankla, Jamieson & Co	Grand Rapids, Mich	William Mackenzie	335 Broadway
Transatlantic Fire Ins. Co	Hamburg, Germany	Ernest Harbers	60 Liberty
Transatlantic Life Ins. Co	Hamburg, Germany	Hall & Henshaw	54 William
Trans-Continental Assn	St. Louis, Mo	James F. Fuller	280 Broadway
Traub & Co	Vienna, Austria	Ignatz Strauss	428 Broome
Traut & Hine Co	New Britain, Conn		487 Broadway
Travelers' Life & Accident Ins. Co.	Hartford, Conn	Richard M. Johnson	140 Broadway
Tredogar Co	Richmond, Va	John Fey	47 Broadway
Trenton China Co	Trenton, N. J	H. G. Angell & Co	17 Murray
Trenton Spring Mattress Co	Trenton, N. J	Frederick Barber	171 Canal
Trenton Watch Co	Trenton, N. J	Quincy Walker	177 Broadway
Tribot A., Fils & Co	Cognac, France	Julius Wile, Brother & Co	51 Murray
Trojan Shirt & Collar Co	Troy, N. Y	Clinton H. Smith	857 Broadway
Tropical American Telephone Co. (Ltd.)	Boston, Mass	Henry W. Bates	18 Cortlandt
Trounstine A. & J. & Co	Cincinnati, O		21 White
Trout Brook Mills	Mumford, N. Y	A. Augustus Hyneman	87 Worth
Troy Steel & Iron Co	Troy, N. Y	Herman P. Schuyler	26 Broadway
Tuchfarber F., Co	Cincinnati, O	William J. Moore	99 Water
Tucker & Cook Mfg. Co	Springfield, Mass	S. A. Castle & Co	60 Leonard
Tucson, Globe & Northern R. R. Co.	Tucson, Ariz. Ter	Moses M. Broadwell	11 Wall
Tuerk Hydraulic Power Co	Sycamore, Ill	William H. Marsh	12 Cortlandt
Turkey Creek Mines Co	San Miguel, Colo	William L. Church	17 Cortlandt
Turnbull Gregor & Co	Glasgow, Scotland	George Christall	46 Exchange pl.
Turnbull, Stewart & Co	Trinidad, West Indies	George Christall	45 Exchange pl.
Turner & Seymour Mfg. Co	Torrington, Conn	Luther G. Turner	79 Chambers
Turner, Day & Woolworth Mfg. Co.	Sandusky, O. & Louisville, Ky.	William B. McCullough	82 Chambers
Turpin & Co	Indianapolis, Ind	Samuel T. Turpin	88 Walker
Twitchell R. & Son	Union City, Conn	Osborne & Co	29 White
Tynecastle Co	Edinburgh, Scotland	W. Stewart Morton	74 W. 23d
Ullman M. M. & Co	Natchez, Miss		512 Broadway
Ullman Brothers	Talladega, Ala		657 Broadway
Ullman Brothers	Williamsport, Pa		516 Broadway
Ullman & Co	Anderson, Ala		657 Broadway
Ullman Carl & Co	Bamberg, Bavaria	Sigmund Ullmann	80 Whitehall
Ulman, Goldsborough Co	Baltimore, Md	A. H. & Charles Derongé	19 S. William
Underhill Edge Tool Co	Nashua, N. H	Harmon & Dixon	118 Chambers
Underwood Mfg. Co	Tolland, Conn	Oliver H. Merrill	74 Cortlandt
Union Carpet Lining Co	Boston, Mass	Joseph H. Beale	83 White
Union Central Life Ins. Co	Cincinnati, O	John O. Bach	18 Cortlandt
Union Distilling Co	Cincinnati, O	Albert M. Dalberg	16 S. William
Union Elastic Goods Co	Ansonia, Conn	C. E. Conover Co	101 Franklin
Union Eyelet Co	Providence, R. I	Frank G. Dexter	338 Broadway

TYPEWRITING DONE BY THE TROW CITY DIRECTORY CO., 11 University Place.

Name.	Home Office.	Agent or Representative.	New York Office.
Union Hardware Co	Torrington, Conn	Tower & Lyon	95 Chambers
Union Ins. Co	Philadelphia, Pa		16 Exchange pl.
Union Ins. Co	San Francisco, Cal.	Roosevelt & Boughton	44 Pine
Union Knitting Co	Hudson, N. Y	W. Frank Holsapple	200 Church
Union Line of Steamers	Hamburg, Germany	Funch, Edye & Co	27 S. William
Union Loan & Trust Co	Cleveland, O	Osmer W. Roper	40 Broadway
Union Mfg. Co	New Britain, Conn	Wilbur F. Cards	103 Chambers
Union Marine Ins. Co	Liverpool, Eng	Jones & Whitlock	51 Wall
Union Metallic Cartridge Co	Bridgeport, Conn	Hartley & Graham	17 Maiden la.
Union Mining Co	Mount Savage, Md	Benjamin F. Johnston	115 Broadway
Union Mutual Accident Assn	Chicago, Ill	Coburn & Pagu	140 Nassau
Union Mutual Life Ins. Co	Portland, Me	John M. Crane	96 Broadway
Union Nut Co	Unionville, Conn.	Thaddeus Smith & J. Leonard Varick.	99 Chambers
Union Pacific Railway Co	Boston, Mass	Rensselaer Ten Broeck	257 Broadway
Union Porcelain Works	Brooklyn, N. Y	Thomas C. Smith	48 Murray
Union Publishing House	Chicago, Ill	John B. Crofoot	31 Broadway
Union Rattan Mfg. Co	Brooklyn, N. Y	Frank K. Cowperthwait	125 Chambers
Union Special Sewing Machine Co.	Chicago, Ill.	William H. Boyer	47 Leonard
Union Steamboat Co	Buffalo, N. Y	Augustus Demarest	108 Wall
Union Switch & Signal Co	Swissvale, Pa	John T. Cade	15 Cortlandt
Union Tubing Co	Providence, R. I	P. Christie Ackerman	18 Cortlandt
Union Wadding Co	Pawtucket, R. I	John Maxwell	49 Leonard
United Fire Re-Insurance Co. (Ltd.)	Manchester, Eng	William Wood	82 Nassau
United Firemen's Ins. Co	Philadelphia, Pa	Charles M. Peck & Co	33 Pine
United Gas Improvement Co.	Philadelphia, Pa		10 Wall
United Gas Lamp Co	Philadelphia, Pa	Chester F. Hardon	825 Broadway
United Indurated Fibre Co	Portland, Me	Cordley & Hayes	175 Duane
United N. J. R. R. & Canal Co.	Trenton, N. J	Alfred L. Dennis	100 Broadway
United Straw Pulp Mfg. Co, (Ltd.)	Dresden, Germany	George Hamilton	91 Wall
U. S. Brush Co	Columbus, O	J. Finley Smith	107 Chambers
U. S. Cartridge Co	Lowell, Mass	Wallace & Sons	20 Chambers
U. S. Credit System Co	Newark, N. J	Julius Stein	531 Broadway
U. S. Watch Co	Waltham, Mass	Frank S. Baker	101 Broadway
Universal Button & Novelty Co.	Philadelphia, Pa	Ostheimer Brothers	406 Broadway
Universal Inter-Oceanic Panama Canal Co.	Paris, France	Xavier Boyard	18 Broadway
Universal Joint Co	Philadelphia, Pa	Charles K. Ellery	30 Broad
Universal Marine Ins. Co.(Ltd.)	London, Eng	James Lawson	4 Hanover
Usher Andrew & Co	Edinburgh, Scotland	George S. Nicholas	43 Beaver
Vacheron & Constantin	Geneva, Switzerland	Charles Leo Abry	41 Maiden la.
Valentine Knitting Co	Bennington, Vt	Abner S. Haight	110 Franklin
Van Antwerp, Bragg & Co	Cincinnati, O	Joseph K. Butler	28 Bond
Vanbenthuysen Charles & Sons.	Albany, N. Y	William M. Thayer	64 College pl.
Vanbergen A. & Co	Paris, France	John Heydenreich	261 Broadway
Van Dulken, Weiland & Co	Rotterdam, Holland	Emil Schultze & Co	38 Bower
Vanhouten C. J. & Zoon	Weesp, Holland	Adolphus D. Rohrer	106 Reade
Van Oppen & Co	London, Eng	R. F. Downing & Co	20 Exchange pl.
Vanschaack K. G. & Co	Chicago, Ill	Clarence S. Siermayer	84 W. B'way
Van Zandt, Jacobs & Co	Troy, N. Y	Walter H. Staude	744 Broadway
Voit & Co	Gablonz, Austria	Rudolph Epstein	18 Cortlandt
Vellor & Holcomb	Montreal, Can		966 Ninth av.
Venetian Blind Co	Burlington, Vt	George D. Wright	18 Cortlandt
Verdier G. & Co	San Francisco, Cal.	Thomas McKee	486 Broadway
Victor Knitting Mills Co	Cohoes, N. Y	Henry D. Hammond	51 Leonard
Vienna Pressed Yeast Co	Buffalo, N. Y	W. Dean Smith	309 E. 27th
Vincent & Co	New Orleans, La	Thomas A. Fulton	90 Walker
Viola Co. (Ltd.)	London, Eng	Nathaniel Witherell	20 Nassau
Violet Simon & Cie	Thuir, France	Comptoirs Commerciaux Français	46 University pl.
Vionnet & Co	Havana, Cuba	George Harang	132 Pearl
Virginia Electric Light & Power Co.	Richmond, Va	George E. Fisher / Louis C. Spencer	63 Wall
Virginia Tide Water Coal Co	Richmond, Va	Walter Hamilton	141 Broadway
Virginia, Tennessee & Georgia Air Line	Knoxville, Tenn	Thomas Pinckney	393 Broadway
Vivian & Sons	London, Eng	Willett & Gray	91 Wall
Vogeler, Son & Co	Baltimore, Md	William T. Esler	75 Leonard
Vogelsang's J., Sons	Haida, Bohemia	Ernst Wolf	47 Barclay
Von Borries & Co	Louisville, Ky		69 Worth
Voorhees, Miller & Ruppel	Cincinnati, O		502 Broadway
Vonga & Co	Geneva, Switzerland	Charles Vonga	205 Broadway
Wachtel Charles & Co	Macon, Ga		670 Broadway
Wachtel & Weihl	Cincinnati, O		96 Franklin
Wachusett Shirt Co	Leominster, Mass	James H. Marley	75 Franklin
Wacamuth L. C. & Co	Chicago, Ill	William H. Stiles	86 Thomas
Wade, Davis & Co	Plainville, Mass	Charles A. Whiting	198 Broadway
Wadsworth W. C. & Co	Davenport, Iowa	Thomas Howard	112 Leonard
Wahl John & Co	St. Louis, Mo	George W. Clark	22 Burling sl.
Wainwright Mfg. Co	Boston, Mass	Frederick B. Aspinwall	112 Liberty
Wakefield Rattan Co	Boston, Mass	Daniel Dunne / Simon M. Merrill.	8 Park pl. / 924 Broadway
Wakefield Water Co	Wakefield, R. I.	James Gamble	68 Wall

THADDEUS DAVIDS CO., WRITING INKS, SEALING WAX, MUCILAGE
MAKE THE BEST

WAL 383 WEL

Name.	Home Office.	Agent or Representative.	New York Office.
Wald Lewis & Co.	Cincinnati, O.		63 White
Walker George H. & Co.	Boston, Mass.	Frank J. Barnes	1162 Broadway
Walker Gum Co.	London, Eng.	Gilbert Potter & Co.	164 Front
Walker James H. & Co.	Chicago, Ill.	John G. Crawford	99 Franklin
Walker B. & Co.	Nottingham, Eng.	John McKean	86 Leonard
Walker E. W. & Co.	Boston, Mass.	Charles S. Goodwin	8 Union sq. E.
Wallace R. & Sons Mfg. Co.	Wallingford, Conn.	John W. Sisson	8 Park pl.
Wallace & Co.	Bradford, Eng.	Hicks Brothers	43 White
Wallenstein & Cohen	Wichita, Kan.		46 White
Wallerstein Brothers	Paducah, Ky.		650 Broadway
Walling R. R. & Co.	Frederick, Md	William H. Jacobus	90 Chambers
Wallis Iron Works	Jersey City, N. J.	Richard E. Haslam	102 Broadway
Wallis John & Co.	Nottingham, Eng.	Stephen Wallis	291 Church
Walpert Fred. & Co.	Baltimore, Md	Philip F. Hertzog	416 Broadway
Walpole Dye & Chemical Co.	Boston, Mass.	J. A. & W. Bird & Co.	19 Cedar
Walter Brothers	San Francisco, Cal.	Moritz Walter	88 W. B'way
Walworth Mfg. Co.	Boston, Mass.	Eugene P. Keane	54 Gold
Wamsutta Mills.	New Bedford, Mass	Grinnell Willis	41 Thomas
Wanamaker & Brown	Philadelphia, Pa.	William Dittmar jr.	234 Centre
Ward Marcus & Co. (Ltd.)	London, Eng. & Belfast, Ireland.	John Glenn	784 Broadway
Ward & Payne	Sheffield, Eng.	David B. McIlwaine	97 Chambers
Ward, Lock & Co	London, Eng.	Lancelot Knight	35 Bond
Wardlow S. & C	Sheffield, Eng.	Frank S. Pilditch	95 John
Wardwell Edward H., Co	Newark, N. J.	Edward H. Wardwell	10 Warren
Warne Frederick & Co	London, Eng.	P. Charles Leadbeater	3 Cooper Union
Warne William & Co	London, Eng.	Herman Isaac	280 Broadway
Warner Bellah Co.	Boston, Mass.	Wilbur H. Townsend	63 Broadway
Warner William R. & Co.	Philadelphia, Pa.	Edward Fuhr	18 Liberty
Warner Brothers & Co	Buffalo, N. Y.		76 Leonard
Warner, Jellnek & Warner	Buffalo, N. Y.		83 White
Warren Featherbone Co.	Three Oaks, Mich.	J. V. Farwell & Co.	115 Worth
Warren Foundry & Machine Co.	Phillipsburg, N. J.	William Runkle	160 Broadway
Warren Glass Works	Uniontown, Pa.	William H. Bryant	72 Murray
Warren J. J., Co	Worcester, Mass	George H. Young	401 Broadway
Warren Thread Co	Ashland, Mass	Stephen G. Carpenter	8 Greene
Warrick Frères	Grasse, France	Harry Warrick	84 Church
Wartor & May	Oporto, Portugal & London, Eng.	Anthony Oechs	81 Warren
Warwick Valley Milk Assn. & Co.	Warwick, N. Y.	Nicholas N. Ryerson	1279 Broadway
Washburn Car Wheel Co.	Hartford, Conn.	William H. Price	10 Wall
Washburn Mill Co.	Minneapolis, Minn.	Rice, Quinby & Co.	114 Produce Ex.
Washburn, Crosby Co.	Minneapolis, Minn.	Robert O. N. Ford	17 Moore
Washington Loan & Trust Co.	Walla Walla, Wash.	Alfred J. Taylor	287 Broadway
Washington Mills Co	Lawrence, Mass.	Duncan H. Currie	89 Worth
Wasson H. P. & Co	Indianapolis, Ind.	John A. Donahue	335 Broadway
Waterbury Brass Co.	Waterbury, Conn.	John Sherman	296 Broadway
Waterbury Button Co	Waterbury, Conn.	John C. Smith	48 Howard
Waterbury Clock Co.	Waterbury, Conn.	George M. Vandeventer	10 Cortlandt
Waterbury Malleable Iron Co.	Waterbury, Conn.	Pancoast & Rogers	29 Platt
Waterbury Watch Co.	Waterbury, Conn.	George Merritt	04 Liberty
Waterhouse & Lester	San Francisco, Cal.	Horace A. Waterhouse	151 Front
Waterman, Star & Co.	Denison, Tex.	Charles Waterman	687 Broadway
Watertown Indurated Fibre Co.	Watertown, Mass	Cortley & Hayes	172 Duane
Watjen D. H. & Co.	Bremen, Germany.	William Toel	70 Broad
Watkins J. B., Land Mortgage Co.	Lawrence, Kan.	Henry Dickinson	810 Broadway
Watson, Armstrong & Co	Portadown, Ireland.	George E. Armstrong	128 Franklin
Watson, Newell & Co	Attleboro, Mass.	John M. Dayton	200 Broadway
Wattson Thomas & Sons	Philadelphia, Pa	Wattson & Farr	140 Pearl
Waxelbaum S. & Son	Macon, Ga.		89 Worth
Wear & Boogher Dry Goods Co.	St. Louis, Mo	Robert D. Sparks	56 Worth
Weaver Mailing Envelope & Box Co.	Philadelphia, Pa.	George F. Nock	176 Fulton
Weber F. & Co.	Hamburg, Germany.	Charles H. Knoche	81 Broad
Webster & Horsfall	Birmingham, Eng.	Alfred Field & Co.	93 Chambers
Weed Sewing Machine Co.	Hartford, Conn.	Augustus H. Tennis	26 Union sq. E.
Woodsport Skirt & Dress Co.	Woodsport, N. Y.	Robert Ferguson	51 Mercer
Weidmann Silk Dyeing Co.	Paterson, N. J	Charles M. Miller	100 Grand
Well D. & Co.	Nashville, Tenn.		512 Broadway
Well M. & T. & Co.	San Francisco, Cal.	Theodore Well	55 Leonard
Well & Rosenbaum	Harvard, Neb		102 Franklin
Well Brothers & Co	Philadelphia, Pa.	Louis N. Meyer	529 Broadway
Well Brothers & Co.	San Francisco, Cal.	Moses Well	34 Thomas
Well, Baer & Co.	San Francisco, Cal.		33 Thomas
Well, Dreyfus & Co.	Boston, Mass.	Alexander Jacobs	538 Broadway
Weill Elie & Co.	Paris, France	Alphonse D. Well	13 Walker
Weille B. & Son.	Paducah, Ky.		50 Broadway
Weinstein I. H. & Brother	Birmingham, Ala.	Herman Gardner	302 Church
Weinstock, Lubin & Co.	Sacramento, Cal.	Edward Bonnheim	56 Worth
Weir Frog Co.	Cincinnati, O.	William H. Price	10 Wall
Weir J. D. & Co.	Belfast, Ireland & Glasgow, Scotland	James D. Weir	78 Franklin
Weis Brothers.	Galveston, Tex.	K. Mandell & Co.	26 Howard
Weitzenkorn A. & Sons.	Pottstown, Pa.		705 Broadway
Welch E. N., Mfg. Co.	Forestville, Conn.	James H. Welch	6 Warren
Welch H. L., Hosiery Co.	Waterville, Conn.	H. Lee Mallory	128 Franklin

COMPILED WITH ACCURACY AND DESPATCH. } **CLASSIFIED BUSINESS LISTS.** { THE TROW CITY DIRECTORY CO. 11 University Place.

WEL 384 WHI

Name.	Home Office.	Agent or Representative.	New York Office.
Wells & French Co.	Chicago, Ill.	Edward A. Meysenburg	85 Broadway
Wells & Hope Co.	Philadelphia, Pa.	Edmund H. Sentenne.	132 Nassau
Welsbach Incandescent Gas Light Co.	Philadelphia, Pa.	George A. Tarbell.	71 University pl.
Wendel & Co.	Hayange, Germany.	Welz, Rogers & Co.	45 Broadway
Werner J. & Co.	Mannheim, Germany	Schwartz & Wedde.	40 Stone
Wernse William F. & Co.	St. Louis, Mo.	David M. Bright.	11 Wall
Wernway & Dawson	Philadelphia, Pa.	Frank R. Masters.	45 Leonard
Wertheim A. & Co.	Hamburg & Cassel, Germany	Siegfried Wertheim.	41 Park row
Wessel L. & Co.	Nebraska City, Neb.	—	296 Church
West Cumberland Iron & Steel Co. (Ltd.)	Workington, Eng.	Stroud & Co.	104 John
West Publishing Co.	St. Paul, Minn.	Jay R. Shipley.	84 Nassau
West Shore Line	Chicago, Ill.	J. Bolles Smith.	363 B'way
W. Va. Central & Pittsburgh Railway Co.	Baltimore, Md.	Stephen B. Elkins.	1 B'way
W. Va. Fire Brick Co.	New Cumberland, W. Va.	Thomas G. Boyle & Co.	45 Broadway
West I, S. & Co.	New Orleans, La.	—	56 Worth
West & Sessions	Syracuse, N. Y.	Charles Wolf.	212 Mercer
Western Associated Press.	Chicago, Ill.	William H. Smith	195 Broadway
Western Assurance Co.	Toronto, Can.	Carpinter & Baker, Roosevelt & Boughton	4 Hanover, 44 Pine
Western Dakota Loan & Trust Co.	Deadwood, S. Dak.	Louis C. Schliep.	10 Wall
Western Electric Co.	Chicago, Ill.	Henry B. Thayer.	142 G'wich
Western Express	Buffalo, N. Y.	Edwin T. Douglass.	91 Wall
Western Farm Mortgage Co.	Aberdeen, S. Dak.	Blanchard, Gay & Phelps.	154 Nassau
Western Farm Mortgage Trust Co.	Lawrence, Kan.	William T. Pratt.	40 Wall
Western File Co.	Beaver Falls, Pa.	Alfred Field & Co.	93 Chambers
Western Indurated Fibre Co.	Winona, Minn.	Cordley & Hayes.	173 Duane
Western Ins. Co.	Pittsburgh, Pa.	Frame & Shade.	200 Broadway
Western Newspaper Union	Des Moines, Iowa.	Wagar H. Remington	154 Nassau
Western Patent Overall Co.	Dubuque, Iowa.	Solomon Friend.	21 White
Western Publishing House.	Chicago, Ill.	Frank B. Olmstead.	10 E. 16th
Western States Line	Philadelphia, Pa.	Horace S. Nichols.	76 Wall & Pier 6 E. R.
Western Transit Co.	Buffalo, N. Y.	Edwin T. Douglass.	91 Wall & Pier 7 E. R.
Western Wheel Works.	Chicago, Ill.	R. L. Coleman & Co.	35 Barclay
Westervelt J. B. & Co.	Fort Scott, Kan.	James C. Cleveland.	84 W. B'way
Westhead J. P. & Co. (Ltd.)	Manchester, Eng.	Innes R. Macpherson.	486 Broadway
Westinghouse Air Brake Co.	Pittsburgh, Pa., St. Louis, Mo.	Westinghouse, Church, Kerr & Co., John B. Gray	17 Cortlandt, 160 Broadway
Westinghouse Machine Co.	Pittsburgh, Pa.	Westinghouse, Church, Kerr & Co.	17 Cortlandt
Westray's Point Land & Improvement Co.	Westray's Point, N.J.	A. Bell Malcomson.	132 Nassau
Wetherell Brothers.	Boston, Mass.	James V. Davis.	98 Liberty
Wetherill S. P., Co. (Ltd.)	Philadelphia, Pa.	William Baltuch.	112 John
Wetter & Co.	St. Gall, Switzerland	John McKean	80 Leonard
Wex & Sons.	Chemnitz, Germany.	Schuurr & Delius.	115 Worth
Weyman & Brother	Pittsburgh, Pa.	William A. Robinson.	18 Broadway
Wheatley George W. & Co.	London, Eng.	Morris European & Am. Express Co. (Ltd.)	18 Broadway
Wheeler Brothers	London, Eng.	Daniel Forsdike.	10 W. 23d
Wheeler & Co. (Ltd.)	Belfast, Ireland.	Daniel T. McCullis.	60 Broad
Wheeling Bridge & Terminal Railway Co.	Wheeling, W. Va.	George P. Bissell.	48 Wall
Whitaker Iron Co.	Wheeling, W. Va.	Herman C. Mechling.	81 Fulton
White Cross Line	Antwerp, Belgium	Funch, Edye & Co.	27 S. William
White George & Co.	Des Moines, Iowa.	—	63 Leonard
White Sewing Machine Co.	Cleveland, O.	Edwin M. Young.	22 Union sq. E.
White Star Mining Co.	Portland, Me.	Joseph H. H. Williams.	32 Broadway
White J. D. & Brothers (Ltd.)	London, Eng.	Marolai & Co.	36 Broadway
White J. B. & Co.	Augusta, Ga.	James Aitkin.	5 Walker
White J. H. & Co.	Uniontown, Ala.	—	470 Broadway
White R. H. & Co.	Boston, Mass.	James H. Kehoe.	89 Grand
White W. E. & Co.	Providence, R. I.	Samuel A. Baldwin.	26 Maiden ln.
White Brothers	Winchendon Springs, Mass.	Percival W. White.	51 Leonard
White, Hentz & Co.	Philadelphia, Pa.	D. Lieber & Co.	17 S. William
White, Smith & Co.	Boston, Mass.	Bennett & Maguire.	8 E. 17th
White's Isaac, Sons.	Albany, N. Y.	—	60 Worth
Whitehall Lumber Co.	Whitehall, N. Y.	Brackett W. Burleigh.	1 Broadway
Whitehill Motor Co.	Milwaukee, Wis.	Dwight Ripley.	60 Laight
Whitehill & Cleveland	Newburgh, N. Y.	William H. Crawford.	23 Walker
Whitchurch Brothers	London, Eng.	Henry C. Connell.	r 47 Lafayette pl.
Whiting Paper Co.	Holyoke, Mass.	John M. Tate.	150 Duane
Whiting F. M. & Co.	N, Attleboro, Mass.	Frank M. Whiting.	507 Broadway
Whitlock Machine Co.	Birmingham, Conn.	Carl F. Ahlstrom.	8 Spruce
Whitman Stephen F. & Son	Philadelphia, Pa.	Eugene W. Dunstan.	8 College pl.
Whitney Glass Works	Glassboro, N. J.	Walter B. Wills.	35 Murray
Whitney A. & Sons.	Philadelphia, Pa.	Henry H. Mansfield	52 Wall
Whitney W. M. & Co.	Albany, N. Y.	Thomas Harbison.	386 Broadway

Name.	Home Office.	Agent or Representative.	New York Office.
Whitney Brothers & Co	Boston, Mass.	Charles G. Nichols	81 Water
Whittier Machine Co	Boston, Mass.	Mulford Helmer	103 Liberty
Whittier, Fuller & Co.	San Francisco, Cal.	William B. Weir	72 Broadway
Whytlaw H. A., Son & Co.	Glasgow, Scotland	William A. McCreary	90 Franklin
Wickes Refrigerator Co	Chicago, Ill.	James H. Briggs	9 W. 26th
Widnes Alkali Co.	Widnes, Eng.	Edward Hill's Son & Co.	27 Cedar
Wightman & Hough	Providence, R. I.	Walter H. Tarlton	196 Broadway
Wigton R. M. & Sons	Philadelphia, Pa.	James B. Geisinger	50 Broadway
Wilber Mercantile Agency	Chicago, Ill.	William O. Campbell	90 Nassau
Wilber D. & Son	Oneonta, N. Y.	Charles L. Neumann	19 Whitehall
Wilbur H. O. & Sons	Philadelphia, Pa	Paul Sutorius	125 Chambers
Wilcox Silver Plate Co	Meriden, Conn.	Clarence E. Breckenridge	6 Maiden la.
Wilcox William, Mfg. Co.	Middletown, Conn	Norwalk Lock Co.	82 Chambers
Wilcox & Matthews Co	Waterbury, Conn.	Abner M. Wilcox	42 Murray
Wilcox, Crittenden & Co.	Middletown, Conn.	Frank Baldwin	38 South
Wildt H. & Co	Bradford, Eng.	William Quarmbusch	47 Leonard
Wile M. & Co	Buffalo, N. Y.		75 Leonard
Wile, Brickner & Wile	Rochester, N. Y.	Max Brickner	780 Broadway
Wiley & Russell Mfg. Co.	Greenfield, Mass.	Cooke & Co.	22 Cortlandt
Wilkes & Co	Buenos Ayres, Argentine Republic	E. W. Ketcham	284 Pearl
Willard Mfg. Co	St. Albans, Vt.	Charles Schweizer	712 Broadway
Willard Tract Repository	Boston, Mass.	Joseph E. Jewett	77 Bible h.
Williams Frank & Co.	Buffalo, N. Y.	Arthur H. Williams	110 Broad
Williams J. B., Co	Glastonbury, Conn.	Gustavus R. Lyons	95 Reade
Williams John & Co	Liverpool, Eng.	Charles W. Whitney	63 Fulton
Williams & Co	Nashua, N. H.	William H. Ramsdell	90 Ann
Williams, Hoyt & Co	Rochester, N. Y.	H. Edgar Hoyt	142 Duane
Williams, Page & Co	Boston, Mass.	Joseph Barre & Co.	71 Fulton
Williams, Wells & Co.	New Haven, Conn.	Williams & Peters	1 Broadway
Williamsburgh Color Works	Brooklyn, N. Y.	Charles H. Bromley	1325 Broadway
Williamson & Foster	Harrisburg, Pa.		705 Broadway
Willimantic Linen Co	Willimantic, Conn	Theodore M. Ives	100 Worth
Willis P. J. & Brother	Galveston, Tex.	Thomas L. Rushmore	84 Thomas
Willis & Dunham	Minneapolis, Minn.	Marshall Dunham	531 Broadway
Willoughby, Hill & Co	Chicago, Ill.		696 Broadway
Wilmarth W. H. & Co.	Attleboro, Mass.	William P. Stowe	176 Broadway
Wilson Line of Steamers	Hull, Eng.	Sanderson & Son	22 State & Pier 5-l (now) N. R.
Wilson W. J. & Brother	Green Cove Springs, Fla.	J. C. Thompson & Co	9 Walker
Wilson Brothers	Chicago, Ill.	George W. Tompkins	486 Broadway
Wilson & Bradbury	Philadelphia, Pa.	Henry B. Patterson	95 Franklin
Wilson & McCallay Tobacco Co.	Middletown, O.	Weber & Erskine	110 Reade
Wilson, Frank & Horner	Baltimore, Md.	Owen F. Dalley & Upton B. Sinclair	94 Bleecker
Winchester Repeating Arms Co	New Haven, Conn.	Philip G. Sanford	312 Broadway
Windsor Silver Plate & Cutlery Co.	Boston, Mass.	George W. Wollerman	7 Murray
Wing Woh Cheng & Co.	Hong Kong, China.	Wing Woh Cheng	34 Pell
Winkelmann & Brown Drug Co.	Baltimore, Md	Alfred Stubbe	22 Gold
		Edward S. Lockwood	51 Mercer
Winsted Hosiery Co.	Winsted, Conn.	Valentine & Flagler	90 Franklin
Winsted Silk Co.	W. Winsted, Conn.	Paul V. Kelley	402 Broadway
Wirbel H. A. & Co	Hanau, Germany.	Johannes E. W. Granck	86 Walker
Wisconsin Central Co.	Milwaukee, Wis.	George R. Fitch	310 Broadway
Wisconsin Iron & Steel Co	Hurley, Wis.	Hildreth K. Bloodgood	42 New
Wisdom & Warter	Xerez, Spain & London, Eng.	Anthony Oechs	51 Warren
Wisner Shoe Co.	Bridgeport, Conn.	Whiting R. Smith	128 Duane
Witherbees, Sherman & Co	Port Henry, N. Y.	George B. Wilkinson	40 Wall
Witz, Biedler & Co	Baltimore, Md.		102 Franklin
Wolf B. & Co.	Greenville, Miss.		479 Broadway
Wolf H. & Brother	Thomasville, Ga.		8 W. 3d
Wolf J. L. & Brother	St. Louis, Mo		104 Bleecker
Wolf M. & Sons	Cincinnati, O.		90 Franklin
Wolf & Co.	Philadelphia, Pa.		456 Broadway
Wolf & Brother	Little Rock, Ark		56 Worth
Wolf & Marks	New Orleans, La.	Marcus A. Marks	473 Broadway
Wolf & Wertz	Carlisle, Pa.		479 Broadway
Wolff L. M., Son & Thomas	Johnstown, Pa.		705 Broadway
Wolff & Glaserfeld	Berlin, Germany	Adolph Rosenfeld	42 E. 14th
Wolff & Marx	San Antonio, Tex.	Morris Gonsenheim	18 Lispenard
Wolfson Brothers & Co	Cincinnati, O		21 White
Wood Julius J., Starch Co	Columbus, O.	Henry M. Anthony	100 Reade
Wood Mfg. Co.	St. Joseph, Mo.	Henry S. Hart	339 Broadway
Wood William & Co.	Philadelphia. Pa.	Robert M. Moore	51 Leonard
Wood R. D. & Sons.	Philadelphia, Pa.	Townsend S. Hunn	106 Franklin
Woodburn J. & R. H	Franklin, Pa.	Charles Walker	51 Leonard
Woodcock Brothers	Germantown, Pa	Frederick A. Schmidt	57 Leonard
Woodrough & Clemson	Montvale, Mass.	C. F. Guyon & Co.	99 Reade
Woods, Sherwood & Co.	Lowell, Mass.	James F. Stephens	176 Fulton
Woodward & Lothrop.	Washington, D. C.	Samuel Grosscock	415 Broadway
Woodworth C. B. & Sons.	Rochester, N. Y.	Jonas Langfeld	336 Broadway
Woolworth & Cowles	Sandusky, O.	William R. McCullough	82 Chambers
Woonsocket Rubber Co.	Providence, R. I.	Willett A. Eldridge	72 Reade
Wootton, Mosley & Clifton (Ltd.)	Nottingham, Eng.	Robert Martin	45 White

TYPEWRITING DONE BY THE TROW CITY DIRECTORY CO., 11 University Place.

Name.	Home Office.	Agent or Representative.	New York Office.
Worcester Carpet Co	Worcester, Mass	A. C. Sweeton & Co	108 Worth
Wright J. K. & Co	Philadelphia, Pa	George W. Plumley jr	22 Spruce
Wright & Peters	Rochester, N. Y	Joseph M. King	84 Reade
Wright & Taylor	Louisville, Ky	Charles H. Knoche	81 Broad
Wurtt Electro Plate Co	Berlin & Geislingen, Germany	Leopold Stern	41 Malden la.
Wylur, Ackerland & Co	Cincinnati, O		21 White
Wyman Charles H. & Co	St. Louis, Mo	R. F. Downing & Co	20 Exchange pl.
Wyman, Mullin & Co	Minneapolis, Minn		50 Worth
W's Muller & Co	Paris, France	Richard H. Walker	835 Broadway
Yale & Bowling	New Orleans, La		56 Worth
Yale & Towne Mfg. Co	Stamford, Conn	Thomas F. Kenting	84 Chambers
Yalovitz Brothers & Weinborg	Atlanta, Ga	J. Yalovitz & Brother	4 Walker
Yaryan Co	Hartford, Conn	Augustus G. Paine	5 Bookman
Yee Long & Co	Yokohama, Japan	Chu Cam	47 W. 23d
Yokohama Specie Bank (Ltd.)	Yokohama, Japan	Teissku Tatski	7 Warren
York Haven Paper Co	York Haven, Pa	William B. Dillon	38 Park row
York Iron Co	Milwaukee, Wis	William Schlesinger	45 Wall
York Street Flax Spinning Co. (Ltd.)	Belfast, Ireland	Robert McBrutney	120 Franklin
Young Charles B. & Co	Boston, Mass	Gardiner R. Wright	86 Worth
Young James & Robert	Ballymena, Ireland	Braman, Ash & Barker	105 Franklin
Young & Farrel Diamond Stone Sawing Co	Chicago, Ill	James Hamilton Young	Railroad av. n E. 138th
Younker Brothers	Des Moines, Iowa	Herman Younker	689 Broadway
Ypsilanti Dress Stay Mfg. Co	Ypsilanti, Mich	John H. Goodbody	74 Grand
Zeckendorf L. & Co	Tucson, Ariz	Louis Zeckendorf	34 Thomas
Ziegler John Hastings & Co	Liverpool, Eng	J. E. Grote Higgins	57 Beaver
Zion Co-operative Mercantile Institution	Salt Lake City, Utah		134 Grand
Zweig, Frankfurter & Co	Vienna, Austria	Weiller, Strauss & Co	387 Broadway

THE FOURTH NATIONAL BANK
OF THE CITY OF NEW YORK.

J. EDWARD SIMMONS, President.
CORNELIUS N. BLISS, Vice-Pres't.   C. H. PATTERSON, Cashier.
JAMES G. CANNON, Vice-Pres't.   J. A. HILTNER, Ass't Cashier.

STATEMENT.
January 2d, 1890.

RESOURCES.

Loans and Discounts,	$16,903,745.88
United States 4 per cent. bonds, at par,	200,000.00
Other Bonds,	178,377.83
Real Estate,	600,000.00
Exchanges, National Bank Notes, Etc.,	8,713,739.03
Specie and United States Notes,	4,771,885.00
Due from Banks and Treasurer U. S.,	1,128,981.50
	$32,496,729.24

LIABILITIES.

Capital Stock,	$3,200,000.00	
Surplus Fund,	1,280,000.00	
Undivided Profits, net,	135,099.44	$ 4,615,099.44
Circulation,		180,000.00
Dividends Unpaid,		133,736.18
Deposits,		27,567,893.62
		$32,496,729.24

NEW YORK, January 2d, 1890.

Inviting attention to the above Statement, we solicit the accounts of Banks, Bankers, Corporations, Firms, and Individuals.

Respectfully,

J. EDWARD SIMMONS, *President.*

DIRECTORS.

J. EDWARD SIMMONS, President,
14 Nassau Street, New York.

FREDERICK MEAD,
Of Frederick Mead & Co., Importers and Jobbers of Teas, 104 Water and 188 Pearl Streets, New York.

CORNELIUS N. BLISS,
Of Bliss, Fabyan & Co., Dry Goods Commission, 117 and 119 Duane Street, New York, and Boston and Philadelphia.

CHARLES S. SMITH,
President of the Chamber of Commerce. Late of Smith, Hogg & Gardner, Dry Goods Commission, 115 and 117 Worth Street, New York, and Boston.

JOHN H. INMAN,
of Inman, Swann & Co., Cotton Factors and Commission Merchants, Cotton Exchange Building, New York.

ROBERT W. STUART,
Of J. & J. Stuart & Co., Bankers, 33 Nassau Street, New York.

RICHARD T. WILSON,
Of R. T. Wilson & Co., Bankers and Commission Merchants, 2 Exchange Court, New York.

MARCUS A. BETTMAN,
Of Herman Bernheimer, Son & Co., Importers of Woolens, etc., 75 Leonard Street, New York.

JAMES G. CANNON,
Vice-President, 14 Nassau Street, New York.

THE NATIONAL PARK BANK

OF NEW YORK,

214 & 216 Broadway.

ORGANIZED 1856.

CAPITAL, - - -	$2,000,000
SURPLUS, - - - -	2,000,000
DEPOSITS, - - -	25,000,000

V. MUMFORD MOORE, President.
　　EBENEZER K. WRIGHT, Vice-President.
　　　　GEORGE S. HICKOK, Cashier.
　　　　　　EDWARD J. BALDWIN, Assistant Cashier.

DIRECTORS.

ARTHUR LEARY,	V. MUMFORD MOORE,	CHARLES SCRIBNER,
EUGENE KELLY,	STUYVESANT FISH,	EDWARD C. HOYT,
EBENEZER K. WRIGHT,	GEORGE S. HART,	EDWARD E. POOR,
FRANCIS H. LEGGETT,	JAMES H. PARKER,	W. ROCKHILL POTTS,
JOSEPH T. MOORE,	CHARLES STEINBACH,	DAVID L. WALLACE.

Having very extensive correspondence throughout the United States, our collection facilities are unsurpassed by any similar institution in this country.

A SAFE DEPOSIT VAULT

of superior convenience and security, is provided for the use of depositors and others. Open from 9 A.M. to 4 P.M., except on holidays.

$129,000,000 PAID POLICY-HOLDERS.

New-York Life
Insurance Co.,

346 & 348 BROADWAY, NEW YORK.

WILLIAM H. BEERS, President.

ASSETS, OVER $105,000,000.

IF YOU WISH TO KNOW

HOW IT PAID SO MUCH,

HOW IT GREW SO LARGE,

AND WHAT IT NOW OFFERS,

Send Your Address and Date of Birth to the Home Office as above.

Fac-simile (half-size) of MEDAL Awarded to NEW-YORK LIFE Insurance Co., at PARIS EXPOSITION of 1889.

EDWARD J. SWEENY,

302 Greenwich St., NEW YORK.

TELEPHONE CALL
MURRAY 311.

INSURANCE

AGENT

AND

BROKER,

The placing of Insurance for "Estates" a Specialty.

THE
WESTERN
NATIONAL BANK

OF THE

CITY OF NEW YORK,

120 Broadway.

Capital, $3,500,000.

C. N. JORDAN, President.
CHARLES J. CANDA, Vice-President.
F. BLANKENHORN, Cashier.
H. A. SMITH, Asst. Cashier.

THE
U. S. and Brazil Mail Steamship Co.,
AMERICAN LINE.

H. K. THURBER, PRESIDENT.   C. P. HUNTINGTON, VICE-PRESIDENT.
J. M. LACHLAN, GENERAL MANAGER.

HEAD OFFICE, MILLS BUILDING, NEW YORK.

RUNNING BETWEEN

NEW ❋ YORK

(VIA NEWPORT NEWS, VA.)

AND

ST. Thomas, Martinique, Barbados, West India Islands.

S. S. FINANCE,   S. S. ADVANCE,   S. S. ALLIANCA,
2,600 Tons.   2,600 Tons.   3,200 Tons.
S. S. SEGURANCA, 4,500 Tons.   S. S. VIGILANCIA, 4,500 Tons.
(NOW BUILDING.)   (NOW BUILDING.)

THE
NEW WINTER RESORT,
THE MARINE HOTEL, BARBADOS.

This fine House is located at Hastings, about two miles from the Steamship landing of Bridgetown, Barbados, and facing the broad Ocean, which rolls upon the beautiful beach, but 300 feet distant.

The Marine Hotel is built of stone, with walls thirty inches thick, rendering it cool and pleasant, even in the warmest season. Its broad piazzas are fanned by the N. E. trade wind, which blows continuously (but gently) from October to March, from off the tropical seas, which surround this delightful Island.

The building is 360 feet long and 80 feet wide, accommodating 300 persons. The rooms are large, airy, and well ventilated, overlooking the sea, where vessels of all nations are passing to and from all parts of the world, Barbados being the great port of call for the shipping of the Western Hemisphere.

CONNECTING FOR WEST INDIES, CENTRAL AMERICA, ETC.

Para, Maranham, Pernambuco, Bahia, Rio de Janeiro and Santos;

Connecting for Paranagua, Antonina, Santa Catharina, Rio Grande do Sul, Pelotas, Porto Alegre,

MONTEVIDEO AND BUENOS AYRES.

In point of climate and varied scenery no other trip can approach this. After a few days out from the North American coast it is unusual to have any but clear, balmy weather, and smooth water all the way. The immense advantages of this trip to those seeking health are therefore apparent.

☞ This is the ONLY Steamship Line CARRYING PASSENGERS from the U. S. to the East Coast of South America.

Dictated to and Transcribed from the Phonograph.

314 Broadway, New York, January 30th, 1890.

Gentlemen:—

As there are many people who do not quite understand the uses of the Phonograph and the Graphophone, it may serve a good purpose if I should say to you that from practical experience I consider these machines of the greatest possible value. For an overworked business man like myself I consider that no greater boon could be furnished, than to have beside him a silent but ever ready receptacle for what he has to dictate or say. I am using one of the Phonographs in my own house, and often when I am pressed with correspondence or with some literary work, I turn to it and dictate what I have to convey to my friends, then bringing the cylinders to the city with me, an expert typewriter interprets their contents. At my side at my business in the city a Graphophone is always ready, and the piles of correspondence which crowd my desk are disposed of in no time at all.

I look forward to the period when one-half the correspondence of the country will be not only dictated to the Phonograph, but absolutely conveyed by cylinders in boxes through the mails from one part of the country to the other.

It will not be long before every hotel will have a half-dozen of these machines into which the guests can talk, and for a mere trifle buy a cylinder, transmit it by mail to his home or to his office.

There is no limit to the use of this useful addenda and instrumentality of business. Like many other things in this age in the line of invention, one can double their capacity for usefulness and achievement. I am glad to be able to bear this testimony of a practical nature to the usefulness of the great device, and to say that this is an entirely voluntary statement of my own.

Yours truly,

ERASTUS WIMAN.

Full information in regard to these instruments for use in New York City and State can be obtained from

THE METROPOLITAN AND NEW YORK PHONOGRAPH COMPANIES,
257 5th Avenue, New York.

NORTH RIVER
SAFE DEPOSIT VAULTS,

Cor. Dey and Greenwich Sts.

THE LARGEST, AND BEST ADAPTED BOX

FOR PAPERS, BANK BOOKS, Etc.

$5.00 Per Year.

Inspection Solicited Before Renting Elsewhere.

STORAGE FOR VALUABLES AT CHEAPEST RATES.

NATHANIEL JOHNSON,

MANUFACTURER OF

Church and School Furniture

No. 127 Clinton Place (8th St.), N. Y.

PATENT NE PLUS ULTRA DESK.

CLOSED.   OPEN.

This is the Best and Most Popular Desk made and is in use in all the Public Schools in the City of New York.

OPERA AND CHURCH SEATING

A SPECIALTY.

IDEN & CO.,
MANUFACTURERS OF
GAS AND ELECTRIC LIGHT FIXTURES,

University Place,
9th and 10th Streets, - - NEW YORK.

CATALOGUE

OF

DIRECTORIES IN THE LIBRARY

OF

The Trow City Directory Co.

UNITED STATES AND CANADIAN DIRECTORIES.

Akron, Ohio.
ALABAMA STATE.
Albany, N. Y.
Allegheny, Pa.
Allentown, Pa.
Alpena, Mich.
Amsterdam, N. Y.
Ansonia, Conn.
ARKANSAS STATE.
Asbury Park, N. J.
Atlanta, Ga.
Auburn, Me.
Auburn, N. Y.
Augusta, Ga.
Austin, Tex.
Baltimore, Md.
Bangor, Me.
Bay City, Mich.
Beverly, Mass.
Binghamton, N. Y.
Birmingham, Ala.
Birmingham, Conn.
Bloomfield, N. J.
Bordentown, N. J.
Boston, Mass.
Bridgeport, Conn.
Bridgeton, N. J.
BRITISH COLUMBIA, Province.
Brooklyn City & Business, N. Y.
Buffalo, N. Y.
Burlington, N. J.
Burlington, Vt.
CALIFORNIA STATE.
Cambridge, Mass.
Camden, N. J.
Canton, Ohio.
Charleston, S. C.
Chattanooga, Tenn.
Chelsea, Mass.
Chicago, Ill.
Chicopee, Mass.
Cincinnati, Ohio.
Cleveland, Ohio.
Cohoes, N. Y.
COLORADO STATE.
Columbia, District of.
Columbus, Ohio.
Concord, N. H.
CONNECTICUT STATE.
Council Bluffs, Iowa.
Covington, Ky.
Cumberland County, N. J.
Dallas, Tex.
Danbury, Conn.
Danvers, Mass.
Dayton, Ohio.
DELAWARE STATE.
Denver, Col.
Derby, Conn.
Des Moines, Iowa.
Detroit, Mich.
Duluth, Minn.
East Saginaw, Mich.

Eau Claire, Wis.
Elizabeth, N. J.
Elmira, N. Y.
Erie, Pa.
Evansville, Ind.
Fall River, Mass.
Fitchburg, Mass.
FLORIDA STATE.
Fort Scott, Kan.
Fort Wayne, Ind.
Fort Worth, Tex.
Galveston, Tex.
Glens Falls, N. Y.
Gloucester, Mass.
Gloversville, N. Y.
Grand Rapids, Mich.
Halifax, N. S.
Harrisburg, Pa.
Hartford, Conn.
Haverhill, Mass.
Hoboken, N. J.
Holyoke, Mass.
Hoosick Falls, N. Y.
Houston, Tex.
IDAHO TERRITORY.
ILLINOIS STATE.
INDIANA STATE.
Indianapolis, Ind.
IOWA STATE.
Ithaca, N. Y.
Jacksonville, Fla.
Jamestown, N. Y.
Jeffersonville, Ind.
Jersey City, N. J.
Johnstown, N. Y.
Kansas City, Mo.
KANSAS STATE.
KENTUCKY STATE.
Key West, Fla.
Kingston, N. Y.
Knoxville, Tenn.
Lancaster, Pa.
Lansingburgh, N. Y.
Lawrence, Mass.
Leadville, Col.
Leavenworth, Kan.
Lewiston, Me.
Lexington, Ky.
Lincoln, Neb.
Little Rock, Ark.
Lockport, N. Y.
London, Ont.
Long Island, N. Y.
Los Angeles, Cal.
Louisville, Ky.
Lowell, Mass.
Lynchburg, Va.
Lynn, Mass.
MAINE STATE.
Manchester, N. H.
Marblehead, Mass.
MARYLAND STATE.
MASSACHUSETTS STATE.
Memphis, Tenn.
Meriden, Conn.

MICHIGAN STATE.
Middletown, Conn.
Millville, N. J.
Milwaukee, Wis.
Minneapolis, Minn.
MINNESOTA STATE.
MISSOURI STATE.
Mobile, Ala.
MONTANA STATE.
Montclair, N. J.
Montreal, Canada.
Mount Holly, N. J.
Muskegon, Mich.
Nashua, N. H.
Nashville, Tenn.
NEBRASKA STATE.
New Albany, Ind.
New Bedford, Mass.
New Britain, Conn.
New Brunswick, N. J.
NEW ENGLAND STATES BUSINESS.
NEW HAMPSHIRE STATE.
New Haven, Conn.
NEW JERSEY STATE.
New Orleans, La.
NEW YORK STATE BUSINESS
Newark, N. J.
Newark, Ohio.
Newport, Ky.
Newport, R. I.
Newton, Mass.
Norfolk, Va.
NORTH CAROLINA STATE.
North Adams, Mass.
NORTH DAKOTA STATE.
Norwich, Conn.
Oakland, Cal.
OHIO STATE.
Omaha, Neb.
ONTARIO PROVINCE, Canada.
Orange, N. J.
OREGON STATE.
Oswego, N. Y.
Ottawa, Canada.
Paterson, N. J.
Peabody, Mass.
PENNSYLVANIA STATE.
Peoria, Ill.
Petersburg, Va.
Philadelphia City and Business, Pa.
Pittsburgh, Pa.
Pittsfield, Mass.
Plainfield, N. J.
Portland, Me.
Portland, Oregon.
Portsmouth, Va.
Pottsville, Pa.
Poughkeepsie, N. Y.
Providence, R. I.
Quebec, Canada.
Quincy, Ill.
Rahway, N. J.

Raleigh, N. C.
Reading, Pa.
RHODE ISLAND STATE.
Richmond, Va.
Rochester, N. Y.
Rome, N. Y.
Rutland, Vt.
Sacramento, Cal.
St. John, N. B.
St. Joseph, Mo.
St. Louis, Mo.
St. Paul, Minn.
Salem, Mass.
Salt Lake City, Utah.
San Antonio, Tex.
Sandusky, Ohio.
San Francisco, Cal.
San Jose, Cal.
Saratoga Springs, N. Y.
Savannah, Ga.
Schenectady, N. Y.
Scranton, Pa.
Sing Sing, N. Y.
Sioux City, Iowa.
SOUTH CAROLINA STATE.
SOUTH DAKOTA STATE.
South Hadley Falls, Mass.
Springfield, Ill.
Springfield, Mass.
Springfield, Mo.
Staten Island, N. Y.
Syracuse, N. Y.
Tacoma, Wash.
Taunton, Mass.
TENNESSEE STATE.
Terre Haute, Ind.
TEXAS STATE.
Toledo, Ohio.
Topeka, Kan.
Toronto, Canada.
Trenton, N. J.
Troy, N. Y.
UTAH TERRITORY.
Utica, N. Y.
VERMONT STATE.
Vineland, N. J.
VIRGINIA STATE.
Washington, D. C.
WASHINGTON STATE.
Waterbury, Conn.
Watertown, N. Y.
Westfield, Mass.
WEST VIRGINIA STATE.
Wheeling, W. Va.
Wichita, Kan.
Wilkes-Barre, Pa.
Williamsport, Pa.
Wilmington, Del.
WISCONSIN STATE.
Worcester, Mass.
Yonkers, N. Y.
Youngstown, Ohio.
Zanesville, Ohio.

FOREIGN DIRECTORIES.

Barbadoes, W. I.
Central America.
Cuba.
Dublin.

Frankfort, Germany.
French Departments.
Glasgow.
Hamburg.

Hanover.
Liverpool.
London, Eng.
Melbourne.

Mexico.
Paris.
South America.
Sydney.

UNITED STATES TRUST COMPANY OF NEW YORK,

Nos. 45 and 47 Wall Street.

CAPITAL AND SURPLUS,
EIGHT MILLION DOLLARS.

This Company is a legal depository for moneys paid into Court, and is authorized to act as guardian or trustee.

INTEREST ALLOWED ON DEPOSITS,

which may be made at any time and withdrawn after five days' notice, and will be entitled to interest for the whole time they may remain with the Company.

Executors, Administrators, or Trustees of Estates, and Women unaccustomed to the transaction of business, as well as Religious and Benevolent Institutions, will find this Company a convenient depository for money.

JOHN A. STEWART, *President.* GEORGE BLISS, *Vice-President.*
JAMES S. CLARK, *Second Vice-President.*

TRUSTEES.

WILSON G. HUNT,	ERASTUS CORNING, Albany,	CHARLES S. SMITH,
CLINTON GILBERT,	JOHN HARSEN RHOADES,	WM. ROCKEFELLER,
DANIEL D. LORD,	ANSON PHELPS STOKES,	ALEXANDER E. ORR,
SAMUEL SLOAN,	GEORGE HENRY WARREN,	WILLIAM H. MACY, Jr.
JAMES LOW,	GEORGE BLISS,	WM. D. SLOANE,
WM. WALTER PHELPS,	WILLIAM LIBBEY,	GUSTAV H. SCHWAB,
D. WILLIS JAMES,	JOHN CROSBY BROWN,	FRANK LYMAN, B'klyn,
JOHN A. STEWART,	EDWARD COOPER,	GEORGE F. VIETOR.
HENRY E. LAWRENCE,	W. BAYARD CUTTING,	

HENRY L. THORNELL, *Secretary.* LOUIS G. HAMPTON, *Assistant Secretary.*

Manhattan Trust Company.

CAPITAL - - - $1,000,000.
No. 10 Wall St., New York.

A Legal Depository for Trust and Court Funds and General Deposits.

LIBERAL RATES OF INTEREST PAID ON BALANCES.

THE COMPANY is authorized to act as EXECUTOR, ADMINISTRATOR, GUARDIAN, RECEIVER, and TRUSTEE; as FISCAL and TRANSFER AGENT, and as REGISTRAR of STOCKS and BONDS.

The Company offers to Executors and Trustees of Estates and to Religious and Benevolent Institutions, Exceptional Facilities for the Transaction of their Business.

OFFICERS.

FRANCIS ORMOND FRENCH, PRESIDENT. JOHN I. WATERBURY, VICE-PRESIDENT.
CHAS. W. HASKINS, SECRETARY. A. T. FRENCH, TREASURER.

DIRECTORS.

F. O. FRENCH, N. Y.	C. C. BALDWIN, N. Y.	JAMES O. SHELDON, N. Y.
R. J. CROSS, N. Y.	CHARLES F. TAG, N. Y.	A. S. ROSENBAUM, N. Y.
H. L. HIGGINSON, Boston.	HENRY FIELD, Chicago.	EX NORTON, N. Y.
AUGUST BELMONT, Jr., N. Y.	H. W. CANNON, N. Y.	SAMUEL R. SHIPLEY, Philadelphia.
E. D. RANDOLPH, N. Y.	JOHN R. FORD, N. Y.	R. T. WILSON, N. Y.
H. O. NORTHCOTE, N. Y.	T. J. COOLIDGE, Jr., Boston.	JOHN I. WATERBURY, N. Y.

JOHN L. CADWALADER, COUNSEL. STRONG & CADWALADER, ATTORNEYS.

ALL MATTERS OF ACCOUNTS.

WILLIAM WADDELL,

PUBLIC ACCOUNTANT AND AUDITOR.

Qualfd as an expert accountant by special training and examination, nd by twenty years' continuous practical experience in all branches of accounting and bookkeeping.

55 BEAVER STREET,

Telephone, Pearl 463.

Assisted by qualified staff of 18 expert accountants and bookkeepers.

Experts supplied at low terms in or out of city.

JOHN F. B. SMYTH,
REAL ESTATE,
Aucioneer, Broker and Appraiser,
No. 69 LIBERTY ST., NEW YORK.

Within one door of the Real Estate Exchange.

MONEY TO LOAN IN AMOUNTS TO SUIT AT THE LOWEST RATES.

Rents Collected.   Estates Managed.   Real Estate Sold at Public or Private Sale.
No Charges Made unless actual Sale is effected.
NOTARY PUBLIC.   Telephone, John 350.
Sales at Ation of Furniture and Household Effects conducted on Premises.

ames of 30,000 Investors in the United States can be had of the TROW CITY DIRECTORY CO

THE SAFETY
INSULATED WIRE AND CABLE CO.,
MANUFACTURERS OF
SEAMLESS
Insulated Wires & Cables.
HIGH INSULATION GUARANTEED.

234 West 29th Street,
NEW YORK.

38TH YEAR CO-PARTNERSHIP 1890 CORPORATION DIRECTORY OF NEW YORK CITY

THE DELAWARE RIVER IRON SHIP-BUILDING AND ENGINE WORKS.

Iron Steamship Builders.   Steam Machinery of Every Description.
Chester, Pa., and Morgan Iron Works, foot of E. 9th St., N. Y.

NETTLETON & MILLS,
ATTORNEYS AT LAW AND NOTARIES PUBLIC.
COMMISSIONERS OF DEEDS
FOR ALL THE STATES
115 BROADWAY,
New York City.

The Trow City Directory Co., 11 UNIVERSITY PLACE.
CIRCULARS ADDRESSED. TRADE LISTS FURNISHED. MODERATE PRICES.

ESTERBROOK'S PENS.

www.ingramcontent.com/pod-product-compliance
Lightning Source LLC
Chambersburg PA
CBHW051745300426
44115CB00007B/695